Scotland

THE ROUGH GUIDE

There are more than one hundred and fifty Rough Guide titles
covering destinations from Amsterdam to Zimbabwe

Forthcoming titles include

Bejing • Cape Town • Croatia • Ecuador • Switzerland

Rough Guide Reference Series

Classical Music • Drum 'n' Bass • English Football
European Football • House • The Internet • Jazz • Music USA
Opera • Reggae • Rock Music • World Music

Rough Guide Phrasebooks

Czech • Dutch • Egyptian Arabic • European Languages• Dutch • French
German • Greek • Hindi & Urdu • Hungarian • Indonesian • Italian
Japanese • Mandarin Chinese • Mexican Spanish • Polish • Portuguese
Russian • Spanish • Swahili • Thai • Turkish • Vietnamese

Rough Guides on the Internet

www.roughguides.com

ROUGH GUIDE CREDITS

Text editor: Helena Smith
Series editor: Mark Ellingham
Editorial: Martin Dunford, Jonathan Buckley, Jo Mead, Kate Berens, Amanda Tomlin, Ann-Marie Shaw, Paul Gray, Judith Bamber, Orla Duane, Olivia Eccleshall, Ruth Blackmore, Sophie Martin, Geoff Howard, Claire Saunders, Gavin Thomas, Alexander Mark Rogers, Polly Thomas, Joe Staines, Lisa Nellis, Andrew Tomičić, Claire Fogg, Richard Lim, Duncan Clark, Peter Buckley (UK); Andrew Rosenberg, Mary Beth Maioli (US)
Production: Susanne Hillen, Andy Hilliard, Link Hall, Helen Ostick, Julia Bovis, Michelle Draycott,
Katie Pringle, Robert Evers, Neil Cooper
Cartography: Melissa Baker, Maxine Repath, Nichola Goodliffe, Ed Wright
Picture research: Louise Boulton, Sharon Martins
Online editors: Kelly Cross (US)
Finance: John Fisher, Gary Singh, Edward Downey, Mark Hall, Tim Bill
Marketing & Publicity: Richard Trillo, Niki Smith, David Wearn, Jemima Broadbridge (UK); Jean-Marie Kelly, Myra Campolo, Simon Carloss (US)
Administration: Tania Hummel, Charlotte Marriott, Demelza Dallow

···

READERS' LETTERS

We would like to sincerely thank the following readers, who wrote with comments, suggestions and helpful advice:

Stephen Ainsleigh Rice and Jennifer Halliday; Chloë Anderton-Brown; Peter Atkinson; A.J. Barclay; Dorothy Baxter; Perry Bramlett; Michael Briggs; James and Catherine Cape; Nicola Cheyne; Kim Church; Lisette Cohen; Celia Couslon; Sue and Dick Courchée; David A. Crerar and Julia E. Lawn; Karen Cunningham; April Darsch; Sandra Day; Jane and Mark Eaton; Carolyn Ellenberger; Louise Fournier and Roger Simard; Diane Frazer; Anita Garside; Carole Gray and Jane Thompson; John Guest; Colin and Jennifer Hawksworth; Linda Dalrymple Henderson; Sarah Holtom; W.G. Hopkin; Mrs A. Hughson; Richard Ingamells; A. Johnston; Helen Jones; Helen Kara; Karine (from Oslo); A. Kemph; Lynn Kopac; Julia E. Lawn; Mark Leach; Alice Lear; Suzanne Lenton; Richard D. Lysons; Josephine Maltby; Doreen McCarthy; Scott Mcmenomey; Julie McMillan; Dr Shayne Mitchell; Ann Ohlenschlager; Catriona Picken; Max Rathmell; Diana Rawnsley; Elizabeth Raymont; Liz Raynort; Kevin Reagan; Peter Richards; Mrs S.M. Salter; Kay Sayer; Iain Stewart; Claire Stolk; Maxy Stone; Alan Thwaite; Mr G. Tite; Marco Varenkamp; Caroline Ward; Susan Bartlett Weber; Philippa Whittaker; M. Williams; Nathan Williams; Elizabeth Wilson; Amanda Wood; David Wood; Gavin Yamey.

···

PUBLISHING INFORMATION

This fourth edition published January 2000 by Rough Guides Ltd, 62–70 Shorts Gardens, London, WC2H 9AB.
Distributed by the Penguin Group:
Penguin Books Ltd, 27 Wrights Lane, London W8 5TZ
Penguin Books USA Inc., 375 Hudson Street, New York 10014, USA
Penguin Books Australia Ltd, 487 Maroondah Highway, PO Box 257, Ringwood, Victoria 3134, Australia
Penguin Books Canada Ltd, 10 Alcorn Avenue, Toronto, Ontario, Canada M4V 1E4
Penguin Books (NZ) Ltd, 182–190 Wairau Road, Auckland 10, New Zealand
Typeset in Linotron Univers and Century Old Style to an original design by Andrew Oliver.
Printed in England by Clays Ltd, St Ives Plc
Illustrations in Part One and Part Three by Edward Briant.
Illustrations on p.1 and p.623 by Henry Iles.

The image of the National Museum of Scotland, printed on p.623, was kindly provided courtesy of
© Trustees of the National Museums of Scotland.
No part of this book may be reproduced in any form without permission from the publisher except for the quotation of brief passages in reviews.
720pp – Includes index
A catalogue record for this book is available from the British Library
ISBN 1-85828-508-9

··

Scotland

THE ROUGH GUIDE

written and researched by

Rob Humphreys, Donald Reid
and Paul Tarrant

with additional contributions by

Pete Heywood, Geoff Howard
and Colin Irwin

THE ROUGH GUIDES

TRAVEL GUIDES • PHRASEBOOKS • MUSIC AND REFERENCE GUIDES

 We set out to do something different when the first Rough Guide was published in 1982. Mark Ellingham, just out of university, was travelling in Greece. He brought along the popular guides of the day, but found they were all lacking in some way. They were either strong on ruins and museums but went on for pages without mentioning a beach or taverna. Or they were so conscious of the need to save money that they lost sight of Greece's cultural and historical significance. Also, none of the books told him anything about Greece's contemporary life – its politics, its culture, its people, and how they lived.

So with no job in prospect, Mark decided to write his own guidebook, one which aimed to provide practical information that was second to none, detailing the best beaches and the hottest clubs and restaurants, while also giving hard-hitting accounts of every sight, both famous and obscure, and providing up-to-the-minute information on contemporary culture. It was a guide that encouraged independent travellers to find the best of Greece, and was a great success, getting shortlisted for the Thomas Cook travel guide award,

and encouraging Mark, along with three friends, to expand the series.

The Rough Guide list grew rapidly and the letters flooded in, indicating a much broader readership than had been anticipated, but one which uniformly appreciated the Rough Guide mix of practical detail and humour, irreverence and enthusiasm. Things haven't changed. The same four friends who began the series are still the caretakers of the Rough Guide mission today: to provide the most reliable, up-to-date and entertaining information to independent-minded travellers of all ages, on all budgets.

We now publish more than 150 titles and have offices in London and New York. The travel guides are written and researched by a dedicated team of more than 100 authors, based in Britain, Europe, the USA and Australia. We have also created a unique series of phrasebooks to accompany the travel series, along with an acclaimed series of music guides, and a best-selling pocket guide to the Internet and World Wide Web. We also publish comprehensive travel information on our Web site:

www.roughguides.com

HELP US UPDATE

We've gone to a lot of effort to ensure that the fourth edition of The Rough Guide to Scotland is accurate and up-to-date. However, things change – places get "discovered", opening hours are notoriously fickle, restaurants and rooms raise prices or lower standards. If you feel we've got it wrong or left something out, we'd like to know, and if you can remember the address, the price, the time, the phone number, so much the better.

We'll credit all contributions, and send a copy of the next edition (or any other Rough Guide if you prefer) for the best letters. Please mark letters: "Rough Guide Scotland Update" and send to:
Rough Guides, 62–70 Shorts Gardens, London WC2H 9AB, or Rough Guides, 375 Hudson St, 9th floor, New York NY 10014. Or send email to: mail@roughguides.co.uk
Online updates about this book can be found on Rough Guides' Web site at www.roughguides.com

THE AUTHORS

Rob Humphreys joined the Rough Guides in 1989, having worked as a failed actor, taxi driver and male model. He has spent some part of every year in Scotland since he was nowt but a lad in rural Yorkshire. He has also travelled extensively in central and eastern Europe, writing guides to Prague, the Czech and Slovak Republics and St Petersburg, as well as London.

Donald Reid was born and brought up in Glasgow, studied law at Edinburgh University and left the country soon afterwards to avoid the threat of an office. Having worked on an island in the Caribbean and as a trawler fisherman in Australia, he floated into Cape Town one misty December morning in 1993 and took a notion to hang around, working on books, magazines and newspapers in South Africa for the next three years. He returned to Scotland and now lives in Edinburgh working as a freelance writer and editor. He is the co-author of the *Rough Guide to South Africa*.

Paul Tarrant is co-author of the *Rough Guide to New England*, and author of *Americans in Britain – A Survival Guide*, a spoof travel guide for US visitors to the UK. He has written travel features for publications as diverse as *Take a Break* and *The Church Times*, and has recently returned – along with his golden retriever Tess – to his native Dorset from Scotland, where he lived for the past three years.

ACKNOWLEDGEMENTS

Thanks to everyone who contributed to previous editions of this book: Dave Abram, Wayne Alderson, Donald Greig, Alastair Hamilton, Phil Lee, Catherine Logie, Gordon McLachlan, Mike Parker, Sophie Pragnall, Helena Smith, Tania Smith and Julian Ward. At Rough Guides, many thanks go to Michelle Draycott for hunting down new pictures, Robert Evers and Anna Wray for typesetting, Maxine Repath for the maps, Louise Boulton for the cover and Gillian Armstrong for proofreading.

The authors would like to thank the National Trust for Scotland and Historic Scotland; Caledonian MacBrayne, P&O Scottish Ferries and Orkney Ferries for help getting around the islands; and Helena Smith for her fine touch, skilful organization and good-humoured and enduring patience, and for basically staying cool.

Rob Humphreys would also like to thank: Alasdair Enticknap for helpful hints on updating the Outer Hebs; Dick and Sue Courchée for B&B tips; Val and Gordon for enthusiastic updates for Skye and elsewhere; Val (again) for further trips beyond the call of duty; and Kate, Stan and Josh for groundwork in the snow and sun in Islay, Mull and Orkney.

Donald Reid would also like to thank: all those who smoothed the way with information, assistance, good leads, beds, meals, opinions and enthusiasm, particularly Sally Munro of the Highlands and Islands Tourist Board; Jenni Steele of Edinburgh and Lothians Tourist Board; Moira Dyer of Glasgow and Clyde Valley Tourist Board; Beverley Tricker of Aberdeen and Grampian Tourist Board; Fran and Chris at Rua Reidh; Gavin and Nicola at Aite Cruinnichidh; Frank and Kate at Rogat; Peter Collingridge; and Mo for chumming me above and beyond.

Paul Tarrant would also like to thank: Stewart Asquith; Elizabeth Turner; Joy Dawson; Colin Blair; Derek Trotter; Jean and Colin Hill; David Lawson; and the staff of the local and regional tourist offices, especially at Eyemouth, St Andrews, Perth and Stirling.

CONTENTS

Introduction xii

• CHAPTER 3: GLASGOW AND THE CLYDE 190–240

• CHAPTER 4: CENTRAL SCOTLAND 241–299

● CHAPTER 5: ARGYLL

● CHAPTER 6: SKYE AND THE WESTERN ISLES

• CHAPTER 7: NORTHEAST SCOTLAND

• CHAPTER 8: THE HIGHLANDS

• CHAPTER 9: ORKNEY AND SHETLAND

PART THREE CONTEXTS 623

LIST OF MAPS

MAP SYMBOLS

Railway		Abbey
Motorway		Stately home
Road		Museum
Tunnel		Gardens
Pedestrianized street		Battlefield
One-way street		Campsite
Steps		Accommodation
Footpath		Hostel
Ferry route		Airport
Waterway		Underground station
Chapter division boundary		Bus stop
International boundary		Parking
Highland boundary fault		Tourist office
Point of interest		Post office
Peak		Telephone
Hill		Whisky distillery
Viewpoint		Building
Rocks		Church
Lighthouse		Park
Waterfall		National park
Cave		Forest
Ruins/archeological site		Beach
Castle		

INTRODUCTION

D espite the best efforts of an unreliable climate, **Scotland** is, quite simply, a wonderfully rewarding and diverse country to visit, encompassing everything from the rolling countryside of the Borders to the wild and weather-beaten islands that arc around its west and north coasts. Many parts of the mainland are surprisingly accessible, with remote lochs, glens and Highland mountains lying less than two hours' travel from Edinburgh and Glasgow, two of Britain's most complex and intriguing cities.

For centuries Scotland was a divided nation, with Gaelic-speaking, cattle-raising clans concentrated to the north and west, and Lowland Scots, distinguished by their Norman-style feudal loyalties and allegiances, dominant to the south and east. These two linguistically distinct Scotlands developed along separate lines, their mutually antagonistic populations creating the first of several overlapping sources of national tension. After the Reformation, religion became another flashpoint, not just between Catholic and Protestant, but also amongst a host of reformist sects. Later still, industrialization divided the rural from the urban, generating the class-conscious, socialist-minded cities of central and eastern Scotland. Such tensions are still apparent today in the complex relationships between incomers and natives, between the landed and the stranded, and between the progressive core of the cities and the drug-ridden poverty of their fringes.

In the background lurks Scotland's problematic relationship with England. In 1707, the Act of Union united the English and Scottish parliaments, ending centuries of political strife and, shortly afterwards, in 1745, the failure of Bonnie Prince Charlie's Jacobite rebellion gave the English and their Scottish allies the chance to bring the Gaels to heel. However, the union only partly integrated the two nations, with Scotland retaining separate legal and education systems, and, to this day, its relationship with its southern neighbour remains anomalous. During the Conservative rule of the 1980s and 1990s, many Scots were left feeling disenfranchized by and resentful of the Westminster government. However, with the Labour party victory in the 1997 general election came manifesto promises of dramatic constitutional reform, endorsed in September of that year by a referendum in which Scots voted resoundingly in favour of their own parliament, with control over issues such as health, education, law and order and the environment. Elections for the historic Parliament, the first to be convened in Scotland for nearly 300 years, were held in May 1999, and it was officially vested with power by the Queen in an inspiring ceremony in Edinburgh on July 1, 1999. As the new Scottish government begins to make its mark on the day-to-day running of the country, larger questions about the future of the United Kingdom linger. The debate remains fierce, both within the new Parliament and without, over whether this quasi-federal devolution of power or complete independence within the European Union will better serve Scotland, and while most Scots welcome the way in which recent events have heightened their sense of identity and importance, they also acknowledge the challenges inherent in converting expectation and optimism into tangible progress.

Where to go

If you're short of time, you can still sample a little of everything by starting at either – or both – of the country's great cities, Glasgow and Edinburgh, before moving on up the west coast, where stunning land and seascapes are studded with reminders of Scotland's long and fractious history.

Travelling around mainland Scotland is comparatively easy: the **road** network reaches almost every corner of the country, **trains** serve the major towns and an extensive **bus** system links all but the most remote villages. **Hikers** are well served, too: all of the

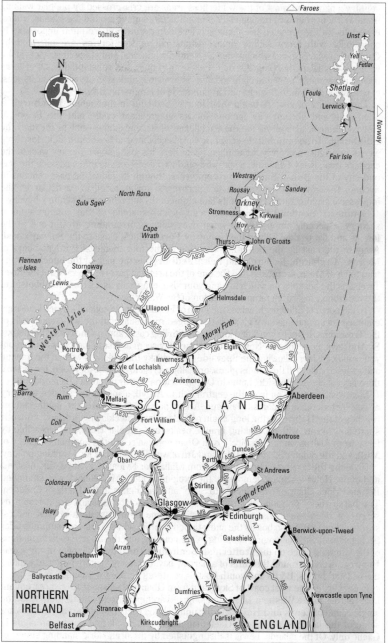

country's parks and most of the wilderness areas are crisscrossed by popular walking trails. Without your own transport it's more difficult to move around the islands, where, especially on the Western Isles, bus services deteriorate and are often impossible to coordinate with ferry sailing times. Almost all of the **ferries** are operated by Caledonian MacBrayne, who provide a splendidly punctual and efficient service, along with various island-hopping discount tickets to reduce the substantial costs of ferry travel. Reasonably priced accommodation is available almost everywhere, at its least expensive in the youth hostels, and in hundreds of family-run B&Bs.

The majority of visitors begin their tour of Scotland in the capital, **Edinburgh**, a handsome and ancient city famous for its magnificent castle and the Palace of Holyroodhouse, as well as for the excellence of its museums – not to mention the **Edinburgh International Festival**, a world-acclaimed arts shindig held for three weeks in August and early September. From here it's just a short journey west to the capital's rival, lively **Glasgow**, a sprawling industrial metropolis that was once the second city of the British Empire. In recent years, though its industrial base remains in decline, Glasgow has done much to improve its image, aided in particular by the impressive architectural legacy of its late eighteenth- and nineteenth-century heyday.

Southern Scotland, often underrated, features some of the country's finest scenery, especially among the elevated river valleys surrounding **Moffat** and in the forests and flat-peaked hills of the **Galloway Forest Park**, close to the **Solway coast**. Away to the east lie the better-known ruins of the four medieval Border abbeys of Melrose, Dryburgh, Jedburgh and Kelso. **Jedburgh** is the pick of the bunch, but the trim town of **Melrose**, tucked into the one of the prettiest parts of the valley of the River Tweed, is the best peg on which to hang your visit, especially as it's close to Abbotsford, the intriguing, treasure-crammed mansion of Sir Walter Scott.

To the north of Edinburgh, across the Firth of Forth, Central Scotland's varied landscape embraces deep and shadowy glens, jagged-edged mountains and the well-walked hills of the **Trossachs**. It's here you'll find impressive **Stirling** castle and, on the coast, prosperous **St Andrews**, home of golf. Northeast Scotland may seem at first to have less to offer, but you could consider following the **Speyside** malt whisky trail, taking a walk in the tranquil and majestic valleys of the **Angus glens**, or making a visit to oil-rich **Aberdeen**, the nation's third largest city, or **Deeside**, home to Queen Victoria's "dear paradise", Balmoral.

Most visitors move on from the central belt to **Argyll**, a sparsely populated territory of sea lochs and mountains. Mainland Argyll points out towards the southernmost reaches of the **Hebrides**, the long chain of rocky islands necklacing Scotland's Atlantic shoreline. **Arran**, with its striking granite peaks, and popular **Bute**, are accessible by ferry from Ardrossan in Ayrshire. From Oban you can reach the gorgeous scenery of **Mull**, and the quieter islands of **Islay** and **Jura**, wonderful places for a walking holiday.

Up along the coast, reached by boat from Mallaig or Kyleakin, is **Skye**, the most visited of the Hebrides, made famous by the exploits of Flora MacDonald, who smuggled Bonnie Prince Charlie "over the sea to Skye" after his defeat at the Battle of Culloden. The harsh rocky promontories that make up the bulk of the island are serrated by scores of deep sea lochs, together creating some of the western coast's fiercest scenery. The island also boasts the snow-tipped **Cuillin**, whose clustered summits offer perhaps the most challenging climbing in the country, and the bizarre rock formations of the Quiraing ridge on the **Trotternish peninsula**. The only settlement of any size is **Portree**, draped around the cliffs of a narrow bay, but many visitors prefer to explore the isolated hotels, B&Bs and youth hostels scattered across the island.

From Uig, on the west coast of Skye, and from Oban and Ullapool, there are frequent boats across to the **Western Isles**, an elongated archipelago extending south from the single island of **Lewis and Harris**, to the uninhabited islets below **Barra**. The Isles are some of the last bastions of the Gaelic language, and you'll find most road signs in Gaelic only. Of the islands, Lewis is distinguished by the prehistoric standing stones of

Calanais (Callanish), one of the best-preserved monuments of its type in Europe, while North Harris possesses a remarkably hostile landscape of forbiddingly bare mountains giving way to the wide sandy beaches and lunar-like hills of South Harris.

Back on the mainland, the **Highlands**, whose multitude of mountains, sea cliffs, glens and lochs cover the northern two-thirds of the country, is the region which best represents the tourist image of wild Scotland. Its great popularity belies its stark remoteness, despite a number of internationally known sights, not least **Loch Ness**, midway along the Great Glen and home to the eponymous monster. Inverness, near the site of the **Battle of Culloden**, is an obvious base for exploring the region, although **Fort William**, at the opposite end of the Great Glen close by **Ben Nevis**, Scotland's highest peak, is a possible alternative, especially if you're heading west.

In the far north, boats leave for the cluster of islands that make up the agricultural **Orkney Islands**. By far the most picturesque town is the port of **Stromness**, the main point of arrival for those coming by boat, while the capital, **Kirkwall**, boasts a magnificent medieval cathedral. Further on, 200 miles north of Aberdeen, are the much more rugged **Shetland Islands**, where the bustling and historic harbour at Lerwick shelters craft from every corner of the North Atlantic. Orkney and Shetland, both with a rich Norse heritage, differ not only from each other, but also quite distinctly, in dialect and culture, from mainland Scotland. These far-flung, sea- and wind-buffeted islands offer some of the country's wildest scenery, finest bird-watching and most fascinating archeological remains.

When to go

The pressure systems rolling in off the Atlantic pretty much control Scotland's volatile **climate**, especially on the west coast, where a bright, sunny morning can soon turn into a wet and windy afternoon. The west coast is appreciably wetter than the rest of the country, but milder in winter, due to the moderating influence of the Gulf Stream. There's no way of predicting when the fine weather will arrive, though spring and early autumn have proved good bets in recent years: you just have to trust your luck and be well prepared, even in high summer. Always pack warm and waterproof clothing – and an umbrella.

SCOTLAND'S CLIMATE												

Average daily maximum temperatures in °C and monthly rainfall in mm

	Jan	Feb	Mar	Apr	May	June	July	Aug	Sept	Oct	Nov	Dec
Dumfries												
°C	5.6	6.0	8.2	11.2	14.4	17.3	18.3	18.1	15.9	12.9	8.6	6.8
mm	103	72	66	55	71	63	77	93	104	106	109	104
Edinburgh												
°C	6.2	6.4	8.5	11.2	14.2	17.1	18.4	18.2	16.3	13.3	9	71
mm	47	39	39	38	49	45	69	73	57	56	58	56
Fort William												
°C	6.3	6.7	8.6	11.2	14.5	16.6	17.2	17.3	15.4	12.8	8.8	7.3
mm	200	132	152	111	103	124	137	150	199	215	220	238
Lerwick												
°C	5.1	4.9	6	7.8	10	12.5	13.7	14	12.5	10.3	7.4	6
mm	127	93	93	72	64	64	67	78	113	119	140	147
Perth												
°C	5.7	6	8.4	11.8	14.9	18	19.1	18.6	16.2	12.9	8.5	6.6
mm	70	52	47	43	57	51	67	72	63	65	69	82
Tiree												
°C	7.2	7	8.3	10.3	12.7	14.8	15.8	16.1	14.7	12.6	9.6	8.2
mm	120	71	77	60	56	66	79	83	123	125	123	123
Wick												
°C	5.6	5.7	7.3	9.3	11.3	14.2	15.4	15.4	14.1	11.8	8.2	6.5
mm	81	58	55	45	47	49	61	74	68	73	90	82

PART ONE

THE

BASICS

GETTING THERE FROM THE USA AND CANADA

The majority of airlines fly from the USA and Canada to London with connections to any number of Scottish airports (see p.4). However, if you are planning on travelling throughout the British Isles you might want to fly into London and take a slower, more scenic route up to Scotland, either by rail or road.

Only **Glasgow** is served by nonstop direct flights from North America. Flights to **Edinburgh** tend to route through London or Dublin; to get to **Aberdeen** or **Inverness** you can fly to London or Manchester and hop on a British Airways, British Midland, or Air UK shuttle. Aberdeen is also well served with flights from Paris, Amsterdam and Scandinavia. For the **Scottish Islands** there are many internal flights from Glasgow and Edinburgh, or you can take any of a number of ferries from the west coast or from Aberdeen. See p.11 for the full picture on flying to Scotland from other parts of Britain.

Figure on seven hours' flying time nonstop from New York to Glasgow, or seven hours to London with an extra hour and a quarter to Glasgow or Edinburgh (not including stopover time). Add an extra four or five hours to travel from the West Coast. Most eastbound flights cross the Atlantic overnight, reaching Britain the next morning, although a few flights from the East Coast leave early in the morning, landing late the same evening.

SHOPPING FOR TICKETS

Barring special offers, the absolute cheapest of the airlines' published fares is a winter **Super Apex** ticket, sometimes known as a "Eurosaver". However, these are only available at certain times of the year and on certain routes, and your stay is limited to between seven and 21 days. You're more likely, therefore, to get an **Apex** ticket, which also carries certain restrictions: you have to book – and pay – at least 21 days before departure, spend at least seven days abroad (maximum stay three months), and you tend to get penalized if you change your schedule. Some airlines also issue **Special Apex** tickets to people younger than 24, often extending the maximum stay to a year. In addition, many airlines offer youth or student fares to **under-26s**; a passport or driving licence are sufficient proof of age, though these tickets are subject to availability and can have eccentric booking conditions. It's worth remembering that most cheap return fares involve spending at least one Saturday night away and that many tickets will only permit you a percentage refund if you need to cancel or alter your journey, so make sure you check the restrictions carefully before buying a ticket.

You can normally cut costs further by going through a **specialist flight agent** – either a **consolidator**, who buys up blocks of tickets from the airlines and sells them at a discount, or a **discount agent**, who in addition to selling discounted flights may also offer special student and youth fares and a range of other travel-related services such as insurance, rail passes, car rentals, tours and the like. Bear in mind, though, that these companies make their money by dealing in bulk – don't expect them to answer lots of questions, and remember that the penalties for changing your plans can be stiff. Some agents specialize in **charter flights**, which may be cheaper than anything available on a scheduled flight, but again departure dates are fixed and withdrawal penalties are high (check the refund policy). If you travel a lot, **discount travel clubs** are another option – the annual membership fee may be worth it for benefits such as cut-price air tickets and car rental.

However, you shouldn't automatically assume that tickets purchased through a travel specialist will be cheapest – once you get a quote, check with the airlines and you may turn up an even better deal. **Students** might be able to find cheaper flights through the major student travel agencies, such as STA Travel, Nouvelles Frontières and, for Canadian students, Travel CUTS.

A further possibility is to see if you can arrange a **courier flight**, although the hit-or-miss nature of these makes them most suitable for the single traveller who travels light and has a very flexible schedule. In return for shepherding a parcel through customs and possibly giving up your baggage allowance, you can expect to get a heavily discounted ticket. For information about courier flights you could contact Now Voyager (☎212/431-1616) in New York. For more options, consult *A Simple Guide to Courier Travel* (Pacific Data Sales Publishing).

If you are travelling to Scotland as part of a much longer journey, you might want to consider

AIRLINES IN NORTH AMERICA

Air Canada ☎1-800/776-3000; in Canada ☎1-888/247-2262; *www.aircanada.ca*

Air France ☎1-800/237-2747; in Canada ☎1-800/667-2747; *www.airfrance.fr*

American Airlines ☎1-800/433-7300; *www.americanair.com*

British Airways ☎1-800/247-9297; in Canada ☎1-800/668-1059; *www.british-airways.com*

British Midland ☎1-800/788-0555; *www.iflybritishmidland.com*

Continental Airlines ☎1-800/231-0856; *www.flycontinental.com*

Delta Airlines ☎1-800/241-4141; in Canada ☎1-800/221-1212; *www.delta-air.com*

Iberia ☎1-800/772-4642; *www.iberia.com*

Icelandair ☎1-800/223-5500; *www.icelandair.is*

Lufthansa ☎1-800/645-3880; in Canada ☎1-800/563-5954; *www.lufthansa.com*

Sabena ☎1-800/955-2000; *www.sabena-usa.com*

Swissair ☎1-800/221-4750; in Canada ☎1-800/267-9477; *www.swissair.com*

TWA ☎1-800/892-4141; *www.twa.com*

United Airlines ☎1-800/538.2929; *www.ual.com*

US Airways ☎1-800/662-1015; *www.usairways.com*

Virgin Atlantic Airways ☎1-800/862-8621; *www.fly.virgin.com*

buying a **Round-the-World (RTW) ticket**. Some travel agents can sell you an "off-the-shelf" RTW ticket that will have you touching down in about half a dozen cities (London is easily arranged, but a Scottish connection will probably have to be added on separately); others will have to assemble one for you, which can be tailored to your needs but is likely to be more expensive.

The newest tool for finding low price air fares is the **World Wide Web**. There are a number of new sites, where you can look up fares and even book tickets. You can search in the travel sections of your Web browser, or try one of the following locations: Travelocity at *www.travelocity.com*; Travel Information Service at *www.ibm.tiss.com*; or FLIFO Cyber Travel Agent at *www.flifo.com*. In addition, you could link up with Discount Airfares Worldwide On-Line at *www.etn.nl/discount.htm*, which is a hub of consolidator and discount agent Web links, maintained by the non-profit European Travel Network.

Regardless of where you buy your ticket, **fares** will depend on the season. Fares to Scotland are highest from around early June to mid-September, when the weather is best; they drop during the "shoulder" seasons – mid-September to early November, and mid-April to early June – and you'll get the best prices during the low season, November through to April, when only a few hardy souls feel like vacationing in Scotland (excluding Christmas and New Year when prices are hiked up and seats are at a premium). Note also that flying at the weekend

ordinarily adds up to $50 to the round-trip fare; price ranges quoted below assume midweek travel.

FLIGHTS FROM THE USA

There are several daily **nonstop flights to Glasgow** from US cities: British Airways flies from New York, American from Chicago, and Northwest from Boston. You can also fly to London on any of those airlines, as well as on Virgin, TWA, Continental and Delta, and take a connecting flight to Scotland.

Low-season **Apex** fares to Glasgow from New York and other East Coast cities cost $400–500, and from the West Coast $500–600. During the shoulder season prices rise to $500–550 from New York, $700–800 from Los Angeles, and in the summer fares can reach $700–950 from New York and up to $1100 from Los Angeles.

For direct flights to London, British Airways, British Midland, Air UK, EasyJet and Ryanair offer the greatest selection of onward connections to Scotland (see p.11). Aer Lingus also serves Edinburgh, and United can ticket you straight through to several Scottish destinations on British Midland. Flying to Manchester in the north of England is another possibility, though this won't be any cheaper than the direct Apex fare to Glasgow.

FLIGHTS FROM CANADA

Air Canada flies daily nonstop to **Glasgow from Toronto** in summer (four times a week in winter).

From other Canadian cities you can fly via London on Air Canada or British Airways (see p.10 for details of onward travel to Scotland), or alternatively fly to Chicago, New York or Boston and pick

DISCOUNT TRAVEL COMPANIES IN THE USA AND CANADA

Air Brokers International, 323 Geary St, Suite 411, San Francisco, CA 94102 (☎1-800/883-3273 or ☎ 415/397-1383, *www.airbrokers.com*). Consolidator and specialist in RTW and Circle Pacific tickets.

Air Courier Association, 15000 W. 6th Ave., Suite 203, Golden, CO 80401 (☎1-800/282-1202 or ☎303/278-8810, *www.aircourier.org*). Courier flight broker. Annual fee $64 ($25 membership fee plus $39 annual fee).

Airhitch, 2641Broadway, New York, NY 10025 (☎1-800/326-2009 or ☎212/864-2000, *www.airhitch.org*). Standby-seat broker: For a set price, they guarantee to get you on a flight as close to your preferred destination as possible, within a week.

Council Travel, 205 E 42nd St, New York, NY 10017 (☎1-888-COUNCIL, *www.counciltravel.com*), and branches in many other US cities. Student/budget travel agency.

Discount Airfares Worldwide On-Line (*www.etn.nl/discount.htm*). A hub of consolidator and discount agent Web links, maintained by the nonprofit European Travel Network.

Educational Travel Centre, 438 N Frances St, Madison, WI 53703 (☎1-800/747-5551 or ☎608/256-5551, *www.edtrav.com*). Student/youth and consolidator fares.

High Adventure Travel, 442 Post St., Suite 400, San Francisco, CA 94102 (☎1-800/350-0612 or ☎415/912-5600, *www.highadv.com*). Round-the-world and Circle Pacific tickets. The Web site features an interactive database called "Farebuilder" that lets you build your own RTW itinerary.

International Association of Air Travel Couriers, 220 S. Dixie Hwy, #3, Lake Worth, FL 33460 (☎561/582-8320, *www.courier.org*). Courier flight broker. Membership $45 per year.

International Travel Network/Airlines of the Web (*www.itn.net/airlines*). Online air travel info and reservations site.

New Frontiers/Nouvelles Frontières, 12 E 33rd St, New York, NY 10016 (☎1-800/366-6387 or ☎212/779-0600, *www.new-frontiers.com*); 1000 Sherbrook East, Suite 720, Montréal, H2L 1L3 (☎514/526-8444); and other branches in LA, San Francisco and Québec City. French discount travel firm.

Now Voyager, 74 Varick St, Suite 307, New York, NY 10013 (☎212/431-1616, *www.nowvoyagertravel.com*). Lesbian and gay-friendly courier flight broker and consolidator.

Skylink, 265 Madison Ave, 5th floor, New York, NY 10016 (☎1-800/AIR-ONLY or ☎212/599-0430) with branches in Chicago, Los Angeles, Montréal, Toronto, and Washington DC. Consolidator.

STA Travel, Head Office: 5900 Wiltshire Blvd, Suite 2110, Los Angeles, CA 90036 (☎1-800/777-0112, *www.sta-travel.com*), and other branches in the New York, San Francisco, Boston, Miami, Chicago, Seattle, Philadelphia and Washington DC areas. Worldwide discount travel firm specializing in student/youth fares; also student IDs, travel insurance, car rental, rail passes, etc.

Student Flights, 5010 E Shea Blvd, Suite 104A, Scottsdale, AZ 85254 (☎1-800/255-8000 or ☎602/951-1177, *www.isecard.com*). Student/youth fares, student IDs.

TFI Tours International, 34 W 32nd St, 12th floor, New York, NY 10001 (☎1-800/745-8000 or ☎212/736-1140). Consolidator.

Travac Tours, 989 6th Ave, 16th floor, New York NY 10018 (☎1-800/872-8800 or 212/563-3303, *www.travac.com*). Consolidator and charter broker. They will fax current fares from their fax line: 1/888-872-8327.

Travel Avenue, 10 S Riverside Plaza, Suite 1404, Chicago, IL 60606 (☎1-800/333-3335 or ☎312/876-6866, *www.tipc.com*). Full-service travel agent that offers discounts in the form of rebates.

Travel CUTS, 187 College St, Toronto, ON M5T 1P7 (☎1-800/667-2887 or ☎416/979-2406, *www.travelcuts.com*), and other branches all over Canada, including San Francisco (☎415/247-1800). Organization specializing in student fares, IDs and other travel services.

Travelocity (*www.travelocity.com*). Online consolidator.

UniTravel, 11737 Administration Dr, Suite 120, St Louis, MO 63146 (☎1-800/325-2222 or ☎314/569-2501, *www.unitravel.com*). Consolidator.

Worldtek Travel, 111 Water St, New Haven, CT 06511 (☎1/800-243-1723, *www.worldtek.com*) Discount travel agency for worldwide travel.

Worldwide Discount Travel Club, 1674 Meridian Ave, Suite 206, Miami Beach, FL 33139 (☎305/534-2082) Discount travel club.

SPECIALIST TOUR OPERATORS

Abercrombie & Kent (☎1-800/323-7308, www.abercrombiekent.com). Land and rail tours of Scotland.

Above the Clouds Trekking (☎1-800/233-4499, www.gorp.com/abvclds.htm). Week-long walking tours of the Highlands.

British Coastal Trails (☎1-800/473-1210, www.bctwalk.com). Walking trips in the Borders and Western Isles.

British Travel International (☎1-800/327-6097). Offers self-catering country cottages and B&B accommodation in Scotland and can arrange air tickets, rail and bus passes.

CIE Tours International (☎1-800/243-8687 or 973/292-3899, www.cietours.com). Escorted bus tours and deluxe castle tours of Scotland.

Especially Britain (☎1-800/869-0538). Fly-drives and independent rail tours with accommodation in B&Bs, country houses and castles.

Golf International Inc (☎800/833-1389). Scottish golf vacation specialist.

Himalayan Travel (☎1-800/225-2380, www.gorp.com/himtravel.htm). Hiking and walking tours of Scotland.

Home At First (☎1-800/523-5842). Rents out cottages and flats in Scotland.

Jerry Quinlan's Celtic Golf (☎1-800/535-6148 or 609/884-8090, www.jqcelticgolf.com). Customized golf tours of Scotland's best links.

Lord Addison Travel (☎1-800/326-0170, www.lordaddison.com). Small escorted specialist tours, including garden tours and history tours, such as the "Bonnie Prince Charlie tour".

Prestige Tours (☎1-800/890-7375). A variety of Scottish tours.

Sterling Tours (☎1-800/727-4359, www.sterlingtours.com). Scottish specialist offering a variety of independent itineraries, some packages.

up a nonstop flight to Glasgow from there. In addition, Air Canada also has direct flights from Toronto to Manchester.

Low-season midweek Apex fares from Toronto and Montréal to Glasgow should set you back CAN$600–700, and from Vancouver CAN$800–900. During the shoulder seasons fares are CAN$650–750 from Toronto, CAN$850–950 from Vancouver, and in high season expect to pay $750–950 from Toronto and $950–1150 from Vancouver.

PACKAGES AND INCLUSIVE TOURS

Although you may want to see Scotland at your own speed, you shouldn't dismiss out of hand the idea of a **package deal**. Many agents and airlines put together very flexible deals, sometimes amounting to no more than a flight plus car or train pass and accommodation, which can actually work

out to be better value than the same arrangements made on arrival, especially in the case of fly-drive deals, as car rental is expensive in Britain.

There are also many tour operators that specialize in travel to Scotland. Most can do packages of the standard highlights, and many also organize **walking or cycling trips** through the countryside, with any number of theme tours based around Scotland's literary heritage, history, pubs, gardens, golf – you name it. A few possibilities are listed in the box below, and a good travel agent will be able to point out others. For further listings, contact the British Tourist Authority (☎1-800/462-2748) or check out the Scottish Tourist Board's Web site at www.holiday.scotland.net. Be sure to examine the fine print of any deal, and make sure the operator is a member of the United States Tour Operator Association (USTOA) or approved by the American Society of Travel Agents (ASTA).

GETTING THERE FROM AUSTRALIA AND NEW ZEALAND

There are no direct flights to Scotland from Australia or New Zealand, and mostly you will have to route through London then get an onward flight north. Travelling time is nearly twenty-four hours, so you might be better off including a stopover – and a good night's sleep – in your itinerary. Fares obviously depend on the time of the year: low-season rates run from mid-January to the end of February and October to mid-November; high season is mid-May to August, and December to mid-January; and shoulder season is the rest of the year. Tickets purchased direct from the airlines tend to be more expensive, while travel agents can offer better deals and have the latest information on special offers and stopovers – the best discounts are often available through Flight Centres, STA and travel.com.au who can also advise on visa regulations. Students and under-26s can usually get a further ten percent off published prices.

All the fares quoted below are from Australia's east coast, unless otherwise stated, to London. From Perth you'll pay A$200–400 less on flights routed through Asia and Africa, and the same amount more for flights via the Americas. In addition, you'll need to add on an extra A$80–200, depending on the season, for the flight to Glasgow or Edinburgh; most travel agents will be able to book this leg for you in advance, though you may find it cheaper to wait and pick up a low-cost flight in London (see p.10 for details). Alternatively, you may prefer to travel overland from London by bus or train. BritRail train passes can be good value if you intend to do a lot of travelling in the UK, but must be bought before you leave home (see p.26 for full details).

The cheapest scheduled flights to London are **via Asia** with Gulf Air or Thai Airways, which charge A$1350–1500 in low season, and A$1760 in high season, and involve a transfer in the carrier's hub city. For A$1600 in low season to A$1815 in peak season, you can fly with Virgin Atlantic and either Malaysia Airlines via Kuala Lumpur or Ansett via Hong Kong. In the mid-range, Lufthansa and Singapore Airlines all fly direct to London for A$1700–1900, while British Airways and Qantas quote published through fares to Edinburgh or Glasgow of A$1760 in low season up to A$2195 in high season. From Perth, Royal Brunei Airlines offer a fare to London of A$1455 year-round. Many of the airlines also offer fly-drive packages and stopovers in their hub cities for no extra cost; Qantas, for example, flies from all major Australian cities daily, including a stopover in Asia and thirteen-day car hire in London, with fares starting at A$1799 in low season to A$2199 in peak season.

Via Africa, the lowest fares start at A$1999, with South African Airways via Johannesburg to London. Qantas/British Airways include a free stopover in Perth and Johannesburg or Harare on the way out, and Asia on the return, for A$2019–2600.

Flights are pricier **via North America**, with United Airlines offering the cheapest deal via Los Angeles and either New York, Washington or Chicago for A$1950–2430, while Air New Zealand via Auckland and Los Angeles, and Canadian Airlines via Toronto or Vancouver, both charge around A$1975–2450.

Currently the best fare of all on offer is the Britannia Airways or Airtours **charter flights** which run several times a month to Gatwick and Manchester via Singapore and Bahrain. Fares start at A$1099 in low season and range up to A$1759 in high season, though the flight only runs between November and March and is definitely a "no-frills" service. For extra money they offer the option of upgrading to a better quality of in-flight meals.

From New Zealand, the cheapest scheduled flights to London Heathrow (with an extra NZ$150–250 for flights to Edinburgh and

AIRLINES IN AUSTRALIA AND NEW ZEALAND

Air New Zealand, Australia ☎132476; New Zealand ☎09/357 3000; *www.airnz.co.nz*. Daily direct flights to London Heathrow from major Australian cities via Asia and from major New Zealand cities via Los Angeles.

Airtours/Britannia Airways, Australia ☎02/9247 4833. Several flights a month from Sydney, Adelaide, Brisbane, Melbourne, Perth and Auckland to London Gatwick and once a week from Sydney to Manchester via Singapore and Bahrain; flights only run between November and March.

British Airways, Australia ☎02/8904 8800; New Zealand ☎09/356 8690; *www.british-airways.com*. Daily direct flights from Sydney to London Heathrow via Singapore/Los Angeles, and twice-weekly via Harare or Johannesburg; daily flights from Auckland via Los Angeles, with onward connections to Scotland.

Canadian Airlines, Australia ☎1300/655 767; New Zealand ☎09/309 0735; *www.british-airways.com*. Several flights a week to London Heathrow via Vancouver/Toronto from Sydney, Melbourne and Auckland.

Cathay Pacific, Australia ☎131747; New Zealand ☎09/379 0861; *www.british-airways.com*. Several flights a week to London and Manchester from Brisbane, Sydney, Melbourne, Perth, Cairns and Auckland, via Hong Kong.

Gulf Air, Australia ☎02/9244 2199; *www.british-airways.com*. Several flights weekly from Sydney to London via Singapore and Bahrain or Abu Dhabi.

Japanese Airlines (JAL), Australia ☎02/9272 1111; New Zealand ☎09/379 9906. Daily flights to London Heathrow via Tokyo or Osaka from Brisbane and Sydney, and several weekly flights from Cairns and Auckland: onward connections to Edinburgh on British Midland.

KLM, Australia ☎02/9231 6333 or 1-800/505 747; *www.klm.com*. Twice-weekly flights from Sydney to London Heathrow via Amsterdam and Singapore.

Korean Air, Australia ☎02/9262 6000; New Zealand ☎09/307 3687. Several flights a week to London from Sydney, Brisbane, Auckland and Christchurch, via Seoul.

Malaysia Airlines (MAS), Australia ☎13 2627; New Zealand ☎09/373 2741. Several flights a week to London Heathrow from Sydney, Melbourne, Perth and Auckland via Kuala Lumpur.

Qantas, Australia ☎131313; New Zealand ☎09/357 8900 or 0800/808 767; *www.qantas.com.au*. Daily flights from major Australasian cities to London Heathrow via Singapore, Bangkok or Hong Kong.

Royal Brunei Airlines, Australia ☎07/3221 7757. Three flights weekly to London from Brisbane, and two weekly from Darwin and Perth, via Abu Dhabi and Brunei.

Singapore Airlines, Australia ☎131011; New Zealand ☎09/379 3209. Daily flights to London Heathrow and Manchester from Brisbane, Sydney, Melbourne, Perth and Auckland via Singapore.

South African Airways (SAA), Australia ☎02/9223 4402; New Zealand ☎09/309 9132; *www.qantas.com.au*. Flights to London from major Australian cities via Perth and Johannesburg/Harare: code-shares with Qantas.

Thai Airways, Australia ☎1300/651960; New Zealand ☎09/377 3886; *www.thaiair.om*. Several flights a week to London Heathrow via Bangkok from Brisbane, Sydney, Melbourne, Perth and Auckland.

United Airlines, Australia ☎131777; New Zealand ☎09/379 3800; *www.ual.com*. Daily flights to London Heathrow and Manchester via Los Angeles, Chicago, New York or Washington from Sydney, Melbourne and Auckland. Code-share arrangements with Malaysia Airlines and Alitalia.

Virgin Atlantic, Australia ☎02/9244 2747; *www.flyvirgin.com/atlantic/*. Daily flights to London Heathrow via Kuala Lumpur from Sydney, Melbourne, and Adelaide: code-shares with Malaysia Airlines and Ansett.

Glasgow) are with Korean Air, Thai Airways (in conjunction with KLM) or JAL, all of whom fly via their respective home cities for around NZ$2050–2280. British Airways' daily flight from Auckland costs from NZ$2780 (low season) to NZ$3170 (high season), including a connecting flight to Edinburgh or Glasgow. The most direct

route to London is via North America with United Airlines, stopping in Los Angeles and Chicago, for NZ$2770 (low season) to NZ$3170 (high season). As with Australia, the cheapest fare of all is on Britannia Airways' charter flight from Auckland to Gatwick and Manchester, which runs several times a month from November to March. Fares

DISCOUNT AGENTS IN AUSTRALIA AND NEW ZEALAND

Anywhere Travel, 345 Anzac Parade, Kingsford, Sydney (☎02/9663 0411, *anywhere@ozemail.com.au*).

Budget Travel, 16 Fort St, Auckland, plus branches around the city (☎09/366 0061 and ☎0800/808 040).

Destinations Unlimited, 3 Milford Rd, Auckland (☎09/373 4033).

Flight Centres, 82 Elizabeth St, Sydney, plus branches nationwide (☎13 1600); 205 Queen St, Auckland (☎09/309 6171), plus branches nationwide.

STA Travel (*www.statravelaus.com.au*), 702 Harris St, Ultimo, Sydney; 256 Flinders St, Melbourne, plus offices in state capitals and major universities (fastfare telesales ☎1300/360 960; nearest branch 131776); 10 High St, Auckland, plus branches in Wellington, Christchurch, Dunedin, Palmerston North, Hamilton and at major universities (telesales ☎09/366 6673).

Status Travel, 22 Cavenagh St, Darwin (☎08/8941 1843).

Student Uni Travel, 92 Pitt St, Sydney (☎02/9232 8444) plus branches in Melbourne, Darwin, Brisbane, Cairns and Perth.

Thomas Cook, 175 Pitt St, Sydney; 257 Collins St, Melbourne, plus branches in other state capitals (telesales ☎1800/063 913; nearest branch 131771); Level 5, Telstra Business Centre, Auckland (☎09/359 5200).

Trailfinders, 8 Spring St, Sydney (☎02/9247 7666).

Travel.com.au (*www.travel.com.au*), 80 Clarence St, Sydney (☎02/9290 1500).

Usit Beyond, corner of Shortland and Jean Batten Place, Auckland (☎09/379 4224) plus branches in Christchurch, Hamilton, Palmerston North and Wellington.

UK Flight Shop (*www.ukflightshop.com.au*), 7 Macquarie Place, Sydney (☎02/9247 4833) plus branches in Melbourne and Perth.

SPECIALIST TOUR AGENTS

Adventure Specialists, 69 Liverpool St, Sydney (☎02/9261 2927). Offers a selection of walking and cycling holidays throughout Scotland.

Adventure Travel Company, 164 Parnell Rd, Parnell, East Auckland (☎09/379 9755). New Zealand agents for Peregrine Adventures.

Adventure World, 73 Walker St, North Sydney (☎02/9956 7766 and 1800/221 931), plus branches in Adelaide, Brisbane, Melbourne and Perth; 101 Great South Rd, Remuera, Auckland (☎09/524 5118). Based in London, but with an extensive variety of tours throughout Scotland.

Best of Britain, 352a Military Rd, Cremorne, Sydney (☎02/9909 1055). Can arrange flights, accommodation, car rental, tours, canal boats and B&Bs throughout Scotland.

Explore Holidays, 55 Blaxland Rd, Ryde NSW 2112 (☎02/9857 6200). Wholesaler of guesthouse, B&B and hotel accommodation throughout Scotland, as well as Military Tattoo packages.

Peregrine Adventures (*www.peregrine.net.au*), 258 Lonsdale St, Melbourne (☎03/9663 8611), plus offices in Brisbane, Sydney, Adelaide and Perth. Adventure travel company specializing in small-group walking and cycling holidays in Scotland, with travel between main points by minibus.

Sundowners, Suite 15, 600 Lonsdale St, Melbourne (☎03/9600 1934 or 1800/337 089). Russian and Trans-Siberian Railway specialists; escorted group tours and independent travel by train to Scotland via Moscow.

Wiltrans/Maupintour, Level 10, 189 Kent St, Sydney (☎02/9255 0899).
Fully escorted tours around Scotland's historic homes and gardens, staying in upmarket accommodation.

YHA Travel Centre, 422 Kent St, Sydney (☎02/9261 1111); 205 King St, Melbourne (☎03/9670 9611); 38 Sturt St, Adelaide (☎08/8231 5583); 154 Roma St, Brisbane (☎07/3236 1680); 236 William St, Perth (☎08/9227 5122); 69 Mitchell St, Darwin (☎08/8981 2560); 28 Criterion St, Hobart (☎03/6234 9617).
Organizes budget accommodation throughout England, Wales and Scotland for YHA members.

from Auckland are NZ$1620 low season to NZ$2110 in high season.

If you're visiting Scotland as part of a longer trip, a **round-the-world (RTW) ticket** can work out very good value. Currently the best deals on offer are the Qantas/British Airways "Global Explorer" or "One World" tickets allowing four stops (including Glasgow or Edinburgh) costing from A$1895/NZ$3070. The "Star Alliance" between Ansett, Air New Zealand, United Airlines, Thai Airways, Varig, SAS, Lufthansa and Air Canada allows at least six stopovers worldwide, and starts at A$2699/NZ$3300. Note that, while it's easy

enough to include London on a round-the-world itinerary, a stop in Scotland may involve back-tracking and can be harder to arrange; you may find it cheaper to buy the London to Scotland leg separately, or to travel overland (see p.12 for details).

GETTING THERE FROM BRITAIN, IRELAND AND EUROPE

Crossing the border from England into Scotland is straightforward, with train and bus services forming part of the British national network. Trains from London to Glasgow or Edinburgh take between four and six hours, while coaches take at least eight hours. Flying will obviously save you an enormous amount of time, particularly if you're heading out to the Highlands and Islands, though fares are only really competitive on popular routes such as London to Edinburgh. You can also reach mainland Scotland direct by ferry, in under an hour from Ireland, and in twenty-four hours from Norway. On the whole, the cheapest and quickest way to reach Scotland from the rest of Europe is by plane.

BY PLANE

You can fly direct to Scotland's **main airports** – Edinburgh, Glasgow and Aberdeen – in an hour or so, from all three major London airports (Heathrow, Gatwick and Stansted), as well as from Luton and various other provincial airports. There are also

direct flights from Belfast, Dublin and numerous other major European airports. If you're flying on to any of Scotland's smaller airports, you'll need to change planes in order to do so (see p.30 for more details on flights within Scotland).

There are flights almost hourly to Edinburgh and Glasgow from **London**, and nearly as many to Aberdeen. As a broad guide to what you're likely to pay, reckon on around £30 for a rock-bottom one-way ticket and £50 for a return, from airlines such as EasyJet or Ryanair. These flights tend to leave from airports such as Luton and Stansted, and are often subject to rigid restrictions, but the savings can make the extra effort well worthwhile. Go, British Airways' low-cost airline, also fly from Stansted to Edinburgh, and offer competitive fares, from £70 return. The other three main carriers – British Airways, British Midland and KLM Air UK – all have special offer fares from time to time. Again, ticket prices depend very much on the restrictions. The cheaper tickets usually have to be bought at least a week in advance, apply to only a very few mid-week flights, must include a Saturday night stayover, and are either non-refundable or only partially refundable, and non-exchangeable. For a flexible, refundable fare, you're looking £100 one-way London to Glasgow, and double that for a return.

Note, too, that **airport tax**, currently £10, is levied for each single or return ticket on all domestic flights to Scotland. The tax may or may not be included in the price, and you'll almost certainly have to pay a passenger surcharge (£10) on top of that. Anyone under 26 should also check out specialist agencies such as Campus Travel or STA Travel, who offer **youth deals**, including Domestic Air Passes (also known as Hopper Passes) on British Airways flights, which can get you to Inverness and the Hebrides for a fraction of the

AIRLINES IN BRITAIN AND IRELAND

Aer Lingus (Eire ☎01/844 4777, UK ☎0645/737747, *www.aerlingus.ie*). Dublin to Edinburgh or Glasgow.

British Airways (UK ☎0345/222111; Eire ☎0141/222 2345, *www.british-airways.com*). BA fly direct to Edinburgh, Glasgow and Aberdeen from all three London airports, as well as Belfast, Birmingham, Bristol, Cardiff, Manchester and Southampton. They also fly Gatwick to Inverness, Leeds/Bradford to Aberdeen, and from Jersey to Edinburgh and Glasgow.

British Midland (UK ☎0345/554554, Eire ☎01/283 8833, *www.iflybritishmidland.com*). East Midlands to Edinburgh, Glasgow and Aberdeen, Heathrow to Edinburgh and Glasgow, and Amsterdam to Edinburgh.

EasyJet (☎01582/702900, 0870/600 0000, *www.easyjet.com*). Luton to Edinburgh, Glasgow, Aberdeen and Inverness.

Go (☎0845/605 4321, *www.go-fly.com*). BA's low-cost airline currently offers direct flights from Stansted to Edinburgh.

KLM Air UK (UK ☎0990/074074, Eire ☎0345/445588, *www.klm.com*). Amsterdam to Edinburgh, Glasgow and Aberdeen; Stansted to Glasgow and Aberdeen; London City to Edinburgh; and Norwich to Aberdeen.

Ryanair (Eire ☎01/609 7800; UK ☎0541/569569). Dublin and Stansted to Glasgow (Prestwick).

DISCOUNT AGENTS IN BRITAIN AND IRELAND

Council Travel, 28a Poland St, London W1V 3DB; (☎0171/437 7767, *www.destination-group.com*). Flights and student discounts.

North South Travel, Moulsham Mill Centre, Parkway, Chelmsford CM2 7PX (☎01245/492882). Friendly, competitive travel agency, whose profits are used to support projects in the developing world.

STA Travel (*www.statravel.co.uk*), 86 Old Brompton Rd, London SW7 3LH; 117 Euston Rd, London NW1 2SX; 38 Store St, London WC1E 7BZ; 11 Goodge St, London W1P 1FE (UK/Europe ☎0171/ 361 6161); 38 North St, Brighton, BN1 1RH (☎01273/728282); 25 Queens Rd, Bristol BS8 1QE (☎0117/929 4399); 38 Sidney St, Cambridge CB2 3HX (☎01223/366966); 75 Deansgate, Manchester M3 2BW (☎0161/834 0668); 88 Vicar Lane, Leeds LS1 7JH (☎0113/244 9212); 9 St Mary's Place, Newcastle-upon-Tyne NE1 7PG (☎0191/233 2111); 36 George St, Oxford OX1 2OJ (☎01865/792800); and branches on university campuses in London, Birmingham, Brighton, Bristol, Cambridge, Canterbury, Cardiff, Coventry, Durham, Leicestershire, Leeds, Loughborough, Nottingham, Manchester, Oxford, Sheffield and Warwick. Specialists in low-cost flights and tours for students and under-26s, though other customers welcome.

Usit Campus (*www.campustravel.co.uk*), 52 Grosvenor Gardens, London SW1W 0AG (UK/Europe ☎0171/730 3402); 541 Bristol Rd, Selly Oak, Birmingham B29 6AU (☎0121/414 1848); 61 Ditchling Rd, Brighton BN1 4SD (☎01273/570226); 37–39 Queen's Rd, Clifton, Bristol BS8 1QE (☎0117/929 2494); 5 Emmanuel St, Cambridge CB1 1NE (☎01223/324283); 166 Deansgate, Manchester M3 3FE (☎0161/833 2046, telesales 273 1721); 105–106 St Aldates, Oxford OX1 1BU (☎01865/242067), Fountain Centre, College St, Belfast BT1 6ET (☎01232/324 073); 10–11 Market Parade, Patrick St, Cork (☎021/270 900); 33 Ferryquay St, Derry (☎01504/371 888); 19 Aston Quay, Dublin 2 (☎01/602 1777 or 677 8117, Europe and UK ☎01/602 1600 or 679 8833, long-haul ☎01/602 1700); Victoria Place, Eyre Square, Galway (☎091/565 177); Central Buildings, O'Connell St, Limerick (☎061/415 064); 36–37 Georges St, Waterford (☎051/872 601). Student/youth travel specialists, with branches also in YHA shops and on university campuses all over Britain.

published fare. Addresses for discount agents are listed above.

Coming from **Ireland**, the best deals are with Ryanair, who operate three flights a day from Dublin to Glasgow Prestwick. Their cheapest fares are around IR£60 return (with an additional IR£20 airport tax), though special offers for less crop up from time to time. A fully flexible fare with Aer Lingus can cost three or four times that amount, but will allow you to change your ticket or claim a refund. From **Belfast**, your only option is British Airways, who have several daily flights to Edinburgh, Glasgow and Aberdeen; the cheapest fare is around £70 return.

BY TRAIN

Glasgow and Edinburgh are both served by frequent direct **train** services from London, and are easily reached from other main English towns and cities, though you may have to change trains en route. Two separate companies operate direct services **from London** to Scotland: GNER trains depart from King's Cross and run up the east coast to Edinburgh, while Virgin trains depart from Euston and go to Glasgow via the west coast. The **fares** of both companies are fiendishly complex; the restrictions and conditions are outlined in detail below. You can book rail tickets online via *www.thetrainline.com*, *www.gner.co.uk* and *www.virgintrains.co.uk*.

Journey times from London can be as little as 4hr 30min to Edinburgh and 5hr to Glasgow; from Manchester, reckon on around 2hr 30min to Edinburgh and 3hr to Glasgow. From either of these two points allow another 2hr 30min to Aberdeen and 3hr 30min to Inverness. Edinburgh, Glasgow, Aberdeen, Inverness and Fort William are all served by overnight **sleeper trains** from London Euston, run by ScotRail.

Eurostar operates frequent train services through the **Channel Tunnel** to London Waterloo from Lille (2hr), Paris (3hr) and Brussels (2hr 40min). You then have to change trains, and stations, to Euston or King's Cross for the onward journey. If you are driving from mainland Europe, you might want to take the frequent train service – Eurotunnel – that carries you and your car from Calais to Folkestone in 35 minutes; fares range from £84 to £169 per carload, and depend on whether you book in advance, and whether you're prepared to travel at anti-social hours.

TICKETS AND PASSES

The most flexible ticket is a **Saver** return, which can be used on all trains on the outward and return journeys. **SuperSavers**, which cost slightly less, cannot be used on a Fridays (nor on a dozen other specified days of the year), and are not valid for any peak-hour services. Saver and SuperSaver tickets are valid for a month (outward travel has to be on the date of issue), and can be used to cross from one mainline station to another via the London Underground. A variety of advance purchase tickets are issued in limited numbers on certain services: **SuperAdvance** tickets must be booked before 2pm, the day before the date of travel; **Apex** tickets have to be booked at least seven days before travelling; and **SuperApex** tickets have to be booked at least fourteen days in advance. Each of the railway companies also offer various other promotional fares from time to time, or offer the above tickets under a different name.

To take the **GNER London–Edinburgh service** as an example: a Saver return costs £79, a SuperSaver £69, a SuperAdvance £59, an Apex £49, and a SuperApex just £36. For all these tickets you should book as far in advance as you possibly can – many Apex and SuperApex are sold out weeks before the travel date, especially around Christmas and Easter. A **seat reservation** is included in all advance purchase tickets, but not with Savers and SuperSavers, though one can be booked in advance for £1 a seat. If you find yourself without a seat on a weekend or bank holiday long-distance service, you can often upgrade to first-class by paying a £10 supplement.

If you're travelling up from London it's definitely worth considering taking one of the **Caledonian Sleepers**, run by ScotRail, daily except Saturday nights from Euston. A sample Apex return fare to Edinburgh or Glasgow is £79, which includes a bed in a two-person berth; first-class customers enjoy the luxury of a single-berth cabin. Note, however, that there are no discounts for railcard holders; children pay full price, unless you go for a Family Ticket, which costs £199 return to Edinburgh or Glasgow for one adult and three children, or two adults and two children. You can usually board the train an hour before departure, and if your final destination is Edinburgh or Glasgow, you don't have to vacate the cabins until 8am, more than an hour after the train has arrived.

Although it is still theoretically possible to have your car transported via **Motorail** (☎0990/502309), the price is prohibitive. To have your car transported from London to Glasgow, for example, costs £165 one-way and £295 return (Caledonian Sleeper customers get a £50 discount). It's also extremely inconvenient, as pick up and delivery takes place at the airports and not at the train stations.

RAIL ENQUIRIES	
Eurostar	☎0990/186186
Eurotunnel	☎0990/353535
GNER	☎0345/225225
National Rail Enquiries	☎0345/484950
Rail Europe	☎0990/848848
ScotRail	☎08457/550033
Virgin	☎08457/222333

Three discount **passes**, all valid for a year, are available in Britain to nationals and foreign visitors alike. The **Young Person's Railcard** costs £18 and gives reductions of a third on all standard, Saver and SuperSaver fares to full-time students studying in Britain and anyone who is between 16 and 26 years of age. A **Senior Citizens' Railcard**, also £18 and offering reductions of a third on many tickets, is available to all those aged 60 or over. For both passes you'll need to show proof of age (for foreign visitors your passport is preferred) and provide two passport-size photographs. Foreign students will need to show proof of full-time study in Britain.

Children aged 5–15 pay half the adult fare on most journeys, but there are no discounts on Apex and SuperApex tickets. Under-fives travel free, but are not entitled to their own seat on crowded trains. The best option if you're travelling with kids is to buy a **Family Railcard**, which costs £20 and gives a variety of discounts (from a fifth to a third) for up to four adults, travelling with children (visitors will need to show their passports). Even more enticingly, it allows up to four children aged 5–15 to travel anywhere in the country for a flat fare of £2 each (which includes a seat reservation). If all your children are under five, you must buy at least one £2 fare to qualify for the discount.

If you've been resident in a European country other than the UK for at least six months, an **InterRail** pass might be a cost-effective way to travel, if Scotland is part of a longer European trip. If bought outside the UK, the passes offer a month's unlimited train travel within Britain, plus discounts on cross-Channel ferries and Eurostar – the only restriction is that they are not valid in the country of purchase. InterRail passes are now zonal: an all-zone pass costs £349 for a month (£259 for under-26s); three zones cost £309 (£229 for under-26s); two zones cost £279 (£209 for under-26s); and one zone costs £229 (£159 for under-26s), but is only valid for 22 days.

BY BUS

Inter-town **bus** services (known as **coaches** in Scotland and the rest of Britain) duplicate many train routes, often at half the price or less. The frequency of service is usually comparable to the train, and in some instances the difference in journey time isn't that great; buses are also reasonably comfortable, and on longer routes often have drinks and sandwiches available on board.

Two of the main operators between England and Scotland are National Express (☎0990/808080) and its sister company Scottish Citylink (☎0990/505050). If you're a full-time student, under 25 or over 50, you can buy a **Coach Card** for £8, valid for one year, which will get you a thirty percent discount on all fares. Children normally travel for half price, but if you buy a **Lone Parent Coach Card**, which costs £8 and lasts for a year, one child can travel for free; the £15 **Family Card** allows two children to travel for free with two adults. See "Getting around" (p.25) for details of bus and train passes for within Scotland.

Direct buses run from most provincial British cities to **Edinburgh**, **Glasgow**, **Aberdeen** and **Inverness**. Tickets are widely available from bus stations and hundreds of agents throughout England. Typical fares from London to Glasgow and Edinburgh (journeys of around eight hours) are £30 return on National Express. You can travel during the day or overnight, thus saving you the cost of overnight accommodation. The journeys to Aberdeen and Inverness take around eleven and twelve hours respectively, with the ticket to both costing under £50 return. There's also a 25 percent **discount** on bookings made seven days in advance.

If you're going to do quite a bit of travelling by bus, it might be worth buying a **Tourist Trail Pass**, which gives you unlimited travel within Britain on National Express and Scottish Citylink coaches. Passes start at £49 for two days' travel out of three; £85 for five days out of ten; £120 for seven days out of twenty-one; £187 for fourteen days out of thirty. Coach Card holders can get discounts on these prices. The passes can be bought both from major travel agents, at Gatwick and Heathrow airports and at the British Travel Centre, 1 Regent St, London W1 (walk-in service only). In Scotland, outlets include St Andrew Square Bus Station, Edinburgh, and Buchanan Street Bus Station, Glasgow, as well as other local bus stations. In **North America** these passes are available from British Travel International (☎1-800/327-6097, *www.britishtravel.com*) and US National Express (☎540/298-1395).

A fun alternative for travellers wishing to take in some of the highlights of England and Wales en route to Scotland is the popular Haggis Backpackers' London–Edinburgh **minibus tour**. Beginning in London, the bus takes three to six days to reach Edinburgh, via Bath, Stratford,

Snowdonia, Chester, York and the Lake District. Tickets cost £75 for the three-day tour and £119 for the six-day jaunt, and cover only the travel and guided tours, but not accommodation or entry to attractions. There are up to two departures a week in summer, departing from outside the OVC (Overseas Visitors' Club), 41 Longridge Rd, London SW5. For more details, contact Haggis in Edinburgh (☎0131/557 9393, *www. haggis-backpackers.com*).

BY CAR

If you're **driving** to Scotland from the south, the two main routes are up the east of England on the A1, or up the west side of the country using the M6, A74 and M74. The latter route offers at least dual-carriageway driving the whole way. It takes the best part of a day to get from London to Edinburgh or Glasgow by car. If you drive flat out and encounter no road-work delays, you can get to either city in around eight hours. If you prefer a slower, more scenic route, head off the A1 up the A68 which takes the hilly but scenic route over the border at Carter Bar, and adds an hour or so to the journey time.

BY FERRY

The only way to get to Scotland direct by **ferry from Europe** is on the Smyril Line service which links Shetland with Norway, the Faroe Islands and Iceland (mid-May to early Sept only). The most direct route is from **Bergen (Norway)** to Lerwick in Shetland and then on to Aberdeen with P&O

Scottish Ferries. The first leg of the journey to Lerwick (1 weekly) takes twelve hours, with the crossing to Aberdeen (6 weekly) taking fourteen hours. Special through fares from Bergen to Aberdeen are available for around £100 single for each passenger and another £100 if you want to take a car, plus another £50 per person if you want a berth in a cabin.

There's a greater choice of ferry services from Europe to ports in England, the most convenient being those to Newcastle, less than an hour's drive from the Scottish border, or Hull in the northeast, two hours' drive from Scotland. Tariffs on the ferries are bewilderingly complex: prices vary with the month, day or even hour at certain times of the year, not to mention how long you're staying and the size of your car. The highest prices are usually for daytime sailings in July and August, the lowest for night journeys out of season. You can often get further reductions through special offers, or by booking in advance – a sensible precaution in any case as ferries can get booked solid in peak months. Prices given below are for one-way peak period daytime sailings.

P&O North Sea Ferries sail daily to Hull from **Rotterdam and Zeebrugge** (14–15hr; £50 single for foot passengers, £120 with a small car). From Scandinavia, Fjord Line sail to Newcastle from **Bergen** and/or **Stavanger** (1–3 times weekly; 20–27hr depending on whether it's direct).

Scandinavian Seaways runs one service a week all year round from **Gothenburg (Sweden)** to Newcastle (26hr), costing £115 per person, with an extra £65 for a car. From May to

---

FERRY COMPANIES

Argyll & Antrim Steam Packet Company (UK ☎0990/523523). Ballycastle to Campbeltown.

Fjord Line (UK ☎0191/296 1313; Bergen ☎5554 8600; Stavanger ☎5152 4545). Bergen and Stavangar to Newcastle.

Hoverspeed (UK ☎0990/240241; France ☎0800/901777). Dieppe to Newhaven, Boulogne to Folkstone, and Calais or Ostend to Dover.

P&O European Ferries (Portsmouth Services ☎0870/600 3300; Irish services ☎0870/242 4777; Cherbourg ☎02/33.88.65.70). Bilbao, Cherbourg or Le Havre to Portsmouth; Larne to Cairnryan.

P&O North Sea Ferries (Hull ☎01482/377177; Rotterdam ☎01812/55555; Zeebrugge ☎050/54.34.30). Rotterdam or Zeebrugge to Hull.

P&O Scottish Ferries (Aberdeen ☎01224/572615). Lerwick and Stromness to Aberdeen.

P&O Stena Line (UK ☎0990/980222; Calais ☎03/21.46.04.40). Calais to Dover.

Scandinavian Seaways (Harwich ☎0191/293 6262; Amsterdam ☎25/553 4546; Gothenburg ☎031/650650; Hamburg ☎040/389 0371). Gothenburg or Ijmuiden (Amsterdam) to Newcastle, and Hamburg to Newcastle or Harwich.

SeaCat (UK ☎0990/523523). Belfast to Stranraer or Troon.

Smyril Line (Aberdeen ☎01224/572615; Torshavn, Faroe ☎01/5900). Bergen or Faroe to Lerwick.

Stena Line (Belfast ☎01232/747747). Belfast to Stranraer.

September they also operate a **Hamburg** to Newcastle service (21hr), four times a week, costing around £85 per person, plus another £50 for cars. The same company also runs from **Ijmuiden (Amsterdam)** to Newcastle (14hr), which costs roughly £55 per person and £60 for a car.

A further alternative is to take Eurotunnel (see p.12), or one of the very frequent ferries to England from the **French ports**; there's a greater choice of sailings this way, though the drive up to Scotland from the south coast can easily take a full day. Hoverspeed and P&O Stena Line offer regular sailings from Calais to Dover (the shortest route), for which the lowest fare for a foot passenger is £25 single (or £100 and upwards for small car). For full details of ferry routes and prices call the ferry companies direct; telephone numbers are listed in the box opposite.

From Ireland, P&O European Ferries runs several crossings daily from **Larne to Cairnryan**

(2hr by ferry; 1hr by jetliner); fares for foot passengers are £20–25 single, and £100–120 with a car. Stena Line operates numerous conventional ferries and a high-speed service daily on the **Belfast to Stranraer** route (1hr 45min–3hr 15min), at £25 single for foot passengers, and £85–130 for a car. In addition, there are daily SeaCat catamarans on this route, (just 1hr 30min), and costing £25 single for foot passengers, £85 with a car. SeaCat also run catamarans from Belfast to Troon, just outside Ayr (2hr 30min), with prices only very slightly higher. There's also a new ferry link run by the Argyll & Antrim Steam Packet Company from **Ballycastle to Campbeltown** (mid-June to Sept only; 2hr 45min), which runs twice daily. Single fares are roughly £25 for a foot passenger, and £90 for a small car. All the ferry companies also offer much cheaper five-day return fares, as well as rock-bottom day-return fares. For more details, call the companies.

RED TAPE

Citizens of all European countries – except **Albania, Bosnia, Bulgaria, Macedonia, Romania, Slovakia, Yugoslavia and all the former Soviet republics (other than the Baltic states) – can enter Britain with just a passport, generally for up to three months. US, Canadian, Australian and New Zealand citizens can stay for up to six months, providing they have a return ticket and adequate funds**

to cover their stay. Citizens of most other countries require a visa, obtainable from the British consular or mission office in the country of application. All overseas consulates in Scotland are detailed in the listings sections for Edinburgh (p.125) and Glasgow (p.231).

Details of British immigration and visa requirements are listed on the Foreign and Commonwealth Office's **Web site** (*www.fco. gov.uk*), from which you can download the full range of application forms and information leaflets. In addition, an independent charity, the **Immigration Advisory Service** (IAS), County House, 190 Great Dover St, London SE1 4YB (☎0171/357 6917, *www.vois.org.uk*), offers free and confidential advice to anyone applying for entry clearance into the UK.

LONG STAYS AND WORK PERMITS

For stays of longer than six months, US, Canadian, Australian and New Zealand citizens can apply to the British Embassy (see box on p.16) in person or by post for an **Entry Clearance Certificate**. Unless you're a resident of an EU country, you need a **permit** to work legally in the UK, although without the backing of an established employer or company this can be very difficult to obtain. People aged between 17 and 27 may, however, apply for a **Working Holiday-Maker Entry Certificate**, which entitles you to stay in the UK for up to two years and to do casual work. The certificates are only available abroad, from British embassies and consulates, and when you apply you must have proof of a valid return or onward ticket, and the means to support yourself while you're in Britain. Note, too, that the certificates are valid from the date of entry into Britain – you won't be able to recoup time spent out of the country during the two-year period.

In North America, full-time, bona fide college students can get temporary work or study permits through the **Council of International Education Exchange** (CIEE), 205 E 42nd St, New York, NY 10017 (☎212/822 2600, *www.ciee.org*). In addition, Commonwealth citizens with a parent or grandparent born in the UK can apply for a **Certificate of Entitlement to the Right of Abode**, which permits them to work in Britain. If you're unsure about whether or not you may eligible for one of these, contact your nearest British mission (embassy, high commission or consulate), or the Foreign and Commonwealth Office in London (☎0171/270 1500 or 238 4633).

CUSTOMS AND TAX

Travellers from **EU countries** coming into Britain do not have to make a declaration to customs at their place of entry. The current limits for duty-paid goods from within the EU are 800 cigarettes or 1kg of tobacco, 110 litres of beer, 90 litres of wine, 20 litres of fortified wine and 10 litres of spirits. Duty-free shopping was phased out in 1999. **Travellers from non-EU countries** are only allowed to bring in 200 cigarettes or 250g of tobacco, 2 litres of wine, plus 1 litre of spirits or 2 litres of fortified wine.

There are **import restrictions** on a variety of articles and substances, from firearms to furs derived from endangered species, none of which should bother the average tourist. However, if you need any clarification on British import regulations, contact HM Customs and Excise, Dorset House, Stamford St, London SE1 9PJ (☎0171/928 3344, *www.hmce.gov.uk*). You cannot bring pets into Britain on holiday, as tight quarantine restrictions apply to animals brought from overseas (except for Ireland).

Many goods in Britain, with the chief exceptions of books and food, are subject to **Value Added Tax** (VAT), which currently increases the cost of an item by 17.5 percent. Visitors from non-EU countries can save a lot of money through the Retail Export Scheme, which allows a refund of VAT on goods to be taken out of the country. EU nationals will usually save very little, if anything, however, because of their own VAT rates. Note that not all shops participate in this scheme – those doing so display a sign to this effect – and that you cannot reclaim VAT charged on hotel bills or other services.

BRITISH EMBASSIES ABROAD

Australia (High Commission) Commonwealth Ave, Yarralumla, Canberra, ACT 2600 (☎1902/941 555, *www.uk.emb.gov.au*).

Canada (High Commission) 80 Elgin St, Ottawa K1P 5K7 (☎613/237-1530, *www.bis-canada.org*).

Ireland 29 Merrion Rd, Ballsbridge, Dublin 4 (☎01/205 3822).

Netherlands Koningslaan 44, 1075AE Amsterdam (☎676 43 43).

New Zealand (High Commission) 44 Hill St, Wellington (☎04/472 6049, *www.brithighcomm.org.nz*).

South Africa (High Commission) 91 Parliament St, Cape Town 8001 (☎461 7220).

USA 3100 Massachusetts Ave NW, Washington, DC 20008 (☎202/462-1340, *www.britain-info.org*).

MONEY, BANKS AND COSTS

The basic unit of currency in Britain is the pound sterling (£), divided into 100 pence (p). Coins come in denominations of 1p, 2p, 5p, 10p, 20p, 50p, £1 and £2. Bank of England banknotes are legal tender in Scotland; in addition the Bank of Scotland, the Royal Bank of Scotland and the Clydesdale Bank issue their own banknotes in denominations of £1, £5, £10, £20, £50 and £100 – legal tender in the rest of Britain, no matter what shopkeepers south of the border might say. Shopkeepers will carefully scrutinize any £20 or £50 notes, as forgeries are widespread, and you'd be well advised to do the same. The quickest test is to hold the note up to the light to make sure there's a thin wire filament running from top to bottom; this is by no means foolproof, but it will catch most fakes.

CARRYING MONEY

There are no exchange controls in Britain, so you can bring in as much money as you like. The easiest and safest way to carry your money is in **travellers' cheques**, available for a small commission (usually one percent) from any major bank. The most commonly accepted travellers' cheques are American Express (Amex), followed by Visa and Thomas Cook – most cheques issued by banks will be one of these brands. You'll usually pay commission again when you cash each cheque, normally another one percent or so, or a flat rate, though no commission is payable on Amex cheques exchanged at Amex offices. Make

sure you keep a record of the cheques as you cash them, so that you'll be able to get the value of all uncashed cheques refunded immediately if you lose them.

Most hotels, shops and restaurants in Scotland accept the major **credit cards** (Access/MasterCard, Visa and Amex), although they're less useful in rural areas; smaller establishments all over the country, such as B&Bs, will often accept cash only. You can get cash advances from certain **ATMs** – call the issuing bank or credit company to get a list of locations in Scotland. In addition, you may be able to make withdrawals using your ATM cash card, if you have a **PIN number** designed to work overseas.

Visa and Access/MasterCard holders can use Bank of Scotland, Clydesdale and Royal Bank of Scotland ATMs – known in Britain as **cashpoint** machines. If you have an account with a high-street bank in England or Wales, you can simply take your cashpoint card with you. Bank of Scotland and Royal Bank of Scotland cashpoints take Lloyds and Barclays cash cards, while Clydesdale takes HSBC/Midland and National Westminster cards. Bank of Scotland, Clydesdale and most building society cashpoints are in the Link network and accept all affiliated cards.

BANKS

In every sizeable town in Scotland and, surprisingly, in some small places, you'll find a branch of at least one of the big highstreet **banks**: Bank of Scotland, Royal Bank of Scotland, Clydesdale and TSB Scotland. However, on some islands, and in remoter parts, you may find there is only a mobile bank that runs to a timetable, usually available from the local post office. General opening hours are Monday to Friday from between 9am and 9.30am to between 4pm and 5pm, though some branches are open until slightly later on Thursdays. Almost everywhere, banks are the best places in which to change money and cheques. Outside banking hours you'll have to use a **bureau de change**, found in most city centres and often at train stations or airports. Avoid changing money or cheques in hotels, where the rates are normally very poor.

If, as a foreign visitor, you run out of money or there is some kind of emergency, the quickest way to get money sent out is to have the cash **wired** to the nearest bank via Western Union (☎0800/833833) or Moneygram (☎0800/894887). Both charge on a sliding scale: for example, it will cost you around £15 to wire out £100, but only £80 to wire out £2500. You should get the money within twenty minutes. You can do the same thing through Thomas Cook or American Express if there's a branch nearby, but it usually takes a day or two. Your bank may also have reciprocal arrangements with a Scottish bank, but again its money transfer will take a day or so.

COSTS

Scotland is an expensive place to visit, although in general it is marginally less pricey than England. The minimum expenditure, if you're camping, cycling or hitching and preparing most of your own food, is in the region of £25 a day, rising to around £35 a day if you're using the hostelling network, some public transport and eating the odd meal out. Couples staying at budget B&Bs, eating at unpretentious restaurants and visiting a fair number of tourist attractions, are looking at around £50 each per day; if you're renting a car, staying in comfortable B&Bs or hotels and eating well, you should reckon on at least £80 a day per person. Single travellers should budget on spending around sixty percent of what a couple would spend (single rooms cost more than half a double). If you're visiting **Edinburgh**, which can be pricey, allow at least an extra £10 or so a day to get full pleasure out of the place.

TIPPING

There are no fixed rules for **tipping** in Scotland. If you think you've received good service, particularly in restaurants or cafés, you may want to leave a tip of ten to fifteen percent, but check first that service has not already been included. It is not normal, however, to leave tips in pubs, although bar staff are sometimes offered drinks, which they may accept in the form of money (the assumption is they'll spend this on a drink after closing time). Taxi drivers, on the other hand, will expect tips on long journeys – ten percent is the norm. The other occasion when you'll be expected to tip is in upmarket hotels where, in common with most other countries, porters, bellboys and table waiters rely on being tipped to bump up their often dismal wages.

YOUTH AND STUDENT DISCOUNTS

Various official youth/student ID cards are widely available and most will soon pay for themselves in savings. Full-time students are eligible for the **International Student ID Card** (ISIC), which entitles the bearer to special fares on local transport, and discounts at museums, theatres and other attractions. For Americans, there's also a health benefit, providing up to US$3000 in emergency medical coverage and US$100 a day for sixty days in the hospital, plus a 24-hour hotline to call in the event of a medical, legal or financial emergency. The card, which costs US$20 for Americans, CAN$30 for Canadians, A$15 for Australians and NZ$17 in New Zealand, is available from branches of Council Travel, STA and Travel CUTS (see p.5 and p.9 for addresses).

You only have to be 25 or younger to qualify for the **Go-25 Card**, which costs the same as the ISIC and carries the same benefits. It can be purchased through Council Travel in the US and around the world, Hostelling International in Canada (see "Accommodation", p.33) and STA in Australia and New Zealand.

INSURANCE AND HEALTH

Wherever you're travelling from, it's a good idea to have some kind of travel insurance, which covers you for loss of possessions and money, as well as the cost of all medical and dental treatment. If you're travelling to Scotland from elsewhere in Britain, you may well be covered by your domestic insurance policy.

The amount of cover you get varies according to the premium, but a standard policy should always cover the cost of cancellation and curtailment of flights, medical expenses, travel delay, accident, missed departures, lost baggage, lost passport, personal liability and legal expenses. Policies tend to weigh in at under £30 per month, though it's always worth shopping around to get the best price. Good companies to phone for quotes include Columbus Direct (☎0171/375 0011) or Endsleigh Insurance (☎0171/436 4451). Some companies refuse to cover travellers over 65, or stop at 69 or 74 years of age, and most that do charge hefty premiums. The best policies for **older travellers**, with no upper age limit, are offered by Age Concern (☎01883/346964).

Whatever your policy, if you have anything stolen, get a copy of the police report of the incident, as this is essential to substantiate your claim.

NORTH AMERICAN COVER

Before buying an insurance policy, check that you're not already covered. **Canadian provincial health plans** typically provide some overseas medical coverage, although they're unlikely to pick up the full tab in the event of a mishap. Holders of official **student/teacher/youth cards** (see p.18) are covered for accident coverage and hospital in-patient benefits, and the annual membership fee is far less than the cost of comparable insurance. **Students** may also find that their student health coverage extends during the vacations and for one term beyond the date of last enrolment. Bank and **credit cards** (particularly American Express) often provide certain levels of medical or other insurance, and travel insurance may also be included if you use a major credit or charge card to pay for your trip. In addition, **homeowners' or renters'** insurance often covers theft or loss of documents, money and valuables while overseas.

If you do need to purchase a separate travel insurance **policy**, be aware that they can vary hugely: some are comprehensive, while others cover only certain risks (accidents, illnesses, delayed or lost luggage, cancelled flights and so on). In particular, ask whether the policy pays medical costs up front or reimburses you later, and whether it provides for medical evacuation to your home country. For policies that include lost or stolen luggage, check exactly what is and isn't covered, and make sure the per-article limit will cover your most valuable possessions. A specialist travel insurance company (see the box on p.20) can give you advice about various policies and ensure that you get one suited to your needs.

The lowest **premiums** are usually available through student/youth travel agencies: for example, ISIS policies (for students of any age) for eight to fifteen days cost $60 with medical coverage, and $45 without; for a month you'll pay $110 and $85 respectively; and for two months the charge is $165 with medical coverage, $135 without. Non-students will pay a bit more: Travel Assistance International, for example, offers a fifteen-day policy including medical cover for $75–95, and a thirty-day plan for $105–130. If you're planning to do any "dangerous sports" (skiing and mountaineering for example), check whether these activities are covered: some companies levy a surcharge.

Most North American travel policies apply only to items lost, stolen or damaged while in the custody of an identifiable, responsible third party such as a hotel porter, an airline or luggage

TRAVEL INSURANCE COMPANIES IN NORTH AMERICA

Access America (☎1-800/284-8300).
Carefree Travel Insurance (☎1-800/323-3149).
Council Travel (☎1/888/COUNCIL, *www. counciltravel.com*)
Desjardins Travel Insurance (Canada only ☎1-800/463-7830).
International Student Insurance Service (ISIS), available through STA Travel (☎1-800/777-0112, *www.sta-travel.com*).

Travel Assistance International (☎1-800/821-2828)
Travel Guard (☎1-800/826-1300, *www.noelgroup.com*).
Travel Insurance Services (☎1-800/937-1387).
Worldwide Assistance (☎1-800/821-2828)

consignment. Even in these cases you will have to contact the local police within a certain time limit to have a complete report made out so that your insurer can process the claim.

AUSTRALIAN AND NEW ZEALAND COVER

Travel insurance policies in Australia and New Zealand tend to be put together by airlines and travel agent groups, and are all fairly similar in terms of coverage and price. A typical policy for the UK covering medical costs, lost baggage and personal liability will cost around A$140/NZ$150 for two weeks, A$190/NZ$210 for one month, and A$300/NZ$330 for two months.

The following companies offer some of the widest cover available and can be arranged direct or through most travel agents: Ready Plan, 141 Walker St, Dandenong, Melbourne (☎03/9791 5077 or 1300/555 017) and 10/63 Albert St, Auckland (☎09/300 5333); and Cover More, Level 9, 32 Walker St, North Sydney, (☎02/9202 8000 or 1800.251 881), with branches also in Victoria, Queensland, and at 57 Simon St, Auckland (☎09/377 5958).

HEALTH

No vaccinations are required for entry into Britain. **EU** citizens are entitled to free medical treatment at National Health Service hospitals on production of an **E111** form. Australia, New Zealand and several non-EU European countries have reciprocal health-care arrangements with Britain. Citizens of other countries will be charged for all medical services except those administered by Accident and Emergency units at National Health Service hospitals. In other words, if you've just been hit by a car, you would not be charged if the injuries simply required stitching and setting in the emergency unit, but would if admission to a hospital ward were necessary. Health insurance is therefore extremely advisable for all non-EU nationals.

Pharmacists can dispense only a limited range of drugs without a doctor's prescription. Most are open standard shop hours, though in large towns some may close as late as 10pm – local newspapers carry lists of late-opening pharmacies, or contact the local police for current details. **Doctors' surgeries** tend to be open from about 9am to noon and then for a couple of hours in the evening; outside surgery hours, you can turn up at the casualty department of the local hospital for complaints that require immediate attention – unless it's an emergency, in which case ring for an ambulance ☎999.

EMERGENCIES

For the most part the Scottish police are approachable and helpful to visitors. If you're lost in a major town, asking a police officer is generally the quickest way to get help – alternatively, you could ask a traffic warden, a much-maligned species of law enforcer responsible for parking restrictions and other vehicle-related matters. Traditionally their uniform includes a flat cap with a yellow band, though a variety of different uniforms has been introduced during the 1990s. Police officers on street duty wear a peaked flat hat with a black and white chequered band, and are generally armed with a truncheon (baton).

As with any country, Scotland's major towns and cities have their danger spots, but these tend to be inner-city housing estates where no tourist has any reason to roam. The chief urban risk is **pickpocketing**, so carry only as much money as you need, and keep all bags and pockets fastened. Out in the Highlands and Islands, crime levels are very low indeed. Should you have anything stolen or be involved in some incident that requires reporting, go to the local police station (addresses in the major cities are listed in this guide); the ☎999 number should only be used in emergencies. For information on wiring money, see pp.17-18.

EMERGENCIES

For **police**, **fire brigade**, **ambulance** and, in certain areas, mountain rescue or coastguard, dial ☎**999**.

INFORMATION AND MAPS

If you want to do a bit of research before arriving in Scotland, you should contact the **British Tourist Authority (BTA)** in your country or write direct to the main office of the **Scottish Tourist Board (STB)**, marking your letter "Information Department" – the addresses are given below – or email the STB (*info@stb.gov.uk*). The BTA and STB will send you a wealth of free literature, some of it just rose-tinted advertising copy, but much of it extremely useful – especially the maps, city guides and event calendars. If you want more hard facts on a particular area, approach the area tourist boards, which are listed on p.24, or visit one of the Web sites suggested on p.24.

Tourist offices (sometimes called Tourist Information Centres) exist in virtually every Scottish town – you'll find their phone numbers and opening hours in the relevant sections of the guide. Opening hours vary from month to month, with offices in many areas closing completely in the winter season. All centres offer information on accommodation (and can usually book rooms – see p.31), local public transport, attractions and restaurants, as well as selling books, local guides, maps and souvenirs. In many cases their services are free, though some offices make a small charge for an accommodation list or a town guide with an accompanying street plan.

MAPS

Many bookshops will have a selection of maps of Scotland and Britain in general, but see the box opposite for a list of travel specialists. Virtually every service station in Scotland stocks one or more of the big **road atlases**. The best of these are the large-format ones produced by the AA, RAC, Collins and Ordnance Survey, which cover all of Britain at around three miles to one inch, and include larger-scale plans of major towns. You could also invest in the excellent **fold-out maps** published by Michelin and Bartholomew; the latter includes clear town plans of the major cities. Another option is the official tourist map series published by Estate Publications, perfect if you're driving or cycling round one particular region since it marks all the major tourist sights as well as youth hostels and campsites. These are available from just about every tourist office in Scotland.

SCOTTISH TOURIST BOARDS

Scotland 23 Ravelston Terrace, Edinburgh EH4 3EU (☎0131/332 2433).

England 19 Cockspur St, London SW1 5BL (☎0171/930 8661 or 8662 or 8663).

BRITISH TOURIST AUTHORITY OFFICES ABROAD

Australia Level 16, Gateway, 1 Macquarie Place, Sydney, NSW 2000 (☎02/9377 4400).

Canada 5915 Airport Rd, Suite 120, Mississauga, Toronto, Ontario L4V 1T1 (☎905/405 1840; 1-888-VISIT-UK).

Netherlands Aurora Gebouw (5e), Stadhouderskade 2, 1054 ES Amsterdam (☎020/607 0002).

New Zealand 17th floor, Fay Richwhite Building, 151 Queen St, Auckland 1 (☎09/303 1446).

South Africa Lancaster Gate, Hyde Park Lane, Hyde Park 2196, Johannesburg (☎011/325 0342).

USA 7th floor, 551 Fifth Ave, New York, NY 10176-0799 (☎ 212/986 2200; 1-800-GO-2-BRITAIN); 10880 Wilshire Blvd, Suite 570, Los Angeles, CA 90024 (☎310/470 2782).

MAP OUTLETS

ENGLAND

Blackwell's Map and Travel Shop, 53 Broad St, Oxford OX1 3BQ (☎01865/792792; www.bookshop.blackwell.co.uk).

Heffers Map Shop, 3rd floor, in Heffers Stationery Department, 19 Sidney St, Cambridge, CB2 3HL (☎01223/568467, www.heffers.co.uk).

The Map Shop, 30a Belvoir St, Leicester, LE1 6QH (☎0116/2471400).

Newcastle Map Centre, 55 Grey St, Newcastle upon Tyne, NE1 6EF (☎0191/261 5622).

Stanfords, 12–14 Long Acre, London WC2E 9LP (☎0171/836 1321, sales@stanfords.co.uk). Other branches within Campus Travel at 52 Grosvenor Gardens, London SW1W 0AG (☎0171/730 1314); within the British Airways offices at 156 Regent St, London W1R 5TA (☎0171/434 4744); and at 29 Corn St, Bristol BS1 1HT (☎0117/929 9966).

IRELAND

Easons Bookshop, 40 O'Connell St, Dublin 1 (☎01/873 3811).

Fred Hanna's Bookshop, 27–29 Nassau St, Dublin 2 (☎01/677 1255).

Hodges Figgis Bookshop, 56–58 Dawson St, Dublin 2 (☎01/677 4754).

Waterstone's, Queens Bldg, 8 Royal Ave, Belfast BT1 1DA (☎01232/247 355); 7 Dawson St, Dublin 2 (☎01/679 1415); 69 Patrick St, Cork (☎021/276 522).

NORTH AMERICA

Adventurous Traveler Bookstore, PO Box 1468, Williston, VT 05495 (☎1-800/282-3963, www.AdventurousTraveler.com).

Book Passage, 51 Tamal Vista Blvd, Corte Madera, CA 94925 (☎415/927-0960).

The Complete Traveler Bookstore, 199 Madison Ave, New York, NY 10016 (☎212/685-9007).

The Complete Traveler Bookstore, 3207 Fillmore St, San Francisco, CA 94123 (☎415/923-1511).

The Globe Corner Bookstore, 28 Church St, Cambridge, MA 02138 (☎617/497-6277); 500 Bolyston St, Boston, MA 02116.

Map Link, 30 S La Petera Lane, Unit #5, Santa Barbara, CA 93117 (☎805/692-6777).

The Map Store Inc, 1636 1st St, Washington DC, 20006 (☎202/628-2608).

Open Air Books and Maps, 25 Toronto St, Toronto, ON M5R 2C1 (☎416/363-0719).

Phileas Fogg's Books & Maps, #87 Stanford Shopping Center, Palo Alto, CA 94304 (☎1-800/533-FOGG).

Rand McNally, 444 N Michigan Ave, Chicago, IL 60611 (☎312/321-1751); 150 E 52nd St, New York, NY 10022 (☎212/758-7488); 595 Market St, San Francisco, CA 94105 (☎415/777-3131); call ☎1-800/234-0679 for other locations, or for maps by mail order.

Sierra Club Bookstore, 6014 College Ave, Oakland, CA 94618 (☎510/658-7470).

Travel Books & Language Center, 4931 Cordell Ave, Bethesda, MD 20814 (☎1-800/220-2665).

Traveler's Bookstore, 22 W 52nd St, New York, NY 10019 (☎212/664-0995).

Ulysses Travel Bookshop, 4176 St-Denis, Montréal (☎514/843-9447).

World Wide Books and Maps, 736 Granville St, Vancouver, BC V6Z 1E4 (☎604/687-3320).

AUSTRALIA AND NEW ZEALAND

Mapland, 372 Little Bourke St, Melbourne, VIC 3000 (☎03/9670 4383).

The Map Shop, 16a Peel St, Adelaide, SA 5000 (☎08/8231 2033).

Perth Map Centre, 891 Hay St, Perth, WA 6000 (☎08/9322 5733).

Speciality Maps, 58 Albert St, Auckland (☎09/307 2217).

Travel Bookshop, shop 3, 175 Liverpool St, Sydney, NSW 2000 (☎02/9261 8200).

Worldwide Maps and Guides, 187 George St, Brisbane, Queensland (☎07/3221 4330).

If you're after more detail, the most comprehensive **maps** of Scotland are produced by the **Ordnance Survey** series – renowned for its accuracy and clarity. The 204 maps in their 1:50,000 (a little over a mile to an inch) Landranger series cover the whole of Britain and show enough detail to be useful for most walkers. There's more detail still in the 1:25,000 Pathfinder series, which also covers the whole of Britain, though it is currently being replaced by the new Explorer series, drawn to the same scale. The full Ordnance Survey range is only available at a few big-city stores, although in any walking district of Scotland you'll find the relevant maps in local shops or tourist offices.

SCOTLAND ONLINE

TOURISM

www.aboutscotland.co.uk
Useful for accommodation, easy to use and linked to holiday activities.

www.holiday.scotland.net
The official Scottish Tourist Board site, with sections on transport, accommodation, sight-seeing and outdoor activities.

www.nts.org.uk
Web site of the National Trust for Scotland which is constantly updated; you can check current opening hours and events.

www.rampantscotland.co.uk
Well worth looking at its index of links to everything Scottish if you're searching for something specific.

www.scotland-info.co.uk
A big site covering the whole of the country, with a commercial bent – links to shops, hotels and so on – but good on information for individual areas.

www.travelscotland.co.uk
Run in association with the STB, this is a lively magazine-format site, with features and reviews.

EDINBURGH

www.edinburgh-galleries.co.uk
Lists all the exhibitions on in Edinburgh and is updated monthly; links with Festival exhibitions when appropriate.

www.edinburgh.org
Tourist board site for Edinburgh and Lothians; some good kids pages as well as all the usual stuff.

GLASGOW

www.clyde-valley.com/glasgow
Fairly comprehensive and regularly updated Web site covering all the sights of Glasgow.

THE ISLANDS

www.hebrides.com
Absorbing site on the islands off the west coast of Scotland, with masses of pages and links.

www.orknet.co.uk
Run by the Orkney tourist board and council, covering tourism, business, community and heritage. Lots of information and easy to use.

www.shetland-tourism.co.uk
Excellent Shetland tourist board site, covering almost everything you could possibly want to know – well linked and well illustrated.

SPORT

http://aviemore.org
Site run by local chamber of commerce with good information on skiing holidays and facilities, accommodation and outdoor sports, from trout fishing to four-wheel, off-road driving.

REGIONAL TOURIST BOARDS IN SCOTLAND

Aberdeen & Grampian Tourist Board, 27 Albyn Place, Aberdeen AB10 1YL (☎01224/632727).

Angus & City of Dundee Tourist Board, 21 Castle St, Dundee DD1 3AA (☎01382/527527).

Argyll, The Isles, Loch Lomond, Stirling & Trossachs Tourist Board, Old Town Jail, St John St, Stirling (☎01786/470945).

Ayrshire & Arran Tourist Board, Burns House, Burns Statue Square, Ayr KA7 1UT (☎01292/288688).

Dumfries and Galloway Tourist Board, 64 Whitesands, Dumfries DG1 2RS (☎01387/253862).

Edinburgh and the Lothians Tourist Board, 4 Rothesay Terrace, Edinburgh EH3 7RY (☎0131/473 3800).

Greater Glasgow and Clyde Valley Tourist Board, 11 George Square, Glasgow G2 1DY (☎0141/204 4480).

Highlands of Scotland Tourist Board, Peffery House, Strathpeffer IV14 9HA (☎01463/421160).

Kingdom of Fife Tourist Board, 7 Haig House, Haig Business Park, Markinch KY7 6AQ (☎01592/750066).

Orkney Tourist Board, 6 Broad St, Kirkwall, Orkney KW15 1NX (☎01856/872856).

Perthshire Tourist Board, Lower City Mills, West Mill St, Perth PH1 5QP (☎01738/627958).

Scottish Borders Tourist Board, Shepherd Mills, Whinfield Rd, Selkirk TD7 5DT (☎01750/20555).

Shetland Island Tourism, Market Cross, Lerwick, Shetland ZE1 0LU (☎01595/693434).

Western Isles Tourist Board, 4 South Beach, Stornoway, Isle of Lewis HS1 2XY (☎01851/703088).

www.golfscotland.co.uk
A real must for golf fanatics: it lists all the courses and gives their details, organizes tours for the Open and is updated with the latest golfing news.

THE ENVIRONMENT

www.geo.ed.ac.uk/home/scotland/scotland/html
Produced by the Geography Department of Edinburgh University – an introduction to all things Scottish, history, geography and politics.

Excellent background information with a myriad of links.
www.scotlandthegreen.co.uk
Green travel, accommodation and shopping; as yet it's not very comprehensive, but it's getting there.

MUSIC

www.ceolas.org
A very informative Celtic music site, both historical and contemporary, with lots of music to listen to.

GETTING AROUND

The majority of Scots live in the central belt, which spreads from Glasgow in the west to Edinburgh, virtually on the east coast. Public transport here is efficient and most places are easily accessible by train and bus. To the south and north it can be a different story: off the main routes, public transport services are few and far between, particularly in more remote parts of Argyll, and the Highlands and Islands. With careful planning, however, practically everywhere is accessible and you'll have no trouble getting to the main tourist destinations. In most parts of Scotland, especially if you take the scenic backroads, the low level of traffic makes driving wonderfully unstressful.

BY TRAIN

Scotland has a modest railway network, at its densest in the central belt, at its most skeletal in the Highlands, and all but nonexistent in the islands. **ScotRail** runs the majority of train services, reaching all the major towns, sometimes on lines rated as among the great scenic routes of the world. For a rundown of the different fares available in getting to Scotland by train, see p.12.

You can buy **tickets** for ScotRail trains at stations, from major travel agents, or over the phone with a credit card. For busy long-distance routes, it's a good idea to make sure you have a seat. **Seat reservations** to Edinburgh, Glasgow, Aberdeen or Inverness are included in the price of the ticket if you book in advance. The ticket offices at many rural and commuter stations are closed in the evenings and at weekends; in these instances there's sometimes a **ticket machine** on the platform. If the machine isn't working, or there simply isn't one, you can buy your ticket on board. However, if you've embarked at a station that does have a ticket office open or a machine, and you haven't bought a ticket, there's a spot fine of £10.

In addition to the British Rail passes outlined on p.26, ScotRail offers a couple of **travel passes** worth considering. The most flexible is the **Freedom of Scotland Travelpass**, which gives unlimited train travel within Scotland. It's also valid on all CalMac ferry links on the west coast (see ferry information on p.29), as well as on various buses in the remoter regions where the railway network is non-existent. You also get up to a third off P&O ferries to Orkney and Shetland. The pass currently costs £69/A$205/NZ$246 for four out of eight days' travel, £99/A$295/NZ$354 for eight days out of fifteen, or £119/A$354/NZ$424 for twelve days out of fifteen, and comes complete with timetables, a map and a card giving discounts at tourist attractions, shops and restaurants throughout Scotland.

The **Highland Rover** is more limited in its scope, allowing unlimited travel on trains within

---

RAIL CONTACTS

BRITAIN

National Rail Enquiries ☎0345/484950, *www.railtrack.co.uk*. Gives details of timetables, fares and other information on rail travel within Scotland.

ScotRail ☎08457/550033, *www.scotrail.co.uk*. For booking tickets and seats on all trains within Scotland, and sleeper trains to Scotland.

NORTH AMERICA

BritRail Travel International ☎1-888/274-8724 or 212/575-2667, *www.britrail.com/us*
CIT Eurail ☎1-800/223-7987
DER Travel Services ☎1-800/421-2929
McFarland Ltd ☎1-800/437-2687; *www.reveretvl.com*

Online Travel ☎1-800/660-5300, *www.online@eurorail.com*
Rail Europe USA, ☎1-800/438-7245; Canada, ☎1-800/361-7245; *www.raileurope.com*

AUSTRALIA
Rail Plus ☎1300/555 003.

NEW ZEALAND
Rail Plus ☎09/303 2484.

---

the Highland region, plus the West Highland Line (Glasgow–Oban), and travel between Aberdeen and Aviemore. It also allows free travel on buses between Oban, Fort William and Inverness. However, it does not cover travel from Glasgow to Inverness or Aberdeen, so you have to be canny about your route planning. The Highland Rover currently costs £49 and is valid for four out of eight consecutive days. The Freedom of Scotland and the Highland Rover passes are both available from ScotRail telesales (see below).

If you plan to do a lot of travelling around the UK, your best bet is to buy one of the range of passes which allow unlimited travel in Scotland, England and Wales. The only one of these passes that can be bought in the UK is the **All-Line Rail Rover**, which costs £275 for seven consecutive days' travel, or £450 for fourteen days. All other BritRail passes are only available for purchase before you leave your home country, through local travel agents or the specialist companies listed below. The **BritRail Consecutive Pass** allows unlimited standard-class travel for four consecutive days for A\$268/NZ\$321; eight days costs US\$265/A\$383/NZ\$459; fifteen days costs US\$400/A\$574/NZ\$688; 22 days costs US\$505/A\$727/NZ\$872; and one month for US\$600/A\$861/NZ\$1033. Under-26s pay A\$215/NZ\$258 for four days; US\$215/A\$307/NZ\$368 for eight days; US\$280/A\$402/NZ\$482 for fifteen days;

US\$355/A\$509/NZ\$610 for 22 days; or US\$420/A\$603/NZ\$723 for one month. Seniors (aged 60+ and only available for first-class travel) pay A\$342/NZ\$410 for four days US\$340/A\$488/NZ\$585 for eight days, US\$510/A\$732/ NZ\$878 for fifteen days, US\$645/A\$927/ NZ\$1112 for 22 days, or US\$765/A\$1098/ NZ\$1317 for one month.

Better value if you're not travelling every day is the **BritRail Flexipass**, which allows four days of travel within a two-month period for US\$235/A\$336/NZ\$403; eight days out of two months for US\$340/A\$487/NZ\$584; or fifteen days out of two months for US\$515/A\$739/NZ\$886. Under-26s pay US\$185/A\$269/NZ\$323 for four days out of two months, US\$240/A\$341/NZ\$409 for eight days in two months, or US\$360/A\$517/NZ\$620 for fifteen days out of two months. For Seniors (60+ and only available for first-class travel) the prices are US\$300/A\$428/NZ\$513 for four days out of two months; US\$435/A\$621/NZ\$745 for eight days in two-months; and US\$655/A\$942/NZ\$1130 for fifteen days in a two-month period.

A great bargain for **travellers with children** allows one free child pass for each paying adult, and, if four adults are travelling together on a BritRail pass, two of the four can purchase the pass for half-price. BritRail Pass holders can also get special rates on the London to Paris Eurostar, and the passes are valid on Airport Links services plus the Heathrow Express service.

BY BUS

Travelling around Scotland by **bus** may take a little longer than using the train, but works out considerably cheaper. There's a plethora of regional companies, but by far the biggest national operator is **Scottish Citylink** (☎0990/505050), a subsidiary company of National Express. With train travel being so expensive, bus services have become very popular, so for busy routes and at weekends and holidays it's a good idea to buy a "reserved-journey ticket", which guarantees you a seat.

If you're under 26, a full-time student, or 50 and over, it's worth buying a **Smart Card**, which costs £5 for a year, £12 for three, saving you thirty percent on all adult fares. Children normally pay half fare, but with a **Parent & Child Saver Card** (£5 a year), one child can travel free; the **Family Saver Card** (£10 a year) allows two children to travel free with two adults.

If you plan to do a lot of travelling by bus, it may be worth buying a **Explorer Pass**, which offers unlimited travel on the Scottish Citylink network: it costs £30 for three consecutive days; £60 for any five days within ten; £90 for any eight within sixteen; and £120 for any fifteen within thirty. Smart Card holders can get a third off the above prices. However, if you're travelling a lot in England and Wales, too, you might be better off with a National Express Tourist Trail Pass, details of which appear on p.13.

The SYHA also sells its own **Explore Scotland** bus pass, which allows free travel on Citylink buses. You also get a Historic Scotland Scottish Explorer pass (see p.39), free SYHA membership and several nights of free hostel accommodation. The pass costs £165 for five out of ten days' travel, with seven nights' accommodation, or £280 for eight days' travel out of sixteen, with fourteen nights' accommodation.

Local bus services are run by a bewildering array of companies, and it's increasingly the case that private companies duplicate the busiest routes in an attempt to undercut the commercial opposition, leaving the remoter spots neglected. As a general rule, the further away from urban areas you get, the less frequent and more expensive bus services become.

Some rural areas, particularly in the Highlands and Islands, are only served by the **postbus** network, which operates 140 minibuses carrying mail and three to ten fare-paying passengers. They set off early in the morning – usually around 8am

from the main post office and collect mail (or deliver it) from/to the nether regions. It's a sociable, though often excruciatingly slow, way to travel, and may well be the only means of reaching hidden-away B&Bs and the like. You can get a booklet of routes and timetables from the Royal Mail Communications (☎0131/228 7407), or the Scottish Tourist Board (see p.22).

BUS TOURS

If you're backpacking, a cheap, flexible and fun way of travelling around Scotland is on one of the popular "**jump-on-jump-off**" minibus services that operate out of Edinburgh. The leading operator at the moment is Haggis Backpackers, whose minibus calls at Pitlochry, Inverness, Loch Ness, Ullapool, Kyleakin and Isle of Skye, Fort William, Oban, Loch Lomond and Glasgow before returning to Edinburgh. It runs every day except Sunday, throughout the year, stopping at independent hostels along the route – which saves you the hassle of lugging of your bags around – and you can spend as long as you like at each place. The Flexitour pass for one complete circuit costs £85; for further details, contact Haggis Backpackers, at 11 Blackfriars St, Edinburgh EH1 1NB (☎0131/557 9393, *www.haggis-backpackers.com*).

Haggis also run backpackers' **minibus tours** of Scotland. Prices start at £75 for a three-day round-trip from Edinburgh, taking in Loch Ness, Skye, Glen Coe and other Highland highlights, while a six-day guided tour, combining most of Scotland's main tourist destinations, costs £139; these fares do not include food and accommodation, but the tour companies can help with hostel booking. Several other companies run similar guided tours, including the popular Rabbie's Trail Burners tours, which also start in Edinburgh (207 High St, Edinburgh; ☎0131/226 3133, *www.rabbies.com*), and offer a range of tours led by knowledgeable driver-guides. If you're pushed for time and want to do a whistlestop tour of England and Wales en route to Scotland, another option worth considering is the Haggis Backpackers London to Edinburgh trip, outlined in "Getting there" on p.13.

BY CAR

If you want to cover a lot of the country in a short time, or just want more flexibility, you'll need your own transport. In order to **drive** in Scotland you must have a current driving licence; foreign nationals will need to supplement this with an

DRIVING ORGANIZATIONS

American Automobile Association (AAA; *www.aaa.com*). Each state has its own club – check the phone book for local addresses and phone numbers. The AAA can refer members to overseas auto associations, and can provide international drivers' licences and *carnets de passage* (for those planning to transport cars across certain international boundaries).

Australian Automobile Association, 212 Northbourne Ave, Canberra ACT 2601 (☎02/6247 7311).

Automobile Association, PO Box 126, Basingstoke, Hants RG21 4BA (☎0990/448866, *www.theaa.co.uk*).

Canadian Automobile Association (**CAA**). Each region has its own club – check the phone book for local addresses and phone numbers. Benefits are comparable to the AAA's (see above), and membership rates vary.

New Zealand Automobile Association, PO Box 5, Auckland (☎09/377 4660).

Royal Automobile Club, RAC House, PO Box 700, Bristol BS99 1RB (☎0800/550550, *www.rac.co.uk*).

CAR RENTAL FIRMS

BRITAIN

Avis ☎0990/900500
Budget ☎0800/181181
Europcar ☎0345/222525
Hertz ☎0990/996699

Holiday Autos ☎0990/300400
National Car Rental ☎0990/365365
Thrifty ☎0990/168238

AUSTRALIA

Avis ☎1800/225 533
Budget ☎1300/362 848
Hertz ☎1800/550 067

NEW ZEALAND

Avis ☎09/526 2847
Budget ☎09/375 2222
Hertz ☎09/367 6350

NORTH AMERICA

Alamo ☎1-800/522-9696, *www.goalamo.com*
Auto Europe ☎1-800/223-5555, *www.wrld.com/ae*
Avis ☎1-800/331-1084, *www.avis.com*
Budget ☎1-800/527-0700, *www.budgetrentacar.com*
Dollar ☎1-800/421-6868, *www.dollarcar.com*
Enterprise Rent-a-Car ☎1-800/325-8007, *www.pickenterprise.com*
Europe by Car ☎1-800/223-1516, *www.europebycar.com*

Hertz ☎1-800/654-3001; in Canada ☎1-800/263-0600, *www.hertz.com*
Holiday Autos ☎1-800/422-7737, *www.holiday/colauto.com*
National ☎1-800/CAR-RENT, *www.nationalcar.com*
Thrifty ☎1-800/367-2277, *www.thrifty.com*
US Rent-a-Car ☎1-800/777-9377.
Value ☎1-800/468-2583.

international driving permit, available from state and national motoring organizations for a small fee. If you're bringing your own car into the country you should also carry your vehicle registration or ownership document at all times. Furthermore, you must be adequately insured, so be sure to check your existing policy.

In Scotland, as in England, you drive on the left, which can lead to a few tense days of acclimatization for many overseas drivers. **Speed limits** are 30 or 40mph (50 or 65kmph) in built-up areas, 70mph (110kmph) on motorways and dual carriageways, and 60mph (100kmph) on most other roads. As a rule, assume that in any area with street lighting the speed limit is 30mph (50kmph), unless otherwise stated. In the Highlands and Islands, there are still plenty of **single-track roads** with passing places – these should also be used to enable cars to overtake you. In these remoter regions, the roads are littered with sheep which are entirely oblivious to cars, so slow down and edge your way past – should you kill one, it is your duty to inform the local farmer.

The three major motoring organizations, the Automobile Association (AA), the Royal Automobile Club (RAC) and Green Flag Emergency Assistance, all operate 24-hour emergency **breakdown** services. The AA and RAC also provide many other motoring services, including a reciprocal arrangement for free assistance through many overseas motoring organizations – check the situation with yours before setting out. On motorways, the AA and RAC can be called from roadside booths. Elsewhere, ring ☎0800/887766 for the AA; ☎0800/828282 for the RAC; and ☎0800/400600 for Green Flag. In remote areas, however, particularly in the Highlands and Islands, you may have a long wait for assistance. You can ring these emergency numbers even if you are not a member of the respective organization, although a substantial fee will be charged.

It may also be worth investing in a policy with **home-relay**, as spare parts can be hard to get hold of in the Highlands, and most standard policies will only get you to the nearest garage, where you can find yourself stranded for days until the part you need is sent from Inverness or Glasgow. If you're touring the remoter parts of Scotland, bear in mind, too, that some regions of the country, particularly the far north, have comparatively few garages and petrol stations.

Like the rest of Britain, it's inadvisable for anyone travelling alone to **hitch** in Scotland, even in the central region where there's a good motorway network and a lot of traffic. In remote areas, especially in the Highlands, there's a long tradition of giving lifts, but you may have to wait a long time before you're picked up.

CAR RENTAL

Car rental in Scotland is expensive, and, especially if you're travelling from North America, you'll probably find it cheaper to arrange things in advance through one of the multinational chains. If you do rent a car, the least you can expect to pay is around £135 a week – the rate for a small hatchback from Holiday Autos, one of the most competitive rental agencies. The multinationals charge around £40 per day, and you may well find that you can save a considerable sum by using a local firm, particularly over the course of a week.

Most companies prefer you to pay with a credit card, otherwise you may have to leave a deposit

of over £100. There are very few automatics at the lower end of the price scale – if you want one, you should book well ahead. To rent a car you need to show your driving licence; few companies will rent to drivers with less than a year's experience and most will only rent to people between 21 and 70 years of age.

Motorbike rental is ludicrously expensive, at around £50 a day/£220 a week for a 500cc machine, and around £90/£325 for a one-litre tourer, including insurance, helmets and luggage.

BY FERRY

Scotland has 61 inhabited islands, according to the last census, and 49 of them have scheduled ferries. Ferries, therefore, play an important part in travelling around the country. Most ferries carry cars and vans, and the vast majority can be booked in advance. In fact, if you're taking a vehicle on a ferry, you should book ahead as far in advance as possible, whatever the time of year, as places can get filled up months in advance.

Caledonian MacBrayne (abbreviated by most people, and throughout this book, to CalMac) has a virtual monopoly on services on the River Clyde and those to the Inner and Outer Hebrides, sailing to 21 islands altogether. They aren't cheap, but they do have two types of reduced-fare pass. The **Island Hopscotch** offers a range of economy fares for cars and passengers on a number of preset routes and is valid for one month from the date of the first journey. It's the best option for anyone planning to make several short ferry trips between islands, though you do have to follow a set itinerary. Much more flexible is the **Island Rover**, which entitles you to eight or fifteen consecutive days' unlimited ferry travel. It does not, however, guarantee you a place on any ferry, so you still need to book ahead. The eight-day pass costs £41 for passengers and £199 for cars, while the fifteen-day pass costs £59 and £299 respectively. CalMac schedules are highly complicated, but you can get details from the address given in the box on p.30.

P&O Scottish Ferries run car ferries to Orkney and Shetland. For Orkney, you can depart either from Aberdeen (1–2 weekly; 8–10hr) or from Scrabster, near Thurso (1–3 daily; 2hr). Fares from Aberdeen are roughly £80 return for a foot passenger, plus £140 for a car; from Scrabster passengers pay £30 return, plus £80 for a car. There's also a summer-only passenger ferry from John O' Groats to Orkney (May–Sept 2–4 daily;

FERRY COMPANIES IN SCOTLAND

Caledonian MacBrayne, The Ferry Terminal, Gourock PA19 1QP (☎0990/650000; *reservations@calmac.co.uk*).

Orkney Ferries, Shore St, Kirkwall KW15 1LG (☎01856/872044).

P&O Scottish Ferries, PO Box 5, Jamieson's Quay, Aberdeen AB11 5NP (☎01224/572615; *passenger@poscottishferries.co.uk*).

Western Ferries, Hunter's Quay, Dunoon, Argyll PA23 8HG (☎01369/704452).

45min), run by **John O' Groats Ferries** (see p.559). P&O run an overnight ferry from Aberdeen to Shetland (14–20hr), which runs daily except Saturday night in summer. Fares work out around £115 return for a foot passenger, plus £175 return for a small car. On all routes you should book in advance if you are taking a vehicle.

The various Orkney islands are linked to each other by services run by **Orkney Ferries**; Shetland's inter-island ferries are run in conjunction with the local council, so contacting the local tourist board is your best bet. There are also numerous small operators round the Scottish coast that run day-excursion trips; their phone numbers are listed in the relevant chapters of this guide.

It's possible to book ferry tickets in advance in **North America**, if you're organized enough to know exactly when you'll be making the crossing. For sailings to/from France, Belgium or the Netherlands, contact BritRail Travel International (☎1-888/274-8724) or Scots American (☎1-201/768-1187); to/from Scandinavia, contact Bergen Line (☎1-800/323-7436) or Scandinavian Seaways (☎1-800/533-3755). In **Australia** and **New Zealand**, you can book ferry tickets in advance at branches of Thomas Cook (see p.9).

BY PLANE

Apart from the three major airports of Glasgow, Edinburgh and Aberdeen, Scotland has numerous minor airports, many of them on the islands, some little more than gravel airstrips. Internal **flights** are pretty expensive on the whole: a single fare from Glasgow to Islay will set you back around £75, and there are very few discounted tickets available. However, if you are short on time, the extra expense may well be worth it. Most flights are operated by British Airways or Loganair, though the majority of flights can be booked directly through British Airways (☎0345/222111). For inter-island flights in Shetland (excluding Fair Isle), you need to book direct through Loganair (☎01595/840246).

The main Scottish airports are listed below; call them, or British Airways, for timetable information, or pick up a BA schedule from a travel agent. BA should also be able to fill you in on any cost-cutting special tickets available. The **Highland Rover**, for example, costs just £169, and allows you to take any five flights within seven days (flights to and between Orkney and Shetland are covered, but not services within either of those two archipelagos).

AIRPORTS IN SCOTLAND			
Aberdeen	☎01224/722331	**Islay**	☎01496/302361
Barra	☎01871/890283	**Kirkwall**	☎01856/872421
Benbecula	☎01870/602310	**Stornoway**	☎01851/702256
Campbeltown	☎01586/552571	**Sumburgh**	☎01950/460654
Dundee	☎01382/643242	**Tingwall**	☎01595/840246
Edinburgh	☎0131/333 1000	**Tiree**	☎01879/220456
Glasgow	☎0141/887 1111	**Unst**	☎01957/711620
Inverness	☎01463/232471	**Wick**	☎01955/602215

ACCOMMODATION

In common with the rest of Britain, accommodation in Scotland is expensive. Budget travellers are well catered for with numerous hostels, and those with money to spend will relish the country's upmarket hotels, many of which are converted feudal seats. Just about every tourist office can help you find the right sort of accommodation to suit, whatever your budget. This can be easily arranged on arrival, but you'll find a much greater choice if you book in advance; tourist offices usually make a small fee for booking rooms. In some areas you will pay a deposit that's deducted from your first night's bill (usually ten percent), while in others the office will take a percentage or flat-rate commission – on average around £3. Another useful service operated by the majority of tourist offices is the "Book-a-

Bed-Ahead" service, which reserves accommodation for you in your next port of call, and costs £3 per booking.

HOTELS AND B&BS

The STB operates a nationwide system for grading **hotels**, **guest houses** and **B&Bs**, which is updated annually. Although the STB cover a huge number of places, by no means everyone participates, and you shouldn't assume that a particular B&B is no good simply because it's not on the STB books. Within the STB system, the most important element is the new **star awards**, from one to five. These reflect the quality of welcome, service and hospitality, and not simply the level of facilities – these are separately assessed and graded in three categories: Approved, Commended and Highly Commended. The AA and the RAC have their own star system, independent of, and slightly more subjective than, the STB.

Hotels come in all shapes and sizes, and, at the lower end of the scale, merge almost imperceptibly into B&Bs and guest houses. These range from private houses with a couple of bedrooms set aside for paying guests and a dining room for the consumption of a rudimentary breakfast, to rooms as well furnished as those in hotels costing twice as much, with delicious home-prepared breakfasts, and an informal hospitality that a larger place couldn't match.

There's no hard and fast correlation between standards and price. However, at the bottom end of the **price scale** (though not necessarily the quality scale) you'll probably pay around £40 per night for a double room at a B&B, rising to

ACCOMMODATION PRICE CODES

Throughout this book, accommodation **prices** have been graded with the numbers below, according to the cost of the least expensive double room in high season. Although costs will rise slightly overall within the life of this edition, the relative comparisons should remain valid. The bulk of the recommendations will fall in categories ② to ⑤; those in the highest categories are limited to places that are especially attractive. Bear in mind that many of the chain hotels slash their tariffs at the weekend, and that many of the cheaper places will also have more expensive rooms. Note that in our accommodation listings, price codes are not given for youth hostels – all youth hostel accommodation costs under £10 per person per night, except in the odd rare case, where we have quoted the price in the review.

① under £40	④ £60–70	⑦ £110–150
② £40–50	⑤ £70–90	⑧ £150–200
③ £50–60	⑥ £90–110	⑨ over £200

around £70 in a very comfortable guest house, and from £110 and upwards in an established, award-winning hotel. For a full explanation of the price codes used in this book, see the box on p.31.

Many B&Bs, even the pricier ones, have only a few rooms, so **advance booking** is recommended. This is especially true in the Islands, where the number of options is limited. You might also want to book in for dinner, bed and breakfast (not to mention packed lunch), as many islands have limited, or no, eating and drinking options. Another important point to remember is that outside of the main towns and cities, many places are only open for the summer season, roughly from Easter to October. You'll always find somewhere to stay outside this period, but the choice may be pretty limited.

HOSTELS

The network of the **Scottish Youth Hostels Association (SYHA)** consists of some eighty properties, usually offering bunk-bed accommodation in single-sex dormitories or smaller rooms. Most youth hostels have moved away from the ethic of former days, when you had to perform chores before leaving. Some of the bigger city hostels are more like bed and breakfast places, offering private facilities and even evening meals. However, the more rural hostels retain some of the old ways – you're certainly expected to leave the place looking spick and span, and an 11.30pm curfew is still the norm.

All the hostels referred to as "youth hostels" in the guide are official SYHA properties unless stated otherwise. For Scottish residents, adult membership costs £6, and can be obtained either via the **SYHA National Office** (7 Glebe Crescent, Stirling FK8 2JA; ☎01786/891400), or at the first SYHA hostel you book into. SYHA membership gives you automatic membership to **Hostelling International (HI)**, as does membership of any of the seventy HI-affiliated hostelling associations around the world. Don't worry if you arrive in Scotland without HI membership, as you can join up at virtually any SYHA hostel. HI membership costs £9, though you can pay in £1.50 instalments, spread out over the first six nights – that way it makes no odds if you only end up staying in a couple of nights in hostels. It's also worth noting that youth hostel members are entitled to half-price entry to all National Trust for Scotland properties (see p.39).

Hostels in Scotland are generally cheaper than those in the rest of Britain: the majority charge between £6.50 and £10 a night, with only a few top-grade establishments (normally those in large cities) charging more than this. The cost of hostel **meals**, where available, is low: breakfast is around £2.50, and evening meals start at £5. Nearly all hostels have kitchen facilities, for those who prefer self-catering. If you need to check any tariffs in advance, phone the hostel, or consult the current *SYHA Handbook*, which comes free when you pay your membership subscription.

At any time of the year, particularly in the popular city hostels, **advance booking** is recommended, and just about essential at Easter, Christmas and from May to August. You can book by post, telephone or, sometimes, fax, and your bed will be held until 6pm on the day of arrival. If you have a credit card, you can also use HI's **International Booking Network** (IBN) to book beds as far as six months in advance – there is a small booking fee for this service which varies from country to country. Even if you haven't booked, always phone ahead – phone numbers are given in the guide. Not all hostels are open all year round, and many close during the day, so it's worth getting hold of a copy of the current SYHA Handbook in order to check the details.

Allied to the SYHA, the **Gatliff Hebridean Hostels Trust** is a charitable organization that rents out very simple croft accommodation in the Western Isles. Accommodation is very basic, almost primitive, and many of these hostels have no phone, but the settings are invariably spectacular. In Shetland, camping böds, operated by the **Shetland Amenity Trust**, offer similarly simple accommodation: you need all your usual camping equipment, except, of course, a tent. For more details about Gatliff hostels and camping böds, see the relevant chapters in the guide.

In addition, the **Independent Backpackers Hostels of Scotland**, is an association of independent hostels, mainly situated in the Highlands and Islands, though including a few in Edinburgh. These are usually laid-back places with no membership, fewer rules and no curfew. Housed in buildings ranging from croft houses to converted churches, they all have dormitories, hot showers, common rooms and self-catering kitchens, while many organize a range of outdoor activities. Prices hover at around £10 per person per night. Detailed reviews of most independent hostels in Scotland are featured in the relevant sections of

YOUTH HOSTEL ASSOCIATIONS

Australia Australian Youth Hostels Association, 422 Kent St, Sydney (☎02/9261 1111).

Canada Hostelling International Canada, Room 400, 205 Catherine St, Ottawa, ON K2P 1C3 (☎1-800/663-5777 or ☎613/237-7884). Annual membership adults $26.75, free for under-18s when accompanied by parents; two-year memberships cost $35.

England and Wales Youth Hostel Association (YHA), Trevelyan House, 8 St Stephen's Hill, St Albans, Herts AL1 2DY (☎01727/855215, www.yha/england/wales.org.uk).

Ireland An Óige, 61 Mountjoy St, Dublin 7 (☎01/830 4555, www.irelandyha.org).

New Zealand Youth Hostels Association of New Zealand, PO Box 436, Christchurch 1 (☎03/3799970).

Northern Ireland Youth Hostel Association of Northern Ireland, 22 Donegal Rd, Belfast BT12 5JN (☎01232/324733).

Scotland Scottish Youth Hostel Association (SYHA), 7 Glebe Crescent, Stirling, FK8 2JA (☎01786/451181, www.syha.org.uk).

USA Hostelling International-American Youth Hostels (HI-AYH), 733 15th St NW, Suite 840, PO Box 37613, Washington, DC 20005 (☎202/783-6161, www.hostel.com). Annual membership adults $25, youths (under 18) $10, seniors (55 or over) $15, families $35.

---

this book, and in more detail in the excellent *Independent Hostels Guide* by Sam Dalley, which is updated annually and published by Backpacker Press (for details, contact the distributors Cordee Books and Maps, 3a De Montfort St, Leicester LE1 7HD; ☎0116/254 3579).

CAMPING AND SELF-CATERING

There are hundreds of **campsites** in Scotland, most of which are open from April to October. The most expensive sites, which charge about £10 to pitch a tent, are usually well equipped, with shops, a restaurant, a bar and, occasionally, sports facilities. At the other end of the scale, farmers sometimes offer pitches on their land for as little as £2.50 per night. The AA lists and grades campsites in its publication *Camping and Caravanning in Britain and Ireland*, and the area tourist boards can all supply lists of their recommended sites.

In the most popular parts of rural Scotland – especially in the Highlands and Islands – tents have to share space with **caravans**. The great majority of these are permanently moored nose-to-tail in the vicinity of some of Scotland's finest scenery; others are positioned singly in back gardens or amidst farmland. Some can be booked as self-catering caravans, either by the week, or for shorter periods. With prices hovering around £100 a week, this can work out as one of the cheapest options if you're travelling with kids in tow.

For **North Americans** planning to do a lot of camping, an international camping carnet is a sound investment, available from home motoring organizations, or from Family Campers and RVers

(FCRV), 4804 Transit Rd, Building 2, Depew, NY 14043 (☎1-800/245-9755). The carnet is good for discounts at member sites and serves as useful identification. FCRV annual membership costs $25, and the carnet an additional $10.

You may prefer more robust **self-catering** accommodation, and there are thousands of STB-approved properties for rent by the week, ranging from city penthouses to secluded cottages. The least you can expect to pay for four-berth self-catering accommodation in summer is around £150 per week, but for something special – such as a well-sited coastal cottage – you should budget for more than twice that amount. In the guide we give summer rates for self-catering accommodation, but note that rates tend to fall dramatically out of season. A good source of accommodation is the STB's self-catering guide. Updated annually, this full-colour brochure lists over 1200 properties, ranging from cottages and chalets to luxurious apartments, with colour photographs of most places included. Copies can be bought or ordered through any Scottish tourist office (see p.24).

Another cheap self-catering option, especially if you're staying a week or more, is **campus accommodation**. The universities of Glasgow, Strathclyde, Edinburgh, Stirling, St Andrews and Dundee all open their halls of residence to overseas visitors during the summer break, with some also offering rooms during the Easter and Christmas vacations. Rooms vary from tiny single rooms in long, lonely corridors, to relatively comfortable places in small shared apartments. Prices per night for bed and breakfast tend to be no

---

SELF-CATERING ACCOMMODATION

Finlayson Hughes, 45 Church St, Inverness IV1 1DR (☎01463/224343). Fifty or so properties mainly in the Highlands and Islands, everything from castles to bothies, from around £200 a week upwards.

Forest Holidays, Forestry Commission, 231 Corstorphine Rd, Edinburgh EH12 7AT (☎0131/334 0303). Only two sites, at Loch Awe, and Strathyre near Callander: purpose-built cabins in beautiful woodland areas, sleeping five or six people. Prices start from around £150 for three nights in June, though during school holidays, you must book the cabins for at least a week.

Highland Hideways, 5/7 Stafford Street, Oban, Argyll PA34 5NJ (☎01631/526056). A range of

self-catering properties, mainly on the Highlands and Islands, which range from a former bank in Oban to a converted boathouse on Loch Awe. Free colour brochure.

Landmark Trust, Shottesbrook, Maidenhead, Berkshire SL6 3SW (☎01628 825925). The Landmark Trust has fifteen upmarket historical properties in Scotland. Their brochure costs £9.50, redeemable when you book a holiday.

National Trust for Scotland, 5 Charlotte Square, Edinburgh EH2 4DU (☎0131/226 5922). The NTS owns 34 converted historic cottages and houses around Scotland, with prices starting at around £250 week in high season.

---

cheaper than local B&Bs, but per week for self-catering, you can pay as little as £50 per person.

Phone the British Universities Accommodation Consortium (☎0115/950 4571) for a brochure.

FOOD AND DRINK

The quality of Scottish food has improved by leaps and bounds in recent years. Scottish produce – particularly the country's meat, fish, seafood and game – is of outstanding quality and has to some extent been rediscovered of late. Bear in mind, too, that in the larger cities the presence of various immigrant communities has led to a fine array of ethnic restaurants.

In many hotels and B&Bs you'll be offered a **Scottish breakfast**, similar to its English counterpart of sausage, bacon and egg, but with the addition of black pudding (blood and gristle) and potato scones. Porridge is another likely option – properly made with genuine oatmeal and traditionally eaten with salt rather than sugar, though the latter is always on offer. You may also be served kippers (smoked herring) or Arbroath smokies (smoked haddock), or a large piece of haddock eaten with a poached egg on top. Oatcakes (plain, slightly salty biscuits) and a "buttery" – a butter-enriched bread related to the French croissant – might feature. Scotland's staple drink, like England's, is **tea**, drunk strong and with milk, though **coffee** is just as readily available everywhere.

The quintessential Scots dish is **haggis**, a sheep's stomach bag stuffed with spiced liver, offal, oatmeal and onion and traditionally eaten with bashed neeps (mashed turnips) and chappit tatties (mashed potatoes). The humble haggis has become rather trendy in recent years, and you can, in the big cities, get a vegetarian version. Other staples include steak and kidney pie and shepherd's pie (minced beef covered with mashed potato and baked), as well as **stovies**, a tasty mash of onion and fried potato heated up with minced beef. In this cold climate, home-made soup is often welcome; try **Scots broth**, made with combinations of lentil, split pea, mutton stock or vegetables and barley.

Scots **beef** is delicious, especially the Aberdeen Angus breed; menus will specify if your steak falls into that fine category. **Venison**, the meat of the red deer, also features large – low in cholesterol and very tasty, it's served roasted or in casseroles, often flavoured with juniper or with a whisky sauce. If you like **game** and can afford it, splash out on grouse, the most highly prized of all game birds, strong, dark and succulent, best eaten with bread sauce. Pheasant is also worth a try and is less rich than other game, more like a tasty chicken – you can eat it stuffed with oatmeal or with a mealie pudding, a kind of vegetarian black pudding made from onion, oatmeal and spices.

Scotland has a huge variety of fresh **fish** to choose from. In the coastal towns, prawns, mussels, oysters, crab and scallops are always available, while inland salmon is a must, especially the more delicately flavoured wild salmon – though this will always cost more than the farmed variety. Both are served either hot with melted butter, small new potatoes and a creamy Hollandaise sauce, or cold in a salad. Trout is also farmed in Scotland, often fried in oatmeal and eaten with bacon. Look out especially for the wild brown trout, whose firm pink flesh is nearly as good as salmon.

Puddings, often smothered in butterscotch sauce or syrup, are taken very seriously in Scotland. One traditional favourite is Cranachan, made with toasted oatmeal steeped in whisky and folded into whipped cream flavoured with fresh raspberries; on the same lines, Atholl Brose, related to English syllabub, is made with oatmeal, whisky and cream. For the ultimate dessert decadence, try the clootie dumpling, a sweet, stodgy fruit pudding soaked in a cloth for hours. If it all sounds a bit rich you might prefer the black bun, a peppery fruitcake encased in a thin pastry and traditionally eaten at New Year, or the many home-made shortbreads – far superior to the commercial varieties.

One Scottish institution that satisfies the Scots' sweet tooth is **high tea**, consisting of a cooked main course and a plethora of cakes, washed down with tea or coffee and eaten between about 5pm and 6.30pm.

As for **fast food**, fish and chips is as popular in Scotland as in England and "**chippies**" abound, serving battered fish (invariably known as a "fish supper" even if eaten at lunchtime), haggis, oatmeal-based numbers such as black and mealie puddings, and artery-clogging, battered, deep-fried Mars bars. For alternative fast food, the major towns feature all the usual **pizza**, **burger** and **baked potato** outlets.

WHERE TO EAT

For **budget food** in Scotland you'll find **cafés** ranging from the most basic "greasy spoons" to French-style **brasseries**, where you can have anything from a glass of wine to a cup of coffee, as well as a simple meal. Even the smallest place will have a **tearoom** of sorts, where you can sample Scottish baking. Some of the cheapest places to eat in Scotland are the **pubs** or **hotel bars** – indeed, in the smallest villages these might be your only option. Bar food ranges from the very ordinary – scampi and chips – to food that equals the à la carte dishes served in the adjacent hotel restaurant.

As for **restaurants**, standards vary enormously, but Scotland has an ever-increasing number of top-class chefs producing superb dishes with a Scottish slant that certainly rival their English and European counterparts. Outside Edinburgh and Glasgow, many of these are found in hotels but are happy to serve non-residents. You could easily end up paying £25–50 a head.

In central Scotland, particularly in Edinburgh and Glasgow, the **Indian** and **Chinese** communities ensure there is a good choice of restaurants, offering quality meals at fair prices. Some of the **French** restaurants in Edinburgh are excellent, and Scotland's large **Italian** community means there are numerous good trattorias. On the whole, though, you won't find the range of choice that exists south of the border, and outside the big cities **vegetarians** are still looked on somewhat askance, though the situation is slowly improving.

The restaurant listings in the guide include a mix of high-quality and budget establishments. (If you're primarily on a culinary pilgrimage, you might consider getting hold of a copy of *A Taste of Scotland* (David Frame Creative), the country's top annual foodie guide.) To help give an idea of costs, each place listed in this guide is placed in one of three **price categories**: inexpensive (under £10 a head), moderate (£10–20) and expensive (£20–30). Prices do not include alcohol.

DRINKING

As in the rest of Britain, Scottish **pubs**, which originated as travellers' hostelries and coaching inns, are *the* great social institution. The pub crawl, a drunken stagger through as many pubs as possible in one night, is a national pastime in large towns and cities. The focal points of any community, Scottish pubs vary hugely, from old-fashioned inns, with heaps of atmosphere and open fires, to raucous theme pubs, with jukeboxes and satellite TV. Most city pubs are owned by large breweries who favour their own cask-conditioned real ales served from the distinctive Scottish tall font (for more on types of beer, see below). Many of them, especially outside the big cities, are no-nonsense spit-and-sawdust public bars with an almost exclusively male clientele, making some visitors, especially women, feel highly uncomfortable. Out in the Islands, pubs are few and far between, with most drinking taking place in the local hotel bar. In Edinburgh and Glasgow, by contrast, you'll find traditional pubs supplemented by upbeat, trendy café-bars.

Scotland has all-day **opening hours**, and pubs are generally open from Monday to Saturday 11am to 11pm, with "last orders" called by the bar staff about fifteen minutes before closing time. On Sunday the hours are reduced; many pubs are closed in the afternoon and last orders are called at 10.30pm. In general, you have to be 16 to enter a pub unaccompanied, though some places have special family rooms for people with children, and beer gardens where younger kids can run free. The legal drinking age is 18.

BEER

Beer is the staple drink in Scotland's pubs, the indigenous variety a thick, dark ale, known as **heavy**, served at room temperature with a full head in pints or half-pints. Scottish beers are graded by the shilling: a system used since the 1870s and indicating the level of potency – the higher the shilling mark, the stronger or "heavier" the beer. A pint costs anything from £1.50 to

£2.20, depending on the brew and the locale of the pub.

Scotland's biggest-name breweries are McEwan's and Younger's, part of the mighty Scottish and Newcastle group, and Tennents, owned by the English firm Bass. The beers produced by these companies tend to be heavier, smoother and stronger than their English equivalents, especially McEwan's Export, a mass-produced, highly potent brew, and Tennents' Fowler's Wee Heavy, a famously tasty smooth ale. Younger's Tartan, though less flavoursome, is Scotland's biggest seller.

However, if you really want to discover how good Scottish beer, once renowned throughout the world for its strength, can be, look out for the products of the small **local breweries** scattered throughout Scotland. Edinburgh's Caledonian Brewery makes nine good cask beers, and operates from Victorian premises using much of their original equipment, including the only direct-fired coppers left in Britain. Others to look out for are Bellhaven, brewed in Dunbar near Edinburgh, whose 80-shilling Export is a typical Scottish ale; Maclays, a hoppy, lightish ale brewed in Alloa; and Traquair, in the Borders, which does a wonderfully smooth House Ale. The dry, fruity Alice Ale, brewed in Inverness, and the Orkney Brewery's Raven Ale, can be life-savers in the north, where good beer is hard to come by.

WHISKY

Scotland's national drink is **whisky** – *uisge beatha*, or the "water of life" in Gaelic – sometimes drunk in pubs as a sort of chaser with a half-pint of beer on the side, a combination known as a "nip and a hauf". A standard single measure is 50ml.

Whisky has been produced in Scotland since the fifteenth century, but only really took off in popularity after the 1780 tax on claret made wine too expensive for most people. The taxman soon caught up with whisky distilling, however, and drove the stills underground. Today, many distilleries operate on the site of simple cottages that once distilled the stuff illegally. In 1823, Parliament revised its Excise Laws, in the process legalizing whisky production, and today the drink is Scotland's chief export. There are two types of whisky: single malt, made from malted barley, and grain whisky, which (relatively cheap to produce), is made from maize and a small amount of malted barley in a continuous still. **Blended**, which accounts for more than ninety percent of all sales, is as the name suggests, a blend of the two types.

Grain whisky forms about seventy percent of the average bottle of blended whisky, but the distinctive flavour of the different blends comes from the malt whisky which is added to the grain in different quantities. The more expensive the blend, the higher the proportion of skilfully chosen and aged malts that have gone into it. Among many brand names, Johnnie Walker, Bells, Teachers and The Famous Grouse are some of the most widely available. All have a similar flavour, and are often drunk with mixers such as lemonade or mineral water.

Despite the dominance of the blended whiskies, **single malt whiskies** are infinitely superior, and best drunk neat (or with a little water) to appreciate their distinctive flavours. Malt whisky is made by soaking barley in water for two or three days until it swells, after which it is left to germinate for up to twelve days, allowing the starch in the barley seed to become soluble. The malted barley is dried with peat, mashed with hot water and fermented with yeast to convert the sugar into crude alcohol, which is then twice distilled and the vapours condensed as a spirit, aged for a minimum of three years (usually much longer) in oak casks. Single malts vary enormously depending on the peat used for drying, the water used for mashing, and the type of oak cask used in the maturing process, but they fall into four distinct groups: Highland, Lowland, Campbeltown and Islay, with the majority in the Highland category and being produced largely on Speyside. You can get the best-known blends – among them Glenlivet, Glenmorangie, MacAllan, Talisker, Laphroaig, Highland Park and Glenfiddich, the top seller – in most pubs.

Most distilleries have a highly developed nose for PR and offer guided tours that range from slick and streamlined to small and friendly. All of them offer visitors a "wee dram" as a finale, and those distilleries that charge an entrance fee often give you your money back if you buy a bottle at the end – though prices are no lower at source than in the shops.

NON-ALCOHOLIC DRINKS

Scotland produces a prodigious amount of **natural mineral water**, which is mainly exported, as the tap water tends to be chill and clean. In addition, Scotland has the distinction of being the only country in the world where neither Coke nor Pepsi is the most popular fizzy drink. That accolade belongs to Irn-Bru, a fizzy, orange, sickly sweet concoction sold in just about every shop in the country.

POST AND PHONES

In towns and cities across Scotland, most post offices are open Monday to Friday 9am to 5.30pm and Saturday 9am to 12.30pm or 1pm. However, in small communities you'll find sub-post offices operating out of a shop, shed, or even a private house. Hours can vary enormously, but the post office counter won't be open longer hours even if the shop is.

Stamps can be bought at post-office counters, from vending machines outside, or from an increasing number of newsagents. A first-class letter to anywhere in the UK currently costs 26p and should – in theory – arrive the next day; sec-

ond-class letters cost 19p, and take from two to four days. Airmail letters of less than 20g (0.7oz) cost 30p to EU and non-EU countries. Letters to other overseas destinations cost from 44p for 10g, and 63p for 20g. Pre-stamped aerogrammes conforming to overseas airmail weight limits of under 10g can be bought for 37p only from post offices. For more information about Royal Mail postal services, phone ☎0345/740740.

Most public **payphones** in Scotland are still operated by British Telecom (BT) and, in towns, at least, are widespread. Many BT payphones take all coins from 10p upwards, although some only accept **phonecards**, available from post offices and newsagents which display the BT logo. These cards come in denominations of £2, £3, £5, £10 and £20; some BT phones accept credit cards too. Calls are cheapest between 6pm and 8am from Monday to Friday and all day on Saturday and Sunday, though for Australia and New Zealand, calls are cheapest between midnight and 7am, and between 2.30pm and 7.30pm, daily. Throughout this guide, every phone number is prefixed by the area code, separated from the subscriber number by an oblique slash. You don't have to dial the prefix if you're in the same area code. Any number with the prefix ☎0800 is free; ☎0345 numbers are charged at the local rate; ☎0990 numbers at the national rate.

OPERATOR SERVICES AND PHONE CODES

Operator ☎100
Directory assistance ☎192

International operator ☎155
Overseas directory assistance ☎153

INTERNATIONAL CALLS

To **telephone Scotland** from overseas dial ☎011 from the US and Canada, ☎0011 from Australia and ☎00 from New Zealand, followed in all cases by 44, then the area code minus its initial zero, and then the number.
To call **overseas from Scotland** dial ☎00, followed by the country code, the area code (minus the zero if there is one), and then the number. Country codes include:

Australia ☎61	New Zealand ☎64	USA and Canada ☎1
Ireland ☎353	South Africa ☎27	

OPENING HOURS, HOLIDAYS AND ENTRANCE CHARGES

Traditionally, shop hours in Scotland have been Monday to Saturday 9am to 5.30pm or 6pm. In the bigger towns and cities, many places now stay open on Sundays and late at night, with Thursday or Friday the favoured evenings. Large supermarkets, and out-of-town shopping complexes also tend to stay open until 8pm or 9pm from Monday to Saturday, and for six hours on a Sunday. However, in the Highlands and Islands, you'll find precious little open on a Sunday, with many small towns also retaining an "early closing day" when shops close at 1pm – Wednesday is the favourite.

Unlike in England, Scotland's **Bank Holidays** mean just that: they are literally days when the banks are closed, rather than general public holidays, and they vary from year to year. They include January 2; the Friday before Easter; the first and last Monday in May; the last Monday in August; St Andrew's Day (November 30); Christmas Day (December 25); and Boxing Day (December 26).

New Year's Day, January 1, is the only fixed **Public Holiday**, but all Scottish towns and cities have a one-day holiday in both spring and autumn – dates vary from place to place but normally fall on a Monday. If you want to know the exact dates, you can get a booklet detailing them from the Glasgow Chamber of Commerce, 30 George Square, Glasgow G2 1EQ.

MUSEUMS AND MONUMENTS

Apart from the really big museums, and a number of attractions high on the tourist trail, Scotland's **tourist season** runs from Easter to October, and outside this period many indoor attractions are shut – though ruins, parks and gardens are normally accessible year-round. We've given full details of opening hours and admission charges in the guide.

Many of Scotland's most treasured sights – from castles and country houses to islands, gardens and tracts of protected landscape – come under the control of the privately run **National Trust for Scotland**, 5 Charlotte Square, Edinburgh EH2 4DU (☎0131/226 5922), or the state-run **Historic Scotland**, Longmore House, Salisbury Place, Edinburgh EH9 1SH (☎0131/668 8600), shown respectively as the "NTS" or "HS" in the guide. Both organizations charge an entry fee for most

places, and these can be quite high, especially for the more grandiose NTS estates. If you think you'll be visiting more than half a dozen owned by the NTS, or more than a dozen owned by HS, it's worth taking **annual membership** (NTS £26, family £42; HS £24, one-parent family £27, two-parent family £42), which allows free entry to their properties.

In addition, both the NTS and HS offer short-term passes that give discounts on admission prices. The **National Trust Touring Pass**, which costs £16 for an adult and £26 for a family, is valid for seven days and gives free admission to all NTS properties; the fourteen-day pass costs £24 and £42 respectively. The HS **Scottish Explorer** seven-day ticket allows free entry to seventy monuments, castles and other properties and costs £13.50 or £28 for a family; a two-week equivalent costs £18 and £36 respectively. **HI Members** (see p.32) are automatically eligible for half-price entry into all NTS properties.

A lot of Scottish **stately homes** remain in the hands of the landed gentry, who tend to charge around £5 for admission to edited highlights of their domain. Many other old buildings, albeit rarely the most momentous structures, are owned by local authorities, and admission is often cheap and sometimes free. Municipal art galleries and museums are usually free, as are most of the **state-owned museums**, although "voluntary" donations may be solicited.

The majority of fee-charging attractions in Scotland give 25–50 percent **reductions** for senior citizens, the unemployed, full-time students and children under 16, with under-5s being admitted free almost everywhere. Proof of age will be required in most cases. The entry charges quoted in the guide are the full adult charges.

North Americans can buy the Scottish Explorer and National Trust Touring passes at travel agents or directly from Especially Britain (see p.6). A further option, only open to overseas visitors, is the **Great British Heritage Pass**, which gives free admission to some 600 sites throughout Britain, including many which are not run by the NTS or HS. Costing $45 for seven days, around $70 for 15 days and $90 for a month, it can be purchased through most travel agents at home, on arrival at any large UK airport, from British Airways offices and the British Travel Centre, 1 Regent St, London W1 (walk-in service only).

THE MEDIA

The principal British daily newspapers are all available in Scotland. The tabloids are as popular as in England, and many appear in a specific Scottish edition – among them Rupert Murdoch's sex-and-scandal *Sun*, the self-consciously ridiculous *Daily Sport*, and the vaguely left-wing *Daily Mirror*, the only tabloid that manages anything approximating an antidote to the *Sun's* reactionary politics. The biggest seller in the "quality" end of the market is the staunchly Conservative *Daily Telegraph*, followed by the Murdoch-owned *Times*. The political centre is occupied by *The Independent*, which strives to live up to its name, despite being owned by the Mirror Group, and *The Guardian*, which inhabits a niche marginally left of centre.

All the above-mentioned "qualities", however, are justifiably seen in Scotland as being London newspapers. The **Scottish press** produces two major serious daily newspapers: Edinburgh's liberal-left *The Scotsman* and Glasgow's centre-right *Daily Herald*. Both offer good coverage of the current issues affecting Scotland, along with British and foreign news, sport, arts and lifestyle pages. Scotland's biggest-selling daily paper, though, is the downmarket *Daily Record*, from the same stable as the *Daily Mirror*. The provincial daily press is more widely read than its English counterpart, with the two biggest-selling regional titles being Aberdeen's famously parochial *Press and Journal*, widely read in the northeast, the Highlands and the Islands, and the right-wing *Dundee Courier*, mostly sold in Perth, Angus, Tayside and Fife. For an insight into life in the Highlands and islands, there's the weekly *Oban Times*, a staid paper compared with the more radical, campaigning weekly *West Highland Free Press*, printed on Skye. All carry articles in Gaelic as well as English. Further north, the lively *Shetland Times* and the sedate *Orcadian* are essential weekly reads.

Many national **Sunday newspapers** have a Scottish edition north of the border, although again Scotland has its own Sunday "heavies": *Scotland on Sunday*, from the *Scotsman* stable, and the *Sunday Herald*, complementing its eponymous daily. Both have heavyweight political analysis bulked out by exhaustive sports sections and energetic arts and lifestyle supplements. Far more fun and widely read, is the anachronistic *Sunday Post*, published by Dundee's mighty Thomson and Legg publishing

group and read by just under half the population. It's a wholesome paper, uniquely Scottish, and has changed little since the 1950s, since when its two long-running cartoon strips, *Oor Wullie* and *The Broons*, have acquired something of a cult status.

When it comes to **specialist periodicals**, the best-selling national weekly news magazine is the dry, centre-right *Economist*. The earnest centre-left alternative, the *New Statesman*, has considerably fewer readers, while the satirical bi-weekly *Private Eye* is a much-loved institution that prides itself on printing the stories the rest of the press won't touch, and on surviving the consequent stream of libel suits. The above three publications are all London-based, whereas the lively, weekly *Big Issue*, produced by homeless people and sold by vendors on every city street, has a separate Scottish edition and often carries features by well-known writers.

Scottish **monthlies** include the *Scottish Field*, a lowbrow version of England's *Tatler*, covering the interests and pursuits of the landed gentry, and the widely read *Scots Magazine*, an old-fashioned middle-of-the-road publication which promotes family values and lots of good fresh air. For visitors to Glasgow and Edinburgh, the fortnightly **listings magazine** *The List* is a must, covering all events in both cities and featuring lively interviews and articles.

USA Today is the most widely available **North American paper**, though only the larger newsagents will stock it; you can also find *Time* and *Newsweek* in quality bookstores and newsagents.

TELEVISION AND RADIO

In Scotland there are five main **television channels**: the state-owned BBC1 and BBC2, and the independent commercial channels, ITV, Channel Four and Channel 5. Though assailed by government critics of late, the **BBC** is just about maintaining its worldwide reputation for in-house quality productions, ranging from expensive costume dramas to intelligent documentaries – split between the avowedly mainstream BBC1 and the more rarefied fare of BBC2. Three companies, the populist STV, which serves most of southern Scotland and parts of the West Highlands, the Aberdeen-based Grampian, and Border Television which transmits from Carlisle, form the **ITV** network in Scotland. This is complemented by the more eclectic and less mainstream broadcasting of the partly subsidized **Channel Four**, and downmarket **Channel 5**, which can't yet be received in many parts of Scotland. A plethora of **satellite** and, in the cities, **cable stations**, are also available, though the dominant force is still Rupert Murdoch's **Sky**, which offers unlimited news, movies, soaps, home shopping and game shows, along with increasing amounts of British sport, which plays wall-to-wall in pubs the length of the country. For the time being, however, the old terrestrial stations still attract the majority of viewers.

Market forces are also eating away at the **BBC radio** network, which broadcasts six main channels in Scotland, though most of them originate largely from London. Radio One plays almost exclusively mainstream pop music; Radio Two specializes in MOR music; Radio Three broadcasts predominantly classical music; Radio Four is a blend of current affairs, arts and drama; and Radio Five Live, the newest station, transmits a mix of sport and news. The award-winning BBC Radio Scotland offers a Scottish perspective on news, politics, arts, music, travel and sport, and provides a Gaelic network in the northwest with local programmes in Shetland, Orkney, the north and the borders.

A web of **local commercial radio** stations stretches from Shetland to the Borders, mostly mixing rock and pop music with news, but a few tiny community-based stations such as Lochbroom FM in Ullapool – famed for its daily midge count – transmit documentaries and discussions on local issues. The most populated areas of Scotland also receive UK commercial radio: Classic FM lures listeners from Radios 2 and 3, Virgin Radio competes head to head with Radio 1 and Talk Radio UK competes with Radio 5 Live for sports coverage, phone-ins and chat.

SCOTTISH RADIO STATIONS

BBC Radio Scotland 92–95FM, 810MW. Nationwide news, sport, music, current affairs and arts.

Clyde 1 102.5FM. Glasgow's main contemporary rock and pop station. The slightly mellower Clyde 2 is at 1152MW.

Lochbroom FM 102.2FM. Britain's smallest radio station, broadcasting to the world and the Ullapool area.

Moray Firth 99.4FM, 1107MW. Award-winning independent station for the Inverness area.

Nevis Radio 96.6FM. From the slopes of Ben Nevis, all that's happening in Fort William and surrounds.

North Sound 96.9FM, 1035MW. Pumps out the latest tunes to the Aberdeen area.

Scot FM 100.3–101.1FM. Mainstream pop and shock-jocks for the central belt.

SIBC 96.2FM Shetland's very own independent radio station.

Radio Forth 97.3FM. Rock and pop for Edinburgh and around. Max AM at 1548MW is their easier listening stablemate.

Radio Tay 96.4–102.8FM, 1161MW. Dundee's local radio.

EVENTS AND SPECTATOR SPORTS

Scotland offers a huge range of organized annual events, reflecting both vibrant contemporary culture and well-marketed heritage. Many tourists will want to home straight in on Highland Games and other tartan-draped theatricals, but it's worth bearing in mind that there's more to Scotland than this: numerous regional celebrations perpetuate ancient customs, and the fabulous Edinburgh Festival is an arts celebration unrivalled in size and variety in the world.

A few of the smaller, more obscure events, particularly those with a pagan bent, are in no way created for tourists, and indeed do not always welcome the casual visitor. If in doubt, check at the local tourist office. The STB publishes a weighty and complete list of Scottish events in December: it's free and you can get it from area tourist offices or direct from their headquarters.

HIGHLAND GAMES

Despite their name, **Highland Games** are held all over Scotland, from May until mid-September: they vary in size and differ in the range of events they offer. Although the most famous are at Oban, Cowal and especially Braemar, often the smaller ones are more fun. They probably originated in the fourteenth century as a means of recruiting the best fighting men for the clan chiefs, and were popularized by Queen Victoria to encourage the traditional dress, music, games and dance of the Highlands; various royals still attend the

Games at Braemar. The most distinctive events are known as the "**heavies**" – tossing the caber, putting the stone, and tossing the weight over the bar – all of which require prodigious strength and skill. Tossing the caber is the most spectacular, when the athlete must run carrying an entire tree trunk and attempt to heave it end over end in a perfect, elegant throw. Just as important as the sporting events are the **piping competitions** – for individuals and bands – and **dancing competitions**, where you'll see girls as young as three tripping the quick, intricate steps of dances such as the Highland Fling.

FOOTBALL

Football (soccer), is far and away Scotland's most popular spectator sport, and one of the areas of Scottish life that has remained truly independent from the English. A potent source of pride for Scots everywhere, the national team (always accompanied by its distinctive and vocal supporters, known as the "Tartan Army") has consistently managed to hold its own in international competitions, qualifying for every World Cup but one since 1974, though at the same time cornering the market in gallant failure by failing to progress to the second round on every occasion.

Behind Scotland's footballing success is a thriving league, established in 1874, and dominated from the start by the two Glasgow teams, **Rangers** and **Celtic** (known collectively as the "Old Firm") – the former traditionally representing the city's Protestant community, and the latter its Catholics. The sectarian, and occasionally violent, rivalry between these two is one of the least attractive aspects of Scottish life, and Rangers' and Celtic's stranglehold over the Premier Division has arguably been just as damaging. Although the 1980s saw Dundee United and Aberdeen break the deadlock between the two teams, the old pattern has reasserted itself during the 1990s, with Rangers winning nine titles in a row, and Celtic being the only other side to come anywhere close. During the past few seasons, calls have been mounting for both clubs to join the English Premiership, which would give them the kind of tough opposition they need to achieve greater success at international level. However, the loss of the two flagship

EVENTS CALENDAR

December 31 and January 1: Hogmanay and Ne'er Day. Traditionally more important to the Scots than Christmas, known for the custom of "first-footing", when groups of revellers troop into neighbours' houses at midnight bearing gifts – the first foot should ideally be a dark-haired stranger carrying coal and salt (so the house won't lack for warmth or food), and a bottle of whisky (for obvious reasons). More popular these days are huge and highly organized street parties, most notably in Edinburgh, but also held in Aberdeen, Glasgow and other centres.

January 1: Stonehaven fireball ceremony. Locals swing fireballs on long sticks to welcome New Year and ward off evil spirits.

January 1: Kirkwall Boy's and Men's Ba' Games, Orkney. Mass, drunken football game through the streets of the town, with the castle and the harbour the respective goals – as a grand finale the players jump into the harbour.

January 11: Burning of the Clavie, Burghead, Moray. A burning tar barrel is carried through the town and then rolled down Doorie Hill. Charred fragments of the Clavie offer protection against the evil eye.

Mid- to late January: Celtic Connections, Glasgow. A celebration of Celtic and folk music held in venues across Glasgow.

Last Tuesday in January: Up-Helly-Aa, Lerwick, Shetland. Norse fire festival culminating in the burning of a specially built Viking longship. Visitors will need an invite from one of the locals, or you can buy a ticket for the Town Hall celebrations; see p.597.

January 25: Burns Night. Burns suppers all over Scotland. Dinners held to commemorate Scotland's greatest poet, involving haggis, whisky and lots of poetry recital.

February: Scottish Curling Championship held in a different (indoor) venue each year.

February: Aberdeen Angus Bull Sales at Perth.

February–March: Six Nations Rugby Tournament. Scotland's home games are played at Murrayfield stadium in Edinburgh.

March 1: Whuppity Scourie at Lanark. Local children race round the church beating each other with home-made paper weapons as they go: a representation (it's thought) of the chasing away of winter or the warding off of evil spirits.

March or April: Shoots and Roots folk music festival, Edinburgh.

April: Scottish Grand National at Ayr. Not quite as testing as the English equivalent steeplechase but an important event on the Scottish racing calendar.

April: Rugby Sevens (seven-a-side rugby tournament) in full swing all over the Borders.

April: Kate Kennedy procession at St Andrews. An exclusively male university tradition in honour of distinguished figures in the town and university's history. The role of Kate, niece of the founder of the university, and mythologized as a great beauty, is always played by a first-year student.

April: Spirit of Speyside Scotch Whisky Festival.

April: Shetland Folk Festival.

May 1: Beltane Fire Festival on Calton Hill in Edinburgh.

May: Scottish FA Cup Final in Glasgow.

Late May: Atholl Highlanders Parade at Blair Castle, Perthshire. The annual parade and inspection of Britain's last private army by their colonel-in-chief, the Duke of Atholl.

Late May: Scottish Hebridean Islands Peak Race. The biggest combined sailing and fell-running competition in the world.

June–August: Riding of the Marches in the border towns of Hawick, Selkirk, Annan, Dumfries, Duns, Peebles, Jedburgh, Langholm and Lauder. The Rides originated to check the boundaries of common land owned by the town and also to commemorate warfare between the Scots and the English. Nowadays individual Ridings have their own special ceremonies, though they all start with a parade of pipes and brass bands.

June: Shinty Camanachd Cup Final. The climax of the season for Scotland's own stick-and-ball game, normally held in one of the main Highland towns.

June: Royal Highland Agricultural Show, Ingliston, near Edinburgh. Scotland's biggest and best.

June: Beginning of the Highland Games season across the Highlands, northeast and Argyll.

June: St Magnus Festival, Orkney. Classical and folk music, drama, dance and literature celebrating the Orkney Islands.

July: Scottish Open Golf Championship, held at a different venue each year.

July: Glasgow International Jazz Festival.

July: T in the Park. Scotland's biggest outdoor music event, with a star-studded line-up of contemporary bands.

July: Highland Games at Caithness, Elgin, Glengarry, North Uist, Inverness, Inveraray, Mull, Lewis, Durness, Lochaber, Dufftown, Halkirk.

Early August: The Lammas Fair at St Andrews. The oldest medieval market in the country, which runs for two days.

EVENTS CALENDAR continued

August: Edinburgh International Festival and Fringe. One of the world's great arts jamborees, described in full on p.120.

August: Edinburgh Military Tattoo, held on the castle esplanade. Massed pipe bands and drums by floodlight.

August: World Pipe Band Championship at Glasgow.

August: Horse festival on South Ronaldsay in Orkney. Small children dress as horses and drag decorative wooden ploughs along the beach in a competition to turn the straightest furrows.

August: Highland Games at Dunoon (Cowal), Mallaig, Skye, Dornoch, Aboyne, Strathpeffer, Assynt, Bute, Glenfinnan, Argyllshire, Glenurquhart and Invergordon.

Early September: Highland Games at Braemar.

September: Ben Nevis Race (for amateurs), to the top of the highest mountain in Scotland and back again.

Late September: Doors Open Day. The one weekend a year when many public and private buildings are open to the public. Actual dates vary in different parts of Scotland.

October: The National Mod Competitive festival of all aspects of Gaelic performing arts, held in various venues.

October: Glenfiddich Piping Championships at Blair Atholl for the world's top ten solo pipers.

October: Aberdeen Alternative Festival. Aberdeen's pitch at an arts and culture fest.

November: St Andrew's Day celebrations at St Andrews.

clubs would lead to the Scottish league no longer remaining a credible European contender, and serve an undeserved deathblow to the nation's rich footballing tradition.

With a couple of exceptions (notably Jock Stein's legendary Celtic sides of the 1970s), Scottish soccer has traditionally been renowned less for its great teams than for its outstanding individuals – **players** such as Denis Law of Manchester United, Kenny Dalglish of Celtic and Liverpool, Billy Bremner at Leeds and Graeme Souness in the famous Liverpool side of the early 1980s, as well as **managers** of near-mythical status like Jock Stein, Sir Matt Busby, Bill Shankly and, of course, Sir Alex Ferguson, present manager of Manchester United. These days, as in England, foreign players have flooded the league, to the extent that home-grown players are the exception rather than the rule in the Rangers and Celtic teams. However, talented local players still have a stage on which to perform, and the new blend of continental sophistication mixed with Scottish passion and ruggedness makes for a distinctive spectacle which will appeal to soccer enthusiasts, who should definitely take in a game or two while they're here.

The **season** begins in early August and ends in mid-May, with Saturday afternoon fixtures kicking off at 3pm; you can also often watch live matches on television on Wednesday evenings and Sunday afternoons. Match **tickets** are a little less expensive in Scotland than England, ranging from £10 to £20 for big games; the major clubs operate

telephone credit-card booking services (see the relevant listings section for details). For a quick overview of the Scottish soccer scene, check out the *Daily Mail*'s Soccernet **Web site**, at *www.soccernet.com*, which features the homepages of each Scottish Premier Division club, with news and match-report archives.

RUGBY UNION

Rugby gets its name from Rugby public school in England, where the game mutated from football (soccer) in the nineteenth century. A rugby match may at times look like a bunch of weightlifters grappling each other in the mud – as the old joke goes, rugby is a hooligan's game played by gentlemen, while football is a gentleman's game played by hooligans – but it is in reality a highly tactical and athletic game.

Although rugby has always lived under the shadow of football in Scotland, it still ranks as one of the country's major sports, and the national team has achieved some major successes on the international stage. Indeed, weekends when the national team is playing a home international at **Murrayfield** stadium in Edinburgh are colourful occasions, with kilted masses filling the capital's pubs and lining the streets leading to the ground. Internationals take place in the first few months of the year, when Scotland take on the other home nations, along with France and Italy, in the annual Six Nations tournament, although there are always fixtures in the autumn against international touring teams such as New Zealand, Australia and South Africa. Tickets for all big games are hard to come by; phone the Scottish Rugby Union (SRU) (☎0131/346 5000) for an indication of where and when tickets are available for any particular fixture.

The **club rugby** scene in Scotland is in a certain amount of disarray, with many of the country's top players finding better offers to play in England or France. The one area where the traditions run deepest, however, is in the Borders, where towns such as Hawick, Kelso and Galashields can be gripped by the fortunes of their team on a Saturday afternoon. The Borders are also the home of **seven-a-side rugby**, an abridged version of the game which was invented in Melrose in the 1890s and is now played around the world, most notably at the glamorous annual event in Hong Kong. The Melrose Sevens is still the biggest tournament of the year in Scotland, although you'll find events at one or other of the Border towns through the spring, most going on right through an afternoon and invoking a festival atmosphere in the large crowd. For details contact the Melrose Rugby Club (☎0891/884 511).

SHINTY

Played throughout Scotland but with particular strongholds in the West Highlands and Speyside, the game of **shinty** (the word derives from the Gaelic *sinteag*, meaning "leap") arrived in the country from Ireland around 1500 years ago. Until the latter part of the nineteenth century, it was played on an informal basis and teams from neighbouring villages had to come to an agreement about rules before matches could begin. However, in 1893, the sport's governing body, the

Camanachd Association – from the Gaelic word for "shinty", *camanachd* – was set up to formalize the rules. The first **Camanachd Cup Final** was held in Inverness in 1896, with Glasgow Cowal going down 2:0 to Kingussie.

Today, shinty is still fairly close to its Irish roots in the game of hurling, with each team having twelve players including a goalkeeper, and each goal counting for a point. The game, sometimes described as "hockey with injuries", isn't for the faint-hearted; it's played at a furious pace, with sticks – called camans or cammocks – flying alarmingly in all directions. Support is enthusiastic and vocal, and if you're in the Highlands during the season – roughly parallel with the soccer season – it's well worth trying to catch a match: check with tourist offices or the local paper to see if there are any local fixtures.

CURLING

The one winter sport which enjoys a strong Scottish identity is **curling**, occasionally still played on a frozen outdoor rink, or "pond", though most commonly these days seen in indoor ice-rinks found in many sizeable Scottish towns. The game, which involves sliding smooth-bottomed 18kg discs of granite called "stones" across the ice towards a target circle, is said to have been invented in Scotland, although its earliest representation is in a sixteenth-century Flemish painting. Played by two teams of four, curling is a highly tactical and skilful sport, enlivened by team-members using brushes to sweep the ice in front of a moving stone to help it travel further and straighter. If you're interested in seeing curling being played, go along to the ice-rink in places such as Perth, Hamilton or Aviemore on a winter evening.

OUTDOOR PURSUITS

A large number of visitors to Scotland come specifically to enjoy a landscape that's perfect for outdoor pursuits at all levels of fitness and ambition. Within striking distance of Glasgow and Edinburgh there are vast stretches of glens and moorland and spectacular mountains, which in winter can provide great skiing. Throughout the country, numerous marked trails range from hour-long ambles to coast-to-coast treks. The shoreline, lochs and rivers give opportunities for fishing as well as sailing and watersports, including surfing, and there are plenty of fine beaches. Scotland, of course, is also the "home of golf": it's relatively cheap to play here, and there are proportionally more courses than anywhere else in the world.

WALKING AND CLIMBING

The whole of Scotland offers superb opportunities for **hill walking**, from the smooth, grassy hills and moors of the **Southern Uplands** to the wild and rugged country of the northwest. Scotland has several **Long Distance Footpaths** (LDPs) which will take days to walk, though you can, of course, just do a section of them. The **Southern Upland Way**, which crosses the country from coast to coast in the south, is, at 212 miles, the longest. The best known, however, is the **West Highland Way**, a 95-mile hike from Glasgow to Fort William via Loch Lomond and Glen Coe. The gentler **Speyside Way**, in Aberdeenshire, leads for 45 miles from the Cairngorms to the Moray Firth past a number of whisky distilleries. The green signposts of the Scottish Rights of Way Society point to these and many other cross-country routes, which include "drove roads", long-established paths through the hills along which clansmen once led their cattle to or from markets held in the larger settlements.

Scotland's main climbing areas are in the **Highlands**, which boast many challenging peaks as well as great hill walks. There are 284 mountains over 3000ft (914m) in Scotland, known as **Munros** after the man who first classified them: many walkers "collect" or "bag" them, and it's possible to chalk up several in a day. Serious climbers will probably head for **Glen Coe** or **Torridon**, which offer difficult routes in spectacular surroundings. These and some of the other finest Highland areas (Lawers, Kintail, West Affric) are in the ownership of the National Trust for Scotland, while Blaven on Skye and Ladhar Bheinn (Knoydart) are John Muir Trust properties; both allow year-round

THE MIDGE

Despite being only just over a millimetre long, and enjoying a life span on the wing of just a few weeks, the **midge** (culicoides) – a tiny biting fly prevalent in the Highlands (mainly the west coast) and Islands – is considered to be second only to the weather as the major deterrent to tourism in Scotland. There are more than thirty varieties of midge, though only half of these actually bite humans. Ninety percent of all midge bites are down to the female culicoides impunctatus or Highland midge (the male does not bite). With two sets of jaws and twenty teeth in each, the female needs a good meal of blood in order to produce eggs.

To some, these persistent creatures are merely a nuisance; others have a violent allergic reaction when bitten. The easiest way to avoid midges is to visit in the winter, since they only appear between April and October. Midges also favour still, damp, overcast or shady conditions and are at their meanest around sunrise and sunset. Direct sunlight, heavy rain, noise and smoke discourage them to some degree, though the most effective deterrent is, undoubtedly, wind. You'll soon notice if they're near; cover up arms and legs and try to avoid wearing dark colours, which attract the creatures. Various **repellents** are worth a try. Recommendations include Autan and Jungle Formula (widely available from pharmacists), the herbal remedy citronella, and Skin So Soft by Avon, which is said to be very effective, despite not being designed to fend off midges. An alternative to repellents for protecting your face, especially if you are walking or camping, is the midge net, which you secure by tucking under your hat. Although they appear ridiculous at first, midge nets are commonplace and extremely useful.

USEFUL ADDRESSES FOR WALKERS

Assynt Guided Holidays, Birchbank, Knockan, Elphin, Sutherland (☎ & fax 1854/666215). Mountain walks, and glen and lochside ambles, and fishing trips, with one of Scotland's most knowledgeable guides.

C-N-Do Scotland WS, Unit 32, Stirling Enterprise Park, Stirling FK7 7RP (☎01786/445703; *cndo.scotland@btinternet.com*). Munro-bagging for novices and experts, in small groups and with qualified leaders, as well as day-long winter skills and navigation courses.

Cordee (Book Distributors), 3a de Montfort St, Leicester LE1 7HD (☎0116/254 3579). Produces extensive lists of walking books, and distributes all Scottish Mountaineering Club publications.

Glen Coe Mountain Sport, 37 Park Rd, Ballachulish, Glen Coe, Argyll PA39 4JB (☎01855/811472, *www.glencoe-mountain-sport.co.uk*). Year-round programme of gentle walks and scrambles on Skye, and around Glen Coe and Ben Nevis.

John Muir Trust, Freepost, Musselburgh, Midlothian EH21 7BR (☎0131/665 0596). An organization that purchases land for conservation and public access and can give details of public rights of way.

Mountaineering Council of Scotland, 4a St Catherine's Rd, Perth, Perthshire PH1 5SE (☎01738/638227). The representative body for all mountain activities, which publishes details of estate boundaries and contact phone numbers to help climbers and walkers check on estate activities before setting out.

National Trust for Scotland, 5 Charlotte Square, Edinburgh EH2 4DU (☎0131/226 5922). Guided ranger walks in Torridon and Glencoe.

North-West Frontiers, 18a Braes, Ullapool, Ross-shire IV26 2SZ (☎ & fax 01854/612628, *www.nwfrontiers.com*). Guided mountain trips with small groups in the northwest Highlands, starting in Inverness; May to October only.

Ossian Guides, Sanna, Newtonmore, Inverness-shire PH20 1DG (☎01540/673402). Walking, scrambling and photo-treks with qualified leaders throughout the Highlands.

Ramblers Association Scotland, 23 Crusader House, Haig Business Park, Markinch, Fife KY7 6AQ (☎01592/611177).

Rua Reidh Lighthouse, Melvaig, Gairloch, Wester Ross (☎01445/771263; *ruaeidh@netcomuk.co.uk*). Accompanied and self-guided wilderness walks on the west coast, from three-night to one-week itineraries. Family multi-activity holidays also available.

Scottish Rights of Way Society, John Cotton Business Centre, 10–12 Sunnyside, Edinburgh EH7 5RA (☎0131/652 2937). A campaigning organization which is strong on providing access for walkers.

Scottish Youth Hostel Association, 7 Glebe Crescent, Stirling FK8 2JA (☎01786/451181).

Walkabout Scotland, 2 Rossie Place, Edinburgh EH7 5SG (☎0774/703 2300). A great way to get a taste of walking in the Highlands, with guided day-trips from Edinburgh – they tackle a different hill, of different grades, for each day of the week. All transport included in price (£30 per person).

---

access. Elsewhere, the accepted freedom to roam in wilder parts of the countryside allows extensive walking and climbing, although there may be restricted access during lambing (dogs are particularly unwelcome in April and May) and deerstalking seasons (mid-August to the third week in October). The booklet *Heading for the Scottish Hills* (published by the Scottish Mountaineering Club or SMC) provides such information on all areas.

Numerous short walks (from accessible towns and villages) and several major walks are touched on in this guide. However, you should only use these notes as general outlines and always in conjunction with a good map. Where possible, we have given details of the best maps to use – in most cases one of the excellent and reliable Ordnance Survey (OS) Landranger series (see p.23). You should never attempt walks beyond your abilities and always follow the guidelines below. Other useful sources for information on walks are listed in the box above. If you decide to follow one of the walks and haven't got a map with you, head for the nearest tourist office which will usually supply OS and other local maps, safety advice and guidebooks/leaflets, as will shops in most areas. Among the many **guidebooks** available for serious walking and climbing, the SMC's series of District Guides offer blow-by-blow accounts of climbs written by professional mountaineers – for other good walking guides see the "Books" section of Contexts (p.666). These, as well as a wide range of maps, are available from most of the good **outdoor stores** scattered around the country. These shops are normally staffed by experienced climbers and walkers, who are a good source of candid advice about the equipment you'll need and favourite hiking areas. The best stores for this are Tiso and Nevisport, which have various branches in Scotland.

MOUNTAIN SAFETY

Due to rapid weather changes, the Scottish mountains are potentially extremely dangerous and should be treated with respect. Every year, in every season, climbers and walkers die on Scottish mountains. If the weather looks as if it's closing in, get down fast. It is essential that you are properly equipped – even for what appears to be an easy expedition in apparently settled weather – with proper warm, brightly coloured and waterproof layered clothing, supportive footwear and adequate maps, a compass (which you should know how to use), food, water and a whistle. Always leave word of your route and what time you expect to return, and remember to contact the person again to let them know that you are back.

WINTER SPORTS

Skiing, including **snowboarding**, takes place at five different locations in Scotland – Glen Coe, the Nevis Range beside Fort William, Glenshee, the Lecht and the Cairngorms near Aviemore – but as none of these can offer anything even vaguely approaching an alpine experience it is as well not to come with high expectations. They can go for months on end through the winter with insufficient snow, then see the approach roads suddenly made impassable by a glut of the stuff.

All the resorts have a combination of chairlifts and tows – Nevis Range boasts a gondola – and equipment can always be hired nearby. Expect to pay up to £20 for a standard day pass at one of the resorts, or £55 for a three-day pass; hire of skis or snowboard comes in at around £15 per day, with reductions for multi-day hire. At weekends, in good weather with decent snow, expect the slopes to be packed with trippers from the central belt, although midweek usually sees queues dissolving and the experience improving immeasurably. We've given details for each of the resorts in the appropriate place in the text, including telephone numbers to use to find out ski conditions; for more general information contact Snowsport Scotland in Edinburgh (☎0131/317 7280) or get hold of the STB's Ski Scotland brochure (*www.ski.scotland.net*).

Nordic, or cross-country, skiing, is found in a few places around Scotland, notably around Braemar near Glenshee and the Cairngorms. This can be a great way to free yourself from the crowds of the resorts and explore the Highland wilderness made pristine by the snow, although the demands on fitness and navigational abilities are higher. The best way to get started or to find out about good routes is to contact an outdoor pursuits company who offer Nordic hire and instruction – try Cairnwell Ski School in Glenshee (☎01250/885255) or Huntly Nordic Ski Centre in Huntly, Aberdeenshire (☎01466/794428; *hnsc@rocketmail.com*).

PONY TREKKING AND HORSE RIDING

Pony trekking as an organized leisure activity originated in Scotland; the late Lieutenant Commander Jock Kerr Hunter set up the first **riding school** here fifty or so years ago, to encourage people to explore the country via its old drove roads. Since then, equestrian centres have mushroomed, and miles of the most beautiful lochsides, heather-clad moorland and long sandy beaches are now accessible on horseback, to novices as well as experienced riders.

The Scottish Tourist Board produces a glossy brochure listing around sixty **riding centres** across the country, all of them approved by either the Trekking and Riding Society of Scotland (TRSS) or the British Horse Society (BHS). Membership of these schemes ensures that the centre is inspected each year, the horses are well looked after, and the staff are properly qualified. As a rule, any centre will offer the option of **pony trekking** (leisurely ambles on sure-footed Highland ponies), **hacking** (for experienced riders who want to go for a short ride at a fastish pace), and **trail riding** (over longer distances, for riders who feel secure at a canter). In addition, a network of special **horse and rider B&Bs** in Scotland means you can ride independently on your own horse.

A four-day route – the **Buccleuch Country Ride** – was recently inaugurated in the Borders region, using private tracks, open country and quiet bridleways. For more information about this, and the B&B network for riders, contact the

Scottish Borders Tourist Board (☎01835/863435), or the BRS/TRSS, Boreland, Fearnan, Aberfeldy, Perthshire PH15 2PG (☎01887/830274).

CYCLING AND MOUNTAIN BIKING

Despite the recent boom in the sale of mountain bikes, **cyclists** are still treated with notorious neglect by many motorists and by the people who plan the country's traffic systems. Very few of Scotland's towns have proper cycle routes, but if you're hellbent on tackling the congestion, pollution and aggression of city traffic, get a **helmet** and a secure **lock** – cycle theft in Scotland is an organized and highly effective racket. The rural backroads are infinitely more enjoyable, particularly in the gentle landscape of the south of the country, where generally amiable gradients and a decent density of pubs and B&Bs make it a perfect area for cycle touring. Your main problem out in the countryside will be finding spare parts – anything more complex than inner tubes or tyres can be very hard to come by.

Cycling is popular in the Highland walking areas, but cyclists should always keep to tracks where a right to cycle exists, and pass walkers at considerate speeds. Footpaths, unless otherwise marked, are for pedestrian use only. The Forestry Commission has recently established 1150 miles of excellent off-road routes all over the country, which are detailed in numerous *Cycling in the Forest* leaflets (available from Forest Enterprise offices listed below, and from most tourist offices). Waymarked and graded, these are best attempted on **mountain bikes** with multi-gears, although many of the gentler routes may be tackled on hybrid and standard road cycles.

Transporting your bike by train is a good way of getting to the interesting parts of Scotland without a lot of hard pedalling. Bikes are allowed on the main GNER and Virgin Intercity trains (subject to availability of space) for a £3 charge: you should book the space as far in advance as possible. Bikes are carried free on ScotRail services, but again, subject to availability (call ScotRail bookings ☎08457/550033). Bus and coach companies, including National Express and Scottish Citylink rarely accept cycles unless they are dismantled and boxed. One notable exception is the Bike Bus Company (☎0131/229 6274), which operates a minibus and trailer service out of Edinburgh for cyclists.

Bike rental is available at shops in most large towns and many tourist centres, although only a few more enlightened establishments offer much more than pretty heavy and basic standard models – OK for a brief spin, but not for any serious touring. Expect to pay £10–20 per day; most rental outlets also give good discounts for multi-day hire.

Another option is to shell out on a **cycling holiday package**. These take many forms, but generally include transport of your luggage to each stop, prebooked accommodation, detailed route instructions, a packed lunch and backup support. Most holiday companies offer some budget packages, with

USEFUL ADDRESSES FOR CYCLISTS

Bespoke Highland Tours, The Bothy, Camusdarach, Arisaig, Inverness-shire PH39 4NT (☎01687/450272, *www.scotland-info.co.uk/tours*). Organizes cycle touring in the Highlands and Islands, using a reliable and long-standing network of B&Bs and hostels, and arranges transport links and baggage transfer.

Cyclists' Touring Club, 69 Meadrow, Godalming, Surrey GU7 3HS (☎01483/417217). Britain's largest cycling organization, and a good source of general advice; their handbook has lists of cyclist-friendly B&Bs and cafés in Scotland. Annual membership costs £25 for adults.

Forest Enterprise, 21 Church St, Inverness, Invernesshire IV1 1EL (☎01463/232811). The best source of information on Scotland's extensive network of forest trails – ideal for mountain biking at all levels of ability.

Scottish Border Trails, Venlaw High Rd, Peebles EH45 8RL (☎01721/722934, *arthur@trails.scotborders.co.uk*).

Scottish Cyclists' Union, The Velodrome, Meadowbank Stadium, London Rd, Edinburgh EH7 6AY (☎0131/652 0187). This organization produces an annual handbook and calendar of cycling events (£4.50) – mainly road, mountain-bike and track races.

Scottish Cycle Safaris, 29 Blackfriars St, Edinburgh EH1 1NB (☎0131/556 5560). Fully organized cycle tours at all levels from camping to country house hotels, with a good range of bikes available for hire, from tandems to childrens' bikes.

Scottish Youth Hostel Association: Breakaway Holidays, 7 Glebe Crescent, Stirling FK8 2JA (☎01786/891400).

hostel instead of hotel or B&B accommodation, and the cost-cutting option of using your own bike. A week-long tour starts at around £250 per person for hostel accommodation, including bike hire. For a list of recommended cycling holiday specialists, see the box on p.49.

Britain's biggest **cycling organization**, the Cycle Touring Club or CTC (see box on p.49), provides lists of tour operators and rental outlets in Scotland, and supplies members with touring and technical advice, as well as insurance. As a gen[...] [...] Tourist Board's *Cycling in Scotland* brochure is worth sending off for, with practical advice and suggestions for itineraries around the country. The STB's recently introduced "Cyclists Welcome" scheme gives guest houses and B&Bs around the country a chance to advertise that they're cyclist-friendly, and able to provide such things as an overnight laundry service, a late meal or a packed lunch. Recommended as a more detailed guide is *Cycling in Scotland & North East England* by Philip Routledge (available from Sigma Leisure, 1 South Oak Lane, Wilmslow, Cheshire SK9 6AR; £7.95 plus £2 p&p), which crams dozens of maps, route details and general information into 220 pages.

GOLF

There are over 400 **golf courses** in Scotland, where the game is less elitist and more accessible than anywhere else in the world. Golf in its present form took shape in the fifteenth century on the dunes of Scotland's east coast, and today you'll find some of the oldest courses in the world on these early coastal sites, known as "links". If you want a round of golf, it's often possible just to turn up and play, though it's sensible to phone ahead and book, and essential for the championship courses (see below).

Public courses are owned by the local council, while **private** courses belong to a club. You can play on both – occasionally the private courses require that you are a member of another club, and the odd one asks for introductions from a member, but these rules are often waived for overseas visitors and all you need to do is pay a one-off fee. The cost of one round will set you back around £10 on a small nine-hole course, and more than £40 for eighteen holes. Simply pay as you enter and play. In remote areas the courses are sometimes unstaffed – just put the admission fee into the honour box. Most courses have **resident professionals** who give lessons, and some rent equip-

ment at reasonable rates. Renting a caddie car will add an extra few pounds to the cost.

Scotland's **championship** courses, which often host the British Open tournament, are renowned for their immaculately kept greens and challenging holes and, though they're favoured by serious players, anybody with a valid handicap certificate can enjoy them. **St Andrews** (☎01334/475757) is *the* destination for golfers: it's the home of the Royal and Ancient [...] worldwide controlling body that regulates the rules of the game. Of its five courses, the best known is the Old Course (£75), a particularly intriguing ground with eleven enormous greens and the world-famous "Road Hole". If you want to play, there's no introduction needed, but you'll need to book months in advance and have a handicap certificate – handicap limits are 24 for men and 36 for women. You could also enter your name for the daily right-to-play lottery – contact the club before 2pm on the day you'd like to play. One of the easiest championship courses to get into is **Carnoustie** in Angus (☎01241/853789; £52), venue of the British Open in 1999, though you should still try to book as far ahead as possible. No handicap certificate is required for play here before 1.30pm on Saturday and 11am on Sunday. Other championship courses include **Gleneagles** in Perthshire (☎01764/663543; £85), **Royal Dornoch** in Sutherland (☎01862/810219; £45), and **Turnberry** in Ayrshire (☎01655/331000; £120). In addition to the high fees, you'll be expected to tip your caddie. In Gullane, near Edinburgh, Muirfield (☎01620/842255; £70) is considered by professional players to be one of the most testing grounds in the world and is also one of the most elitist – women can only play if accompanied by a man and aren't allowed into the clubhouse.

Worth shelling out for if you're coming to Scotland primarily to play golf, is a ticket which gives you access to a number of courses in any one region – **Golf Pass Scotland** (☎0990/133206) covers four different Tourist Board areas, including Lothians and Edinburgh.

FISHING

Scotland's serrated coastline – with the deep sea lochs of the west, the firths of the east and the myriad offshore islands – encompasses the full gamut of marine habitats, and ranks among the cleanest coasts in Europe. Combine this with an abundance of **salmon**, **sea trout**, **brown trout** and **pike**, acres of open space and easy access, and you have an angler's paradise. Whether you're into game-, coarse- or sea-fishing, you'll be spoilt for choice. The only element in short supply is company; Scotland may offer wonderful fishing, but its unpolluted, open waters don't attract anywhere near the numbers of anglers you'd expect.

Nor will you get bogged down in fishing bureaucracy. No licence is needed to fish in Scotland, although nearly all land is privately owned and its fishing therefore controlled by a landlord/lady or his/her agent. Permission, however, is usually easy to obtain: **permits** can be bought without hassle at local tackle shops, or through fishing clubs in the area – if in doubt, ask at the nearest tourist office. The other thing to bear in mind is that salmon and sea trout have strict **seasons**, which vary between districts but usually stretch from late August to late February. Once again, individual tourist offices will know the precise dates, or you can check in the Scottish Tourist Board's excellent *Fish Scotland* brochure (free from any tourist office or by post; see p.24). It provides a rough introduction to game-, coarse- and sea-angling, with tips on how to find the famous sea marks and salmon beats, and a rundown of less-well-known fishing spots. Other sources of useful information are the Scottish Federation of Sea Anglers, Brian Burn, Flat 2, 16 Bellevue Rd, Ayr KA7 2SA (☎01292/264735), and the Scottish Anglers National Association, Caledonia House, South Gyle, Edinburgh EH12 9DQ (☎0131/339 8808).

BEACHES

Scotland is ringed by fine **beaches** and bays, most of them clean and many of them deserted even in high summer – perhaps hardly surprising, given the bracing winds and chilly water. Few people come to Scotland for a beach holiday, but it's worth sampling one or two, even if you never shed as much as a sweater. A rash of slightly melancholy seaside towns lies within easy reach of Glasgow, while on the east coast the relatively low cliffs and miles of sandy beaches are ideal for walking. Bizarrely enough, given the low temperature of the water, the beaches in the northeast are beginning to figure on surfers' itineraries, attracting enthusiasts from all over Europe (see below). Perhaps the most beautiful beaches of all are to be found on Scotland's islands: endless, isolated stretches that on a sunny day can be paradisal.

In order to comply with EU directives on bathing-water quality, Scotland's 23 dirtiest beaches have been monitored over the past decade for pollution, and measures implemented to ensure they clean up their act. In 1999 the Tidy Britain Group awarded their top award, a Blue Flag, to only one Scottish beach, Silver Sands at Aberdour, and while great strides have been made over the past few years, a handful of bathing beaches, including Girvan and South Beach, Ayr, remain on the blacklist.

SURFING

Unlikely though it may seem, Scotland is fast gaining a reputation as a **surfing** destination, with a good selection of excellent quality breaks. It may not have the sunshine of Hawaii, and the water is generally steely-grey rather than turquoise-blue, but there are world-class waves to be found. **Thurso** is the number-one spot on the **north coast**, and boasts one of the finest reef breaks in Europe. In addition, the rest of this coastline – Sango Bay, Torrisdale, Farr Bay and Armadale, in particular – offers waves comparable to those in Hawaii, Australia and Indonesia. However, Scotland's northern coastline lies on the same latitude as Alaska and Iceland, so the water temperature is very low: even in midsummer it rarely exceeds 15°C, and in winter can drop to as low as to 7°C. The one vital accessory, therefore, is a good wet suit (ideally a 5/3mm steamer) wetsuit boots and, outside of summer, gloves and a hood, too.

In addition to Thurso, there are several other excellent breaks, many of which lie within easy reach of large cities, such as **Pease Bay** near Edinburgh, and **Fraserburgh** near Aberdeen. The beaches of the **Moray Firth** also offer a good North Sea swell. Of the islands, the west coasts of **Coll**, **Tiree** and **Islay** get great swell from the Atlantic and have good beaches, while the spectacular west coast offers numerous possibilities, in particular one of Britain's most isolated beaches, **Sandwood Bay**. In the Outer Hebrides, the best breaks are to be found along the northern coastline of **Lewis**, near Carloway and Bragar.

Many of these beaches are surrounded by stunning scenery, and you'd be unlucky to encounter another surfer for miles. However, this isolation – combined with the cold water and big, powerful waves – means that, in general, much of Scottish surf is best left to **experienced surfers** (see box on p.54). If you're a beginner, get local

TOP TEN SCOTTISH BREAKS

*Thurso East, just below the castle; see p.536. One of the best right-hand reef breaks in Europe.

*Brimm's Ness, five miles west of Thurso; see p.536. A selection of reef breaks that pick up the smallest of swells.

Pease Bay, near Dunbar, 26 miles east of Edinburgh; see p.135. A popular break suited to all abilities; can get very crowded.

Fraserburgh, 39 miles north of Aberdeen; see p.465. A number of beach and reef breaks – beginners should stick to the beach.

*Skirza Harbour, three miles south of John O'Groats; see p.538. An excellent left-hand reef break on the far northeast tip of Scotland.

Sandside Bay, on the north coast, ten miles west of Thurso; see p.536. Reef and beach breaks, but dubious water quality due to the proximity of the Dounreay nuclear power station.

*Torrisdale Bay, Bettyhill, on the north coast of the Highlands; see p.535. An excellent right-hand river-mouth break.

Sandwood Bay, a day's hike south of Cape Wrath in Sutherland; see p.533. Beach breaks on one of the most scenic and remote shorelines in Britain, only accessible on foot.

Machrihanish Bay, Mull of Kintyre; see p.345. Four miles of beach breaks on one of Scotland's loneliest peninsulas.

*Valtos, on the Uig peninsula, Lewis; see p.397. A break on one of the Outer Hebrides' most exquisite shell-sand beaches.

*Experienced surfers only.

---

advice before you go in, and be aware of your limitations; remember, if you get caught in a current off the west coast the next stop might be Iceland.

The popularity of surfing in Scotland has led to a spate of **surf shops** opening up, all of which rent or sell equipment, and provide good information about the local breaks and events on the surfing scene. The last two listed also offer surfing lessons. Clan, 45 Hyndland St, Partick, Glasgow (☎0141/339 6523); Boardwise, 1146 Argyle St, Glasgow (☎0141/334 5559); ESP, 6 Greyfriars St, Elgin (☎01343/550129); Granite Reef, 45 Justice St, Aberdeen (☎01224/621193); and Momentum, 22 Bruntsfield Place, Edinburgh (☎0131/229 6665). Two further sources of information are *Surf UK* by Wayne "Alf" Alderson (Fernhurst Books; £13.95), with details on over 400 breaks around Britain, and the bimonthly *Surf* magazine (£3), which is good for grassroots information on the Scottish surfing scene.

TRAVELLERS WITH DISABILITIES

Scotland has numerous specialist tour operators catering for disabled travellers, and the number of non-specialist operators who welcome clients with disabilities is increasing. For more information on these operators, you should get in touch with **Disability Scotland, Princes House, 5 Shandwick Place, Edinburgh EH2 4RG** (☎0131/229 8632; *dis_scot.gcal.ac.uk*). It has a comprehensive computer database covering all aspects of disabled holidays in Scotland and publishes a full directory. See also the box below for other useful organizations in Britain.

Should you go it alone, you'll find that Scottish attitudes towards travellers are far behind advances towards independence made in North America and Australia. Access to theatres, cinemas and other public places has improved recently, but **public transport** companies rarely make any effort to help disabled people, though some ScotRail InterCity services now accommodate

wheelchair users in comfort. Wheelchair users and blind or partially sighted people are automatically given thirty–fifty percent reductions on train fares, and people with other disabilities are eligible for the **Disabled Persons Railcard** (£14 per year), which gives a third off most tickets. There are no bus discounts for the disabled, and of the major **car-rental** firms only Hertz offers models with hand controls at the same rate as conventional vehicles, and even these are only available in the more expensive categories. Its the same story for **accommodation**, with modified suites for people with disabilities available only at higher-priced establishments and perhaps the odd B&B.

Useful **publications** include RADAR's annually updated *Holidays in the British Isles: A Guide for Disabled People*. Another publications to look out for is *The World Wheelchair Traveller* by Susan Abbott and Mary Ann Tyrrell (AA Publications), which includes basic hints and advice.

ADDRESSES FOR TRAVELLERS WITH DISABILITIES

BRITAIN AND IRELAND

Access Travel, 16 Haweswater Ave, Astley, Lancashire M29 7BL (☎01942/888844). Tour operator that can arrange flights, transfer and accommodation. This is a small business which personally checks out places before recommendation.

Disability Action Group, 2 Annadale Ave, Belfast BT7 3JH (☎01232/491011).

Holiday Care Service, 2nd floor, Imperial Building, Victoria Rd, Horley, Surrey RH6 7PZ (☎01293/774535; Minicom ☎01293/776943). Provides free lists of accessible accommodation abroad – European, American and long-haul destinations – plus a list of accessible attractions in the UK. Information on financial help for holidays available.

Irish Wheelchair Association, Blackheath Drive, Clontarf, Dublin 3 (☎01/833 8241; *iwa@iol.ie*).

RADAR (Royal Association for Disability and Rehabilitation), 12 City Forum, 250 City Rd, London EC1V 8AF (☎0171/250 3222; Minicom ☎0171/250 4119, *www.radar.org.uk*). A good source of advice on holidays and travel. They produce an annual holiday guide for the UK (£7.50, includes p&p), which includes some information on Scotland.

Tripscope, The Courtyard, Evelyn Rd, London W4 5JL (☎0181/994 9294). This registered charity provides a national telephone information service offering free advice on UK and international transport and travel for those with a mobility problem.

continues overleaf . . .

ADDRESSES FOR TRAVELLERS WITH DISABILITIES continued

NORTH AMERICA

Directions Unlimited, 720 N Bedford Rd, Bedford Hills, NY 10507 (☎1-800/533-5343). Tour operator specializing in custom tours for people with disabilities.

Jewish Rehabilitation Hospital, Laval, Canada (☎514/688-9550; *axis@musica.mcgill.ca*). Friendly service providing general advice about travelling abroad with disabilities. Will reply to email queries.

Mobility International USA, PO Box 10767, Eugene, OR 97440 (voice and TDD: ☎503/343-1284). Information and referral services, access guides, tours and exchange programmes. Annual membership $25 (includes quarterly newsletter).

Society for the Advancement of Travel for the Handicapped (SATH), 347 5th Ave, Suite 610, New York, NY 10016 (☎212/447-7284). Non-profit travel-industry referral service that passes queries onto its members as appropriate; allow plenty of time for a response.

Travel Information Service, Moss Rehabilitation Hospital, 1200 W Tabor Rd, Philadelphia, PA 19141 (☎215/456-9600; TTY for the hearing impaired: ☎215/456-9602, *www.mossresourcenet.com*). Telephone information and referral service.

Twin Peaks Press, Box 129, Vancouver, WA 98666 (☎360/694-2462 or 1-800/637-2256). Publisher of the *Directory of Travel Agencies for the Disabled* ($19.95), listing more than 370 agencies worldwide; *Travel for the Disabled* ($19.95); the *Directory of Accessible Van Rentals* ($9.95); and *Wheelchair Vagabond* ($14.95), loaded with personal tips.

Wheels Up! (☎1-800/389-4335). Provides discounted airfare, tour and cruise prices for disabled travellers, and also publishes a free monthly newsletter.

AUSTRALIA AND NEW ZEALAND

ACROD, PO Box 60, Curtin, ACT 2605 (☎02/6282 4333). Compiles lists of organizations, accommodation, travel agencies and tour operators.

Barrier Free Travel, 36 Wheatley St, North Bellingen NSW 2454 (☎02/6655 1733)

Disabled Persons Assembly, 173–175 Victoria St, Wellington (☎04/811 9100).

DIRECTORY

Electricity In Britain the current is 240V AC. North American appliances need a transformer and adapter; Australasian appliances need only an adapter.

Gaelic In some areas of Scotland, particularly in the Highlands and Hebrides, road signs are bilingual English/Gaelic. In the guide, the Gaelic translation is given (in italics and parentheses) the first time any village or island is mentioned, after which the English name is used. The main exception to this rule is in the Western Isles, where signposting is exclusively in Gaelic – we've reflected this in the main text by giving the Gaelic first and putting the English in parentheses. Thereafter we've used the Gaelic, except for the islands and ferry ports which are more familiar in the English, as they appear on CalMac timetables.

Laundry Coin-operated laundries are found in nearly all Scottish cities and towns, and are open about twelve hours a day from Monday to Friday, less on weekends. A wash followed by a spin or tumble dry costs about £2.50; a "service wash" (your laundry done for you in a few hours) costs about £1 extra. In the remoter regions of Scotland, you'll have to rely on hostel and campsite laundry facilities.

Smoking The last decade has seen a dramatic change in attitudes towards smoking, and a significant reduction in the consumption of cigarettes. Smoking is now outlawed from just about all public buildings and on public transport, and many restaurants and hotels have become totally non-smoking. Smokers are advised, when booking a table or a room, to check their vice is tolerated there.

Time Greenwich Mean Time (GMT) is used from late October to late March, after which the clocks go forward an hour for British Summer Time (BST). GMT is five hours ahead of the US Eastern Standard Time and ten hours behind Australian Eastern Standard Time.

Toilets Public loos are found at all train and bus stations and signposted on town high streets; a fee of 10p or 20p is sometimes charged.

Videos Visitors from North America planning to use their video cameras in Britain should note that Betamax video cassettes are less easy to obtain in Scotland, where VHS is the commonly used format, so bring a supply with you.

PART TWO

THE
GUIDE

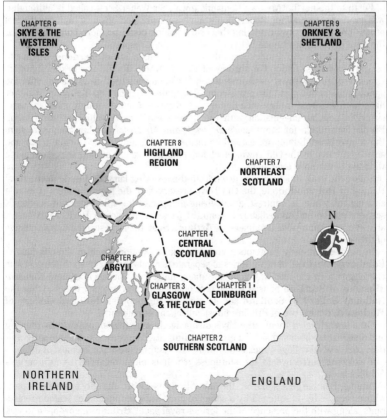

CHAPTER 6
SKYE & THE WESTERN ISLES

CHAPTER 9
ORKNEY & SHETLAND

CHAPTER 8
HIGHLAND REGION

CHAPTER 7
NORTHEAST SCOTLAND

CHAPTER 4
CENTRAL SCOTLAND

CHAPTER 5
ARGYLL

CHAPTER 3
GLASGOW & THE CLYDE

CHAPTER 1
EDINBURGH

CHAPTER 2
SOUTHERN SCOTLAND

N

NORTHERN IRELAND

ENGLAND

CHAPTER ONE

EDINBURGH AND AROUND

W ell-heeled **EDINBURGH**, the showcase capital of Scotland, is a cosmopolitan and cultured city. The setting is wonderfully striking; the city is perched on a series of extinct volcanoes and rocky crags which rise from the generally flat landscape of the Lothians, with the sheltered shoreline of the Firth of Forth to the north. "My own Romantic town", Sir Walter Scott called it, although it was another native author, Robert Louis Stevenson, who perhaps best captured the feel of his "precipitous city", declaring that "No situation could be more commanding for the head of a kingdom; none better chosen for noble prospects."

The centre has two distinct parts, divided by **Princes Street Gardens**, which run roughly east–west under the shadow of **Castle Rock**. To the north, the dignified, Grecian-style **New Town** was immaculately laid out during the Age of Reason, after the announcement of a plan to improve conditions in the city. The **Old Town**, on the other hand, with its tortuous alleys and tightly packed closes, is unrelentingly medieval, associated in popular imagination with the underworld lore of schizophrenic Deacon Brodie, inspiration for Stevenson's *Dr Jekyll and Mr Hyde*, and the body snatchers Burke and Hare. Edinburgh earned its nickname of "Auld Reekie" for the smog and smell generated by the Old Town, which for centuries swam in sewage tipped out of the windows of cramped tenements.

Set on the crag which sweeps down from the towering fairytale **Castle** to the royal **Palace of Holyroodhouse**, the Old Town preserves all the key reminders of its role as a capital, while, in contrast, a tantalizing glimpse of the wild beauty of Scotland's scenery can be had immediately beyond the palace in **Holyrood Park**, an extensive area of open countryside dominated by **Arthur's Seat**, the largest and most impressive of the volcanoes.

In August and early September, around a million visitors flock to the city for the **Edinburgh Festival**, in fact a series of separate festivals that make up the largest arts extravaganza in the world. Among the many museums, the exciting new **National Museum of Scotland** houses 10,000 of Scotland's most precious artefacts, while the **National Gallery of Scotland** and its offshoot, the **Scottish National Gallery of Modern Art**, have two of Britain's finest collections of paintings.

On a less elevated theme, the city's distinctive howffs (pubs), allied to its brewing and distilling traditions, make it a great **drinking** city. The presence of three **universities**, plus several colleges, means that there is a youthful presence for most of the year – a welcome corrective to the stuffiness which is often regarded as Edinburgh's Achilles heel.

Among Edinburgh's suburbs, the most lively is **Leith**, the city's medieval port, whose seedy edge is softened by a series of great bars and upmarket seafood restaurants, along with the presence of the former royal yacht **Britannia**, now open to visi-

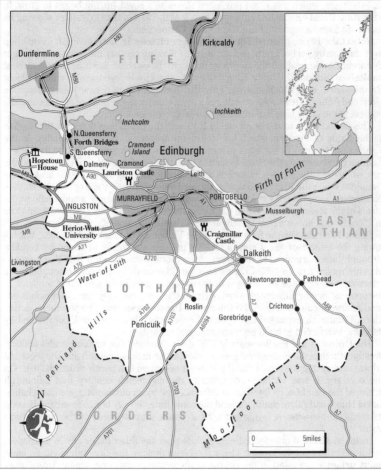

© Crown copyright

tors. Elsewhere around Edinburgh the **Pentland Hills** offer attractive countryside for hikers or mountain-bikers, while, of the Midlothian villages, **Roslin** is the most visited, for its mysterious fifteenth-century chapel. To the northwest of the city, the dramatic curves of the **Forth Rail Bridge** are best seen by walking across the parallel road bridge, starting at **South Queensferry**.

Some history

It was during the **Dark Ages** that the name of Edinburgh – at least in its early forms of Dunedin or Din Eidyn ("fort of Eidyn") – first appeared. Castle Rock, a strategic fort atop one of the volcanoes, served as the nation's **southernmost border post** until 1018, when King Malcolm I established the River Tweed as the permanent frontier. In the reign of Malcolm Canmore, the Castle became one of the main seats of the court, and the town, which was given privileged status as a **royal burgh**, began to grow. In 1128 King David established Holyrood Abbey at the foot of the slope, later allowing its monks to found a separate burgh, known as **Canongate**.

Robert the Bruce granted Edinburgh a **new charter** in 1329, giving it jurisdiction over the nearby port of **Leith**, and during the following century the prosperity brought by foreign trade enabled the newly fortified city to establish itself as the permanent **capital of Scotland**. Under King James IV, the city enjoyed a short but brilliant **Renaissance era**, which saw not only the construction of a new palace alongside Holyrood Abbey, but also the granting of a royal charter to the College of Surgeons, the earliest in the city's long line of academic and professional bodies.

This period came to an abrupt end in 1513 with the calamitous defeat by the English at the Battle of Flodden, which led to several decades of political instability. In the 1540s, King Henry VIII's attempt to force a royal union with Scotland led to the sack of Edinburgh, prompting the Scots to turn to France: French troops arrived to defend the city, while the young queen Mary was dispatched to Paris as the promised bride of the Dauphin. While the French occupiers succeeded in removing the English threat, they themselves antagonized the locals, who had become increasingly sympathetic to the ideals of the **Reformation**. When the radical preacher John Knox returned from exile in 1555, he quickly won over the city to his Calvinist message.

James VI's rule saw the foundation of the University of Edinburgh in 1582, but following the **Union of the Crowns** in 1603 the city was totally upstaged by London: although James promised to visit every three years, it was not until 1617 that he made his only return trip. In 1633 Charles I visited Edinburgh for his coronation, but soon afterwards precipitated a crisis by introducing episcopacy to the Church of Scotland, in the process making Edinburgh a bishopric for the first time. Fifty years of religious turmoil followed, culminating in the triumph of **Presbyterianism**. Despite these vicissitudes, Edinburgh expanded throughout the seventeenth century and, constrained by its walls, was forced to build both upwards and inwards.

The **Union of the Parliaments** of 1707 dealt a further blow to Edinburgh's political prestige, though the guaranteed preservation of the national church and the legal and educational systems ensured that it was never relegated to a purely provincial role. On the contrary, it was in the second half of the eighteenth century that Edinburgh achieved the height of its intellectual influence, led by an outstanding group, including David Hume and Adam Smith. Around the same time, the city began to expand beyond its medieval boundaries, laying out a **New Town**, a masterpiece of the Neoclassical style.

Industrialization affected Edinburgh less than any other major city in the nation, and it never lost its white-collar character. Nevertheless, the city underwent an enormous **urban expansion** in the course of the century, annexing, among many other small burghs, the large port of Leith.

In 1947 Edinburgh was chosen to host the great **International Festival** which served as a symbol of the new peaceful European order; despite some hiccups, it has flourished ever since, in the process helping to make tourism a mainstay of the local economy. In 1975 the city carried out another territorial expansion, moving its boundaries westwards as far as the old burgh of South Queensferry and the Forth Bridges. Four years later, an inconclusive referendum on Scottish devolution delayed Edinburgh's revival of its role as a governmental capital, and Glasgow, previously the poor relation but always a tenacious rival, began to challenge the city's status as a cultural centre.

However, while the 1990s have seen Glasgow establish a clear lead in driving Scotland's contemporary arts scene, they have also seen the return of power and influence to Edinburgh. Following the general election of May 1997, Britain's new Labour government immediately implemented its promise of a referendum, in which Scotland voted resoundingly in favour of its own **parliament** with tax-levying powers. Elections to the parliament were held in May 1999, with the Labour party winning the largest share of the seats, and the Scottish National Party (SNP) establishing itself as the second largest party. The leader of the Labour group, Donald Dewar, was elected First Minister, and the parliament, sitting in its temporary home in the twin-towered Church of Scotland Assembly Halls on the Mound, was formally opened by the Queen on July 1, 1999. With real political power over domestic issues being wielded from Edinburgh for the first time in nearly 300 years, the city has every right to feel and act like a proper capital again. Meanwhile, construction teams are at work on the modernist Parliament building, which will take its place opposite the ancient Palace of Holyroodhouse at the foot of the Royal Mile.

Arrival, information and transport

Although Edinburgh occupies a large area relative to its population – less than half a million people – most places worth visiting lie within the compact city centre, which is easily explored on foot. This is divided clearly and unequivocally between the maze-like **Old Town**, which lies on and around the crag linking the Castle and the Palace, and the **New Town**, laid out in a symmetrical pattern on the undulating ground to the north.

Edinburgh International Airport (☎0131/333 1000) is at Turnhouse, seven miles west of the city centre, close to the start of the M8 motorway to Glasgow. Regular shuttle buses (£3.60) connect to Waverley Station in the town centre; taxis charge around £14 for the same journey. Conveniently situated at the eastern end of Princes Street in the New Town, **Waverley Station** (timetable and fare enquiries ☎0345/484950) is the terminus for all mainline trains. The main central exits take you out onto Waverley Bridge, where the Castle appears dramatically ahead of you and the Old Town skyline is to the south, with Princes Street to the north. The northern exit from Waverley leads up a stairway to Princes Street itself, while the southern exit leads to Market Street, the outer fringe of the Old Town.

There's a second mainline train stop, **Haymarket Station**, just under two miles west on the lines from Waverley to Glasgow, Fife and the Highlands, although this is only really of use if you're staying nearby.

The bus terminal for local and intercity services is on St Andrew Square, two minutes' walk from Waverley Station, on the opposite side of Princes Street. One of the major bus companies, First Edinburgh, has a shop (☎0131/557 5061) at the southeastern corner of the bus station, where timetables are kept and tickets sold for a number of the local bus operators.

Information

Edinburgh's main **tourist office** is found on top of Princes Mall near the northern entrance to the station (Sept–June Mon–Fri 9am–5.30pm, Sat 9am–4.30pm, Sun 9.30am–2.30pm; July Mon–Fri 9am–6pm, Sat 9am–5.30pm, Sun 9.30am–5pm; Aug Mon–Fri 9am–7pm, Sat 9am–6pm, Sun 9am–5pm; call centre ☎0131/473 3800). Although inevitably flustered at the height of the season, it's efficiently run, with scores of free leaflets; when the office is closed, there's a 24-hour computerized information service at the door. The much smaller **airport branch** is in the main concourse, directly opposite Gate 5 (April–Oct daily 6.30am–10.30pm; Nov–March daily 7.30am–9.30pm). For backpacker-related information head to the **Haggis Office** at 60 High St (daily 9am–6pm; ☎0131/557 9393). Although their main function is to run minibus tours of Scotland, they're a good source of general information about the backpacker scene around Scotland and you can book both SYHA and independent hostels in Edinburgh from here. For up-to-date maps of the city head for one of the major book stores – Waterstones, 13–14 Princes St, is the nearest to Waverley Station.

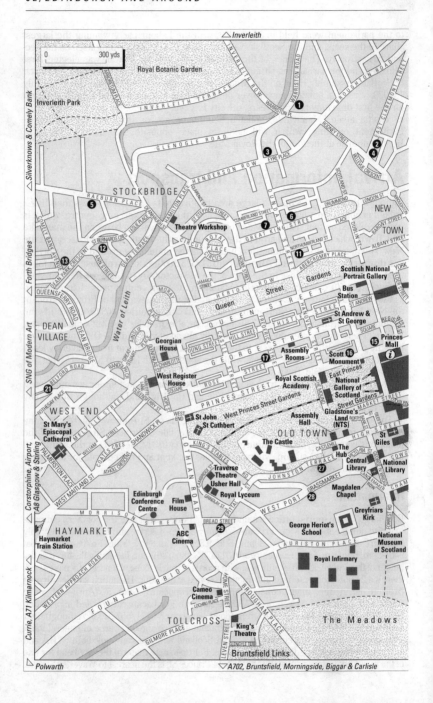

△ *Inverleith*

0 ___ 300 yds

Royal Botanic Garden

Inverleith Park

◁ Silverknows & Comely Bank

◁ Forth Bridges

INVERLEITH TERRACE

WARRISTON ROW

WARRISTON ROAD

BROUGHTON ROAD

EAST CLAREMONT STREET

GLENOGLE ROAD

EYRE PLACE

HENDERSON ROW

SCOTLAND STREET

LONDON STREET

BARONY STREET

ALBANY STREET

DUBLIN STREET

STOCKBRIDGE

RAEBURN PLACE

NEW TOWN

Theatre Workshop

CUMBERLAND STREET

GREAT KING STREET

DRUMMOND PLACE

NORTHUMBERLAND ST

ABERCROMBY PLACE

ST BERNARDS CRES

ANN STREET

DEAN TERRACE

ROYAL CIRCUS

HOWE STREET

JAMAICA STREET

Gardens

Scottish National Portrait Gallery

YORK PLACE

◁ DEAN DARK CRESCENT

DEAN BRIDGE

DEAN VILLAGE

Water of Leith

MORAY PLACE

HERIOT ROW

Queen Street

QUEEN STREET

Gardens

Bus Station

ST ANDREW

St Andrew & St George

ST ANDREW SQUARE

REGISTER ST

Princes Mall

◁ SNG of Modern Art

QUEENSFERRY ROAD

Georgian House

HILL STREET

YOUNG STREET

GEORGE STREET

Assembly Rooms

Scott Monument

East Princes Street Gardens

National Gallery of Scotland

BELFORD ROAD

West Register House

CHARLOTTE SQUARE

ROSE STREET

PRINCES STREET

West Princes Street Gardens

Royal Scottish Academy

Gladstone's Land (NTS)

HIGH

◁ Corstorphine, Airport, A8 Glasgow & Stirling

WEST END

St Mary's Episcopal Cathedral

MELVILLE STREET

WILLIAM STREET

COATES CRES

SHANDWICK PL

ATHOLL CRESCENT

WEST MAITLAND ST

St John

St Cuthbert

WEST END

KING'S STABLES RD

The Castle

Assembly Hall

OLD TOWN

CASTLEHILL

The Hub

CASTLE TERRACE

St Giles

National Library

JOHNSTON TERRACE

Central Library

◁ Currie, A71 Kilmarnock

Haymarket Train Station

MORRISON STREET

Edinburgh Conference Centre

Film House

Traverse Theatre

Usher Hall

Royal Lyceum

CAMBRIDGE ST

GRINDLAY ST

WEST PORT

GRASSMARKET

Magdalen Chapel

Greyfriars Kirk

George Heriot's School

FORREST ROAD

National Museum of Scotland

HAYMARKET

Haymarket Train Station

ABC Cinema

BREAD STREET

SPITTAL ST

LAURISTON PLACE

Royal Infirmary

WESTERN APPROACH ROAD

FOUNTAIN BRIDGE

Cameo Cinema

LOCHRIN PLACE

HOME STREET

BROUGHAM PLACE

The Meadows

TOLLCROSS

GILMORE PLACE

King's Theatre

LEVEN STREET

Bruntsfield Links

△ Polwarth

▽ *A702, Bruntsfield, Morningside, Biggar & Carlisle*

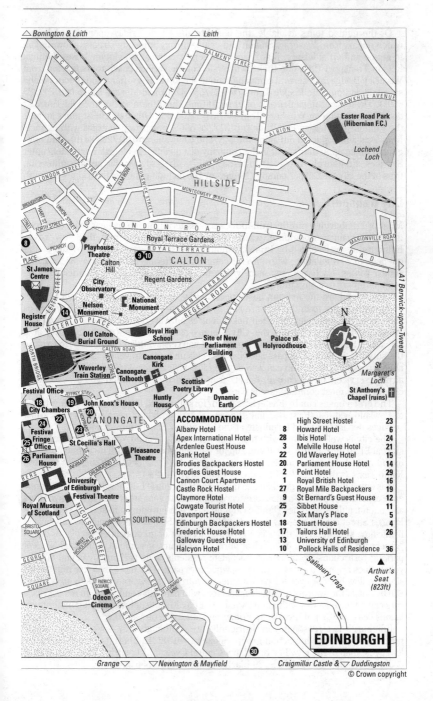

Easter Road Park
(Hibernian F.C.)

Lochend
Loch

HILLSIDE

LONDON ROAD

Royal Terrace Gardens
ROYAL TERRACE
9 10 CALTON

MARIONVILLE ROAD

Playhouse
Theatre
Calton
Hill

Regent Gardens

St James
Centre

City
Observatory

Nelson
Monument

National
Monument

Register
House

14

Old Calton
Burial Ground

Royal High
School

Site of New
Parliament
Building

Palace of
Holyroodhouse

St
Margaret's
Loch

Waverley
Train Station

Canongate
Tolbooth

Canongate
Kirk

St Anthony's
Chapel (ruins)

Festival Office

John Knox's House

Scottish
Poetry Library

Huntly
House

Dynamic
Earth

City Chambers
18   19   20   CANONGATE

22

24

Festival
Fringe
Office

23

St Cecilia's Hall

Pleasance
Theatre

25
Parliament
26 House

University
of Edinburgh

Festival Theatre

Royal Museum
of Scotland

SOUTHSIDE

ACCOMMODATION

Albany Hotel	8	High Street Hostel	23
Apex International Hotel	28	Howard Hotel	6
Ardenlee Guest House	3	Ibis Hotel	24
Bank Hotel	22	Melville House Hotel	21
Brodies Backpackers Hostel	20	Old Waverley Hotel	15
Brodies Guest House	2	Parliament House Hotel	14
Cannon Court Apartments	1	Point Hotel	29
Castle Rock Hostel	27	Royal British Hotel	16
Claymore Hotel	9	Royal Mile Backpackers	19
Cowgate Tourist Hotel	25	St Bernard's Guest House	12
Davenport House	7	Sibbet House	11
Edinburgh Backpackers Hostel	18	Six Mary's Place	5
Frederick House Hotel	17	Stuart House	4
Galloway Guest House	13	Tailors Hall Hotel	26
Halcyon Hotel	10	University of Edinburgh	
		Pollock Halls of Residence	36

Salisbury Crags

Arthur's
Seat
(823ft)

Odeon
Cinema

30

EDINBURGH

Of the guided tours available, the best are the Guide Friday open-topped buses, which depart from Waverley Station and cruise through the city streets, allowing you to get on and off at leisure. MacTours do much the same, with vintage buses, Lothian Region Transport (LRT) do their own version of the various coach tours leaving from Waverley Bridge, and several companies along the Royal Mile offer walking tours of the street, including Auld Reekie Tours (☎0131/557 4700) and Mercat Tours (☎0131/225 6591). These two companies also offer night-time ghost tours around the Old Town, as does the entertaining Witchery Tour (☎0131/225 6745). Other specialist tours include the Edinburgh Literary Pub Tour (☎0131/226 6665) mixing a pub crawl with extracts from local authors acted out along the way, and Geowalks (☎0131/228 2410), who offer guided walks up Arthur's Seat in the company of a qualified geologist. Forth Helicopter Services, Edinburgh Airport (☎0131/339 8877), offer spectacular aerial sightseeing trips of the city for £29 per person (10min), or £45 including the Forth Bridges (15min).

City transport

Most of Edinburgh's **public transport** services terminate on or near Princes Street, the city's main thoroughfare, which divides the Old Town from the New Town. Edinburgh is well-served by **buses**, although even locals are confused by the consequences of deregulation, with several companies offering competing services along similar routes. Each bus stop usually lists the different companies together with the route numbers that stop there.

Most useful are the maroon buses operated by Lothian Regional Transport (LRT); all buses referred to in the text are run by them unless otherwise stated. Timetables and passes are available from their ticket centres on Waverley Bridge or 27 Hanover St (☎0131/554 4494), or from the City Council-run Traveline (☎0800/232323) at 2 Cockburn St. A good investment, especially if you're staying far out or want to explore the suburbs, is the £10.50 pass allowing a week's unlimited travel on LRT buses; you'll need a passport photo. You can also buy an LRT day pass for £2.40 (£4.20 including the airport service), or, of course, tickets from the driver, for which you'll need exact change – the most common fare is 65p.

The green buses run by Eastern Scottish/First Bus, and the green and yellow buses of Lowland Scottish/First Bus link the capital with outlying towns and villages. Most services depart from and terminate at the St Andrew Square bus station.

The city is well endowed with taxi ranks, especially around Waverley Bridge. Costs start at £1.20 for the first 340yd and 20p for each additional 240yd. The phone numbers of the main local cab companies are: Capital Castle Cabs (☎0131/228 2555), Central Radio Taxis (☎0131/229 2468) and City Cabs (☎0131/228 1211).

It is emphatically not a good idea to take a **car** into central Edinburgh: despite the presence of several expensive multi-storey car parks, finding somewhere to park involves long and often fruitless searches. Traffic calming has been introduced in several key areas – Princes Street is now one-way for cars and Charlotte Square has adopted a complicated traffic-flow system – and there is a growing network of green-painted bus lanes called "greenways", which must be left clear during rush hours. In addition, Edinburgh's street parking restrictions are famously draconian: residents' zone parking areas and double-yellow lines are no-go areas at all times, while cars parked for more than five minutes on single yellow lines or overdue parking-meter-controlled areas are very likely to be fined £20 by one of the swarms of vehicle inspectors who patrol day and night. In severe cases cars can be towed away, with a retrieval fee of £120. Most ticket and parking-meter regulations cease at 6.30pm Monday to Friday, and at 1.30pm on Saturday.

Edinburgh is a reasonably cycle-friendly city – although hilly – with several **cycle paths**. The local cycling action group, Spokes (☎0131/313 2114), publishes an excellent cycle map of the city. For rental, try Central Cycles, 13 Lochrin Place (☎0131/228 6333) or Scottish Cycle Safaris, 29 Blackfriars St (☎0131/556 5560).

Accommodation

As befits its status as a top tourist city, Edinburgh has a greater choice of **accommodation** than any other place in Britain outside London. The highest concentration of places to stay can be found in the streets immediately north of Haymarket Station, Royal Terrace and the lower reaches of the New Town, and to the south, the inner suburbs of Bruntsfield and Newington, where numerous hotels and guest houses line the major roads into the city.

In addition to Edinburgh's **hotels**, hundreds of **private houses** offer B&B deals at low rates, but in order to protect the guest-house trade from excessive competition, they are only open between Easter and October. There is also a decent choice of both official and private **hostels**, and three **campsites** attached to caravan parks. Surprisingly, the wide range of **campus accommodation** is neither as cheap nor as convenient as might be expected. **Self-catering** is an alternative, and is extremely cost-effective for groups intending to stay a week or more, with some enticing addresses available for let.

Advance reservations are very strongly recommended during the Festival: turning up on spec entails accepting whatever is left (which is unlikely to be good value) or else commuting from the suburbs. The **tourist office** (see p.61) sends out accommodation lists for free, and can reserve any type of accommodation in advance for a non-refundable £5 fee: call in personally when you arrive or write in advance to Edinburgh Marketing Central Reservations Department, 3 Princes St, Edinburgh EH2 2QP (☎0131/473 3800, *www.edinburgh.org*), stating requirements. In Waverley Station, Capital Holidays runs an accommodation reservation service (daily 9am–5pm; ☎0131/556 0030) which makes no charge for bookings but requires the first night to be paid in full in advance by credit card.

The centrally located accommodation options we've listed are shown on the map on p.62.

Hotels

In the centre of the city, Edinburgh's **hotels** tend to fall into two categories: grand and traditional at the upper end of the market, and modern, continental-style hotels in the middle price range. While a number of stylish upmarket hotels have recently arrived around the edges of the city centre, in the suburbs and beyond the country-house hotel style dominates. Smaller hotels have generally been included in the Guest House section below.

Old Town

Apex International Hotel, 31–35 Grassmarket (☎0131/300 3456, *mail@apexhotels.co.uk*). Large new business-orientated hotel, with great access to the bars and restaurants of the Grassmarket. Upper rooms have views across to the Castle. ⑥.

ACCOMMODATION PRICE CODES

Throughout this book, accommodation **prices** have been graded with the codes below, according to the cost of the least expensive double room in high season. Price codes are not given for campsites, most of which charge under £10 per person. Almost all hostels charge less than £10 a night for a bed – the few exceptions to this rule have the prices quoted in the text. For a full account of the accommodation price codes, see p.31.

① under £40	④ £60–70	⑦ £110–150
② £40–50	⑤ £70–90	⑧ £150–200
③ £50–60	⑥ £90–110	⑨ £200 and over

Bank Hotel, 1 South Bridge (☎0131/556 9043). Unique location in a 1920s bank at the crossroads of the Royal Mile and South Bridge, with Logie Baird's bar downstairs and nine unusual but comfortable rooms upstairs in the theme of famous Scots. ⑤.

Ibis Hotel, 6 Hunter Square (☎0131/240 7000). French economy hotel chain, offering smart if uncharacterful rooms right at the centre of the Old Town. ③.

Point Hotel, 34–59 Bread St (☎0131/221 5555). Chic, thoroughly modern conversion of a former supermarket, with a popular style bar and excellent restaurant at street level. ⑥.

Tailors Hall Hotel, 139 Cowgate (☎0131/622 6800). Stylish and modern en-suite rooms in a recently converted 1621 trades hall and brewery in otherwise dingy Cowgate, linked to the lively mock-Gothic *Three Sisters Bar*. ⑥.

New Town

Albany Hotel, 39–43 Albany St (☎0131/556 0397). Georgian listed building with many period features and comfortable rooms in a quiet street a couple of minutes' walk south of the bus station. ⑦.

Frederick House Hotel, 42 Frederick St (☎0131/226 1999, *frederickhouse@ednet.co.uk*). A smart, well-priced hotel in a superb location just off George Street in the New Town. Continental breakfasts served across the road at *Café Rouge*. ④.

Howard Hotel, 34 Great King St (☎0131/557 3500, *reserve@thehoward.com*). Top-of-the-range elegant town-house hotel. Lavishly decorated and serving classy modern Scottish food. ⑨.

Melville House Hotel, 3 Rothesay Terrace (☎0131/225 5084). One of Edinburgh's grandest Victorian dwellings, with some exquisite internal features and decent rooms, some with outstanding views over Dean village and the city skyline. ⑥.

Old Waverley Hotel, 43 Princes St (☎0131/556 4648). Large, recently refurbished, grand hotel in an ideal location, right across from Waverley Station and with sweeping city views. ⑧.

Parliament House Hotel, 15 Calton Hill (☎0131/478 4000). Smart new hotel in great central location halfway up Calton Hill; includes three rooms for disabled visitors. ⑧.

Royal British Hotel, 20 Princes St (☎0131/556 4901). Swanky hotel with a prime location on Edinburgh's main street, offering stunning views. ⑦.

Leith

Malmaison, 1 Tower Place (☎0131/468 5000, *edinburgh@malmaison.com*). Chic modern hotel in a converted harbourside building with bright, bold original designs in each room, as well as CD players and cable TV. Also has gym, room service, Parisian brasserie and café-bar serving lighter meals. ⑦.

South of the centre

Allison House Hotel, 15–17 Mayfield Gardens, Mayfield (☎0131/667 8049, *dh007ljh@msn.com*). Well-run and recently expanded hotel with an "honesty" bar – guests serve themselves and pay on departure. ④.

Braid Hills Hotel, 134 Braid Rd, Braid Hills (☎0131/447 8888, *bookings@braidhillshotel.co.uk*). Old-fashioned baronial-style hotel in a residential area up in the hilly southern outskirts, with fine views (a ten-minute drive from the city). ⑦.

Bruntsfield Hotel, 69–74 Bruntsfield Place, Bruntsfield (☎0131/229 1393, *bruntsfield@queensferry-hotels.co.uk*). Large, comfortable and peaceful hotel overlooking Bruntsfield Links, a mile south of Princes Street. ⑦.

Prestonfield House Hotel, Priestfield Road, Bruntsfield (☎0131/668 3346). Luxury hotel in a seventeenth-century mansion set in its own park below Arthur's Seat. A new wing, sympathetic to the old building, has been added, raising the number of rooms from a tiny five to a still trim 31. Peacocks strut around on the lawns and Highland cattle low in the adjacent fields. ⑦.

West of the centre

Jarvis Ellersly Country House Hotel, 4 Ellersly Rd, Corstorphine (☎0131/337 6888). Edwardian country mansion set in a walled garden in quiet suburban Corstorphine, between the city centre and the airport. Predominantly business clientele. ⑦.

Norton House Hotel, Ingliston (☎0131/333 1275). Country house with spacious rooms and a conservatory restaurant, set in extensive parkland a mile from the airport; owned by the Virgin group. ⑧.

Guest houses

Edinburgh's innumerable **guest houses** and **small hotels** generally offer much better value for money, and are far more personal places to stay, than the larger city hotels.

New Town

Ardenlee Guest House, 9 Eyre Place (☎0131/556 2838). Welcoming, non-smoking guest house, with exceptionally comfortable and spacious rooms. Breakfast includes some vegetarian options, and private parking is available. ③.

Brodies Guest House, 22 E Claremont St (☎0131/556 4032, *rose.olbert@saqnet.co.uk*). Friendly B&B in a Victorian town house on the eastern edge of the New Town. ④.

Claymore Hotel, 6 Royal Terrace (☎0131/556 2693). Small, family-run hotel on Calton Hill, located on one of the city's most desirable streets, with views to the north over the Forth. ⑤.

Davenport House, 58 Great King St (☎0131/558 8495, *davenporthouse@btinternet.com*). A grand, regally decorated guest house in an attractive New Town town house; a well-priced and intimate alternative to some of the nearby hotels. ④.

Galloway Guest House, 22 Dean Park Crescent (☎0131/332 3672). Friendly, family-run place in elegant Stockbridge, within walking distance of the centre. ②.

Halcyon Hotel, 8 Royal Terrace (☎0131/556 1032). A very reasonably priced, unpretentious hotel, in a prime location on the north side of Calton Hill. ④.

St Bernard's Guest House, 22 St Bernard's Crescent (☎332 2339). Well located in Georgian Stockbridge, with pink rooms. ②.

Sibbet House, 26 Northumberland St (☎0131/556 1078, *sibbet.house@zetnet.co.uk*). Small, sumptuous family guest house, with beautifully decorated rooms and high standards. Breakfast is communal and often lively. Non-smoking throughout. ⑥.

Six Mary's Place, Raeburn Place (☎0131/332 8965, *sixmarysplace@btinternet.com*). Collectively run "alternative" guest house; has a no-smoking policy and offers excellent home-cooked vegetarian meals. ③.

Stuart House, 12 E Claremont St (☎0131/557 9030, *stuartho@globalnet.co.uk*). Homely, bright refurbished Georgian house in eastern New Town, a few minutes' walk from the bus station. No smoking. ④.

South of the centre

Ashdene House, 23 Fountainhall Rd, Grange (☎0131/667 6026, *Ashdene_House_Edinburgh@compuserve.com*). Well-run, non-smoking and environmentally friendly guest house in the quiet southern suburbs. ③.

Glenfield House, 21 Mayfield Gardens, Mayfield (☎0131/667 3641). Victorian mansion on the south side of the city, with a pleasant first-floor lounge and luxurious conservatory. ⑤.

Hopetoun Guest House, 15 Mayfield Rd, Mayfield (☎0131/667 7691, *hopetoun@aol.com*). Bright, friendly non-smoking guest house with just three rooms. Great views of Arthur's Seat and Blackford Hill. ②.

International Guest House, 37 Mayfield Gardens, Mayfield (☎0131/667 2511). One of the best of the Mayfield guest houses, with comfortable well-equipped rooms. ③.

The Stuarts B&B, 17 Glengyle Terrace, Bruntsfield (☎0131/229 9559, *reservations@the-stuarts.com*). A five-star bed and breakfast in central Edinburgh, with three comfortable and well-equipped rooms in a basement beside Bruntsfield Links. ⑥.

Teviotdale House Hotel, 53 Grange Loan, Grange (☎0131/667 4376, *teviotdale.house@btinternet.com*). Peaceful non-smoking hotel, offering luxurious standards at reasonable prices. Particularly good (and huge) home-cooked Scottish breakfasts. ③.

Leith and Inverleith

A-Haven Town House, 180 Ferry Rd, Leith (☎0131/554 6559, *reservations@a-haven.co.uk*). A terrifically friendly place – among the best of a number of guest houses on one of Edinburgh's main east–west arteries. ⑤.

Ashlyn Guest House, 42 Inverleith Row, Inverleith (☎0131/552 2954). Right by the Botanic Garden, and within walking distance of the centre. Non-smoking. ③.

Bar Java, 48–50 Constitution St, Leith (☎0131/467 7527, *www.scoot.co.uk/bar_java/*). Simple but brightly designed rooms above one of Leith's funkiest bars. Great breakfasts served, and food and drink available till late in the bar itself. ②.

Camore Hotel, 7 Links Gardens, Leith (☎0131/554 7897). A Georgian house with many attractive original features including marble fireplaces. Also has great views over Leith Links, Calton Hill and Arthur's Seat. ③.

Ravensdown Guest House, 248 Ferry Rd, Inverleith (☎0131/552 5438). Another place on Ferry Road, with a fine panoramic view across Inverleith playing fields to the city centre. ②.

East of the centre

Devon Guest House, 2 Pittville St, Portobello (☎0131/669 6067). Pleasant rooms and good breakfasts at this family-run guest house, only two minutes from the shore. ②.

Joppa Turrets Guest House, 1 Lower Joppa, Joppa (☎0131/669 5806, *stanley@joppaturrets.demon. co.uk*). The place to come if you want an Edinburgh holiday by the sea: a quiet establishment right by the beach in Joppa, five miles east of the city centre. ②.

Stra'ven Guest House, 3 Brunstane Rd North, Joppa (☎0131/669 5580). Splendid lounge and friendly service in an elegant well-kept guest house. No smoking. ②.

Self-catering apartments

Canon Court Apartments, 20 Canonmills (☎0131/474 7000, *www.canoncourt.co.uk*). All mod cons available in these smart, comfortable apartments on the northern edge of the New Town, near the Water of Leith. Prices start at £64 a night for one person and rise to £624 for six people for a week.

Crosswoodhill Farm, West Calder, West Lothian (☎01501/785205). Located eighteen miles from the centre of Edinburgh, this rural farm has two self-catering properties (one sleeps five people and one six) and is surrounded by attractive countryside and farm animals. Prices start from £230 a week in low season, up to £500 in high season.

National Trust for Scotland, 5 Charlotte Square (☎0131/243 9331). Has a two-room apartment in Gladstone's Land (the finest house on the Royal Mile) available for rent. Minimum period one week in summer and three nights in winter. Sleeps two and costs from £350 per week.

No. 5 Self Catering Apartments, 5 Abercorn Terrace (☎0131/669 1044). These Georgian houses in Portobello have apartments for three people for £125–360 per week, for two at £85–225 and single units at £60–95. Reduced rates for longer stays.

Rosslyn Castle, Roslin, Midlothian (☎01628/825925). For a very special holiday, this fifteenth-century castle is dramatically sited on a rock high above the River Esk and just five minutes' walk from Rosslyn Chapel (seven miles from city centre). Sleeps up to seven people and costs £650–1269 a week; minimum three nights.

West End Apartments, c/o Brian Matheson, 2 Learmonth Terrace, Comely Bank (☎0131/332 0717 or 226 6512, *brian@sias.co.uk*). Five apartments in a West End town house; minimum let two nights. Sleeps up to five and costs £200–800 per week.

Campus accommodation

Heriot-Watt University Riccarton Campus, Currie (☎0131/451 3669). Rather inconveniently sited at the extreme western fringe of the city, but comfortable, en-suite rooms are available all year and simpler student accommodation during university holidays. Transport links include trains from Curriehill and buses #22/22A, #45 and #65. ②–③.

Jewel and Esk Valley College, 24 Milton Rd E, Joppa (☎0131/657 7222). Again the location, about five miles east of the centre, is not ideal, but it's served directly by bus #44 and lies just beyond the terminus of bus #5. Open Jan–Nov. ③.

Napier University, 219 Colinton Rd, Merchiston (☎0131/455 4291). Halls of residence (①) in a reasonable location in the southern inner suburbs, but open July to mid-Sept only. Minimum stay two nights. Buses #23 and #37 will take you to Princes Street. Also available during same period are three–five person self-catering flats (☎0131/455 4427) in more central locations near Haymarket. Minimum stay one week; from £300 per week.

University of Edinburgh Pollock Halls of Residence, 18 Holyrood Park Rd, Newington (☎0131/651 2011). Unquestionably the best setting of any of the campuses, right beside the Royal Commonwealth Pool and Holyrood Park, but also quite expensive for its type (though rates are for bed and breakfast). Open Easter and late June to mid-Sept only. ⑤.

Hostels

Edinburgh now has a wealth of **hostels**, including two grand SYHA-run establishments and a cluster of independent outfits on or near the Royal Mile. Competition is fierce, so be prepared for a bit of enthusiastic marketing when you make an enquiry.

Argyle Backpackers Hotel, 14 Argyle Place, Marchmont (☎0131/667 9991, *iolaire@sol.uk*). Quieter, less intense version of the typical backpackers' hostel, with small dorms with single beds and a dozen double/twin rooms. Located near Meadows in studenty Marchmont.

Belford Hostel, 6–8 Douglas Gardens, West End (☎0131/225 6209; booking hotline 0800/096 6868, *info@hoppo.com*). Housed in a converted Arts and Crafts church, just west of the centre close to St Mary's Cathedral and the Gallery of Modern Art. The dorms are in box rooms with the vaulted church ceiling above. No curfew. Open all year.

Brodies Backpackers Hostel, 12 High St, Old Town (☎0131/557 8800). Tucked down a typical Old Town close, with four fairly straightforward dorms and limited communal areas. Centrally situated and no curfew. Open all year.

Bruntsfield Hostel, 7 Bruntsfield Crescent, Bruntsfield (☎0131/447 2994, central reservations 0541/553255). Large SYHA youth hostel overlooking Bruntsfield Links a mile south of Princes Street; take bus #11, #15 or #16. There's a 2am curfew, and breakfast is included in price. Note that as well as the similarly sized Eglinton hostel (see below), SYHA also take over two wonderfully central student residences during July and August – one on The Pleasance and one on Cowgate; both have over 100 single bedrooms for £16 per night (☎0131/337 1120 or book on the central reservations line).

Castle Rock Hostel, 15 Johnston Terrace, Old Town (☎0131/225 9666). Busy 200-bed hostel tucked below the Castle ramparts. Dorms are large but bright, and the communal areas include a games room with pool and ping-pong tables. No curfew. Open all year.

Cowgate Tourist Hostel, 112 Cowgate, Old Town (☎0131/226 2153). Basic, excellent-value accommodation in small apartments with kitchens, in the heart of the Old Town. Laundry facilities. Open July–Sept only; no curfew.

Edinburgh Backpackers Hostel, 65 Cockburn St, Old Town (☎0131/539 8695; booking hotline 0800/0966868; *info@hoppo.com*). Big hostel with a great central location in a side street off the Royal Mile. Accommodation is mostly in large but bright dorms, although a few doubles are available. No curfew. Open all year.

Eglinton Hostel, 18 Eglinton Crescent, Haymarket (☎0131/337 1120; central reservations 0541/55 32 55). Slightly more expensive but the more central of the two main SYHA hostels, in a characterful town house west of the centre, near Haymarket Station. The curfew is 2am; breakfast is included in price.

High Street Hostel, 8 Blackfriars St, Old Town (☎0131/557 3984). Large but lively and well-known hostel in a sixteenth-century building just off the Royal Mile. Linked to Castle Rock and Royal Mile Backpackers. Open 24hr, all year.

Royal Mile Backpackers, 105 High St, Old Town (☎0131/557 6120). Small, friendly hostel popular with longer-term residents, with limited communal areas but shared facilities with the nearby *High Street Hostel*. No curfew; open all year.

Campsites

Drummohr Caravan Park, Levenhall, Musselburgh (☎0131/665 6867). A large, pleasant site in this coastal satellite town to the east of Edinburgh, with excellent transport connections to the city, including buses #15, #15A, #26, #44, #66 (SMT) and #85. Open March–Oct.

Mortonhall Caravan Park, 38 Mortonhall Gate, Frogston Rd E (☎0131/664 1533). A good site, five miles out, near the Braid Hills; take bus #11 from Princes Street. Open March–Oct.

Silverknowes Caravan Site, Marine Drive, Silverknowes (☎0131/312 6874). Pleasant campsite close to the shore in the north-western suburbs, a thirty-minute ride from the centre by bus #14. Open year-round.

The Old Town

The **OLD TOWN**, although only about a mile long and 300yd wide, represents the total extent of the twin burghs of Edinburgh and Canongate for the first 650 years of their existence, and its general appearance and character remain indubitably medieval. Containing as it does the majority of the city's most famous tourist sights, it makes by far the best starting point for your explorations.

In addition to the obvious goals of the **Castle**, the **Palace of Holyroodhouse** and **Holyrood Abbey**, scores of historic buildings along the length of the **Royal Mile** link the two. Inevitably, much of the Old Town is sacrificed to hard-sell tourism, and can be uncomfortably crowded throughout the summer, especially during the Festival. Yet the area remains at the heart of Edinburgh, with daily business of the greatest importance being conducted in **Parliament House**, home of the Scottish Parliament until 1707 and now the location of Scotland's highest Law Courts, and in the **Assembly Hall**, temporary home of the new Scottish Parliament, formed in 1999. It's well worth while extending your explorations to the area immediately to the south of the Royal Mile, and in particular to the stunning new **National Museum of Scotland**.

It's possible to touch upon the highlights of the Old Town in the course of a single day, but a thorough visit requires several days. No matter how pressed you are, make sure you spare time for the wonderfully varied scenery and breathtaking vantage points of **Holyrood Park**, an extensive tract of open countryside on the eastern edge of the Old Town.

The Castle

The history of Edinburgh, and indeed of Scotland, is indissolubly bound up with its **Castle** (daily: April–Oct 9.30am–6pm; Nov–March 9.30am–5pm; £6.50), which dominates the city from its lofty seat atop an extinct volcanic rock. It requires no great imaginative feat to comprehend the strategic importance that underpinned the Castle's, and hence Edinburgh's, importance in Scotland: from Princes Street, the north side rears high above an almost sheer rockface; the southern side is equally formidable; the western, where the rock rises in terraces, only marginally less so. Would-be attackers, like modern tourists, were forced to approach the Castle from the crag to the east on which the Royal Mile runs down to Holyrood.

The Castle's disparate styles reflect its many changes in usage, as well as advances in military architecture: the oldest surviving part, **St Margaret's Chapel**, is from the twelfth century, while the most recent additions date back to the 1920s. Nothing remains from its period as a seat of the Scottish court in the reign of Malcolm Canmore; indeed, having been lost to (and subsequently recaptured from) the English on several occasions, the defences were dismantled by the Scots themselves in 1313, and only rebuilt in 1356 when the return of King David II from captivity introduced a modicum of political stability. Thereafter, it gradually developed into Scotland's premier castle, with the dual function of fortress and royal palace. It last saw action in 1745, when the Young Pretender's forces, fresh from their victory at Prestonpans, made a half-hearted attempt to storm it. Subsequently, advances in weapon technology diminished the Castle's importance, but under the influence of the Romantic movement it came to be seen as a great national monument. A grandiose "improvement" scheme, which would have transformed it into a bloated nineteenth-century vision of the Middle Ages, was considered, but fortunately only a few elements of it were actually built.

Though you can easily take in the views and wander round the Castle yourself, you might like to join one of the somewhat overheated **guided tours**, with their talk of war, boiling oil and the roar of the cannon. Alternatively, **audio guides** with personal headphones and a black box into which you punch different numbers depending on which part of the Castle you're in, are available from a booth just inside the gatehouse. Both the guided tours and audio guides are included in the entrance price.

The Esplanade

The Castle is entered via the **Esplanade**, a parade ground laid out in the eighteenth century and enclosed a hundred years later by ornamental walls, the southern one commanding fine views towards the Pentland Hills. Each evening during the Festival (see p.120), the Esplanade is the setting for the city's most shameless and spectacular demonstration of tourist kitsch, the Edinburgh Military Tattoo. Despite opposition from traditionalists, plans have been mooted to move the Tattoo to a permanent auditorium in Princes Street Gardens, which will reduce the cost of erecting and dismantling the spectators' grandstands each year.

Dotted around are several military monuments, including an equestrian **statue of Field Marshal Earl Haig**, the controversial Edinburgh-born commander of the British forces in World War I, whose trench warfare strategy of sending men "over the top" led to previously unimaginable casualties.

The lower defences

The **Gatehouse** to the Castle is a Romantic-style addition of the 1880s, complete with the last drawbridge ever built in Scotland. It was later adorned with appropriately heroic-looking statues of Sir William Wallace and Robert the Bruce.

Rearing up behind is the most distinctive and impressive feature of the Castle's silhouette, the sixteenth-century **Half Moon Battery**, which marks the outer limit of the actual defences. Continuing uphill, you pass through the **Portcullis Gate**, a handsome Renaissance gateway of the same period, marred by the addition of a nineteenth-century upper storey equipped with anachronistic arrow slits rather than gunholes.

Beyond is the six-gun **Argyle Battery**, built in the eighteenth century by Major-General Wade, whose network of military roads and bridges still forms an essential part of the transport infrastructure of the Highlands. Further west on **Mill's Mount Battery**, a well-known Edinburgh ritual takes place – the daily firing of the one o'clock gun. Originally designed for the benefit of ships in the Firth of Forth, it's now used as a time signal by city-centre office workers. Both batteries offer wonderful panoramic views over Princes Street and the New Town to the coastal towns and hills of Fife across the Forth.

Up the tortuously sloping road, the **Governor's House** is a 1740s mansion whose harled masonry and crow-stepped gables are archetypal features of vernacular Scottish architecture. It now serves as the officers' mess for members of the garrison, while the governor himself lives in the northern side wing. Behind stands the largest single construction in the Castle complex, the **New Barracks**, built in the 1790s in an austere Neoclassical style. The road then snakes round towards the enclosed citadel at the uppermost point of Castle Rock, entered via **Foog's Gate**.

St Margaret's Chapel

At the eastern end of the citadel, **St Margaret's Chapel** is the oldest surviving building in the Castle, and probably also in Edinburgh itself. Used as a powder magazine for 300 years, this tiny Norman church was rediscovered in 1845 and was eventually rededicated in 1934, after sympathetic restoration. Externally, it is plain and severe, but the interior preserves an elaborate zigzag archway dividing the nave from the sanctuary. Although once believed to have been built by the saint herself, and mooted as the site of her death in 1093, its architectural style suggests that it actually dates from about thirty years later, and was thus probably built by King David I as a memorial to his mother.

The battlements in front of the chapel offer the best of all the Castle's panoramic views. They are interrupted by the **Lang Stairs**, which provide an alternative means of access from the Argyle Battery via the side of the Portcullis Gate. Just below the battlements there's a small **cemetery**, the last resting place of the **soldiers' pets**: it is kept in immaculate condition, particularly when contrasted with the dilapidated state of some of the city's public cemeteries. Continuing eastwards, you skirt the top of the Forewall and Half Moon Batteries, passing the 110-foot **Castle Well** en route to **Crown Square**, the highest, most secure and most important section of the entire complex.

The Palace

The eastern side of Crown Square is occupied by the **Palace**, a surprisingly unassuming edifice built round an octagonal stair turret heightened last century to bear the Castle's main flagpole. Begun in the 1430s, the Palace's present Renaissance appearance is thanks to King James IV, though it was remodelled for Mary, Queen of Scots and her consort Henry, Lord Darnley, whose entwined initials (MAH), together with the date 1566, can be seen above one of the doorways. This gives access to a few historic rooms, the most interesting of which is the tiny panelled bedchamber at the extreme southeastern corner, where Mary gave birth to James VI. Along with the rest of the Palace, the room was revamped for James's triumphant homecoming in 1617, though this was to be the last time it served as a royal residence.

Another section of the Palace has recently been refurbished with a detailed audiovisual presentation on the **Honours of Scotland**, the originals of which are housed in the Crown Room at the very end of the display. Though you might be put off by the slow-moving, claustrophobic queues that shuffle past the displays, the interest in them is justified: these magnificent crown jewels – the only pre-Restoration set in the United Kingdom – serve as one of the most potent images of Scotland's nationhood. They were last used for the Scottish-only coronation of Charles II in 1651, an event which provoked the wrath of Oliver Cromwell, who made exhaustive attempts to have the jewels melted down. Having narrowly escaped his clutches by being smuggled out of the Castle and hidden in a rural church, the jewels later served as symbols of the absent monarch at sittings of the Scottish Parliament before being locked away in a chest following the Union of 1707. For over a century they were out of sight and eventually presumed lost, before being rediscovered in 1818 as a result of a search initiated by Sir Walter Scott.

Of the three pieces comprising the Honours, the oldest is the **sceptre**, which bears statuettes of the Virgin and Child, St James and St Andrew, rounded off by a polished globe of rock crystal: it was given to James IV in 1494 by Pope Alexander VI, and refashioned by Scottish craftsmen for James V. Even finer is the **sword**, a swaggering Italian High Renaissance masterpiece by the silversmith Domenico da Sutri, presented to James IV by the great artistic patron Pope Julius II. Both the hilt and the scabbard are engraved with Julius's personal emblem, showing the oak tree and its acorns, the symbols of the Risen Christ, together with dolphins, symbols of the Church. The jewel-encrusted **crown**, made for James V by the Scottish goldsmith James Mosman, incorporates the gold circlet worn by Robert the Bruce and is surmounted by an enamelled orb and cross.

The glass case containing the Honours has recently been rearranged to create space for its newest addition, the **Stone of Destiny** (see box). This remarkably plain object now lies incongruously next to the opulent Crown Jewels.

Around Crown Square

The south side of **Crown Square** is occupied by the **Great Hall**, built under James IV as a venue for banquets and other ceremonial occasions. Until 1639 the meeting place of the Scottish Parliament, it later underwent the indignity of conversion and subdivi-

THE STONE OF DESTINY

Legend has it that the **Stone of Destiny** (also called the Stone of Scone) was "Jacob's Pillow", on which he dreamed of the ladder of angels from earth to heaven. Its real history is obscure, but it is known that it was moved from Ireland to Dunadd by missionaries, and thence to Dunstaffnage, from where Kenneth MacAlpine, king of the Dalriada Scots, brought it to the abbey at Scone in 838. There it remained for almost five hundred years, used as a coronation throne on which all kings of Scotland were crowned.

In 1296, an over-eager Edward I stole what he believed to be the Stone and installed it at Westminster Abbey, where, apart from a brief interlude in 1950 when it was removed by Scottish nationalists and hidden in Arbroath for several months, it remained for seven hundred years. All this changed in December 1996 when, after an elaborate ceremony-laden journey from London, the Stone returned to Scotland, in one of the doomed attempts by the Conservative government to convince the Scottish people that the Union was a good thing. Much to the annoyance of the people of Perth and the curators of Scone Palace (see p.289), and to the general indifference of the people of Scotland, the Stone was placed in Edinburgh Castle.

However, speculation surrounds the authenticity of the Stone, for the original is said to have been intricately carved, while the one seen today is a plain block of sandstone. Many believe that the canny monks at Scone palmed this off onto the English king, and that the real Stone of Destiny lies hidden in an underground chamber, its whereabouts a mystery to all but the chosen few.

sion, firstly into a barracks, then a hospital. During this time, its hammerbeam roof – the earliest of three in the Old Town – was hidden from view. It was restored towards the end of the last century, when the hall was decked out in the full-blown Romantic manner.

On the west side of the square, the eighteenth-century **Queen Anne Barracks** house part of the **Scottish United Services Museum**, with displays on each of the different Scottish military regiments, plus the navy and air force. Note the model of the ship *The Great George*, made by French prisoners incarcerated in the Castle during the eighteenth and early nineteenth centuries.

In 1755, the castle church of St Mary on the north side of the square was replaced by a barracks, which in turn was skilfully converted into the quietly reverential **Scottish National War Memorial** in honour of the 150,000 Scots who fell in World War I.

The rest of the complex

From Crown Square, you can descend to the **Vaults**, a series of cavernous chambers erected by order of James IV to provide an even surface for the showpiece buildings above. They were later used as a prison for captured foreign nationals, who have bequeathed a rich legacy of graffiti. One of the rooms houses the famous fifteenth-century siege gun, **Mons Meg**, which could fire a 500-pound stone nearly two miles. A seventeenth-century visitor, the London poet, John Taylor, commented: "It is so great within, that it was told me that a child was once gotten there." In 1754, Mons Meg was taken to the Tower of London, where it stayed till Sir Walter Scott persuaded George IV, on the occasion of his 1822 state visit to Scotland, to return it.

Directly opposite the entrance to the Vaults is the **Military Prison**, built in 1842, when the design and function of jails was a major topic of public debate. The cells, though designed for solitary confinement, are less forbidding than might be expected. Finally, beyond the Governor's House, and overlooking the two-tier western defences, the late nineteenth-century **Hospital** is a continuation of the Scottish United Services Museum.

The Royal Mile

The **Royal Mile**, the name given to the ridge linking the Castle with Holyrood, was described by Daniel Defoe, in 1724, as "the largest, longest and finest street for Buildings and Number of Inhabitants, not in Bretain only, but in the World". Almost exactly a mile in length, it is divided into four separate streets – Castlehill, Lawnmarket, High Street and Canongate. From these, branching out in a herringbone pattern, a series of tightly packed closes and steep lanes are entered via archways known as pends. After the construction of the New Town, the Royal Mile degenerated into a notorious slum, but has since shaken off that reputation, becoming once again a highly desirable place to live. Although marred somewhat by rather too many tacky tourist shops and the odd misjudged new development, it is still among the most evocative parts of the city, and one that particularly rewards detailed exploration.

Castlehill

The narrow uppermost stretch of the Royal Mile is known as **Castlehill**. The first building on the northern side of the street as you leave the Castle Esplanade is the former reservoir for the Old Town, which has been converted into the **Edinburgh Old Town Weaving Centre** (Mon–Sat 9am–5.30pm, Sun 10am–5pm). Very much a commercial enterprise, the centre contains various large shops selling kilts, rugs and other tartan adornments while noisy looms rhymically churn the stuff out on the floors below. You can see these up close and try your hand at weaving on a self-guided tour (£4), or for £7 dress up in rather ridiculous-looking ancient tartan dress and have your photo snapped.

On the corner of the wall of the Weaving Centre facing the Castle, a pretty Art Nouveau **Witches' Fountain** commemorates the three hundred or more women burnt at the spot on charges of sorcery, the last of whom died in 1722. Rising up behind is **Ramsay Gardens**, surely some of the most picturesque city-centre flats in the world. The oldest part is the octagonal Goose Pie House, home of the eighteenth-century poet Allan Ramsay, author of *The Gentle Shepherd* and father of the better-known portrait painter of the same name, while the rest dates from the 1890s and was the brainchild of Patrick Geddes, a pioneer of the modern town-planning movement, who created these desirable apartments in an attempt to regenerate the Old Town.

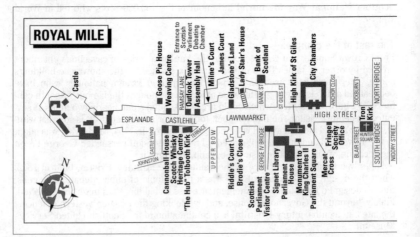

Opposite the Weaving Centre at the top of the southern side of Castlehill, the so-called **Cannonball House** takes its name from the cannonball embedded in its masonry, which according to legend was the result of a poorly targeted shot fired by the Castle garrison at Bonnie Prince Charlie's encampment at Holyrood. The truth is far more prosaic: the ball marks the gravitation height of the city's first piped water supply. Alongside, the **Scotch Whisky Heritage Centre** (daily: June–Sept 9.30am–6pm; Oct–May 10am–5.30pm; tours £3.25 and £4.95) gives the lowdown on all aspects of Scotland's national beverage, featuring a gimmicky ride in a "barrel" through a series of uninspiring historical tableaux and a free dram (a measure) of whisky at the end. The longer tour also offers a detailed explanation of aspects of production and blending, although there's little on offer here which you won't find done rather better on a tour of a real distillery. For whisky novices, it's worth popping into the shop, whose stock gives an idea of the sheer range and diversity of the drink, with dozens of different brands on sale.

Across the street, the **Outlook Tower** (April–Oct Mon–Fri 9.30am–6pm, Sat & Sun 10am–6pm; Nov–March 10am–5pm; £3.95) has been one of Edinburgh's top tourist attractions since 1853, when the original seventeenth-century tenement was equipped with a **camera obscura**. It makes a good introduction to the city: live images are beamed through a periscope mounted at the highest point of the tower onto a white table in the auditorium, accompanied by a running commentary. For the best views, visit at noon when there are fewer shadows. The viewing balcony is one of Edinburgh's best vantage points, and there are exhibitions on pinhole photography, holography, Victorian photographs of the city, and topographic paintings made between 1780 and 1860.

A few doors further on is the **Assembly Hall**, normally used as the meeting place of the annual General Assembly of the Church of Scotland but, since May 1999, the home of the **Scottish Parliament** while it awaits more permanent accommodation (see p.82). The Hall is nothing to look at from the Royal Mile side; at its northern entrance, however, on Mound Place, are the twin towers which feature so prominently on vistas of the Old Town skyline from the New Town. It is possible to visit the debating chamber of the Parliament by going to the public entrance in Milne's Court, one of the closes off the Royal Mile just past the Assembly Hall (open Mon–Fri 10am–noon & 2–4pm;

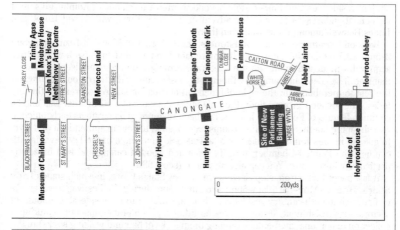

free). When Parliament is in session, you can sit and watch the **debates** from the large public gallery – tickets are available on an ad hoc basis either from the desk at the public entrance or from the Scottish Parliament **Visitor Centre** on the corner of George IV Bridge and High Street, although they can also be booked (☎0131/348 5000) up to a week before the date you wish to attend. The Visitor Centre will tell you when Parliament is in session, and which debates are taking place on particular days. If Parliament is not in session, it is still possible to view the empty debating chamber from the public gallery, where stewards are on hand to answer questions.

The imposing black church building opposite the Assembly Hall at the foot of Castlehill is **The Hub** (daily 8am–late), which in 1999 became the first permanent home of the Edinburgh International Festival; it is open year round, providing performance, rehearsal and exhibition space, a ticket centre and a café. It also acts as a ticket centre for other **festivals** held in Edinburgh, including the Hogmanay celebrations and the Science Festival. During August and early September, the upstairs of The Hub is the home of the **Festival Club** (daily from 10am–2am; membership £5 per day or £25 per week), a highly-charged daily social gathering of the great and the good of the Festival scene. The building itself was constructed in 1845 to designs by James Gillespie Graham and Augustus Pugin, one of the co-architects of the Houses of Parliament in London – a connection obvious from the superb neo-Gothic detailing and the sheer presence of the building, whose spire is the highest in Edinburgh. It was built as an Assembly Hall for the Church of Scotland, and became a parish church when the assembly moved to the United Free Church hall across the road. On the ground floor level is the *Hub Café* (daily 8am–11pm), which serves drinks, coffees and a small selection of tasty snacks and meals in a vivid yellow interior space as well as on the large terrace area outside. Also worth checking out is the main hall upstairs, where the original neo-Gothic woodwork and high-vaulted ceiling is enlivened with a fabulous fabric design in Rastafarian colours. Permanent works of art have been incorporated into the centre, including over 200 delightful foot-high sculptures by Scottish sculptor Jill Watson, depicting Festival performers and audiences.

Lawnmarket

Below the Tolbooth Kirk, the Royal Mile opens out into the broader expanse of **Lawnmarket**, which, as its name suggests, was once a marketplace. At its northern end is the entry to **Milne's Court**, whose excellently restored tenements now serve as student residences, and immediately beyond, **James Court**, one of Edinburgh's most fashionable addresses prior to the advent of the New Town, with David Hume and James Boswell among those who lived there.

Back on Lawnmarket itself, **Gladstone's Land** (April–Oct Mon–Sat 10am–5pm, Sun 2–5pm; £3.20) takes its name from the merchant Thomas Gledstane (sic), who in 1617 acquired a modest dwelling on the site, transforming it into a magnificent six-storey mansion. The Gledstane family are thought to have occupied the third floor, renting out the rest to merchants, in the style of tenement occupation still widespread in the city today. The arcaded ground floor, the only authentic example left of what was once a common feature of Royal Mile houses, has been restored to illustrate its early function as a shopping booth. Several other rooms have been kitted out in authentic period style to give an impression of the lifestyle of a well-to-do household of the late seventeenth century; the Painted Chamber, with its decorated wooden ceiling and wall friezes, is particularly impressive. You can also stay here (see p.68).

A few paces further on, steps lead down to Lady Stair's Close, in which stands **Lady Stair's House** (Mon–Sat 10am–5pm; also Sun 2–5pm during the Festival; free), another fine seventeenth-century residence, albeit one subject to a considerable amount of Victorian refurbishment. It now serves as Edinburgh's literary museum, featuring a collection of personal mementoes (among them locks of hair and walking sticks) of the three lions of Scottish literature – Robert Burns, Sir Walter Scott and Robert Louis Stevenson. In the courtyard outside, called the **Makars' Court** after the Scots word for the "maker" of poetry or prose, look out for quotations by twelve of Scotland's most famous writers and poets inscribed on paving stones.

On the south side of Lawnmarket is **Riddle's Court**, actually a double courtyard, each with its own pend. Further down the street, **Brodie's Close** is named after the father of one of Edinburgh's most morbid characters, Deacon William Brodie, burglar by night and apparent pillar of society by day. Following his eventual capture, he managed to escape to Holland, but was betrayed, brought back to Edinburgh and hanged in 1788 on gallows of his own design. His ruse of trying to cheat death by secretly wearing an iron collar under his shirt failed.

The High Kirk of St Giles

Across George IV Bridge is the third section of the Royal Mile, known as the **High Street**, which occupies two blocks either side of the intersection between North Bridge and South Bridge. The dominant building of the southern side of the street is the **High Kirk of St Giles** (April–Sept Mon–Fri 9am–7pm, Sat & Sun 9am–5pm; Oct–March Mon–Sat 9am–5pm, Sun 1–5pm; free) which closes off Parliament Square from High Street. The sole parish church of medieval Edinburgh, where John Knox (see box on p.78) launched and directed the Scottish Reformation, the Kirk is almost invariably referred to as a cathedral, although it has only been the seat of a bishop on two brief and unhappy occasions in the seventeenth century. According to one of the city's best-known legends, the attempt in 1637 to introduce the English prayer book, and thus Episcopal government, so incensed a humble stallholder named Jenny Geddes that she hurled her stool at the preacher, prompting the rest of the congregation to chase the offending clergy out of the building. A tablet in the north aisle marks the spot from where she let rip.

In the early nineteenth century, St Giles received a much-needed but over-drastic restoration, covering most of the Gothic exterior with a smooth stone coating that gives it a certain Georgian dignity while sacrificing its medieval character almost completely. The only part to survive this treatment is the late fifteenth-century tower, whose resplendent crown spire is formed by eight flying buttresses. The **interior** has survived in much better shape. Especially notable are the four massive piers supporting the tower, which date back, at least in part, to the church's Norman predecessor. In the nineteenth century, St Giles was adorned with a whole series of funerary monuments in order to give it the character of a national pantheon on the model of Westminster Abbey. It was also equipped with several Pre-Raphaelite stained-glass windows. The best of these, designed by Edward Burne-Jones and William Morris, showing Old Testament prophets and the Israelites crossing the River Jordan, can be seen on the facade wall of the **north aisle**. Alongside is the great **west window**, whose dedication to Robbie Burns in 1985 caused enormous controversy – as a hardened drinker and womanizer, the national bard was far from being an upholder of accepted Presbyterian values. Look out, also, for an elegant bronze relief of Robert Louis Stevenson on the south side of the church.

At the southeastern corner of St Giles, the **Thistle Chapel** was built by Sir Robert Lorimer in 1911 as the private chapel of the sixteen knights of the Most Noble Order of the Thistle, the highest chivalric order in Scotland. Self-consciously derivative of St George's Chapel in Windsor, it's an exquisite piece of craftsmanship, with an elaborate ribbed vault, huge drooping bosses, and extravagantly ornate stalls.

Parliament Square

The rest of **Parliament Square** is dominated by the continuous Neoclassical facades of the **Law Courts**, originally planned by Robert Adam (1728–92), one of four brothers in a family of architects (their father William Adam designed Hopetoun House; see

JOHN KNOX

The Protestant reformer **John Knox** has been alternately credited with, or blamed for, the distinctive national culture that emerged from the Calvinist Reformation, which has cast its shadow over Scottish history and the Scottish character right up to the present.

Little is known about Knox's early years: he was born between 1505 and 1514 in East Lothian, and trained for the priesthood at St Andrews University under John Major (sic), author of a *History of Great Britain* that advocated the union of Scotland and England. Ordained in 1540, Knox then served as a private tutor, in league with Scotland's first significant Protestant leader, **George Wishart**. After Wishart was burnt at the stake for heresy in 1546, Knox became involved with the group who had carried out the revenge murder of the Scottish primate, Cardinal David Beaton, subsequently taking over his castle in St Andrews. The following year this was captured by the French, and Knox was carted off to work as a galley slave.

He was freed in 1548, as a result of the intervention of the English, who invited him to play an evangelizing role in the spread of their own Reformation. Following successful ministries in Berwick-upon-Tweed and Newcastle-upon-Tyne, Knox turned down the bishopric of Rochester, less from an intrinsic opposition to episcopacy than from a wish to avoid becoming embroiled in the turmoil he guessed would ensue if the Catholic Mary Tudor acceded to the English throne. When this duly happened in 1553, Knox fled to the Continent, ending up as minister to the English-speaking community in Geneva, which was then in the grip of the theocratic government of the Frenchman **Jean Calvin**. Knox was quickly won over to his radical version of Protestantism, declaring Geneva to be "the most perfect school of Christ since the days of the Apostles".

In exile, Knox was much preoccupied with the question of the influence wielded by political rulers, believing that the future of the Reformation in Europe was at risk because of the opposition of a few powerful sovereigns. This prompted him to write his most infamous treatise, *The First Blast of the Trumpet Against the Monstrous Regiment of Women*, a specific attack on the three Catholic women then ruling Scotland, England and France, which has made his name synonymous with misogyny ever since.

When Knox was allowed to return to Scotland in 1555, he took over as spiritual leader of the Reformation, becoming minister of St Giles in Edinburgh, where he established a reputation as a charismatic preacher. However, the establishment of Protestantism as the official religion of Scotland in 1560 was dependent on the forging of an alliance with Elizabeth I, which Knox himself rigorously championed: the swift deployment of English troops against the French garrison in Edinburgh dealt a fatal blow to Franco-Spanish hopes of re-establishing Catholicism in both Scotland and England. Although the return of Mary, Queen of Scots the following year placed a Catholic monarch on the Scottish throne, reputedly Knox was always able to retain the upper hand in his famous disputes with her.

Before his death in 1572, Knox began mapping out the organization of the Scots Kirk, sweeping away all vestiges of Episcopal control and giving lay people a role of unprecedented importance. He also proposed a nationwide education system, to be compulsory for the very young and free for the poor, though lack of funds meant this could not be implemented in full. His final legacy was the posthumously published *History of the Reformation of Religion in the Realm of Scotland*, a justification of his life's work.

For all his considerable influence, Knox was not responsible for many of the features which have created the popular image of Scottish Presbyterianism – and of Knox himself – as austere and joyless. A man of refined cultural tastes, he did not encourage the iconoclasm that destroyed so many of Scotland's churches and works of art: indeed, much of this was carried out by English hands. Nor did he promote the unbending Sabbatarianism, the obsessive work ethic or even the inflexible view of the doctrine of predestination favoured by his far more fanatical successors. Ironically, though, by fostering an irrevocable rift in the "Auld Alliance" with France, he did do more than anyone else to ensure that Scotland's future was to be linked irrevocably with that of England.

p.106) whose work helped imbue the New Town with much of its grace and elegance. Because of a shortage of funds, the present exteriors were built to designs by Robert Reid (1776–1856), the designer of the northern part of New Town, who faithfully quoted from Adam's architectural vocabulary without matching his flair. The mentor of William Playfair (see p.650), William Stark was flamboyant in his design, and his **Signet Library**, which occupies the west side of the square, is one of the most beautiful interiors in Edinburgh, its sumptuous colonnaded hall a perfect embodiment of the ideals of the Age of Reason. Unfortunately it can only be seen by prior written application, except on very occasional open days.

Around the corner, facing the southern side of St Giles, is **Parliament House**, built in the 1630s for the Scottish Parliament, a role it maintained until the Union, when it passed into the hands of the legal fraternity. To enter the impressive main hall go through the entrance lobby (Mon–Fri 9am–5pm); the most notable feature is the extravagant hammerbeam roof and the delicately carved stone corbels from which it springs – in addition to some vicious grotesques, they include accurate depictions of several castles, including Edinburgh. In the far corner is a small exhibition explaining the history of the building and courts, but it's more fun simply to watch the every day business, with solicitors and bewigged advocates in hushed conferrals, often following the time-honoured tradition of pacing up and down the main hall to prevent their conversation being overheard by anyone sitting on the benches around the walls. Most of the court rooms have public galleries, which you can sit in if you're interested – ask one of the attendants in the lobby to point you in the right direction.

Outside on the square, an imposing equestrian **monument to King Charles II** depicts him in fetching Roman garb. Back on the High Street, beside a bloated memorial to the fifth Duke of Buccleuch, the brickwork pattern set in the pavement is known as the **Heart of Midlothian**. Immortalized in Scott's novel of the same name, it marks the site of a demolished tollbooth; you may see passers-by spitting on it for luck. Public proclamations have traditionally been read from the **Mercat Cross** at the back of St Giles. The present structure, adorned with coats of arms and topped by a sculpture of a unicorn, looks venerable enough, but most of it is little more than a hundred years old, a gift to the city from nineteenth-century prime minister William Ewart Gladstone.

Upper High Street

The first main building on the northern side of the **High Street** after crossing the intersection of George IV Bridge and Bank Street is the High Court of Justiciary, Scotland's highest criminal court, outside which is a statue of David Hume, the philosopher and one of Edinburgh's greatest sons, who looks decidedly wan and chilly dressed in nothing but a Roman toga. A little further on, opposite the Mercat Cross, the U-shaped **City Chambers** were designed by John Adam, brother of Robert, as the Royal Exchange. Local traders never warmed to the exchange, however, so the town council established its headquarters there instead. Beneath the City Chambers lies **Mary King's Close**, one of Edinburgh's most unusual attractions. Built in the early sixteenth century, it was closed off for many years after the devastation of the 1645 plague, before being entirely covered up by the chambers in 1753. Brief tours of this rather spooky "lost city" are run regularly through the day by Mercat Tours (☎0131/225 6591). A little further down the High Street is **Anchor Close**, site of the printing works of William Smellie, who published the first ever edition of the *Encyclopaedia Britannica* there in 1768.

Across the road is the **Tron Kirk**, best known as the focal point for hardy Hogmanay revellers. The church was built in the 1630s to accommodate the Presbyterian congregation ejected from St Giles when the latter became the seat of a bishop; the spire is an 1820s replacement for one destroyed by fire. The Tron remained in use as a church until 1952. It was then closed for forty years, during which time excavations revealed sections of an old close, Marlin's Wynd, which ran from High Street down to the

Cowgate. Today the building houses the **Old Town Information Centre** (Easter–May Thurs–Mon 10am–1pm & 2–5pm, daily June–Sept 10am–7pm), where you can peruse information boards on the buildings of the Old Town and look down from raised walkways on the Marlin's Wynd excavations.

Lower High Street

Beyond the intersection of North Bridge and South Bridge back on the northern side of High Street is **Paisley Close**, above whose entrance is a bust of a youth with the inscription "Heave awa' chaps, I'm no' dead yet", uttered in 1861 by a boy trapped by rubble following the collapse of a tenement in the close, and who was subsequently dug out by rescue workers.

In Chalmers Close, just to the west, **Trinity Apse** is a poignant reminder of the fifteenth-century Holy Trinity Collegiate Church, formerly one of Edinburgh's most outstanding buildings, but demolished in 1848 to make way for an extension to Waverley Station. The stones were carefully numbered and stored on Calton Hill so that it could be reassembled at a later date, but many were pilfered before sufficient funds became available, and only the apse could be reconstructed on this new site. A few years ago, it was transformed into a **Brass Rubbing Centre** (Mon–Sat 10am–5pm; Sun 2–5pm during the Festival only; last rubbing sold 1hr before closing; free), where you can rub your own impressions from Pictish crosses and medieval church brasses from £1.20 upwards.

On the other side of High Street, the noisy **Museum of Childhood** (Mon–Sat 10am–5pm; also Sun 2–5pm during the Festival; free) was, oddly enough, founded by an eccentric local councillor who heartily disliked children. Although he claimed that the museum was a serious social archive for adults, and dedicated it to King Herod, it has always attracted swarms of kids, who delight in the dolls' houses, teddy bears, train sets, marionettes and other paraphernalia.

Almost directly opposite is what's thought to be the city's oldest surviving dwelling, the early sixteenth-century **Moubray House** (closed to the public). The uses of the four-storey house have included tavern, bookshop and even, towards the end of the nineteenth century, temperance hotel. It also served as Daniel Defoe's office during his stay as an English government representative in 1707. Next door lies the picturesque **John Knox's House** (Mon–Sat 10am–4.30pm; £1.95), built some thirty years later. With its outside stairway, biblical motto, and sundial adorned with a statue of Moses, it gives a good impression of how the Royal Mile must have once looked. Whether or not it was ever really the home of Knox is debatable: he may have moved here for safety at the height of the religious troubles. The house did, however, once belong to goldsmith James Mosman, son of the designer of the Scottish crown, who was executed for his dogged loyalty to Knox's *bête noire*, Mary, Queen of Scots. The rather bare interiors, which give a good idea of the labyrinthine layout of Old Town houses, display explanatory material on Knox's life and career. The house is linked to the neighbouring **Netherbow Arts Centre**, a busy venue during the Festival which displays paintings and photography throughout the year and has a popular lunchtime café selling wholesome soups and light meals.

Canongate

For over seven hundred years, the district through which Canongate runs was a burgh in its own right, officially separate from the capital. In recent decades, it has been the subject of some of the most ambitious restoration programmes in the Old Town, two notable examples of which can be seen at the top of the street. On the south side is the residential **Chessel's Court**, a mid-eighteenth-century development with fanciful Rococo chimneys. It was formerly the site of the Excise Office, scene of the robbery that led to the arrest and execution of Deacon Brodie. Over the road the **Morocco Land** is a reasonably faithful reproduction of an old tenement, incorporating the original bust of a Moor from which its name derives.

Dominated by a turreted steeple, the late sixteenth-century **Canongate Tolbooth**, a little further down the north side of the street, has served both as the headquarters of the burgh administration and as a prison, and now houses **The People's Story** (Mon–Sat 10am–5pm, during the Festival also Sun 2–5pm; free), a lively museum devoted to the everyday life and work of Edinburgh people down the centuries, with sounds and tableaux on various aspects of city living – including a typical Edinburgh pub. Next door, **Canongate Kirk** was built in the 1680s to house the congregation expelled from Holyrood Abbey when the latter was commandeered by James VII (James II in England) to serve as the chapel for the Order of the Thistle. It's a curiously archaic design, still Renaissance in outline, and built to a cruciform plan wholly at odds with the ideals and requirements of Protestant worship. Its churchyard, one of the city's most exclusive cemeteries, commands a superb view across to Calton Hill. Among those buried here are Adam Smith, Mrs Agnes McLehose (better known as Robert Burns' "Clarinda") and Robert Fergusson, regarded by some as Edinburgh's greatest poet, despite his death at the age of 24; his headstone was donated by Burns, a fervent admirer, who also wrote the inscription.

Opposite the church, the local history museum in **Huntly House** (Mon–Sat 10am–5pm; Sun 2–5pm during the Festival only; free) includes a quirky array of old shop signs, some dating back to the eighteenth century, as well as displays on indigenous industries such as glass, silver, pottery and clockmaking, and on the dubious military career of Earl Haig. Also on view is the original version of the National Covenant of 1638; modern science has failed to resolve whether or not some of the signatories signed with their own blood, as tradition has it.

Among the several fine seventeenth-century mansions on the easternmost stretch of Canongate, **Panmure House** was for a time the home of Adam Smith, father of the science of political economy and unwitting guru of latter-day Conservatism. At the very foot of the street, the entrance to the residential **Whitehorse Close** was once the site of the inn from where stagecoaches began the journey to London. Stridently quaint, it drips with the characteristic features of Scottish vernacular architecture: crow-stepped gables, dormer windows, overhanging upper storeys and curving outside stairways.

Holyrood

At the foot of Canongate lies **Holyrood**, Edinburgh's royal quarter, the **legend** of whose foundation in 1128 is described in a fifteenth-century manuscript which is still kept there. The story goes that King David I, son of Malcolm Canmore and St Margaret, went out hunting one day and was suddenly confronted by a stag who threw him from his horse and seemed ready to gore him. In desperation, the king tried to protect himself by grasping its antlers, but instead found himself holding a crucifix, whereupon the animal ran off. In a dream that night, he heard a voice commanding him to "make a house for Canons devoted to the Cross"; he duly obeyed, naming the abbey Holyrood (rood being an alternative name for a cross). A more prosaic explanation is that David, the most pious of all Scotland's monarchs, simply acquired a relic of the True Cross and decided to build a suitable home for it.

Holyrood soon became a favoured **royal residence**, its situation in a secluded valley making it far more agreeable than the draughty Castle. At first, monarchs lodged in the monastic guest house, to which a wing for the exclusive use of the court was added during the reign of James II. This was transformed into a full-blown palace for James IV, which in turn was replaced by a much larger building for Charles II, although he never actually lived there. Indeed, it was something of a white elephant until Queen Victoria started making regular trips to her northern kingdom, a custom that has been maintained by her successors.

ADMISSIONS TO HOLYROOD

Guided tours of Holyrood only take place from November to March; at other times of the year, visitors are free to move at their own pace. It is worth remembering that Holyrood is still a working palace, so the buildings are closed to the public for long periods during state functions; you won't be able to visit for a fortnight in the middle of May, and during the annual royal visit which usually takes place in the last two weeks of June and the first in July.

The precincts

On the north side of **Abbey Strand**, which forms a sort of processional way linking Canongate with Holyrood, Abbey Lairds is a four-storey sixteenth-century mansion which once served as a home for aristocratic debtors and is now occupied by royal flunkies during the summer seat of the court.

Legend has it that Mary, Queen of Scots used to bathe in sweet white wine in the curious little turreted structure nearby known as **Queen Mary's Bath House**; it is more likely, however, that it was either a summer pavilion or a dovecote. Its architecture is mirrored in the **Croft an Righ**, a picturesque L-shaped house in a quiet, generally overlooked corner beside the eastern wall of the complex.

The Scottish Parliament site

Immediately opposite Abbey Strand, the massive construction site is where the new **Scottish Parliament** is being built. For decades, campaigners for home rule for Scotland lifted their eyes to the Old Royal High School building on Calton Hill (see p.95) as the ideal place for a Scottish parliament to sit. In the run-up to devolution becoming a reality, however, the Scottish office unexpectedly announced that the Old Royal High School was too small to accommodate the proposed parliament and its offices, and various alternative sites were suggested, including the empty docklands at Leith. Eventually a disused brewery at the foot of the Royal Mile was identified as the ideal location, and a competition to design the brand new Parliament building was won by Catalan architect Enric Miralles, in association with Edinburgh-based architects RMJM. Their concept, a model of which can be viewed in the Scottish Parliament Visitor Centre on George IV Bridge, centres on a series of petal-shaped buildings which have been compared (both favourably and unfavourably) to upturned boats. The structure will cost something in the region of £100 million, and is due to be ready by 2002, until which time the parliament is sitting in the Church of Scotland Assembly Hall on the Mound (see p.75).

The Palace of Holyroodhouse

In its present form, the **Palace of Holyroodhouse** (April–Oct daily 9.30am–5.15pm; Nov–March daily 9.30am–3.15pm; £5.50) is largely a seventeenth-century creation, planned for Charles II. However, the tower house of the old palace was skilfully incorporated to form the northwestern block, with a virtual mirror image of it erected as a counterbalance at the other end. The three-storey **courtyard** is an early exercise in Palladian style, exhibiting a punctiliously accurate knowledge of the main Classical orders to create a sense of absolute harmony and unity.

Inside, the **State Apartments**, as Charles II's palace is known, are decked out with oak panelling, tapestries, portraits and decorative paintings, all overshadowed by the magnificent white stucco **ceilings**, especially in the Morning Drawing Room. The most eye-catching chamber, however, is the **Great Gallery**, which takes up the entire first floor of the northern wing. During the 1745 sojourn of the Young Pretender this was the setting for a banquet, described in detail in Scott's novel *Waverley*, and it is still used for big ceremonial occasions. Along the walls are 89 portraits commissioned from the seventeenth-century Dutch artist Jacob de Wit to illustrate the royal lineage of Scotland from its mythical origins in the fourth century BC; the result is unintentionally hilarious, as it is clear that the artist's imagination was taxed to bursting point by the need to paint so many different facial types without having an inkling as to what the subjects actually looked like. In the adjacent **King's Closet**, de Wit's *The Finding of Moses* provides a biblical link to the portraits, the Scottish royal family claiming descent from Scota, the Egyptian pharaoh's daughter, who discovered Moses in the bulrushes.

The oldest parts of the palace, the **Historical Apartments**, are mainly of note for their associations with Mary, Queen of Scots and in particular for the brutal murder, organized by her husband, Lord Darnley, of her private secretary, David Rizzio, who was stabbed 56 times and dragged from the small closet, through the Queen's Bedchamber, and into the Outer Chamber. Until a few years ago, visitors were shown apparently indelible bloodstains on the floor of the latter, but these are now admitted to be fakes, and have been covered up. A display cabinet in the same room shows some pieces of **needlework** woven by the deposed queen while in English captivity; another case has an outstanding **miniature portrait** of her by the French court painter, François Clouet.

Holyrood Abbey

In the grounds of the Palace are the wonderfully evocative ruins of **Holyrood Abbey**. Of King David's original Norman church, the only surviving fragment is a doorway in the far southeastern corner. Most of the remainder dates from a late twelfth- and early thirteenth-century rebuilding in the Early Gothic style.

The surviving parts of the **west front**, including one of the twin towers and the elaborately carved entrance portal, show how resplendent the abbey must once have been. Unfortunately, its sacking by the English in 1547, followed by the demolition of the transept and chancel during the Reformation, all but destroyed the building. Charles I attempted to restore some semblance of unity by ordering the erection of the great east window and a new stone roof, but the latter collapsed in 1768, causing grievous damage to the rest of the structure. By this time, the Canongate congregation had another place of worship, and schemes to rebuild the abbey were abandoned.

Dynamic Earth

Although the largest, the New Parliament Building is by no means the only newcomer to this historic area. On the Holyrood Road side of the construction site, beneath a pincushion of white metal struts which make it look like a miniature version of London's controversial Millennium Dome, is **Our Dynamic Earth** (April–Oct daily 10am–6pm; Nov–March Wed–Sat 10am–5pm; £5.95, children £3.50, families £16.50), a hi-tech attraction aimed mainly at families. Although James Hutton, the Edinburgh-born "Father of Geology", lived nearby in the eighteenth century, there are few specific links to Edinburgh or Scotland, as you're taken in a "time machine" elevator to a room where the creation of the universe, 15 billion years ago, is described using wide-screen video graphics, eerie music and a deep-throated commentary. Subsequent galleries describe the formation of the earth and continents with crashing sound-effects and a shaking floor, the calmer grandeur of glaciers and oceans being explored through magnificent large-screen landscape footage. The "Casualties and Survivors" gallery describes the history of life on earth, from primordial swamps to life-size models of some of the odd creatures who once inhabited the earth, while, further on, the polar regions – complete with a real iceberg – and tropical jungles are imaginatively recreated, with interactive computer screens and special effects at every turn.

Holyrood Park

Holyrood Park – or Queen's Park – a natural wilderness in the very heart of the modern city, is unquestionably one of Edinburgh's main assets, as locals (though relatively few tourists) readily appreciate. Packed into an area no more than five miles in diameter is an amazing variety of landscapes – mountains, crags, moorland, marshes, glens, lochs and fields – representing something of a microcosm of Scotland's scenery. The park is a great place for outdoor activities, with toddlers, cyclists and rock-climbers all being catered for. A single tarred road, the **Queen's Drive**, circles the park, enabling many of its features to be seen by car, though you really need to stroll around to appreciate it fully. Two of the most rewarding walks begin opposite the southern gates of the Palace: one, a pathway nicknamed the Radical Road, traverses the ridge immediately below the **Salisbury Crags**, one of the main features of the Edinburgh skyline, while you can also walk along the top of the basalt crags, from where there are excellent views of the Palace of Holyroodhouse and Holyrood Abbey.

From the Palace gates, the best way to follow Queen's Drive is in a clockwise direction. Soon you arrive at **St Margaret's Loch**, a nineteenth-century man-made pond, above which stand the scanty ruins of **St Anthony's Chapel**, another fine vantage point. From here, the road's loop is one-way only, ascending to **Dunsapie Loch**, again an artificial stretch of water, which makes an excellent foil to the crag behind.

This is the usual starting point for the ascent of **Arthur's Seat**, a majestic extinct volcano rising 823ft above sea level. The Seat is Edinburgh's single most prominent landmark, resembling a huge crouched lion when seen from the west. The climb from Dunsapie, up a grassy slope, followed by a rocky path near the summit, is considerably less arduous than it looks, and is a fairly straightforward twenty-minute walk, though there are several other, somewhat longer and more taxing ways up from other points in the park. The views from the top are all you'd expect, covering the entire city and much of the Firth of Forth; on a clear day, you can even see the southernmost mountains of the Highlands. The composer, Felix Mendelssohn, climbed Arthur's Seat in July 1829, noting: "It is beautiful here! In the evening a cool breeze is wafted from the sea, and then all objects appear clearly and sharply defined against the gray sky; the lights from the windows glitter brilliantly." As there is little reason to associate it with the British king of the Holy Grail legends, there's no satisfactory story to explain the name.

From Dunsapie Loch, Queen's Drive continues round beneath the summit to meet itself again at a roundabout near the southern point of the Salisbury Crags. At a second roundabout the second exit leads out of the park; the first exit takes you beneath **Samson's Ribs**, a group of basalt pillars strikingly reminiscent of the Hebridean island of Staffa (see p.327), and onto **Duddingston Loch**, the only natural stretch of water in the park, now a bird sanctuary. Perched above it, just outside the park boundary, **Duddingston Kirk** dates back in part to the twelfth century and is the focus of one of the most unspoilt old villages within modern Edinburgh.

The rest of the Old Town

Although most visitors to the Old Town understandably concentrate on the Royal Mile, the area has many other intriguing, and less commercial, corners, notably the **Grassmarket**, famous as the site of public executions in previous centuries, and the area around the University, where the excellent **National Museum of Scotland** is found.

Cowgate

At the bottom of the valley immediately south of the Royal Mile, and following a roughly parallel course from the Lawnmarket to St Mary's Street, is **Cowgate**. One of

Edinburgh's oldest surviving streets, it was also formerly one of the city's most prestigious addresses. However, the construction of the great **viaducts** of George IV Bridge
and South Bridge entombed it below street level, condemning it to decay and neglect
and leading the nineteenth-century writer, Alexander Smith, to declare that "the condition of the inhabitants is as little known to respectable Edinburgh as are the habits of
moles, earthworms, and the mining population". In the last decade or so Cowgate has
experienced something of a revival, with various nightclubs and Festival venues establishing themselves, though few tourists venture here and the contrast with the neighbouring Royal Mile remains stark.

At the corner with Niddry Street, which runs down from the High Street near its
junction with North Bridge and South Bridge, the unprepossessing **St Cecilia's Hall**
(Wed & Sat 2–5pm; £3) was built in the 1760s for the Musical Society of Edinburgh.
Inside, Scotland's oldest and most beautiful concert room, oval in shape and set under
a shallow dome, makes a perfect venue for concerts of Baroque and early music, held
during the Festival and occasionally at other times of the year. The building is primarily worth visiting for the **Russell Collection** of antique keyboard instruments.

Towards the western end of Cowgate stands the **Magdalen Chapel** (Mon–Fri
9.30am–4.30pm; free), a sixteenth-century almshouse under the jurisdiction of the
Incorporation of Hammermen, a guild to which most Edinburgh workers, other than
goldsmiths, belonged. A few years later, as one of the focal points of the Reformation,
it was probably the setting for the first ever General Assembly of the Church of
Scotland. The Hammermen added a handsome tower and steeple in the 1620s, and
later transformed the chapel into their guildhall, which was suitably adorned with fine
ironwork. However, the main feature of the interior is the only significant pre-
Reformation stained glass in Scotland still in its original location. That it escaped the
iconoclasts is probably due to the fact that it is purely heraldic.

Grassmarket and George IV Bridge

At its western end, Cowgate opens out into the **Grassmarket**, which has played an
important role in the murkier aspects of Edinburgh's turbulent history. The public gallows were located here, and it was the scene of numerous riots and other disturbances
down the centuries. It was here, in 1736, that Captain Porteous was lynched after he
had ordered shots to be fired at the crowd watching a public execution. The notorious
duo William Burke and William Hare had their lair in a now-vanished close just off the
western end of Grassmarket, luring to it victims whom they murdered with the inten-
tion of selling their bodies to the eminent physician Robert Knox. Eventually, Hare
betrayed his partner, who was duly executed in 1829, and Knox's career was finished
off as a result. Today, Grassmarket can still be seamy, though the cluster of busy bars
and restaurants along its northern side are evidence of a serious attempt to clean up its
image.

At the northeastern corner of Grassmarket are five old tenements of the old **West
Bow**, which formerly zigzagged up to the Royal Mile. The rest of this was replaced in
the 1840s by the curving **Victoria Street**, an unusual two-tier thoroughfare, with arcaded shops below, and a pedestrian terrace above. This sweeps up to **George IV Bridge**
and the **National Library of Scotland** which holds a rich collection of illuminated
manuscripts, early printed books, historical documents, and the letters and papers of
prominent Scottish literary figures, displayed in regularly changing thematic exhibitions (usually Mon–Sat 10am–5pm, Sun 2–5pm; free).

Greyfriars and around

The **statue of Greyfriars Bobby** at the southwestern corner of **George IV Bridge**
must rank as Edinburgh's most sentimental tourist attraction. Bobby was a Skye terri-

er acquired as a working dog by a police constable named John Gray. When John Gray died in 1858, Bobby began a vigil on his grave which he maintained until he died fourteen years later. In the process, he became an Edinburgh celebrity, fed and cared for by locals who gave him a special collar (now in the Huntly House Museum; see p.81) to prevent him being impounded as a stray. His statue, originally a fountain, was modelled from life, and erected soon after his death; his story has gained international renown, thanks to a spate of cloying books and tear-jerking movies.

The grave Bobby mourned over is in the **Greyfriars Kirkyard**, which among its clutter of grandiose seventeenth- and eighteenth-century funerary monuments boasts the striking mausoleum of the Adam family of architects. Greyfriars is particularly associated with the long struggle to establish Presbyterianism in Scotland: in 1638, it was the setting for the signing of the National Covenant, while in 1679 some 1200 Covenanters were imprisoned in the enclosure at the southwestern end of the yard. Set against the northern wall is the Martyrs' Monument, a defiantly worded memorial commemorating all those who died in pursuit of the eventual victory.

The graveyard rather overshadows **Greyfriars Kirk** itself, completed in 1620 as the first new church in Edinburgh since the Reformation. It's a real oddball in both layout and design, having a nave and aisles but no chancel, and adopting the anachronistic architectural language of the friary that preceded it, complete with medieval-looking windows, arches and buttresses.

At the western end of Greyfriars Kirkyard is one of the most significant surviving portions of the **Flodden Wall**, the city fortifications erected in the wake of Scotland's disastrous military defeat of 1513. When open, the gateway beyond offers a short cut to **George Heriot's Hospital**, otherwise approached from Lauriston Place to the south. Founded as a home for poor boys by "Jinglin Geordie" Heriot, James VI's goldsmith, it is now one of Edinburgh's most prestigious fee-paying schools; although you can't go inside, you can wander round the quadrangle, whose array of towers, turrets, chimneys, carved doorways and traceried windows is one of the finest achievements of the Scottish Renaissance.

The National Museum of Scotland

Immediately opposite Greyfriars Bobby, on the south side of Chambers Street, stands the striking honey-coloured sandstone **National Museum of Scotland** (Mon–Sat 10am–5pm, Tues 10am–8pm, Sun noon–5pm; £3, £5 for one-year season ticket, free Tues 4.30–8pm). Opened in 1998 to deserved acclaim, both for its elegant design and for its respectful but imaginative treatment of the nation's treasures, this is undoubtedly Scotland's premier museum. The fresh, open atmosphere of the building is combined with terrific features: specially commissioned art works; the **Discovery Centre**, specifically aimed at 5–14-year-olds; the **exhibIT** computer bank with databases of the museum's collections; and the **Tower Restaurant**, a sleek, stylish place with fabulous views which is also open in the evenings (for a review, see p.110).

The lack of a figurehead national museum had been keenly felt for decades, but it wasn't until the late 1980s that funding was made available, with construction beginning in 1996. Designed by the architects Benson & Forsyth, and built principally from sandstone quarried near Elgin in northeast Scotland, the most obvious feature of the exterior is the cylindrical entrance tower, which breaks up the angular, modern lines of the building and deliberately echoes the shape of the Half Moon Battery of Edinburgh Castle. Tall windows reveal glimpses of the interior, an effect continued inside, where unexpected views of the floors above and below, as well as out on to the street, emphasise the interconnectedness of the layers of Scotland's history.

The main entrance to the museum is at the base of the tower (although it is also possible to enter through the neighbouring Royal Museum of Scotland; see p.88). Make your way to the information desk in **Hawthornden Court**, the central atrium of the museum and a useful orientation point; on this level you'll also find the museum shop, the sound guide desk and access to the Royal Museum café. The glossy **brochure** on sale (£4.99) is more a photographic souvenir than a guidebook, but free guided tours on different themes take place through the day, and audio headsets (free) give detailed information on artefacts and displays.

BEGINNINGS AND EARLY PEOPLE

To get to the first section, "**Beginnings**", take the lift or stairs from Hawthornden Court down to Level 0. Here, Scotland's story before the arrival of man is presented with audio-visual displays, artistic recreations and a selection of rocks and fossils, including some Lewisian gneiss, the oldest rock in Europe, and "Lizzie" (*Westlothiana lizziae*), the oldest known fossil reptile in world.

The second section, "**Early People**", also on Level 0, covers the period from the arrival of the first people to the end of the first millennium AD. This, in many ways, is the most engrossing section of the entire museum, an eloquent testament to the remarkable craftsmanship, artistry and practicality of Scotland's early people. The best way to approach this section is from the doors of the main lift, where you are confronted by eight giant bronze figures in the distinctive post-industrial style of Edinburgh-born sculptor **Sir Eduardo Paolozzi**. His trademark incorporation of geometric shapes into the human form allows the figures to "wear" different artefacts such as prehistoric bracelets and necklaces in small display compartments. The innovative use of contemporary art is continued with installations by the environmental artist **Andy Goldsworthy**, who shapes natural materials into sinuously beautiful geometrical patterns. Look out for *Hearth*, created from pieces of wood found on the construction site of the new museum, and *Enclosure*, four curved walls of slate roof tiles and four panels of cracked clay. Among the artefacts on display, highlights are the **Trappain treasure** hoard, 20kg of silver plates, cutlery and goblets found buried in East Lothian; the **Cramond Lioness**, a sculpture from a Roman tombstone found recently in the Firth of Forth (see p.104); and the beautifully detailed gold, silver and amber **Hunterston brooch**, dating from around 700AD.

THE KINGDOM OF THE SCOTS

The "**Kingdom of the Scots**" on Level 1 covers the period between Scotland's development as a single independent nation and the union with England in 1707. At the entrance to the section in Hawthornden Court is the **Dupplin Cross**, a symbol of the different peoples who united under king Kenneth MacAlpin to form a single kingdom in 843. Many famous Scots are represented here, including Robert the Bruce, Mary Queen of Scots and her son James VI, under whom the crowns of Scotland and England became united in 1603. Star exhibits include the **Monymusk reliquary**, an intricately decorated box said to have carried the remains of St Columba; the **Lewis chessmen**, exquisitely idiosyncratic twelfth-century pieces carved from walrus ivory; and the "**Maiden**", an early form of the guillotine. The section on the church is of interest not only for the craftsmanship of some of the objects, most notably the silver gilt **St Fillan's crozier**, but also because just outside the window you can glimpse Greyfriars Kirkyard, where the National Covenant – the document which demanded a Presbyterian rather than Episcopalian form of worship in Scotland and provoked numerous battles in the sixteenth and seventeenth centuries – was signed in 1638.

SCOTLAND TRANSFORMED

Level 3 shows exhibits under the theme "**Scotland Transformed**", covering the century or so following the Union of Parliaments in 1707. This was the period which saw the last of the Highland uprisings under Bonnie Prince Charlie (whose silver travelling canteen is on display), yet also witnessed the expansion of trade links with the Americas and developments in industries such as weaving and iron and steel production. Dominating the floor is a reconstructed steam-driven **Newcomen engine**, which was still being used to pump water from a coal mine in Ayrshire in 1901. Alongside it, in contrast, is part of a thatched, cruck-frame house of the 1720s of a type in which many Scots still lived during this time.

INDUSTRY AND EMPIRE

Following the early innovations of steam and mechanical engineering, Scotland went on to pioneer many aspects of heavy engineering, with ship and locomotive production to the fore. Largest of the exhibits in "**Industry and Empire**" on Level 4 is the steam locomotive *Ellesmere*. As well as industrial progress, other fields are covered too, including domestic life, leisure activities and the influence of Scots around the world, both as a result of emigration, and through such luminaries as James Watt, Charles Rennie Mackintosh and Robert Louis Stevenson.

THE TWENTIETH CENTURY GALLERY

For the **Twentieth Century Gallery** on Level 6, a range of Scots, from schoolchildren to celebrities, were asked to pick a single object to represent the twentieth century. Choices are intriguing, controversial and unexpected, from computers to football strips, cans of Irn Bru to a black Saab convertible. Tony Blair, who went to Fettes school in Edinburgh, chose a guitar, and former Edinburgh "milkie" Sean Connery a milk bottle. The obvious challenge is implicitly made: what would you choose, and why? Other features worth taking in here include a small **cinema** showing black-and-white documentary films about life in Scotland in the 1930s, and the **roof garden**, accessed by a lift. Up here, sweeping views open out to the Firth of Forth, the Pentland hills, and across to the Castle and Royal Mile skyline.

The Royal Museum of Scotland

Interlinked with the National Museum, though also with its own entrance, is the Royal Museum of Scotland (same hours), a dignified Venetian-style palace with a cast-iron interior modelled on that of the Crystal Palace in London. Intended as Scotland's answer to the museum complex in London's South Kensington, the Royal Museum has been an Edinburgh institution for over 100 years. It contains an extraordinarily eclectic range of exhibits, from exotic stuffed animals to colonial loot – the neat slogan used to describe the different roles of the sister museums is that the National Museum shows Scotland to the world, and the Royal Museum shows the world to Scotland.

The **sculpture** in the lofty entrance hall begins with a superb Assyrian relief from the royal palace at Nimrud, and ranges via Classical Greece, Rome and Nubia to Buddhas from Japan and Burma and a totem pole from British Columbia. Also on the ground floor are collections of stuffed animals and birds, and the **Power Collections**, with a double-action beam engine designed by James Watt in 1786 alongside a section of the Inchkeith lighthouse and the control desk from Hunterston A nuclear reactor. Upstairs there's a fine array of Egyptian mummies, ceramics from ancient Greece to the present day, costumes, jewellery, natural-history displays and a splendid selection of European decorative art, ranging from early medieval liturgical objects via Limoges enamels and sixteenth-century German woodcarving to stunning **French silverware** made during the reign of Louis XIV. Finally, on the top floor, you'll come to a distinguished collection of historic scientific instruments, a small selection of arms and armour, plus sections on geology, fossils, ethnology, and the arts of Islam, Japan and China.

The University of Edinburgh

Immediately alongside the Royal Museum is the earliest surviving part of the **University of Edinburgh**, variously referred to as Old College or Old Quad, although nowadays it houses only a few University departments; the main campus colonizes the streets and squares to the south.

The Old College was designed by Robert Adam, but was built after his death in a considerably modified form by William Playfair (1789–1857), one of Edinburgh's greatest architects. Playfair built just one of Adam's two quadrangles (the dome was not added until 1879) and his magnificent Upper Library is now mostly used for ceremonial occasions. The **Talbot Rice Art Gallery** (Tues–Sat 10am–5pm; free), housed in the Old College, includes many splendid seventeenth-century works from the Low Countries, with Teniers, Steen and van de Velde well represented. There are also some outstanding bronzes, notably the *Anatomical Horse* by an unknown Italian sculptor of the High Renaissance, and *Cain Killing Abel* by the Dutch Mannerist Adrian de Vries. The first and largest exhibition hall displays temporary shows of contemporary art.

The New Town

The **NEW TOWN**, itself well over two hundred years old, stands in total contrast to the Old Town: the layout is symmetrical, the streets broad and straight, and most of the buildings are Neoclassical. Originally intended to be residential, the entire area, right down to the names of its streets, is something of a celebration of the Union, which was then generally regarded as a proud development in Scotland's history. Today the New Town is the bustling hub of the city's professional, commercial and business life, dominated by shops, banks and offices.

The existence of the New Town is chiefly due to the vision of **George Drummond**, who made schemes for the expansion of the city soon after becoming Lord Provost in 1725. Work began on the draining of the Nor' Loch below the Castle in 1759, a job that was to last some sixty years. The North Bridge, linking the Old Town with the port of Leith, was built between 1763 and 1772 and, in 1766, following a public competition, a plan for the New Town by 22-year-old architect **James Craig** was chosen. Its gridiron pattern was perfectly matched to the site: central George Street, flanked by showpiece squares, was laid out along the main ridge, with the parallel Princes Street and Queen Street on either side below, and two smaller streets, Thistle Street and Rose Street in between the three major thoroughfares to provide coach houses, artisans' dwellings and shops. Princes and Queen streets were built up on one side only, so as not to block the spectacular views of the Old Town and Fife. Architects were accordingly afforded a wonderful opportunity to play with vistas and spatial relationships, particularly well exploited by Robert Adam, who contributed extensively to the later phases of the work. The First New Town, as the area covered by Craig's plan came to be known, received a whole series of extensions in the first few decades of the nineteenth century, all carefully in harmony with the Neoclassical idiom.

In many ways, the layout of the New Town is its own most remarkable sight, an extraordinary grouping of squares, circuses, terraces, crescents and parks with a few set pieces such as **Register House**, the north frontage of **Charlotte Square** and the assemblage of curiosities on and around **Calton Hill**. However, it also contains an assortment of Victorian additions, notably the **Scott Monument**, as well as two of the city's most important public collections – the **National Gallery of Scotland**, and the **Scottish National Gallery of Modern Art**.

Princes Street

Although only allocated a subsidiary role in the original plan of the New Town, **Princes Street** had developed into Edinburgh's principal thoroughfare by the middle of the nineteenth century, a role it has retained ever since. Its unobstructed views across to the Castle and the Old Town are undeniably magnificent. Indeed, without the views, Princes Street would lose much of its appeal; its northern side, dominated by ugly department stores, is almost always crowded with shoppers, and few of the original eighteenth-century buildings remain.

It was the coming of the railway, which follows a parallel course to the south, that ensured Princes Street's rise to prominence. The tracks are well concealed at the far end of the sunken **gardens** that replaced the Nor' Loch, which provide ample space to relax or picnic during the summer. Thomas de Quincey (1785–1859), author of the classic account of drug addiction, *Confessions of an English Opium Eater* (published in 1821), spent the last thirty years of his life in Edinburgh and is buried in the graveyard of St Cuthbert's Church, beneath the Castle at the western end of the gardens.

The East End

Register House (Mon–Fri 10am–4pm; free), Princes Street's most distinguished building, is at its extreme northeastern corner, framing the perspective down North Bridge, and providing a good visual link between the Old and New Towns. Unfortunately, the majesty of the setting is marred by the **St James Centre** to the rear, a covered shopping arcade now regarded as the city's worst ever planning blunder. Register House was designed in the 1770s by Robert Adam to hold Scotland's historic records, a function it has maintained ever since. Its exterior is a model of restrained Neoclassicism; the interior, centred on a glorious Roman rotunda, has a dome lavishly decorated with plasterwork and antique-style medallions.

Opposite is one of the few buildings on the south side of Princes Street, the **Balmoral Hotel**, formerly known as the *North British*. Among the most luxurious hotels in the city, it has always been associated with the railway, and the timepiece on its bulky clock tower is always kept two minutes fast in order to encourage passengers to hurry to catch their trains. Alongside the hotel, **Princes Mall** is a fairly sensitive modern commercial development. The open-air piazza on its street-level roof is home to Edinburgh's tourist office (see p.61), and a favourite haunt of street theatre groups and other performing artists during the Festival.

The Scott Monument and the Royal Scottish Academy

Facing the Victorian shopping emporium Jenners, and set within East Princes Street Gardens, the 200ft-high **Scott Monument** (March–May daily 10am–6pm; June–Sept Mon–Sat 9am–8pm, Sun 10am–6pm; Oct daily 10am–6pm; Nov–Feb daily 10am–4pm; £2.50) was erected in memory of the writer by public subscription within a few years of his death. The largest monument in the world to a man of letters, its magisterial, spire-like design was created by George Meikle Kemp, a carpenter and joiner whose only building this is; while it was still under construction, he stumbled into a canal one foggy evening and drowned. The architecture is closely modelled on Scott's beloved Melrose Abbey (see p.144), while the rich sculptural decoration shows 16 Scottish writers and 64 characters from the *Waverley* novels. Underneath the archway is a **statue** of Scott with his deerhound Maida, carved from a thirty-ton block of Carrara marble.

The monument's rather mottled appearance is a result of a recent project aimed at preserving the eroded, crumbling condition of some of the stonework. The result is largely a happy one: the monument is fully on view again and visitors are able to use the tightly winding internal spiral staircase to climb up to some inspiring – if heady – vistas of the city below and hills and firths beyond.

The Princes Street Gardens are bisected by the **Mound**, which provides a road link between the Old and New Towns. Its name is an accurate description: it was formed in the 1780s by dumping piles of earth brought from the New Town's building plots. At the foot of the Mound, nearest to Princes Street, Playfair's **Royal Scottish Academy** (Mon–Sat 10am–5pm, Sun 2–5pm; price varies) is a Grecian-style Doric temple used somewhat infrequently for temporary exhibitions during the year, notably for the RSA annual exhibition held from April to July.

The National Gallery of Scotland

To the rear of the Royal Scottish Academy, the less elaborate **National Gallery of Scotland** (Mon–Sat 10am–5pm, Sun 2–5pm; free) is another Playfair construction, built in the 1850s and now housing a choice display of Old Masters, many of which belong to the Duke of Sutherland. The knowledgeable staff wear tartan trousers, one of a series of innovations introduced by the flamboyant English director, Timothy Clifford. A few years ago, and more controversially, the original Playfair rooms on the ground floor were restored to their 1850s appearance, with the pictures hung closely together, often on two levels, and intermingled with sculptures and *objets d'art* to produce a deliberately cluttered effect (some lesser works, which would otherwise languish in the vaults, are a good 15ft up). Two small, late nineteenth-century works in Room 12 – one anonymous, the other by A.E. Moffat – show the gallery as it was in the nineteenth century, with paintings stacked up even higher than at present.

Though individual works are frequently rearranged, the layout is broadly chronological, starting in the upper rooms above the entrance, and continuing clockwise around the ground floor. The upper part of the rear extension is devoted to smaller panels of the eighteenth and nineteenth centuries, while the basement contains the majority of the Scottish collection. There are no guided tours; instead, audio guides (£2) provide commentaries on the gallery's more important works.

EARLY NETHERLANDISH AND GERMAN WORKS

Among the gallery's most valuable treasures are the *Trinity Panels*, the remaining parts of the only surviving pre-Reformation altarpiece made for a Scottish church. Painted by **Hugo van der Goes** in the mid-fifteenth century, they were commissioned for the Holy Trinity Collegiate Church by its provost Edward Bonkil, who appears in the company of organ-playing angels in the finest and best preserved of the four panels. On the reverse sides are portraits of James III, his son (the future James IV) and Queen Margaret of Denmark. Their feebly characterized heads, which stand in jarring contrast to the superlative figures of the patron saints accompanying them, were modelled from life by an unknown local painter after the altar had been shipped to Edinburgh.

Of the later Netherlandish works, **Gerard David** is represented by the touchingly anecdotal *Three Legends of St Nicholas*, while the *Portrait of a Notary* by **Quentin Massys** is an excellent early example of northern European assimilation of the forms and techniques of the Italian Renaissance. Many of his German contemporaries developed their own variations on this style, among them **Cranach**, by whom there is a splendidly erotic *Venus and Cupid*, and **Holbein**, whose *Allegory of the Old and New Testaments* is a Protestant tract painted for an English patron.

ITALIAN RENAISSANCE WORKS

The Italian section includes a wonderful array of **Renaissance** masterpieces. Of these, *The Virgin Adoring the Child* is a beautiful composition set against a ruined architectural background shown in strict perspective: although known to have been painted in the workshop of the great Florentine sculptor **Andrea del Verrocchio**, its authorship remains a mystery. Equally graceful are the three works by **Raphael**, particularly *The*

Bridgewater Madonna and the tondo of *The Holy Family with a Palm Tree*, whose strik-ing luminosity has been revealed after recent restoration.

Of the four mythological scenes by **Titian**, the sensuous *Three Ages of Man*, an alle-gory of childhood, adulthood and old age, is one of the most accomplished composi-tions of his early period, while the later *Venus Anadyomene* ranks among the great nudes of Western art, notwithstanding its rough state of preservation. The companion pair of *Diana and Acteon* and *Diana and Calisto*, painted for Philip II of Spain, show the almost impressionistic freedom of his late style. **Bassano**'s truly regal *Adoration of the Kings*, a dramatic altarpiece of *The Descent from the Cross* by **Tintoretto**, and several other works by **Veronese**, complete a fine Venetian collection.

SEVENTEENTH-CENTURY SOUTHERN EUROPEAN WORKS

Among the seventeenth-century works is the gallery's most important sculpture, **Bernini**'s *Bust of Monsignor Carlo Antonio dal Pozzo*. **El Greco**'s *A Fable*, painted dur-ing his early years in Italy, takes a mysterious subject whose exact meaning is unclear, while *The Saviour of the World* is a typically intense, visionary image from his mature years in Spain. Indigenous Spanish art is represented by **Velázquez**'s *An Old Woman Cooking Eggs*, an astonishingly assured work for a lad of nineteen, and by **Zurbaran**'s *The Immaculate Conception*, part of his ambitious decorative scheme of the Carthusian monastery in Jerez. There are two small copper panels by the short-lived but enor-mously influential Rome-based German painter **Adam Elsheimer**; of these, *Il Contento*, showing Jupiter's descent to earth to punish the ungodly, is a *tour de force* of technical precision.

The series of *The Seven Sacraments* by **Poussin** are displayed in their own room, whose floor and central octagonal seat repeat some of the motifs in the paintings. Based on the artist's extensive research into biblical times, the series marks the first attempt to portray scenes from the life of Jesus and the early Christians in an authentic manner, rather than one overlaid by artistic conventions. The result is profoundly touching, with a myriad of imaginative and subtle details. Poussin's younger contemporary **Claude**, who also left France to live in Rome, is represented by his largest canvas, *Landscape with Apollo, the Muses and a River God*, which radiates his characteristically idealized vision of Classical antiquity.

SEVENTEENTH-CENTURY FLEMISH AND DUTCH WORKS

Rubens' *The Feast of Herod* is an archetypal example of his grand manner, in which the gory subject matter is overshadowed by the lively depiction of the delights of the table; the painting's rich colours have been revived by recent restoration. Like all his large works, it was executed with extensive studio assistance, whereas the three small *mod-ellos*, including the highly finished *Adoration of the Shepherds*, are all from his own hand. The trio of large upright canvases by **Van Dyck** date from his early Genoese peri-od; of these, *The Lomellini Family* shows his mastery in creating a definitive dynastic image.

Among the four canvases by **Rembrandt** is a poignant *Self-Portrait Aged 51*, and the ripely suggestive *Woman in Bed*, which probably represents the biblical figure of Sarah on her wedding night, waiting for her husband Tobias to put the devil to flight. *Christ in the House of Martha and Mary* is the largest and probably the earliest of the thirty or so surviving paintings by **Vermeer**; as the only one with a religious subject, it inspired a notorious series of forgeries by Han van Meegeren. By **Hals** are a typical pair of portraits plus a brilliant caricature, *Verdonck*. There's also an excellent cross-sec-tion of the specialist Dutch painters of the age, highlights being the mischievous *School for Boys and Girls* by **Jan Steen**, and the strangely haunting *Interior of the Church of St Bavo in Haarlem* by **Pieter Saenredam**, which was one of the gallery's most expen-sive purchases.

EUROPEAN WORKS OF THE EIGHTEENTH AND NINETEENTH CENTURIES
Of the large-scale eighteenth-century works, **Tiepolo**'s *The Finding of Moses*, a gloriously bravura fantasy (the Pharaoh's daughter and her attendants appear in sixteenth-century garb) stands out; despite its enormous size, it has lost a sizeable portion from the right-hand side. Other decorative compositions of the same period are **Goya**'s *The Doctor*, a cartoon for a tapestry design, and the three large upright pastoral scenes by **Boucher**. However, the gems of the French section are the smaller panels, in particular **Watteau**'s *Fêtes Vénitiennes*, an effervescent Rococo idyll, and **Chardin**'s *Vase of Flowers*, a copybook example of still-life painting. One of the gallery's most recent major purchases is **Canova**'s 1817 statue, *The Three Graces* – saved at the last minute from the hands of the J. Paul Getty Museum in California. However, as part of the purchase agreement it is on loan to the Victoria and Albert Museum in London until 2006.

There's also a superb group of Impressionist and Post-Impressionist masterpieces, including a particularly good showing of the works of **Degas**, not least his seminal *Portrait of Diego Martelli*, depicting the Florentine critic who was one of the most fervent early champions of Impressionism. Also on display are three outstanding examples of **Gauguin**'s work, set respectively in Brittany, Martinique and Tahiti, **Cézanne**'s *The Tall Trees* – a clear forerunner of modern abstraction, and one of **Monet**'s famous haystacks series.

ENGLISH AND AMERICAN WORKS
The gallery has relatively few English paintings, but those here are impressive. **Hogarth**'s *Sarah Malcolm*, painted in Newgate Prison the day the murderess was executed, once belonged to Horace Walpole, who also commissioned **Reynolds**' *The Ladies Waldegrave*, a group portrait of his three great-nieces. **Gainsborough**'s *The Honourable Mrs Graham* is one of his most memorable society portraits, while **Constable** himself described *Dedham Vale* as being "perhaps my best". There are two prime Roman views by **Turner**, by whom the gallery owns a wonderful array of watercolours, faithfully displayed each January, when the light is at its weakest.

More unexpected than the scarcity of English works is the presence of some exceptional American canvases: **Benjamin West**'s Romantic fantasy, *King Alexander III Rescued from a Stag*; **John Singer Sargent**'s virtuoso *Lady Agnew of Lochnaw*; and **Frederic Edwin Church**'s *View of Niagara Falls from the American Side*. The latter, having been kept in store for decades, was put back on display when the "rediscovery" of the artist in the late 1970s prompted astronomical bids from American museums keen to acquire the only work by the artist owned by a European gallery.

SCOTTISH WORKS
On the face of it, the gallery's Scottish collection, which shows the entire gamut of Scottish painting from seventeenth-century portraiture to the Arts and Crafts movement, is something of an anticlimax. There are, however, some important works displayed within a broad European context; **Gavin Hamilton**'s *Achilles Mourning the Death of Patroclus*, for example, painted in Rome, is an unquestionably arresting image. **Allan Ramsay**, who became court painter to George III, is represented by his intimate *The Artist's Second Wife* and *Jean-Jacques Rousseau*, in which the philosopher is shown in Armenian costume.

Of **Sir Henry Raeburn**'s large portraits, note the swaggering masculinity of *Sir John Sinclair* or *Colonel Alistair MacDonell of Glengarry*, both of whom are shown in full Highland dress. Raeburn's technical mastery was equally sure when working on a small scale, as shown in one of the gallery's most popular pictures, *The Rev Robert Walker Skating on Duddingston Loch*.

Other Scottish painters represented include the versatile **Sir David Wilkie**, whose huge history painting, *Sir David Baird Discovering the Body of Sultan Tippo Saib*, is in marked contrast to the early documentary and genre scenes displayed in the basement, and **Alexander Nasmyth**, whose tendency to gild the lily can be seen in his *View of Tantallon Castle and the Bass Rock*, where the dramatic scenery is further spiced up by the inclusion of a shipwreck. More recent Scottish work is best represented in works such as Sir William McTaggart's *The Storm*, and James Guthrie's *A Hind's Daughter*, along with Phoebe Anna Traquair's exquisite Arts and Crafts panels.

George Street

The street parallel to Princes Street to the north is **George Street**, rapidly changing its role from a thoroughfare of august financial institutions to a highbrow version of Princes Street, where the deals are done in designer-label shops. George Street was designed to be the centrepiece of the First New Town, joining two grand squares. At its eastern end lies **St Andrew Square**, in the middle of which is the Melville Monument, a statue of Lord Melville, Pitt the Younger's Navy Treasurer. On the eastern side of the square stands a handsome eighteenth-century town mansion, designed by Sir William Chambers. Headquarters of the Royal Bank of Scotland since 1825, the palatial mid-nineteenth-century banking hall is a symbol of the success of the New Town. On the south side of the street, the oval-shaped church of **St Andrew** (now known as St Andrew and St George) is chiefly famous as the scene of the 1843 Disruption led by Thomas Chalmers, which split the Church of Scotland in two. Famous visitors to George Street have included Percy Bysshe Shelley, who stayed at no. 60 with the sixteen-year-old Harriet Westbrook during the summer of 1811, and Charles Dickens, who gave a number of readings of his works in the Assembly Rooms in the 1840s and 1850s.

At the western end of the street, **Charlotte Square** was designed by Robert Adam in 1791, a year before his death. For the most part, his plans were faithfully implemented, an exception being the domed and porticoed church of St George, which was simplified on grounds of expense. Its interior was gutted in the 1960s and refurbished as **West Register House**; like its counterpart at the opposite end of Princes Street, it features changing documentary exhibitions (Mon–Fri 10am–4pm; free).

The **north side** of the square has deservedly become the most exclusive address in the city. Number 6 is the official residence of the First Minister of the Scottish Parliament, and also where Scottish cabinet meetings take place, while the upper storeys of no. 7 are the home of the Moderator of the General Assembly, the annually elected leader of the Church of Scotland. Restored by the NTS, the lower floors are open to the public under the name of the **Georgian House** (April–Oct Mon–Sat 10am–5pm, Sun 2–5pm; £4.40), whose contents give a good idea of what the house must have looked like during the period of the first owner, the head of the clan Lamont. The rooms are decked out in period furniture, including a working barrel organ which plays a selection of Scottish airs, and hung with fine paintings, including portraits by Ramsay and Raeburn, seventeenth-century Dutch cabinet pictures, and a beautiful *Marriage of the Virgin* by El Greco's teacher, the Italian miniaturist Giulio Clovio. In the basement are the original wine cellar, lined with roughly made bins, and a kitchen, complete with an open fire for roasting, and a separate oven for baking; video reconstructions of life below and above stairs are shown in a nearby room.

Queen Street

Queen Street, the last of the three main streets of the First New Town, is bordered to the north by gardens, and commands sweeping views across to Fife. Much the best preserved of the area's three main streets, its principal attraction is the excellent portrait gallery.

The Scottish National Portrait Gallery

At the far eastern end of Queen Street is the **Scottish National Portrait Gallery** (Mon–Sat 10am–5pm, Sun 2–5pm; free). The building is itself a fascinating period piece, its red sandstone exterior, modelled on the Doge's Palace in Venice, encrusted with statues of famous Scots – a theme taken up in the stunning entrance hall, which has a mosaic-like frieze procession by William Hole of great figures from Scotland's past, with heroic murals by the same artist of stirring episodes from the nation's history adorning the balcony above.

Temporary exhibitions are displayed in the galleries on the ground floor; elsewhere on this floor are the gallery shop and **café** (which closes 30min before the gallery), a favourite spot with locals.

The permanent exhibitions are located on the two floors above, and are devoted to **portraits**, accompanied by potted biographies, of famous Scots – a definition stretched to include anyone with the slightest Scottish connection. Taken as a whole, the gallery offers an engaging procession through Scottish history, with familiar images of famous Scots such as Bonnie Prince Charlie, Mary Queen of Scots and Robert Burns. The gallery in fact owns two portraits of Prince Charlie (not always shown at the same time), one by Antonio David showing him as an aristocratic, rosy-cheeked twelve-year-old; the other, by Maurice-Quentin de la Tour, depicting him as an older, dashing warrior in armour, was purchased by the prince himself. From the seventeenth century, there's an excellent Van Dyck portrait of Charles Seton, second Earl of Dunfermline, and the tartan-clad Lord Mungo Murray, who died in the disastrous attempt to establish a Scottish colony in Panama. Eighteenth-century highlights include portraits of the philosopher-historian David Hume by Allan Ramsay, and the bard Robert Burns by his friend Alexander Nasmyth, plus a varied group by Raeburn: subjects include Sir Walter Scott, the fiddler Niel Gow and the artist himself. The star portrait from the nineteenth century is that of physician Sir Alexander Morison by his patient, the mad painter **Richard Dadd** – Edinburgh's fishing port of Newhaven is in the background. Twentieth-century portraits on the first floor include a very angular Alec Douglas-Home, briefly prime minister in the 1960s, Sean Connery depicted by the Scottish artist John Bellany, and photomontages of sporting stars Stephen Hendry and Alex Ferguson.

Calton

Of the various extensions to the New Town, the most intriguing is **Calton**, which branches out from the eastern end of Princes Street and encircles a volcanic hill. For years the centre of a thriving **gay** scene (see p.119), it is an area of extraordinary showpiece architecture, dating from the time of the Napoleonic Wars or just after, and intended as an ostentatious celebration of the British victory. While the predominantly Grecian architecture led to Calton being regarded as a Georgian Acropolis, it is, in fact, more of a shrine to local heroes.

Waterloo Place forms a ceremonial way from Princes Street to Calton Hill. On its southern side is the sombre and overgrown **Old Calton Burial Ground**, in which you can see Robert Adam's plain, cylindrical memorial to David Hume and a monument, complete with a statue of Abraham Lincoln, to the Scots who died in the American Civil War. Hard up against the cemetery's eastern wall, perched above a sheer rockface, is a picturesque castellated building which many visitors arriving at Waverley Station below imagine to be Edinburgh Castle itself. In fact, it's the only surviving part of the **Calton Gaol**, once Edinburgh's main prison. Next door is the massive **St Andrew's House**, built in the 1930s to house civil servants.

Further on, set majestically in a confined site below Calton Hill, is one of Edinburgh's greatest buildings, the Grecian **Old Royal High School**, which for many years was assumed to be where Scotland's new parliament would sit. Less than a year before the first elections, however, it was announced that the building was too small for the parliament envisaged, and that a brand new building would be commissioned (see p.82), while the Church of Scotland Assembly Hall (see p.75) would act as a temporary home. Previously in the Old Town, the new site for Edinburgh's oldest school – alma mater to, among others, Robert Adam, Walter Scott and Alexander Graham Bell – was built by Thomas Hamilton, himself an old boy. Across the road, Hamilton also built the **Burns Monument**, a circular Corinthian temple modelled on the Monument to Lysicrates in Athens, as a memorial to the national bard.

Robert Louis Stevenson reckoned that **Calton Hill** was the best place to view Edinburgh, "since you can see the Castle, which you lose from the Castle, and Arthur's Seat, which you cannot see from Arthur's Seat". Though the panoramas from ground level are spectacular enough, those from the top of the **Nelson Monument** (April–Sept Mon 1–6pm, Tues–Sat 10am–6pm; Oct–March Mon–Sat 10am–3pm; £2, or £4 joint ticket with Scott Monument) are even better. Begun just two years after Nelson's death at Trafalgar, this is one of Edinburgh's oddest buildings, resembling a gigantic spyglass.

Alongside, the **National Monument** was begun in 1822 by Playfair to plans by the English architect Charles Cockerell. Had it been completed, it would have been a reasonably accurate replica of the Parthenon, but funds ran out with only twelve columns built. Various later schemes to finish it similarly foundered, earning it the nickname "Edinburgh's Disgrace". At the opposite side of the hill, the grandeur of Playfair's Classical **Monument to Dugald Stewart** seems totally disproportionate to the stature of the man it commemorates – a now-forgotten professor of philosophy at the University.

Playfair also built the **City Observatory** for his uncle, the mathematician and astronomer John Playfair, whom he honoured in the cenotaph outside. Because of pollution and the advent of street lighting, which impaired views of the stars, the observatory proper had to be relocated to Blackford Hill before the end of the century, though the equipment here continues to be used by students. At the opposite end of the complex is the **Old Observatory**, one of the few surviving buildings by James Craig, designer of the New Town. New schemes for the development of Calton Hill, either grandiose or foolish (or both), are proposed on a regular basis: with the possibility of cash from the Lottery Fund, one of these may some day be carried out.

Elsewhere in the New Town

The **Northern New Town** was the earliest extension to the First New Town, begun in 1801, and today roughly covers the area north of Queen Street between India Street to the west and Broughton Street to the east, and as far as Fettes Row to the north. This has survived in far better shape than its predecessor: with the exception of one street, almost all of it is intact, and it has managed to preserve a predominantly residential character. One of the area's most intriguing buildings is the neo-Norman **Mansfield Place Church**, on the corner of Broughton and East London streets, designed in the late nineteenth century for the strange, now defunct Catholic Apostolic sect. Having lain redundant and neglected for three decades, it has suddenly acquired cult status, its preservation the current obsession of local conservation groups. The chief reason for this is its cycle of **murals** by the Dublin-born **Phoebe Anna Traquair**, a leading light in the Scottish Arts and Crafts movement. She laboured for eight years on this decorative scheme, which has all the freshness and luminosity of a medieval manuscript, yet it was almost lost due to leaks and rot in the fabric of the building in recent decades. It was only when the building was acquired by a trust in 1998 that its future was secured and the precious murals saved. While the basement is currently used regularly as a nightclub (*Café Graffiti*; see p.119 for review), sometime in 2000 the whole building will undergo major refurbishment, with the basement being turned into a centre for Scottish voluntary groups and the upper level beside the murals being used as a large performance and exhibition space.

Dean Village and Stockbridge

Work began on the western end of the New Town in 1822, in a small area of land north of Charlotte Square and west of George Street. Instead of the straight lines of the earlier sections, there were now the gracious curves of Randolph Crescent, Ainslie Place and the magnificent twelve-sided Moray Place, designed by the vainglorious James Gillespie Graham who described himself, with no authority to do so, as "architect in Scotland to the Prince Regent". Round the corner from Randolph Crescent, the four-arched **Dean Bridge**, a bravura feat of 1830s engineering by Thomas Telford, carries the main road high above Edinburgh's placid little river, the **Water of Leith**. Down to the left lies **Dean Village**, an old milling community that is one of central Edinburgh's most picturesque yet oddest corners, its atmosphere of terminal decay arrested by the conversion of some of the mills into designer flats. The riverside path into Stockbridge passes **St Bernard's Well**, a pump room covered by a mock Roman temple. Commissioned in 1788 by Lord Gardenstone to draw mineral waters from the Water of Leith, it has recently been restored, and is occasionally open to the public (contact Water of Leith Conservation Trust; ☎0131/445 7367).

Stockbridge, which straddles both sides of the Water of Leith on the other side of Dean Bridge, is another old village which has retained its distinctive identity, in spite of its absorption into the Georgian face of the New Town, and is particularly renowned for its antique shops and "alternative" outlets. The residential upper streets on the far side of the river were developed by Sir Henry Raeburn, who named the finest of them **Ann Street**, which after Charlotte Square is the most prestigious address in Edinburgh (writers Thomas de Quincey and J.M. Ballantyne were residents); alone among New Town streets, its houses each have a front garden.

The West End

The western extension to the New Town was the last part to be built, deviating from the area's overriding Neoclassicism with a number of Victorian additions. Because of this, the huge **St Mary's Episcopal Cathedral**, an addition of the 1870s, is less intrusive than it would otherwise be, its three spires forming an eminently satisfying landmark for the far end of the city centre. The last major work of Sir George Gilbert Scott, the cathedral is built in imitation of the Early English Gothic style and was, at the time of its construction, the most ambitious church built in Britain since the Reformation.

The Scottish National Gallery of Modern Art

Set in spacious wooded grounds at the far northwestern fringe of the New Town, about ten minutes' walk from either the cathedral or Dean Village, the **Scottish National Gallery of Modern Art** on Belford Road (Mon–Sat 10am–5pm, Sun 2–5pm; free), was established as the first collection in Britain devoted solely to twentieth-century painting and sculpture. The grounds serve as a sculpture park, featuring works by Jacob Epstein, Henry Moore and Barbara Hepworth, while inside the display space is divided between temporary loan exhibitions and selections from the gallery's own holdings; the latter are arranged thematically, but are almost constantly moved around. What you get to see at any particular time is therefore a matter of chance, though the most important works are nearly always on view.

French painters are particularly well represented, beginning with **Bonnard's** *Lane at Vernonnet* and **Vuillard's** jewel-like *Two Seamstresses*, and by a few examples of the Fauves, notably **Matisse's** *The Painting Lesson* and **Derain's** dazzlingly brilliant *Collioure*; there's also a fine group of late canvases by **Leger**, notably *The Constructors*.

Among some striking examples of German Expressionism are **Kirchner**'s *Japanese Theatre*, **Feininger**'s *Gelmeroda III*, and a wonderfully soulful wooden sculpture of a woman by **Barlach** entitled *The Terrible Year, 1937*. Highlights of the Surrealist section are **Magritte**'s haunting *Black Flag*, **Miró**'s seminal *Composition* and **Giacometti**'s contorted *Woman with her Throat Cut*, while Cubism is represented by **Picasso**'s *Soles* and **Braque**'s *Candlestick*.

Of works by Americans, **Roy Lichtenstein**'s *In the Car* is a fine example of his Pop Art style, while **Duane Hanson**'s fibreglass *Tourists* is typically unflinching. English artists on show include Sickert, Nicholson, Spencer, Freud and Hockney, but, as you'd expect, considerably more space is allocated to Scottish artists. Of particular note are the Colourists – **S.J. Peploe, J.D. Fergusson, Francis Cadell** and **George Leslie Hunter** – whose works are attracting fancy prices on the art market, as well as ever-growing posthumous critical acclaim. Although they did not form a recognizable school, they all worked in France and displayed considerable French influence in their warm, bright palettes. Also worth exploring is the vivid realism of the more recent Edinburgh School, whose members include **Anne Redpath, Sir Robin Philipson** and **William Gillies**. The gallery also shows works by many contemporary Scots, among them **John Bellany**, a portraitist of striking originality, and the poet-artist-gardener **Ian Hamilton Finlay**.

The Dean Gallery

Opposite the Modern Art Gallery on the other side of Belford Road is the latest addition to the National Galleries of Scotland, the **Dean Gallery** (same hours; free), housed in an equally impressive Neoclassical building completed in 1833. The interior of the gallery, built as an orphanage and later an education centre, has been dramatically refurbished specifically to make room for the work of Edinburgh-born sculptor **Sir Eduardo Paolozzi**, partly assembled from a bequest by Gabrielle Keiller (of the marmalade family), and partly from a gift of the artist himself, which included some 3000 sculptures, 2000 prints and drawings, and 2000 books.

Visitors are given an awesome introduction to Paolozzi's work by the huge *Vulcan*, a half-man, half-machine which squeezes into the Great Hall immediately opposite the main entrance. No less persuasive of Paolozzi's dynamic creative talents are the rooms to the right of the main entrance, where his London studios have been expertly recreated, right down to the clutter of half-finished casts and empty pots of glue. Hidden amongst this chaos is a large part of his bequest, with half-finished casts piled four or five deep on the floor and designs stacked randomly on shelves. In the adjoining room a much smaller selection of his sculptures and drawings are exhibited more formally.

Also on the ground floor is the **Roland Penrose Gallery**, which houses an impressive collection of Dada and Surrealist art; Penrose was a close friend and patron of many of the movements' leading figures. **Marcel Duchamp, Max Ernst** and **Man Ray** are all represented in the gallery, and look out also for **Dali**'s *The Signal of Anguish* and **Magritte**'s *Magic Mirror* along with work by **Picasso** and **Miró**, including the former's montage *Head* – all hung on crowded walls with an assortment of artefacts and ethnic

---

APPROACHES TO THE MODERN ART AND DEAN GALLERIES

One of the most pleasant ways of arriving at the neighbouring Modern Art and Dean galleries is along the **Water of Leith walkway**, which can be picked up at Stockbridge or the Dean Village. Alternatively, a **free bus** runs on the hour (Mon–Sat 10am–5pm, Sun 2–5pm) from outside the National Gallery on the Mound, stopping at the National Portrait Gallery on the way. The only regular **public transport** running along Belford Road is bus #13, which leaves from the western end of George Street.

souvenirs gathered by Penrose and his artist companions while travelling. In the adjoining **Gabrielle Keiller Library**, which is open to all and contains a unique collection of surrealist literature, manuscripts and correspondence, there is a wonderful pen and ink caricature of Picasso by **De Chirico**, as well as a series of Picasso's own cartoons satirizing General Franco. The rooms upstairs are normally given over to special exhibitions, which usually carry an entrance charge.

The suburbs

Edinburgh's principal sights are by no means confined to the city centre: indeed, at least three of its most popular tourist draws – the **Royal Botanic Garden**, the **Zoo** and the **Royal Observatory** – are out in the suburbs. Other major attractions in the outskirts include **Craigmillar Castle** and the southern hill ranges, the **Braids** and the **Pentlands**. Additionally, there are several districts with their own very distinct identity, among them the academic enclave of the **Southside**, the seaside resort of **Portobello** and the fashionable port area of **Leith**.

The Royal Botanic Garden

Just beyond the northern boundaries of the New Town, with entrances on Inverleith Row and Arboretum Place, is the seventy-acre site of the **Royal Botanic Garden** (daily: March & Sept 9.30am–6pm; April–Aug 9.30am–7pm; Oct & Feb 9.30am–5pm; Nov–Jan 9.30am–4pm; free), particularly renowned for the rhododendrons, which blaze out in a glorious patchwork of colours in April and May. In the heart of the grounds a group of hothouses designated the **Glasshouse Experience** (daily: March–Oct 10am–5pm; Nov–Feb 10am–3.30pm; free, but donation requested) displays orchids, giant Amazonian water lilies, and a 200-year-old West Indian palm tree, the latter being in the elegant 1850s glass-topped Palm House. Many of the most exotic plants were brought to Edinburgh by the aptly named George Forrest, who made seven expeditions to southwestern China between 1904 and 1932. There is also a major new Chinese-style garden, featuring a pavilion, waterfall and the world's biggest collection of Chinese wild plants outside China.

The southwest

The area **southwest** of the Old Town was formerly known as **Portsburgh**, a theoretically separate burgh outside the city walls that was nonetheless a virtual fiefdom of Edinburgh. Since the 1880s and the construction of the **Royal Lyceum Theatre** on Grindlay Street, the area has gradually developed into something of a theatre district, although more recently the derelict ground immediately to the west has seen a good deal of construction, most prominently two large financial headquarters and the Edinburgh Conference Centre. The **Museum of Fire** (by appointment only; ☎0131/228 2401; free) situated on Lauriston Place next to the Art School, records the history of the oldest municipal fire brigade in Britain, formed in 1824. It contains a small collection of well-preserved manual, horse-drawn and motorized fire appliances. At its southern edge, the open parkland areas of the **Meadows** and **Bruntsfield Links** mark the transition to Edinburgh's genteel Victorian villa suburbs. South of the Meadows, a plaque on the wall of Sciennes Hill House in Sciennes House Place records the only known meeting, in 1787, of Robert Burns and Sir Walter Scott. On the opposite side of the street is a tiny Jewish graveyard. Prominent among the suburbs is **Morningside**, whose prim and proper outlook, accompanied by an appropriately plummy accent, was immortalized in Muriel Spark's *The Prime of Miss Jean Brodie*, and remains a favourite target for ridicule.

The Southside

The New Town was not the only mid-eighteenth-century expansion of Edinburgh: the city also spread in the opposite direction, creating a tenement suburb which became known as the **Southside**. Since the 1950s, this has developed into a lively academic quarter, having been progressively colonized by the overspill of University buildings.

On Nicolson Street, the southern extension of South Bridge, is **Surgeons' Hall**, a handsome Ionic temple built by Playfair as the headquarters of the Royal College of Surgeons. Most of it is accessible to the public only one day a year, an exception being the **museum**, entered from 9 Hill Square (Mon–Fri 2–4pm; free), which has intriguing, if somewhat specialist exhibits on the history of medicine. Across the street is the glass-fronted **Festival Theatre**, a refurbished music hall which opened in 1994, giving the city a long-awaited venue for presenting opera and dance on a large scale.

Craigmillar Castle

Craigmillar Castle (April–Sept daily 9.30am–6pm; Oct–March Mon–Wed & Sat 9.30am–4pm, Thurs 9.30am–noon, Sun 2–4pm; £1.80), where the murder of Lord Darnley, second husband of Mary, Queen of Scots was plotted, lies in a green belt five miles south-east of the centre. It's one of the best-preserved medieval fortresses in Scotland, and before Queen Victoria set her heart on Balmoral, it was being considered as her royal castle north of the border, a possibility which seems odd now given its proximity to the ugly council housing scheme of Craigmillar, one of Edinburgh's most deprived districts.

The oldest part of the complex is the L-shaped **tower house**, which dates back to the early 1400s: it remains substantially intact, and the great hall, with its resplendent late Gothic chimneypiece, is in good enough shape to be rented out for functions. A few decades after Craigmillar's completion, the tower house was surrounded by a quadrangular wall with cylindrical corner towers pierced by some of the earliest surviving gunholes in Britain. The west range was remodelled as an aristocratic mansion in the mid-seventeenth century, but its owners abandoned the place a hundred years later, leaving it to picturesque decay. Take bus #30, #33 or #82, or any bus heading for Hawick or Jedburgh, from the city centre to the district called Little France, from where the castle is a ten-minute walk along Craigmillar Castle Road.

The southern hills

The **hills** in Edinburgh's southern suburbs offer good, not overly demanding, walking opportunities, with plenty of sweeping panoramic views. The **Royal Observatory** (Mon–Sat 10am–5pm, Sun noon–5pm; £3) stands at the top of Blackford Hill, just a short walk south of Morningside, or accessible by buses #24 and #41 direct from the centre. The visitor centre here seeks to explain the mysteries of the solar system by means of various hands-on exhibits and CD-Roms, and you also get to see the observatory's two main telescopes.

At the foot of the hill, the bird sanctuary of Blackford Pond is the starting point for one of the many trails running through the **Hermitage of Braid** local nature reserve, a lovely shady area along the course of the Braid Burn. The castellated eighteenth-century mansion along the burn, after which the reserve is named, now serves as a visitor centre (April–Oct Mon–Fri 10am–4pm, Sun noon–5pm; Oct–March daily 11am–4pm; café Sun only noon–4pm). Immediately to the south are the **Braid Hills**, most of whose area is occupied by two golf courses, which are closed on alternate Sundays in order to allow access to walkers.

Further south are the **Pentland Hills**, a chain some eighteen miles long and five wide. Numerous walks, from gentle strolls along well-marked paths to a ten-mile tra-

ROBERT LOUIS STEVENSON

Though **Robert Louis Stevenson** (1850–94) is sometimes dismissed for his deceptively simple manner, he was undoubtedly one of the best-loved writers of his generation, and one whose travelogues, novels, short stories and essays remain enormously popular a century after his death.

Born in Edinburgh into a distinguished family of engineers, Stevenson was a sickly child, with a solitary childhood dominated by his governess, Alison "Cummie" Cunningham, who regaled him with tales drawn from Calvinist folklore. Sent to the University to study engineering, Stevenson rebelled against his upbringing by spending much of his time in the lowlife howffs and brothels of the city, and eventually switching to law. Although called to the bar in 1875, by then he had decided to channel his energies into literature: while still a student, he had already made his mark as an **essayist** – he eventually had over a hundred essays published, ranging from light-hearted whimsy to trenchant political analysis. A set of topographical pieces about his native city was later collected together as *Edinburgh: Picturesque Notes*, which conjure up nicely its atmosphere, character and appearance – warts and all.

Stevenson's other early successes were two **travelogues**, *An Inland Voyage* and *Travels with a Donkey in the Cevennes*, kaleidoscopic jottings based on his journeys in France, where he went to escape Scotland's weather, which was damaging his health. It was there that he met Fanny Osbourne, an American ten years his senior, who was estranged from her husband and had two children in tow. His voyage to join her in San Francisco formed the basis for his most important factual work, *The Amateur Emigrant*, a vivid first-hand account of the great nineteenth-century European migration to the United States.

Having married the now-divorced Fanny, Stevenson began an elusive search for an agreeable climate that led to Switzerland, the French Riviera and the Scottish Highlands. He belatedly turned to the novel, achieving immediate acclaim in 1881 for **Treasure Island**, a highly moralistic adventure yarn that began as an entertainment for his stepson and future collaborator, Lloyd Osbourne. In 1886, his most famous short story, **Dr Jekyll and Mr Hyde**, despite its nominal London setting, offered a vivid evocation of Edinburgh's Old Town: an allegory of its dual personality of prosperity and squalor, and an analysis of its Calvinistic preoccupations with guilt and damnation. The same year saw the publication of the historical romance **Kidnapped**, an adventure novel which exemplified Stevenson's view that literature should seek above all to entertain.

In 1887 Stevenson left Britain for good, travelling first to the United States where he began one of his most ambitious novels, *The Master of Ballantrae*. A year later, he set sail for the **South Seas**, and eventually settled in Samoa; his last works include a number of stories with a local setting, such as the grimly realistic *The Ebb Tide* and *The Beach of Falesà*. However, Scotland continued to be his main inspiration: he wrote *Catriona* as a sequel to *Kidnapped*, and was at work on two more novels with Scottish settings, *St Ives* and *Weir of Hermiston*, a dark story of father and son confrontation, at the time of his sudden death from a brain haemorrhage in 1894. He was buried on the top of Mount Vaea overlooking the Pacific Ocean.

verse of the hills and moors, are outlined on a pamphlet available from the Regional Park Information Centre at **FLOTTERSTONE**, ten miles south of the city centre on the A702, an old staging post on the route south. There's been an inn since the seventeenth century; the present *Flotterstone Inn* is a good spot for a drink or a pub meal after your exertions (see box on p.102). The best entry point from within Edinburgh is **SWANSTON**, an unspoiled, highly exclusive hamlet of whitewashed thatched roof dwellings separated from the rest of the city by almost a mile of farmland. **Robert Louis Stevenson** (see below) spent his boyhood summers in Swanston Cottage, the largest of the houses, immortalizing it in the novel *St Ives*. To get a taste of the scenery of the Pentlands, the simplest way is to set off from the car park by the ski centre at **Hillend** at the northeast

EDINBURGH'S PENTLAND HILLS

Ordnance Survey Landranger map no. 66.

Allow four hours for this walk. Exit the city on the A702 and look out for the **Flotterstone Inn** where there is a car park and small interpretative centre. A pleasant sideroad leads up to Glencorse Reservoir, a lochan, then swings round it to go through a tight pass and on to Loganlee Reservoir, a quite remote area that feels far away from city life. The more energetic can set off from Flotterstone onto Turnhouse Hill and cross Carnethy Hill (1890ft) to come down to the Howe, at the loch's west end.

A path leads on through a short pass to come out on the far side of the Pentland range, where the large expanse of Thriepmuir Reservoir stretches out in front of you. Cross a bridge over a "neck" in the reservoir; the path heads inland for a while, but take the first right to return to the reservoir and then follow it along Harlaw Reservoir beyond.

At the far end of this is another small ranger centre and car park – here, take the path going over flat moorland and back into the hills through the pass between Bell's Hill and Harbour Hill. The path runs down the burn to rejoin Glencorse Reservoir.

For more walking and biking routes in the Pentlands pick up the leaflets available at the ranger centre at Flotterstone. There are also several books and special maps about the Pentlands, *25 Walks, Edinburgh and Lothian* (HMSO, 1995) being the best option.

end of the range; take the path up the right-hand side of the dry ski slopes, turning left shortly after crossing a style to reach a point with outstanding views over Edinburgh and Fife. If you're feeling energetic, the views get even better higher up, and you'll get more of an idea of the unexpected green emptiness of the Pentland range running away to the south. Alternatively, there's a **chair lift** from the ski centre (Mon–Fri 1–9pm, Sun 10am–7pm; £1.20), which is connected with the city centre by buses #4 and #15, while the hourly Lowland Omnibus #315 carries on to Flotterstone.

Portobello

Among Edinburgh's least expected assets is its **beach**, most of which falls within **POR-TOBELLO**, once a lively **seaside resort** but now a forlorn kind of place, its funfairs and amusement arcades decidedly down-at-heel. Nonetheless, it retains a certain faded charm, and – on hot summer weekends at least – the beach can be a mass of swimmers, sunbathers, surfers and pleasure boats. A walk along the promenade is a pleasure at any time of the year. Portobello is about three miles east of the centre of town, and can be reached on buses #15, #26, #46 or #86.

Leith

For several hundred years, **LEITH** was separate from Edinburgh. As Scotland's major east coast port, it played a key role in the nation's history, even serving as the seat of government for a time, and in 1833 finally became a burgh in its own right. In 1920, however, it was incorporated into the capital and, in the decades that followed, went into seemingly terminal decline: the population dropped dramatically, and much of its centre was ripped out, to be replaced by grim housing schemes.

The 1980s, however, saw an astonishing turnaround. Against all the odds, a couple of waterfront bistros proved enormously successful; competitors followed apace, and by the end of the decade the port had acquired arguably the best concentration of restaurants and pubs in Edinburgh (see p.114 and 118 for reviews). The surviving historic monuments were spruced up and a host of housing developments built or restored, a renaissance crowned by the completion of a vast new building housing civil servants from the Scottish Office. The most recent developments have focused on the old harbour itself, with a huge shopping and entertainment complex being built alongside the berth where the former royal yacht **Britannia** is now settling into retirement.

To reach Leith from the city centre, take one of the many buses going down Leith Walk, near the top end of which is a statue of Sherlock Holmes, whose creator, Sir Arthur Conan Doyle, was born nearby. Otherwise, it's a brisk walk of around twenty minutes, or you can travel on from Portobello by bus #2.

Around the port

While you're most likely to come to Leith for the bars and restaurants, the area itself warrants exploration; though the shipbuilding yards have gone, it remains an active port with a rough-edged character. Most of the showpiece Neoclassical buildings lie on or near **The Shore**, the tenement-lined road along the final stretch of the Water of Leith, just before it disgorges into the Firth of Forth. Note the former **Town Hall**, on the parallel Constitution Street, now the headquarters of the local constabulary, immortalized in the tongue twister, "The Leith police dismisseth us"; the Classical Trinity House on Kirkgate, built in 1816; and the massive Customs House on Commercial Street. To the west, set back from The Shore, is **Lamb's House**, a seventeenth-century mansion comparable to Gladstone's Land in the Old Town. Built as the home of the prosperous merchant Andro Lamb, it currently functions as an old people's day centre.

Leith Links is an area of predominantly flat parkland, just east of the police station. Documentary evidence suggests that The Links was a golf course in the fifteenth century, giving rise to Leith's claim to be regarded as the birthplace of the sport: in 1744 its first written rules were drawn up here, ten years before they were formalized in St Andrews.

Britannia

A little to the west of The Shore, moored alongside Ocean Drive near the huge Chancelot flour mills, is one of the world's most famous ships, **Britannia** (daily 10.30am–4.30pm; bookings advised ☎0131/555 5566; £7.50). Launched in 1953 at John Brown's shipyard on Clydeside, *Britannia* was used by the royal family for 44 years for state visits, diplomatic functions and royal holidays. Leith acquired her following decommission in 1997, against the wishes of many of the royal family, who felt that scuttling would have been a more dignified end.

Visits to *Britannia* begin in a purpose-built **visitor centre**, which uses the royal barge and a reconstructed sergeant's mess to display royal holiday snaps and video clips of *Britannia*'s most famous moments, which included the evacuation of Aden and the British handover of Hong Kong in 1997. An audio handset is then handed out and you are allowed to roam around the yacht: the **bridge**, the **admiral's quarters**, the **officers' mess** and a large part of the **state apartments**, including the state dining and drawing rooms and the (separate) cabins used by the Queen and the Duke of Edinburgh, viewed through a glass partition. The ship has been largely kept as she was when she was in service, with a well-preserved 1950s dowdiness which the audio guide loyally attributes to the Queen's good taste and astute frugality in the lean post-war years. Certainly the atmosphere is a far cry from the opulent splendour which many expect, but it's by no means warm and homely – it's perhaps a reflection on the royal lot that *Britannia* was the one place where the Queen said she was could truly relax.

The audio guide also reveals quirkier aspects of *Britannia*'s history: a full Marine Band was always part of the 300-strong crew; hand signals were used by the sailors to communicate orders as shouting was forbidden; and a special solid mahogany rail was built onto the royal bridge to allow the Queen to stand on deck as *Britannia* came into port, without fear of a gust of wind lifting the royal skirt.

Regular shuttle buses operated by both Guide Friday and LRT run between Waverley Bridge and *Britannia*; otherwise, buses #10 and #16 from Princes Street and #22 from St Andrews Square run down Leith Walk to the junction of Commercial Street and North Junction Street, from where it's a five-minute walk down to the visitor centre.

Newhaven

To the west of Leith lies the village of **NEWHAVEN**, built by James IV at the start of the sixteenth century as an alternative shipbuilding centre to Leith: his massive warship, the *Michael*, capable of carrying 120 gunners, 300 mariners and 1000 troops, and said to have used up all the trees in Fife, was built here. It has also been a ferry station and an important fishing centre, landing some six million oysters a year at the height of its success (in the 1860s). Today, although a few boats still operate from the harbour, the fish market is no more and the last of the colourfully dressed fishwives has long since retired. A variety of costumes and other memorabilia of the village's only industry can be found in the small **Newhaven Heritage Museum** (daily noon–5pm; free), a fascinating collection staffed by enthusiastic members of local fishing families.

The Zoo

Edinburgh Zoo (daily: April–Sept 9am–6pm; Oct & March 9am–5pm; Nov–Feb 9am–4.30pm; £6) lies three miles west of Princes Street on an eighty-acre site on the slopes of Corstorphine Hill (buses from town: #2, #26, #31, #36, #69, #85, #86). Here you can see over 1000 animals, including a number of endangered species such as white rhinos, red pandas, pygmy hippos and Madagascar tree boas. Making the most of the space offered by Corstorphine Hill, the **African Plains Experience** and a new **Lion Enclosure** have walkways leading you out over the animals to viewing platforms, while other popular new additions include the Magic Forest, showcasing smaller primates, and a water-filled Evolution Maze. However, the zoo's chief claim to fame is its crowd of penguins (the largest number in captivity anywhere in the world), a legacy of Leith's whaling trade in the South Atlantic. The **penguin parade**, which takes place daily at 2pm from April to September, and on sunny March and October days, has gained something of a cult status.

Lauriston Castle and Cramond

Lauriston Castle (40min obligatory guided tours April–Oct daily except Friday 11am–1pm & 2–5pm; Nov–March Sat & Sun 2–4pm; £4.50) is a country mansion set in its own parkland overlooking the Firth of Forth, about five miles west of the centre. The original sixteenth-century tower house forms the centrepiece of what is otherwise a neo-Jacobean structure, which in 1902 became the retirement home of a prosperous local cabinet-maker. He decked out the interior with his private collection of furniture and antiques, which includes Flemish tapestries and ornaments made of Blue John from Derbyshire. The castle can be reached from the city centre by bus #40.

One mile further west, **CRAMOND** is one of the city's most atmospheric – and poshest – old villages. The enduring image of Cramond is of step-gabled whitewashed houses rising uphill from the waterfront, though it also boasts the foundations of a Roman fort, a medieval bridge and tower house, and a church, inn and mansion, all from the seventeenth century. In December 1996, a wonderful Roman sculpture of a lioness devouring a man was discovered in the River Almond: it is thought that it was simply thrown into the river after the departure of the Romans. It is now on display in the National Museum of Scotland on Chambers Street (see p.86). There are a number of interesting **short walks** in the area: across the causeway at low tide to the uninhabited (except for seabirds) **Cramond Island**; eastwards along the seafront towards the gasometers of **Granton** with sweeping views out to sea; upstream along the River Almond past former mills and their adjoining cottages towards the sixteenth-century **Old Cramond Brig**; and, after a short ferry crossing, through the Dalmeny estate to **Dalmeny House** (see below). Apart from the last one, which is just a little longer, these walks should take around an hour each.

Dalmeny

In 1975, Edinburgh's boundaries were extended to include a number of towns and villages which were formerly part of West Lothian. Among them is **DALMENY**, two miles west of Cramond and accessible directly from the city centre by bus (#43 SMT) or train. Another option is to take the coastal path from Cramond, which passes through the estate of **Dalmeny House** (July & Aug Mon & Tues noon–5.30pm, Sun 1–5.30pm; £3.80), the seat of the Earls of Rosebery. Built in 1815 by the English architect William Wilkins, it was the first stately home in Scotland in the neo-Gothic style, vividly evoking Tudor architecture in its picturesque turreted roofline, and in its fan vaults and hammerbeam ceilings. The family portraits include one of the fourth Earl (who commissioned the house) by Raeburn, and of the fifth Earl (a former British prime minister) by Millais; there are also likenesses of other famous society figures by Reynolds, Gainsborough and Lawrence. Among the furnishings are a set of tapestries made from cartoons by Goya, and the Rothschild Collection of eighteenth-century French furniture and objets d'art. There's also a fascinating collection of memorabilia of Napoleon Bonaparte – notably some items he used during his exile in St Helena – amassed by the fifth Earl, who wrote a biography of the French emperor.

Dalmeny **village** is a quiet community built around a spacious green. Its focal point is the mid-twelfth-century **St Cuthbert's Kirk**, a wonderful Norman church that has remained more or less intact. Although very weather-beaten, the south doorway is particularly notable for its depictions of strange beasts. More vivaciously grotesque carvings can be seen inside on the chancel corbels and arch.

South Queensferry and around

Less than a mile of countryside separates Dalmeny from **SOUTH QUEENSFERRY**, a compact little town used by St Margaret as a crossing point for her frequent trips between her palaces in Edinburgh and Dunfermline. The **High Street**, squeezed into the narrow gap between the seashore and the hillside above, is lined by a picturesque array of old buildings, among them an unusual two-tiered row of shops, the roofs of the lower level serving as the walkway for the upper storey. The small **museum**, 53 High St (Mon & Thurs–Sat 10am–1pm & 2.15–5pm, Sun 2–5pm; free), contains relics of the town's history and the building of the two bridges.

Everything in South Queensferry is overshadowed, quite literally, by the two great bridges, each about a mile and a half in length, which traverse the Firth of Forth at its narrowest point. The cantilevered **Forth Rail Bridge**, built from 1883 to 1890 by Sir John Fowler and Benjamin Baker, ranks among the supreme achievements of Victorian engineering. Some 50,000 tons of steel were used in the construction of a design that manages to express grace as well as might. Derived from American models, the suspension format chosen for the **Forth Road Bridge** makes a perfect complement to the older structure. Erected between 1958 and 1964, it finally killed off the 900-year-old ferry, and now attracts a heavy volume of traffic. It's well worth walking (or cycling) across its footpath to Fife (see the Central Scotland chapter) for tremendous views of the rail bridge and the Forth estuary.

Inchcolm

From South Queensferry's Hawes Pier, just west of the rail bridge, pleasure boats leave for a variety of cruises on the Forth (Easter, May & June Sat & Sun; July to mid-Sept daily; ☎0131/331 4857; £7.50–10). Be sure to check in advance as sailings are always subject to cancellation in bad weather.

The most enticing destination is the island of **Inchcolm**, whose beautiful ruined **Abbey** was founded in 1123 by King Alexander I in gratitude for the hospitality he received from a hermit (whose cell survives at the northwestern corner of the island) when his ship was forced ashore in a storm. The best-preserved medieval monastic complex in Scotland, the abbey's surviving buildings date from the thirteenth to the fifteenth centuries, and include a splendid octagonal chapterhouse. Although the church is almost totally dilapidated, its tower can be ascended for a great aerial view of the island, which is populated by a variety of nesting birds and a colony of grey seals.

Hopetoun House

Immediately beyond the western edge of South Queensferry, just over the West Lothian border, **Hopetoun House** (April–Sept daily 10am–5.30pm, Oct Sat & Sun 10am–5.30pm; £5 house and grounds, £2.80 grounds only) is one of Scotland's grandest stately homes. The original house was built at the turn of the eighteenth century for the first Earl of Hopetoun by Sir William Bruce, the architect of Holyroodhouse. A couple of decades later, William Adam carried out an enormous extension, engulfing the house in a curvaceous main facade and two projecting wings – superb examples of Roman Baroque pomp and swagger. The scale and lavishness of the Adam interiors, most of whose decoration was carried out by his sons after the architect's death, make for a stark contrast with the intimacy of those designed by Bruce. Particularly impressive are the Red and Yellow Drawing Rooms, with their splendid ceilings by the young Robert Adam. Among the house's furnishings are seventeenth-century tapestries, Meissen porcelain, and a distinguished collection of paintings, including portraits by Gainsborough, Ramsay and Raeburn. The grounds of Hopetoun House are also open, with magnificent walks along the banks of the Forth and great opportunities for picnics.

Midlothian

Immediately south of Edinburgh lies the old county of **MIDLOTHIAN**, once called Edinburghshire. It's one of the hilliest parts of the Central Lowlands, with the Pentland chain running down its western side, and the Moorfoots defining its boundary with the Borders to the south. Though predominantly rural, it contains a belt of former mining communities, which are struggling to come to terms with the recent decline of the industry. Such charms as it has are mostly low-key, with the exception of the riotously ornate chapel at **Roslin**.

Dalkeith and around

Despite its Victorian demeanour, **DALKEITH**, eight miles southeast of central Edinburgh – to which it is linked by very regular buses (#3, #30, #82) – grew up in the Middle Ages as a baronial burgh under the successive control of the Douglases and Buccleuchs. Today it's a bustling shopping centre, with an unusually broad High Street at its heart.

At the far end of the street is the entrance to **Dalkeith Country Park** (April–Oct daily 10am–6pm; £2), the estate of the Dukes of Buccleuch, whose seat, the early eighteenth-century **Dalkeith Palace**, can only be seen from the outside. You can, however, visit its one-time chapel, now the Episcopalian parish church of **St Mary**, adorned inside with extremely rich furnishings. Further north, Robert Adam's **Montagu Bridge** straddles the River North Esk in a graceful arch; beyond are some derelict but once wonderfully grandiose garden follies. There is also a large woodland playground, suitable for all but the youngest children.

A mile or so south of Dalkeith is **NEWTONGRANGE**, whose Lady Victoria Colliery is now open to the public as the **Scottish Mining Museum** (Feb–Nov daily 10am–5pm; £4), with a 1625-foot shaft, and a winding tower powered by Scotland's largest steam engine. A brand-new visitor centre brings the life of the mine and the local community to life, helped by some entertaining innovation, including "magic helmets", with which you can go on shift and experience a virtual reality tour of life below ground.

Roslin

The tranquil village of **ROSLIN** lies seven miles south of the centre of Edinburgh, from where it can be reached by bus #87A or by regular Eastern Scottish services from St Andrew Square. An otherwise nondescript place, the village has two unusual claims to fame: it was near here, at the Roslin Institute, that the world's first cloned sheep, Dolly, was created in 1997; and it also boasts the mysterious, richly decorated late-Gothic **Rosslyn Chapel** (Mon–Sat 10am–5pm, Sun noon–4.45pm; £3). Only the choir, Lady Chapel and part of the transepts were built of what was intended to be a huge collegiate church dedicated to St Matthew: construction halted soon after the founder's death in 1484, and the vestry built onto the facade nearly four hundred years later is the sole subsequent addition. After a long period of neglect, a massive restoration project has recently been undertaken: a canopy has been placed over the chapel which will remain in place for several years in order to dry out the saturated ceiling and walls, and other essential repairs are due to be carried out within the chapel.

The outside of the chapel bristles with pinnacles, gargoyles, flying buttresses and canopies, while inside the foliage carving is particularly outstanding, with botanically accurate depictions of over a dozen different leaves and plants. Among them are cacti and Indian corn, providing fairly convincing evidence that the founder's grandfather, the daring sea adventurer Prince Henry of Orkney, did indeed, as legend has it, set foot in the New World a century before Columbus. The rich and subtle figurative sculptures have given Rosslyn the nickname of "a Bible in stone", though they're more allegorical than literal, with portrayals of the Dance of Death, the Seven Acts of Mercy and the Seven Deadly Sins.

The greatest and most original carving of all is the extraordinary knotted **Prentice Pillar** at the southeastern corner of the Lady Chapel. According to local legend, the pillar was made by an apprentice during the absence of the master mason, who killed him in a fit of jealousy on seeing the finished work. A tiny head of a man with a slashed forehead, set at the apex of the ceiling at the far northwestern corner of the building, is popularly supposed to represent the apprentice, his murderer the corresponding head at the opposite side. The entwined dragons at the foot are symbols of Satan, and were probably inspired by Norse mythology.

A number of books have been published in recent years about Rosslyn Chapel, drawing on everything from Freemasons and the Turin Shroud to the True Gospels and the regular sightings of UFOs over Midlothian. Conspiracy theories notwithstanding, the chapel is very definitely worth a visit.

Cafés and restaurants

Style, sophistication and good taste are breaking out all over in Edinburgh. **Café culture** has hit the centre of the city, with tables spilling onto the pavements in the summer.

Small **diners** and **bistros** predominate, many adopting a casual French style and offering good-value set menus. Traditional **Scottish cooking**, using fresh local produce, can still be found at some of the more formal restaurants, but it's worth keeping an eye out for contemporary Scottish places, which have a more unusual modern slant. There are plenty of **fish** specialists – seafood fans should head to **Leith**, whose waterside restaurants serve consistently good food.

The city's ethnic communities, despite their small size, ensure that the perennial favourites are well represented, in particular with some great **Italian** trattorias and a host of excellent **Indian** restaurants serving regional dishes. **Vegetarians** and vegans are well catered for, while influences from around the world, from Spain to Southeast Asia, can all be found. Most of Edinburgh's restaurants serve from noon to 2.30pm and 6pm to 11pm and close on Sundays, except where otherwise stated in our reviews. During the Festival, however, the majority of restaurants stay open all day until the early hours. It's worth bearing in mind that most **pubs** (which are covered in the following section) serve food, and that many have restaurants attached.

Old Town and Tollcross

Terrific cafés and most of the upmarket Scottish and French restaurants are concentrated in the atmospheric streets of the **Old Town**, with a wide range of other cuisines on offer, including vegetarian. **Tollcross**, handy for the city's theatres, also has a sprinkling of good restaurants, including some notable Chinese options.

Cafés and diners

blue, 10 Cambridge St (☎0131/221 1222). Stunning glass and pale-wood decor in the same building as the avant-garde Traverse Theatre, and equally impressive food – original and tasty dishes for under £10 per main course. Open later than most – till midnight Sun & Mon, and 1am Tues–Sat. Inexpensive–moderate.

Clarinda's, 69 Canongate (☎0131/557 1888). Spruce olde-worlde café serving home-cooked breakfasts and light lunches. Closed evenings. Inexpensive.

Common Grounds, 2–3 North Bank St (☎0131/226 1146). American-style coffee shop on two levels, non-smoking upstairs. The menu includes filled croissants, quiches and a good range of coffees – anyone struggling to stay awake through a session of the nearby Parliament should try the "Keith Richards", which contains four shots of espresso. Open till 10pm, and live music most evenings. Inexpensive.

Deacon's House Café, Brodies Close (☎0131/226 1894). Quiet licensed café off the Royal Mile, claiming to have been the workshop of the infamous Deacon Brodie. It serves light snacks, home baking and even a nip of whisky. Daily 9am to around 6pm, later during the Festival. Inexpensive.

Elephant House, 21 George IV Bridge (☎0131/220 5355). Attractive and popular café with a large selection of coffees, teas, sandwiches and cakes and wonderful views of the Castle from the cavernous back room. Mon–Sat 8am–11pm, Sun 10am–8pm. Inexpensive.

Lower Aisle, in the High Kirk of St Giles, High Street (☎0131/225 5147). Popular with bewigged advocates from the High Court, this café in the crypt serves good-value light lunches, with excellent home baking. Closed evenings. Inexpensive.

Ndebele, 57 Home St (☎0131/221 1141). Colourful African café offering tasty sandwiches, delicious fruit juices and a great selection of teas and coffees. Open daily till 10pm. Inexpensive.

Netherbow Café, Netherbow Arts Centre, 43 High St (☎0131/556 9579). Excellent wholefood and vegetarian soups and light meals, with a courtyard for sunny days. Lunchtimes only. Inexpensive.

Patisserie Florentin, 8–10 St Giles St (☎0131/225 6267). French-style café off High Street whose extended opening hours and fabulous cakes and pastries make it a popular late-night rendezvous. Open daily 7am–11pm, closes 3am during the Festival. Inexpensive.

Chinese

Jasmine, 32 Grindlay St (☎0131/229 5757). Good-value restaurant, with a strong line in fresh fish. Across the street from the Lyceum and the Usher Hall. Moderate.

Oriental Dining Centre, 8–14a Morrison St, Tollcross (☎0131/221 1288). Three distinct restaurants, the most popular being the *Ho-Ho-Mei Noodle Shak*. Also contains the *Rainbow Arch Gourmet Restaurant* – try the three-course banquet for two for around £20 – and *Henry's Dim Sum Cellar*, which also has a popular bar. All inexpensive–moderate.

French

La Bagatelle, 22a Brougham Place, Tollcross (☎0131/229 0869). Fine French food in an authentic atmosphere, with a good-value three-course lunch for £8.50. Closed Sun. Expensive.

Bleu, 36–38 Victoria St (☎0131/226 1900). From the creator of the original *Pierre Victoire* comes a newer, trendier way to eat French – *bouchées* (mouthfuls), which are bigger than a starter and smaller than a main. Moderate.

Chez Jules, 1 Craigs Close, off Cockburn St (☎0131/225 7007). French food in a fine, no-frills establishment. Open daily 5.30–10.30pm. Moderate.

Le Sept, Old Fishmarket Close (☎0131/225 5428). Long-established French brasserie tucked down a cobbled close off the Royal Mile. Three-course set lunch for £6, with three-course set evening meal for around £15 Sun–Thurs; a la carte only Fri–Sun. Moderate.

Pierre Victoire, 10 Victoria St (☎0131/225 1721). The PV phenomenon started here, and lives on despite a recent brush with the bankers, doing what it does best – great French food in an easygoing atmosphere, at decent prices. Moderate.

Indian

Shamiana, 14 Brougham Place, Tollcross (☎0131/228 2265). Established, first-class North Indian and Kashmiri restaurant located midway between the King's and Lyceum theatres. One of the more expensive places in this category, and an oddly stark interior, but well worth it. Mon–Sat 6–9.30pm, Sun 6–8pm. Moderate.

Italian

Caffe Sardi, 18–20 Forrest Rd (☎0131/220 5553). Fresh food, with original twists given to the usual Italian stand-bys. Three-course evening set menu for around £10. Closed Sun. Moderate.

Lazio's, 95 Lothian Rd (☎0131/229 7788). Pick of the family-run trattorias on this block, handy for a late-night meal after a show in the nearby theatre district. Closes 1.30am daily. Moderate.

Mamma's, 30 Grassmarket (☎0131/225 6464). The best pizzas in this part of town, popular with students and larger groups, with outside tables in the summer and reasonably priced wine. Open till 11pm Sun–Thurs, midnight Fri & Sat. Inexpensive–moderate.

Mexican

Viva Mexico, 10 Anchor Close, off Cockburn Street (☎0131/226 5145). Long-standing restaurant, with plenty of choice for vegetarians, and bargain options at lunchtimes; check out the *tacos, burritos* and refreshing *margaritas*. Moderate.

Scottish and seafood

The Atrium, 10 Cambridge St (☎0131/228 8882). This award-winning restaurant is considered by many to be the city's best, serving innovative nouvelle food and focusing on high-quality Scottish produce. The chunky tables are made from railway sleepers, and the place is lit by flaming torches. Closed Sunday. Very expensive.

Creelers, 3 Hunter Square (☎0131/220 4447). Excellent seafood restaurant priding itself on fresh produce brought in from a sister restaurant/fish shop on Arran. A bistro section is located at the front, with a more expensive restaurant at the back. Moderate–expensive.

Point Hotel, 34 Bread St (☎0131/221 5555). A classy feel with modernist decor, white linen tablecloths and smartly dressed waiters, and great food based on fresh local fish and meat, yet one of the best-value deals in town: a three-course set menu is just £12. Moderate.

Stac Polly, 8a Grindlay St (☎0131/229 5405). Unusual mix of traditional and contemporary Scottish fare, with an emphasis on game, fish and meat. Evenings only. Expensive.

The Tower, Museum of Scotland, Chambers Street (☎0131/225 3003). Unique setting on Level 5 of the new Museum of Scotland; at night you are escorted along the empty corridors to the restaurant, where spectacular views to the floodlit Castle are revealed. Modern Scottish food in a self-consciously chic setting. Expensive.

The Witchery by the Castle, 352 Castlehill, Royal Mile (☎0131/225 5613). The restaurant that only Edinburgh could create, with Gothic panelling, tapestries and heavy stonework only a broomstick-hop from the Castle. The superb fish and game dishes are pricey, but you can steal a sense of it all with a pre- or post-theatre set menu (£10). Expensive.

Spanish

Igg's, 15 Jeffrey St (☎0131/557 8184). A Spanish-owned hybrid, offering tapas snacks and Mediterranean dishes, plus traditional Scottish food. Good lunchtime tapas for around £5. Closed Sun. Expensive.

Vegetarian

Bann's Vegetarian Café, 5 Hunter Square (☎0131/226 1112). Reliable, informal café, halfway up the Royal Mile, with a frequently changing but always original and appealing menu. Daily 10am–11pm. Moderate.

Black Bo's, 57 Blackfriars St (☎0131/557 6136). Inventive non-meat diner with an earthy atmosphere and friendly service. Open after 11pm for drinks only. Closed Sun lunch. Moderate.

New Town and Stockbridge

With everything from Japanese and North African to organic Scottish food, the **New Town** and its satellites **Stockbridge** and **Broughton** have a number of very good places to eat, with prices often cheaper than in the Old Town.

Cafés and diners

Bell's Diner, 7 St Stephen St, Stockbridge (☎0131/225 8116). Unpretentious little diner tucked away in Stockbridge. Good, inexpensive burgers, plus a wide choice of steaks and pancakes. Open daily until 11pm. Moderate.

Cyberia, 88 Hanover St, New Town (☎0131/220 4403). Bright Internet café with fifteen computers (£2.50 per 30min; *manager@cybersurf.co.uk*), and a wide range of snacks. Inexpensive.

The Gallery Café, Scottish National Gallery of Modern Art, Belford Road, Dean (☎0131/332 8600). Far more than a standard refreshment stop for gallery visitors, with its cultured setting and strong menu attracting reassuring numbers of locals. Serves salads, filled croisants, light meals, coffee and cakes. Open Mon–Sat 10am–4.30pm, Sun 2–4.30pm. Moderate.

Glass & Thompson, 2 Dundas St, New Town (☎0131/557 0909). An unusually airy deli with huge bowls of olives and an extensive cheese counter; scattered tables and chairs mean you can linger over a made-to-order sandwich, an irresistible cake and coffee. Closed evenings. Inexpensive.

Laigh Bake House, 117a Hanover St, New Town (☎0131/225 1552). Long-established, homely New Town café with a flagstone floor and cast-iron stoves. Good salads and soups, but best known for its wonderful home-baked scones and cakes. Closed evenings and all day Sun. Inexpensive.

L'Alba d'Oro, 5 Henderson Row, Canonmills (☎0131/557 2580). Italian voices throng the air in this classic takeaway, with fish and chips served on one side and pizzas, filled Italian rolls and ready-made pasta dishes on the other. Open till midnight. Inexpensive.

Lost Sock Diner, 11 East London St, Broughton (☎0131/557 6097). Fill up on burgers, wraps and blackboard specials, all at surprising low prices, while your dirty clothes take a spin in the adjacent laundrette. Try the parsnip chips. Open till 10pm Tues–Sat. Inexpensive.

Starbucks Coffee, Waterstone's, 128 Princes St, New Town (☎0131/226 3610). The bookstore/coffee shop idea isn't that original these days, but this one is made memorable by excellent coffee and the fantastic views across Princes Street Gardens to the Castle. Inexpensive.

Terrace Café, Royal Botanic Garden, Inverleith (☎0131/552 0616). Superior spot with outside tables offering stunning views of the city skyline, though the food is not that exciting. Their changing menu includes hot dishes, sandwiches and cakes. Inexpensive.

Valvona and Crolla, 19 Elm Row, Leith Walk (☎556 0616). Café at the back of this exquisite Italian deli, serving authentic and delicious breakfasts, lunches and snacks. The best advert for the café is the walk through the shop – which has food stacked from floor to ceiling, with display cabinets full of sublime olives, meats and cheeses. Open Mon–Sat 8am–5pm. Moderate.

Chinese

Bamboo Garden, 57a Frederick St, New Town (☎0131/225 2382). Many of Edinburgh's Chinese inhabitants gather in this inexpensive place for great *dim sum* on Sunday lunchtime. Get the waiter to explain the choices rather than rely on the limited English-language menu. Moderate.

Loon Fung. 2 Warriston Place, Canonmills (☎0131/556 1781). Something of a trailblazer for Cantonese cuisine in Scotland, near the eastern entrance to the Botanic Garden. Moderate.

French

Café St Honoré, 3–4 Thistle St Lane, New Town (☎0131/226 2211). New Town brasserie serving good, traditional French food, with fabulous pastries and coffee. Closed Sun. Expensive.

La Cuisine d'Odile, French Institute, 13 Randolph Crescent, West End (☎0131/225 5685). Genuine French home cooking in a West End basement. Lunch only (noon–2pm). Closed Sun, Mon & July. Inexpensive.

La P'tite Folie, 61 Frederick St, New Town (☎0131/225 7983). Another by-product of the Pierre Victoire school of reliable French cuisine in an uncomplicated, lively setting. Set lunches (£6) and an à la carte evening menu. Moderate.

Indian

Indian Cavalry Club, 3 Atholl Place, West End (☎0131/228 3282). Upmarket but moderately priced West End Indian restaurant with a pseudo-Raj decor and mildly spiced food. Five-course evening banquets for around £17. Moderate.

Lancers, 5 Hamilton Place, Stockbridge (☎0131/332 3444). Aficionados rate the primarily Bengali and Punjabi curries at this moderately priced restaurant as the best in Scotland. Moderate.

Italian

Cosmo, 58a N Castle St, New Town (☎0131/226 6743). Straightforward, delicious Italian cuisine in a long-established trattoria. Main courses start at around £10. Closed Sun. Expensive.

Est Est Est, 135 George St, New Town (☎0131/225 2555). Pale wood, clever lighting and high ceilings give this popular modern Italian an irresistibly stylish feel. The big menu offers old favourites with all the designer touches, from squid ink to flakes of parmesan. Open daily till 1am. Moderate.

Giuliano's, 18–19 Union Place, Broughton (☎0131/554 5272). Raucous trattoria across from the Playhouse, much favoured for family and office nights out. Does its best to conjure up the full Italian atmosphere. Closes midnight. Moderate.

Pizza Express, 1 Deanhaugh St, Stockbridge (☎0131/332 7229). The chain with the winning formula for smart interiors and decent pizzas combines with a terrific location in a clocktower building overlooking the Water of Leith. Open till midnight. Inexpensive–moderate.

Japanese

Tampopo, 25a Thistle St, New Town (☎0131/220 5254). Budget noodle bar offering filling meals from around £5. Open Mon–Sat noon–2.30pm & 6–9pm. Inexpensive.

Mexican

Blue Parrot Cantina, 49 St Stephen's St, Stockbridge (☎0131/225 2941). Cosy Stockbridge basement restaurant, with a small, frequently changing menu which dares to deviate from the Mexican clichés. Moderate.

Tex Mex, 47 Hanover St, New Town (☎0131/225 1796). Authentic, reasonably priced Mexican *burritos* and steaks; if you're in between 4 and 7pm ask for the good value (£12.50) three-course pre-theatre menu. Moderate.

North African

Marrakech, 30 London St, Broughton (☎0131/556 4444). Scotland's only Moroccan restaurant and very reasonably priced, dishing up superb, authentic couscous, and *tajine*, plus a range of soups, fresh bread and pastries. Unlicensed, but you can take your own bottle and there's no corkage charge. Moderate.

Scottish

Duck's at Le Marché Noir, 2–4 Eyre Place, just off Dundas Street, Canonmills (☎0131/558 1608). Adventurous Scottish menu, featuring such delicacies as haggis in filo pastry. Half the restaurant is non-smoking. Closed lunchtime Sat & Sun. Expensive.

Martin's, 70 Rose St North Lane, New Town (☎0131/225 3106). The emphasis is on organic, unfarmed ingredients – salmon, venison, unpasteurized cheeses – in this long-standing restaurant hidden in an unlikely looking backstreet. It's at its priciest in the evenings, but well worth the money. Closed Sun & Mon. Expensive.

Stac Polly, 29–33 Dublin St, New Town (☎0131/556 2231). Very much a carnivore's eating place, with good game, fish and meat dishes. Closed lunchtimes Sat & Sun. Expensive.

36, 36 Great King St, New Town (☎0131/556 3636). The decor may be minimalist but the top-quality Scottish food is given lavish attention. Meat dishes dominate, surrounded by sculpted vegetables and superb sauces. Very expensive.

Seafood

Café Royal Oyster Bar, 17a W Register St, New Town (☎0131/556 4124). Splendidly ornate Victorian interior featured in *Chariots of Fire* – look out for the stained-glass windows showing sportsmen. Classic seafood dishes, including freshly caught oysters, served in a civilized, chatty atmosphere. Very expensive.

Mussel Inn, 61–65 Rose St, New Town (☎0131/225 5979). The tightly packed tables remind you that there's a double entendre in the name, but after feasting on a kilo of mussels and a basket of chips for under £10 you'll realise why there's a demand to get in. Owned by two west-coast shellfish farmers, which ensures that the time from sea to stomach is minimal. Closed Sun. Moderate.

Spanish

The Tapas Tree, 1 Forth St, Broughton (☎0131/556 7118). Authentic, lively and extremely friendly tapas bar, featuring Spanish guitar music on Wednesday evenings and flamenco on Thursday evenings. Moderate.

Thai

Siam Erewan, 48 Howe St, New Town (☎0131/226 3675). Excellent Thai restaurant, serving a three-course lunch for £6.95 and evening banquets from £15.95 per person upwards. Closed Sun. Moderate.

Vegetarian

Henderson's Salad Table, 94 Hanover St, New Town (☎0131/225 2131). Self-service vegetarian basement restaurant, recently attractively renovated, with freshly prepared hot dishes, plus a great choice of salads, soups, sweets and cheeses. An Edinburgh institution, so arrive early for lunch or be prepared to queue. Light jazz every evening. Open Mon–Sat 8am–10.30pm. Inexpensive. *Henderson's Bistro*, next door at 25 Thistle St (☎0131/225 2605) offers equally delicious, moderately priced bistro-style meals, is only open during the day, and Thurs–Sat evenings.

Southside

The **Southside** has plenty of well-priced restaurants aimed at the local student population, as well as some of the city's most unusual international eateries.

Cafés and diners

Brattisani's, 85–87 Newington Rd, Newington (☎0131/667 5808). The capital's oldest Italo-Scottish chippy, with choice of sit-down or carry-out meals. Daily 9.30am–midnight. Inexpensive.

Buffalo Grill, 14 Chapel St, Newington (☎0131/667 7427). Chargrilled steaks are the speciality in this popular and busy diner facing the main University campus. Moderate.

Café Q, 87 Clerk St, Newington (☎0131/668 3456). In the Queen's Hall, a respected music and arts venue, this café serves well-prepared salads, vegetarian dishes, soups and puddings as well as some decent wines and beers. Open Mon–Sat 9.30am–5pm. Inexpensive.

Kaffe Politik, 146–148 Marchmont Rd, Marchmont (☎0131/446 9837). Café culture hits the student fiefdom of deepest Marchmont, in a relaxed and stylish venue serving coffees and substantial snacks. Open till 10pm. Inexpensive.

Mango & Stone, 165a Bruntsfield Place, Bruntsfield (☎0131/229 2987). A juice bar serving colourful and wickedly healthy freshly squeezed fruit cocktails. Also has sandwiches and coffee. Closed evenings. Inexpensive.

Maxies, 32 W Nicolson St (☎0131/667 0845). Large basement brasserie and wine bar with regular live music and some good vegetarian offerings. Popular with students and University staff. Closed Sun. Moderate.

Metropole, 33 Newington Rd, Newington (☎0131/668 4999). Non-smoking Art Deco café with a good selection of coffees and excellent cakes. Open 9am–10pm. Inexpensive.

Nicolson's, 6a Nicolson St (☎0131/557 4567). Spacious, unpretentious first-floor restaurant opposite the Festival Theatre. Expensive. By day caffeine cures and snacks can be had at the downstairs *Black Medicine* café.

Parrots, 3 Viewforth, Bruntsfield (☎0131/229 3252). Rather heavy velvety decor and a bizarre parrot theme, but it's a great place for friendly service and a satisfying, old-fashioned feed based on stews, curries and stodgy puddings. An antidote to the chargrilled goats cheese and rocket brigade. No smoking. Closed Sun & Mon. Inexpensive–moderate.

Chinese

Chinese Home Cooking, 34 West Preston St (☎0131/668 4946). Very reasonably priced BYOB café: three-course lunch for £4.50, with daily chef's specials in the evening. Inexpensive.

Szechuan House, 12 Leamington Terrace (☎0131/229 4655). Unassuming setting in a Bruntsfield hotel, but a real find for lovers of genuine spicy Chinese food. BYOB. Closed Mon. Moderate.

French

La Bonne Mer, 113 Buccleuch St (☎0131/662 9111). Easy going BYOB bistro serving seafood and other Gallic favourites for reasonable prices. Moderate.

La Bonne Vie, 49 Causewayside, Newington (☎0131/667 1110). Very popular French restaurant serving a £15 set dinner. Moderate.

Indian

Ann Purna, 45 St Patrick Square (☎0131/662 1807). Excellent-value restaurant serving authentic Gujarati and southern Indian cuisine (so mainly vegetarian) – try the three-course lunch for £4.95. Moderate.

Kalpna, 2 St Patrick Square (☎0131/667 9890). Outstanding vegetarian restaurant serving authentic Gujarati dishes. Offers a good-value eat-as-much-as-you-like lunchtime buffet for £5, and a gourmet buffet on Wednesday evenings for £8.95. Closed Sun. Moderate.

Khushi's, 16 Drummond St (☎0131/556 8996). More a café than a restaurant, with only the basic comforts, but the food is reliable and cheap. Bring your own drink. Closed Sun. Inexpensive.

King's Balti, 79 Buccleuch St (☎0131/662 9212). Edinburgh's best balti establishment is very popular with students and features an evening banquet for £25.95. You can bring your own bottle, but 50p corkage per person is charged. Moderate.

Suruchi, 14a Nicolson St (☎0131/556 6583). Popular establishment serving genuine south Indian dishes – the menu is written in bizarre but entertaining broad Scots. The emphasis is on rice and vegetables, with a few splendid poultry dishes. The set lunches go for £3.50–6.50. Moderate.

North African

Phenecia, 55–57 W Nicolson St (☎0131/662 4493). A basic joint beside the main University campus, serving mostly Tunisian food but drawing on a variety of Mediterranean cuisines; the three-course lunch for £4.40 is very good value. Moderate.

Scottish

Howies, 75 St Leonard's St (☎0131/668 2917); 208 Bruntsfield Place, Bruntsfield (☎0131/221 1777). Dependable brasserie-style Scottish cooking with some interesting combinations. No alcohol served, but you can bring your own bottle. Moderate.

Kelly's, 46b W Richmond St (☎0131/668 3847). Enjoys virtual cult status among Edinburgh foodies, serving modern Scottish food and scrumptious desserts. Closed Mon lunch & Sun. Expensive.

Sweet Melinda's, 11 Rosneath St, Marchmont (☎0131/229 7953). Highly regarded, friendly restaurant serving seafood and Scottish fare. On Tuesday nights the deal is that you pay only what you think the food is worth. Closed Sun & Mon. Moderate.

Vegetarian

Engine Shed, 19 St Leonard's Lane (☎0131/662 0040) Spacious, friendly vegetarian restaurant with a bakery on the premises. Lunchtime only. Inexpensive.

Susie's Diner, 51 W Nicolson St (☎0131/667 8729). Popular café serving inventive soups, savouries and puddings, and a range of vegan food, to crowds of students. Inexpensive.

Leith and Newhaven

The most fashionable place to eat in the city, **Leith** is packed with high-quality restaurants and waterfront brasseries, and is particularly good for seafood.

Brasseries and cafés

Bar Sirius, 10 Dock Place (☎0131/555 3344). Seriously cool bar named after a locally built ship in the heart of Leith. All muted colours and low tables. Pasta and salad snacks, and Thai stir-fry or chicken couscous for something more substantial. Open Mon–Wed & Sun 11.30am–1am, Thurs–Sat 11.30am–2am. Moderate.

Daniel's, 88 Commercial St (☎0131/553 5933). Top-grade bistro in an attractive setting on the ground floor of a converted warehouse in Leith. Food is from the Alsace region of France; the *tarte flambée*, one of the specialist dishes, is a sort of pizza with a French name and German ingredients. Moderate.

Malmaison Café Bar, 1 Tower Place (☎0131/468 5001). Successful attempt to create the feel of a French café, serving excellent steak and chips and great fish dishes, plus incredibly rich mashed potato. Expensive.

Ship on the Shore, 24–26 The Shore (☎0131/555 0409). The homeliest and least expensive of the waterfront brasseries, serving good fresh fish and with a changing range of cask ales. Moderate.

The Shore, 3 The Shore (☎0131/553 5080). Non–smoking bar/restaurant with good fish dishes and decent wines. Great views at sunset, and live jazz and folk in the adjoining bar. Moderate.

Skippers, 1a Dock Place (☎0131/554 1018). Across the Water of Leith from *The Shore*, with a vaguely nautical atmosphere and a superb – if expensive – fish-oriented menu that changes according to what's fresh. Closed Sun. Expensive.

Waterfront Wine Bar, 1c Dock Place (☎0131/554 7427). Housed in the former lock-keeper's cottage with outdoor seating overlooking the waterfront, this popular wine bar/restaurant serves up fish dishes and good wines. Moderate.

Chinese

Joanna's Cuisine, 42 Dalmeny St (☎0131/554 5833). Homely little place, on a side street leading east off the middle of Leith Walk. The menu includes wonderful Pekinese specialities, notably delicious duck. Moderate.

French

Restaurant Martin Wishart, 52 The Shore (☎0131/553 3557). Scotland's latest "it-chef" wows the gourmets with French-influenced Scottish food right by the Water of Leith. Closed Sun & Mon. Expensive.

The Vintner's Rooms, 87 Giles St (☎0131/554 6767). Splendid restaurant in a seventeenth-century warehouse, which is well worth the high prices. The bar in the cellar has a sombre, candlelit ambience and a coal fire; the ornate Rococo dining room serves expertly prepared food, using ingredients of the highest quality and is especially strong on fish and Gallic dishes. Closed Sun. Very expensive.

Indian

Raj, 89–91a Henderson St (☎0131/553 3980). An excellent ethnic alternative to the waterfront brasseries, serving Bangladeshi and north Indian dishes, but few vegetarian choices. Moderate.

Italian

Tinelli, 139 Easter Rd (☎0131/652 1932). Long-standing, very popular restaurant in an unlikely part of town, reputed to be Edinburgh's best Italian. Specializes in northern Italian food – try the spinach and pumpkin-stuffed pasta. Closed Sun. Moderate.

Umberto's, 2 Bonnington Road Lane, Bonnington (☎0131/554 1314). The best place in Edinburgh for anyone with children. Play areas, sympathetic staff and the food's good as well. Moderate.

Japanese

Daruma-Ya, 82 Commercial St (☎0131/554 7660). A smart, stylish interior, with the best sushi and sashimi in Edinburgh. Closed Sun. Moderate–expensive.

Scottish

(Fitz)henry, 19 Shore Place (☎0131/555 6625). Individual and stylish contemporary brasserie which has already won a Michelin Red M. Expect the unexpected, with pig's head, sweetmeats and innovative vegetarian dishes competing for attention on the menu. Closed Sun. Expensive.

Seafood

Harry Ramsden's, 5 Newhaven Place (☎0131/551 5566). Just west of Leith in Newhaven, this branch of the Yorkshire chain offers substantial portions of fish and chips in an attractive harbourside setting. Inexpensive.

Marinette, 52 Coburg St (☎0131/555 0922). A slightly insalubrious location only serves to give this well-regarded seafood restaurant even more of a Leith feel. French flair, an informal ambience and great food. Closed Sun & Mon. Expensive.

Swiss

Denzlers, 121 Constitution St (☎0131/554 3268). A genuine Central European eating experience, big on meat and melted cheese, but a high standard is maintained and the surroundings are attractive, with decent comtemporary paintings adorning the walls. Three-course set menu in the evenings for under £15. Closed Sun & Mon. Moderate.

Pubs and bars

Many of Edinburgh's **pubs**, especially in the Old Town, have histories that stretch back centuries, while others, particularly in the New Town, are unaltered Victorian or Edwardian period pieces that rank among Edinburgh's outstanding examples of interior design. Add in the plentiful supply of trendy modern bars, and there's a variety of styles and atmospheres to cater for all tastes. The standard licensing hours are 11am–11pm (12.30–11pm on Sundays), but many honest howffs stay open later and, during the Festival especially, it's no problem to find bars open till at least 1am.

Currently, Edinburgh has three **breweries**, including the giant Scottish and Newcastle (who produce McEwan's and Younger's). The small independent Caledonian Brewery uses old techniques and equipment to produce some of the best beers in Britain, and there's also the tiny Rose Street Brewery, which has its own pub. The Caledonian Brewery, Slateford Road (☎0131/337 1286) runs tours at 11.30am and 2.30pm (Mon–Fri), though it's best to phone ahead before you visit.

Once upon a time Edinburgh's main drinking strip was the near-legendary **Rose Street**, a pedestrianized lane tucked between Princes and George streets, and the ultimate Edinburgh pub crawl was to drink a half-pint in each of its dozen or so establishments – plus the two in West Register Street, its eastern continuation. Things are a bit more sophisticated these days, with **George Street** itself taking a lead: various former financial institutions have been converted into bars, with a predictable invasion of suits by day and style by night. Most of the **student pubs** are in and around Grassmarket, with a further batch on the Southside, an area overlooked by most tourists. **Leith** has a nicely varied crop of bars, ranging from the rough spit-and-sawdust places to polished pseudo-Victoriana, while two of the city's best and most characterful pubs are further west along the seafront in **Newhaven**.

A fun way to explore Edinburgh's pubs is to take the **McEwan's 80 Shilling Edinburgh Literary Pub Tour**, a pub crawl with culture around Old and New Town watering holes. Led by professional actors, the tour introduces you to the scenes, characters and words of the major figures of Scottish literature, including Burns, Scott and MacDiarmid. The tour starts from the *Beehive Inn*, 18–20 Grassmarket (March–May & Oct Thurs–Sun 7.30pm; June & Sept daily 6pm & 8.30pm; July & Aug daily 2pm, 6pm & 8.30pm; Nov–Feb Fri 7.30pm; £7).

The Old Town and Tollcross

Bannermans, 212 Cowgate. The best pub in the street, formerly a vintner's cellar, with a labyrinthine interior and good beer on tap. On weekdays, tasty veggie lunches are on offer at rock-bottom prices; breakfasts are served at weekends 11am–4pm. Open daily till 1am.

Bar Kohl, 54 George IV Bridge. Trendy vodka bar with a choice of more than two hundred ways to give yourself a fearsome hangover. Open Mon–Sat till 1am. Closed Sun.

Bennets Bar, 8 Leven St, Tollcross. Edwardian pub with mahogany-set mirrors and Art Nouveau stained glass; gets packed in the evening, particularly when there's a show at the King's Theatre next door. Mon–Sat serves lunch and opens till midnight.

Blue Blazer, 2 Spittal St. Traditional Edinburgh howff with oak-clad bar and church pews; serves a good selection of ales. Open till midnight Wed & Thurs, 1am Fri & Sat.

Bow Bar, 80 West Bow. Old wood-panelled bar that won an award as the best drinkers' pub in Britain a few years back. Choose from among nearly 150 whiskies, an almost equally wide range of other spirits, and a changing selection of first-rate Scottish and English cask beers. Closed Sun afternoons.

City Café, 19 Blair St (☎0131/220 0125). Longstanding but determinedly trendy bar on the street linking the Royal Mile to the clubbers' hub along the Cowgate. Serves candies behind the American-style bar.

Doric Tavern, 15 Market St. Long-established upstairs wine bar (open till 1am) is a favoured watering hole of journalists and artists. The downstairs *McGuffie's Tavern* is a traditional Edinburgh howff, while the brasserie beside the wine bar serves reliable good quality Scottish food.

EH1, 197 High St (☎0131/220 5277). Wrought iron and cool aqua colours dominate in this contemporary Royal Mile bar, popular with a pre-club set. Serves up good food throughout the day, plus pitchers of vividly coloured cocktails. Open till 1am.

Fiddlers Arms, 9–11 Grassmarket. Traditional bar serving excellent McEwan's 80 Shilling. The walls are adorned with forlorn, stringless violins, though you can hear fiddlers playing on Monday nights. Open Mon–Thurs till 11.30pm, Fri & Sat 1am.

Greyfriars Bobby, 34 Candlemaker Row. Long-established favourite with both students and tourists, named after the statue outside. Open till 1am.

Hebrides Bar, 17 Market St. Home from home for Edinburgh's Highland community; there's a ceilidh atmosphere with lots of jigs, strathspeys and reels, but no tartan kitsch.

International Bar, 15 Brougham Place. Good Tollcross pub offers toasted sandwiches to go with your pint and footie on the telly. Open till 1am.

Jolly Judge, 7a James Court. Atmospheric, low-ceilinged bar in a close just down from the Castle. Cosy in winter and pleasant outside in summer.

Last Drop, 74–78 Grassmarket. The "Drop" refers to the Edinburgh gallows, which were located in front, and whose former presence is symbolized in the red paintwork of the exterior. Cheapish pub food, and, like its competitors in the same block, patronized mainly by students. Open till 1am.

Malt Shovel, 11–15 Cockburn St. Dimly lit, comfortable bar with an excellent range of cask beers and single malt whiskies, and serving big portions of chilli and haddock and chips at lunchtime. Open Sun–Thurs 11am–12.30am, Fri & Sat 11am–1am.

Sandy Bell's, 25 Forrest Rd. A folk music institution, hosting regular impromptu sessions, as well as the city's favourite chess-playing pub. Small but busy with an impressive selection of beers and whiskies. Open until 12.30am Mon–Sat.

Traverse Bar Café, Traverse Theatre, 10 Cambridge St. Spacious modern bar with a lively, sophisticated crowd which dispels any notion of a quiet interval drink. Good food available in the bar and also at *blue* upstairs.

New Town and Stockbridge

Abbotsford, 3 Rose St. Large-scale pub whose original Victorian decor, complete with wood panelling and "island bar", is among the finest in the city. Good range of ales, including a house ale brewed by Broughton. The restaurant upstairs serves hearty Scottish food. Closed Sun.

Baillie Bar, 2 St Stephen St, Stockbridge. Traditional basement bar at the corner of Edinburgh's most self-consciously Bohemian street. English and Scottish ales are available, including some from the Caledonian Brewery. Open Mon–Thurs till midnight; Fri & Sat till 1am; Sun till 11pm.

The Basement, 10a Broughton St, Broughton. Packed out, especially at the weekends, with a preclub crowd, this trendy bar is run by young and enthusiastic staff and serves cheap Mexican food till 10pm every day. Open till 1am.

Bert's Bar, 29 William St, West End and 2–4 Raeburn Place, Stockbridge. The former fills up with the office lunchtime crowd, the latter at night with Stockbridge yuppies. Both have excellent beer, good food and strive to be authentic, non-theme-oriented pubs, though the telly rarely misses any sporting action.

Café Royal Circle Bar, 17 W Register St. The pub part of this stylish Victorian restaurant, and worth a visit just for its decor, notably the huge elliptical "island" counter and the tiled portraits of renowned inventors. Thurs open until midnight, Fri & Sat till 1am. Upstairs, the *Café Royal Bistro Bar* is an unlovely rugby-themed affair.

Cumberland Bar, 1 Cumberland St. Mellow and highly regarded New Town bar with no jukebox, no TV and a wide variety of ales. There's a garden in the summer and good, reasonably priced food is served from noon to 2pm.

The Dome Bar and Grill, 14 George St. Opulent conversion of a massive New Town bank, thronging with minor local celebrities. Probably the most impressive bar interior in Edinburgh, though the ultra-chic atmosphere can be a bit intense. Sun–Thurs open till 11.30pm, Fri & Sat till 1am.

Guildford Arms, 1–5 W Register St. Excellent selection of ales, reasonable food and a mixed clientele in this splendidly Baroque bar just off Princes Street.

Indigo Yard, 7 Charlotte Lane, West End. Designer chic hits Edinburgh's West End: great for those who want Thai fish cakes with their draught beer. Daily till 1am.

Kay's Bar, 39 Jamaica St. Small, civilized one-time wine shop, warmed by a roaring log fire in winter, and serving fine cask ales. Mon–Thurs till midnight, Fri & Sat till 1am.

Kenilworth, 152–154 Rose St. Attractive high-ceilinged pub dating from 1899, with good beer and food. There's a family room at the back, with a special children's menu. Open till 1am Fri & Sat.

Mathers, 25 Broughton St, Broughton. Relaxed, old-fashioned pub which attracts a mixed crowd and gets noisy during big TV sporting occasions. Open till midnight Mon–Thurs, and 12.30am Fri & Sat.

Milne's Bar, 35 Hanover St. Cellar bar once beloved of Edinburgh's literati, earning the nickname "The Poets' Pub" courtesy of Hugh MacDiarmid et al. Serves a good range of cask beers, including McEwan's 80 Shilling.

Oxford Bar, 8 Young St. Traditional city bar, unpretentious and somewhat of a shrine for rugby fans and off-duty policemen. Good Scottish pub food is available: try the Forfar bridies (similar to Cornish pasties) and mutton pies. Open until 1am.

Po-Na-Na, 43b Frederick St. Trendy and very popular "souk" bar, offering simple snacks. On Thurs (£2) and Fri & Sat (£3), admission is charged after 11pm. Open daily 8pm–3am.

Rose Street Brewery, 55 Rose St. Edinburgh's only micro-brewery, whose equipment can be inspected in the upstairs restaurant; the two beers made there are also on tap in the ground-floor bar.

The Standing Order, 62–66 George St. A former bank which has had the chain makeover, but the vast central hall is worth a peek, and you can nestle into a comfy chair in the library. Real ales and good-value meals available. Open till 1am.

The Southside

Peartree House, 36 W Nicolson St. Fine bar in an eighteenth-century house with a courtyard, one of Edinburgh's very few beer gardens; serves decent bar lunches. Open Mon–Wed & Sun until midnight, Thurs–Sat until 1am.

Southsider, 3–5 W Richmond St. Genuine local pub with a superb range of draught and imported bottled beers. Open till midnight Mon–Thurs, 1am Fri & Sat.

Stewart's, 14 Drummond St. A Southside institution since the beginning of the century, and seemingly little changed since then; popular with lecturers and students. Open till midnight Mon–Sat.

Leith

Carriers Quarters, 42 Bernard St, Leith. Intimate pub that dates back to 1775, and is still preserved in its original state with a blazing log fire. Specializes in high-quality cask beers.

Kings Wark, 36 The Shore, Leith. Real ale and good food in a restored eighteenth-century pub.

Malt and Hops, 45 The Shore, Leith. Real-ale pub offering basic bar snacks. Open till 1am Fri & Sat.

Starbank Inn, 64 Laverockbank Rd, Newhaven. Fine old stone-built pub overlooking the Forth with a high reputation for cask ales and bar food. Open till midnight Thurs–Sat.

Ye Olde Peacock Inn, Lindsay Road, Newhaven (☎0131/552 8707). Serves cheap, homely food, including the best fish and chips in the city. Advance reservations are advisable for the main bar and restaurant; otherwise try for a table in the small lounge. Don't miss the gallery displaying prints of the pioneering Hill and Adamson calotypes of Newhaven fishwives.

Elsewhere in the city

Athletic Arms (The Diggers), 1 Angle Park Terrace, Polwarth. Out in the western suburbs, near Tynecastle football ground and Murrayfield rugby stadium; the pub's nickname comes from the cemetery nearby. For decades it has had the reputation of being Edinburgh's best pub for serious ale drinkers. Open Mon–Sat till midnight; Sun till 6pm.

Caley Sample Room, 58 Angle Park Terrace, Polwarth. Showpiece pub for the cask ales of the nearby Caledonian Brewery. Open Mon–Thurs & Sun till midnight, Fri & Sat till 1am.

Canny Man's (Volunteer Arms), 237 Morningside Rd, Morningside. Atmospheric and idiosyncratic pub/museum adorned with anything that can be hung on the walls or from the ceiling. Mon–Sat open until midnight.

Hawes Inn, Newhalls Road, S Queensferry. Famous old whitewashed tavern virtually under the Forth Rail Bridge, immortalized by Stevenson in *Kidnapped*. The bar serves a wide range of food and drink and the rambling complex also includes a hotel and restaurant (☎0131/319 1120).

Sheep Heid Inn, 43 The Causeway, Duddingston. This eighteenth-century inn with a family atmosphere makes an ideal refreshment stop at the end of a tramp through Holyrood Park. Decent home-cooked meals are available at the bar, and more substantial fare in the upstairs restaurant, while the old-fashioned skittle alley is always popular with students.

Nightlife and entertainment

Inevitably, Edinburgh's **nightlife** is at its best during the Festival (see p.120), which can make the other 49 weeks of the year seem like an anticlimax. However, at any time the city has a lot to offer, especially in the realm of **performing arts** and **concerts**.

The **nightclub** scene is lively, with some excellent venues hosting a changing selection of one-nighters. In the bigger venues, you may find different clubs taking place on each floor. Most of the city-centre clubs stay open till around 3am. While you can normally hear **live jazz**, **folk** and **rock** every evening in one or other of the city's pubs, for the really big rock events, ad hoc venues – such as the Castle Esplanade, Murrayfield Stadium or the exhibition halls of the Royal Highland Show at Ingliston, which hosts occasional **raves** – are often pressed into service.

With an estimated homosexual population of around 15,000–20,000, Edinburgh has a dynamic **gay** culture, for years centred round the top of Leith Walk and Broughton Street, where the first gay and lesbian centre appeared in the 1970s. Since the start of the 1990s, more and more gay enterprises, especially cafés and nightclubs, have moved into this area, now dubbed the "Pink Triangle", and there is a constant stream of new places and old ones changing name.

The best way to find out **what's on** is to pick up a copy of *The List*, a fortnightly listings magazine covering both Edinburgh and Glasgow (£1.95). Alternatively, get hold of the *Edinburgh Evening News*, which appears daily except Sunday: its listings column gives details of performances in the city that day, hotels and bars included. Information on nightclubs can be found on posters and piles of leaflets distributed to most of the pre-club bars around town. Box offices of individual halls and theatres are likewise liberally supplied with promotional leaflets about forthcoming music and theatre, and some are able to sell tickets for more than one venue.

Nightclubs

The Bongo Club, 14 New St (☎0131/556 5204). Great venue above a car park near Waverley Station, attracting some of the most interesting DJs around. Look out for the mighty Messenger Sound System on Saturday nights.

Café Graffiti, Mansfield Place Church, at the foot of Broughton Street (☎0131/557 8003). Great venue in a church basement, with Latin and jazz playing at the weekend. Usually sells out very quickly, so arrive before 11.30pm.

The Cavendish, W Tollcross (☎0131/228 3252). Slightly dingy but still a packed venue for roots, ragga and reggae night on Friday; *The Mambo Club* on Saturday plays African and Latin rhythms.

Club Mercado 36–39 Market St (☎0131/226 4224). Cheesy music night on Friday starts at 5pm for the after-work crowd, while sharp clothes are required to get in to Saturday's busy thumping house nights.

Honeycomb, 36–38a Blair St (☎0131/220 4381). A great sound system plays thumping house, hip-hop and garage music Thurs–Sun. Live jazz Mon–Wed.

La Belle Angèle, 11 Hasties Close (☎0131/225 2774). A rotating selection of Latin, soul, hip-hop and jazz. Edinburgh's best drum'n'bass club on Fridays, while house rules on Saturdays. Occasionally hosts important touring bands.

Rocking Horse, Cowgate (☎0131/225 3326). Rock nights including heavy metal, Goth-rock and grunge.

The Venue, 15 Calton Rd (☎0131/557 3073). Each of the three levels hosts a variety of different one-nighters specializing in house, funk and garage. Friday nights see the long-running popular *Pure* with techno and live acts, and Saturdays alternate between 1970s disco and *Tribal Funktion* house and garage soul.

Wilkie House Cowgate (☎0131/225 2935). *Sublime*, held on alternate Fridays, is a busy techno and trance event, while *Joy*, a popular gay night, takes place monthly on Saturdays.

Gay clubs and bars

Blue Moon Café, 1 Barony St (☎0131/556 2788). Coffee, drinks and light meals available at this stylish café-bar which attracts a mixed crowd. Mon–Fri 11am–12.30am; Sat & Sun 9am–12.30am.

CC Bloom's, 23 Greenside Place (☎0131/556 9331). Big dance floor, stonking rhythms and a young, friendly crowd.

THE EDINBURGH FESTIVAL

The **Edinburgh Festival**, now the largest arts festival in the world, first took place in August 1947. Driven by a desire for reconciliation and escape from postwar austerity, the Austrian Rudolf Bing, who was administrator of the Glyndebourne opera, brought together a host of distinguished musicians from the war-ravaged countries of central Europe. The symbolic centrepiece of his vision was the emotional reunion of Bruno Walter, a Jewish refugee from Nazi tyranny, and the Vienna Philharmonic Orchestra. At the same time, eight theatrical groups, both Scottish and English, turned up in Edinburgh, uninvited, performing in an unlikely variety of local venues, thus establishing the Fringe. Today more than a million people come to the city during August and early September to see several separate festivals, each offering a bewildering variety of artists and events – everything is on show, from the word's finest orchestras to controversial body-mutilating circus acts.

The legacy of Rudolf Bing's Glyndebourne connections ensured that for many years the official **Edinburgh International Festival** was dominated by opera, but, in the 1980s, efforts were made to involve locals and provide a broader cultural mix of international theatre, dance and classical music. The International Festival now has a prominent year-round base at **The Hub** on the Royal Mile (see p.76), which has a café, performance space and a ticket centre. The **programme** is published in April by the Edinburgh International Festival Society, 21 Market St, EH1 1BW (☎0131/473 2000, *www.edinburghfestivals.co.uk*); booking begins shortly afterwards.

For many years largely the domain of student revues – notable exceptions include Joan Littlewood's distinguished Theatre Workshop, with their early 1950s production of *The Other Animal*, about life in a concentration camp, and work by the great Spanish playwright, Lorca – the **Festival Fringe** began to really take off in the 1970s and it is now far and away the largest component of what many people think of as the Edinburgh Festival. Despite the arrival of nearly 1000 acts – from national theatre groups to stand-up comedians – using around two hundred venues, the Fringe remains loyal to its original open policy and there is still no vetting of performers. This means that the shows range from the inspired to the truly diabolical and ensures a highly competitive atmosphere, in which one bad review in a prominent publication means box-office disaster. Certain venues, such as the Assembly Rooms, the Pleasance and the Gilded Balloon are reliable places to start if you're looking for a wide range of good-quality shows, though, with their corporate sponsorship, slick marketing and high luvvie quotient, many would argue that these places have simply become "official Fringe", and that you should look elsewhere for the true spirit of the event. Many unknowns rely on self-publicity, taking to the streets to perform highlights from their show, or pressing leaflets into the hands of every passer-by. Performances go on round the clock: if so inclined, you could sit through twenty shows in a day. The full programme is usually available in June from the Festival Fringe Office, 180 High St, EH1 1QS (☎0131/226 5257, *www.edfringe.com*). Postal and telephone bookings (☎0131/226 5138) can be made immediately afterwards, while during the Festival tickets can be bought from the office or at various locations around the city. Each day during the Fringe, a free daily guide is published listing everything showing that day.

Over the years in both the official Festival and the Fringe, there has been a remarkable choice of both performers and venues: both Jean-Louis Barrault (star of the 1945 movie *Les Enfants du Paradis*) and Richard Burton as Hamlet; Grace Kelly reading the works of early American poets; 65-year-old Marlene Dietrich in cabaret; *Macbeth* on Inchcolm Island in the Firth of Forth; and *2001: A Space Odyssey* performed to an audience sitting in a Hillman Avenger. The 1980s saw the anarchic circus performers Archaos, whose publicity involved sawing up cars outside the Fringe office. Although now disbanded, their spirit lives on in a number of ever more shocking shows, including recently a troupe of naked lesbian trapeze artists.

Edinburgh in August is also, of course, the place to witness the emergence of new **stars**, from actors Donald Pleasance and Penelope Keith in the 1950s, to the *Beyond the*

Fringe comedy team of Alan Bennett, Jonathan Miller, Peter Cook and Dudley Moore in 1960 and, in the 1980s and 1990s, contemporary stars such as comedians Harry Enfield, Lee Evans and the late Bill Hicks, and actress Emma Thompson.

The **Film Festival** also began at the same time as the main Festival, making it the longest-running film festival in the world. After a period in the doldrums, it has become a respected fixture on the international circuit, incorporating both mainstream and independent new releases and presenting a series of valuable retrospectives from Sam Fuller to Shohei Immamura. It also hosts interviews and discussions with film directors; in recent years visitors have included Kenneth Anger, the Coen brothers, Clint Eastwood and Steve Martin. A particular feature has been the high profile support given to Scottish film, from Bill Douglas's austere and brilliant *Childhood* trilogy, through the lighter style of Bill Forsyth, to the recent hits, *Shallow Grave* and *Mrs Brown*. Tickets and information are available from the main venue, the Filmhouse, 88 Lothian Rd, EH3 9BZ (☎0131/228 2688, *www.edfilmfest.org.uk*). The programme is usually ready by late June, when bookings start.

Meanwhile, other Festivals have emerged: the **Jazz Festival**, which has attracted the likes of Teddy Wilson and Benny Waters, takes place in the first week of August (programme available at the end of May from the office at 29 St Stephen's St, EH3 5AN; ☎0131/225 2202, *www.jazzmusic.co.uk*); and the **Book Festival**, which evolved from meet-the-author sessions to become a burgeoning and important annual jamboree held in the *douce* setting of a marquee-covered Charlotte Square. Hundreds of established authors from throughout the English-speaking world come to take part in readings, lectures, panel discussions and audience question-and-answer sessions, and there's a particularly strong programme of children's events. For further information, contact the Scottish Book Centre, 137 Dundee St, EH11 1BG (☎0131/228 5444, *www.edbookfest.co.uk*). The **Television Festival** is largely an in-house event, surfacing in the public consciousness only briefly as the keynote speaker indulges in the sport of deriding the latest changes at the BBC.

Although officially a separate event, the **Edinburgh Military Tattoo**, held in a splendid setting on the Castle Esplanade, is very much part of the Festival scene and an unashamed display of the kilt-and-bagpipes view of Scottish culture. Pipes and drums form the kernel of the programme, but performing animals, gymnastic and daredevil displays, plus at least one guest regiment from abroad, provide variety. Tickets for the Tattoo are like gold dust during August and it's best to get hold of them in advance: contact the Tattoo Office, 32 Market St, EH1 1QB (☎0131/225 1188, *www.edintattoo.co.uk*).

Although the Festival is dubbed irrelevant and inconvenient by some locals, one-third of the tickets are sold to local people and there's little doubt that it is one of the city's greatest assets, and a cornerstone in Edinburgh's claims to be one of Europe's great capital cities. Aside from providing a substantial boost to the city's economy, the Festival stages two events which regularly bring in huge crowds of townspeople: Fringe Sunday, when Holyrood Park is taken over for a vast open-air party; and the massive firework display and concert, held in Princes Street Gardens with the Castle as a backdrop, held on the final Sunday of the International Festival. And there are, of course, the annual Festival **rituals**: celebrity-spotting at the Assembly Rooms; newspaper gossip revolving around fears of imminent financial catastrophe for a major venue, if not the Festival itself; and the constant, raging debate about the strengths or otherwise of the Scottish element. Above all, though, there is a buzz to the city: the rumoured visit of a superstar, or even a soap star, the best and worst shows in towns, and the hot tips for the winners of the plethora of awards up for grabs, all become matters of supreme importance. By the Sunday following the end of the Festival, the performers have all departed, the winners to London for the various "Pick of the Fringe" seasons, and the losers back home to dream of next year. The church halls and Masonic lodges are locked up, the traders and hoteliers count their takings and the city streets are restored to respectability.

For information on other festivals in the city, see p.122.

Newtown Club Bar, 26b Dublin St (☎0131/538 7775). Men-only, with a high number of professionals. The raunchy *Intense Cellar Bar* downstairs is particularly good fun and opens Wed–Sun 9pm–late.

Nexus Café, 60 Broughton St (☎0131/478 7069). Light meals, snacks and drinks in a relaxed atmosphere at the Edinburgh Gay, Lesbian and Bisexual Centre. Open 11am–11pm.

Planet Out, 6 Baxter's Place (☎0131/556 5991). Loud and outrageous bar beside the Playhouse Theatre.

Live music pubs and venues

Canon's Gait, 232 Canongate (☎0131/556 4481). Local folk and jazz in a Royal Mile basement bar, which serves good beer.

Cas Rock, 104 W Port (☎0131/229 4341). A mixture of sedate folk and raucous punky sounds.

Cellar No.1, 1 Chambers St. Traditional cellar bar which sways to jazz, salsa or flamenco every night of the week. Open till 1am.

Kulu's Jazz Joint, 8 Morrison St, off Lothian Road (☎0131/221 1288). Edinburgh's premier jazz and hiphop venue, with live music every night and regular top performers.

La Belle Angèle, 11 Hasties Close (☎0131/225 2774). A home to both indie bands and Latin divas.

The Liquid Room, 9c Victoria St (☎0131/225 2528). Good-sized venue frequented by visiting indie and local R&B bands.

Negociants, 45–47 Lothian St (☎0131/225 6313). An upstairs brasserie serves food from 8am till 2.30am, and specializes in Belgian fruit beers. The downstairs bar hosts varied live bands and DJs and is popular with students. Open until 3am.

The Queen's Hall, 37 Clerk St (☎0131/667 2019). Housed in a former Southside church, with some pews still in place, hosting African, funk and rock bands, as well as smaller jazz, folk concerts and comedy nights with well-established comedians.

Sandy Bell's, 25 Forrest Rd (☎0131/225 2751). A friendly bar and a reliable place to find folk music every night of the week.

Tron Ceilidh House, 9 Hunter Square (☎0131/226 0931). Busy, huge complex of bars on different levels, with regular jazz and folk nights. Comedy on Friday nights.

The Venue, 15 Calton Rd (☎0131/557 3073). Small, intimate sweaty club hosting up-and-coming indie bands.

EDINBURGH'S OTHER FESTIVALS

Quite apart from the Edinburgh Festival, the city is now promoting itself as a year-round festival city, beginning with **Edinburgh's Hogmanay** (contact the tourist office ☎0131/473 3800 or the Hub ☎0131/473 2010), one of the world's largest New Year street parties, involving torchlight processions, folk and rock concerts and fireworks galore. The **Shoots and Roots** folk festival has sessions in April and November (☎0131/557 1050), drawing local and international performers, while the **Science Festival**, also in April (☎0131/530 2001), incorporates hands-on children's events as well as numerous lectures on a vast array of subjects. There is a **Puppet and Animation Festival** in March (☎0131/556 9579), and a **Children's Festival** in May (☎0131/225 8050), with readings, magicians and so on. In the summer, a series of concerts (usually free), ranging from tea dances to world music, is held in the **Ross Bandstand** in Princes Street Gardens. The Caledonian Brewery, 42 Slateford Rd, runs its own German-style **beer festival** in early June.

The **Doors Open Day**, around late September, is an opportunity to visit a number of noteworthy buildings, otherwise closed to the public. In recent years, these have included private homes in the New Town, the High Court and the Central Mosque. Contact the **Cockburn Association** (☎0131/557 8686) for details. The **Filmhouse** (☎0131/228 2688) also has a number of annual seasons of international cinema, notably French (in November) and Italian (April), and a gay season (June).

The useful Web site *www.edinburghfestivals.co.uk* has links to the sites of most of Edinburgh's main festivals.

Theatre and comedy

Assembly Rooms, 54 George St (☎0131/220 4349). Varied complex of small and large halls. Used all year, but really comes into its own during the Fringe, featuring large-scale drama productions and mainstream comedy.

Bedlam Theatre, 2a Forrest Rd (☎0131/225 9893). Housed in a converted Victorian church and used predominantly by student groups.

W.J. Christie & Son, 27–31 West Port (☎0131/228 3765). Small, intense cellar bar with raw nightly comedy spots and some of the better local acts Thurs–Sun.

Festival Theatre, Nicolson Street (☎0131/529 6000). The largest stage in Britain, principally used for Scottish Opera's appearances in the capital and other major orchestral performances, but also for everything from the children's show *Singing Kettle* to Engelbert Humperdinck.

Gilded Balloon Theatre, 233 Cowgate (☎0131/226 6550). Fringe comedy venue, noted for the Late 'n' Live (1–4am) slot which gives you the chance to see top comedians whose main show elsewhere may be booked out. Also puts on regular comedy shows throughout the year.

King's Theatre, 2 Leven St (☎0131/228 5955). Stately Edwardian civic theatre that offers the most eclectic programme in the city – includes major touring theatre companies, Shakespeare, pantomime and comedy.

Netherbow Arts Centre, 43 High St (☎0131/556 9579). Small auditorium used heavily through the Festival but with an adventurous year-round programme concentrating on childrens' and Scottish theatre.

Playhouse Theatre, 18–22 Greenside Place (☎0131/557 2590). The most capacious theatre in Britain, formerly a cinema. Recently refurbished, and used largely for extended runs of popular musicals and occasional rock concerts.

Pleasance Theatre, 60 The Pleasance (☎0131/556 6550). Fringe Festival venue. Cobbled courtyard with stunning views across to Arthur's Seat, and an array of auditoria used for a varied programme.

Royal Lyceum Theatre, 30 Grindlay St (☎0131/229 9697). Fine Victorian civic theatre with compact auditorium. The city's leading year-round venue for mainstream drama.

St Bride's Centre, 10 Orwell Terrace, Dalry (☎0131/346 1405). Neo-Gothic church converted into an intimate stage that can be adapted for theatre in the round.

The Stand Comedy Club, 5 York Place (☎0131/558 7272). The city's top comedy spot, with a different act on every night and some of the UK's top comics headlining at the weekends. The bar itself is a great place to eat and drink, even if the stage is quiet.

Theatre Workshop, 34 Hamilton Place (☎0131/226 5425). Enticing programmes of international innovative theatre and performance art all year round.

Traverse Theatre, 10 Cambridge St (☎0131/228 1404). A byword in experimental theatrical circles, and unquestionably one of Britain's premier venues for new plays. Going from strength to strength in its new custom-built home beside the Usher Hall, with a great bar downstairs and the inventive *blue* café-bar upstairs.

Concert halls

Queen's Hall, 89 Clerk St (☎0131/667 2019). Converted Georgian church with a capacity of around eight hundred, though many seats have little or no view of the platform. Home base of both the Scottish Chamber Orchestra and Scottish Ensemble, and much favoured by jazz, blues and folk groups. Also hosts established comedians.

Reid Concert Hall, Bristo Square (☎0131/650 2423). Narrow, steeply pitched Victorian hall owned by the University, and hosting classical concerts.

St Cecilia's Hall, corner of Cowgate and Niddry Street (☎0131/650 2805). A Georgian treasure that is again university-owned and not used as frequently as it deserves to be.

Usher Hall, corner of Lothian Road and Grindlay Street (☎0131/228 1155). Edinburgh's main civic concert hall, seating over 2500. Excellent for choral and symphony concerts, but less suitable for solo vocalists. The upper circle seats are cheapest and have the best acoustics; avoid the back of the grand tier and the stalls, where the sound is muffled by the overhanging balconies.

Cinemas

ABC Filmcentre, 120 Lothian Road (info line ☎0131/228 1638; credit card bookings ☎0131/229 3030). Mainstream cinema.

Cameo, 38 Home St, Tollcross (info line ☎0131/228 2800; bookings ☎0131/228 4141). New arthouse and more challenging mainstream releases and cult late-nighters. Tarantino's been here and thinks its great.

Dominion, 18 Newbattle Terrace, Morningside (☎0131/447 4771). Latest releases.

Filmhouse, 88 Lothian Rd (☎0131/228 2688). Eclectic programme of independent, arthouse and classic films.

The Lumière, Royal Museum of Scotland (enter from Lothian Street; ☎0131/247 4219). Arthouse movies grouped into special themes and seasons. Open Fri–Sun only.

Odeon, 7 Clerk St (☎0131/667 0971; info and credit card bookings ☎0870/505 0007). Five-screen cinema showing the latest releases.

UCI, Kinnaird Park, Newcraighall Rd, Niddrie (☎0131/669 0777; credit card bookings ☎0990/888990). Multiplex 4.5 miles southeast of the city; use buses #14, #32 and #C3.

Shopping

Despite the relentless advance of the big chains, central Edinburgh remains an enticing place for **shopping**, with many of its streets having their own distinctive character. **Princes Street**, though dominated by standard chain outlets, retains a number of independent emporia. At the eastern end is the underground **Princes Mall**, a mall of specialist shops, while **Cockburn Street** is a hub for trendy clothes and record shops. Along the **Royal Mile** are several distinctly offbeat places among the tacky-souvenir sellers, and down **Victoria Street** and in and around the **Grassmarket** you'll find an eclectic range of antique and arts and crafts shops plus some antiquarian booksellers. The main concentration of general, academic and remainder bookshops is in the area stretching from **South Bridge** to **George IV Bridge**. For antique shops the two best areas are **St Stephen Street** in Stockbridge and **Causewayside** in Southside.

Bagpipes Bagpipe Centre, 49 Blackfriars St (☎0131/557 3090); Clan Bagpipes, 13a James Court, Lawnmarket (☎0131/225 2415).

Books Bauermeisters, 19 George IV Bridge (☎0131/226 5561), is a row of separate bookshops selling general and academic books, music, stationery and paperbacks. James Thin is located at 53–59 South Bridge (☎0131/556 6743) and 57 George St (☎0131/225 4495): the first is a huge, rambling general and academic shop, the second smaller and more genteel, with a good café. Waterstone's is at 128 Princes St (☎0131/226 2666), 13–14 Princes St (☎0131/556 3034) and 83 George St (☎0131/225 3436). There's a good selection of antiquarian bookshops in the city: Peter Bell, 68 West Port (☎0131/229 0562); Castle Books, 20 Rankeillor St (☎0131/667 5174); West Port Books, 147 West Port (☎0131/229 4431); and McNaughtan's Bookshop 3a–4a Haddington Place, Leith Walk (☎0131/556 5897). The best of the secondhand bookshops are: Broughton Books, 2a Broughton Place (☎0131/557 8010), and Second Edition, 9 Howard St (☎0131/556 9403).

Clothes (secondhand) Anna's, 2a Tarvit St (☎0131/229 9126); Wm Armstrong, 313 Cowgate (☎0131/556 5977), 81–83 Grassmarket (☎0131/220 5557), 64 Clerk St (☎0131/667 3056); Echo, 66 West Port (☎0131/229 6344); Herman Brown, 151 West Port (☎0131/228 2589); Paddy Barass, 15 Grassmarket (☎0131/226 3087); Elaine's, 55 St Stephen St; and Flip, 60–62 South Bridge (☎0131/556 4966).

Haggis Charles MacSween & Son, Dryden Rd, Bilston Glen, Loanhead (☎0131/440 2555), has an international reputation, and also makes a tasty vegetarian version; buy it from the factory or various outlets around Edinburgh, such as the Food Hall in Jenners at 48 Princes St, or Peckhams, 155–9 Bruntsfield Place.

Maps Carson Clark, 181–3 Canongate (☎0131/556 4710), sells antique maps, charts and globes.

Records Avalanche, 17 West Nicolson St (☎0131/668 2374), 28 Lady Lawson St (☎0131/228 1939) and 63 Cockburn St (☎0131/225 3939) for indie music; Coda, 12 Bank St (☎0131/622 7246) for contemporary Scottish folk and roots music; Fopp, 55 Cockburn St (☎0131/220 0133) for a wide range of CDs; Ripping Records, 91 South Bridge (☎0131/226 7010); Underground Solu'shun, 9 Cockburn St (☎0131/226 2242) for house, garage, techno and drum'n'bass vinyl; and Vinyl Villains, 5 Elm Row (☎0131/558 1170), for secondhand records, tapes and ephemera.

Tartan Celtic Craft Centre, 101 High St (☎0131/556 3228); Kinloch Anderson, on the corner of Commercial and Dock streets, Leith (☎0131/555 1390); James Pringle Woollen Mill, 70 Bangor Rd, Leith (☎0131/553 5161), which has an archive computer which tells you if you're entitled to wear a clan tartan, and gives full historic information; Geoffrey Tailor, 57–59 High St (☎0131/557 0256).

Tweed Romanes and Paterson, 62 Princes St (☎0131/225 4966).

Whisky Royal Mile Whiskies, 379–381 High St (☎0131/225 3383); William Cadenhead, 172 Canongate (☎0131/556 5864).

Woollen goods Bill Baber Knitwear, 66 Grassmarket (☎0131/225 3249), designs and makes the garments on the premises; Ragamuffin, 276 Canongate (☎0131/557 6007), for Skye knitwear; Shetland Connection, 491 Lawnmarket (☎0131/225 3525) for Shetland knitting wool, lace and cobweb.

Listings

Airlines British Airways, 32 Frederick St (☎0345/222111); British Midland, Edinburgh Airport (☎0131/344 5600); EasyJet (booking line ☎0870/600 0000); Ryanair (☎0541/569569).

American Express, 139 Princes St (Mon–Fri 9am–5.30pm, Sat 9am–4pm; ☎0131/225 9179).

Banks Bank of Scotland, The Mound (head office), 38 St Andrew Square, 103 George St; Barclays, 1 St Andrew Square; Clydesdale, 20 Hanover St; Lloyds, 113–115 George St; Midland, 76 Hanover St; NatWest, 80 George St; Royal Bank of Scotland, 36 St Andrew Square; TSB, 109 George St.

Bike rental Central Cycles, 13 Lochrin Place (☎228 6333), Scottish Cycle Safaris, 29 Blackfriars St (☎556 5560).

Car rental Arnold Clark, Lochrin Place (☎0131/228 4747); Avis, 100 Dalry Rd (☎0131/337 6363); Budget, 111 Glasgow Rd (☎0845 606 6669); Carnies, 46 Westfield Rd (☎0131/346 4155); Europcar, 24 E London St (☎0131/557 3456); Hertz, Waverley Station (☎0131/557 5272); Mitchells, 32 Torphichen St (☎0131/229 5384); Thrifty Car Rental, 24 Haymarket Terrace (☎0131/313 1613).

Consulates Australia, 37 George St (☎0131/624 3333); Canada, 30 Lothian Rd (☎0131/220 4333); Denmark, 4 Royal Terrace (☎0131/556 4263); France, 11 Randolph Crescent (☎0131/225 7954); Germany, 16 Eglington Crescent (☎0131/337 2323); Italy, 32 Melville St (☎0131/226 3631); Netherlands, 53 George St (☎0131/220 3226); Norway, 86 George St (☎0131/226 5701); Poland, 2 Kinnear Rd (☎0131/552 0301); Spain, 63 N Castle St (☎0131/220 1843); Sweden, 22 Hanover St (☎0131/220 6050); Switzerland, 66 Hanover Place (☎0131/226 5660); USA, 3 Regent Terrace (☎0131/556 8315).

Dentist The National Health Service Line ☎0800 224488 will tell you where your nearest surgery is. For emergencies go to Edinburgh Dental Institute, Lauriston Place (☎0131/556 4913) or the Western General Hospital, Crewe Rd South (☎0131/537 1338).

Exchange Thomas Cook, 28 Frederick St (Mon–Sat 9am–5.30pm; ☎0131/465 7600); currency exchange bureaus in the main tourist office (Mon–Wed 9am–5pm, Thurs–Sat 9am–6pm & Sun 10am–5pm) and beside platform 1 at Waverley Station (Sept–June Mon–Sat 7.30am–9pm, Sun 8.30am–9pm; July–Aug Mon–Sat 7am–10pm, Sun 8am–10pm). To change money after hours, try one of the upmarket hotels – but expect to pay a hefty commission charge.

Football Edinburgh has two Scottish Premier Division teams, who are at home on alternate Saturdays. Heart of Midlothian (or Hearts) play at Tynecastle Stadium, Gorgie Road, a couple of miles west of the centre; Hibernian (or Hibs) play at Easter Road Stadium, a similar distance east of the centre. Between them, the two clubs dominated Scottish football in the 1950s, but neither has won more than the odd trophy since, though one or the other periodically threatens to make a major breakthrough. Tickets from £12.

Gay and lesbian contacts Gay & Lesbian Switchboard (☎0131/556 4049); Edinburgh Gay Escorts (☎0131/558 1011).

Genealogical research Scots Ancestry Research Society, 29a Albany St (☎0131/556 4220); Scottish Genealogy Society, 15 Victoria Terrace (☎0131/220 3677); Scottish Roots, 16 Forth St (☎0131/477 8214).

Golf Edinburgh is awash with fine golf courses, but most of them are private. The best public courses are the two on the Braid Hills (☎0131/447 6666); others are Carrick Knowe (☎0131/337 1096), Craigentinny (☎0131/554 7501) and Silverknowes (☎0131/336 3843).

Hospital Royal Infirmary, 1 Lauriston Place (☎0131/536 1000), has a 24hr casualty department.

Internet cafés Cyberia, 88 Hanover St (Mon–Sat 10am–10pm, Sun noon–7pm; ☎0131/220 4403; *www.cybersurf.co.uk*); Web 13, 13 Bread St (Mon–Wed & Fri 9am–5.30pm, Thurs 9am–7pm, Sat 9am–6pm, Sun 11am–5pm; ☎0131/229 8883; *www.web13.co.uk*).

Laundry Capital Launderette, 208 Dalkeith Rd, Newington; Sundial Launderette at 7–9 East London St, Broughton; Tarvit Launderette, 7–9 Tarvit St, Tollcross.

Left luggage Lockers available at Waverley Station (Mon–Sat 7am–11pm, Sun 8am–11pm) and St Andrew Square bus station (Mon–Sat 6.35am–10pm, Sun 8am–10pm).

Libraries Central Library, George IV Bridge (Mon–Thurs 10am–8pm, Fri 10am–5pm, Sat 9am–1pm; ☎0131/225 5584). In addition to the usual departments, there's a separate Scottish section, plus an Edinburgh Room which is a mine of information on the city. The National Library of Scotland, George IV Bridge (Mon–Fri 9.30am–8.30pm, Sat 9.30am–1pm; ☎0131/226 4531), a magnificent copyright library, is for research purposes only, although accreditation is necessary to use the facilities. There is freer access to an annex which contains the Map Room, 33 Salisbury Place (Mon–Fri 9.30am–5pm, Sat 9.30am–1pm).

Lost property Edinburgh Airport (☎0131/333 1000); Edinburgh Police HQ (☎0131/311 3141); Lothian Regional Transport (☎0131/554 4492); Scotrail (☎0141/332 9811).

Motoring organizations AA, 18–22 Melville St (☎0990/989989); RAC, 35 Kinnaird Park (☎0990/722722).

Pharmacy Boots, 48 Shandwick Place (Mon–Fri 8am–9pm, Sat 8am–7pm, Sun 10am–5pm; ☎0131/225 6757) has the longest opening hours.

Police In an emergency call 999. Otherwise contact Lothian and Borders Police HQ, Fettes Ave (☎0131/311 3131); or local police station at Queen Charlotte St, Leith (☎0131/554 9350); St Leonard's St, Southside (☎0131/662 500); or Torphichen Place, West End (☎0131/229 2323).

Post office 8–10 St James Centre (Mon 9am–5.30pm, Tues–Fri 8.30am–5.30pm, Sat 8.30am–6pm; ☎0345/223344).

Rape crisis centre ☎0131/556 9437.

Rugby Scotland's international fixtures are played at Murrayfield Stadium, a couple of miles west of the city centre. Phone the stadium on ☎0131/346 5000 for advice on ticket sales, but be warned that tickets can be very hard to come by for the big games.

Sports stadium Meadowbank Sports Centre and Stadium, 139 London Rd (☎0131/661 5351), is Edinburgh's main venue for most spectator and participatory sports. Facilities include an athletics track, a velodrome and indoor halls.

Swimming pools The city has one Olympic-standard modern pool, the Royal Commonwealth Pool, 21 Dalkeith Rd (☎0131/667 7211), and a number of considerably older pools at Caledonian Crescent (☎0131/313 3964), Glenogle Road (☎0131/343 6376), 15 Bellfield St, Portobello (☎0131/669 6888), and 6 Thirlestane Rd (☎0131/447 0052).

Taxis Airport Taxis (☎0131/344 3344); Central Radio Taxis (☎0131/229 2468); City Cabs (☎0131/228 1211).

Travel agents USIT/Campus Travel (student and youth specialist), 53 Forrest Rd (☎0131/225 6111) and 5 Nicolson Square (☎0131/668 3303); Edinburgh Travel Centre (student and youth specialist), 196 Rose St (☎0131/226 2019) and 3 Bristo Square (☎0131/668 2221). For three- and six-day coach trips to the Highlands, try Haggis Backpackers, 11 Blackfriars St (☎0131/558 1177) or MacBackpackers, 105 High St (☎0131/558 9900).

travel details

Trains

Edinburgh to: Aberdeen (hourly; 2hr 40min); Aviemore (5 daily; 3hr); Birmingham (6 daily; 5hr 30min); Crewe (6 daily; 3hr 30min); Dundee (hourly; 1hr 45min); Fort William (change at Glasgow, 3 daily; 4hr 55min); Glasgow (2–4 hourly; 50min); Inverness (4 daily; 3hr 50min); London (20 daily; 4hr 30min); Manchester (4 daily, direct; 4hr: 7 daily, change at Preston; 4hr); Newcastle upon Tyne (27 daily; 1hr 30min); Oban (3 daily, change at Glasgow; 4hr 10min); Perth (6 daily; 1hr 15min); Stirling (every 30min; 45min); York (24 daily; 2hr 30min).

Buses

Edinburgh St Andrew Square bus station to: Aberdeen (22 daily; express 3hr, standard 3hr 50min); Birmingham (2 daily; 6hr 50min); Dundee (22 daily; express 1hr 25min–2hr); Fort William (2 daily direct; 5hr); Glasgow (44 daily; 1hr 10min); Inverness (13 daily; 3hr–4hr); London (6 daily; 7hr 50min); Newcastle upon Tyne (3 daily; 3hr 15min); Oban (3 daily; 5hr); Perth (21 daily; 1hr 20min); Pitlochry (13 daily; 2hr); York (1 daily; 5hr).

Flights

Edinburgh to: Birmingham (Mon–Fri 9 daily, Sat & Sun 4 daily; 1hr); London Gatwick (Mon–Fri 5 daily, Sat & Sun 3 daily; 1hr 15min); London Heathrow (Mon–Fri 20 daily, Sat & Sun 15 daily;1hr); Manchester (Mon–Fri Mon–Fri 9 daily, Sat & Sun 2 daily; 50min); Stansted (Mon–Fri 13 daily, Sat & Sun 7 daily; 1hr 10min).

CHAPTER TWO

SOUTHERN SCOTLAND

Although Southern Scotland doesn't have the high tourist profile of other areas, the bulk of visitors who whizz past on their way to Edinburgh, Glasgow or the Highlands are missing out on a region that is in many ways the very heart of the country. Its inhabitants bore the brunt of long wars with the English, its farms have fed Scotland's cities since industrialization, and two of the country's literary icons, Sir Walter Scott and Robbie Burns, lived and died here. If you make the effort to get off the main north–south highways there's plenty to see, from the ruins of medieval castles and abbeys to well-preserved market towns and rural villages set within a wild, hilly, intensely atmospheric countryside.

Geographically, Southern Scotland is dominated by the **Southern Uplands** – a chain of bulging flat-peaked hills and weather-beaten moorland punctuated by narrow glens, fast-flowing rivers and blue-black lochs – extending south and west from an imaginary line drawn between Peebles and Jedburgh in central southern Scotland over to the Ayrshire coast. It's in the west, in the **Galloway Forest Park**, that they are at their most dramatic, with peaks soaring over 2000ft, and criss-crossed by many popular **walking** trails.

North of the inhospitable Cheviot Hills, which straddle the border with England, a clutch of tiny towns in the **Tweed River Valley** – including delightful **Melrose** – form the nucleus of the Borders, inspiration for countless folkloric ballads telling of bloody battles with the English and clashes between the notorious warring families, the Border Reivers. East of **Kelso**, one of four abbeys founded on the Borders by the medieval Canmore kings, the Tweed Valley widens to form the Merse basin, an area of flat farmland that boasts a series of grand stately homes, principally **Floors Castle**, **Manderston**, **Paxton** and **Mellerstain House**. These feature the work of the Adam family – William, and two of his four sons, John and Robert, whose fine skills are also displayed at Ayr's **Culzean Castle**.

North of the Tweed, a narrow band of foothills – the **Pentland**, **Moorfoot** and **Lammermuir** ranges – forms the southern edge of the Central Lowlands. These Lowlands spread west beyond Edinburgh, but here they constitute the slender coastal plain of **East Lothian**, which rolls down towards a string of fine sandy beaches. Further east, the coastline becomes more rugged, its cliffs and rocky outcrops harbouring a series of desolate ruined castles, while inland, the flatness of the terrain is interrupted by the occasional extinct volcano.

The gritty town of **Dumfries** is the gateway to **southwest Scotland**, where on the marshy Solway coast you can visit charming **Kirkcudbright** and explore the magnificent remains of **Caerlaverock Castle**. Pastoral **Ayrshire** also rewards a visit for its strong associations with Robert Burns, especially at Ayr, the county town, and **Alloway**, the poet's birthplace, as well as for its gentle coastline and sandy beaches.

There's a **train** line along both coasts, and a good **bus** service linking all the major towns and many of the villages. It's excellent **walking** country; there are two marked treks for the ambitious hiker. The new **St Cuthbert's Way** follows a sixty-mile trail from Melrose, where St Cuthbert started his ministry, to Lindisfarne (the Holy Isle), south of the English border, where he died. The **Southern Upland Way**, a 212-mile hike, stretches from Portpatrick on the west to Cockburnspath on the east coast. You

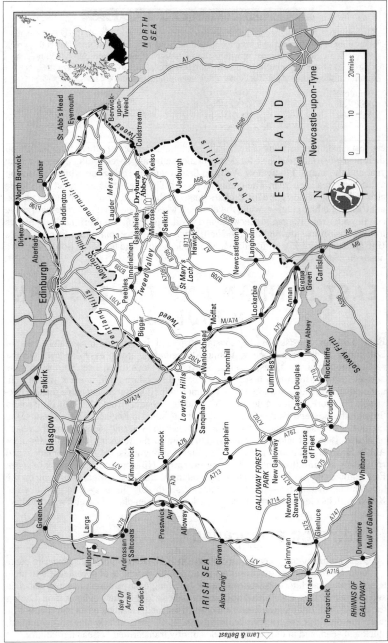

© Crown copyright

ACCOMMODATION PRICE CODES

Throughout this book, accommodation **prices** have been graded with the codes below, according to the cost of the least expensive double room in high season. Price codes are not given for campsites, most of which charge under £10 per person. Almost all hostels charge less than £10 a night for a bed – the few exceptions to this rule have the prices quoted in the text. For a full account of the accommodation price codes, see p.33.

① under £40	④ £60–70	⑦ £110–150
② £40–50	⑤ £70–90	⑧ £150–200
③ £50–60	⑥ £90–110	⑨ £200 and over

---

can just do shorter sections of both walks – all the major tourist offices have leaflets on their nearest stretch. Ask also for details of the many **ranger-led walks** throughout the year and the annual **Festival of Walking** (late August to early Sept) which focuses on a different area each year. The combination of rolling landscape and quiet backroads also makes the region good for **cyclists**: many of the forested hills have mountain-biking tracks and hire centres, while the 88-mile Tweed Cycleway runs through attractive countryside from Biggar to Berwick-on-Tweed. Meanwhile, **golfers** can buy passes from tourist offices throughout the south, such as the Freedom of the Fairways pass (£46 for three days; £70 for five days), which allows access to ten of the Border region's nineteen courses.

EAST LOTHIAN AND THE EASTERN BORDERS

East Lothian consists of the coastal strip and hinterland immediately east of Edinburgh. Its western reaches, around Musselburgh, are an easy day-trip from the capital; the remainder takes a couple of overnight stays to explore. The prosperous market town of **Haddington** serves as a base for exploring the interior, where rich, undulating farmland gives way to the Lammermuir Hills. But most people make a beeline for the shore, the fifty miles or so of coastline extending from **Aberlady** right round through the **Eastern Borders** to Berwick-upon-Tweed in England. There's something for most tastes here, from the wide sandy beaches and volcanic islets around the resort of **North Berwick** and neighbouring **Dirleton**, to the towering, jagged cliffs of **St Abb's Head**, and a number of ruined medieval strongholds, the most dramatic – and romantic – at **Tantallon**. Inland, the **Lammermuir Hills** cross the boundary between East Lothian and the Borders to form the northern edge of the Merse, centring on the unassuming market town of **Duns**. Further south still, the busy Georgian town of **Kelso**, with its elegant main square, is the key attraction of the **Lower Tweed Valley**.

Haddington and around

The East Lothian gentry keep a careful eye on **HADDINGTON**, their favourite country town. Its compact centre preserves an intriguing ensemble of seventeenth- to nineteenth-century architectural styles where everything of any interest has been labelled and plaqued. Yet the town's staid appearance belies a long history of innovation. During the early 1700s, Haddington became a byword for modernization as its merchants supplied the district's progressive landowners with all sorts of new-fangled equipment, stock and seed, and in only a few decades utterly transformed Lothian agriculture.

Haddington was also the birthplace of **John Knox**, the fiery sixteenth-century religious reformer who led the Protestant assault on Scotland's Catholic Church. He laid the foundations of the Presbyterian movement, but is mainly remembered for his treatise of 1558 entitled *The First Blast of the Trumpet Against the Monstrous Regiment of Women*: a specific attack on Mary of Guise, regent of Scotland; Mary, Queen of England; and Catherine de Medici. It didn't endear him to Queen Elizabeth I or Mary Stuart either (see p.78).

The Town

Haddington's centre is best approached from the west, where tree-trimmed **Court Street** ends suddenly with the soaring spire, stately stonework and dignified Venetian windows of the **Town House**, designed by William Adam in 1748. Close by, to the right and next door to a fine Italianate facade, the **Jane Welsh Carlyle House** (April–Sept Wed–Sat 2–5pm; £1.50) was the childhood home of the wife of essayist and historian Thomas Carlyle (see p.159). The dining room – the only part of the house open to the public – has been restored to its early nineteenth-century appearance and sports pictures of the influential personalities of the day, while the lovely garden is pretty much as Jane would have known it. Carrying straight on, **High Street** is distinguished by its pastel-painted gables and quaint pends, a tad prettier than those in neighbouring **Market Street**. Keep an eye open for **Mitchell's Close** on Market Street, a recently restored seventeenth-century close with crow-stepped gables, rubble masonry and the narrowest of staircase towers.

Heading east from the town centre along High Street, it's a brief walk down Church Street – past the hooped arches of **Nungate Bridge** – to the hulking mass of **St Mary's Church** (Mon–Sat 10am–4pm, Sun 1–4pm; free), Scotland's largest parish church. Built close to the reedy River Tyne, the church dates from the fourteenth century but it's a real hotch-potch of styles, the squat grey tower uneasy above clumsy buttressing and pinkish-ochre stone walls. Inside, on the **Lauderdale Aisle**, a munificent tomb features the best of Elizabethan alabaster carving, moustached knights and their ruffed ladies lying beneath a finely ornamented canopy. In stark contrast, a plain slab in the choir is inscribed with Thomas Carlyle's beautiful tribute to his wife, who died on April 21, 1866, after forty years of marriage. Carlyle rounds the inscription off: "Suddenly snatched away from him, and the light of his life as if gone out." The church also offers brass rubbing, has a good tearoom and hosts internationally acclaimed concerts organized by the Lamp of Lothian Collegiate Trust (call ☎01620/825111 for details). At nearby Haddington House, on Sidegate, the seventeenth-century medicinal gardens of **St Mary's Pleasance** (open during daylight hours; free) merit a brief stroll.

Practicalities

Fast and frequent **buses** connect Haddington with Edinburgh, fifteen miles to the west, and with North Berwick on the east coast, with all services stopping on High Street. There's no **tourist office**, but orientation is easy and *A Walk Around Haddington* (£1), detailing every building of any conceivable consequence, is available from local newsagents.

There are several central **B&Bs**, including Mrs Richards' well-kept Georgian town house at 19 Church St (☎01620/825663; ②), and the *Plough Tavern*, 11 Court St (☎01620/823326; ⑤), a traditional inn in the town centre. Alternatively, try the more luxurious *Brown's Hotel*, 1 West Rd (☎01620/822254; ⑧), which occupies a fine Regency town house. The *Monks' Muir Caravan Park* (☎01620/860340), on the eastern edge of town by the A1, also takes tents.

For **daytime snacks** and light lunches, it's hard to beat *Simply Scrumptious*, next to the Town House, whose imaginative menu outshines its main rival, the *Golden Grain* café, 13 High St, while *Peter Potter* at 10 The Sand serves coffee and snacks and is attached to a craft shop where you can watch the artist in residence at work. The best place for an **evening meal** is the *Waterside Bistro* (☎1620/825674), on the far side of Nungate Bridge, justifiably popular for its delicious seafood and varied vegetarian dishes. Alternatively, try *Poldrate's Restaurant* (☎01620/826882) at Poldrate Mill on Gifford Road, where the menu changes daily, or the restaurant at *Brown's Hotel*, though you'll need to book in advance. Decent bar meals are available at the *Victoria Inn* in Court Street, while real-ale fans should head to *The Pheasant* in Poldrate, rumoured to serve the best pint in East Lothian.

Around Haddington

A thorough exploration of Haddington will only take two or three hours, but there are several other attractions in its vicinity. If you're heading north to the coast on the A6137, stop off at Byres Hill, where you can climb up to the Hopetoun Monument for sweeping views over the Firth of Forth. Hidden away four miles or so northeast of Haddington, the **Museum of Flight** (April–June, Sept & Oct daily 10.30am–5pm; July & Aug daily 10.30am–6pm; Nov–March Mon–Fri 11am–3pm; £3) on the B1347 at East Fortune airfield, is one of Britain's largest museums. Its many exhibits include a Vulcan bomber, a Comet airliner, a Spitfire and a Tigermoth, all displayed in World War II hangars.

A mile south of Haddington, **Lennoxlove House** (Easter–Oct Wed, Sat & Sun 2–5pm; £3.50), a sprawling pile incorporating a medieval tower house, displays a splendid fine and applied art collection belonging to the Duke of Hamilton. An hour-long tour takes in portraits of the family, French furniture, porcelain and damask wall hangings, with the highlight being the death mask of Mary, Queen of Scots, and a silver casket in which she kept the letters that allegedly proved her involvement in Darnley's murder.

A further three miles south along the B6369 on the edge of the Lammermuir Hills, the pretty hamlet of **Gifford**, whose eighteenth-century estate cottages edge a trim whitewashed church, was the birthplace (in 1723) of the Reverend John Witherspoon, a signatory of the American Declaration of Independence. The hamlet makes a good base for walkers, with several footpaths setting out across the surrounding red-soiled farmland for the Lammermuir Hills, while longer trails connect with the Southern Upland Way. If you want **to stay**, try the traditional and well-reputed *Tweeddale Arms* (☎01620/810240; ⑥), which has a fine **restaurant**, or *Eaglescairne Mains* (☎01620/810491; ④), a huge country house with open fires and a tennis court. You can also eat at the *Goblin Ha Hotel*, Main Street (☎01620/810244), which has a wonderful beer garden and serves excellent healthy country fare. Alternatively you may prefer to make up a picnic of freshly baked breads, pizza and sandwiches from the deli-style *Little Bread Shop* opposite the green.

The east coast to the Lammermuir Hills

Skirting the southern shore of the Firth of Forth before curving down along the North Sea coast, this fifty-mile section of the **east coast** begins at **ABERLADY**, an elongated conservation village of Gothic-style cottages and mansions, just sixteen miles from the capital. The village served as Haddington's port until its river silted up in the sixteenth century, the costly stained-glass windows of the honey-coloured medieval church acting as a reminder of more affluent times. The salt marshes and sand dunes of the adjacent **Aberlady Bay Nature Reserve**, a bird-watchers' haven, mark the site of the old harbour.

From the nature reserve, it's a couple of miles to **GULLANE**, the location of the famous shoreline links of **Muirfield Golf Course** (see p.52), established in the late 1800s, as well as the fine sandy **beaches** of Gullane Bay. Other than golf, Gullane's main claim to fame is the almost legendary *La Potinière* restaurant on Main Street (☎01620/843214), an intimate place with exceptional cooking and an extensive wine list. Dinner is served on Friday and Saturday nights only, and you're likely to have to book several weeks in advance. A half-mile detour off the Aberlady to Gullane Road takes you to the **Myreton Motor Museum** (Easter–Oct daily 10am–6pm; Nov–Easter daily 10am–5pm; £3), a small stash of vintage cars, motorbikes, military vehicles and motoring memorabilia.

Two miles east of Gullane lies the genteel hamlet of **DIRLETON**, where a pair of triangular greens are bordered by tastefully refurbished cottages with thriving gardens. **Dirleton Castle** (April–Sept daily 9.30am–6.30pm; Oct–March daily 9.30am–4.30pm; £2.50) has lovely gardens too, leading to a volcanic knoll crowned by Cromwell-shattered ruins. Scrambling round the castle is fun, and if the weather's good you can take the mile-long path from the village church to the sandy, rock-framed beach at **Yellowcraigs**, which overlooks **Fidra Island**, a large lump of basalt that's home to thousands of (noisy) seabirds. It's said that R.L. Stevenson modelled Spyglass Hill in *Treasure Island* on the hill that rises from the trees along the shore. Also near the beach, the *Yellowcraig Caravan Club Site* (☎01620/850217; April–Sept), with pleasant woodland walks to the shore, is the only budget place to **stay**; the splendid *Open Arms Hotel* opposite the castle (☎01620/850241; ⑨), on the other hand, has every luxury, including a fantastic restaurant serving moderate to expensive dinners from a varied and imaginative menu. Across the green, the *Castle Inn* (☎01620/850221; ④), an old coaching inn, falls somewhere in between and serves decent afternoon teas from 3pm to 5pm on Sundays.

North Berwick

NORTH BERWICK has a great deal of charm and a somewhat faded, old-fashioned air, its guest houses and hotels extending along the shore in all their Victorian and Edwardian sobriety. Set within sight of two volcanic heaps – the **Bass Rock** and **North Berwick Law** – the resort's pair of wide and sandy **beaches** are the main attraction. These fall either side of a narrow headland harbour that's an extension of Victoria Road, itself an extension of Quality Street. The only other attraction is the town's small **museum** on School Road (April–Oct daily 11am–5pm; free), housed in the old school house and displaying local curios, such as the old town stocks, though a new **Scottish Seabird Centre** on the harbour is due for completion in 2000.

Little now remains of the original medieval town, but the fragmentary ruins of the **Auld Kirk**, next to the harbour, bear witness to one of the most extraordinary events of sixteenth-century Scotland. In 1590, while **King James VI** spent the summer in Denmark wooing his prospective wife, the **Earl of Bothwell**, Francis Stuart, was plotting against him. On hearing of the king's imminent return, Bothwell, a keen practitioner of the "black arts", summoned the witches of Lothian to meet the Devil in the Auld Kirk. Bothwell turned up disguised as the Devil and instructed his 200 acolytes to raise a storm that would shipwreck the king. To cast the spell, they opened a few graves and engaged in a little flagellation before kissing the bare buttocks of the "Devil" – reportedly "as cold as ice and as hard as iron" as it hung over the pulpit. Despite these shenanigans, the king returned safely – when rumours reached him of Bothwell's treachery he refused to believe them, and the earl went unpunished, possibly because James was reassured by his failure. After all, if the Devil himself was unable to harm him, he must surely be blessed by God, a belief the monarch was later to elaborate as the "Divine Right of Kings".

Bass Rock

Resembling a giant molar, the **Bass Rock** rises 350ft above the sea some three miles east of North Berwick. This massive chunk of basalt was bought by the government in

1671 and served as a prison, a fortress and a monastic retreat, with a natural tunnel running east to west under the chapel building. Now it is home to millions of nesting seabirds, with Scotland's second-largest gannet colony after St Kilda in tight competition with razorbills, terns, puffins, guillemots and fulmars. Weather permitting, there are regular ninety-minute **boat trips** round the island from North Berwick harbour (Easter to early Oct daily; £3.50), but only Fred Marr (☎01620/892838) has landing rights. It's not to everyone's taste – as William Dunbar, a fifteenth-century poet, described it:

> *The air was dirkit with the fowlis*
> *That cam with jammeris and with youlis*
> *With shrykking, shrieking, skyrmming scowlis*
> *And meikle noyis and showtes.*

North Berwick Law

The other volcanic monolith, 613ft-high **North Berwick Law**, which dominates the Lothian landscape for miles around, is about an hour's walk from the beach (take Law Road off High Street and follow the signs). On a clear day, the views out across the Firth of Forth, Fife and the Lammermuirs make the effort worthwhile, and at the top you can see the remains of a Napoleonic watchtower and an arch made from the jawbone of a whale.

Practicalities

It's a ten-minute walk east from North Berwick **train station**, with its frequent services from Edinburgh, to the town centre along Abbey Road, Westgate and High Street. **Buses** from Edinburgh (every 30min) run along the coast via Aberlady, Gullane and Dirleton and stop on High Street, while the hourly service from Haddington and Dunbar terminates outside the **tourist office**, on Quality Street (April & May Mon–Sat 9am–6pm; June & Sept Mon–Sat 9am–6pm, Sun 11am–4pm; July Mon–Sat 9am–7pm, Sun 11am–6pm; Aug Mon–Sat 9am–8pm, Sun 11am–6pm; Oct–March Mon–Fri 9am–5pm; ☎01620/892197).

Several excellent **B&Bs** are open from April to September, including *Windrow*, at 20 Marmion Rd (☎01620/892066; ③), a Victorian house within easy walking distance of the sea, and Mrs McQueen's modern bungalow at 5 West Bay Rd (☎01620/894576; ①), next to the golf course while *Glebe House*, Law Road (☎01620/892608; ④), is a beautiful eighteenth-century manse in its own secluded grounds overlooking the sea; alternatively, try Mrs Ralph's, at 13 Westgate (☎01620/892782; ③), a spacious Victorian house. Of the **guest houses**, the seafront *Craigview*, 5 Beach Rd (☎01620/892257; ④), has four-poster beds and serves good vegetarian breakfasts, while *Point Garry*, 20 West Bay Rd (☎01620/892380; ⑤; April–Oct), is an upmarket **hotel** with a great cocktail bar. The nearest **campsite**, *Tantallon Rhodes Caravan Park* (☎01620/893348, *TantallonP@aol.com*; March–Oct), occupies a prime clifftop location a couple of miles east of the centre – take the Dunbar bus (Mon–Sat 6 daily, Sun 2 daily).

Several little cafés, such as the *Buttercup* on the High Street sell cheap **food**; for an evening meal, there's the usual array of takeaways or decent bar meals at *The Grange*, *The County Hotel* (both on High Street) or the *Tantallon Inn* on Marine Parade.

East of North Berwick

The melodramatic ruins of **Tantallon Castle** (April–Sept daily 9.30am–6.30pm; Oct–March Mon–Wed & Sat 9.30am–4.30pm, Thurs 9.30am–noon, Sun 2–4.30pm; £2.50), three miles east of North Berwick, on the A198, stand on the precipitous cliffs facing the Bass Rock. This pinkish sandstone edifice with its imposing cylindrical towers protected the powerful "Red" Douglases, the Earls of Angus, from their enemies for over three hundred years. With a sheer drop down to the sea on three sides and a sequence of moats and ditches on the fourth, the castle's desolate invincibility is daunting, especially when the wind howls over the remaining battlements and the surf crashes on the rocks far below. In fact, the setting is more striking than the ruins: Cromwell's army savaged the castle in 1651 and only the impressive 50ft-high and 14ft-thick curtain wall has survived relatively intact. To reach Tantallon Castle from North Berwick, a fifteen-minute trip, take the Dunbar **bus** (Mon–Sat 6 daily, Sun 2 daily).

Claiming to be the sunniest and driest place in all Scotland, **DUNBAR** is in much the same vein as North Berwick, twelve miles away, with a wide, recently spruced-up High Street graced by several grand old stone buildings. One of the oldest is the **Town House** (April–Oct daily 12.30–4.30pm; free), formerly a prison and now home to a small archeology room and local-history centre. Of greater significance is the three-storey **John Muir House**, 128 High St (June–Sept Mon–Sat 11am–1pm & 2–5pm, Sun 2–5pm; free), birthplace of the explorer and naturalist who created the United States national park system. The house has been refurbished in period detail and contains a tiny museum dedicated to the pioneer's life and work. A **country park** in Muir's honour, embracing Belhaven Bay and a rugged stretch of coast, can be reached by a pleasant five-minute walk from the harbour in town. The delightfully intricate double **harbour** merits a stroll itself, with its narrow channels, cobbled quays and roughened rocks, set beside the shattered remains of the castle. The town's only other claim to fame is as the home of **Belhaven beers**, which are still made on the original site of the monks' brewery, signposted off the Edinburgh road (guided tours can be arranged; phone ☎01368/864488 for details).

South of the town, two giant industrial plants rise out of the gentle, pastoral landscape. You pass the first of these, a vast cement works, before reaching the second: the massive **Torness Power Station**, a nuclear facility that provides about a quarter of Scotland's electricity. The station, accessible from the A1, is open for guided tours (March–Sept daily 9.30–4.30; call ☎0800/250255 in advance to book guided tour; free).

If you want to stay in Dunbar, the **tourist office**, 143 High St (May Mon–Sat 9am–6pm; June, July & Sept Mon–Sat 9am–7pm, Sun 11am–6pm; Aug Mon–Sat 9am–8pm, Sun 11am–6pm; ☎01368/863353) will help with **accommodation**. Alternatively, try the pleasant bay-windowed *Overcliffe Guest House*, 11 Bayswell Park (☎01368/864004; ③), a short walk west from the castle, or *Muirfield* B&B, 40 Belhaven Rd (☎01368/862289; ③; March–Oct). The nearest **campsite** is *Belhaven Bay Caravan and Camping Park*, in the John Muir Park, just off the A1087 (☎01620/893348; March–Oct), while the Camping and Caravanning Club maintain a site at *Barns Ness*, just off the A1 (☎01368/866536; March–Oct). For a light **lunch**, *The Food Hamper* and *William Smith's* on the High Street do good sandwiches, while the best evening meal options are *The Creel* (☎01368/863279) on Victoria Street, which specializes in steaks and seafood, *The Starfish* (☎01368/865384), a brightly painted quayside hostelry overlooking the old harbour with a great choice of hearty, freshly caught fish, and *Umberto's* (☎01368/862354), at 119 High St, is the place for Italian food.

St Abb's Head

Heading south from Dunbar, it's around seven miles to tiny Cockburnspath, where the Southern Upland Way reaches its conclusion about a mile from the coast – though there's now a five-mile extension which takes hikers from Cockburnspath square, underneath the A1 and down along the coast via Pease Bay, to **PENMANSHEIL**, back beside the A1. Nearby, the A1107 cuts off the main road for **ST ABBS**, a remote fishing village stuck onto the steepest of seashores. Flanked by jagged cliffs, St Abbs has a dramatic setting, with old fishermen's cottages tumbling down to the surf-battered harbour. The village is named after Ebba, a seventh-century Northumbrian princess who struggled ashore here after being shipwrecked and promptly founded a nunnery. From the harbour, you can take sea angling, sub-aqua diving, birdwatching and regular sightseeing **boat trips** with local guide, Peter Gibson (☎01890/771681) or with St Abb's Marine Services (☎01890/771412). It's also an ideal base for visiting **St Abb's Head Nature Reserve**, reached from the tearoom and car park just half a mile back along the road, where there's a small **visitor centre** and the Kittiwake Gallery (☎01890/771504), with a display of watercolours featuring local birdlife. Owned by the NTS, the Reserve comprises 200 acres of wild and rugged coastline with sheer, seabird-encrusted cliffs rising 300ft above the water. An easy-to-follow walking trail ends at the lighthouse, a mile or so from the car park, but if you continue downhill along the lane that leads back to Northcliffe Farm, you'll be rewarded with a spectacular view of the rugged Berwickshire coast – especially at high tide on a stormy day.

Twice daily the Edinburgh/Dunbar to Berwick-upon-Tweed **bus** passes through Coldingham on the A1107, where a **taxi-bus** service connects to St Abbs, a mile away down the B6438; connections are, however, only guaranteed for prebooked passengers (Mon–Fri 9am–4pm; ☎01289/308719). Buses south from St Abbs to Eyemouth run hourly. There are three places to **stay** in St Abbs: the excellent *Castle Rock Guest House*, Murrayfield (☎01890/771715; ②; Easter–Oct), a Victorian manse whose spick-and-span bedrooms and gingerbread woodwork look out along the sea cliffs; the highly recommended *Ebba Strand B&B*, Brierydean (☎01890/771717; ①), an architect-designed house with sweeping views over the sea where they serve particularly good breakfasts; and *Wilma Wilson's B&B*, a former fisherman's cottage at 7 Murrayfield (☎01890/771468; ①).

Coldingham itself is unremarkable, but a second minor road leaves here for the mile-long trip down to the coast at **COLDINGHAM SANDS**, where intrepid surfers gather. This pint-sized resort has a fine sandy beach and a **youth hostel** (☎018907/71298; March–Nov) in a large Victorian villa on a hill overlooking the seashore; the **B&B** *Cul-Na-Sithe* (☎018907/71565, *culnasithe@clara.co.uk*; ②; Feb–Nov) nearby also overlooks the sands. For **camping**, the *Scoutscroft Holiday Centre* (☎018907/71338) is just off the St Abb's road, very close to the beach at Coldingham Sands, and has a full range of facilities plus a **dive shop** for equipment rental and courses, should you wish to take advantage of one of the east coast's best diving locations.

Eyemouth

Almost the entire 3500 population of **EYEMOUTH**, a few miles south of St Abbs – and accessible from there via a pleasant two-hour coastal walk – is dependent on the fishing industry, started by the thirteenth-century Benedictine monks of Coldingham Priory. Consequently, the town's slender harbour is very much the focus of activity, its waters packed with deep sea and inshore fleets and its quay strewn with tatters of old net, discarded fish and fish crates. It even boasts two annual fishy events, the week-long **Herring Queen Festival** in July and the weekend **Seafood Festival** on the second weekend in June.

Eyemouth's tiny centre, to the west of the harbour, is drearily modern, despite the town's medieval foundation. But the **Eyemouth Museum**, in the Auld Kirk on the Market Place (April–June & Sept Mon–Sat 10am–5pm, Sun 2–4pm; July & Aug Mon–Sat 10am–6pm, Sun 1–6pm; Oct Mon–Sat 10am–12.30pm & 1.30–4.30pm; £1.75) is just about worth a visit for the **Eyemouth Tapestry**, a recent composition commemorating the east coast fishing disaster of 1881 when a freak storm destroyed most of the inshore fleet: 129 local men were lost, a tragedy of extraordinary proportions for a place of this size. Nearby, along High Street, in the old **cemetery**, a stone memorial surmounted by a broken mast also pays tribute to the dead. Years before, in 1849, the inhabitants had to raise the level of the cemetery by 6ft to cope with the victims of a cholera epidemic. However, the work was for nothing, as the site was soon abandoned (hence the lack of gravestones); but they did use the old tombstones to build the ghoulish **watch house** – a precaution against body snatchers – which you can still see today.

The elegant **Gunsgreen House**, standing alone on the far side of the harbour, was designed by James Adam (one of the famous family of architects) in the 1750s. Despite its respectable appearance – in keeping with its present use by the golf club – the house was once used by smugglers, with secret passages and underground tunnels leading back into town. This illicit trade in tobacco and booze peaked in the late eighteenth century, with local fishermen using their knowledge of the coast to regularly outwit the excise.

Two miles inland from Eyemouth, the village of Ayton and the surrounding landscape is dominated by the eccentric, red sandstone **Ayton Castle** (mid-May to mid-Sept Sun 2–5pm; £2). Built in 1846 on the site of an earlier fortification, local legend has it that it was built without plans or architect, which would certainly account for its erratic architecture, though in fact it was designed by Gillespie Graham. A couple of miles southeast, down a steep side valley, the pretty seaside village of **Burnmouth Harbour** is home to a small fleet of fishing boats and a cluster of picturesque cottages. The *Gull's Nest* pub, right on the A1, does excellent sandwiches with crab caught fresh from local boats and contains a fascinating display of old seafaring photographs and marine antiquities, while the neighbouring *Flemington Inn* serves hearty fare in a tiny restaurant just off the main bar.

In the unlikely event that you'll want to **stay** in Eyemouth overnight, the tourist office in the Auld Kirk (April–June & Sept Mon–Sat 10am–5pm, Sun 2–4pm; July & Aug Mon–Sat 10am–6pm, Sun 1–6pm; Oct Mon–Sat 10am–12.30pm & 1.30–4.30pm; ☎01890/750678) can recommend **B&Bs** in the area: the only two in town are Mrs MacKay's (☎01890/750463; ③) and Mrs McGovern's at Ebba House (☎01890/750350; ③). (Note that when dialling a telephone number locally in Eyemouth, you should use only the last five digits). For **food**, a sprinkling of tawdry hotels along the harbour serve fish and standard bar fodder, but for snacks and great cakes try the licensed *Old Bakehouse* on Manse Road, across from the Auld Kirk. Underwater enthusiasts should head to the Eyemouth Diving Centre on Fort Road (☎01890/751202), which rents out **dive equipment**, charters boats and runs diving courses. Leaving town, regular **buses** from the stop opposite the old cemetery run north along the coast, west to Chirnside/Duns and south across the border to Berwick-upon-Tweed, eight miles away. If you're driving north, take the scenic A1107 for coastal views as far as Cockburnspath where you can rejoin the faster A1 to Dunbar and Edinburgh.

Duns

Heading inland from Eyemouth, the B6355 and then the A6105 cross the fertile farmland of the Merse to the little-visited market town of **DUNS**, birthplace of John Duns Scotus, a medieval scholar, from whose name the word "dunce" was derived. A more modern hero was also born here: Jim Clark, a farmer-turned-motor-racing ace whose brilliant career ended in death on the track at Hockenheim in Germany in 1968, is commemorated at the **Jim Clark Room**, 44 Newtown St (Easter–Oct Mon–Sat 10am–1pm & 2–5pm, Sun 2–5pm; £1). There's little else to do in Duns, but it's only a twenty-minute walk to the top of **Duns Law** (take North Castle Street and follow the signs). Most people make the trek up to the 714ft-high summit for the view, some to see the **Covenanters' Stone**, marking the spot where Alexander Leslie's army camped in 1639. Leslie assembled his troops on the Law to watch for Charles I's mercenaries, who had been sent north to crush the Covenanters. In the event, the royalist army faded away without even forcing a battle, and the king, by refusing to accept defeat, took one more step towards the Civil War. Other local **walks** are detailed in the leaflet *Walks Around Duns*, available from The Cherry Tree, a jeweller's shop on Market Square, with a good tearoom at the back.

Duns is well connected by **bus** to all the major settlements of the east Borders, so you don't have to stay the night. However, the town does have half a dozen **B&Bs**, such as the central *St Albans*, Clouds (☎01361/883285; ④), a former eighteenth-century manse. The wooden bar of the *Whip and Saddle* in Market Square is the best place for a **drink** and a traditional bar **meal**, but, if you fancy a splurge, the villages to the southeast of Duns boast two award-winning **restaurants**: the *Wheatsheaf Hotel* at Swinton (☎01890/860257; ③), overlooking the village green, and *Chirnside Hall Country House* (☎01890/818219, *jea@globalnet.co.uk*; ⑥), both of which merit a detour. Located right on the Southern Uplands Way, the plant-filled *Riverside Restaurant* (☎01890/840312), ten miles north of Duns in the idyllic village of Abbey St Bathans, serves a good selection of soups, salads and mains.

Manderston House

Manderston House (May–Sept Thurs & Sun 2–5.30pm; £4), two miles east of Duns on the A6105, is the very embodiment of Edwardian Britain. Between 1871 and 1905, the Miller family spent most of their herring and hemp fortune on turning their home into a prestigious country house, with no expense spared as architect John Kinross added entire suites of rooms in the Classical Revival style. It's certainly a staggering sight, from the intricate plasterwork ceilings to the inlaid marble floor in the hall and the extravagant silver staircase, the whole lot sumptuously furnished with trappings worthy of a new member of the aristocracy: James Miller married Eveline Curzon, the daughter of Lord Scarsdale, in 1893. When you've finished inside the house, stroll round the fifty or so acres of garden, noted for their rhododendrons and azaleas.

The Lammermuir Hills and Lauder

Leaving Duns to the north, it's about three miles to the edge of the **Lammermuir Hills**, a slender, east–west chain whose flat-topped summits and quiet streams are a favourite haunt of ramblers. The hills are criss-crossed with footpaths, some of which follow ancient carting and droving trails as they slice from north to south. In the other direction, tracking along the body of the Lammermuirs between Lauder in the west and Cockburnspath on the coast, is the Southern Upland Way. If you're keen to sample a portion, leave Duns on the A6112, turn left along the B6355 and then follow the minor road to Abbey St Bathans, a hamlet beside the Whiteadder (pronounced "Whitta-der") Water with a tiny **youth hostel** (☎01361/840245) and a pretty and undemanding ten-mile stretch of the trail which leads down to the sea. Alternatively, you could carry on up to East Lothian's Gifford (see p.132), some twenty miles from Duns on the other side of the Lammermuirs.

It is also easy to join the Southern Upland Way on the western edge of the Lammermuir Hills in **LAUDER**, a grey market town twenty miles west of Duns on the A68. Lauder's only attraction is **Thirlestane Castle** (May–Oct daily except Sat 11am–5pm; £4.50), an imposing pile on the eastern edge of town: the main entrance is half a mile south of Lauder, but pedestrians can take the signposted footpath from The Avenue, effectively the main square about halfway along High Street. Owned by the Maitland family since the sixteenth century, the castle has been refashioned and remodelled on several occasions, but its impressive reddish turrets and castellated towers appear as a cohesive whole nevertheless. The interior is disappointing, with little to see beyond the delicate plasterwork of the Restoration ceilings: most of the original furnishings were carted off to London in the 1840s to be replaced by inferior Victoriana.

The Lower Tweed Valley

Rising in the hills far to the west, the River Tweed snakes its way across the Borders until it reaches the North Sea at Berwick-upon-Tweed. The eastern reaches of the river, constituting the **Lower Tweed Valley**, run from Kelso to the coast and for the most part form the boundary between Scotland and England. This is a gentle, rural landscape of farmland and wooded river banks where the occasional military ruin, usually on the south side of the border, serves as a reminder of more violent days. For the English, the eastern Borders were the quickest land route to the centre of Scotland, and time and again they launched themselves north, destroying everything in their way. Indeed, the English turned Berwick-upon-Tweed into one of the most heavily guarded frontier towns in northern Europe, and the massive fortifications survive today. The region also witnessed one of the most devastating of medieval battles when the Scots, under James IV, were decimated at **Flodden Field** in 1513. The heavily armoured Scottish noblemen got stuck in the mud at the bottom of a hill near Branxton, south of the border near Coldstream, and their over-long pikes and lances were simply no match for the shorter and sturdier English halberds.

Nowadays, the Lower Tweed Valley has one town of note, **Kelso**, a busy agricultural centre distinguished by the Georgian elegance of its main square and its proximity to Floors Castle (also Mellerstain House; see p.148). Perhaps surprisingly, Kelso is often visited for its abbey, even though the ruins of the colossal twelfth-century foundation, whose abbots claimed precedence over St Andrews, are scant indeed. Further downstream, close to Berwick-upon-Tweed, is the district's other main attraction, Georgian **Paxton House**.

Paxton House

Built for Patrick Home in the middle of the eighteenth century, **Paxton House** (mid-April to Oct daily 10am–5pm; £4.50), some five miles west of Berwick-upon-Tweed along the B6461, was the last act of a would-be matrimonial fiasco. Resident in Germany, the young Scot had been a great success at the court of Frederick the Great, even seducing the king's only daughter, Charlotte de Brandt. The affair became public and Home was forced to leave Berlin, but not before the lovers "plighted their troth". Back in Scotland, Home built Paxton for his putative bride, but she never appeared – much to Frederick's dynastic satisfaction.

The building, designed by John and James Adam, is a grand neo-Palladian mansion, with a carefully contrived facade focused on the main house, whose imposing centrepiece comprises temple-like columns rising two storeys to an equally impressive pediment. This geometrical simplicity is continued inside, where a particular highlight of the guided tour is the contrast between John and James's Rococo and their more famous brother Robert's Neoclassical plasterwork. Also on display is a stunning collection of Chippendale and Regency rosewood furniture. Finally, the expansive **Picture Gallery**, completed in the 1810s, blends aspects of earlier Neoclassicism into a more austere design, with most of the plasterwork moulded to look like masonry. The National Gallery of Scotland uses this room as an outstation, displaying some of its lesser works here and changing the exhibits frequently.

The grounds (April–Oct 10am–sunset), eighty acres of mixed parkland and woodland abutting the Tweed, boast gentle footpaths, a salmon-fishing museum and a hide, from where you can spy on red squirrels.

THE BORDER REIVERS

From the thirteenth to the early seventeenth centuries, the wild, inhospitable border country stretching from the Solway Firth in the west to the Tweed Valley in the east, well away from the power bases of both the Scottish and English monarchs, was overrun by outlaws known as the **Border Reivers**, *reive* being a Scots word for plunder. As George MacDonald Fraser put it in his book *The Steel Bonnets*, "the great border tribes of both Scotland and England feuded continuously among themselves. Robbery and blackmail were everyday professions; raiding, arson, kidnapping, murder and extortion were an accepted part of the social system." This, then, was no cross-border dispute, but an open struggle for power among the tribes of the region. Those who "shook loose the Border" included people from all walks of life – agricultural labourers, gentleman farmers, small-holders, even peers of the realm – for whom theft, raiding, tracking and ambush became second nature.

The source of this behaviour was the destruction and devastation brought upon the region by virtually continual warfare between England and Scotland, and the "slash and burn" policy of the era. With many residents no longer able to find sustenance from the land, crime became the only way to survive. Cattle-rustling, blackmail and kidnapping led to an anarchical mind set, where feuding families would wreak havoc and devastation on each other almost as a way of life.

The legacy of the Border Reivers can still be seen today in the fortified farms and churches of the region's architecture; in the Common Riding traditions of many border towns (see p.143); in the language – the words "blackmail" and "bereaved" have their roots in the destructive behaviour that was so characteristic of this period; and in the great family names such as Armstrong, Graham, Kerr and Nixon, which once filled the hearts of Borderers with dread.

Coldstream

The small town of **COLDSTREAM** sits tight against the Tweed, its long High Street part of the trunk road linking Newcastle across the border and Edinburgh. Entering Coldstream from the south you cross Smeaton's handsome five-arched bridge on the site of the original ford across the **River Tweed** which marks the border with England. It was here that Edward I and his army invaded Scotland in 1296, Robert Burns first ventured "abroad" some five hundred years later and the Stone of Destiny re-entered Scotland in 1996. These events aside, the town's principal claim to fame is its association with the **Coldstream Guards**. General George Monck billeted his Cromwellian soldiers here in the winter of 1659–60, just before they were persuaded to discard their parliamentary allegiance and march on London to restore Charles II to the throne. Monck's regiment was thereafter recognized as the "Coldstream Guards" and the general became the first Duke of Albemarle – a handsome payoff for his timely change of heart. Oddly enough, in the sort of detail beloved of military historians, the Coldstreamers still sport the crownless tunic buttons they first wore as part of Cromwell's Model Army. The regiment's deeds are recorded in the **Coldstream Museum** (April–June & Sept Mon–Sat 10am–4pm; July & Aug daily 10am–5pm; Oct Mon–Sat 1–4pm; £1), on the attractively old-fashioned (and traffic-free) Market Square, just off High Street. Near the huge obelisk dedicated to an obscure nineteenth-century MP at the east end of town, is the bridge **Toll House**, an eighteenth-century building where "irregular marriages" were granted to runaway English couples as an alternative site to Gretna Green.

Coldstream's outdoor attractions include the pocket-size **Henderson Park**, opposite the tourist office, an aromatic garden for the blind with signs in braille. Slightly further afield, on the western side of Coldstream, you can visit the 3000-acre **Hirsel estate** (grounds open all year during daylight hours; parking £2). Hirsel House is not open to the public but you can walk around the attractive grounds, complete with lake, picnic area and rhododendron woods, which are particularly resplendent in early summer. A museum, housed in the old homestead outhouses, shows the workings of the estate, past and present (Mon–Fri 10am–5pm Sat & Sun noon–5pm; free).

Practicalities

Coldstream's **tourist office** is in the old town hall, about halfway down the High Street (April–June & Sept Mon–Sat 10am–5pm, Sun 10am–1pm; July & Aug Mon–Sat 10am–6pm, Sun 10am–2pm; Oct Mon–Sat 10am–12.30pm & 1.30–4.30pm; ☎01890/882607). It has a comprehensive supply of brochures and booklets on the Borders as well as a list of local **B&Bs**. The best of these is the trimly kept *Attadale*, just off Market Square at 1 Leet St (☎01890/883047; ①); alternatively, try *Kengarth Guest House*, 7 Market St (☎01890/882477; ①), or *Hirsel Law*, a converted old school just outside the town (☎01890/882139; ①). For daytime **snacks**, there's home baking in abundance at the little *Candy's Kitchen* on the High Street, while the *Castle Hotel*, 11 High St, offers substantial and reasonably priced **meals**. The best bet for a **drink** is the *Besom Inn*, next to the tourist office, a cosy pub decked out with all sorts of military mementoes.

Kelso and around

Compact **KELSO**, at the confluence of the Tweed and Teviot, grew up in the shadow of its now-ruined abbey, once the richest and most powerful in southern Scotland. The abbey was founded in 1128 during the reign of King David (1124–53), whose policy of encouraging the monastic orders had little to do with spirituality. The bishops and monks David established here, as well as at Melrose, Jedburgh and Dryburgh, were the frontiersmen of his kingdom, helping to advance his authority in areas of doubtful allegiance. This began a long period of relative stability across the region which enabled its abbeys to flourish, until frequent raids by the English, who savaged Kelso three times in the early sixteenth century (in 1522, 1544 and 1545) brought ruin. The last assault – part of the "Rough Wooing" led by the Earl of Hertford when the Scots refused to ratify a marriage treaty between Henry VIII's son and the infant Mary Stuart – was the worst. Such was the extent of the devastation – compounded by the Reformation – that the surviving ruins of **Kelso Abbey** (April–Sept Mon–Sat 9.30am–6pm, Sun 2–6pm; Oct–March Mon–Fri 9.30am–4pm, Sun 2pm–4pm; free) are disappointing: a heavy central tower and supporting buttresses represent a scant memorial to the massive Romanesque original that took over eighty years to build. Enough remains, however, to make out the two transepts and towers which give the abbey the shape of a double cross, unique in Scotland. Just behind the abbey, notice the Old Parish Church, constructed in 1773 to an octagonal design that excited universal execration. "It is", wrote one contemporary, "a misshapen pile, the ugliest Parish Church in Scotland, but it is an excellent model for a circus."

From the abbey, it's a couple of minutes' walk along Bridge Street to **The Square**, a cobbled expanse where the columns and pediments of the **Town Hall** are flanked by a splendid ensemble of three-storey eighteenth- and nineteenth-century pastel buildings. Beyond the general air of elegance, there's little to see, though if you're around the abbey, pop into the Kelso Pottery (Mon–Sat 10am–1pm & 2–5pm), beside the big car park at The Knowes, to see the ceramics which are fired in a large outdoor pit kiln.

Kelso has one other diversion. Leaving The Square along Roxburgh Street, take the alley down to the **Cobby Riverside Walk**, where a brief stroll leads to Floors Castle. En route, but hidden from view by the islet in the middle of the river, is the spot where the Teviot meets the Tweed. This junction has long been famous for its salmon fishing, with permits booked years in advance irrespective of the cost: currently around £5000 per rod per week. Permits for fishing other (less expensive) reaches of the Tweed and Teviot are available from Tweeside Fishing Tackle, 36 Bridge St (☎01573/225306). Details of last-minute fishing lets are available from the Tweedline on ☎01891/666412; for fishing catches and prospects, phone ☎01891/666410.

Six miles or so north of town lie the ruins of **Hume Castle**, one of the earliest types of Scottish castle, built on a rectangular plan. While the recently constructed folly on the ruined site gives you little idea of the life that existed within its walls, it's worth a visit for the panoramic views alone.

Floors Castle

There's nothing medieval about **Floors Castle** (April–Oct daily 10am–4.30pm; £5), a vast castellated mansion overlooking the Tweed about a mile northwest of Kelso. The bulk of the building was designed by William Adam in the 1720s, and, picking through the Victorian modifications, much of the interior demonstrates his uncluttered style. However, you won't see much of it, as just ten rooms and a basement are open to the public. Highlights include Hendrick Danckert's splendid panorama of Horse Guards Parade in the entrance hall; the Brussels tapestries in the ante and drawing rooms; paintings by Augustus John and Henri Matisse in the Needle Room; and all sorts of snuff boxes and cigarette cases in the gallery.

Floors remains privately owned, the property of the tenth Duke of Roxburgh, whose arrogant features can be seen in a variety of portraits. The duke is a close friend of royalty: it was here, apparently, that Prince Andrew proposed to Sarah Ferguson in 1986.

Practicalities

With good connections to Melrose and Jedburgh to the west and a less regular service to Coldstream and Duns, Kelso **bus station** on Roxburgh Street is a brief walk from The Square, where you'll find the **tourist office** in the elegant Town Hall building (April–June & Sept Mon–Sat 10am–5pm, Sun 10am–1pm; July & Aug Mon–Sat 9.30am–6.30pm, Sun 10am–6pm; Oct Mon–Sat 10am–4.30pm, Sun 10am–1pm; ☎01573/223464).

Other than during Kelso's main festivals – the Border Union Dog Show in late June, the Border Union Agricultural Show in late July, the Kelso Rugby Sevens in early September and the Ram Sales a week or so later – **accommodation** is not a problem. The best B&Bs in town are the convenient *Wester House*, 155 Roxburgh St (☎01573/224428; ①); *Duncan House*, on Chalkheugh Terrace (☎01573/225682; ①), which is more basic but has river views; and *Abbey Bank*, The Knowes (☎01573/226550; ②), a mansion house with large double beds. There's also a couple of rather special hotels that are both ideal for a splurge: *Ednam House*, on Bridge Street near The Square (☎01573/224168; ⑥), a splendid Georgian mansion with antique furnishings and fittings whose gardens abut the Tweed (make sure you're not put in the modern extension); and *The Roxburghe* ☎01573/450331; ⑧) a luxury hotel two miles south of Kelso on the A698 at Heiton, owned by the Duke and Duchess of Roxburghe. There's a **campsite** at *Springwood Caravan Park* (☎01573/224596, *springwood-estate@lineone.net*; March–Oct) overlooking the Tweed on the St Boswells road.

Most **eating** places are dotted around The Square: for snacks, try the cheap *Hazel Lodge Tea Room* on Horsemarket, with tables outside, or the quaint non-smoking *Cottage Garden*, opposite the abbey, which serves a wide range of home-made goodies. For something more substantial, *Cobbles* restaurant, tucked away in the alley off The Square, and *The Horse & Wagon* in the street linking Horsemarket and Woodmarket, offer reasonable bar-type meals, while *The Queen's Head* on Bridge Street, has an imaginative menu using fresh produce. The area boasts two upmarket restaurants: the traditional *Ednam House* hotel (see above) and the outstanding *Sunlaws Restaurant* at the *Roxburghe Hotel*; in both cases, top-quality food and service are matched by high prices.

Kirk Yetholm and Town Yetholm

Six miles southeast of Kelso along the B6352, Yetholm, perched on the edge of the Cheviot Hills, is actually two separate places, **KIRK YETHOLM** and **TOWN YETHOLM**, lying a quarter of a mile apart. The villages, accessible by bus from Kelso (4–8 daily; 20min), lie at the northern end of the **Pennine Way**, a long-distance footpath which travels the length of northern England finishing at the Kirk Yetholm **youth hostel** (☎01573/420631; late March to Sept). The hostel also marks the end of the second leg of **St Cuthbert's Way** (see p.145). Walkers who have completed the Pennine Way clutching a copy of Wainwright's guidebook are entitled to a celebratory free half-pint at the *Border Hotel* (☎01573/420637) in Kirk Yetholm, which serves good food, too. You'll find cheaper **accommodation** at *Spring Valley B&B* on the green in Kirk Yetholm (☎01573/420253; ③), or at the friendly *Plough Hotel* in Town Yetholm (☎01573/420215; ③).

CENTRAL SOUTHERN SCOTLAND

Central southern Scotland encompasses a rough rectangle of land sandwiched between the Cheviot Hills on the English border and the chain of foothills – the Pentland and Moorfoot ranges – to the south of Edinburgh. The region incorporates some of the finest stretches of the **Southern Uplands**, with bare, rounded peaks and heathery hills punctuated by valleys.

Most of the roads stick assiduously to the valleys, and the main problem is finding a route that avoids endless to and froing. Whichever way you're travelling, be sure to take in the section of the **Tweed Valley** stretching from **Melrose** (the best base for your explorations) to **Peebles**, where you'll find a string of attractions, from the ruins of **Dryburgh** and **Melrose Abbey** to the eccentricities of Sir Walter Scott's mansion at **Abbotsford** and the intriguing Jacobite past of **Traquair House**. The extensive medieval remains of the abbey at **Jedburgh**, just south, also merit a visit.

Along with semi-industrialized Selkirk and Galashiels, these towns form the heart of the **Borders** region, whose turbulent history was, until the Act of Union, characterized by endless clan warfare and Reivers' raids. Consequently, the countryside is strewn with ruined castles and keeps, while each major town celebrates its agitated past in the **Common Ridings**, when locals – especially the "Callants", the young men – dress up in period costume and ride out to check the burgh boundaries. It's a boisterous business, performed with pride and matched only by the local love of **rugby union**, which reaches a crescendo with the **Melrose Sevens** tournament in April.

The Southern Uplands assume a wild aspect in **Liddesdale**, southwest of Jedburgh, and along the **Yarrow Water** and **Moffat Water** connecting Selkirk with Moffat. Choose either of these two routes for the scenery, using the old spa town of **Moffat** as a base.

Travelling around the region by **bus** takes some forethought: pick up timetables from any tourist office and plan your connections closely – it's often difficult to cross between valleys. Some relief is, however, provided by the Harrier Scenic Bus Service, which threads its way between the more noteworthy towns from early July to September: again, the tourist office has schedules (see "Travel Details" at the end of the chapter).

Melrose

Tucked in between the Tweed and the Eildon Hills, minuscule **MELROSE** is the most beguiling of towns, its narrow streets trimmed by a harmonious ensemble of styles, from pretty little cottages and tweedy shops to high-standing Georgian and Victorian facades. Most of the year it's a sleepy little place, but as the birthplace of the **Rugby**

Sevens in 1883, it swarms during Sevens Week (second week in April), and again in early September when it hosts the **Melrose Music Festival**, a popular weekend of traditional music attracting folkies from afar.

Behind the town square, the pink- and ochre-tinted stone ruins of **Melrose Abbey** (April–Sept daily 9.30am–6.30pm; Oct–March Mon–Sat 9.30am–4.30pm, Sun 2–4.30pm; HS; £3.50) soar above their riverside surroundings. The abbey, founded in 1136 by David I, grew rich selling wool and hides to Flanders, but its prosperity was fragile: the English repeatedly razed Melrose, most viciously under Richard II in 1385 and the Earl of Hertford in 1545. Most of the present remains date from the intervening period, when extensive rebuilding abandoned the original austerity for an elaborate, Gothic style inspired by the abbeys of northern England.

The site is dominated by the **Abbey Church**, where the elegant window arches of the nave approach the **monk's choir**, whose grand piers are disfigured by the masonry of a later parish church. The adjacent **presbytery** is better preserved, its dignified lines illuminated by a magnificent perpendicular window pointing piously high into the sky, with the capitals of the surrounding columns sporting the most intricate of curly kale carving. The legend that the heart of Robert the Bruce is buried here beneath the window was proven to be true when the cask containing it was publicly exhumed in 1996, although the burial location was not in accordance with Bruce's wishes. In 1329, the dying king told his friend, James Douglas, to carry his heart on a Crusade to the Holy Land in fulfilment of an old vow – "Seeing therefore, that my body cannot go to achieve what my heart desires, I will send my heart instead of my body, to accomplish my vow." Douglas tried his best, but was killed fighting the Moors in Spain – and Bruce's heart ended up in Melrose.

In the **south transept**, another fine fifteenth-century window sprouts yet more delicate, foliate tracery and the adjacent cornice is enlivened by angels playing musical instruments, though these figures are badly weathered. This kind of finely carved detail is repeated everywhere you look. Outside, all sorts of **gargoyles** frolic along the majestic lines of the church, from peculiar crouching beasts to the pig playing the bagpipes on the roof on the south side of the nave.

The fragmentary ruins of the old monastic buildings edge the church and lead across to the **Commendator's House** (same times as the abbey), which displays a modest collection of ecclesiastical bric-a-brac in the house of the abbey's sixteenth-century lay administrators. Next door to the abbey in the opposite direction is the delightful **Priorwood Garden** (April–Sept Mon–Sat 10am–5.30pm, Sun 1.30–5.30pm; Oct–Dec Mon–Sat 10am–4pm, Sun 1.30–4pm; NTS; free), whose walled precincts, owned by the NTS, are given over to an orchard and flowers that are suitable for drying – there's a dried flower shop, too.

Melrose's other museum, the **Trimontium Exhibition**, just off Market Square (April–Oct daily 10.30am–4.30pm; £1.25), is a quirky little centre that merits a browse. Its displays include Celtic bronze axe heads excavated from the Eildon hills, dioramas, models and the odd archeological find outlining the three Roman occupations of the region. For further Roman adventures, the four-mile circular **Trimontium Walk** (March–Oct Thurs 1.20–4.45pm; ☎01896 822651 for details; £2.50) visits various Roman sites in the area, including the Leaderfoot viaduct, and the most northerly amphitheatre in the Roman Empire. The walk includes a guide and tea in Newstead, the site of the Trimontium fort (Three Hills), whose remains are on display in the National Museum of Scotland in Edinburgh (see p.86).

Practicalities

Buses to Melrose stop in Market Square, a brief walk from both the abbey ruins and the adjacent **tourist office** (March–May Mon–Sat 10am–5pm, Sun 10am–1pm; June

WALKING IN THE EILDONS AND ST CUTHBERT'S WAY

Ordnance Survey Landranger map No. 73

From the centre of Melrose, it's a vigorous three-mile walk to the top of the **Eildon Hills**, whose triple volcanic peaks are the Central Borders' most distinctive landmark. The tourist office sells a leaflet detailing the hike, which begins about 90yd south of – and up the hill from – Market Square, along the B6359 to Lilliesleaf. The path is signposted to the left and leads to the saddle between the North and Mid Hills. To the right of the saddle are **Mid Hill**, the highest summit at 1385ft, and further south, **West Hill**; to the left **North Hill** is topped by the scant remains of an Iron Age fort and a Roman signal station. There are several routes back to town: one heading down from the northeast picks up a path to Newstead and you can return to Melrose by the river.

The hills have been associated with all sorts of legends, beginning with their creation by the wizard-cum-alchemist Michael Scott (1175–1230) who, in the words of Sir Walter Scott, "cleft the Eildon Hills in three". It was here that the mystic Thomas the Rhymer received the gift of prophecy from the Faerie Queen, and Arthur and his knights are reckoned to lie asleep deep within the hills, victims of a powerful spell. The ancient Celts, who revered the number three, also considered the site a holy place and maintained their settlements on the slopes long after the Romans' departure.

Melrose is also the starting point for the popular **St Cuthbert's Way**, a sixty-mile walk which finishes at Lindisfarne (Holy Island of Northumberland) on the east coast. The tourist office can give details of the walk, though the trail is well marked by yellow arrows from the abbey up over the Eildons to the pretty village of **Bowden**, where you can make a detour to see a twelfth-century kirk, half a mile down the hill from the square.

Mon–Sat 10am–6pm, Sun 10am–2pm; July & Aug Mon–Sat 9.30am–6.30pm, Sun 10.00am–6.00pm; Sept Mon–Sat 10am–6pm, Sun 10am–2pm; Oct Mon–Sat 10am–5pm, Sun 10am–1pm; ☎01896/822555).

Melrose has a clutch of **hotels**, including the smart and tidy *Burts Hotel*, on Market Square (☎01896/822285, *burtshotel@aol.com*; ⑤); the neat, ten-bedroom *Bon Accord* (☎01896/822645; ④) just across the street; and the far less expensive – but rather humdrum – *Station Hotel* (☎01896/822038; ②), up the hill from Market Square. It's among Melrose's **B&Bs**, however, that you'll get the real flavour of the place, most notably at the easy-going and comfortable *Braidwood*, on Buccleuch Street (☎01896/822488; ①), a stone's throw from the abbey, and the equally agreeable *Dunfermline House* (☎01896/822148; ②) opposite – advance booking is recommended at both during the summer. Other nearby options include *Little Fordel*, Abbey Street (☎01896/822206; ②), and the basic *Orchard House*, High Street (☎01896/822005; ①). The town also has a **youth hostel** (☎01896/822521) in a sprawling Victorian villa overlooking the abbey from beside the access road into the bypass. The *Gibson Caravan Park* (☎01896/822969) is at the foot of the High Street, opposite the Greenyards rugby grounds.

Melrose offers a reasonable variety of **eating** options: *Marmion's Brasserie* (☎01896/822245), on Buccleuch Street serves well-prepared meals from an imaginative menu, while *Melrose Station* (☎01896/822546), in the old train station above the square, has a good range of daily specials featuring local produce. The busy *Burts Hotel* does excellent bar meals, although their attitude to backpackers can be a bit snooty. If you're feeling energetic, walk across the old suspension bridge to Gattonside, where the *Hoebridge Inn* (☎01896/823082), once a bobbin mill and now one of the Borders' best restaurants, serves home-made Italian and British food in relaxed, low-key surroundings. If you want a light lunch or snack, head to *Russel's* on Market Square; *Graham's*, just opposite Priorwood Gardens, for home-made ice cream and fudge; or *Haldane's Fish & Chip Shop* (closed Wed), just off the square. For **pubs**, try the friendly *King's*

Arms on the High Street, or the *Ship Inn*, on East Port at the top of the square, the liveliest in town, especially during the Folk Festival and on Saturday afternoons when the Melrose rugby union team have played at home.

Around Melrose

Melrose makes a great base for exploring the middle reaches of the **Tweed Valley**. The rich, forested scenery inspired Sir Walter Scott, and the area's most outstanding attractions – the elegiac ruins of **Dryburgh Abbey** and lonely **Smailholm Tower**, not to mention Scott's purpose-built creation, **Abbotsford House** – bear his mark. Perhaps fortunately, Scott died before the textile boom industrialized parts of the Tweed Valley, turning his beloved **Selkirk** and **Galashiels** into mill towns. Allow time, too, for a visit to **Mellerstain House**, an example of the work of William and Robert Adam.

A comprehensive network of **bus** services connects Melrose with its surroundings and footpaths line much of the river's length. However, if you have your own transport or **bikes** – Gala Cycles, 58 High St, Galashiels (☎01896/757587), and Herbert Cycles, 5 Bridge Place, Galashiels (☎01896/755340), both rent mountain bikes – you can explore the surrounding lush farmlands dotted with attractive villages which have remained almost unchanged for centuries.

Dryburgh Abbey

Hidden away on a bend in the Tweed a few miles east of Melrose, the remains of **Dryburgh Abbey** (April–Sept daily 9.30am–6.30pm; Oct–March Mon–Sat 9.30am–4.30pm, Sun 2–4.30pm; HS; £2.50) occupy an idyllic position against a hilly backdrop, with ancient cedar trees and wide lawns flattering the reddish hues of the stonework. The Premonstratensians, or White Canons, founded the abbey in the twelfth century, but they were never as successful – or apparently as devout – as their Cistercian neighbours in Melrose. Their chronicles detail interminable disputes about land and money – in one incident, a fourteenth-century canon called Marcus flattened the abbot with his fist. Later, the abbey attained its own folklore: Scott's *Minstrelsy* records the tale of a woman who lived in the vaults with a sprite called Fatlips. She only came out after dark to beg from her neighbours and was variously thought mad or demonic.

The abbey, demolished and rebuilt on several occasions, incorporates several architectural styles, beginning in the shattered **church** where the clumsy decoration of the main entrance contrasts with the spirited dog's-tooth motif around the east processional doorway. The latter leads through to the **monastic buildings**, a two-storey ensemble that provides an insight into the lives of the monks. Bits and pieces of several rooms have survived, but the real highlight is the barrel-vaulted **chapterhouse**, complete with low stone benches, grouped windows and carved arcade. The room was used by the monks for the daily reading of a chapter from either the Bible or their rule book, and was, as they prospered, draped with expensive hangings.

Finally, back in the church, the battered north transept contains the grave of **Sir Walter Scott**; close by lies Field Marshal Haig, the World War I commander whose ineptitude cost thousands of soldiers' lives.

Practicalities

If you're driving from Melrose to Dryburgh, you can either take the scenic route along the B6360 through Gattonside or go up the bypass to the A68 and turn right after the Leaderfoot viaduct following the back roads to the abbey. Either way, you'll pass the much-visited **Scott's View** overlooking the Tweed Valley, where writer and friends

SIR WALTER SCOTT

Walter Scott (1771–1832) was born in Edinburgh to a solidly bourgeois family whose roots were in Selkirkshire. As a child he was left lame by polio and his anxious parents sent him to recuperate at his grandfather's farm in Smailholm, where the boy's imagination was fired by his relatives' tales of derring-do, the violent history of the Borders retold amidst the rugged landscape that he spent long summer days exploring. Scott returned to Edinburgh to resume his education and take up a career in law, but his real interests remained elsewhere. Throughout the 1790s he transcribed hundreds of old Border ballads, publishing a three-volume collection entitled *Minstrelsy of the Scottish Borders* in 1802. An instant success, *Minstrelsy* was followed by Scott's own *Lay of the Last Minstrel*, a narrative poem whose strong story and rose-tinted regionalism proved very popular.

More poetry was to come, most successfully *Marmion* (1808) and *The Lady of the Lake* (1810), not to mention an eighteen-volume edition of the works of John Dryden and nineteen volumes of Jonathan Swift. However, despite having two paid jobs, one as the Sheriff-Depute of Selkirkshire, the other as clerk to the Court of Session in Edinburgh, his finances remained shaky. He had become a partner in a printing firm, which put him deeply into debt, not helped by the enormous sums he spent on his mansion, Abbotsford. From 1813, Scott was writing to pay the bills and thumped out a veritable flood of historical novels using his extensive knowledge of Scottish history and folklore. He produced his best work within the space of ten years: *Waverley* (1814), *The Antiquary* (1816), *Rob Roy* and *The Heart of Midlothian* (both 1818), as well as two notable novels set in England, *Ivanhoe* (1819) and *Kenilworth* (1821). In 1824 he returned to Scottish tales with *Redgauntlet*, the last of his quality work.

A year later Scott's money problems reached crisis proportions after an economic crash bankrupted his printing business. Attempting to pay his creditors in full, he found the quality of his writing deteriorating with its increased speed and the effort broke his health. His last years were plagued by illness, and in 1832 he died at Abbotsford and was buried within the ruins of Dryburgh Abbey.

Although Scott's interests were diverse, his historical novels mostly focused on the Jacobites, whose loyalty to the Stuarts had riven Scotland since the "Glorious Revolution" of 1688. That the nation was prepared to be entertained by such tales was essentially a matter of timing: by the 1760s it was clear the Jacobite cause was lost for good and Scotland, emerging from its isolated medievalism, had been firmly welded into the United Kingdom. Thus its turbulent history and independent spirit was safely in the past, and ripe for romancing – as shown by the arrival of King George IV in Edinburgh during 1822 decked out in Highland dress. Yet, for Sir Walter the romance was tinged with a genuine sense of loss. Loyal to the Hanoverians, he still grieved for Bonnie Prince Charlie; he welcomed a commercial Scotland but lamented the passing of feudal ties, and so his heroes are transitional, fighting men of action superseded by bourgeois figures searching for a clear identity.

With the 1997 televised serial of *Ivanhoe*, British interest in Scott has been revived, and although many of his works are currently out of print, Edinburgh University Press has recently begun a long-term project to issue proper critical editions of the Waverley novels for the first time, correcting hitherto heavily corrupted texts and restoring passages and endings that had been altered – often drastically – by the original publishers. See "Books" on p.666 for details of works by Scott currently in print.

often picnicked and where Scott's horse stopped out of habit during the writer's own funeral procession. The scene inspired Joseph Turner's *Melrose 1831*, now on display in the National Gallery of Scotland (see p.91). Getting to Dryburgh by public transport, the only direct service is with the four-seater **postbus** (Mon–Fri 1 daily; 25min), but this doesn't make a return trip. Alternatively, you can take the Jedburgh **bus** (Mon–Sat hourly, Sun 8 daily; 10min) as far as St Boswells, then walk north from the village back along the main road and take the third right down the mile-long lane that leads to a footbridge and Dryburgh. Dryburgh has just one **place to stay**, the commodious **Dryburgh Abbey Hotel** (☎01835/822261, *enquiries@dryburgh.co.uk*; ⑧), a sprawling red-sandstone building right next to the ruins.

Smailholm Tower

Crossing the Tweed after St Boswells on the B6404, you'll pass **Mertoun Gardens** on the right-hand side of the road (April–Sept Sat, Sun, Mon & public holidays 2–6pm; HS; £1.50), a 26-acre bird- and flower-filled garden that sprawls beside the Tweed like a tribute to Monet. In marked contrast is the craggy **Smailholm Tower** (April–Sept daily 9.30am–6.30pm; £1.80), perched on a rocky outcrop a few miles further on. A remote and evocative fastness recalling Reivers' raids and border skirmishes, the fifteenth-century tower was designed to withstand sudden attack. The rough rubble walls average 6ft thick and both the entrance – once guarded by a heavy door plus an iron yett (gate) – and the windows are disproportionately small. These were necessary precautions. On both sides of the border, clans were engaged in endless feuds, a violent history that stirred the imagination of a "wee, sick laddie" who was brought here to live in 1773. The boy was Walter Scott and his epic poem *Marmion* resounds to the clamour of Smailholm's ancient quarrels:

> [The forayers], *home returning, fill'd the hall*
> *With revel, wassel-rout, and brawl.*
> *Methought that still with trump and clang,*
> *The gateway's broken arches rang;*
> *Methought grim features, seam'd with scars,*
> *Glared through the window's rusty bars.*

Inside, ignore the inept costumed models and press on up to the roof, where two narrow **wall-walks**, jammed against the barrel-vaulted roof and the crow-stepped gables, provide panoramic views. On the north side the watchman's seat has also survived, stuck against the chimney stack for warmth and with a recess for a lantern.

Mellerstain House

Mellerstain House (May–Sept daily except Sat 12.30–5pm; £4.50) is about four miles east of Smailholm via a series of signposted byroads, and six miles northwest of Kelso along the A6089. The house represents the very best of the Adams' work: William designed the wings in 1725, and his son Robert the castellated centre fifty years later. Robert's love of columns, roundels and friezes culminates in a stunning sequence of plaster-moulded, pastel-shaded ceilings, from the looping symmetry of the library ceiling, adorned by medallion oil paintings of *Learning* and *Reading* on either side of *Minerva*, to the whimsical griffin and vase pattern in the drawing room. It takes an hour to tour the house; afterwards you can wander the formal Edwardian gardens, which slope down to the lake.

Abbotsford House

Abbotsford House (March–May & Oct Mon–Sat 10am–5pm, Sun 2–5pm; June–Sept daily 10am–5pm; £3.50) was designed to satisfy the Romantic inclinations of Sir Walter Scott, who lived here from 1812 until his death twenty years later. Built on the site of a farmhouse Scott bought and subsequently demolished, Abbotsford took twelve years to evolve, with the fanciful turrets and castellations of the Scots Baronial exterior incorporating copies of medieval originals: the entrance porch imitates that of Linlithgow Palace and the screen wall in the garden echoes Melrose Abbey's cloister. Scott was proud of his creation, writing to a friend, "It is a kind of conundrum castle to be sure [which] pleases a fantastic person in style and manner."

Inside, visitors start in the wood-panelled **study**, with its small writing desk made of salvage from the Spanish Armada. The **library** boasts Scott's collection of more than 9000 rare books and an extraordinary assortment of Scottish memorabilia, including Rob Roy's purse and *skene dhu* (knife), a lock of Bonnie Prince Charlie's hair and his *quaich* (drinking cup), Flora Macdonald's pocketbook, the inlaid pearl crucifix that accompanied Mary, Queen of Scots to the scaffold, and even a piece of oatcake found in the pocket of a dead Highlander at Culloden. You can also see Henry Raeburn's famous portrait of Scott hanging in the **drawing room**, and all sorts of weapons – notably Rob Roy's sword, dagger and gun – in the **armoury**. In the barbaric-looking **entrance hall**, hung with elk and wild cattle skulls, is a cast of the head of Robert the Bruce.

Abbotsford is sandwiched between the Tweed and the B6360, about three miles west of Melrose. The fast and frequent Melrose–Galashiels bus provides easy access: ask for the Tweedbank island on the A6091 and walk up the road from there, for about ten minutes.

Selkirk and around

Whichever way you're heading, it's likely you'll pass through the royal burgh of **SELKIRK**, a textile town of high stone houses that spreads along the hillside above Ettrick Water about four miles south of Abbotsford. The **tourist office** at the west end of High Street, off Market Square (April–Oct Mon–Sat 10am–5pm, Sun 2–4pm; July & Aug Mon–Sat 10am–6pm, Sun 2–5pm; ☎01750/20054), shares a building with **Halliwell's House Museum** and **The Robson Gallery** (same hours as tourist office; both free). The museum features an old-style hardware shop and an informative exhibit on the industrialization of the Tweed Valley, while the gallery hosts a series of temporary exhibitions of paintings and ceramics. Also in Market Square, you can visit **Sir Walter Scott's Courtroom** (April–Sept Mon–Sat 10am–4pm; July & Aug Mon–Sat 10am–4pm, Sun 2–4pm; Oct–March Mon–Sat 1–4pm; free), where he served as Sheriff for 33 years. At the other end of High Street, the statue of **Mungo Park**, the renowned explorer and anti-slavery advocate born in Selkirkshire in 1771, displays two finely cast bas-reliefs depicting his exploits along the River Niger, which came to an end with his accidental drowning in 1805. The bronze life-size figures of *Peace, War, Slavery* and *Home Life in the Niger* were added in 1913, after several petitions and newspaper editorials demanded that he be further commemorated.

The imposing greystone woollen mills by the riverside are mostly boarded up now, an eerie reminder of a once prosperous era, though a few function as tweed and tartan outlets. In contrast, **Selkirk Glass** on the A7 to Galashiels (Mon–Fri 9am–4.30pm, Sat 11am–4.30pm, Sun noon–4pm; free), is a thriving craft industry which draws visitors by the coachload to watch glass-blowers making intricate paperweights. It has a bright showroom and café; glass-blowing displays only take place on weekdays.

Practicalities

There are frequent **buses** to Selkirk from most other border towns, but out-of-season transport along the Yarrow Valley takes you only as far as the *Gordon Arms Hotel* and then turns north to Traquair and Peebles. Details of local **accommodation** are posted on the window of Halliwell's House Museum: among them is the upmarket eighteenth-century *Philipburn Country House Hotel* (☎01750/720747, *100414.1237@compuserve.com*; ⑥), noted for its fine cuisine, and the white-turreted

Woodburn House Hotel, with pleasant gardens (☎01750/20816; ②), a sharp left turn up from the road to Ettrick at Heatherlie Park. **Camping** facilities (☎01750/20897; April–Oct) are available beside the river, next to the swimming pool at *Victoria Park*, though the campsites in the Ettrick Valley are far more scenic (see p.151). **Eating** in Selkirk is confined to average bar meals and hotel restaurants: the *Woodburn House Hotel* serves a good range of food at reasonable prices. Other than that, you can snack on the traditional Selkirk Bannock fruit bread available from the *Courthouse Coffee Shop* in Market Place, or *Chatterbox* at West Port.

Bowhill House and the Yarrow Valley

Three miles west of Selkirk on the A708, nineteenth-century **Bowhill House** (July daily 1–4.30pm; £4.50) is the property of the Duke of Buccleuch and Queensberry, a seriously wealthy man. Beyond the mansion's grand and extensive facade is an outstanding collection of French antiques and European paintings: in the **dining room**, for example, there are portraits by Reynolds and Gainsborough and a Canaletto cityscape, while the **drawing room** boasts Boulle furniture, Meissen tableware, paintings by Ruysdael, Leandro Bassano and Claude Lorraine, as well as two more family portraits by Reynolds. Look out also for the **Scott Room**, which features another splendid portrait of Sir Walter by Henry Raeburn, and the **Monmouth Room**, commemorating James, Duke of Monmouth, the illegitimate son of Charles II, who married Anne of the Buccleuchs. After several years in exile, Monmouth returned to England when his father died in 1685, hoping to wrest the crown from James II. He was defeated at the battle of Sedgemoor in Somerset and subsequently sent to the scaffold: among other items, his execution shirt is on display.

The wooded hills of **Bowhill Country Park** adjoining the house (April–June & Aug daily except Fri noon–5pm; July daily noon–5pm; £2) are crisscrossed by scenic footpaths and cycle trails: **mountain bikes** can be rented from the visitor centre. Getting to Bowhill by **public transport** is difficult. The Peebles bus, leaving Selkirk daily at 2pm, will drop you at General's Bridge (10min), from where it's a 1.5-mile walk through the grounds to the house. In addition, from July to late September, there's a weekly Harrier Scenic Bus Service from Selkirk and Melrose in the morning, returning in the afternoon.

A few miles beyond Bowhill on the A708, at the head of the **Yarrow Valley**, the roadside *Broadmeadows* **youth hostel** at Yarrowford (☎01750/76262; April–Sept) is a convenient starting point for some good hill walks. From here, you can reach the hilltop cairns of **The Three Brethren**, whose 1530-ft summit offers excellent views over the Borders. You can also link up with stretches of the Southern Upland Way by heading east down through Yair Forest, or by following an old drove road west to the Cheese Well at Minchmoor (so called because of offerings left by travellers for the faerie folk), and ending up at Traquair House near Innerleithen.

Aikwood Tower

Aikwood Tower (April–Sept Tues, Thurs & Sun 2–5pm; £1.50), four miles west of Selkirk on the B7009, is a sixteenth-century fortified tower house, whose stern rubble walls stand surrounded by forests of the Ettrick Water Valley. Inside, an exhibition explores the life and work of Sir Walter Scott's friend, **James Hogg**, known as the "Ettrick Shepherd". Born locally, in sheep-farming Ettrick Valley, self-taught Hogg was a poet of some contemporary renown who spent several years living among the Edinburgh literary elite. Today he's largely forgotten which – if you read any of his work – is not entirely surprising. The old byres adjoining the tower are given over to temporary displays of local artists' work and during the summer months sculpture is exhibited in the gardens. Incidentally, Aikwood is also the home of the Speaker of the Scottish Parliament, Sir David Steel.

Ettrick Water and Eskdalemuir

Running alongside **Ettrick Water** towards Langholm (see p.157), the B7009 passes through some of the Borders' loveliest scenery, from gentle, open hills dotted with the occasional sheep farm to the progressively bleak moors of Eskdalemuir. After Aikwood Tower, the hamlet of Ettrickbridge, like every border town, boasts a *Cross Keys Inn* (☎01750/52224; ②), a seventeenth-century coaching inn with a cosy, oak-beamed bar. A few miles further on, just north of Ettrick, birthplace of Hogg in 1770, you'll find the picturesque *Angecroft Caravan Park* (☎01750/62251, *kevinnewton@compuserve.com*; mid-Feb to mid-Jan) and *Honey Cottage Caravan Park* (☎01750/62246; all year).

Nine miles further along the B709, the fluttering prayer flags, scarlet-robed Buddhists and golden temple domes of one of the only **Tibetan monasteries** outside Tibet make a surreal sight against the bleak expanse of **ESKDALEMUIR**. Visitors are welcome to look round the impressive Samye Ling temple, and to attend courses on Buddhist meditation and Eastern philosophy (☎013873/73232 for further details). Accommodation and a basic vegetarian canteen are available for people staying on retreats or attending courses, and there's a small shop and café for passing visitors.

The Tweed Valley: Galashiels to Peebles

There's a wide choice of routes on from Melrose; one of the more popular options is to travel 22 miles west along the **Tweed Valley** to the pleasant country town of **Peebles**. On the way, savour the wooded scenery and drop into **Traquair House**, just off the main road at **Innerleithen**. Public transport is no problem: frequent buses along the valley are supplemented by the seasonal Harrier Scenic Bus Service (see p.187). Just west of Peebles, the River Tweed curves south towards Tweedsmuir, from where it's just a few miles further to Moffat (see p.160).

Galashiels

Four miles west of Melrose, it's probably best to avoid **GALASHIELS**, a workaday textile town and home to the Scottish College of Textiles, spread along the valley of the Gala Water near its junction with the Tweed. You may, however, have to pass through the region's principal bus station, close to (and across the river from) the town centre. If you're delayed you could take a stroll along the main drag, High, then Bank, Street, whose eastern end is cheered by a melodramatic statue of a mounted Border Reiver. The long-demolished New Gala House, a mansion which stood at the top of the town, was taken over during World War II by an Edinburgh girls' school, St Trinnean's – Ronald Searle met two of the pupils in 1941, inspiration for the unruly schoolgirls in his St Trinian's novels. Galashiels **tourist office**, 3 St John's St, is across the square from the statue (April–June & Sept Mon–Sat 10am–5pm, Sun 2–4pm; July & Aug Mon–Sat 10am–6pm, Sun 1–5pm; Oct Mon–Sat 10am–12.30pm & 1.30–4.30pm; ☎01896/755551).

Walkerburn and Innerleithen

Ten miles west of Galashiels on the A72, tiny **WALKERBURN** is home to the pint-sized **Museum of Woollen Textiles** (Mon–Sat 9am–5.30pm; April–Nov also Sun 11am–5pm; free). Some of the early wool and cloth patterns are of interest, but it won't be long before you're moving on the mile or so west to **INNERLEITHEN**, a rural village which gained prominence in the 1700s and 1800s as a mill town and spa centre. Aside from its main attraction, wonderful Traquair House (see below), the town boasts **Robert Smail's Printing Works** (Easter & May–Sept Mon–Sat 10am–1pm & 2–5pm, Sun 2–5pm; Oct Sat 10am–1pm & 2–5pm, Sun 2–5pm; NTS; £2.50), a working museum with original nineteenth-century machinery where you can try your hand at typesetting, and the visitor centre at **St Ronan's Wells** (April–Oct daily 2–5pm; free), where Walter Scott used to imbibe the sulphur waters.

Most visitors make Peebles their base, but there are a few places **to stay** in Innerleithen, such as the central *Traquair Arms Hotel*, on Traquair Road (☎01896/830229, *traquair.arms@scotborders.co.uk*; ③), and the *Caddon View Guest House*, 14 Pirn Rd (☎01896/830208; ②), though you have to book early during the Traquair Fair each August. Campers should head for the *Tweedside Caravan Park* on Montgomery Street (☎01896/831271; April–Oct), while **mountain bikes** can be rented from Bikesport on Peebles Road (☎01896/830880), if you feel like checking out the many graded cycle routes through Glentress, Cardrona, or the Elibank and Traquair forests.

Traquair House

Peeping out from the trees a mile or so south of Innerleithen on the B709, **Traquair House** (April, May & Sept daily 12.30–5.30pm; June–Aug daily 10.30am–5.30pm; Oct Fri–Sun 2–5pm; £5; grounds only £2) is the oldest continuously inhabited house in Scotland, with the present owners – the Maxwell Stuarts – having lived here since 1491. The first of the line, **James**, first Laird of Traquair, inherited an elementary fortified tower, which his powerful descendants gradually converted into a mansion, visited, it is said, by 27 monarchs including Mary, Queen of Scots. Persistently Catholic, the family paid for its principles: the fifth earl got two years in the Tower of London for his support of Bonnie Prince Charlie, Protestant mill workers repeatedly attacked their property, and by 1800 little remained of the family's once enormous estates – certainly not enough to fund any major rebuilding.

Consequently, Traquair's main appeal is in its ancient shape and structure. The whitewashed facade is strikingly handsome, with narrow windows and trim turrets surrounding the tiniest of front doors – an organic, homogeneous edifice that's a welcome change from other grandiose stately homes. Inside, the house has kept many of its oldest features. You can see original vaulted cellars, where locals once hid their cattle from raiders; the twisting main staircase as well as the earlier medieval version, later a secret escape route for persecuted Catholics; a carefully camouflaged priest's hole; and even a **priest's room** where a string of resident chaplains lived in hiding until the Catholic Emancipation Act freed things up in 1829. Of the furniture and fittings, the carved oak door at the foot of the stairs is outstanding, as are the Dutch trompe l'oeil carvings in the **still room** and the bright-yellow four-poster of the **king's room**, with a bedspread allegedly embroidered by Mary, Queen of Scots. That said, it's not any particular piece that impresses, but rather the accumulation of family possessions that give a real insight into the Maxwell Stuarts' revolving-door fortunes and eccentricities. In the **museum room** there are several fine examples of Jacobite or **Amen glass**, inscribed with pictures of the Bonnie Prince or verses in his honour; a handful of personal items thought to have been owned by Mary, Queen of Scots; and the cloak worn by the fourth earl during his dramatic escape from the Tower of London. Under sentence of death for his part in the Jacobite Rising of 1715, the earl was saved by his wife, Lady Winifred Herbert, who got his jailers drunk and smuggled him out disguised as a maid.

It's worth sparing time for the surrounding **gardens** where you'll find a maze, several craft workshops and a **working brewery** dating back to 1566 which had lain unused for 150 years. The present owner restored it and opened it to the public in 1965, claiming it to be the only British brewery that still ferments totally in oak. You can taste the ales in the Brewery House (April & May daily 12.30–5.30pm; June–Aug daily 10.30am–5.30pm; Oct Fri–Sun 12.30–5.30pm), and buy them from the laid-back tearoom and gift shop. There's also a redundant avenue which leads to the locked **Bear Gates**; Bonnie Prince Charlie departed the house through the gates, and the then owner promised to keep them locked till a Stuart should ascend the throne.

Peebles

Straddling the Tweed and circled by hills, the royal burgh of **PEEBLES** has a genteel, relaxed air, its wide High Street bordered by houses in a medley of architectural styles, mostly dating from Victorian times. A stroll around town should include a visit to the **Tweedale Museum & Picture Gallery** (April–Oct Mon–Fri 10am–1pm & 2–5pm, Sat 10am–noon, Sun 2–4pm; Nov–March Mon–Fri only; free), housed in the Chambers Institute on High Street. William Chambers, a local worthy, presented the building to the town in 1859, complete with an art gallery dedicated to the enlightenment of his neighbours. He stuffed the place with casts of the world's most famous sculptures and, although most were lost long ago, today's "Secret Room", once the Museum Room, boasts two handsome friezes: one a copy of the Elgin marbles taken from the Parthenon; the other of the Triumph of Alexander, originally cast in 1812 to honour Napoleon. The **Old Parish Church** (daily 10am–4pm) dominates the High Street and has some unusual features in its elegant oak, bronze and engraved-glass entrance screen and 22 modern oil paintings illustrating the scriptures. Suspended from the ceiling are tattered Napoleonic flags, emblems of 1816, the year the Peeblesshire Militia disbanded.

Practicalities

Buses to Peebles from Selkirk, Galashiels and Edinburgh stop outside the post office, a few doors down from the well-stocked **tourist office** on the High Street (April & May Mon–Sat 10am–5pm, Sun 10am–2pm; June Mon–Sat 10am–5.30pm, Sun 10am–4pm; July & Aug Mon–Sat 9am–7pm, Sun 10am–6pm; Sept Mon–Sat 10am–5.30pm, Sun 1–4pm; Oct Mon–Sat 10am–4.30pm, Sun 10am–2pm; Nov & Dec Mon–Sat 10am–12.30pm & 1.30–4.30pm; ☎01721/720138), where you can buy the useful leaflet, *Peebles Town Walk* (25p). Peebles boasts more than twenty **B&Bs**; try the trim, pint-sized *Rowanbrae*, on Northgate, a turning off the east end of High Street

---

WALKS AND CYCLING AROUND PEEBLES

A series of **footpaths** snake through the hills surrounding Peebles with their rough-edged burns, bare peaks and deep woods. The main local tracks are listed in the *Popular Walks Around Peebles* leaflet available from the tourist office. The five-mile **Sware Trail** is one of the easiest and most scenic, weaving west along the north bank of the river and looping back to the south. On the way, it passes **Neidpath Castle** (Easter–Sept Mon–Sat 11am–5pm, Sun 1–5pm; £2.50), a gaunt medieval tower house perched high above the river on a rocky buff. It's a superb setting, and the interior possesses a pit prison, while displayed in the great hall are stunning batik wall hangings, depicting the life of Mary, Queen of Scots. The walk also goes by the splendid skew rail bridge, part of the Glasgow line which was finished in 1850. Other, longer footpaths follow the old **drove tracks**, like the thirteen-mile haul to St Mary's Loch or the fourteen-mile route to Selkirk via Traquair House (see p.152). For either of these, you'll need an Ordnance Survey map, a compass and proper hiking gear (see "Outdoor pursuits" in Basics). A more gentle stroll is the 2.5-mile amble to the privately owned **Kailzie Gardens** (daily: April to mid-Oct 11am–5.30pm; £2; mid-Oct to March daylight hours; £1; ☎01721/720007), whose fifteen acres include a walled garden, trout pond (fishing costs £5 a day; fly-fishing tackle is available for rent), a lovely wood-panelled tearoom, a souvenir shop and small gallery.

From Peebles, you can link up to the clearly signposted ninety-mile **Tweed Cycleway**: mountain bikes can be rented from George Pennel Cycles, 3 High St (☎01721/720844), or Scottish Border Trails (☎01721/722934), at the entrance to Glentress Forest two miles east of town on the A72. If you need four bikes or more, the latter deliver free within a ten-mile radius.

(☎01721/721630; ①); the *Minniebank Guest House*, Greenside (☎01721/722093; ②), a Victorian villa set beside the river by the main bridge; or *Viewfield*, 1 Rosetta Rd (☎01721/721232; ①), an attractive Victorian house a ten-minute walk west of the bridge – take the Old Town road (the A72) and follow it round, turning right up Young Street. The best of the upmarket **hotels** is *The Park Hotel*, just east of the town centre on Innerleithen Road, with views of the Cademuir Hills (☎01721/720451; ⑤), with cheaper alternatives including the mundane *Green Tree Hotel*, 41 Eastgate (☎01721/720582; ③), and the relaxing *Kingsmuir Hotel*, south of the river on Springhill Road (☎01721/720151, *chrisburn@kingsmuir.scotborders.co.uk*; ④). For **camping**, the *Rosetta Caravan and Camping Park* (☎01721/720770; April–Oct) is a fifteen-minute walk north of the High Street (directions as for *Viewfield* B&B), while the *Crossburn Caravan Park* is located on Edinburgh Road (☎01721/720501, *xburncaravans@martex.co.uk*).

The best places for **food** are the *Crown Hotel* on the High Street, featuring good daily specials, the *Kingsmuir Hotel*, Springhill Road (☎01721/720151), with more expensive but excellent bar meals, or the *Tontine Hotel* (☎01721 720892), on the High Street, which has a spacious lounge and restaurant serving good food. Other options on the High Street include the *Prince of India Tandoori Restaurant* (☎01721/724455), and, during the day, the cheap-and-cheerful *Tatler Café* for good-value fish and chips, or the *Olive Tree* delicatessen for superb, imaginative sandwiches.

Jedburgh

Just ten miles north of the border with England, **JEDBURGH** nestles in the valley of the Jed Water near its confluence with the Teviot out on the edge of the wild Cheviot Hills. During the interminable Anglo-Scottish Wars, it was the quintessential frontier town, a heavily garrisoned royal burgh incorporating a mighty castle and abbey. Though the **Castle** was destroyed by the Scots in 1409 to keep it out of the hands of the English, its memory has been kept alive by stories: in 1285, for example, King Alexander III was celebrating his wedding feast in the Great Hall when a ghostly apparition predicted his untimely death and a bloody civil war; sure enough, he died in a hunting accident shortly afterwards and chaos ensued. Today the ruined **Abbey** is the main event though a stroll round Jedburgh's old town centre is a pleasant way to while away an hour or two.

The Town

The remains of **Jedburgh Abbey** (April–Sept Mon–Sat 9.30am–6.30pm, Sun 2–6.30pm; Oct–March Mon–Sat 9.30am–4.30pm, Sun 2–4.30pm; HS; £3), right in the centre of town, date from the twelfth century. Benefiting from King David's patronage, the monks developed an extravagant complex on a sloping site next to the Jed Water, the monastic buildings standing beneath a huge sandstone church. All went well until the late thirteenth century, when the power of the Scots kings waned following the death of Alexander III and a prolonged war. The abbey was subsequently burnt and badly damaged on a number of occasions, the worst being inflicted by the English in 1544–45. The monastic way of life, however, had already fallen prey to corruption and only a few canons remained living in the ruins of the abbey, until the monastery closed in 1560 with the Reformation. However, the Abbey Church remained a parish kirk for another three centuries and has survived particularly well preserved.

Entry to the site is through the bright **visitor centre** at the bottom of the hill (arrangements can be made for wheelchair access), whose explanation of the abbey's history uses both contemporary quotations and "mood music" – chanting monks and the like. Next to the centre are the scant remains of the cloister buildings and chapter room, where day-to-day affairs were administered. The **Abbey Church**, lying on an east–west axis, is entered through the East Processional doorway, remarkably still in its original condition. Behind the doorway lies the splendidly proportioned three-storey nave, a fine example of the transition from Romanesque to Gothic design, with pointed window arches surmounted by the round-headed arches of the triforium, which, in turn, support the lancet windows of the clerestory. This delicacy of form is, however, not matched at the east end of the church, where the squat central tower is underpinned by the monumental circular pillars and truncated arches of the earlier, twelfth-century choir. On close inspection you can see the three places where the sculptor, Thomas Cranston, carved his initials and insignia.

It's a couple of minutes' walk from the abbey round to the tiny triangular **Market Place**. Up the hill from here, at the top of Castlegate, **Jedburgh Castle Jail and Museum** (April–Oct Mon–Sat 10am–4.45pm, Sun 1–4pm; £1.25) exhibits displays on prison life throughout the ages. The prison buildings themselves are, for the period, remarkably comfortable, reflecting the influence of reformer John Howard. Finally, **Mary, Queen of Scots' House** (April–Oct Mon–Sat 10am–4.45pm, Sun 10am–4.30pm; March & Nov Mon–Sat 10.30–3.45pm, Sun 1–4pm; £2), situated at the opposite end of the town centre, is something of a misnomer; the owner was actually her protector, Sir Thomas Kerr, ancestor of the present Lord Lothian of Ferniehurst Castle. It's true that Mary stayed here in this castle house during the assizes of 1566, but she didn't stay long and there's little on show connected with her visit. The attempt to unravel her complex life is cursory, the redeeming features being a copy of Mary's death mask and one of the few surviving portraits of the Earl of Bothwell. One curious feature of all Kerr houses is that the staircases spiral to the left for ease of sword-drawing, giving rise to the Scottish term for left-handedness, "kerry haunded" or "kerry fisted".

Practicalities

Jedburgh's **bus station**, a few yards from the abbey, is the starting point for a wide range of services around the Borders. Footsteps away on Murray's Green, the **tourist office** (April, May & Oct Mon–Sat 10am–5pm, Sun noon–4pm; June & Sept Mon–Sat 9.30am–6pm, Sun noon–4pm; July & Aug Mon–Fri 9am–8.30pm, Sat 9am–7pm, Sun 10am–7pm; Nov–March Mon–Fri 10am–4.30pm; ☎01835/863435) has a vast array of information, pamphlets detailing three circular walks and a town trail, and a comprehensive list of local **accommodation**. Try the *Kenmore Bank Guest House*, Oxnam Road (☎01835/862369; ②), a Victorian villa overlooking the Jed Water five minutes' walk south of the abbey, or *Glenfriars Hotel*, The Friars (☎01835/862000; ④), a big old house in its own grounds near the north end of High Street. Alternatively, there are several **B&Bs** among the pleasant and antique row houses of Castlegate, notably Mrs Poloczek's, at no. 48 (☎01835/862504; ①). A mile south of town on the A68, you'll find *Hundalee House* (☎01835/863011, *sheilawhittaker@btinternet.com*; March–Oct; ③), a historic mansion house in open grounds. The *Jedwater Caravan and Camping Park* (☎01835/840219; April–Oct) occupies a riverside site four miles south of town on the A68, while the *Elliot Park* caravan and **campsite** (☎01835/863393; March–Sept) is beside the Edinburgh road about a mile north of the centre. For **horse riders**, there are both stables and accommodation at *Ferniehurst Mill Lodge*, two miles south of Jedburgh on the A68 (☎01835/863279; ②), from where experienced riders can venture out into the Cheviot hills.

During the day there are enough places **to eat** in Jedburgh, although evening meal choices are more limited. *Simply Scottish* (☎01835/864696), on the High Street, serves quality Scottish meals and snacks all day, while *Brown Sugar* coffee bar, by Market Place, offers sandwiches, salads and cakes. The *Castlegate Tea Room and Restaurant* (☎01835/862592) around the corner has an evening menu as well, and the friendly

---

JEDBURGH FESTIVALS

Jedburgh is at its busiest during the town's two main **festivals**. The **Common Riding**, or Callants' Festival, takes place in late June/early July, when the young people of the town – especially the lads – mount up and ride out to check the burgh boundaries, a reminder of more troubled days when Jedburgh was subject to English raids. In similar spirit, early February sees the day-long **Jedburgh Hand Ba'** game, an all-male affair between the "uppies" (those born above Market Place) and "downies" (those born below). In theory the aim of the game is to get hay-stuffed leather balls – originally representing the heads of English men – from one end of town to the other, but there's more at stake than that: macho reputations are made and lost during the two two-hour games.

Cookie Jar (☎01835/863982), popular by day with locals and smokers, metamorphoses by night into an Italian restaurant. Other evening options are *The Wayfarer* (☎01835/863503), down the High Street, whose German owners offer a variety of mainly meat dishes, and bar meals at *The Carter's Rest*, across from the abbey. Try the local speciality, Jethart Snails, which are sticky boiled sweets invented by a French POW in the 1700s and on sale everywhere.

Teviotdale, Ewes Water and Liddesdale

If you're heading southwest from Jedburgh, there are two clearly defined routes. The first, along the A698 and then A7, tracks up **Teviotdale** to **Hawick**, before slipping through the dramatic uplands which stretch as far as the English border. En route you change dales – joining **Ewes Water** at the Dumfries boundary.

The route down **Liddesdale**, along the B6357, is slower but even more picturesque, on a remote road flanked by dense forests, barren moors and secluded heaths. If you do come this way, stop off at solitary **Hermitage Castle**, a well-preserved fourteenth-century fortress.

The Galashiels to Carlisle **bus** travels the length of Teviotdale and Ewes Water (Mon–Sat 7 daily, Sun 3 daily), with buses from Jedburgh connecting with this service at Hawick. There are no buses along the length of Liddesdale – the best you'll do is the occasional, school-term-only service from Langholm to Canonbie and Newcastleton; ring Telfords Coaches (☎013873/75677) for details.

Hawick to Langholm and Liddesdale

Fourteen miles from Jedburgh, the unprepossessing mill town of **HAWICK** (pronounced "Hoyk") hit the headlines in 1996, when two local women attempted to join a traditional all-male ride-out which takes place each June. Having been refused permission to ride on grounds of their sex, the women took their case to the Equal Opportunities Commission. The Sheriff Court ruled that the ban was illegal under the Sex Discrimination Act, and the subsequent furore split the town. Controversy aside, Hawick is known for its many factory outlets which swarm with visitors, bearing witness to its history as centre of the region's knitwear and hosiery industry. Hawick's **tourist information office** is in **Drumlanrig Tower** (Easter–May & Oct Mon–Sat 10am–5pm, June & Sept 10am–5.30pm, Sun noon–5.30pm, July & Aug Mon–Sat 10am–6pm, Sun noon–6pm; ☎01450/372547) and doubles as a **museum** (times as for tourist office; £2.25), telling the story of the tower from the sixteenth century. The **Hawick Museum & Scott Gallery**, Wilton Lodge Park (April–Sept Mon–Fri 10am–noon & 1.30–5pm, Sat & Sun 2–4.45pm; Oct–March Mon–Fri 1–4pm, Sun

2–4pm; £1.25), has displays reflecting the manufacturing life of the area – it was a major producer of woollens. There's also a gallery housing nineteenth- and twentieth-century Scottish art; more exciting, though, are the regular travelling exhibitions which, surprisingly, Hawick seems to attract.

Beyond Hawick, the road twists its way south between the bulging heathery hills that shadow the river to **TEVIOTHEAD**, home of the **Johnnie Armstrong Gallery** and the workshops of the Moffat family who make gold and silver jewellery, specializing in Celtic, Viking and Scottish designs (daily 9am–7pm; ☎01450/850237). The museum is named after a local hero and defender of Scotland, who, in 1529, annoyed Henry VIII so much that he persuaded James V of Scotland to get rid of him – James then invited Johnnie Armstrong to a truce and had him murdered.

At Teviothead the road leaves the dale to cross over into Dumfries, where the **Ewes Water** tumbles down to **LANGHOLM**, a quiet, stone-built mill town at the confluence of the Esk, Ewes and Wauchope waters, which flourished during the eighteenth-century textile boom, and is still dominated by the industry. This was the birthplace in 1892 of the poet **Hugh MacDiarmid**, a co-founder of the Scottish National Party and a key player in the literary renaissance that fired the nationalist movement between the two world wars. MacDiarmid, born Christopher Murray Grieve, looked to the Scotland of the eighteenth century, lionizing Walter Scott and Robbie Burns while heaping scorn on the anglicized gentry. This didn't go down well with some of the burghers of Langholm, who, when MacDiarmid died in 1978 at the age of 86, tried to prevent him being buried in the local churchyard. If you're passing through town, stop off at the **Armstrong Museum and Clan Centre**, at Castle Holm (Easter to end Sept Tues–Sun 1.30–4.30pm; £1), for further stories of the clan, or follow the MacDiarmid Trail round town.

The **tourist office** (April, May & Sept Mon–Sat 10.30am–4.30pm; June–Aug daily 10am–5pm; ☎013873/80976), on the main road leading into Langholm from the north, can provide details of **accommodation**, or try the convenient *Eskdale Hotel*, Market Place (☎013873/80357; ②), the *Reivers Rest*, High Street (☎013873/81343, *paul@reivers-rest.demon.co.uk*; ②), or one of the town's two **campsites**.

On from Langholm

Four roads lead out of Langholm, the most stunning being the narrow country lane that snakes its way east over the empty hills to **Newcastleton** in Liddesdale. Otherwise, choose between the rustic thirty-mile journey west to **Dumfries** (see p.165) via Lockerbie; the far slower trip northwest up **Eskdale** for Selkirk and the Tweed Valley (see p.151); or the shorter journey south past Canonbie to **Gretna Green**.

If you're travelling by **bus** from Langholm, it takes about three hours to get to Dumfries, changing at Lockerbie (4 buses weekly), whilst Gretna Green can be reached via the better-served Carlisle route. Buses to Selkirk (6–7 daily; 1hr) go along the A7 via Hawick – there aren't any services along Eskdale and only an occasional bus to Newcastleton (see p.158).

Liddesdale

Heading south out of Jedburgh on the A68, it's about a mile to the B6357, a narrow byroad that leads over the moors to the hamlet of Bonchester Bridge. From here, the road cuts south through Wauchope Forest and carries on into **Liddesdale**, whose wild beauty is at its most striking between Saughtree and Newcastleton. In between the two, take the turning to **Hermitage Castle** (April–Sept Mon–Sun 9.30am–6.30pm; Oct–March Sat 9.30am–4.30pm, Sun 2–4.30pm; HS; £1.80), a bleak and forbidding fastness bedevilled by all sorts of horrifying legends: one owner, William Douglas, starved his prisoners to death; whilst Lord de Soulis, another occupant, engaged the help of demons to fortify the castle in defiance of the king, Robert the Bruce. Not entirely trusting his demonic assistants, Soulis also drilled holes into the shoulders of his vassals, the better to yoke them to sledges of building materials. Bruce became so tired of the complaints that he exclaimed, "Boil him if you please, but let me hear no more of him." Bruce's henchmen took him at his word and ambushed the rebellious baron. Convinced, however, that Soulis had a pact with his demonic familiar, Redcap, that made him difficult to kill ("ropes could not bind him, nor steel weapons touch"), they bound him with ropes of sifted sand, wrapped him in lead and boiled him slowly.

From the outside, the castle remains an imposing structure, its heavy walls topped by stepped gables and a tidy corbelled parapet. However, the apparent homogeneity is deceptive: certain features were invented during a Victorian restoration, a confusing supplement to the ad hoc alterations that had already transformed the fourteenth-century original. The ruinous interior is a bit of a letdown, but look out for the tight Gothic doorways and gruesome dungeon.

It's a short journey on to **NEWCASTLETON**, a classic estate village built for the hand-loom weavers of the third Duke of Buccleuch in 1793. The gridiron streets fall either side of a long main road that connects three geometrically arranged squares – nice enough to while away the odd hour. You can **stay** the night at the *Liddesdale Hotel* (☎013873/75255; ②) and sample some local trout or pheasant, or try the comfortable *Borders Honey Farm* B&B (☎013873/76737; ②), four miles north of Newcastleton on the B6357, but if you plan to stay during the hugely popular **Newcastleton Folk Festival** in July, book ahead. For **food**, try the *Copshaw Kitchen Restaurant* (☎01387/375250), Hermitage Street (closed Tues), provided you don't mind dining in an antique shop.

The road leaves Liddesdale ten miles southwest of Newcastleton at Canonbie. Around here, sandwiched between the **Esk** and the **Sark**, was what was known as the "**Debateable Land**", a pocket-sized territory claimed – but not controlled – by both England and Scotland from the fourteenth to the early eighteenth centuries. In the prevailing chaos, the Border Reivers flourished, and famed outlaws like Kinmont Willie, Jock o' the Side and Clym of the Cleugh established fabulous reputations for acts of cruelty and kindness in equal measure.

Annandale: Gretna Green to Moffat

Cutting through **Annandale**, the M/A74 connects Carlisle with Glasgow. This is the fastest way to cross southern Scotland but it's an unpleasantly busy road, jam-packed with trucks and lorries. You could break your journey by stopping off at **Gretna Green**, whose name is synonymous with elopements and quick weddings, before travelling the thirty miles north to the charming market town of **Moffat**, bypassed by the main road, which makes an ideal base for exploring the surrounding uplands. Bus services along Annandale are quick and frequent.

Gretna to Lockerbie

There's not much to the twin villages of **GRETNA GREEN** and **GRETNA** except their curious history, the result of the quirks of the British legal system. Up until 1754 English couples could buy a quick and secret wedding at London's Fleet Prison, bribing imprisoned clerics with small amounts of money. The Hardwicke Marriage Act brought an end to this seedy wheeze, enforcing the requirement of a licence and a church ceremony. However, in Scotland, a marriage declaration made before two witnesses remained legal. The consequences of this difference in the law verged on farce: hundreds of runaway couples dashed north to Scotland, their weddings witnessed by just about anyone who came to hand – ferrymen, farmers, tollgate keepers and even self-styled "priests" who set up their own "marriage houses".

Gretna and Gretna Green, due to their position beside the border on the main turnpike road to Edinburgh, became the most popular destination for the fugitives. In their rush, many people tied the knot at the first place to hand after dismounting from the stagecoach, which happened to be a blacksmith's shop situated at the crossroads, though the better-off maintained class distinctions, heading for the staging post at Gretna Hall. The association with blacksmiths was strengthened by one of the first "priests", the redoubtable Joseph Paisley, a 25-stone Goliath who – in business from 1754 to 1812 – gave a certain style to the ceremony by straightening a horseshoe, a show of strength rather than a symbolic act. His melodramatic act led to stories of Gretna weddings being performed over the blacksmith's anvil, and later "priests" were more than happy to act out the rumour. Both villages boomed until the marriage laws were further amended in 1856, but some business continued right down to 1940, when marriage by declaration was made illegal. The **Gretna Hall Blacksmith's & Crafts Shop** now houses a museum, shops, workshops, restaurants, a pub and the **tourist office** (daily: April & Oct 10am–4.30pm; May, June & Sept 10am–5pm; July & Aug 10am–6pm; ☎01461/337834; museum fee 80p); year-round information is also available from the tourist office at the Gretna Services on the A74. Confusingly, the *Gretna Hall Hotel* (☎01461/338257; ⑤) also has a **Blacksmith's Shop and Museum** (April–Sept daily 9am–5pm; Oct–March Tues–Sat 10am–4pm; £1) containing a diverting collection of romantic bygones.

There are lots of places to **stay** in and around Gretna and Gretna Green and all the hotels serve **bar meals**. The tourist office has the full list, but the nicest options are in Gretna: try either of two modernized farmhouses, the *Surrone Guest House*, on Annan Road (☎01461/338341; ②), or *The Beeches*, Loanwath Road (☎01461/337448; ②; Feb–Dec), which has just two (non-smoking) rooms.

Ecclefechan and Lockerbie

It's about nine miles from Gretna to the tidy hamlet of **ECCLEFECHAN**, birthplace of the historian and essayist **Thomas Carlyle** (1795–1881). Born into a strongly Calvinist family, Carlyle's highly successful account of the *French Revolution* (1837) set out his theory of history as "Divine Scripture": the French aristocracy had reaped the rewards of their corruption and indulgence. However, with no clearly defined political ideology his radicalism soon began to wane – reinforced by the failure of contemporary activist movements to live up to his idealistic expectations. Disillusioned, Carlyle was eventually to become the strongest voice for the moral concerns of the Victorian bourgeoisie, and as such a litmus paper of his age. His long marriage was turbulent, but when his wife died in 1866 he never recovered and was a semi-recluse for many years before his death. His old home, the whitewashed **Arched House** (May–Sept daily except Sat 1.30–5pm; NTS; £1.80), is now a tiny museum, featuring among the personal memorabilia a bronze cast of his hands, old smoking caps and his cradle. There are several **hotels** and **B&Bs** in Ecclefechan, including *Carlyle House*, opposite the museum (☎01576/300322; ②), the *Cressfield Country House Hotel*, Townfoot (☎01576/300281; ③), designed by Carlyle's father – as well as the well-serviced *Hoddom Castle Campsite* nearby on the B725 (☎01576/300251).

The quiet country town of **LOCKERBIE**, eight miles from Ecclefechan, was catapulted into the headlines on Wednesday December 21, 1988, when a Pan-Am jumbo jet, flying from Frankfurt to New York via Heathrow, was blown up by a terrorist bomb concealed in a transistor radio. All the crew and passengers died and the plane's fragments crashed down on Lockerbie, killing a further eleven. After many attempts to extradite those who planted the bomb, allegedly Arab terrorists residing in Libya, the suspects are to face trial under Scottish law in a specially-created court in the Netherlands. Local people have set up a Remembrance Garden on the outskirts of town, but this is no place for the casual visitor.

Moffat

Encircled by hills and dales, **MOFFAT** is a good-looking market town, its wide and elegant **High Street** flanked by Georgian mansions and streets of colourful brick cottages. The former hark back to the eighteenth century, when Moffat was briefly a modish spa, its sulphur springs attracting the rich and famous. One disappointed customer suggested they smelt of bilge water – but they were good enough for Robbie Burns and James Boswell, who came to "wash off the scurvy spots".

Moffat is no longer so fashionable, despite being winner of the "best kept small country town" in 1996, but boasts such low-key attractions as the John Adam-designed **Moffat House Hotel** and the neighbouring **Colvin Fountain**, whose sturdy bronze ram was accidentally cast without any ears. Not far away, the dark shadows of the **Black Bull** pub once quartered John Graham of Claverhouse as he planned his persecution of the Covenanters on behalf of Charles II. For details of the town's history, pop into the **museum**, at Church Gate (Easter–Sept Mon–Sat except Wed 10.30am–1pm & 2.30–5pm, Sun 2.30–5pm; £1). The tourist office (see below) has a helpful compendium of local **walks**, one of the best being the short but brisk hike up to the top of Gallow Hill, from where there are great views out over Annandale: allow a couple of hours. For a more gentle stroll round the outskirts of the town by the River Annan, follow the "waterside walk" sign opposite Station Park. More strenuous walking is within reach in the Lowther Hills (see p.162), and nearby Beattock marks the midway point of the Southern Upland Way.

Practicalities

Buses to Moffat drop passengers on High Street near the **tourist office** (daily: April, May, Sept & Oct 10am–5pm; June–Aug 9.30am–6.30pm; ☎01683/220620). There is no shortage of accommodation in town: several **hotels** line the High Street, the best being the opulent *Moffat House Hotel*, High Street (☎01683/220039; ⑤). Some alternatives include the palatable *Buccleuch Arms* (☎01683/220003; ④), a former coaching inn, and the *Star Hotel* (☎01683/220156; ②), which claims the dubious distinction of being Britain's narrowest free-standing hotel; both are on the High Street. For **B&Bs**, try along Beechgrove, a five-minute walk from the town centre: head north along High Street, continue down Academy Road, and turn beside Moffat Academy. Here you'll find an array of places to stay including *Queensberry House* (☎01683/220538; ①; March to mid-Jan), *Alba House* (☎01683/220418; ②; April–Oct), and *Gilbert House* (☎01683/220050; ①). The fourteen-acre *Hammerland's Farm* **camping and caravan** site (☎01683/220436; March–Nov) sits beside the Selkirk road, about half a mile east of Moffat.

The *Buccleuch Arms* serves the best **bar meals** in town: alternatively, choose from two Italian restaurants, *Valle Verde Trattoria* (closed Wed) further up High Street for filling, cheap pizzas, and *Claudio's* in the old police station at Burnside for popular home cooking. You'll find a few cafés along High Street, including *Pacitti's* which serves great coffee, or go for the afternoon teas (May–Sept) at the *Moffat House Hotel*. If you've got a real sweet tooth, try the home-made fudge and local Moffat toffee from the sweet shop in the High Street.

Around Moffat

From Moffat, there are three beautiful routes you can take through the most dramatic parts of the Southern Uplands. Of the three, the finest is the A708 between Moffat and

Selkirk (see p.149), via **Moffat Water** and **Yarrow Water**. On the way, the Grey Mare's Tail Waterfall provides the opportunity for an exhilarating ramble and St Mary's Loch gives easy access to an especially stimulating section of the Southern Upland Way. Further west, the second route uses the A701, which climbs over the hills at the head of Annandale, cuts down **Tweeddale**, and joins the Tweed Valley near Peebles (see p.153). The third option begins at Elvanfoot on the M/A74, where the B7040 leaves the main road to cross the **Lowther Hills**. Passing through the former lead-mining villages of **Leadhills** and **Wanlockhead**, this road reaches Nithsdale north of Drumlanrig Castle (see p.168).

Travelling these routes by **bus** remains difficult. The only service along the A708 is the Harrier Scenic Bus Service, which runs from Moffat to Melrose once weekly between July and late September. The Harrier also links Moffat and Peebles via the A701 once a week during the summer. The only way to reach Leadhills and Wanlockhead is on the once- or twice-daily service from Sanquhar in Nithsdale.

Moffat Water and Yarrow Water

Heading northeast from Moffat, the A708 snakes its way through the forests and hills along the lower stretches of **Moffat Water**. Before long the road climbs to wilder terrain, tracking along the bottom of a gloomy gully surrounded by desolate moorland. Beyond, ten miles from town, the 200ft **Grey Mare's Tail Waterfall** (NTS) tumbles down a rocky crevasse – it's one of Dumfries's best-known beauty spots. The base of the falls is approached by a precipitous footpath along the left side of the stream, a ten-minute clamber each way from the road. There's a longer hike, too, up the steep right-hand bank, past the head of the falls and on to the remote **Loch Skeen**, where you can fish without permits.

Back on the road, and crossing over into the Borders, it's a few miles further to the pair of icy lakes that mark the start of **Yarrow Water**. Tiny **Loch of the Lowes** to the south and the larger **St Mary's Loch** to the north are separated by a slender isthmus and magnificently set beneath the surrounding hills. This spot was popular with the nineteenth-century Scottish literati, especially Walter Scott and his friend James Hogg, the "Shepherd poet of Ettrick", who wrote:

Oft had he viewed, as morning rose
the bosom of the lonely Lowes.
Oft thrilled his heart at close of even
to see the dappled vales of heaven
with many a mountain, moor and tree
asleep upon Saint Mary.

The pair gathered to chew the fat at **Tibbie Shiels Inn** on the isthmus (☎01750/42231; ②), which takes its name from Isabella Shiel, a formidable and, by all accounts, amusing woman who ruled the place till her death in 1878 at the age of 96. Today, the inn is a famous watering hole on the Southern Upland Way and serves a limited range of bar meals. For a short and enjoyable walk, follow the footpath from the inn along the east side of St Mary's Loch into **Bowerhope Forest**. Alternatively, the Southern Upland Way heads across the moors north to Traquair House and south to the valley of the Ettrick Water, both strenuous hikes that require an Ordnance Survey map, a compass and proper clothing (see "Outdoor pursuits" in Basics).

East of St Mary's Loch, the A708 is crossed by the B709 going north through the hills to Innerleithen or southeast to Hawick. The junction is marked by *The Gordon Arms Hotel* (☎01750/82232; ②), reputedly the last meeting place of Scott and Hogg, where framed fragments of letters from Scott are on display in an otherwise basic bar serving meals and real ale. From the hotel, which offers a transport service and a cheap bunkhouse dormitory for walkers, you can follow the course of the lovely Yarrow Water further east for about seventeen miles to Selkirk (see p.149).

Tweeddale

Just north of Moffat, the A701 ascends the west side of **Annandale** to skirt the impressive box canyon at its head. Best viewed from the road about six miles from town, the gorge – the **Devil's Beef Tub** – takes its name from the days when rustling Reivers hid their herds here. Walter Scott described the place aptly: "It looks as if four hills were laying their heads together to shut out daylight from the dark hollow place between them." The gorge was also a suitably secret hideaway for persecuted Covenanters during Charles II's "Killing Times".

Beyond the Tub, the road crosses over into **Tweeddale** and soon reaches tiny **Tweedsmuir**, where an alternative route turns right over the Tweedsmuir Hills to St Mary's Loch (see above). The eleven-mile single-track road, inaccessible in winter, climbs at a twenty percent gradient past Talla Reservoir, where many men lost their lives constructing a water supply for Edinburgh in 1905. Fishing permits for Talla and the neighbouring Megget Reservoir are available from *Tibbie Shiels Inn* at St Mary's Loch.

Back on the A701, a mile north of Tweedsmuir, you'll pass *The Crook Inn* (☎01899/880272; ⑤), one-time watering hole of Robbie Burns and a good base for climbing Broad Law, Southern Scotland's second highest hill. Behind the hotel, there's a small workshop and craft centre, where you can watch glass-blowing displays. Continuing north along the widening Tweeddale, you'll reach the village of **BROUGHTON**, where, inside the old Free Church, **The John Buchan Centre** (May to mid-Oct daily 2–5pm; £1) commemorates the novelist, who spent his childhood holidays in the district. Three miles down the road in pretty Holmswater Glen, the *Glenholm Centre* (☎01899/830408, *glenhom@dircon.co.uk*; ②) is a working farm with a cosy four-room guesthouse.

The Lowther Hills

West of Moffat, sandwiched between the M74/A74 and Nithsdale, the **Lowther Hills** offer a wild landscape of tightly clustered peaks, bare until the heather blooms, hiding fast-flowing burns and narrow valleys – a dramatic terrain once known as "God's Treasure House" on account of its gold and silver ores. These mineral deposits were much sought after by the impoverished kings of Scotland, who banned their export and claimed a monopoly – draconian measures that only encouraged smuggling. There was lead here too, mined from Roman times right up to the 1950s, and used in the manufacture of pottery and glass.

Leadhills and Wanlockhead

Twenty-one miles north of Moffat, tiny **LEADHILLS** has a disconsolate air born of its wilderness surroundings. The terraced cottages of this classic "company town" were built by the mine owners for their employees, but the boom years ended in the 1830s, since when the village has been left pretty much to itself.

A couple of miles away, remote and windswept **WANLOCKHEAD**, at 1500ft the highest village in Scotland, is even smaller than its neighbour. It shares Leadhills' mining history, but Wanlockhead's attempts to lure the tourists have made the villages very different. The **Scottish Lead Mining Museum** (April–Oct daily 11am–4.30pm; £3.50) deserves a good hour or two, beginning with the spruce **visitor centre**, which traces the development of the industry and its workforce. Afterwards, highlights of the open-air site include a guided tour of the underground **Loch Nell Mine** and of a couple of restored miners' cottages. There's also a rare example of a wooden **beam engine** and all sorts of industrial bits and pieces, mostly dating from the late 1950s when government grants sponsored a brief revival in lead mining; the earlier workings were closed in the 1930s. Sometimes the eighteenth-century **library** is open too (early May to late Sept Wed, Sat & Sun 2–4pm), its books purchased from the voluntary subscriptions of its members: at its height, the library had a stock of 2000 volumes.

Wanlockhead straddles the Southern Upland Way, and is thus blessed with a **youth hostel** (☎01659/74252; April–Oct), sited in the old mine surgeon's house, while the museum's visitor centre can give details of a couple of cheap **B&Bs**.

Biggar and around

Five miles north of the Leadhills turning on the M/A74, Edinburgh traffic leaves the motorway to head northeast along the A702. Most people shoot straight through to the capital – it's only about forty miles – but, if you're looking to break your journey, the old market town of **BIGGAR** warrants an hour or two. Start your visit at the **Moat Park Heritage Centre** (April–Oct Mon–Sat 10am–5pm, Sun 2–5pm; £2), which occupies a grand neo-Romanesque church near the foot of Kirkstyle (off High Street). Inside, a well-presented exhibition traces the history of Upper Clydesdale, and on the upper floor you can see a display of extraordinary table covers made by local tailor Menzies Moffat (1828–1907). Don't miss the banquet-sized Royal Crimean Hero Tablecloth, which sets a cartoon strip of notable figures alongside scenes from Scottish country life. The heritage centre can also give details of **Hugh MacDiarmid's Cottage**, three miles from Biggar on the Edinburgh road, which can be visited by appointment only.

Biggar has four other museums: the nearest, the **Gladstone Court Museum** (April–Oct Mon–Sat 10am–12.30pm & 2–5pm, Sun 2–5pm; £2), across Kirkstyle on North Back Road, boasts a shop-lined Victorian street illustrating different aspects of nineteenth-century life, from the telephone exchange and classroom to the bank and the cobblers. Returning to Kirkstyle, walk over the hill to the footpath beside Biggar burn. To the right is the **Greenhill Covenanters' Museum** (April to mid-Oct daily 2–5pm; £1), which explores the development of the Covenanting movement and the religious conflicts that ensued. To the left along the burn lies **Biggar Gasworks Museum** (June–Sept daily 2–5pm; £1). Before North Sea gas was piped across the UK, small coal-based gasworks like this one were common. Most were demolished in the 1970s, but Biggar's has survived and even manages to look quite spick-and-span. Lastly, on Broughton Road, the unusual **Puppet Museum** (Easter–Sept Mon–Sat 10am–5pm, Sun 2–5pm; £2.50; ☎01899/220631 for details of shows), set up by the touring company Purves Puppets, features marionettes from around the world with regular workshops and shows held in the museum's Victorian theatre. Backstage tours cost £4.

Back up High Street, the **sundial** outside the tourist office is the work of local poet-artist Ian Hamilton Finlay, a founder of the "concrete poetry" movement; you can see more of his work in Edinburgh's National Gallery of Modern Art (see p.97).

Practicalities

Regular **bus** services to Biggar arrive from a wide range of towns including Edinburgh, Peebles, Moffat and Dumfries. They stop on High Street, near the **tourist office** (Easter–Oct daily 10am–5pm; ☎01899/221066). There's a **B&B**, *Daleside*, 165 High St (☎01899/220097; ①) a stone's throw away, and **camping** is available at *Biggar Caravan*

Park on Broughton Road (☎01899/220319). For **food**, both the *Elphinstone Hotel* and the *Crown*, on High Street, have good daily specials.

Around Biggar

Six miles west of Biggar along the A72/73, near the village of Thankerton, the solitary peak of **Tinto Hill** was the site of Druidic festivals in honour of the sun-god Baal, or Bel. It's relatively easy to walk the footpath up to the 2320ft summit, from where the views are splendid – you'll also see a Druidic Circle and a Bronze Age burial cairn. A regular **bus** links Biggar with Thankerton.

Just north of Biggar on the A702 lie the southern extremities of the **Pentland Hills**, the narrow belt of upland extending into the suburbs of Edinburgh. The hills are best visited from the capital, but the pretty medieval village of **WEST LINTON**, straddling the Lyne Water twelve miles from Biggar, gives ready access to several rambles across the neighbouring hills. If you want to **stay**, try the large Victorian country house of Mrs McCallum, on Carlops Road (☎01968/660795; ④; April–Oct), while the best **food** around is at *The Old Mill Inn* (☎01721/752220) in nearby Blyth Bridge. Its extensive menu specializes in local fare with excellent home-made puddings, and a free pick-up/drop-home service is available if you're based further afield (a minimum of six people; book in advance).

Nothing more than an unassuming row of whitewashed weavers' cottages, **CAR-LOPS**, three miles on from West Linton, gives access to some excellent walks along the farm tracks of rural hamlets hidden between the A702 and A701. The poet Alan Ramsey, father of the artist, hailed from here; the *Alan Ramsey Hotel* (☎01968/660258; ②) serves standard bar fare and has an open fire.

SOUTHWEST SCOTLAND

Up until the eleventh century, the whole of **southwest Scotland** was known as Galloway, where independent chieftains maintained close contacts with the Vikings rather than the Scots. Gradually, this autonomy was whittled away and by the late thirteenth century the region, which comprises the rough triangle of land between the Solway Firth, the Firth of Clyde and the stretch from Dumfries to Kilmarnock, was integrated into Scotland. Indeed, it was here that both Robert the Bruce and William Wallace launched their wars against the English. Later on, from around the seventeenth century, the ports of the Solway coast prospered with the expansion of local shipping routes over to Ireland and, later still, the towns along the Firth of Clyde benefited from the industrialization of Glasgow. The region subsequently experienced economic decline as trade routes changed, turning busy ports into sleepy backwaters, and these days southwest Scotland is agreeably laid-back, not crossed by motorway and – with most travellers skipping past on their way to the Highlands and Islands – suffering little of the tourist crush familiar further north.

Robert Burns lived and died in this part of Scotland, a fact much exploited by the tourist offices. **The Burns Heritage Trail**, a motorist's route across much of the region, passes every conceivable place with which he had any connection, but frankly, unless you're particularly devoted, stick to the Burns sights in **Dumfries**, Ayr and Alloway. Extending southwest of Dumfries, the low-lying **Solway coast** boasts the delightfully tranquil township of **Kirkcudbright** and a handful of splendid medieval ruins, principally **Caerlaverock Castle** and **Sweetheart Abbey**. Crisscrossed by walking trails that cater for every level of athleticism and any amount of time, the **Galloway Hills** rise just to the north of the coast, their beautiful moors, mountains, lakes and rivers centred on the 150,000-acre **Galloway Forest Park**. After this come the rolling hills of the **Ayrshire Coast**, whose mostly agricultural landscapes are enlivened by a string of wide, flat sandy beaches and the occasional strip of coastal cliff. Here you'll also find the diverting town of **Ayr**, noteworthy for its Burns attractions and beach, and the district's other main resort, **Largs**, with its agreeable setting between hills and sea.

Travelling the region by **bus** presents few problems and there's a good **train** service from Glasgow along the Ayrshire coast to Stranraer. It's also easy to travel on from southwest Scotland by **ferry**, from Stranraer to Belfast and Larne, in Northern Ireland, and from the port of Ardrossan, north of Ayr, to the Isle of Arran, where you can hopscotch on up the Western Isles.

If you are keen to pursue a particular interest while visiting the area, Dumfries and Galloway Tourist Board has produced an excellent range of leaflets on local activities such as birdwatching, fishing and cycling, which are available from tourist offices.

Dumfries and around

With a population of 30,000, bustling **DUMFRIES** crowds the banks of the River Nith a few miles from the Solway Firth. Long known as the "Queen of the South", the town flourished as a medieval seaport and trading centre, its success attracting the attention of many English armies. The invaders managed to polish off most of the early settlement in 1448, 1536 and again in 1570, but Dumfries survived to prosper with its light industries supplying the agricultural hinterland. The town planners of the 1960s badly damaged the town, reducing it to an architectural hotchpotch, with – as the prime

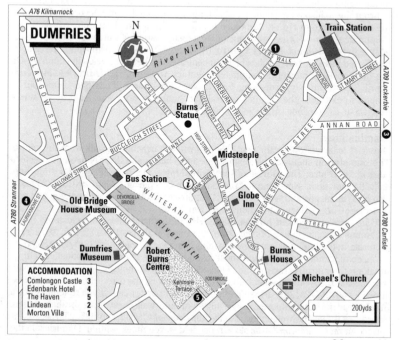

© Crown copyright

example – the graceful fifteenth-century lines of Devorgilla Bridge set against cereal-box apartment blocks. Nevertheless, the town makes a convenient base for exploring the Solway coast, and is at least worth a visit for its associations with Burns, who spent the last five years of his life here.

The Town

Hemmed in by the river to the north and west, the snout-shaped centre of Dumfries radiates out from the pedestrianized **High Street**, which runs roughly parallel to the Nith. At its northern edge is the **Burns Statue**, a fanciful piece of Victorian frippery featuring the great man holding a posy in one hand, whilst the other clutches at his heart. They haven't forgotten his faithful hound either, who lies curled around his feet.

Heading south down High Street, it's a couple of minutes' walk to **Midsteeple**, the old prison-cum-courthouse, and the narrow alley that leads to the smoky, oak-panelled *Globe Inn*, one of Burns' favourite drinking spots, and still a tavern. Continuing down the street, follow the signs to the **Burns' House** (April–Sept Mon–Sat 10am–5pm, Sun 2–5pm; Oct–March Tues–Sat 10am–1pm & 2–5pm; free), a simple sandstone building where the poet died of rheumatic heart disease in 1796. Inside, there's a collection of Burns memorabilia – manuscripts, letters and the like – and one of the bedroom windows bears his signature, scratched with his diamond ring.

Burns was buried in a simple grave beside **St Michael's Church**, a monstrous eighteenth-century heap just south of his house. Twenty years later, though, he was dug up and moved across the graveyard to a purpose-built Neoclassical **Mausoleum**, whose bright white columns hide a statue of Burns being accosted by the Poetic Muse. All around, in contrasting brownstone, stand the tombstones of the town's bourgeoisie, including many of the poet's friends; a plan indicates exactly where each is interred.

From the mausoleum, saunter back along the Nith and cross Devorgilla Bridge to the tiny **Old Bridge House Museum** (April–Sept Mon–Sat 10am–1pm & 2–5pm, Sun 2–5pm; free) of local bric-a-brac – including a teeth-chattering range of Victorian dental gear – and the **Robert Burns Centre** (April–Sept Mon–Sat 10am–8pm, Sun 2–5pm; free), sited in an old water mill, which concentrates on the poet's years in Dumfries. On the hill above, occupying an eighteenth-century windmill, the **Dumfries Museum** (April–Sept Mon–Sat 10am–5pm, Sun 2–5pm; Oct–March Tues–Sat 10am–1pm & 2–5pm; free) traces the region's natural and human history and features a camera obscura on its top floor (April–Sept; £1.20).

Practicalities

Dumfries train station, on the east side of town, is a five-minute walk from the centre. The **bus station** stands at the top of Whitesands beside the River Nith on the western edge of the centre. The **tourist office** (April, May & Oct daily 10am–5pm; June–Sept daily 9.30am–6pm; Nov–March Mon–Sat 10am–4.30pm & 2–5pm; ☎01387/253862), also on Whitesands at the corner with Bank Street, can book accommodation and give information about Burns attractions and town trails.

There are lots of **guest houses** and **B&Bs** in the handsome villas clustered round the train station, including *Morton Villa*, 28 Lovers Walk (☎01387/255825; ③), a large Victorian house with a pleasant garden, and *Lindean*, 50 Rae St (☎01387/251888; ①), a clean, comfortable red-sandstone house in a quiet street. For a more distinctive setting, try along Kenmure Terrace, a short block of attractive old houses overlooking the Nith from beside the footbridge below the Burns Centre. Of the three choices, *The Haven*, at no. 1 (☎01387/251281; ①), should be your first port of call. If you're looking for a **hotel**, head for Laurieknowe, a five- to ten-minute walk west from the bus station, where you'll find the welcoming, family-run *Edenbank Hotel* (☎01387/252759; ④), or splash out on *Comlongon Castle* at Clarencefield, seven miles south of Dumfries on the

A75 (☎01387/870283; ⑦), an atmospheric manor house adjacent to a fourteenth-century castle.

For **food**, try the child-friendly *Ben Venuto*, 42 Eastfield Rd, which serves Italian and seafood meals, or the *Station Hotel*, 49 Lovers Walk, specializing in fish and game dishes. The *Cairndale Hotel* (☎01387/254111), English Street, offers a "Taste of Burns Country" menu and hosts Sunday-night ceilidhs (May–Oct). The cheapest meals in town are provided by the popular YMCA café *Grapevine*, behind the Burns Statue on Castle Street (Mon–Fri 10am–3pm, Sat 10am–2.30pm), while *Bruno*'s fish and chip shop on Balmoral Road claims to sell the best chips in the southwest. Two of Burns' favourite drinking places are still in operation: the *Hole in the Wa'* **pub**, down an alley opposite Woolworth's on High Street, serves reasonable bar food, but for somewhere with a bit more atmosphere, make for the earthy *Globe Inn* on the High Street, which is crammed with memorabilia connected with the poet but is otherwise little changed since his time. Grierson and Graham, 10 Academy St (☎01387/259483), offer **bike rental**, useful for reaching the nearby Solway coast.

Around Dumfries: the east Solway coast and Nithsdale

The magnificent **Caerlaverock Castle** and the fine early Christian cross at **Ruthwell** are to be found on the shores of the Solway Firth southeast of Dumfries, from where a regular **bus** service runs to both. Alternatively, if you're heading north, the A76 travels the length of **Nithsdale** (there are also regular buses along this route), whose gentle slopes and old forests hide one major attraction: the massive, many-turreted seventeenth-century mansion of **Drumlanrig Castle**.

Caerlaverock Castle and Wildlife Centre

The remote and lichen-stained **Caerlaverock Castle**, eight miles from Dumfries (April–Sept daily 9.30am–6.30pm; Oct–March Mon–Sat 9.30am–4.30pm, Sun 2–4.30pm; HS £2.50), is shaped like a dramatic triangle with a mighty gatehouse at the apex. Built around 1270, it clearly impressed medieval chroniclers. During the siege of 1300, Edward I's balladeer, Walter of Exeter, commented: "In shape it was like a shield, for it had but three sides round it, with a tower at each corner . . . and good ditches filled right up to the brim with water. And I think you will never see a more finely situated castle."

Nowadays, close inspection reveals several phases of construction, which reflect Caerlaverock's turbulent past: time and again, the castle was attacked and damaged, each subsequent rebuilding further modifying the late thirteenth-century original. For instance, the fifteenth-century machicolations of the gatehouse top earlier towers that are themselves studded with wide-mouthed gunports from around 1590. This confusion of styles continues inside, where the gracious Renaissance facade of the **Nithsdale Apartments** was added by the first earl in 1634. Nithsdale didn't get much value for money: just six years later he was forced to surrender his castle to the Covenanters, who proceeded to wreck the place. It was never inhabited again.

Three miles further on you'll find the **Caerlaverock Wildfowl and Wetlands Centre** (daily 10am–5pm; £3.25, with concessions for those arriving by public transport, bicycle or on foot), 1350 acres of protected salt marsh and mud flat edging the Solway Firth. A National Nature Reserve and a Wildfowl and Wetlands Trust Refuge, the centre is equipped with screened approaches that link the main observatory to a score of well-situated birdwatchers' hides. It's famous for the 12,000 or so barnacle geese which return here in winter. Between May and August, when the geese are away, walkers along a wetlands trail may glimpse the rare natterjack toad. Throughout the year at 2pm daily, the wild swans are fed and the wardens run free wildlife safaris. A varied **birdwatching and wildlife** programme is also on offer – call ☎01387/770200 for up-to-date details. Both the castle and the centre are reached along the B725; this is the route the bus takes, mostly terminating at the castle but sometimes continuing to the start of the two-mile lane leading off the B725 to the centre.

The Ruthwell Cross

From the nature reserve it's about seven miles east along the B725 to both the village of **RUTHWELL** and the B724, the minor Dumfries–Annan road which trims its northern edge. Here you should turn down the short, signposted lane to the modest country church. The keys are kept at one of the houses at the foot of the lane; just look for the notice. Inside the church is the impressive **Ruthwell Cross**, an extraordinary early Christian monument dating from the late seventh century when Galloway was ruled by the Northumbrians. The eighteen-foot cross reveals a striking diversity of influences, with Germanic and Roman Catholic decoration and, running round the edge, a poem written in both runic figures and Northumbrian dialect. But it's the biblical carvings on the main face that really catch the eye, notably Mary Magdalene washing the feet of Jesus.

If you want to **stay**, your best bet is the comfortable *Kirkland Country House Hotel* (☎01387/870284; ③), next to the church.

Nithsdale

North of Dumfries, the A76 runs along the southern reaches of Nithsdale, a pastoral scene with the Forest of Ae and the Lowther Hills brooding in the distance. The road passes **Ellisland Farm** (April–Sept daily 10am–1pm & 2–5pm; Oct–March Tues–Sat 10am–1pm & 2–5pm; £1.50), built by Robert Burns and now housing a museum displaying many of his personal effects. After fourteen miles you reach the antiquated cottages of tiny **Thornhill**, where you can turn off onto the A702 to the conservation village of **MONAINE**, which nestles between several glens and offers lovely walks and cycle rides. Stay at *Bainoon* B&B (☎01848/200266; ②) for huge cooked breakfasts, or the excellent *Craigdarroch Arms Hotel* (☎01848/200205; ④).

Back on the A76, three miles north of Thornhill lies **Drumlanrig Castle** (May–Aug daily 10am–4pm; £6 or £2.50 for grounds only), not in fact a castle at all, but the grandiose stately home of the Duke of Buccleuch and Queensberry. The impressive driveway sweeps along an avenue of trees to the pink sandstone house with its cupolas, turrets and towers, surrounding an interior courtyard. The front is graced by a charming horseshoe-shaped stairway – a welcome touch of informality to the stateliness of the structure behind.

Inside, a string of luxurious rooms witness the immense wealth of the family. Among the priceless hoard of antique furnishings and fittings – which include a few mementoes dating from the overnight visit of Bonnie Prince Charlie in 1745 – are a trio of famous paintings exhibited in the **staircase hall**. These are Rembrandt's *Old Woman Reading*, a sensual composition dappling the shadow of the subject's hood against her white surplice, Holbein's formal portrait of *Sir Nicholas Carew*, and the *Madonna with the Yarnwinder* by Leonardo da Vinci. Other works are by Joost van Cleef, Breughel, Jan Grossaert (otherwise Mabuse) and Van Dyck, and there are endless family portraits by Allan Ramsay and Godfrey Kneller. Also look out for a striking 1950s portrait of the present duchess, all debutante coiffure and high-society shoulders, by John Merton and, in the serving room, John Ainslie's *Joseph Florence the Chef*, a sharply observed and dynamic portrait much liked by Walter Scott.

As well as the house, Drumlanrig offers a host of attractions, including a forested **country park** crisscrossed by footpaths and cycle routes (mountain bikes are available for rent), an adventure playground, a cycle museum, craft workshops, a gift shop, a tearoom and a bird of prey collection with demonstrations at 1pm and 3pm daily (except Thursdays). If you're heading here by bus from Dumfries or Ayr, bear in mind it's a 1.5-mile walk from the road to the house.

Leaving Drumlanrig, the A76 slips through the wooded hills of Nithsdale, passing the turning to Wanlockhead (see p.162) en route to **SANQUHAR**, a trim market town which boasts the oldest working post office in Britain, dating from 1712 and now also home to the **tourist office** (Easter–May & Sept 10.30am–4.30pm; June–Aug 10am–5pm; ☎01659/50185). Pressing on, the mining village of **Kirkconnel** prefigures the industrial settlements further north, one of them being **Cumnock**, for many years the home of James Keir Hardie, whose bronze bust stands outside the Town Hall. At Cumnock, there's a choice of routes. The A76 ploughs on to Kilmarnock, whilst the A70 crosses the Ayrshire hills to reach the coast of Ayr.

The Solway coast to the Galloway Hills

The creeks, bays and peninsulas of the **Solway coast** string along the Solway Firth, a shallow estuary wedged between Scotland and England. Edged by tidal marsh and mud bank, much of the shoreline is flat and eerily remote, but there are also some fine rocky bays sheltering beneath wooded hills, most notably at **Rockcliffe**, about twenty miles west of Dumfries. **Kirkcudbright** and **Gatehouse of Fleet** were once bustling ports thronged with sailing ships, but they were bypassed by the Victorian train network and so slipped into economic decline, which in effect preserved their handsome eighteenth- and early nineteenth-century town houses and workers' cottages. Both these towns are popular with – but not crowded by – tourists, as are **Sweetheart Abbey**, whose splendid Gothic remains are near Dumfries, and **Threave Castle**, a gaunt tower house perched on an islet just outside Castle Douglas.

Within comfortable striking distance of the coast are the **Galloway Hills**, whose forested knolls and grassy peaks flank lochs and tumbling burns – classic Southern Upland scenery – with scores of trails within **Galloway Forest Park**.

New Abbey

NEW ABBEY, a tidy hamlet eight miles south of Dumfries, is home to the red sandstone ruins of **Sweetheart Abbey** (April–Sept daily 9.30am–6.30pm; Oct–March Mon–Wed & Sat 9.30am–4.30pm, Thurs 9.30am–1pm, Sun 2–4.30pm; HS; £1.20). Founded by Cistercians in 1273, Sweetheart takes its name from the obsessive behaviour of its patron, Devorgilla de Balliol, who carried her husband's embalmed heart around with her for the last sixteen years of her life. The site is dominated by the remains of the Abbey Church, a massive structure that abandons the austere simplicity of earlier Cistercian foundations. The grand, high-pointed window arches of the nave, set beneath the elaborate clerestory, draw the eye to a mighty central tower with a battlemented parapet and flamboyant corbels. The opulent style reflects the monks' wealth, born of their skill in turning the wastes and swamps of Solway into productive farmland. Next door to the abbey, the **Abbey Cottage** tearooms serve great coffee and home-made cake, while the nearby *Criffel Inn* (☎01387/850305; ②) is a fine village pub with good beer. Alternatively, try the *Abbey Arms* (☎01387/850489; ②), opposite in the main square; both do food at lunch and dinner.

Just outside New Abbey on the Dumfries road, **Shambellie House** (April–Oct daily 11am–5pm; £2.50), set in beautiful gardens, houses a costume museum of dress and accessories from the late eighteenth century to the early twentieth century. One and a half miles south of New Abbey, Ardwell Mains Farm marks the start of the walk up **Criffel**, a 1871ft peak which offers great views of the Borders and the Lake District. A couple of miles further on at Kirkbean, a small turning on the left leads to **John Paul Jones Cottage** (April–June & Sept Tues–Sun 10am–5pm; July & Aug daily 10am–5pm; £2), birthplace of the founder of the US navy, although interestingly he also fought for the Russians.

The Colvend coast: Rockcliffe and Kippford

South of New Abbey, the A710 cuts across a handsome landscape of rolling farmland following the **Colvend coast** past the aptly named **Sandyhills beach**, before heading inland to Dalbeattie. Along the road, you'll see turnings first to **ROCKCLIFFE**, a beguiling little place nestled around a beautiful cove, and then to **KIPPFORD**, a cosy yachting centre strung out along the Urr estuary. A pleasant thirty-minute coastal stroll, the Jubilee Path, links the two villages, passing the Celtic hill fort of the **Mote of Mark** en route. At low tide you can walk over the Rough Firth causeway from Kippford across the mud flats to **Rough Island**, a humpy twenty-acre bird sanctuary owned by the National Trust for Scotland, though it's out of bounds in May and June when the terns and oystercatchers are nesting.

Either of these villages would make a pleasant base for exploring the local countryside and beaches, or for tackling some of the excellent local walks: Rockcliffe has the bigger choice of accommodation, while Kippford is the more lively. In Rockcliffe, try the attractive *Albany* **B&B** (☎01556/630355; ①), right on the seafront, or nearby *Millbrae House* (☎01556/630217; ②). The only **hotel** in the village is the grand *Barons Craig* (☎01556/630225; ⑥), a splendid Victorian mansion on the hill above the bay, but there are several cottages available for rent by the week – try *Westlin* (☎01556/630212; 4 people; £120–215 per week; April–Oct), overlooking the bay, or the charming *Port Donnell* cottage rented out by the NTS (☎0131/243 9331; £240–390 per week). If you prefer to camp, there's the *Castle Point Caravan Site* (☎01556/630248; March–Oct). The best place to stay, and eat, in Kippford is the *Anchor Hotel* (☎01556 620205; ③), on the seafront, which serves excellent bar meals. There are a few lovely places to stay along the main A710 – both *Cairngill House* (☎01387/780681; ③) and *Craigbittern House* (☎01387/780247; ②) have stunning views of the coast at Sandyhills, and a couple of miles further on at Colvend is *Clonyard House* (☎01556/630372; ③), with wooded grounds and resident birds. Additional **campsites** in the area include the attractive *Kippford Caravan Park* (☎01556/620636) and *Sandyhills Leisure Park* (☎01557/870267) on the beach at Sandyhills.

Beyond Kippford the A710 heads north to Dalbeattie, where you'll find the local **tourist office** (April, May & Sept Mon–Sat 10.30am–4.30pm; June–Aug daily 10am–5pm; ☎01556/610117) and a reasonable range of shops and supermarkets. From here, you can continue west along the attractive coastal road, the A711, to Kirkcudbright (see p.171), taking a brief signposted detour en route down a narrow country lane to see the evocative remains of **Orchardton Tower** (free), a mid-fifteenth-century fortified tower house, unusual in its circular design.

Around Castle Douglas

The eighteenth-century streets of **CASTLE DOUGLAS**, eleven miles north of Rockcliffe, were designed by the town's owner, William Douglas, a local lad who made a fortune trading in the West Indies. Douglas had ambitious plans to turn his town into a prosperous industrial and commercial centre, but, like his scheme to create an extensive Galloway canal system, it didn't quite work.

You'll only need to hang around town long enough to get your bearings as the district's two attractions are well outside the centre, but you might consider renting a **bike** here – at Ace Cycles, 11 Church St (Mon–Sat 9am–5pm; ☎01556/504542). The **tourist office** (April–June, Sept & Oct 10am–4.30pm; July & Aug 10am–6pm; ☎01556/502611) is at the end of the long main drag, King Street. Buses stop at the other end, on the lochside road to **Threave Garden** (daily 9.30am–5.30pm; NTS; £4.40), which can also be reached direct from the A75 – the signposted turning is at the roundabout on the west side of town. The garden features a magnificent spread of flowers and woodland, sixty acres subdivided into more than a dozen areas, from the bright, old-fashioned blooms of the Rose Garden to the brilliant banks of rhododendrons in the Woodland Garden and the ranks of primula, astilbe and gentian in the Peat Garden. In springtime, thousands of visitors turn up for the flowering of more than two hundred types of daffodil and, from late May onwards, the herbaceous beds are the main attraction, with most of them arranged like islets in a sea of lawn (so that they can be viewed from all sides). The exception is the more formal beds of the Walled Garden which adjoin the greenhouses and the nursery.

Threave Garden was developed by the National Trust for Scotland as a teaching arena for its School of Horticulture, whose students occupy Threave House, the hulking Victorian mansion that was the residence of the last laird. The **visitor centre** (April to late Oct daily 9.30am–5.30pm) has maps of and an exhibition about the garden and the surrounding estate (also NTS property), though the restaurant's (10am–5pm) fruit pies are more immediately satisfying.

To reach **Threave Castle** (April–Sept daily 9am–6.30pm; HS; £1.80), return to the A75 roundabout, where you'll see signs to the Open Farm and Threave Wildfowl Refuge, and cut straight across, down the mile-long country lane which brings you to the start of the footpath to the River Dee. It's a lovely ten-minute walk down to the river, where you ring a brass bell for the boat over to the stern-looking stronghold, stuck on a flat and grassy islet. Built for a Black Douglas, Archibald the Grim, in around 1370, the fortress was among the first of its kind, a sturdy, rectangular structure completed shortly after the War of Independence when clan feuding spurred a frenzy of castle-building. The bleak lines of the original structure are, however, partly obscured by a rickety, fifteenth-century curtain wall, thrown up as a desperate – and unsuccessful – attempt to defend the castle against James II. Determined to crush the Black Douglases, the king personally murdered the eighth earl after dinner in Stirling and subsequently appropriated his estate. The Covenanters wrecked the place in the 1640s, but enough remains of the interior to make out its general plan, beginning with the storage areas and spitefully gloomy prison in the basement. Up above, the first – and entrance – floor was once reached from the outside by removable timber stairs, while inside a spiral staircase ascended to the upper floors – you can still make out its course. The roof was flat to accommodate stone-throwing machinery, with projecting wooden galleries to enable the defenders to drop everything harmful onto the heads of the attackers – from the outside you can still discern the holes where the timber supports were lodged.

From Castle Douglas you can head north on the A713 which runs alongside **Loch Ken** to New Galloway (see p.175). The wooded banks of the loch are particularly stunning in autumn, and the area is a haven for the watersports fans, with waterskiing, powerboating, rowing, sailing, windsurfing, angling, birdwatching and more on offer. Contact Loch Ken Marina and Water Sports Club (☎01644/470220) for the action sports or Galloway Sailing Centre (☎01644/420626) for the non-powered variety; angling permits and boats are available from all the marinas and caravan parks. The village of Parton, halfway up the loch, is home to the **Scottish Alternative Games**, which takes place in early August and features the World Gird and Cleek Championships, amongst others.

There is a variety of **accommodation** available including the pleasant *Lochside* campsite on the Threave road (☎01556/502949), and several B&Bs in Castle Douglas itself: try the friendly and welcoming *Craigvar House* (☎01556/503515; ②) at 60 St Andrews St, or *Balmaghie House* (☎01556/670234; ②), a huge mansion in its own grounds, with great home cooking. For considerably more luxury, head thirteen miles south of Castle Douglas to Auchencairn, where the award-winning *Balcary Bay Hotel* (☎01556/640217; ⑦) boasts a stunning location at the water's edge.

Kirkcudbright

KIRKCUDBRIGHT (pronounced "Kirkcoobrie"), hugging the muddy banks of the Dee ten miles southwest of Castle Douglas, has a quaint harbour and the most attractive of town centres, a charming medley of simple brick cottages with medieval pends,

Georgian villas and Victorian town houses, many attractively painted. This is the setting for **MacLellan's Castle** (April–Sept daily 9.30am–6pm; Oct–March Sat 9.30am–4.30pm, Sun 2–4.30pm; HS; £1.50), a sullen pink-flecked hulk towering above the harbourside. Part fortified tower house and part spacious mansion, the castle was built in 1577 for the then-Provost, Sir Thomas MacLellan of Bombie, when a degree of law and order permitted the aristocracy to relax its former defensive preoccupations and satisfy its increasing desire for comfort and domestic convenience. As a consequence, chimneys have replaced battlements at the wall-heads and windows begin at the ground floor. Nevertheless, the walls remain impressively thick, and there are a handful of wide-mouthed gun loops, though these are haphazard affairs designed to deter intruders rather than beat off an invading army. Inside, it's easy to pick out the vaulted basement – which accommodated the kitchen and storerooms – underpinning three upper storeys, home to a rabbit warren of well-appointed domestic apartments. Also, keep an eye out for a real curiosity, the laird's lug, or peephole, behind the fireplace of the Great Hall. Sir Thomas MacLellan is buried in the neighbouring **Greyfriars Church**, where his tomb is an eccentrically crude attempt at Neoclassicism – it even incorporates parts of someone else's gravestone.

Close by, on the L-shaped High Street, **Broughton House** (April–Oct daily 1–5.30pm; NTS; £2.40) was once the home of Edward Hornel, an important member of the late nineteenth-century Scottish art establishment. Hornel and his buddies – The Glasgow Boys (see p.212) – established an artists' colony in Kirkcudbright, and some of their work, impressionistic in style, is on display here. Hornel's paintings of Japan, a country he often visited, are bright and cheery, and the house itself a delight. Hornel had the Georgian mansion he bought in 1901 modified to include a studio and a mahogany-panelled gallery decked out with a frieze of the Elgin marbles. He also designed the lovely **Japanese garden**.

A couple of minutes' walk away is the church-like **tollbooth**, which once served as court house, prison and town hall. Its clock faces are off-set so that they can be viewed down both parts of High Street. The building now houses the **Tolbooth Art Centre** (March, April & Oct–Feb Mon–Sat 11am–4pm; May & June Mon–Sat 11am–5pm & Sun 2–5pm; July & Aug Mon–Sat 10am–6pm, Sun 2–5pm; £1.50), featuring work by Hornel and his associates, whose history is detailed in an explanatory video. The studios on the upper floor are leased to artists and craftworkers, whom you can sometimes watch at work. The town's artistic connections are furthered by its several art galleries, including the picturesque **Harbour Cottage Gallery**, which hosts a variety of temporary exhibitions (March–Nov 10.30am–12.30pm & 2–5pm; 50p).

WALKS AROUND KIRKCUDBRIGHT

There are several easy and popular walks around Kirkcudbright including the seven-mile round-trip up the Dee to **Tongland Power Station** (May–Sept Mon–Sat 4 guided tours daily; bookings ☎01557/330114; £1), whose turbines and generators are housed in a fine Art Deco building. Another option is the five-mile trek southeast along narrow country roads to **Dundrennan**, an appealing little village hiding the greystone ruins of **Dundrennan Abbey**, where Mary, Queen of Scots spent her last night on Scottish soil (April–Sept Mon–Wed & Sat–Sun 9.30am–6pm, Thurs 9.30am–1.30pm; £1.50). Enough remains of this twelfth-century Cistercian foundation to be able to appreciate its architectural simplicity, in contrast to the more ornate style adopted by its daughter house, Sweetheart at New Abbey (see p.169). **Bus** service #501 connects Kirkcudbright and Dundrennan (Mon–Fri 4 daily, Sat 2 daily). Another eight-mile walk will take you along the coast through the **Stell** to **Nun Mill Bridge** looping back through the **Dhoon**. Further details of these and other local walks are available from the Kirkcudbright tourist office, and are contained in the leaflet, *Walks Around Kirkcudbright*.

Don't miss the **Stewartry Museum** on St Mary Street (same hours as the Tolbooth Arts Centre; £1.50), where, packed into a purpose-built Victorian building, hundreds of local exhibits illuminate the life and times of the Solway coast. It's an extraordinary collection, cabinets crammed with anything from glass bottles, weaving equipment, pipes, pictures and postcards to stuffed birds, pickled fish and the tricornered hats once worn by town officials. There are also examples of book jackets designed by Jessie King and E.A. Taylor, two of Hornel's coterie.

Practicalities

Buses to Kirkcudbright stop by the harbour, next to the **tourist office** (April–June, Sept & Oct daily 10am–5pm; July & Aug daily 9.30am–6pm; ☎01557/330494), where you can get help finding accommodation, a service you will probably need in high season. The town has several quality **hotels** – the best among them being the *Gladstone House*, a renovated Georgian town house at 48 High St (☎01557/331734; ④), and the *Selkirk Arms*, an attractively refurbished eighteenth-century hotel just up the road (☎01557/330402; ⑤). For convenient **B&Bs**, try the bright, modern house run by Mrs Durok, 109a High St (☎01557/331279; ①; March–Sept); *Baytree* at 110 High St (☎01557/330824; ③), a recently restored Georgian town house with lovely rooms and a beautiful garden with sundeck; or Mrs Black at 1 Gordon Place, in a terrace of attractive whitewashed houses just off the High Street (☎01557/330472; ②). *Silvercraigs* caravan and **campsite** (☎01557/331079; Easter to late Oct) is on a bluff overlooking town at the end of St Mary's Place, five to ten minutes' walk from the centre, and at Brighouse Bay the *Seaward* caravan park includes a full range of facilities in a new leisure complex (☎01557/870319; March–Oct). The town is also a popular spot for residential **painting courses**: contact Gracefield Arts Centre (☎01387/262084) or Kirkcudbright Painting Holidays (☎01557/330274) for details.

Kirkcudbright is light on **restaurants**, but the cheap-and-cheerful *Belfry*, up along St Cuthbert Street from the tourist office, offers filling daytime snacks, while the *Selkirk Arms* serves excellent bar meals. The *Auld Alliance*, 5 Castle St (☎01557/330569), is a superior, if pricey, restaurant offering an imaginative mixture of French and Scottish cuisine. For a **drink**, the busy *Masonic Arms*, on Castle Street, pulls a reasonable pint.

Gatehouse of Fleet

The quiet streets of **GATEHOUSE OF FLEET**, easily reached by bus from Kirkcudbright ten miles to the east, give no clue that for James Murray, the eighteenth-century laird, this spot was to become the "Glasgow" of the Solway coast – a centre of the cotton industry whose profits had already made him immeasurably rich. Yorkshire mill owners provided the industrial expertise, imported engineers, designed aqueducts to improve the water supply, and dispossessed crofters – and their children – contributed the labour. Between 1760 and 1790, Murray achieved much success, but his custom-built town failed to match its better-placed rivals. By 1850 the boom was over, the mills slipped into disrepair, and nowadays tiny Gatehouse is sustained by tourism and forestry.

It's the country setting that appeals rather than any particular sight, but there are some graceful Georgian houses along High Street, which also has an incongruous, granite clock tower and the **Mill on the Fleet Museum** (March–Oct daily 10am–5.30pm; £2.75), which traces the history of Gatehouse and Galloway from inside an old bobbin mill – check out its café with an attractive terrace overlooking the river. The nearby **tourist office** (daily: March, April & Oct 10am–4.30pm; May, June & Sept 10am–5pm; July & Aug 10am–6pm; ☎01557/814212) sells an excellent leaflet on local walks. One of them starts from the tourist office and heads along Old Military Road, passing through deciduous woodland before circling back to visit the stark remains of **Cardoness Castle** (April–Sept daily 9.30am–6.30pm; Oct–March Sat 9.30am–4.30pm, Sun 2–4.30pm; HS; £1.80), with its colourful and violent history. Perched on a hill, this late fifteenth-century stronghold is a classic example of the fortified tower house, with dense walls and tiny windows. It once edged the Water of Fleet river, but this was canalized long ago and today Cardoness overlooks the minor road linking Gatehouse with the A75, with stunning views of Fleet Bay in the distance. Another walk loops southeast from Gatehouse through the forests beside the Water of Fleet river on towards the Solway Firth. En route, you can't miss James Murray's country mansion, converted into the sumptuous *Cally Palace Hotel* (☎01557/814341, *cally@cphotel.demon.co.uk*; ⑦; closed Jan), though if you stay here make sure you are in the old house rather than the ugly modern extension. **Accommodation** in Gatehouse includes the *Murray Arms Hotel* (☎01557/814207; ⑤), a refurbished nineteenth-century mansion close to the clock tower, and some more affordable and convenient **B&Bs**, such as the *Bay Horse B&B*, 9 Ann St (☎01557/814073; ③; March–Oct). Farm accommodation is available in the surrounding countryside at *High Auchenlarie Farm* (☎01557/840231; ②; March–Oct), six miles west, off the A75, and *Holecroft Farm* (☎01557/840250; ①), half a mile or so further on. The *Murray Arms* serves delicious bar **meals** all day and has a very smart restaurant, as well as dispensing advice and permits for **fishing** locally.

Newton Stewart and Glen Trool

To the west of Gatehouse, the A75 skirts the mud flats of Wigtown Bay before cutting up to **NEWTON STEWART**, an unassuming market town beside the River Cree, famous for its **salmon and trout fishing**. The excellent **Creebridge House Hotel** (☎01671/402121, *creebridge.hotel@daelnet.co.uk*; ⑦), in an old hunting lodge near the main bridge, arranges fishing permits for around £15 per day, can provide personal gillies (guides) for a further £25 daily, and at a pinch they'll even rent you all the tackle. The season runs from March to mid-October.

With its plentiful supply of accommodation (see below) and good bus connections along the A75, Newton Stewart has also become a popular base for **hikers** heading for the nearby **Galloway Hills**, most of which are enclosed within **Galloway Forest Park**. Many hikers aim for the park's **Glen Trool** by following the A714 north for about ten miles to Bargrennan, where a narrow lane twists the five miles over to the glen's **Loch Trool**. Halfway up the loch stands one of the area's two **Bruce's Stones**, this one marking the spot where Robert the Bruce ambushed an English force in 1307 after routing the main body of the army at Solway Moss. From here, there's a choice of magnificent hiking trails, including access to Merrick, at 2746ft the biggest hill in the southwest, as well as lesser tracks laid out by the Forestry Commission. Several longer routes curve round the grassy peaks and icy lochs of the Awful Hand and Dungeon ranges, whilst another includes part of the **Southern Upland Way**, which threads through the Minnigaff hills to Clatteringshaws Loch, beside the A712, the road that links Newton Stewart with New Galloway.

Practicalities

Newton Stewart is easily accessible by bus, with services from Dumfries, Ayr and Stranraer, but reaching Loch Trool by **bus** is a bit of a pain: service #359 makes the twenty-minute trip from Newton Stewart to Glentrool village between three and six times daily, but you have to walk the final four miles. For the more adventurous **trails**, you'll need to be properly equipped; the Newton Stewart **tourist office** (April & Oct 10am–4.30pm; May, June & Sept 10am–5pm; July & Aug 10am–6pm; ☎01671/402431), just off the main street opposite the bus station, has bags of helpful literature. If you mean business, be sure to buy the relevant Ordnance Survey maps and *The Galloway Hills: A Walker's Paradise* by George Brittain (£2.50). In addition, the Forestry Commission produces leaflets on its various walks and other activities in the Forest Park: for further details, call ☎01671/402420.

The tourist office will provide a full list of local **accommodation** and book a bed on your behalf. In town, the cheapest choice is the convenient Minnigaff **youth hostel** (☎01671/402211; April–Sept) in an old schoolhouse 650 yards from the main street, near the bridge. Alternatively – apart from the *Creebridge House Hotel* – you could try the **B&Bs** along Corvisel Road, a quiet residential street of Victorian brownstone houses near the tourist office – *Kilwarlin* at no. 4 (☎01671/403047; ①; April–Oct) is one of the best. On the southeast outskirts of town near the A75/A712 junction, there's the luxurious *Kirroughtree Hotel* (☎01671/402141, *mcmhotel@mcmhotel.demon.co.uk*; ⑦; Feb–Dec), a splendid eighteenth-century mansion surrounded by beautiful gardens of azaleas and rhododendrons. Nearby are the well-appointed, two-bedroomed log chalets of the *Conifers Leisure Park* (☎01671/402107; £160–500 for four people depending on season; minimum stay three nights), with its own health centre. In Glen Trool village, the *House O'Hill Hotel* (☎01671/840243; ②) provides basic accommodation, beer, food and, occasionally, great music, while *Caldons Campsite* (☎01671/402420; April–Oct) is near the car park at the western tip of Loch Trool, and the Forestry Commission's *Talnotry Campsite* (☎01671/402420; April–Sept), close to the Queen's Way, is a picturesque spot with excellent views.

The best place **to eat** in Newton Stewart is the *Creebridge* (☎01671/402121), which has a wonderful but pricey restaurant as well as serving great pub food with its beers. A cheaper alternative is *Chatterbox* on the main street, which serves good snacks and cakes.

The Queen's Way: New Galloway and The Glenkens

The twenty-mile stretch from Newton Stewart to New Galloway, known as the **Queen's Way**, cuts through the southern periphery of **Galloway Forest Park**, a landscape of glassy lochs, wooded hills and bare, rounded peaks. You'll pass all sorts of **hiking trails**, some the gentlest of strolls, others long-distance treks. For a short walk, stop at the **Talnotry Campsite** (☎01671/402420; April–Oct), about seven miles from Newton Stewart, where the Forestry Commission has laid out three trails between two and four miles long: each delves into the pine forests beside the road, crossing gorges and burns. The campsite itself occupies an attractive spot among the wooded hills of the park; you can also buy fishing permits here. A few miles further on is **Clatteringshaws Loch**, a reservoir surrounded by pine forest, with a fourteen-mile footpath running right round. This runs past a second **Bruce's Stone**, a huge boulder where Robert the Bruce is supposed to have rested after victory over the English. The trail also connects with the Southern Upland Way as it meanders north towards the **Rhinns of Kells**, the bumpy hill range marking the park's eastern boundary.

From the loch, it's seven miles further to **NEW GALLOWAY**, nestling in the river valley at the northern tip of Loch Ken. Although little more than one long street lined by neat and attractive stone houses, it provides further easy access to the Southern Upland Way and the Rhinns of Kells, as does the neighbouring village of **DALRY** – which straddles the Southern Upland Way – a couple of miles upstream. New Galloway is in the valley of **The Glenkens**, which extends south to Castle Douglas via Loch Ken, and north along the river as far as Carsphairn, a desolate hamlet surrounded by wild moors. Midway between New Galloway and Carsphairn, you can visit the **Polmaddy**

Settlement, a reconstructed Galloway village dating from before the Clearances. Continuing along the A713 through the attractive Doon Valley towards the coast at Ayr, you'll pass the old ironworks at **WATERSIDE**, which has been turned into a large, open-air **museum** portraying life for the workers of the iron industry a hundred years ago (April–Oct daily 10am–5pm; £2).

Practicalities

Connecting with services from Dumfries and Kirkcudbright, the fast and frequent Castle Douglas to Ayr **bus** stops in New Galloway. There's no official tourist office, but **The Smithy Teashop**, on High Street (daily: March, April & Sept 10am–8pm; May–Aug 10am–9pm; Oct 10am–6pm), provides all the essential information, rents out **bikes** and sells tasty oatcakes. The village has several **hotels** and **B&Bs** strung along the main drag: try the agreeable *Leamington Hotel* (☎01644/420327; ①), or *The Smithy* itself (☎01644/420269; ①; March–Oct). If you want to stay in Dalry, head for the attractive *Lochinvar Hotel* (☎01644/430210; ②). The nearest **youth hostel** is at Kendoon (☎01786/891400; mid-May to Sept), five miles north of Dalry along the B7000, near the Southern Upland Way. It's about fifteen minutes' walk from the A713; if you're travelling there on the Castle Douglas–Ayr bus, ask the driver to tell you when to get off.

The Machars

The Machars, the name given to the peninsula of rolling farmland and open landscapes south of Newton Stewart, is a neglected part of the coastline, with a somewhat disconsolate air. Just six miles off the A75 is **WIGTOWN**, a modest country town whose spacious main street and square occupy a hill above Wigtown Bay. It's a five-minute walk from the square to the tidal flats below, where a simple stone obelisk commemorates two Covenanter martyrs, Margaret McLachlan and Margaret Wilson, who in 1685 were tied to stakes on the flats and drowned by the rising tide.

Whithorn

From Wigtown, it's a further eleven miles south to **WHITHORN**, with its sloping, airy high street of pastel-painted cottages. This one-horse town occupies an important place in Scottish history, for it was here in 397 AD that **St Ninian** founded the first Christian church north of Hadrian's Wall. Ninian daubed his tiny building in white plaster and called it **Candida Casa**, translated as "Hwiterne" (White House), hence Whithorn, by his Pictish neighbours. Ninian's life is shrouded in mystery, but he does seem to have been raised in Galloway and was a key figure in the Christianization of his country. Indeed, his tomb became a popular place of pilgrimage and, in the twelfth century, a priory was built to service the shrine. For generations the rich and the royal made the trek here, but this ended with the Reformation – and the prohibition of pilgrimages in 1581.

Halfway down the main street, the **Whithorn Dig** (April–Oct daily 10.30am–5pm; £2.70) explores these ecclesiastical connections. A video gives background details and a handful of archeological finds serves as an introduction for a stroll round the dig. Be sure to take up the complimentary guide service – you won't make much sense of the complex sequence of ruins without one. Beyond the dig the meagre remains of the priory fail to inspire, unlike the adjacent **Whithorn Museum**, whose impressive assortment of early Christian memorials includes a series of standing crosses and headstones, the earliest being the Latinus Stone of 450 AD. For **lunch**, the *Diner*, near the Dig, offers basic meals.

The pilgrims who crossed the Solway to visit St Ninian's shrine landed at the **ISLE OF WHITHORN**, four miles south of Whithorn. Not an island at all, it's an antique and

Edinburgh Castle

Victoria Street, Edinburgh

Street entertainers, Edinburgh

Scott's View, the Borders

Kippford and Rockcliffe on the Solway coast

"The Armadillo", Clydeside, Glasgow

Glasgow School of Art, designed by Charles Rennie Mackintosh

Drummond Castle Gardens, Perthshire

Scotland's favourite drink

Statue of "Progress and Posterity"
Kelvingrove Park, Glasgow

tiny seaport hiding the minuscule remains of the thirteenth-century **St Ninian's Chapel**. You can still follow in the pilgrims' footsteps by walking, cycling or riding the marked **Pilgrim Way** in a hundred-mile round-trip, starting from Glenluce and winding along paths and quiet roads to the Isle of Whithorn. For the less energetic, there's a pleasant twelve-mile round-walk between Whithorn and the Isle of Whithorn, which takes in St Ninian's Cave, the spot where the saint first put foot on Scottish soil. These and other shorter routes are detailed in a leaflet available from local tourist offices.

If you want to **stay** in the area, try the unassuming *Steam Packet Inn* (☎01988/500334; ②), right on the quay in Isle of Whithorn, or one of two farmhouses in Whithorn itself – *Baltier Farm* (☎01988/600241; ①) or *Clugston Farm* (☎01671/830338; ①). The owner of the *Queens Arms Hotel* (☎01988/500369; ②), in Isle of Whithorn, has a boat and takes people out on sea-angling trips.

Glenluce Abbey and Castle Kennedy Gardens

Heading west from Whithorn, the main road follows the wild and windy shore of Luce Bay on its way back to the A75 near the turning for **Glenluce Abbey** (April–Sept daily 9.30am–6.30pm; Oct–March Sat 9.30am–4.30pm, Sun 2–4.30pm; HS; £1.80), whose ruins lie in a gentle valley a couple of miles north of the main road. There are no direct buses to the abbey, but the Glenluce–Newton Stewart bus will drop you off along the main road and you can walk from there. Founded in 1192, Glenluce prospered from the diligence of its Cistercian monks who drained the surrounding marshes, creating prime farmland. The brothers' fifteenth-century Chapter House has survived pretty much intact, and with its ribbed vault ceiling generates the clearest of acoustics – opera singers practise here. Notice, too, the green man motif carved into the corbels and bosses. Popularized in the twelfth century, these grotesques have human or cat-like faces, with large, glaring eyes, frowning foreheads and prominent teeth or fangs. All have greenery sprouting from their faces – a feature that originated with pagan leaf masks and the Celtic concept of fertility. The thirteenth-century wizard and alchemist **Michael Scott** lived here, supposedly luring the plague into a secret vault where he promptly imprisoned it. Scott, one-time magician to the court of the Emperor Frederick in Sicily, appears in Dante's *Inferno*.

Seven miles from Glenluce and three miles east of Stranraer, **Castle Kennedy & Lochinch Gardens** (April–Sept daily 10am–5pm; £2) flank the shattered, ivy-clad remains of a medieval fortress, situated on a narrow isthmus between two lochs. The 75-acre gardens are noted for their monkey puzzle trees, magnolias, rhododendrons and a huge lily pond.

The Rhinns of Galloway

West of the Machars, the **Rhinns of Galloway** is a hilly, hammer-shaped peninsula at the end of the Solway coast, encompassing two contrasting towns, the grimy port of Stranraer, from where there are regular ferries over to Northern Ireland, and the beguiling resort of **Portpatrick**. Between the two, a string of tiny farming villages lead down to the **Mull of Galloway**, the windswept headland at the southwest tip of Scotland.

Stranraer

No one could say that **STRANRAER** was beautiful, though it has a nice feel to it and, if you're heading to (or coming from) Northern Ireland, you'll find everything's convenient. The **train station** is close to the Stena Sealink **ferry terminal** (☎0990/707070) on the Ross Pier, where boats depart for Larne; a couple of minutes' walk away, on Port

Rodie, is the town's **bus station**; and nearby, further round the bay, Seacat **catamaran** services (☎0345/523523) leave from the West Pier to Belfast. Less handy, however, is the P&O ferry (☎0990/980777) to Larne, which leaves from the port of **CAIRNRYAN**, some five miles away.

Although a little dishevelled in parts, Stranraer has a pleasant walk from the recently renovated harbour area to a nearby beach. The main street, variously Charlotte, George and High streets, takes in the town's one specific attraction, a medieval tower which is all that remains of the **Castle of St John** (April–Sept Mon–Sat 10am–1pm & 2–5pm; £1). Inside, an exhibition traces the history of the castle down to its use as a police station and prison in the nineteenth century. Features of the castle include the old exercise yard on the roof and an interesting outdoor sculpture by Sibylle von Halem. If you've time to kill, pop into the **Stranraer Museum** in the Old Town Hall on George Street (Mon–Sat 10am–5pm; free) for a brief foray into the history of the area.

The **tourist office**, 28 Harbour St (April–June, Oct & Nov Mon–Sat 9.30am–5.30pm, Sun 10am–4pm; July–Sept daily 9.30am–6pm; Dec–March Mon–Sat 10am–4pm; ☎01776/702595) can arrange **accommodation**; alternatively, you could try the excellent family-run *Old Manse* on Lewis Street (☎01776/702135; ①), or *Fernlea*, on the same street (☎01776/703037; ①). For a real splurge, head to *Corsewall Lighthouse Hotel* at Kirkcolm on the peninsula eleven miles north of Stranraer (☎01776/853220, *Jim-Neilson@msn.com*; ⑦). You'll need your own transport to get to this converted lighthouse set in twenty acres of garden, though the owners will collect from the town, if you book in advance. For **camping**, *Aird Donald Camp & Caravan Park* (☎01776/702025) is ten minutes' walk east of the town centre along London Road.

Stranraer has plenty of basic **snack bars**, but it's well worth paying a little extra to enjoy a **meal** at the *Apéritif* (☎01776/702991) just up the hill from the bus station along Bellevilla Road. The *Ark House* on Church Street serves excellent (though fairly pricey) food in its nautically-themed bar. The *Marine House Hotel* (☎01776/703161) on the seafront is a cheaper alternative.

Portpatrick and south

Perched on the west shore of the Rhinns, the pastel houses of **PORTPATRICK** spread over the craggy coast above the slender harbour. Until the mid-nineteenth century, when sailing ships were replaced by steamboats, this was the main embarkation point for Northern Ireland, with coal, cotton and British troops heading in one direction, Ulster cattle and linen in the other. Nowadays, Portpatrick is a quiet, comely resort enjoyed for its rugged scenery and coastal hikes, including the twenty-minute stroll (take the steep steps near the garages beyond the lighthouse then follow the public footpath) along the sea cliffs to the shattered ruins of **Dunskey Castle**, an L-shaped tower house dating from the early sixteenth century. Portpatrick also has several intriguing and competitively priced craft-antique shops – check out the Old Lighthouse Pottery and the Smugglers Cove, around the harbour area – and offers excellent **sea fishing**; in summer, daily trips cost £8 for three hours. Walkers can tackle the first thirteen miles of the 212-mile coast-to-coast **Southern Upland Way**. It's a good day's walk past Castle Kennedy Gardens, and you can return by bus via Stranraer, but check the times first.

Portpatrick has several good **hotels** and **guest houses**, the best of which is the *Portpatrick Hotel* (☎01776/810333; ⑧), a grand turreted Edwardian mansion on the hill above the harbour. Other options include the *Mount Stewart Hotel* (☎01776/810291; ②) with great food and good views of the harbour, the comfortable *Carlton Guest House*, beside the harbour on South Crescent (☎01776/810253; ①), and, close by, the bright, white *Knowe Guest House* (☎01776/810441; ①). There are three caravan and **campsites** in a row on the hill overlooking Portpatrick and Dunskey Castle. They are quite a distance from town, but it's a pleasant walk along the disused railway and clifftop trail – the *Galloway* (☎01776/810561; Easter–Oct) is the largest and has its own restaurant and shop, but the other two – the *Castle Bay* (☎01776/810462) and the *Sunnymeade* (☎01776/810293) also have good facilities and nice views. The best place in Portpatrick for a **meal** and a **drink** is the *Crown* pub, on the seafront, or the *Auld Acquaintance* coffee shop nearby.

South to the Mull of Galloway

The remoter reaches of the Rhinns of Galloway, extending about twenty miles south from Portpatrick, consist of gorse-covered hills and pastureland crossed by narrow country lanes and dotted with farming hamlets. Of the two shorelines, the west has a sharper, rockier aspect and it's here, near the village of Port Logan, you'll find the uncrowded **Logan Botanic Garden** (March–Oct daily 10am–6pm; £3), an outpost of Edinburgh's Royal Botanic Garden. There are three main areas: a peat garden, a woodland and a walled garden noted for its tree ferns and cabbage palms. The Gulf Stream keeps the Rhinns almost completely free of frost, allowing subtropical species to grow, including plants from South and Central America, southern Africa, Australasia and the Mediterranean.

It's a further twelve miles south to the **Mull of Galloway**, a bleak and precipitous headland where wheeling birds (guillemots, razorbills and kittiwakes) and whistling winds circle a bright whitewashed lighthouse. On clear days you can see over to Cumbria and Ireland.

The South Ayrshire coast

Fifty miles from top to bottom, the **South Ayrshire coast** between Stranraer and Ayr is easily seen from the winding A77 coastal road which leaves Stranraer to trim thirty miles of low, rocky shore before reaching **Girvan**, a low-key seaside resort where boats depart for **Ailsa Craig**, in the Firth of Clyde. Back on shore, the A77 presses on through the village of **Turnberry**, home to one of the world's most famous golf courses, where the A719 branches off for eighteenth-century **Culzean Castle** (pronounced "Cullane"). From the castle, it's twelve miles further to **Ayr**. Alternatively, if you keep to the main road, you'll pass by the medieval remains of **Crossraguel Abbey** on the way to the old market town of **Maybole**, just nine miles from Ayr. The whole area is steeped in links with its famous son, **Robert Burns**, and the association is exploited to the full. There's a reasonable **bus** service along the coast, a better one between Culzean and Ayr – plus a **train** line from Stranraer to Girvan, Maybole and Ayr.

Girvan and Ailsa Craig

Set beneath a ridge of grassy hills, **GIRVAN** is at its prettiest round the harbour, a narrow slit beside the mouth of the Girvan Water. Here, overlooked by old stone houses, the fishing fleet sets about its business, and, for a moment, it's possible to ignore the amusement arcades and seaside tat elsewhere in town. The long beaches around Girvan's otherwise rugged coastline are great for seaside strolls, though clambering down the cliff to the caves where the legendary Sawney Bean and his cannibal family lived is not recommended.

There are regular **bus** services from Stranraer and Ayr to Girvan, which is also on the Glasgow–Stranraer **train** line. The **tourist office**, on Bridge Street, just up from the harbour (Easter–May Mon–Fri 11am–1pm & 2–5pm, Sat & Sun 11am–5pm; June daily 11am–6pm; July & Aug daily 10am–7pm; Sept daily 11am–5pm; first two weeks of Oct daily noon–4pm; ☎01465/714950) has a full list of **accommodation**, or try one of the attractive Victorian villas along the seafront, such as the neat and tidy *Thistleneuk Guest House*, 19 Louisa Drive (☎01465/712137, *reservations@thistleneuk.freeserve.co.uk*; ②), or *St Oswalds*, 5 Golf Course Rd (☎01465/713786; ①), with views out to Ailsa Craig. If you have money to burn and want to play the famous course which hosts the Open Golf Championship every few years, stay at the luxurious *Turnberry Hotel* (☎01655/331000; ⑦), five miles north of Girvan.

Ailsa Craig

From late May to September, boats leave Girvan harbour for the ten-mile excursion west to the **Ailsa Craig**, "Fairy Rock" in Gaelic – though the island looks more like an enormous muffin than a place of enchantment. It would certainly have been less than enchanting for the persecuted Catholics who escaped to the island during the Reformation. With its jagged cliffs and 1114ft summit, Ailsa Craig is now a privately owned bird sanctuary that's home to thousands of gannets. The best time to make the trip is at the end of May and in June when the fledglings are trying to fly. Several companies cruise round the island, but only Mark McCrindle, who also organizes sea-angling trips, is licensed to land (once- or twice-daily sailings cost £10 per person for six hours, £9 for four; bookings required on ☎01465/713219). It takes about an hour to reach the island, so you've enough time to walk up to the summit of the rock and watch the birds – weather permitting.

Culzean Castle

The impressive NTS-maintained **Culzean Castle** and its surrounding **country park** (both April–Oct daily 10.30am–5pm; Nov–March park open 9am–sunset; NTS; £7 for both, £5 for park only) is Ayrshire's premier tourist attraction. The best place to start is at the **visitor centre** in the modernized Home Farm buildings. Here, you can pick up free maps – as well as wildlife leaflets – that help you get your bearings, the layout of the place being rather confusing, or you can take a guided tour (castle daily 3.30pm; also July & Aug 11am: grounds April–June 2.30pm; July–Sept daily 11am & 2.30pm). From the visitor centre it's a few minutes' walk over to the **Castle**, whose towers and turrets rise high above the sea cliffs. Nothing remains of the original fifteenth-century structure, since, in 1777, David Kennedy, the tenth Earl of Cassillis, commissioned **Robert Adam**, the highly successful Scottish architect, to remodel the family home.

The work took fifteen years to complete, and, although the exterior, with its arrow slits and battlements, preserves a medieval aspect, the interior exemplifies the harmonious Classical designs Adam loved. On the ground floor, the subtle greens of the old eating room are enlivened by vine-leaf-and-grape plasterwork along the cornice, a motif continued in the adjacent dining room. Nearby, there's the brilliantly conceived oval staircase, where tiers of Corinthian and Ionic columns lead up to a huge cupola allowing light to stream down. All this is a fitting prologue to the impressive circular saloon, whose symmetrical flourishes deliberately contrast with the natural land and seascapes on view through the windows. Further on, a small exhibition celebrates President Eisenhower's military and civilian career as well as his association with Culzean; Ike stayed here on several occasions and the castle's top floor was given to him by the old owners, the Kennedys, for his lifetime. Nowadays, the top floor accommodates six double bedrooms done out in a comfortably genteel style. Guests eat together in the shared dining room and the chef comes in to do breakfast as well. Although hard to imagine a more distinctive setting, it's at a price: the smallest rooms cost £140 for bed and breakfast per night, the biggest £265 (reservations on ☎01655/760274).

Leave time for an exploration of the **country park**, whose 565 acres spread out along the seashore. A web of wooded trails lead you through the park, taking in cliffs, a beach, a walled garden, where the blooms are at their best in July and August, and the occasional reminder of earlier days – the laird's boat house and gun battery, the old ice and powder houses. Guided tours, craft shows, country dancing and a "fascinating fungi" walk are laid on throughout the year – details from the visitor centre and nearby tourist offices.

Places to **stay** nearby include *Nether Culzean Farm* (☎01655/882269; ①), an eighteenth-century farmhouse just west of Maybolem on the B7023, and *Homelea* (☎01655/882736; ①), a family-run B&B in a Victorian villa. For campers, the *Culzean Bay Holiday Park* (☎01292/500444) is located by Croy Shore on the A77 coast road.

Crossraguel Abbey

Leaving Turnberry on the A77, it's a couple of miles to the hamlet of **KIRKOSWALD** and **Souter Johnnie's Cottage** (Easter–Sept daily 11.30am–5pm; Oct Sat & Sun 11.30am–5pm; NTS; £1.80), the simple thatched house that was once the home of John Davidson, the boon companion of Robert Burns and original Souter (cobbler) Johnnie of the poet's *Tam o' Shanter*. To the rear of the house, the restored alehouse has life-sized stone figures of Johnnie, Tam himself (called after his boat, Shanter being his farm) and other Burnsian characters, all of whom are buried in the nearby graveyard.

The substantial remains of **Crossraguel Abbey** (April–Sept Mon–Sat 9.30am–6.30pm; Sun 2–6.30pm; HS £1.80), a further three miles along the main road, are mostly overlooked – something of a surprise considering their singularity. Founded as a Cluniac monastery in the thirteenth century, Crossraguel benefited from royal patronage, with its abbots holding land "for ever in free regality". The abbots took the temporal side of their work seriously and became powerful local lords. By the early sixteenth century, they had constructed an extensive private compound complete with a massive gatehouse and sturdy tower house. Both still stand – behind what remains of the abbey church – recalling the corruption of the monastic ideal that prodded the Reformation. Behind the gatehouse, you'll also spot the well-preserved dovecote, a funnel-shaped affair that was a crucial part of the abbey's economy; the monks not only ate the doves but also relied on them for eggs.

Ayr and around

With a population of around 50,000, **AYR**, the largest town on the Firth of Clyde coast, was an important seaport and trading centre for many centuries, and rivalled Glasgow in size and significance right up until the late seventeenth century. In recognition, Cromwell made it a centre of his administration and built an enormous fortress here, long since destroyed. With the relative decline of its seaborne trade, Ayr developed as a market town, praised by Robert Burns, who was born in the neighbouring village of **Alloway** (see p.184), for its "honest men and bonny lasses". In the nineteenth century, Ayr became a popular resort for middle-class Victorians, with a new town of wide streets and boulevards built behind the beach immediately southwest of the old town. Nowadays, Ayr is both Ayrshire's commercial centre and a holiday resort, its long sandy beach (and prestigious racecourse) attracting hundreds of Scotland's city dwellers.

The Town

The cramped, sometimes seedy streets and alleys of Ayr's **old town** occupy a wedge of land between Sandgate to Alloway Place in the west, and the south bank of the treacly River Ayr to the east. Almost all the medieval buildings were knocked down by the Victorians, but the **Auld Brig**, with its cobbles and sturdy breakwaters, has survived

ACCOMMODATION
Bona Lea cottage 6
Dargil Guest House 3
Daviot House 5
Grasmere Guest house 1
Queens 4
Thornton 2
Stamore 8
Youth hostel 7

© Crown copyright

from the thirteenth century. The bridge was saved by Robert Burns or, rather, by his poem *Twa Brigs*, which made it too famous to demolish; an international appeal raised the capital necessary for its refurbishment in 1907.

The bridge connects with High Street, where you should turn left and subsequently left again down Kirk Port, a narrow lane leading to the **Auld Kirk** (July & Aug Tues & Thurs only; phone ☎01292/262580 for further details), the church funded by Cromwell as recompense for the one he incorporated into his stronghold. At the lych gate, a plan of the graveyard shows where some of Burns' friends are buried. Notice also the mort-safe (heavy grating) on the wall of the lych gate. Placed over newly dug graves, these mort-safes were a sort of early nineteenth-century corpse security system meant to deter body snatchers at a time when dead bodies were swiftly bought up by medical schools with no questions asked. The church's dark and gloomy interior retains the original pulpit. Retracing your steps along High Street, take the first left down pedestrianized Newmarket Street, leading onto Sandgate, with the elegant spire of the **Town Buildings**, down towards the New Bridge.

Extending southwest of Sandgate to the Esplanade and the **beach**, the wide, gridiron streets of the Victorian **new town** contrast with the crowded lanes of old Ayr. It was the opening of the Glasgow to Ayr train line in 1840 that brought the first major influx of holiday-makers, and Ayr remains a busy resort today, with many visitors heading for the plethora of trim guest houses concentrated around **Wellington Square**, whose terraces flank the impressive County Buildings dating from 1820. The new town extends north towards the river, with its comfortable villas spreading over what remains of the walls of Cromwell's fort. It's here, off Bruce Crescent, that you'll find St John's Tower, all that's left of the church Cromwell used as his armoury. The northern perimeter of the fortress once overlooked the harbour, which is now the place to go for either a summer **sea-angling trip** (details from the Sea Angling Centre, ☎01292/285297), or a **cruise** on the *Waverley*, the last seagoing paddle steamer in the world (July 8–Aug 27 Tues & Wed only 10am; ☎0141/221 8152). In addition, you can go on various excursions round the islands off the west coast, including those around Ailsa Craig (see p.180); the tourist office has details.

Practicalities

Ayr **bus station** is at the foot of Sandgate, a ten-minute walk west of both the **train station** and the **tourist office**, on Burns Statue Square (June & Sept to early Oct Mon–Sat 9.15am–6pm, Sun 10am–6pm; July & Aug Mon–Sat 9.15am–7pm, Sun 10am–7pm; Oct–May Mon–Sat 9.15am–5pm; ☎01292/288688). They can help with accommodation, a particularly useful service at the height of the season and during important race meetings.

At other times, head straight for the cluster of **hotels** and **guest houses** around Wellington Square, a couple of minutes' walk south of Sandgate along Alloway Place. In particular, try Queen's Terrace where, among others, there's the *Dargil Guest House*, no. 7 (☎01292/261955; ①), *Queens*, no. 10 (☎01292/265618; ②), and the *Daviot*, no. 12 (☎01292/269678; ②). There's another cluster of B&Bs among the attractive Victorian villas of Eglinton Terrace, a short walk north of Wellington Square. These include the *Grasmere Guest House*, no. 2 (☎01292/611033; ①; March–Oct) and the *Thornton* at no. 9 (☎01292/262948; ①). Cheaper accommodation is available at *Stamore*, 41 St Leonards Rd (☎01292/262597; ①), or at Ayr **youth hostel**, 5 Craigweil Rd (☎01292/262322; March–Oct), which occupies a grand neo-Gothic mansion behind the beach, a twenty-minute walk south of the town centre along Alloway Place (turn right down Blackburn Road – it's signposted). The *Heads of Ayr Leisure Park* (☎01292/442269; March–Nov), five miles south of town along the coastal A719, accepts **caravans** and **tents**, as does *Culzean Bay Holiday Park* (☎01292/500444; March–Oct), eight miles south of Ayr. If you prefer to stay out of town, try *Bona Lea Cottage* (☎01292/500233; ①), five miles south in the tiny village of **Dunure**, which consists of a couple of rows of cottages, a pub with decent food, an old harbour and the dramatic ruins of Dunure Castle.

The best **restaurant** in Ayr is *Fouters*, 2a Academy St, in a cellar off Sandgate (☎01292/261391); steaks and seafood are its specialities. Another good choice, which uses local produce, is the *Boathouse*, 4 South Harbour St, beside the river at the foot of Fort Street. For filling and more reasonably priced meals, try *Littlejohn's*, 231 High St, *Petit Pierre*, 4 River Terrace (☎01292/282087), or the *Stables Restaurant*, at 41 Sandgate. If you fancy Italian food, head to *Bonfantis* at 64 Sandgate, or the *Royal Cafe*, 11 New Rd, for seriously good ice cream. The *Tudor Restaurant*, 8 Beresford Terrace, is famed for home baking and its Scottish "high teas" (5–6pm). The most enjoyable **pub** in town is the thatched *Tam o' Shanter*, on the High Street, whose ancient walls sport quotes from Robert Burns. There are also several lively bars on and around Burns Statue Square, including *O'Briens*, which frequently showcases Irish folk bands.

Public transport to and from Ayr is easy, with plenty of buses and trains from Glasgow, Stranraer and Dumfries, as well as good local bus services. An open-topped bus, "The Burns Country Tour", leaves Ayr bus station (mid-June to mid-Sept hourly

ROBERT BURNS

The first of seven children, **Robert Burns**, the national poet of Scotland, was born in Alloway on January 25, 1759. His father, William, was employed as a gardener until 1766 when he became a tenant farmer at Mount Oliphant, near Alloway, moving to Lochlie farm, Tarbolton, eleven years later. A series of bad harvests and the demands of the landlord's estate manager bankrupted the family, and William died almost penniless in 1784. These events had a profound effect on Robert, leaving him with an antipathy towards political authority and a hatred of the landowning classes.

With the death of his father, Robert became head of the family and they moved again, this time to a farm at Mossgiel, near Mauchline. Burns had already begun writing poetry and prose at Lochlie, recording incidental thoughts in his *First Commonplace Book*, but it was here at Mossgiel that he began to write in earnest, and his first volume, *Poems Chiefly in the Scottish Dialect*, was published in Kilmarnock in 1786. The book proved immensely popular, celebrated by ordinary Scots and Edinburgh literati alike, with the satirical trilogy *Holy Willie's Prayer*, *The Holy Fair* and *Address to the Devil* attracting particular attention. The object of Burns' poetic scorn was the kirk, whose ministers had obliged him to appear in church to be publicly condemned for fornication – a commonplace punishment in those days.

Burns spent the winter of 1786–87 in the capital, lionized by the literary establishment. Despite his success, however, he felt trapped, unable to make enough money from writing to leave farming. He was also in a political snare, fraternizing with the elite, but with radical views and pseudo-Jacobite nationalism that constantly landed him in trouble. His frequent recourse was to play the part of the unlettered ploughman-poet, the noble savage who might be excused his impetuous outbursts and hectic womanizing.

Burns had, however, made useful contacts in Edinburgh and as a consequence was recruited to collect, write and rearrange two volumes of songs set to traditional Scottish tunes. These volumes, James Johnson's *Scots Musical Museum* and George Thomson's *Select Scottish Airs*, contain the bulk of his songwriting, and it's on them that Burns' international reputation rests, with works like *Auld Lang Syne*, *Scots, Wha Hae*, *Coming Through the Rye* and *Green Grow the Rushes, O*. At this time, too, though poetry now took second place, he produced two excellent poems: *Tam o' Shanter* and a republican tract, *A Man's a Man for a' That*.

In 1788, Burns married Jean Armour and moved to Ellisland Farm, near Dumfries. The following year, he was appointed excise officer and could at last leave farming, moving to Dumfries in 1791. Burns' years of comfort were short-lived, however. His years of labour on the farm, allied to a rheumatic fever, damaged his heart, and he died in Dumfries on July 21, 1796, aged 37.

Burns' work, inspired by a romantic nationalism and tinged with a wry wit, has made him a potent symbol of "Scottishness". Ignoring the Anglophile preferences of the Edinburgh elite, he wrote in Scots vernacular about the country he loved, an exuberant celebration that filled a need in a nation culturally colonized by England. Today Burns Clubs all over the world mark every anniversary of the poet's birthday with the Burns' Supper, complete with Scottish totems – haggis, piper and whisky bottle.

10am–5pm; £3) for the round-trip to Alloway and the coast, stopping at Burns attractions en route: you can get on and off as often as you like.

Alloway

There's little else but Burnsiana in **ALLOWAY**, formerly a small village but now part of Ayr's spreading suburbs, and a key stop on the **Burns Heritage Trail** (see p.164). The first port of call in Alloway is the whitewashed **Burns Cottage and Museum** (April–Oct daily 9am–6pm; Nov–March Mon–Sat 10am–4pm, Sun noon–4pm; £1.70) for a peep at the poet's birthplace, a dark and dank thatched cottage where animals and people lived under the same roof. The two-room museum boasts all sorts of memorabilia – the family Bible, letters and manuscripts – plus a potted history of his life, illuminated by contemporaneous quotes.

The modern, faceless building housing the **Tam o' Shanter Experience** (April–Oct daily 9am–6pm; Nov–March daily 9am–5pm; £2.80 for each video), a few minutes further down the road, belies a marginally more interesting interior. Two videos recount the life of Burns, and you can watch a dramatic enactment of the poem *Tam o' Shanter* in a three-screen cinema. There is a large souvenir shop selling the works of Burns amid every other conceivable thing you could produce on the poet.

Across the road from here are the plain, roofless ruins of **Alloway Church**, where Robert's father William is buried. Burns set much of *Tam o' Shanter* here. Tam, having got drunk in Ayr, passes "By Alloway's auld haunted kirk" and stumbles across a witches' dance, from which he's forced to flee for his life over the **Brig o' Doon**, a humpbacked bridge. The dance was a riotous affair:

> *But hornpipes, jigs, strathspeys and reels,*
> *Put life and mettle in their heels.*
> *A winnock-bunker in the east* [window recess],
> *There sat auld Nick, in shape o' beast;*
> *A towzie tyke, black, grim and large* [shaggy dog],
> *To gie them music was his charge:*
> *He screw'd the pipes and gart them skirl* [made; scream],
> *Till roof and rafters a' did dirl* [vibrate].

Across the street from the church, the thirteenth-century bridge still stands, curving gracefully over the river below the **Burns Monument** (April–Oct only, same hours and ticket as Cottage), a striking Neoclassical temple in a small carefully manicured garden and housing yet another museum. True Burns junkies might want to stay here at the newly restored *Brigadoon House Hotel* on the banks of the River Doon (☎01292/442466; ③), reputed to be another of Burns' drinking haunts, where you can sleep with his verse above your bed.

The North Ayrshire coast

The **North Ayrshire coast** extends some thirty miles or so from Ayr up to **Largs**, easily the area's most agreeable resort. The busy coastal road (the A78) cuts across this disparate shoreline, where rolling farmland is interrupted by the pockmarks of industrialization. Leaving Ayr, the road trims the outskirts of Prestwick, the site of an international airport, before bypassing **Troon**, an uninspiring resort with a seaside golf course.

IRVINE, the next settlement along, was once the principal port for Glasgow, its halcyon days recalled by the enjoyable **Scottish Maritime Museum** (April–Oct daily 10am–5pm; £2) down at the old harbour, a mile or so southwest of the town centre. The assortment of craft, which you can board, is moored to the museum docks and includes a dredger, a fishing skiff, a lifeboat, a tug and a "puffer" boat, used as an inshore supply vessel along the Clyde and between the islands. The history of the puffers forms part of the museum's well-presented display on Clydeside shipping. Close by, there's the Magnum Leisure Centre (daily 9am–10pm), with a swimming pool, cinemas and other leisure facilities and – at the mouth of the river – a sandy beach. Back on the west edge of the town centre, Irvine's **tourist office** (July & Aug Mon–Sat 9am–6pm, Sun noon–5pm; Sept–June Mon–Sat 9am–5pm, Sun noon–5pm; ☎01294/313886) adjoins the train and bus stations as well as the giant shopping centre which leads to High Street. Here a couple of narrow side alleys hint at the town's antiquity, amid the prevailing architectural gloom. One, **Seagate**, boasts ancient cottages and the sturdy remains of Irvine's castle; the other – **Glasgow Vennel** – features the house, no. 10, where Burns learnt to dress flax (he didn't enjoy it much), and his lodgings at no. 4. You're unlikely to want **to stay** in Irvine, but if you do, Kilwinning Road is the best place to head for – try *The Conifers Guest House* at no. 40 (☎01294/278070; ③), or *Laurelbank* at no. 3 (☎01294/277153; ③).

Inland from Irvine on the A759, you can visit **Dundonald Castle** (April–Sept 1–4pm; HS; £1.50), which dates from the 1370s, although there's evidence that other structures existed on the site previously. Five miles further east, **KILMARNOCK**, a shabby manufacturing town, is known principally for being the home of **Johnnie Walker** whisky.

North from Irvine, it's just eight miles to **ARDROSSAN**, where Caledonian MacBrayne ferries (☎0990/650000) leave for Brodick on the Isle of Arran (see p.349), and another twelve miles to Largs, from where you can catch a ferry across to the nearby island of **Great Cumbrae**, a low-key but popular holiday spot.

Largs and Great Cumbrae

Tucked in between the hills and the sea, **LARGS** remains a traditional family resort, its guest houses and B&Bs spreading out behind an elongated seaside promenade. There's a tiny pier, too, set beside an unpretentious town centre that conceals one real surprise: **Skelmorlie Aisle** (June–Aug Mon–Fri 2–5pm; keys from the museum next door; free), a Renaissance gem hidden away beside the old graveyard off Main Street. Once the north transept of a larger church, the aisle was converted into a mausoleum for Sir Robert Montgomerie, a local bigwig, in 1636. Carved by Scottish masons following Italian patterns, the tomb is decorated with Montgomerie's coat of arms as well as symbols of mortality such as the skull, winged hourglass and inverted torch. Up above, the intricate paintwork of the barrel-vaulted ceiling includes the signs of the zodiac, biblical figures and texts, and – in tiny detail on the painted corbels – the legendary coats of arms of the tribes of Israel.

Back outside on the promenade, it's about a mile south along the shoreline footpath to the **Pencil Monument**, a modern obelisk commemorating the Battle of Largs of 1263. The battle was actually an accident, forced on King Hakon's Vikings when their longships were blown ashore by a gale. The invaders were attacked by the Scots as they struggled through the surf, and, although both sides claimed victory, the Norwegians retreated north, and abandoned their territorial claims to the Western Isles three years later. The Viking connection is exploited in the **Vikingar** exposition (April–Sept daily 10.30am–5.30pm; Oct–March 10.30am–4.30pm; £3.75), a five-minute walk north of the pier, which traces the history of the Vikings in Scotland with dramatic mood music, dioramas and videos.

Alternatively, you can venture out on the Firth of Clyde, with Clyde Marine **cruises** of Greenock (Mon–Fri; ☎01475/721281), or on the old paddle steamer, the *Waverley*, which visits Largs on its Tuesday trips during the summer (☎0141/221 8152). Caledonian MacBrayne (daily except Sat; ☎01475/674134) also operates from here to the islands just off the west coast – principally Bute and Cumbrae; Largs tourist office has all the details.

Largs practicalities

There are excellent connections to Ayr and Glasgow from Largs' **bus** and adjacent **train station**, on Main Street, a short stroll from the pier where **ferries** leave for Great Cumbrae. Beside the pier, the **tourist office** (Easter–June Mon–Sat 9.15am–5pm, Sun

10am–5pm; July & Aug closes 6pm; Sept–Oct Mon–Sat 9.15am–5pm, Sun 11am–4pm; Oct to Easter Mon–Fri 9.15am–5pm, Sat 9.15am–1pm & 2–5pm; ☎01475/673765) has heaps of free literature and will help with accommodation. Being a holiday town, Largs has no shortage of **guest houses** and **B&Bs**. There is a cluster along Aubery Crescent, a short side street overlooking the coast a few minutes' walk north of the pier. Choose from the *Old Rectory B&B* at no. 2 (☎01475/674405; ①), or the *Ardmore Guest House* at no. 16 (☎01475/672516; ①; April–Oct), both with excellent views over to Cumbrae and Arran. The cheapest place in town is the *Largs Tourist Hostel*, 110 Irvine Rd (☎01475/672851; ①), with doubles, family rooms and dorms available, whilst, at the other end of the scale, about three miles north of the centre on the A78, you can stay in the *Manor Park Hotel* (☎01475/520832; ⑥), a grand Victorian pile set in fifteen-acre grounds and looking out over the seashore; Churchill and Eisenhower met here to plan D-day landings. *South Whittlieburn Farm Campsite* (☎01475/675881) lies about three miles northeast of town on a working farm, and *Skelmorlie Mains Campsite* is about four miles north on the A78 (☎01475/520794; March–Oct).

For **food**, the *Green Shutter Tearoom*, along the seafront just south of the pier, serves excellent meals, while the *Bagel Basket*, on Main Street, is cheap and simple. And no visit to the town is complete without trying one of the amazing ice creams from *Nardini's* on the Promenade, just north of the pier, which sports unadulterated 1950s decor and has a lively buzz.

Great Cumbrae Island

Immediately offshore from Largs lies **Great Cumbrae**, a plump, hilly island roughly four miles long and half as wide. The only settlement of any size is **MILLPORT**, which curves around an attractive hilly bay on the south coast. The town possesses Britain's smallest cathedral, the **Cathedral of The Isles** (daily 11am–4pm except during services), which was completed in 1851 to a design by William Butterfield, an enthusiastic member of the High Church Oxford Movement and one of the leading Gothic revival architects of the day, responsible for several high-profile buildings such as Keble College, Oxford. A mile or so away, along the south shore to the east, is the **Marine Life Museum** (Mon–Fri 9.30am–12.15pm & 2–4.45pm; June–Sept also Sat) of the universities of Glasgow and London. The aquarium is excellent, but you're more likely to remember the view of the nuclear power station and iron-ore terminal back on the mainland. Get away from this depressing sight by heading inland either on foot or by bike to enjoy the peaceful countryside, or head round the coast away from the mainland for some good beaches. **Bike rental** is available in Millport from Mapes on Guildford Street (☎01475/530444).

It takes fifteen minutes to cross by ferry from Largs to the island's northeast tip, where a connecting **bus** travels on to Millport. Caledonian MacBrayne **ferries**

SCENIC BUS ROUTES

Harrier Scenic Bus Services (with several bus companies involved in running this service it's best to contact tourist offices for details) run round-trip tours from July to September once a week along the following routes:

Melrose–Moffat via Galashiels, Selkirk, Bowhill House, Yarrow, St Mary's Loch (Thurs only; 2hr each way).

Selkirk–Eyemouth via Galashiels, Melrose, Kelso, Coldstream, Berwick-upon-Tweed (Tues only; 2hr 10min each way).

Hawick–Eyemouth via Denholm, Jedburgh, Town Yetholm, Berwick-upon-Tweed (Fri only; 2hr each way).

(☎0990/650000) run every fifteen minutes from June to August between 6.45am and 8.45pm, and every thirty minutes in the winter, so there's no need to overnight on the island, but if you decide **to stay** be sure to book a room beforehand at Largs' or Millport **tourist office** (Easter–May Sat & Sun 10am–5pm; June & Sept daily 11am–5pm; July & Aug daily 10am–6pm; first two weeks of Oct Sat & Sun 11am–4pm; ☎01475/530753). For something a bit different, the *College of the Holy Spirit* (☎01475/530353, *tccumbrae@argylll.anglican.org*; ③) in Millport is an Anglican retreat house adjacent to the cathedral, which provides accommodation and food in a very peaceful setting, while the *Millerstone Guest House* (☎01475/530480; ③) offers more conventional B&B. The return ferry fare is £2.95 per person, £12.65 per car, which increases to £14.90 and £3.40 respectively for Saturdays from May to September (discounts on Day Saver returns Tues–Fri); bikes cost £2 return. Little Cumbrae, the islet opposite Millport, is privately owned.

travel details

Trains

Ayr to: Glasgow (approx every 30min; 50min); Stranraer (5–7 daily; 1hr 20min).

Dumfries to: Carlisle (5–15 daily; 35min); Glasgow (2–7 daily; 1hr 40min); Kilmarnock (2–7 daily; 1hr 5min).

Edinburgh to: Dunbar (Mon–Fri 7 daily, Sat 6 daily, Sun 4 daily; 20min); Musselburgh (Mon–Sat hourly, Sun 5 daily; 6 min); North Berwick (Mon–Sat hourly, Sun 5 daily; 30min).

Glasgow to: Ardrossan Harbour (5 daily; 50min); Ayr (every 30min; 50min); Carlisle (2–7 daily; 2hr 15min); Dumfries (2–7 daily; 1hr 40min); Kilmarnock (2–9 daily; 35min); Largs (hourly; 1hr); Stranraer (3–5 daily; 2hr).

Kilmarnock to: Carlisle (2–7 daily; 1hr 40min); Dumfries (2–9 daily; 1hr 5min); Glasgow (2–9 daily; 35min).

Largs to: Glasgow (hourly; 1hr).

Stranraer to: Ayr (5 daily; 1hr 20min); Glasgow (3–5 daily; 2 hr).

Buses

Ayr to: Castle Douglas (Mon–Sat 2 daily; 2hr); Culzean Castle (hourly; 30min); Girvan (every 30min; 1hr); Glasgow (hourly until 5.30pm; 55min); Largs (hourly; 1hr 10min); New Galloway (Mon–Sat 2 daily; 1hr 20min); Stranraer (10 daily; 2hr).

Dumfries to: Caerlaverock (Mon–Sat 5 daily; 35min); Carlisle (hourly; 50min); Castle Douglas (2–4 daily; 45min); Edinburgh (2 daily; 2hr 20min);

Gatehouse of Fleet (2 daily; 55min); Glasgow (4 daily; 2hr); Gretna (6 daily; 1hr); Kirkcudbright (2 daily; 1hr 10min); Lockerbie (hourly; 35min); Newton Stewart (2 daily; 1hr 20min); Rockcliffe (2 daily; 1hr 10min); Sanquhar (4 daily; 50min); Stranraer (2 daily; 2hr); Thornhill (6 daily; 30min).

Edinburgh to: Aberlady (every 30min; 55min); Berwick-upon-Tweed (7–11 daily; 2hr); Carlisle (3 daily; 3hr 25min); Dirleton (every 30min; 1hr 5min); Dumfries (2 daily; 2hr 20min); Dunbar (hourly; 1hr 22min); Eyemouth (5–7 daily; 1hr 40min); Galashiels (hourly; 1hr 25min); Haddington (hourly; 55 min); Jedburgh (Mon–Sat 6 daily, Sun 4 daily; 2hr); Melrose (hourly; 2hr 15min); North Berwick (every 30min; 1hr 20min); Peebles (hourly; 1hr).

Galashiels to: Berwick-upon-Tweed (8–11 daily; 1hr 40min); Canonbie (Mon–Sat 6–7 daily, Sun 3 daily; 1hr 30min); Carlisle (6–7 daily; 2hr); Hawick (9–10 daily; 40min); Langholm (Mon–Sat 6–7 daily, Sun 3 daily; 1hr 15min); Selkirk (every 30min; 17min).

Haddington to: Gifford (hourly; 20min); North Berwick (Mon–Sat 10 daily, Sun 4 daily; 45min).

Jedburgh to: Hawick (hourly; 35 min); Kelso (3–6 daily; 30min).

Kelso to: Coldstream (3–8 daily; 20min); Kirk Yetholm (6 daily; 20min); Melrose (8 daily; 35min).

Largs to: Ayr (hourly; 1hr 10min).

Leadhills to: Wanlockhead (2 daily; 5min).

Lockerbie to: Dumfries (hourly; 35min); Langholm (4 weekly; 35min).

Melrose to: Duns (7 daily; 50min); Eyemouth (3 daily; 1hr 25min); Galashiels (hourly; 15min); Hawick (Wed & Fri 3 daily, Sat 2 daily; 40min); Jedburgh (hourly; 30min); Kelso (8 daily; 35min); Lauder (5–7 daily; 30min); Peebles (7 daily; 1hr 10min); Selkirk (Mon–Sat hourly, Sun 4 daily; 40min).

Moffat to: Dumfries (7–9 daily; 55min); Lockerbie (2 daily; 20min).

Newton Stewart to: Ayr (2–5 daily; 2hr 15min); Bargrennan (2–5 daily; 20min); Girvan (2–5 daily; 1hr 20min); Glentrool (2–5 daily; 25min); Stranraer (2–9 daily; 40min); Wigtown (Mon–Sat 10 daily, Sun 3 daily; 15min); Whithorn (3–8 daily; 50min); Isle of Whithorn (3–6 daily; 1hr).

Peebles to: Biggar (4–6 daily; 40min); Edinburgh (hourly; 1hr); Melrose (7 daily; 1hr 10min).

Selkirk to: Carlisle (Mon–Sat 6–7 daily, Sun 3 daily; 1hr 45 min); Hawick (Mon–Sat 6–7 daily, Sun 3 daily; 20min); Langholm (Mon–Sat 6–7 daily, Sun 3 daily; 1hr).

Stranraer to: Drummore (1–2 daily; 45min); Port Logan (1–2 daily; 35min); Portpatrick (5 daily; 25min).

Ferries

Arran: Ardrossan–Brodick (up to 5 daily; 55min).

Belfast: Stranraer–Belfast (hydrofoil 5 daily; July & Aug Sat & Sun 8 daily; 1hr 35min: Seacat 4 daily; 1hr 30min).

Great Cumbrae Island: Largs-Millport (summer every 15min, winter every 30min; 15min).

Larne: Cairnryan-Larne (Jetliner 6 daily; 1 hr: Ferry 3 daily; 2hr 15min

CHAPTER THREE

GLASGOW AND THE CLYDE

R ejuvenated, upbeat **Glasgow**, Scotland's largest city, has not traditionally enjoyed the best of reputations. Once an industrial giant set on the banks of the mighty River Clyde, it can still initially seem a grey and depressing place, with the M8 motorway screeching through the centre and crumbling slums on its outskirts. However, in recent years Glasgow has undergone a remarkable overhaul, set in motion in the 1980s by a self-promotion campaign featuring a fat yellow creature called Mr Happy, beaming beatifically that "Glasgow's Miles Better". The city proceeded to generate a brisk tourist trade, reaching a climax after beating Paris, Athens and Amsterdam to the title of European City of Culture in 1990.

The epithet is still apt: Glasgow has some of the best-financed and most imaginative museums and galleries in Britain – among them the showcase **Burrell Collection** of art and antiquities – and nearly all of them are free. There's also a robust social scene and nightlife that is remarkably diverse, with a host of clubs and excellent live-music venues as well as a full calendar of theatre, opera and classical music. Its **architecture** is some of the most striking in the nation, from the restored eighteenth-century warehouses of the **Merchant City** to the hulking Victorian prosperity of George Square. Most distinctive of all is the work of local luminary Charles Rennie Mackintosh, whose elegantly streamlined Art Nouveau designs appear all over the city, reaching their apotheosis in the **School of Art**, and newly showcased in the Lighthouse building, the focus of Glasgow's most recent cultural jamboree, when it reigned as the **City of Architecture and Design** in 1999.

Despite all the upbeat hype, however, Glasgow's gentrification has passed by deprived inner-city areas such as the **East End**, home of the **Barras market** and some staunchly change-resistant pubs. This area, along with isolated housing schemes such as Castlemilk and Easterhouse, needs more than a facelift to resolve its complex social and economic problems, and has historically been the breeding ground for the city's much-lauded **socialism**.

Glasgow has also had a long-standing belief in the power of popular culture. Main attractions include the **People's Palace**, a celebrated social history museum, founded in 1898 to extol ordinary lives and achievements, and the **Citizens' Theatre**, formed in 1942 by playwright James Bridie to promote indigenous work for local people, whose innovative productions still cost next to nothing to see. In addition, Glasgow seems to sustain a remarkable number of cultural events – particularly music festivals – by tapping into the enthusiasm and commitment of its residents.

Quite apart from its own attractions, the city makes an excellent base from which to explore the **Clyde Valley and coast**, made easily accessible by the region's reliable rail service. Of the small communities in the Clyde Valley, **Lanark** is probably the best suited for overnight stays, as well as being the home of the remarkable eighteenth-century **New Lanark** mills and workers' village. Beyond that, most of the inland towns (as well as the coastal resorts) are best approached on day-trip from Glasgow.

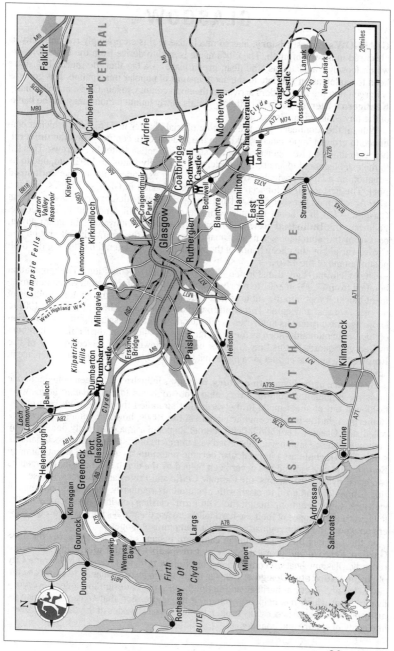

© Crown copyright

GLASGOW

GLASGOW's earliest **history**, like so much else in this surprisingly romantic city, is obscured in a swirl of myth. The city's name is said to derive from the Celtic *Glas-cu*, which loosely translates as "the dear, green place" – a tag that the tourist board are keen to exploit as an antidote to the sooty images of popular imagination. It is generally agreed that the first settlers arrived in the sixth century to join Christian missionary **Kentigern** – later to become St Mungo – in his newly founded monastery on the banks of the tiny Molendinar Burn.

William the Lionheart gave the town an official charter in 1175, after which it continued to grow in importance, peaking in the mid-fifteenth century when the **university** was founded on Kentigern's site – the second in Scotland after St Andrews. This led to the establishment of an archbishopric, and hence city status, in 1492, and, due to its situation on a large, navigable river, Glasgow soon expanded into a major **industrial port**. The first cargo of tobacco from Virginia offloaded in Glasgow in 1674, and the 1707 Act of Union between Scotland and England – despite demonstrations against it in Glasgow – led to a boom in trade with the colonies until American independence. Following the **Industrial Revolution** and James Watt's innovations in steam power, coal from the abundant seams of Lanarkshire fuelled the ironworks all around the Clyde, worked by the cheap hands of the Highlanders and, later, those fleeing the Irish potato famine of the 1840s.

The Victorian age transformed Glasgow beyond recognition. The population boomed from 77,000 in 1801 to nearly 800,000 at the end of the century, and new tenement blocks swept into the suburbs in an attempt to cope with the choking influxes of people. Two vast and stately **International Exhibitions** were held in 1888 and 1901 to showcase the city and its industries to the outside world, necessitating the construction of huge civic monoliths such as the Kelvingrove Art Gallery and the Council Chambers in George Square. At this time Glasgow became known as the "**Second City of the Empire**" – a curious epithet for a place that today rarely acknowledges second place in anything.

By the turn of the **twentieth century**, Glasgow's industries had been honed into one massive shipbuilding culture. Everything from tugboats to transatlantic liners were fashioned out of sheet metal in the yards that straddled the Clyde from Gourock to Rutherglen. In the harsh economic climate of the 1930s, however, unemployment spiralled, and Glasgow could do little to counter its popular image as a city dominated by inebriate violence and, having absorbed vast numbers of Irish emigrants, sectarian tensions. The **Gorbals** area in particular became notorious as one of the worst slums in Europe. The city's image has never been helped by the depth of animosity between its two great rival football teams: the Catholic **Celtic** and Protestant **Rangers**, whose warring armies of fans used to clash with monotonous regularity. Nowadays, post-match violence is less common, though the "Old Firm" clashes continue passionately on the field, even if the hopes of their die-hard followers are these days pinned to foreign players on whom the clubs regularly spend vast amounts of money.

In the Eighties the self-promotion campaign began, snowballing towards the 1988 **Garden Festival** and year-long party as **European City of Culture** in 1990. More recently, Glasgow beat off competition from Edinburgh and Liverpool to become **City of Architecture and Design** in 1999, an event which strove valiantly to showcase the city's rich architectural heritage and highlight the role of design in modern everyday living. All of which has helped to reinforce the impression that Glasgow, despite its many problems, has successfully broken the industrial shackles of the past and evolved into a city of stature and confidence.

Arrival, information and transport

Glasgow is a sprawling place, built upon some punishingly steep hills, and with no really obvious focus, although, as most transport services converge on the area around **Argyle Street** and, 200yd to the north, **George Square**, this pocket of the city is the most obvious candidate for city-centre status. However, with the renovated upmarket **Merchant City** immediately to the east and the main business and commercial areas to the west, the centre, when the term is used, actually refers to a large swathe from **Charing Cross** and the M8 in the west through to **Glasgow Green** in the **East End**. Although run-down, the latter boasts a wonderful social history museum, the People's Palace, and is close to Glasgow Cathedral at the city's medieval heart. Outside the city centre, the **West End** begins just over a mile west of Central station, and covers most of the area west of the M8. In the nineteenth century, as the East End tumbled into poverty, the West End ascended the social scale with great speed, a process crowned by the arrival of the **University**. Today, this is still very much the student quarter of Glasgow, exuding a decorous air, with graceful avenues, parks and cheap, interesting shops and cafés. It's also well connected with the city centre by Underground. The suburbs of Govan and the Gorbals, neither of which hold much for visitors, lie south of the Clyde, as does the area known as **South Side**, a relaxed version of the West End. Here the leafy enclaves of **Queen's Park** are home to the national football stadium, Hampden Park; the main attraction, though, has to be **Pollok Park** and the **Burrell Collection**. None of the sights here are within walking distance of the city centre, but can easily be reached by train or bus.

Arrival

Glasgow's **airport** (☎0141/887 1111) is out at Abbotsinch, eight miles southwest of the city – not to be confused with Glasgow Prestwich Airport (see p.185), which is near Ayr. To get into town, go to bus stop number two and take a Citylink or Airport Link bus (both £2.70), which run to **Buchanan Street** bus station (☎0141/332 7133), north of George Square on the other side of the massive Buchanan Galleries shopping mall, every fifteen minutes during the day. From stop number three, regular buses run to **Paisley Gilmour Street** train station, from where you can catch a fast train into **Glasgow Central**, the terminus for trains from anywhere south of Glasgow.

Central station sits over Argyle Street, one of the city's main shopping thoroughfares. A **shuttle bus** (50p) from the front entrance on Gordon Street travels every fifteen minutes to **Queen Street station**, at the corner of George Square, for trains to Edinburgh and the north. The walk between the two takes about ten minutes.

Information

The city's efficient **tourist office**, at 11 George Square (May Mon–Sat 9am–6pm, Sun 10am–6pm; June & Sept Mon–Sat 9am–7pm, Sun 10am–6pm; July & Aug Mon–Sat 9am–8pm, Sun 10am–6pm; Oct–April Mon–Sat 9am–6pm; ☎0141/204 4400) provides a wide array of maps and leaflets, and an accommodation-booking service (£2 fee). You can also buy travel passes, theatre tickets and organize car rental. Ask for the free *Guide to Getting Around Glasgow*, which contains brief details about public transport and an excellent fold-out map of the city centre and West End. If you're staying for longer, or want to explore the tiny streets and alleys that are invariably airbrushed off the tourist maps, it's probably worth investing in a *Bartholomew Glasgow Streetfinder* (£2.99). The *Guide to Getting Around Glasgow* is also available at the neo-Gothic hut of the **Strathclyde Travel Centre** (Mon–Sat 8.30am–5.30pm; ☎0141/332 7133), located a couple of hundred yards southwest above the St Enoch Underground station, where you can pick up sheaves of maps, leaflets and bus timetables.

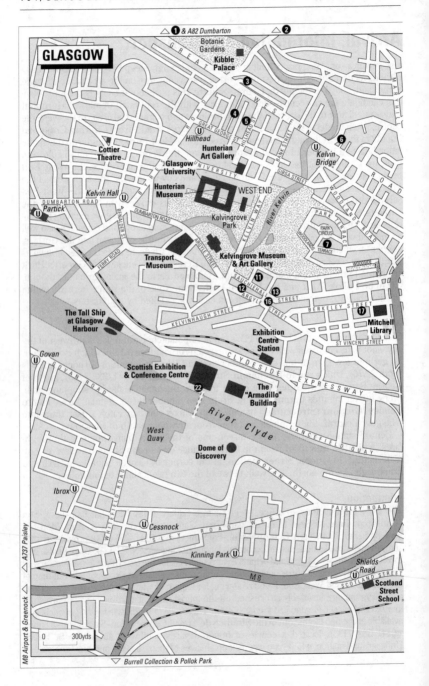

GLASGOW

△ ❶ & A82 Dumbarton

△ ❷

Botanic Gardens

Kibble Palace

❸

Cottier Theatre

❹

❺

Hillhead

Hunterian Art Gallery

Glasgow University

Hunterian Museum

WEST END

Kelvin Bridge

❻

Kelvin Hall

Partick

DUMBARTON ROAD

Kelvingrove Park

Kelvingrove Museum & Art Gallery

Park Circus

❼

Transport Museum

❶❶

❶❷ ❶❸

❶❻

Mitchell Library

❶❼

The Tall Ship at Glasgow Harbour

Exhibition Centre Station

Govan

Scottish Exhibition & Conference Centre

❷❷

The "Armadillo" Building

River Clyde

West Quay

Dome of Discovery

Ibrox

Cessnock

PAISLEY ROAD WEST

Kinning Park

Shields Road

Scotland Street School

M8

0   300yds

▽ Burrell Collection & Pollok Park

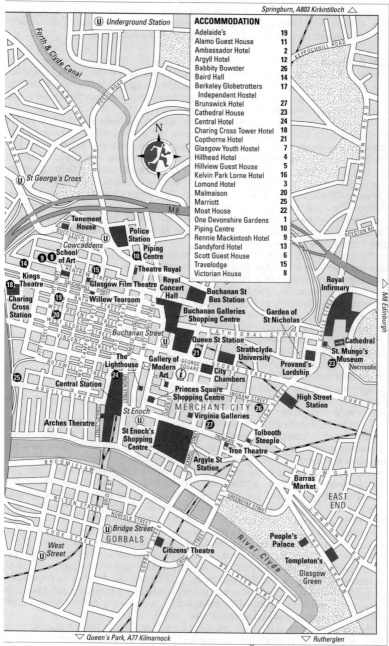

Springburn, A803 Kirkintilloch △

ACCOMMODATION

Adelaide's	19
Alamo Guest House	11
Ambassador Hotel	2
Argyll Hotel	12
Babbity Bowster	26
Baird Hall	14
Berkeley Globetrotters Independent Hostel	17
Brunswick Hotel	27
Cathedral House	23
Central Hotel	24
Charing Cross Tower Hotel	18
Copthorne Hotel	21
Glasgow Youth Hostel	7
Hillhead Hotel	4
Hillview Guest House	5
Kelvin Park Lorne Hotel	16
Lomond Hotel	3
Malmaison	20
Marriott	25
Moat House	22
One Devonshire Gardens	1
Piping Centre	10
Rennie Mackintosh Hotel	9
Sandyford Hotel	13
Scott Guest House	6
Travelodge	15
Victorian House	8

▽ Queen's Park, A77 Kilmarnock   ▽ Rutherglen

© Crown copyright

There is also a tourist office in the **airport** (daily 7.30am–5pm except Sun Oct–April 8am–3.30pm; ☎0141/848 4440), located in the international arrivals hall. They can help out with transport arrangements and make accommodation bookings.

City transport

Although it can be tough negotiating the steep hills, **walking** is the best way of exploring any one part of the city. However, as the main sights are scattered – the West End, for example, is a good thirty-minute walk from the centre – you'll probably need to use the comprehensive **public transport** system.

The best way to get between the city centre, southern suburbs and the West End is to use the city's **Underground**, whose stations are marked with a large orange U. Affectionately known as the "Clockwork Orange" (there's only one, circular route and the trains are a garish bright orange), the service is extremely easy to use. There's a flat fare of 80p, or you can buy a **day ticket** for £2.50; a **multi-journey ticket** gives ten journeys for £5.40 or twenty for £10. From Monday to Saturday, the whole system opens at 6.30am, and shuts down at 10.30pm. On Sundays, trains run from 11am to 5.30pm. The main stations are **Buchanan Street**, near George Square and connected to Queen Street train station by a moving walkway, and **St Enoch**, at the junction of Buchanan Street pedestrian precinct and Argyle Street, while **Hillhead** is bang in the heart of the West End, near the University.

If you're travelling beyond the city centre or the West End, you may need to use the bus and train networks. After deregulation, the city was besieged by a horde of **bus** companies in hot competition. First Bus won the tender, operating under its own name and those of Greater Glasgow and Kelvin Buses – unfortunately there's no easy guide to using them other than picking up individual timetables at the Travel Centre on St Enoch's Square, though you could try calling First Bus on ☎0141/636 3195. Information on relevant services is given at some bus stops.

The suburban **train network** is swift and convenient. Suburbs south of the Clyde are connected to Glasgow Central mainline station, while trains from Queen Street head into the northeast. The grim but functional **cross-city line**, which runs beneath Argyle Street (and includes a low-level stop below Central station), connects northwestern destinations with southeastern districts as far out as Lanark. Trains on both the Queen Street and Central station lines go through **Partick** station, west of the city centre; this is also an Underground stop.

If you are in the city for at least a week, it's worth investing in a **Zonecard**, which covers all public transport networks, and is valid for seven days or a month. Costs depend on the number of zones that you want to travel through – a two-zone card, for example, which gets you from Partick in the west to Rutherglen in the east, and as far as the Burrell Collection in the south, will set you back £11, although a Zonecard giving you access to all zones within Greater Glasgow is only £14.40. The Strathclyde Travel Centre (see above) can give further details and help demystify the system. There is also a **Day-Tripper-Ticket**, which covers all the transport networks, going beyond the city zones, and costs £7.50 for one adult and up to two children, or £13 for two adults and up to four children, although you'd need to spend a very busy day sightseeing to make it worthwhile. Additionally, the **Roundabout Glasgow Ticket** (£3.50) gives unlimited travel for a day on the Underground and rail services from Milngavie in the north to Motherwell in the south. If you want to see the sights, the rival **Discovering Glasgow** and **Guide Friday** open-topped tour buses (both April–Oct Mon–Sat 9.30am–4pm; £6.50) leave on the hour and half-hour from George Square and run a continuous route around all the major attractions in the city centre and West End, allowing you to get on and off as you please.

Should you want to avoid public transport altogether, you can hail a black **cab** from anywhere in the city centre. There are also taxi ranks at Central and Queen Street train stations and Buchanan Street bus station. Taxis run all day and night, and are very reasonable; the minimum fare is £1.60 and the journey from Central station to Pollok Park and the Burrell Collection (about three miles) costs £7–8.

As for **driving**, the M8 motorway runs right through the heart of Glasgow, making it one of the country's most car-friendly cities, with plenty of parking meters and 24-hour multistorey car parks at Waterloo Street, Mitchell Street, Oswald Street and Cambridge Street. Parking tariffs per day in the city centre are expensive, significantly less so in the outskirts.

Accommodation

There's a good range of **accommodation** in Glasgow, from an excellent youth hostel in the leafy West End through to some top international hotels in the centre. Most of the rooms are in the city centre, the West End or down in the southern suburb of Queen's Park. Glasgow's speciality is its profusion of converted Victorian **town houses** in the middle of town, many of which are now privately run B&Bs that offer excellent value for money. In general, prices are significantly lower than in Edinburgh, and given that many hotels are business-oriented, you can often negotiate good deals at weekends.

Hotels and guest houses

During summer it's worth **booking ahead** to ensure a good room – at any time of year the tourist office (*tourismglasgow@ggcvtb.org.uk*) can help secure you somewhere to stay, though they charge a fairly hefty £2 fee plus a deposit of ten percent of the cost of the room, of which only the deposit is offset against your bill. It also publishes a useful brochure of bargain weekend breaks.

City centre

Adelaide's, 209 Bath St (☎0141/248 4970). Eight well-appointed rooms in a beautifully restored church building in a central location, with pleasant staff and an attractive café (breakfast from 7.30am). ②.

Babbity Bowster, 16–18 Blackfriars St (☎0141/552 5055). A traditional and very lively hotel, bar and restaurant that makes much of its Scottishness, yet is set right in the heart of the fashionable Merchant City. Rooms are straightforward but smart and comfortable. ⑤.

Baird Hall, 460 Sauchiehall St (☎0141/553 4148). The most distinctive student halls of residence in the country, in a lavish Art Deco building near the School of Art and the upper end of Sauchiehall Street, with rooms available in summer (June to mid-Sept). ①.

Brunswick Hotel, 106 Brunswick St (☎0141/552 0001, *brunhotel@aol.com*). In the heart of the Merchant City, a fashionable but good-value designer hotel with minimalist furniture and a smart bar and restaurant. ③.

ACCOMMODATION PRICE CODES

Throughout this book, accommodation **prices** have been graded with the codes below, according to the cost of the least expensive double room in high season. Price codes are not given for campsites, most of which charge under £10 per person. Almost all hostels charge less than £10 a night for a bed – the few exceptions to this rule have the prices quoted in the text. For a full account of the accommodation price codes, see p.31.

① under £40	④ £60–70	⑦ £110–150
② £40–50	⑤ £70–90	⑧ £150–200
③ £50–60	⑥ £90–110	⑨ £200 and over

Cathedral House, 28 Cathedral Square (☎0141/552 3519). Located in the oldest part of the city near the cathedral, this intriguing red sandstone Victorian building with turrets and high chimney stacks has comfortable modern rooms and a good restaurant. ④.

Central Hotel, Gordon Street (☎0141/221 9680). Formerly *the* hotel in the city in the heart of the action adjacent to Central railway station, now part of a chain, but still a comfortable place to stay, with its own leisure centre. ⑥.

Charing Cross Tower Hotel, Elmbank Gardens (☎0141/221 1000, *cxt@cims.co.uk*). Functional, well-equipped rooms in a large hotel in a refurbished office block The top-floor rooms give excellent views of the city. ⑦.

Copthorne Hotel, George Square (☎0141/332 6711). Large and impressive eighteenth-century hotel occupying the entire northwestern corner of George Square; rooms are bright and flouncy, and prices rocket at the weekend. There's a popular bar in the ground-floor glass veranda. ⑥.

Malmaison, 278 West George St (☎0141/572 1000, *glasgow@malmaison.com*). Easily the most stylish hotel in the city centre, with large, elegant rooms and contemporary designer touches everywhere. ⑨.

Marriott, 500 Argyle St (☎0141/226 5577). Large and luxurious chain hotel with a popular health centre. Ask for a room out of earshot of the M8. Considerable reductions available at weekends. ⑤.

Piping Centre, 30–34 McPhater St (☎0141/353 0220). Eight (fortunately) soundproofed, hotel-grade rooms attached to the piping centre; a decent restaurant serves Scottish dishes. ④.

Rennie Mackintosh Hotel, 218–220 Renfrew St (☎0141/333 9992). An obvious theme, but the "Mockintosh" is elegant rather than tacky, and the hotel is small, smart and intimate. ③.

Travelodge, 5–11 Hill St (☎0141/333 1515). Flimsy but functional and inexpensive chain hotel, just to the north of the city centre. ③.

Victorian House, 212 Renfrew St (☎0141/332 0129). Smart but friendly terraced guest house with sixty rooms: its rates are among the lowest in the city centre. ②.

West End

Alamo Guest House, 46 Gray St (☎0141/339 2395). Good-value, family-run boarding house next to Kelvingrove Park. Small but comfortable rooms. ②.

Ambassador Hotel, 7 Kelvin Drive (☎0141/946 1018). Smallish and comfortable, family-run hotel in lovely surroundings next to the River Kelvin and Botanic Gardens. ③.

Argyll Hotel, 973 Sauchiehall St (☎0141/337 3313, *argyll_angus.hotel@virgin.net*). Well-placed, newly refurbished hotel near Kelvingrove Museum and Art Gallery with neat rooms and friendly staff. ③.

Hillhead Hotel, 32 Cecil St (☎0141/339 7733, *hillhotel@aol.com*). Quiet, welcoming guest house in a student area only a couple of minutes' stroll from Hillhead Underground and excellent local pubs and restaurants. ②.

Hillview Guest House, 18 Hillhead St (☎0141/334 5585). Unassuming and peaceful small guest house near the University and Byres Road. ②.

Kelvin Park Lorne Hotel, 923 Sauchiehall St (☎0141/314 9955). Dependable, if slightly sterile, international hotel with food to match. Offers good weekend rates. ⑥.

Lomond Hotel, 6 Buckingham Terrace (☎0141/339 2339). Discreet guest house in a beautifully restored Victorian terrace near the Botanic Gardens and Byres Road. ②.

Moat House, Congress Rd (☎0141/306 9988). Slick, 300-room riverside hotel towering above the SECC; most rooms have good views of the Clyde. ⑦.

One Devonshire Gardens, 1 Devonshire Gardens, Great Western Road (☎0141/339 2001). Glasgow's most exclusive and exquisite small hotel, a ten-minute walk up the Great Western Road from the Botanic Gardens. Also well-known for its expensive gourmet restaurant. ⑨.

Sandyford Hotel, 904 Sauchiehall St (☎0141/334 0000). A clean, comfortable mid-sized hotel, well located for Kelvingrove Park and the SECC. ③.

Scott Guest House, 417 Woodside Rd (☎0141/339 3750). Friendly B&B, well situated close to Kelvinbridge underground station. ①.

South Side

Boswell Hotel, 27 Mansionhouse Rd (☎0141/632 9812). Informal, relaxing Queen's Park hotel with a superb real-ale bar. ④.

Drambuie Scottish Chefs Centre, 62 St Andrews Drive (☎0141/427 1106). Scotland's top school for chefs set in a lovely large Victorian mansion, with a number of great-value guest house rooms available. The chefs demonstrate their newly acquired skills in the restaurant (Fri and Sat evenings). ②.

Ewington Hotel, 132 Queen's Drive (☎0141/423 1152, *ewington@aol.com*). Comfortable and peaceful upmarket hotel facing Queen's Park, with an excellent, moderately priced subterranean restaurant. ⑦.

Reidholme Guest House, 36 Regent Park Square (☎0141/423 1855). Small and friendly guest house that was designed by Alexander "Greek" Thomson (see p.203), in a quiet side street. ②.

Queen's Park Hotel, 10 Balvicar Drive (☎0141/423 1123). Faintly shabby, but very welcoming and with good views over the hill of Queen's Park. Attracts regular return visitors. ③.

Hostels

Glasgow doesn't have nearly as many hostels as Edinburgh: the best bet is the SYHA's **Glasgow Youth Hostel**, 7–8 Park Terrace (☎0141/332 3004, central reservations ☎0541/553255, *glasgow@syha.org.uk*), located in a large town house in one of the West End's grandest terraces. It's a ten-minute walk south from Kelvinbridge Underground station, or take First Bus #11, #44 or #59 from the city centre, and then a short stroll west up Woodlands Road. Bed and breakfast costs £13.25 per person in July and August and £12.25 from September to June; the hostel is very popular, with a decent number of four-bed dorms, so book in advance.

In less magnificent surroundings, the **Berkeley Globetrotters Independent Hostel**, 63 Berkeley St (☎0141/221 7880) provides a slightly cheaper alternative to the youth hostel, with dorm beds for £10.50 and twin-bedded rooms for £11.25 per person. The #57 Greater Glasgow bus from the city centre runs straight past the door, or take a low-level train from Queen Street Station to Charing Cross – it's a five-minute walk west from there.

Campsite

The only **campsite** within a decent distance of Glasgow is **Craigendmuir Park**, Campsie View, Stepps (☎0141/779 4159), four miles northeast of the city centre, a fifteen-minute walk from Stepps train station. It has adequate facilities with showers, a laundry and a shop, but there are only ten pitches.

Self-catering

Low-priced **self-catering** rooms and flats are available at the **University of Glasgow** (☎0141/330 5385) from June to mid-September. The **University of Strathclyde** has various sites available during the same period, most of which are gathered around the cathedral. Bed-and-breakfast accommodation in single rooms is available near the main campus in Cathedral Street starting at £18.50 per person per night, though you can pick up rooms for as little as £10 if you have your own bedding and you don't want breakfast (☎0141/553 4148). The **YMCA** at 33 Petershill Drive, Balornock (☎0141/558 6166), three miles northeast of the city centre (a 10min walk from Barnhill train station), offers clean, if rather lifeless self-catering flats (①) sleeping between four and six people which are available all year round; there are no dorms.

The City Centre

Glasgow's large **City Centre** is ranged across the north bank of the River Clyde. At its geographical heart is **George Square**, a nineteenth-century municipal showpiece crowned by the enormous **City Chambers** at its eastern end. Behind this lies one of the 1980s' greatest marketing successes, the **Merchant City**, an area which blends magnificent Victorian architecture with yuppie conversions. The grand buildings and trendy cafés cling to the borders of the run-down **East End**, a strongly working-class district that chooses to ignore its rather showy neighbour. The oldest part of Glasgow, around the **Cathedral**, lies immediately north of the East End.

Called by John Betjeman "the greatest Victorian city in the world", Glasgow's commercial core spreads west of George Square, and is mostly built on a large grid system – possibly inspired by Edinburgh's New Town – with ruler-straight roads soon rising up severe hills to grand, sandblasted buildings. The main shopping areas here are **Argyle Street**, running parallel to the river, and **Buchanan Street**, which links Argyle Street to the pedestrianized shopping thoroughfare, **Sauchiehall Street**. Just to the north-west of here is Rennie Mackintosh's famous **Glasgow School of Art**. Lying between the commercial bustle of Argyle and Sauchiehall streets, and to the immediate west of Buchanan Street, are the contours of an Ice Age drumlin (one of three main drumlins in the area), now known as **Blythswood Hill**. The tightly packed grid of streets piled on its slopes are lined by Georgian buildings filled with offices. In comparison with the bustling shopping parades surrounding it on three sides, this area is remarkably quiet and reserved, crowned by neat Blythswood Square.

George Square

Now hemmed in by the city's grinding traffic, the imposing architecture of **George Square** reflects the confidence of Glasgow's Victorian age. Rising high above the centre of the square is an eighty-foot column topped by a statue of Sir Walter Scott, although his links with Glasgow were, at best, sketchy. Haphazardly dotted around the great writer's plinth are a number of dignified statues of assorted luminaries, ranging from Queen Victoria to Scots heroes such as James Watt and wee Robbie Burns. The florid splendour of the **City Chambers**, opened by Queen Victoria in 1888, occupies the entire eastern end of the square. Built from wealth gained by colonial trade and heavy industry, it epitomizes the aspirations and optimism of late-Victorian city elders. Its intricately detailed facade includes high-minded friezes typical of the era: the four nations (England, Ireland, Scotland, Wales) of the then United Kingdom at the feet of the throned queen, the British colonies and allegorical figures representing Religion, Virtue and Knowledge. It's worth taking a free guided tour (Mon–Fri 10.30am & 2.30pm; ☎0141/227 4017) of the labyrinthine interior to get a look at the acres of intricate gold leaf and Italian marble.

Equally opulent is the **Merchant's House** opposite Queen Street station (entry by appointment only; ☎0141/221 8272; free), where the grand Banqueting Hall and silk-lined Directors' Room are highlights. Even if you don't get inside, look out for the golden square-rigged ship on a globe perched on the top of the building.

The Gallery of Modern Art

Queen Street leads south from George Square to Royal Exchange Square, where the focal point is the graceful mansion built in 1780 for tobacco lord William Cunninghame. It was the most ostentatious of the Glasgow merchants' homes and, having served as the city's Royal Exchange and central library, now houses the **Gallery of Modern Art**

(Mon–Sat 10am–5pm, Sun 11am–5pm; free). Surrounded by controversy from the day it opened, the gallery has pleased the punters more than the critics, who have damned the place for putting more emphasis on presentation than on content. The presentation is certainly unusual: the main part of the gallery is divided into four levels, named Fire, Earth, Water and Air, though these themes bear only a tenuous link to the work displayed. A mirrored reception area (inhabited by an irreverent fibreglass model of the Queen picking up milk bottles from her doorstep, which unsurprisingly wasn't in place when she opened the gallery in 1996) leads you straight into the **Earth Gallery**, a spacious zone that effortlessly absorbs large-scale socially committed works by the "Glasgow Pups" – Peter Howson, Adrian Wiszniewski, Ken Currie and Stephen Campbell. Felipe Linares' beautifully painted papier-mâché skeletons, exploring the seven deadly sins, shine defiantly from the end of the gallery, along with the evocative photographs of Sebastião Salgado, whose work records the plight of the world's economic underclasses.

Downstairs is the **Fire Gallery**, a dark place packed with interactive creations, while upstairs you'll find the **Water Gallery**, a brightly lit room dealing with the flow of life and death through art that ranges from Andy Goldsworthy's sun-baked and cracked red clay floor to intricate Aboriginal paintings on canvas and bark. The blinding-white **Air Gallery** is a perfect setting for such displays of optical fireworks as *Punjabi*, an eye-shattering study in red, white, violet and green by Bridget Riley, and *Jubilee* by Patrick Hughes, a witty exercise in visual deception. A small set of stairs at the far end of the gallery leads down to an area filled with examples of well-designed everyday objects, from nappies to bookshelves. Don't miss the top-floor **café** (see p.220), where a huge mural by Adrian Wiszniewski competes with the view of rooftops below.

The Merchant City

The grid of streets that lies immediately east of the City Chambers is known as the **Merchant City**, an area of eighteenth-century warehouses and homes once bustling with cotton, tobacco and sugar traders, which in the last decade or so has been sandblasted and swabbed clean with greater enthusiasm and municipal money than any other part of Glasgow in an attempt to bring residents back into the city centre. The expected flood of yuppies, however, was more like a trickle, and the latest efforts to woo them revolve around New York-style loft apartments. Yet the expensive designer shops, style bars and bijou cafés continue to flock here, giving the area a pervasive air of sophistication and chic.

At the junction of Ingram and John streets, look out for the **Italian Centre**, a revitalized eighteenth-century warehouse now housing lively cafés, outdoor sculpture and some of the city's most fashionable boutiques – Versace established his first shop in Britain here. Immediately opposite across John Street is the delicate white spire of the National Trust for Scotland's regional headquarters, **Hutcheson Hall**, at 158 Ingram St (Mon–Sat 10am–5pm). The NTS has a shop on the ground floor and visitors can see the ornately decorated hall upstairs. In the shop you can pick up a Merchant City Trail leaflet, which guides you around a dozen of the most interesting buildings in the area.

Almost opposite in the other direction, a little way down Glassford Street, the Robert Adam-designed **Trades House** (visits by appointment only; ☎0141/552 2418; free) is easily distinguished by its neat, green copper dome. Purpose-built in 1794, it still functions as the headquarters of the Glasgow trade guilds. Its history can be traced back to 1605 when fourteen societies of well-to-do city merchants, who were the forerunners of the trade unions, first incorporated. These included a Bakers' Guild, and societies for Hammermen, Gardeners, Bonnet Makers, Wrights and Weavers, although today they have limited connections to their respective trades and act as charitably minded associations of (mostly) men from all sections of Glasgow's busi-

GLASGOW'S ARCHITECTURE

Glasgow, founded on religion, built on trade and now well established as a cultural centre, has become recognized as an architectural hot-spot, from its medieval cathedral to the modern glass-lined galleries of the Burrell Collection. Most dominant, however, is the legacy of the **Victorian age**, when booming trade and industry allowed merchants to commission the finest architects of the day. As World War II bombing was focused on the shipbuilding centre of Clydebank, most of the city's fine sandstone buildings have survived intact. The celebrated work of **Charles Rennie Mackintosh** (1868–1928) took Glasgow architecture to the forefront of early twentieth-century design, a final flowering of homespun genius before economic conditions effectively stopped the architectural trade in its tracks.

Glasgow's great expansion was initiated in the eighteenth century by wealthy tobacco merchants who, in an attempt to bask in the reflected glory of Classical times, built the grand edifices of public and municipal importance that still make up much of the **Merchant City**. One of the finest Merchant City views is down Garth Street, where the Venetian windows and Ionic columns of **Trades House**, designed by Robert Adam in 1791, close the vista with a flourish. **Hutcheson Hall**, closing off Hutcheson Street, is another fine monument of civic pride, with a five-bay facade and elegant tower that moves from a square through octagonals to a drum – an early nineteenth-century architectural nod to the Renaissance by the architect David Hamilton.

Further west, **Royal Exchange Square** is one of the best examples of a typical Glasgow square: treeless, bare and centred around a building of importance, the 1829 **Royal Exchange**, now housing the Gallery of Modern Art. The square itself is an excellent example of integrated municipal design, with closely matching Georgian buildings unifying the area into a harmonious whole. Further north, off Queen Street, the open space of **George Square** holds the emphatically Victorian **City Chambers**, its Venetian splendour a testimony to the confidence of the wealthy merchants, built only a couple of years after the crash of the Glasgow bank in 1878.

As workers piled into the centre of Glasgow in the early nineteenth century, filling up the already bursting tenements, wealthy residents began moving west. This expansion was completely uncontrolled and so the gridded streets that line **Blythswood Hill** (mostly developed after 1820) hold an eclectic range of buildings. However, a harmonious streetscape was created by the predominance of two- or three-storey terraces, their porches and heavy cornices providing textural relief to the endless sandstone monotony. The dignified proportions and design of **Blythswood Square** are a highlight of this area; at no. 5 the later Art Nouveau doorway designed by Charles Rennie Mackintosh sits incongruously amongst the Georgian solidity. Above all, the long streets provide a beautiful selection of open-ended views, one moment leading into the heart of the city, the next filled with distant hills and sky.

Now desiring to surround themselves with trees and fields, the well-to-do continued their migration west; in the early 1830s, beyond Charing Cross, the Woodlands Hill development was completed – a leafy parkland area in contrast to the treeless town squares of the city centre. Here **Woodside Crescent**, leading into Woodside Terrace, is

ness community. The former civic pride and status of the guilds is still evident, however, from the rich assortment of carvings and stained-glass windows, with a lively pictorial representation of the different trades in the silk frieze around the walls of the first-floor banqueting hall.

On Virginia Street, parallel to Glassford Street, the **Virginia Galleries** sit behind the intricate wrought-iron gate of no 33. Formerly the city's nineteenth-century tobacco and sugar trading house, the graceful market hall is now a sedate place, filled with a variety of shops selling everything from secondhand clothing to African artefacts.

a severe line of buildings, with splendid Doric porches and neatly organized gardens. **Park Circus**, on the other hand, is a parade of uninterrupted Georgian magnificence, with delicate detail – such as narrow window slots on either side of the doors – enhancing the dignified crescent. Now predominantly commercial, it's an excellent example of grand planning.

Long since overshadowed by Charles Rennie Mackintosh (see p.208), the design of **Alexander "Greek" Thomson**, in the latter half of the nineteenth century, though well respected in its time, has been sadly neglected. As his nickname suggests, his work took the principles of Greek architecture, but reprocessed them in a highly unique manner. Energetic and talented, he designed buildings from the lowly tenement to grand suburban villas. The St Vincent Street Church (1857), his best work, has a massive simplicity and serenity lightened by the use of exotic Egyptian and Hindu motifs, particularly in the tower with its decorated egg-shaped dome. This fusion of the Classical and the Eastern stands out for its originality at a time when Gothic Revival or Renaissance work was all the rage. Thanks in part to a major retrospective of his work during Glasgow's year as City of Architecture and Design in 1999, Thomson's buildings are now coming to the prominence they deserve, though some were tragically torn down in the municipal clearances of the 1970s. Most recently, the National Trust has opened his finest domestic dwelling, Holmwood House, on the south side, to the public (see p.219).

West from Park Circus lies **Glasgow University** (1866–86), its Gothic Revivalism – the work of Sir George Gilbert Scott – representing everything that Greek Thomson despised; he called it "sixteenth-century Scottish architecture clothed in fourteenth-century French details". Scottish features abound, such as crow-stepped gables, round turrets with conical caps and the top-heavy central tower. Inside, cloisters and quadrants sum up a suitably scholastic severity.

Originally conceived as a convenient way to house the influx of workers in the late 1800s, the Glasgow **tenement** design became more refined as the wealthy middle classes began to realize its potential. Tenements were built by private landlords, the majority constructed in a remarkably short space of time, from around 1860 to 1910. In general these buildings are three to five storeys with two or three apartments per floor. Important rooms are picked out with bay windows, middle storeys are emphasized by architraves or decorated panels below sill or above lintel, and street junctions are given importance by swelling bay windows, turrets and domes. West of the University, the streets off **Byres Road** are lined with such grand tenement buildings, in particular the Baronial red sandstone of Great George Street.

World War I put an end to the glorious century of Glasgow building, and the Depression years did little to enhance the city. More recently, glassy office buildings have sprung up, their mirrored walls basking in the reflected glory of the surrounding buildings to disguise their banality of design. More notable modern constructions include the **Burrell Collection** and **St Mungo's Museum**, both successfully designed to suit their surroundings, and the unmistakeable giant silver Clyde Auditorium, better known as the "**Armadillo**", beside the Scottish Exhibition and Conference Centre (SECC), that now dominates the Clydeside.

From Trongate to the East End

Before 1846, **Glasgow Cross** – the junction of **Trongate**, Gallowgate and the High Street – was the city's principal intersection, until the construction of the new train station near George Square shifted the city's emphasis west. The turreted seventeenth-century **Tolbooth Steeple** still stands here, although the rest of the building has long since disappeared, and today the stern tower is little more than a traffic hazard at a busy junction. Further east, down Gallowgate, beyond the train lines, lies the **East End**, the district that perhaps most closely corresponds to the old perception of Glasgow. Hemmed in by Glasgow Green to the south, and the old university to the west, this densely packed industrial area essentially created the city's wealth. The Depression caused the closure of many factories, leaving communities stranded in an industrial wasteland. Today isolated pubs, tatty shops and cafés sit amidst this dereliction, in sharp contrast to the gloss of the Merchant City only a few blocks to the west.

Three hundred yards down either London Road or Gallowgate, **The Barras** is Glasgow's largest and most popular weekend market (Sat & Sun 9am–5pm). Red iron gates announce its official entrance, but boundaries are breached as the stalls – selling household goods, bric-a-brac, secondhand clothes and records – spill out into the surrounding cobbled streets. The fast-talking traders are sharp-witted and friendly, and there are plenty of bargains to be had, but you'll be in strong competition with locals vying for the goods.

Between London Road and the River Clyde are the wide and tree-lined spaces of **Glasgow Green**. Reputedly the oldest public park in Britain, the Green has been common land since at least 1178, when it was first mentioned in records. Glaswegians hold it very dear, considering it to be an immortal link between themselves and their ancestors, for whom a stroll on the Green was a favourite Sunday afternoon jaunt. It has also been the site of many of the city's major political demonstrations – the Chartists in the 1830s and Scottish republican campaigners in the 1920s – and was the traditional culmination of the May Day marches until the 1950s, when the celebrations were moved to Queen's Park. Various memorials (some in bad states of disrepair) are dotted around the lawns: the 146-foot **Nelson Monument**; the ornate but derelict terracotta **Doulton Fountain**, rising like a wedding cake to a pinnacle where forlorn Queen Victoria oversees her crumbling Empire; and the stern monument extolling the evils of drink and the glory of God that was erected by the nineteenth-century Temperance movement – today, quite a meeting place for local drunks.

The People's Palace

On the northern end of Glasgow Green, the **People's Palace** (Mon–Sat 10am–5pm, Sun 11am–5pm; free) is a wonderfully haphazard evocation of the city's history. This squat, red-brick Victorian building, with a vast semicircular glasshouse tacked on the back, was purpose-built as a museum back in 1898 – almost a century before the rest of the country caught on to the fashion for social history collections.

On the top floor, glowing murals by local artist Ken Currie powerfully evoke the spirit of radical Glasgow, from the Carlton Weavers strike in 1787 to the Red Clydesiders of the 1920s (a radical Independent Labour Party formed during the post-World War I economic slump), and look down upon a potted history of Glasgow's social and economic development. Decorated by Suffragette flags and trade union banners, the room contains a host of memorabilia including the desk of John MacLean, who became consul to the Bolshevik Government in 1918. The west wing looks at famous Glasgow products through history, with displays of everything from cast-iron railings and biscuit wrappers to a giant portrait of Billy Connolly. In the East Gallery, an entertaining sound-and-light show reconstructs a "single-end" or one-roomed house, the focus of the daily life of hundreds of thousands of Glasgow people through the years. On the first floor, various themes with a particular resonance in Glasgow are explored, including alcohol, the traditional holiday excursion "Doon the Water" by steamer to various Clyde coastal resorts, and some guidance to understanding "the Patter", Glasgwegians' individual version of the Queen's English.

The glasshouse at the back of the palace contains the **Winter Gardens**, whose café, water garden, twittering birds and assorted tropical plants and shrubs make a pleasant place in which to pass an hour or so. These were unfortunately damaged recently by fire, but should be fully restored and reopened some time in 2000.

The Cathedral area

Rising north up the hill from the Tolbooth Steeple at Glasgow Cross is Glasgow's **High Street**. In British cities, the name is commonly associated with the busiest central thoroughfare, and it's a surprise to see how forlorn and dilapidated Glasgow's version is, long superseded by the grander thoroughfares further west. The High Street leads up to the **Cathedral**, on the site of Glasgow's original settlement.

Glasgow Cathedral

Built in 1136, destroyed in 1192 and rebuilt soon after, stumpy-spired **Glasgow Cathedral** (April–Sept Mon–Sat 9.30am–6pm, Sun 2–5pm; Oct–March Mon–Sat 9.30am–4pm, Sun 2–4pm) was not completed until the late fifteenth century, with the final reconstruction of the chapterhouse and the aisle designed by Robert Blacader, the city's first archbishop. Thanks to the intervention of the city guilds, it is the only Scottish mainland cathedral to have escaped the hands of religious reformers in the sixteenth century. The cathedral is dedicated to the city's patron saint and reputed founder, St Mungo, about whom four popular stories are frequently told – they even make an appearance on the city's coat of arms. These involve a bird that he brought back to life, the bell with which he summoned the faithful to prayer, a tree that he managed to make spontaneously combust and a fish that he caught with a repentant adulterous queen's ring on its tongue.

Because of the sloping ground on which it is built, at its east end the cathedral is effectively on two levels, the crypt being part of the lower church. On entering, you arrive in the impressively lofty nave of the **upper church**, with the lower church entirely hidden from view. Most of this upper church was completed under the direction of Bishop William de Bondington (1233–58), although later design elements came from Blacader. Either side of the nave, the narrow **aisles** are illuminated by vivid stained-glass windows, most of which date from this century. Threadbare Union flags and military pennants hang listlessly beneath them, serving as a reminder that the cathedral is very much a part of the Unionist Protestant tradition. Beyond the nave, the **choir** is hidden from view by the curtained stone pulpit, making the interior feel a great deal smaller than might be expected from the outside. In the choir's northeastern corner, a small door leads into the cathedral's gloomy **sacristy**, in which Glasgow University was first founded over five hundred years ago. Wooden boards mounted on the walls detail the alternating Roman Catholic and Protestant clergy of the cathedral, testimony to the turbulence and fluctuations of the Church in Scotland.

Two sets of steps from the nave lead down into the **lower church**, where you'll see the dark and musty **chapel** surrounding the tomb of St Mungo. The saint's relics were removed in the late Middle Ages, although the tomb still forms the centrepiece. The chapel itself is one of the most glorious examples of medieval architecture in Scotland, best seen in the delicate fan vaulting rising up from the thicket of cool stone columns. Scots designer Robert Stewart was commissioned in 1979 to produce a tapestry detailing the four myths of St Mungo, which can be illuminated using the button at the bottom of the north-side stairs to reveal its swirl of browns and oranges. Also in the lower church, the spaciously light **Blacader Aisle** was originally built as a two-storey extension; today only this lower section survives, where the bright, and frequently gory, medieval ceiling bosses stand out superbly against the simple whitewashed vaulting.

Outside, the atmospheric **Necropolis** rises above the cathedral. Inspired by the Père Lachaise cemetery in Paris, developer John Strong created a garden of death in 1833, filled with Doric columns, gloomy catacombs and Neoclassical temples reflecting the vanity of the nineteenth-century industrialists buried here. From the summit, next to the column topped with an indignant John Knox, there are superb views over the cathedral and its surrounding area.

Cathedral Square

Back in Cathedral Square, the **St Mungo Museum of Religious Life and Art** (Mon–Sat 10am–5pm, Sun 11am–5pm; free) focuses on objects, beliefs and art from Christianity, Buddhism, Judaism, Islam, Hinduism and Sikhism. Portrayals of Hindu gods are juxtaposed with the stunning Salvador Dali painting *Christ Upon the Cross* – moved here from Kelvingrove Art Gallery – that draws the viewer into its morose depths. In addition to the main exhibition there is a small collection of photographs, papers and archive material looking at religion in Glasgow, the power and zealotry of the nineteenth-century Temperance movement and Christian missionaries (local boy David Livingstone in particular). Outside is Britain's only permanent "dry stone" Zen Buddhist garden, with slabs of rock, white gravel and moss arranged to suggest the forms of land and sea.

Across the square, the oldest house in the city, the **Provand's Lordship** (Mon–Sat 10am–5pm, Sun 11am–5pm; free) dates from 1471, and has been used, among other things, as an ecclesiastical residence and an inn. Many of the rooms have been kitted out with period furniture, including a recreation of the fifteenth-century chamber of cathedral clerk Cuthbert Simon, who is seen as a contemplative bewigged wax dummy living in comparative luxury for the age. As a reminder of the manse's earthier history, the upper floor contains pictures of assorted lowlife characters, such as the notorious drunkards and prostitutes of eighteenth- and nineteenth-century Glasgow.

Behind this building lies the small **Garden of St Nicholas**, a herb garden contrasting medieval and Renaissance aesthetics and approaches to medicine, with muddled clusters of herbs amid stone carvings of the heart and other organs, and a controlled arrangement of plants around a small ornate fountain. The garden, bordered by sandstone walkways where you can sit, is an aromatic and peaceful haven away from the High Street.

From Buchanan Street to Sauchiehall Street

The huge grid of streets that runs from **Buchanan Street** to the M8 a mile to the west, is home to Glasgow's main shopping district as well as its financial and business corporations, piling up the slopes of drumlins shaped by the receding glaciers of the last Ice Age. The **St Enoch Shopping Centre**, south of George Square, sandwiched between Argyle and Howard streets, is a lofty glass pyramid built around a redundant train station. Here you can wander amongst the glossy shops or sip a cappuccino whilst choosing from the array of stalls in the large food court area. A short walk north, on Buchanan Street, **Princes Square**, hollowed out of the innards of a soft sandstone building, is one of the most stylish and imaginative shopping centres in the country. The interior, all recherché Art Deco and ornate ironwork, has lots of pricey, highly fashionable shops, the whole place set to a soothing background of classical music.

Glaswegians' voracious appetite for shopping is fed further at the northern end of Buchanan Street, just beyond the Underground station, where the recently completed **Buchanan Galleries** is a bewilderingly vast shopping mall of some 600,000 square feet which includes the largest Habitat store in Europe. Next door, almost anonymous beside its massive neighbouring auditorium of consumerism, is the £30-million **Royal Concert Hall**, with only three huge flagpoles protruding to proclaim that this is, in fact, a building of note. The showpiece hall does, however, have an excellent auditorium which plays host to world-class musical events from touring orchestras to rock acts, while the lobbies are used for temporary art exhibitions. These can be seen for free, or you can take a guided tour of the huge hall and its backstage areas (Tues & Thurs 2pm, Sat 11am; ☎0141/332 6633; £1.50).

The Lighthouse

At 11 Mitchell Lane, an otherwise nondescript alleyway between Buchanan Street and Union Street, is **The Lighthouse** (Mon, Wed, Fri & Sat 10.30am–6pm, Tues 11am–6pm, Thurs 10.30am–8pm, Sun noon–5pm; free), a spectacularly converted Charles Rennie Mackintosh building which has found new life as Scotland's Centre for Architecture, Design and the City. The 1895 building was Mackintosh's first public commission, and housed the offices of the *Glasgow Herald* newspaper; despite glass and sandstone additions by architects Page & Park, it retains many original features, including the distinctive tower from which the building takes its name. The venue played a central role in Glasgow's reign as City of Architecture and Design in 1999, and acts as a permanent legacy of the year, mounting temporary exhibitions on design and architecture alongside the permanent **Mackintosh Interpretation Centre** (£2.50), a great place to come if you want to learn more about the man and his work. It features plans, models, photographs, original objects and computer and video displays which explore many of Mackintosh's unique buildings and interiors, while the Lighthouse Tower itself gives fantastic views out over the city skyline to a number of his important buildings, including the School of Art and Scotland Street School.

Sauchiehall Street

Sauchiehall Street runs in a straight line west past some unexciting shopping malls, leading to a few of the city's most interesting sights. Charles Rennie Mackintosh fans should head for the **Willow Tea Rooms**, 217 Sauchiehall St (its not all that easy to spot at first, above a jewellery shop), a faithful reconstruction (opened in 1980 after over fifty years of closure) on the site of the 1904 original, which was created for Kate Cranston, one of his few contemporary supporters in the city. Everything from the fixtures and fittings right down to the teaspoons and menu cards were designed by Mackintosh. Taking inspiration from the word *Sauchiehall*, which means "avenue of willow", he chose the willow leaf as a theme to unify the whole structure from the tables to the mirrors and the ironwork. The motif is most apparent in the stylized linear panels of the bow window which continues into the intimate dining room as if to surround the sitter, like a willow grove, and is echoed in the distinctively high-backed silver-and-purple chairs. These elongated forms were used to enhance the small space and demonstrate Mackintosh's superb ability to fuse function with decoration. Tea is served here from 9.30am until 5pm (see p.221 for review).

One block west are the **McLellan Galleries**, 270 Sauchiehall St (daily 10am–6pm, open till 8pm Thurs; charges for some exhibitions), the temporary home of the **Centre for Contemporary Arts**, whose eclectically internationalist exhibitions and performances have taken refuge here while their usual home along the road at no. 350 is given a major remodelling. Despite its inauspicious frontage and the avant-garde nature of the CCA's programme, inside, the building is as soothing an example of classical architecture as anywhere in the city. A grand staircase sweeps you up into the main exhibition space, lit naturally by beautiful pedimented windows.

Glasgow School of Art

Rising above Sauchiehall Street to the north is one of the city centre's steepest hills, where Dalhousie and Scott streets veer up to Renfrew Street. Here, at no. 167, you'll find Charles Rennie Mackintosh's **Glasgow School of Art** (guided tours Mon–Fri 11am & 2pm, Sat 10.30 & 11.30am; Sun 10.30 & 11.30am July & August only; booking advised; ☎0141/353 4526; £5), one of the most prestigious in the country, with such notable alumni as artists Robert Colquhoun and Robert Macbryde and, more recently, Steven Campbell, Ken Currie and actor Robbie Coltrane. Widely considered to be the pinnacle of Mackintosh's work, the school is a characteristically angular building of warm sandstone which, due to financial constraints, had to be constructed in two sections (1897–99 and 1907–09). There's a clear change in the architect's style from the earlier severity of the mock-Baronial east wing to the softer lines of the western half.

The only way to see the school is to take one of the student-led daily guided tours, the extent of which are dependent on curricular activities. You can, however, be sure of seeing at least some of the differences between the two halves and a handful of the most impressive rooms. All over the school, from the roof to the stairwells, Mackintosh's unique touches recur – light Oriental reliefs, tall-backed chairs and stylized Celtic illuminations. Even before entering the building up the gently curving stairway, you cannot fail to be struck by the soaring height of the north-facing windows, which light the art studios and were designed, in the architect's inimitable style, to combine aesthetics with practicality.

In the main entrance hall, the school shop sells tour tickets and a good selection of Mackintosh books, posters and cards. Hanging in the hall stairwell is the artist's highly personal wrought-iron version of the "bird, bell, tree, ring and fish" legend of St Mungo. You'll see excellent examples of his early furniture in the tranquil **Mackintosh Room**, flooded with soft, natural light, while the **Furniture Gallery**, tucked up in the

---

CHARLES RENNIE MACKINTOSH

The work of the architect **Charles Rennie Mackintosh** (1868–1928), has come to be synonymous with the image of Glasgow. Whether his work was a forerunner of the Modernist movement or merely a sunset of Victorianism, he undoubtedly created buildings of great beauty, idiosyncratically fusing Scots Baronial with Gothic, Art Nouveau and modern design. Though the bulk of his work was conceived at the turn of the century, since the postwar years Mackintosh's ideas have become particularly fashionable, giving rise to a certain amount of ersatz "Mockintosh" in his home city, with his distinctive lettering and small design features used time and again by shops, pubs and businesses. Fortunately, there are also plenty of examples of the genuine article, making the city something of a pilgrimage centre for art and design students from all over the world.

Although his family did little to encourage his artistic ambitions, as a young child Mackintosh began to cultivate his interest in drawing from nature during walks in the countryside, taken to improve his health. This talent was to flourish when he joined the **Glasgow School of Art** in 1884, where the vibrant new director, Francis Newbery, encouraged his pupils to create original and individual work. Here he met Herbert MacNair and the sisters Margaret and Frances MacDonald, whose work seemed to be sympathetic with his, fusing the organic forms of nature with a linear, symbolic Art Nouveau style. Nicknamed "The Spook School", the four created a new artistic language, using extended vertical design, stylized abstract organic forms and muted colours, reflecting their interest in Japanese design and the work of Whistler and Beardsley. However, it was architecture that truly challenged Mackintosh, allowing him to use his creative artistic impulse in a three-dimensional and cohesive manner.

His big break came in 1896, when he won the competition to design a new **art school** (see p.207). This is his most famous work, but a number of smaller buildings created during his tenure with the architects Honeyman and Keppie, which began in 1889, document the development of his style. One of his earliest commissions was for a new building to house the Glasgow Herald headquarters on Mitchell Lane, off Argyle Street. A massive tower rises up from the corner, giving the building its popular name of **The Lighthouse**; it now houses the Mackintosh Interpretation Centre (see p.207).

In the 1890s Glasgow went wild for tearooms, where the middle classes could play billiards and chess, read in the library or merely chat over some fine dining. The imposing Miss Cranston, who dominated the Glasgow teashop scene, running the most elegant

eaves, shelters an Aladdin's cave of designs that weren't able to be housed elsewhere in the school – numerous tall-backed chairs, a semicircular settle designed for the Willow Tea Rooms, domino tables, a chest of drawers with highlighted silver panels and two bedroom suites. Around the room are mounted building designs including the House for an Art Lover, which Mackintosh submitted to a German competition in 1901. This building – which never saw the light of day during his lifetime – was recently constructed exactly to Mackintosh's specifications and now stands in the South Side's Bellahouston Park, providing offices and study areas for the Glasgow School of Art, with rooms open for public viewing.

You can peer down from the Furniture Gallery into the school's most spectacular room, the glorious two-storey **Library**. Here, sombre oak panelling is set against angular lights adorned with primary colours, dangling down in seemingly random clusters. The dark bookcases sit precisely in their fitted alcoves, while of the furniture, the most unusual feature is the central periodical desk, whose oval central strut displays perfect and quite beautiful symmetry.

The school also puts on various exhibitions through the year, which you can view without going on a tour. For details of these check up-to-date listings or phone ☎0141/353 4500.

establishments, gave Mackintosh great freedom of design, and in 1896 he started to plan the interiors for her growing business. Over the next twenty years he designed articles from teaspoons to furniture and, finally, as in the case of the **Willow Tea Rooms** (see p.207), the structure itself.

Mackintosh designed few **religious buildings**: the Queens Cross Church of 1896, still at the junction of Garscube and Maryhill roads in the northwest of the city, is the only completed one standing. Hallmarks include the sturdy box-shaped tower and asymmetrical exterior with complex heart-shaped floral motifs in the large chancel window. To give height to the small and peaceful interior, he used an open-arched timber ceiling, enhanced by carved detail and an oak pulpit decorated with tulip-form relief. It isn't the most unified of structures, but shows the flexibility of his distinctive style.

The spectre of limited budgets was to haunt Mackintosh throughout his career, and he never had the chance to design and construct with complete freedom. However, these constraints didn't manage to dull his creativity, as demonstrated by the **Scotland Street School** of 1904, near the Burrell Collection, (see p.218). Here, the two main stairways that frame the entrance are lit by glass-filled bays that protrude from the building. It is his most symmetrical work, with a whimsical nod to history in the Scots Baronial conical tower roofs and sandstone building material. Mackintosh's forceful personality and originality did not endear him to construction workers – he would frequently change his mind or add details at the last minute, often running a budget overboard. This lost him the support of local builders and architects, despite being admired on the continent, and prompted him to move to Suffolk in 1914, to escape the "philistines" of Glasgow and to re-evaluate his achievements. Indeed, the building which arguably displays Mackintosh at his most flamboyant was one he never saw built, the **House for an Art Lover** (see p.218), constructed in Bellahouston Park in 1996, 95 years after plans for it were submitted to a German architectural competition.

Having moved away from Glasgow, he now made use of his natural ability to draw flora and fauna, often in botanical detail and coloured with delicate watercolour washes. Whilst living in Port Vendres in 1923–27, on the Mediterranean side of the Franco-Spanish border, he produced a series of still-lifes and landscape works which express something of his architectural style. Here, houses and rocks are painted in precise detail with a massive solidity and geometric form, and bold colours unite the patterned texture of the landscape, within an eerie stillness unbroken by human activity. These are a final flowering of his creative talent, a delicate contrast to the massive legacy of stonework left behind in the city that he loved.

The Tenement House

Just a few hundred yards northwest of the School of Art – on the other side of the sheer hill that rises and falls down to Buccleuch Street – is the **Tenement House** at no. 145 (March–Oct daily 2–5pm; Nov–Feb by appointment only; NTS; £3.20). This is the perfectly preserved home of the habitually hoarding Agnes Toward, who moved here with her mother in 1911, changing nothing and throwing very little out until she was hospitalized in 1965. On the ground floor, the NTS has constructed a fascinating display on the development of the humble tenement block as the bedrock of urban Scottish housing, with a display of relics – ration books, letters, bills, holiday snaps and so forth – from Miss Toward's life. Upstairs you have to ring the doorbell to enter the living quarters, which give every impression of still being inhabited, with a roaring hearth and range, kitchen utensils, recess beds, framed religious tracts and sewing machine all untouched. The only major change since Miss Toward left has been the reinstallation of the flickering gas lamps she would have used in the early days.

The Piping Centre

Behind the hulking Royal Scottish Academy for Music and Drama, the immaculate **Piping Centre**, at 30–34 McPhater St, prides itself on being a national centre for the promotion of the bagpipe. Equipped with rehearsal rooms, performance halls, conference centre, accommodation, museum and an attractive café, it is a meeting place for fans and performers from all over the world. For the casual visitor, the **museum** (daily 10.30am–4.30pm; £2) is of most interest, with a collection of instruments and artefacts from the fourteenth century to the present day. Headsets provide a taped commentary with musical examples at relevant stages. The commentary is available in a number of languages (Gaelic included) and the museum shop contains a stack of related material, from tapes and videos to manuscripts and piping accessories.

The West End

The urbane veneer of the **West End**, an area which contains many of the city's premier museums, seems a world away from Glasgow's industrial image. In the 1800s, the city's focus moved west as wealthy merchants established huge estates away from the soot and grime of city life, and in 1870 the ancient university was moved from its cramped home near the cathedral to a spacious new site overlooking the River Kelvin. Elegant housing swiftly followed, the Kelvingrove Art Gallery was built to house the 1888 International Exhibition and, in 1896, the Glasgow District Subway – today's Underground – started its circuitous shuffle from here to the city centre.

The hub of life in this part of Glasgow is **Byres Road**, running down from the straight Great Western Road past Hillhead Underground station. Shops, restaurants, cafés, some enticing pubs and hordes of roving young people, including thousands of students, give the area a sense of style. Glowing red sandstone tenements and graceful terraces provide a suitably upmarket backdrop to this cosmopolitan district.

Straddling the banks of the cleaned-up River Kelvin, the slopes, trees and statues of **Kelvingrove Park** are framed by a backdrop of the Gothic towers and turrets of **Glasgow University** and the **Kelvingrove Museum and Art Gallery**, off Argyle Street in the park.

Kelvingrove Museum and Art Gallery

Founded on donations from the city's chief industrialists, the huge, red-brick fantasy castle of **Kelvingrove Museum and Art Gallery** (Mon–Sat 10am–5pm, Sun 11am–5pm; free) is a brash statement of Glasgow's nineteenth-century self-confidence.

> At the time of going to press, the Kelvingrove Museum and Art Gallery was on the point of securing a grant for a complete **refurbishment** of the building in time for its centenary in 2001. This would mean that the museum would be closed to the public from spring 2000 for around a year. For an update, contact the tourist office on ☎0141/332

On the ground floor, the central hall is an impressive, airy introduction to the style of the place. On summer Sundays, the organ, which also dates from the 1901 exhibition, leaps to life with recitals by Scotland's top organists. In the east wing off the main atrium a fairly dusty hall contains the **Scottish Natural History** display, where local and global events are marked in the rings of a slice of ancient Douglas fir. On the opposite side of the main hall sits an unremarkable exhibition of European and Scottish weapons.

However, it's the art collections, the majority of which are upstairs, that are of most interest. **Room 22** contains some superb Italian paintings, notably Botticelli's delicate *Annunciation*, Giorgione's rich and vibrant *The Adulteress Brought Before Christ*, and some fervent landscapes by Salvator Rosa. Further down the gallery, Rembrandt's symbolic portrayal of a crucified ox stands out darkly, along with his quiet portrait, *The Man in Armour*. Continuing from the seventeenth century and leading up to the early nineteenth century, **Room 23** contains predominantly British work. The space is dominated by two paintings by Jacob More, a Scottish artist who worked in the elegiacally classical style of Claude; the spread of classicism in eighteenth-century Europe is also attested by pieces such as *Vestals Attending the Sacred Fire*, by David Allan, whose figures languish amongst ancient temples.

Room 24 is filled with quality work from Scottish and European artists from the eighteenth century to the early twentieth century. Among the biggest non-British names here are Courbet, Corot, Degas and Monet. As for the Scots, the angelic face of *Mrs William Urquhart* is testimony to Sir Henry Raeburn's skill as an informal portraitist, while the meticulous detail of *South and North Western View from Ben Lomond* – a dramatic pair of paintings by John Knox – makes a striking contrast with Turner's radiant *Modern Italy – The Pifferari*, a picture that glows amongst the dark glens and sombre portraits. Catching up on the twentieth century, **Room 26** contains such continental luminaries as Bonnard, Pissarro, Vuillard, Braque and Derain, and more excellent work by undervalued Scottish artists. *The Pink Parasol* by J.D. Fergusson, for example, reveals what he learned from Matisse and Cézanne, and the grittier *Two Children* by Joan Eardley makes use of collage and thick paint to convey the energy of Gorbals children in the 1960s.

Crossing over to the east wing, take time to look at some of the superb sculptures and busts arrayed around the balcony overlooking the main hall. In the east wing, **The Scottish Gallery** is entirely devoted to native artists. Here Raeburn's magnificent *Mr and Mrs Robert N. Campbell of Kailzie* almost overwhelms the room, the golden, life-size figures emerging from the loosely brushed background. A statue of Sir Walter Scott gazes upon a row of paintings depicting the romantic, Victorian view of Scotland, as exemplified by Horatio McCullochs' depiction of *Loch Maree*. On the far wall hangs the famous portrait of *Robert Burns* by Alexander Naysmyth, now found on biscuit tins the world over.

The **Glasgow Style** room is dedicated to the era when Charles Rennie Mackintosh was in his prime: this marvellous collection of furniture is crowned by a pair of domino tables and chairs designed by Mackintosh for the tearooms of Miss Cranston (see p.207). The **Glasgow Boys** are well represented, with the decoratively patterned *In a Japanese Garden* by George Henry balanced by the bovine tranquillity of Crawhall's *Landscape with Cattle*. Works by Guthrie, Hornel and Lavery are also on display.

THE GLASGOW BOYS

The traditional rivalry between Glasgow and Edinburgh was alive and kicking in the late nineteenth century when the Royal Scottish Academy resolutely refused to accept the work of any west coast artist. That was soon to change, however, when in the 1870s a group of painters formed a loose association, centred in Glasgow, that was to invest Scottish painting with a fresh approach inspired by contemporary European trends (in particular the *plein air* painting of the Impressionists). Derisively nicknamed "The Glasgow Boys", only in later years did their work come to be seen as quintessentially Glaswegian and reclaimed with considerable pride. The group was dominated by five men – Guthrie, Lavery, Henry, Hornel and Crawhall – who, despite coming from very different backgrounds, all violently rejected the eighteenth-century conservatism which spawned little other than sentimental, anecdotal renditions of Scottish history peopled by "poor but happy" families, in a detailed, exacting manner. They called these paintings "gluepots" for their use of megilp, an oily substance that gave the work the brown patina of age, and instead began to experiment with colour, liberally splashing paint across the canvas. The content and concerns of the paintings, often showing peasant life and work, were as offensive as their style to the effete art establishment – until then most of Glasgow's public art collections had been accrued by wealthy tobacco lords and merchants.

Sir James Guthrie spent his summers in the countryside, surrounded by like-minded artists, painting in the outdoors and observing everyday life. Instead of happy peasants, his work shows individuals staring out of the canvas, detached and unrepentant, painted with rich tones but without undue attention to detail or the play of light. Typical of his finest work during the 1880s, *A Highland Funeral* (on display in St Mungo's Museum; see p.206) was hugely influential for the rest of the group, who found inspiration in its restrained emotional content, colour and unaffected realism. Seeing it persuaded **Sir John Lavery**, then studying in France, to return to Glasgow. Lavery was eventually to become an internationally popular society portraitist, his subtle use of paint revealing his debt to Whistler, but his earlier work, depicting the middle class at play, is filled with fresh colour and figures in motion. In 1888 he documented the Glasgow International Exhibition and went on to paint a number of large-scale works, one of which – a massive depiction of Queen Victoria's visit to Glasgow – hangs in the Royal Concert Hall.

Rather than a realistic aesthetic, an interest in colour and decoration united the work of friends **George Henry** and **E.A. Hornel**. The predominance of colour, pattern and design in Henry's *Galloway Landscape*, for example, is remarkable, while their joint work *The Druids* (both on display in the Kelvingrove; see p.210), in thickly applied impasto, is full of Celtic symbolism. In 1893 both artists set off for Japan, funded by Alexander Reid and later William Burrell, where their work used vibrant tone and texture for expressive effect and took Scottish painting to the forefront of European trends.

Newcastle-born **Joseph Crawhall** was, by all accounts, a reserved and quiet individual. He combined superb draughtsmanship and simplicity of line with a photographic memory to create watercolours of an outstanding naturalism and freshness. Unlike the forceful Guthrie and Lavery, who craved wealth and success, Crawhall was a shy man who enjoyed hunting and riding in the countryside and was quite happy to paint delicate animal studies throughout his career. William Burrell was an important patron, and a good collection of Crawhall's works resides at the Burrell Collection.

The school reached its height by 1900, and once its members had achieved the artistic respect – and for some the commercial success – they craved, it began to disintegrate and did not outlast World War I. However, the influence of their work cannot be underestimated, shaking the foundations of the artistic elite and inspiring the next generation of Edinburgh painters, who are now known as the "Colourists".

The Transport Museum

Twin-towered **Kelvin Hall** is home to the excellent and enormous city **Transport Museum**, a collection of trains, cars, trams, circus caravans and prams, along with an array of old Glaswegian ephemera (Mon–Sat 10am–5pm, Sun 11am–5pm; free). Just inside the Bunhouse Road entrance, "Kelvin Street" is a re-created 1950s cobbled street featuring an old Italian coffee shop, a butcher (complete with plastic meat joints dangling in the window), a bakery (where labels claim that the buns were provided by the university's taxidermy department) and an old-time Underground station. A cinema shows fascinating films – mostly on themes based loosely around transport – of old Glasgow life, with crackly footage of Sauchiehall Street packed solid with trams and shoppers and hordes of pasty-faced Glaswegians setting off for their annual jaunts down the coast. The Clyde Room displays intricate models of ships forged in Glasgow's yards – everything from tiny schooners to ostentatious ocean liners such as the QE2.

Glasgow University and the Hunterian bequests

Dominating the West End skyline, the gloomy turreted tower of Glasgow's **University**, designed by Sir Gilbert Scott in the mid-nineteenth century, overlooks the glades of the River Kelvin (see "Glasgow architecture", p.202). Access to the main buildings and museums is from University Avenue, running east from Byres Road. In the dark neo-Gothic pile under the tower you'll find the **University Visitor Centre** (Mon–Sat 9.30am–5pm; May–Sept also Sun 2–5pm), which, as well as giving information for potential students, distributes leaflets about the various university buildings and the statues around the campus. From May to September **tours** (£2) of the campus are run from here on Wednesdays, Fridays and Saturdays at 11am and 2pm.

Next door to the University Visitor Centre, the collection of the **Hunterian Museum** (Mon–Sat 9.30am–5pm; free), Scotland's oldest public museum dating back to 1807, was donated to the university by ex-student William Hunter, a pathologist and anatomist whose eclectic tastes form the basis of a fairly diverting zoological and archeological museum. Exhibitions include Scotland's only dinosaur, a look at the Romans in Scotland – the furthest outpost of their massive empire – and a vast coin collection.

The Hunterian Art Gallery

On the other side of University Avenue is Hunter's more frequently visited bequest: the **Hunterian Art Gallery** (Mon–Sat 9.30am–5pm; free), best known for its wonderful works by James Abbott McNeill Whistler – only Washington DC has a larger collection. Whistler's breathy landscapes are less compelling than his portraits of women, which give his subjects a resolute strength in addition to their fey and occasionally winsome qualities: look out especially for the trio of full-length portraits, *Harmony of Flesh Colour* and *Black, Pink and Gold – the Tulip* and *Red and Black – the Fan*.

The gallery's other major collection is of nineteenth- and twentieth-century Scottish art, including the quasi-Impressionist Scottish landscapes of William McTaggart, a forerunner of the Glasgow Boys movement, itself represented here by Guthrie and Hornel. Taking the aims of this group one step further, the monumental dancing figures of J.D. Fergusson's *Les Eus* preside over a small collection of work by the Scottish Colourists, such as Peploe, Hunter and Cadell, who left a vibrant legacy of thickly textured, colourful landscapes and portraits. A small selection of French Impressionism includes works by Boudin and Pissarro, with Corot's soothing *Distant View of Corbeil* being a highlight from the Barbizon school.

A side gallery leads to the **Mackintosh House**, a re-creation of the interior of the now-demolished Glasgow home of Margaret and Charles Rennie Mackintosh. An introductory display contains photographs of the original house sliding irrevocably into terminal decay, from where you are led into an exquisitely cool interior that contains over sixty pieces of Mackintosh furniture on three floors. Among the highlights are the Studio Drawing Room, whose cream and white furnishings are bathed in expansive pools of natural light, and the Japanese-influenced guest bedroom in dazzling, monochrome geometrics.

The Botanic Gardens

At the top of Byres Road, where it meets the Great Western Road, is the main entrance to the **Botanic Gardens** (daily 7am–dusk; free). The best-known glasshouse here, the hulking, domed **Kibble Palace** (daily summer 10am–4.45pm; winter 10am–4.15pm), originally known as the Crystal Palace, was built in 1863 for wealthy landowner John Kibble's estate on the shores of Loch Long, where it stood for ten years, before he decided to transport it into Glasgow, drawing it up the Clyde on a vast raft pulled by a steamer. For over two decades it was used not as a greenhouse but as a Victorian pleasure palace, before the gardens' owners put a stop to the drunken revels that wreaked havoc with the lawns and plant beds. Today the palace is far more sedate, housing a damp, musty collection of swaying palms from around the world, along with an unremarkable but well-placed **café**. The smell is much sweeter on entering the **Main Range Glasshouse** (summer Mon–Fri 10am–4.45pm, Sat 1–4.45pm Sun noon–4.45pm; winter closes 4.15pm), home to lurid and blooming flowers and plants – including stunning orchids, cacti, ferns and tropical fruit – luxuriating in the humidity. Between the two in the old curator's house is a small **visitor centre** (daily 11am–4pm; free) with an interactive computer aimed at younger visitors. In addition to the area around the main glasshouses, the Botanic Gardens have some beautifully remote paths that weave and dive along the closely wooded banks of the gorged River Kelvin, linking up with the walkway which runs alongside the river all the way down to Dumbarton Road, near its confluence with the Clyde.

The SECC and Glasgow Harbour

Down by the riverside, fifteen minutes' walk from Kelvingrove Park – and not strictly part of the West End – is the harshly re-landscaped **Scottish Exhibition and Conference Centre (SECC)**. It was built in 1985 to kick-start the revival of the Riverbank: two vast adjoining red and grey sheds that make a dutifully utilitarian venue for travelling fairs, mega-concerts and anonymous bars and cafés. However, the sparkling new Clyde Auditorium now draws the eye: nicknamed "the Armadillo", it resembles a poor man's version of the Sydney Opera House but nevertheless stands as an architectural landmark, giving a bit of character to the riverside. The gleaming hotel alongside, and the expensive restaurants in the nearby rotunda – one of two access shafts to a long-closed tunnel under the Clyde – are reasonably successful, but the rotunda's twin on the opposite bank, the **Dome of Discovery**, once a hands-on science museum and showpiece of the 1988 Glasgow Garden Festival site, didn't survive much longer than it took for the grass of the gardens to wither and die. However, construction is now underway of the Glasgow Science Centre, an ambitious project which will combine a 100-foot tower, an IMAX cinema and a glass-fronted "theatre of discovery" containing a planetarium and hands-on technology displays.

The various regeneration projects underway along the river beside the SECC have recently been drawn together under the banner of "Glasgow Harbour". For the moment the most obvious and attractive point of interest is **The Tall Ship at Glasgow Harbour** (daily 10am–6pm; £3.50), an impressive three-masted barque, the *Glenlee*, moored beside the square Pumphouse tower at Yorkhill Quay a few hundred yards downstream from the SECC. The *Glenlee*, launched on the river in 1896 and now only one of five large sailing vessels built on Clydeside still afloat, offers a poignant reminder of the days when Glasgow was the greatest shipbuilding centre in the world. Everyone would follow the progress of the skeleton ships under construction in the riverside yards, cheering them on their way down the Clyde when they were launched. The last of the great liners to be built on the Clyde was the *QE2* in 1967, and now only one yard, at Clydebank, remains open, albeit tenuously. Visitors can look around the restored *Glenlee*, and at the changing exhibitions mounted in the Pumphouse Visitor Centre on the story of the ship and the local shipbuilding industry.

South of the Clyde

The southern bank of the Clyde, facing the city centre, is home to the notoriously deprived districts of **Govan**, a community yet to find its niche after the shipbuilding slump, and the **Gorbals**, associated with the razor gangs of old. On the southern side of Govan the vast bowl of **Ibrox Stadium**, home to the overwhelmingly Protestant Rangers football team, proudly displays the Union flag. This Unionist fortress was totally overhauled following the disaster on January 2, 1971, towards the end of a match against bitter arch-rivals Celtic, when hundreds of early-leavers turned to try to get back into the stadium after an unlikely last-minute goal, crushing 66 fans to death when the railings of a stairway collapsed.

Inner-city decay fades into altogether gentler and more salubrious suburbs, commonly referred to as **South Side**. These include Queen's Park, a residential area which is home to Hampden Park football stadium, and the rural landscape of **Pollok Park**, three miles southwest of the city centre, which contains two of Glasgow's major museums: the **Burrell Collection** and **Pollok House**. Buses #34 and #34A from Govan Underground station stop outside the gate nearest to the Burrell. An easier option from the city centre is to Pollokshaws West station (don't confuse with Pollokshields West), served by regular trains from Glasgow Central, or to nearby bus stops on the Pollokshaws Road: take Greater Glasgow buses #45, #48 or #57 from Union Street. From the park gates a free half-hourly minibus runs between 10am and 4.30pm to both the Burrell and Pollok House. In addition, as Pollok Park is only three miles from the city centre, a taxi to the Burrell is an inexpensive option. A further reason to venture south is to see the latest attractions on the Glasgow architect's trail: Charles Rennie Mackintosh's **House for an Art Lover** in Bellahouston Park and Alexander "Greek" Thomson's **Holmwood House** in the Cathcart district.

The Burrell Collection

The lifetime collection of shipping magnate Sir William Burrell (1861–1958), the outstanding **Burrell Collection** (Mon–Sat 10am–5pm, Sun 11am–5pm; free) is, for some, the principal reason for visiting Glasgow. Unlike many other art collectors, Sir William's only real criterion for buying a piece was whether he liked it or not, enabling him to buy many "unfashionable" works, which cost comparatively little, and subsequently proved their worth. He wanted to leave his collection of art, sculpture and antiquities for public display, but stipulated in 1943 that they should be housed "in a rural setting far removed from the atmospheric pollution of urban conurbations, not less than sixteen miles from the Royal Exchange". For decades, these conditions proved too difficult to meet, with few open spaces available and a pall of industrial smoke ruling out any city site. However, by the late 1960s, after the nationwide Clean

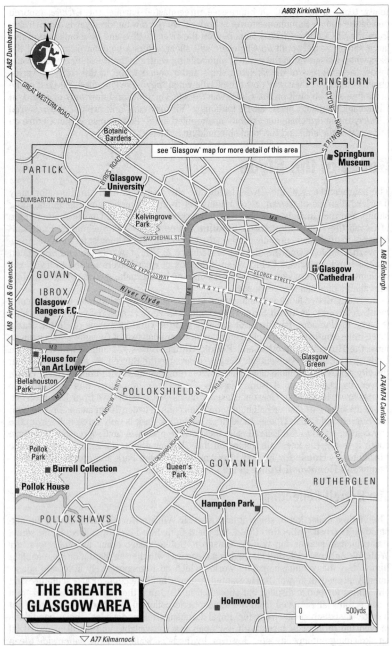

Air Act had reduced pollution, and the vast land of Pollok Park, previously privately owned, had been donated to the city, plans began for a new, purpose-built gallery, which finally opened in 1983. Today the simplicity and clean lines of the Burrell building are its greatest assets, with large picture windows giving sweeping views over woodland and serving as a tranquil backdrop to the objects inside. The sculpture and antiques are on the ground level, arranged in six sections that overlap and occasionally backtrack, while a mezzanine above displays most of the paintings.

On entering the building, head past the information desk and shop to an airy covered courtyard where the most striking piece, by virtue of sheer size, is the **Warwick Vase**, a huge bowl containing fragments of a second-century AD vase from Hadrian's Villa in Tivoli. Next to it are the first of a series of sinewy and naturalistic bronze casts of Rodin sculptures, among them *The Age of Bronze*, *A Call to Arms* and the famous *Thinker*. Beyond the entrance hall, on three sides of a courtyard, a trio of dark and sombre panelled rooms have been re-erected in faithful detail from the Burrells' Hutton Castle home, their heavy tapestries, antique furniture and fireplaces displaying the same eclectic taste as the rest of the museum.

From the courtyard, go through the massive sandstone portal and door from Hornby Castle which was incorporated into the design of the building, to the start of the **Ancient Civilizations** collection – a catch-all title for Greek, Roman and earlier artefacts – which includes an exquisite mosaic Roman cockerel from the first century BC and a 4000-year-old Mesopotamian lion's head. The bulk of it is Egyptian, however, with rows of inscrutable gods and kings. Nearby, also illuminated by enormous windows, the **Oriental Art** forms nearly one-quarter of the complete collection, ranging from Neolithic jades through bronze vessels and Tang funerary horses to cloisonné. The earliest piece, from around the second century BC, is a loveable earthenware watchdog from the Han Dynasty, but most dominant is the serene fifteenth-century *Lohan* (disciple of Buddha), who sits cross-legged and contemplative up against the window and the trees of Pollok Park. Near Eastern art is also represented, in a dazzling array of turquoise- and cobalt-decorated jugs, and a swathe of intricate carpets.

Burrell considered his **Medieval and Post-Medieval European Art**, which encompasses silverware, glass, textiles and sculpture, to be the most valuable part of his collection. Ranged across a maze of small galleries, the most impressive sections are the sympathetically lit stained glass – note the homely image of a man warming his toes by the fire – and the numerous tapestries, among them the riotous fifteenth-century *Peasants Hunting Rabbits with Ferrets*. Among the church art and reliquary are simple thirteenth-century Spanish wooden images and cool fifteenth-century English alabaster, while a trio of period interiors span the period from the Gothic era to the eighteenth century. This is interrupted by a selection from Burrell's vast art collection, the highlight of which is one of Rembrandt's evocative early self-portraits.

Upstairs, the cramped and comparatively gloomy mezzanine is probably the least satisfactory section of the gallery, not the best setting for its sparkling array of paintings. The selection incongruously leaps from a small gathering of fifteenth-century religious works to Géricault's darkly dynamic *Prancing Grey Horse* and Degas's thoughtful and perceptive *Portrait of Émile Duranty*. Pissarro, Manet and Boudin are also represented, along with some exquisite watercolours by Glasgow Boy Joseph Crawhall, revealing his accurate and tender observations of the animal world.

Pollok House

A quarter of a mile away down rutted tracks lies the lovely eighteenth-century **Pollok House** (April–Oct daily 9.30am–5pm; Nov–March daily 10am–4pm; NTS; £3.20; free access to house Nov–March and to café and gardens all year), the manor of the Pollok Park estate and once home of the Maxwell family, local lords and owners of most of southern Glasgow until well into this century. Designed by William Adam in the mid-1700s, the house is typical of its age: graciously light and sturdily built, looking out onto the pristine raked and parterre gardens, whose stylized daintiness contrasts with the heavy Spanish paintings inside, among them two El Greco portraits and works by Murillo and Goya.

After many years being run by Glasgow Museums, the house recently came under the management of the National Trust of Scotland – a happy reunion, as it was in the upstairs smoking room in 1931 that the then owner, Sir John Stirling Maxwell, held the first meetings with the 8th Duke of Atholl and Lord Colquhoun of Luss that led to the formation of a National Trust for Scotland. The Trust has made a deliberate effort to return the house to the layout and style it would have enjoyed when the Stirling Maxwells were living here in the 1920s and 1930s. As a result, the **paintings** range from the Spanish masterpieces in the Morning Room and some splendid Dutch hunting scenes in the Dining Room to Sir John's own worthy but noticeably amateur efforts which line the upstairs corridors. Generally the rooms have the flavour of a well-to-do but unstuffy country house, with the odd piece of attractive furniture and some pleasant rooms, but little that can be described as outstanding. The servants' quarters downstairs do manage to capture the imagination – a virtually untouched labyrinth of tiled Victorian parlours and corridors that includes a good tearoom in the old kitchen. Free tours of the house are available from the front desk, or you can wander around at your own pace.

Scotland Street School Museum of Education

A mile and a half northeast of the Burrell Collection is another great Mackintosh monument, the **Scotland Street School Museum of Education** (Mon–Sat 10am–5pm, Sun 2–5pm; free), slap opposite the Shields Road Underground station. Opened as a school in 1906 to Mackintosh's distinctively angular design, it closed in 1979, since when it has been refurbished as an entertaining education museum, housing a fascinating collection of memorabilia related to life in the classroom. There are reconstructed classrooms from the Victorian and Edwardian eras, World War II and the 1960s, as well as changing rooms, a primitive domestic science room and recreations of a headmaster's office, the school matron's sanatorium and a janitor's lair. If you visit on a weekday during term time, you may stumble on a period lesson going on, local schoolkids struggling with their ink blotters, gas masks and archly unsympathetic teachers. Even the faint smell of antiseptic will conjure up memories of scuffed knees and playground tantrums.

House for an Art Lover

Northwest of Pollok Park lies the smaller Bellahouston Park, home to Charles Rennie Mackintosh's **House for an Art Lover** (April–Sept daily 10am–4pm, closed Fri; Oct–March daily 10am–4pm but closed occasionally for functions – ☎0141/353 4449; £3.50), which was designed in 1901 for a German competition but not built until nearly a century later. In 1996, after years of detailed research and painstaking work, the building opened as a centre for Glasgow School of Art postgraduate students, with a limited number of rooms open to the public.

On the first floor, you can watch a video giving a detailed account of the building's construction, then pass into the delicate **Oval Room**, intended for women to retire to after dinner. From here, a small corridor leads into the main **hallway**, where massive windows cast a cool light upon an area designed for large parties. In direct contrast, the dazzling, white **Music Room** has bow windows opening out to a large balcony, though the garden view is marred by an artificial ski slope. The **Dining Room** is decorated with darkened stained wood and enhanced by some beautiful gesso tiles.

On the ground floor, the **café** is dotted with massive sofas, which are particularly popular with locals on Sunday mornings; there's an attractive menu, and it's open through the day and also in the evenings (Mon–Thurs; ☎0141/353 4779). To reach the house, take the Underground to Cessnock station and turn right at Paisley Road West which runs up to the park. If you're coming by train, get off at Dumbreck, cross the road and continue straight on until you reach the park.

Holmwood House

Four miles south of the city centre in the suburb of Cathcart, the finest domestic design by rediscovered Glasgow architect Alexander "Greek" Thomson, **Holmwood House** (April–Oct daily 1.30–5.30pm; NTS; £3.20), has recently been restored and opened to the public. A commission by James Couper, co-owner of a paper mill on the nearby River Carth, the house shows off Thomson's bold Classical concepts, with exterior pillars on two levels and a raised main door, as well as his detailed and highly imaginative interiors. The restoration is on-going, as you'll see from the patches of exquisite stencilling revealed beneath the wallpaper, and the fact that the rooms are unfurnished. An audio guide comes as part of the entrance charge and provides some background information and explanation in each of the rooms. One room upstairs is given over to a series of displays about Thomson and the history of the house; also on the upper floor is the **drawing room** – look out for the white marble fireplace and the night-time star decorations on the ceiling, which contrast with a black marble fireplace and sunburst decorations in the room immediately underneath on the downstairs level, the **parlour**, which also boasts a delightful round bay window. Across the corridor, the **dining room** has a frieze of scenes from the *Iliad*, along with a skylight at the back of the room designed to allow the Greek Gods to peer down on the feasts being consumed inside. One unusual feature not designed by Thomson is the small hatch cut in the interconnecting door between the dining room and the butler's pantry. The house was last occupied by a sisterhood of nuns, who used the dining room as a chapel and created the small hatch for use as a confessional.

Cafés and restaurants

Glasgow's renaissance has seen an explosion of fine restaurants and European-style bars and cafés, which, with its diverse and ethnically mixed population, make eating possibilities pretty wide: the city's **restaurants** cover an impressively international spectrum, with everything from tapas to sushi on offer. Traditional **Scottish cuisine** has become very trendy in recent years, with an upsurge in the number of outlets that serve local specialities. There is a handful of exclusively **vegetarian** restaurants, although most places – especially around the Merchant City – have good, imaginative vegetarian choices.

For **budget food**, cafés range from the cheapest, greasiest cholesterol-hole through to bars offering reasonable snacks all day, and frequently into the evening. Unlike in staid Edinburgh, where a lot of places close on Sunday, most of Glasgow's restaurants are open seven days a week.

City centre

The **Merchant City** is where you'll find the largest concentration of designer brasseries and some very pricey restaurants, although with office workers to give them trade by day, cafés, bars and restaurants are spread across the wide swathe of the city centre. The shopping precincts of **Buchanan** and **Sauchiehall streets** feature the familiar line-up of fast-food chains, while the area around **Charing Cross**, where a number of clubs are situated, is a good place to head if you're searching for food after 10pm.

Cafés, diners and pubs

Brunswick Café Bar, 106–8 Brunswick St (☎0141/552 0001). Attached to the most self-consciously trendy hotel in town, this bistro isn't overpowered by the high design of its decor or its clientele, offering an eclectic menu ranging from Scottish meats to Japanese sushi, including a good range of lighter meals. Open daily 8am–midnight. Moderate.

Café Gandolfi, 64 Albion St (☎0141/552 6813). An enduring Merchant City favourite, this is a café-bar which Glaswegians could boast about in Paris, or Bohemia. With beautifully distinctive wooden furniture ("sculpture in disguise" its creator, Tim Stead, calls it) and stained glass, *Café Gandolfi* serves up good-quality soup, salads and fish dishes, or you can just come in for a coffee or a beer. Mon–Sat 9am–11.30pm, Moderate.

Gallery of Modern Art Café, Queen St (☎0141/221 7484). Worth visiting for the mural alone and the view over the rooftops. Serves light lunches – the salads are good – and cakes and coffee at other times. Daily 10am–4.30pm. Inexpensive.

GLC Café-Bar, 11 Dixon St (☎0141/400 1008). In the Glasgow Gay and Lesbian Centre, this colourful and relaxed establishment, tucked in a side street behind the St Enoch Centre, has a varied menu that includes soups, salads and sandwiches, as well as three-course specials in the evening. Food served daily 11am–10pm, bar open till midnight. Inexpensive.

Granary, 82 Howard St (☎0141/226 3770). Well situated near the St Enoch Centre, an affordable café serving quiches, lasagne and other vegetarian favourites complemented by a good variety of salads. Open daily till 5pm. Inexpensive.

Kings Café, 71 Elmbank St, off Sauchiehall Street. Good fish-and-chip shop near Charing Cross with seating at the back, serving generous helpings of traditional greasy fare plus quality pasta. Mon–Fri 7am–midnight, Sat 7am–5am, Sun 10am–midnight. Inexpensive.

October Café, top floor, Princes Square Shopping Centre. A variety of different dishes, including some vegetarian options, served on the wraparound verandah peering down into the swish designer-shopping paradise. Mon–Sat 11am–midnight, Sun 12.30–5pm. Moderate.

Pipers' Tryst, 30–34 McPhater St (☎0141/353 0220). Decorated with their very own tartan, this small, bright café in the Piping Centre uses fresh produce to create a variety of Scottish dishes including a hearty all-day breakfast. Mon–Sat 10.30am–9pm. Moderate.

13th Note, corner King St & Osborne St (☎0141/553 1638). This Merchant City bar stands out for its all-vegan menu, from vegeburgers to chilli, with daily specials on an international theme. Food served daily noon–10.30pm. Inexpensive.

Toast, 84–86 Albion St (☎0141/552 3044). A coffee shop in the heart of the Merchant City which is far too stylish just to offer plain or pan-cooked, rare, medium or well-done, so you'll find focaccia, ciabatta and muffins and plenty of yummy fillings, as well as a classic all-day breakfast. Mon–Sat 8am–8pm, Sun 10am–6pm.

Tron Theatre, 63 Trongate (☎0141/552 8587). Two atmospheres prevail here – the trendy wrought-iron café-bar caters for the quick-lunch and coffee crowd (daily noon–9pm), while the recently made-over but still old-fashioned Victorian bar is perfect for a laid-back lunch or dinner. Mon–Sat noon–10pm, Sun 10.30am–4pm. Moderate.

Tun Ton, 157 Hope St (☎0141/572 1230). A very hip arrival on the Glasgow restaurant scene, with 1970s throwbacks in the design, dazzling light and a creative buzz. The food is "fusion" – food from around the world but leaning to the East and lots of fresh veggies and fruit. Moderate.

Vegville Diner, 93 St Georges Rd (☎0141/572 1160). Good quality and value for money is the name of the game in this relaxed diner. The menu consists of innovative and tasty vegetarian dishes with several international options. Mon–Sat 10am–1am, Sun 12.30–11pm. Inexpensive.

Willow Tea Rooms, 217 Sauchiehall St and 97 Buchanan St. Refined elevenses, lunches and afternoon tea in Mackintosh-designed splendour. Of the two, the Sauchiehall Street branch is more authentic. Open till 4.30pm. Inexpensive.

Chinese

Amber Regent, 50 West Regent St (☎0141/331 1655). Decisively Western decoration matched with authentic Chinese food characterizes this small, quality restaurant. The menu is extensive with half-price meals every Monday and Tuesday evening. Mon–Fri noon–2.15pm & 5.30–11pm, Sat noon–midnight. Moderate.

Canton Express, 407 Sauchiehall St, opposite *The Garage* nightclub. Open from noon until 4am every day, this formica palace is popular with shoppers and late-night clubbers alike, tempted by the Chinese and Sichuan fast food and good prices. Inexpensive.

Ho Wong, 82 York St, just off Argyle Street west of Central station (☎0141/221 3550). Secluded restaurant offering a top-class range of Cantonese and Sichuan food – well worth the high prices. Mon–Sat noon–2pm & 6–11.30pm, Sun 6–11.30pm. Expensive.

Loon Fung, 417 Sauchiehall St (☎0141/332 1240). Long-established Cantonese with great *dim sum* but lacking in vegetarian options. Daily noon–11.30pm. Moderate.

Indian

Kama Sutra, 331 Sauchiehall St (☎0141/332 0055). Thick velvet curtains, wrought ironwork and a designer interior give a new twist to the Glaswegians' love of curry. An unusual and wide-ranging menu including dishes from the northeast frontier plus low-fat, healthy options. Mon–Thurs noon–midnight, Fri & Sat noon–1am, Sun 5pm–midnight. Moderate.

Taj Mahal, 573–581 Sauchiehall St (☎0141/226 5030). Pleasant restaurant serving huge portions of delicious Indian food – check out the enormous nan breads. Mon–Thurs noon–2.30pm & 5pm–midnight, Fri & Sat noon–midnight, Sun 2pm–midnight. Moderate.

Wee Curry Shop, 7 Buccleuch St. Tiny Indian cafe, serving tasty, filling, well-priced food, with an open kitchen so you can watch the cooking while you wait. Mon–Sat noon–2pm & 5.30–10.30pm, Sun 5.30–10.30pm. Inexpensive.

Italian

Fire Station, 33 Ingram St (☎0141/552 2929). Merchant City restaurant housed in a huge old fire station, dating from 1900 and walled with municipal cast-off marble tiling. The excellent food, especially the pasta and the indulgent puddings, is good value, and the half-price pasta from 5pm to 7pm is a real bargain. Mon–Thurs noon–2.30pm & 5–9.30pm, Fri noon–2.30pm & 5–10.30pm, Sat noon–10.30pm, Sun 11am–9pm. Moderate.

Fratelli Sarti, 133 Wellington St (☎0141/248 2228) and 121 Bath St (☎0141/204 0440). Authentic and popular, the frantic Wellington Street café also has a deli (9am–6pm) serving delicious takeaway pizza and pastas. The Bath Street restaurant (next door) is larger with the same quality menu; both café and restaurant open Mon–Sat 8am–10pm, Sun noon–11pm. Moderate.

O'Sole Mio, 34 Bath St (☎0141/331 1397). A superb and affordable city-centre restaurant for unusual pasta dishes, as well as pizzas from their log-fired oven. Go from 5pm to 6.30pm for extra-cheap food. Mon–Thurs noon–2.30pm & 5–11pm, Fri noon–2.30pm & 5pm–midnight, Sat noon–midnight, Sun 5–11pm. Moderate.

Japanese

Ichiban Noodle Café, 50 Queen St (☎0141/204 4200). Authentic Japanese noodle bar with long benches and an open kitchen which can make for compulsive viewing. The staple is a huge bowl of noodle soup with meat or veg topping, to which you can add substantial side orders of fish, salad or dumplings if you're hungry. Mon–Fri noon–4pm & 5.30–11pm, Sat noon–11pm, Sun 1–10pm. Inexpensive.

Mexican

Cantina Del Rey, 10 Kings Court (☎0141/552 4044). Behind the St Enoch Centre in a converted railway vault, this spacious restaurant serves authentic Mexican cuisine including *fajitas, burritos* and frozen *margaritas* at reasonable prices. Open Sun–Thurs 5–10pm, Fri & Sat till 11pm. Moderate.

Scottish and seafood

Babbity Bowster, 16–18 Blackfriars St (☎0141/552 5055). Atmospheric and popular Merchant City bar on the ground level serving excellent Scottish food – anything from hearty broths to haggis, salmon and kippers. The restaurant upstairs is pricier, and more sedate, serving venison, fresh fish and the like. Open Mon–Sat till 10.30pm. Moderate.

Buttery, 652 Argyle St (☎0141/221 8188). A fine, if slightly snooty, restaurant serving lavish, imaginative and expensive food, with lots of tarted-up traditional Scottish dishes. Downstairs is the more informal, moderately priced *Belfry* bistro. Open Mon–Sat till 10.30pm.

City Merchant, 97 Candleriggs (☎0141/553 1577). Popular restaurant in the Merchant City that serves good food using Scottish produce, from Dingwall haggis to fresh lobster. Open daily till 10.30pm. Expensive.

Gamba, 225a West George St (☎0141/572 0899). A stylish, upmarket basement restaurant with nods to Spain in both the decor and seafood-dominated menu. Tempting starters include a wonderful fish soup or a *sahimi* platter, while the mains include shellfish and daily specials depending on what's available at the fish market. Closed Sun. Expensive.

Rab Ha's, 83 Hutcheson St (☎0141/572 0400). Underneath this popular Merchant City bar lies a restaurant offering a version of the "Auld Alliance" with a combination of French and Scottish cuisine at reasonable prices. Daily 5.30–10.30pm. Expensive.

Rogano, 11 Exchange Place, near Buchanan Street (☎0141/248 4055). Although the food here is not solely Scottish, the *Rogano* is a Glasgow institution, an absolutely superb but shockingly expensive fish restaurant decked out as a replica of the 1930s Cunard liner, the *Queen Mary*. *Café Rogano*, in the basement, is cheaper but not so deliciously ostentatious. Café Sun–Thurs noon–11pm, Fri & Sat noon–11.30pm; moderate. Restaurant daily noon–2.30pm & 6.30–10.30pm. Very expensive.

Thai

Pattaya, 437 Sauchiehall St (☎0141/572 0071). The atmosphere can be a bit stiff but the prices are reasonable and the food tasty and well-presented. Plenty of choice, including some excellent fish and vegetarian dishes. Open Mon–Thurs noon–2pm & 5–11pm, Fri & Sat till midnight, Sun 6–11pm. Moderate.

VEGETARIAN EATING

Vegetarians will not have a hard time finding something to eat in Glasgow. Most restaurants and cafés have at least one vegetarian dish on their menus, whilst those listed below are either exclusively vegetarian, or offer a very good selection of meat-free dishes.

Bay Tree, see p.223
Café Alba, see p.223
Granary, see p.220

The 13th Note, see p.220
Vegville Diner, see p.221

West End

Predominantly due to the large local student population, the **West End** is the best area for cheap, stylish restaurants and cafés, and bars serving food, especially along Byres Road. There's a particular concentration near the Hillhead Underground station, with some reliable eateries tucked down **Ruthven Lane**, while **Ashton Lane** is always live-ly, with some good restaurants and packed bars.

Cafés, diners and pubs

Air Organic, 36 Kelvingrove St (☎0141/564 5200). With moulded plastic seats and minimalist decor, this funky eatery (and club downstairs) has been picking up design awards ever since it opened in 1998. The menu is dominated by delicious organic offerings, veggies and meat, cooked with flair and flavour. Organic beer and wine also on offer. Sun–Thurs 11am–11pm, Fri & Sat 11am–midnight. Expensive.

Back Alley, 8 Ruthven Lane (☎0141/334 7165). Deservedly popular spot serving great burgers smothered in assorted toppings, washed down with good beer and finished off with calorific pud-dings. Try the Mon–Thurs early-evening happy hour for good meal deals. Mon–Sat noon–midnight, Sun 11am–11pm. Inexpensive.

Bay Tree, 403 Great Western Rd (☎0141/334 5898). This small café offers a decent selection of veg-eburgers, salads and soups with good daily specials. Try the sugar-free cakes for a guilt-free pud-ding. Mon–Sat 8.30am–9pm, Sun 10am–8pm. Inexpensive.

Café Alba, 61 Otago St (☎0141/337 2282). Situated just off Gibson Street, this popular café sells a good selection of vegetarian food and the best home baking in the west. Mon–Sat 10am–5pm. Inexpensive.

Grosvenor Café, 31 Ashton Lane (☎0141/339 1848). Small, traditional Italo-Scots café tucked behind Hillhead Underground station with a die-hard clientele, addicted to the no-nonsense food (pizzas, fried food, burgers) served at unbelievably low prices. Slightly more upmarket menu in the evening, but lacking in quality. Mon open till 7pm, Tues–Sat till 11pm, Sun till 5.30pm. Inexpensive.

Jinty McGinty's, 21–29 Ashton Lane. Wood-panelled and frosted-glassed Irish pub that, as well as serving excellent stout, maintains a small menu of Irish favourites such as bacon and cabbage, steak and Guinness pie or hearty soups. Inexpensive.

Insomnia, 38–42 Woodlands Rd. This 24hr café lies conveniently on the path from the city centre to the West End and gets very crowded once the pubs close. Choose from soups, sandwiches, pas-tries and coffee to beat those late-night blues. Inexpensive.

Tinderbox, 189 Byres Rd. A great place for coffee and a snack, even if it's so fashionable it can hard-ly breathe. It's all a bit different here: you stand in line to get served, they don't put chocolate on your cappuccino, there are CD listening posts and scooters parked outside. Daily 8am–10pm.

University Café, 87 Byres Rd. One of the last of a dying race of "caffs", dearly loved by generations of students, with formica tables and high glass counters, which serves up fish'n'chips or mince'n'-tatties, rounded off with ice-cream in a cone. Open till 10pm every night. Inexpensive.

French

Cul de Sac, 44 Ashton Lane (☎0141/334 4749). Informal, relaxed restaurant, underneath an endur-ingly popular bar. A small menu with delicious half-price crepes and burgers during the week from 5–7pm. Mon–Thurs & Sun noon–11pm, Fri & Sat noon–midnight. Moderate.

Indian

Ashoka, 19 Ashton Lane (☎0141/337 1115). More traditional but lively West End *dhosa* house and Indian restaurant, popular with local students. Mon–Sat noon–midnight, Sun 5pm–midnight. Moderate.

Crème de la Crème, 1071 Argyle St (☎0141/221 3222). In Glasgow, curry houses are different, and this is no exception. Located in a former cinema, the huge main restaurant downstairs serves à la carte favourites, while the buffet on the balcony is great value (especially Sun–Thurs). A large video screen shows cartoons and cheesy movies. Open daily till midnight. Moderate.

Mother India, 28 Westminster Terrace, off Sauchiehall St (☎0141/221 1663). Good-quality food at affordable prices in the refreshingly laid-back surroundings of this friendly Indian restaurant. It's unlicensed, so bring your own alcohol: small corkage fee. Mon–Thurs noon–2pm & 5.30–11pm, Fri & Sat till 11.30pm, Sun 5.30–11pm. Moderate.

Murphy's Pakora Bar, 1287 Argyle St (☎0141/334 1550). Even picky eaters are spoilt for choice here, with over seventy varieties of pakora available as a light snack or mountainous meal. Close to the Kelvingrove Museum and open daily till midnight. Inexpensive.

Italian

The Big Blue, 445 Great Western Rd (☎0141/357 1038). Whitewashed walls and colourful upholstery characterize this low-level bar and restaurant that serves simple but tasty pasta dishes. Food served till 10pm every day. Moderate.

Café Antipasti, 337 Byres Rd. Two-tier bistro near the Botanic Gardens serving tasty and well-priced pastas and salads. No bookings, so you sometimes have to queue for a table on busy nights. Sun–Thurs 9am–11pm, Fri & Sat 9am–midnight.

Di Maggio's, 61 Ruthven Lane (☎0141/334 8560). Extremely popular West End pizzeria and pasta joint, usually packed solid with bargain-hungry students. Frantic atmosphere with occasional live music. Open daily until midnight. Inexpensive.

Stazione, 1051 Great Western Rd (☎0141/576 7576). Its setting in a grand sandstone railway building a mile or so west of the heart of the West End gives this Mediterranean-oriented bistro a dignified but relaxed ambience. *Mezze* platters and pizzas are both on the menu, along with mussels and a Pasta "Scozzese", with local smoked haddock and cream. Moderate.

Japanese

Fusion, 41 Byres Rd (☎0141/339 3666). The sushi bar that New York and London have but not Edinburgh. Individual sushi or sashimi pieces are priced between £1.50 and £3.50, but there are folk on hand to help you sort out your *nigiri* from your *temaki*. Open till midnight Tues–Sun, closed Mon. Moderate.

Mexican

Salsa, 184 Dumbarton Rd (☎0141/337 1416). A smaller version of the *Cantina Del Rey* (see p.222), this West End branch serves the same good-quality food in a colourful and laid-back atmosphere. Open Sun–Thurs till 10pm, Fri & Sat till 11pm. Moderate.

Scottish and seafood

Nairn's, 13 Woodside Crescent (☎0141/353 0707). Showcase restaurant in a smartly redesigned town house run by Scotland's celebrity chef Nick Nairn. Expect highly original combinations of food, beautifully presented dishes, and a hefty but not outrageous bill. Expensive.

Stravaigin, 28 Gibson St (☎0141/334 2665). You can get selections from the menu served in the busy upstairs bar, or more substantial dishes in the downstairs restaurant. Local meats and fish are given a cosmopolitan make-over with roast vegetables or a shitake mushroom sauce. Restaurant open till 10.30pm, bar till 11pm Sun–Thurs, midnight Fri & Sat. Moderate upstairs, expensive downstairs.

Two Fat Ladies, 88 Dumbarton Rd (☎0141/339 1944). Named after the bingo-call for "88", and hardly large enough to fit more than a couple of well-proportioned opera singers, this is the best fish restaurant in Glasgow. The blackboard menu reminds you that everything is fresh, and is likely to include oysters and shellfish as well as the catch of the day. Closed Sun & Mon. Expensive.

Ubiquitous Chip, 12 Ashton Lane (☎0141/334 5007). Splendid West End restaurant with a covered patio that resembles an indoor forest. Glasgow's most delicious Scottish food – game, seafood and local cheeses, and occasionally oatmeal ice cream and venison haggis. Daily till 11pm. Very expensive.

South Side

Although the range isn't as great as elsewhere, the **South Side** is a quieter and less studenty alternative to the centre or the West End, with a couple of notable Greek and Italian restaurants.

Cafés, diners and pubs

Boswell Hotel, 27 Mansionhouse Rd, Queen's Park (☎0141/632 9812). Unusually cheap and extensive bar-food menu with some offbeat house specialities – a good complement to the wide selection of real ales. Food served until 9pm. Inexpensive.

Cul de Sac, 1179 Pollockshaws Rd (☎0141/649 1819). Relaxing rather than fashionable, where crepe is about the toughest French word on the menu, but you'll find comforting, moderately priced meals which are half-price from 5–7pm. The bar is on ground level, the bistro above. Moderate.

Stoat and Ferret, 1534 Pollokshaws Rd (☎0141/632 0161). Wood-panelled real-ale pub close to Pollok Park. Bar meals including steak pie, pasta and haggis until 6pm, baked potatoes and lighter snacks until 9pm. Inexpensive.

Chinese

Wok Way, 2 Burnfield Rd, Giffnock (☎0141/638 2244). The place to come with a party, when this tiny venue is always odds-on to turn into a cabaret of karaoke and dancing, all wilfully encouraged by the proprietors. The food can be overwhelmed by other events, but you'll find familiar Chinese dishes and more original specials. Closed Mon. Moderate.

Greek

Café Serghei, 67 Bridge St (☎0141/429 1547). One of the few authentic Greek restaurants in Glasgow, serving traditional food in a lively atmosphere. Mon–Sat noon–2.30pm & 5–11pm, Sun 6–11pm. Moderate.

The Taverna, 780 Pollokshaws Rd, near Queen's Park train station (☎0141/424 0858). Busy Greek restaurant serving authentic dishes, with a popular real-ale bar next door. Mon–Sat noon–2.30pm & 5–10.30pm. Moderate.

Italian

Buongiorno, 1012 Pollockshaws Rd (☎0141/649 1029). An instant hit with all who uncover this little gem, not just for its intimacy and friendliness, but also for home-cooked pasta and pizzas at rock-bottom prices. Inexpensive.

Di Maggio's, 1038 Pollokshaws Rd, Queen's Park (☎0141/632 4194). Less studenty than the West End branch, offering the same selection of gargantuan pizzas and hefty pasta dishes. Mon–Fri noon–2.30pm & 5pm–midnight, Sat noon–midnight, Sun 12.30pm–midnight. Inexpensive.

Scottish

Art Lovers' Café, House for an Art Lover, Bellahouston Park, Dumbrech Rd (☎0141/353 4779). Open for classy lunches including goat's cheese or poached salmon salads through the week, the restaurant stays open on Saturday night when a live jazz band plays and you can wander freely through this incredible Rennie Mackintosh house. Moderate.

Ewington, at the *Ewington Hotel*, 132 Queen's Drive (☎0141/423 1152). Facing Queen's Park, this sedate suburban hotel has a cellar restaurant whose very pink and flouncy decor is compensated for by the fine mix of traditional Scottish and continental cuisine. Food daily 6–8.45pm. Expensive.

Pubs and bars

Not so many years ago, Glasgow's rough image was inextricably associated with its **pubs**, widely thought of as no-go areas for any visitor. Although much of this reputation was exaggerated, there was an element of truth in it. Nowadays, however, you're much more likely to spend an evening in a succession of open and airy café-bars than encounter a dark, threatening, nicotine-stained pub. On Friday and Saturday night, Glaswegians like to dress to the nines and head for town, homing in on the ultra-hip bars which have opened in the last few years. If you tire of the glossy **Merchant City**, head for the **East End**, where some of the local spit-and-sawdust establishments make a welcome change.

Inevitably there will be some overlap between bars, cafés and restaurants, with many pubs serving good food, restaurants having good bars, and cafés being lively places to drink. If a pub serves particularly good food, we have included it in our eating section; conversely, if we recommend it for its convivial drinking atmosphere, rather than its food, we have included it in the pubs and bars section.

All in all, though, the liveliest area (once again) has to be the **West End**, where students mix with fun-seeking locals. Most pubs and bars in Glasgow stay open until midnight, although some will close at 11pm from Sunday to Thursday. After that, your only option is to head to a nightclub (see below), some of which stay open until as late as 5am.

City centre

Babbity Bowster, 16–18 Blackfriars St. Lively hangout at the heart of the Merchant City, with a much more Scottish feel than many places nearby.

Balsa, 71 Renfield St. One of a now bewildering range of seriously cool Glasgow "style bars", with retro 1970s-style decor, attracting a young, hip, pre-club crowd.

Bargo, 80 Albion Street. Winner of pub design awards with a spacious wood and stainless-steel interior, where the local Merchant City crowd and trendy set pose elegantly behind the massive glass frontage.

Bar 91, 91 Candleriggs. Well-designed Merchant City bar, using wrought iron to evoke a stylish atmosphere.

Bay Horse, 19 Bath St. Ordinary Glasgow pub, serving malt whisky, pies and peas.

Buddha, 142 St Vincent St. Despite its name the theme here is Arab bazaar, though the deep sofas and elegant crowd make this a good place to kick back and watch the world.

Buzzy Wares, Princes Square Shopping Centre. Glossy bar, popular at weekends as a pre-club stop.

Corinthian, 191 Ingram St. Reminiscent of a grand 1920s London gentlemen's club, this exquisite renovation of an old bank, complete with huge glass dome, is worth experiencing for cocktails or a light meal in the grill room: dress smartly.

Corn Exchange, 88 Gordon St. Slap opposite Central station, this bar has successfully re-created the feel of a traditional Victorian Glaswegian pub.

The Griffin, 226 Bath St. Friendly, if faintly tacky, three-bar pub with a firm crowd of regulars – mostly students.

Horseshoe Bar, 17 Drury St. Traditional old pub, reputedly Glasgow's busiest – loud, frantic and great fun, with a very mixed clientele. Karaoke upstairs, with a downstairs bar for quiet conversation. The horseshoe-shaped bar is the longest in the UK.

McChuill's, 40 High St. Glasgow's skateboarders wheel into this brick-lined bar for the Wednesday hip-hop evenings and, with live music most other nights, it attracts a faithful crowd.

Mitre Bar, 12–16 Brunswick St. Tucked away in a small side street between Wilson Street and Trongate, this unpretentious retreat sells decent beer to a mixed bag of locals.

Monkey Bar, 100 Bath St. Another city-centre style bar, with office staff making it loud at lunchtimes and the pre-club crowd thronging in at weekends.

Nico's, 375–379 Sauchiehall St. Trendy without being painfully so, the ambience in this popular bar strives towards a French flavour – prices, especially for the bottled beer, are steep.

RG's, 73 Queen St. Nostalgia-soaked bar that serves as a focus for Glasgow's rock music heritage – hence the large portraits of local musical luminaries that adorn the walls. A bit cramped, but a fun atmosphere. Incongruously, the downstairs section, *Bar Sauza*, is all funky Latin and margaritas.

Saracen Head, 209 Gallowgate (opposite the Barras market). Unchanged East End pub that offers an enjoyably beery, sawdust-floored wallow. Even the faintly threatening atmosphere is pure Glasgow. Look out for the tax demand from Robbie Burns displayed on the wall, from the days when he was the local tax officer.

Scotia Bar, 112 Stockwell St. Laid-back bar popular with writers and artists. Occasional live folk music – Billy Connolly began his career here, telling jokes in between singing folk songs.

Solid Rock Café, 19 Hope St. Glasgow's top rock pub, with heavy-rock DJs from Thurs–Sun.

Ten, 10 Mitchell St. In a tiny lane connecting Buchanan and Mitchell streets, *Ten* was designed by the same crew as Manchester's legendary *Hacienda* club. As you'd expect, it's suitably chic, though with a healthy dose of Glaswegian humour to take off the posey edge.

Variety Bar, 401 Sauchiehall St. Crowded bar with faded Art Nouveau appeal frequented by local art school students.

Victoria Bar, 157–159 Bridgegate. Basic, folksy pub serving a wide selection of real ales.

West End

The Aragon, 131 Byres Rd. Old-fashioned bar with mixed crowd. The main attraction here is the vast beer selection, which includes European fruit beers and weekly guest ales.

Attic, 44–46 Ashton Lane. Proof that New York doesn't have a monopoly on creative loft conversions, this bar above the *Cul-de-Sac* restaurant is the smart place to drink on busy Ashton Lane.

Bonham's, 194 Byres Rd. Tall, spacious bar with splendid stained-glass windows. Popular, unpretentious, and serving reasonable daytime food.

Br-el, 39–43 Ashton Lane. If *The Attic* across the way is a taste of Manhattan, *Br-el* is the European alternative. Slim and tastefully designed bar with a wide range of Belgian beers, and an eating section serving up big pans of mussels and frites.

Brewery Tap, 1055 Sauchiehall St. Well-known for its excellent selection of real ales and imported lager, this pub caters for students and locals alike with seating outside for those long summer evenings.

Firebird, 1321 Argyle St. Located near the Kelvingrove Art Gallery, the plate-glass walls expose a hip drinking spot with a wood-stoked pizza oven producing some tasty snacks, while downstairs guest DJs keep the clubbing crowd entertained.

The Halt, 106 Woodlands Rd. Great beer and a vast selection of whiskies in this relaxed music pub, spiritual home of Glasgow cartoon character Lobey Dosser, whose statue is opposite. Regular live bands.

Living Room, 5–9 Byres Rd. Hotbed for the young and hip, at the southern end of Byres Road. Wrought iron and candles enhance the pre-club atmosphere.

Lismore, 206 Dumbarton Rd. Decorated with stained-glass panels depicting scenes from the Highland Clearances, this friendly pub is a meeting point for the local Gaels, who come here to chat, relax and listen to the impromptu music sessions.

Mitchell's, 157 North St. Next to the domed Mitchell's Library, a comfortable pub with a scholarly atmosphere. Good beer and an excellent refuge.

Tennent's, 191 Byres Rd. No-nonsense, beery den, a refreshing antidote to all the designer paradises nearby. Large and very popular, especially with real-ale aficionados.

Uisge Beatha, 232 Woodlands Rd. The plain frontage is far from indicative of the eclectic interior, where a lively mixed crowd relish the re-created Scottish atmosphere – all kilts, piped music and stripped wood. The name, by the way, is Gaelic for whisky, the "water of life".

The Western Bar, 80 Dumbarton Rd. A world apart from the student haunts nearby, this genuinely friendly working-class stronghold has walls that read like a city social-history treatise, with lots of old photographs and faded memorabilia.

Whistler's Mother, 116–122 Byres Rd. Combines a relaxed restaurant with the more basic bar, which is deservedly popular with students and legions of young people.

South Side

Boswell Hotel, 27 Mansionhouse Rd. Lively Queen's Park pub with great atmosphere and occasional live music. Good selection of real ales, including some unusually potent local brews. Fine bar food (see p.225).

Brazen Head, 1–3 Cathcart Rd. Close to the Citizens' Theatre and decorated with football strips, this Irish-Italian bar is a local haunt and well endowed with Guinness and Gillespies.

Church on the Hill, 16 Algie St. Perched on the hill behind Queen's Park, the wood panelling and brass fittings give an old time atmosphere to the bar and restaurant, which serves American-style food. Seating outside for sunny evenings.

Cul de Sac Southside, 1179 Pollokshaws Rd. Comfortable, trendy bar that serves food during the day. The pricier restaurant above has dishes with a Scottish-French influence for around £9.

The Granary, 10 Kilmarnock Rd, ten-minute walk south from Queen's Park. Friendly bar, with a busy restaurant that serves a good selection of burgers, steaks and Mexican food.

M.J. Heraghty, 708 Pollokshaws Rd. Tiny pub on the corner of Pollokshaws and Nithsdale roads. A rough working-men's hangout, particularly crowded when Celtic play, and so masculine that they don't even have a women's toilet – you have to go next door.

Samuel Dow's, 69–71 Northside Rd, close to Pollokshields West train station. This South Side favourite offers cheap bar meals and occasionally live music to a welcoming crowd. Ceilidhs every Sunday and poetry readings on the first Monday of every month.

Nightlife and entertainment

Glasgow's streets can seem incredibly busy between midnight and 1am, especially on Friday and Saturday nights, but the impression is a little distorted by the city's unique **licensing laws**, which mean that the pubs close up at midnight, and that no-one is allowed into a club after 1am. Most locals, however, are now quite used to these migration patterns, and certainly don't let them stand in the way of having a good time. As a result the **clubbing scene** is highly rated, with one or two large, mainstream venues; Glasgow consistently attracts some of the top DJs from around the world and can easily provide a good night out.

Most of Glasgow's nightclubs are in the heart of the main shopping areas off Argyle and Buchanan streets, with a further concentration on Sauchiehall Street near Charing Cross. Establishments are pretty mixed, and although there's still a stack of outdated mega-discos with rigorous dress codes, the last couple of years have seen the arrival of far more stylish haunts. Hours hover from around 11pm to 3am, though some are open until 5am, and cover charges are variable – expect to pay around £3 during the week, and up to £10 at the weekend. Drinks are usually about thirty percent more expensive than in the pubs.

While the city's cultural programme doesn't these days match those of the heady 1980s and early 1990s, it has maintained an impressive breadth of art, theatre, film and music, firmly established as the home of both Scottish Opera and the Royal Scottish National Orchestra. The majority of the larger **theatres**, **cinemas** and showpiece **concert halls** are around the shopping streets of the city centre, while the West End is home to student-oriented venues such as the quirky Grosvenor cinema. The city's two trendiest theatres, the Citizens' and the Tramway, are both South Side. You can find **details** of the city's events in the *Herald* or *Evening Times* newspapers, or the comprehensive fortnightly listings magazine, *The List* (£1.95), which also covers Edinburgh. To book **tickets** for theatre productions or big concerts, call at the Ticket Centre, City Hall, Candleriggs, on the Trongate end of Argyle Street (Mon–Sat 9am–6pm, Sun noon–5pm; phone bookings Mon–Sat 9am–9pm, Sun noon–6pm; ☎0141/287 5511).

Nightclubs

Archaos, 25 Queen St (☎0141/204 3189). Massive nightclub with designer decor, and a mixed, young crowd. Weekends are balanced between dance, hip-hop and garage.

The Arches, 30 Midland St (☎0141/221 4001). Deservedly popular weekend club pounding out predominantly dance and rave-oriented music in converted railway arches, under Central station, off Jamaica Street.

Fury Murray's, 96 Maxwell St, behind the St Enoch Centre (☎0141/221 6511). Student-oriented and lively, with music spanning from the 1960s to rave and techno.

The Garage, 490 Sauchiehall St (☎0141/332 1120). Medium-sized club at the heavier end of the rock spectrum; features some dance nights but lacks atmosphere.

Lime, 5 Scott St (☎0141/332 0712). Busy, studenty club with mainstream music and Seventies and Eighties classics midweek.

Riverside Club, Fox Road, off Clyde Street (☎0141/248 3144). Regular weekend ceilidh that gets packed out with good-natured, drunken Scottish dancers. Great fun, with a live band and callers involving everyone from seasoned ceilidh dancers to visiting novices. Get there early (8–9pm) to ensure a place.

Sub Club, 22 Jamaica St (☎0141/248 4600). Well-established nightclub aimed squarely at the dance and rave end of the market. Weekend nights are very trendy.

Tin Pan Alley, Mitchell Street (☎0141/248 7377). Large dance club attracting a mixed crowd, with rave music dominating at the weekend.

Trash, 197 Pitt St. Three-room venue playing house and garage, though the popular Sly on Thursday nights draws in a party crowd with cheesy favourites from the Seventies and Eighties.

The Tunnel, 84 Mitchell St (☎0141/204 1000). Stylish club with arty decor, though now a bit faded; the gents' toilet has cascading waterfall walls.

The Velvet Rooms, Sauchiehall Street (☎0141/332 0755). Consists of a small bar with postage-stamp dance area for the posing set, and a larger bar above playing mainstream dance, garage and soul.

Gay clubs and bars

Bennett's, 90 Glassford St, Merchant City (☎0141/552 5761). Glasgow's main gay club, predominantly male, fairly old-fashioned but enjoyable nonetheless. Straight nights on Tues.

Caffe Latte, 58 Virginia St. Café serving food by day, and a trendy bar by night, and very popular with the gay crowd, although the clientele is usually very mixed.

Del Monica's, 68 Virginia St. Glasgow's liveliest and most stylish gay bar, very near George Square, with a mixed and hedonistic crowd.

Polo Lounge, 84 Wilson St, off Glassford Street. The original decor in this converted insurance office – all marble tiles and open fires – and the dark pounding nightclub underneath attract a mixed crowd.

The Waterloo Bar, 306 Argyle St. Very central, garish but enjoyable gay bar, which gets packed at weekends. Mainly men.

Live music pubs and venues

Barrowlands, 244 Gallowgate (☎0141/552 4601). Legendary East End dance hall, complete with spinning glitterball, that hosts some of the sweatiest, liveliest gigs you will ever encounter. Has a capacity of a couple of thousand, so tends to attract bands that are just breaking into the big time, though many big names still come back for the amazing atmosphere.

Curlers, 256 Byres Rd (☎0141/334 1284). Part of this landmark Byres Road pub, *Jock Tamson's*, hosts folk bands on Friday and Saturday nights.

The Garage, 490 Sauchiehall St (☎0141/332 1120). Good-size venue for bands that are just about to make it big.

King Tut's Wah Wah Hut, 272a St Vincent St (☎0141/221 5279). One of the city's best programmes of bands at this splendid city-centre live music pub. Famous as the place where Oasis were discovered. Good bar downstairs if you want to sit out the sweaty gig above.

Nice'n'Sleazy, 421 Sauchiehall St (☎0141/333 9637). Alternative bands most nights in the somewhat cramped downstairs bar.

Scotia Bar, 112 Stockwell St, near the St Enoch Centre (☎0141/552 8681). The folkies' favourite, a mellow musical pub that acts as a magnet for folk players and followers. Regular live gigs and frequent jam sessions.

The 13th Note Café, 50–60 King St (☎0141/553 1638). This relaxed bar and vegetarian restaurant with Art Deco styling is the place to sample local music talent, including jazz and r'n'b; the club of the same name at 260 Clyde St is a bit louder and livelier.

Theatre and comedy

The Arches, 30 Midland St (☎0141/221 4001). Trendy base for performances by touring theatre and contemporary dance groups.

Blackfriars, 36 Bell St (☎0141/552 5924). The city's premier comedy and cabaret venue, well sited in the Merchant City and renowned for its good-value Sunday-night line-ups. Also live music at the weekend, particularly jazz.

Citizens' Theatre, 119 Gorbals St (☎0141/429 0022). "The Citz" has grown from profound working-class roots to become one of the most respected and adventurous theatres in Britain. Three stages, with truly bargain prices for students and the unemployed, together with free preview nights. Their Christmas plays, as distinct from pantomimes, are a must for kids.

Cottier Theatre, 935 Hyndland St (☎0141/357 3868). Small theatre in old West End church which hosts touring shows and regular music gigs. The adjoining bar and beer garden is a favourite on long summer evenings.

King's Theatre, 294 Bath St (☎0141/287 5511). Large, grand theatre featuring mainstream shows and comedy, south of Sauchiehall Street.

Mitchell Theatre, 6 Granville St, Charing Cross (☎0141/287 5511). Small but popular venue for touring groups located at the back of the huge reference library.

Tramway Theatre, 25 Albert Drive, off Pollokshaws Road (☎0141/227 5511). Good venue for experimental theatre, dance, music and regular art exhibitions.

Tron Theatre, 63 Trongate (☎0141/552 4267). Varied repertoire of mainstream and experimental productions from visiting companies, together with one of the city's most laid-back bars.

Concert halls

Royal Concert Hall, 2 Sauchiehall St (☎0141/287 5511). Some big-name rock and soul stars, as well as middle-of-the-road music hall acts, enjoy the acoustics and intimate feel of this relatively new venue. Also features big-name touring orchestras and is home to the Royal Scottish National Orchestra.

Scottish Exhibition and Conference Centre, Finnieston Quay (☎0141/248 3000). Soulless and overpriced huge shed with the acoustics and atmosphere of an aircraft hangar, but, unfortunately, the only venue in Glasgow (often the only venue in Scotland) visited by megastars on their world tours.

Theatre Royal, 282 Hope Street (☎0141/332 9000). The opulent home of Scottish Opera and regular host to visiting classical orchestras, opera companies, theatre blockbusters and occasional comedy.

Cinemas

ABC Filmcentre, 326 Sauchiehall St (☎0141/332 9513). Five-screen mainstream multiplex.

City Centre Odeon, 56 Renfield St (☎0141/332 3413). Multiscreen cinema with similar programming to the ABC.

Glasgow Film Theatre, 12 Rose St (☎0141/332 8128). The city's main arthouse and independent cinema.

Grosvenor, Ashton Lane (☎0141/339 4298). Eclectic mix of mainstream and arthouse movies on two screens in this tiny West End alley. Occasional theme nights and frequent lates for local students.

Listings

Airlines Aer Lingus, 19 Dixon St (☎0645/737747); British Airways, 66 Gordon St (☎0345/222111); British Airways Express, Glasgow Airport (☎0141/889 1311); Icelandair, Glasgow Airport (☎0345/581111); Lufthansa, 78 St Vincent St (☎0345/737747); Northwest, 177 W George St (☎0141/226 4991); Qantas, 395 King St (☎0345/747767).

Airport enquiries ☎0141/887 1111.

American Express 115 Hope St (Mon–Fri 8.30am–5.30pm, Sat 9am–noon; ☎0141/221 4366).

Banks Bank of Scotland, 110 Queen St, 63 Waterloo St, 235 Sauchiehall St and 55 Bath St; Clydesdale Bank, 14 Bothwell St, 7 St Enoch Square, 30 St Vincent Place, 344 Argyle St and 120 Bath St; Royal Bank of Scotland, 98 Buchanan St, 22 St Enoch Square, 140 St Vincent St and 393

Sauchiehall St. English banks in Glasgow include Barclays, 90 St Vincent St; Lloyds, 12 Bothwell St and National Westminster, 14 Blythswood Square.

Bike rental see box on p.219.

Books John Smith's, 57 St Vincent St; Waterstone's, 132 Union St, Dillons, 104–108 Argyle St, and the vast Borders, 98 Buchanan St, all have extensive sections on Glasgow.

Bus enquiries Buchanan Street bus station. For local buses, call ☎0141/332 7133; for national ones, ☎0990 505050.

Car rental Arnold Clark, 10–24 Vinnicomb St (☎0141/334 9501); Avis, 161 North St (☎0141/221 2827); Budget, 101 Waterloo St (☎0141/226 4141); Europcar, 38 Anderston Quay (☎0141/248 8788). Car-rental firms at the airport include Avis (☎0141/887 2261); Budget (☎0141/887 0501); Eurodollar (☎0141/887 7915); and Europcar (☎0141/887 0414).

Consulates Germany, 158 W Regent St (☎0141/221 0304); Italy, 24 St Enoch Square (☎0141/226 3000); Norway, 80 Oswald St (☎0141/204 1353); Spain, 389 Argyle St (☎0141/221 6943); Sweden, 16 Robertson St (☎0141/221 7845).

Dentist Glasgow Dental Hospital, 378 Sauchiehall St (☎0141/211 9600); J McDonald and Assocs, 2 Lansdowne Cres, (☎0141/339 0873); Smile Dental Care, 128 Great Western Road (☎0141/331 1366).

Exchange Outside banking hours you can change money at Thomas Cook in Central station (Mon–Wed & Sat 8am–7pm, Thurs & Fri 8am–8pm, Sun 10am–6pm; ☎0141/204 4496).

Football Of the two big Glasgow teams, you can see Celtic at Celtic Park, 95 Kerrydale St, off the A749 London Road (☎0141/551 8653), and bitter rivals Rangers at the mighty Ibrox stadium, Edminston Drive (☎0141/427 8800). Glasgow's other, lesser teams include Partick Thistle in Firhill stadium, Firhill Road (☎0141/945 4811), or, on the South Side, lowly Queen's Park at the national stadium Hampden Park, Mount Florida (☎0141/632 1275). Tickets from £10 depending on the opposing team and match status.

Gay and lesbian contacts Lesbian and Gay Switchboard (daily 7–10pm; ☎0141/332 8372); Glasgow Women's Library, 4th floor, 109 Trongate (Tues–Fri 1–6pm, Sat 2–5pm; ☎0141/552/8345); Glasgow Lesbian and Gay Centre, 11 Dixon St (Mon–Fri 10am–1pm, answer-machine message outside these hours; ☎0141/221 7203).

Hospital 24hr casualty department at the Royal Infirmary, 84 Castle St (☎0141/211 4000).

Internet *Café Internet*, 2nd floor, Waterstones Bookshop, 153–7 Sauchiehall St (☎0141/353 2484, *glasgow@cafeinternet.co.uk*); *Link Café*, 569 Sauchiehall St (☎0141/564 1052, *info@linkcafe.co.uk*).

Laundry 1110 Argyle St (☎0141/339 6530), 39 Bank St (☎0141/339 8953); 161 Great Western Road (☎0141/353 2965).

Left luggage Staffed office available at Buchanan Street bus station (daily 6.30am–10.30pm) and 24hr lockers at both Central and Queen Street train stations.

Pharmacies Munroes', 693 Great Western Rd (daily 9am–9pm; ☎0141/339 0012), and Superdrug, Central station (Mon–Wed 8am–8pm, Thurs–Sat 8am–9pm, Sun 10am–8pm; ☎0141/221 8197).

Police Cranstonhill Police Station, 945 Argyle St (☎0141/532 3200); and Stewart Street station, Cowcaddens (☎0141/532 3000).

Post office 47 St Vincent St (Mon–Fri 8.30am–5.45pm, Sat 9am–5.50pm; ☎0345/223344), with branch offices at 85–89 Bothwell St, 228 Hope St and 533 Sauchiehall St.

Taxis TOA Taxis (☎0141/332 7070).

Train enquiries ☎0345/484 950.

Travel agents Campus Travel, The Hub, Hillhead St (☎0141/357 0608), and 122 George St (☎0141/553 1818); Glasgow Flight Centre, 143 W Regent St (☎0141/221 8989).

THE CLYDE

The temptation to speed through the **Clyde Valley** is considerable, especially since the raw beauty of the Highlands, the islands and lakes of Argyll and the urbane sophistication of Edinburgh are all within easy reach of the city. Although many of the towns and villages surrounding Glasgow are decidedly missable, some receive far fewer visitors than they deserve, being tarnished with the frequently redundant reputation of being dejected industrial towns clinging to the coat tails of Glasgow.

From the city, regular trains dip down the southern bank of the Clyde to **Paisley**, where the distinctive cloth pattern gained its name, before heading up to the Firth of Clyde. Along the northern bank, the train rattles through some of Glasgow's oldest shipbuilding communities before arriving in the ancient Strathclyde capital of **Dumbarton**, whose twin-peaked **castle** dominates the flat estuary for miles around.

Heading southeast out of Glasgow, the river's industrial landscape gives way to a far more attractive scenery of gorges and towering castles. Here you can see the stoic town of **Lanark**, where eighteenth-century philanthropists built their model workers' community around the mills of **New Lanark**, and the spectacular **Falls of Clyde**, a mile upstream.

North of the city lies some wonderful upland countryside. Trains terminate at tiny **Milngavie** (pronounced "Mull-gay"), which makes great play of its status as the start of the long-distance walk, the **West Highland Way**, for details of which, see p.505. Nearby, the rolling beauty of the **Campsie Fells** provides excellent walking and stunning views down onto Glasgow and the glinting river that runs through it (see p.253 of "Central Scotland" for the full story).

The Firth of Clyde

The shipbuilding industry forged the **Firth of Clyde**, though only the last remnants of it can be seen by the banks of the river as you head west out of the city, through the north Clyde communities of **Clydebank**, **Yoker** and **Dalmuir**. The A82 and the rail line run along this northern bank, hemmed into the shore by the **Kilpatrick Hills** that rise sharply above.

These days, the two river banks are connected by the concrete parabola of the **Erskine Bridge**, dominating the landscape in a way that even Dumbarton Castle has never managed. The bridge disgorges its traffic onto the M8, which runs out from Glasgow along the south side of the river past the textile centre of **Paisley** – billed rather meaninglessly as "Scotland's largest town". West of the Erskine bridge, the M8/A8 and the main train line cling to the shipyard-lined estuary edge, passing the shipbuilding centre of **Greenock**, the old-fashioned seaside resort of **Gourock**, and **Wemyss Bay**, the ferry port for Argyll and Bute. Of the three, Greenock is by far the most interesting, with an excellent town museum that examines the life and achievements of local boy James Watt.

Paisley

Founded in the twelfth century as a monastic settlement around an abbey, **PAISLEY** expanded rapidly after the eighteenth century as a linen manufacturing town, specializing in the production of highly fashionable imitation Kashmiri shawls. Paisley quickly eclipsed other British centres producing the cloth, eventually lending its name to the swirling pine-cone design.

South of the train station, down Gilmour or Smithills streets, lies the bridge over the White Cart Water and the borough's ponderous **Town Hall**, seemingly built back to front as its municipal clock and mismatched double towers loom incongruously over the river instead of facing onto the town. Opposite the town hall, the **Abbey** (Mon–Sat 10am–3.30pm; free) was built on the site of the town's original settlement and was massively overhauled in the Victorian age. The unattractive, fat grey facade of the church does little justice to the renovated interior, which is tall, spacious and elaborately decorated, the elongated choir, rebuilt extensively throughout the last two centuries, illuminated by jewel-coloured stained glass from a variety of ages and styles. The abbey's oldest monument is the tenth-century Celtic cross of St Barochan, which lurks like a gnarled old bone at the eastern end of the north aisle.

Paisley's tatty **High Street** leads from the town hall to the west and towards two churches that make far more of an impression on the town's skyline than the modest abbey. The steep cobbles of Church Hill rise away from the High Street up to the grand steps and five-stage spire of the **High Church**, while, beyond the civic museum at the bottom of the High Street, the **Thomas Coats Memorial Church** (May–Sept Mon, Wed & Fri 2–6pm; free) is a Victorian masterpiece of hugely overstated grandeur. Sitting squat like a giant red predator waiting to pounce, the church is one of the most opulent Baptist centres in Britain, with huge tower-top buttresses and an interior of seemingly endless marble and alabaster.

Between the two churches, Paisley's civic **Museum and Art Gallery** (Tues–Sat 10am–5pm, Sun 2–5pm; free) shelters behind pompous Ionic columns that face the grim buildings of Paisley University. The local history section, nearest the entrance, contains an interesting collection of local artefacts, from song sheets and spinning threads to the death warrant and executioner's contract for the last public hanging in Paisley in 1858. The most popular part of the museum, which deals with the growth and development of the Paisley pattern and shawls, shows the familiar pine cone (or teardrop) pattern from its simplistic beginnings to elaborate later incarnations. The Upper Gallery houses a small art collection including works by Glasgow Boys Hornel, Guthrie and Lavery (see p.212).

On Oakshaw Street, which runs along the crest of the hill above the Art Gallery, the **Coats Observatory** (Tues–Sat 10am–5pm, Sun 2–5pm; free) has recorded astronomical and meteorological information since 1884. Today it houses a ten-inch telescope under its dome, and a couple of small exhibition areas display seismic recorders that documented the horrendous San Francisco earthquake of 1906. The telescopes are used for public viewing on Thursday evenings from the last Thursday in October until the last Thursday in March (7.30–9.30pm, weather permitting).

To bring you back down to earth, the harsh reality of eighteenth-century life is re-created in the **Sma' Shot Cottages** (April–Sept Wed & Sat 1–5pm; free) in George Place, off New Street. Each of these old houses has individual themes, and contains perfect re-creations of eighteenth- and nineteenth-century daily life, complete with bone cutlery and ancient looms. The nineteenth-century artisan's home is filled with artefacts, from ceramic hot-water bottles to period wallpaper, and leads you into a cosy tearoom where you can enjoy some home baking.

Practicalities

Regular **trains** from Glasgow Central connect with Paisley's Gilmour Street station in the centre of town. First Bus **buses** #39, #53 and #54 stop at Paisley Abbey; however, the train is faster and more convenient. Buses leave Paisley's Gilmour Street forecourt every ten minutes for Glasgow Airport, two miles north of the town. The **tourist office** (April & May Mon–Fri 9am–1pm & 2–5pm; June–Sept Mon–Sat 9am–6pm; ☎0141/889 0711) is a five-minute walk east from the Town Hall, tucked inside the unremarkable Lagoon Leisure Centre, on Mill Street.

Few people bother to stay in Paisley, except those catching an early flight, and **accommodation** in the town tends to be overpriced. If you do need to stay, the faded but comfortable *Brabloch Hotel*, at 62 Renfrew Rd (☎0141/889 5577, *stay@brablochhotel.co.uk*; ⑤), is the nicest option. **B&Bs** include *Ardgowan House*, 92 Renfrew Rd (☎0141/889 4763; ②), and *Greenlaw*, 12 Greenlaw Drive, off the Glasgow road (☎0141/889 5359; ①). Lunchtime and early-evening bar **meals**, together with a reasonably convivial atmosphere, can be found in *Gabriel's Bar* at 33 Gauze St, near the abbey, and *O'Neills'*, a large Irish theme pub on New Street. Close by, the Paisley Arts

Centre has a small bar with seating outside, while the *Last Post* pub in the old Post Office building in County Square is lively in the evenings, and serves a range of bar meals.

From Port Glasgow to Wemyss Bay

PORT GLASGOW is the first of a string of unprepossessing towns that sprawl along the southern coast of the Firth of Clyde. A small fishing village until 1688, when the burghers of Glasgow bought it and developed it as their main harbour, it's a grim place, with nothing to detain you. The train line splits here, one branch heading west along the industrialized coast to Greenock and Gourock and the other heading inland before curving round to the ferry port at Wemyss Bay. You can get hourly City Link buses to Greenock and Gourock from Buchanan Street bus station.

Greenock and Gourock
GREENOCK was the site of the first dock on the Clyde, founded in 1711, and the community has grown on the back of shipping ever since. Despite its ranks of anonymous tower blocks and sterile shopping centres, the town still retains a few features of interest.

From the Central train station, it's a short walk down the hill to **Cathcart Square**, where an exuberant 245-foot Victorian tower looms high over the elegant Council House. Directly opposite, in rather shabbier surroundings, lies the **tourist office** (Mon–Fri 8.45am–4.45pm, Sat 9.30am–12.30pm; ☎01475/722007) for both Greenock and Gourock. On the dockside, reached by crossing the dual carriageway behind the square, the Neoclassical **Custom House** has an informative museum (Mon–Fri 10am–4pm; free) featuring the work of the Customs and Excise departments, with a display on illicit whisky distilleries and a computer game in which you search a ship for contraband. From the dock in front, tens of thousands of nineteenth-century emigrants departed for the New World. On a happier note, **Clyde Marine Cruises** (May–Sept; ☎01475/721281) operates from Princes Pier, past the Tesco superstore, with daily sailings to Dunoon, Largs, Rothesay, Millport and Tighnabruaich, allowing you to admire stunning scenery and explore local towns. If you make arrangements beforehand, they offer a free pick-up service from the train or bus station.

Greenock's town centre has been disfigured by astonishingly unsympathetic developments. More attractive, and indicative of the town's wealthy past, is the western side of town, with its mock-Baronial houses, graceful churches and quiet, tree-lined avenues. This area can be reached either via Greenock West station, or by taking a ten-minute walk up the High Street from the Council House. A hundred yards from the well-proportioned **George Square**, close to Greenock West station, the **McLean Museum and Art Gallery** in Union Street (Mon–Sat 10am–5pm; free) contains pictures and contemporary records of the life and achievements of Greenock-born James Watt, prominent eighteenth-century industrialist and pioneer of steam power, as well as featuring exhibits on the shipbuilding industry and other local trades. The upper gallery houses a curious exhibition that purports to show the district's internationalism through its trading links, with a random selection of oddments from, among others, Japan, Papua New Guinea, India, China and Egypt. The small art gallery on the ground floor contains work by Glasgow Boys Hornel and Guthrie plus Colourists Fergusson, Cadell and Peploe.

Accommodation is particularly scarce in Greenock, so it's advisable to book ahead. *The Tontine Hotel* in Ardgowan Square, a few minutes' walk west of the Art Gallery, is expensive, but provides a pleasant atmosphere for afternoon tea or an evening meal (☎01475/723316; ⑤); smaller and more intimate, though the rooms are large, the classical-style *Lindores Guest House* lies further west, at 61 Newark St (☎01475/783075; ②). The *James Watt Halls of Residence* (☎01475/731360; all-year) Customhouse Quay, offer clean and tidy single rooms with views across the water for £25 per person. *Morgan's* brasserie on West Blackhall Street, west of the shopping centre, serves a decent selection of soups, sandwiches and pasta dishes, while further west, *L'Arlecchino*, an Italian **restaurant**, is the best option for reasonably priced evening meals. In the town centre, on Cathcart Street, the old post office is now a popular bar, *The James Watt*, serving a wide range of beers and bar meals.

On the train line between Greenock and Gourock, **Fort Matilda** station perches below **Lyle Hill**, an invigorating 450-foot climb that is well worth the effort for the astounding views over the purple mountains of Argyll and the creeks and lochs spilling off the Firth of Clyde. West of here lies the dowdy old resort of **GOUROCK**, from where CalMac ferries (☎01475/650100 for enquiries, ☎0990/650000 for ticket sales) head across to Dunoon and Kilcreggan on the Cowal peninsula (see p.304). Generations of Glaswegians have holidayed here, but today the place is more or less a stopoff point for the ferry terminal. There's an enjoyable seafront **swimming pool** (May–Sept Mon–Fri 10am–8pm, Sat & Sun 10am–5pm; £1.80) with a spectacular backdrop of the Argyll mountains, which can be seen in their full glory from Tower Hill, reached from John Street, past the Health Centre. It's a steep climb but the view makes the effort worthwhile.

Wemyss Bay

The southern branch of the train line from Port Glasgow heads inland, clipping the edge of Greenock before curling around the mountains and moors, playing a flirtatious game of peek-a-boo with the Clyde estuary. The terminus station, at **WEMYSS BAY**, is a startling wrought-iron and glass reminder of the great glory days, when thousands of Glaswegians would alight for their steamer trip "doon the watter". Today, Wemyss Bay station is far quieter, as the ferries chug their way from its exit over to Rothesay, capital of the Island of Bute (see p.308).

Dumbarton

Founded in the fifth century, today the town of **DUMBARTON** is a brutal concrete sprawl, fulfilling every last cliché about postwar planning and architecture. Avoid the town itself – though Talking Heads fans might be interested to know that David Byrne, of big suits fame, was born here – and head one mile southeast to **Dumbarton Castle** (April–Sept Mon–Sat 9.30am–6pm, Sun 2–6pm; Oct–March Mon–Wed & Sat 9.30–4pm, Thurs 9.30am–1pm, Sun 2–4pm; £1.50), sitting atop a twin plug of volcanic rock overlooking the Clyde. It is best reached from Dumbarton East train station, from where you turn right and take the second left, Victoria Street, continuing straight for just over half a mile. As a natural site, Dumbarton Rock could not be bettered – surrounded by water on three sides and with commanding views. First founded as a Roman fort, the structure was expanded in the fifth century by the Damnonii tribe, and remained Strathclyde's capital until its absorption into the greater kingdom of Scotland in 1034. The castle then became a royal seat, from which Mary, Queen of Scots sailed for France to marry Henri II's son in 1548, and to which she was attempting to escape when she and her troops were defeated twenty years later at the Battle of Langside. Since the 1600s, the castle has been used as a garrison and artillery fortress to guard the approaches to Glasgow – most of the current buildings date from this period.

The solid eighteenth-century Governor's House lies at the base of the rock, from where you enter the castle complex proper by climbing the steep steps up into the narrow cleft between the two rocks, crowned by the oldest remaining structure in the complex, a fourteenth-century portcullis arch. Vertiginous steps ascend to each peak – to see both you must climb more than five hundred steps. The eastern rock is the highest, with a windy summit that affords excellent views over to the lakes, rivers and mountains beyond Dumbarton town.

If you have a particular interest in shipbuilding, you may want to visit the **Denny Tank** (Mon–Sat 10am–4pm; £1.50), the world's oldest working ship-model experiment tank: at around 110yd long, it's used to test scale models of ships prior to the expensive business of construction. Explanatory panels cover the whole process from wax modelling to the experiments themselves. It is on Castle Street, three streets west of Victoria Street.

Practicalities

Regular **trains** run from Glasgow's Queen Street station to Dumbarton East and Dumbarton Central stations. Take the first stop for access to the castle and accommodation. The **tourist office** (daily: Nov–April 10am–4pm; May & Oct 10am–5pm; June & Sept 10am–6pm; July & Aug 10am–7pm; ☎01389/742306) is situated out of town on the A82 and mainly caters for the vast number of car-bound tourists on their way to the Highlands. Likewise, most **accommodation** is clustered around this artery of traffic and the busy Glasgow Road, that leads into Dumbarton proper. The *Dumbuck House Hotel*, Glasgow Road (☎01389/734336; ⑤), offers spacious and comfortable rooms, while *Kilmalid House*, 17 Glenpath, is a quiet **B&B** (☎01389/732030; ①), off Barnhill Road and opposite the conventional *Abbotsford Hotel*. To reach this area from Dumbarton East train station, turn left at the exit and continue until you reach Greenhead Road, which will take you straight up to the A82. Closer to Dumbarton Central, Mrs Valentine (☎01389/732819; ①), at 87 Glasgow Rd, also offers inexpensive B&B. There is the usual selection of takeaways focused on the High Street in the centre of town or, for decent **pub food** during the day, try the *Burgh Bar* on the High Street.

The Clyde valley

The landscape becomes more rural as the River Clyde heads east out of Glasgow, passing the last of a string of shipbuilding yards in Rutherglen, and criss-crossing the M74 as both river and road head southeast into Lanarkshire. Less than ten miles from central Glasgow, **Bothwell Castle** lies about a mile northeast from the **Blantyre** tenement, in which the explorer David Livingstone was born. Two miles further upstream, the valley's largest settlements, **Motherwell** and **Hamilton**, straddle either side of the river and motorway. Motherwell is a depressed town, hard-hit by the closure of its steel works in 1992 and, although Hamilton fancies itself as more upscale, there is little for the visitor in either place. Sandwiched between the two, the enormous **Strathclyde Country Park** features a glassy 200-acre man-made loch, the focus of many sports and outdoor pursuits.

From here the river winds through lush market gardens and orchards that bloom far below the austere lines of **Craignethan Castle**, before passing beneath the sturdy little town of **Lanark**, probably the best base from which to explore the valley. **New Lanark**, on the river bank, is a remarkable planned village dreamed up by eighteenth-century industrialists, David Dale and his son-in-law, Robert Owen. Travel around the area is relatively simple, with good train and bus services. Frequent low-level trains leave Central station for Lanark via Motherwell and Hamilton via Blantyre. At Buchanan Street bus station, First Bus operates a regular service to Hamilton, buses #255, #263 or #267, as well as an express bus, #X1; for Blantyre take #263 and #267; and for Bothwell, #255 or services #55, #61, #62 operated Coakley Bus Company. To Lanark, it's best to take the train, as there's only a very limited commuter bus service.

From Hamilton to Craignethan Castle

Although the town of **HAMILTON** itself has little to offer the visitor, it lies under the watchful gaze of an old hunting lodge built in 1732 for the aristocratic Hamilton family. Designed by Scots architect William Adam, this building is the centrepiece of Chatelherault Park (daily: lodge 10am–4.30pm, park until 9pm; free), a pleasant area with walks that follow the Avon water and wind through the surrounding countryside, past the ruins of Cadzow Castle and some 600-year-old oaks. To reach the park, take bus #253 or #254 from Hamilton Central train station, both of which stop at the entrance.

BLANTYRE, now a colourless suburb of Hamilton, was a remote Clydeside hamlet when explorer and missionary David Livingstone was born there in 1813. From Blantyre station, a right turn brings you to a quiet country lane. The entire tenement block at the bottom of the lane, now painted a brilliant white, has been taken over by the **David Livingstone Centre** (Mon–Sat 10am–5.30pm, Sun 12.30–5.30pm; during winter hours may be reduced, phone ☎01698 823140 to check; NTS; £2.95), exploring his life from early years as a mill worker up until his death in 1873 when he was searching for the source of the River Nile. In 1813, the block consisted of 24 one-room tenements, each occupied by an entire family. Today the Livingstone family room shows the claustrophobic conditions under which he was brought up; all the others feature slightly defensive exhibitions on the missionary movement with tableaux of scenes from his life in Africa, including the famous meeting with Stanley. Unfortunately, due to vandalism, the thatched huts donated by the government of Malawi which housed changing exhibitions on African themes have had to be removed. Smaller exhibitions on Blantyre and the Clyde valley area are now held inside the main "Africa Pavilion" building.

A mile or so from Blantyre, **Bothwell Castle** (April–Sept daily 9.30am–6.30pm; Oct–March Sat–Wed 9.30am–4pm, Thurs 9.30am–12.30pm, Sun 2–4.30pm; HS; £1.80) is one of Scotland's most dramatic citadels, its great red sandstone bulk looming high above a loop in the river. The oldest section is the solid donjon, or circular tower, at the western end, built by the Moray family in the late 1200s to protect themselves against the English king Edward I during the Scottish wars of independence. Such was the might of the castle, Edward only finally succeeded in capturing it in September 1301 after ordering the construction and deployment of a massive siege engine, wheeled from Glasgow to Bothwell in order to lob huge stones at the castle walls. Over the next two centuries, the castle changed hands numerous times and was added to by each successive owner, with the last section, the Great Hall, in the grassy inner courtyard. Despite its jigsaw construction, today the overwhelming impression is of the almost impenetrable strength of the castle, its solid red towers – whose walls reach almost sixteen feet thick in places – standing firm centuries after their construction. **Bus** #255 from Glasgow to Hamilton will drop you off on the Bothwell Road, near the castle entrance. By car, it is best approached from the B7071 Bothwell–Uddingston road.

Once known as the "Steelopolis" of Scotland, the small town of **MOTHERWELL**, a few miles east of Blantyre, has little to offer except the informative **Motherwell Heritage Centre** (Mon–Wed & Fri–Sat 10am–5pm, Thurs 10am–7pm, Sun noon–5pm; free), looming above the station on the High Road. The entrance foyer holds changing exhibitions on local themes, whilst the **multimedia exhibition** takes you through the history of the town. Reconstructed streets, cinemas and exhibits document the lives of the local community, and the future of Motherwell is explored with optimism despite widespread unemployment. On the first floor the **local history lab** contains books, maps and photos of the area, as well as databases on Lanarkshire and Motherwell Football Club. From the top of the glass tower, there are spectacular views across Lanarkshire.

The section of the Clyde Valley southeast from Hamilton to Lanark has appropriately become known as "Greenhouse Glen", where the winding road, lined with small stone villages and inordinate numbers of garden centres, gives occasional glimpses of the river through the trees. Buses #17 and #217 from Hamilton and Lanark stop off at **CROSSFORD**, five miles short of Lanark, where the River Nethan forks off from the Clyde. From here you can either climb a difficult mile through the wooded Nethan valley up to the gaunt clifftop ruins of **Craignethan Castle** (April–Sept daily 9.30am–6.30pm; Oct & Nov Mon–Wed & Sat 9.30am–4.30pm, Thurs 9.30am–12.30pm, Sun 2–4.30pm; HS; £1.80), or, if driving, take the extremely tortuous three-mile signposted route. The last major castle to be built in Scotland, Craignethan was constructed by Sir James Hamilton of Finnart, Master of Works to James V, in 1530. Hamilton, inspired by new styles of artillery fortification in Italy, built a unique *caponier*, a dank vault wedged into the dry moat between the two sections of the castle. From here, defenders could spray the ditch with small-arms fire from behind the safety of walls five feet thick. It was from Craignethan, owned by loyalist James Hamilton, that Mary, Queen of Scots left on May 13, 1568, ultimately for defeat at Langside, followed by exile and imprisonment in England. The castle, like so many others in Scotland, is said to be inhabited by her ghost, as Craignethan was probably the last time she was ever amongst true friends. Whatever the truth, Craignethan does have a spooky quality about it, its stillness only interrupted by the shriek of circling crows. The most intact parts of the castle are the gloomy *caponier* and the musty cellars underneath the vast main tower, from which gun holders still protrude.

Lanark and New Lanark

The neat little market town of **LANARK** is an old and distinguished burgh, sitting in the purple hills high above the River Clyde, its rooftops and spires visible for miles around. Beyond the world's oldest bell, cast in 1130 and visible in the Georgian Church of St Nicholas, there's little to see in town and most people make their way to the village of **NEW LANARK**, a mile below the main town on Braxfield Road, whose importance as a centre of social and industrial innovation has recently been recognised by its nomination as a World Heritage Site.

Although New Lanark is served by an hourly bus from the train station, it's well worth the steep downhill walk to get there. The first sight of the village, hidden away down in the gorge, is unforgettable: large broken curving walls of honeyed warehouses and tenements, built in Palladian style, lined up along the turbulent river's edge. The community was founded by David Dale and Richard Arkwright in 1785 to harness the power of the Clyde waterfalls in their cotton-spinning industry, but it was Dale's son-in-law, Robert Owen, who revolutionized the social side of the experiment in 1798, creating a "village of unity". Believing the welfare of the workers to be crucial to industrial success, Owen built adult educational facilities, the world's first day nursery and playground, and schools in which dancing and music were obligatory and there was no punishment or reward.

While you're free to wander around the village, to get into any of the exhibitions (all open daily 11am–5pm) you need to get hold of a passport ticket (£3.75, though family tickets are available, as is one including the return train and bus trip from Glasgow). The Neoclassical building at the very heart of the village was opened by Owen in 1816 under the utopian title of **The Institute for the Formation of Character**. With a library, chapel and dance hall, the Institute became the main focus of the community, and today you can see an introductory video about New Lanark and its founders in the spacious congregational hall. Of the three vast old mill buildings open to visitors, one houses the **Annie McLeod Experience**, where a chair lift whisks visitors through a social history of life here from the imaginary perspective of a young mill girl. With a plethora of special effects – low light diffused through aromatic fog, holograms and lasers – the ten-minute journey portrays an honest and unsentimental picture of village life. Other exhibits in the mills include huge spinning wheels and a massive steam engine.

The village itself is just as fascinating: everything, from the co-operative store to the workers' tenements and workshops, was built in an attempt to prove that industrialism need not be unaesthetic. You can wander through the 1920s shop, and find out how the workers lived from the 1820s to the 1920s in the **New Buildings**, then poke around the domestic kitchen, study and living areas of **Robert Owen's House**. Situated in the Old Dyeworks, **The Scottish Wildlife Trust Visitor Centre** (Feb, March & Oct–Dec Sat & Sun 1–5pm; April–Sept Mon–Fri 11am–5pm, Sat & Sun 1–5pm; £1) provides information about the history and wildlife of the area. Friendly rangers give details of the walks around the tree-lined valley; the longest is an eight-mile round-trip. Further on, beyond the visitor centre, a path along the Clyde leads you past the small falls of green water on which the Lanark project was first founded, and the Bonnington hydroelectric station to the major **Falls of The Clyde**, where at the stunning tree-fringed **Cora Linn**, the river plunges 90ft in three tumultuous stages. It is a marker point for the Clyde Walkway, a path that follows the river from Glasgow Green to this valley forest.

Practicalities

Lanark is the terminus on the **train** line from Glasgow Central station. The town's **tourist office** (May–Sept Mon–Sat 10am–6pm, Sun noon–5pm; Oct–April Mon–Sat 10am–5pm; ☎01555/661661) is housed in a circular building in the Horsemarket, next to Somerfields supermarket, 100yd west of the station.

By far the most original **accommodation** options in the area, at both ends of the market, make use of reconstructed mill buildings in New Lanark: the **youth hostel** (☎01555/666710) has sixteen four-bed rooms in the cutely named Wee Row on Rosedale Street, and is an excellent spot for enjoying the surrounding countryside in peace, while the *New Lanark Mill Hotel* (☎01555/6672000, *hotel@newlanark.org*; ④) is a four-star hotel with good views and lots of character, as well as a brasserie serving some tasty dishes.

Elsewhere, accommodation varies from the spectacular wooded surroundings of the *Cartland Bridge Hotel* on the town's edge just off the A73 Glasgow Road (☎01555/664426; ⑤), to faintly seedy town-centre pubs such as the *Royal Oak*, opposite the train station at 39 Bannatyne St (☎01555/665895; ②). The best of the **B&Bs** are a little out of town; try Mrs Somerville at Covanhill Farm (☎01555/811219; ①), or Mrs Findlater at Jerviswood Mains Farm (☎01555/663987; ①). There are plenty of cheap **cafés** and takeaways on High Street, and the *Courtyard Restaurant*, at 3 Castlegate, has a quiet patio to enjoy lunch away from the road. There are some more pricey Indian and Italian **restaurants** along Wellgate, while the far less pretentious *Crown Tavern*, a quiet drinking haunt in Hope Street, does reasonable food until 9.30pm. Other good local pubs include the *Horse and Jockey* in High Street and the *Wallace Cave* in Bloomgate. The current favourite amongst young people is the *Woodpecker Inn*, tucked behind High Street off the tiny Wide Close alley.

travel details

Trains

Glasgow Central to: Ardrossan (every 30min; 45min); Ayr (every 30min; 50min); Birmingham (5 daily; 3hr 50min); Blantyre (every 30min; 20min); Carlisle (hourly; 2hr 25min); Crewe (6 daily; 3hr 35min); Dumbarton (every 20min; 25min); East Kilbride (Mon–Sat every 30min; 30min); Gourock (every 30min; 47min); Greenock (every 30min; 40min); Hamilton (every 30min; 25min); Kilmarnock (hourly; 40min); Lanark (Mon–Sat hourly; 50min); Largs (hourly; 1hr); London (10 daily; 5hr 45min); Manchester (1 daily; 3hr 50min); Motherwell (every 20min; 30min); Newcastle-upon-Tyne (8 daily; 2hr 30min); Paisley (every 15min; 10min); Port Glasgow (every 15min; 30min); Queen's Park (every 15min; 6min); Rutherglen (every 20min; 10min); Stranraer (4 daily; 2hr 10min); Wemyss Bay (hourly; 55min); York (7 daily; 3hr 30min).

Glasgow Queen Street to: Aberdeen (hourly; 2hr 35min); Aviemore (3 daily; 2hr 40min); Balloch (Mon–Sat every 30min; 45min); Dundee (hourly; 1hr 20min); Edinburgh (every 15min; 50min); Fort William (3 daily; 3hr 40min); Helensburgh (every 30min; 45min); Inverness (3 daily; 3hr 25min); Mallaig (3 daily; 5hr 15min); Milngavie (Mon–Sat every 30min; 22min); Oban (3 daily; 3hr); Perth (hourly; 1hr); Springburn (Mon–Sat every 30min; 13min); Stirling (hourly; 30min).

Buses

Glasgow to: Aberdeen (20 daily; 4hr 15min); Aviemore (hourly; 3hr 30min); Campbeltown (4 daily; 4hr 20min); Dundee (hourly; 2hr 15min); Edinburgh (every 15min; 1hr 15min); Fort William (4 daily; 3hr); Glen Coe (4 daily; 2hr 30min); Inverness (hourly; 4–5hr); Kyle of Lochalsh (3 daily; 5hr); Lochgilphead (3 daily; 2hr 40min); Loch Lomond (hourly; 45min); London (5 daily; 7hr 30min); Newcastle-upon-Tyne (2 daily; 4hr); Oban (4 daily; 3hr); Perth (hourly; 1hr 35min); Pitlochry (hourly; 2hr 20min); Portree (3 daily; 6hr); Stirling (hourly; 45min); York (1 daily; 6hr 30min).

Flights

Glasgow to: Aberdeen (2 daily; 50min); Birmingham (Mon–Fri 11 daily, Sat & Sun 6 daily; 1hr); Inverness (Mon–Fri 4 daily; 55min); Islay (Mon–Fri 2 daily; 40min); London Heathrow (Mon–Fri 20 daily, Sat & Sun 12 daily; 1hr 30min); London Gatwick (Mon–Fri 6 daily, Sat & Sun 4 daily; 1hr 30min); London Stansted (Mon–Fri 4 daily, Sat 1 daily, Sun 4 daily; 1hr 30min); Manchester (Mon–Fri 10 daily, Sat 3 daily, Sun 2 daily; 1hr); Shetland (Mon–Fri 3 daily Sat & Sun 1 daily; 2hr 20min); Stornaway (Mon–Fri 2 daily, Sat 1 daily; 1hr).

CHAPTER FOUR

CENTRAL SCOTLAND

Within easy reach of Edinburgh and Glasgow, **central Scotland** is a much-visited area, not least for its spectacular and varied countryside, ranging from the picture-postcard beauty of the Central Lowlands to the wilder, more challenging terrain of the Highlands, which officially begin here. The **Highland Boundary Fault**, the dramatic physical divide running southwest to northeast across the region, has rendered central Scotland – from medieval to modern times – the main stage for some of the most important events in Scottish history. Today the landscape is not only littered with remnants of the past – well-preserved medieval towns and castles, royal residences and battle sites – but also coloured by the many romantic myths and legends that have grown up around it.

At the heart of the **Central Lowlands**, above the industrial belt around Falkirk and Grangemouth, is venerable **Stirling**, its imposing castle perched high above the town. Historically one of the most important bridging points across the River Forth, it was the site of two of the most famous battles fought under Robert the Bruce during the **Wars of Independence** (1296–1328). To the west and north of Stirling the magnificent scenery centres on the fabled mountains, glens, lochs and forests of the **Trossachs**, a unique and beautiful area of high peaks and steep-sided glens that stretches west from **Callander** to the eastern banks of Loch Lomond. The geography and history of the area caught the imagination of **Sir Walter Scott**, who took so much delight in the tales of local clansman **Rob Roy** MacGregor, the notorious seventeenth-century outlaw, that he set them down in his novel of the same name. Visitors flocked to the Trossachs and, according to one contemporaneous account, after Scott's *Lady of the Lake* was published in 1810, the number of carriages passing Loch Katrine rose from 50 the previous year to 270. Thanks to Scott and to William and Dorothy Wordsworth's effusive praise, Queen Victoria decided to visit, placing the area firmly on the tourist map. Today, however, the trappings of tourism – evident in twee shops and tearooms in every small town – don't impinge too much on the experience.

Lying to the east of the Central Lowlands is **Fife**, the only one of Scotland's seven original Pictish kingdoms to survive relatively intact. Neither Norse nor Norman influence found its way to this independent corner, and nine and a half centuries later, when the government at Westminster redrew local boundaries in 1975 and again in 1995, the Fifers stuck to their guns and successfully opposed any changes. Here you'll find coastal fishing villages and sandy beaches and the self-assured town of **St Andrews**, inextricably linked in the public consciousness with **golf**.

North of St Andrews on the west bank of the River Tay is the ancient town of **Perth**, surrounded by beautiful rugged country. At nearby **Scone**, Kenneth Macalpine established the capital of the kingdom of the Scots and the Picts in 846. When this settlement was washed away by floods in 1210, William the Lion founded Perth as a royal burgh and it stood as Scotland's capital until 1452. The four great monasteries of Perth reflected the town's political and religious importance, but were all destroyed during the Reformation following a sermon by John Knox at St John's Church. North of Perth, the Highlands begin in earnest. From **Loch Tay** onwards, beyond the agreeable town of **Aberfeldy**, the countryside becomes more sparsely populated and more spectacular, with the **Grampian Mountains** to the east offering wonderful walks,

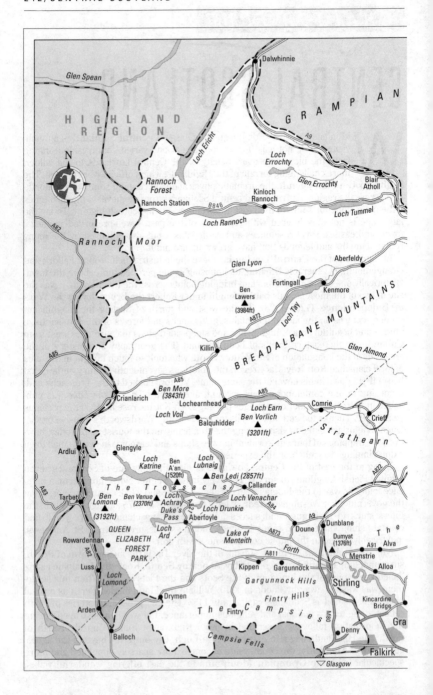

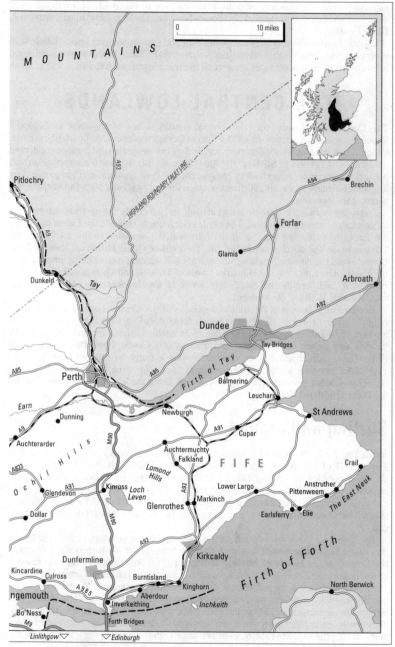

0   10 miles

M O U N T A I N S

HIGHLAND BOUNDARY FAULT LINE

Pitlochry

A93

A9

A94   Brechin

Dunkeld   *Tay*   Forfar

Glamis

Arbroath

A92

Perth   Dundee

Tay Bridges

Firth of Tay   Balmerino

A85   Leuchars

Earn   A85   Newburgh   St Andrews

Dunning   A91   Cupar

Auchterarder   M90   Auchtermuchty

Ochil Hills   Falkland   F I F E   Crail

A823   *Lomond Hills*   A92   Anstruther

Glendevon   A91   Kinross   Lower Largo   Pittenweem

Dollar   *Loch Leven*   Markinch   *The East Neuk*

Glenrothes   Earlsferry   Elie

M90

A92

Dunfermline   Kirkcaldy   *Firth of Forth*

Kincardine   Culross   Burntisland

ngemouth   A985   Aberdour   Kinghorn   North Berwick

Bo'Ness   Inverkeithing   *Inchkeith*

M9   Forth Bridges

▽ *Linlithgow*   ▽ *Edinburgh*

© Crown copyright

especially around **Pitlochry**, and the wild expanses of **Rannoch Moor** to the west. This northerly part of the region also boasts Scotland's most popular tourist attraction, **Blair Castle**.

Central Scotland is easy to **get around**. Scotland's two main train lines – Glasgow to Inverness and Edinburgh to Aberdeen – cut straight through the region, and good intercity and local bus services connect all the main towns and villages.

THE CENTRAL LOWLANDS

The **Central Lowlands** were, for several centuries, one of the most strategically important areas in Scotland. In 1250, a map of Britain was compiled by Matthew Paris, a monk of St Albans, which depicted Scotland as two separate land masses connected only by the thin band of **Stirling Bridge**. Although this figurative interpretation was not strictly accurate, nevertheless lying at the heart of Scotland and surrounded by inhospitable marshy terrain, Stirling was once the only gateway from the north to the south of the country.

Today the town is a tourist attraction in itself, its fine **castle** the perfect vantage point to look far out across the region. The castle rock plunges down to the **Carse of Forth**, the flat plain extending west, with the little-visited **Campsies** to the south and the **Trossachs** to the north. East of the city, the gentler **Ochil Hills** run towards Loch Leven. From the castle's heights you can trace the winding course of the once naviga-ble **Forth River**, linking the industrial towns of **Falkirk** and **Grangemouth** with the rural west, and identify the great blunt tower of **Cambuskenneth Abbey** and the unmistakable **Wallace Monument**.

Alongside the beauty of the hills and villages of the Central Lowlands, there are a range of other diversions all within an hour's drive of Stirling, from the wonderful island monastery of **Inchmahome** in the Lake of Menteith in the Trossachs, to the Forth Valley's airy palace of **Linlithgow** and atmospheric **Castle Campbell** in the Ochil Hills. These attractions can be combined with a range of outdoor activities; the Trossachs provide great walking country, and the area is traversed by the **Glasgow–Loch Lomond–Killin cycleway** and, along the length of Loch Lomond, by the **West Highland Way**.

Stirling and around

Straddling the River Forth a few miles upstream from the estuary at Kincardine, at first glance **STIRLING** appears like a smaller version of Edinburgh. With its crag-top cas-tle, steep, cobbled streets and mixed community of locals and students, it's an appeal-ing place, though it lacks the cosmopolitan edge of Edinburgh or Glasgow. It's historic, due to its former importance as a much coveted river crossing, but – geographically trapped between Scotland's two main cities – Stirling remains at heart decidedly provin-cial.

The town was the scene of some of the most significant developments in the evolu-tion of the Scottish nation. It was here that the Scots under William Wallace defeated the English at the **Battle of Stirling Bridge** in 1297, only to fight – and win again – under Robert the Bruce just a couple of miles away at the **Battle of Bannockburn** in 1314. Stirling enjoyed its golden age in the fifteenth to seventeenth centuries, most notably when its castle was the favoured residence of the Stuart monarchy and the set-ting for the coronation in 1543 of the young Mary, future Queen of Scots. By the early eighteenth century the town was again besieged, its location being of strategic impor-tance during the Jacobite rebellions of 1715 and 1745.

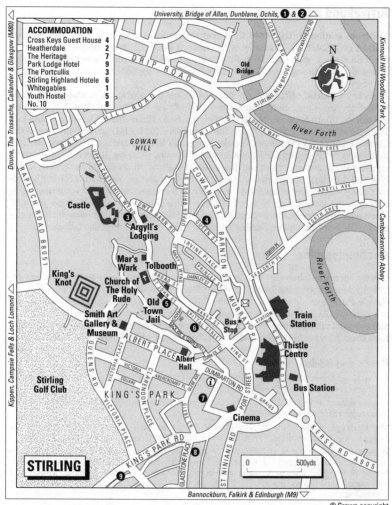

STIRLING

ACCOMMODATION
Cross Keys Guest House	4
Heatherdale	2
The Heritage	7
Park Lodge Hotel	9
The Portcullis	3
Stirling Highland Hotele	6
Whitegables	1
Youth Hostel	5
No. 10	8

© Crown copyright

Today Stirling is known for its **Castle** – just as beautiful as its Edinburgh counterpart – and the lofty **Wallace Monument**, a mammoth Victorian monolith high on Abbey Craig to the northeast. The **University**, also, has helped to maintain the town's profile.

Stirling is at its liveliest during the summer, with buskers and street artists jostling for performing space in the pedestrianized centre. If you get decent weather – which isn't all that uncommon despite the proliferation of surrounding hills – there's very much a holiday air about the place, with kids rushing around the castle ramparts, backpackers struggling up the steep hill to the youth hostel, and students, many of whom choose to stay here over the summer, spilling out of the cafés.

Arrival and information

The **train station** (☎0345/484950) is near the centre of town on Station Road; the **bus station** (☎01324/613777) nearby on Goosecroft Road. To reach the town centre from the train station, walk up Station Road and turn left at the mini-roundabout; from the bus station cut through the Thistle Shopping Centre opposite to reach the main drag, Port Street.

Stirling's **tourist office** is in the heart of the town centre at 41 Dumbarton Rd (June Mon–Sat 9am–6pm, Sun 10am–4pm; July & Aug Mon–Sat 9am–7.30pm, Sun 9.30am–6.30pm; Sept Mon–Sat 9am–6pm, Sun 10am–4pm; Oct–May Mon–Sat 10am–5pm; ☎01786/475019), and is the main office for Loch Lomond, Stirling and the Trossachs, with a wide range of books, maps and leaflets, and a free accommodation-booking service. Further information about the town can be gleaned from personal stereo guides, available from the Stags Audio Walk shop, 24 Broad St (£2.50), which cover all the major attractions, spiced up with ghost stories. Because of Stirling's compact size – barely five miles from the centre to the outermost fringes – sightseeing is best done on foot, though to avoid the steep hills you can take the "hop on, hop off" **Heritage Bus** service (June–Sept 10am–5pm; £6), whose circular route includes the castle, Wallace Monument, Stirling University, and the bus and train stations.

Accommodation

If you're in Stirling between May and October, you'll need to book your **accommodation** by lunchtime at the latest, or you're likely to be stranded. A good option is the **King's Park** area – immediately south of the tourist office – an opulent Victorian suburb built for Glasgow industrialists and merchants and composed of tree-lined avenues and splendid villas, some wonderfully Italianate with towers and balconies. There is a high concentration of **B&Bs** on Causewayhead Road which leads to the University.

Hotels and B&Bs

Cross Keys Guest House, 3 Queen St (☎01786/448435). Comfortable accommodation above a traditional town centre pub. Close to the attractions. ①.

Heatherdale, 2 Dumyat Rd (☎01786/473574). Small family-run B&B located near the Wallace Monument, castle and university. ②.

The Heritage, 16 Allan Park (☎01786/473660). On the northern edge of King's Park, the pretty rooms look up at the castle, and there's a good Scottish/French restaurant too (see p.250). ③.

Highland Hotel, Spittal St (☎01786/272727, *andrews@scottishhighlandhotels.co.uk*). Upmarket if rather pretentiously genteel hotel in an handsome Victorian Gothic building that once housed Stirling High School. It features comfortable rooms, good leisure facilities – including a pretty pool with saunas – and two restaurants. The location, in the old town and just 500 yards from the castle, is excellent. ⑦.

ACCOMMODATION PRICE CODES

Throughout this book, accommodation **prices** have been graded with the codes below, according to the cost of the least expensive double room in high season. Price codes are not given for campsites, most of which charge under £10 per person. Almost all hostels charge less than £10 a night for a bed – the few exceptions to this rule have the prices quoted in the text. For a full account of the accommodation price codes, see p.31.

① under £40	④ £60–70	⑦ £110–150
② £40–50	⑤ £70–90	⑧ £150–200
③ £50–60	⑥ £90–110	⑨ £200 and over

No. 10, 10 Gladstone Place (☎01786/472681). Modernized Victorian home providing friendly and pleasant B&B accommodation. ②.

Park Lodge Hotel, 32 Park Terrace (☎01786/474862). Magnificently sited and luxurious, overlooking the park and castle and with a *haute cuisine* restaurant. ⑤.

Portcullis, Castle Wynd (☎01786/472290). Located in an imposing two-hundred-year-old building that's recently been refurbished, and is adjacent to the castle at the top of the town. ⑤.

Whitegables, 112 Causewayhead Rd (☎01786/479838). A friendly B&B with TVs in all the rooms and excellent breakfasts. ②.

Youth hostel, campsite and campus accommodation

At the top of the town (a strenuous trek with a backpack), the cheapest option is the **youth hostel** in a recently converted church on St John Street (☎01786/473442). All rooms have showers and toilets en suite, and continental breakfast is included; the high-season price is £11.95 per person.

If you prefer to stay out of town, try the **campus accommodation** at Stirling University (☎01786/467141; ③; June–Aug), a couple of miles north of the town centre. Regular buses (#53 and #58) leave from Murray Place at the end of the main street (last services around 10.45pm). You can also rent Scandinavian-style **chalets** in the University's landscaped grounds (6 people; around £340 per week; June–Aug). Also on campus is the new Stirling Management Centre (☎01786/451666; ⑦; open year round), with luxurious en-suite rooms looking out at the Wallace Monument. There's a **campsite**, the *Witches Craig* at Blairlogie, three miles east of the town off the A91 road to St Andrews (☎01786/474947; April–Oct), which has the distinction of holding the 1997 Loo of the Year award.

The Town

Stirling evolved from the top down, starting with its castle and gradually spreading south and east onto the low-lying flood plain. At the centre of the original **Old Town**, Broad Street was the main thoroughfare, with St John Street running more or less parallel, and St Mary's Wynd forming part of the original route to Stirling Bridge below. In the eighteenth and nineteenth centuries, as the threat of attack decreased, the centre of commercial life crept down towards the River Forth, with the modern town growing on the edge of the plain over which the castle has traditionally stood guard.

Stirling Castle

Stirling Castle (daily: April–Sept 9.30am–6.30pm; Oct–March 9.30am–5pm; HS; £5 including entry to Argyll's Lodging) must have presented would-be invaders with a formidable challenge. Its impregnability is most daunting when you approach the town from the west, from where the sheer, 250ft drop down the side of the crag is most obvious. The rock was first fortified during the Iron Age, though what you see now dates largely from the fifteenth and sixteenth centuries. The castle is presently undergoing a massive restoration scheme (due to be completed in 2001), and parts of it may be inaccessible when you visit.

The **visitor centre** (same times as castle) on the esplanade shows an introductory film giving a potted history of the castle, but the best place to get an impression of its gradual expansion is in the courtyard known as the **Upper Square**. Here you can see the magnificent **Great Hall** (1501–3) which, with its lofty dimensions and huge fireplaces, is perhaps the finest medieval secular building in Scotland. The exterior of the **Palace** (1540–42) is richly decorated with grotesque carved figures and Renaissance sculpture, including, in the left-hand corner, the glaring bearded figure of James V in the dress of a commoner. Inside in the royal apartments are the **Stirling Heads**, 56 elegantly carved oak medallions, which once comprised the ceiling of the Presence Chamber, where visitors were presented to royalty. Otherwise the royal apartments are bare, their emptiness emphasizing the fine dimensions and wonderful views. The **Chapel Royal** (1594) was built by James VI for the baptism of his son, and replaced an earlier chapel, not deemed sufficiently impressive. The interior is lovely, with a seventeenth-century fresco of elaborate scrolls and patterns.

The castle also houses the impressive Argyll and Sutherland Highlanders **museum**, with its collection of well-polished silver and memorabilia, including a seemingly endless display of Victoria Crosses won by the regiment. The restored castle **kitchens**, complete with regulation unconvincing life-size figures, re-creates the preparations for the spectacular Renaissance banquet given by Mary, Queen of Scots for the baptism of the future James VI. As well as an audiovisual display describing how delicacies for the feast were procured and an abundance of stuffed animals in various stages of preparation (who, we are assured, died natural deaths), the kitchens feature *faux* recipe books with such delights as sugar wineglasses, golden steamed custard and dressed peacock.

From the **Douglas Gardens** you can see the surprisingly small window from which the eighth Earl of Douglas, suspected of treachery, was thrown by James II in 1452. There is a bird's-eye view down to the **King's Knot**, a series of grassed octagonal mounds which in the seventeenth century were planted with box trees and ornamental hedges.

The Old Town

Leaving the castle, head downhill into the old centre of Stirling, fortified behind the massive, whinstone boulders of the **town walls**, built in the mid-sixteenth century and intended to ward off the advances of Henry VIII, who had set his sights on the young Mary as a wife for his son, Edward. The walls now constitute some of the best-preserved town defences in Scotland, and can be traced by following the path known as **Back Walk**. This circular walkway was built in the eighteenth century and in the upper reaches encircles the castle, taut along the edge of the crag, offering panoramic views of the surrounding countryside.

Five minutes' walk down the hill from the castle's visitor centre, you'll find **Argyll's Lodging** (daily: April–Sept 9.30am–6.30pm; Oct–March 9.30am–5pm; HS; £2.80), a romantic Renaissance mansion built by Sir William Alexander of Menstrie. Inside, an informative exhibition takes you through the history of the building in its various incarnations, from its period as the home of the first Earl of Stirling, Sir William Alexander, and the ninth Earl of Argyll amongst others, to its later uses as military hospital and youth hostel. The oldest part of the building, marked by low ceilings and tiny windows, is the Great Kitchen, whose enormous fireplace comes complete with a special recess for salt, while the Drawing Room, hung with lavishly decorated purple tapestries, contains the ninth earl's imposing chair of state. An adjoining smaller room for his wife, Anna, contains her personal chamber pot, an ornate affair in purple.

Further down Castle Wynd at the top of Broad Street, a richly decorated facade hides the dilapidated **Mar's Wark**, a would-be palace which the first Earl of Mar, Regent of Scotland and hereditary Keeper of Stirling Castle, started in 1570. His dream house was never to be realized, however, for he died two years later and what had been built was left to ruin, its degeneration speeded up by extensive damage during the 1745 Jacobite Rebellion. Behind here is the **Church of the Holy Rude** (May–Sept Mon–Fri 10am–5pm; Sat times vary; Sunday service), a fine medieval structure, the oldest parts of which, including the impressive oak hammerbeam roof, date from the early fifteenth century. Go in during the day and imagine the ceremony that was held here in 1567 for the coronation of the infant James VI – later the first monarch of the United Kingdom – and come back in the evening to the atmospheric graveyard, from where you can watch the sun set. Just south of the church on the edge of the crag, the grand E-shaped **John Cowane's Hospital** was built as a 1649 almshouse for "decayed [unsuccessful] members of the Guild of Merchants". Above the entrance, John Cowane, the wealthy merchant who founded the hospital, is commemorated in a statue which, it is said, comes alive at Hogmanay.

A short walk down St John Street, a sweeping driveway leads up to the impressive **Old Town Jail** (April–Sept daily 9.30am–6pm; daily Oct–March 9.30am–4pm; guided tours every 30min; £2.75), a formidable building rescued from dereliction in 1992 and superbly refurbished. Tours are brought to life by enthusiastic actors who change costumes and character a number of times, and there's a working example of the dreaded crank, a lever which prisoners had to turn 14,400 times per day for punishment. Take the glass lift up to the prison roof to admire spectacular views across Stirling and the Forth Valley.

Back on the ground, **Broad Street** was the site of the marketplace and centre of the medieval town. Many of its buildings have been restored in recent years, and preservation work continues. Down here, past the **Mercat Cross** (the unicorn on top is known, inexplicably, as "the puggy"), the **Tolbooth**, sandwiched between Broad and St John streets (with the entrance on Broad Street), was built in 1705 by Sir William Bruce, who designed the Palace of Holyroodhouse in Edinburgh. It was used as both a courthouse and, after 1809, a prison, from where the unfortunate were led to execution in the street outside. **Darnley's House**, at the bottom of Broad Street, was where Mary, Queen of Scots' husband is believed to have lodged while she lorded it up in the castle; it now houses a coffee shop (see below).

The Lower Town

The further downhill you go in Stirling's Lower Town, the more recent the buildings become. Follow St John Street into Spittal Street, and then on down into King Street, where austere Victorian facades block the sun from the cobbled road. Stirling's main **shopping** area is down here, along Port Street and Murray Place, while the **Smith Art Gallery and Museum** (Tues–Sat 10.30am–5pm, Sun 2–5pm; free) is a short walk west up Dumbarton Road. Founded in 1874 with a legacy from local painter and collector Thomas Stuart Smith, it houses a permanent exhibition relating the history of Stirling, and a range of changing displays of arts and crafts, contemporary art and photography.

The fifteenth-century **Old Bridge** over the Forth lies to the north on the edge of the town centre (a 20min walk from Murray Place). Although once the most important river crossing in Scotland – the lowest bridging point on the Forth until the new bridge was built in 1831 – it now stands virtually forgotten, an almost incidental reminder of Stirling's former importance. An earlier, wooden **bridge** nearby was the focus of the Battle of Stirling Bridge in 1297, where William Wallace defeated the English.

Eating

The elegant three-storey *Darnley Coffee House* on Bow Street (the continuation of Broad Street) serves reasonably priced lunches and teas, in an impressive barrel-vaulted interior, while on Albert Place, the *Café Albert* lodged in the Victorian grandeur of *Albert Hall*, is a good, well-priced place to lunch. More upmarket is *Hermann's* at 32 St John St (☎01786/450632), with its handsomely austere interior; the downstairs brasserie is open at lunchtime and their Austrian/Scottish evening main courses start at £8. *Italia Nostra*, close by at 25 Baker St (☎01786/473208), serves good well-priced Italian food and is very lively, especially at weekends, while *The Heritage*, 16 Allan Park

(☎01786/473660), has established a good reputation for French/Scottish cuisine, served up in a sumptuous dining room in an elegant Georgian town house that's also a hotel. At the *East India Club*, 7 Viewfield Place, a five-minute walk from the centre (☎01786/471330), you can enjoy fabulous Indian food, "Raj" decor, and the friendliest service in town – their buffet (Sun–Thurs) costs around £10 per person for three courses and as much as you can eat. Slightly more expensive is the delicious and elegantly served Cantonese food at *The Regent*, 30 Upper Craigs (☎01786/472513).

If you're planning a high-class **picnic**, head to Clive Ramsay Delicatessen and Fine Foods at 28 Henderson St, Bridge of Allan (buses #51 and #52 from Murray Place).

Nightlife and entertainment

Nightlife in Stirling revolves around **pubs** and **bars** and is dominated by the student population. The lively *Barnton Bar and Bistro*, on Barnton Street, serves a good selection of beers and food in a setting of wrought-iron and marble tables. Try to visit in the morning (from 10.30am) to sample one of their huge breakfasts. Also popular with students is the real ale at the *Settle Inn*, 91 St Mary's Wynd, Stirling's oldest alehouse; built in 1733, with a barrel-vaulted roof, its patina testifies to centuries of smoking and drinking. The *Hog's Head*, at the top of Friars Street, has a fairly convincing "old world" feel, even though it's a relatively recent addition, and a good range of real ales, while *The Meadowpark* pub, on Kenilworth Road near the university, is especially lively in term time.

If you want to carry on after the pubs close, you could try *Rainbow Rocks*, a mainstream **nightclub** off Baker Street, or *Fubars* in Murray Place for a blast of house (see the *Stirling Observer* for weekly details). From June to September, **ceilidhs** take place in the wonderful venue of John Cowane's Hospital, near the castle (usually on Mon at 8pm, but check with the tourist office; £3.50). Although geared to tourists rather than locals, the ceilidhs can be fun and often singers and professional dancers feature. The larger Albert Hall is a good venue for classical and pop/rock **concerts**, and recently summer rock concerts have been held on the castle esplanade; contact the tourist office for details.

The main venue for **theatre** and **film** is the excellent MacRobert Arts Centre (☎01786/461081) on the university campus (see below), which shows a good selection of drama and mainstream and arthouse films.

Around Stirling

North of Stirling, a ten-minute walk from the fine Victorian spa town of **BRIDGE OF ALLAN**, **Stirling University** was, until 1992 (when all British colleges and polytechnics acquired university status), the youngest university in Scotland, and once one of the most radical. The university exemplifies successful 1960s architecture, and the landscaped grounds are beautiful – resplendent with daffodils in spring, rhododendrons along the sides of the artificial Airthrey Loch in summer, and the rich colours of the Ochil Hills as a backdrop in autumn. Stranded on the northern edge, **Airthrey Castle** is a prepossessing late-eighteenth-century affair built by Robert Adam, now housing CELT (the Centre for English Language Teaching). The Pathfoot building displays in its main corridor a rich collection of portraits and landscapes by J.D. Fergusson (see p.288), given to the university by his widow. Frequent **buses** run to the university from Murray Place in Stirling, including the Heritage bus service (see p.246).

Overlooking the university one mile to the southwest is the prominent 1860s **Wallace Monument** (daily: March–May & Oct 10am–5pm; June & Sept 10am–6pm; July & Aug 9.30am–6.30pm; Nov & Dec 10am–4pm; £3.25), a rocket-like tribute to Sir

William Wallace ("the hammer and scourge of the English"), who was portrayed by Mel Gibson in the wildly inaccurate *Braveheart*. It was from the nearby Wallace's Pass that the Scottish hero led his troops down to defeat the English at the Battle of Stirling Bridge in 1297. Exhibits inside the monument include Wallace's long steel sword and the Hall of (Scottish) Heroes, a row of stern white marble busts featuring John Knox and Adam Smith, as well as a life-size "talking" model of Wallace, who tells visitors about his preparations for the battle. If you can manage the climb – up 246 spiral steps – there are superb views across to Fife and Ben Lomond from the top of the 220ft tower. A shuttle bus (75p return) runs from the base of the hill to the tower every ten minutes, allowing you to avoid the initial steep walk; the Heritage bus service also calls here. If, however, you use the car park, you can't fail to notice a second, more recent tribute to Wallace: a statue which bears a striking resemblance to Mel Gibson.

A woodland path weaves its way from the monument to the ruins of **Cambuskenneth Abbey**, about a mile east of Stirling (ruins April–Sept; grounds all year; HS; free). Founded in 1147 by David I on the site of an Augustinian settlement, the abbey is distinguished by its early fourteenth-century bell tower, though there's little else to see there now. Its history, however, makes it worth a brief look; the Scots parliament met here in 1326 to pledge allegiance to Robert the Bruce's son David, James III (1451–88) and his wife, Queen Margaret of Denmark, are both buried in the grounds, their graves marked by a nineteenth-century monument erected at the insistence of Queen Victoria.

Above the university on the edge of the Ochil Hills (see p.264) are the wild moors of **Sheriffmuir**, where the Earl of Mar fought the crown forces in 1715. Access to the area is by car up steep single-track roads, but the splendid hills are worth the effort. In summer you can take "hacks" from the **Drumbrae Farm Riding Centre** (☎01786/832247), whose ponies are plump and reliable. The *Sheriffmuir Inn*, sitting in glorious isolation (follow the signs from Dunblane), serves food and is particularly popular in summer.

Frequent trains, bus #58 (and bus #358 in term time) make the journey four miles north of Stirling to **DUNBLANE**, indissolubly linked with the horrific massacre of March 1996, when Thomas Hamilton entered a local primary school and shot dead fifteen children and their teacher, before turning the gun on himself. Prior to that atrocity, this small, attractive city was renowned for being an ecclesiastical centre since the seventh century, when the Celts founded the Church of St Blane here. **Dunblane Cathedral** (April–Sept Mon–Sat 9.30am–6.30pm, Sun 2–6pm; Oct–March Mon–Sat 9.30am–4.30pm, Sun 2–4pm; HS; free) dates mainly from the thirteenth century, and restoration work carried out a century ago has returned the cathedral to its Gothic splendour. Inside, note the delicate blue-purple stained glass, and the exquisitely carved pews, screen and choir stalls, all crafted in the early twentieth century. Also of interest is the little alcove with its narrow stained-glass window, thought to be a hermit's cell, the tenth-century Celtic cross and a worn thirteenth-century double effigy of the fifth Earl of Strathearn and his countess. The cathedral, praised in the highest terms by John Ruskin ("I know not anything so perfect in its simplicity, and so beautiful, in all the Gothic with which I am acquainted"), stands serenely amid a clutch of old-world buildings, among them the seventeenth-century Dean's House, which houses the tiny cathedral **museum** (May–Oct Mon–Sat 10am–12.30pm & 2–4.30pm; free) with exhibits on local history. Close by, the oldest private library in Scotland, **Leighton Library** (May–Oct Mon–Fri 10am–12.30pm & 2–4.30pm; donation), houses 4500 books in ninety languages printed between 1500 and 1840; visitors can browse through some of the country's rarest books, including a first edition of Sir Walter Scott's *Lady of the Lake*.

On a hill overlooking the city, the luxurious **Dunblane Hydro**, a great Victorian *palazzo* run by the Stakis Hotel group (☎01786/822551; ⑨), offers tennis and archery lessons and walks in a 44-acre woodland setting. Four miles north of Dunblane, off the A9 through Kinbuck village on the B8033, is *Cromlix House* (☎01786/822125, *cromlix@bestloved.com*; ⑨), a sumptuous late Victorian pile that's perfect for an upmarket but leisurely meal (£18 for two lunch courses; £25 for three), followed by a peek into the lovely chapel and a stroll in the grounds. The rooms themselves are plush and comfortable, and croquet, tennis, riding and fishing are on offer for guests.

Five miles northwest of Stirling (Mon–Sat buses #59 and #211), the **Blair Drummond Safari Park** (April–Oct daily 10am–5.30pm; £8), attempts to recreate the African bush in the Scottish countryside. The only wildlife park in the country, it's good for a family day out, with everything from big cats to sea lions and Scotland's only elephants. There's also a pet farm, chimp island and waterfowl cruise, pedal boats and a small bus (50p) to visit the areas where lions, camel and bison roam free. The unlikely background to the park is **Blair Drummond Castle**, a Victorian Baronial extravaganza, now a Rudolf Steiner residential home. Just north past the safari park on the right hand side of the road to Doune is a secluded **graveyard**, the final resting place of the Home Drummond family, who owned Blair Drummond Castle, and their servants. One faithful retainer, as a stone records, served the family all his life, and to within an hour of his death.

DOUNE, eight miles northwest of Stirling, is a sleepy village with a violent past. The ruined, fourteenth-century **Castle** (April–Sept Mon–Sat 9.30am–6pm, Sun 2–6pm; Oct–March Mon–Wed & Sat 9am–4pm, Sun 2–4pm; HS; £2.30) is a marvellous pile standing on a small hill in a bend of the River Teith. Built by Robert, Duke of Albany, it eventually ended up in the hands of the Earls of Moray (whose descendants live there), following the execution of the Albany family by James I. In the sixteenth century it belonged to the second earl, James Stewart – son of James V and half-brother of Mary, Queen of Scots – murdered in 1592 and immortalized in the ballad, the *Bonnie Earl of Moray*. Today the most prominent features of the castle are its mighty 95ft gatehouse, with spacious vaulted rooms, and the kitchens, complete with medieval rubbish chute. Close to the castle, **accommodation** is provided in the excellent *Glenardoch House*, Castle Road (☎01786/841489; ②), an eighteenth-century country-house B&B with two comfortable en-suite rooms and a beautiful riverside garden.

The present earl has a fabulous collection of flash vintage cars, which are on show one mile northwest of town in the **Doune Motor Museum** (April–Nov daily 10am–5pm; £3) off the A84. Among the examples of gleaming paintwork and tanned upholstery you can see legendary models of Bentley, Lagonda, Jaguar, Aston Martin and the second-oldest Rolls Royce in the world (built in 1905). To get to Doune from Stirling, take bus #59 which leaves hourly – every two hours on Sunday.

Bannockburn

A couple of miles south of Stirling, just north of the village of **BANNOCKBURN**, the **Bannockburn Heritage Centre** (April–Oct daily 10am–5.30pm; March, Nov–Dec daily 11am–3pm; NTS; £2.30) stands close to where Robert the Bruce won his mighty victory over the English at the **Battle of Bannockburn** on June 24, 1314. It was this battle, the climax of the Wars of Independence, which united the Scots under Bruce and led to independence under the Declaration of Arbroath (1320) and the Treaty of Northampton (1328).

Outside, a concrete rotunda encloses a cairn near the spot where Bruce planted his standard after beating Edward II. Of the original bore stone, only a fragment remains, safely on display in the visitor centre. Over-eager visitors used to chip pieces off, and the final straw came when a particularly zealous enthusiast attempted to blast enough of it away to make two curling stones. Pondering the scene is an equestrian statue of Bruce, on the spot from where he is said to have commanded the battle, which was fought on the boggy carse down towards the burn. To reach Bannockburn, buses #51 and #52 leave from Stirling every half-hour.

The Campsies: hills and villages

Southwest of Stirling, the **Campsies**, an area of gently rolling hills and fertile farmland, include the Gargunnock and Fintry hills and villages and, further south, the **Campsie Fells**. Although the area is often overlooked in the rush to reach the more spectacular Trossachs, it's worth taking a detour here for the fine walks and fishing on offer and the many quiet and pretty hamlets, most notably Fintry. To the north, the Campsies are bordered by the flat swath of the **Carse of Forth**, which separates it from the Trossachs. The carse, blocked in the east by the volcanic crag on which Stirling Castle is perched, partly accounts for Stirling's historical importance: for politicians, soldiers and merchants, the treacherous path north, edged by deep marshes and moss, was only accessible from the town. Finally drained in the eighteenth century by local landowners, the carse was transformed into lush and productive farmland, now traversed by the main road west from Stirling to the heart of the Trossachs, the A811. Heading this way, you'll see the long stretch of the Gargunnock Hills to your left, which derive their distinctive stepped look from ancient lava flows. You can also approach and explore the area from the south from Falkirk, or Glasgow along the A803/A891, which winds along the northern edges of Glasgow's commuter belt, where almost every view is spoilt by industrial blight. Beyond **Lennoxtown**, however, the Campsie Fells are interrupted by nothing but sheep and waterfalls, the roads narrow and winding, and there are few signs of habitation. In winter it's an eerie sight, with the mists rolling in from the moors.

Hikers might want to follow the **Campsie Fells Trail** (for information, call ☎01786/475019 or ☎0141/204 4400), which links the Campsie villages (these include Fintry, Kippen, Gargunnock, Balfron and Lennoxtown), or the **Forth and Clyde Canal** walk which gives access to the second-century **Antonine Wall** (see p.261). The area also encompasses part of the West Highland Way, which starts in Milngavie (see p.505), and there are various options for coarse and game fishing (you can get details from Stirling's tourist office; see p.246). Plenty of **buses** run through the region from Stirling (#10, #107, #210; three or four daily, fewer at weekends), and a **postbus** service (Mon–Sat 9.55am only) operates from **Denny**, five miles south of Stirling (reached from Stirling bus station on buses #39, #81 or #81A). The postbus stops at **Fintry**, from where two buses (Mon–Sat) head further west to Balfron, the birthplace of architect Alexander "Greek" Thomson, who designed many of Glasgow's finest Victorian buildings (see p.203).

Gargunnock and Kippen

Six miles west of Stirling and just off the A811, **GARGUNNOCK**, mainly composed of eighteenth-century cottages, has a seventeenth-century grey crow-stepped church at its centre. The village is home to the oldest **agricultural show** in Scotland which has been held here every summer since 1795; the views over the great green of the carse and across to the mountains of the Trossachs are spectacular. To the east of the village in rolling parkland is handsome **Gargunnock House**, ancestral home of the Stirlings; Chopin is reputed to have spent two weeks here improving the family's keyboard skills. Recently restored and renovated, the house was begun in 1580, with pediments and a Classical facade added in 1794. It sleeps sixteen people, and can be rented from the Landmark Trust (☎01628/825925) for around £2000–2500 a week, depending on the season. More affordable accommodation is provided by *McNair House* in the main square, a charmingly pretty eighteenth-century cottage with an open fire, which can be rented on a weekly basis (☎ 01786/860668; £225–375). There is one **pub** in the centre of the village, the *Gargunnock Inn*, which serves upmarket bar meals.

The attractive village of **KIPPEN** can be reached by a lovely unmarked walk (1hr 30min). The track leads from the west of Gargunnock – the village is a dead-end –

through a path of beech trees and into the Leckie Estate, at the heart of which is the privately owned **Leckie Castle**, a sixteenth-century Laird's House where the Lady of Leckie entertained Bonnie Prince Charlie in 1745. Following the farm road to the left as you look down at Leckie Castle, you will eventually come to the Burnton of Boqhuan, a row of eighteenth-century red-stone cottages; take the left-hand fork past the Burnton, until the track comes to a steep field. Cross the field to the far gate and continue up the track and you soon begin the descent into Kippen. You can have a good **lunch** at *The Cross Keys*, an eighteenth-century hotel-pub on the main street (☎01786/870293; ③). There is little to do in Kippen other than wander along its pretty cobbled street of eighteenth-century houses, into the beautifully restored **smithy** (entry by arrangement only; NTS; ☎01738/631296), and round the adjoining ruined church and graveyard. Midland buses #10, #210 and #212 take you back to Stirling.

Fintry

The key settlement in the Campsies is **FINTRY**, a picture-postcard village at the head of Strathendrick valley and at the centre of the Campsie Fells Trail, that is a regular winner of the "Best Kept Small Village in Scotland" award. There are a couple of **places to stay**: if you're feeling flush, try the wonderful *Culcreuch Castle Hotel* (☎01360/860555; ⑥), a fourteenth-century thick-walled and parapeted pile on the northern side of the village. The castle is set in a country park which contains eight small wooden lodges, available for rent for £169–429 per week. The *Fintry Inn* (☎01360/860224; ①), a pretty white building on Main Street, offers pub food plus B&B accommodation.

Drymen

At the western end of the Campsie Fells, all roads meet at the small village of **DRYMEN**, which sits peacefully in the hills overlooking the winding Endrick water as it nears Loch Lomond. Although once you've seen the pretty eighteenth-century parish church there's nothing more to do, Drymen's reputation as the "gateway to east Loch Lomondside" means it gets extremely busy during the summer. If you want **to stay**, the no-frills *Winnock Hotel* (☎01360/660245; ⑤) has a restaurant and is prettily sited on the village green, while those wanting to follow the Loch Lomond cycleway can **rent bikes** from Lomond Activities, 64 Main St (☎01360/660066; £10 per day). Ten miles southeast of the village in the Blane Valley, Lang Brothers' **Glengoyne Distillery** (April–Nov Mon–Sat 10am–4pm, Sun noon–4pm; £2.50) offers interesting guided tours of the whisky-making processes.

Loch Lomond

Loch Lomond is the largest stretch of fresh water in Britain (about 24 miles long and up to five miles wide), and is almost as famous as Loch Ness, thanks to the ballad about its "bonnie, bonnie banks". The song was said to be have been written by a Jacobite prisoner captured by the English, who, sure of his fate, wrote that his spirit would return to Scotland on the low road much faster than his living compatriots on the high road. However, all is not bonnie at the loch nowadays, especially on its overdeveloped west side, fringed by the A82 which brings hoards of day-trippers from Glasgow, just thirty miles away. On the water itself, speedboats tear up and down on summer weekends, destroying the tranquillity which so impressed, among others, Queen Victoria, the Wordsworths and Sir Walter Scott.

Nevertheless, the west bank of the loch is an undeniably beautiful stretch of water, and despite the crowds gives better views than the heavily wooded east side. **LUSS**, the setting for the Scottish TV soap *High Road*, is the prettiest village, though its picturesque streets can become unbearably crowded in summer. The **visitor centre**

BEN LOMOND

Ordnance Survey Landranger map no. 56

Ben Lomond (3192ft), the most southerly of the "Munros", is one of the most frequently climbed hills in Scotland, its commanding position above Loch Lomond affording amazing views of both the Highlands and Lowlands. You should allow five to six hours for the climb.

The tourist route starts in Rowardennan at the car park at the rear end of the public road just beyond *Rowardennan Hotel*. The route rises through forest and crosses open moors to gain the southern ridge, which leads to the final pyramid. The path zigzags up, then rims the crags of the northeast corrie to reach the summit.

You can return the same way or start off westwards, then south, to traverse the subsidiary top of Ptarmigan down to the youth hostel in Rowardennan (see below) and then along the track to the start.

(Easter–Oct 10am–6pm; ☎01436/860601) adjacent to the main village car park, and run by the **Loch Lomond Park Authority**, gives a fascinating glimpse into the loch's landscape, wildlife and history as well as the environmental pressures it faces. **BALLOCH**, a brash holiday resort with a glut of moderately-priced hotels at the loch's southern tip, is the place to head for if you want to take a **boat trip**. Various operators offer cruises around the 33 islands scattered near the shore: Mullens Cruises, Riverside (☎01389/751481), operate daily trips on the *Lomond Duchess* and the *Lomond Maid* (£5); and Sweeney's Cruises, Riverside (☎01389/752376), run one-hour cruises departing hourly (starting at £4.50). Their daily Balloch to Luss cruise leaves at 2.30pm (£7), and ninety-minute evening cruises operate daily during July and August only, leaving at 7.30pm (£6).

The tranquil east bank is far better for walking than the west, and is traversed in its entirety by the West Highland Way footpath, from where you can head on in through **Queen Elizabeth Forest Park** (see p.259), or take the stiff but hugely rewarding five-to six-hour hike from **ROWARDENNAN** to the summit of Ben Lomond, the subject of the Scottish proverb "Leave Ben Lomond where it stands" – just let things be.

Practicalities

The West Highland **train** – the line from Glasgow to Mallaig, with a branch line to Oban – joins Loch Lomond seventeen miles north of Balloch at **TARBET**, and has one other station further on at **ARDLUI**, at the mountain-framed head of the loch. There are plenty of **buses** along the shore from Balloch.

Loch Lomond's **tourist office** (daily: April–June, Sept & Oct 10am–5pm; July & Aug 9.30am–7.30pm; ☎01389/753533) is above the marina in Balloch. They'll reserve a room for you without charge at one of the many local **hotels** and **B&Bs**, such as the comfortable *Balloch Hotel*, Balloch Road (☎01389/752579; ④), which also has a decent restaurant, or the friendly *Gowanlea Guest House* on Drymen Road (☎01389/752456; ②). A couple of miles up the west side of the loch at minuscule **ARDEN** is Scotland's most beautiful **youth hostel**, a turreted building complete with ghost (☎01389/850226). Caravan parks abound on the west side of the loch, and in Balloch itself there's the year-round *Tullichewan Caravan Park*, Old Luss Road (☎01389/759475), which also rents out **bikes**; tents are best pitched at the secluded Forestry Commission **campsite** (☎01360/870234; April–Oct) two miles south of Rowardennan at Cashel on the eastern shore of the loch.

Passenger ferries cross between Inverbeg and Rowardennan, where there's an eponymous **hotel** (☎01360/870273; ⑤) and a wonderfully situated **youth hostel**

(☎01360/870259; March–Oct), right on the West Highland Way. On the northeast shore of the loch is the *Inversnaid Lodge* (☎01877/386254; ⑥); once the hunting lodge of the Duke of Montrose, it now has a photography centre with instruction and workshops from guest tutors. There is no road from Rowardennan up the east of the loch to Inversnaid; you have to take the B829 west from Aberfoyle. From Inversnaid you can take the mile-long loch-side walk to Rob Roy's cave, a hideout which is said to have given shelter to both Rob Roy and Robert the Bruce.

As for **eating**, on the west side of the loch, the *Inverbeg Inn* (signposted off the A82), is the most convenient place to stop, with bar snacks and outdoor seating from which to view the loch, as well as a few comfortable **rooms** (☎01436/860678; ⑦). On the east side, there's little option but to take a picnic.

The Trossachs

Often described as the Highlands in miniature, the **Trossachs** area boasts a magnificent diversity of scenery, with dramatic peaks and mysterious, forest-covered slopes that live up to all the images ever produced of Scotland's wild land. This is Rob Roy country, where every waterfall, hidden cave and barely discernible path was once frequented by the seventeenth-century Scottish outlaw who led the Clan MacGregor. Strictly speaking, the name "Trossachs", normally translated as either "bristly country" or "crossing place", originally referred only to the wooded glen between **Loch Katrine** and Loch Achray, but today it is usually taken as being the whole area from **Callander** in the east to Queen Elizabeth Forest Park in the west, right up to the eastern banks of Loch Lomond.

This is fabulous walking territory. **Ben Venue** and **Ben A'an**, on the southern shores of Loch Katrine, and **Ben Ledi**, just northwest of Callander, especially, offer challenging climbs and, on clear days, stunning views. The weather, however, is unpredictable, and every year there are fatalities in the Trossachs Mountains, so be sure to follow the necessary safety precautions (see p.48). Less taxing walks can be made from the **Queen Elizabeth Park Visitor Centre**, on the A821 north of Aberfoyle. It's a good idea to consult the Bartholomew guide *Walk Loch Lomond and the Trossachs*, which grades walks according to difficulty. The **Trossachs Trundler** (June–Sept Mon–Fri & Sun; contact any tourist office for details) is a gleaming vintage bus which takes a circular route linking Callander, Loch Katrine and Aberfoyle, stopping at various points en route. The bus is timed to connect with sailings of the SS *Sir Walter Scott* on Loch Katrine, and costs £4.50 for a day-pass or £7.40 including the bus fare from Stirling to Callander.

The Trossachs' high tourist profile was largely attributable in the early days to Sir Walter Scott, whose *Lady of the Lake* and *Rob Roy* were set in and around the area. Since then, neither the popularity – nor beauty – of the region have waned, and in high season the place is jam-packed. Autumn is a better time to come, when the hills are blanketed in rich, rusty colours and the crowds are thinner. In terms of where to stay, **Aberfoyle** has a slightly dowdy air, even at the height of summer, so it is better to opt for the romantic seclusion of the **Lake of Menteith**, or the handsome country town of **Callander**.

Aberfoyle and the Lake of Menteith

Like Brigadoon waking once a year from a mist-shrouded slumber, each summer the sleepy little town of **ABERFOYLE**, twenty miles west of Stirling, dusts itself down for the annual influx of tourists. Its position in the heart of the Trossachs is ideal, with **Loch Ard Forest** and **Queen Elizabeth Forest Park** stretching across to **Ben**

Lomond and **Loch Lomond** to the west, the long curve of Loch Katrine and **Ben Venue** to the northwest, and **Ben Ledi** to the northeast.

Don't come here for lively nightlife or entertainment, but for a good, healthy blast of the outdoors. The town itself is well equipped to lodge and feed visitors (though booking is recommended), and is an excellent base for walking and pony trekking, or simply wandering the hills. You might like to wander to Doon Hill to the north of Aberfoyle; cross the bridge over the Forth, continue past the cemetery and then follow signs to the **Fairy Knowe** (knoll). A toadstool marker points you through oak and holly trees to the summit of the Knowe where there is a pine tree, said to contain the unquiet spirit of the Reverend Robert Kirk, who studied local fairy lore and published his inquiries in *The Secret Commonwealth* (1691). Legend has it that, as punishment for disclosing supernatural secrets, Robert Kirk was forcibly removed to fairyland where he has languished ever since, although his mortal remains can be found in the nearby graveyard. This short walk should preferably be made at dusk, when it is at its most atmospheric.

About four miles east of Aberfoyle towards Doune, the **Lake of Menteith** is a superb fly-fishing centre and Scotland's only lake (as opposed to loch), so named due to a historic mix-up with the word *laigh*, the Scots for "low-lying ground", which applied to the whole area. To rent a **fishing boat**, contact the Lake of Menteith Fisheries (☎01877/385664; April–Oct). From the northern shore of the lake you can take a little ferry (April–Sept Mon–Sat 9.30am–6.30pm, Sun 2pm–6.30pm; £3) to the **Island of Inchmahome**, and explore the lovely ruin of the Augustine abbey. Founded in 1238, **Inchmahome Priory** (HS) is perhaps the most beautiful island monastery in Scotland, its remains rising tall and graceful above the trees. The masons employed to build the Priory are thought to be those who built Dunblane Cathedral (see p.251); certainly the western entrance there resembles that at Inchmahome. The nave of the church is roofless, but in the choir are preserved the graves of important families from the surrounding area. Most touching is a late thirteenth-century double effigy depicting Walter, the first Stewart Earl of Menteith, and his Countess Mary who, feet resting on lion-like animals, turn towards each other and embrace. Also buried at Inchmahome is Robert Bontine Cunninghame Graham (1852–1936), the adventurer, scholar, socialist and Scottish nationalist, who was Liberal MP for northwest

---

ROB ROY

"Rob Roy, hero or villain?" ponders the tourist literature, in the great spirit of inquiry. Given that Rob Roy's clan, the MacGregors, may be the source of the term blackmail (from the levying of black meal through protection rackets), and that Rob Roy himself achieved fame through cattle rustling and thieving, the evidence seems to point to the "villain" thesis. His life, though, dramatizes the clash between the doomed clan culture of the Gaelic-speaking Highlanders, and the organized feudal culture of lowland Scots, which effectively ended with the defeat of the Jacobites at Culloden in 1746.

Rob Roy (meaning "Red Robert" in Gaelic) was born in 1671 in Glengyle just north of Loch Katrine and started life as a cattle farmer, supported by the powerful Duke of Montrose. When the Duke withdrew his support, possibly having been robbed of £1000 by Rob Roy, the latter became a bankrupt and a brigand, plundering the rich carse land and avenging himself on the duke. He was present at the Battle of Sherrifmuir in 1715, ostensibly as a Jacobite but probably as an opportunist – the chaos would have made cattle raiding easier. Eventually captured and sentenced to transportation, Rob Roy was pardoned and returned to Balquhidder, where he remained until his death in 1734. His life has been much romanticized, from Sir Walter Scott's 1818 version of the story in his novel *Rob Roy*, to the 1995 film of the same name starring Liam Neeson.

Lanarkshire for 25 years and the first president of the National Party of Scotland. A pal of Buffalo Bill in Mexico as well as an intimate friend of the novelist Joseph Conrad, Cunninghame Graham had a ranch in Argentina, where he was affectionately known as "Don Roberto".

Five-year-old **Mary, Queen of Scots** was hidden at Inchmahome in 1547 before being taken to France; there's a knot garden in the west of the island known as Queen Mary's bower, where legend has it, the child Queen played. Traces remain of an orchard planted by the monks, but the island is thick now with oak, ash and Spanish chestnut. On an nearby but inaccessible island is the ruined castle of **Inchtalla**, the home of the Earls of Menteith in the sixteenth and seventeenth centuries.

Seven miles east of Aberfoyle on the A873 to Callander, the **Farm Life Centre** (April–Oct daily 10am–6pm; £3.50) makes an entertaining stop for children on a rainy day. Kids can pet a host of animals, make oatcakes, milk goats and ride tractors on this converted farm; there's also a picnic area, tearoom and small museum.

Practicalities

Regular **buses** from Stirling to Aberfoyle pull into the car park on Main Street. The **tourist office**, directly next door, has full details of local accommodation, sights and outdoor activities (daily: March–June, Sept & Oct 10am–5pm; July & Aug 9.30pm–7pm; ☎01877/382352). The nearby **Scottish Wool Centre** (Easter–Oct daily 9.30am–6pm; Nov–Easter daily 10am–4.30pm) sells all the usual jumpers and woolly toys as well as featuring shows of sheep-shearing and sheep dog trials, and is a popular stopoff point with tour buses.

For **accommodation**, there are scores of **B&Bs** in Aberfoyle, including the comfortable Tudor-style *Craigend*, 1 Craiguchty Terrace (☎01877/382716; ②; March–Oct), and many dotted around the surrounding countryside, among them *Creag-Ard House* (☎01877/382297; ②) in the pretty village of Milton, two miles west of Aberfoyle. It looks out on Ben Lomond and Loch Ard, to which it has fishing and boating rights. At Kinlochard, five miles west of Aberfoyle, is the deluxe *Forest Hills Hotel* (☎01877/387277; ⑦), set in 25 acres of woodland, with excellent food and a leisure centre. More atmospheric than Aberfoyle, the **Lake of Menteith** is a beautiful place to stay – the *Lake Hotel and Restaurant* (☎01877/385258; ⑥) at Port of Menteith has a lovely lakeside setting next to the Victorian Gothic parish church, and a classy restaurant, or there are the handsome *Lochend Chalets* (☎01877/385268) on the lake, which sleep four to six people, and cost £240–650 per week.

A couple of miles south of Aberfoyle on the edge of Queen Elizabeth Forest Park, *Cobleland Campsite* (☎01877/382392; April–Oct), run by the Forestry Commission, covers five acres of woodland by the River Forth (little more than a stream here). Further south the excellent family-run *Trossachs Holiday Park* (☎01877/382614; April–Oct), is twice the size and has **bikes** for rent.

For food, there's a range of decent eating places in the centre of Aberfoyle; try the *Forth Inn* (☎01877/382372) or *The Coach House* (01877 382822), both on Main Street.

Duke's Pass

Even if you have to walk it, don't miss the twelve-mile trip from Aberfoyle to Callander, which for part of the way takes you along the **Duke's Pass** (so called because it once belonged to the Duke of Montrose), as it weaves through the **Queen Elizabeth Forest Park** to just south of Loch Katrine.

The A821 twists up out of Aberfoyle, following the contours of the hills and snaking back on itself in tortuous bends. About halfway up is the park's excellent **visitor cen-**

THE QUEEN ELIZABETH FOREST PARK

Covering 75,000 acres on the edge of the Highlands, the **Queen Elizabeth Forest Park** is a spectacular tract of wilderness bordering Loch Lomond, and incorporating Loch Ard, Loch Achray and Loch Lubnaig, as well as Ben Venue, Ben A'an and Ben Ledi. Managed by the Forestry Commission, it is used partly for leisure and recreation and is criss-crossed by waymarked paths and trails, including part of the **West Highland Way** and, on the western side, access to **Ben Lomond** (3192ft). Among its varied wildlife habitats are the forests north of Balmaha, which are home to red and roe deer, as well as wild goats. The park **visitor centre** is just outside **Aberfoyle** in the Trossachs (see p.256).

Accommodation in the park is available at two **campsites** – one on the banks of Loch Lomond at Cashel, near Rowardennan (see p.255), and the other beside the River Forth at Cobleland, south of Aberfoyle (☎01877/382392). There are also **log cabins** on the shores of Loch Lubnaig in Strathyre, south of Lochearnhead (cabins for five cost £350 per week; ☎0131/334 0303).

Full details about the park are available from the **Forest Enterprise**, Aberfoyle, Stirling FK8 3UX (☎01877/382258), and the **Countryside Ranger Service**, Enviromental Services, Viewforth, Stirling FK8 2ET (☎01786/432363).

---

tre (April–Oct daily 10am–6pm; Nov–March Sat & Sun only 10am–4pm; ☎01877/382258; car park fee £1), which gives detail on the local fauna and flora. From here various marked paths wind through the forest, giving splendid views over the low-lands and surrounding hills. About five miles further on, a track to the right marks the start of the **Achray Forest Drive**, a worthwhile excursion by car, foot or mountain bike which leads through the forest and along the western shore of **Loch Drunkie**, before rejoining the main road. After another couple of miles, a road branches off to the left, leading to the southern end of **Loch Katrine** at the foot of **Ben Venue** (2370ft, a stren-uous walk), from where the historic steamer, the SS *Sir Walter Scott*, has been plying the waters since 1900, chugging up the loch to Stronachlachar and the wild country of Glengyle (April–Oct Sun–Fri 4 daily, Sat 2 daily; £3.70). To climb **Ben A'an** (1520ft), start from the *Trossachs Hotel* on the north bank of Loch Achray. No longer a hotel, it retains the splendid exterior designed by the outlandishly named Lord Willoughby d'Eresby in 1852.

The final leg of the pass is along the tranquil shores of **Loch Venachar** at the south-ern foot of Ben Ledi. Look out for the small **Callander Kirk** in a lovely setting at the edge of the loch, where services are still held on the first Sunday of each month at 3pm – presumably because it takes all morning to get there.

Callander and around

CALLANDER, on the eastern edge of the Trossachs, sits quietly on the banks of the River Teith roughly ten miles north of Doune, at the southern end of the **Pass of Leny**, one of the key routes into the Highlands. Larger than Aberfoyle, it is an even more pop-ular summer holiday base and a convenient springboard for exploring the surrounding area. Its wide main street recalls the influence of the military architects who designed the town after Bonnie Prince Charlie's Jacobite Rebellion of 1745.

Callander first came to fame during the "Scottish Enlightenment" of the eighteenth and nineteenth centuries, when the glowing reports given by Sir Walter Scott and William Wordsworth prompted the first tourists to venture into the wilds by horse-drawn carriage. Development was given a boost when Queen Victoria chose to visit, and then by the arrival of the train line – long since closed – in the 1860s.

The present community has not been slow to capitalize on the town's appeal, establishing a plethora of restaurants and tearooms, antique shops, secondhand bookstores, and shops selling local woollens and crafts. The chief formal attraction is the **Rob Roy and Trossachs Visitor Centre** at Ancaster Square on the main street (Jan & Feb Sat & Sun only 11am–4.30pm; March–May & Oct–Dec daily 10am–5pm; June daily 9.30am–6pm; July & Aug daily 9.30am–10pm; Sept 10am–6pm; £2.50), which gives an entertaining and partisan account of the life of the diminutive redhead.

Practicalities

Callander's **tourist office** is in the Rob Roy and Trossachs Visitor Centre (same times; ☎01877/330342), and can book **accommodation**. The best options include *The Priory*, on Bracklinn Road (☎01877/330001; ③), a highly recommended Victorian house in its own gardens with good views; the handsome Victorian *Brook Linn Country House*, Leny Feus (☎01877/330103; ③; March–Nov), set above the town; and the family-run *Ben A'an Guest House* (☎01877/330317; ③), 158 Main St. A couple of miles out of town – cross the river at Bridge Street, follow the A81, turn right at the Invertrossachs Junction and continue for a mile – you'll find *Trossachs Backpackers* (☎01877 331200, *trosstel@aol.com*), a sparkling new thirty-bed **hostel** and activity centre with self-catering dorms, family rooms and **bike rental** (☎01877/331100). For more luxury, try the *Roman Camp Country House Hotel*, signposted off the main street (☎01877/330003; ⑧), a turreted and romantic seventeenth-century hunting lodge in twenty-acre gardens on the River Teith, or the *Invertrossachs Country House* (☎01877/331126; ⑥), west of Callander on the southern shores of Loch Venachar, a plush Edwardian mansion offering superior B&B. Despite its popularity, there are few **restaurants** worth recommending in Callander. The best place is in the *Roman Camp Hotel*, which serves splendid Scottish produce in refined surroundings. For good pub food, try the *Myrtle Inn* on the eastern edge of Callander, or the *Lade Inn* in Kilmahog, two miles west of the town.

North to Lochearnhead

On each side of Callander, pleasant and less-than-arduous walks wind north through a wooded gorge to the **Falls of Leny** and **Bracklinn Falls** – both distances of only a mile or so. Longer **walks** of varying degrees of exertion thread their way through the surrounding countryside, the most challenging being that to the summit of **Ben Ledi** (2857ft), for which you should be well shod and well prepared (see p.48).

North of town, you can walk or ride the scenic six-mile **Callander to Strathyre Cycleway**, which forms part of the network of cycleways between the Highlands and Glasgow. The route is based on the old Caledonian train line to Oban, which closed in 1965, and runs along the western side of **Loch Lubnaig**. To the north, Rob Roy is buried in the small yard behind the ruined church at tiny **BALQUHIDDER**, where he died in 1734. Oddly enough, considering the Rob Roy fever that plagues the region, his grave – marked by a rough stone carved with a sword, cross and a man with a dog – is remarkably underplayed. If you want to **stay** in Balquhidder, avoid the plethora of Rob Roy-themed places, and try the award-winning *Monachyle Mhor* hotel (☎01877/384622; ⑦), an eighteenth-century farmhouse which has a terrific restaurant specializing in local game and has the added bonus of lovely views out to Loch Voil.

Watersports are the life force of the village of **Lochearnhead** (see p.292), at the western head of Loch Earn, a substantial body of water running east into Perthshire and fed by waters from the slopes of **Ben Vorlich** (3201ft) to the south. For a more impressive stretch of water, though, head to **Loch Tay**, about fifteen miles north of Callander, which points northeastwards for fourteen miles towards Aberfeldy (see p.295).

The Forth Valley

The **Forth Valley** stretches some forty miles southeast of Stirling along the Firth of Forth. The area has long been known for its industry, historically for the famous – but now redundant – Carron Ironworks near **Falkirk**, which were founded in 1759 and manufactured "carronades" (small cannons) for Nelson's fleet, and more recently produced iron for BP's gargantuan petrochemical plant at **Grangemouth**. The lights and fires of the refineries are spectacular at night, and inspired Bertrand Tavernier to make the dour 1979 sci-fi film *Death Watch* in Scotland.

Given the lack of good accommodation in the Forth Valley, the area is best seen as a day-trip from either Stirling or Edinburgh. Unless you are particularly interested in steam trains – in which case definitely visit **Bo'ness** – the only unmissable outing is to **Linlithgow Palace**.

If you're coming from the east, across the Kincardine Bridge, you may want to pop into the signposted **tourist office** at Pine'N'Oak Layby, Kincardine Bridge (April, May & Sept Mon–Sat 10am–4pm, Sun noon–4pm; June–Aug daily 10am–5pm; ☎01324/831422). The regular train service between Stirling and Edinburgh makes Falkirk and Linlithgow easily accessible; for other destinations you'll have to rely on the comprehensive network of buses.

Falkirk and around

FALKIRK, the Forth Valley's main commercial centre, was the site of two major battles, one in 1298, when William Wallace fell victim to the English under Edward I, and the other in 1746, when Bonnie Prince Charlie, retreating northwards, sent the Hanoverians packing in one of his last victories over government troops. Traditionally a livestock centre, Falkirk was transformed in the eighteenth century by the construction of first the Forth and Clyde Canal, allowing easy access to Glasgow, and then the Edinburgh and Glasgow Union Canal, which continued the route through to Edinburgh. Just twenty years later, the trains arrived, and the canals became obsolete. However, a £78 million millennium project is currently under way to renovate the canal link to Glasgow – ultimately linking the North Sea to the Atlantic – with a massive canal interchange at Falkirk itself, using waterwheel technology to raise and lower boats between the locks. The wide network of old industrial canals in the area surrounding Falkirk offers good opportunities for **boating**, **canoeing**, easy **cycling** and **walks**.

The town itself is a busy local shopping centre, whose only formal attraction, set in Callendar Park, is **Callendar House** (Mon–Sat 10am–5pm, Sun 2–5pm; £1.80), which was owned by the staunchly Jacobite Livingston family. Though more geared to conference guests than tourists, the house's fabulous Georgian kitchens are worth a look, with gleaming utensils, a huge mechanized spit and a costumed kitchen maid who dispenses information about life below stairs whilst chopping apples, while the **Historical Research Centre** (Mon–Fri 10am–12.30pm & 1.30–5pm; free) will gladly help you delve into local family history.

In **BONNYBRIDGE**, five miles west of Falkirk (take bus #37 from Falkirk), is **Rough Castle**. Built in 142 AD, this was one of the forts which were set up, at two-mile intervals, to defend the entire length of the Roman **Antonine Wall**. In the opposite direction, the industrial town of **GRANGEMOUTH** sits at the edge of the Forth, its huge chimneys spewing out smoke visible for miles around. If industrial heritage is your scene, head for the **museum** on Bo'ness Road in the Charing Cross area of town (Mon–Sat 10am–12.30pm & 1.30–5pm; free), which tells the history of Grangemouth as one of Scotland's first planned industrial towns.

The Pineapple, north of Falkirk (turn off the A905 onto the B9124, or take bus #75), qualifies as one of Scotland's most exotic and eccentric buildings, a 45ft-high stone pineapple built as a garden folly in the 1770s for the fourth Earl of Dunmore. The folly was an elaborate joke on Lord Dunmore's part; returning from a spell as Governor of Virginia, where sailors would put a pineapple on a gatepost to announce their return, he chose to signal his homecoming on a grand scale. The folly is now owned by the NTS, and the outhouse can be rented for holidays (see below).

Practicalities

Falkirk's centrally located **bus** station is at Callender Riggs. Regular **trains** run from Glasgow Queen Street, Edinburgh and Stirling to Falkirk Grahamston Station (as opposed to Falkirk High Station, which is further from the centre), from where it's a five-minute walk to the **tourist office**, 2–4 Glebe St (April & May daily 9.30am–5pm; June, July, Sept & Oct daily 9.30am–6pm; Aug daily 9.30am–7pm; Nov–March Mon–Sat 9.30am–12.30pm & 1.30–5pm; ☎01324/620244). If you want to **stay**, the best bet is the elegant *Darroch House B&B*, on Camelon Road at the west end of town (☎01324/623041; ③), with large and peaceful gardens. The outhouse of **The Pineapple** folly can be rented through the Landmark Trust (☎01628/825925); it sleeps four, and costs around £550 per week.

You can **eat** Mexican food and hear **live music** at *Behind the Wall* (☎01324 633338), 14 Melville St, a brasserie-style café with a beer garden and conservatory, while *Finn MacCools*, 1 Princess St, serves good bar meals. There's also an upmarket French **restaurant**, *Pierre's* (☎01324/635843), serving classic Gallic cuisine using fresh local produce, near the town centre at 140 Graham's Rd.

Linlithgow

Roughly equidistant (fifteen miles) from Falkirk and Edinburgh is the ancient royal burgh of **LINLITHGOW**. The town itself has largely kept its medieval layout, but development since the 1960s has sadly stripped it of some fine buildings, notably close to the **Town Hall** and **Cross** – the former marketplace – on the long High Street.

You should head straight for **Linlithgow Palace** (April–Sept daily 9.30am–6.30pm; Oct–March Mon–Sat 9.30am–4.30pm, Sun 2–4.30pm, last admissions half an hour before closing; HS; £2.50), a splendid fifteenth-century ruin romantically set on the edge of Linlithgow Loch and associated with some of Scotland's best-known historical figures – including the ubiquitous Mary, Queen of Scots, who was born here in 1542. A royal manor house is believed to have existed on this site since the time of David I. Fire razed the manor in 1424, after which James I began construction of the present palace, a process that continued through two centuries and the reign of no fewer than eight monarchs. From the top of the northwest tower, Queen Margaret looked out in vain for the return of James IV from the field of Flodden in 1513. The ornate octagonal **fountain** in the inner courtyard, with its wonderfully intricate figures and medallion heads, flowed with wine for the wedding of James V and Mary of Guise. Bonnie Prince Charlie visited during the 1745 rebellion, and one year later the palace was burnt, probably accidentally, whilst occupied by General Hawley's troops.

This is a great place to take children: the rooflessness of the castle creates unexpected vistas and the elegant rooms with their intriguing spiral staircases seem labyrinthine. The galleried **Great Hall** is magnificent, as is the adjoining kitchen, which has a truly cavernous fireplace. Don't miss the dank downstairs **brewery**, which produced vast quantities of ale; 24 gallons was apparently a good nightly consumption in the sixteenth century.

St Michael's Church, adjacent to the palace, is one of Scotland's largest pre-Reformation churches, consecrated in the thirteenth century. The present building was completed three hundred years later, with the exception of the hugely incongruous aluminium spire, tacked on in 1946. Inside, decorative woodcarving around the pulpit depicts queens Margaret, Mary and Victoria.

A foil to the romantic historicism of the palace, the **Linlithgow Story** (March–Oct Mon & Wed–Sat 10am–5pm, Sun 1–4pm; £1), 143 High St, takes a realistic look at the town's transition from royal burgh via industrial centre to suburban backwater, with items such as a sword reputedly used at the Battle of Stirling Bridge and fifteenth-century coins on display. The second floor looks at local industries from paper mills to tanneries, where, it is said, the use of materials derived from animals was so efficient that "only the moo was left".

Running through Linlithgow is part of the **Union Canal**, the 31-mile artery opened in 1822, which linked Edinburgh with Glasgow via Falkirk. On summer weekends the Linlithgow Union Canal Society runs short trips on the *Victoria* (£2), a diesel-powered replica of a Victorian steam packet boat, and longer trips to the Avon Aqueduct on the *St Magdalene*, an electric canal boat (£6). The boats depart from the Manse Road canal basin, uphill from the train station at the southern end of town (☎01506/842575). An eighteen-mile walk along the canal towpath leads eventually to the centre of Edinburgh, but involves negotiating a path across a section of the Edinburgh ring road.

Practicalities

Frequent **buses** between Stirling and Edinburgh stop at the Cross, and the town is on the main train routes from Edinburgh to both Glasgow Queen Street and Stirling; the **train station** is at the southern end of town. From the station head downhill for High Street, where the **tourist office** is in the Burgh Halls building at the Cross (May & Sept daily 10am–5pm; June daily 10am–5pm; July & Aug daily 10am–6pm; Oct–April Tues–Sat 10am–4pm; ☎01506/844600).

For **accommodation** try *The Star and Garter*, 1 High St (☎01506/846362; ③), at the east end of town, a comfortable old coaching inn that also serves inexpensive bar meals. The Victorian *Pardovan House* is an excellent **B&B** (☎01506/834219; ②; May–Sept) at Philipstoun, a couple of miles west of Linlithgow, or you could try the friendly *Belsyde Farm*, Lanark Road (☎01506/842098; ①), a late-eighteenth-century house on a sheep and cattle farm beside the Union Canal. There are very few places to **eat** in Linlithgow, but for good pub food try *The Four Marys*, opposite the Cross on High Street, or, at the opposite end of the street, the smaller, more basic *West Port Hotel*, 18–20 West Port (☎01506/847456; ③), with a popular downstairs **bar** which also serves food. For more expensive Scottish cuisine, *Livingstone's* (☎01506/846505) on the High Street serves meals in a small garden observatory.

The only official **campsite** in the area is at *Beecraigs Caravan Park* (☎01506/844516), about four miles south of town and part of the larger Beecraigs Country Park. There are only 39 pitches, however, so get there early or phone first.

Around Linlithgow

The small hillside town of **BO'NESS**, roughly four miles north of Linlithgow – which has traditionally looked down its nose at its pint-sized neighbour – sprawls in a less than genteel fashion down to the Forth, where a riverside path is separated from the road by a strip of scrub. On a clear day there are good views across the Forth to Culross (see p.268). The **Bo'ness and Kinneil Railway**, whose headquarters are in the old station at the eastern end of the waterfront road, is Scotland's largest vintage train centre, and in summer (July & Aug Tues–Sun; April–Oct Sat & Sun; ☎01506/822298) runs lovingly kept steam trains to Birkhill, just over three miles away (£3.90 return). Here, you can wander along the wooded Avon Gorge, or take a guided tour through the **Birkhill Fireclay Mine** (four tours a day coincide with train times; £2.90), where 300 million-year-old fossils still line the walls. There's a small **tourist office** at Hamilton's Cottage (March & April Mon–Fri 9.30am–5.30pm; May & June Mon–Sat 9.30am–5.30pm, Sun 2–5pm; July–Sept Mon–Sat 9am–5.45pm, Sun 11am–5pm; Oct Mon–Fri 10am–5pm; ☎01506/826626), but if you can't find it – even some of the locals don't know it's there – ask at the post office on the waterfront road. If you want to **stay the night**, the best option is the *Richmond Park Hotel*, 26 Linlithgow Rd (☎01506/823213; ⑤), which has comfortable rooms and offers good views across the Forth to the Fife hills. The moderately priced **restaurant** serves a fair choice of dishes, including some vegetarian.

Further down the coast from Bo'ness and four miles northeast of Linlithgow, boldly positioned on a rocky promontory in the Forth, lies the village of **BLACKNESS**, once Linlithgow's seaport but now known for the fifteenth-century **Blackness Castle** (April–Sept Mon–Sat 9.30am–6.30pm, Sun 9.30am–6.30pm; Oct–March Mon–Sat 9.30am–4.30pm, Thurs 9.30am–noon, Sun 2–4.30pm; HS; £1.80), which, after the Treaty of Union in 1707, was one of only four castles in Scotland to be garrisoned. Said to be built in the shape of a galleon, the castle offers grand views of the Forth bridges from the narrow gun slits in its northern tower.

General Tam Dalyell, the seventeenth-century Scottish royalist, spent part of his youth at the **House of the Binns** (May–Sept daily except Fri 1.30–5pm; grounds open year-round 10am–dusk; NTS; £3.90), occupying a hilltop site about two miles east of Linlithgow. Today it's the home of the veteran Labour MP Tam Dalyell. Inside you can see ornate plaster ceilings, paintings, period furniture and family relics not much changed since (the original) Tam's day.

The Ochils

The rugged **Ochil Hills** stretch for roughly forty miles northeast of Stirling, along the northern side of the Firth of Forth, forming a steep-faced range which drops down to the flood plain of the Forth Valley and is sliced by a series of deep-cut, richly wooded glens. Although they provide a dramatic backdrop for the region's towns, villages and castles, this is gentler country than, say, the Trossachs, with the hills gradually giving way to the pastoral landscape of Fife.

The area has been at the centre of Scotland's wool production for centuries, rivalled only by the Borders. The cottage industry of **Clackmannanshire**, immediately east of Stirling, capitalized on the technological advances of the Industrial Revolution, and by the mid-nineteenth century there were more than thirty mills in a fifteen-mile stretch.

Recent times have seen a change in the industry, with the old family firms and hand-knitters unable to compete with modern technology. Nonetheless, you can still see traditional producers at work in shops and private houses, especially on the **Mill Trail** that starts in **Alva** and links the main towns, historic sites and modern mill shops. A glimpse of a different past is offered by various fortified tower houses – Clackmannanshire was a convenient base from which the country's powerful families could keep abreast of developments at the Royal Court at Stirling. None of them are open to the public at present, but substantial remains can still be seen at the Bruce house at Clackmannan and the Erskine's at **Alloa**, which has recently been restored. Above the picturesque town of **Dollar** (once Dolour) is a wooded glen which you ascend, with the Burn of Sorrow and the Burn of Care rushing by, to reach **Castle Campbell**, once called Castle Gloom. Despite the preponderance of mournful names, the town, the walk and the castle make for a wonderful outing. Beyond Dollar the road runs south along the Devon Valley to Kinross, on the shores of Loch Leven.

There are no trains to destinations in the Ochils, but regular **buses** shuttle between Stirling and Yetts o' Muckhart (northeast of Dollar), and from Alloa to Tillicoultry.

The Ochil foothills

Three miles or so northeast of Stirling, the small and appealing village of **BLAIR-LOGIE** sits amidst orchards and gardens below a private castle; it also features an attractive campsite (see p.247). **Logie Old Kirk**, a ruined church and graveyard dating from the late seventeenth century, is beautifully sited by Logie Burn. Immediately to the rear looms **Dumyat** (pronounced "Dum-eye-at"), which offers spectacular views from its 1376ft summit.

MENSTRIE, a mile east, is noted for **Menstrie Castle** (May–Sept Sat & Sun 2–4pm; free), a much-restored sixteenth-century stone-built mansion on Castle Road, which is totally at odds with the housing estate that now hems it in. The castle was the birth-place of Sir William Alexander, first Earl of Stirling, who in 1621 set off to found a Scots colony in Nova Scotia. There's little to see now, except an exhibition room displaying the coats of arms of the 109 subsequent baronets of Nova Scotia.

As well as a strong tradition of weaving, **ALVA**, five miles further on, was also known for its silver mining – an industry long since gone. From here you can follow **Alva Glen**, a hearty mile-and-a-half walk dipping down through the hills, which takes in a number of waterfalls. The **Mill Trail** starts from Glentana Mills, on Stirling Street, which doubles as a **visitor centre** (Jan–June & Oct–Dec daily 10am–5pm; July–Sept daily 9am–6pm; ☎01259/769696; free).

A few miles south of Alva on the A907, the nondescript town of **ALLOA** is home to the beautifully restored **Alloa Tower** (May–Sept daily 1.30–5.30pm; NTS; £2.30). Ancestral home of the Earls of Mar for four centuries, it's now incongruously sur-rounded by housing estates, though the parapet walk offers lovely views of the Forth. The only other reason to visit Alloa is to **stay** in or eat at the luxurious *Gean House* (☎01259/219275; ⑦), an elegant Edwardian mansion set in twenty acres of parkland, with a plush walnut-panelled **restaurant**, which serves simple, high-qual-ity food.

Dollar

Nestling in a fold of the Ochils on the northern bank of the small River Devon where mountain waters rush off the hills, affluent **DOLLAR** is known for its Academy, found-ed in 1820 with a substantial bequest from local lad John MacNabb, and now one of Scotland's most respected private schools – its pupils and staff account for around a third of the town's population. Above the town, the dramatic chasm of **Dollar Glen** is commanded by **Castle Campbell** (April–Sept daily 9.30am–6.30pm; Oct–March Mon–Wed & Sat 9.30am–4.30pm, Thurs 9.30am–noon, Sun 2–4.30pm; NTS/HS; £2.50), formerly, and still unofficially, known as Castle Gloom – a fine and evocative tag but, prosaically, a derivation of an old Gaelic name. A one-and-a-half-mile road leads up from the main street, but becomes very narrow, very steep, and stops short of the castle, with only limited parking at the top. There is a marked walk through the glen to the cas-tle, past mossy crags and rushing streams (see below).

The castle came into the hands of the Campbells in 1481, who changed its name from Castle Gloom in 1489. John Knox preached here in 1556, although probably from with-in the castle rather than from the curious archway in the garden as is traditionally claimed. In 1654 the castle was burnt by Cromwell's troops; the remains of a graceful seventeenth-century loggia and a roofless hall bear witness to the destruction. However, the oldest part of the castle, the fine fifteenth-century tower built by Sir Colin Campbell, survived the fire; look out for the claustrophobic pit-prison just off the Great Hall and the latrines with their vertiginous views. You can also walk round the roof of the tower, where there's a wonderful vista of the hills behind the castle, and down the glen to Dollar.

WALKING ABOVE DOLLAR

Ordnance Survey Landranger map no. 58

The River Devon rises far in the Ochils but does a huge loop round Glendevon and the crook of Devon before turning to flow along the valley below the Ochil scarp. A walk combining the glen with **Castle Campbell** and **Dollar Hill** is highly recommended, and takes around three hours. A shorter (2hr) walk is possible, if you miss out the hill.

Walk up the Burnside from the town centre (clock tower) and then along a footpath from the top bridge beside the burn to pass an open area and reach the wooded glen (NTS). Keep an eye on small children, as in some places the path is steep and unfenced. Other bridges eventually lead you out near Castle Campbell, perched between the Burn of Care and the Burn of Sorrow.

You can return to Dollar by the small tarred road, which stops just short of the castle. But if you want to venture further Dollar Hill (Bank Hill on the OS map) is easily accessible by going up the burn to a bridge over the Sorrow. From here there's a direct descent to Dollar via the golf course. There is also an old drovers' road through to Glendevon, but you'll need to arrange transport back to Dollar from there. Leaving the castle the road dips, then climbs to a cottage (start of the track to Glendevon) and a car park (good view of the keep), before descending steeply to the town below.

If you're tempted to **stay** at Dollar, try the modern *Tigh Ur*, 4 Hillfoots Rd (☎0374/182799; ①), or the comfortable *Castle Campbell Hotel* on Bridge Street (☎01259/742519; ④). The *Strathallen Hotel* on Chapel Road is a good spot for a pub **lunch** with real ale and outside seating, while three miles east of town, on the Tillicoultry road, the *Harvieston Inn* offers reasonably priced Scottish food.

The Devon Valley

Beyond Dollar, the A91 leads through the hills to Kinross and runs along the southern edge of the **Devon Valley**, passing through the hamlets of **Pool o' Muckhart** and **Yetts o' Muckhart**.

The scenic A823 cuts up from Yetts o' Muckhart through the valley itself, where there's a large **campsite** with good facilities (☎01259/781246) just beyond **GLENDEVON**. The village is also home to a simple **youth hostel** (☎01259/781206; April–Oct), which organizes pony trekking from mid-June to September, and can give advice on walks in the area. The road continues from here to **Gleneagles**, with its famous hotel and golf course (see p.291).

In the other direction, south of Yetts o' Muckhart, the same road crosses the River Devon at **Rumbling Bridge** – effectively two bridges; the newer one, built in the early nineteenth century, sweeping over the top of the old one, which dates from 1713. The observation point offers breathtaking views of the magnificent, 120ft-deep **gorge**, and you can follow a shady path along the river, through the lush vegetation flourishing in the damp, limestone walls of the chasm.

Kinross and Loch Leven

Although still by no means a large place, **KINROSS**, on the A977 a mile west of the loch, has been transformed in the last couple of decades by the construction of the nearby M90 Edinburgh–Perth motorway. The old village is still there, at the southern end of the main street, but apart from the views of Loch Leven its charm has been eroded by amorphous splodges of modern housing, which threaten to nudge it into the loch itself. The best time to visit is on Sunday, when the stalls of a large and lively **covered**

market spring up on the southern edge of town, pulling in crowds who rifle through everything from kitsch ornaments to leather jackets.

During the summer a **ferry** departs regularly to ply the trout-filled waters of **Loch Leven**. In recent years the loch has become a National Nature Reserve and the location of international fishing competitions, and it also features **Castle Island**, where Mary, Queen of Scots was imprisoned for eleven months in 1567–68. On the island, the ruined fourteenth-century **Loch Leven Castle** (April–Sept Mon–Sat 9.30am–6pm, Sun 2–6pm; HS; £3) stands forlorn, little more than a tower. Nevertheless, it's easy to imagine the isolation of the incarcerated Mary, who is believed to have miscarried twins while here. She managed to charm the eighteen-year-old son of Lady Douglas into helping her escape: he stole the castle keys, secured a boat in which to row ashore, locked the castle gates behind them and threw the keys into the loch – from where they were retrieved three centuries later.

FIFE

The ancient Kingdom of **Fife**, designated as such by the Picts in the fourth century, is a small area (barely fifty miles at its widest point), but one which has a definite identity, inextricably bound with the waters which surround it on three sides – the Tay to the north, the Forth to the south, and the cold North Sea to the east. That the Fifers managed to retain their "Kingdom" when local government was reorganized in 1975 and 1995, is perhaps testimony to their will.

Despite its small size, Fife encompasses several different areas, with a marked difference between the semi-industrial south and the rural north. In the **south**, the recent closure of the coal mines has left local communities floundering to regain a foothold, and the squeeze on the fishing industry may well lead to further decline. In the meantime, many of the villages have capitalized on their unpretentious appeal and welcomed tourism in a way that has enhanced rather than degraded their natural assets; the perfectly preserved town of **Culross** is unmissable. East of Culross is **Dunfermline**, an overdeveloped town with the stunning remains of the first Benedictine priory in Scotland.

Central Fife is dominated in the south by **Kirkcaldy**, the region's largest town, and in the north by **Cupar**, Fife's capital. Although only separated by twenty miles, they couldn't be more different: the former is something of an industrial blackspot in an otherwise green area, while the latter is a charming market town set in the rolling scenery for which central Fife is known.

Tourism and agriculture are the economic mainstays of the **northeast** corner of Fife, where the landscape varies from the gentle hills in the rural hinterland, to the windswept cliffs, rocky bays and sandy beaches on which scenes from the film *Chariots of Fire* were shot. The fishing industry is still prominent, as is evident in the beautiful and ancient villages lining the shore of the East Neuk from Crail on the eastern tip down to Earlsferry. **St Andrews**, Scotland's oldest university town, and the home of the world-famous Royal and Ancient Golf club, is on the northeast coast. Development here has been cautious, and the hills and hamlets of the surrounding area retain an appealing and old-fashioned feel.

The main **transport route** through the region is the M90 from Edinburgh to Perth, which edges Fife's western boundary. The coastal route is more attractive, however, and also affords relatively easy access into the centre of Fife. The train line follows the coast as far north as Kirkcaldy and then cuts inland, towards Dundee, stopping at Cupar and Leuchars (catch a bus from here to St Andrews) on the way. Exploration of the eastern and western fringes by public transport requires some thought as there is no train service, and buses are few and far between.

The south coast

Although the **south coast** of Fife is predominantly industrial – with everything from cottage industries to the refitting of nuclear submarines – thankfully only a small part has been blighted by insensitive development. Even in the old coal-mining areas, disused pits and left-over slag heaps have either been well camouflaged through landscaping or put to alternative use as recreation areas. If you're driving, it's tempting once you've crossed the river to beat a path directly north up the M90 motorway; however, if you do decide to stop off, you'll find the area has much to offer.

Culross was once a lively port, which enjoyed a thriving trade with Holland, the Dutch influence obvious in the lovely gabled houses. After a period of about two hundred years of decline, the town has been lovingly restored this century. It was from **Dunfermline** that Queen Margaret ousted the Celtic Church from Scotland in the eleventh century; her son, David I, founded an abbey here in the twelfth century, which acquired vast stretches of land for miles around. Today, even though the lands no longer belong to the town, Dunfermline remains the chief town and focus of the coast.

Fife is linked to Edinburgh by the two **Forth bridges**. You used to be able to take guided walks across the historic rail bridge, whose boldness of concept was all the more remarkable for coming so hard on the heels of the Tay Bridge disaster of 1879 (see p.284); today, however, you'll have to be satisfied with seeing it from a train or a boat (for more on the Forth bridges, see p.105). The towns and villages of the south coast are connected by **trains** from Edinburgh via the Forth Rail Bridge, and there is a good local **bus** service.

Culross

Crossing the Forth Road Bridge from the south, with unattractive views of the shipyard at Inverkeithing and the naval dock at Rosyth, the A985 heads west along the Forth before approaching **CULROSS** (pronounced "Cooros"), one of Scotland's most picturesque settlements. The town's development began in the fifth century with the arrival of St Serf on the northern side of the Forth at "Holly Point", or Culenros, and it is said to be the birthplace of St Mungo, who travelled west and founded Glasgow cathedral. The town today is in excellent condition, thanks to the work of the NTS, which has been renovating its whitewashed, red-tiled buildings since 1932. Buses from Glasgow via Stirling and Alloa stop here, and there are also services from Dunfermline and Falkirk.

Make your first stop the **National Trust Visitor Centre** (Easter–Sept daily 11am–5pm; combined ticket for Town House, Palace and Study £4.40), in the **Town House** on the main road in the centre of Culross, for an excellent introduction to the burgh's history. On the upper floor of the house, some of the 4000 witches executed in Scotland between 1560 and 1707 were tried and held while awaiting execution in Edinburgh. Behind the ticket office is a tiny prison with built-in manacles, where people were locked up as punishment for minor offences. The focal point of the community is the ochre-coloured **Culross Palace** (Easter–Sept daily 11am–5pm), built by wealthy coal merchant George Bruce in the late sixteenth century. In fact, it's not a palace at all – its name comes from the Latin *palatium*, or "hall" – but a grand and impressive house, with lots of small rooms and connecting passageways. Inside, well-informed staff point out the wonderful painted ceilings, pine panelling, antique furniture and curios; outside, dormer windows and crow-stepped gables dominate the walled court in which the house stands. The garden is planted with grasses, herbs and vegetables of the period, carefully grown from seed. The café serves home-made food, and is open from 10.30am to 4.30pm.

A cobbled alleyway known as **Back Causeway**, complete with a raised central aisle formerly used by noblemen to separate them from the commoners, leads up behind the Town House to the **Study** (Easter–Sept daily 1.30–5pm), a restored house that takes its name from the small room at the top of the corbelled projecting tower, reached by a turnpike stair. Built in 1610, its oak panelling in Dutch Renaissance style dates from around twenty years later. Further up the hill lie the remains of **Culross Abbey**, founded by Cistercian monks on land given to the Church in 1217 by the Earl of Fife. The nave of the original building is a ruin, a lawn studded with great stumps of columns. Although it is difficult to get a sense of what the abbey would have looked like, the overall effect is of grace and grandeur. A ladder leads to a vaulted chamber, now exposed to the elements on one side, which feels as if it is suspended in mid-air. This adjoins the fine seventeenth-century **manse**, hung with clematis, and the choir of the abbey, which became the **Parish Church** in 1633. Inside, wooden panels detail the donations given by eighteenth-century worthies to the parish poor, and a tenth-century Celtic cross in the north transept is a reminder of the origins of the abbey – there was a Celtic church here in 450. Alabaster figures of Sir George Bruce, his lady, three sons and five daughters decorate the splendid family tomb, the parents lying in state and the children lined up and kneeling in devotion. A brass plaque tells the story of Edward, Lord Bruce of Kinloss, who was defeated by Sir Edward Sackville in a duel fought in Bergen in Holland in 1613. The luckless lord had been buried in Holland, but a persistent rumour that his heart had been taken back to Scotland was proved true when it was found during building work in the church in 1808, embalmed in a "silver casket of foreign workmanship".

The graveyard of the church is fascinating. Many of the graves are eighteenth-century, with symbols depicting the occupation of the person who is buried; the gravestone of a gardener has a crossed spade and rake and an hourglass with the sand run out – the latter a symbol of mortality used on many of the graves. Note the Scottish custom, still continued, of marking women's graves with maiden names, even when they are buried with their husbands.

Beyond Culross, the B9037 continues west to **Kincardine**, where the **Kincardine Bridge** provides a second crossing point over the Forth before the Old Bridge at Stirling.

Dunfermline

Scotland's capital until the Union of the Crowns in 1603, **DUNFERMLINE** lies seven miles inland east of Culross, north of the Forth bridges. This "auld, grey toun" is built on a hill, dominated by the abbey and ruined palace at the top. Up until the late nineteenth century, Dunfermline was one of Scotland's foremost linen producers, as well as a major coal-mining centre, and today the town is a busy place, its ever-increasing sprawl attesting to a booming economy. At the heart of the town is the imposing abbey, and the dramatic skeleton of the palace.

In the eleventh century, **Malcolm III** (Canmore) offered refuge here to Edgar Atheling, heir to the English throne, and his family, who while fleeing the Norman Conquest were shipwrecked in the Forth. Malcolm married Edgar's sister, the Catholic Margaret, in 1067, and in so doing started a process of reformation that ultimately supplanted the Celtic Church. Margaret, an intensely pious woman who was canonized in 1250, began building a Benedictine priory in 1072, the remains of which can still be seen beneath the nave of the present church; her son, **David I**, raised the priory to the rank of abbey in the following century. In 1303, during the first of the **Wars of Independence** (1296–1328), the English king Edward I occupied the palace, conducting a military campaign which culminated in the siege of Stirling Castle the following year. He had the church roof stripped of lead to provide ammunition for his army's catapults, and also appears to have ordered the destruction of most of the monastery buildings, with the exception of the church and some of the monks' dwellings. **Robert the Bruce** helped rebuild the abbey, and when he died of leprosy was buried here 25 years later, although his body went undiscovered until building began on a new parish church in 1821. His heart, which was first taken on crusade to Spain by Sir James Douglas, now lies in Melrose Abbey in southern Scotland (see p.143).

The Town

Dunfermline's **centre**, at the top of the hill around the abbey and palace, holds an appeal of its own, with its narrow, cobbled streets, pedestrianized shopping areas and gargoyle-adorned buildings. One of the best of these, the **city chambers** on the corner of Bridge and Bruce streets, is a fine example of late nineteenth-century Gothic Revival style. Among the ornate porticoes and grotesques of dragons and winged serpents which adorn the exterior are the sculpted heads of Robert the Bruce, Malcolm Canmore, Queen Margaret and Elizabeth I.

Dunfermline Abbey (April–Sept Mon–Sat 9.30am–6.30pm, Sun 2–6.30pm; Oct–March Mon–Wed & Sat 9.30am–4.30pm, Thurs 9.30am–12.30pm, Sun 2–4.30pm; HS; £1.80) is comprised of the twelfth-century nave of the medieval monastic church, with an early nineteenth-century parish church spliced on. A plaque beneath the pulpit marks the spot where Robert the Bruce's remains were laid to rest for the second time, while Malcolm and his queen, Margaret, who died of grief three days after her husband in 1093, have a shrine outside. The enormous stonework graffiti, "King Robert the Bruce", at the top of the tower is attributable to an overexcited architect thrilled by the discovery of Bruce's remains. The nearby pink harled **Abbot House** (daily 10am–5pm; £3), possibly fourteenth-century, is best seen from the outside. This building, variously used as an iron foundry, an art school and a doctor's surgery, has been recently restored, although nothing remains of the original interior, and there are no interesting artefacts on display. The upstairs rooms consist of "exhibitions", every square inch painted with scenes of Dunfermline life, medieval and modern, with sinister life-size models of local figures dotted about. You can visit the witches'-coven-style café with a patio garden first to decide if you are willing to pay the entrance fee to see more.

The guest house of Margaret's Benedictine monastery, south of the abbey, became the **Palace** (same times as abbey; £1.80) in the sixteenth century under James VI, who gave both it and the abbey to his consort, Queen Anne of Denmark. Charles I, the last monarch to be born in Scotland, entered the world here in 1600. All that is left of it today is a long, sandstone facade, especially impressive when silhouetted against the evening sky. The four redundant walls next to the palace are those of the refectory, connected via the gatehouse to the kitchen, which was tacked on at the palace's eastern end.

Pittencrieff Park, known to locals as "the Glen", covers a huge area in the centre of town. Bordering the ruined palace, the 76-acre park used to be owned by the Lairds of Pittencrieff, whose 1610 estate house, built of stone pillaged from the palace, still stands within the grounds. In 1902, however, the entire plot was purchased by the local rags-to-riches industrialist and philanthropist Andrew Carnegie, who donated it to his home town. This was just as much sweet revenge as beneficent public-spiritedness: the young Carnegie had been banned from the estate, according to a former laird's edict that no Morrison would pass through the gates. Since his mother had been a Morrison, Carnegie could do little but gaze through the bars on the one day a year that the estate was open to the rest of the public. Today **Pittencrieff House** (April–Sept daily 11am–5pm, Oct–March daily 11am–4pm; free) displays exhibits on local history, the glasshouses are filled with exotic blooms, and the Pavilion coffee shop offers refreshment. In the centre of the park are the remains – little more than the foundations – of **Malcolm Canmore's Tower**, which may be the location of Malcolm's residence, known to have been somewhere to the west of the abbey. Dunfermline – meaning "fort by the crooked pool" – takes its name from the tower's location: *Dun* meaning "hill or fort"; *Fearum* "bent or crooked" and *Lin* (or *Lyne/Line*) "a pool or running water".

Just beyond the southeast corner of the park, the modest little cottage at the bottom of St Margaret Street is **Andrew Carnegie's Birthplace** (April–May, Sept–Oct Mon–Sat 11am–5pm, Sun 2–5pm; June–Aug Mon–Sat 10am–6pm; Nov–March daily 2–4pm; £1.50). The son of a weaver, the young Carnegie (1835–1919) lived upstairs with his family, while the room below housed his father's loom shop. Following the family's emigration to America in 1848, he worked on the railroads before becoming involved with the iron and then the steel industries. From 1873 he began his acquisition of steel-production firms, later to be consolidated into the Carnegie Steel Company; when he retired in 1901 to devote himself to philanthropy, Carnegie was a multi-millionaire. His house has been preserved as it was at the end of the last century, and the adjacent Memorial Hall details his life and work.

Just north of the park, the holy shrine of **St Margaret's Cave** (Easter–Sept daily 11am–4pm; free) lies incongruously buried beneath the Glen Bridge car park. A dimly lit passageway descends deep into the ground, past displays and information panels that document the pious life of Margaret, who prayed here on a daily basis. At the bottom, the sparse stone praying area is small and damp, though in Margaret's day it would have been decorated with crosses and candles.

Practicalities

Trains from Edinburgh connect with Dunfermline, whose **train station** is southeast of the centre, halfway down the long hill of St Margaret's Drive. It's a fifteen-minute walk up the hill from here to the **tourist office**, on Maygate, next to Abbot House (April–Sept Mon–Sat 9.30am–5.30pm, Sun 11am–4pm; Oct–March Mon–Sat 9.30am–5.30pm; ☎01383/720999). An hourly bus from Edinburgh and two-hourly services from Glasgow, Perth and Dundee come in at the **bus station**, in the Kingsgate Centre, on the north side of town. If you want to **stay**, try the comfortable *Davaar House Hotel*, 126 Grieve St (☎01383/721886; ⑤), in a tastefully furnished Victorian town house, or the nearby B&B at 59 Buffies Brae (☎01383/733677; ①), which offers a warm welcome. There are some good, well-priced ethnic **restaurants** in Dunfermline, including *Blossom's*, 6–8 Chalmers St (☎01383 623092), for Chinese food, or *Khan's* (☎01383 739478), 33 Carnegie Drive, for Indian cuisine. Cheap-and-cheerful French cooking is on offer at *Café René* (☎01383 623798), also on Carnegie Drive, while, for great traditional Italian food, there's *Il Pescatore* (☎01383/872999; ⑤) on the coast at Limekilns (about five miles south of the town on the B9156), which also offers reasonable accommodation and boasts of patronage by Prince Andrew and his naval chums. If you want a drink in town, try the *Watering Hole*, New Row.

East of the bridges

Fife's **south coast** curves sharply north at the mouth of the Forth, exposing the towns and villages to an icy east wind that somewhat undermines the sunshine image of their beaches. If you've got the time, though, or fancy an alternative route to St Andrews, after crossing the bridge, cut off to the east along the A921, following the train line as it clings to the northern shore of the mouth of the Forth. Here you'll find a straggle of Fife fishing communities which have depended on the crop of the sea for centuries, and now make popular, although not especially attractive, holiday spots. The **train** line from Inverkeithing and twice-hourly **buses** (#7 and #7A) from Dunfermline run along the coast, stopping at all the following towns.

North Queensferry

Cowering beneath the bridges is **NORTH QUEENSFERRY**, a small fishing village, which, until the opening of the road bridge, was the northern landing point of the ferry across the Forth, and a nineteenth-century bathing resort. Built on a rocky outcrop, the place is comparatively well preserved for somewhere which takes such a battering from the elements, and there are good views across the Forth and of the bridges. The massive spans of the rail bridge – inspiration for Iain Banks' postmodern novel, *The Bridge* – loom frighteningly large from such close range. Today, an ambitious programme to strip the old paint and replace it with a high-tech, long-lasting coating will render redundant the old saying for a seemingly endless task: "It's like painting the Forth Bridge." Also here is the popular **Deep-Sea World** (April–June daily 10am–6pm; July & Aug daily 10am–6.30pm; Nov–March Mon–Fri 11am–5pm; £6.15), a huge aquarium that boasts the world's largest underwater viewing tunnel, through which you glide on a moving walkway while sharks, conger eels and all manner of creatures from the deep swim nonchalantly past.

Inverkeithing

The North Queensferry peninsula gives way to Inverkeithing Bay and **INVERKEITHING**, a medieval watering place established by David I in the twelfth century and granted a charter by William I around 1165, thanks to its strategic location and safe harbour. Modern Inverkeithing is unprepossessing, with housing estates sprawling around the more attractive old town centre. The **Parish Church of St Peter**, on Church Street near the train station, began as a wooden Celtic church before Queen Margaret set to work, and ended up as a Norman stone structure bequeathed to Dunfermline Abbey in 1139. The oldest part of it today is the fifteenth-century tower, the rest having been razed by fire in 1825.

Aberdour

Beyond Inverkeithing, **ABERDOUR** clings tight to the walls of its **Castle** (April–Sept daily 9.30am–6pm; Oct & Nov Mon–Sat 9.30am–4pm, Sun 2–4pm; Dec–March Mon–Wed & Sat 9.30am–4pm, Sun 2–4pm; HS; £1.80) at the southern end of the main street. Once a Douglas stronghold, the castle is on a comparatively modest scale, with gently sloping lawns, a large enclosed seventeenth-century garden and terraces. The fourteenth-century tower is the oldest part of the castle, the other buildings having been added in the sixteenth and seventeenth centuries, including the well-preserved dovecote. Worth more perusal is **St Fillan's Church**, also in the castle grounds, which dates from the twelfth century, with a few sixteenth-century additions, such as the porch restored from total dereliction earlier this century. There's little else to see here apart from the town's popular **silver sands** beach, which, along with its watersports, golf and sailing, has earned Aberdour the rather optimistic tourist board soubriquet the "Fife Riviera". From Aberdour you can take a ferry to Inchcolm Island to see its ruined medieval abbey.

For **accommodation**, the real gem is *Hawkcraig House*, Hawkcraig Point (☎01383/860335; ③), a guest house with a good restaurant in an old ferryman's house overlooking the harbour. Alternatively, you could try the friendly *Aberdour Hotel* on High Street (☎01383/860325; ④), which also has an inexpensive **restaurant** downstairs.

Burntisland

From Aberdour it's three miles to the large holiday resort of **BURNTISLAND** (pronounced "Burnt Island") with its fine stretch of sandy beach. The busy High Street runs the length of the waterfront, hemmed in by buildings at the western end, where you'll find the unkempt **train station**. Offices now occupy **Rossend Castle** (beyond the west end of High Street), a fifteenth-century tower with sixteenth-century additions, sadly not open to the public. Mary, Queen of Scots stayed in 1563 and Pierre de Chastelard, an eager French poet, was discovered in her bedchamber. Chastelard, having been warned once already about hiding in the young queen's private rooms at Holyrood Palace, was whisked off to St Andrews where, proclaiming "Adieu, thou most beautiful and most cruel Princess in the world", he was executed.

Although almost every house along the Links, just beyond High Street, sports a **B&B** sign, the choice of **hotels** is limited to four. The *Inchview Hotel*, 69 Kinghorn Rd (☎01592/872239; ⑤), a listed Georgian building looking out across the sea, and *Kingswood Hotel*, Kinghorn Road (☎01592/872329; ⑤), are the most comfortable. The latter, in a leafy road just north of town, will also organize fishing and shooting trips for guests, and offers good bar meals, high teas and dinners. Other **eating** options include *The Smugglers Inn*, 14 Harbour Place, which does snacks and bar meals and has a good vegetarian selection. If you want to make up a picnic, *Delicate Essen*, 83 High St, is the place to go for bread, cheese, cakes and beer.

Kinghorn

Shortly before reaching **KINGHORN**, the coastal road from Burntisland passes a **Celtic cross** commemorating Alexander III, the last of the Celtic kings, who plunged over the cliff near here one night in 1286, when his horse stumbled. The ancient settlement of Kinghorn is today a popular but not too crowded holiday centre, with few formal attractions but a good beach. The ugly brown pebble-dashed **parish church**, looking over the beach and whipped by wintry winds at the land's edge, dates from 1894, though the site has been used as a church for centuries and the small graveyard is filled with lichen-covered, semi-legible tombstones from the eighteenth century. At the opposite (southern) end of town, a hill lined with Spanish-style villas leads down to the waterfront and the beach at **Pettycur Bay**, where fishing boats cluster round the small harbour and brightly coloured lobster nets dot the sands.

Regular trains from Edinburgh and Dundee arrive at Kinghorn's **train station**, just off High Street. The best place **to stay** is the *Longboat Inn*, 107 Pettycur Rd (☎01592/890625; ②), overlooking the River Forth, just above the beach at Pettycur Bay. Ask for a room with a balcony, from where you'll get good views across to Edinburgh and the Lothians. Cheaper B&Bs include *Craigo-er*, 45 Pettycur Rd (☎01592/890527; ①), and *The Anchorgate* further down the road at no. 55 (☎01592/890245; ①). Decent bar meals are available in the wine bar of the *Longboat Inn*, and full meals in its moderately priced **restaurant**.

Kirkcaldy and around

The ancient royal burgh of **KIRKCALDY** (pronounced "Kirkcawdy") is familiarly known as "The Lang Toun" for its four-mile-long esplanade which stretches the length of the waterfront. The esplanade was built in 1922–23 – not just to hold back the sea, but also to alleviate unemployment – and runs parallel for part of the way with the shorter High Street. If you're here in mid-April, you'll see the historic **Links Market**, a week-long funfair that dates back to 1305 and is possibly the largest street fair in Britain.

Incidentally, though there's little to show for it today, architect brothers Robert and James Adam were born in Kirkcaldy, as was the eighteenth-century scholar, philosopher and political economist Adam Smith, whose great work *The Wealth of Nations* (1776) established political economy as a separate science.

The Town

Kirkcaldy doesn't hold a great deal of interest for the visitor, its charms largely obliterated by overdevelopment. However, a stroll along the promenade is pleasant on a sunny day and there's a good range of the major chain stores in the town centre. The town's history is chronicled in its **Museum and Art Gallery** (Mon–Sat 10.30am–5pm, Sun 2–5pm; free) in the colourful War Memorial Gardens between the train and bus stations. The museum covers everything from archeological discoveries to the tradition of the local Wemyss Ware pottery and the evolution of the present town. Since its inception in 1925, the gallery has built up its collection to around three hundred works by some of Scotland's finest painters from the late eighteenth century onwards, including works by the fine portraitist Sir Henry Raeburn, the historical painter Sir David Wilkie, the Scottish "Colourists", the "Glasgow Boys" and William McTaggart. For a town which is known primarily for linoleum production and whose reputation is firmly rooted in the prosaic, the art gallery is an unexpected boon.

Just beyond the northern end of the waterfront, Ravenscraig Park is the site of the substantial ruin of **Ravenscraig Castle**, a thick-walled, fifteenth-century defence post, which occupies a lovely spot above a beach. The castle looks out over the Forth, and is flanked on either side by a flight of steps – the inspiration, apparently, for the title of John Buchan's novel, *The Thirty-Nine Steps*. Sir Walter Scott also found this a place worthy of comment, using it as a setting for the story of "lovely Rosabella" in *The Lay of the Last Minstrel*.

Beyond Kirkcaldy lies the old suburb of **Dysart**, where tall ships once arrived bringing cargo from the Netherlands, setting off again with coal, beer, salt and fish. Well restored, and retaining historic street names such as Hot Pot Wynd (after the hot pans used for salt evaporation), it's an atmospheric place of narrow alleyways and picturesque old buildings. In Rectory Lane, the birthplace of John McDouall Stuart (who in 1862 became the first man to cross Australia from the south to the north) now holds the **McDouall Stuart Museum** (June–Aug daily 2–5pm; NTS; free), giving an account of his emigration to Australia in 1838 and his subsequent adventures.

Practicalities

Kirkcaldy's **train** and **bus stations** are in the upper part of town – keep heading downhill to get to the centre. For the **tourist office**, 19 Whytecauseway (Mon–Fri 10am–5pm, Sat 10am–1pm & 2–5pm; ☎01592/267775), follow the road for about ten minutes round to the right from the bus station. If you want to stay in Kirkcaldy, the office's accommodation booking service is a life-saver; there are few places **to stay** in the centre, and the layout of the rest of the town is not easy to follow because of the way it falls across the hillside. In Kirkcaldy town centre the *Parkway Hotel*, Abbotshall Road (☎01592/262143; ④), offers smart rooms and traditional breakfasts, while the smaller, more refined *Dunnikier House Hotel*, Dunnikier Park, Dunnikier Way (☎01592/268393; ④), serves fine local food and is set in pleasant grounds. The *Strathearn Hotel*, 2 Wishart Place, on Dysart Road (☎01592/652210; ③), is a welcoming place set in its own gardens, a couple of miles north of the centre of town. You can get cheaper rooms along the road in **Dysart**, at the *Royal Hotel*, Townhead (☎01592/654112; ②), which occupies one of the village's historic buildings.

The *Royal Hotel* is a good place for **eating**, as is the *Old Rectory Inn*, West Quality Street, also in Dysart. In Kirkcaldy itself, try *Giovanni's*, 66 Dunnikier Rd (☎01592/200659), for traditional Italian food, or *Maxin*, 5 High St (☎01592/263406), for Chinese.

There's a good **arts cinema** with a restaurant and bar, which is housed in the Adam Smith Theatre on Bennochy Road in the town centre (☎01592/260498).

Around Kirkcaldy

Inland from Kirkcaldy, the old **mining towns** of Cowdenbeath, Kelty, Lochgelly and Cardenden huddle together, their fires virtually extinguished by a blanket of economic depression. These are neglected places, and indeed are rarely even seen by visitors shooting up to St Andrews on the coastal route or zooming along the M90 to Perth. Take the train, however, and you'll weave through this forlorn stretch as the line leaves the coast and heads inland.

Ten miles inland from Kirkcaldy, **GLENROTHES** is a new town in much the same mould as any other. Stark, concrete and utilitarian, it is the European headquarters of the Californian company Hughes Microelectronics, who, along with similar operations, have given the town much-needed wealth and self-confidence. Until recently, a sign at Markinch train station to the west (Glenrothes' nearest station) boldly announced, "Welcome to Glenrothes, the Capital of Fife". So outraged at this audacity were the residents of Cupar, Fife's real capital for centuries, that the sign had to be removed.

If you have even a passing interest in castles and their construction, try to visit **Balgonie Castle**, two miles east of Glenrothes on the B921 off the A911. Set above the River Leven, this splendid castle with its fourteenth-century keep and fine open courtyard has a somewhat unkempt appearance from the outside; only a small plaque stating that it is home to the Laird and Lady of Balgonie suggests it's inhabited. Don't be put off by the huge, but docile, Scottish deerhounds, or by the fact that you may have to wait some time at the door of the keep before anyone hears your knock. Once inside, you are guaranteed a uniquely personal tour from the laird or a member of his family; the castle has the distinction of being open every day of the year (roughly 10am–5pm; £3) except when the fourteenth-century chapel is being used for candlelit weddings. The tour gives in-depth information on the architecture of the castle and its owners and occupiers, including Rob Roy who stayed here with 200 clansmen in 1716. Balgonie was partly restored in 1971 and the present laird, who hails from the West Midlands but is always attired in a kilt, has continued the process.

The Howe of Fife

Completely different from the industrial landscape of Kirkcaldy and Glenrothes, the **Howe of Fife**, north of Glenrothes, is a low-lying stretch of ground ("howe") at the foot of the twin peaks of the heather-swathed **Lomond Hills** – West Lomond (1696ft) and East Lomond (1378ft). The area makes an ideal stopping point on the way to St Andrews, with wonderful **Falkland Palace** and the handsome market town of **Cupar** along the way. Frequent **buses** run throughout the area, with regular services threading their way towards Dundee from Kirkcaldy. The **train** also comes this way, stopping at Cupar and Leuchars before crossing the Tay Bridge to Dundee.

Falkland

Nestling in the lower slopes of East Lomond, the narrow streets of **FALKLAND** are lined with fine and well-preserved seventeenth- and eighteenth-century buildings. The village grew up around **Falkland Palace** (April–Oct Mon–Sat 11am–5.30pm, Sun 1.30–5.30pm; NTS; £5, gardens only £2.30), which stands on the site of an earlier castle, home to the Macduffs, the Earls of Fife. James IV began the construction of the present palace in 1500; it was completed and embellished by James V, and became a favoured royal residence. Charles II stayed here in 1650, when he was in Scotland for his coronation, but after the Jacobite rising of 1715 and temporary occupation by Rob Roy the palace was left to ruin, remaining so until the late nineteenth century when the keepership was acquired by the third Marquess of Bute. He restored the palace entirely, and today it is a stunning example of Early Renaissance architecture, complete with corbelled parapet, mullioned windows, round towers and massive walls. A **guided tour** (40min) takes in a cross-section of public and private rooms in the south and east wings. The former is better preserved and includes the stately drawing room, the Chapel Royal (still used for Mass) and the Tapestry Gallery, swathed with splendid seventeenth-century Flemish hangings. Outside, the **gardens** are also worth a look, their well-stocked herbaceous borders lining a pristine lawn, and they feature the oldest tennis court in Britain – built in 1539 for James V and still used.

Falkland is also a good base for **walks**, with several leading from the village; but for the more serious hikes to the summits of East and West Lomond, you have to start from Craigmead car park about two miles west of the village (follow the usual safety precautions; see p.48).

If you want to **stay** in Falkland, try the **youth hostel**, Back Wynd (☎01337/857710; March–Sept; Nov–Feb Sat only), or, for B&B, the attractive *Oakbank Guest House*, The Pleasance (☎01337/857287; ①). Both the *Hunting Lodge Hotel*, on High Street, directly opposite the palace (☎01337/857226; ③), and the *Covenanter Hotel* (☎01337/857224; ③), just up the road, are comfortable.

Cupar and around

Straddling the small River Eden and surrounded by gentle hills, **CUPAR**, (pronounced "Kew-par") the capital of Fife, has retained much of its medieval character – and its self-confident air – from the days when it was a bustling market centre. A livestock auction still takes place here every week. In 1276 Alexander III held an assembly in the town, bringing together the Church, aristocracy and local burgesses in an early form of Scottish parliament. For his troubles he subsequently became the butt of Sir David Lindsay's biting play, *Ane Pleasant Satyre of the Thrie Estaitis* (1535), one of the first great Scottish dramas.

Situated at the centre of Fife's road network, Cupar's main street, part of the main road from Edinburgh to St Andrews, is plagued with thundering traffic. The **Mercat Cross**, stranded in the midst of the lorries and cars which speed through the centre, now consists of salvaged sections of the seventeenth-century original, following its destruction by an errant lorry some years ago.

One of the best reasons for stopping off at Cupar is to visit the **Hill of Tarvit** (Easter–Sept daily 1.30–5.30pm; NTS; £3.90; gardens open April–Oct 9.30am–9pm, Nov–March 9.30am–4.30pm; £1 donation), an Edwardian mansion two miles south of town remodelled by Sir Robert Lorimer from a late seventeenth-century building. The estate, formerly the home of the geographer and cartographer Sir John Scott, includes the five-storey, late sixteenth-century **Scotstarvit Tower**, three-quarters of a mile west of the present house (keys available from the house during season only). Set on a little mound, Scotstarvit is a fine example of a Scots tower house, providing both fortification and comfort. The entire estate was bequeathed to the NTS in 1949 (part of which they rent out; see below), and the house contains an impressive collection of eighteenth-century Chippendale and French furniture, Dutch paintings, Chinese porcelain and a restored Edwardian laundry.

Practicalities

Cupar's **train station** is immediately south of the centre; **bus** #23 from Stirling to St Andrews stops outside. If you want to **stay**, try the friendly *Eden House Hotel*, 2 Pitscottie Rd (☎01334/652510, *lv@eden.u-net.com*; ④), which also serves good inexpensive Scottish food, or *Rathcluan* B&B on Carslogie Road (☎01334/657857, *reservations@rathcluan.co.uk*; ③). You can rent the small cottage at the foot of the Scotstarvit Tower from the NTS for around £250–340 per week (☎0131/243 9331). If money is no object, head for one of the luxury hotels out of the centre: *Balbirnie House Hotel*, Balbirnie Park (☎01592/610066; ⑦), is a magnificent Georgian mansion five miles southwest of town, complete with 416 acres of parkland; and five miles north of Cupar in **Letham**, the *Fernie Castle Hotel* (☎01337/810381; ⑥) occupies a real fourteenth-century castle and offers bar meals as well as a more expensive à la carte menu. There is no shortage of good **restaurants** in the area; try the excellent *Ostler's Close*, 25 Bonnygate (☎01334/655574), or take the B940 east to the renowned *Peat Inn* (see p.281). For drinks and bar food, try *Watts* on Coal Road.

Around Cupar

To the west of Falkland are a couple of attractions particularly suitable for children. The **Scottish Deer Centre** (Easter–Oct daily 10am–6pm; Nov–Easter daily 10am–5pm; £3.50), three miles from Cupar on the A91, specializes in the rearing of red deer, and is also home to species of sika, fallow and reindeer. The tamer animals can be petted and there are falconry displays three times a day, as well as play and picnic areas and guided nature trails. A couple of miles further west along the A91, more unusual creatures are on show at the **Ostrich Kingdom** (daily 10am–5pm; £3.85), next to Birnie Loch Nature Reserve. Children will enjoy watching the giant birds cavort, and looking at chickens, goats and pot-bellied pigs in the children's farm.

A couple of miles southeast of Cupar, **CERES**, set around a village green, is home to the **Fife Folk Museum** (mid-May to Oct daily except Fri 2–5pm; £2). Occupying several well-preserved seventeenth- to nineteenth-century buildings, it exhibits all manner of historical farming and agricultural paraphernalia. The pillory that used to restrain miscreants on market days still stands at the entrance of the old burgh tollbooth, and at the village crossroads is an unusual seventeenth-century stone carving of a man in a three-cornered hat with a toothy grin and a beer glass on his knee, said to be a depiction of a former provost.

Continuing east on the B939, you soon come to **Magnus Muir**, halfway between Cupar and St Andrews, site of the murder of the controversial and oppressive Episcopalian Archbishop of St Andrews by a band of Covenanters in 1679. During the struggle, Archbishop Sharp's daughter, Isabella, was wounded trying to protect him. One of the culprits, Hackston of Rathillet, was captured in Edinburgh and gruesomely executed; his hands were buried in Cupar's graveyard.

St Andrews and around

Confident, poised and well groomed, if a little snooty, **ST ANDREWS**, Scotland's oldest university town and a pilgrimage centre for golfers from all over the world, is on a wide bay on the northeastern coast of Fife. It's often referred to in tourist literature as "the Oxford or Cambridge of the North" and, by and large, St Andrews *is* its university.

According to legend, the town was founded, pretty much by accident, in the fourth century. St Rule – or Regulus – a custodian of the bones of St Andrew on the Greek island of Patras, had a vision in which an angel ordered him to carry five of the saint's bones to the western edge of the world, where he was to build a city in his honour. The conscientious courier set off, but was shipwrecked on the rocks close to the present harbour. Struggling ashore with his precious burden, he built a shrine to the saint on what subsequently became the site of the cathedral; St Andrew became Scotland's patron saint and the town its ecclesiastical capital.

Local residents are proud of their town, with its refined old-fashioned ambience. Thanks to a strong and well-informed local conservation lobby, many of the original

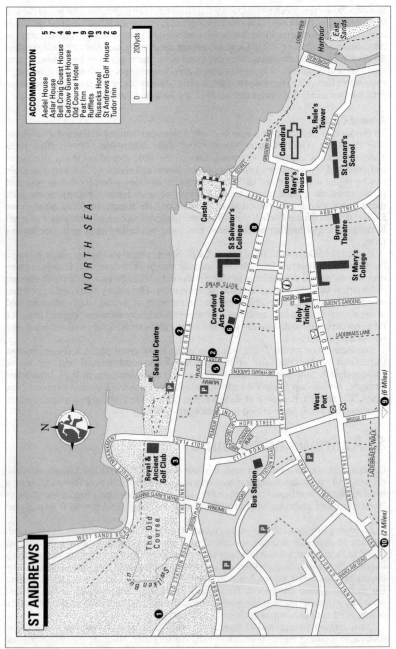

ST ANDREWS

ACCOMMODATION
Aedel House 5
Aslar House 7
Bell Craig Guest House 4
Cadzow Guest House 8
Old Course Hotel 1
Peat Inn 9
Rufflets 10
Rusacks Hotel 3
St Andrews Golf House 2
Tudor Inn 6

0 — 200yds

NORTH SEA

West Sands Road
The Old Course
Swilken Burn
Bruce Embankment
Grannie Clark's Wynd
The Links
Gibson Place
Old Station Road
Golf Place
Royal & Ancient Golf Club
Windmill Road
Guardbridge Road
Bus Station
Station Road
City Road
Hope Street
Pilmour Terrace
Murray Place
The Scores
Sea Life Centre
Castle
East Scores
Castle Street
Gregory Place
Cathedral
St Rule's Tower
Long Pier
Harbour
East Sands
Shorehead
Fends Road
St Leonard's School
Queen Mary's House
Abbey Street
Byre Theatre
St Salvator's College
Butts Wynd
North Street
Crawford Arts Centre
Market Street
St Mary's College
Church St
Holy Trinity
Queen's Gardens
South Street
Ladebraes Lane
Greyfriars Gardens
Bell Street
St Mary's Place
Greenside Place
Howard Place
West Port
Bridge St
Abbey Walk
Ladebraes Walk
Double Dykes Road
Argyle Street
A915 (6 Miles)
A917 (2 Miles)
Kennedy Gardens
Nan'kar Brae
B965

N

© Crown copyright

buildings have survived. Almost the entire centre consists of listed buildings, while the ruined castle and cathedral have all but been rebuilt in the efforts to preserve their remains. If you're here in early August, don't miss the two-day **Lammas Fair**, Scotland's oldest surviving medieval market, complete with town crier. The other main event in the St Andrews calendar is the **Kate Kennedy Pageant**, usually held on the third Saturday in April, which involves an all-male procession of students taking to the streets dressed as characters associated with the university, from Kate Kennedy herself, niece of one of the university founders, to Mary, Queen of Scots.

There are two main excursion areas from St Andrews. The most popular, with its beaches and little fishing villages, is the **East Neuk**, stretching from Fife Ness to Largo Bay; the other is the **Tay coast**, which runs around Fife's northeast headland and along the Tay estuary almost to Perth. **Bus** #95 runs from Leven up the coast to Dundee.

Arrival and information

St Andrews is not on the train line. The nearest **train station** is on the Edinburgh–Dundee–Aberdeen line at **Leuchars**, five miles northwest across the River Eden, from where regular (but not always connecting) buses make the fifteen-minute trip into town. The price of the rail ticket to Leuchars does not include the bus trip to St Andrews. Frequent **buses** from Edinburgh and Dundee terminate at the bus station on City Road at the west end of Market Street. The **tourist office**, 70 Market St (April & May Mon–Sat 9.30am–6pm, Sun 11am–4pm; June Mon–Sat 9.30–7pm, Sun 11am–6pm; July & Aug Mon–Sat 9.30am–8pm, Sun 11am–6pm; Sept to mid-Oct Mon–Sat 9.30am–7pm, Sun 11am–6pm; mid-Oct to March Mon–Sat 9.30am–5pm; ☎01334/472021), holds comprehensive information about St Andrews and northeast Fife. If you're **driving**, the town's fiendish **parking** system requires vouchers (35p per hour) which you can get from the tourist office and some local shops. Scratch out the month, day, date and hour from the card, display it in your car, and cross your fingers that you've worked it out correctly.

Accommodation

Although rooms in St Andrews cost more than in the surrounding area, they often get booked up in the summer, when advance reservations are strongly recommended. Most of the **guest houses** are around Murray Place and Murray Park between The Scores and North Street. Good ones include *Aedel House*, 72 Murray Place (☎01334/472315; ③), and *Bell Craig Guest House* at 8 Murray Park (☎01334/472962; ②). On North Street, try *Aslar House*, at no. 120 (☎01334/473460, *pardoe@aslar.u-net.com*; ③), or *Cadzow Guest House*, at no. 58 (☎01334/476933; ②). Between June and September, the **university** (☎01334/462000; ③) rents out about 200 rooms in various locations, all on a B&B basis with dinner optional. More upmarket are the various **hotels** lining The Scores, beyond the eastern end of the Old (golf) Course, overlooking the bay. The *St Andrews Golf Hotel*, at no. 40 (☎01334/472611, *thegolfhotel@standrews.co.uk*; ⑦), occupies a three-storey town house, with chintzy, comfortable bedrooms – those at the front have great views – good food and an extensive wine list, while the luxurious *Old Course Hotel* (☎01334 474371; ⑨), is famously located by the seventeenth hole of the Old Course.

As you come into town from Leuchars, you'll see the entrance to the swanky *Rusacks Hotel*, 16 Pilmour Links (☎01334/474321; ⑦), on the left. From the airy lobby to its spacious rooms, this is a refined place whose old-fashioned style is in keeping with the town's air of respectability. A little further up the road is the *Tudor Inn*, 129 North St (☎01334/474906; ③) – its uncharacteristic black-and-white facade more English than Scottish. Although less luxurious than the above hotels, this is good value as long as you're not sleeping above the noisy downstairs bar. A couple of miles west of St

Andrews on the B939 to Ceres is *Rufflets* (☎01334/472594; ⑧), an elegant 1920s country house, whose garden provides much of the produce for the hotel's restaurant. The *Peat Inn* hotel (☎01334/840206; ⑦), five miles south of town on the A915 and then one mile west on the B940 in a village named after it, has plush suites in a modern building tucked behind the old coaching inn, and is renowned for its wonderful restaurant (see p.281).

The Town

The centre of St Andrews still follows the medieval layout. On its three main thoroughfares, North Street, South Street and Market Street, which run west to east towards the ruined Gothic cathedral, are several of the original university buildings from the fifteenth century. Narrow alleys connect the cobbled streets, attic windows and gable ends shape the rooftops, and here and there you'll see old wooden doors with heavy knockers and black iron hinges.

The ruin of the great **St Andrews Cathedral** (visitor centre April–Sept Mon–Sat 9.30am–6pm, Sun noon–6pm; Oct–March Mon–Sat 9.30am–4pm, Sun 2–4pm; £1.80, joint ticket with St Andrew's Castle £3.50: grounds Sun only 9am–6.30pm; HS; free), at the east end of town, gives only an idea of the former importance of what was once the largest cathedral in Scotland. Though founded in 1160, it was not finished and consecrated until 1318, in the presence of Robert the Bruce. On June 5, 1559, the Reformation took its toll, and supporters of John Knox, fresh from a rousing meeting, plundered the cathedral and left it to ruin. Stone was still being taken from the cathedral for various local building projects as late as the 1820s.

Standing above the harbour where the land drops to the sea, the cathedral site can be a blustery place, with the wind whistling through the great east window and down the stretch of turf that was once the central aisle. In front of the window a slab is all that remains of the high altar, where the relics of St Andrew were once enshrined. Previously, it is believed that they were kept in **St Rule's Tower**, the austere Romanesque monolith next to the cathedral, which was built as part of an abbey in 1130. From the top of the tower (a climb of 157 steps), there's a good view of the town and surroundings, and of the remains of the monastic buildings which made up the priory. Around the entire complex is a sturdy wall dating from the sixteenth century, over half a mile long and with three gateways.

Southwest of the cathedral enclosure lies **the Pends**, a huge fourteenth-century vaulted gatehouse which marked the main entrance to the priory, and from where the road leads down to the harbour, passing prim **St Leonard's**, one of Scotland's leading private schools for girls. The sixteenth-century, rubble-stonework building on the right as you go through the Pends is **Queen Mary's House**, where she is believed to have stayed in 1563. The house was restored in 1927 and is now used as the school library.

Down at the **harbour**, gulls screech above the fishing boats, keeping an eye on the lobster nets strewn along the quay. If you come here on a Sunday morning, you'll see students parading down the long pier, red gowns billowing in the wind, in a time-honoured after-church walk. The beach, **East Sands**, is a popular stretch, although it's cool in summer and positively biting in winter. A path leads south from the far end of the beach, climbing up the hill past the caravan site and cutting through the gorse; this makes a pleasant walk on a sunny day, taking in hidden coves and caves.

North of the beach, the rocky coastline curves inland to the ruined **St Andrew's Castle** (April–Sept Mon–Sat 9.30am–6pm, Sun 9.30am–4pm; Oct–March Mon–Sat 9.30am–4pm, Sun 2–4pm; HS; £2.50), with a drop to the sea on three sides and a moat on the fourth. Founded around 1200 and extended over the centuries, it was built as part of the Palace of the Bishops and Archbishops of St Andrews and was consequently the scene of some fairly grim incidents at the time of the Reformation. There's not a great deal left of the castle, since it fell into ruin in the seventeenth century, and most of what can be seen dates from the sixteenth century, apart from the fourteenth-century Fore Tower.

Protestant reformer George Wishart was burnt at the stake in front of the castle in 1546, as an incumbent Cardinal Beaton looked on. Wishart had been a friend of John Knox's, and it wasn't long before fellow reformers sought vengeance for his death. Less than three months later, Cardinal Beaton was stabbed to death and his body displayed from the battlements before being dropped into the "bottle dungeon", a 24ft pit hewn out of solid rock which can still be seen in the Sea Tower. The perpetrators then held the castle for over a year, and during that time dug the secret passage which can be entered from the ditch in front. Outside the castle, the initials "GW" are carved in stone.

St Andrews University is the oldest in Scotland, founded in 1410 by Bishop Henry Wardlaw. The nominal founder is James I to whom the bishop was tutor, and the king was certainly a great benefactor of the university. The first building was on the site of the Old University Library and by the end of the Middle Ages three colleges had been built: St Salvator's (1450) on North Street, St Leonard's (1512) on The Pens, and St Mary's (1538) on South Street. At the time of the Reformation, St Mary's became a seminary of Protestant theology, and today it houses the university's Faculty of Divinity. The **quad** here has beautiful gardens and some magnificent old trees, perfect for flopping under on a warm day. A **guided tour** of the University buildings starts from the International Office, Butts Wynd, near St Salvator's Chapel (June–Aug Mon–Sat 11am & 2.30pm, 4.30pm on request; £3), or you can wander freely around the buildings at your own pace.

If you've got children in tow you may want to visit the huge **Sea Life Centre** (daily 10am–6pm; July & Aug closes 7pm; £4.25), on The Scores, at the west end of town close to the golf museum (see below). Here, you can see marine life of all shapes and sizes with displays, observation pools and underwater walkways. Also good for children is the fifty-acre **Craigtoun Country Park** (April–Sept daily 10.30am–6.30pm; £2), a couple of miles southwest of town on the B939. As well as several landscaped gardens there is a miniature train, trampolines, boating, crazy golf and picnic areas, and a country fair each May with craft stalls, wildlife exhibits and showjumping displays.

To escape the bustle of the town, head to the **Botanic Gardens** on Canongate (daily May–Sept 10am–7pm; Oct–April 10am–4pm; £1.50: glasshouses all year Mon–Fri 10am–4pm; £1.50), a peaceful retreat just ten minutes' walk south of South Street.

Eating and drinking

St Andrews has no shortage of **restaurants** and **cafés**. In town, *Littlejohns*, at the east end of Market Street, serves hearty burgers and steaks, while *The Vine Leaf Restaurant*, 131 South St (☎01334/477497; closed Sun), is known for its well-priced, good-quality dishes made from local produce and a good range of seafood.

Brambles, 5 College St, offers inexpensive homebaking, as does *The Merchant's House*, 49 South St, which also has good vegetarian options. The *Victoria Café*, 1 St Mary's Place, is a popular student haunt serving baked potatoes and toasted sandwiches, and a good place to have a few drinks in the evening. *Ma Belle's*, 40 The Scores, in the basement of the *St Andrews Golf Hotel*, is a lively pub serving cheap food and catering for locals as much as students. For the best views of the Old Course, *Rusacks Lounge Bar*, 16 Pilmour Links, has huge comfy chairs, where you can watch golfers through huge windows and sip pricey drinks.

For truly great food, head for the *Peat Inn* (☎01334/840206; see p.280), one of Britain's top restaurants, serving a varied menu of local specialities. The dining area is

GOLF IN ST ANDREWS

St Andrew's **Royal and Ancient Golf Club** (or "R&A") is the governing body for golf the world over, dating back to a meeting of 22 of the local gentry in 1754, who founded the Society of St Andrews Golfers, being "admirers of the ancient and healthful exercise of golf". It acquired its current title after King William IV agreed to be the society's patron in 1834.

The game itself has been played here since the fifteenth century. Those early days were instrumental in establishing Scotland as the home of golf, for the rules were distinguished from those of the French game by the fact that participants had to manoeuvre the ball into a hole, rather than hit an above-ground target. (Early French versions were, in fact, more like croquet.) The game developed, acquiring popularity along the way – even Mary, Queen of Scots was known to have the occasional round. It was not without its opponents, however, particularly James II who, in 1457, banned his subjects from playing since it was distracting them from archery practice.

St Andrews' status as a world-renowned **golf** centre is obvious as you enter the town from the west, where the approach road runs adjacent to the famous **Old Course**. At the eastern end of the course lies the strictly private **clubhouse**, a stolid, square building dating from 1854. The first British Open Championship was held here in 1873, having been inaugurated in 1860 at Prestwick in Ayrshire, and since then the British Open has been held here regularly, pulling in enormous crowds. The eighteenth hole of the Old Course is immediately in front of the clubhouse, and has been officially christened the "Tom Morris", after one of the world's most famous golfers. Pictures of Nick Faldo, Jack Nicklaus and other golfing greats, along with clubs and a variety of memorabilia which they donated, are displayed in the admirable **British Golf Museum** on Bruce Embankment, along the waterfront below the clubhouse (April–Oct daily 9.30am–5.30pm; Nov–March Thurs–Mon 11am–3pm; £3.75). There are also plenty of hands-on exhibits, including computers, video screens and footage of British Open championships, tracing the development of golf through the centuries.

intimate without being cramped, and a three-course meal – perhaps featuring lobster broth, venison or roast monkfish – will set you back at least £40 per head.

With its big student population, St Andrews has lots of good **pubs**. Locals and tourists mix with the students at the *Tudor*, 129 North St, which has a late-night licence on Thursdays and Fridays and live bands from time to time. The *Central* on Market Street serves huge pies and a powerful beer brewed by Trappist monks. *Firkins*, St Mary's Place, at the bottom of Market Street, is a popular real-ale bar whose extensive beer selection attracts a young crowd.

The East Neuk

Extending south of St Andrews as far as Largo Bay, the **East Neuk** (*neuk* is Scots for "corner") is a region of quaint fishing villages, all crow-stepped gables and tiled roofs, the Flemish influence in the architecture indicating a history of strong trading links with the low countries. Inland, gently rolling hills provide some of the best farmland in Scotland, with quiet country lanes more redolent of parts of southern England than north of the border.

Perhaps the prettiest of the coastal communities is **Crail**, with a picturesque pottery near the harbour, but the best beaches are at the resorts of **Elie** and **Earlsferry**, which lie next to each other about twelve miles south of St Andrews, and at **Lower Largo**, where you can also see a statue of Alexander Selkirk, the young Scots sailor who was immortalized by Daniel Defoe as *Robinson Crusoe*. The other villages between St Andrews and Lower Largo fall into two distinct types: either scattered higgledy-piggledy up the hillside like **St Monans**, between **Pittenweem** and Elie, or neatly lined along the harbour like **Anstruther**, between Crail and Pittenweem.

For **eating** in the East Neuk, your best options are the *Seafood Restaurant*, 16 West End, in the village of St Monans (☎01333/730327), which has an excellent reputation for contemporary Scottish cuisine, or the *Bouquet Garni* restaurant in Elie (☎01333/330374), which specializes in fresh seafood and game.

Crail

CRAIL consists of a maze of streets lined with a higgledy-piggledy mixture of cottages leading down to one of the most picturesque harbours in Fife. Among the attractions is the twelfth-century **St Mary's Church**, where legend has it that the large blue stone by the gate was tossed there by the devil, all the way from the offshore Isle of May. You can trace the history of the town at the fascinating **Crail Museum and Heritage Centre** at 62 Marketgate (Easter–Sept daily 10am–1pm 2pm–5pm, Sun 2–5pm; free), which also doubles up as the town's **tourist information centre**, while at 75 Nethergate, the **Crail Pottery** (Mon–Fri 8am–5pm, weekends 10am–5pm), is worth a visit for the wide range of locally-made pottery on display, some of which is for sale.

If you want to **stay** in Crail, choices include the *Hazelton Guest House* (☎01333/450250; ②), 29 Marketgate, a small establishment with comfortable rooms and excellent breakfasts, the *Caiplie Guest House*, 53 High St (☎01333/450564; ②), where some of the rooms have sea views and the home cooking is superb, and the *Honeypot Guest House* (☎01333/450935; ①), 6 High St, a small, inexpensive place that's right in the centre of things.

Anstruther

ANSTRUTHER is home to the wonderfully unpretentious **Scottish Fisheries Museum** (April–Oct Mon–Sat 10am–5.30pm, Sun 10am–5pm; Nov–March Mon–Sat 10am–4.30pm, Sun 2–4.30pm; £3.20; ☎01333/310628), quite in keeping with the no-frills integrity of the area in general. Set in a complex of sixteenth- to nineteenth-century buildings on a total of eighteen different floors, it chronicles the history of the fishing and whaling industries with ingenious displays. Anstruther's helpful **tourist office** (Easter to mid-Sept Mon, Fri & Sat 10am–5pm, Tues–Thurs 10am–1pm & 2–5pm, Sun noon–5pm; ☎01333/311073) is next to the museum.

Several miles offshore from Anstruther on the rugged **Isle of May**, you can see a lighthouse, erected in 1816 by Robert Louis Stevenson's grandfather, as well as the remains of Scotland's first lighthouse, built in 1636, which burnt coals as a beacon. The island is now a nature reserve and bird sanctuary, and can be reached by boat from Anstruther (May–Sept; ☎01333/310103; one sailing daily; £12). Between April and July the dramatic sea cliffs are covered with breeding kittiwakes, razorbills, guillemots and shags, while inland there are thousands of puffins and eider duck. Grey seals also make the occasional appearance. Check up on departure times, as crossings vary according to weather and tide, and allow between four and five hours for a round-trip: an hour each way, and a couple of hours there. Take plenty of warm, waterproof clothing.

At the end of a graceful avenue of trees, **Kellie Castle** (May–Oct daily 1.30–5.30pm; £3.50; garden and grounds all year daily 9.30am–sunset; NTS; £1), a couple of miles northeast of Anstruther on the B9171, has an unusual but harmonious mix of twin sixteenth-century towers linked by a seventeenth-century building. Abandoned in the early nineteenth century, the castle was discovered in 1878 by Professor James Lorimer, the distinguished political philosopher, who took on the castle as an "improving tenant". The professor, his artist wife and their children restored the building and made it their home, the family atmosphere evident in an upstairs nursery crammed with Victorian toys. The wonderful gardens, where space is broken up by arches,

SCOTLAND'S SECRET BUNKER

Inland between St Andrews and Anstruther on the B940 (bus #61 takes you to within two miles) is **Scotland's Secret Bunker** (April–Oct daily 10am–5pm; £5.95), as idiosyncratic a tourist attraction as you are likely to find. Just off the official secrets list, the bunker was opened to the public in 1994, though part of the complex is still operational, and remains secret. Entrance is through an innocent-looking farmhouse, then you walk down a vast ramp to the bunker, which is 100ft below ground and encased in 15ft of reinforced concrete. In the event of a nuclear war the bunker was to have become Scotland's new administrative centre, from where government and military commanders would have coordinated firefighting and medical help for Scotland (the equivalent centres in England and Wales aren't open to the public). The bunker, which could house 300 people, was due to be equipped with air filters, a vast electricity generator, its own water supply, and a switchboard room with 2800 phone lines. The best of 1950s technology, today it has a rather kitsch James Bond feel about it. A single concession to entertainment was a couple of cinemas, which now show 1950s newsreel giving painfully inadequate instructions to civilians in the event of nuclear war. Appropriately, the bunker has not been spruced up for tourists, and remains uncompromisingly spartan.

alcoves and paths which weave between profuse herbaceous borders, were designed by the Professor's son Robert aged just sixteen. Later Sir Robert Lorimer, he became a well-known architect specializing in restorations and war memorials; among his restoration works is the Hill of Tarvit in Cupar (see p.276).

Anstruther makes a pretty and peaceful base for exploring the surrounding area, and there are plenty of good **B&Bs**; try the lovely *Hermitage Guest House* (☎01333/310909; ②) on Ladywalk; the *Beaumont Lodge Guest House* (☎01333/310315; ②) and *The Spindrift* (☎01333/310573, *spindrift@east-neuk.co.uk*; ③), both on Pittenweem Road; or *The Sheiling* (☎01333/310697; ①) at 32 Glenogil Gardens. The *Sauchope Links* (☎01337/450460) is a very pleasant **campsite**, a few miles north at Crail. There is a fine **fish restaurant** in Anstruther, the *Cellar*, East Green (☎01333/310378), in one of the village's oldest buildings, once a cooperage and smokehouse. For tasty fish and chips, try the *Anstruther Fish Bar*, The Shore, reputed to be the best in Fife.

The Tay coast

Looking across to Dundee and Perthshire, the **Tay coast**, a peaceful wedge of rural hinterland on the edge of the River Tay, offers little in the way of specific attractions, but a lot of undiscovered hideaways. Gentle hills fringe the shore, sheltering the villages – several of which only acquired running water and streetlights in the past decade or two – that lie in the dips and hollows along the coast.

LEUCHARS, five miles north of St Andrews, is known for its RAF base, from where low-flying jets screech over the hills, appearing out of nowhere and sending sheep, cows and horses galloping for shelter. There is a beautiful twelfth-century church in the village, with fine Norman stonework. Romantic **Earlshall Castle** (private), just east of Leuchars, is the home of the Baron and Baroness of Earlshall, whose ancestor, Sir William Bruce, built the castle in 1546.

Northeast of Leuchars, **Tentsmuir Forest** occupies the northeasternmost point of the Fife headland, and is also a nature reserve with a good beach and peaceful woodland walks – so peaceful that you would never guess it's only five miles or so from the **Tay bridges** with Dundee just the other side (80p toll charge on the road bridge). The current Tay **rail bridge** is the second to span the river on this spot, the first having collapsed in a terrifying disaster during a storm on December 28, 1879, which claimed the lives of around a hundred people in a train crossing the bridge at the time. The event was recorded by the poet, William McGonagall, who has gone down in history as being responsible for some of the most banal verse ever written, including some memorably trite rhyme about the disaster:

So the train mov'd slowly along the Bridge of Tay,
Until it was about midway,
Then the central girders with a crash gave way,
And down went the train and passengers into the Tay!
The storm Fiend did loudly bray,
Because ninety lives had been taken away,
On the last Sabbath day of 1879,
Which will be remember'd for a very long time.

There's a **camping** and **caravan** site at **TAYPORT**, a popular resort a couple of miles east of the bridge, from where one of Scotland's oldest ferries once ran across the river. Here the "silvery Tay" more than justifies this traditional description, shimmering in the light whatever the season. There are good views across the river from the shingly cove at **BALMERINO**, a quaint hamlet five miles further on, just below the ruin of **Balmerino Abbey** (daily dawn–dusk; NTS; £1), surrounded by venerable old trees, including an enormous gnarled Spanish chestnut, which has stood here for four centuries. The Cistercian abbey was founded in 1229 by Alexander II and his mother Ermengarde, who is buried here, and built by monks from the abbey at Melrose in the Borders. Destroyed by the English in 1547, reconstruction work was halted for good by the Reformation. Unfortunately, the only substantial part remaining is unsafe and inaccessible.

Lindores Abbey, seven miles or so further west along the coast, dates from the century before and was a Benedictine settlement. The west tower still stands, silhouetted against the sky, and there are views down to nearby **NEWBURGH**, stunning on a summer evening, with the setting sun lighting up the mud flats below and skimming across the Tay. Newburgh itself is a fairly quiet, slightly rough-edged place. Originally a fishing village, it evolved due to its proximity to the abbey, and is now known for the admirable **Laing Museum** (April–Sept Mon–Fri 10am–5pm, Sat & Sun 2–5pm; Oct–March Wed & Fri noon–4pm, Sun 2–5pm; free). The collection, donated by the banker and historian Dr Alexander Laing in 1892, includes a fine array of antiques and geological specimens gathered in the area.

PERTH AND THE HIGHLANDS

Genteel **Perthshire**, although now officially part of Perthshire and Kinross, still retains its own identity: an area of scenic valleys and glens, rushing rivers and peaceful lochs, it's the long-established domain of Scotland's country-club set. First settled over 8000 years ago, it was taken by the Romans and then the Picts, before Celtic missionaries established themselves here, enjoying the amenable climate, fertile soil and ideal defensive and trading location.

The hub of the region is the port of **Perth**, which for centuries has benefited from its inland position on the River Tay. Salmon, wool and, by the sixteenth century, whisky – Bell's, Dewar's (which has now moved to Glasgow) and the Famous Grouse whiskies all hail from this area – were exported from here, while a major import was Bordeaux claret. Today, perhaps Perth's greatest attraction is the fine **Fergusson Gallery**.

A place of magnificent natural beauty, where the snow-capped peaks fall away to forested slopes and long, deep lochs, the area is dominated by the western **Grampian Mountains**, a mighty range that controls transport routes, influences the weather and tolerates little development. The **Breadalbane Mountains** run between **Loch Tay** and

Loch Earn; as well as providing walking and watersports, the area is dotted with fine towns and villages, like **Aberfeldy** at the western tip of Loch Tay and **Dunkeld** with its eighteenth-century whitewashed cottages and lovely ruined cathedral. Among the wealth of historical sites in Perthshire are the splendid Baronial **Blair Castle** north of Pitlochry, and the breathtaking Italianate gardens at **Drummond Castle** near Crieff.

Transport connections in the region are at their best if you head straight north from Perth, along the train line to Inverness, but buses – albeit often infrequent – also trail the more remote areas. Keep asking at bus stations for details of services, as the further you get from the main villages the less definitive timetables become.

Perth

Surrounded by fertile agricultural land and beautiful scenery, **PERTH** was for several centuries Scotland's capital. Viewed from the hills to the south, the town still justifies Sir Walter Scott's glowing description of it in the opening pages of his novel *The Fair Maid of Perth*. Scott writes of approaching Perth from the south:

> . . . *the town of Perth with its two large measures or inches, its steeples and towers; the hills of Moncreiff and Kinnoul faintly rising into picturesque rocks, partly clothed with woods; the rich margin of the river studded with elegant mansions; and the huge Grampian Mountains, the northern screen of this exquisite landscape.*

During the reign of James I, Parliament met here on several occasions, but its glory was short-lived: the king was murdered in the town's Dominican priory in 1437 by the traitorous Sir Robert Graham, who was captured in the Highlands and tortured to death in Stirling. During the Reformation, on May 11, 1559, John Knox preached a rousing sermon in St John's Church, which led to the destruction of the town's four monasteries (by those Knox later condemned as "the rascal multitude") and quickened the pace of reform in Scotland. Despite decline in the seventeenth century, the community expanded in the eighteenth and has prospered ever since – today it is a finance centre, and still an important and bustling market town. Its long history in **livestock trading** is continued throughout the year, notably with the Aberdeen Angus shows and sales from June to September, and the Perthshire Agricultural Show in August.

Arrival, information and accommodation

Perth is on the main train lines north from Edinburgh and Glasgow and is well connected by bus; the **bus** and **train** stations are on opposite sides of the road at the west end of town where Kings Place runs into Leonard Street. The **tourist office**, 45 High St (April–June, Sept & Oct Mon–Sat 9am–6pm, Sun 11am–4pm; July & Aug Mon–Sat 9am–8pm, Sun 11am–6pm; Nov–March Mon–Sat 9am–5pm; ☎01738/638353), is a ten-minute walk away.

Of the numerous **hotels** in Perth's town centre, try the *Quality Hotel Station*, on Leonard Street (☎01738/624141, *admin@gb628-u-net.com*; ⑤), right by the station, or *Stakis Perth*, West Mill Street (☎01783/628281; ⑤). The spick-and-span *Salutation Hotel*, 34 South St (☎01738/630066; ⑤), claims to be one of Scotland's oldest hotels, having been established in 1699. There are **B&Bs** and guest houses all over town, notably on the approach roads from Crieff and Stirling. In the centre, Marshall Place, overlooking the South Inch, is the place to look. Of the many possibilities along here *Kinnaird House*, 5 Marshall Place (☎01738/628021; ②), offers a warm welcome in a lovely town house, with well-equipped en-suite rooms. In an elegant Georgian terrace facing the park is the *Park Lane Guest House*, 17 Marshall Place (☎01738/637218, *park-lane@sol.co.uk*; ②). On the other side of the river, there's the friendly *Ballabeg*, 14 Keir

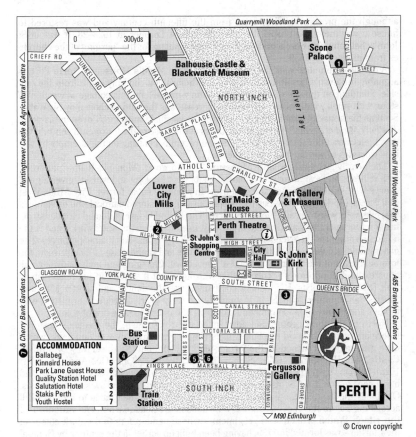

© Crown copyright

St (☎01738/620434; ①), with spacious and comfortable rooms but shared facilities. The **youth hostel** is housed in an impressive old mansion with 64 rooms, at 107 Glasgow Rd (☎01738/623658; March–Oct) beyond the west end of York Place. It's a fair walk from the bus station – if you've got a heavy rucksack you might want to take bus #7.

The Town

Perth's compact **centre** occupies a small area, easily explored on foot, on the west bank of the Tay. Two large areas of green parkland, known as the North and South Inch, flank the centre. The **North Inch** was the site of the Battle of the Clans in 1396, in which thirty men from each of the clans Chattan and Quhele (pronounced "Kay") met in a battle, while the **South Inch** was the public meeting place for witch-burning in the seventeenth century. Both are now used for more civilized public recreation, with sports matches to the north, and boating and putting to the south.

A good variety of shops line **High Street** and **South Street**, as well as filling **St John's** shopping centre on King Edward Street. Opposite the entrance to the centre, the imposing **City Hall** is used by Scotland's politicians for party conferences. Behind here lies **St John's Kirk** (daily 10am–noon & 2–4pm; free), founded by David I in 1126, although the present building dates from the fifteenth century and was restored to house a war memorial chapel designed by Robert Lorimer in 1923–28. It was in St John's that John Knox preached his fiery sermon calling for the "purging of the churches from idolatry" in 1559.

A couple of minutes' walk north of here, the **Fair Maid's House**, on North Port, is arguably the town's best-known attraction, although you can only see it from the outside. Standing on the site of a thirteenth-century monastery, this cottage of weathered stone with small windows and an outside staircase was the setting chosen by Sir Walter Scott as the house of Simon Glover, father of the virginal Catherine Glover, in his novel *The Fair Maid of Perth*. Set in turbulent times at the close of the fourteenth century, the novel tells a traditional story of love, war and revenge, centring on the attempts by various worthies to win the hand of Catherine.

The nearby **Art Gallery and Museum**, 78 George St (Mon–Sat 10am–5pm; free), with exhibits on local history, art, natural history, archeology and whisky, gives a good overview of local life through the centuries. In similar vein, at **Lower City Mills**, West Mill Street (April–Nov Mon–Sat 10am–5pm; £1.50), a restored oatmeal mill driven by a massive waterwheel recalls Victorian Perth. The Round House, a domed circular structure on Marshall Place at the edge of the Tay, used to house the waterworks, and is the unlikely setting for the excellent **Fergusson Gallery** (Mon–Sat 10am–5pm; free). The gallery holds a collection of the paintings, drawings and sculpture of J.D. Fergusson, the foremost artist of the Scottish "Colourist" movement. Changing and imaginative exhibitions explore Fergusson's preoccupation with light and the sea, and his relationships with fellow modernists. His lifelong companion was the dancer and painter Margaret Morris; her summer schools, held annually for forty years, provided Fergusson with models and inspired his monumental paintings of bathers, in pure bright colours.

North of the town centre, and adjacent to the North Inch, the elegantly restored Georgian terraces beyond the Fair Maid's House give way to newer buildings, which have gradually encroached on the former territory of the fifteenth-century **Balhousie Castle**, off Hay Street (May–Sept Mon–Sat 10am–4.30pm; Oct–April Mon–Fri 10am–3.30pm; free). The castle sits incongruously in a peaceful residential area and has been restored in Scots Baronial style with turrets and crow-stepped gables. Originally the home of the Earls of Kinnoull, who have lent their name to Kinnoull Hill across the Tay to the east of Perth, it now houses the headquarters and **museum of the Black Watch**. This historic regiment – whose name refers to the dark colour of their tartan – was formed in 1739, having been built up earlier in the century by General Wade, who employed groups of Highlanders to keep the peace. The museum chronicles its history through a good display of paintings, uniforms, documents, weapons and photographs.

A number of attractions lie around Perth. A mile north of the town on the A9, in the Inveralmond Industrial Estate, is the **Caithness Glass** factory (April–Oct Mon–Sat 9am–5pm, Sun 10am–5pm; Nov–March Mon–Sat 9am–5pm, Sun noon–5pm; free), with a viewing area where you can watch glass-blowing (take bus #4 from Mill Street in Perth).

For outdoor distractions, head for **Bell's Cherrybank Gardens** (April–Oct daily 9am–5pm; £2), a mile west of the centre, where you'll find eighteen acres of well-kept gardens, including the largest collection of heathers in Britain, interspersed with a waterfall, pools, aviary and children's play area. On the other side of the Tay, the **Branklyn Gardens**, 116 Dundee Rd (March–Oct daily 9.30am–sunset; NTS; £2.50), comprise an astonishing collection of Alpine plants and dwarf rhododendrons, spread across a compact two acres of hillside. Looking over the gardens from the north is **Kinnoull Hill**, which also offers splendid views of Perth, the Tay and the surrounding area from its 783ft summit (a 20min walk from the car park on Braes Road). Pick up a leaflet from Perth's tourist office for details of the hill's various woodland walks.

Eating and drinking

There's a fair selection of decent **eating places** in Perth: many ethnic restaurants and pubs offer cheap and satisfying food and there are several upmarket options. Within striking distance of the youth hostel is a good basic Indian restaurant, the *Café Kamran*, 13 York Place. The *Good Luck Food Palace*, 181 South St, serves well-priced Chinese cuisine, while the best choice for a classier meal is *Number Thirty Three*, 33 George St (☎01738/633771), a stylish Art Deco fish restaurant, whose oyster bar serves delicious snacks, while the à la carte restaurant has more substantial fish dishes and good puds. *Strangeways*, 24 George St, is a popular bar and bistro, or, for delicious wholefood, home baking and coffee, try *The Lemon Tree*, 29–41 Skinnergate, just behind the tourist office (closes at 5pm). In addition, there are numerous little **coffee shops** in town like *Brambles*, 11 Princes St, and *Willows*, 12 St John's Place. An Irish **pub** in the town centre, *Mucky Mulligans*, 97 Canal St, claims to be the first "Dublin cottage-style" pub in Scotland and serves specialities like Irish stew all day, with live Irish folk music nightly. Nearby, *Twa Tams*, on Scott Street, and *Brennans*, on St John Street, have inexpensive meals and regular live music.

North of Perth

Just a couple of miles north of Perth on the A93 (bus #58 from South Street in Perth every 20min), on the eastern side of the Tay, **Scone Palace** (pronounced "Scoon") is worth every penny of the admission charge levied by its owners, the Earl and Countess of Mansfield, whose family has owned it for almost four centuries (mid-April to mid-Oct daily 9.30am–5.15pm; £5.40). The two-storey building is stately but not overpowering; it is far more a home than an untouchable monument, and the rooms, although full of priceless antiques and lavish furnishings, feel lived in and used.

Restored in the nineteenth century, the palace today consists of a sixteenth-century core surrounded by earlier buildings, most built of red sandstone, complete with battlements and the original gateway. The abbey that stood here in the sixteenth century, and where all Scottish kings until James I were crowned, was one of those destroyed following John Knox's sermon in Perth. In the extensive grounds which surround the palace lies the Moot Hill, which was once the site of the famous Coronation **Stone of Destiny** (see p.73).

Inside, a good selection of sumptuous rooms are open to visitors, including the library, which now houses an outstanding collection of porcelain, one of the foremost in the world, with items by Meissen, Sèvres, Chelsea, Derby and Worcester. Look out too for the beautiful papier-mâché dishes, Marie Antoinette's writing desk, and John Zoffany's exquisite eighteenth-century portrait of the *Lady Elizabeth Murray* [daughter of the second earl] *with Dido*. You could easily spend a morning here, enjoying strutting peacocks in the gardens, the roaming Highland cattle, donkey park, children's playground and the fragrant pine garden planted in 1848 with exotic conifers.

Huntingtower Castle

Nothing like as grand as Scone, but nonetheless worth a visit, is **Huntingtower Castle** (April–Sept daily 9.30am–6pm; Oct–March Mon–Wed & Sat 9.30am–4.30pm, Sun 2–4.30pm; HS; £1.80), three miles northwest of Perth on the A85 (bus #14, #15 or #55 from Scott Street in Perth). Two three-storey towers formed the original fifteenth- and sixteenth-century tower house, and these were linked in the seventeenth century by a range to provide more room. Formerly known as Ruthven Castle, it was here that the Raid of Ruthven took place in 1582, when the sixteen-year-old James VI, at the request of William, fourth Earl of Ruthven, came to the castle only to be held captive by a group of conspirators demanding the dismissal of favoured royal advisers. The plot failed and the young James was released ten months later. Today the castle's chief attractions are its splendid sixteenth-century painted walls and ceilings – you'll see them in the main hall in the east tower.

Dunkeld and Birnam

DUNKELD, twelve miles on from Perth up the A9 (trains from Perth to Inverness stop here; buses #23 and #27, Sun #22), was proclaimed Scotland's ecclesiastical capital by Kenneth MacAlpine in 850. Its position at the southern boundary of the Grampian Mountains made it a favoured meeting place for Highland and Lowland cultures, but in 1689 it was burnt to the ground by the Cameronians – fighting for William of Orange – in an effort to flush out troops of the Stuart monarch, James VII. Subsequent rebuilding, however, has created one of the area's most delightful communities, and it's well worth at least a brief stop to view its whitewashed houses and lovely cathedral. The **tourist office** is at The Cross in the town centre (April–June, Sept & Oct Mon–Sat 9.30am–5.30pm, Sun 11am–4pm; July & Aug Mon–Sat 9am–7.30pm, Sun 11am–7pm; Nov & Dec Mon–Sat 9.30am–1.30pm; ☎01350/727688).

Dunkeld's partly ruined **cathedral** is on the northern side of town, in an idyllic setting amid lawns and trees on the east bank of the Tay. Construction began in the early twelfth century and continued throughout the next two hundred years, but the building was more or less ruined at the time of the Reformation. The present structure, in Gothic and Norman style, consists of the fourteenth-century choir and the fifteenth-century nave. The choir, restored in 1600 (and several times since), now serves as the parish church, while the nave remains roofless apart from the clock tower. Inside, note the leper's peep near the pulpit in the north wall, through which lepers could receive the sacrament without contact with the congregation. Also look out for the great effigy of "The Wolf of Badenoch", Robert II's son, born in 1343. The Wolf acquired his name and notoriety when, after being excommunicated from the Church for leaving his wife, he took his revenge by burning the towns of Forres and Elgin and sacking Elgin cathedral. He eventually repented, did public penance for his crimes and was absolved by his brother Robert III.

Dunkeld is linked to its sister community, **BIRNAM**, by Thomas Telford's seven-arched bridge of 1809. This little village has a place in history thanks to Shakespeare, for it was on "Dunsinane Hill" to the southeast of the village that Macbeth declared: "I will not be afraid of death and bane/Till Birnam Forest come to Dunsinane", only to be told by a messenger:

> *As I did stand my watch upon the Hill,*
> *I look'd toward Birnam, and anon me thought*
> *The Wood began to move . . .*

The **Perthshire Visitor Centre** just south of Birnam, down the A9 at Bankfoot (March–Oct daily 9am–8pm; Nov–Feb Mon–Fri 9am–7pm, Sat & Sun 9am–7.30pm; £2) offers "The Macbeth Experience", which documents – on film and through talking dummies – the true story of Macbeth, who in real life was quite the opposite of Shakespeare's scheming villain. Several centuries later another literary personality, Beatrix Potter, drew inspiration from the area, recalling her childhood holidays here when penning the *Peter Rabbit* stories. The **Beatrix Potter Garden** in Birnam celebrates the connection.

There are several large **hotels** in Dunkeld, including the *Atholl Arms Hotel*, Tay Terrace (☎01350/727219; ④), the *Royal Dunkeld*, Atholl Street (☎01350/727322; ④), and the Victorian Gothic *Birnam House Hotel* on Perth Road (☎01350/727462; ⑤). Just to the north, the luxurious *Stakis Dunkeld* (☎01350/727771; ⑨) is set at the end of a long drive which winds through the hotel's lush estate, where you can fish, shoot, cycle and stroll. For **B&B**, try the non-smoking *Bheinne Mhor* (☎013502/727779; ②), Birnam Glen, Dunkeld, or the friendly *Heatherbank* (☎01350/727413; ①), on St Mary's Road in Birnam. There are a few mediocre **eating places** on Dunkeld's main street; the best food options are lunch at the *Atholl Arms* or a more expensive dinner at the *Stakis Dunkeld*.

Driving north on the A9 to Pitlochry, you can stop off and walk the mile and a half to **The Hermitage** (buses from Perth to Pitlochry stop near here), set in the wooded gorge of the River Braan. This pretty eighteenth-century folly, also known as Ossian's Hall, was once mirrored to reflect the water, but the mirrors were smashed by Victorian vandals and the folly more tamely restored. The hall, appealing yet incongruous in its splendid setting, neatly frames a dramatic waterfall.

Strathearn

Strathearn – the valley of the River Earn – stretches west of Perth, across to **Loch Earn** and the watersports centre at **Lochearnhead**. Agricola was here around two thousand years ago, trying to establish a foothold in the Highlands; later the area was frequented by Bonnie Prince Charlie and Rob Roy, both bound up in the north–south struggle between Highlands and Lowlands.

South of Strathearn, the small town of **AUCHTERARDER** sees its fair share of visitors, many of whom come to play golf at the swanky **Gleneagles Hotel** nearby (☎01764/662231, *ressales@guinness.com*; ⑨). There is a **tourist office** on High Street (April–June, Sept & Oct Mon–Sat 9.30am–5.30pm, Sun 11am–4pm; July & Aug Mon–Sat 9am–6pm, Sun 11am–5pm; Nov–March Mon–Fri 9.30am–1.30pm; ☎01764/663450).

Dunning

Just southeast of the valley, it is worth taking a detour from the busy A9 to the quiet village of **DUNNING**, five miles east of Auchterarder on the B8062, which has an impressive history. The village was once the capital of the Picts and was the place where Kenneth I, King of the Picts and Scots, died in 860. Dunning was destroyed by the Jacobites and subsequently rebuilt, which accounts for its homogeneous appearance, the houses all being late eighteenth and early nineteenth century. Only **St Serf's** survived, a rugged church with a Norman tower and arch. Just west of the village is an extraordinary monument, a pile of stones surmounted by a cross, and scrawled with the words: "Maggie Wall, Burnt here, 1657". Maggie Wall was burnt as a witch, and rumour has it that local women replenish the white writing on the monument every year.

Crieff and around

At the heart of the valley is the old spa town of **CRIEFF**, in a lovely position on a south-facing slope of the Grampian foothills. Cattle traders used to come here in the eighteenth century, since this was a good location – between the Highlands and the Lowlands – for buying and selling livestock, but Crieff really came into its own with the arrival of the railway in 1856. Shortly after that, Morrison's Academy, now one of Scotland's most respected schools, took in its first pupils, and in 1868 the grand old *Crieff Hydro* (☎01764/655555; ⑧), then known as the *Strathearn Hydropathic*, opened its doors. It's still the nicest place to stay in town, despite being dry (of alcohol). Cheaper **B&B** options include *Eastview Guest House*, 98 East High St (☎01764/652132; ①), and the *Comely Bank Guest House*, 32 Burrell St (☎01764/653409, *bookings@comely-bank .demon.co.uk*; ①). Crieff consists of a pleasing mixture of Edwardian and Victorian houses, with a busy little centre which still retains something of the atmosphere of the former spa town. The **Crieff Visitor Centre** (daily 9am–5pm) is a "craftsy" place, crammed with pottery and paperweights. The **tourist office** is in the town hall on High Street (April–June, Sept & Oct Mon–Sat 9.30am–5.30pm, Sun 11am–4pm; July & Aug Mon–Sat 9am–7pm, Sun 11am–6pm; Nov–March Mon–Fri 9.30am–5pm, Sat 9.30am–1.30pm; ☎01764/652578).

From Crieff, it's a short drive or a twenty-minute walk to the **Glenturret Distillery** (March–Dec Mon–Sat 9.30am–6pm, Sun noon–6pm, last tour 4.30pm; Jan & Feb Mon–Fri 11.30am–4pm, last tour 2.30pm; free; guided tour £3.50, tasting tour £7.50), just off the A85 to Comrie. To get there on public transport, catch any bus going to Crieff, Comrie or St Fillans and ask the driver to drop you at the bottom of the Glenturret Distillery road, from where it's a five-minute walk. This is Scotland's oldest distillery, established in 1775, and a good one to visit, if only for its splendid isolation. Four miles southeast of Crieff on the B8062 (Crieff/Auchterarder bus) is the **Innerpeffray Library** (Feb–Nov Mon–Wed, Fri & Sat 10am–12.45pm & 2–4.45pm, Sun 2–4pm; £2). Founded in 1691, it is the oldest library in Scotland, and is a must for bibliophiles, with mainly theological and classical books.

Even if you have no specialist interest in gardens, on no account miss the **Drummond Castle Gardens** (May–Oct daily 2–6pm; £3) near Muthill, two miles south of Crieff on the A822 (bus #47 from Crieff towards Muthill, then a mile and a half walk up the castle drive). The approach to the garden is extraordinary, up a dark avenue of trees; crossing the courtyard of the castle to the grand terrace, you can view the garden in all its symmetrical glory. It was laid out by John Drummond, second Earl of Perth, in 1630, and shows clear French and Italian influence, although the central structural feature of the parterre is a St Andrews cross. Italian marble statues punctuate the long lines of the cross, and the overall effect is of exceptional harmony and grace. Beyond the formal garden, everything from corn to figs and grapes grows in the Victorian greenhouse and kitchen garden. The castle itself (closed to the public) is a wonderful mixture of architectural styles, a blunt fifteenth-century keep on a rocky crag adjoining a much modified Renaissance mansion house.

Comrie

COMRIE, a pretty conservation village another five miles along the River Earn, has the dubious distinction of being the location where more seismic tremors have been recorded than anywhere else in Britain, due to its position on the Highland Boundary Fault. Earthquake readings are still taken at **Earthquake House**, about 600yd off the A85, on the south side of the river. The building itself is not open to the public, but there are information panels outside, and if you're really keen you can look through the windows at a model of the world's first seismometer, set up here in 1874.

If you've got children, an excellent place to take them is the **Auchingarrich Wildlife Centre** (daily 10am–dusk; £4), a couple of miles south of Comrie on the B827 (bus #15 from Crieff to Comrie, then a two-mile walk). Recently established in a blustery hillside location, it covers 100 acres and provides lots of opportunities for you to pet the farm animals and admire the rare and ornamental birds.

Loch Earn

At the eastern edge of Strathearn is **Loch Earn**, a gently lapping Highland loch dramatically edged by mountains. The A85 runs north along the loch shore from the village of **ST FILLANS**, at the eastern tip, to the main settlement, **LOCHEARNHEAD**, at the western edge of the loch. This wide tranquil expanse is ideal for **watersports**, and particularly good for beginners. Lochearnhead Watersports (☎01567/830330) organizes and teaches a wide variety of activities, including water-skiing, windsurfing, Canadian canoeing and kayaking. Lochearnhead is also a good base for **walking**, and the watersports centre runs "heritage rambles". For **accommodation**, try the *Clachan Cottage Hotel* (☎01567/830247; ③), or the cheaper and terrifically friendly *Earnknowe* B&B (☎01567/830238; ②), both on Lochside, Lochearnhead. There are also some good **self-catering** options in the area: from *Earnknowe* you can rent attractive stone cottages close to Lochearnhead village (2–6 people; £120–355 per week). In addition, there are some Scandinavian-style wooden chalets with good facilities (6 people; £280–355 per week; ☎01567/830211), or a nice little whitewashed cottage in St Fillans (2–4 people; £240 per week; ☎0131/313 0467 or 01764/670004). Perhaps the best choice for the area as a whole, though, is the chalet-like *Four Seasons Hotel* (☎01764/685333; ⑤) in St Fillans, with its wonderful loch-side location. It's also the best choice for **eating**; indeed, there are few other options in the area.

Around Loch Tay

The mountains and valleys of **Glenalmond**, north of Strathearn, give way to the fourteen-mile-long, freshwater **Loch Tay**, just north of which is moody **Ben Lawers** (3984ft), Perthshire's highest mountain; from the top there are incredible views towards both the Atlantic and the North Sea. The ascent – which should not be tackled without all the right equipment (see p.48) – takes around three hours from the NTS **visitor centre** (mid-April to Sept daily 10am–5pm; ☎01567/820397), which is at 1300ft and reached by a track off the A827 along the northern side of the loch. The centre has an audio-visual show, slides of the mountain flowers – including the rare Alpine flora found here – and a nature trail with accompanying descriptive booklet.

The **mountains of Breadalbane** (pronounced "Bread-*al*bane"), named after the Earls of Breadalbane, loom over the southern end of Loch Tay. Glens Lochay and Dochart curve into the north and south respectively from the small town of **KILLIN**, where the River Dochart comes rushing out of the hills and down the frothy **Falls of Dochart**, before disgorging into Loch Tay. There's little to do in Killin itself, but it makes a convenient base for some of the area's best walks. The **tourist office** is located by the falls (March–May & Oct daily 10am–5pm; June & Sept daily 9.30am–6pm; July & Aug daily 9am–6pm; Nov, Dec & Feb Sat & Sun 10am–4pm), next to the **Breadalbane Folklore Centre** (same times as tourist office; £1). The centre explores the history and mythology of Breadalbane and holds the thirteen-hundred-year-old "healing stones" of St Fillan, an early Christian missionary who settled in Glen Dochart. Twelve miles west of Killin, **CRIANLARICH** is a veritable crossroads, the confluence of the main railway lines from Oban and Fort William as they head south, the meeting-point of roads leading to Oban, Fort William and Pitlochry, and a staging post on the West Highland Way (see p.294).

Killin is littered with B&Bs, but one of the more unusual places **to stay** is the *Dall Lodge Hotel*, Main Street (☎01567/820217, *wilson@dalllodgehotel.co.uk*; ⑤), which is filled with all manner of exotic Far Eastern bits and pieces, and has a dining room serving fine local produce. There is also a **youth hostel** (☎01567/820546; April–Oct), in a fine old country house just beyond the northern end of the village, with views out over the loch.

Around six miles further north, the village of **TYNDRUM**, on the A82, is dotted with some rather ugly hotels which owe their existence to a minor (and very short-lived) gold rush, but today is famous primarily for its **Green Welly Shop** (☎01838/400271), where you can purchase a pair of the old dependables from the vast selection of clothing, boots and other outdoor gear on display.

North of the loch

Beyond Breadalbane, the mountains tumble down into **Glen Lyon** – at 34 miles long, the longest enclosed glen in Scotland – where, legend has it, the Celtic warrior Fingal

THE WEST HIGHLAND WAY

Opened in 1980, the spectacular **West Highland Way** was Scotland's first long-distance footpath, stretching some 95 miles from Milngavie (six miles north of central Glasgow), to Fort William, where it reaches the foot of Ben Nevis, Britain's highest mountain.

The route follows ancient drove roads, along which Highlanders herded their cattle and sheep to market in the lowlands, as well as military roads built by troops to control the Jacobite insurgence in the eighteenth century, old coaching roads and even disused railway lines. In addition to the stunning scenery, increasingly dramatic as the path heads north, walkers may see some of Scotland's rarer wildlife, including red deer, feral goats – ancestors of those left behind after the Highland clearances – and, soaring over the highest peaks, golden eagles.

Passing through the lowlands north of Glasgow, the West Highland Way runs along the eastern shores of Loch Lomond, over the Highland Boundary Fault Line, then round Crianlarich, crossing open heather moorland across the Rannoch Moor wilderness area. It passes close to Glencoe, notorious for the massacre of the MacDonald clan, before reaching Fort William. This is wild, remote country: north of Rowardennan on Loch Lomond, the landscape is increasingly spare and exposed, and you should be well prepared for sudden and extreme weather changes.

Though this is emphatically not the most strenuous of Britain's long-distance walks – it passes between lofty mountain peaks, rather than over them – a moderate degree of fitness is required as there are some steep ascents. If you're looking for an added challenge, you could work a climb of Ben Lomond or Ben Nevis into your schedule. You might choose to walk individual sections of the Way (the eight-mile climb from Glencoe up the Devil's Staircase is particularly spectacular), but to tackle the whole thing you need to set aside at least seven days – avoid a Saturday start from Milngavie and you'll be less likely to be walking with hordes of people, and there'll be less pressure on accommodation. Most walkers tackle the route from south to north, and manage between ten and fourteen miles at a time, staying at hotels, B&Bs and bunkhouses en route. Camping is permitted at recognized sites.

Although the path is clearly waymarked, you may want to check the official guide, published by the HMSO, which includes Ordnance Survey maps as well as descriptions of the route, with detailed cultural, historical, archeological and wildlife information. It's available from bookshops or from the HMSO, 72 Lothian Rd, Edinburgh EH3 9AZ. Further details about the Way, including an accommodation list, can be obtained from the West Highland Way ranger, Balloch Castle, Balloch, Dunbartonshire G53 8LX (☎01389/758216), or from the very useful West Highland Way Web site at *www.west-highland-way.co.uk*. As well as giving comprehensive accommodation listings, the Web site has links to tour companies and transport providers, who will take your luggage from one stopping point to the next.

built twelve castles. Access to the glen is usually impossible in winter, but the narrow roads are passable in summer. You can either take the road from Killin up past the **Ben Lawers Visitor Centre**, four miles up Loch Tay, and continue going, or take the road from Fortingall, which is a couple of miles north of the loch's northern end. The two roads join up, making a round-trip possible, but bear in mind there is no road through the mountains to Loch Rannoch further north. **FORTINGALL** itself is little more than a handful of thatched cottages, although locals make much of their 3000-year-old yew tree – believed (by them at least) to be the oldest living thing in Europe. The village also lays claim to being the birthplace of Pontius Pilate, reputedly the son of a Roman officer stationed here.

On a slight promontory at Loch Tay's northern end and overlooking the River Tay, **KENMORE**'s whitewashed houses and well-tended gardens cluster around the gate to **Taymouth Castle** – built by the Campbells of Glenorchy in the early nineteenth century and now a private golf club. Also in Kenmore, the **Scottish Crannog Centre** (April–Oct Mon–Fri 10am–5pm, Sat & Sun 10am–6pm; £2.80), perched above the loch on stilts, is an authentic reconstruction of a Bronze Age defensive house complete with sheepskin rugs and wooden bowls. There are various **boat rental** places around this end of the loch, as well as **Croft-na-Caber** (☎01887/830588), an impressive **outdoor pursuits** complex on the southern bank of the loch, where you can try water-skiing, fishing, hill walking, cross-country skiing, river sledging, rafting and jet biking. The complex also offers comfortable **accommodation** either in its own hotel (☎01887/830236; ④) or in well-equipped chalets overlooking the loch (2–6 people; £210–590 per week). You don't have to stay here to use the facilities, however, and tuition or equipment rental is available by the hour, half-day, full day or longer. As an example of prices, a day's sailing or windsurfing instruction costs around £50. You can also stay at the overwhelmingly Scottish *Kenmore Hotel*, in the village square (☎01887/830205; ⑤), a descendant of Scotland's oldest inn, established here in 1572, or at *Ben Lawers Hotel* (☎01567/820436; ③), about half way between Kenmore and Killin, where the food is particularly good. Meanwhile *Mrs Jolly's B&B* (☎01567/830353; ②), Lower Dualin Croft, is another good place to sample traditional Scottish hospitality in a tranquil location.

Aberfeldy

A largely Victorian town six miles or so to the east, along the A827, **ABERFELDY** makes a good base for exploring the area. The **tourist office** at The Square in the town centre (April–June, Sept & Oct Mon–Sat 9.30am–5.30pm, Sun noon–4pm; July & Aug Mon–Sat 9am–7pm, Sun 11am–6pm; Nov–March Mon–Fri 9.30am–5pm, Sat 9.30am–1.30pm; ☎01887/820276) gives details of the so-called Locus Project, a local initiative whereby a series of looped trails has been devised to take in all the main sights.

Aberfeldy sits at the point where the Urlar Burn – lined by the silver birch trees celebrated by Robert Burns in his poem *The Birks of Aberfeldy* – flows into the River Tay. The Tay is spanned by **Wade's Bridge**, built by General Wade in 1733 during his efforts to control the trouble in the Highlands, and, with its humpback and four arches, regarded as one of the general's finest remaining crossing points. Overlooking the bridge from the south end is the **Black Watch Monument**, a pensive, kilted soldier, erected in 1887 to commemorate the peacekeeping troop of Highlanders gathered together by Wade in 1739.

The small town centre is a busy mixture of craft and tourist shops, its main attraction the superbly restored early nineteenth-century **Aberfeldy Water Mill** (Easter–Oct Mon–Sat 10am–5pm, Sun 11am–5pm; £2), which harnesses the water of the Urlar to turn the wheel that stone-grinds oatmeal in the traditional Scottish way.

One mile west of Aberfeldy, across Wade's Bridge, **Castle Menzies** (April to mid-Oct Mon–Sat 10.30am–5pm, Sun 2–5pm; £2.30) is an imposing, Z-shaped, sixteenth-century tower house, which until the middle of this century was the chief seat of the Clan Menzies. With the demise of the Menzies line the castle was taken over by the Menzies Clan Society, which since 1971 has been involved in the lengthy process of restoring it. Now the interior, with its wide stone staircase, is refreshingly free of fixtures and fittings, restored to authentic austerity.

If you want to **stay** in Aberfeldy, head for *Moness House Hotel and Country Club*, Crieff Road (☎01887/820446, *moness@btinternet.com*; ④), a whitewashed country house which also offers luxurious **self-catering** cottages (2–6 people; £245–500 per week), as well as fishing, golf and watersports. Alternatively, there's *Guinach House*, by the Birks (☎01887/820251, *100127.222@compuserve.com*; ⑤), a tastefully decorated place in pleasant grounds near the famous silver birches, with a good dining room, or *Farleyer House* (☎01887/820332; ⑧), a mile out of Aberfeldy on the B846, which is highly recommended as a hotel and **restaurant**. For B&B, try *Novar*, 2 Home St (☎01887/820779; ①), or *Mavisbank*, Taybridge Drive (☎01887/820223; ①; March–Oct), both attractive stone cottages.

Pitlochry

Surrounded by hills just north of the confluence of the Tummel and Tay rivers at Ballinluig, **PITLOCHRY** spreads gracefully along the eastern shore of the Tummel, on the lower slopes of Ben Vrackie (see box opposite). Even after General Wade built one of his first roads through here in the early eighteenth century, Pitlochry remained little more than a village. Queen Victoria's visit in 1842 helped put the area on the map, but it wasn't until the end of the century that Pitlochry established itself as a popular holiday centre.

Today the busy main street is a constant flurry of traffic, both locals and tourists. Beyond the train bridge at the southern end of the main street (Atholl Road leading to Perth Road) is Bells' **Blair Atholl Distillery**, Perth Road (Oct–Easter Mon–Fri 9am–5pm; Easter–Sept also Sat 9am–5pm, Sun noon–5pm; tours every 10min; £3 including tastings), where the excellent visitor centre illustrates the process involved in making the Blair Atholl Malt. Whisky has been produced on this site since 1798, in which time production has been stepped up to around two million litres a year, making this a medium-sized distillery.

A perfect contrast to Blair Atholl is the **Edradour Distillery** (March–Oct Mon–Sat 9.30am–5pm, Sun noon–5pm; Nov & Dec Mon–Sat 10am–4pm; Dec group bookings only), Scotland's smallest, in an idyllic position tucked into the hills a couple of miles east of Pitlochry on the A924. A whistle-stop audiovisual presentation covering more than 250 years of production precedes the tour of the distillery itself.

On the western edge of Pitlochry, just across the river, lies Scotland's renowned "Theatre in the Hills", the **Pitlochry Festival Theatre** (☎01796/472680; Easter–early Oct). Set up in 1951, the theatre started in a tent on the site of what is now the town curling rink, before moving to the banks of the river in 1981. Backstage tours, covering all aspects of theatre production (generally Thurs & Fri 2pm; £3; booking essential), are on offer during the day, while a variety of productions – both mainstream and offbeat – are staged in the evening.

A short stroll upstream from the theatre is the **Pitlochry Power Station and Dam**, a massive concrete wall which harnesses the water of the man-made Loch Faskally, just north of the town, for hydroelectric power. Although the visitor centre (April–Oct daily 10am–5.30pm; £1.90) explains the ins and outs of it all, the main attraction here, apart from the views up the loch, is the **salmon ladder**, which the salmon leap up on their annual migration – a sight not to be missed.

Practicalities

Access to Pitlochry is easy by public transport, thanks to its position on the main train line to Inverness, and regular buses running from Perth. The **bus** stop and the **train** station are on Station Road, at the north end of town, ten minutes' walk from the centre and the **tourist office**, 22 Atholl Rd (April to mid-May & Oct Mon–Sat 9am–6pm, Sun noon–6pm; mid-May to Sept daily 9am–8pm; Nov–April Mon–Fri 9am–5pm, Sat 9am–1.30pm; ☎01796/472215). The office gives out an informative free guide of walks in the surrounding area, and also offers an **accommodation** booking service.

Birchwood Hotel, East Moulin Road (☎01796/472477, *birchwoodhotel@msn.com*; ⑤), occupies a lovely Victorian country house at the top of town, set in four acres of grounds, and has a particularly good restaurant. South of the hotel, the magnificent and much pricier *Pitlochry Hydro*, Knockard Road (☎01796/472666; ⑦), looks out over the Tummel Valley. Five miles west of Pitlochry on the B8019, at Strathtummel, the *Queens View Hotel* (☎01796/473291, *queensviewhotel@compuserve.com*; ⑤) has lovely views,

WALKS AROUND PITLOCHRY

Ordnance Survey Landranger maps Nos. 43 & 52

Pitlochry is surrounded by good walking country. The biggest lure has to be **Ben Vrackie** (2733ft), which provides a stunning backdrop for the Festival Theatre and deserves better than a straight up-and-down walk; however, the climb should only be attempted in settled weather conditions, with the right equipment and following the necessary safety precautions (see p.48). A good circular walk goes via the quiet Loch Faskally to **Killiecrankie Visitor Centre** (refreshments available) and then heads up the hill by a seldom-used route before returning via Moulin. Allow a full day for the complete walk.

Head through Pitlochry northwards and branch off to pass the *Green Hotel* to reach attractive Loch Faskally. You could walk right round it, but for the purposes of this walk, follow the shore and take the signs up the River Garry to go through the **Pass of Killiecrankie**. This is looked after by the NTS, which has a visitor centre with interpretive displays, books and souvenirs for sale. To get this far takes a couple of hours.

From the NTS centre walk north up the old A9 and branch off on the small tarred road signposted **Old Faskally**, which twists up under the new A9 and past a house and the gates of Old Faskally. Keep on the tarred road until you reach a diversion sign which leads up the embankment above the road onto a lesser track and through a kissing gate at the top of the field. Continue from here until you finally leave the cultivated land through the hill dyke.

The track zigzags up heathery pasture to an old wall and a gate in a fence just beyond: go through the gate then bear right across the open hillside, crossing the **Allt Eachainn**, the burn that drains this corrie, before heading up the hill opposite in another series of bends, clearly seen from below. Also visible from below is a footpath bearing off left as the slope gets steeper, which you should follow through the heather towards the pass. It goes over the saddle of a dark heathery prow and, 220yd beyond, brings you to the pass looking down on **Loch a' Choire**. The track from Pitlochry/Moulin crosses below the dam on the loch and heads directly up the peak. This steep track can be seen from the col; skirt north of the loch to join it. As Ben Vrackie is an isolated summit, the weather can change quickly and clouds render route-finding difficult, so Loch a' Choire may be a better place to picnic. The descending path from Loch a' Choire is clear and runs across the moors to reach forest level. A stile crosses the fence into the birch and pine woods that lead down to a small car park. Follow the minor road from it down to the hamlet of **Moulin** and on to Pitlochry.

good bar meals and a fine restaurant. In the town centre, there are a number of cheaper hotels along the main street, including the comfortable *McKays Hotel*, 138 Atholl Rd (☎01796/473888; ④), and many guest houses and **B&Bs**. Try *Craigroyston House*, 2 Lower Oakfield (☎01796/472053; ③); *Comar House*, Strathview Terrace (☎01796/473531; ②); or *Ferryman's Cottage* (☎01796/473681; ②), Port-na-Craig, in a beautiful position next to the River Tummel. The **youth hostel** (☎01796/472308) is a fine stone mansion on Knockard Road at the top of town.

Pitlochry is the domain of the tearoom and pitifully short of **restaurants** and pubs; the best option is the *Killiecrankie Hotel* (☎01796/473220, *killiecrankie.hotel@btinternet.com*; ⑤) at Killiecrankie, three miles north on the A9, where the meals are hearty and well priced. In town, try the popular restaurant at the Festival Theatre, or the nearby *Port-na-craig Inn & Restaurant*, both of which have beautiful riverside locations. For a pub lunch with spectacular views over the water, it's worth driving ten miles west to the *Loch Tummel Inn* (☎01882/634272; ④), halfway along Loch Tummel. Its restaurant is also highly recommended and booking ahead is essential for dinner.

Loch Tummel and Loch Rannoch

Between Pitlochry and Loch Ericht lies a sparsely populated, ever-changing panorama of mountains, moors, lochs and glens. Venturing into the hills is difficult without a car – unless you're walking – but infrequent local buses run from Pitlochry to the outlying communities, and the train to Inverness runs parallel to the A9.

West of Pitlochry, the B8019/B846 twists and turns along the Grampian mountain-sides, overlooking **Loch Tummel** and then **Loch Rannoch**. These two lochs, celebrated by Harry Lauder in his famous song *The Road to the Isles*, are joined by Dunalastair Water, which narrows to become the River Tummel at the western end of the loch of the same name. This is a spectacular stretch of countryside and one which deserves leisurely exploration. **Queen's View** at the eastern end of Loch Tummel is a fabulous vantage point, looking down the loch across the hills to the misty peak of Schiehallion (3520ft) or the "Fairy Mountain", whose mass was used in early experiments to judge the weight of the Earth. The Forestry Commission's **visitor centre** (April–Oct daily 10am–6pm; ☎01350/727284) interprets the fauna and flora of the area, and also has a café.

Beyond Loch Tummel, marking the eastern end of Loch Rannoch, the small community of **KINLOCH RANNOCH** is popular with backpackers, who stock up at the local store before taking to the hills. You can **stay** here in the converted eighteenth-century croft *Cuilimore Cottage* (☎01882/632218; ②), with a rustic atmosphere and delicious food, or try *Bunrannoch House* (☎01882/632407; ②), a Victorian former shooting lodge with lovely views. The road follows the loch to its end and then heads six miles further into the desolation of **Rannoch Moor**, where **Rannoch Station**, a lonely outpost on the Glasgow–Fort William West Highland train, marks the end of the route. The only way back is by the same road as far as Loch Rannoch, where it's possible – but not always advisable, depending on conditions – to return on a (very) minor road along the south side of the lochs. The round-trip is roughly seventy miles.

Blair Atholl to Loch Ericht

Four miles north of Pitlochry, the A9 cuts through the **Pass of Killiecrankie**, a breath-taking wooded gorge which falls away to the River Garry below. This dramatic setting was the site of the **Battle of Killiecrankie** in 1689, when the Jacobites quashed the forces of General Mackay. Legend has it that one soldier of the Crown, fleeing for his life, made a miraculous jump across the 18ft **Soldier's Leap**, an impossibly wide chasm halfway up the gorge. Queen Victoria, visiting here 160 years later, contented herself with recording the beauty of the area in her diary. Exhibits at the slick NTS **visitor centre** (April–Oct daily 10am–5.30pm; ☎01796/473233; £1) recall the battle and examine the gorge in detail.

Before leading the Jacobites into battle, Graham of Claverhouse, Viscount ("Bonnie") Dundee, had seized **Blair Castle** (April–Oct daily 10am–6pm; £6), three miles up the road at Blair Atholl. Seat of the Atholl dukedom, this whitewashed, tur-reted castle, surrounded by parkland and dating from 1269, presents an impressive sight as you approach up the drive. A piper may be playing in front of the castle: he is one of the Atholl Highlanders, a select group retained by the duke as his private army – a privilege afforded to him by Queen Victoria, who stayed here in 1844. Today the duke is the only British subject allowed to maintain his own force.

A total of 32 rooms are open for inspection, and display a selection of paintings, fur-niture and plasterwork that is sumptuous in the extreme, although the vast number of stuffed animals may not be to everyone's liking. The Tapestry Room, on the top floor of the original Cumming's Tower, is hung with Brussels tapestries and contains an out-rageous four-poster bed, topped with vases of ostrich feathers which originally came from the first duke's suite at Holyrood Palace in Edinburgh. The ballroom, also, with its timber roof, antlers and melange of portraits, is Baronial Scotland at its best.

Highland cows graze the ancient landscaped grounds and peacocks strut in front of the castle. There is a **riding stable** from where you can take treks, and formal wood-land walks have been laid out – don't miss the neglected, walled Japanese water garden. There is also a well-equipped **caravan park** (☎01796/481263) in the grounds.

Beyond Blair Atholl, the A9 follows the line of **Glen Garry** and the River Garry through the Grampian Mountains. The road climbs continuously, sweeping past the eastern end of **Glen Errochty**, on towards the barren **Pass of Drummochter** and to the bleak little village of Dalwhinnie at the northern end of **Loch Ericht**. The scenery is marvellous all the way, but there is literally nothing here apart from the mountains and moors.

travel details

Trains

Falkirk Grahamston to: Edinburgh (every 30min; 35min); Glasgow Queen Street (every 30min; 25min); Linlithgow (every 30min; 13min).

Kirkcaldy to: Aberdeen (hourly; 2hr); Dundee (hourly; 40min–1hr); Edinburgh (23 daily; 40min); Perth (7 daily; 40min); Pitlochry (4 direct daily; 1hr 15min; 4 indirect, change at Perth; 1hr 25min).

Linlithgow to: Edinburgh (hourly; 20min); Falkirk Grahamston (every 30min; 13min); Glasgow Queen Street (hourly; 30min).

Perth to: Aberdeen (hourly; 1hr 40min); Dundee (hourly; 25min); Edinburgh (9 daily; 1hr 25min); Glasgow Queen Street (hourly; 1hr 5min); Kirkcaldy (7 daily; 40min); Pitlochry (8 daily; 30min).

Pitlochry to: Edinburgh (5 daily; 2hr); Glasgow Queen Street (3 daily; 1hr 45min); Kirkcaldy (4 direct daily; 1hr 15min; 1 indirect, change at Perth; 1hr 45min); Perth (8 daily; 30min); Stirling (3–5 daily; 1hr 15min).

Stirling to: Aberdeen (hourly; 2hr 15min); Dundee (hourly; 1hr); Edinburgh (hourly; 1hr); Falkirk Grahamston (hourly; 28min); Glasgow Queen Street (hourly; 30min); Linlithgow (hourly; 35min); Perth (hourly; 30min); Pitlochry (3–5 daily; 1hr 15min).

Buses

Bo'ness to: Edinburgh (5 daily; 45min); Stirling (3 daily; 35min).

Dundee to: Glenrothes (every 30min; 1hr 10min); St Andrews (every 20min; 35min); Kirkcaldy (10 daily; 1hr 30min); Stirling (12 daily; 1hr 30min).

Dunfermline to: Edinburgh (2 daily; 40min); Glenrothes (15 daily; 1hr 5min); Kirkcaldy (hourly; 1hr); St Andrews (11–13 daily; 2hr).

Glenrothes to: Dundee (every 30min; 1hr 10min); Dunfermline (15 daily; 1hr 10min); Kirkcaldy (hourly; 20min); St Andrews (hourly; 45min).

Kirkcaldy to: Dundee (10 daily; 1hr 30min); Dunfermline (hourly; 1hr); Glenrothes (hourly; 20min); St Andrews (16 daily; 1hr).

Perth to: Dunblane (every 30min; 35min); Dunfermline (every 30min; 50min); Edinburgh (hourly; 1hr 20min); Glasgow (20 daily; 1hr 35min); Gleneagles (18 daily; 25min); Inverness (10 daily; 2hr 30min); London (4 daily; 9hr); Stirling (20 daily; 50min).

St Andrews to: Dundee (every 20min; 40min); Dunfermline (Mon–Sat 11–13 daily; 2hr); Edinburgh (12 daily; 2hr); Glasgow (6 daily; 2hr 50min); Glenrothes (hourly; 45min); Kirkcaldy (16 daily; 1hr); Stirling (6 daily; 2hr).

Stirling to: Aberfoyle (4 daily; 45min); Bo'ness (3 daily; 35 min); Callander (11 daily; 45min); Dollar (13 daily; 35min); Doune (14 daily; 30min); Dunblane (20 daily; 1hr 15min); Dundee (12 daily; 1hr 30min); Dunfermline (13 daily; 50min); Edinburgh (hourly; 1hr 35min); Falkirk (every 45min; 30min); Glasgow (34 daily; 1hr 10min); Gleneagles (16 daily; 30min); Inverness (12 daily; 3hr 30min); Killin (2 daily; 2hr); Linlithgow (hourly; 1hr); Lochearnhead (2 daily; 1hr 40min); Perth (20 daily; 50min); Pitlochry (2 daily; 1hr 30min); St Andrews (6 daily; 2hr).

CHAPTER FIVE

ARGYLL

Cut off for centuries from the rest of Scotland by the mountains and sea lochs that characterize the region, Argyll remains remote, its scatter of offshore islands forming part of the Inner Hebridean archipelago (the remaining Hebrides are dealt with in Skye and the Western Isles). Geographically, as well as culturally, this is a transitional area between Highland and Lowland, boasting a rich variety of scenery, from lush, subtropical gardens warmed by the Gulf Stream to flat and treeless islands on the edge of the Atlantic. It's in the folds and twists of the countryside and the views out to the islands that the strengths and beauties of mainland Argyll lie – the one area of man-made sights you shouldn't miss is the cluster of Celtic and prehistoric sites near Kilmartin. The overall population is tiny; even Oban, Argyll's chief ferry port, has just seven thousand inhabitants, while the prettiest, Inveraray, boasts a mere four hundred.

The eastern duo of **Bute** and **Arran** are the most popular of Scotland's more southerly islands, the latter – now strictly speaking part of North Ayrshire – justifiably so, with spectacular scenery ranging from the granite peaks of the north to the Lowland pasture of the south. Of the Hebridean islands covered in this chapter, mountainous **Mull** is the most visited, though it is large enough to absorb the crowds, many of whom are only passing through en route to the tiny isle of **Iona**, a centre of Christian culture since the sixth century. **Islay**, best known for its distinctive malt whiskies, is fairly quiet even in the height of summer, as is neighbouring **Jura**, which offers excellent walking opportunities. And for those seeking further solitude, there's the island of **Colonsay**, with its golden sands, and the more remote islands of **Tiree** and **Coll**, which, although swept with fierce winds, boast more sunny days than anywhere else in Scotland.

The region's name derives from *Aragaidheal*, which translates as "Boundary of the Gaels", the Irish Celts who settled here in the fifth century AD, and whose **kingdom of Dalriada** embraced much of what is now Argyll. Known to the Romans as *Scotti* – hence Scotland – it was the Irish Celts who promoted Celtic Christianity, and whose Gaelic language eventually became the national tongue. After a brief period of Norse invasion and settlement, the islands (and the peninsula of Kintyre) fell to the immensely powerful Somerled, who became King of the Hebrides and Lord of Argyll in the twelfth century. Somerled's successors, the MacDonalds, established Islay as their headquarters in the 1200s, but were in turn dislodged by Robert the Bruce. Of Bruce's allies, it was the **Campbells** who benefited most from the MacDonalds' demise and, eventually, as the dukes of Argyll, gained control of the entire area – even today they remain one of the largest landowners in the region.

In the aftermath of the Jacobite uprisings, Argyll, like the rest of the Highlands, was devastated by the **Clearances**, with thousands of crofters evicted from their homes in order to make room for profitable sheep farming – "the white plague" – and cattle rearing. More recently forestry plantations have dramatically altered the landscape of Argyll, while purpose-built marinas have sprouted all around the heavily indented coastline. Today the traditional industries of fishing and farming are in deep crisis, as is the modern industry of fish-farming, leaving the region ever more dependent on tourism, EU grants and a steady influx of new settlers to keep things going, while

Gaelic, once the language of the majority in Argyll, retains only a tenuous hold on the outlying islands of Islay, Coll and Tiree.

It's on Argyll's west coast that the unpredictability of the **weather** can really affect your holiday. If you can, avoid July and August, when the crowds on Mull, Iona and Arran are at their densest – there's no guarantee the weather will be any better than during the rest of the year, and you might have more chance of avoiding the persistent Scottish midge (for more on which see p.46). **Public transport** throughout Argyll is minimal, though buses do serve most major settlements, and the train line reaches all the way to Oban. In the remoter parts of the region and on the islands, you'll have to rely on a combination of walking, shared taxis and the postbus. If you're planning to take a car across to one of the islands, it's essential that you book both your outward and return journeys as early as possible, as the ferries get very booked up. And lastly, a word on **accommodation**: a large proportion of visitors to this part of Scotland come here for a week or two and stay in self-catering cottages. On some islands and in more remote areas, this is often the most common form of accommodation available – in peak season, you should book several months in advance (for more on self-catering, see p.33)

Gare Loch

Most people approach Argyll from Glasgow, from where there's a choice of two routes: the most popular is along Loch Lomond (see p.252); a quieter route (and the one which the train takes for some of the way) is along the shores of **Gare Loch** and Loch Long to Arrochar, which marks the beginning of Argyll proper. Apart from **Helensburgh**, there's little to see along the shores of either loch, though the road is appealingly winding. Both shores are littered with decaying industrial remains, including the nuclear submarine base at Faslane on Gare Loch and the oil tanks at Finnart on Loch Long. Only occasionally is it possible to glimpse the unspeakably beautiful landscape described by eighteenth-century travellers.

Helensburgh

HELENSBURGH, twenty miles or so northwest of Glasgow, is a smart, Georgian grid-plan settlement laid out in an imitation of Edinburgh's New Town and overlooking the Clyde estuary. In the eighteenth century it was a well-to-do commuter town for Glasgow and a seaside resort, whose bathing-master, **Henry Bell**, invented one of the first steamboats, the *Comet*, to transport Glaswegians "doon the watter". Today Helensburgh is a stop on the route of the **Waverley**, the last seagoing paddle steamer in the world, which ploughs up and down the Firth of Clyde in the summer months, and occasionally does a longer zigzag tour of the Inner Hebrides. In addition, there's a **passenger-only ferry** service across the Clyde from Helensburgh to Gourock (see p.235) – pick up timetables for both the above services from the tourist office.

The inventor of TV, John Logie Baird, was born here, as was Charles Rennie Mackintosh, who in 1902 was commissioned by the Glaswegian publisher Walter Blackie to design **Hill House** (Easter–Oct daily 1.30–5pm; NTS; £6), on Upper Colquhoun Street. You won't see the house advertised in any National Trust or tourist board literature, because it's already so popular it can barely cope with the current visitor numbers. Without doubt the best surviving example of Mackintosh's domestic architecture, the house – right down to light fittings – is stamped with his very personal interpretation of Art Nouveau, characterized by his sparing use of colour and stylized floral patterns. The effect is occasionally overwhelming – it's difficult to imagine actually living in such an

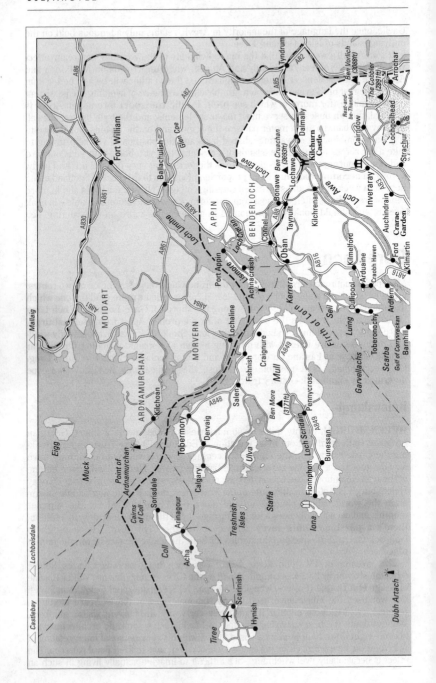

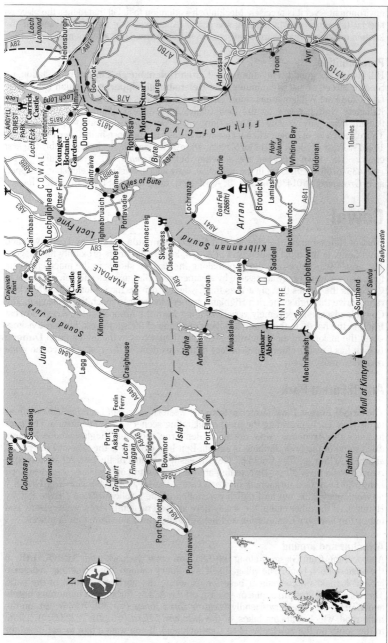

© Crown copyright

environment – yet it is precisely Mackintosh's attention to detail that makes the place so special (for more on Mackintosh, see p.208). After exploring the house, head for the kitchen quarters, which have been sensitively transformed into a tearoom.

Practicalities

Hill House is a good twenty-minute walk from **Helensburgh Central** train station, up Sinclair Street, or just five minutes from **Helensburgh Upper** train station (where the Oban and Fort William trains stop). The **tourist office** is on the ground floor of the old Italianate church tower by the loch (daily: April & May 10am–5pm; June & Sept 9.30am–6pm; July & Aug 9.30am–7pm; early Oct 10am–4.30pm; ☎01436/672642). There's not a lot of choice when it comes to **hotels**: the purpose-built *Commodore Hotel*, 112–117 West Clyde St (☎01436/676924; ④), overlooking the loch, is probably the first choice. The town's **B&Bs** are a better bet: *Lethamhill*, 20 West Dhuhill Drive (☎01436/676016; ③), is set in the attractive, leafy villa district near Helensburgh Upper, as is *Greenpark* (☎01436/671545; ②; April–Oct), on Charlotte Street, near Hill House.

Cowal

West of Helensburgh, the claw-shaped **Cowal peninsula**, formed by Loch Fyne and Loch Long, is the most visited part of Argyll, largely due to its proximity to Glasgow. The area's seaside resorts developed along the eastern shores in the nineteenth century, as they were easily accessible by steamer from Glasgow. It's still quicker to get to Cowal via the ferries that ply across the Clyde; car drivers have a long, though exhilarating drive through some rich Highland scenery in order to reach the same spot. The Cowal landscape is extremely varied, ranging from the Munros of the **Argyll Forest Park** in the north, to the gentle low-lying coastline of the southwest, but most visitors – and the majority of the population – confine themselves to the area around **Dunoon** (which has Cowal's chief tourist office) in the east, leaving the rest of the countryside relatively undisturbed.

Argyll Forest Park

The **Argyll Forest Park** stretches from the western shores of Loch Lomond south as far as Holy Loch, providing the most exhilarating scenery on the peninsula. The park includes the **Arrochar Alps**, north of Glen Croe and Glen Kinglas, whose Munros offer some of the best climbing in Argyll: Ben Ime (3318ft) is the tallest of the range, and Ben Arthur or "The Cobbler" (2891ft) easily the most distinctive. All are for experienced walkers only. Less threatening are the peaks south of Glen Croe, between Loch Long and Loch Goil (branching off Loch Long), known as **Argyll's Bowling Green** – no ironic nickname but an English corruption of the Gaelic *Baile na Greine* (Sunny Hamlet). At the other end of the scale, there are several gentle forest walks clearly laid out by the Forestry Commission and helpful leaflets available from tourist offices.

Arrochar and around

Approaching from Glasgow along the A83, you enter the park from **ARROCHAR**, at the head of Loch Long. The village itself is ordinary enough, but the setting is dramatic, and it makes a convenient base for exploring the northern section of the park. There's a **train station**, a mile or so east, off the A83 to Tarbet, and numerous **hotels** and **B&Bs** – try the very friendly *Lochside Guest House* (☎01301/702467; ①), on the main road, which rents out bikes, or the *Mansefield Hotel* (☎01301/702282; ②), a little to the south on the quieter A814 to Garelochhead. If you want a bite **to eat**, head for the *Village Inn*, near the *Mansefield*; the local nightlife revolves around *Callum's Bar*, two doors down from *Lochside Guest House*.

Two miles beyond Arrochar at **ARDGARTAN**, there's a loch-side Forestry Commission **campsite** (☎01301/702293; Easter–Oct), an SYHA **hostel** (☎01301/702362; Feb–Dec) and, a little further down the road, a **visitor centre** (daily: April–June, Sept & Oct 10am–5pm; July & Aug 10am–6pm; ☎01301/702432), run jointly by the tourist board and the Forestry Commission. It's a great source of advice on weather conditions and wildlife, and organizes various nature activities, ranging from hill climbing to deer spotting, though advance booking is essential. There are also waymarked walks starting from the centre.

Rest-and-be-Thankful, Cairndow and Lochgoilhead

Approaching Cowal from the east, you're forced to climb **Glen Croe**, a strategic hill pass whose saddle is called – for obvious reasons – **Rest-and-be-Thankful**. Here the road forks, with the single-track B828 heading down to **LOCHGOILHEAD**, overlooking Loch Goil. The setting is difficult to beat, but the village has been upstaged by the *Drimsynie Holiday Resort*, whose triangular chalets pockmark the landscape for a mile to the west. A road tracks the west side of the loch, petering out after five miles at the ruins of **Carrick Castle**, a classic tower-house castle built around 1400 and used as a hunting lodge by James IV.

If you'd rather skip Lochgoilhead, continue along the A83 from the Rest-and-be-Thankful down the grand Highland sweep of Glen Kinglas to **CAIRNDOW**, at the head of Loch Fyne. Just behind the village, off the main road, you'll find the **Ardkinglas Woodland Garden** (daily dawn–dusk; £2) which contains exotic rhododendrons, azaleas and a superb collection of conifers, some of which rise to over 200ft. A mile or so further along on the A83 around the head of the loch at Clachan is the famous **Loch Fyne Oyster Bar** (☎01499/600264), which sells more oysters than anywhere else in the country, plus lots of other fish and seafood treats. You can easily assemble a gourmet picnic here, and the moderately expensive restaurant is excellent.

Loch Eck and around

If you're heading south into Cowal from Cairndow, take the A815 which follows the loch southwest to **STRACHUR**, where the church has medieval graveslabs set into its walls and there's a restored smiddy. Just to the north of the village stands the famous *Creggans Inn*, belonging to the son of Sir Fitzroy Maclean (☎01369/860279; ⑥); even if the rooms and restaurant are too pricey, you can pop into the bar or the all-day coffee shop.

The road divides at Strachur, with the A815 heading inland to **Loch Eck**, an exceptionally narrow freshwater loch, squeezed between steeply banked woods, and a

---

ACCOMMODATION PRICE CODES

Throughout this book, accommodation **prices** have been graded with the codes below, according to the cost of the least expensive double room in high season. Price codes are not given for campsites, most of which charge under £10 per person. Almost all hostels charge less than £10 a night for a bed – the few exceptions to this rule have the prices quoted in the text. For a full account of the accommodation price codes, see p.31.

① under £40	④ £60–70	⑦ £110–150
② £40–50	⑤ £70–90	⑧ £150–200
③ £50–60	⑥ £90–110	⑨ £200 and over

favourite spot for trout fishing. At the southern tip of Loch Eck are the beautifully laid-out **Younger Botanic Gardens** (mid-March to mid-Oct daily 10am–6pm; £3), an offshoot of Edinburgh's Royal Botanic Gardens, famed for their rhododendrons and especially striking for their avenue of Great Redwoods, planted in 1863 and now over 100ft high. There's an excellent inexpensive café by the entrance, open in the season, with an imaginative menu – you can eat there without visiting the gardens if trees aren't your thing. If you're feeling energetic, you could combine a visit here with one of the most popular of the local **forest walks**, a leisurely stroll up the rocky ravine of **Puck's Glen**; the walk begins from the car park a mile south of the gardens (1hr 30min round-trip). The *Stratheck* **campsite** at the southern end of Loch Eck (☎01369/840472; March–Dec) enjoys a nice situation.

Before heading south to Dunoon, it's worth taking a trip down the north shores of Holy Loch, the former site of the US nuclear submarine base which closed in 1992, to **KILMUN**, where there's a fascinating church with a mausoleum where many a Duke of Argyll is buried – alas closed to the public – several good stained glass windows and an organ driven by tap water (teas and tours in the summer). There's also an arboretum at Kilmun, through which the Forestry Commission has laid out several walks, which make for a pleasant stroll. You can get some good **food** in the village at the *Fern Grove Bistro*, which does takeaway and a couple of **rooms** as well (☎01369/840334; ②; April–Oct). Further up the coast, round the corner and overlooking Loch Long, there's more choice of accommodation: the *Gairletter Caravan Park* **campsite** (☎01369/810208; April–Oct), at Blairmore, which enjoys an idyllic lochside spot, and, further on still, *Ardentinny* (☎01369/810209; ④), a whitewashed eighteenth-century **hotel** on a spit of land jutting out into the loch.

Dunoon

In the nineteenth century, Cowal's capital, **DUNOON**, grew from a mere village to a major Clyde seaside resort and favourite holiday spot for Glaswegians. Nowadays, tourists tend to arrive by ferry from Gourock and, though their numbers are smaller, Dunoon remains by far the largest town in all Argyll, with 13,000 inhabitants. Apart from its practical uses and its fine pier, however, there's little to tempt you to linger in Dunoon.

The centre of town is dominated by a grassy lump of rock known as **Castle Hill**, crowned by Castle House, built in the 1820s by a wealthy Glaswegian, and the subject of a bitter dispute with the local populace over closure of the common land around his house. The people eventually won, and the grounds remain open to the public to this day, as does the house, which is now home to the local **museum** (June–Oct Mon–Sat 10am–4.30pm; £1.50). There's some good hands-on nature stuff for kids, an excellent section on the Clyde steamers and details about **Highland Mary**, whose statue is in the grounds. Betrothed to Robbie Burns, who seems conveniently to have ignored the fact that he already had a pregnant wife, Highland Mary nursed the poet through typhus while they planned to elope to the West Indies, only to die tragically from the disease herself. Another more violent scene in local history is commemorated by a memorial on a nearby rock: at least 36 men of the Lamont clan were executed by their rivals, the Campbells, who hanged them from "a lively, fresh-growing ash tree" in 1646. The tree couldn't take the strain, and had to be cut down two years later – tradition has it that blood gushed from the roots when it was felled.

With an hour or so to spare, you could visit the **Cowal Bird Garden** (April–Oct daily 10.30am–6pm; £3), one mile northwest along the A885 to Sandbank, and wander through their woodland amid exotic caged birds as well as free-roaming peacocks, macaws and pot-bellied pigs. If the weather's fine, take the **Ardnadam Heritage Trail**, a mile further up the road, to the wonderful Dunan viewpoint looking out to the Firth of Clyde; if the weather's bad, you could head for Dunoon Ceramics, on Hamilton Street, which produces various styles of high-quality porcelain and bone china, and offers tours around the factory (Mon–Thurs 10am–4pm, Fri 10am–3pm).

Practicalities

It's a good idea to take advantage of Dunoon's **tourist office** (the main one in Cowal) on Alexandra Parade (April & Oct Mon–Fri 9am–5.30pm, Sat 10am–5.30pm, Sun 11am–3pm; May, June & Sept Mon–Fri 9am–5.30pm, Sat & Sun 10am–5pm; July & Aug Mon–Fri 9am–7pm, Sat 10am–7pm, Sun 10am–5pm; Nov–March Mon–Thurs 9am–5.30pm, Fri 9am–5pm; ☎01369/703785). The shorter, more frequent of the two **ferry crossings** across the Clyde from Gourock to Dunoon is the half-hourly Western Ferries service to Hunter's Quay, a mile north of the town centre; CalMac has the prime position, however, on the main pier, and has better transport connections if you're on foot.

If you need to **stay** the night, there's an enormous choice of B&Bs: try *Cedars* (☎01369/702425; ②), which is better than average and central, or the town's landmark *Argyll Hotel*, opposite the pier (☎01369/702059; ②), which is not as plush as you might expect. For real class, though, head for the highly reputable *Ardfillayne House*, West Bay (☎01369/702267; ③), its welcoming next door neighbour *Abbot's Brae* (☎01369/705021, *enquiry@abbotsbrae.ndirect.co.uk*; ③), or, topping the lot, the luxurious *Enmore Hotel* (☎01369/702230, *enmorehotel@btinternet.com*; ⑤), an eighteenth-century villa on Marine Parade, near Hunter's Quay. The good news for hostellers is that there's a **hostel** due to open in 2000 on Alexandra Parade, run by the Baptist Church (for the latest, phone ☎01369/706665).

Chatters, 58 John St (March–Dec Wed–Sat), is Dunoon's best **restaurant**, offering delicious Loch Fyne seafood and Scottish beef; for something a bit less pricey, the *Argyll* does decent, filling bar snacks. Dunoon boasts a two-screen cinema (a rarity in Argyll) on John Street, but the town's most famous entertainment by far is the **Cowal Highland Gathering**, the largest of its kind in the world, held here on the last weekend in August, and culminating in the awesome spectacle of the massed pipes and drums of more than 150 bands marching through the streets. For **bike rental**, head for the Highland Stores on Argyll Street, or the *Argyll Hotel*; for **pony trekking** contact the Velvet Path Riding and Trekking Centre (☎01369/830580) at Inellan, four miles south of Dunoon.

Southwest Cowal

The mellower landscape of **southwest Cowal**, in complete contrast to the bustle of Dunoon or the Highland grandeur of the Argyll Forest Park, becomes immediate as soon as you head west along the scenic B836 to Loch Striven, and then on to Loch Soch Riddon, where, from either side, there are few more beautiful sights than the **Kyles of Bute**, the thin slithers of water that separate the bleak bulk of north Bute from Cowal, and constitute some of the best sailing territory in Scotland.

COLINTRAIVE, on the eastern Kyle, marks the narrowest point in the Kyles – barely more than a couple of hundred yards – and is the place from which the small CalMac car ferry departs to Bute (possibly the most expensive ferry journey in the world mile for mile). However, the most popular spot from which to appreciate the Kyles is the A8003 as it rises dramatically above the sea lochs before descending to the peaceful, loch-side village of **TIGHNABRUAICH**, best known for its excellent **sailing school** (☎01700/811396), which offers week-long courses from beginners to advanced. Boat trips still call at the pier and the village is thriving, boasting a bank, a post office and several shops as well as a good inexpensive place to eat – the *Burnside Bistro*. The *Royal Hotel* (☎01700/811239, *royalhotel@btinternet.com*; ⑤), by the waterside, serves exceptionally good bar meals, but it's a lot cheaper to stay in neighbouring **KAMES** at the

Kames Hotel (☎01700/811489; ②), which has wonderful views over the Kyles. Close by Kames pier is the tank landing site where troops practised for the D-Day invasion of France in the Second World War.

The Kyles can get busy in July and August, but you can escape the crowds by heading for Cowal's deserted west coast, overlooking Loch Fyne. The one brief glimpse of habitation en route is the luxurious, whitewashed *Kilfinan Hotel* (☎01700/821201; ⑤; closed Feb), set back from a sandy bay seven miles along the B8000 from Tighnabruaich. The road rejoins the coast at **OTTER FERRY**, which has a small sandy beach, a wonderful pub and an oyster restaurant, *The Oystercatcher*, with tables outside if the weather's good. There was once a ferry link to Lochgilphead from here, though the "otter" part is not derived from the furry beast but from the Gaelic *an oitir* (sandbank), which juts out a mile or so into Loch Fyne. If you're heading for Kintyre, Islay or Jura, you can avoid the long haul around Loch Fyne – some seventy miles or so – by using the **ferry service to Tarbert** from Portavadie, three miles southwest of Kames.

The faster road north from Portavadie and the Kyles is the A886 which runs through the lovely forested Glendaruel. En route, the road passes the pretty village of **CLACHAN OF GLENDARUEL**, whose riverside churchyard preserves several medieval grave slabs. **Accommodation** is available at the homely *Glendaruel Hotel* (☎01369/820274; ③), which does the unusual bar snacks, and there's a prize-winning **campsite** in the forest just up the road (☎01369/820267; April–Oct) at *Glendaruel Caravan Park*.

Isle of Bute

The island of **Bute** is in many ways simply an extension of the Cowal peninsula, from which it is separated by the merest slither of water. Until 1975, it formed its own county, along with the Isle of Arran, to the south, but it's now be thrown in with Argyll. Thanks to its consistently mild climate and its ferry link with Wemyss Bay (see p.235), **Bute** has been a popular holiday and convalescence spot for Clydesiders – particularly the elderly – for over a century. Its chief town, **Rothesay**, rivals Dunoon as the major seaside resort on the Clyde, and easily surpasses the latter thanks to the two superb castles in its vicinity. Most of Bute's inhabitants are centred around the two wide bays on the east coast of the island which resembles one long seaside promenade. Consequently, it's easy enough to escape the crowds by heading for the sparsely populated west coast, which, in any case, has much the sandiest beaches.

Rothesay

Bute's one and only town, **ROTHESAY** is a handsome Victorian resort, set in a wide sweeping bay, backed by green hills, with a classic palm-tree promenade and 1920s pagoda-style Winter Gardens. It creates a much better general impression than Dunoon, with its period architecture and the occasional flourishes of wrought-iron-work. Even if you're just passing through, you must pay a visit to the ornate **Victorian toilets** (daily: Easter–Oct 8am–9pm; Nov–Easter 9am–5pm; 10p) on the pier, which were built by Twyfords in 1899 and have since been declared a national treasure. Men have the best time as the porcelain urinals steal the show, but women can ask for a guided tour, if the coast is clear, and learn about the haunted cubicle. While you're on the harbour front, look out for the wrought-iron arch marking the **Highland Boundary Fault**, which cuts the island (and Rothesay) in two: the view in one direction looks out on the Highlands and in the other to the Lowlands.

Rothesay also boasts the militarily useless, but architecturally impressive, moated ruins of **Rothesay Castle** (April–Sept daily 9.30am–6.30pm; Oct–March Mon–Wed

9.30am–4.30pm, Thurs 9.30am–noon, Sat 9.30am–4.30pm; £1.80), hidden amid the town's back streets but signposted from the pier. Built around the twelfth century, it was twice captured by the Vikings in the 1200s; such vulnerability was the reasoning behind the unusual, almost circular curtain wall, with its four big drum towers, only one of which remains fully intact.

In rainy weather you could hide inside the **Bute Museum** (Oct–Mar Tues–Sat 2.30–4.30pm; April–Sept Mon–Sat 10.30am–4.30pm, Sun 2–4.30pm; £1.20) behind the castle, whose local history section has some shining imperial weights and measures and a triple mousetrap. More interesting, though, is the fourteenth-century **St Mary's Chapel**, beside the High Kirk on the outskirts of town up the High Street; it houses a couple of impressive canopied medieval tombs and, in the churchyard, the mausoleum of the Marquesses of Bute and the grave of Napoleon's niece, who married a Sheriff of Lancaster.

A real little gem in summer is **Ardencraig Gardens** (May–Sept Mon–Fri 10am–4.30pm, Sat & Sun 1–4.30pm; free), up the hill opposite Craigmore Pier, where the Victorian hothouses are a riot of blooms and the garden is technicolour, with flowers in the midst of aviaries full of exotic birds; there is even a decent tearoom with mouthwatering home-made cakes. More horticultural delights are to be found out along the road to Mount Stuart (see below) at the **Ascog Fernery and Garden** (April to mid-Oct Wed–Sun 10am–5pm; £2.50), an unusual Victorian fernery that has been lovingly restored and boasts an ancient fern, reputed to be a thousand years old.

Practicalities

Rothesay's **tourist office**, opposite the pier at 15 Victoria St (April & Oct Mon–Fri 9am–5.30pm, Sat 10am–5.30pm, Sun 11am–3pm; May, June & Sept Mon–Fri 9am–5.30pm, Sat & Sun 10am–5pm; July & Aug Mon–Fri 9am–7pm, Sat 10am–7pm, Sun 10am–5pm; Nov–March Mon–Thurs 9am–5.30pm, Fri 9am–5pm; ☎01700/502151) can help with **accommodation**, though there's no shortage of B&Bs all along the seafront from Rothesay north to Port Bannatyne. One of the most attractive hotels on the bay is *Cannon House* (☎01700/502819; ④), close to the pier on Battery Place, while the nearby *Commodore* (☎01700/502178; ②) is a more modest choice. Another very comfortable option, set in its own grounds out in Ardbeg, is *Ardmory House* (☎01700/502346; ⑤), which is also one of the best places to eat in town. At the quiet end of town on Mountstuart Road try the very friendly *Bayview Hotel* (☎01700/505411; ②), or, further out in Ascog, B&B at *Ascog Farm* (☎01700/503372; ①) that's exceptionally good value. Finally *New Farm* (☎01700/831646; ②), just one mile from Mount Stuart, has a few rooms in a lovely converted farmhouse, above a moderately expensive **restaurant** which uses local ingredients and produces its own delicious bread; it's popular, so be sure to make a reservation. A good **self-catering** option at Port Ballantyne is the six Victorian cottages in the grounds of Kames Castle (☎01700/504500, *kames-castle@easynet.co.uk*).

The best **food** options in Rothesay itself are *Oliver's*, on Victoria Street, which serves decent pasta and steak (and occasionally local seafood), and the waterfront bistro, *Fowlers* (closed Tues), in the Winter Gardens, which offers a good-value menu and a superb view of the bay. For Rothesay's finest fish and chips head for the *West End Café* on Gallowgate. You can't miss the many Zavaroni cafés, part of the subculture of Italian cafés in the Clyde area; the most famous member of the family was, of course, the late Lena Zavaroni, a child pop star in the 1970s. If you want to check your email, the *Harbour Café* on the seafront combines coffee and cakes and surfing.

It's worth noting that Rothesay has a **cinema** in the Winter Gardens. Bute also holds its own **Highland Games** on the last weekend in August – Prince Charles as Duke of Rothesay occasionally attends – plus an international **folk festival** on the third weekend in July, and a (mainly trad) **jazz festival** during May Bank Holiday. There are several golf courses, **pony trekking** at Kingarth Trekking Centre (☎01700/831673), near Kilchattan Bay, and **bike rental** from the Mountain Bike Centre, 24 East Princes St, or Calder Bros, 7 Bridge St, both of which are open daily.

Mount Stuart

One very good reason for coming to Bute is to visit **Mount Stuart** (Easter & May to mid-Oct Mon, Wed & Fri–Sun 11am–5pm; £6 house and gardens), a fantasy Gothic house set amidst acres of lush woodland gardens, overlooking the Firth of Clyde just three miles south of Rothesay. Home of the obscenely wealthy seventh Marquess of Bute, the building was created by the marvellously eccentric third Marquess after a fire in 1877 had destroyed the family seat. With little regard for expense, the marquess shipped in tons of Italian marble, building a railway line to transport it down the coast and employing craftsmen who had worked with the great William Burges on the marquess's earlier medieval concoctions at Cardiff Castle. The building was by no means finished when the third Marquess died in 1900, and work continues even today, though subsequent family members haven't had quite the inspirational taste of their predecessor.

A bus runs from Rothesay approximately every 45 minutes to the gates of Mount Stuart, while the house itself is a pleasant fifteen-minute walk through the gardens from the ticket office; if it's raining it might be worth taking the shuttle service provided. Inside the building, the showpiece is the columned **Marble Hall**, its vaulted ceiling and stained-glass windows decorated with the signs of the zodiac, reflecting the marquess's taste for mysticism. The marquess was equally fond of animal and plant imagery, hence you'll find birds feeding on berries in the dining-room frieze and monkeys reading (and tearing up) books and scrolls in the library. Look out also for the unusual heraldic plaster ceiling in the drawing room. After the heavy furnishings of the ground-floor rooms, you can seek aesthetic relief in the **Marble Chapel**, built entirely out of dazzling white Carrara marble, with a magnificent Cosmati floor pattern. Upstairs is less interesting, with the notable exception of the **Horoscope Room**, where you can see a fine astrological ceiling and adjacent observatory.

Although the sumptuous interior of Mount Stuart is not to everyone's taste, it's worth coming here if only to picnic and explore the wonderfully mature **gardens** (same hours as house, but open at 10am; £3 gardens only), established in the eighteenth century by the third Earl of Bute, who had a hand in London's Kew Gardens. Before you leave Mount Stuart, take a look at the planned village of **Kerrycroy**, just beyond the main exit, built by the second Marquess in the early nineteenth century for the estate workers. Semi-detached houses – alternately mock-Tudor and whitewashed stone – form a crescent overlooking a pristine village green and, beyond, the sea.

The rest of Bute

The Highland–Lowland dividing line passes through the middle of Bute, which is all but sliced in two by the freshwater Loch Fad. As a result, the northern half of the island is hilly, uninhabited and little-visited, while the southern half is made up of Lowland-style farmland. The two highest peaks on the island are **Windy Hill** (913ft) and **Torran Turach** (746ft), both in the north; from the latter there are fine views of the Kyles, but for a gentler overview of the island you can simply walk up **Canada Hill**, a few miles east of Rothesay.

A site well worth visiting, which recalls Bute's early monastic history, is **St Blane's Chapel**, a twelfth-century ruin beautifully situated in open countryside on the west coast, close to the island's southernmost tip. The medieval church stands amidst the foundations of an earlier Christian settlement established in the sixth century by Saint Catan, uncle to the local-born Saint Blane. In a rather peculiar arrangement, the upper graveyard was reserved for the men of the parish while the women were consigned to the lower one.

Four miles up the west coast is the sandy strand of **Scalpsie Bay** while, further on, beyond the village of Straad, lies **St Ninian's Point**, where the ruins of a sixth-century chapel overlook another fine sandy strand and the uninhabited island of **Inchmarnock**, to which, according to tradition, alcoholics were banished in the last century. Bute's finest sandy beach, however, is **Ettrick Bay**, with an excellent tearoom (April–Oct) at the north end. On the road from Ettrick Bay to Rothesay, you can still see traces of the tramlines which brought visitors to the beach in its heyday.

Inveraray and around

A classic example of an eighteenth-century planned town, **INVERARAY** was built on the site of a ruined fishing village in 1745 by the third Duke of Argyll, head of the powerful Campbell clan, in order to distance his newly rebuilt castle from the hoi polloi in the town and to establish a commercial and legal centre for the region. Today Inveraray, an absolute set-piece of Scottish Georgian architecture, has a truly memorable setting, the brilliant white arches of Front Street reflected in the still waters of Loch Fyne, which separate it from the Cowal peninsula.

The Town

Squeezed onto a promontory some distance from the duke's new castle, there's not much more to Inveraray's "New Town" than its distinctive **Main Street** (set at a right angle to Front Street), flanked by whitewashed terraces, whose window casements are picked out in black. At the top of the street, the road divides to circumnavigate the town's Neoclassical church, originally built in two parts: the southern half served the Gaelic-speaking community, while the northern half – still in use and worth a peek for its period wood-panelled interior – served those who spoke English.

East of the church is **Inveraray Jail** (daily: April–Oct 9.30am–6pm; Nov–March 10am–5pm; £4.50), whose attractive Georgian courthouse and grim prison blocks ceased to function in the 1930s. The jail is now an imaginative and thoroughly enjoyable museum, which graphically recounts prison conditions from medieval times up until the nineteenth century – and even brings it up to date by including a picture of life in Barlinnie Prison. You can also sit in the beautiful semicircular courthouse and listen to the trial of a farmer accused of fraud.

Moored at the town pier is the **Arctic Penguin** (daily: April–Oct 9.30am–6pm; Nov–March 10am–5pm; £3), a handsome, triple-masted schooner built in Dublin in 1911 – it has some nautical knick-knacks and displays on the maritime history of the Clyde, but is only really worth a wander round in wet weather. During the replanning of the town, the fifteenth-century **Inveraray Cross** was moved to its present position on Front Street by the loch; a more interesting cross (from the island of Tiree) can be found in the castle gardens (see below), featuring a crucifixion scene on one side, and a stag-hunting scene on the reverse.

For a panoramic view of the town, castle and loch, you can climb the **Bell Tower** (May–Sept daily 10am–1pm & 2–5pm; £1.50) of All Saints' Church, accessible via the peaceful avenue of trees through the screen arches on Front Street. Built after World War I as a memorial to the fallen Campbells by the tenth Duke of Argyll, the tower contains a ringing peal of ten bells, which are apparently the second heaviest in the world – it takes four hours to ring a complete peal.

Inveraray Castle

A ten-minute walk north of the New Town, the neo-Gothic **Inveraray Castle** (April–June, Sept & Oct Mon–Thurs & Sat 10am–1pm & 2–6pm, Sun 1–6pm; July & Aug Mon–Sat 10am–6pm, Sun 1–6pm; £4) remains the family home of the Duke of Argyll. Built in 1745 by the third duke, it was given a touch of the Loire with the addition of dormer windows and conical roofs in the nineteenth century. Inside, the most startling feature is the armoury hall, whose displays of weaponry – supplied to the Campbells by the British government to put down the Jacobites – rise through several storeys (look out for Rob Roy's rather sad-looking sporran and dirk handle, the traditional dagger worn in Highland dress).

Gracing the extensive **castle grounds** (daily dawn–dusk; free) is the aforementioned Celtic cross from Tiree, and one of three elegant bridges built during the re-landscaping of Inveraray (the other two are on the road from Cairndow). Of the walks marked out in the grounds, the most strenuous takes you to the tower atop **Dùn na Cuaiche** (813ft), from which there's a spectacular view over the castle, town and loch. Back at sea level, in the old stables, the **Combined Operations Museum** (April–Oct Mon–Thurs & Sat 11am–6pm, Sun 1–6pm; £1.25) in the old stables, recalls the intriguing wartime role of Inveraray as a training centre for the D-Day landings, during which over half a million troops practised secret amphibious manoeuvres around Loch Fyne.

Around Inveraray

If you've got children in tow, the **Argyll Wildlife Park** (daily 10am–5pm; £3.50), two miles south of Inveraray, along the A83 to Campbeltown, provides some light relief, allowing children to come face to face with Scotland's indigenous fauna, from sika deer to wildcats.

Three miles further on, the **Auchindrain Folk Museum** (April–Sept daily 10am–5pm; £3) is in fact a fascinating old township of around twenty thatched buildings which give an idea of life here before the Clearances, and before the planning of towns like neighbouring Inveraray. Original furniture, straw on the floors, and hens wandering in and out of the houses, give the place a lived-in feel, and the informative visitor centre has a good bookshop and a tearoom, whose water comes from the same spring that served the original township.

Another four miles down the road is **Crarae Garden** (daily: March–Oct 9am–6pm; Nov–Feb dawn–dusk; £2.50), laid out earlier this century as a "Himalayan ravine" in a deep glen that tumbles down into Loch Fyne. It is this dramatic setting that sets Crarae apart from the innumerable other gardens of Argyll, and provides the scenic backdrop for the gardens, with over 400 rhododendrons, azaleas and wide variety of eucalyptus and conifers. There's also a visitor centre and tearoom open in summer.

Practicalities

Inveraray's **tourist office** is on Front Street (April & mid-Sept to Oct Mon–Sat 9am–5pm, Sun noon–5pm; May & June Mon–Sat 9am–5pm, Sun 11am–5pm; July to mid-Sept daily 9am–6pm; Nov–March Mon–Fri 11am–4pm, Sat & Sun noon–4pm; ☎01499/302063), as is the town's chief **hotel**, the historic and very comfortable *Argyll* (☎01499/302466; ④), formerly the *Great Inn*, where Dr Johnson and Boswell stayed. A cheaper, but equally well-appointed alternative is the Georgian *Fernpoint Hotel* (☎01499/302170; ①) round by the pier; otherwise there's a convenient **B&B** called *Lorona* (☎01499/302258; ①; April–Oct), on Main Street, *Creag Dhubh* (☎01499/302430; March–Nov; ①) is set in a large garden overlooking Loch Fyne, up the Lochgilphead road, or for a more secluded position try *Breagha Lodge* (☎01499/302061; ③) by the golf course. Four miles south of the town, try the friendly farm cottages or house of *Kilean House* (☎01499/302474; ①). The **youth hostel** (☎01499/302454; mid-March to Oct) is in a modern building just up Dalmally Road (A819), while the old Royal Navy base, two miles down the A83, is now the excellent, fully equipped *Argyll Caravan Park* (☎01499/302285; April–Oct). The **bar** of the *George Hotel* in the middle of town is the liveliest spot, while for tea and cakes head for *The Poacher*. However, by far the best place to sample Loch Fyne's delicious fresh fish and seafood is the superb, moderately-priced restaurant of the *Loch Fyne Oyster Bar* (see p.305), six miles back up the A83 towards Glasgow.

Loch Awe and Taynuilt

Legend has it that **Loch Awe** – at more than 25 miles in length the longest stretch of fresh water in the country – was created by a witch and inhabited by a monster even more gruesome than the one at Loch Ness. The northwestern shores of the loch are the most peaceful, with gentle hills and the magnificent **Inverliever Forest**, where the Forestry Commission has laid out a series of none-too-strenuous **forest walks** around Dalavich. The most spectacular of these is the hour-long circular walk from Inverinan up to the Royal Engineers' wooden footbridge which takes you over a pretty waterfall.

Dotted around the north of the loch, where it's joined by the A819 from Inveraray, the A85 from Tyndrum and the railway from Glasgow, are several tiny islands sporting picturesque ruins. On **Inishail** you can see a crumbling thirteenth-century chapel which once served as a burial ground for the MacArthur clan; the ruined castle on **Fraoch Eilean** dates from the same period. Fifteenth-century **Kilchurn Castle**, strategically situated on a rocky spit – once an island – at the head of the loch and once a Campbell stronghold, has been abandoned to the elements since being struck by lightning in the 1760s, and is now one of Argyll's most photogenic loch-side ruins.

During the summer you can sail around Kilchurn Castle as part of an hour-long steamboat cruise that sets off from the pier at **LOCHAWE**, right by the village's train station. A mile further along the A85, it's worth pausing at **St Conan's Kirk**, an unusual architectural work fashioned in a sort of home-made Norman/Gothic style. The original church was built in the 1880s, but the version you see now was begun in 1907 by Walter Campbell and completed by his sister Helen. The church contains a fair amount of historical bric-a-brac, from a piece of Robert the Bruce to fragments from Iona Abbey and Eton College, but by far the finest sections are the ambulatory, with its tall, clear windows overlooking Loch Awe, and the dinky lead-roofed cloisters.

Further west, gorged into the giant granite bulk of Ben Cruachan (3695ft), is the underground **Cruachan Power Station** (daily: Easter–June & Sept–Nov 9.30am–5pm; July & Aug 9.30am–6pm; £3), built in 1965. Half-hour guided tours set off every hour from the newly refurbished **visitor centre** by the loch, taking you to a viewing platform above the generating room deep inside the "hollow mountain". Using the water from an artificial loch high up on Ben Cruachan to drive the turbines, the power station can become fully operational in less than two minutes, supplying electricity during surges on the National Grid. Sadly it takes ten percent more electricity to pump the water back up into the artificial loch, so the station only manages to make a profit by buying cheap off-peak power and selling during daytime peak demand. If you're keen to go, make sure you get there before the queues start to form, particularly in summer.

In order to maintain the right level of water in Loch Awe itself, a dam was built at the mouth of the loch, which then had to be fitted with a special lift to transport the salmon – for which the loch is justly famous – upriver to spawn. From the dam, the River Awe squeezes through the mountains via the gloomy rock-walled **Pass of Brander** (which means "ambush" in Gaelic), where Robert the Bruce put to flight the MacDougall clan in 1308, cutting them down as they fought with one another to cross the river and escape.

There are two particularly luxurious **hotels** on the northwestern shores of Loch Awe: the *Taychreggan Hotel* (☎01866/833211; ⑥), an old drovers' inn by the loch, to the southeast of Kilchrenan, and the *Ardanaiseig Hotel* (☎01866/833333; ⑦; Feb–Dec), a palatial Scottish Baronial pile four miles to the northeast down a dead-end track. Both these hotels have superb, though expensive, restaurants, and the *Ardanaiseig* also has its own glorious gardens (daily 9.30am–dusk), worth visiting even if you're not staying here. Considerably easier to reach is the *Loch Awe Hotel* (☎01838/200261; ⑨; Feb–Dec), another Scots Baronial hotel, on the busy A85, along the north shore of the loch. The nicest **B&Bs** are on the more peaceful western shores: try the comfortable *Thistle-Doo* B&B (☎01866/833339; ③) at Kilchrenan. Further south, at Dalavich, there are Forestry Commission **chalets** for rent by the loch; you must stay a minimum of three nights, and book through Forest Holidays (☎0131/334 0303). Loch Awe is stocked full of trout, pike and salmon, and there are **boats for hire** (and fishing tackle) from Donald Wilson (☎01866/833256), based at Ardbrecknish, southwest of Cladich on the east shore, though he will deliver boats to any other point on the loch for a fee.

Taynuilt and Loch Etive

TAYNUILT, where the River Awe flows into Loch Etive, is a small but sprawling village, best known for its iron-smelting works. To reach this industrial heritage site, follow the signpost off the A85 to **Bonawe Iron Furnace** (April–Sept Mon–Sat 9.30am–6.30pm, Sun 2–6.30pm; HS; £2.50), which was originally founded by Cumbrian ironworkers in 1753. It was clearly cheaper, in those days, to import iron ore from south of the border, rather than transport charcoal to the Lake District, since several iron furnaces were established in the area, of which Bonawe was the most successful. A whole series of buildings in various states of repair are scattered across the factory site, which employed 600 people at its height, and eventually closed down in 1876.

From the pier beyond the iron furnace, **boat cruises** (May–Sept Mon–Fri 10.30am & 2pm, Sat & Sun 2pm; April & early Oct daily 2pm; £8) explore the otherwise inaccessible reaches of Loch Etive; phone Loch Etive Cruises (☎01866/822430) for more details. Before you reach Taynuilt from Loch Awe, a sign to the right invites you to visit the **Inverawe Fisheries and Smokery** (March–Dec daily 8am–dusk), where you can buy traditionally smoked local fish and mussels, learn how to fly-fish, check out the exhibition on traditional smoking techniques, or go for a stroll down to nearby Loch Etive with your picnic.

Oban and around

The solidly Victorian resort of **OBAN** enjoys a superb setting – the island of Kerrera providing its bay with a natural shelter – distinguished by a bizarre granite amphitheatre, dramatically lit at night, on the hilltop above the town. Despite a population of just 8500, it's by far the main port in northwest Scotland, the second-largest town in Argyll, and the main departure point for ferries to the Hebrides. If you arrive late, or are catching an early boat, you may have to spend the night here (there's no real need otherwise); if you're staying elsewhere, it's a useful base for wet-weather activities and shopping, although it does get uncomfortably crowded in the summer.

Oban lies at the centre of the coastal region known as Lorn, named after the Irish Celt Loarn, who, along with his brothers Fergus and Oengus, settled here around 500 AD. Given the number of tourists that pass through or stay in the area, it's hardly surprising that a few out-and-out tourist attractions have developed, which can be handy to know about if it's raining and/or you have children with you. The mainland is very picturesque, although its beauty is no secret – to escape the crowds, head off and explore the islands, like **Lismore** or **Kerrera**, just offshore.

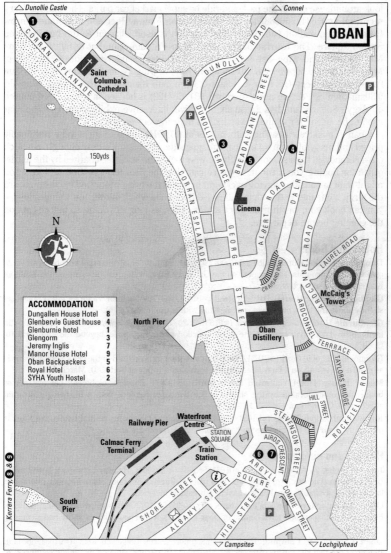

△ Dunollie Castle △ Connel

OBAN

Saint Columba's Cathedral

DUNOLLIE ROAD

BREADALBANE STREET

DUNOLLIE TERRACE

CORRAN ESPLANADE

0 150yds

❶
❷

❸
❺
❹

Cinema

GEORGE STREET

ALBERT ROAD

DALRIACH ROAD

CRAIGARD ROAD

ARDCONNEL ROAD

LAUREL ROAD

McCaig's Tower

N

ACCOMMODATION

Dungallen House Hotel	8
Glenbervie Guest house	4
Glenburnie hotel	1
Glengorm	3
Jeremy Inglis	7
Manor House Hotel	9
Oban Backpackers	5
Royal Hotel	6
SYHA Youth Hostel	2

North Pier

Oban Distillery

ARDCONNEL TERRACE

TAYLORS BRIDGE

ROCKFIELD ROAD

HILL STREET

Railway Pier

Waterfront Centre

STATION SQUARE

Calmac Ferry Terminal

Train Station

STEVENSON STREET

AIRDS CRESCENT

❻ ❼

ARGYLL SQUARE

COMBIE STREET

△ Kerrera Ferry, ❽ & ❾

South Pier

SHORE STREET

ALBANY STREET

HIGH STREET

ℹ

▽ Campsites ▽ Lochgilphead

© Crown copyright

Arrival and accommodation

Arriving in Oban **by car** can be a bit of a nightmare in the summer. If you're heading straight for the ferry, either make sure you leave an extra hour to allow for sitting in the tailbacks, which can stretch for more than a mile back along the A85, or try and approach the town from the south along the A816. If you're just coming into town to look around, use one of the park-and-ride or supermarket car parks. The CalMac **ferry terminal** (☎01631/566688) for the islands is on Railway Pier and is a stone's throw from the train station (☎01631/563083), which is itself adjacent to the bus stops on Station Square. The **tourist office** (April Mon–Fri 9am–5pm, Sat & Sun noon–5pm; May to mid-June Mon–Sat 9am–5.30pm, Sun 10am–5pm; late June & early Sept Mon–Sat 9am–6.30pm, Sun 10am–5pm; July & Aug Mon–Sat 9am–9pm & Sun 9am–7pm; late Sept–Oct Mon–Sat 9am–5.30pm, Sun 10am–4pm; Nov–March Mon–Fri 9.30am–5pm, Sat & Sun noon–4pm; ☎01631/563122) is housed in a converted church on Argyll Square, and has a visually attractive, interactive exhibition where the altar used to be, useful for whiling away half an hour in wet weather.

Oban is positively heaving with **hotels** and **B&Bs**, most of them very reasonably priced and many of them on or near the quayside. Although it's easy enough to search out a vacancy, in high season it might be wise to pay the small fee charged by the tourist office for finding you a room. If you're catching the 6am ferry to Coll or Tiree, you might want to consider staying overnight in one of the two- or four-bed berths on board the ferry, a cheaper option than a local B&B and one which allows you a longer lie-in – you can book your berth from any CalMac office, as long as you do so before 6pm on the evening before departure.

Hotels and B&Bs

Dungallen House Hotel, Gallanach Road (☎01631/563799). Solid Victorian villa hotel set in its own woodland grounds, hidden away on the Gallanach Road, with great views across the Sound of Kerrera. ⑤. Closed Feb & Nov.

Glenbervie Guest House, Dalriach Road (☎01631/564770). Superior Victorian guest house set slightly above the town on a quiet road heaving with accommodation. ①.

Glenburnie Hotel, Corran Esplanade (☎01631/562089, *glanburnie8@hotmail.com*). Efficiently-run medium-sized Victorian hotel on the quieter section of the Esplanade, beyond the Cathedral. ③. Open April–Oct.

Glengorm, Dunollie Road (☎01631/565361). If you want a cheap B&B in the centre of town, this is as good a bet as any, on a busy street replete with similarly priced B&Bs. ①. March–Nov.

Manor House Hotel, Gallanach Road (☎01631/562087). Beautiful eighteenth-century manor house, peacefully located by the shores of the Sound of Kerrera, with a top-notch restaurant attached. ④. Closed Jan.

Royal Hotel, Argyll Square (☎01631/563021). The best of Oban's big central hotels, the *Royal* is pleasantly plush and has been recently refurbished; all rooms are en suite. ⑤.

Hostels and campsites

Jeremy Inglis, 21 Airds Crescent (☎01631/565065 or 563064). Halfway between a hostel and a B&B, with an eccentric proprietor who also runs *McTavish's Kitchens*. Shared rooms, doubles or family rooms available, plus kitchen facilities; breakfast included.

Oban Backpackers, Breadalbane Street (☎01631/562107, *hostels@scotlands-top-hostels.com*). Friendliest. Cheapest and most central of Oban's hostels, with a pool table, real fire and a communal kitchen.

Oban Caravan & Camping Park, Gallanachmore Farm, Gallanach Road (☎01631/566425). Bigger of the two sites, with caravans for hire, plus ten pitches, situated two miles southwest of Oban along the Gallanach Road beside the Sound of Kerrera. Open April to mid-Oct.

Oban Divers Caravan Park, Glenshellach Road (☎01631/562755). A mile and a half south of the ferry terminal. Kids' playground, but no dogs allowed. Open March–Nov.

SYHA Hostel, Corran Esplanade (☎01631/562025, *reservations@syha.org.uk*). Converted Victorian house, with the purpose-built *Oban Lodge* annexe behind, both a fair trek from the ferry terminal along the Corran Esplanade, just beyond the Catholic cathedral. Breakfast included.

The Town

The only truly remarkable sight in Oban is the town's landmark, **McCaig's Folly**, a stiff ten-minute climb from the quayside. Built in imitation of Rome's Colosseum, it was the brainchild of a local businessman a century ago, who had the twin aims of alleviating off-season unemployment among the local stonemasons and creating a museum, art gallery and chapel. Originally, the plan was to add a 95ft central tower, but work never progressed further than the exterior granite walls before McCaig died. In his will, McCaig gave instructions for the lancet windows to be filled with bronze statues of the family, though no such work was ever undertaken. Instead, the folly has been turned into a sort of walled garden, and simply provides a wonderful seaward panorama, particularly at sunset.

Down in the centre of town, you can pass a few hours admiring the boats in the harbour and looking out for inquisitive seals in the bay. If the weather's bad, you can shelter in the ugly **Waterfront Centre**, beside the equally cheerless new train station (the Victorian one was demolished in 1988). Caithness Glass have a shop outlet and small exhibition in the centre, though you can no longer watch glass-blowing demonstrations. Another option is to take a forty-minute guided tour of the **Oban Distillery** (Mon–Fri 9.30am–5pm; Easter–Oct also Sat; July–Sept Sat until 8.30pm; £3), in the centre of town off George Street, which ends with a dram of whisky (and a refund of the admission fee if you buy a bottle).

A pleasant half-hour evening stroll can be had by walking north along the Corran Esplanade, past the modern, Roman Catholic **Cathedral of St Columba** – built in the 1920s by Sir Giles Gilbert Scott, architect of Battersea Power Station – to the rocky ruins of **Dunollie Castle**, a MacDougall stronghold on a very ancient site, successfully defended by the laird's Jacobite wife during the 1715 uprising but abandoned after 1745.

Anyone looking for the **World in Miniature** (April–Oct daily 10am–6pm; £2.50), which used to reside on Oban's North Pier, now has to travel seven miles south along the A816 to view the museum's assortment of minute "dolls' house" rooms. However, folks with kids would probably be better off heading just a couple of miles out of Oban, east along Glencruitten Road, to the **Oban Rare Breeds Farm Park** (daily: late March to Oct 10am–5.30pm; mid-June to Aug 10am–7.30pm; £4), which displays rare but indigenous species of deer, cattle, sheep and so forth – they can meet the baby animals at the children's corner.

A host of private **boat operators** can be found around the harbour, on the North, South and Railway piers: their excursions – to Mull, Iona, Staffa, Seal Island and the Treshnish Isles – are worth considering, particularly if you're pushed for time, or have no transport. Gordon Grant Tours (☎01681/700338), on Oban's Railway Pier, offers a whole range of trips, including an entire day's cruise around the Treshnish Isles. **Boat hire** is available from Borro Boats, on the Gallanach Road (☎01631/563292), and you can **rent bikes** from Oban Cycles, 9 Craigard Rd (☎01631/566996).

Eating, drinking and nightlife

Oban doesn't hold a lot of treats for visitors or locals. If you're only here to catch a ferry, you might as well grab a quick bite to eat at the excellent **take away** seafood counter by the side of the CalMac terminal. Venturing further into town, you can't miss *McTavish's Kitchens*, on George Street, a local institution serving unexceptional soups, burgers, grills and sandwiches. More promising is the nearby *Kitchen Garden* deli's mezzanine **café**, or *F'Eats*, a new place on John Street offering delicious toasted panini and good cappuccino. Oban's best **restaurant** is, without doubt, *The Gathering* (☎01631/565421; Easter–Christmas daily from 5pm) on Breadalbane Street, which excels in, among other things, moderately expensive local fish and seafood. The inexpensive *Box Tree* restaurant, on George Street, is your next best bet, with a wide choice of veggie dishes and seafood on offer. And of course, there's always fish and chips: try *Onorio's*, 86 George St (closed Sun).

Oban's only half-decent **pub** is the *Oban Inn* opposite the north pier, with a classic dark-wood-flagstone-and-brass bar downstairs and lounge bar with stained-glass upstairs. The town's nightlife doesn't bear thinking about (though you can read all about it in the *Oban Times*). It's worth noting, however, that Oban is one of the few places in Argyll with a **cinema**, confusingly known as The Highland Theatre (☎01631/562444), at the north end of George Street. You should be able to catch some **live music** at the weekend at *O'Donnell's* Irish pub, underneath *The Gathering*, or in the bar of the *Royal Hotel*, on Argyll Square, and occasionally (concert-style) at the Corran Halls, along the Esplanade. The annual **Argyllshire Gathering** takes place on the last weekend in August, featuring piping competitions, and Highland Games.

Isle of Kerrera

One of the best places to escape from the crowds that plague Oban is the low-lying island of **Kerrera**, which shelters Oban Bay from the worst of the westerly winds. Measuring just five miles by two, the island is easily explored on foot, and gives panoramic views from its highest point, Càrn Breugach (620ft), over to Mull, the Slate Islands, Lismore, Jura and beyond.

The ferry lands by the lobster factory, roughly halfway down the east coast, at the north end of **Horseshoe Bay**, where King Alexander II died in 1249. If the weather's fine and you feel like lazing by the sea, head for the island's finest sandy beach, **Slatrach Bay**, on the west coast, one mile northwest of the ferry jetty. Otherwise, the most rewarding trail is down to **Gylen Castle**, a clifftop ruin on the south coast, built in 1582 by the MacDougalls and burnt to the ground by the Covenanter General Leslie in 1647. You can head back to the ferry via the Drove Road, where cattle from Mull and other islands were once herded to be swum across the sound to the market in Oban.

The passenger and bicycle **ferry** departs daily from the mainland two miles down the Gallanach road from Oban (phone ☎01631/563665 for the latest schedule; £3 return). Kerrera has a total population of fewer than thirty – and no shop – so if you're day-tripping, make sure you bring enough supplies with you. Alternatively, you can eat at the *Kerrera Teagarden* (daily 10am–5pm), in Lower Gylen, which serves home-made, often organic, veggie snacks. You can also stay at Lower Gylen in the *Kerrera Bothy*, a converted eighteenth-century stable building (☎01631/570223, *email@landlign.demon.co.uk*; April–Oct) – ring ahead if you need transport from the ferry.

Dunstaffnage Castle and Connel

Just beyond the northern satellite suburbs of Oban, on a strategic promontory over-looking the important water crossroads at the mouth of Loch Etive, lie the ruins of **Dunstaffnage Castle** (April–Sept daily 9.30am–6.30pm; Oct–March Mon–Wed, Sat & Sun 9am–4pm, Thurs HS; £1.80). Originally built as a thirteenth-century MacDougall fort, the castle was captured by Robert the Bruce in 1309, and remained in royal hands until it was handed over to the Campbells in 1470. Garrisoned by government forces during the 1745 rebellion, it served as a temporary prison for Flora MacDonald, and was eventually destroyed by fire in 1810. The approach, through a housing estate, is a bit unsettling, but, with the castle's substantial curtain wall battlements partially intact, Dunstaffnage makes for a fun and safe place to explore, and gives great views across to Lismore and Morvern.

A couple of miles further up the A85, at **CONNEL**, you can't fail to admire the majestic steel cantilever **Connel Bridge**, built in 1903 to take the old branch rail line across the sea cataract at the mouth of Loch Etive, north to Fort William. The name "Connel" comes from the Gaelic *conghail* (tumultuous flood), which refers to the rapids, clearly visible from the bridge, and caused by the water at low ebb rushing over a ledge of rock between the two shores of the loch. The A828 now crosses Connel Bridge to take you onto Benderloch (see below).

Benderloch

On the north side of the Connel Bridge lies the hammerhead peninsula of **Benderloch** (from *beinn eadar da loch*, "hill between two lochs"), on whose northern shores you'll find **Barcaldine Castle** (Easter & late May to Sept daily 11am–5.30pm; £3.25), an early seventeenth-century Campbell tower house. The house was abandoned by the Campbells in favour of Barcaldine House, three miles northeast, and eventually sold in 1842. Bought back by the family as a ruin in 1896 and restored, it is now occupied and run by the current heir, London-born and bred Roderick, and his wife Caroline. There are no real treasures here, but the castle has a pleasant, lived-in feel, and is fun to explore, with dungeons and hidden staircases. To help balance the books, the Campbells also offer **B&B** at the castle (☎01631/720598; ③). Those with rather larger budgets might prefer to stay at Argyll's most exclusive hotel, the *Isle of Eriska*, a luxury, turreted, Scottish Baronial pile, run by the Buchanan-Smiths on their own 300-acre island, off the northern point of Benderloch (☎01631/720371, *office@eriska-hotel.co.uk*; ⑨; March–Dec), with an acclaimed and very expensive dining room (open to non-residents in the evening).

Since the weather in this part of Scotland can be bad at almost any time of the year, it's as well to know about the **Oban Sea Life Centre** (April–June daily 9am–6pm; July & Aug daily 9am–7pm; call ☎01631/720386 for winter opening times; £5.50), which is, in actual fact, to be found on the A828, along the southern shores of Loch Creran. Here you can see locally caught sea creatures at close quarters – look out for the octopus and stingray, and the wonderful "herring ring" – before they are returned to the sea at the end of the season. The centre's self-service *Shoreline* restaurant features a small oyster bar.

Appin

With the new Creagan Bridge in place – the old wrought-iron railway bridge sadly having been demolished – there's no need to circumnavigate Loch Creran in order to reach the district of **Appin**, best known as the setting for Robert Louis Stevenson's *Kidnapped*, a fictionalized account of the "Appin Murder" of 1752, when Colin Campbell was shot in the back, allegedly by one of the disenfranchised Stewart clan. However, the new bridge also means than the eastern reaches of the loch, and **Glen Creran** itself are now even more peaceful and secluded. The lovely dead-end single-track road through the woods to Fasnacloich shelters several wonderful B&B retreats such as *Lochside Cottage* (☎01631/730216; ②), a large white house with a garden sloping down to a freshwater loch. At the end of the road there's a seven-mile forest walk over to Ballachulish (see p.506).

The name "Appin" derives from the Gaelic *abthaine*, meaning "Lands belonging to the Abbey", in this case the one on the island of Lismore (see p.320), which is linked to the peninsula by passenger ferry from **PORT APPIN**, a pretty little fishing village at the westernmost tip of the peninsula. Overlooking a host of tiny little islands, dotted around Loch Linnhe, with Lismore and the mountains Morvern and Mull in the background, this is, without doubt, one of Argyll's most picturesque spots. The *Pierhouse Hotel* (☎01631/730302; ⑦), nicely situated right by the ferry, has a popular bar, and an expensive, but excellent and very popular seafood restaurant (prices are slightly lower at lunchtimes). Alternatively, you could eat at the *Pierhouse*, but stay in the friendly *Rhugarbh Croft* (☎01631/730309; ②), up the road in North Shian, and enjoy homemade bread and free-range eggs for breakfast.

One of Argyll's most romantic ruined castles, the much-photographed **Castle Stalker**, occupies a tiny rock island to the north of Port Appin. Built by the Stewarts of Appin in the sixteenth century and gifted to King James IV as a hunting lodge, it inevitably fell into the hands of the Campbells after 1745. The current owners open the castle to the public for a very short period only each year; ring ☎01631/730234 or ask at Oban tourist office for this year's opening times. If you're looking for **outdoor pursuits** in Appin, head for the Linnhe Marine Water Sports Centre (☎01631/730401; May–Sept), in Lettershuna (just north of Castle Stalker), which rents out boats of all shapes and sizes, offers sailing and windsurfing lessons, not to mention water-skiing, clay-pigeon shooting and even pony trekking.

Isle of Lismore

Lying in the middle of Loch Linnhe, to the north of Oban, and barely rising above a hillock, the narrow island of **Lismore** offers wonderful gentle walking or cycling opportunities, with unrivalled views, in fine weather, across to the mountains of Morvern, Lochaber and Mull. Legend has it that saints Columba and Moluag both fancied the skinny island as a missionary base, but as they raced towards it Moluag cut off his finger and threw it ashore ahead of Columba, claiming the land for himself. Of Moluag's sixth-century foundation nothing remains, but from 1236 until 1507 the island served as the seat of the Bishop of Argyll. It was a judicious choice, as Lismore is undoubtedly one of the most fertile of the Inner Hebrides – its name, coined by Moluag himself, derives from the Gaelic *lios mór*, meaning "great garden" – and at one time it supported nearly 1400 inhabitants; the population today is around a tenth of that figure.

The ferry from Oban lands at **ACHNACROISH**, roughly halfway along the eastern coastline. To get to grips with the history of the island and its Gaelic culture (and have a cup of tea), head inland until you catch the signs for the nearby **Comann Eachdraidh Lios Mór**, or Lismore Historical Society (Easter & May–Sept Mon–Sat 10am–5pm; £1). The island post office and shop are along the main road between Achnacroish and **CLACHAN**, a couple of miles northeast, where the diminutive, white-washed former **Cathedral of St Moluag** stands. All that remains of the fourteenth-century cathedral is the choir, which was reduced in height and converted into the parish church in 1749; inside you can see a few of the original seats for the upper clergy, a stone basin in the south wall, and several medieval doorways. Due east of the church – head north up the road and take the turning signposted on the right – the circular **Tirefour Broch**, over two thousand years old, occupies a commanding position and boasts walls almost 10ft thick in places. West of Clachan are the much more recent ruins of **Castle Coeffin**, a twelfth-century MacDougall fortress once believed to have been haunted by the ghost of Beothail, sister of the Norse prince Caiffen. A few other places worth exploring are **Sailean**, an abandoned quarry village further south along the west coast, with its disused kilns and cottages, the ruins of **Achanduin Castle**, in the southwest, where the bishops are thought to have resided, and Barr Mór (416ft), the island's highest point.

Two **ferries** serve Lismore: a small CalMac car ferry from Oban to Achnacroish (Mon–Sat 2–4 daily; 50min), and a shorter passenger- and bicycle-only crossing from Port Appin to the island's north point (daily every 2hr; 5min). There's a **postbus** round the island (Mon–Sat; pick up a timetable from Oban tourist office). **Accommodation** on the island is limited to a handful of B&Bs: try the budget B&B at Clachan Farm

Culross on the Firth of Forth

Tobermory harbour, Mull

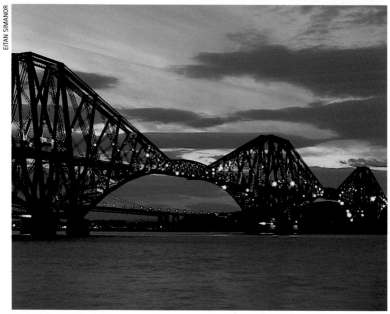

The Forth bridges

Celtic cross on the Isle of Oronsay

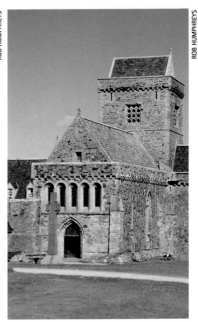
Iona Abbey

McCaig's Folly from Oban harbour

Autumn around Loch Tummel

Calanais Standing Stones, Lewis

Trotternish, Isle of Skye

EDMUND NÄGELE

Kilnave Chapel, Islay

JOHN NOBLE

Fingal's Cave, Isle of Staffa

EDMUND NÄGELE

Croft house in North Uist

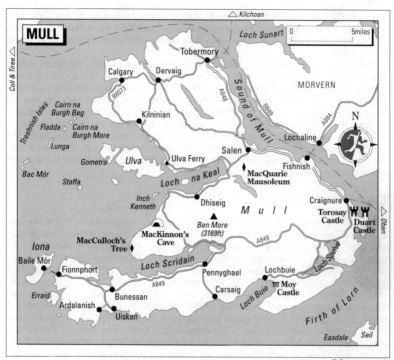

© Crown copyright

(☎0631/760271; ①), or the *Schoolhouse* (☎01631/760262; ①), north of Clachan, which also serves evening meals. **Bike rental** is available from Island Bike Hire (☎01631/760213) for around £10 a day.

Isle of Mull

The second largest of the Inner Hebrides, **Mull** is by far the most accessible: just forty minutes from Oban by ferry. As so often, first impressions largely depend on the weather – it is the wettest of the Hebrides (and that's saying something) – for without the sun the large tracts of moorland, particularly around the island's highest peak, Ben More (3196ft), can appear bleak and unwelcoming. There are, however, areas of more gentle pastoral scenery around **Dervaig** in the north and **Salen** on the east coast, and the indented west coast varies from the sandy beaches around **Calgary** to the cliffs of Loch na Keal. The most common mistake is to try and "do" the island in a day or two: flogging up the main road to the picturesque capital of **Tobermory**, then covering the fifty-odd miles between there and Fionnphort, in order to visit **Iona**. Mull is a place that will grow on you only if you have the time and patience to explore.

Historically, crofting, whisky distilling and fishing supported the islanders (*Muileachs*), but the population – which peaked at 10,000 – decreased dramatically in the nineteenth century due to the Clearances and the 1846 potato famine. On Mull, it is a trend that has been reversed, mostly due to the large influx of settlers from elsewhere in the country which has brought the current population up to over 2500. One of the main reasons for this resurgence is, of course, tourism – more than half a million visitors come here each year – although oddly enough, there are very few large hotels or campsites.

Craignure is the main entry point to Mull, with a frequent daily **car ferry** link to Oban; if you're taking a car over, it's advisable to book ahead for this service. A much smaller car ferry crosses daily from Lochaline on the Morvern peninsula (see p.509) to the slipway at Fishnish, six miles northwest of Craignure; another even smaller car ferry connects Kilchoan on the Ardnamurchan peninsula (see p.509) with Tobermory, 24 miles northwest of Craignure. Both of these two smaller ferries run on a first-come-first-served basis. **Public transport** on Mull is not too bad on the main A849, but there's more or less no service along the west coast. Those with **cars** should note that the roads are still predominantly single-track, with passing places, which can cause serious congestion on the main road in summer.

Craignure and around

CRAIGNURE is little more than a scattering of cottages, though there is a CalMac and **tourist office** – the only one on the island open all year round – situated opposite the pier (April to mid-June & Sept to mid-Oct Mon–Thurs 9am–7pm, Fri 9am–5pm, Sat 9am–6.30pm, Sun 10.30am–5pm; mid-June to Aug Mon–Thurs 9am–7pm, Fri 9am–5pm, Sat 9am–8.15pm, Sun 10.30am–7pm; mid-Oct to March Mon–Sat 9am–5pm, Sun 10.30am–5pm; ☎01680/812377). The *Craignure Inn* (☎01680/812305; ③), just a minute's stroll up the road towards Fionnphort, is a snug **pub** to hole up in, if you need one. There's also a well-equipped **campsite** (☎01680/812496; April–Oct) on the south side of Craignure Bay, behind the new village hall, run by Sheiling Holidays. The campsite offers hostel or private accommodation in "carpeted cottage tents", bike rental and other outdoor activities. The best **guest house** in the area, *Old Mill Cottage* (☎01680/812442; ③), is three miles south in Lochdon; it also has a small and highly recommended restaurant attached.

Bus connections with Fionnphort (Mon–Sat 3–4 daily, Sun 1 daily; 1hr 10min) and Tobermory (Mon–Sat 4–5 daily, Sun 3 daily; 50min) are infrequent, so check with Oban tourist office before you catch the ferry. The other method of transport available at Craignure is the diminutive, narrow-gauge Mull and West Highland Railway, commonly known as **Mull Rail** (Easter to mid-Oct; phone ☎01680/812494 for full details; £3.30 return), the only working railway in the Scottish Islands. The Craignure station is situated beyond the Sheiling Holidays campsite, and the line stretches southeast for about a mile and a half to Torosay Castle (see below). If you prefer to take the train one-way only, it's an easy half-hour walk along the coast. The company use diesel and steam locomotives, so ring ahead if you want to be sure of a steam-driven train.

Torosay and Duart Castle

Two castles lie immediately southeast of Craignure. The first, **Torosay Castle** (Easter to mid-Oct daily 10.30am–5pm; £4.50), is a full-blown Scottish Baronial creation. The house itself is stuffed with memorabilia relating to the present owners, the Guthries, all of it amusingly captioned but of no great import, with the possible exception of the belongings of the late David Guthrie-James, who was something of an adventurer and a POW in Colditz. Torosay's real highlight, however, is the magnificent **gardens** (open all year daily 10.30am–5.30pm; gardens only £3.50) with their avenue of eighteenth-century Venetian statues, Japanese section, and views over to neighbouring Duart. If the admission price puts you off Torosay, head for the silversmiths or the workshop of the **Mull Weavers** (Mon–Sat 9am–5pm; April–Oct also Sun; free), in the castle grounds, where you can watch the old-fashioned dobby loom in the workshop weave tartan.

Lacking the gardens, but on a picturesque spit of rock a couple of miles east of Torosay, **Duart Castle** (May to mid-Oct daily 10.30am–6pm; £3.50) is clearly visible from the Oban–Craignure ferry. Headquarters of the once-powerful MacLean clan from the thirteenth century, it was burnt down by the Campbells and confiscated after the 1745 rebellion. Finally in 1911, the 26th clan chief, Fitzroy MacLean (1835–1936) – not to be confused with the Scottish writer of the same name – managed to buy it back and restore it. You can peek at the dungeons, climb up to the ramparts, study the family photos, and learn about the world scout movement – the 27th clan chief became Chief Scout in 1959. After your visit, you can enjoy home-made cakes and tea at the castle's excellent tearoom.

Tobermory

Mull's chief town, **TOBERMORY**, is easily the most attractive fishing port on the west coast of Scotland, its clusters of brightly coloured houses and boats sheltering in a bay backed by a steep bluff. Founded in 1788 by the British Society for Encouraging Fisheries, it never really took off as a fishing port and only survived due to the steady influx of crofters evicted from other parts of the island during the Clearances. With a population of more than 700, it is, without doubt, the capital of Mull, and if you're staying any length of time on the island you're bound to end up here.

Information and accommodation

The **tourist office** (April & mid-Sept to Oct Mon–Sat 9am–5pm, Sun 10.30am–5pm; May & June daily 9am–5pm; July to mid-Sept daily 9am–6pm; ☎01688/302182) is in the same building as the CalMac ticket office at the far end of Main Street. If you want to rent a **bike**, head for the youth hostel (see below), or Tom-a'Mhuillin (☎01688/302164) on the Salen road. The island's only permanent **bank**, the Clydesdale, is on Main Street (a mobile one tours the island; ask at the tourist office for details).

The tourist office can book you into a **B&B** for a small fee – not a bad idea in high season when the places on Main Street tend to get booked up fast, and the rest are a stiff climb from the harbour. The small, friendly **SYHA hostel** is on Main Street (☎01688/302481; late Feb to Oct) and has laundry facilities. The nearest **campsite** is *Newdale* (☎01688/302306; April–Nov), nicely situated one and a half miles outside Tobermory on the B8073 to Dervaig.

Baliscate Guest House, Salen Road (☎01688/302495). Imposing whitewashed Victorian guest house, with a large garden, set back from the road to Salen, just outside Tobermory. ②.

Failte Guest House, Main Street (☎01688/302495). Very comfortably and pleasantly furnished en suite rooms, some of which have views out over the harbour. Open March–Oct. ②.

Glengorm Castle, near Tobermory (☎01688/302321). Rambling Baronial mansion in a superb, secluded setting, four miles northwest of Tobermory, overlooking the sea. Guests get use of the castle's huge public rooms; self-catering cottages are available, too. ⑥.

Harbour Guest House, Main Street (☎01688/302209). Spacious, clean rooms, some great views and big breakfasts. ①.

Highland Cottage, Breadalbane Street (☎01688/302030). Superior guest house, plushly furnished, fully en suite and boasting excellent home cooking. ⑤.

Western Isles Hotel (☎01688/302012, *wihotel@aol.com*). Tobermory's most distinguished hotel, a grandiose Scottish Baronial pile high above the harbour, with terrific views. ⑤.

The town

The harbour – known as **Main Street** – is one long parade of multicoloured hotels, guest houses, restaurants and shops, and you could happily spend an hour or so pottering around: Mull Pottery and the Mull Silver Company are both worth a browse, as is The Gallery, a converted church more of interest for its architecture than the tartan

THE TOBERMORY TREASURE

The most dramatic event in Tobermory's history was in 1588 when a ship from **the Spanish Armada** sank in mysterious circumstances while having repairs done to its sails and rigging. The story goes that one of the MacLeans of Duart was taken prisoner, but when the ship weighed anchor, he made his way to the powder magazine and blew it up. However, several versions of the story exist, and even the identity of the ship has been hotly disputed: for many years it was thought to be the treasure-laden Spanish galleon *Almirante di Florencia*, but it now seems more likely that it was the rather more prosaic troop carrier *San Juan de Sicilia*. Nevertheless, the possibility of precious sunken booty at the bottom of Tobermory harbour has fired the greed of numerous lairds and kings – in the 1950s Royal Navy divers were engaged by the Duke of Argyll in the seemingly futile activity of diving for treasure, and in 1982 another unsuccessful attempt was made.

and shortbread on sale. One of Tobermory's endearing features is the incessant chiming of its diminutive **Clock Tower**, erected by the author Isabella Bird in 1905 in memory of her sister who died of typhoid on the island in 1880. Close by is a polychrome watery cherub, donated by the local water-supply contractors in 1883.

A recent arrival on Main Street is the **Hebridean Whale and Dolphin Trust** (April–Oct Mon–Fri 10am–6pm, Sat & Sun 11am–5pm; Nov–March Mon–Fri 11am–5pm; free), run by a welcoming bunch of enthusiasts. The small office has lots of information on how to identify marine mammals, and on recent sightings. They're very child-friendly, too, and will keep kids amused for an hour or so with computer marine games, word searches and a bit of artwork. Sea Life Surveys (☎01688/302787), who offer a variety of whale- and dolphin-watching trips from Tobermory, are run from the same office.

Another good wet weather retreat is the **Mull Museum** (Easter to mid-Oct Mon–Fri 10.30am–4pm, Sat 10am–1pm; £1), further along Main Street, which packs in a great deal of information and artefacts (including a few objects salvaged from the *San Juan*) in one tiny room. Alternatively, there's the minuscule **Tobermory Distillery** (Easter–Oct Mon–Fri 10.30am–4pm; £2.50) at the south end of the bay, founded in 1795 but closed down three times since then. Today, it's back in business and offers a guided tour (every 30min), rounded off with a tasting.

A stiff climb up Back Brae will bring you to the island's new arts centre, **An Tobar** (Tues–Sat 10am–4pm; free), housed in a converted Victorian schoolhouse. The centre hosts exhibitions, a variety of live events, and contains a café with comfy sofas set before a real fire. The rest of the upper town is laid out on a classic grid-plan, and merits a stroll, if only for the great views over the bay.

Eating and drinking

Main Street is heaving with **places to eat**. You can get inexpensive fry-ups and fish and chips at *Gannets* or huge bar meals in the lounge bar at the *Mishnish*. For more imaginative local seafood and meat dishes, however, you need to go to *Back Brae* (evenings only), which does filling, moderately expensive set menus, or to the *Western Isles Hotel*, which serves superior bar food in the conservatory overlooking the Sound of Mull, as well as more expensive à la carte dishes in the dining room. Fresh fish and seafood is available from the Tobermory Fish Mart shop, on Main Street, and would do for **picnic** fodder, supplemented, perhaps, by bread and goodies from the excellent Island Bakery, also on the harbour front.

If you want to know what there is in the way of **entertainment** in Tobermory (or anywhere else on Mull), be sure to pick up the free monthly newsletter *Round & About*, and/or buy a copy of *Am Muileach*, the monthly island newspaper. The lively bar of the

Mishnish Hotel has been the most popular local drinking hole for many years, and features live music at the weekend, It's also the focus of Mull's annual **Traditional Music Festival**, a feast of Gaelic folk music held on the last weekend in April. Unfortunately, the *Mishnish* lost much of its character after a recent facelift, and some of its custom, after competition arrived in the shape of *MacGochan's*, a purpose-built, though pleasant enough, pub, which also offers occasional live music, on the opposite side of the harbour near the distillery. Mull's other major musical event, after the folk festival, is the annual **Mendelssohn on Mull Festival**, held over ten days in early July, which commemorates the composer's visit here in 1829.

Dervaig and Calgary

The gently undulating countryside west of Tobermory, beyond the freshwater Mishnish lochs, provides some of the most beguiling scenery on the island. Added to this, the road out west, the B8073, is exceptionally dramatic, with fiendish switchbacks much appreciated during the annual Mull Rally, which takes place each October.

The only village of any size is **DERVAIG**, which nestles beside narrow Loch Chumhainn, just eight miles southwest of Tobermory, distinguished by its unusual pencil-shaped church spire and dinky whitewashed cottages set in twos along its main street. Dervaig is best known as the home of **Mull Theatre**, one of the smallest professional theatres in the world, which puts on an adventurous season of plays adapted for a handful of resident actors (April–Sept; booking recommended ☎01688/400245). The theatre lies within the grounds of the Victorian *Druimard Country House* (☎01688/400345; ⑦; late March–Oct), which has a decent bar, and offers top-class, expensive pre-theatre dinners. A cheaper spot of refreshment is available from *Coffee and Books*, which offers just that (and a few provisions) from its premises opposite the *Bellacroy Hotel*, whose bar is a great place to shelter for the day in bad weather.

Dervaig has a wide choice of **places to stay**, aside from the aforementioned *Druimard*. The best of the B&Bs are the vegetarian-friendly *Glen Bellart House* (☎01688/400282; ①; Easter–Oct) in one of the whitewashed houses on the main street, *Glenview* (☎01688/400239; ②; April–Oct), a really lovely 1890s house on the edge of the village, the excellent *Cuin Lodge* (☎01688/400346; ②; March–Oct), northwest of the village overlooking the loch, or *Balmacara* (☎01688/400363; ③), a modern and extremely luxurious hillside house. A little beyond Dervaig, the **Old Byre Heritage Centre** (Easter–Oct daily 10.30am–6.30pm; £2) is better than many of its kind, with a video on the island's history and a passable tearoom.

The road continues cross-country to **CALGARY**, once a thriving crofting community, now an idyllic holiday spot boasting Mull's finest sandy bay, backed by low-lying dunes and machair, with wonderful views over to Coll and Tiree. There's just one hotel, the delightful *Calgary Farmhouse* (☎01688/400256; ④; April–Oct), whose excellent, moderately priced restaurant, *The Dovecote*, is (unsurprisingly) housed in a converted dovecote. The south side of the beach is a favourite spot for **camping** rough, though the only facilities are the public toilets. For the record: the city of Calgary in Canada does indeed take its name from this little village, though it was not so named by Mull emigrants, but by one Colonel McLeod of the North West Mounted Police, who once holidayed here.

Salen and around

SALEN, on the east coast halfway between Craignure and Tobermory, lies at the narrowest point on the island. As such it makes a good central base for exploring the island, though it has none of Tobermory's charm. There are, however, several decent places to stay, ranging from the **hostel** accommodation of *Arle Farm Lodge* (☎01680/300343; ②), a well-equipped modern lodge on a working farm, four miles up the A848, to the *Victorian Gruline Home Farm B&B* (☎01680/300581; ③), four miles to the southwest, set in its own beautiful grounds near the MacQuarie Mausoleum (see below); the moderately expensive five-course dinners are absolutely excellent. Those with even more money can head three miles west to the shores of the Loch na Keal, where the award-winning *Killiechronan Hotel* (☎01680/300403; ⑦; March–Oct) offers dinner and bed and breakfast only; a set menu dinner for non-residents is £25 a head. Salen itself has only a couple of very ordinary eating options, though it does have **bike rental** from On Yer Bike (☎01680/300501), who also have child trailers for hire. The nearest **campsite** is the well-equipped site at *Balmeanach Park* (☎01680/300342; March–Oct), five miles southeast by the Sound of Mull at Fishnish.

The most unusual sight near Salen is the **MacQuarie Mausoleum**, a simple but-tressed tomb, set within a walled clearing surrounded by pine trees and rhododen-drons, and lovingly maintained by the National Trust for Scotland, on behalf of the National Trust of Australia. Within lies the body of Lachlan MacQuarie (1761–1824), the "Father of Australia", who, as the effusive epitaph explains, was appointed by the British as Governor of New South Wales in 1809, to replace the unpopular William Bligh, formerly of the *Bounty*. However, the enlightened MacQuarie was equally unpop-ular with the Aussie settlers, primarily for instituting liberal penal reforms, and also had to be recalled in 1820.

Isle of Ulva

A chieftain to the Highlands bound
Cries "Boatman, do not tarry!
And I'll give thee a silver pound
To row us o'er the ferry!"
"Now who be ye, would cross Lochgyle
This dark and stormy water?"
"O I'm the chief of Ulva's isle,
An this, Lord Ullin's daughter."

Lord Ullin's Daughter, Thomas Campbell (1777–1844)

Around the time poet laureate Campbell penned this tragic poem, **Ulva**'s population was a staggering 850, sustained by the huge quantities of kelp which were exported for glass and soap production. That was before the market for kelp collapsed and the 1846 potato famine hit, after which the remaining population was brutally evicted. Nowadays barely thirty people live here, and the island is littered with ruined crofts, not to men-tion a church, designed by Thomas Telford, which would once have seated over three hundred parishioners. It's great walking country, however, with several clearly marked paths criss-crossing the rocky heather moorland interior – and you're almost guaran-teed to spot some of the abundant wildlife: at the very least deer, if not buzzards, gold-en eagles and even sea eagles, with seals and divers offshore. Those who like to have a focus for their wanderings should head for the ruined crofting villages, and basalt columns similar to those on Staffa; along the island's southern coastline, for the island's highest point, Beinn Chreagach (1027ft); or along the north coast to Ulva's tidal neigh-bour, Gometra, off the west coast.

To get to **Ulva** (from the Norse *ulv øy* or "wolf island") which lies just 100yd or so off the west coast of Mull, follow the signs for "Ulva Ferry" from Salen – if you've no trans-port, a postbus can get you there, but not back. From **Ulva Ferry**, a small bicycle/pas-senger-only ferry is available on demand (Mon–Fri 9am–5pm; June–Aug also Sun; at other times by arrangement; £2.50 return); look out for the ferryman's dog, who is famous for his cartwheels. *The Boathouse*, near the ferry slip on Ulva, serves as a licensed **tearoom** selling cakes, snacks, Guinness and Ulva oysters; evening meal boat trips are a new feature (phone ☎01688/500241 to book). You can learn more about the history of the island from the **Heritage Centre** exhibition upstairs, soon to be supplemented with more displays in nearby **Sheila's Cottage**, a newly restored thatched crofthouse. There's no accommodation, but with permission from the present owners (☎01688/500264, *ulva@zetnet.co.uk*) you can **camp** rough overnight.

Isle of Staffa and the Treshnish Isles

Five miles southwest of Ulva, **Staffa** is the most romantic and dramatic of Scotland's many uninhabited islands. On its south side, the perpendicular rockface features an imposing series of black basalt columns, known as the Colonnade, which have been cut by the sea into cathedralesque caverns, most notably **Fingal's Cave**. The Vikings knew about the island – the name derives from their word for "Island of Pillars" – but it wasn't until 1772 that it was "discovered" by the world. Turner painted it, Wordsworth explored it, but Mendelssohn's *Die Fingalshöhle*, inspired by the sounds of the sea-wracked caves he heard on a visit here in 1829, did most to popularize the place – after which Queen Victoria gave her blessing, too. The geological explanation for these polygonal basalt organ pipes is that they were created by a massive subterranean explosion some sixty million years ago. A huge mass of molten basalt ejaculated onto land and, as it cooled, solidified into what are, essentially, crystals. Of course, confronted with such artistry, most visitors have found it difficult to believe that their origin is entirely natural – indeed, the various Celtic folk tales, which link the phenomenon with the Giant's Causeway in Ireland, are certainly more appealing.

To **get to Staffa**, join one of the many boat trips from Oban, Dervaig, Ulva Ferry or Fionnphort, weather permitting. Staffa-only trips start at £10 per person on the MB *Iolaire* (☎01681/700358; £10 return) which sails out of Fionnphort, and with *Turus Mara* (☎01688/400242, *turus.mara@dial.pipex.com*), operating out of Ulva Ferry. However, Inter-Island Cruises (☎01688/400264), which run from Dervaig, is worth the extra money.

Several outfits such as Turus Mara, Inter-Island Cruises, and the whale-watching Sea Life Surveys (see p.324), also offer boat trips around the archipelago of uninhabited volcanic islets that make up the **Treshnish Isles** northwest of Staffa. None of them are more than a mile across, the most distinctive being **Bac Mór**, shaped like a Puritan's hat and popularly dubbed the Dutchman's Cap. Most trips include a stop-over on **Lunga**, the largest island, and a nesting place for hundreds of seabirds, in particular guillemots, razorbills (mid-May to July) and puffins (late April to mid-Aug), as well as a breeding ground for common seals (June) and Atlantic greys (early Sept). The two most northerly islands, **Cairn na Burgh More** and **Cairn na Burgh Beag**, have the remains of ruined castles, the first of which served as a lookout post for the Lords of the Isles and was last garrisoned in the Civil War; Cairn na Burgh Beag hasn't been occupied since the 1715 Jacobite uprising.

Ben More and the Ardmeanach peninsula

From the southern shores of Loch na Keal, which almost splits Mull in two, rise the terraced slopes of **Ben More** (3169ft) – literally "big mountain" – a mighty extinct volcano, and the only Munro in the Hebrides outside of Skye. It's most easily climbed from Dhiseig, halfway along the loch's southern shores, though an alternative route is to climb up to the col between Beinn Fhada and A'Chioch, and approach via the mountain's eastern ridge. Further west along the shore the road carves through spectacular overhanging cliffs before heading south past the Gribun rocks which face the tiny island of **Inch Kenneth**, where Unity Mitford lived until her death in 1948. There are great views out to Staffa and the Treshnish Isles as the road leaves the coast behind, climbing over the pass to Loch Scribain, where it eventually joins the equally dramatic Glen More road (A848) from Craignure.

If you're properly equipped for walking, however, you can explore the **Ardmeanach peninsula**, to the west of the road, on foot. On the north coast, a mile or so from the road, is **Mackinnon's Cave** – at 100ft high, one of the largest caves in the Hebrides, and accessible only at low tide. As so often, there's a legend attached to the cave, which tells of an entire party, led by a lone piper, who were once devoured here by evil spirits. Starting from the south coast, it's a longer, rougher six-mile hike from the road to **MacCulloch's Tree**, a 40ft-high 50-million-year-old fossil tree trunk embedded in the cliffs at Rubha na h-Uambha at the western tip of the peninsula. You'll need a good map and, again, you need to time your arrival with low tide; the area is NTS-owned and you should call in at Burg farm on the way to make your presence known (and get directions).

The Ross of Mull

Stretching for twenty miles west as far as Iona is Mull's rocky southernmost peninsula, the **Ross of Mull**, which, like much of Scotland, appears blissfully tranquil in good weather, and desolate and bleak in bad. Most visitors simply drive through the Ross en route to Iona, but, if you have the time, it's definitely worth considering exploring, or even staying, in this little-visited part of Mull.

The most scenic spots on the Ross are hidden away on the south coast. If you're approaching the Ross from Craignure, the first of these is signposted even before you've negotiated the splendid Highland pass of Glen More, which brings you to the Ross itself. **LOCHBUIE**, situated above a peaceful, sandy bay six miles off the main A849, is dominated by the fifteenth-century ivy-strewn ruins of **Moy Castle**, an old MacLean stronghold. North of the castle is one of the few **stone circles** in the west of Scotland, with eight stones all about 6ft high and dating from the second century BC. The best-value accommodation in the vicinity is at *Barrachandroman* (☎01680/814220, *spelve@aol.com*; ②), a converted barn overlooking Loch Spelve, a couple of miles east of Lochbuie.

A popular and fairly easy walk is the five-mile hike west along the coastal path to the tiny village of **CARSAIG**, where the Inniemore School of Painting enjoys an idyllic setting, at the end of a dead-end road, three miles south of Pennyghael (see below), on the A849. An even finer walk is possible to the west of Carsaig, where the coastal path takes you past, first the **Nun's Cave**, where nuns from Iona are alleged to have hidden during the Reformation, and then, after four miles or so, at Malcolm's Point, the spectacular **Carsaig Arches**, formed by eroded sea caves, which are linked to basalt cliffs.

The main A849 road, single-track, for the most part, and plagued by the large number of coaches that steam down it en route to Iona, hugs the northern coastline of the Ross. The welcoming and comfortable *Pennyghael Hotel* (☎01681/704288; ③; Easter–Oct), which has a good restaurant, and a decent bar, overlooks Loch Scridain and Ben More, from the hamlet of **PENNYGHAEL**. However, if your budget stretches to it, there are two, much more exceptional hotels, near **BUNESSAN**, the largest village on the peninsula, roughly two-thirds of the way along the Ross. The *Assapol House Hotel* (☎01681/700258; ⑥; Easter–Oct) is a former eighteenth-century manse overlooking its own freshwater loch, two miles southeast of Bunessan; room prices include dinner and breakfast. Two miles west of Bunessan, stands *Ardfenaig House* (☎01681/700210; ⑥; April–Oct), an old shooting lodge with its own jetty and a self-catering converted coach house.

Bunessan itself has a few useful shops, plus the remarkable **Angora Rabbit Farm** (Easter–Oct daily except Sat 11am–5pm; £2), just east of town on the A849. Here, an eccentric couple keep comical, long-haired bunnies in order to harvest their incredibly soft fleeces as yarn. Whatever time you arrive, you'll get a guided tour, and the kids will get to stroke the rabbits, but if you arrive at noon, you can watch their fur being clipped, and at 3pm you can observe a spinning demonstration. If the weather's good, it might be worth heading off for the two adjacent sandy beaches, at **UISKEN** and neighbouring **ARDALANISH**. Either of these can be enjoyed by staying at *Uisken Croft* (☎01681/700307; ①; April–Oct) or at *Ardalanish Farm* (☎01681/700265; ①), both of which are highly recommended.

The road ends at **FIONNPHORT**, facing Iona, probably the least attractive place to stay on the Ross, though it has a nice sandy bay backed by pink granite rocks to the north of the ferry slipway. Partly to ease congestion on Iona, and to give their neighbours a slice of the tourist pound, Fionnphort was chosen as the site for the **Columba Centre** (mid-May to Sept Mon–Sat 10am–6pm, Sun 11am–6pm; £2), which opened in 1997 on the 1400th anniversary of the saint's death; inside, a small museum tells the story of Columba's life (for more on which, see below) using a combination of special effects and original artefacts.

If you're in need of a bed in Fionnphort, try the granite-built *Seaview* (☎01681/700235; ②), or the whitewashed *Staffa House* (☎01681/700677; ②), both of which are close to the ferry, and have views over to Iona. The basic *Fidden Farm* **campsite** (☎01681/700427; April–Sept), a mile south along the Knockvologan road by Fidden beach, is the nearest to Iona. Fidden beach looks out to the **Isle of Erraid**, accessible across the sands at low tide. Robert Louis Stevenson is believed to have written *Kidnapped* (its hero, David Balfour, gets shipwrecked here) in one of the island's cottages, overlooking the Torran Rocks, out to sea to the south, where his father and uncle built the Dubh Artach lighthouse in 1862. The island is now in Dutch ownership, and cared for by the Findhorn Community (see p.470).

Isle of Iona

> *Ross:*   *Where is Duncan's body?*
> *MacDuff:* *Carried to Colme-kill,*
>   *The sacred storehouse of his predecessors,*
>   *And guardian of their bones.*

Macbeth (Act II, Scene IV), William Shakespeare

Less than a mile off the southwest tip of Mull, **Iona** – just three miles long and not much more than a mile wide – has been a place of pilgrimage for several centuries, and a place of Christian worship for more than 1400 years. For it was to this flat Hebridean island that St Columba fled from Ireland in 563 and established a monastery which was responsible for the conversion of more or less all of pagan Scotland as well as much of northern England. This history and the island's splendid isolation have lent it a peculiar religiosity; in the much-quoted words of Dr Johnson, who visited in 1773, "that man is little to be envied . . . whose piety would not grow warmer among the ruins of Iona". Today, however, the island can barely cope with the constant flood of day-trippers, so to appreciate the special atmosphere and to have time to see the whole island, including the often-overlooked west coast, you should plan on staying at least one night.

Some history

Legend has it that **St Columba** (Colum Cille), born in Donegal some time around 521, was a direct descendant of the semi-legendary Irish king, Niall of the Nine Hostages. A scholar and soldier priest, who founded numerous monasteries in Ireland, he is thought to have become involved in a bloody dispute with the king when he refused to hand over a copy of the *Book of Psalms* copied illegally from the original owned by St Finian of Moville. This, in turn, provoked the Battle of Cúl Drebene (Cooldrumman) – also known as the **Battle of the Book** – at which Columba's forces won, though with the loss of over 3000 lives. The story goes that, repenting this bloodshed, Columba went into exile with twelve other monks, eventually settling on Iona in 563, allegedly because it was the first island he encountered from which he couldn't see his homeland. The bottom line, however, is that we know very little about Columba, though he undoubtedly became something of a cult figure after his death in 597. He was posthumously credited with miraculous feats such as defeating the Loch Ness monster – it only had to hear his voice and it recoiled in terror – and banishing snakes (and, some say, frogs) from the island. He is also famously alleged to have banned women and cows from Iona, banishing them to Eilean nam Ban (Woman's Island), just north of Fionnphort, for, as he believed, "where there is a cow there is a woman, and where there is a woman there is mischief".

Whatever the truth about Columba's life, in the sixth and seventh centuries, Iona enjoyed a great deal of autonomy from Rome, establishing a specifically **Celtic Christian** tradition. Missionaries were sent out to the rest of Scotland and parts of England, and Iona quickly became a respected seat of learning and artistry; the monks compiled a vast library of intricately **illuminated manuscripts** – most famously the *Book of Kells* (now on display in Trinity College, Dublin) – while the masons excelled in carving peculiarly intricate crosses. Two factors were instrumental in the demise of the Celtic tradition: a series of Viking raids, the worst of which was the massacre of 68 monks on the sands of Martyrs' Bay in 806; and relentless pressure from the established church, beginning with the Synod of Whitby in 664, which chose Rome over the Celtic church, and culminated in the suppression of the Celtic church by King David I in 1144.

In 1203, Iona became part of the mainstream church with the establishment of an **Augustinian nunnery** and a **Benedictine monastery** by Reginald, son of Somerled, Lord of the Isles. During the Reformation, the entire complex was ransacked, the contents of the library burnt and all but three of the island's 360 crosses destroyed. Although plans were drawn up at various times to turn the abbey into a Cathedral of the Isles, nothing came of them until in 1899, when the then owner, the eighth Duke of Argyll, donated the abbey buildings to the **Church of Scotland**, who restored the abbey church for worship over the course of the next decade. Iona's modern resurgence began in 1938, when **George MacLeod**, a minister from Glasgow, established a group of ministers, students and artisans to begin rebuilding the remainder of the monastic buildings. What began as a mostly male, Gaelic-speaking, strictly Presbyterian community is today a lay, mixed and ecumenical retreat. The entire abbey complex has been successfully restored and the island, apart from the church land and a few crofts, now belongs to the NTS.

Baile Mór

The passenger ferry from Fionnphort drops you off at the island's main village, **BAILE MÓR** (literally "large village"), which is in fact little more than a single terrace of cottages facing the sea. Just inland lie the extensive pink granite ruins of the **Augustinian nunnery**, disused since the Reformation. A beautifully maintained garden now occupies the cloisters, and if nothing else the complex gives you an idea of the state of the present-day abbey before it was restored. Across the road to the north, housed in a manse built, like the nearby parish church, by the ubiquitous Thomas Telford, is the **Iona Heritage Centre** (April–Oct Mon–Sat 10.30am–4.30pm; £1.50), with displays on

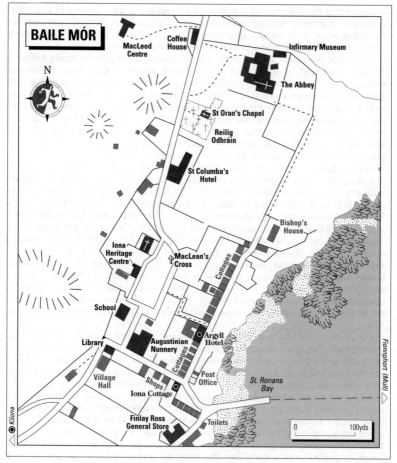

BAILE MÓR

N

Kilona

MacLeod Centre

Coffee House

Infirmary Museum

The Abbey

St Oran's Chapel

Reilig Odhráin

St Columba's Hotel

Bishop's House

Iona Heritage Centre

MacLean's Cross

Cottages

School

Library

Augustinian Nunnery

Cottages

Argyll Hotel

Post Office

St. Ronans Bay

Village Hall

Shops

Iona Cottage

Finlay Ross General Store

Toilets

Fionnphort (Mull)

0   100yds

© Crown copyright

the social history of the island over the last 200 years, including the Clearances which nearly halved the island's population of 500 in the mid-nineteenth century. At a bend in the road, just south of the manse and church, stands the fifteenth-century **MacLean's Cross**, a fine late-medieval example of the distinctive, flowing, three-leaved foliage of the Iona school.

Iona Abbey

At the main entrance to the **abbey** complex, there's a small information hut, where you're asked to give a £2 donation and can pick up a plan of the abbey. No buildings remain from Columba's time: the present abbey dates from the arrival of the Benedictines in around 1200, was extensively rebuilt in the fifteenth and sixteenth centuries, and restored virtually wholesale this century. Iona's oldest building, the plain-looking **St Oran's Chapel**, lies south of the abbey, to your right, and boasts a Norman door dating from the eleventh century. Legend has it that the original chapel could only be completed through human sacrifice. Oran, one of the older monks in Columba's entourage, apparently volunteered to be buried alive, and was found to have survived the ordeal when the grave was opened a few days later. Declaring that he had seen hell and it wasn't all bad, he was promptly reinterred for blasphemy.

Oran's Chapel stands at the centre of Iona's sacred burial ground, **Reilig Odhráin** (Oran's Cemetery), which is said to contain the graves of sixty kings of Norway, Ireland, France and Scotland, including Duncan and Macbeth. The best of the early Christian gravestones and medieval effigies which once lay in the Reilig Odhráin have unfortunately been removed to the Infirmary Museum, behind the abbey (see below), and to various other locations within the complex. The graveyard is still used as a cemetery by the island, however, and the grave that many visitors now head for is that of the short-lived leader of the Labour Party, **John Smith** (1938–94), who was a frequent visitor to Iona, though he himself was born in the town of Ardrishaig.

Approaching the abbey itself, from the main entrance, you cross an exposed section of the evocative medieval **Street of the Dead**, whose giant red marble cobbles once stretched from the abbey, past St Oran's Chapel, to the village. Beside the road stands the most impressive of Iona's Celtic high crosses, the eighth-century **St Martin's Cross**, smothered with figural scenes – the Virgin and Child at the centre, Daniel in the lion's den, Abraham sacrificing Isaac and David with musicians in the shaft below. The reverse side features Pictish serpent-and-boss decoration. Standing directly in front of the abbey are the base of St Matthew's Cross (now in the Infirmary Museum) and, to the left, a replica cast of the eighth-century **St John's Cross**, decorated with serpent-and-boss and Celtic spiral ornamental panels. Before you enter the abbey, take a look inside **St Columba's Shrine**, a small steep-roofed chamber to the left of the main entrance. Columba is believed to have been buried either here or under the rocky mound to the west of the abbey, known as Tórr an Aba.

The **Abbey** itself has been simply and sensitively restored, to incorporate the original elements. You can spot many of the medieval capitals in the south aisle of the choir and in the south transept, where the white marble effigies of the eighth Duke of Argyll and his wife, Ina, lie in a side chapel – an incongruous piece of Victorian pomp in an otherwise modest and tranquil place. The finest pre-Reformation effigy is that of John MacKinnon, the last abbot of Iona, who died around 1500, and now lies on the south side of the choir steps. For reasons of sanitation, the **cloisters** were placed, contrary to the norm, on the north side of the church (where running water was available); entirely reconstructed in the late 1950s, they now shelter lots of medieval grave slabs, a useful historical account of the abbey's development, and the abbey bookshop. There are free daily guided tours of the abbey (the times are posted up inside the west door). If you want to see some more medieval grave slabs from Reilig Odhráin, the rest of St Matthew's Cross and the original fragments of St John's Cross, you should walk round the back of the abbey to the **Infirmary Museum**, which also contains the stone pillow allegedly used by Columba himself.

Practicalities

There's no **tourist office** on Iona, and as demand far exceeds supply you should organize **accommodation** well in advance. Of the island's two **hotels**, the stone-built *Argyll* (☎01681/700334; ⑨; April–Oct), in the terrace of cottages overlooking the Sound of Iona, is by far the nicest. As for **B&Bs**, *Iona Cottage* (☎01681/700569; ①; Easter–Oct) is an attractive whitewashed cottage right by the pier; for a more secluded location, try *Kilona* in Sithean (☎01681/700362; ③), a mile from the ferry, on the peaceful west side of the island. **Camping** is not permitted on Iona, and there is no youth hostel. If you want to stay with the **Iona Community**, contact the *MacLeod Centre* (☎01681/700404, *ionacomm@iona.org.uk*), popularly known as the "Mac". Hostel accommodation is provided and you must be prepared to participate fully in the daily activities, prayers and religious services.

Visitors are not allowed to bring cars onto the island, but **bikes** can be rented from the Finlay Ross general store (☎01681/700357). **Food** options are limited: the eclectic bar menu of the *Argyll* is probably your best option, or for something lighter, head for the *Coffee House*, run by the Iona Community, just west of the abbey, which serves home-made soup and delicious cakes.

Coll and Tiree

Coll and **Tiree** are among the most isolated of the Inner Hebrides, and if anything have more in common with the outlying Western Isles than with their closest neighbour, Mull. Each is roughly twelve miles long and three miles wide, both are low-lying, tree-less and exceptionally windy, with white sandy beaches and the highest sunshine records in Scotland. Like most of the Hebrides, they were once ruled by Vikings, and didn't pass into Scottish hands until the thirteenth century. Coll's population peaked at 1440, Tiree's at a staggering 4450, but both were badly affected by the Clearances, which virtually halved their populations in a generation. Coll was fortunate to be in the hands of the enlightened MacLeans, but they were forced to sell in 1856 to the Stewart family, who sold two-thirds of the island to a Dutch millionaire in the 1960s. Tiree was ruthlessly cleared by its owner, the Duke of Argyll, who sent in the marines in 1885 to evict the crofters. After the passing of the Crofters' Act the following year, the island was divided into crofts, though it remains a part of the Duke of Argyll's estate. Both islands have strong Gaelic roots, but the percentage of English-speaking newcomers is rising steadily.

The CalMac **ferry** from Oban calls at Coll (2hr 40min) and Tiree (3hr 40min) every day except Thursdays and Sundays throughout the year. Tiree also has an **airport** with daily flights (Mon–Sat) to and from Glasgow. The majority of visitors on both islands stay for at least a week in self-catering accommodation (see p.33), though there are B&Bs and hotels on the islands. However, choice is limited so it's as well to book as far in advance as possible (and that goes for the ferry crossing, too). The only **public transport** is on Tiree, which has an infrequent postbus service (Mon–Sat only), plus a shared taxi system (☎01879/220311 or 220419).

Isle of Coll

The fish-shaped rocky island of **Coll** (population 175) lies less than seven miles off the coast of Mull. The CalMac ferry drops off at Coll's only real village, **ARINAGOUR**, whose whitewashed cottages dot the western shore of Loch Eatharna. Half the island's population lives in the village, and it's here you'll find the island's post office, churches, school and handful of shops; two miles northwest along the Arnabost road, there's even a golf course. The island's petrol pump is also in Arinagour, and is run on a volunteer basis – it's basically open when the ferry arrives.

On the southwest coast there are two edifices, both confusingly known as **Breachacha Castle**, and both built by the MacLeans. The oldest, at the head of Loch Breachacha, is a fifteenth-century tower house with an additional curtain wall, recently restored, and is now a training centre for Project Trust overseas aid volunteers. The "new castle", to the northwest, is made up of a central block built around 1750 and two side pavilions added a century later. It was here that Dr Johnson and Boswell stayed in 1773 after a storm forced them to take refuge en route to Mull – they considered the place to be "a mere tradesman's box". The whole area around the castles, and to the west where a strip of rabbit-infested **giant sand dunes** links Calgary Point (the southwesternmost tip of Coll) with the rest of the island, is now owned by the RSPB on account of its precious corncrake population.

For an overview of the whole island, you can follow in Boswell's footsteps and take a wander up **Ben Hogh** – at 339ft, Coll's highest point – two miles west of Arinagour, close to the shore. The island's northwest coast boasts the finest sandy beaches, though they take the full brunt of the Atlantic winds. When the Stewart family took over the island in 1856, and raised the rents, the island's population moved wholesale from the more fertile southeast, to this part of the island. However, overcrowding led to widespread emigration; a few of the old crofts in Bousd and Sorisdale, at Coll's northernmost tip, have more recently been restored. From here, there's an impressive view over to the headland and the islands beyond, which in turn obscure the small crop of tidal rocks, known as the Cairns of Coll, a mile or so north of the headland.

In Arinagour, the small, family-run *Coll Hotel* (☎01879/230334; ③) can provide **accommodation**; otherwise there's the comfortable, modern *Taigh Solas* (☎01879/230333; ①), overlooking the bay. *Achamore* (☎01879/230430; ①), a traditional nineteenth-century farmhouse B&B, lies two miles west of Arinagour, and also has a self-catering caravan for hire. The island's official **campsite** (☎01879/230374; April–Oct), which offers basic facilities, is on Breachacha Bay, in the old walled gardens of the new castle; you can also stay in the adjacent *Garden House* B&B (phone as for campsite; ③; open all year). The *Coll Hotel* doubles as the island's social centre, does good bar meals and has a more expensive dining room. For a change from hotel **food**, try the *Lochside* restaurant (April–Oct closed Tues lunch & Sun), also in Arinagour. For **bike rental** phone ☎01879/230382.

Isle of Tiree

Tiree, as its Gaelic name *tir-iodh* (land of corn) suggests, was once known as the breadbasket of the Inner Hebrides, thanks to its acres of rich machair. Nowadays crofting and tourism are the main sources of income for the resident population of around 800. One of the most distinctive features of Tiree is its architecture, in particular the large numbers of "pudding" or "spotty" houses, where only the mortar is painted white. In addition, there are numerous "white houses" (*tigh geal*) and traditional "blackhouses" (*tigh dubh*); for more on these, see p.371. Wildlife lovers can also have a field day on Tiree, with lapwings, wheatears, redshank, greylag geese and large, laid-back brown hares in abundance. And with no shortage of wind, Tiree's sandy beaches attract large numbers of windsurfers for the Tiree Wave Classic every October.

The CalMac ferry calls at Gott Bay Pier, close to the village of **SCARINISH**, home to a post office, a butcher's, a bank, a petrol pump, and a supermarket, next door to which is the island's new cultural centre, An Iodhlann (Tues–Fri 2–5pm; £2), which houses a small local museum and puts on temporary exhibitions. To the east is **Gott Bay**, backed by a two-mile stretch of sand. It's just one mile across the island from Gott to Vaul Bay, on the north coast, where the well-preserved remains of a drystone broch, **Dun Mor** – dating from the first century BC – lie hidden in the rocks to the west of the bay. From here it's another two miles west along the coast to the *Clach a'Choire* or **Ringing Stone**, a huge glacial boulder decorated with mysterious prehistoric markings, which when struck with a stone gives out a metallic sound. The story goes that, should the Ringing Stone ever be broken in two, Tiree will sink beneath the waves. A mile further west you come to the lovely **Balephetrish Bay**, where you can watch waders feeding in the breakers, and look out to sea to Skye and the Western Isles.

The most intriguing sights, however, lie in the bulging western half of the island, where Tiree's two landmark hills rise up. The highest of the two, **Ben Hynish** (463ft), is unfortunately occupied by a "golf-ball" radar station which tracks incoming transatlantic flights; the views from the top, though, are great. Below Ben Hynish, to the east is **HYNISH**, with its recently restored **harbour**, designed by Alan Stevenson in the 1830s to transport building materials for the magnificent 140ft-tall **Skerryvore Lighthouse**, which lies on a sea-swept reef some twelve miles southwest of Tiree. The harbour features an ingenious reservoir to prevent silting, and up on the hill behind, beside the row of lightkeepers' houses, a stumpy granite signal tower. The tower, whose signals used to be the only contact the lighthouse keepers had with civilization, now houses a **museum** telling the history of the Herculean effort required to erect the lighthouse; weather permitting, you can see the lighthouse from the tower's viewing platform.

On the other side of Ben Hynish, a mile or so across the golden sands of Balephuil Bay, is the spectacular headland of **Ceann a'Mhara** (pronounced "Kenavara"). The cliffs here are home to thousands of seabirds, including fulmars, kittiwakes, guillemots, razorbills, shags and cormorants, with gannets and terns feeding offshore; the islands of Barra and South Uist are also visible on the northern horizon. In the scattered west coast settlement of **SANDAIG**, to the north of Ceann a'Mhara, three thatched white houses in a row have been turned into the **Thatched House Museum** (June–Sept Mon–Fri 2–4pm), which gives an insight into how the majority of islanders lived in the last century.

Practicalities

From the **airport**, about three miles west of Scarinish, you can either catch the postbus, phone for a shared taxi the night before (see p.333, or arrange for your hosts to collect (most will). Transport around the island is limited, though the postbus calls at all the main settlements; **bike rental** is available at the *Tiree Lodge* (see below). Of the island's two **hotels**, the *Tiree Lodge* (☎01879/220368; ②), a mile or so east of Scarinish along Gott Bay, is preferable to the *Scarinish* (☎01879/220308; ②), overlooking the old harbour. Better than both the above, however, are *Kirkapol House* (☎01879/220729; ②), just beyond the *Tiree Lodge*, a great B&B in a converted kirk, and *The Glassary* (☎01879/220684; ③) over on the west coast in Sandaig. *The Sheiling* (☎01879/220503; ①; April–Oct) is a simple B&B that's convenient for the airport. There are no official campsites, but **camping** is allowed with the local crofter's permission.

As for **eating**, apart from bar snacks or à la carte at the *Tiree Lodge*, the best option is *The Glassary* (phone as above) over in Sandaig, an unpretentious, moderately priced restaurant that serves good food, much of it locally produced. The island seriously lacks a tearoom of any description, and the only place you can be sure of getting a cuppa is at *Glebecraft*, off the main road to the north of Scarinish – it's an experience not to be missed, and they've got Jacob Sheep to look at out back. For a map of the island and the daily papers, you need to go to the supermarket at Crossapol.

Isle of Colonsay

Isolated between Mull and Islay, **Colonsay** – eight miles by three at its widest – is nothing like as bleak and windswept as Coll or Tiree. Its craggy, heather-backed hills even support the occasional patch of woodland, plus a bewildering array of plant and birdlife, wild goats and rabbits, and one of the finest quasi-tropical gardens in Scotland. That said, the population is precariously low at around 100, down from a pre-Clearance peak of just under 1000, and the ferry links with the mainland are infrequent: three a week from Oban (Wed, Fri & Sun; 2hr 15min); one a week from Kennacraig via Islay (Wed; 3hr 35min), when a day-trip is possible, giving you around six hours on the island. There's a large number of self-catering cottages, but, with no camping or caravanning and just one hotel, a couple of B&Bs and a bunkhouse, there's no fear of mass tourism taking over.

The CalMac ferry terminal is at **SCALASAIG**, on the east coast, where there's a post office/shop, a petrol pump, a restaurant and the island's hotel. Right by the pier, the old waiting room now serves as the island's heritage centre and is usually open when the ferry docks. Two miles north of Scalasaig, inland at **KILORAN**, is **Colonsay House**, built in 1722 by Malcolm MacNeil. In 1904, the island and house were bought by Lord Strathcona, who made his fortune building the Canadian Pacific Railway (and whose descendants still own the island). He was also responsible for the house's lovely gardens and woods, which are slowly being restored to their former glory. The house and gardens are still off limits, but the outbuildings are now holiday cottages and you're free to wander round the woodland garden to the south, and inspect the strange eighth-century **Riasg Buidhe Cross**, to the east of the house, decorated with an unusually lifelike mug shot (possibly of a monk) east of the house.

To the north of Colonsay House, where the road ends, you'll find the island's finest sandy beach, the breathtaking **Kiloran Bay**, where the breakers roll in from the Atlantic. There's another unspoilt sandy beach backed by dunes at Balnahard, two miles northeast along a rough track; en route, you might spot wild goats, choughs, and even a golden eagle. The island's west coast forms a sharp escarpment, quite at odds with the gentle undulating landscape that characterizes the rest of the island. Due west of Colonsay House around **Beinn Bhreac** (456ft), the cliffs are at their most spectacular and in their lower reaches provide a home to hundreds of seabirds, among them kittiwakes, cormorants and guillemots in spring and early summer.

Isle of Oronsay

Whilst on Colonsay, most folk take a day out to visit the **Isle of Oronsay**, which lies half a mile to the south and contains the ruins of an Augustinian priory. The two islands are separated by "The Strand", a mile of tidal mud flats which act as a causeway for two hours either side of low tide (check locally for timings); you can drive over to the island at low tide, though most people park their cars and walk across. Although legends (and etymology) link saints Columba and Oran with both Colonsay and Oronsay, the ruins actually only date back as far as the fourteenth century. Abandoned since the Reformation and now roofless, you can, nevertheless, still make out the original church and tiny cloisters. The highlight, though, is the **Oronsay Cross**, a superb example of late medieval artistry from Iona which stands to the west of the chapel, and the beautifully carved grave slabs in the Prior's House. It takes about an hour to walk from the tip of Colonsay across the Strand to the priory (wellington boots are a good idea). If you don't have your own picnic, you can get tea, cakes and more substantial food from the *Barn Café* (summer only, daily except Sat) on the Colonsay side of the Strand.

Practicalities

The island's only **hotel**, the *Isle of Colonsay* (☎01951/200316; ⑤), is a cosy eighteenth-century inn at heart, within easy walking distance of the pier in Scalasaig; it serves very decent bar snacks and acts as the island's social centre. The best alternative is to stay at the superb *Seaview* **B&B** (☎01951/200315; ②; April–Oct), run by the charming Lawson family in Kilchattan on the west coast. The budget option is to sleep in the newly established *Backpackers' Lodge* **hostel**, in Kiloran, run by the Colonsay Estate (☎01770/200312). Most people who visit the island, however, stay in **self-catering accommodation**, the majority of which is run by the aforementioned Colonsay Estate (phone as above); who offer a huge choice of cottages and a wide price range. It's also possible to book self-catering places for just a couple of nights, through *Island Lodges* (☎01951/200320; ②).

An alternative to **eating out** at the hotel bar is *The Pantry* (closed Sun), above the pier in Scalasaig, which offers simple home cooking as well as teas and cakes (ring ahead if you want to eat in the evening; ☎01951/200325). All accommodation (and ferry crossings) need to be booked well in advance for the summer; self-catering cottages tend to be booked from Friday to Friday, because of the ferries. Both the hotel, *Seaview* and A. McConnel (☎01951/200355) will rent out **bikes**, and there's a limited **bus** and **postbus** service (Mon–Sat) for those without their own transport. If you need a map or any books on the Highlands and Islands, go to the very well-stocked **bookshop** (and tearoom) right by the hotel.

Mid-Argyll

Mid-Argyll is a vague term which loosely describes the central wedge of land south of Oban and north of Kintyre. Lochgilphead, on the shores of Loch Fyne is the chief town in the area, though it has little to offer beyond its practical use – it has a tourist office, a good supermarket and is the regional transport hub, though, on the whole, public transport is thin on the ground. The highlights of this gently undulating scenery lie along the sharply indented west coast, in particular the rich Bronze Age and Neolithic remains in the Kilmartin valley, one of the most important prehistoric sites in Scotland.

The Slate Islands and the Garvellachs

Just eight miles south of Oban, a road heads off the A816 west to a small group of islands commonly called the **Slate Islands**, which at their peak in the mid-nineteenth century quarried over nine million slates annually. Today many of the old slate villages are sparsely populated, and an inevitable air of melancholy hangs over them, but their dramatic setting amid crashing waves makes for a rewarding day-trip.

Isle of Seil

The most northerly of the Slate Islands is **Seil**, a lush island, now something of an exclusive enclave (Princess Diana's mother, Mrs Shand-Kydd is a resident). It's separated from the mainland only by the thinnest of sea channels and spanned by Thomas Telford's elegant hump-backed **Clachan Bridge**, built in 1793 and popularly known as the "Bridge over the Atlantic". The pub next door to the bridge is the *Tigh na Truish* (House of the Trousers), where kilt-wearing islanders would change into trousers to conform to the post-1745 ban on Highland dress.

The main village on Seil is **ELLENABEICH**, its neat white terraces of workers' cottages – featured in the film *Ring of Bright Water* – crouching below black cliffs on the westernmost tip of the island. This was once the tiny island of Eilean a'Beithich (hence Ellenabeich) separated from the mainland by a slim sea channel until the intensive slate quarrying succeeded in silting it up. Confusingly, the village is often referred to by the same name as the nearby island of Easdale, since they formed an interdependent community based exclusively around the slate industry.

Isle of Easdale

Easdale remains an island, though the few hundred yards that separate it from Ellanabeich have to be dredged to keep the channel open. On the eve of a great storm on November 23, 1881, Easdale, less than a mile across at any one point, supported an incredible 452 inhabitants. That night, waves engulfed the island and flooded the quarries. The island never really recovered, slate quarrying stopped in 1914, and by the 1960s the population was reduced to single figures.

Recently many of the old workers' cottages have been restored: some as holiday homes, others sold to new families (the present population stands at over thirty). One of the cottages now houses the interesting **Easdale Folk Museum** (April–Oct daily 10.30am–5.30pm; £2), near the main square, selling a useful historical map of the island, which you can walk round in about half an hour. The **ferry** from Ellenabeich runs partly to schedule, partly on demand (April–Sept Mon–Sat 7.15am–8.50pm, Sun 9.30am–5.50pm; Oct–March check at Oban tourist office), and there's *The Puffer* **bar/restaurant**, plus a cosy, little whitewashed **B&B** at no. 22 (☎01852/300438; ①).

Isle of Luing

To the south of Seil, across the narrow, treacherous Cuan Sound lies **Luing** (pronounced "Ling"), a long, thin, fertile island which once supported more than 600 people. During the Clearances the population was drastically reduced to make way for cattle; Luing is still renowned for its beef and for the crossbreed named after it. A car **ferry** (Mon–Sat 8am–6pm; mid-June to Aug also Fri & Sat 7.30–10.30pm) crosses the Cuan Sound every half hour or so, though foot passengers can cross until later in the evening (Mon–Thurs until 10pm, Fri & Sat until 11.30pm, Sun 11am–6pm). There's a **postbus** service on Luing itself (Mon–Sat only).

CULLIPOOL, the pretty main village with its post office, and general store, lies a mile or so southwest; quarrying ceased here in 1965, and the place now relies on tourism and lobster fishing. Luing's only other village, **TOBERONOCHY**, lies on the more sheltered east coast, three miles southeast of Cullipool. Its distinctive white cottages, built by the slate company in 1805, nestle below a ruined church, which contains a memorial to the fifteen Latvian seamen who drowned off the nearby abandoned slate island of **Belnahua** during a hurricane in 1936. Other than self-catering cottages, the only **accommodation** available on the island is at *Bardrishaig Farm* (☎01852/314364; ①; mid-Jan to mid-Dec), on the road to Cullipool. For **bike rental**, ring ☎01852/314256 in the evening.

Isle of Scarba and the Garvellachs

Scarba is the largest of the islands around Luing, a brooding 1500ft hulk of slate, not much more than a couple of miles across, inhospitable and wild – most of the fifty or so inhabitants who once lived here had left by the mid-nineteenth century. To the south, between Scarba and Jura, the raging **Gulf of Corrievrechan** is the site of one of the world's most spectacular whirlpools, thought to be caused by a rocky pinnacle below the sea. It remains calm only for an hour or two at high and low tide; between flood and half-flood tide, accompanied by a southerly or westerly wind, water shoots deafeningly some 20ft up in the air. Inevitably there are numerous legends about the place – known as *coire bhreacain* (speckled cauldron) in Gaelic – concerning *Cailleach* (Hag), the Celtic storm goddess. The best place from which to view it is the northern tip of Jura (see p.361).

The string of uninhabited islands visible west of Luing are known collectively as the **Garvellachs**, after the largest of the group, **Garbh Eileach** (Rough Rock), which was inhabited as recently as fifty years ago. The most northerly, **Dún Chonnuill**, contains the remains of an old fort thought to have belonged to Conal of Dalriada, and **Eileach an Naoimh** (Holy Isle), the most southerly of the group, is where the Celtic missionary Brendan the Navigator founded a community in 542, some twenty years before Columba landed on Iona (see p.329). Nothing survives from Brendan's day, but there are a few ninth-century remains, among them a double-beehive cell and a grave enclosure. One school of thought has it that the island is Hinba, Columba's legendary secret retreat, where he founded a monastery before settling on Iona.

If you're interested in taking a **boat trip** to Corrievrechan or the Garvellachs, contact Ruby Cruises (☎01852/500616), who operate out of Ardfern (see opposite), Gemini Cruises (☎01546/830238), who operate from Crinan (see p.342), or Porpoise Charters (☎01852/300203), who are based at Balvicar, just south of the Clachan Bridge.

Arduaine and Craignish

Probably the finest spot at which to stop and have a bite to eat on the main road from Oban to Lochgilphead is the *Loch Melfort Hotel* (☎01852/200233, *lmhotel@aol.com*; ⑨), in **ARDUAINE**, where you can enjoy great bar snacks, sitting out on the hotel lawn, with views over Asknish Bay and out to the islands of Shuna, Luing, Scarba and Jura. Beside the hotel are the **Arduaine Gardens** (daily 9.30am–dusk; NTS; £2.50), which enjoy the same idyllic loch-side location. Gifted as recently as 1992, the gardens are stupendous, particularly in May and June, and have the feel of an intimate private garden, with pristine lawns, lily-strewn ponds, mature woods and spectacular rhododendrons and azaleas. The gardens' disgruntled former owners, the Wright brothers, still live next door and have an equally lovely adjacent garden. Below the hotel and gardens, *Arduaine Caravan and Camping Park* is a lovely loch-side **campsite** (☎01852/200331; Easter–Oct).

A couple of miles south, on the far side of Asknish Bay is the slightly surreal **CRAOBH HAVEN**, a planned holiday village and marina that's reminiscent of a bad film set. There's a fine walk to be had, however, from Craobh Haven along the spine of the **Craignish peninsula** to the southernmost tip some five miles away. Heading back up the single-track road that runs along the shores of Loch Craignish, stop off at the *Galley of Lorne* or pop into the *Crafty Kitchen* (closed Mon), a fair-trade craft shop and café in yachty **ARDFERN**, a real pub and a great place to quench your thirst. There's accommodation close to Craobh Haven, either in the luxurious log-cabin-style *Buidhe Lodge* (☎01852/500291; ②), or in the rambling Baronial pile of *Lunga* (☎01852/500237; ①), run by an eccentric laird. Bike rental is available from Ardfern Cycle Hire (☎01852/500662), based in Ardfern itself.

Kilmartin Glen

The chief sight on the road from Oban to Lochgilphead is the **Kilmartin Glen**, the most important prehistoric site on the Scottish mainland. The most remarkable relic is the **linear cemetery**, where several cairns are aligned for more than two miles, to the south of the village Kilmartin. These are thought to represent the successive burials of a ruling family or chieftains, but nobody can be sure. The best view of the cemetery's configuration is from the Bronze Age **Mid-Cairn**, but the Neolithic **South Cairn**, dating from around 3000 BC, is by far the oldest and the most impressive, with its large chambered tomb roofed by giant slabs.

Close to the Mid-Cairn, the two **Temple Wood stone circles** appear to have been the architectural focus of burials in the area from Neolithic times to the Bronze Age. Visible to the south are the impressively cup-marked **Nether Largie standing stones** (no public access), the largest of which looms over 10ft high. **Cup- and ring-marked rocks** are a recurrent feature of prehistoric sites in the Kilmartin Glen and elsewhere in Argyll. There are many theories as to their origin: some see them as Pictish symbols, others as primitive solar calendars and so on. The most extensive markings in the entire country are at **Achnabreck**, off the A816 towards Lochgilphead.

Kilmartin

Situated on high ground to the north of the cairns is the tiny village of **KILMARTIN**, where a new interpretive centre, **Kilmartin House** (daily 10am–5.30pm; £3.90), is housed in the old manse adjacent to the village church. The fifteen-minute audiovisual is not half as interesting as the excellent museum, which is both enlightening and entertaining. Not only can you learn about the various theories concerning prehistoric crannogs, henges and cairns but you can practise polishing an axe, examine different types of wood and fur, and listen to a variety of weird and wonderful sounds (check out

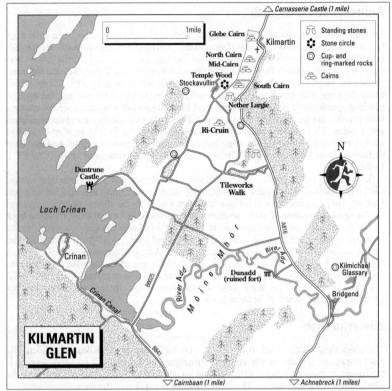

△ *Carnasserie Castle (1 mile)*

0 ___ 1mile

Glebe Cairn   Kilmartin

North Cairn
Mid-Cairn
Temple Wood
Stockavullin   South Cairn

Nether Largie

Ri-Cruin

Duntrune
Castle

Loch Crinan

Tileworks
Walk

Crinan

Crinan Canal

Dunadd
(ruined fort)   Kilmichael
Glassary

Bridgend

**KILMARTIN
GLEN**

	Standing stones
	Stone circle
	Cup- and ring-marked rocks
	Cairns

N

▽ *Cairnbaan (1 mile)*   ▽ *Achnabreck (1 miles)*

© Crown copyright

the Gaelic bird imitations). The **café/restaurant** is equally enticing, with local (often wild) produce on offer, which you can wash down with heather beer.

The nearby church is worth a brief reconnoitre, as it shelters the badly damaged and weathered **Kilmartin crosses**, while a separate enclosure in the graveyard houses a large collection of medieval graveslabs of the Malcolms of Poltalloch. Kilmartin's own castle is ruined beyond recognition; head instead for the much less ruined **Carnasserie Castle**, on a high ridge a mile up the road towards Oban. The castle was built in the 1560s by John Carswell, an influential figure in the Scottish church, who published the first ever book in Gaelic, *Knox's Liturgy*, which contained the doctrines of the Presbyterian faith. Architecturally, the castle is interesting, too, as it represents the transition between fully fortified castles and later mansion houses, and has several original finely carved stone fireplaces, doorways, as well as numerous gun-loops and shot holes.

Mòine Mhór and Dunadd

To the south of Kilmartin, beyond the linear cemetery, lies the raised peat bog of **Mòine Mhór** (Great Moss), now a nature reserve and home to a remarkable plant, insect and bird life. To get a close look at the sphagnum moss and wetlands, head for the newly laid-out Tileworks Walk, just off the A816, which includes a short boardwalk over the bog.

Mòine Mhór is best known as home to the Iron Age fort of **Dunadd**, one of Scotland's most important Celtic sites, occupying a distinctive 176ft-high rocky knoll once surrounded by the sea but currently stranded beside the winding River Add. It was here that Fergus, the first King of Dalriada, established his royal seat, having arrived from Ireland in around 500 AD. Its strategic position, the craggy defences and the view from the top are all impressive, but it's the **stone carvings** between the twin summits which make Dunadd so remarkable: several lines of inscription in ogam (an ancient alphabet of Irish origin), the faint outline of a boar, a hollowed-out footprint and a small basin. The boar and the inscriptions are probably Pictish, since the fort was clearly occupied long before Fergus got there, but the footprint and basin have been interpreted as being part of the royal coronation rituals of the kings of Dalriada. It is thought that the Stone of Destiny was used at Dunadd before being moved to Scone Palace (see p.289), then to Westminster Abbey in London, where it languished until it was returned to Edinburgh in 1996 (see p.73).

Practicalities

Great-value **B&B** is available at *Tibertich* (☎01546/810281; ③; March–Nov), a working sheep farm in the hills to the north of Kilmartin, off the A816. Otherwise, you're best off basing yourself in Crinan rather than Lochgilphead (see below for both). Alternatively, you could hole up in the excellent *Cairnbaan Hotel* (☎01546/603668; ⑤), an eighteenth-century coaching inn overlooking the Crinan Canal; it has a great restaurant and bar meals featuring locally caught seafood – to whip up an appetite you can nip up to the cup- and ring-marked stone behind the hotel. The aforementioned café/restaurant at Kilmartin House is a great lunchtime **eating** option; alternatively *The Cairn* (☎01546/510254; March–Oct), opposite the church in Kilmartin, is also open in the evening, and features moderately expensive Scottish and Mediterranean dishes.

Lochgilphead

The unlikely administrative centre of Argyll and Bute, **LOCHGILPHEAD**, as the name suggests, lies at the head of Loch Gilp, an arm of Loch Fyne. It's a planned town in the same vein as Inveraray, though nothing like as picturesque. If you're staying in the area, however, you're bound to find yourself here at some point, as Lochgilphead has the only bank and supermarket (not to mention swimming pool) for miles. If you're desperate for something to do in wet weather, you could pay a visit to Highbank Pottery, a short distance up the Oban road (A816), where they make grotesque ceramic animals and offer guided tours of the premises (Mon–Fri 10.30am & 2pm; nominal fee). A better idea, in fine weather, is to head for **Castle Riding Centre** (☎01546/603274) at Brenfield Farm, three miles south, which runs highly enjoyable riding courses lasting from a day to a week, plus trekking and pub rides, and even **rents out bikes** and golf equipment. Another fine-weather option is to stroll round **Kilmory Woodland Park**, a couple of miles up the A83 to Inverary, with its Iron Age fort, bird hide and lochside views, and take in the gardens laid out in 1830 around Kilmory Castle (now headquarters of the Argyll and Bute District Council).

The **tourist office**, 27 Lochnell St (April & mid-Sept to Oct Mon–Fri 10am–5pm, Sat & Sun noon–5pm; May & June Mon–Sat 10am–5pm, Sun 11am–5pm; July to mid-Sept Mon–Sat 9.30am–6pm, Sun 10am–5pm; ☎01546/602344), will help you find you **accommodation**, though really you'd be better off in Crinan (see below). If you are looking yourself, the *Stag Hotel* (☎01546/602496; ④) on the main street is the safest option, though it's no bargain. You can also **camp** at the pristinely maintained *Lochgilphead Caravan Park*, a short distance west of town in Bank Park (☎01546/602003; April–Oct); bike rental is available, too. As for **food**, the *Smiddy*, on Smithy Lane (closed Sun), does simple well cooked grub – for high-class picnic fare, call in at the *Alba Smokehouse* in Kilmory, a mile out of town on the Inveraray road in the industrial estate.

Knapdale

Forested **Knapdale** – from the Gaelic *cnap* (hill) and *dall* (field) – forms a buffer zone between the Kintyre peninsula and the rest of Argyll, bounded to the north by the Crinan Canal and to the south by West Loch Tarbert and consisting of three fingers of land, separated by Loch Sween and Loch Caolisport.

Crinan Canal

In 1801 the nine-mile-long **Crinan Canal** opened, linking Loch Fyne, at Ardrishaig south of Lochgilphead, with the Sound of Jura, thus cutting out the long and treacherous journey around the Mull of Kintyre. John Rennie's original design, although an impressive engineering feat, had numerous faults, and by 1816 Thomas Telford was called in to take charge of the renovations. The canal runs parallel to the sea for quite some way before cutting across the bottom of Mòine Mhór and hitting a flight of locks either side of **CAIRNBAAN** (there are fifteen in total); a walk along the towpath is both picturesque and pleasantly unstrenuous.

There are usually one or two yachts passing through the locks, but the most relaxing place from which to view the canal in action is **CRINAN**, the pretty little fishing port at the western end of the canal. Crinan's tiny harbour is, for the moment at least, still home to a small fishing fleet; a quick burst up through Crinan Wood to the hill above Crinan will give you a bird's eye view of the sea-lock and its setting. Every room in the *Crinan Hotel* (☎01546/830261; ⑧) looks across Loch Crinan to the Sound of Jura – one of the most beautiful views in Scotland, especially at sunset when the myriad islets and the distinctive Paps of Jura are reflected in the waters of the loch. If the *Crinan* is beyond your means, try one of the secluded **B&Bs**, such as *Tigh-na-Glaic* (☎01546/830261; ③), perched above the harbour, also with views out to sea. Bar **meals** at the *Crinan* are moderately expensive, but recommended, as is the hotel's expensive seafood restaurant, *Lock 16*, on the third floor, which commands a panoramic view; there's only one sitting, at 8pm, so booking is advisable. Down on the lockside there is a cheaper, cheerful **café** (Easter–Oct), serving mouth-watering home-made cakes and wonderful clootie dumplings. If you want to go on one of the **boat trips** organized by Gemini Cruises (☎01546/830238), however, you need to go to Crinan's other harbour, half a mile further along the coast; from here the waymarked three-mile **Crinan Walk** takes you through the nearby Forestry Commission plantation, with excellent views out to sea.

Knapdale Forest and Loch Sween

South of the canal, **Knapdale Forest**, planted in the 1930s, stretches virtually uninterrupted from coast to coast, across hills sprinkled with tiny lochs. The Forestry Commission has set out several lovely **walks**, the easiest of which is the circular, mile-long path which takes you deep into the forest just past **Achanamara** (five miles south of Crinan). The three-mile route around **Loch Coille-Bharr**, which begins from a bend in the B8025, to Tayvallich, is fairly gentle; the other walk, although half a mile shorter, is more strenuous, starting from the B841 (halfway between Crinan and Lochgilphead), which runs along the canal, and ascending the peak of **Dunardry** (702ft). There are several good cycle routes, from easy to tough, in this area, all clearly waymarked.

Continuing down the western finger of Knapdale you come to the pretty, sheltered village of **TAYVALLICH**, after which the peninsula splits again. The western arm leads eventually to the medieval **Chapel of Keills**, newly roofed, with a display of late medieval carved stones, and the remains of a small port where cattle used to be landed from Ireland. There is also a fine view of the **MacCormaig Islands**, the largest of which, Eilean Mór (currently owned by the Scottish National Party) was previously a retreat of the seventh-century Saint Cormac, but is now a breeding ground for seabirds. The other arm, the **Taynish peninsula**, is a National Nature Reserve and has one of the largest remaining oak forests in Britain, boasting over twenty species of butterfly. If you want to eat round here, then head for the *Tayvallich Inn* for good local food.

Six miles south of Achanamara, on the eastern shores of **Loch Sween** is the "Key of Knapdale", the eleventh-century **Castle Sween**, the earliest stone castle in Scotland, but in ruins since 1647. The tranquillity and beauty of the setting is spoilt by the nearby caravan park, an eyesore which makes a visit pretty depressing. You're better off continuing south to the thirteenth-century **Kilmory Chapel**, also ruined but with a new roof protecting the medieval graveslabs and the well-preserved MacMillan's Cross, an eight-foot fifteenth-century Celtic cross showing the crucifixion on one side and a hunting scene on the other.

The easternmost finger of Knapdale is isolated and fairly impenetrable, but it's worth enduring the twenty miles of single-track road in order to reach **KILBERRY**, where you can **camp** at the *Port Ban Caravan Park* (☎01880/770224; April–Oct), and enjoy the fantastic sunsets, or **stay the night** in comfort at the *Kilberry Inn* (☎01880/770223; ④; Easter to Oct), which guarantees peace and quiet, plus excellent home cooking (Mon–Sat). There's also a church worth viewing in Kilberry and a small collection of carved medieval graveslabs, while the western shores of West Loch Tarbert are usually replete with birdlife.

Kintyre

But for the mile-long isthmus between West Loch Tarbert and the much smaller East Loch Tarbert, **KINTYRE** (from the Gaelic *ceann tire*, "land's end") would be an island. Indeed, in the eleventh century, when the Scottish king, Malcolm Canmore, allowed Magnus Barefoot, King of Norway, to lay claim to any island he could circumnavigate by boat, Magnus succeeded in dragging his boat across the Tarbert isthmus and added the peninsula to his Hebridean kingdom. After the Wars of the Covenant, when the vast majority of the population and property was wiped out by a combination of the 1646 potato blight coupled with the destructive attentions of the Earl of Argyll, Kintyre became a virtual desert until the earl began his policy of transplanting Gaelic-speaking Lowlanders to the region. They probably felt quite at home here, as the southern half of the peninsula lies on the Lowland side of the Highland Boundary Fault.

Getting around Kintyre without your own transport is a slow business, though services have improved. There are regular daily **buses** from Glasgow to Campbeltown, via Tarbert and the west coast, and even a skeleton service down the east coast. Bear in mind, though, if you're driving, that the new west coast road is extremely fast, whereas the single-track east coast road takes more than twice as long. Campbeltown has an **airport**, with regular flights from Glasgow, which is only 40 miles away by air, compared to over 120 miles by road, and there's now a **ferry link with Northern Ireland** from Campbeltown to Ballycastle.

Tarbert

A distinctive rocket-like church steeple heralds the fishing village of **TARBERT** (in Gaelic *An Tairbeart*, meaning "isthmus"), sheltering an attractive little bay backed by rugged hills. Tarbert's herring industry was mentioned in the Annals of Ulster as far back as 836 AD, though right now the local fishing industry is down to its lowest level ever, due to the strict EU quota system. Ironically, it was local Tarbert fishermen, who, in the 1830s, pioneered the method of herring-fishing known as trawling, seining or ring-netting, which eventually wiped out the Loch Fyne herring stocks. Tourism is now an increasingly important source of income, as is the money that flows through the town during the last week in May, when the yacht races of the famous Scottish Series take place.

Of Robert the Bruce's fourteenth-century **castle** above the town to the south, only the ivy-strewn ruins of the keep remain, though the view from the overgrown rubble makes a stroll up here worthwhile. There are steps up to the castle from beside the excellent Ann Thomas bookshop and gallery on the harbour front, and, at the far end of the road, a lovely shell beach. Tarbert's main formal tourist attraction, though, is the **An Tairbeart Heritage Centre** (Easter-Dec daily 10am–5pm; free), five minutes' walk up the Campbeltown road. In addition to a shop selling local produce and a tearoom, there are temporary exhibitions on local history and a child-centred, educative **woodland walk** that gives you the chance to get close to the local wildlife, and takes you to Maggie's House, a nineteenth-century crofthouse, last inhabited in the 1960s, and now slowly being restored. A whole range of activities such as wood turning and sheep shearing are on offer, too, at the centre.

Tarbert's **tourist office** (April Mon–Fri 10am–5pm, Sat & Sun noon–5pm; May & June Mon–Sat 10am–5pm, Sun 11am–5pm; July to mid-Sept Mon–Sat 9.30am–6pm, Sun 10am–5pm; mid-Sept to Oct Mon–Sat 10am–5pm, Sun noon–5pm; ☎01880/820429) is on the harbour. If you need to **stay**, there's no shortage of B&Bs, though none are outstanding – try *Springside* B&B on Pier Road (☎01880/820413; ①). Highly recommended, however, are the wonderfully Victorian *Columba Hotel* further along Tarbert waterfront (☎01880/820808; ④), and, two miles up the A83 to Lochgilphead, *Stonefield Castle Hotel*, a handsome Victorian mansion set in magnificent grounds overlooking Loch Fyne (☎01880/820836; ⑦). The nearest **campsite** is *West Loch Tarbert Caravan Park* (☎01880/820873; April–Oct), two miles south of Tarbert on the A83. **Bike rental** is available from Mr Leitch (☎01880/820287), on the opposite side of the harbour from the tourist office.

The best bar **food** is to be had at the *Victoria Hotel* where you can sit in the conservatory and look out across the harbour. For some excellent fish and seafood, head for the pricey *Anchorage* (☎01880/820881; May–Sept daily; Oct–April Tues–Sat eves only), on the opposite side of the harbour, unforgettable not least for its eccentric proprietor.

Isle of Gigha

Gigha (pronounced "Geeya", with a hard "g") is a low-lying, fertile island, just three miles off the west coast of Kintyre, reputedly occupied for 5000 years. The island's Ayrshire cattle produce over a quarter of a million gallons of milk a year, despite the fact that Gigha's creamery closed down in the 1980s; the island also produces the distinctive fruit-shaped goat's cheese which is one of the main exports. Like many of the smaller Hebrides, Gigha was sold by its original lairds, the MacNeils, and has been put on the market numerous times in recent years, causing great uncertainty amongst the 140 or so inhabitants.

FERRY CONNECTIONS IN AND AROUND TARBERT

One reason you might find yourself staying in Tarbert is its proximity to no fewer than four **ferry terminals**. The small CalMac ferry which connects Kintyre with **Portavadie** on the Cowal peninsula leaves from Tarbert's Pier Road; the busiest terminal, however, is at **Kennacraig**, five miles south along the A83, which runs daily sailings to Islay and a once-weekly service to Colonsay. From Kennacraig, the B8001 cuts across the peninsula to **Claonaig**, where a summer car ferry (April to mid-Oct) runs to Lochranza on Arran; and finally, south of Kennacraig on the A83 the Gigha ferry departs from **Tayinloan**.

The ferry from Tayinloan, 23 miles south of Tarbert, deposits you at the island's only village, **ARDMINISH**, where you'll find the post office and shop and the all-denominations island church with some interesting stained-glass windows, including one to Kenneth Macleod, composer of the well-known ditty *Road to the Isles*. The main attraction on the island is the **Achamore Gardens** (daily 9am–dusk; £2), a mile and a half south of Ardminish. Established by the first postwar owner, Sir James Horlick of hot drink fame, they are best seen in early summer, ablaze with rhododendrons and azaleas. To the south-west of the gardens, the ruins of the thirteenth-century **St Catan's Chapel** are floored with intricately carved medieval gravestones; the ogam stone nearby is the only one of its kind in the west of Scotland. The real draw of Gigha, however, apart from the peace and quiet, is the white sandy beaches, including one at Ardminish itself, that dot the coastline.

Gigha is so small – six miles by one mile – that most visitors come here just for the day. There is no camping allowed, and no hostel, but it is possible **to stay** either with the McSporrans at the *Post Office House* (☎01583/505251; ①), or at the *Gigha Hotel* (☎01583/505254; ⑨; March–Oct), which also runs self-catering flats dotted over the island. The *Gigha Hotel* is also the place to go for tea and cakes, and for bar meals. **Bike rental** is available from the post office, and there's a nine-hole **golf course**.

The west coast

Kintyre's bleak **west coast** ranks among the most exposed stretches of coastline in Argyll. Atlantic breakers pound the shoreline, while the persistent westerly wind forces the trees against the hillside. However, when the weather's fine, and the wind not too fierce, there are numerous deserted sandy beaches to enjoy with great views over to Gigha, Islay, Jura and even Ireland.

There are several **campsites** to choose from along the stretch of coast around **TAYINLOAN**, ranging from the big *Point Sands Caravan Park* (☎01583/441263; April–Oct), two miles to the north, near a long stretch of sandy beach, or the smaller, more informal *Muasdale Holiday Park*, three miles to the south (☎01583/421207; April–Oct). Other **accommodation** options along the coast include the late-Victorian *Balinakill Country House* at Clachan (☎01880/740206; ③), north of Tayinloan, and the *Argyll Hotel* (☎01583/421212, *wmacken759@aol.com*; ③), a clean, fully modernized old Victorian inn overlooking a sandy beach in Bellochantuy. For **food** along the coast try the *Tayinloan Inn*, a cosy pub offering better than average bar meals, or the *North Beachmore Farm*, signposted off the A83, just south of Tayinloan, with superb views over the coast, and good, low-priced meals, tea and cakes.

Two-thirds of the way down the coast you can visit **Glenbarr Abbey** (Easter–Oct daily except Tues 10am–5.30pm; £2.50) an eighteenth-century laird's house filled with tedious memorabilia about the once powerful MacAlister clan, now reduced to augmenting their income by giving personal guided tours of their house to the trickle of tourists that pass this way. Still, there are plenty of musty old sofas to lounge around in, a tearoom, and attractive grounds which provide a brief respite from the Atlantic winds. If you're up for spot of **horse-riding**, get in touch with the nearby Barrglen Equitation Centre, based at Arnicle Farm (☎01583/421397), which offers lessons and longer rides for "the good, the bad and the wobbly".

The only major development along the entire west coast is **MACHRIHANISH**, at the southern end of Machrihanish Bay, the longest continuous stretch of sand in Argyll. There are two approaches to the **beach**: from Machrihanish itself, or from Westport, at the north end of the bay, where the A83 swings east towards Campbeltown; either way, the sea here is too dangerous for swimming. Machrihanish itself was once a thriving salt-producing and coal-mining centre – you can still see the miners' cottages at neighbouring Drumlemble – but now survives solely on tourism. The main draw, apart from the beach, is the exposed championship **golf links** between the beach and Campbeltown airport on the nearby flat and fertile swath of land known as the Laggan. There's also a tiny **seabird observatory** at Uisaed Point, ten minutes' walk west of the village, though it's best visited in the winter months when it provides a welcome shelter for ornithologists trying to spot a rare bird blown off course.

Several of the imposing, detached Victorian town houses overlooking the bay in Machrihanish, such as *Ardell House* (☎01586/810235; ④; March–Oct), offer **accommodation**; there's also a large, fully equipped, and very exposed **campsite** (☎01586/810366; March–Sept) overlooking the golf links. For **nightlife**, *The Beachcomber* bar is the liveliest place in Machrihanish.

Campbeltown

CAMPBELTOWN's best feature is its setting, in a deep bay sheltered by Davaar Island and the surrounding hills. With a population of 6500, it is also one of the largest towns in Argyll and, if you're staying in the southern half of Kintyre, its shops are by far the best place to stock up on supplies. Originally known as Kinlochkilkerran (*Ceann Loch Cill Chiaran*), the town was renamed in the seventeenth century by the Earl of Argyll – a Campbell – when it became one of the main points for immigration from the Lowlands. As is evident from the architecture, Campbeltown's heyday was the Victorian era, when shipbuilding was going strong, coal was shipped by canal from Drumlemble, the fishing fleet was vast and Campbeltown Loch was said to be made of whisky. The decline of all its old industries has left the town permanently depressed, though its geographical isolation has been tempered by the new car-ferry link with Ballycastle in Northern Ireland.

The Town

Nineteenth-century visitors to Campbeltown frequently found the place engulfed in a thick fog of pungent peat smoke from the town's 34 **whisky distilleries**. Today, only Glen Scotia and Springbank are left to maintain this regional subgroup of single malt whiskies which is distinct from Highland, Islay or Lowland varieties (see p.36 for more on whisky). The family-owned Springbank distillery, off Longrow, offers tours by appointment (☎01586/552085; £2.50), and you can buy a guide to Campbeltown's former distilleries from the tourist office; aficionados should also peruse the huge range of whiskies for sale at Eaglesome on Longrow South.

The town's one major sight is the **Campbeltown Cross**, a fourteenth-century blue-green cross with figural scenes and spirals of Celtic knotting, which presides over the main roundabout on the quayside. Until the last war, it used to be rather more impressive in the middle of the main street outside the **Town Hall**, with its distinctive eighteenth-century octagonal clock tower. Back on the palm-tree-dotted waterfront is the "Wee Picture House", a dinky little Art Deco cinema on Hall Street, built in 1913 and now doubling as a bingo hall (Fri), and movie house. Next door is the equally delightful **Campbeltown Museum and Library** (Wed, Fri & Sat 10am–1pm & 2–5pm, Tues & Thurs 10am–1pm & 2–7.30pm; free), built in 1897 in the local sandstone, crowned by a distinctive lantern, and decorated on its harbourside wall with four relief panels depicting each of the town's main industries at the time. Inside, there's a timber-framed ceiling and etched glass partitions to admire, not to mention a rather unusual brass model of the Temple of Solomon (as it might have looked). The museum itself, which you enter through the library, provides a less remarkable rundown on local history; for a more enlightening version, head to the Heritage Centre (described below).

It used to be said that Campbeltown had almost as many churches as it did distilleries, and even today the townscape is dominated by its church spires – in particular, the top-heavy crown spire of **Longrow Church**, on the road to Machrihanish. The former Lorne Street Church, known locally as the "Tartan Kirk", partly due to its Gaelic associations and its stripy bell-cote and pinnacles, has now become the **Campbeltown Heritage Centre** (April–Oct Mon–Sat noon–5pm, Sun 2–5pm; £2). A beautiful wooden skiff from 1906 stands where the main altar once was, and there's plenty on the local whisky industry and Saint Kieran, the sixth-century "Apostle of Kintyre", who lived in a cave – which you can get to at low tide – not far from Campbeltown. A dedicated ascetic, he would only eat bread mixed with one-third sand and a few herbs; he wore chains, had a stone pillow and slept out in the snow – unsurprisingly, at the age of 33, he died of jaundice.

One of the most popular day-trips is to **Davaar Island**, linked to the peninsula at low tide by a mile-long shoal, or *dóirlinn* as it's known in Gaelic. Check the times of the tides from the tourist office before setting out; you have around six hours in which to make the return journey from Kildalloig Point, two miles or so east of town. Davaar is uninhabited and used for grazing (hence no dogs are allowed); its main attraction, besides the wealth of rock flora, is the cave painting of the Crucifixion executed in secret by local artist, Archibald MacKinnon, in 1887, and touched up by him after he'd owned up in 1934; a year later, aged 85, he died.

Practicalities

Campbeltown's **tourist office** is currently on the Old Quay (April Mon–Sat 10am–5pm; May & June Mon–Sat 9am–5pm, Sun noon–5pm; July to mid-Sept Mon–Sat 9am–6.30pm, Sun noon–5pm; mid-Sept to Oct Mon–Fri 10am–5pm, Sun 10am–4pm; Nov–March Mon–Fri 10am–4pm; ☎01586/552056); the new pier for the **ferry** to Ballycastle lies just to the south and the **airport** lies three miles west, towards Machrihanish (there's a bus connection). There's no shortage of **accommodation**, the delightful family-run *Ardshiel Hotel*, on Kilkerran Road (☎01586/552133; ③), being by far the best choice; it's situated on a lovely leafy square, just a block or so back from the ferry terminal, and has a cosy bar, serving food, and a more expensive à la carte restaurant. Another excellent choice is the *Balegreggan Country House Hotel* (☎01586/552062; ④), a fine detached Victorian villa, in the hills to the north of town, off the A83. For a cheap, simple, central B&B, head for *Eagle Lodge*, 56 High Street (☎01586/551359; ①; Feb–Nov).

As for **places to eat**, the *Locarno Café* on Longrow South is a period-piece greasy spoon, one of many in Campbeltown. The best bar meals and restaurant are to be found at the aforementioned *Ardshiel Hotel*, while the *Commercial Inn* on Cross Street is a good drinking hole. You can **rent bikes** at *The Bike Shop*, Longrow (☎01586/554443). If you're here in the middle of August, be sure to check out the **Mull of Kintyre Music & Arts Festival**, which features some great traditional Irish and Scottish bands.

Southend and the Mull of Kintyre

The bulbous, hilly end of Kintyre, to the south of Campbeltown, features some of the most spectacular scenery on the whole peninsula, mixed with large swathes of Lowland-style farmland. **SOUTHEND** itself, a bleak, blustery spot, comes as something of a disappointment, though it does have a wide sandy beach. Below the cliffs to the west of the beach, a ruined thirteenth-century chapel marks the alleged arrival point of Saint Columba prior to his trip to Iona, and on a rocky knoll nearby a pair of footprints carved into the rock are known as **Columba's footprints**, though only one is actually of ancient origin. Jutting out into the sea at the east end of the bay is **Dunaverty Rock**, where a force of 300 Royalists was massacred by the Covenanting army of the Earl of Argyll in 1647 despite having surrendered voluntarily. A couple of miles out to sea from Dunaverty lies **Sanda Island**, which contains the remains of St Ninian's chapel, plus two ancient crosses, a holy well. a lighthouse and lots of seabirds, including puffins; it's now a holiday retreat with self-catering cottages available (☎01586/553134; April–Sept). Back on the mainland, there are even nicer beaches further west at Carskiey Bay, and at Macharioch Bay, three miles east, looking out to distant Ailsa Craig in the Firth of Clyde (see p.180).

Most people venture south of Campbeltown to make a pilgrimage to the **Mull of Kintyre** – the nearest Britain gets to Ireland, whose coastline, just twelve miles away, appears remarkably close on fine days. Although the Mull was made famous by the mawkish number-one hit by sometime local resident Paul McCartney, with the help of the Campbeltown Pipe Band, there's nothing specifically to see in this godforsaken storm-racked spot but the view. The roads up to the **"Gap"** (1150ft) – where you must leave your car – and particularly down to the lighthouse, itself 300ft above the ocean waves, are terrifyingly tortuous. It's about a mile from the "Gap" to the lighthouse (and a long haul back up), though there's a strategic viewpoint just ten minutes' walk from the car park.

There are few places to **stay** in this remote region. Southend's only hotel has been closed for some time and cuts a forlorn figure, set back from the bay; try instead *Ormsary Farm* (☎01586/830665; ①; April–Sept), a small dairy farm up Glen Breakerie, or the **campsite** at *Machribeg Farm* (☎01586/830249; Easter–Sept) right by the beach. If you're interested in **horse riding**, call the Mull of Kintyre Equestrian Centre at Homeston Farm (☎01586/552437), signposted off the B842 to Southend.

The east coast

The **east coast** of Kintyre is gentler than the west, sheltered from the Atlantic winds and in parts strikingly beautiful, with stunning views across to Arran. However, be warned that bus services are very limited up the east coast and, if you're driving the thirty or so miles up to Skipness on the slow, winding, single-track B842, you'll need a fair amount of time.

The ruins of **Saddell Abbey**, a Cistercian foundation thought to have been founded by Somerled in 1160, lie ten miles up the coast from Campbeltown, set at the lush, wooded entrance to Saddell Glen. The abbey fell into disrepair in the sixteenth century, and though the remains are not exactly impressive, they do shelter a collection of medieval graveslabs decorated with full-scale relief figures of knights. Standing by the privately owned shoreline there's a splendid memorial to the last Campbell laird to live at Saddell Castle, which he built in 1774.

Further north lies the fishing village of **CARRADALE**, the only place of any size on the east coast and "popular with those who like unsophisticated resorts", as one 1930s guide put it. The village itself is rather drab, but the tiny, very pretty harbour with its small fishing fleet, and the wide, sandy beach to the south, make up for it. On the east side of the beach is **Carradale Point**, a wildlife reserve with feral goats and a good example of a **vitrified fort** built more than two thousand years ago on a small tidal island off the headland (best approached from the beach). There are several pleasant walks with good views across to Arran laid out in the woods around Carradale, for which the best starting point is the car park at Port na Storm on the road into the village. The best wet-weather option is **Network Carradale Heritage Centre** on the outskirts of the village (Easter to mid-Oct Mon–Sat 10.30am–5pm; Sun 12.30–4pm; £1) which traces the demise of the local herring fleet; it's small in scale but informative and there's good home-baking to be had in the tearoom.

Accommodation is available at the *Carradale Hotel* (☎01583/431223; ③) whose bar is the hub of village social life (and whose food is good). There are several **B&Bs**, the best of which is the big Victorian *Dunvalanree Guest House* (☎01583/431226; ③), overlooking the sheltered little bay of Port Righ, towards Carradale Point; you can also stay at *Mains Farm* (☎01583/431216; ①; April–Oct), a working farm adjacent to *Carradale*

Bay **campsite** (☎01583/431665; Easter–Sept), right by the sandy beach. Carradale also boasts a real baker – try the treacle scones or cookie pudding (bread and butter pudding south of the border). Close by, a little to the south, above a seal-strewn soft shingle beach, the imposing Victorian pile, *Torrisdale Castle*, offers **self-catering** in castle or cottage. (☎01583/431233).

Five miles further up the coast road is **Grogport Tannery** (daily 9am–6pm; free), which produces naturally coloured, organically tanned, fully washable sheepskins (gloves and slippers too). The B842 ends seven miles north of Grogport at **CLAONAIG**, little more than a slipway for the small summer car ferry to Arran. Beyond here, a dead-end road winds its way along the shore a few miles further north to the tiny village of **SKIPNESS**, where the considerable ruins of the enormous thirteenth-century **Skipness Castle** and a chapel look out across the Kilbrannan Sound to Arran. You can sit outside and admire both, whilst enjoying fresh oysters, delicious queenies, mussels and home-baked cakes from the excellent **seafood cabin** (late May to Sept) at *Skipness House*, which also offers **accommodation** in a family home (☎01880/760207; ⑤). There are several gentle walks laid out in the mixed woodland, up the nearby glen.

Isle of Arran

Shaped like a kidney bean, **Arran** is the most southerly (and therefore the most accessible) of all the Scottish islands. The Highland–Lowland dividing line passes right through its centre – hence the tourist board's aphorism about it being like "Scotland in miniature" – leaving the northern half sparsely populated, mountainous and bleak, while the lush southern half enjoys a much milder climate. Despite its immense popularity, the tourists, like the population of around 4500 – many of whom are incomers – tend to stick to the southeastern quarter of the island, leaving the west and the north relatively undisturbed.

There are two big crowd pullers on Arran: **geology** and **golf**. The former has fascinated rock-obsessed students since Sir James Hutton came here in the late eighteenth century to confirm his theories of igneous geology. A hundred years later, Sir Archibald Geikie's investigations were a landmark in the study of Arran's geology, and the island remains a popular destination for university and school field trips. As for golf, Arran boasts seven courses, including three of the eighteen-hole variety at Brodick, Lamlash and Whiting Bay, and a unique twelve-hole course at Shiskine, near Blackwaterfoot.

Although tourism is now by far its most important industry, Arran, at twenty miles in length, is large enough to have a life of its own. While the island's history post-1745 and the Clearances (set in motion by the local lairds, the dukes of Hamilton) are as depressing as elsewhere in the Highlands, in recent years Arran has not suffered from the depopulation which has plagued other, more remote, islands. Once a county in its own right (along with Bute), Arran has been left out of the new Argyll and Bute district in the latest county boundary shake-up, and is coupled instead with mainland North Ayrshire, with which it enjoys year-round transport links, but little else.

Transport on Arran itself is pretty good: daily **buses** circle the island (Brodick tourist office has timetables) and there are two **ferry services** – a year-round one from Ardrossan in Ayrshire to **Brodick**, and a smaller ferry from Claonaig on the Kintyre peninsula to **Lochranza** in the north (April to mid-Oct).

Brodick

Although the resort of **BRODICK** (from the Norse *breidr vik*, "broad bay") is a place of little charm, it does at least have a grand setting in a wide, sandy bay set against a backdrop of granite mountains. Its development as a tourist resort was held back for a

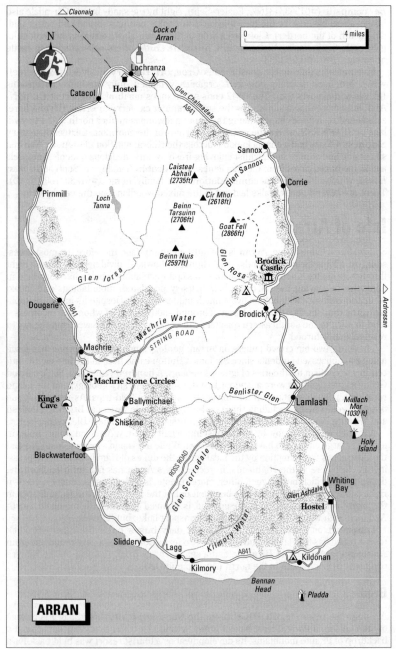

△ *Claonaig*

Cock of Arran

Lochranza

Hostel

Catacol

N

0 — 4 miles

Glen Chalmadale

A841

Sannox

Pirnmill

Loch Tanna

Caisteal Abhail (2735ft) ▲

Cir Mhor (2618ft) ▲

Glen Sannox

Corrie

Beinn Tarsuinn (2706ft) ▲

Goat Fell (2866ft) ▲

Glen Iorsa

Beinn Nuis (2597ft) ▲

Glen Rosa

Brodick Castle

△ *Ardrossan*

Dougarie

A841

Machrie Water

STRING ROAD

Brodick *i*

Machrie

Machrie Stone Circles

Benlister Glen

Lamlash

Mullach Mor (1030 ft) ▲

King's Cave

Ballymichael

Shiskine

A841

Holy Island

Blackwaterfoot

ROSS ROAD

Glen Scorrodale

Glen Ashdale

Whiting Bay

Hostel

Sliddery

Lagg

Kilmory Water

A841

Kildonan

Kilmory

Bennan Head

🕯 *Pladda*

ARRAN

© Crown copyright

long time by its elitist owners, the dukes of Hamilton, though nowadays, as the island's capital and main communication hub, Brodick is by far the busiest town on Arran.

Brodick's sights, such as they are, are clustered on the north side of the bay, a couple of miles from the ferry terminal. The **Arran Heritage Museum** (Easter–Oct Mon–Sat 11am–5pm; £2) is a somewhat dry collection of old tools and furniture in a converted eighteenth-century crofter's farm, and is really only worth visiting to escape from bad weather. It's occasionally enlivened on summer Sundays by a demonstration by the local blacksmith and you can picnic by the river. Other wet weather options lie in the visitor centre at **Home Farm**, also on the road to the castle; here you'll find the Island Cheese Company, where you can see the soft, round *crottins* of goats' cheese being made and taste Brodick and Glenshant blues; Arran Aromatics lets you try your hand at natural soap-making and *Creelers* **smokehouse** offers succulent seafood.

Brodick Castle

Even if you're not based in Brodick, it's worth coming here in order to visit **Brodick Castle** (daily: April–June & Sept–Oct 11am–4.30pm; July & Aug 11am–5pm; NTS; £5), former seat of the dukes of Hamilton on a steep bank on the north side of the bay. Just before the entrance, there's a little sandstone jetty where the duke's wine and ice from Canada was landed. It used to serve the village but the eleventh duke thought the tenants unsightly and had them moved out of sight round the bay. He also closed the barytes mine at Sannox, a vital source of employment for the islanders, on the grounds that it "spoilt the solemn grandeur of the scene".

The bulk of the castle was built in the nineteenth century, giving it a domestic rather than military look, and the **interior** – once you've fought your way past the eighty-seven stags' heads on the stairs – is comfortable but undistinguished. Don't miss the portrait of the eleventh duke's faithful piper who injured his throat on a grouse bone, was warned never to pipe again but did so and died. Probably the most atmospheric room is the copper-filled Victorian kitchen which conjures up a vision of the sweated and sweating labour required to feed the folk upstairs.

Much more attractive, however, are the walled **gardens** (daily 9.30am–dusk; gardens and country park only £2.50) and extensive grounds, a treasury of exotic plants and trees enjoying the favourable climate (including one of Europe's finest collections of rhododendrons), and commanding a superb view across the bay. There is an adventure playground for kids, but the whole area is a natural playground with waterfalls, a giant pitcher plant which swallows thousands of midges daily and a maze of paths. Buried in the grounds there is a bizarre Bavarian-style **summer house** lined entirely with pine cones, one of three built by the eleventh duke to make his wife, Princess Marie of Baden, feel at home. For the energetic there is also a **country park** with eleven miles of scenic trails, starting from a small, informative, hands-on nature centre. In summer there are guided walks with the rangers, but at any time you can be surprised by red squirrels, nightjars and the abundance of fungi. The excellent castle **tearoom** serves traditional food with a local flavour and is highly recommended.

Practicalities

Brodick's **tourist office** (May–Sept Mon–Sat 9am–7.30pm, Sun 10am–5pm; Oct–April Mon–Sat 9am–5pm; ☎01770/302140) is by the CalMac pier, and has reams of information on every activity from pony trekking to paragliding. Unless you've got to catch an early-morning ferry, however, there's little reason to stay in Brodick. Should you do so, the best **rooms** close to the ferry terminal are at the excellent *Dunvegan House Hotel* (☎01770/302811; ④), the Art Deco *Invercloy Hotel* (☎01770/302225, *invercloy-hotel@s.i.co.uk*; ②; March-Oct), or the good-value *Belvedere Guest House* (☎01770/302397, *brachure@visionunltd.force9.co.uk*; ①); closer to the castle is the sandstone *Glen Cloy Farm House* (☎01770/302351, *mvpglencloy@compuserve.com*; ②; March–Nov), has real fires and a warm welcome. For those in search of leisure facilities, the *Auchrannie Country House Hotel* (☎01770/302234, *auchrannie@btinternet .com*; ④), former home of the dowager Duchess of Hamilton, has the lot, including a huge indoor pool, sauna, steam room and gym, all of which are open to non-residents, too. Offering nothing so vulgar as a swimming pool, is the tasteful *Kilmichael Country House Hotel* (☎01770/302219; ⑥), originally built in the seventeenth century and still retaining lots of period features; dinner here is very expensive and very formal, but it's one of the best you'll get on the island. The nearest **campsite** is *Glenrosa* (☎01770/302380), a lovely farm site two miles from town off the B880 to Blackwaterfoot.

For **food**, apart from dinner at the aforementioned *Kilmichael Country House Hotel*, the only place which really stands out is the moderately expensive seafood restaurant *Creelers* (☎01770/302810; mid-March to Oct), by the Arran Heritage Museum on the road to the castle; there are above average bar meals at *Brodick Bar & Brasserie* (☎01770/302169) by the post office; the bar snacks (lunch time only) at *Duncan's Bar* in the *Kingsley Hotel* make a cheaper option and there's real ale too, while, the *Douglas Hotel* features regular **live music** sessions on Sundays. If you want to find out about any other events taking place on Arran, pick up a copy of island's **weekly newspaper**, the *Arran Banner*.

The south

The southern half of Arran is less spectacular, and less forbidding than the north; it's more heavily forested and the land is more fertile, and for that reason the vast majority of the population lives here. The tourist industry has followed them, though with considerably less justification.

Lamlash, Holy Island and Whiting Bay

With its distinctive Edwardian architecture and mild climate, **LAMLASH** epitomizes the sedate charm of southeast Arran. Lamlash Bay has in its time sheltered King Hakon's fleet in 1263 and, more recently, served as a naval base in both world wars. Its major drawback for the visitor, however, is that it is made not of sand but of boulder-strewn mud flats. The monument on the village green marks the spot on which a farewell sermon was given to the eleven families, victims of the Clearances, who, in 1829, sailed from here to Canada.

The best reason for coming to Lamlash is to visit the slug-shaped hump of **Holy Island** which shelters the bay, and is now owned by a group of Tibetan Buddhists who have set up a meditation centre – providing you don't dawdle, it's possible to scramble up to the top of Mullach Mór (1030ft), the island's highest point, and still catch the last ferry back. En route, you might well bump into the island's most numerous residents: feral goats, Highland cattle and rabbits. The Holy Island ferry runs more or less hourly (☎01770/600998; £6 return); alternatively, you might prefer to go **mackerel fishing** – booking essential from the caravan on the pier (☎01770/600349).

If you want to **stay** in style in Lamlash, head for the *Glenisle Hotel* (☎01770/600559; ③; Feb–Dec), or the comfortable *Lilybank* (☎01770/600230; ②; March–Oct), which does good home-made food. You can **camp** at the fully-equipped *Middleton Camping Park* (☎01770/600255; April–Oct), just five minutes' walk south of the centre. Lamlash's best **restaurant** is undoubtedly the *Carraig Mhor* near the pier (☎01770/600453; Mon–Sat eves only), which offers an exclusive and expensive menu featuring fresh local game, fish and seafood. There are a few cheaper options, such as the **bar meals** at the *Pier Head Tavern*, or at the friendly *Drift Inn* by the shore; there's even a Chinese takeaway behind the post office. On the subject of eating, it was a Lamlash man, Donald McKelvie, who made Arran potatoes world famous, breeding in the rich soil of the island Arran Pilot, Arran Chief and Arran Victory, of which Maris Piper is a modern descendant.

Although it has been an established Clydeside resort for over a century now, **WHITING BAY**, four miles south of Lamlash, is actually pretty characterless. However, it's a good base for walking in the southern half of Arran and there are some excellent **places to stay**, including *The Royal* (☎01770/700286; ②; March–Oct), the *Argentine House Hotel*, run (confusingly) by a Swiss couple (☎01770/700662; *argentine.hotel.arran@dial.pipex.com*; ③; closed mid-Jan to mid-Feb), and the *Burlington Hotel* (☎01770/700255; *burlhotel@aol.com*; ③; Easter-Oct) all on Shore Road. At the lower end of the price range, *Norwood* (☎01770/700536; ①; March–Oct), on Smiddy Brae, is the best choice. Whiting Bay also boasts a **youth hostel** (☎01770/700339; March–Oct), at the southern end of the bay. **Eating** options are limited outside of the hotels; the best dining room is at the *Argentine House Hotel*, but it's expensive. Otherwise, you're limited to the snacks at the *Coffee Pot* on the seafront, or the bar meals at the *Cameronia Hotel*. For **bike rental** go to Whiting Bay Hires (☎01770/700382) on the jetty.

Kildonan to Lagg

Access to the sea is tricky along the south coast, but worth the effort, as the sandy beaches here are among the island's finest. One place you can get down to the sea is at **KILDONAN**, an attractive small village south of Lamlash, set slightly off the main road, with a good sandy beach which you share with the local wildlife and, at its east end, a ruined castle looking out to the tiny island of Pladda. Those with kids might like to drop in at the nearby **South Bank Farm Park** (Easter–Sept daily 10am–5pm; £2), to see rare breeds and the occasional sheepdog demonstration (Tues & Thurs 2pm). You can also camp in Kildonan, at the *Breadalbane* **campsite** (☎01770/820210), right on the shore.

KILMORY, four miles west of Kildonan, is the home of the prize-winning **Torrylinn Creamery** (daily 10am–4pm), which produces a cheddary cheese called Arran Dunlop, and where you can watch the whole process from a viewing window. Next door to Kilmory is the picturesque village of **LAGG**, nestling in a tree-filled hollow by Kilmory Water. The friendly village stores has an excellent **tearoom**; those feeling flush should **stay** at the comfortable *Lagg Country House Hotel* (☎01770/870255; ⑤), an eighteenth-century inn set in acres of woodland; for a nice family **B&B** go for the converted seventeenth-century flax mill of *Kilmory House* (☎01770/870342; ①). Scotland's only naturist beach is half a mile west of Lagg, down a rough track at Cleat shore.

Blackwaterfoot and Machrie

BLACKWATERFOOT, on the western end of String Road that bisects the island, is dominated, not to say somewhat spoiled, by the presence of the island's largest hotel. In every other way, Blackwaterfoot is a beguiling little place, which boasts the only twelve-hole golf course in the world. A gentle two-mile walk north along the coast will bring you to the **King's Cave**, one of several where Robert the Bruce is said to have encountered the famously patient arachnid, while hiding during his final bid to free Scotland in 1306. If you want **to stay**, the Victorian *Blackwaterfoot Hotel* (☎01770/860202; ⑤; March–Dec) is the place to hole up, though there are even better B&Bs just up the road in **SHISKINE**, in particular, *The Old House* (☎01770/860302; ②; April–Nov).

North of Blackwaterfoot, the wide expanse of **Machrie Moor** boasts a wealth of Bronze Age sites. No fewer than six **stone circles** sit east of the main road, and, although many of them barely break the peat's surface, the tallest surviving monolith is over 18ft high. The most striking configuration is at Fingal's Cauldron Seat, with two concentric circles of granite boulders; legend has it that Fingal tied his dog to one of them while cooking at his cauldron. If you're feeling peckish, the Machrie golf course **tearoom** (April to mid-Oct) is a welcome oasis in this sparsely populated area.

The north

The desolate **north half of Arran** – effectively the Highland part – features bare granite peaks, the occasional golden eagle and miles of unspoilt scenery, within reach only to those prepared to do some serious hiking. Arran's most accessible peak is also the island's highest, **Goat Fell** (2866ft) – take your pick from the Gaelic, *goath*, meaning "windy", or the Norse, *geit-fjall*, "goat mountain" – which can be ascended in just three hours from Brodick (return journey 5hr), though it's a strenuous hike (for the usual safety precautions, see p.48). From Goat Fell, experienced walkers can follow the horseshoe of craggy summits and descend either from the saddle below Beinn Tarsuinn (2706ft) or from Beinn Nuis (2597ft) itself.

Corrie and Sannox

Another good base for hiking is the pretty little seaside village of **CORRIE**, six miles north of Brodick, where a procession of pristine cottages lines the road to Lochranza. You can **stay** at *Tigh-na-Achaidh* (☎01770/810208; ③), Corrie's finest B&B, while a good budget option is the *North High Corrie Croft* **bunkhouse** (☎01770/302203) above the village on a raised beach; it has one large room for group bookings, and an annexe with eight beds (advance booking advisable). **Bike rental** is available from The Spinning Wheel (☎01770/810640). *Corrie Golf Club*, confusingly in Sannox, offers good-value meals all day in summer.

At **SANNOX**, two miles north, the road leaves the shoreline and climbs steeply, giving breathtaking views over to the scree-strewn slopes around Caisteal Abhail (2735ft). If you make this journey around dusk, be sure to pause in **Glen Chalmadale**, on the other northern side of the pass, to catch a glimpse of the red deer that come down to pasture by the water. Another possibility is to turn off to North Sannox where you can park and walk along the shore to the **Fallen Rocks**, a major rockfall of Devonian sandstone.

Lochranza

On fair Lochranza streamed the early day,
Thin wreaths of cottage smoke are upward curl'd
From the lone hamlet, which her inland bay
And circling mountains sever from the world.
The Lord of the Isles, Sir Walter Scott

The ruined castle which occupies the mud flats of the bay, and the brooding north-facing slopes of the mountains which frame it, make for one of the most spectacular settings on the island – yet **LOCHRANZA**, despite being the only place of any size in this sparsely populated area, attracts far fewer visitors than Arran's southern resorts. Lochranza now boasts the island's first legal whisky **distillery** for more than 150 years, which offers guided tours ending with a free sample (daily 10am–6pm; £2.50), but won't begin to offer its first single malt until 2001; it's housed in an elegant building and boasts the moderately expensive *Harolds* **restaurant**, a state-of-the-art place not to be missed (☎01770/830264; closed Wed eve). If you're just passing through, you can always get a filling snack at the *Pier Tearoom* by the ferry, serving breakfast, lunch, dinner and takeaways from its licensed restaurant, with a magnificent view across to Kintyre.

The finest **accommodation** is to be had at the superb *Apple Lodge* (☎01770/830229; ③), which does excellent home cooking, or at the *Lochranza Hotel* (☎01770/830223; *george@lochranza.co.uk*; ②), whose bar is the centre of the local social scene; the most intriguing of the **B&Bs** is the welcoming *Castlekirk* (☎01770/830202; ①; Feb–Nov) in a converted nineteenth-century church opposite the castle. Lochranza also has a **youth hostel** (☎01770/830631; closed Jan) overlooking the castle, and a well-equipped **campsite** (☎01770/830273, *camp@lochgolf.demon.co.uk*; Easter to mid-Oct) beautifully situated by the golf course on the Brodick Road.

Catacol and Pirnmill

An alternative to staying or drinking in Lochranza is to continue a mile or so southwest along the coast to **CATACOL**, and stay or drink at the friendly *Catacol Bay Hotel* (☎01770/830231, *davecath@aol.com*; ②). It takes the prize as the island's best pub by far, serving good, basic food (with several veggie options) and great beer on tap; there's a small adjoining **campsite**, and seals and shags to view on the nearby shingle. The pub also puts on live music most weeks, and hosts a week-long **folk festival** in early June.

Just past the pub there is a row of striking black-and-white cottages, known as the **Twelve Apostles**, built by the eleventh Duke of Hamilton, and intended to house tenants displaced to make way, not for sheep, but for deer (thanks to Queen Victoria's passion for stalking them), though no one could be persuaded to live in them for two years. You can stay close by at *Fairhaven Guest House* (☎01770/830237; ②; closed Christmas & New Year) a **B&B** with a homely air at the start of the path up Glen Catacol.

From here to the String Road it's very bleak but ideal for spotting wildlife, on hillside and at sea. The next village of any size is neat and tidy **PIRNMILL**, so called because they used to make "pirns" or bobbins for the mills of Paisley here (until they ran out of trees). In summer you can get a snack in the *Anvil Tearoom*.

Isle of Islay

The fertile, largely treeless island of **Islay** (pronounced "eye-la") is famous for one thing – single malt **whisky**. The smoky, peaty, pungent quality of Islay whisky is unique, recognizable even to the untutored palate, and all six of the island's distilleries will happily take visitors on a guided tour, ending with the customary complimentary tipple. Yet, despite the fame of its whiskies, Islay remains relatively undiscovered, much as Skye and Mull were some twenty years ago. Part of the reason, no doubt, is that it takes an expensive, two-hour ferry journey from Kennacraig on Kintyre to reach the island, and once there, you'll find no luxury hotels or fancy restaurants. If you do make the effort, however, you'll be rewarded with a genuinely friendly welcome from islanders proud of their history, landscape and Gaelic culture.

In medieval times, Islay was the political centre of the Hebrides, with **Finlaggan**, near Port Askaig, the seat of the MacDonalds, Lords of the Isles. The picturesque, whitewashed villages you see on Islay today, however, date from the planned settlements founded by the Campbells in the late eighteenth and early nineteenth centuries. Apart from whisky and solitude, the other great draw is the **birdlife**, in particular the scores of white-fronted and barnacle geese who winter here in their thousands. A good time to visit is in late May/early June, when the **Islay Festival** *Feis Ile*, takes place, with whisky tasting, pipe bands, folk dancing and other events celebrating the island's Gaelic roots.

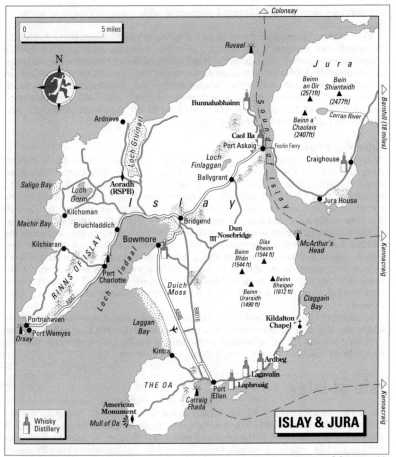

© Crown copyright

Public transport, in the form of buses and postbuses, will get you from one end of the island to the other, but it's as well to know that there is one solitary bus on a Sunday; pick up an island transport guide from the Islay tourist office in **Bowmore**. The **airport**, which lies between Port Ellen and Bowmore, has regular flights to and from Glasgow, and the local bus or postbus will get you to either of the above villages. For a local point of view and news of up-and-coming events, pick up a copy of the fortnightly *Ileach* or visit their Web site (*www.ileach.co.uk*).

Port Ellen and around

Laid out as a planned village in 1821 by Walter Frederick Campbell and named after his wife, **PORT ELLEN** is the busiest port on Islay, with the island's largest fishing fleet, and main CalMac ferry terminal. Arriving at Port Ellen by boat, it's impossible to miss the unusual, square-shaped **Carraig Fhada lighthouse**, at the western entrance to

Kilnaughton Bay, erected in 1832, in memory of Walter Frederick Campbell's afore-mentioned wife, Ellen. The neat terraces along the harbour are pretty enough, but the bay is dominated by the modern maltings, just off the Bowmore road, whose powerful odours waft across the town.

There's really not much point in basing yourself in Port Ellen. The island's main **tourist office** is in Bowmore, and Port Ellen has just an ad hoc office called KOADA, run by volunteers, and therefore open only sporadically. If you need **accommodation** in Port Ellen itself, the best place is *Tighcargaman* (☎01496/302345; ①), set back from the road to Bowmore, half a mile from the ferry. However, you'd be better off heading up the A846 towards the airport, to the excellent *Glenmachrie Farmhouse* (☎01496/302560; ③), which does superb home cooking, or to *Glenegedale House Hotel* (☎01496/302147; ③), a converted farmhouse opposite the airport building, with its own restaurant, *The Heather Hen*. Alternatively, there's a **hostel** at the stone-built *Kintra Farm* (☎01496/302051), three miles northwest of Port Ellen, at the southern tip of Laggan Bay; the farm also does B&B (①) in July and August, has an adjoining **campsite** (April–Sept), and serves food and drink at *The Granary* (late May to Aug evenings only).

Along the coast to Kildalton

From Port Ellen, a dead-end road heads off east along the coastline, passing three distilleries in as many miles. Each tour offers a generous dram, and you usually get your entry fee back if you buy a bottle at the end – though be warned that a bottle of the stuff is no cheaper at source, so expect to pay over £20 for the privilege. Whatever you do, ring first to make sure there's a tour running, as times do change frequently.

First comes **Laphroaig distillery** (☎01496/302418; Mon–Fri 10am & 2.15pm; £2), which produces the most uncompromisingly smoky of the Islay whiskies. As every bottle of Laphroaig tells you, translated from the Gaelic the name means "the beautiful hollow by the broad bay", and, true enough, the whitewashed distillery is indeed in a gorgeous setting by the sea. It's also the first whisky ever to be officially supplied to a member of the royal family (Prince Charles, of course) and each bottle now bears the "By Appointment" stamp. The **Lagavulin distillery** (☎01496/302400; Mon–Fri 10.30am & 2.30pm; £2), a mile down the road, produces a superb sixteen-year-old single malt, while the **Ardbeg distillery** (☎01496/302244; Mon–Fri 10am–4pm; June–Aug also Sat; £2), another mile on, sports the traditional pagoda-style roofs of the malting houses, and has recently been brought back to life by Glenmorangie.

Armed with a bottle of your choice, you could do worse than head down to the shoreline just beyond Lagavulin and have a tot or two beside **Dunyvaig Castle** (*Dún Naomhaig*), a romantic ruin on a promontory looking out to the tiny isle of Texa. There are a handful of **B&Bs** along the rapidly deteriorating road – *Tigh-na-Suil* (☎01496/302483; ①) has a lovely secluded position. A mile beyond this, the simple thirteenth-century **Kildalton Chapel** boasts a wonderful eighth-century Celtic ringed cross made from the local "bluestone", which is, in fact, a rich bottle-green. The quality of the scenes matches any to be found on the crosses carved by the monks in Iona: the Virgin and Child are on the east face, with Cain murdering Abel to the left, David fighting the lion on the top, and Abraham sacrificing Isaac on the right; on the west side amidst the serpent-and-boss work are four elephant-like beasts.

The Oa

The most dramatic landscape on Islay is to be found in the nub of land to the southwest of Port Ellen known as **The Oa** (pronounced "O"), a windswept and inhospitable landscape, much loved by illicit whisky distillers and smugglers over the centuries. Halfway along road, a ruined church is visible to the south, testament to the area's once large population dispersed during the Clearances. The chief target for most visitors to the Oa is the gargantuan **American Monument**, built in the shape of a lighthouse on the clifftop above the Mull of Oa. It was erected by the American National Red Cross in memory of those who died when the *Tuscania* was torpedoed seven miles offshore in February 1918, and when the *Otranto* was shipwrecked off Kilchoman (see p.360) in October of the same year. The memorial is inscribed with the unusual sustained metaphor: "On Fame's eternal camping ground, their silent tents are spread, while glory keeps with solemn round, the bivouac of the dead". If you're driving, you can park in a car park, just before Upper Killeyan farm, and follow the duckboards across the soggy peat. En route, look out for choughs, golden eagles and other birds of prey, not to mention feral goats and, down on the shore, basking seals; for a longer walk, follow the coast round to or from Kintra (see above).

Bowmore

At the northern end of the seven-mile-long Laggan Bay, across the monotonous peat bog of Duich Moss, lies **BOWMORE**, Islay's administrative capital, with a population of around 900. It was founded in 1768 to replace the village of Kilarrow, which was deemed by the local laird to be too close to his own residence. It's a striking place, laid out in a grid-plan rather like Inveraray, with the whitewashed terraces of Main Street climbing up the hill in a straight line from the pier on Loch Indaal to the town's crowning landmark, the **Round Church**, whose central tower looks uncannily like a lighthouse. Built in the round, so that the devil would have no corners in which to hide, it has a plain, wood-panelled interior, with a lovely tiered balcony and a big central mushroom pillar.

A little to the west of Main Street is **Bowmore distillery** (☎01496/810441; Easter–Sept Mon–Fri 10.30am, 11.30am, 2 & 3pm, Sat 10.30am; Oct–Easter Mon–Fri 10.30am & 2pm; £2), the first of the legal Islay distilleries, founded in 1779, and still occupying its original whitewashed buildings by the loch. One of the distillery's former bonded warehouses is now the **MacTaggert Leisure Centre**, whose pool is partially heated by waste heat from the distillery; if you're camping or self-catering, it's as well to know that it has a very useful, minuscule laundrette.

Islay's only official **tourist office** is in Bowmore (April Mon–Sat 10am–5pm; May & June Mon–Sat 9.30am–5pm, Sun 2–5pm; July to mid-Sept Mon–Sat 9.30am–5.30pm, Sun 2–5pm; mid-Sept to Oct Mon–Sat 10am–4.30pm; Nov–March Mon–Fri noon–4pm; ☎01496/810254); it can help you find **accommodation** anywhere on Islay or Jura. Like Port Ellen, Bowmore itself is, in fact, not the best place in which to stay. If you must, however, you're probably better off in one of the town's better B&Bs, such as *Lambeth House* (☎01496/810597; ①), centrally located on Jamieson Street, or *Sheiling* (☎01496/810634; ①) on Flora Street. Of the hotels, the *Lochside Hotel* (☎01496/810390, *alistair@whisky4u.co.uk*; ②), on Shore Street, is reasonable, and has a stupendous array of single malts in the bar. If you're looking for more character and comfort, head out to the *Bridgend Hotel* (☎01496/810960; ⑤), a couple of miles up the road, positioned by the main road junction, but also close to the island's finest patch of deciduous woodland.

Bowmore's cosiest **pub**, however, is the *Harbour Inn* on Main Street, where you can warm yourself by a peat fire; you can get breakfast, lunch or dinner at the inn's outstanding **restaurant**, though it is advisable to book in the evening (☎01496/810330). *The Cottage* (closed Sun) is a cheap and friendly greasy spoon, further up on the same side of the street. Somewhat incredibly there's no fish-and-chip shop in Bowmore, though there is an excellent **bakery**, again on Main Street.

Loch Gruinart

If you're visiting Islay between mid-September and the third week of April, it's impossible to miss the island's staggeringly large wintering population of **barnacle** and

white-fronted geese. During this period, the geese dominate the landscape, feeding incessantly off the rich pasture, strolling by the shores, and flying in formation across the winter skies. In the spring, the geese hang around just long enough to snap up the first shoots of new grass, in order to give themselves enough energy to make the two thousand-mile journey to Greenland, where they breed in the summer. Understandably, many local farmers are none too happy about the geese feeding off their land, and now receive compensation for the inconvenience.

You can see the geese just about anywhere on the island – there are an estimated 20,000 here (and rising) – though they are at their most concentrated in the fields between Bridgend and Ballygrant. In the evening, they tend to congregate in the tidal mudflats and fields around **Loch Gruinart**, which is now an **RSPB nature reserve**. The nearby farm of Aoradh (pronounced "oorig") is now run by the RSPB, and one of its outbuildings contains a **visitor centre** (daily 10am–5pm; free), housing an observation point with telescopes and a CCTV link with the mudflats; there's also a hide across the road looking north over the salt flats at the head of the loch. From the hide, you're more likely to see pintail, widgeon, teal and other waterfowl than geese.

The road along the western shores of Loch Gruinart to Ardnave is a good place to spot **choughs**, members of the crow family, distinguished by their downcurved red beaks and matching legs. Halfway along the road, there's a path off to the ruins of **Kilnave Chapel**, whose working graveyard contains a very weathered, eighth-century Celtic cross. The road ends at Ardnave Loch, beyond which lie numerous sand dunes, where seals often sun themselves, while otters sometimes catch fish offshore. Nature lovers and twitchers should hole themselves up in *Loch Gruinart House* (☎01496/850212; ①) by the reserve, or at the rudimentary *Craigens Farm* **campsite** by the head of the loch (☎01496/850256; April–Oct).

Port Charlotte and the Rinns of Islay

PORT CHARLOTTE, founded in 1828 by Walter Frederick Campbell and named after his mother, is generally agreed to be Islay's prettiest village. Known as the "Queen of the Rinns" (derived from the Gaelic word for promontory), its immaculate white-washed cottages hug a sandy cove overlooking Loch Indaal. On the northern fringe of the village, in a whitewashed former chapel, the imaginative **Museum of Islay Life** (Easter–Oct Mon–Sat 10am–5pm, Sun 2–5pm; £2), has a children's corner, a good library of books about the island, and tantalizing snippets about eighteenth-century illegal whisky distillers. Close by the museum is the spanking new **Islay Cheese Company** (Mon–Fri 10am–4pm, Sat 10am–2pm; free), which has a shop, explanatory panels and a viewing window from which you can see the long curd table where the Dunlop cheese is turned to remove the whey. The **Wildlife Information Centre** (Easter–Oct Mon, Tues, Thurs & Fri 10am–3pm, Sun 2–5pm; £1.80), housed in the former distillery warehouse, is also worth a visit for anyone interested in the island's fauna and flora. Tickets are valid for a week, allowing you to go back and identify things you've seen on your travels.

Port Charlotte is the perfect place in which to base yourself on Islay. The welcoming *Port Charlotte Hotel* (☎01496/850360; *carl@portcharlottehot.demon.co.uk*; ⑤) has the best **accommodation**, and a good (only moderately expensive) restaurant specializing in seafood. For B&B, you're actually better off going for *Octofad Farm* (☎01496/850225; ①; April–Oct), a dairy farm a few miles down the road beyond Nerabus. Port Charlotte itself is also home to the SYHA Islay **hostel** (☎01496/850385; mid-March to Oct), housed in an old bonded warehouse next door to the Wildlife Information Centre. The *Croft Kitchen* (mid-March to mid-Oct; ☎01496/850230), opposite the museum, serves simple **food**, such as sandwiches and cakes, as well as inexpensive seafood, including oysters. The bar of the *Port Charlotte* is very easy-going, while the local crack (and occasional live music) goes on at the *Lochindaal Inn*, down the road.

The main coastal road culminates seven miles south of Port Charlotte at **PORTNA-HAVEN**, a fishing and crofting community since the early nineteenth century. The familiar whitewashed cottages wrap themselves prettily around the steep banks of a deep bay, where seals bask on the rocks in considerable numbers; in the distance, you can see Portnahaven's twin settlement, **PORT WEMYSS**, a mile south. The communities share a little whitewashed church, located above the bay in Portnahaven, with separate doors for each village. A short way out to sea are two islands, the largest of which, Orsay, sports the **Rinns of Islay Lighthouse**, built by Robert Louis Stevenson's father in 1825; ask around locally if you're keen to visit the island.

Those in search of still more solitude should head for the isolated west coast of the Rinns, which is peppered with sandy beaches. The finest of these is the lovely golden beach of **Machir Bay**, backed by great white sand dunes, where an old wreck is visible at low tide. The sea here has dangerous undercurrents, however, and is not safe to swim in (the same goes for the much smaller Saligo Bay, to the north). **Kilchiaran church**, set back from the bay, beneath low rocky cliffs, is in a sorry state of disrepair, but its churchyard contains a beautiful fifteenth-century cross, decorated with interlacing on one side and the crucifixion on the other; at its base there's a wishing stone that should be turned sunwise when wishing. Across a nearby field towards the bay lies the **sailors' cemetery**, containing 75 graves of those drowned when HMS *Otranto* sank in a storm in October 1918; they lie in three neat rows, from the cook to the captain, who has his own much larger graveslab.

Finlaggan and Port Askaig

Just beyond Ballygrant, on the road to Port Askaig, a narrow road leads off north to **Loch Finlaggan**, site of a number of prehistoric crannogs (artificial islands) and, for four hundred years from the twelfth century, headquarters of the Lords of the Isles, semi-autonomous rulers over the Hebrides and Kintyre. The site is evocative enough, but there are, in truth, very few remains beyond the foundations. Remarkably the palace that stood here appears to have been unfortified, a testament perhaps to the prosperity and stability of the islands in those days. Unless you need shelter from the rain, or are desperate to see the head of the commemorative medieval cross found here, you can happily skip the **visitor centre** (Easter & Oct Tues, Thurs & Sun 2–4pm; May–Sept daily except Sat 2.30–5pm; £2), to the northeast of the loch, and simply head on down to the site itself (access at any time), which is dotted with interpretive panels. Duckboards allow you to walk out across the reed beds of the loch and explore the main crannog, **Eilean Mor**, where several carved graveslabs can be seen among the ruins, which seem to support the theory that the Lords of the Isles buried their wives and children, while having themselves interred on Iona. Further out into the loch is another smaller crannog, **Eilean na Comhairle**, originally connected to Eilean Mor by a causeway, where the Lords of the Isles are thought to have held meetings of the Council of the Isles.

Islay's other ferry connection with the mainland, and its sole link with Colonsay and Jura, is from **PORT ASKAIG**, a scattering of buildings which tumble down a little cove by the narrowest section of the Sound of Islay (*Caol Ila*). The only real reason to come here is to catch one of the ferries or go to the hotel bar; if you've time to kill, you can wander round the island's **RNLI lifeboat station** or through the nearby woods of Dunlossit House. Whisky fanatics might want to head half a mile north of Port Askaig to the **Caol Ila distillery** (☎01496/840207; Easter–Sept Mon, Tues, Thurs & Fri 10.30am, 11.15am, 1.30 & 2.45pm, Wed 10.30 & 11.15am; £2), or the **Bunnahabhainn distillery** (tours by appointment Mon–Fri; ☎01496/840646), a couple of miles further on; both enjoy idyllic settings, overlooking the Sound of Islay, though they are no beauties in themselves.

Easily the most comfortable **place to stay** is the lovely whitewashed *Kilmeny Farmhouse* (☎01496/840668; ④), southwest of Ballygrant, a place which richly deserves all the superlatives it regularly receives. A more modest alternative is a room at the secluded B&B at *The Kennels* (☎01496/840237; ①). The *Ballygrant Inn* is a good **pub** in which to grab a pint, as is the bar of the *Port Askaig Hotel*, which enjoys a wonderful position by the pier at Port Askaig, with views over to the Paps of Jura.

Isle of Jura

Twenty-eight miles long and eight miles wide, the long whale-shaped island of **Jura** is one of the wildest and most mountainous of the Inner Hebrides, its entire west coast uninhabited and inaccessible except to the dedicated walker. The distinctive Paps of Jura – so called because of their smooth breast-like shape, though there are in fact three of them – seem to dominate every view off the west coast of Argyll, their glacial rounded tops covered in a light dusting of quartzite scree. The island's name derives from the Norse *dyr-oe* (deer island) and, appropriately enough, the current deer population of five thousand outnumbers the two hundred humans 25:1. With just one road, which sticks to the more sheltered eastern coast of the island, and only one hotel and a smattering of B&Bs, Jura is an ideal place to go for peace and quiet and some great walking.

If you're just coming over for the day from Islay, and don't fancy climbing the Paps, you could happily spend the day in the lovely wooded grounds of **Jura House** (daily 9am–5pm; £2), five miles up the road from Feolin Ferry, where the car ferry from Port Askaig arrives. Pick up a booklet at the entrance to the grounds, and follow the path which takes you down to the sandy shore, a perfect picnic spot in fine weather. Closer

---

GEORGE ORWELL ON JURA

In April 1946, Eric Blair (better known by his pen name of **George Orwell**), intending to give himself "six months' quiet" in which to complete his latest novel, moved to a remote farmhouse called **Barnhill**, on the northern tip of Jura, which he had visited for the first time the previous year. He appears to have relished the challenge of living in Barnhill, fishing almost every night, shooting rabbits, laying lobster pots, and even attempting a little farming. Along with his adopted three-year-old son, Richard, and, later, his sister, Avril, he clearly enjoyed his spartan existence. The book he was writing, under the working title *The Last Man in Europe*, was to become *1984* (the title was arrived at by simply reversing the last two digits of the year in which it was finished, 1948). During his time on Jura, however, Orwell was suffering badly from tuberculosis, and eventually he was forced to return to London where he died in January 1950.

Barnhill, twenty-three miles north of Craighouse is as remote today as it was in Orwell's day. The road deteriorates rapidly beyond Lealt, and, after two miles, is closed to all vehicles, so pilgrims need to walk the last two or three miles to the house itself. Orwell wrote most of the book in the bedroom (top left window as you look at the house) – at present, there is no public access. If you're keen on making the journey out to Barnhill, you might as well combine it with a trip to the nearby **Gulf of Corrievreckan** (see p.338, which lies between Jura and Scarba, to the north. Orwell nearly drowned in the whirlpool during a fishing trip in August 1947, along with his three companions (including Richard): the outboard motor was washed away, and they had to row to a nearby island and wait for several hours before being rescued by a passing fisherman. The best time to see the water whirling is between flood and half-flood tide, with a southerly or westerly wind.

to the house itself, there's an idyllic **walled garden**, divided in two by a natural rushing burn that tumbles down in steps. The garden specializes in Antipodean plants, which flourish in the frost-free climate; in season, you can buy some of the garden's organic produce or take tea in the tea tent.

Anything that happens on Jura happens in the island's only real village, **CRAIGHOUSE**, eight miles up the road from Feolin Ferry. The village enjoys a sheltered setting, overlooking Knapdale on the mainland – so sheltered, in fact, there are even a few palm trees thriving on the seafront. There's a shop/post office, the island hotel and a tearoom, plus the tiny **Craighouse distillery** (tours by appointment; ☎01496/820240), which welcomes visitors.

The family-run *Jura Hotel* in Craighouse is the island's one and only **hotel** (☎01496/820243; ④), not much to look at from the outside, but warm and friendly within, and centre of the island's social scene. The hotel does inexpensive bar meals, and has a shower block and laundry facilities round the back for non-residents. For B&B, go to Dave Gilmour at 8 Woodside (☎01496/820319; ①), a great guy for whom nothing is too much trouble. There's an infrequent **minibus service** on the island (phone ☎01496/820314 to find out when it's running). The **ferry** from Port Askaig occasionally fails to run if there's a strong northerly or southerly wind, so bring your toothbrush if you're coming for a day-trip.

travel details

Trains

Glasgow (Queen St) to: Arrochar & Tarbert (4 daily; 1hr 15min); Dalmally (3 daily; 2hr 15min); Helensburgh Central (every 30min; 45min); Helensburgh Upper (4 daily; 45min); Oban (3 daily; 3hr).

Mainland buses (not including postbuses)

Arrochar to: Carrick Castle (Mon–Sat 3 daily; 1hr); Garelochhead (Mon–Fri 2 daily; 20min); Inveraray (Mon–Sat 5 daily, Sun 2 daily; 35min); Lochgilphead (Mon–Sat 3 daily, Sun 2 daily; 1hr 30min); Lochgoilhead (Mon–Sat 3 daily; 40min).

Campbeltown to: Airport (Mon–Fri 2 daily; 10min); Carradale (Mon–Sat 3–4 daily, Sun 2 daily; 45min); Machrihanish (Mon–Sat 9–11 daily, Sun 3 daily; 15min); Saddell (Mon–Sat 3–4 daily, Sun 2 daily; 25min); Southend (Mon–Sat 5–6 daily, Sun 2 daily; 23min).

Colintraive to: Dunoon (Mon–Fri 1–3 daily, Sat 3 daily; 40min); Tighnabruaich (Mon–Thurs 1–2 daily; 35min).

Dunoon to: Colintraive (Mon–Fri 1–3 daily, Sat 3 daily; 40min); Inveraray (Mon–Fri 5 daily, Sat 3 daily; 1hr 15min); Lochgoilhead (Mon–Fri 0–3 daily; 1hr 15min).

Glasgow to: Arrochar (Mon–Sat 6 daily, Sun 3 daily; 1hr 10min); Campbeltown (Mon–Sat 3 daily, Sun 2 daily; 4hr 25min); Dalmally (Mon–Sat 4 daily, Sun 2 daily; 2hr 20min); Inveraray (Mon–Sat 6 daily, Sun 3 daily; 1hr 45min); Kennacraig (Mon–Sat 2 daily, Sun 1 daily; 3hr 30min); Lochgilphead (Mon–Sat 3 daily, Sun 2 daily; 2hr 40min); Oban (Mon–Sat 4 daily, Sun 2 daily; 3hr); Tarbert (Mon–Sat 3 daily, Sun 2 daily; 3hr 15min); Taynuilt (Mon–Sat 4 daily, Sun 2 daily; 2hr 45min).

Kennacraig to: Claonaig (Mon–Sat 3 daily; 15min); Skipness (Mon–Sat 3 daily; 20min).

Inveraray to: Dalmally (Mon–Sat 3 daily, Sun 1 daily; 25min); Dunoon (Mon–Fri 5 daily, Sat 3 daily; 1hr 15min); Lochgilphead (Mon–Sat 3 daily, Sun 2 daily; 40min); Oban (Mon–Sat 3 daily, Sun 1 daily; 1hr 5min); Tarbert (Mon–Sat 3 daily, Sun 2 daily; 1hr 30min); Taynuilt (Mon–Sat 3 daily, Sun 1 daily; 45min).

Lochgilphead to: Campbeltown (Mon–Sat 4 daily, Sun 2 daily; 1hr 25min); Crinan (Mon–Fri 1–3 daily, Sat 2 daily; 20min); Inveraray (Mon–Sat 3 daily, Sun 2 daily; 40min); Kilmartin (Mon–Sat 1–5 daily; 15–40min); Oban (Mon–Sat 1 daily; 1hr 25min); Tarbert (2–4 daily; 30min).

Oban to: Appin (Mon–Sat 4 daily, Sun 1 daily; 30min); Benderloch (Mon–Sat 10–14 daily, Sun 6 daily; 20min); Ellenabeich (Mon–Sat 2–4 daily; 45min); Kilmartin (Mon–Sat 1 daily; 1hr 10min);

Lochgilphead (Mon–Sat 1 daily; 1hr 30min).

Tarbert to: Campbeltown (Mon–Sat 4 daily, Sun 2 daily; 1hr 10min); Claonaig (Mon–Sat 3 daily; 30min); Kennacraig (Mon–Sat 5 daily, Sun 1 daily; 15min); Skipness (Mon–Sat 3 daily; 35min).

Tighnabruaich to: Portavadie (Mon–Sat 3–4 daily; 25min); Rothesay (Mon–Thurs 1–2 daily; 1hr).

Island buses (not including postbuses)
Arran
Brodick to: Blackwaterfoot (Mon–Sat 16–19 daily, Sun 5 daily; 30min–1hr 20min); Corrie (Mon–Sat 5–6 daily, Sun 4 daily; 20min); Kildonan (Mon–Sat 4–5 daily, Sun 4 daily; 40min); Lagg (Mon–Sat 4–5 daily, Sun 4 daily; 55min); Lamlash (Mon–Sat12–13 daily, Sun 4 daily; 10min); Lochranza (Mon–Sat 5–6 daily, Sun 4 daily; 45min); Pirnmill (Mon–Sat 5–6 daily, Sun 4 daily; 1hr); Whiting Bay (Mon–Sat12–13 daily, Sun 4 daily; 25min).

Bute
Rothesay to: Kilchattan Bay (Mon–Sat 4 daily, Sun 3 daily; 30min); Mount Stuart (1 daily except Tues & Thurs every 45min; 15min); Rhubodach (Mon–Sat 1–2 daily; 20min).

Colonsay
Scalasaig to: Kilchattan (Mon–Fri 2–4 daily; 30min); Kiloran Bay (Mon–Fri 2–3 daily; 12min); The Strand (Mon–Fri 1 daily).

Islay
Bowmore to: Port Askaig (Mon–Sat 8–10 daily, Sun 1 daily; 30–40min); Port Charlotte (Mon–Sat 4–6 daily; 30min); Port Ellen (Mon–Sat 5–7 daily, Sun 1 daily; 20–30min); Portnahaven (Mon–Sat 5–7 daily; 50min).

Mull
Craignure to: Fionnphort (Mon–Sat 4 daily, Sun 1 daily; 1hr 10min); Fishnish (Mon–Sat 4 daily, Sun 3 daily; 10min); Salen (Mon–Sat 4 daily, Sun 2 daily; 25min); Tobermory (Mon–Sat 4 daily, Sun 3 daily; 50min).

Tobermory to: Calgary (Mon–Fri 3–6 daily, Sat 2 daily; 45min); Dervaig (Mon–Fri 3–6 daily, Sat 2 daily; 30min); Fishnish (Mon–Sat 4 daily, Sun 3 daily; 40min).

Car ferries (summer timetable)
To Arran: Ardrossan–Brodick (Mon–Sat 5–6 daily, Sun 4 daily; 55min); Claonaig–Lochranza (10 daily; 30min).

To Bute: Colintraive–Rhubodach (frequently; 5min); Wemyss Bay–Rothesay (every 45min; 30min).

To Campbeltown: Ballycastle (Northern Ireland)–Campbeltown (2 daily; 3hr).

To Coll: Oban–Coll (1 daily except Thurs & Sun; 2hr 40min).

To Colonsay: Kennacraig–Colonsay (Wed 1 daily; 3hr 40min); Oban–Colonsay (Wed, Fri & Sun 1 daily; 2hr 10min); Port Askaig–Colonsay (Wed 1 daily; 1hr 20min).

To Dunoon: Gourock–Dunoon (hourly; 20min); McInroy's Point–Hunter's Quay (every 30min; 20min).

To Gigha: Tayinloan–Gigha (hourly; 20min).

To Islay: Colonsay–Port Askaig (Wed 1 daily; 1hr 20min); Kennacraig–Port Askaig (Mon–Sat 1–2 daily; 2hr); Kennacraig–Port Ellen (1–2 daily except Wed; 2hr 10min); Oban–Port Askaig (Wed 1 daily; 4hr).

To Jura: Port Askaig–Feolin Ferry (Mon–Sat 16 daily, Sun 6 daily; 10min).

To Kintyre: Portavadie–Tarbert (hourly; 25min).

To Lismore: Oban–Lismore (Mon–Sat 2–4 daily; 50min).

To Luing: Cuan Ferry (Seil)–Luing (every 30min; 5min).

To Mull: Kilchoan–Tobermory (Mon–Sat 7–8 daily; July & Aug also Sun 5 daily; 35min); Lochaline–Fishnish (Mon–Sat every 50min, Sun hourly; 15min); Oban–Craignure (Mon–Sat 6 daily, Sun 4–5 daily; 40min).

To Tiree: Oban–Tiree (1 daily except Thurs & Sun; 3hr 40min).

Passenger-only ferries (summer only)
To Helensburgh: Kilcreggan–Helensburgh (Mon–Sat 3 daily; 25min); Gourock–Helensburgh (Mon–Sat 4 daily; 40min).

To Iona: Fionnphort–Iona (Mon–Sat frequently, Sun hourly; 5min).

To Lismore: Port Appin–Lismore (daily every 2hr; 5min).

Flights
Glasgow to: Campbeltown (Mon–Fri 2 daily; 35min); Islay (Mon–Fri 2 daily, Sat 1 daily; 40min); Tiree (Mon–Sat 1 daily; 45min).

CHAPTER SIX

SKYE AND THE WESTERN ISLES

A procession of Hebridean islands, islets and reefs off the northwest shore of Scotland, **Skye and the Western Isles** between them boast some of the country's most alluring scenery. It's here that the turbulent seas of the Atlantic smash up against an extravagant shoreline hundreds of miles long, a geologically complex terrain whose rough rocks and mighty sea cliffs are interrupted by a thousand sheltered bays and, in the far west, a long line of sweeping sandy beaches. The islands' interiors are equally dramatic, a series of formidable mountain ranges soaring high above great chunks of boggy peat moor, a barren wilderness enclosing a host of tiny lakes, or lochans.

Skye and the Western Isles were first settled by Neolithic farming peoples in around 4000 BC. They lived along the coast, where they are remembered by scores of remains, from passage graves through to stone circles – most famously at **Calanais** (Callanish) on Lewis. Viking colonization gathered pace from 700 AD onwards – on Lewis four out of every five place names is of Norse origin – and it was only in 1266 that the islands were returned to the Scottish crown. James VI (and I of England), a Stuart and a Scot, though no Gaelic-speaker, was the first to put forward the idea of clearing the Hebrides, though it wasn't until after the Jacobite uprisings, in which many Highland clans disastrously backed the wrong side, that the **Clearances** began in earnest.

The isolation of the Hebrides exposed them to the whims and fancies of the various merchants and aristocrats who caught "island fever" and bought them up. Time and again, from the mid-eighteenth century to the present day, both the land and its people were sold to the highest bidder. Some proprietors were well-meaning, but insensitive – like **Lord Leverhulme**, who had no time for crofting and wanted to turn Lewis into a centre of the fishing industry in the 1920s – while others were simply autocratic – such as **Colonel Gordon of Cluny**, who bought Benbecula, South Uist, Eriskay and Barra, and forced the inhabitants onto ships bound for North America at gunpoint – but always the islanders were powerless and almost everywhere they were driven from their ancestral homes, robbing them of their particular sense of place. However, their language survived, ensuring a degree of cultural continuity, especially in the Western Isles, where even today the mother tongue of the vast majority is **Gaelic**.

Each island has its own distinct character, though you can split the grouping quite neatly into two. **Skye** and the so-called **Small Isles** – the improbably named Rùm, Eigg, Muck and Canna – are part of the Inner Hebrides, which also include the islands of Argyll (see the Argyll chapter). Beyond Skye, across the unpredictable waters of the Minch, lie the Outer Hebrides or Outer Isles, nowadays known as the **Western Isles**, a 130-mile-long archipelago stretching from Lewis and Harris in the north to Barra in the south.

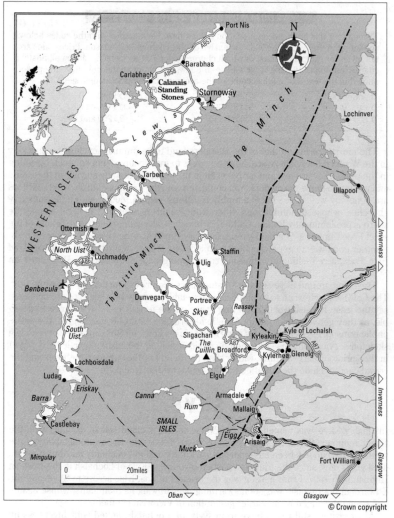

© Crown copyright

Although this area is one of the most popular holiday spots in Scotland, the crowds only become oppressive on Skye, and even here most visitors stick to a well-trodden sequence of roadside sights that leaves the rest of the island unaffected. The main attraction, the spectacular scenery, is best explored on **foot**, following the scores of paths that range from the simplest of cross-country strolls to arduous treks. There are four obvious areas of outstanding natural beauty to aim for: on Skye, the harsh peaks of the **Cuillin** and the bizarre rock formations of the **Trotternish** peninsula, both of which attract hundreds of walkers and mountaineers; on the Western Isles, the mountains of **North Harris** and the splendid sandy beaches that string along the Atlantic seaboard of **South Harris** and the **Uists**.

ACCOMMODATION PRICE CODES

Throughout this book, accommodation **prices** have been graded with the codes below, according to the cost of the least expensive double room in high season. Price codes are not given for campsites, most of which charge under £10 per person. Almost all hostels charge less than £10 a night for a bed – the few exceptions to this rule have the prices quoted in the text. For a full account of the accommodation price codes, see p.31.

① under £40	④ £60–70	⑦ £110–150
② £40–50	⑤ £70–90	⑧ £150–200
③ £50–60	⑥ £90–110	⑨ £200 and over

The tourist world and that of the islanders tend to be mutually exclusive, especially in the Western Isles. There are, however, ways to meet people – not so much by sitting in the pubs (they are few and far between in these parts), than by staying in the B&Bs and getting to know the owners. You could, too, join the locals at church, where visitors are generally welcome. This is a highly **religious region**, dotted with numerous tiny churches, whose denominations differ from island to island. In general terms, the south is predominantly Roman Catholic, while the Calvinist north is a stronghold of the strict Free Church of Scotland – more familiarly known as the "Wee Frees" (see p.389). Another good way to get acquainted with local life is to read the weekly *West Highland Free Press*, a refreshingly vociferous campaigning paper published in Broadford on Skye.

Travelling around Skye and the Western Isles requires some degree of forethought. The CalMac **ferries** run to a complicated timetable, and the **bus** services are patchy to say the least. It's also worth reserving space on the ferries as far in advance as possible, as they get very booked up. Also, in accordance with Calvinist dogma, the entire public transport system of Lewis and Harris closes down on **Sunday**; elsewhere only a skeleton service remains. You should consider visiting the islands (particularly Skye) in the spring or early autumn, rather than the height of the summer, both to avoid the crowds and to elude the attentions of the pesky **midge** (see p.46)

SKYE

Justifiably **Skye** was named after the Norse word for cloud (*skuy*), earning itself the Gaelic moniker, *Eilean a Cheo* (Island of Mist). Yet despite the unpredictability of the weather, tourism has been an important part of the island's economy for almost a hundred years now, since the train line pushed through to Kyle of Lochalsh in the western Highlands in 1897. From here, it was the briefest of boat trips across to Skye, and the Edwardian bourgeoisie was soon swarming over to walk its mountains, whose beauty had been proclaimed by an earlier generation of Victorian climbers.

Most visitors still reach Skye from **Kyle of Lochalsh**, linked with Inverness by train, via the new Skye Bridge on one of the frequent buses over to **Kyleakin**, on the western tip of the island. However, this part of Skye is pretty dull, and the more scenic approach is from the **ferry** port of **Mallaig**, further south on the Morar peninsula (see p.512). Linked by **train** with Glasgow, the Mallaig boat (up to seven daily) takes thirty minutes to cross to **Armadale**, on the gentle southern slopes of the **Sleat peninsula**. A third option is the privately operated car **ferry** which leaves the mainland at Glenelg, south of Kyle of Lochalsh, to arrive at **Kylerhea**, from where the road heads inland towards **Portree**. If you're carrying on to the Western Isles, it's 57 miles from Armadale to the opposite end of Skye, where **ferries** leave Uig for Tarbert on Harris and Lochmaddy on North Uist.

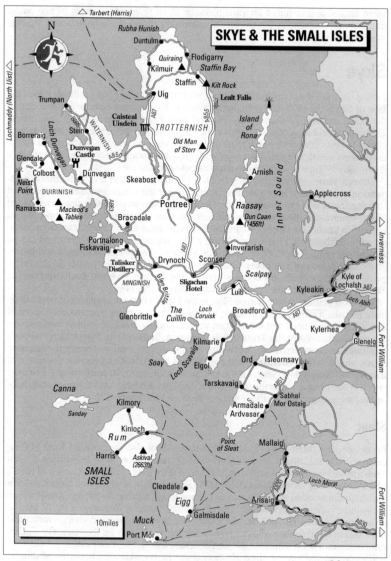

SKYE & THE SMALL ISLES

© Crown copyright

Skye has several substantial **campsites**, and numerous **hostels** or bunkhouses –
all of which recommend advance bookings, particularly in July and August – plenty
of B&Bs and a string of pricey, but excellent **hotels**. Most visitors arrive by car, as
the **bus** services, while adequate between the villages, peter out in the more remote
areas, and virtually close down on Sundays. Accommodation on the Small Isles is

more limited and requires forward planning at all times of the year; formal public transport is nonexistent, but the locals will usually oblige if you have heavy baggage to shift.

Skye

Jutting out from the mainland like a giant wing, the bare and bony promontories of the **Isle of Skye** (An t-Eilean Sgiathanach) fringe a deeply indented coastline that makes the island never more than twenty-five, and sometimes as little as seven, miles wide. This causes problems at the height of the tourist season when the main road system begins to bottleneck with coach tours and minibuses and caravans. Yet Skye is a deceptively large island, and you'll get most out of it – and escape the worst of the crowds – if you take the time to explore the more remote parts of the island.

Though some estimate that only half the island's population are *Sgiathanachs* (pronounced "Ski-anaks"), Skye remains the most important centre for **Gaelic culture** and language outside of the Western Isles. Despite the Clearances, which saw an estimated 30,000 emigrate in the mid-nineteenth century, around forty percent of the population is fluent in Gaelic, the Gaelic college on Sleat is the most important in Scotland, and the extreme Sabbatarian Free Church (see p.389) maintains a strong presence. As an English-speaking visitor, it's as well to be aware of the tensions that exist within this idyllic island, even if you never experience them first-hand. For a taste of the resurgence of Gaelic culture, try and get here in time for the Skye and Lochalsh Festival, *Feis an Eilean*, which takes place over two weeks in mid-July.

The most popular destination on Skye is the **Cuillin** ridge, whose jagged peaks dominate the island during clear weather; to explore them at close quarters you'll need to be a fairly experienced and determined walker. Equally dramatic in their own way are the rock formations of the **Trotternish** peninsula, in the north, from which there are inspirational views across to the Western Isles. If you want to escape the summer crush, shuffle off to **Glendale** and the cliffs of Neist Point or head for the island of **Raasay**, off Skye's east coast. Of the two main settlements, **Broadford** and **Portree**, only the latter has any charm attached to it, though both have tourist offices, and make useful bases, especially for those without their own transport.

Sleat

Ferry services (Mon–Sat 6–7 daily; June to mid-Sept also Sun; 30min) from Mallaig connect with the **Sleat** (pronounced "Slate") **peninsula**, Skye's southern tip, an uncharacteristically fertile area that has earned it the sobriquet "The Garden of Skye". The CalMac ferry terminal is at **ARMADALE** (Armadal), an elongated hamlet stretching along the wooded shoreline. If you've time to kill waiting for the ferry, take a look at the huge variety of Scottish and Irish knitwear on offer at *Ragamuffin* by the pier, or if you need a bite **to eat**, pop into the *Pasta Shed* next door, which does a great seafood pizza (eat-in or takeaway). Alternatively, a few hundred yards up the road, *The Gallery* café/restaurant serves inexpensive and delicious fish and seafood dishes.

If you're leaving Skye on the early-morning ferry, you may need **accommodation** in Armadale: try *Skye Batiks* B&B (☎01471/844396; ③), near the pier, or, better still, head a mile southwest to neighbouring Ardvasar, where the traditional, whitewashed *Ardvasar Hotel* (☎01471/844223; ⑤; March–Dec) has an excellent restaurant specializing in local seafood, and a lively bar. There are three **hostels** on the peninsula: *Armadale SYHA Hostel* (☎01471/844260; mid-March to Sept) is a ten-minute walk up the A851 towards Broadford and overlooks the bay; *Sleat Independent Hostel* (☎01471/844440; open all year) is two miles further up the same road, beyond Sabhal

Mòr Ostaig; while *Hairy Coo Backpackers* (☎01471/833231) is another couple of miles further on, in Toravaig House by Knock Castle. The SYHA hostel **rents bikes**, as does the local petrol station (☎01471/844249), close to the pier.

Just past Armadale youth hostel, you'll find the **Clan Donald Visitor Centre** (April–Oct daily 9.30am–5.30pm; £3.80), housed in the neo-Gothic Armadale Castle, which was built by the MacDonalds as their clan seat in 1815. Part of the castle has been restored to create a touristy museum that traces the history of the Gaels, concentrating on medieval times when the MacDonalds were in their glory as the Lords of the Isles. There's a lot of fairly confusing historical text on the walls, and the romantic sound effects – the cries of sea birds and battle songs – don't really compensate for the lack of original artefacts, but the handsome forty-acre **gardens** (April–Oct, as above; Nov–March free) are the highlight, with guided nature walks in the grounds. There's an attractive café and a library for those who want to chase up their ancestral Donald connections.

A couple of miles up the road in an old MacDonald farm is the **Sabhal Mòr Ostaig** (☎01471/844373), a modern, independent Gaelic college of further education founded by Sir Iain Noble, an Edinburgh merchant banker, who owns a large chunk of the peninsula and is an untiring Gaelic enthusiast. The college runs a variety of extremely popular short courses in Gaelic language, music and culture, and longer full-time courses in Gaelic business, computing and media. If you're looking for a book and tape on beginners' Gaelic, the college bookshop has a good selection.

The loveliest part of the Sleat peninsula, by far, is the west coast: take the fiercely winding single-track road over to the scattered settlement of **TARSKAVAIG**, with its little sandy beach looking out over to Eigg. Further along the coast, through some ancient deciduous woods, you come to **Tokavaig**, where a stony, seaweedy beach overlooked by the ruined Dunscaith Castle boasts views over the entire Cuillin range – this, and neighbouring **ORD**, with a pleasant sandy beach, are the two best places on the whole of Skye from which to view the mountains in fine weather. There are very few places to stay in this area, but there is a B&B with great views in Ord, *Fiordhem* (☎01471/855226; Easter–Oct; ⑨).

Continuing northeast, it's another six miles to **ISLEORNSAY** (Eilean Iarmain), a secluded little village of whitewashed cottages that was once Skye's main fishing port. With the mountains of the mainland on the horizon, the views out across the bay are wonderful, overlooking a necklace of seaweed-encrusted rocks and the tidal **Isle of Ornsay**, which sports a trim lighthouse built by Robert Louis Stevenson's father. You can **stay** at another of Sir Iain Noble's enterprises, the mid-nineteenth-century *Isleornsay Hotel* – also known by its Gaelic name *Hotel Eilean Iarmain* – a pricey place with excellent service, whose **restaurant** serves great seafood (☎01471/833332; ⑥). Also based in Isleornsay is Sir Iain's Gaelic whisky company, Prabann na Linne, which markets a number of unpronounceable Gaelic-named blended and single malt whiskies; the company offers tastings at its head office (phone ☎01471/833266 for opening hours).

Kyleakin and Kylerhea

The aforementioned Sir Iain Noble is also one of the leading advocates of (and investors in) the privately financed **Skye Bridge**, which now links the tidy hamlet of **KYLEAKIN** (Caol Acain – pronounced K*a*l*a*kin, with the stress on the second syllable) with the Kyle of Lochalsh (see p.517), just half a mile away on the mainland. The bridge, welcomed by the vast majority of islanders, was built entirely by Anglo-German contractors for a cool £30 million, which they are currently trying to recoup by charging just around £5 each way for cars and £30 for lorries and coaches, making it the most expensive toll bridge in Europe, and no cheaper than the ferry it replaced. With a new

Scottish Parliament in control, the well-orchestrated campaign by SKAT (Skye and Kyle Against Tolls), 350 of whose members have refused to pay the tolls, may yet succeed in either reducing or abolishing the fee. There's a notice board erected by SKAT just before the bridge giving you an update. Strictly speaking there are two bridges which rest on an island in the middle, **Eilean Ban**, once the home of author and naturalist Gavin Maxwell, which is set to become a wildlife sanctuary.

There's nothing much to see or do in Kyleakin, though you could have a quick look at the scant remains of **Castle Moil**, a fourteenth-century keep poking out into the straits on top of a diminutive rocky knoll, that looks romantic when floodlit. One of its earliest inhabitants, an entrepreneurial Norwegian princess, married to a MacDonald chief, hung a chain across the water and exacted a toll from every passing boat. With its ferry now defunct, Kyleakin has reinvented itself as something of a backpackers' paradise – to the consternation of many villagers – in summer, the population more than doubles. If you're intent on joining the throng, the SYHA **hostel** (☎01599/534585; open all year) is an ugly, modern building a couple of hundred yards from the old pier; nearby *Skye Backpackers* (open all year; ☎01599/534510) is a more laid-back option, as is *Dun Caan Hostel* (open all year; ☎01599/534087). **Bike rental** is available from Skye Bikes (☎01599/534795) on the pier. On the road to Broadford there's the cheery *Crofters Kitchen*, providing homely **food** all day with a local flavour.

You can still avoid crossing the Skye Bridge by taking the ferry service (mid-March to mid-May & Sept to mid-Oct Mon–Sat 9am–6pm; mid-May to Aug Mon–Sat 9am–8.30pm, Sun 10am–6pm; 15min) from Glenelg to **KYLERHEA** (pronounced "Kileray"), a peaceful little place some four miles down the coast from Kyleakin. **Seal trips**, organized by Castle Moil Seal Cruises, also set off from the ferry pier, taking you to view the seal colony on Eilean Mhal (4 daily; ☎01599/534641; £5.50). Alternatively, you can walk half an hour up the coast to the Forestry Commission **Otter Hide**, where, if you're lucky, you may be able to spot one of these elusive creatures.

Broadford

Heading west out of Kyleakin or Kylerhea brings you eventually to the island's second-largest village, charmless **BROADFORD** (An t-Ath Leathann), whose mile-long main street curves round a wide bay. Despite its rather unlovely appearance, Broadford makes a useful base for exploring the southern half of Skye, and something of a wet-weather retreat, with the unusual **Skye Serpentarium** (Easter–Oct Mon–Sat 10am–5pm; July & Aug daily 10am–5pm; £2), full of snakes, lizards and frogs to amuse bored children. You can also go for trips in a glass-bottomed boat from the pier (check the times on ☎01471/822037). For **mountain climbing and walking** contact Skye Highs Mountain Guiding (☎01471/822116).

More pragmatically, Broadford has a **tourist office** (April, May & Sept Mon–Sat 9.30am–5.30pm; June Mon–Sat 9am–6pm; July & Aug Mon–Sat 9am–7pm, Sun 10am–5pm; Oct Mon–Sat 9.30am–5pm; ☎01471/822361), next to the Esso garage on the main road, which also contains a laundry, small shop and *bureau de change*, all open 24 hours. At the west end of the village there's a bank, a bakery, a tearoom and a post office. The SYHA **hostel** is on the west shore of Broadford Bay (☎01471/822442; Feb–Dec), or there's the much smaller, more beautiful and primitive *Fossil Bothy* hostel (☎01471/822297 or 822644, *scu_h.q._mandeville@sprite.co.uk*; open all year), a mile or so east of the bay, in Lower Breakish, off the road to Kyleakin. Two **B&Bs** which stand out are the delightful old croft-house *Lime Stone Cottage*, 4 Lime Park (☎01471/822142; ①), and the modern, comfortable *Ptarmigan* (☎01471/822744; ②), on the main road with views over the bay. Close to the *Fossil Bothy*, the pleasant *Seagull* **restaurant** (Easter–Oct eves & Sun lunch only) serves inexpensive local meat and seafood dishes, while you can **rent bikes** from the SYHA hostel or from *Fairwinds*, another good place to stay (☎01471/822270; ②; March–Oct), just past the *Broadford Hotel*.

Scalpay, Luib and The Braes

The A87 from Broadford to Portree continues to hug the coast for the next ten miles, giving out views across Loch na Cairidh to the **Isle of Scalpay**, a huge heather-backed lump that looks something like a giant scone, rising to 1298ft at the peak of Mullach na Carn. The island is part red-deer farm, part forestry plantation, and is currently owned by a merchant banker. Close by the boat slip in Ard Dorch that serves Scalpay, is *The Picture House* (☎01471/822531, *holidays@picture-house.demon.co.uk*; ①), a **B&B** with stunning views of the Inner Sound, which doubles as a photographic gallery.

As the road twists round into Loch Ainort, there's a turnoff to **Luib Folk Museum** (daily 9am–6pm; £1), a restored **blackhouse**, with a coffee shop next door. Built low against the wind, the house's thick walls are made up of an inner and outer layer of loose stone on either side of a central core of earth, a traditional type of construction which attracted the soubriquet "blackhouse" (*tigh dubh*) around 1850, when buildings with single-thickness walls, known as "white houses" (*tigh geal*), were introduced from the mainland. The Luib museum is run by local museum magnate and restorer, Peter MacAskill, who's also responsible for two other museums in restored blackhouses on the island.

From the head of Loch Ainort, the main road takes a steep short cut across a pass to Loch Sligachan, while a prettier, minor road meanders round the coast – either way, you'll reach **SCONSER**, departure point for the car ferry to Raasay (see below), and home to a nine-hole **golf course**, with superb views. There's a good **B&B** here by the shore in a crofthouse, *Loch Aluinn* (March–Oct; ☎01478/650288; ②) or *The Old Schoolhouse* (☎01478/650313; March–Dec; ①).

On the opposite side of Loch Sligachan are the crofting communities of **The Braes**, whose inhabitants staged a successful rent strike in 1881 against their landlords, the MacDonalds. After eviction summonses were burnt by the crofters, a detachment of fifty Glasgow policemen were drafted in and took part in a "battle" which aroused a great deal of publicity for the crofters' cause (for more on which, see p.375).

Isle of Raasay

Though it takes only fifteen minutes to reach from Skye, the lovely island of **Raasay**, a nature conservancy area with great walks across its bleak and barren hills, remains well off the tourist trail. For much of its history, Raasay was the property of a branch of the Jacobite MacLeods of Lewis, and the island sent 100 men and 26 pipers to Culloden, as a consequence of which it was practically destroyed by government troops in the aftermath of the 1745 uprising. Bonnie Prince Charlie spent a miserable night in a "mean low hut" on Raasay during his flight and swore to replace the burnt turf cottages with proper stone houses (he never did). Not long after the MacLeods were forced to sell up in 1843, the Clearances started in earnest, a period of the island's history immortalized in verse by Raasay poet, Sorley MacLean (Somhairle MacGill Eathain). In 1921, seven ex-servicemen and their families from the neighbouring isle of Rona illegally squatted crofts on Raasay, and were imprisoned, causing a public outcry. As a result both islands were bought by the government the following year. Rona, ancestral home of the family of Billy Graham, the American evangelist, is now uninhabited, and Raasay's population stands at around 160, most of them members of the Free Presbyterian Church (see p.389). Strict observance of the Sabbath – no work or play on Sundays – is the most obvious manifestation for visitors, who should respect the islanders' feelings.

The ferry docks at the southern tip of the island, an easy fifteen-minute walk from **INVERARISH**, a tiny village set within thick woods on the island's southwest coast. If your time is limited there are several walks in these woods: you can follow the miners' trail which traces the route of the railway constructed to carry iron-ore to the jetty, built by German POWs in 1914, most of whom died of influenza in 1918. The grand Georgian mansion of **Raasay House** (now an outdoor centre), was built by the MacLeods in the late 1740s, to be all but ruined by government troops a few years later. The grounds slope down to a tiny old **harbour**, overlooked by two weathered stone mermaids stuck on top of the remains of a battery armed in the Napoleonic era with several cannons. The house's stable clock stopped on the day in 1914 when 36 men of Raasay went to war – only 14 returned; also in the grounds, there are Pictish symbol stones and the charming ruined thirteenth-century Chapel of St Moluag.

The interior of Raasay is starkly barren, a rugged and rocky terrain of sandstone in the south and gneiss in the north, with the most obvious feature being the curiously truncated basalt cap on top of **Dun Caan** (1456ft), where Boswell "danced a Highland dance" on his visit to the island with Dr Johnson in 1773 – you may feel like doing the same if you're rewarded with a clear view over to the Cuillin and the Outer Hebrides. The trail to the top of the peak is fairly easy to follow, a splendid five-mile trek up through the forest and along the burn behind Inverarish. The quickest return is made down the northwest slope of Dun Caan, but – by going a couple of miles further – you can get back to the ferry along the path by the southeast shore, passing the abandoned crofters' village of Hallaig, whose steep incline led mothers to tether their children to stakes to prevent them rolling onto the shore.

If you want to explore the north of the island you really need transport and a fine day to appreciate the views across to the Skye Cuillin, Portree and the Trotternish peninsula. Where the road dips to the east coast the stark remains of **Brochel Castle** stand overlooking the shore. The last two miles of the road to Arnish is known as **Calum's Road**: in the 1960s the council refused to extend the road to the village so Calum MacLeod decided to build it himself; it took him ten years and by the time he'd finished he and his wife were the only people left in the village. You can walk on a boggy path to the north end and onto **Eilean Tigh** at low tide or there's a shorter walk onto **Eilean Fladday** which is also tidal. Raasay is rich in flora and fauna and it's at the north end that you're more likely to see a golden eagle, snipe, orchids and perhaps the unique Raasay vole. Rather than walking, you could always book a guided tour with Heavy Horses Tours (☎01478/660233; Easter–Oct)

Practicalities

The CalMac **car ferry** departs for Raasay from Sconser (Mon–Sat 9–10 daily; 15min). Many visitors go for the day, since there's plenty to do within walking distance of the pier – if you do take a car, be warned there's no petrol on the island. Comfortable **accommodation** in tastefully Bohemian rooms is available at the *Raasay Outdoor Centre* (☎01478/660266, *raasay.house@virgin.net*; ①; March to mid-Oct), where Boswell and Johnson stayed; it also has a café, open to all. You can **camp** in the grounds and, for a daily cost of around £25, join in the centre's activity programme: anything from sailing, windsurfing and canoeing, to climbing and hill walking. Close by is the likeably old-fashioned *Isle of Raasay Hotel* (☎01478/660222; ③), which serves delicious traditional Scottish food and where the view of the Cuillin surpasses any other; in the village is a pleasant Victorian guest house, *Churchton House* (☎01478/660260; ①). A rough track cuts up the steep hillside from the village to Raasay's isolated but beautifully placed SYHA **hostel** (☎01478/660240; mid-May to Sept).

The Cuillin and the Red Hills

For many people the **Cuillin**, whose sharp snowcapped peaks rise mirage-like from the flatness of the surrounding terrain, are Skye's *raison d'être*. When the clouds finally disperse, they are the dominating feature of the island, visible from every other peninsula on Skye. There are basically three approaches to the Cuillin: from the south, by foot or by boat from Elgol; from the *Sligachan Hotel* to the north; or from Glen Brittle to the west of the mountains. Glen Sligachan is one of the most popular routes, dividing as it does the granite of the round-topped **Red Hills** (sometimes known as the Red Cuillin) to the east from the dark, coarse-grained jagged-edged gabbro of the real Cuillin (also known as the Black Cuillin), to the west. With some twenty Munros between them, these are mountains to be taken seriously, and many routes through the Cuillin are for experienced climbers only (for more on safety, see p.473).

Elgol and Loch Coruisk

The road to **ELGOL** (Ealaghol), fourteen miles southwest of Broadford at the tip of the Strathaird peninsula, is one of the most dramatic on the island, leading right into the heart of the Red Hills and then down a precipitous slope, with a stunning view from the top down to Elgol pier. On the way you pass the ruins of a pre-Reformation church and graveyard at Kilchrist where there are also traces of marble quarries which flourished for a while, employing Belgian experts and running the marble on a small railway to Broadford pier. Further down the road at Torrin you'll see the modern quarry with its white gleaming gash in the hillside; the brilliance of the stone has been compared favourably with Carrara but it is too hard to work and mostly graces local drives as chippings. In summer there's a busy stall at Elgol pier, serving burgers and seafood because the chief reason for visiting Elgol is, weather permitting, to take a boat across Loch Scavaig (March–Sept 2–4 daily), past a seal colony, to a jetty near the entrance of **Loch Coruisk** (*coire uish*, "cauldron of water"). An isolated, glacial loch, this needle-like shaft of water, nearly two miles long but only a couple of hundred yards wide, lies in the shadow of the highest peaks of the Black Cuillin, a wonderfully overpowering landscape.

The journey by sea takes 45 minutes and passengers are dropped to spend about one and a half hours ashore; for booking (essential) and details of sailing times, ring the *Bella Jane* (☎0800/7313089). Walkers use the boat on a one-way trip simply to get to Loch Coruisk, from where there are numerous possibilities for hiking amidst the Red Hills, the most popular (and gentle) of which is the eight-mile trek north over the pass into **Glen Sligachan**. Alternatively, you could walk round the coast to the sandy bay of **Camasunary**, over two miles to the east – a difficult walk that involves tricky river crossing and negotiating "The Bad Step", an overhanging rock with a 30ft drop to the sea – and either head north to Glen Sligachan, continue south three miles along the coast to Elgol, or continue east to the Am Mam shoulder, for a stunning view of mountains and the islands of Soay, Rùm and Canna. From Am Mam, the path leads down to the Elgol road, joining it at Kilmarie.

The only public transport is the **postbus** from Broadford (Mon–Fri 2 daily, Sat once), which takes two hours to reach Elgol in the morning (check with the tourist office in Broadford about connections). Rather than stay in Elgol, head for *Rowan Cottage* (☎01471/866287; ①; April–Nov), a lovely **B&B** a mile or so east in Glasnakille, or the larger, more luxurious *Strathaird House* (☎01471/866269, *jkubale@compuserve.com*; ③; April–Sept) just beyond Kilmarie, three miles up the road to Broadford. By far the most popular place to stay, though, is the **campsite** (April–Oct) by the *Sligachan Hotel* (☎01478/650204; ②) on the A87, at the northern end of Glen Sligachan. The hotel's huge *Seamus Bar* serves food for weary walkers until 10pm, and quenches their thirst with the full range of real ales produced by Skye's very own micro-brewery in Uig.

Glen Brittle

Six miles along the A863 to Dunvegan from the *Sligachan Hotel*, a turning signed Carbost and Portnalong quickly leads to the entrance to stony **Glen Brittle**, edging the most spectacular peaks of the Cuillin; at the end of the glen, idyllically situated by the sea is the village of **GLENBRITTLE**. Climbers and serious walkers tend to congregate at the **SYHA hostel** (☎01478/640278; mid-March to Sept) or the fairly basic **campsite** (☎01478/640404; April–Oct), a mile or so further south behind the wide sandy beach at the foot of the glen. During the summer, two buses a day (Mon–Fri; also Sat in July & Aug) from Portree will drop you at the top of the glen, but you'll have to walk the last seven miles; both the youth hostel and the campsite have grocery stores, the only ones for miles.

From the valley a score of difficult and strenuous trails lead east into the **Black Cuillin**, a rough semicircle of peaks rising to about 3000ft, which surround Loch Coruisk. One of the easiest walks is the five-mile round trip from the campsite up **Coire Lagan**, to a crystal-cold lochan squeezed in among the sternest of rockfaces. Above the lochan is Skye's highest peak, **Sgurr Alasdair** (3258ft), one of the more difficult Munros, while Sgurr na Banachdich (3166ft) is considered the most easily accessible Munro in the Cuillin (for the usual walking safety precautions, see p.473). The Mountain Rescue Service has produced a book of walks for those who are not climbers, available locally.

Minginish

If the Cuillin have disappeared into the mist for the day, you could while away an afternoon exploring the nearby **Minginish** peninsula, to the north of Glen Brittle. One wet-weather activity is to visit the **Talisker whisky distillery** (April–Oct Mon–Fri 9am–4.30pm; July & Aug also Sat; Nov–March Mon–Fri 2–4.30pm; by appointment; ☎01478/640314), which produces a very smoky, peaty single malt. Talisker is the island's only distillery, situated on the shores of Loch Harport at **CARBOST** (and not, confusingly, at the village of Talisker itself, which lies on the west coast of Minginish). Hostellers might like to know that there are three year-round **bunkhouses** in Carbost and **PORTNALONG**: the *Waterfront Bunkhouse* (☎01478/640205) is next to the *Old Inn* in Carbost; the *Croft Bunkhouse and Bothies* (☎01478/640254), where you can also **camp**, is signposted just before you get to Portnalong; while the *Skyewalker Independent Hostel* (☎01478/640250, *skyewalker@easynet.co.uk*) is a converted school building beyond Portnalong, en route to Fiskavaig – it also has a campsite and an excellent café which welcomes passers-by.

Dunvegan, Duirinish and Waternish

After the Portnalong and Glen Brittle turning, the A863 slips across bare rounded hills to skirt the bony sea cliffs and stacks of the west coast twenty miles or so north to **DUNVEGAN** (Dùn Bheagain). It's an unimpressive place, strung out along the east shore of the sea loch of the same name, though it does make quite a good base for exploring two interesting peninsulas: Duirinish and Waternish.

The main tourist trap in the village is **Dunvegan Castle** (mid-March to Oct daily 10am–5.30pm; £5.20; gardens only £3.70) which sprawls on top of a rocky outcrop, sandwiched between the sea and several acres of beautifully maintained gardens. It's been the seat of the Clan MacLeod since the thirteenth century, but the present greying, rectangular fortress with its uniform battlements and dummy pepperpots dates from the 1840s. Inside, you don't get a lot of castle for your money and the contents are far from stunning, but there are three famous items: **Rory Mor's Horn**, a drinking vessel made from the horn of a mad bull which each new chief still has to drain at one draught "without setting down or falling down"; the **Dunvegan Cup**, made of bog oak covered in medieval silver filigree believed to have been given to Rory Mor by the O'Neils of Ulster in return for his help against England; and, most intriguing of all, the battered remnants of the **Fairy Flag** in the drawing room. This yellow silken flag from the Middle East may have been the battle standard of the Norwegian king, Harald Hardrada, who had been the commander of the imperial guard in Constantinople. Hardrada died trying to seize the English throne at the Battle of Stamford Bridge in 1066, after which his flag was allegedly carried back to Skye by his Gaelic boatmen. More fancifully, MacLeod family tradition asserts that the flag was the gift of the fairies, blessed with the power to protect the clan in times of danger – as late as World War II MacLeod pilots carried pictures of it for luck. Among the Jacobite mementoes are a lock of hair from the head of Bonnie Prince Charlie (whom the MacLeods, in fact, fought against) and Flora MacDonald's corsets. Elsewhere there's a "virtual" consumptive in the dungeon and an interesting display on the remote archipelago of St Kilda (see p.393), long the fiefdom of the MacLeods.

From the jetty outside the castle there are regular seal-spotting **boat trips** out along Loch Dunvegan, as well as longer and less frequent sea cruises to the small islands of Mingay, Isay and Clett, which were cleared of the last crofters in 1860. Outside in the car park you can buy sandwiches from a kiosk or have a more substantial snack in the castle restaurant. The estate also has a number of **holiday cottages** (☎01470/521206). On a wet day you might scrape up some enthusiasm for Dunvegan's newest tourist attraction, the **Giant Angus MacAskill Museum** (daily 10am–6pm; £1), the weakest of Peter MacAskill's three museums on Skye, housed in a restored thatched smithy. The museum's eponymous hero was, in fact, born in the Outer Hebrides in 1825 and emigrated to Nova Scotia when he was just six years old. Before his untimely death of a fever at the age of 38, he toured with the midget, Tom Thumb, who, it is said, used to dance on his outstretched hand.

Duirinish and Glen Dale

The hammerhead **Duirinish peninsula** lies to the west of Dunvegan, much of it inaccessible to all except walkers prepared to scale or skirt the area's twin flat-topped basalt peaks: Healabhal Bheag (1600ft) and Healabhal Mhor (1538ft). The mountains are better known as **MacLeod's Tables**, for legend has that the MacLeod chief held an open-air royal feast on the lower of the two for James V. The main areas of habitation lie to the north, along the western shores of Loch Dunvegan, and in the broad green sweep of **Glen Dale**, attractively dotted with white farmhouses and dubbed "Little England" by the locals, due to its high percentage of "white settlers", English incomers searching for a better life. Glen Dale's current predicament is doubly ironic given its history, for it was here in 1882 that local crofters, following the example of their brethren in The Braes (see p.371), staged a rent strike against their landlords, the MacLeods. Five locals – who became known as the "Glen Dale Martyrs" – were given two-month prison sentences, and eventually, in 1904, the crofters became the first owner-occupiers in the Highlands.

All this, and a great deal more about nineteenth-century crofting, is told through fascinating contemporary news cuttings at **Colbost Croft Museum** (Easter–Oct daily 10am–6.30pm; £1), the oldest of Peter MacAskill's three Skye museums, situated in a restored blackhouse, four miles up the road from Dunvegan. A guide is usually on hand to answer questions, the peat fire smokes all day, and there's a restored illegal whisky still round the back. A little further up the shores of the loch is **Borreraig Park** (daily 9am–7pm; £1.50), an eccentric mix of a huge open-air museum of traditional horse-drawn farm machinery and a retail outlet for Skye-made crafts.

At **BORRERAIG** itself, where there was once a famous piping college, is the **MacCrimmon Piping Heritage Centre** (Easter to late May Tues–Sun 11am–5.30pm; late May to early Oct daily 11am–5.30pm; £1.50), on the ancestral holdings of the MacCrimmons, hereditary pipers to the MacLeod chiefs for three centuries, until they were sent packing in the 1770s. The plaintive sounds of the *piobaireachd* of the MacCrimmons, the founding family of Scottish piping, fill this illuminating museum – to hear the real thing, go to the annual recital held in Dunvegan Castle early in August.

In the village of **GLENDALE**, at Holmisdale House, an English settler has gathered together mountains of childhood toys and games from the last hundred years, and opened a **Toy Museum** (Mon–Sat 10am–6pm; £2), whose hands-on approach manages to appeal to all ages; it's open on Sundays, too, in wet weather. Beyond Glendale, a bumpy road leads to **RAMASAIG**, and beyond for another five miles to the deserted village of Lorgill where on August 4, 1830, life came to an end when every crofter was ordered to board the *Midlothian* in Loch Snizort to go to Nova Scotia or go to prison (those over the age of seventy were sent to the poorhouse). As a result of such Clearances, the west coast of Duirinish is mostly uninhabited now. For walkers, though, it's a great area to explore, with blustery but easy footpaths leading to the dramatically sited lighthouse on **Neist Point**, Skye's most westerly spot, which features some fearsome sea cliffs, and wonderful views across the sea to the Western Isles – you can even stay at the lighthouse, in one of the three **self-catering** cottages (☎01470/511200; 6–12 people; £495 per week). Alternatively, head north for the sheer 1000ft cliffs of **Biod an Athair** near Dunvegan Head, though there's no path, and it's a bit of a slog.

Waternish

Waternish is a thin and little-visited peninsula to the north of Dunvegan. It's not as spectacular as either Duirinish or Trotternish, but it provides equally great views over to the Western Isles on a good day. Before you can explore the peninsula, however, you have to cross the **Fairy Bridge**, at the junction of the B886, where legend has it that a MacLeod chief, foolishly married to a fairy, was forced to say farewell when she decided to go home to her mother. More likely its significance lies in the fact that it's at the meeting of three roads and was the scene of religious assemblies of the Free Church and, later, of rebellious crofters led by John MacPherson, one of the "Glendale Martyrs".

Waternish's prettiest village is **STEIN**, on the west coast overlooking Loch Bay. Its row of whitewashed cottages was built in 1787 by the British Fisheries Society, but never saw success and by 1837 the village was more or less abandoned. Today, however, it seems to be coming back to life, particularly the pub, the sixteenth-century *Stein Inn*, which is well worth a visit.

At the end of the road is **Trumpan Church**, a medieval ruin on a cliff top looking out to the Western Isles. This peaceful site was the scene of one of the bloodiest episodes in Skye history, when, in 1578, the MacDonalds of Uist set fire to the church, while numerous MacLeods were attending a service inside. Everyone perished except one young girl who escaped by squeezing through a window, severing one of her breasts in the process. She raised the alarm, and the rest of the MacLeods quickly rallied and, bearing their famous Fairy Flag (see p.375), attacked the MacDonalds as they were launching their galleys. Every MacDonald was slaughtered and their bodies were thrown in a nearby dyke. In the churchyard, along with two medieval graveslabs, you can also see the **Trial Stone**, a four-foot-high pillar with a hole drilled in it. Anyone accused of a crime was blindfolded and had to attempt to put their finger in it; success meant innocence, failure death.

Practicalities

Dunvegan is by no means the most picturesque place on Skye, but it's a useful alternative base to Portree. It has a new **tourist office** (Mon–Sat 9am–5.30pm; ☎01470/521581) and boasts several excellent **hotels** and **B&Bs** dotted along the main road, such as the converted traditional croft *Roskhill House* (☎01470/521317, *stay@roskhill.demon.co.uk*; ③). Other possibilities include the beautifully situated *Silverdale* (☎01470/521251; ①) just before you get to Colbost, or the luxurious *Harlosh House* (☎01470/521367; ⑥; April–Oct), four miles south of Dunvegan, plus *Mo Dhachaidh* (☎01470/511210; ①; Easter–Oct) in Glendale itself. There's a basic lochside **campsite** (April–Sept) a short distance west along the head of Loch Dunvegan.

The culinary mecca in the area is the expensive *Three Chimneys* **restaurant** (☎01470/511258; Mon–Sat), located beside Colbost Folk Museum, which serves sublime meals and is renowned for its marmalade pudding. More reasonably-priced meals can be had at *An Strupag* in Lephin (☎01470/511204), deeper into Glen Dale. There are welcoming fires and good food at the sixteenth-century *Stein Inn* (☎01470/592362, *angus.teresa@steininn.demon.co.uk*; ②), in Stein, and outstanding seafood at the *Lochbay Seafood Restaurant* (☎01470/592235; closed Sat & Sun). Eating in Dunvegan is a little problematical, apart from obvious hotel choices, of which *Atholl House Hotel* (☎01470/521219) is probably the best for dinner. However, there is a snug **café** attached to *Dunvegan Bakery* (closed Sat afternoon & Sun) where you can also pick up sandwich components and home-made carrot cake.

Portree

Although referred to by the locals as "the village", **PORTREE** is the only real town on Skye. It's also one of the most attractive fishing ports in northwest Scotland, its deep cliff-edged harbour filled with fishing boats and circled by multicoloured restaurants and guest houses. Originally known as *Kiltragleann* (the church at the foot of the glen), it takes its current name – some say – from *Portrigh* (port of the king), after the state visit James V made in 1540 to assert his authority over the chieftains of Skye.

Information and accommodation

Hours vary enormously at Portree's **tourist office**, just off Bridge Street, so the ones here are just a guideline (April–Oct Mon–Sat 9am–5.30pm, Sun 11am–4pm; Nov–March closed Sun; ☎01478/612137). The office will, for a small fee, book **accommodation** for you – especially useful at the height of the season, when things can get very busy. Accommodation prices tend to be higher in Portree than elsewhere on the island, especially in the town itself, though B&Bs on the outskirts are usually cheaper. Of Portree's year-round **hostels**, the smartest is the *Portree Independent Hostel* (☎01478/613737, *portreeindhostel@hotmail.co.uk*) housed in the Old Post Office on the Green, though the *Portree Backpackers Hostel* (☎01478/613332), ten minutes' walk up the Dunvegan road, enjoys a more secluded location (and will pick you up from town if you ring ahead). Torvaig **campsite** (☎01478/612209; April–Oct) lies a mile and a half north of town off the A855 Staffin road.

Probably the best **hotel** is the comfortable *Cuillin Hills* (☎01478/612003; *office@cuillinhills.demon.co.uk*; ⑤), ten minutes' walk out of town along the northern shore of the bay; if the rooms are too pricey, try the reasonably-priced bar snacks with a splendid view over the harbour or afternoon tea after a walk round the nearby headland. *Viewfield House* (☎01478/612217; ⑤) on the southern outskirts of town, in the possession of the MacDonalds for over 200 years, is worth it for the Victorian atmosphere, stuffed polecats and antiques. The *Bosville Hotel* (☎01478/612846, *bosville@macleodhotels.co.uk*; ④) on Bosville Terrace commands a good view of the harbour, and has a gourmet seafood restaurant. In the lower price range, try *Givendale Guest House* (☎01478/612183; April–Oct; ①), ten minutes' walk up the hill from the town centre on Heron Place, with good views and a warm welcome for walkers and cyclists, or *Conusg*, a B&B in a quiet spot by the *Cuillin Hills Hotel*, originally built for the coachman in the

1880s (☎01478/612426; Easter–Sept; ③). Further still out of Portree, five miles north-west in Skeabost, is the late-Victorian *Skeabost House Hotel* (☎01470/532202, *skeabost@sol.co.uk*; March–Oct; ⑤), which offers golf, fishing and landscaped gardens.

The Town

It's worth strolling down to the **harbour**, whose pier was built by Thomas Telford in the early nineteenth century. Fishing boats still land a modest catch, some of which is sold through Anchor Seafoods (Tues–Fri only) at the end of the pier. The harbour is overlooked by **The Lump**, a steep and stumpy peninsula with a flagpole on it that was once the site of public hangings on the island, attracting crowds of up to 5000; it also sports a folly built by the celebrated Dr Ban, a visionary who wanted to make Portree into a second Oban. Up above the harbour is the spick-and-span town centre, spreading out from **Somerled Square**, built in the late eighteenth century as the island's administrative and commercial centre, and now housing the bus station and car park. The **Royal Hotel** on Bank Street occupies the site of the *McNab's Inn* where Bonnie Prince Charlie took leave of Flora MacDonald (see p.380), and where, 27 years later, Boswell and Johnson had "a very good dinner, porter, port and punch".

A mile or so out of town on the Sligachan road is one of Skye's most successful tourist attractions, the **Aros Centre** (daily 9am–6pm; open later in summer). Here, you can enjoy the Aros Experience (£2.50), a dramatic and unsentimental presentation of episodes of the island's history, with stunning life-size figures and special effects, ending with an audio-visual show. The centre also contains a modern exhibition space, a licensed coffee bar and restaurant, and there's a special play area for small kids. If it's fine, there are waymarked forest walks and a Gaelic alphabet trail starting just outside.

For a view of the contemporary visual art scene, it's well worth seeking out **An Tuireann Arts Centre**, housed in a converted fever hospital on the Struan road (Mon–Sat 10am–6pm; free), which puts on exhibitions, stages concerts, and has an excellent small café where even the counter is a work of art, with an imaginative range of food on offer (Easter–Oct also Wed–Sat eves).

Eating, drinking and nightlife

The best **food** in town is on Bosville Terrace, but it's pricey: the *Bosville Hotel*'s *Chandlery* restaurant serves excellent meals, with its sister *Bosville* restaurant being much cheaper; *Harbour View* has a seafood **restaurant** with candlelit ambience, but better is *Ben Tianavaig*, an excellent veggie and seafood place (evenings only; closed Mon; ☎01478/612152). For good **fish and chips** (including herring in oatmeal), pop into the excellent chippie, next door to the *Lower Deck Seafood Restaurant* on the harbour. For a cuppa and a cake, there's the *Granary* bakery's **tea shop** on Somerled Square. The *Café*, an ice-cream parlour on Wentworth Street, serves real cappuccino and espresso, plus a selection of cakes and snacks. As for **pubs**, the bar of the *Pier Hotel* on the quayside is the fishermen's drinking hole, while the bar of the *Royal Hotel* is also popular with locals.

The aforementioned Aros Centre has a striking new **theatre** which shows films and hosts Gaelic **concerts** (for more details phone ☎01471/613649); concerts and events also go on at An Tuireann (see above), and it's also worth checking out what's on at the Portree Community Centre (☎01478/613736), which hosts ceilidhs and so forth. For **bike rental**, go to Island Cycles (closed Sun; ☎01478/613121) below the Green; for **horse riding** head for Skye Riding Centre (closed Sun; ☎01470/532233), four miles along the Uig road at Borve, or the Portree Riding and Trekking Centre off the B885 to Struan, signposted Peiness (open all year; ☎01478/612945). Day or half-day **boat trips** leave the pier for daily excursions to Raasay and Rona (☎01478/613718); **diving** can be organized through Hebridean Diving Services in Lochbay, towards Dunvegan

(☎01478/592219). You can collect your **email** at Gael Net Ltd on the Dunvegan road (☎01478/613300; closed Sun).

Trotternish

Protruding twenty miles north from Portree, the **Trotternish** peninsula boasts some of the island's most bizarre scenery, particularly on the east coast, where volcanic basalt has pressed down on the softer sandstone and limestone underneath, causing massive landslides. These, in turn, have created sheer cliffs, peppered with outcrops of hard, wizened basalt, which run the full length of the peninsula. These pinnacles and pillars are at their most eccentric in the Quiraing, above Staffin Bay, on the east coast. Trotternish is best explored with your own transport, but an occasional bus service (Mon–Sat 2–4 daily) along the road encircling the peninsula gives access to almost all the coast.

The east coast

The first geological eccentricity on the **Trotternish** peninsula, six miles north of Portree along the A855, is the **Old Man of Storr**, a distinctive column of rock, shaped like a willow leaf, which, along with its neighbours, is part of a massive landslip. Huge blocks of stone still occasionally break off the cliff face of the Storr (2358ft) above and slide downhill. At 165ft, the Old Man is a real challenge for climbers; less difficult is the half-hour trek up the new footpath to the foot of the column from the woods beside the car park.

Five miles further north, there's another turn-off to the **Lealt Falls**, at the head of a gorge which spends most of its day in shadow (and is home to a fiendish collection of midges). Walking all the way down to the falls is fairly pointless, but the views across to Wester Ross from the first stage of the path are spectacular (weather permitting). The coast here is worth exploring, however, especially the track leading to **Rubha nam Brathairean** (Brothers' Point), where the Glasgow provision boat used to put in, and where fossil hunters can also follow the road that turns off at Dunans down to the end and try their luck on the beach at low tide.

Another car park a few miles up the road gives access to **Kilt Rock**, whose tube-like, basaltic columns rise precipitously from the sea, set amongst sea cliffs dotted with nests for fulmars and kittiwakes. There is a spectacular waterfall which drops 300ft to the sea and a small loch by the car park alive with wildlife. Close by, near the turn off to Elishader, is the slate-roofed **Staffin Museum** (sporadic opening hours; £1.25), which contains fossil finds from the area, and a dinosaur bone discovered here in 1994.

Over the brow of the next hill, **Staffin Bay**, where several fossilized dinosaur foot-prints were discovered in 1996, is spread out before you, dotted with whitewashed and "spotty" houses; **STAFFIN** itself is a lively, largely Gaelic-speaking community where crofts have been handed down the generations. A single-track road cuts across the peninsula from the north end of the bay, allowing access to the **Quiraing**, a spectacular forest of mighty pinnacles and savage rock formations. There are two car parks: from the first, beside a cemetery, it's a steep half-hour climb to the rocks; from the second on the saddle it's a longer but more gentle traverse. Once you're in the midst of the rocks, you should be able to make out the Prison, to your right, and the 120ft Needle, to your left; the Table, a great sunken platform where locals used to play shinty, lies above and beyond the Needle, another fifteen-minute scramble up the rocks; legend also maintains that a local warrior named Fraing hid his cattle there from the invading Norsemen.

The **accommodation** on the east coast is among the best on Skye, with most places enjoying fantastic views out over the sea. Just beyond the Lealt Falls there's the very welcoming and comfortable *Glenview Inn* (☎01470/562248; March–Oct; ③), with an

BONNIE PRINCE CHARLIE

Prince Charles Edward Stewart – better known as **Bonnie Prince Charlie** or "The Young Pretender" – was born in Rome in 1720, where his father, "The Old Pretender", claimant to the British throne, was living in exile. At the age of 25, having little military experience, no knowledge of Gaelic, an imperfect grasp of English and a strong attachment to the Catholic faith, the prince set out for Scotland on a French ship, disguised as a seminarist from the Scots College in Paris. He arrived on the Outer Hebridean island of Eriskay on July 23, 1745, and was immediately implored to return to France by the clan chiefs, who were singularly unimpressed by his lack of army. Charles was unmoved and went on to raise the royal standard at Glenfinnan, gather together a Highland army, win the battle of Prestonpans, march on London and reach Derby before finally (and foolishly) agreeing to retreat. Back in Scotland, he won one last victory at Falkirk, before the final disaster at Culloden in April 1746.

The prince spent the following five months in hiding, with a price of £30,000 on his head, and literally thousands of government troops searching for him. He certainly endured his fair share of cold and hunger whilst on the run, but the real price was paid by the Highlanders themselves, who risked their lives (and often paid for it with them) by aiding and abetting the prince. The most famous of these was, of course, 23-year-old **Flora MacDonald**, whom Charles met on South Uist in June 1746. Flora was persuaded – either by his beauty or her relatives, depending on which account you believe – to convey Charles "over the sea to Skye", disguised as an Irish servant girl by the name of Betty Burke. She was arrested just seven days after parting with the prince in Portree, and held in the Tower of London until July 1747. She went on to marry a local man, had seven children and in 1774 emigrated to America, where her husband was taken prisoner during the American War of Independence. Flora returned to Scotland and was reunited with her husband on his release; they re-settled in Skye and she died at the age of 68.

Charles eventually boarded a ship back to France in September 1746, but, despite his promises – "for all that has happened, Madam, I hope we shall meet in St James's yet" – never returned to Scotland, nor did he ever see Flora again. After mistreating a string of mistresses, he eventually got married at the age of 52 to the 19-year-old Princess of Stolberg, in an effort to produce a Stewart heir. They had no children, and she eventually fled from his violent drunkenness; in 1788, a none-too-"bonnie" Prince Charles died in the arms of his illegitimate daughter in Rome. Bonnie Prince Charlie became a legend in his own lifetime, but it was the Victorians who really milked the myth for all its sentimentality, conveniently overlooking the fact that the real consequence of 1745 was the virtual annihilation of the Highland way of life.

excellent adjoining restaurant, and a **campsite** (☎01470/562213; April–Sept) south of Staffin Bay. In fine weather, you can enjoy good bar snacks on the castellated terrace of the stylish *Flodigarry Country House Hotel* (☎01470/552203; ⑥), three miles up the coast from Staffin. Behind the hotel (and now part of it) is the cottage where local heroine Flora MacDonald lived, and had six of her seven children, from 1751 to 1759. If the hotel's rooms are beyond your means, try the neat and attractive *Dun Flodigarry Backpackers' Hostel* (☎01470/552212), a couple of minutes' walk away – you can ring the hostel to arrange transport or catch the local bus.

Duntulm and Kilmuir

Beyond Flodigarry, at the tip of the Trotternish peninsula, by the road to Shulista, a public footpath leads past the ruins of a cleared hamlet to the spectacular sea stacks of **Rubha Hunish**, the most northerly point on Skye. A couple of miles further on the A855 lies **DUNTULM** (Duntuilm), whose heyday as a major MacDonald power base is recalled by the shattered remains of a headland fortress abandoned by the clan in 1732 after a clumsy nurse dropped the baby son and heir from a window onto the rocks below; on these same rocks, it is said, can be seen the keel marks of Viking longships. The imposing *Duntulm Castle Hotel* (☎01470/552213; ②; March–Nov) is close by, and provides good bar meals as well as wonderful views across the Minch to the Western Isles; the hotel also has **self-catering** cottages, including three former coastguard houses (6–10 people; £590 per week).

Heading down the west shore of the Trotternish, it's two miles to the **Skye Museum of Island Life** (Easter–Oct Mon–Sat 9.30am–5.30pm; £1.75), an impressive cluster of thatched blackhouses on an exposed hill overlooking Harris. The museum, run by locals, gives a fascinating insight into a way of life that was commonplace on Skye a hundred years ago. The blackhouse, now home to the ticket office, is much as it was when it was last inhabited in 1957, while the two houses to the east contain interesting snippets of local history. Behind the museum in the cemetery up the hill are the graves of **Flora MacDonald** and her husband. Thousands turned out for her funeral in 1790, creating a funeral procession a mile long – indeed, so widespread was her fame that the original family mausoleum fell victim to souvenir hunters and had to be replaced. The Celtic cross headstone is inscribed with a simple tribute by Dr Johnson, who visited her in 1773: "Her name will be mentioned in history, if courage and fidelity be virtues, mentioned with honour".

If you want an antidote to folk history and have a liking for puns, don't miss **Macurdie's Exhibition** just off the road in **KILMUIR**. It's unattended, open most of the time, and full of spoof artefacts and pseudo-proverbs such as "it's easier to extract a Mars bar from the gullet of a seagull than to clean your shoes with a blade of grass" – the visitors' book proves people will pay an optional 50p for anything on a wet day. The land around Kilmuir used to be called the "Granary of Skye" since every inch was cultivated: even St Columba's Loch, where there are still indistinct remains of beehive cells and a chapel, was drained and the land eagerly reclaimed by crofters. **Accommodation** is available in the attractive *Kilmuir House*, previously the old manse (☎01470/542262; *phelpskilmuirhouseskye@btinternet.com*; ①), and at the warm and friendly *Whitewave Activities* B&B (☎01470/542414; ①), in Linicro; they also organize **windsurfing**, **archery** and **canoeing**, and run a café in season.

Uig

A further four miles south of Kilmuir is the ferry port of **UIG** (Uige), which curves its way round a dramatic, horseshoe-shaped bay, and is the arrival point for CalMac ferries from Tarbet (Harris) and Lochmaddy (North Uist); if you've time to spare while waiting for a ferry, pop into Uig Pottery. The **tourist office** (April–Oct Mon–Sat 8.45am–6.30pm; mid-July to mid-Sept also Sun 8.45am–2pm; ☎01470/542404) is inside the CalMac office on the pier. Most folk come to Uig to take the ferry to the Western Isles, but if you need an inexpensive **B&B** near the ferry terminal, head for *Braeholm* (☎01470/542396; March–Oct; ②), the **campsite** (☎01470/542360; March–Oct), by the shore near the dock, or the **SYHA hostel** (☎01470/542211; mid-March to Oct), high up on the south side of the village, with exhilarating views over the bay. The *Pub at the Pier* offers filling meals, and serves the local Skye beers, which are also on sale in the shop of the nearby brewery (tours by appointment Mon–Fri; ☎01470/542477). **Bike rental** is available from North Skye Bicycle Hire, **pony trekking** from the *Uig Hotel* (☎01470/542205).

The prettiest place for a fair weather stroll and picnic around Uig is the **Fairy Glen**, reached by taking the minor road up to Balnaknock. Another good walk is to the intriguing ruined castle with no door called **Caisteal Uisdein**, built by Hugh Macdonald of Sleat in the seventeenth century. Take the turning to Cuidrach and continue to the end of the road; walk through the village and then follow the posts, but you'll have to climb in through a window – in spring the castle is filled with primroses. When Hugh's clan chief found he'd been plotting against him, he walled him up in here with a piece of salt beef and an empty water jug. Just after this there's a signpost to the small *Glen Hinnisdal* **bunkhouse** (☎01470/552212).

THE SMALL ISLES

The history of the **Small Isles**, which lie to the south of Skye, is typical of the Hebrides: early Christianization, followed by a period of Norwegian rule that ended in 1266 when the islands fell into Scottish hands. Their support for the Jacobite cause resulted in hard times after the failed rebellion of 1745, but the biggest problems came with the introduction of the **potato** in the mid-eighteenth century. The consequences were as dramatic as they were unforeseen: the success of the crop and its nutritional value – when grown in conjunction with traditional cereals – eliminated famine at a stroke, prompting a population explosion. In 1750, there were just a thousand islanders, but by 1800 their numbers had almost doubled.

At first, the problem of overcrowding was camouflaged by the **kelp** boom, in which the islanders were employed, and the islands' owners made a fortune, gathering and burning local seaweed to sell for use in the manufacture of gunpowder, soap and glass. But the economic bubble burst with the end of the Napoleonic Wars and, to maintain their profit margins, the owners resorted to drastic action. The first to sell up was Alexander Maclean who sold Rùm as grazing land for **sheep**, got quotations for shipping its people to Nova Scotia, and gave them a year's notice to quit. He also cleared Muck to graze cattle, as did the MacNeills on Canna. Only on Eigg was some compassion shown: the new owner, a certain Hugh MacPherson, who bought the island from the Clanranalds in 1827, actually gave some of his tenants extended leases.

Since the Clearances each of the islands has been bought and sold several times, though only **Muck** is now privately owned by the benevolent laird, Lawrence MacEwen. **Eigg** hit the headlines in 1997, when the islanders finally managed to buy the island themselves and put an end to more than 150 years of property speculation. The other islands were bequeathed to national agencies: **Rùm**, the largest and most visited of the group, possessing a cluster of formidable volcanic peaks and the architecturally remarkable Kinloch Castle, passed to the Nature Conservancy Council (now

---

GETTING TO THE SMALL ISLES

CalMac run passenger-only ferries to the Small Isles every day except Sunday from Mallaig (☎01687/462403). Day-trips to any one of the four islands are possible only on Saturdays, but involve catching the ferry at 5am. If you take this option, you have a choice of spending around nine hours on Canna, seven hours on Rùm, five on Muck, and just three and a half on Eigg. The CalMac ferry can currently only dock at Canna; on the other three islands, you (and all the island supplies) have to be transferred to an island tender or "flit boat". There is talk of building newer and bigger piers on the other islands in the near future.

From May to September, you can also reach Rùm, Eigg and Muck seven days a week from Arisaig with **Murdo Grant** (☎01687/450224). This is a much more pleasant way to get there as the boat is licensed, takes you right up to the pier on all three islands, and, if any marine mammals are spotted en route, the boat will pause for a bit of whale-watching. Day-trips are possible to Eigg on most days, allowing four to five hours ashore, and to Rùm and Muck on a few days, allowing two to three hours ashore. With careful studying of both CalMac and Murdo Grant timetables, you should be able to organize a visit to suit you, especially as Arisaig and Mallaig are linked by railway.

Be warned, however, that boats to the Small Isles are frequently cancelled in bad weather, so be prepared to holiday for longer than you planned.

Scottish Natural Heritage) in 1957; and **Canna**, in many ways the prettiest of the isles with its high basalt cliffs, has been in the hands of the NTS since 1981.

Rùm

Like Skye, **Rùm** is dominated by its Cuillin, which, though only reaching a height of 2663ft at the summit of Askival, rises up with comparable drama straight up from the sea in the south of the island. The majority of the island's thirty or so inhabitants now live in **KINLOCH**, on the sheltered east coast, and most are employed by Scottish Natural Heritage (SNH), who run the island as a National Nature Reserve. SNH have been re-introducing native woodland to the island, and overseeing a long-term study of the vast red deer population. However, the organization's most notable achievement to date is the successful re-introduction of **white-tailed (sea) eagles**, whose wing span is even greater than that of the golden eagle. These magnificent birds of prey were last known to have bred on the island of Skye in 1916. After an absence of some seventy years, the eagles are back, and have spread from Rùm to neighbouring islands. The resident breeding population is still very small, however, and the exact location of the eyries is kept secret.

Rùm's chief formal attraction is **Kinloch Castle** (Tues & Thurs guided tours at 2pm; £3), a squat red sandstone edifice fronted by colonnades and topped by crenellations and turrets, that dominates the village of Kinloch. Completed at enormous expense in 1900 – the red sandstone was shipped in from Arran and the soil for the gardens from Ayrshire – its interior is a perfectly-preserved example of Edwardian decadence, "a living memorial of the stalking, the fishing and the sailing, the tenantry and plenty of the days before 1914". From the galleried hall, with its tiger rugs, stags' heads and giant Japanese incense burners, to the "Extra Low Fast Cushion" of the Soho snooker table in the Billiard Room, the interior is packed with knick-knacks and technical gismos accumulated by **Sir George Bullough** (1870–1939), the spendthrift son of self-made millionaire, Sir John Bullough, who bought the island as a sporting estate in 1888. As such, it was only really used for a few weeks each autumn, during the "season", yet employed an island workforce of one hundred all year round. Bullough's guests were woken at eight each morning by a piper; later on, an orchestrion, an electrically driven barrel organ (originally destined for Balmoral), crammed in under the stairs, would grind out an eccentric mixture of pre-dinner tunes: *The Ride of the Valkyries* and *Ma Blushin' Rosie* among others (a demo is included in the tour). The ballroom has a sprung floor, the library features a gruesome photographic collection from the Bulloughs' world tours, but the *pièce de résistance* has to be Bullough's **Edwardian bathrooms**, whose baths have hooded walnut shower cabinets, fitted with two taps and four dials, which allow the bather to fire high-pressure water at their body from every angle.

For those with limited time or energy, there are two gentle waymarked **heritage trails**, both of which start from Kinloch, and take around two hours to complete. For longer walks, you must fill in route cards and pop them into the White House (Mon–Fri 9am–12.30pm), where the reserve manager can give useful advice. The island's best beach is at **KILMORY**, to the north (5hr return), though this part of the island is only open to the public on the weekend as it's given over to the study of red deer; it's also closed completely in June, during calving, and October, during rutting. When the island's human head count peaked at 450 in 1791, the hamlet of **HARRIS** on the southwest coast (6hr return), housed a large crofting community – all that remains now are several ruined blackhouses and the extravagant **Bullough Mausoleum**, built by Sir George to house the remains of his father in the style of a Greek Doric temple, overlooking the sea. This is, in fact, the second one to be constructed here; the first was lined with Italian marble mosaics, but when a friend remarked that it looked like a public lavatory, Bullough had it dynamited and the current Neoclassical one erected.

Practicalities

Until Rùm passed into the hands of the SNH, it was known as the "Forbidden Isle" because of its exclusive use as a sporting estate for the rich – nowadays, visitors are made very welcome by the SNH staff. If you plan to stay the night, you do need to book in advance, as **accommodation** is fairly limited. Kinloch Castle was a luxury hotel until the early 1990s, and still lets a few of its four-poster rooms – for which you pay a bit extra – but it's basically run now as an independent **hostel** (☎01687/462037), with dormitories in the old servants' quarters. SNH also run two simple mountain **bothies** (three nights maximum stay), in Dibidil and Guirdil, and basic **camping** on the foreshore near the jetty. You need to book ahead for both by contacting the reserve manager at the *White House* (☎01687/462026).

Wherever you're staying, you can either do self-catering – hostellers can use the hostel kitchen – or eat the unpretentious **food** offered in the hostel's licensed bistro, which serves full breakfasts, offers packed lunches, and charges just over £10 a head for a three-course evening meal. There is also a small shop, off-licence and post office in Kilmory. Finally, bear in mind that Rùm is the wettest of the Small Isles, and is known for having some of the worst **midges** (see p.46) in Scotland – come prepared for both.

Eigg

Eigg is without doubt the most easily distinguishable of the Small Isles from a distance, since the island is mostly made up of a basalt plateau 1000ft above sea level, and a great stump of columnar pitchstone lava, known as An Sgurr, rising out of the plateau another 290ft. It's also by far the most vibrant, populous and welcoming of the Small Isles, with a real strong sense of community. This has been given an enormous boost by the recent island buy-out by the sixty-odd islanders, which ended Eigg's unhappy history of private ownership, most notoriously with the Olympic bobsleigher and gelatine heir Keith Schellenberg.

Visitors arrive in the southeast corner of the island – which measures just five miles by three – at **GALMISDALE**, where **An Laimhrig** (The Anchorage), the island's new community centre stands, housing a shop, post office, tearoom and information centre. The island minibus meets incoming ferries, and will take you to wherever you need to go on the island. Many visitors head off to **CLEADALE**, the main crofting settlement in the north of the island, where the beach, known as the "**Singing Sands**", is comprised of quartz, which squeaks underfoot when dry (hence the name). With the island's great landmark, **An Sgurr** (1292ft), watching over you wherever you go, many folk feel duty bound to climb it, and enjoy the wonderful views over to Muck and Rùm. The easiest approach is to take the path that skirts the summit to the north, and ascend from the saddle to the west; the return trip takes between three and four hours. A large colony of **Manx shearwater** nests in burrows around the summit; to view the birds, you need to be there around dawn or dusk.

The nicest place **to stay** on Eigg is *Kildonan House* (☎01687/482446; full board ③), a beautiful eighteenth-century wood-panelled house where the cooking is superb. Other B&Bs are *Lageorna* (☎01687/482405; full board ④), a crofthouse that also has a couple of self-catering cottages (6 people; £350 per week). As you'll probably notice, as you walk around the island, Eigg has no mains electricity so each house has its own diesel generator.

Muck

Smallest and most southerly of the Small Isles, **Muck** is low-lying, mostly treeless and extremely fertile, and as such shares more characteristics with the likes of Coll and Tiree than its nearest neighbours. Its name derives from *muc*, the Gaelic for "pig" – or, as some would have it, *muc mara*, "sea pig" or porpoise, which abound in the surrounding water – and has long caused much embarrassment to generations of lairds who preferred to call it the "Isle of Monk", because it had briefly belonged to the medieval church.

PORT MÓR, the village on the southeast corner of the island, is where visitors arrive. The prominent memorial in the local graveyard commemorates two islanders and a visiting student who were drowned shooting shags near Eilean nan Each (Horse Island). A road, just over a mile in length, connects Port Mór with the island's main farm, **GALLANACH**, which overlooks the rocky seal-strewn skerries on the north side of the island. The nicest sandy beach is Camas na Cairidh, to the east of Gallanach. Despite being only 452ft above sea level, it really is worth climbing **Beinn Airein**, in the southwest corner of the island, for the 360-degree panoramic view of the surrounding islands; the return journey from Port Mór takes around two hours.

You can **stay** with one of the MacEwen family, who have owned the island since 1896, at *Port Mór House* (☎01687/462365; full board ③); the rooms are pine-clad and enjoy great views, and the food is delicious. Alternatively, you can stay at the island's **bunkhouse** (☎01687/462042); with permission from the landowner you may also **camp rough**, but bring supplies with you as there is no shop. The island's attempt to install wind power in the 1990s failed after the main contractor went bankrupt, but mains electricity is due to arrive in the very near future. A **tearoom** and craftshop in Port Mór springs into life when day-trippers arrive, and serves soup and sandwiches. Willow basket-making courses are an island speciality (contact *Port Mór House* for more details).

Canna

Measuring a mere five miles by one, and with a Catholic population of just twenty, **Canna** is run as a single farm by the National Trust of Scotland. The island enjoys the best harbour in the Small Isles, a horn-shaped haven at its southeastern corner protected by the tidal island of Sanday, now linked to Canna by a footbridge. For visitors, the chief pastime is walking: from the dock it's about a mile across a grassy basalt plateau to the bony sea cliffs of the north shore, which rise to a peak around Compass Hill (458ft) – so called because its high metal content distorts compasses – in the northeastern corner of the island, from where you get great views across to Rùm and Skye. The cliffs of the buffeted western half of the island are a breeding ground for both Manx shearwater and puffin; some seven miles offshore, you can see the **Heiskeir of Canna**, a curious mass of stone columns sticking up 30ft above the water.

Accommodation is extremely limited. With permission from the National Trust for Scotland (NTS), you may **camp rough** on Canna; otherwise the only option is **B&B** with Wendy MacKinnon (☎01687/462465; full board ⑤), or the NTS-owned *Tighard*, a **self-catering** cottage half a mile from the jetty, which sleeps a maximum of ten people. Booking forms are available from Holiday Cottages, NTS, 5 Charlotte Square, Edinburgh (☎0131/226 5922). Remember, however, that there are no shops on Canna (bar the post office), so you must bring your own supplies.

THE WESTERN ISLES

The wild and windy **Western Isles** – also known as the Outer Hebrides or the Long Isle – vaunt a strikingly hostile mix of landscapes from windswept golden sands to harsh, heather-backed mountains and peat bogs. An elemental beauty pervades each of the more than two hundred islands that make up the archipelago, only a handful of which are actually inhabited by a total of just over 30,000 people. The influence of the Atlantic Gulf Stream ensures a mild but moist climate, though you can expect the strong Atlantic winds to blow in rain on two out of every three days even in summer. Weather fronts, however, come and go at such dramatic speed in these parts, that there's little chance of mist or fog settling and few problems with midges.

The most significant difference between Skye and the Western Isles is that here tourism is much less important to the islands' fragile economy, still mainly concentrated around crofting, fishing and weaving, and the percentage of "white settlers" is a lot lower. The Outer Hebrides remain the heartland of **Gaelic** culture, with the language spoken by the vast majority of islanders, though its everyday usage remains under constant threat from the national dominance of English. Its survival is, in no small part, due to the all-pervading influence of the Free Church and its offshoots, whose strict Calvinism is the creed of the vast majority of the population, with the sparsely populated South Uist, Barra and parts of Benbecula adhering to the more relaxed demands of Catholicism.

The interior of the northernmost island, **Lewis**, is mostly peat moor, a barren and marshy tract that gives way abruptly to the bare peaks of **North Harris**. Across a narrow isthmus lies **South Harris**, presenting some of the finest scenery in Scotland, with wide beaches of golden sand trimming the Atlantic in full view of the mountains and a rough boulder-strewn interior lying to the east. Further south still, a string of tiny, flatter islets, mainly **North Uist**, **Benbecula**, **South Uist** and **Barra**, offer breezy beaches, whose fine sands front a narrow band of boggy farmland, which, in turn, is mostly bordered by a lower range of hills to the east.

In direct contrast to their wonderful landscapes, villages in the Western Isles are rarely picturesque in themselves, and are usually made up of scattered, relatively modern crofthouses strung out along the elementary road system. **Stornoway**, the only real town in the Outer Hebrides, is eminently unappealing. Many visitors, walkers and nature watchers forsake the settlements altogether and retreat to secluded cottages and B&Bs, though for this you really need your own transport.

Visiting the Western Isles

British Regional Airlines and Loganair operate fast and frequent **flights** (Mon–Sat only) from Glasgow and Inverness to Stornoway on Lewis, Barra and Benbecula on North Uist. But be warned, the weather conditions on the islands are notoriously changeable, making flights prone to both delay and stomach-churning bumpiness. On Barra, the other complication is that you land on the beach, so the timetable is adjusted with the tides. CalMac **car ferries** run from Ullapool in the Highlands to Stornoway (Mon–Sat only); from Uig, on Skye, to Tarbert and Lochmaddy (Mon–Sat only); and from Oban and Mallaig to South Uist and Barra (daily). There's also an **inter-island ferry** from Leverburgh, on Harris, to Otternish, on North Uist, and between South Uist and Barra (for more on ferry services, see "Travel details" on p.412).

Although travelling around the islands is time-consuming, for many people this is part of their charm. A series of inter-island causeways makes it possible to drive from one end of the Western Isles to the other with just two interruptions – the CalMac **ferry** trip from Harris to North Uist, and the one from South Uist to Barra. The islands boast a distinctly low-key **bus** service, with no buses on Sundays. Note, however, that sever-

---

GAELIC IN THE WESTERN ISLES

Except in Stornoway, and Balivanich on North Uist, **road signs** are now almost exclusively in **Gaelic**, a difficult language to the English-speaker's eye, with complex pronunciation (see p.676), though as a (very) general rule, the English names can often provide a rough pronunciation guide. Particularly if you're driving, it's essential to buy the bilingual Western Isles map, produced by the local tourist board, Bord Turasachd nan Eilean, and available at most tourist offices. To reflect the signposting we've put the Gaelic first in the text, with the English equivalent in brackets. Thereafter we've stuck to the Gaelic names, to try to familiarize readers with their (albeit variable) spellings – the only exceptions are in the names of islands and ferry terminals, where we've stuck to the English names, partly to reflect CalMac's own policy.

---

al local companies offer very reasonable **car rental** – around £100 a week – though you're not permitted to take their vehicles off the Western Isles.

The islands' **hostels** are geared up for the outdoor life, occupying remote locations on or near the coast. Several of them are run by the Gatliff Hebridean Hostels Trust (GHHT), who have renovated some isolated crofters' cottages. None of these has phones, so you can't book in advance, and you really need to bring your own bedding; each has a simple kitchen, so take your own food. If you're after a little more comfort, then the islands have a generous sprinkling of reasonably priced **B&Bs** and **guest houses** – many of which are a lot more inviting than the hotels and can be easily booked over the phone, or through the tourist offices for a small fee.

Lewis (Leodhas)

Shaped rather like the top of an ice-cream cone, **Lewis** is the largest and by far the most populous of the Western Isles and the northernmost island in the Hebridean archipelago. Most of the island's 20,000 inhabitants – two-thirds of the Western Isles' total population – now live in the crofting and fishing villages strung out along the northwest coast, between **Calanais** and **Port Nis**, in one of the most densely populated rural areas in the country. On this coast you'll also find the islands' best-preserved **prehistoric remains** – Dùn Charlabhaigh broch and Calanais standing stones – as well as a smattering of ancient crofters' houses in various stages of abandonment. The landscape is mostly flat peat bog – hence the island's name, derived from the Gaelic *leogach* (marshy) – with a gentle shoreline that only fulfils its dramatic potential around Rubha Robhanais (Butt of Lewis), a group of rough rocks on the island's northernmost tip, near Port Nis. To the south, where Lewis is physically joined with Harris, the land rises to just over 1800ft, providing a more exhilarating backdrop for the excellent beaches that pepper the isolated coastline of **Uig**, to the west of Calanais.

Most visitors use **Stornoway**, on the east coast, as a base for exploring the island, though this presents problems if you're travelling by **bus**. There's a regular service to Port Nis and Tarbert, and although the most obvious excursion – the 45-mile round trip from Stornoway to Calanais, Carlabhagh, Arnol and back – is difficult to complete by public transport, minibus tours make the trip on most days from April to October (see below).

Some history

After Viking rule ended in 1266, Lewis became a virtually independent state, ruled over by the **MacLeod clan** for several centuries. King James VI, however, had other ideas: he declared the folk of Lewis to be "void of religion", and attempted to establish a

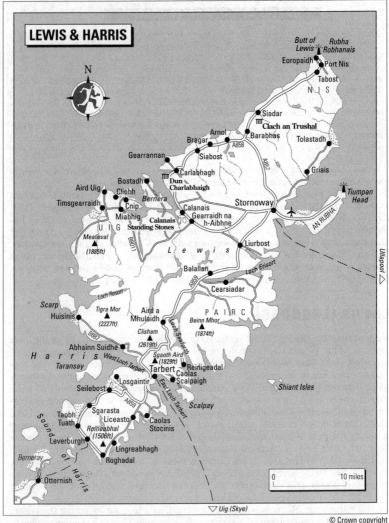

© Crown copyright

colony, as in Ulster, by sending Fife Adventurers to attack Lewis. They were met with armed resistance by the MacLeods so, in retaliation, James VI granted the lands to their arch rivals, the MacKenzies of Kintail. In 1844, the MacKenzies sold Lewis to **Sir James Matheson**, who'd made a fortune from the Chinese opium trade. Matheson invested heavily in the island's infrastructure, though, as his critics point out, he made sure he recouped his money through tax or rent. He was relatively benevolent when the island was hit by potato famine in the mid-1840s, but ultimately opted for solving the problem through eviction and emigration. His chief factor, Donald Munro, was utterly ruthless, and was only removed after the celebrated Bernera Riot of 1874 (see p.397).

The 1886 Crofters Act greatly curtailed the power of the Mathesons; it did not, however, right any of the wrongs of the past. Protests, such as the Pairc Deer Raid of 1887, in which starving crofters killed 200 deer from one of the sporting estates, and the Aignish land raids of the following year, continued against the Clearances of earlier that century.

When **Lord Leverhulme**, founder of the soap empire Unilever, acquired the island (along with Harris) in 1918, he was determined to drag Lewis out of its cycle of poverty by establishing an integrated fishing industry. To this end he founded MacFisheries, a nationwide chain of retail outlets for the fish which would be caught and processed on the islands: he built a cannery, an ice factory, roads, bridges and a light railway; he bought boats, and planned to use spotter planes to locate the shoals of herring. But the dream never came to fruition. Unfortunately, Leverhulme was implacably opposed to the island's centuries-old tradition of crofting which he regarded as inefficient and "an

RELIGION IN THE WESTERN ISLES

It is difficult to overestimate the importance of **religion** in the Western Isles, which are sharply divided – though with little enmity – between the Catholic southern isles of Barra and South Uist, and the Protestant islands of North Uist, Harris and Lewis. Most conflicts arise from the very considerable power the ministers of the Protestant Church, or Kirk, wield in secular life in the north, where the creed of **Sabbatarianism** is very strong. Here, Sunday is the Lord's Day, and virtually the whole community (irrespective of their degree of piety) stops work – all shops close, all pubs close, all garages close and there's no public transport and, perhaps most famously of all, even the swings in the children's playgrounds are padlocked.

The other main area of division is, paradoxically, within the Protestant Church itself. Scotland is unusual in that the national church, the **Church of Scotland**, is presbyterian (ruled by the ministers and elders of the church) rather than episcopal (ruled by bishops). At the time of the main split in the Presbyterian Church – the so-called **1843 Disruption** – a third of its ministers left the Church of Scotland, protesting at the law which allowed landlords to impose ministers against parishioners' wishes, and formed the breakaway **Free Church**. Since those days there has been a partial reconciliation although, in 1893, there was another break, when a minority of the Free Church became the Free Presbyterian Church; meanwhile others slowly made their way back to the Church of Scotland. The remaining rump of the Free Church – better known as the "**Wee Frees**" – has its spiritual heartland on Lewis. To confuse matters further, as recently as 1988 the Free Presbyterian Church split over a minister who attended a requiem mass during a Catholic funeral of a friend – he and his supporters have since formed the break-away Associated Presbyterian Churches. Meanwhile, the Free Church itself is currently in crisis over the "heresies" of Professor Donald MacLeod, one of its more liberal members, who writes a regular column in the *West Highland Free Press*. With a minority within the church determined to force the issue, another split looks inevitable, though as MacLeod himself says, "[Scotland] needs another denomination like it needs a hole in the head".

The various brands and subdivisions of the Presbyterian Church may appear trivial to outsiders, but to the churchgoers of Lewis, Harris and North Uist (as well as much of Skye and Raasay) they are still keenly felt. In part, this is due to social and cultural reasons: Free Church elders helped organize resistance to the Clearances, and the Wee Frees have done the most to help preserve the Gaelic language. A Free Church service is a memorable experience, and in some villages it takes place every evening (and twice on Sundays): there's no set service or prayer book and no hymns, only Biblical readings, plainchant and a fiery sermon all in Gaelic; the pulpit is the architectural focus of the church, not the altar, and communion is taken only on special occasions. If you want to attend one, the Free Church on Kenneth Street in Stornoway has reputedly the largest Sunday evening congregation in the UK, of up to 1500 people.

entirely impossible way of life". He became involved in a long, drawn-out dispute over the distribution of land to returning ex-servicemen, the "land fit for heroes" promised by the Board of Agriculture. In the end, however, it was actually financial difficulties which prompted Leverhulme to pull out of Lewis in 1923, and concentrate on Harris. He generously gifted Lews Castle and Stornoway to its inhabitants and offered free crofts to those islanders who had not been involved in land raids. In the event, few crofters took up the offer – all they wanted was security of tenure not ownership. Whatever the merits of Leverhulme's plans, his departure left a huge gap in the non-crofting economy, and between the wars thousands more emigrated.

Stornoway (Steornabhagh)

In these parts, **STORNOWAY** is a buzzing metropolis, with some 8000 inhabitants, a one-way system, pedestrian precinct with CCTV and all the trappings of a large town. It's a centre for employment, a social hub for the island and, perhaps most importantly of all, home to the **Comhairle nan Eilean Siar** (Western Isles Council), set up in 1974, which has done so much to promote Gaelic language and culture, and try to stem the tide of Anglicization. For the visitor, however, the town is unlikely to win any great praise – aesthetics are not its strong point, and the urban pleasures on offer are limited.

Information and accommodation

The best thing about Stornoway is the convenience of its services. The island's **airport** is four miles east of the town centre, a £5 taxi ride away; the swanky new octagonal CalMac **ferry terminal** is on South Beach, close to the **bus station**. You can get bus timetables, a map of the town and other useful information from the **tourist office**, near North Beach at 26 Cromwell St (April–May & Sept to mid-Oct Mon–Fri 9am–6pm, Sat 9am–5pm; June–Aug Mon, Tues, Thurs & Sat 9am–6pm & 8–9pm, Wed & Fri 9am–8pm; mid-Oct to March Mon–Fri 9am–5pm; ☎01851/703088); they also sell tickets for **minibus tours** to Calanais (Mon–Fri) and for Out and About **wildlife trips** round Lewis and Harris.

Of the **hotels**, the *Royal Hotel* on Cromwell Street (☎01851/702109; ⑤), is your best bet. Another fairly reliable choice is the *Park Guest House* (☎01851/702485; ②) on James Street; the public areas have bags of lugubrious late-Victorian character; the bedrooms significantly less. Of the **B&Bs** along leafy Matheson Road, try *Ravenswood*, at no. 12 (☎01851/702673; ②). The *Stornoway Backpackers* **hostel** is a basic affair about five minutes' walk from the ferry at 47 Keith St (☎01851/703628, *hostel@bayble.demon.co.uk*). The nearest **campsite**, *Laxdale Holiday Park* (☎01851/703234), lies a mile or so along the road to Barabhas, on Laxdale Lane; the campsite has holiday bungalows (three nights' minimum), and a new **bunkhouse**.

The Town

For centuries, life in Stornoway has focused on its **harbour**, whose quayside was filled with barrels of pickled herring, and whose deep and sheltered waters were thronged with coastal steamers and fishing boats in their nineteenth-century heyday, when more than 1000 boats were based at the port. Today, most of the catch is landed on the mainland, and, despite the daily comings and goings of the CalMac ferry from Ullapool, the harbour is a shadow of its former commercial self. The nicest section of the harbour is Cromwell Street Quay, by the tourist office, where the remaining fishing fleet ties up for the night.

Stornoway's commercial centre, to the east, is little more than a string of unprepossessing shops and bars. The one exception is the old **Town Hall** on South Beach, a splendid Scots Baronial building, its rooftop peppered with conical towers, above which a central clocktower rises. On the first floor you'll find the **An Lanntair Art Gallery**

(Mon–Sat 10am–5.30pm; free), whose exhibitions feature the work of local artists, plus a nice tearoom. Anyone remotely interested in Harris Tweed should head for the **Lewis Loom Centre** (Mon–Sat 10am–5pm; £1), run by an eccentric and engaging man and located at the far end of Cromwell Street, in the Old Grainstore off Bayhead. There's an exhibition on the cloth, a shop, and three looms, one of which is a Hattersley, which you may catch going through its paces.

Continuing up the pedestrian precinct into Francis Street, you'll eventually reach the **Museum nan Eilean** (April–Sept Mon–Sat 10am–5.30pm; Oct–March Tues–Fri 10am–5pm, Sat 10am–1pm; free), housed in the old Victorian Nicolson Institute school. The ground floor gallery explores the island's history until the MacKenzie takeover, and is full of artefacts found during peat-cutting, including a lovely Viking dish made from alderwood. There's also a chance to view a Gaelic/English CD-ROM on the Lewis Chessmen (see p.397). The first floor gallery includes lots of information about the herring and weaving industries, and houses an old loom shed with one of the semi-automatic looms introduced by Lord Leverhulme in the 1920s.

To the northwest of the town centre stands **Lews Castle**, a nineteenth-century Gothic pomposity built by Sir James Matheson in 1863. As the former laird's pad, it is seen as a symbol of old oppression by many: it was here, in the house's now defunct conservatory, that Lady Matheson famously gave tea to the Bernera protesters, when they marched on Stornoway prior to the riot (see p.397); when the eccentric Lord Leverhulme took up residence, he had unglazed bedroom windows which allowed the wind and rain to enter, and gutters in the floor to carry off the residue. The current plan is to make it part of the new University of the Highlands and Islands. For the moment, however, its chief attraction is its mature wooded grounds, a unique sight on the Western Isles, for which Matheson had to import thousands of tons of soil from the mainland. If you enter or exit Stornoway via Willowglen Road (A858), you'll see the town **War Memorial**, a castle tower set high above the town amidst gorse bushes, and a good place to take in the sprawl that is Stornoway.

Eating, drinking and nightlife

Decent **food** options are disappointingly limited in Stornoway. One of the best places is the *Thai Café* on Church Street, which serves inexpensive but authentic **Thai** food – as a consequence it's very popular, so book ahead (☎01851/701811). You can get snacks from the *An Lanntair* tearoom, and from *An Leabharlann*, the coffee shop in the new library on Cromwell Street. The *Golden Ocean* **Chinese** restaurant opposite is not a bad choice for lunch, early evening or takeaway, but is otherwise quite expensive. Your best bet for local food is the restaurant of the *Park Guest House*, on James Street (closed Mon & Sun), but it's expensive, unless you go for the "early bird" option. The biggest problem is that all the above places are closed on Sunday. The *Caberfeidh Hotel*, on Macauley Road, is one of the few hotels to serve Sunday lunch, while the *Stornoway Balti House*, near the bus station on South Beach, opens on Sunday evenings.

As for **pubs**, *MacNeills* on Cromwell Street is the liveliest central pub, with a mixed clientele of keen drinkers. *The Criterion*, a tiny wee pub on Point Street, is another option, as is the very pleasant bar of the *Royal Hotel*. Needless to say, all pubs are closed on Sundays, while hotel bars are open for residents only. Last, but not least, Stornoway is home to the Western Isles' only **Internet café**, *Captions*, 27 Church St (Mon–Sat 10am–10pm; *bayble@captions.co.uk*), where you can check your email and enjoy tea and home-made cakes.

Listings

Bakery Stag Bakery, Cromwell St; next door is Nature's Store, a health food shop.
Banks The following banks all have cashpoints: Bank of Scotland, Cromwell St; Clydesdale, South Beach; Lloyds TSB, Francis St; Royal Bank of Scotland, North Beach.

Bike hire Alex Dan's, 67 Kenneth St (closed Sun; ☎01851/704025).

Boat trips Elena C (☎01851/870537) do boat trips to the Shiant Isles and other destinations.

Books Baltic Bookshop, Cromwell Street.

Car rental Lewis Car Hire, 52 Bayhead (☎01851/703760); Mackinnon Self-Drive, southeast of the town centre at 18 Inaclete Rd (☎01851/702984).

Chemist Boots is on the corner of Cromwell St and Point St.

Laundry Erica's Laundrette, Macauley Rd (closed Wed & Sun; last wash 1.40pm). It's situated beyond the second roundabout out of town, and is therefore not central.

Taxis Central Cabs, 20 MacMillan Brae (☎01851/706900).

The road to Tolastadh (Tolsta)

Given the relative paucity of attractions in Stornoway, the dead-end B895 to **TOLAS-TADH**, twelve miles north along the east coast, is a good road to head out on. It boasts several excellent golden beaches and marks the starting point of a lovely coastal walk to Nis.

The legacy of Lord Leverhulme's brief ownership of Lewis is recalled by the striking **Griais Memorial** to the Lewis land raiders, situated by Griais Bridge, above Gress Sands. It was here that Leverhulme's plans came unstuck: he wanted to turn the surrounding crofting land into three big farms, which would provide milk for the workers of his fish-canning factory; the local crofters just wanted to return to their traditional way of life. Such was Leverhulme's fury at the Griais (Gress) and Col (Coll) land raiders, that when he offered to gift the crofts of Lewis to their owners, he made sure the offer didn't include Griais and Col. The stone-built memorial is a symbolic croft split asunder by Leverhulme's interventions.

Further north, beyond Tolastadh, is probably the finest of the coast's sandy beaches, Gheardha (Garry), and the beginning of the footpath to Nis. Shortly after leaving the bay, the path crosses the **"Bridge to Nowhere"**, built by Leverhulme as part of an unrealized plan to forge a new road right along the east coast. A little further along the track, there's a fine waterfall on the Abhainn na Cloich (River of Stones). The makeshift road peters out, but a path continues for another ten miles via the old sheiling village of Diobadail, to Nis (see below).

The road to Barabhas (Barvas) and Nis (Ness)

Northwest of Stornoway, the A857 crosses the vast, barren **peat bog** of the interior, an empty undulating wilderness riddled with stretch marks formed by peat cuttings and pockmarked with freshwater lochans. The whole area was once covered by forests, but these disappeared long ago, leaving a smothering deposit of peat that is, on average, 6ft thick, and is still being formed in certain places. Tourists tend to cross this barren landscape at speed, while ecologists have identified these natural wetlands as important "carbon sinks", whose erosion should be protected. For the people of Lewis, the peat represents a valuable energy resource, with each crofter being assigned a slice of the bog. The islanders spend several very sociable weeks each spring cutting the peat, turning it over and leaving it neatly laid out in the open air to dry, returning in summer to collect the dried sods and stack them outside their houses. Though tempting to take home as souvenirs, these piles are the fruits of hard labour, and remain the island's main source of domestic fuel, its pungent smoke one of the most characteristic smells of the Western Isles.

Twelve miles across the peat bog the road approaches the west coast of Lewis and divides, heading southwest towards Calanais (see p.395), or northeast through **BARABHAS** (Barvas), and a whole string of bleak and fervently Free Church crofting and weaving villages. These scattered settlements have none of the photogenic qualities of Skye's whitewashed villages; the churches are plain and unadorned, the crofters' houses relatively modern and smothered in grey pebble-dash rendering or harling, the stone cottages and enclosures of their forebears often lie half-abandoned in the front garden, while a rusting assortment of discarded cars and vans store peat bags and the like. Just beyond Barabhas, a signpost points to the pleasant **Morven Art Gallery** (Easter–Oct Mon–Sat 11am–5pm; free), with a handy café to hole up in during bad weather. Three miles further up the road, you pass the 20ft monolith of **Clach an Truiseil**, the first of a series of prehistoric sights between the crofting and weaving settlements of **BAILE AN TRUISEIL** (Ballantrushal) and **SIADAR** (Shader). Beyond Siadar, anyone with a passing interest in pottery should visit **Borgh Pottery** (Mon–Sat

OFFSHORE ISLANDS

Though three men dwell on Flannan Isle
To keep the lamp alight,
As we steer'd under the lee, we caught
No glimmer through the night.

Flannan Isle Wilfred Wilson Gibson

On December 15, 1900, a passing ship reported that the lighthouse on the **Flannan Isles**, built the previous year by the Stevensons some 21 miles west of the Butt of Lewis, was not working. Gibson's poem goes on to recount the arrival of the relief boat from Oban on Boxing Day, whose crew found no trace of the three keepers. More mysteriously still, a full meal lay untouched on the table, one chair was knocked over, and only two oilskins were missing. Subsequent lightkeepers doubtless spent many lonely nights trying in vain to figure out what happened, until the lighthouse went automatic in 1971.

Equally famous, but for different reasons, is the tiny island of **Sula Sgeir**, 41 miles due north of the Butt of Lewis. Every August since anyone can remember, the young men of Nis have set sail from Port Nis to harvest the young gannet or guga that nest in their thousands high up on the islet's sea cliffs. It's a dangerous activity, and one that the RSPB has tried its best to stop, but for some unknown reason boiled gannet and potato continues to be a popular Lewis delicacy, and there's never any shortage of eager volunteers for the annual cull.

Somewhat incredibly, the island of **Rona**, less than a mile across and ten miles east of Sula Sgeir, was inhabited on and off until the mid-nineteenth century. The island's St Ronan's Chapel is one of the oldest Celtic Christian ruins in the country. St Ronan was, according to legend, the first inhabitant, moving here in the eighth century with his two sisters, Miriceal and Brianuil, until one day he turned to Brianuil and said, "My dear sister, it is yourself that is handsome, what beautiful legs you have". She apparently replied that it was time for her to leave the island, and made her way to neighbouring Sula Sgeir. Rona is now in the care of Scottish Natural Heritage (☎01870/705258), from whom you must get permission before landing.

The largest of all the offshore islands is the NTS-owned **St Kilda** archipelago, roughly a hundred miles west southwest of the Butt of Lewis and over forty miles from its nearest landfall, Griminish Point on North Uist. The last 36 Gaelic-speaking inhabitants of Hirta, St Kilda's main island, were evacuated at their own request in 1930, ending several hundred years of harsh existence – well recorded in Tom Steel's book *The Life and Death of St Kilda*. Today, the island is partly occupied by the army, who have a missile-tracking radar station here linked to South Uist. The NTS (☎01870/620238) organize week-long volunteer groups, which you can apply to join, though be prepared for a rough, fourteen-hour crossing from Oban. With a calm sea and permission from the NTS – even tour operators have to negotiate long and hard – you may go ashore to visit the museum in the old village, restored by volunteers, and struggle up the massive cliffs, where the islanders once caught puffins, young fulmars and gannets.

9.30am–6pm; free), where you can watch the husband and wife team creating hand-thrown pots.

Nis (Ness)

The main road continues through a string of straggling villages, until you reach the various densely populated settlements that make up the parish of **NIS** (Ness), at the northern tip of Lewis. The folk of Nis are perhaps best known for their annual culling of young gannets on Sula Sgeir (see box on p.393). For an insight into the social history of the area, take a look inside **Comunn Eachdriadh Nis** (Ness Historical Society; Mon–Sat noon–5.30pm; £2), on the left as you pass through **TABOST** (Habost). The museum, housed in an unlikely looking building, contains a huge collection of photographs, but its prize possession is a diminutive sixth- or seventh-century cross from the Isle of Rona (see box on p.393), decorated with a much eroded nude male figure, and thought by some to have been St Ronan's grave-stone. The road terminates at the fishing village of **PORT NIS** (Port of Ness), with a tiny harbour and lovely golden beach.

Shortly before you reach Port Nis, a minor road heads two miles northwest to the hamlet of **EOROPAIDH** (Europie) – pronounced "Yor-erpee". Here, by the road junc-tion that leads to the Butt of Lewis, the simple stone structure of **Teampull Mholuaidh** (St Moluag's Church) stands amidst the runrig fields. Thought to date from the twelfth century, when the islands were still under Norse rule, but restored in 1912 (and now used once a month by the Scottish Episcopal Church for sung Communion), the church features a strange south chapel with only a squint window connecting it to the nave. In the late seventeenth century, the traveller Martin Martin noted "they all went to church. . . and then standing silent for a little time, one of them gave a signal . . . and immediately all of them went into the fields, where they fell a drinking their ale and spent the remainder of the night in dancing and singing, etc". Church services aren't what they used to be.

From Eoropaidh, a narrow road twists to the bleak and blustery northern tip of the island, **Rubha Robhanais** – well known to devotees of the BBC shipping forecast as the **Butt of Lewis** – where a lighthouse sticks up above a series of sheer cliffs and stacks, alive with kittiwakes, fulmars and cormorants, with skuas and gannets feeding offshore, and a great place for marine mammal-spotting. The lighthouse is closed to the public, though a shop and tearoom are planned for the near future. In the meantime, you're better off backtracking half a mile or so, where there's a path down to the tiny sandy bay of **Port Sto**, a more sheltered spot for a picnic than the Butt itself. From Europaidh, you can also gain access to the dunes and machair of the nearby coastline that stretches for two or three miles to the southwest.

Practicalities

There are at least six buses a day from Stornoway to Port Nis, Sundays excepted, and one or two **accommodation** possibilities. The best place to stay is *Galson Farm Guest House* (☎01851/850492; ⑤), an eighteenth-century farmhouse in Gabhsann Bho Dheas (South Galson), halfway between Barabhas and Port Nis, with a **bunkhouse** close by (phone number as above). Another, more modest option is the modern croft of *Eisdean* (☎01851/810240; ①) in Coig Peighinnean (Five Penny Borve), four miles northeast of Barabhas, or *Cross Inn* (☎01851/810378; ①), remark-able primarily for being the only pub in the entire parish. The only **tearoom** (March–Oct; closed Sun) is *Harbour View*, in an old boat-builder's house overlooking Port Nis harbour; it also serves toasted sandwiches and baked potatoes. There are very few shops (other than mobile ones) in these parts, so it's as well to stock up in Stornoway before you set out.

Bru (Brue), Arnol and Siabost (Shawbost)

Heading southwest from the crossroads near Barabhas brings you to several villages that meander down towards the sea. The first is **BRU** (Brue), where you'll find the **Oiseval Gallery** (Mon–Sat 10.30am–5.30pm; free), a photographic gallery that's worth a look. In the neighbouring village of **ARNOL**, the remains of numerous blackhouses lie abandoned in the village, one of which, at the far end of the village, has been restored as a **Black House Museum** (May–Sept Mon–Fri 10am–1pm & 2–5pm, Sat 11am–1pm & 2–5pm; HS; £1.80). Dating from the 1870s and inhabited until 1964, its chimneyless roof is overlaid with grassy sods and oat-straw thatch, lashed down with fish nets and ropes. Beneath, a simple system of wooden tie beams supports the roof, which covers both the living quarters and the attached byre and barn. The postwar wallpaper inside has been removed to reveal sooty rafters above the living room, where, in the centre of the stone and clay floor, the peat fire was the focal point of the house. Today, many visitors look back with nostalgia at the old abandoned blackhouses, but it's as well to remember that they were a breeding ground for disease, and that, essentially, life in the blackhouse was pretty grim.

Returning to the main road, it's about a mile or so to **BRAGAR**, where you'll spot a stark arch formed by the jawbone of a blue whale, washed up on the nearby coast in 1920. The spear sticking through the bone is the harpoon, which only went off when the local blacksmith was trying to remove it, badly injuring him. Another two miles on at **SIABOST** (Shawbost), local school children created the appealingly amateurish **Shawbost Crofting Museum** (Mon–Sat 9am–6pm; free) in 1970. The converted church contains a real hotchpotch of stuff – most of it donated by locals – including a rare Lewis brick from the short-lived factory set up by Lord Leverhulme, an old hand-driven loom and a reconstructed living room with a traditional box bed. Behind the church is the *Eilean Fraoich* **campsite** (☎01851/710504; May–Oct). Just outside Siabost, to the west, there's a sign to the newly restored **Norse Mill and Kiln**. It's a ten-minute walk over a small hill to the two thatched bothies beside a little stream; the nearer one's the kiln, the further the horizontal mill. Mills and kilns of this kind were common in Lewis up until the 1930s, and despite the name are thought to have been introduced here from Ireland as early as the sixth century.

Carlabhagh (Carloway) and Calanais (Callanish)

Five miles on, the landscape becomes less monotonous, with boulders and hillocks rising out of the peat moor, as you approach the parish of **CARLABHAGH** (Carloway), with its scattering of crofthouses. A mile-long road leads off north to the beautifully remote coastal settlement of **GEARRANNAN** (Garenin), where several thatched crofters' houses – the last of which was abandoned in 1973 – have been restored. One blackhouse now serves as a GHHT **youth hostel**, another is for **self-catering** (☎01851/643416, *gearrannan@lews.fc.uhi.ac.uk*; 16 people; £100 per night), while another contains public toilets; **camping** is also permitted. A night here is unforgettable, and there's a beautiful stony beach from which to view the sunset.

Just beyond Carlabhagh, about 400 yards from the road, **Dùn Charlabhaigh Broch** perches on top of a conspicuous rocky outcrop overlooking the sea. Scotland's Atlantic coast is strewn with the remains of over 500 brochs, or fortified towers, but this is one of the best preserved, its drystone circular walls reaching a height of more than 30ft on the seaward side. The broch consists of two concentric walls, the inner one perpendicular, the outer one slanting inwards, the two originally fastened together by roughly hewn flagstones, which also served as lookout galleries reached via a narrow stairwell. The only entrance to the roofless inner yard is through a low doorway set beside a crude and cramped guard cell. As at Calanais (see below), there have been all sorts of theories about the purpose of the brochs, which date from between 100 BC and 100 AD; the most likely explanation is that they were built to provide protection from Roman slave-traders.

Dùn Charlabhaigh now has its very own **Doune Broch Centre** (April–Oct Mon–Sat 10am–6pm; free), situated at a discreet distance, stone-built and sporting a turf roof. It's a good wet-weather retreat, and fun for kids, who can walk through the hay-strewn mock-up of the broch as it might have been. A mile or so beyond the broch, beside a lochan, is the *Doune Braes Hotel* (☎01851/643252, *user@doune-braes.netmedia.co.uk*; ④), a friendly, unpretentious place whose bar serves up the same tasty seafood dishes as its restaurant, only cheaper.

Calanais

Five miles south of Carlabhagh lies the village of **CALANAIS** (Callanish), site of the islands' most dramatic prehistoric ruins, the **Calanais Standing Stones**, whose mono-liths – nearly fifty of them – occupy a serene loch-side setting. There's been years of heated debate about the origin and function of the stones – slabs of gnarled and finely grained gneiss up to 15ft high – though almost everyone agrees that they were lugged here by Neolithic peoples between 3000 and 1500 BC. It's also obvious that the plan-ning and construction of the site – as well as several other lesser circles nearby – was spread over many generations. Such an endeavour could, it's been argued, only be prompted by the desire to predict the seasonal cycle upon which these early farmers were entirely dependent, and indeed many of the stones are aligned with the position of the sun and the stars. This rational explanation, based on clear evidence that this part of Lewis was once a fertile farming area, dismisses as coincidence the ground plan of the site, which resembles a colossal Celtic cross, and explains away the central burial chamber as a later addition of no special significance. These two features have, howev-er, fuelled all sorts of theories ranging from alien intervention to human sacrifice.

A blackhouse adjacent to the main stone circle has been refurbished as a **tearoom** and shop, and it's to this you should head for refreshment rather than the superfluous **Calanais Visitor Centre** (Mon–Sat: April–Sept 10am–7pm; Oct–March 10am–4pm; £1.50) on the other side of the stones (and thankfully out of view), to which all the signs direct you from the road. The centre runs a decent restaurant and a small museum on the site, but with so much information on the panels beside the stones there's little rea-son to visit it. You're politely asked not to walk between the stones, only along the path that surrounds them, so if you want to commune with standing stones in solitude head for the smaller circles in more natural surroundings a mile or two southeast of Calanais, around Gearraidh na h-Aibhne (Garynahine).

If you need a place to stay, there are several inexpensive **B&Bs** in Calanais itself: try Mrs Catherine Morrison, 27 Calanais (☎01851/621392; ①; March–Sept), or an excellent B&B, which caters well for veggies and is run by Debbie Nash (☎01851/621321; ①) in neighbouring Tolastadh a Chaolais (Tolsta Chaolais), or try Kate Kirby for B&B also in Tobstadh a Chaolais (☎01851/621266; ①) three miles north. Calanais also has a modern *Eschol Guest House* (☎01851/621357; ③), no beauty from the outside, but very comfortable within. If it's just **food** you want, *Tigh Mealros* (closed Sun), in Gearraidh na h-Aibhne, serves good, inexpensive lunches and evening meals, featuring local seafood.

Bernera (Bearnaraigh)

From Gearraidh na h-Aibhne, the main road leads back to Stornoway, while the B8011 heads off west to Uig (see below), and, a few miles on, the B8059 sets off north to the island of Great Bernera, usually referred to simply as **Bernera**. Joined to the mainland via a narrow bridge that spans a small sea channel, Bernera is a rocky island, dotted with lochans, fringed by a few small lobster-fishing settlements and currently owned by Comte Robin de la Lanne Mirrlees, the Queen's former Herald.

Bernera has an important place in Lewis history due to the **Bernera Riot** of 1872, when local crofters successfully defied the eviction orders delivered to them by the landlord, Sir James Matheson. In truth, there wasn't much of a riot, but three Bernera men were arrested and charged with assault. The crofters marched on the laird's house, Lews Castle in Stornoway, and demanded an audience with Matheson, who claimed to have no knowledge of what his factor, Donald Munro was doing. In the subsequent trial, Munro was exposed as a ruthless tyrant, and the crofters were acquitted. A stone-built cairn now stands as a memorial to the riot, at the crossroads beyond the central settlement of **BREACLEIT** (Breaclete), which sits beside one of the island's many lochs. Here, you'll find the **Bernera Museum** (April–Sept Mon–Sat 11am–6pm; £1.50), housed in the local community centre. There's a small exhibition on lobster fishing, a St Kilda mail boat, and a mysterious 5000-year-old Neolithic stone tennis ball, but it's hardly worth the entrance fee, unless you're tracing your ancestry.

Much more interesting is the replica **Iron Age House** (Tues–Sat noon–4pm; £1) that has been built above a precious little bay of golden sand beyond the cemetery at **BOSTADH** (Bosta), three miles north of Breacleit – follow the signs "to the shore". In 1992, gale-force winds revealed an entire late Iron Age or Pictish settlement hidden under the sand; due to its exposed position, the site has been refilled with sand, and a full-scale mock-up built instead, based on the "jelly baby" houses – after the shape – that were excavated. Inside, the house is incredibly spacious, and very dark, illuminated only by a central hearth and a few chinks of sunlight. If the weather's fine and you climb to the top of the nearby hills, you should get a good view over the forty or so islands in Loch Roag, and maybe even the Flannan Isles (see p.393) on the horizon.

If you want to stay, there are a couple of comfortable, modern **B&Bs** on the island: *Kelvindale* (☎01851/612347; ①; April–Oct) in Tobson, a couple of miles northwest of Breacleit, and *Garymilis* (☎01851/612341; ①; Feb–Nov), in Circebost (Kirkibost).

Uig

It's a long drive along the partially upgraded B8011 to the remote parish of **Uig**, one of the areas of Lewis that suffered really badly from the Clearances, The landscape here is hillier, and more dramatic than elsewhere, a combination of myriad islets, wild cliff scenery and patches of pristine golden sand.

At the crossroads to **MIABHAIG** (Miavaig), you have a choice of either heading straight for the Uig Sands (see below), or veering off the main road, and heading along a dramatic little road northeast to **CLIOBH** (Cliff). The Atlantic breakers that roll onto the beach below the village are often spectacular, but make it unsafe for swimmers, who should continue another mile to **CNIP** (Kneep), to the southeast of which is **Tràigh na Beirghe**, a glorious strand of shell sand, backed by dunes and machair, in which there's a small primitive **campsite** (mid-April to mid-Sept; ☎01851/672265).

The other route choice from Miabhaig is to continue along the main road through the narrow canyon of Glèann Bhaltois (Glen Valtos) to **TIMSGEARRAIDH** (Timsgarry), which overlooks Tràigh Uuige (**Uig Sands**), the largest and most prized of all the golden strands on Lewis. It was in the nearby village of Eadar dha Fhadhail (Ardroil) in 1831 that a local cow stumbled across the **Lewis Chessmen**, twelfth-century Viking chess pieces carved from walrus ivory that now reside in The National Museum of Scotland in Edinburgh (see p.86) and the British Museum in London. You can see replicas of the chessmen in the **Uig Heritage Centre** (Mon–Sat noon–5pm; £1), housed in Uig School in Timsgearraidh. As well as putting on some excellent temporary exhibitions, the museum has bits and bobs from blackhouses, and is staffed by locals, who are happy to answer any queries you have; there's also a welcome **tearoom** in the adjacent nursery during the holidays.

The most intriguing **place to stay** is *Baile na Cille* (☎01851/672241, *randjgollin@compuserve.com*; ④; April–Sept), in an idyllic setting overlooking the Uig Sands in Timsgearraidh; they also have a couple of **self-catering** cottages (6 people; £350 per week). It's an easy-going place, run by an eccentric couple, who are very welcoming to families – the Blairs have stayed here – and dish up wonderful, though expensive, set menu dinners. An entirely different (but equally unusual) experience is to stay at the old RAF station in **AIRD UIG**, three miles north of Timsgearraidh, which is slowly being transformed by an enterprising Breton. The concrete buildings themselves are something of an eyesore, but the position, overlooking a rocky inlet beside Gallan Head, is superb. The whole complex includes **B&B** (☎01851/672474; ①), **self-catering** (5 people; £250 per week), a **hostel** and the popular *Bonaventure* **restaurant** (closed Mon & Sun) which serves up outstanding food at bargain prices. Boat trips to Bernera and Calanais and elsewhere along the west coast are available from Sea Trek (☎01851/672464), run by Murray MacLeod from Uigean (Uigen), near Miabhaig.

Harris (Na Hearadh)

The "division" between Lewis and **Harris** – they are, in fact, one island – is embedded in a historical split in the MacLeod clan, lost in the mists of time. The border between the two was also a county boundary until 1975, with Harris lying in Inverness-shire, and Lewis belonging to Ross and Cromarty. Nowadays, the dividing line is rarely marked

---

HARRIS TWEED

Far from being a picturesque cottage industry, as it's sometimes presented, the production of **Harris Tweed** is vital to the local economy, with a well-organized and unionized workforce. Traditionally the tweed was made by women, from the wool of their own sheep, to provide clothing for their families, using a 2500-year old process. Each woman was responsible for plucking the wool by hand, washing and scouring it, dyeing it with lichen, heather flowers or ragwort, carding (smoothing and straightening the wool, often adding butter to grease it), spinning and weaving. Finally the cloth was dipped in sheep's urine and "waulked" by a group of women, who beat the cloth on a table to soften and shrink it whilst singing Gaelic waulking songs. Harris Tweed was originally made all over the islands, and was known simply as *clò mór* (big cloth).

In the mid-nineteenth century, the Countess of Dunmore, who owned a large part of Harris, started to sell surplus cloth to her aristocratic friends, thus forming the genesis of the modern industry, which serves as a vital source of employment, though demand (and therefore employment levels) can fluctuate wildly as fashions change. To earn the official Harris Tweed Association trademark of the Orb and the Maltese Cross – taken from the Countess of Dunmore's coat of arms – the fabric has to be hand-woven on the Outer Hebrides from 100 percent pure new Scottish wool, while the other parts of the manufacturing process must take place only in the local mills.

The main centre of production is now Lewis, where the wool is dyed, carded and spun; you can see all these processes by visiting the **Lewis Loom Centre** in Stornoway (see p.391). In recent years there has been a revival of traditional tweed-making techniques, with several small producers, like Anne Campbell at **Clò Mór** in Liceasto (Mon–Fri 9am–5pm; ☎01859/530364), religiously following old methods. One of the more interesting aspects of the process is the use of indigenous plants and bushes to dye the cloth: yellow comes from rocket and broom, green from heather, grey and black from iris and oak, and, most popular of all, reddish brown from crotal, a flat grey lichen scraped off rocks.

even on maps; for the record, it comprises Loch Resort in the west, Loch Seaforth in the east, and the six miles in between. Harris itself is more clearly divided by a minuscule isthmus, into the wild, inhospitable mountains of North Harris and the gentler landscape and sandy shores of South Harris.

Along with Lewis, Harris was purchased in 1918 by **Lord Leverhulme**, and after 1923, when he pulled out of Lewis, all his efforts were concentrated here. In contrast to Lewis, though, Leverhulme and his ambitious projects were broadly welcomed by the people of Harris. His most grandiose plans were drawn up for Leverburgh (see p.402), but he also purchased an old Norwegian whaling station in Bun Abhain Eadara in 1922, built a spinning mill at Geocrab and began the construction of four roads. Financial difficulties, a slump in the tweed industry and the lack of market for whale products meant that none of the schemes was a wholehearted success, and when he died in 1925 the plug was pulled on all of them by his executors.

Since the Leverhulme era, unemployment has been a constant problem in Harris. Crofting continues on a small scale, supplemented by the Harris Tweed industry, though the main focus of this has shifted to Lewis. Shellfish fishing continues on Scalpay, while the rest of the population gets by on whatever employment is available: roadworks, crafts and, of course, tourism. There's a regular **bus** connection between Stornoway and Tarbert, and an occasional service which circumnavigates South Harris (see also "Travel details" on p.412).

Tarbert (Tairbeart)

The largest place on Harris is the ferry port of **TARBERT**, sheltered in a green valley on the narrow isthmus that marks the border between North and South Harris. The town's mountainous backdrop is impressive, and the town is attractively laid out on steep terraces sloping up from the dock. However, it does boast the only **tourist office** (April–Oct Mon–Sat 9am–5pm; also open to greet the ferry; winter hours variable; ☎01859/502011) on Harris, close to the ferry terminal. The office can arrange modest, inexpensive B&B **accommodation** and has a full set of bus timetables, but its real value is as a source of information on local walks.

If you wish to base yourself in Tarbert there's a **hostel**, *Rockview Bunkhouse* (☎01859/502211) on Main Street, which also offers **bike rental**. You'll need to book ahead to stay in Tarbert's two most popular **guest houses**: *Allan Cottage* (☎01859/502146; ③; April–Sept) in the old telephone exchange, and *Leachin House* (☎01859/502157; ⑤), further up the Stornoway road. Another good option is the Victorian B&B *Dunard* (☎01859/502340; ③), or there's the easy-going, old-fashioned *Harris Hotel* (☎01859/502154; ③), five minutes' walk from the ferry. The purpose-built hotel **bar** acts as the local social centre and serves low-grade bar meals; the adjacent *Crofters* **restaurant** serves moderately expensive, fairly ordinary fare. During the day, you're best off heading for the very pleasant *First Fruits* **tearoom** (April–Sept; closed Sun), behind the tourist office, housed in an old stone-built cottage and serving real coffee, home-made cakes, toasties and so forth. The only alternative is the **fish and chip shop** (April–Oct; closed Sun), next to the hostel.

North Harris (Ceann a Tuath na Hearadh)

The A859 north to Stornoway takes you over a boulder-strewn saddle between mighty **Sgaoth Aird** (1829ft) and An Cliseam or the **Clisham** (2619ft), the highest peak in the Western Isles. This bitter terrain, littered with debris left behind by retreating glaciers, offers but the barest of vegetation, with an occasional cluster of crofters' houses sitting in the shadow of a host of pointed peaks, anywhere between 1000ft and 2500ft high. These bulging, pyramidal mountains reach their climax around the dramatic shores of the fjord-like **Loch Seaforth**. Just beyond Aird a' Mhulaidh (Ardvourlie), at the border between Lewis and Harris is a rare patch of woodland, much of it blighted. If you're planning on walking in North Harris, and can afford it, consider using the spectacular *Ardvourlie Castle* (☎01859/502307; ⑥; April–Oct), ten miles north of Tarbert by the shores of Loch Seaforth, as a launch pad. In nearby Bogha Glas (Bowglass), there's also a thatched **self-catering** cottage, *Tigh na Seileach* (☎01859/502411; 4 people; £250 per week).

A cheaper, but equally idyllic spot is the GHHT **youth hostel** (open all year; no phone) in the lonely coastal hamlet of **REINIGEADAL** (Rhenigdale), until recently only accessible by foot or boat. To reach the hostel without your own transport, walk east five miles from Tarbert along the road to Caolas Scalpaigh (Kyles Scalpay). After another mile or so, watch for the sign marking the start of the path which threads its way through the peaks of the craggy promontory that lies trapped between Loch Seaforth and East Loch Tarbert. It's a magnificent hike, with superb views out along the coast and over the mountains, but you'll need to be properly equipped (see p.48) and should allow three hours for the one-way trip.

Scalpay (Scalpaigh)

Caolas Scalpaigh looks out across East Loch Tarbert to the former island of **Scalpay** (Scalpaigh) – from the Norse *skalp-ray* (the island shaped like a boat) – now accessible via the brand-new £6 million single-track bridge. Scalpay's tightly knit prawn-fishing community is surprisingly buoyant, maintaining a relatively large population of around 400. It's a pleasant and fairly easy three-mile hike across the island to the **Eilean Glas** lighthouse which looks out over the sea to Skye. The first lighthouse to be erected in Scotland, in 1788, the current tower was Stevenson-designed and is built out of Aberdeen granite. There are a couple of simple B&Bs on the island: *Suil-Na-Mara* (☎01859/540278; ①; April–Sept) or *Seafield* (☎01859/540250; ①). If you're interested in **diving**, contact Scalpay Diving Services (☎01859/540328).

The road to Huisinis (Hushinish)

The only other road on North Harris is the winding, single-track B887, which clings to the northern shores of West Loch Tarbert, and gives easy access to the awesome mountain range of the (treeless) Forest of Harris to the north. Immediately as you turn down the B887, you pass through **BUN ABHÀINN EADARRA** (Bunavoneadar), where some Norwegians established a short-lived whaling station – the slipways and distinctive red-brick chimney can still be seen. Seven miles further on, the road takes you through the gates of **Amhuinnsuidhe Castle** (pronounced "Avan-soo-ee"), built in Scottish Baronial style in 1868 by the Earl of Dunmore, and right past the front door, much to the annoyance of the castle's owners, who have tried in vain to have the road rerouted. As it is, you have time to admire the lovely salmon-leap waterfalls and pristine castle grounds.

It's another five miles to the end of the road at the small crofting community of **HUISINIS** (Hushinish), where you are rewarded with a south-facing beach of shell sand that looks across to South Harris. A slipway to the north of the bay serves the nearby island of **Scarp**, a hulking mass of rock rising to over 1000ft, once home to more than two hundred people and abandoned as recently as 1971 (it's now just a private holiday hideaway). The most bizarre moment in its history was undoubtedly in 1934, when the German scientist Gerhardt Zucher conducted an experiment with rocket mail, but the letter-laden missile exploded before it even got off the ground and the idea was shelved.

South Harris (Ceann a Deas na Hearadh)

The mountains of **South Harris** are less dramatic than in the north, but the scenery is equally breathtaking. There's a choice of routes from Tarbert to the ferry port of

Leverburgh, which connects with North Uist: the east coast, known as Na Baigh (The Bays), is rugged and seemingly inhospitable, while the west coast is endowed with some of the finest stretches of golden sand in the whole of the archipelago, buffeted by the Atlantic winds. Several buses set off from Tarbert, Sundays excepted, travelling out along the east coast, and returning via all points along the west coast – for more information see "Travel details" at the end of this chapter or contact Tarbert tourist office.

Na Baigh (The Bays)

Paradoxically, most people on South Harris live along the harsh eastern coastline of Bays rather than the more fertile west side. But not by choice – they were evicted from their original crofts to make way for sheep-grazing. Despite the uncompromising lunaresque terrain – mostly bare grey gneiss and heather – the crofters managed to establish "lazybeds" (small labour-intensive raised plots between the rocks fertilized by seaweed and peat), a few of which are still in use even today. The narrow sea lochs provide shelter for fishing boats, while the interior is speckled with freshwater lochans, and the whole coast now served by the endlessly meandering Golden Road (so called because of the expense of constructing it).

There are just a few places to stay along the coast, the most obvious being the hostel (☎01851/511255) three miles south of Tarbert in DRINISIADAR (Drinishader); alternatively, there's *Hillhead* (☎01859/511226; ①; April–Oct), a good tweed-making B&B in SCADABHAGH (Scadabay).

Six miles beyond Liceasto at LINGREABHAGH (Lingarabay), the road skirts the foot of Roineabhal (1508ft), the southernmost mountain of the island and known as *An Aite Boidheach* (The Beautiful Place). The majority of the locals are currently fighting to prevent Redland Aggregates building one of Europe's largest superquarries here, which would demolish virtually the entire mountain over the next seventy years. Environmentalists charge that local fishing grounds would be badly affected, the devout are up in arms over the possibility of Sunday working, and the initial promise of a hundred much-needed new jobs has been reduced on the evidence of a public enquiry to just 25. At the time of writing, the final outcome of the public enquiry was about to be declared.

Roghadal (Rodel)

A mile or so from Rubha Reanais (Renish Point), the southern tip of Harris, is the old port of ROGHADAL (Rodel), where a smattering of ancient stone houses lies among the hillocks surrounding the dilapidated harbour where the ferry from Skye used to arrive. On top of one of these grassy humps, with sheep grazing in the graveyard, is St Clement's Church (Tur Chliamainn), burial place of the MacLeods of Harris and Dunvegan in Skye. Dating from the 1520s – in other words pre-Reformation, hence the big castellated tower – the church was saved from ruination in the eighteenth century, and fully restored in 1873 by the Countess of Dunmore. The bare interior is distinguished by its wall tombs, notably that of the founder, Alasdair Crotach (also known as Alexander MacLeod), whose heavily weathered effigy lies beneath an intriguing backdrop and canopy of sculpted reliefs depicting vernacular and religious scenes – elemental representations of, among others, a stag hunt, the Holy Trinity, St Michael, and the devil and an angel weighing the souls of the dead. Look out, too, for the *sheila-na-gig* halfway up the south side of the church tower; unusually, she has a brother displaying his genitalia, below a carving of St Clement on the west face.

The west coast

The main road from Tarbert into South Harris snakes its way west for ten miles across the boulder-strewn interior to reach the coast. Once there, you get a view of the most stunning beach, the vast golden strand of Tràigh Losgaintir. The road continues to ride above a chain of sweeping sands, backed by rich **machair**, that stretches for nine miles along the Atlantic coast. In good weather, the scenery is particularly impressive, foaming breakers rolling along the golden sands set against the rounded peaks of the mountains to the north and the islet-studded turquoise sea to the west – and even on the dullest day, the sand manages to glow beneath the waves. A short distance out to sea is the island of Taransay (Tarasaigh), which once held a population of nearly a hundred, but was abandoned as recently as 1974.

Nobody bothers much if you **camp** or park beside the dune-edged beach, as long as you're careful not to churn up the machair, and there's the very good B&B, *Moravia* (☎01859/550262; ①; March–Oct), overlooking the sands at **LOSGAINTIR** (Luskentyre). Just south of **BORGH** (Borve), there's a newly-built **self-catering** thatched house by the beach (☎01859/550222; *ofes@zetnet.co.uk*; 4 people; £330 per week), and a stone-built renovated steading (6 people; £295 per week); the *Borvemor* gallery/café (closed Mon, Sat & Sun) serving home-made cakes and real coffee, is attached. The choicest accommodation, though, is five miles further south in **SGARASTA** (Scarista), where one of the first of the Hebridean Clearances took place in 1828, when thirty families were evicted and their homes burned. Here, the Georgian former manse of *Scarista House* (☎01859/550238; *ian@scaristahouse.demon.co.uk*; ⑦; May–Sept) overlooks the nearby golden sands; if you can't afford to stay, it's worth splashing out and booking for dinner, as the meat and seafood served here is among the freshest and finest on the Western Isles.

If you're intrigued by the local machair, you can go on guided walks (mid-May to mid-Sept Mon & Fri 2.30pm; £2) across a particularly magnificent stretch by the golden sands close to the village of **TAOBH TUATH** (Northton), a lovely spot overlooked by the round-topped hill of Chaipabhal at the southwesternmost tip of the island. Taobh Tuath itself is no picture postcard, with the exception of the award-winning **MacGillivray Centre** (open all year at any time), whose design was inspired by the Hebridean blackhouse. However, it's the building that clearly won the accolades and not the centre, which contains precious little information on the naturalist, William MacGillivray (1796–1852), after whom it's named, and only a little on crofting and machair.

Leverburgh (An t-Ob)

From Taobh Tuath the road veers to the southeast to trim the island's south shore, eventually reaching the sprawling settlement of **LEVERBURGH** (An t-Ob), where a series of brown clapperboard houses strikes an odd Scandinavian note. Named after Lord Leverhulme, who planned to turn the place into the largest fishing port on the west coast of Scotland, it's a place that has languished for quite some time, but has picked up quite a bit since the establishment of the CalMac **car ferry** service to Otternish on North Uist. The seventy-minute journey across the skerry-strewn Sound of Harris is one of Scotland's most tortuous ferry routes, with the ship taking part in a virtual slalom race to avoid numerous hidden rocks – it's also a great crossing from which to spot seabirds and sea mammals.

There are several **B&Bs** strung out within a two-mile radius of Leverburgh: try *Caberfeidh House* (☎01859/520276; ①), a lovely stone-built Victorian building by the turn-off to the ferry, or *Sorrel Cottage* (☎01859/520319; ①), which specializes in vegetarian and seafood cooking. A cheaper alternative is the purpose-built timber-clad *An Bothan* **bunkhouse** (☎01859/520251), which has great facilities, and is only a few minutes' walk from the ferry. On the north side of the bay, *An Clachan* co-op store has a **café** (closed Sun) upstairs, and hosts temporary local history exhibitions, while *The Anchorage* (closed Sun), overlooking the ferry slipway, is basically a greasy spoon café.

North Uist (Uibhist a Tuath)

Compared to the mountainous scenery of Harris, **North Uist** – seventeen miles long and thirteen miles wide – is much flatter and for some comes as something of an anti-climax. Over half the surface area is covered by water, creating a distinctive peaty-brown lochan-studded "drowned landscape". Most visitors come here for the trout and salmon fishing and the deerstalking, both of which (along with poaching) are critical to the survival of the island's economy. Others come for the smattering of prehistoric sites and sheer peace of this windy isle, and the solitude of North Uist's vast sandy beaches, which extend – almost without interruption – along the north and west coast.

There are two **car ferry** services to North Uist: the first is from Leverburgh on Harris to Otternish (Mon–Sat 4 daily; 1hr 10min), from where there are regular **buses** to Lochmaddy, the principal village on the east coast; the second is from Tarbert on Harris, via Uig on Skye (Mon–Sat 1–2 daily; 4hr), which docks at Lochmaddy itself. Two or three daily buses leave for Lochboisdale in South Uist along the main road, and several buses travel some way round the coastal road. There is no public transport on Sundays.

Lochmaddy (Loch nam Madadh) and around

Despite being situated on the east coast, some distance away from any beach, the ferry port of **LOCHMADDY** – "Loch of the Dogs" – makes a good base for exploring the island. Occupying a narrow, bumpy promontory, overlooked by the brooding mountains of North Lee and South Lee to the southeast, it's difficult to believe that this sleepy settlement was a large herring port as far back as the seventeenth century. Its most salient feature now is the sixteen incongruous brown weatherboarded houses, which arrived from Sweden in 1948.

If the weather's bad or you've time to kill, take a look round **Taigh Chearsabhagh** (Mon–Sat 10am–5pm; £1), a converted eighteenth-century merchant's house, now home to an excellent local museum, arts centre and café. If the weather's good, take a walk out past the Uist Outdoor Centre, and across the footbridge that leads to the derelict Sponish House. From here a path leads east to Lochmaddy's most intriguing sight, **Both nam Faileas** (Hut of the Shadow), an ingenious drystone, turf-roofed camera obscura recently built by sculptor Chris Drury, that projects the nearby land, sea and skyscape onto its back wall – take time to allow your eyes to adjust to the light, and on the way back look out for otters, who love the tidal rapids hereabouts.

The **tourist office** (mid-April to mid-Oct Mon–Fri 9am–5pm, Sat 9.30am–5.30pm; also open to greet the evening ferry; ☎01876/500321), near the quayside, has local bus and ferry timetables, and can help with **accommodation**. There are a couple of nice Victorian B&Bs, north off the main road: try the *Old Bank House* (☎01876/500275; ①). A little further north lies the *Uist Outdoor Centre* (☎01876/500480), which has **hostel** accommodation in four-person bunk rooms, and offers a wide range of outdoor activities from canoeing round the indented coastline to "rubber tubing".

The **bar** in the *Lochmaddy Hotel* is lively and serves the usual bar meals, but it's currently not a place to recommend staying in. It is, however, a favourite with the **fishing** fraternity – there's even a set of scales in the hotel foyer – and rents out boats and sells permits for brown trout, sea trout and salmon. The island's **bank** is right by the tourist office, though it doesn't have a cashpoint (the nearest one is in Balivanich). There is a small **general store**, petrol and a post office, but the island's nearest large supermarket is in Solas (see below). The only **bike rental** on the island is from Morrison Cycle Hire (☎01876/580211), based nine miles away in Cairinis (Carinish), but they will deliver to Lochmaddy.

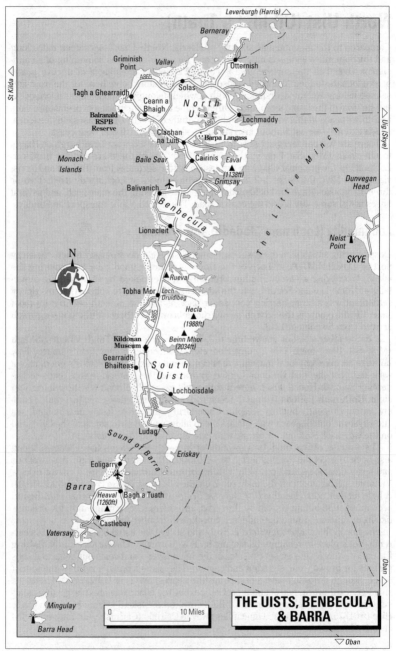

THE UISTS, BENBECULA
& BARRA

© Crown copyright

Nearby Neolithic sites

Several prehistoric sites lie within easy cycling distance of Lochmaddy (or walking distance if you use the bus/postbus for the outward journey). The most remarkable is **Barpa Langass**, a huge chambered burial cairn a short walk from the A867, seven barren miles southwest. The stones are visible from the road and, unless the weather's good, it's not worth making a closer inspection as the chamber has collapsed and is now too dangerous to enter. A mile to the southeast, by *Langass Lodge* (☎01876/500285; ④; closed Feb), whose restaurant and bar snacks feature local seafood, a rough track leads to the small stone circle of **Pobull Fhinn**, which enjoys a much more picturesque location overlooking a narrow loch. The circle covers a large area and, although the stones are not that huge, they occupy an intriguing amphitheatre cut into the hillside. Three miles northwest of Lochmaddy along the A865 you'll find **Na Fir Bhreige** (The Three False Men), three standing stones which, depending on your legend, mark the graves of three spies buried alive or three men who deserted their wives and were turned to stone by a witch.

Berneray (Bhearnaraigh)

For those in search of still more seclusion, there's the low-lying island of **Berneray** – two miles by three, with a population of about 140 – now accessible via a brand new causeway from Otternish, eight miles north of Lochmaddy. The island's main claim to fame is as the birthplace of Giant MacAskill (see p.375) and as the favoured holiday hideaway of that other great eccentric, Prince Charles, lover of Gaelic culture and royal potato picker to local crofter, "Splash" MacKillop. Apart from the sheer peace and isolation, the island's main draw for non-royals is a three-mile-long sandy beach on the west and north coast, backed by rabbit-free dunes and machair. The other great draw is the wonderful GHHT **hostel** which occupies a pair of thatched blackhouses in a lovely spot by a beach, beyond Loch a Bhàigh and the main village. Alternatively you can follow in the prince's footsteps and stay (and help out) at "Splash" MacKillop's *Burnside Croft* **B&B** (☎01876/540235; ②; Feb–Nov), and enjoy "story-telling evenings"; bike rental is also available. There are several **tearooms** currently functioning along the main road, including one in the community centre at the end of the road to Borgh (Borve), all of which serve simple refreshments, and, with the new causeway in place, there's now a **bus** connection with Lochmaddy.

The coastal road via Solas (Sollas)

The A865, which skirts the northern and western shoreline of North Uist for more than thirty miles, takes you through the most scenic sections of the island. Once you've left the boggy east coast and passed the turning to Otternish, the road reaches the parish of **SOLAS** (Sollas), which stands at the centre of a couple of superb tidal strands – sea green at high tide, golden sand at low tide – backed by large tracts of machair that are blanketed with wild flowers in summer. A new memorial opposite the local co-op recalls the appallingly brutal Clearances undertaken by Lord MacDonald of Sleat in Solas. The current laird, Lord Granville, who owns much of North Uist, occupies the large house on the tidal island of **Vallay** (Bhalaigh), which is connected by a road that crosses the largest of the two strands. For a comfortable, friendly **B&B**, with great views across Vallay Strand, head for *Struan House* (☎01876/560282; ①; April–Sept).

Beyond Solas, the rolling hills that occupy the centre of North Uist slope down to the sea. Here, in the northwest corner of the island, you'll find **Scolpaig Tower**, a castellated folly on an islet in Loch Scolpaig, erected as a famine relief project in the nineteenth century – you can reach it, with some difficulty, across stepping stones. A tarmac track leads down past the loch and tower to Scolpaig Bay, beyond which lies the rocky shoreline of **Griminish Point**, the closest landfall to St Kilda (see p.393), which is clearly visible on the horizon in fine weather, looming like some giant dinosaur's skeleton emerging from the sea.

Roughly three miles south of Scolpaig Tower, through the sand dunes, is the **Balranald RSPB Reserve**, one of the last breeding grounds of the corncrake, among Europe's most endangered birds. Sightings are rare, partly because the birds are very good at hiding in long grass, but the males' loud "craking" is relatively easy to hear from May to July. From the excellent new **visitor centre** there's a two-hour walk along the headland, marked out by discreet white pegs, giving you ample opportunity for appreciating the wonderful carpet of flowers that covers the machair in summer, and for spotting corn buntings and arctic terns inland and gannets and Manx shearwaters out to sea – guided walks take place throughout the summer (May–Aug Tues & Fri 2pm; ☎01878/602188).

Children might enjoy a visit to the **Uist Animal Visitors Centre** (daily 11am–7pm; £2), a farm that lies just off the main road, beyond Paible School, in **CEANN A BHAIGH** (Bayhead). Here, you can see Eriskay ponies, Highland cattle, Scottish wild-cats, and other rare Scottish breeds at close quarters; the centre also has a café, and **horse-drawn Romany caravans** for hire (☎01876/510223). Adults might prefer to continue a couple of miles down the main road and pop into the *Westford Inn*, a **pub** in Claddach Chirceboist (Claddach Kirkibost), that occasionally has live music.

Clachan to Grimsay (Griamsaigh)

At **CLACHAN NA LUIB**, by the crossroads with the A867 from Lochmaddy, there's a post office and general store. Offshore, to the south, lie two tidal dune and machair islands, the largest of which is **Baleshare** (Baile Sear), with its fantastic three-mile-long beach, connected by causeway to North Uist. In Gaelic the island's name means "east village", its twin "west village" having disappeared under the sea during a freak storm in the fifteenth or sixteenth century. This also isolated the **Monarch Islands** (sometimes known by their old Norse name of Heisgeir or Heisker), once connected to North Uist at low tide, now eight miles out to sea. The islands, which are connected with each other at low tide, were inhabited until the 1930s when the last remaining families moved to North Uist. In an isolated position, overlooking Baleshare, is *Taigh mo Sheanair* (☎01876/580246), a very welcoming, family-run **hostel**, where you can also **camp**. The hostel is clearly signposted from the main road, from which it's a good fifteen-minute walk.

On leaving North Uist the main road squeezes along a series of single-track causeways, built by the military in 1960, that cross the tidal rapids separating North Uist from Benbecula. The causeways trim the west edge of **Grimsay** (Griomasaigh), a peaceful, little-visited, rocky island that's really quite pretty, especially around **BAGH MOR** (Baymore). The main source of employment is lobster fishing, which takes place at the modern pier in **NA CEALLAN** (Kallin), where there's also a reasonable little B&B, *Glendale* (☎01870/602029; ①).

Benbecula (Beinn na Faoghla)

Blink and you could miss the pancake-flat island of **Benbecula** (put the stress on the second syllable), sandwiched between Protestant North Uist and Catholic South Uist. Most visitors simply trundle along the main road that cuts across the middle of the island in less than five miles – not such a bad idea, since nearly half the island's 1200 population are Royal Artillery personnel, working at the missile range on South Uist, and the noise on both islands can be deafening during practice sessions. Economically, the area has, of course, benefited enormously from the military presence, though the impact on the environment and Gaelic culture (with so many English-speakers around) has been less positive. There is talk of the military pulling out altogether – a devastating prospect for most islanders.

Nearly all the military personnel live in the depressing, barracks-like housing developments of **BALIVANICH** (Baile a Mhanaich), the grim, grey capital of Benbecula in the northwest. The only reason to come here at all is if you happen to be flying into or out of **Benbecula airport** (direct flights to Glasgow, Barra and Stornoway), need to take money out of the Bank of Scotland cashpoint (the only one on the Uists), or stock up on provisions, best done at the old NAAFI store (now a Spar supermarket; open daily), to the west of the post office. There's no tourist office and if you've got your own transport, there's no need **to stay** here, but if you're reliant on public transport, try the modern **hostel** *Taigh-na-Cille* (☎01870/602522), within easy walking distance of the airport, on the road to North Uist. The best thing about Balivanich is *Stepping Stone*, the purpose-built **café/restaurant** situated opposite the post office, a place with an ambivalent character: the café bit is cheap and cheerful, offering filled rolls and chips with everything, while the mezzanine seating area is home to *Sinteag* restaurant, where the four-course lunch for £10 is a bargain, and the evening's à la carte menu is almost twice the price. **Car rental** is available at the airport from Ask Car Hire (☎01870/602818), who are based in neighbouring Uachdar, where you'll also find MacLean's Bakery (closed Sun), useful for amassing a picnic.

The nearest **campsite**, *Shell Bay* (☎01870/602447; April–Oct), is in the south of the island at **LIONACLEIT** (Liniclate). Adjacent is the modern **Sgoil Lionacleit**, the only secondary school (and public swimming pool) on the Uists and Benbecula, and home to a small **museum** which acts as a temporary exhibition space for Museum nan Eilean (Mon, Tues & Thurs 9am–4pm, Wed 9am–12.30pm & 1.30–4pm, Fri 9am–8pm, Sat 11am–1pm & 2–4pm). The island's most comfortable **hotel**, *Dark Island Hotel* (☎01870/602414; ⑤) is also next door, though it's no charmer from the outside. It serves bar meals and has a moderately expensive restaurant, featuring local specialities such as Grimsay lobsters, but you'll get better value for money at the *Orasay Inn*, just across the water in South Uist (see below).

South Uist (Uibhist a Deas)

To the south of Benbecula, the island of **South Uist** is arguably the most appealing of the southern chain of islands. The west coast boasts some of the region's finest machair and beaches – a necklace of gold and grey sand strung twenty miles from one end to the other – while the east coast features a ridge of high mountains rising to 2034ft at the summit of Beinn Mhor. Whatever you do, don't make the mistake of simply driving down the main A865 road, which runs down the centre of the island like a backbone. To reach the beaches (or even see them) you have to get off the main road and pass through the old crofters' villages that straggle along the west coast; to climb the mountains in the east, you need a detailed 1:25,000 map, in order to negotiate the island's maze of lochans. The only blot on South Uist's landscape is the Royal Artillery missile range which occupies the northwest corner of the island, shattering the peace and quiet every so often.

Loch Druidibeg, Tobha Mòr (Howmore) and Kildonan Museum

The Reformation never took a strong hold in South Uist (or Barra), and the island remains Roman Catholic, as is evident from the various roadside shrines and the slender modern statue of *Our Lady of the Isles* that stands by the main road below the small hill of **Rueval**, known to the locals as "Space City" for its forest of aerials and golf balls, which help track the missiles heading out into the Atlantic. To the south of Rueval is the freshwater **Loch Druidibeg**, a breeding ground for greylag geese and a favourite spot for mute swans. The area around the loch is made up of such diverse habitats, from brackish lagoons and peaty moorland to dune and machair, that Scottish National Heritage now manage the place as a National Nature Reserve. At first glance it may not seem to be teeming with wildlife, but it's lovely countryside, and there's a chance of seeing some raptors hunting over the moorland, including hen harriers; there's a way-marked path through the reserve that begins just by the telephone box on the main road in Stadhlaigearraidh (Stilligarry).

One of the best places to gain access to the sandy shoreline is at **TOBHA MÒR** (Howmore), a pretty little crofting settlement with a fair number of restored houses, many still thatched, including one distinctively roofed in brown heather. A GHHT **hostel** (no phone) occupies one such house near the village church, from where it's an easy walk across the flower-infested machair to the gorgeous beach. Close by the hostel are the shattered, lichen-encrusted remains of no fewer than four medieval churches and chapels, and a burial ground now harbouring just a few scattered graves. The sixteenth-century **Clanranald Stone**, carved with the arms of the clan who ruled over South Uist from 1370 until 1839, used to lie here. It's now displayed in the nearby Kildonan Museum (see below), after it was stolen in 1990 and removed to London by a Canadian artist, Lawren Maben. It took three months before anyone noticed it had disappeared. Five years later, it was discovered by the artist's father in a bedsit near Euston Station, as he sorted out his son's belongings, following his "death by misadventure".

There's much more besides the aforementioned stone at the **Kildonan Museum** (Mon–Sat 10am–5pm, Sun 2–5pm; £1.80), on the main road five miles south of Tobha Mor. Mock-ups of Hebridean kitchens through the ages, two lovely box beds, and an impressive selection of old photos are accompanied by a firmly unsentimental yet poetic written text on crofting life in the last two centuries. Among the more unusual exhibits is a pair of ornamental shoes made of deer hooves. The museum also runs a café serving sandwiches and homemade cakes, and has a choice of historical videos for those really wet and windy days. A little to the south of the museum, the road passes a cairn that sits amongst the foundations of **Flora MacDonald**'s childhood home (see p.380); she was born nearby, but the house no longer stands.

Without doubt, the best **hotel** on the Uists is the *Orasay Inn* (☎01870/610298, *orasayinn@btinternet.com*; ③), located in a peaceful spot off the road to Loch a Charnain (Lochcarnan), in the northeastern corner of the island. It's nothing to look at from the outside, but ask for a room looking east out towards the Minch, and you can enjoy a bit of birdwatching from your balcony. The bar meals are good value, the restaurant moderately expensive, and the breakfasts huge. If you're just passing along the main road and need a bit to eat, pop into the *Crofters Kitchen*, an inexpensive **café** near the causeway to Benbecula, serving not only herring in oatmeal, toasted sarnies, tatties and neeps, but also "flaky smoked salmon". This is a speciality you can also buy straight from its source, *Salar* (closed Sat & Sun), further along the road to Loch a Charnain, beyond the *Orasay Inn* turnoff.

Lochboisdale (Loch Baghasdail)

Although South Uist's chief settlement and ferry port, **LOCHBOISDALE**, occupying a narrow, bumpy promontory on the east coast, has, if anything, even less to offer than Lochmaddy, with just the *Lochboisdale Hotel* for somewhere to have a drink and a proper meal. If you're arriving here late at night on the seven-hour boat trip from Oban (or from Castlebay on Barra; 1hr 50min), you should try to book accommodation in advance; otherwise, head for the **tourist office** (Easter to mid-Oct Mon–Sat 9am–5pm; also open to meet the night ferry; ☎01878/700286). Next door to the tourist office is a useful coin-operated shower and toilet block (daily 9am–5pm). There are several small, perfectly ordinary **B&Bs** within comfortable walking distance of the dock, including *Bayview* (☎01878/700329; ②; March–Oct) and *Lochside Cottage* (☎01878/700472; ②), and a few more luxurious ones slightly further afield, such as *The Sheiling* (☎01878/700504; ③), in Gearraidh Sheile (Garryhallie), near Dalabrog (Daliburgh). The shops in Lochboisdale are pretty limited; the nearest supermarket is in Dalabrog.

Perhaps the best place to hole up in this part of South Uist is the *Polochar Inn* (☎01878/700215; ④), eight miles from Lochboisdale, right on the south coast overlooking the Sound of Barra, with its own sandy beach close by. If you're heading for Barra you could take the passenger ferry from **Ludag jetty**, two miles east of the *Polochar Inn*, which lands at Eoligarry on Barra's north coast – and when the causeway to Eriskay is complete in 2001, there are plans to institute a car ferry service to Barra.

Eriskay (Eiriosgaigh)

To the south of South Uist lies the barren, hilly island of **Eriskay**, famous for its patterned jerseys (on sale at the community centre), and a peculiar breed of pony, originally used for carrying peat and seaweed. The island, which measures just over two miles by one, shelters a small fishing community of about 150, and makes a great daytrip from South Uist, as long as the weather's fine. The ferry from Ludag, across the treacherously shallow waters of the Sound of Eriskay, will be made redundant when the new causeway is finished in 2001.

For a small island, Eriskay has had more than its fair share of historical headlines. The island's main beach on the west coast, Coilleag a Phrionnsa (Prince's Cockle Strand), was where **Bonnie Prince Charlie** landed on Scottish soil on July 23, 1745 – the sea bindweed that grows there to this day is said to have sprung from the seeds Charles brought with him from France. The prince, as yet unaccustomed to hardship, spent his first night in a local blackhouse, and ate a couple of flounders, though he apparently couldn't take the peat smoke and chose to sleep sitting up rather than endure the damp bed.

Eriskay's other claim to fame came in 1941 when the 8000-ton **SS Politician** or "Polly" as it's fondly known, sank on its way from Liverpool to Jamaica, along with its cargo of bicycle parts, £3 million in Jamaican currency and 264,000 bottles of whisky, inspiring Compton MacKenzie's book, and the Ealing comedy (filmed on Barra in 1948), *Whisky Galore!* (released as *Tight Little Island* in the US). The real story was somewhat less romantic, especially for the 36 islanders who were charged with illegal possession by the Customs and Excise officers, nineteen of whom were found guilty and imprisoned in Inverness. The ship's stern can still be seen at low tide northwest of Calvay Island in the Sound of Eriskay, and one of the original bottles (and lots of other related memorabilia) is on show in *Am Politician*, the island's purpose-built pub near the two cemeteries on the west coast.

If you're here for the day, the best route to take is to head west from Haun jetty towards **St Michael's Church**, built in 1903 in a vaguely Spanish style on raised ground above the harbour. The most striking features of the church are the bell, which comes from the World War I battle-cruiser *Derfflinger*, the last of the scuttled German fleet to be salvaged from Scapa Flow, and the altar, which is made from the bow of a lifeboat. From here, it's a short walk to the **community centre** (times according to the ferry; closed Sun), which serves tea in the summer, sells jumpers, and occasionally hosts exhibitions. The walk up to the island's highest point, **Ben Scrien** (607ft), is well worth the effort on a clear day, as you can see the whole island, plus Barra, South Uist, and across the sea to Skye, Rùm, Coll and Tiree (2–3hr return from the jetty). On the way up or down, look out for the diminutive Eriskay ponies, who roam free on the hills but tend to graze around Loch Crakavaig, the island's freshwater source.

Until the causeway is complete there are three types of **ferry** to Eriskay from Ludag jetty on South Uist – car ferry, passenger ferry and a rigid inflatable. Which one runs depends on the tides and demand, so get hold of a copy of the monthly timetable from the tourist office or phone the enquiry line (☎01878/720261). You can **camp rough** with permission, or stay (for a minimum of three nights) at the **self-catering** chalet run by Mrs Campbell (☎01878/720274; 4 people; £180 per week).

Barra (Barraigh)

Just four miles wide and eight miles long, **Barra** has a well-deserved reputation of being the Western Isles in miniature. It has sandy beaches, backed by machair, glacial mountains, prehistoric ruins, Gaelic culture, and a laid-back, welcoming Catholic population of just over 1300. Like some miniature feudal island state, it was ruled over for centuries, with relative benevolence, by the MacNeils. Unfortunately, however, the family sold the island in 1838 to Colonel Gordon of Cluny, who had also bought Benbecula, South Uist and Eriskay. The colonel deemed the starving crofters "redundant", and offered to turn Barra into a state penal colony. The government declined, so the colonel called in the police and proceeded with some of the most cruel forced Clearances in the Hebrides. In 1937, the 45th chief of the MacNeil clan bought back most of the island, and the island returned with relief to its more familiar, feudal roots.

Castlebay (Bagh a Chaisteil)

The only settlement of any size is **CASTLEBAY** (Bagh a Chaisteil), which curves around the barren rocky hills of a wide bay on the south side of the island. It's difficult to imagine it now, but Castlebay was a herring port of some significance back in the nineteenth century, with up to 400 boats in the harbour and curing and packing factories ashore. Barra's religious allegiance is immediately announced by the large Catholic church, Our Lady, Star of the Sea, which overlooks the bay; to underline the point, there's a Madonna and Child on the slopes of **Heaval** (1260ft), the largest peak on Barra, and a fairly easy hike from the bay.

As its name suggests, Castlebay has a castle in its bay, the medieval islet-fortress of **Kisimul Castle** (Mon, Wed & Sat tours at 2pm; £3; ☎01871/810336), ancestral home of the MacNeil clan. The castle burnt down in the eighteenth century, but when the 45th MacNeil chief – conveniently enough an architect by training – bought the island back in 1937, he set about restoring the castle. You can take a tour round it by catching the ferry from the slipway at the bottom of Main Street (☎01871/810449).

To learn more about the history of the island, and about the postal system of the Western Isles, it's worth paying a visit to **Barra Heritage Centre** (Mon–Fri 11am–5pm; £1), housed in an unprepossessing block on the road that leads west out of town.

North to Cockle Strand and Eoligarry

Following the west coast round will bring you to the island's finest sandy beaches, particularly those at Halaman Bay and near the village of **ALLATHASDAL** (Allasdale). At **BAILE NA CREIGE** (Craigston), between the two, a dead-end road leads inland to the **Black House Museum** (June–Oct Mon–Fri 11am–5pm; £1), an isolated thatched crofthouse, half a mile's walk from the end of the metalled road, which remains much as it was when last inhabited in the 1970s.

One of Barra's most fascinating sights is, in fact, its **airport**, on the north side of the island, where planes land and take off from the crunchy shell sands of Tràigh Mhór, better known as **Cockle Strand**; the exact timing of the flights depends on the tides since at high tide the beach (and therefore the runway) is covered in water. As its name suggests, the strand is also famous for its cockles and cockleshells, the latter being used to make harling (the rendering used on most Scottish houses). In 1994, mechanical cockle extraction using tractors was introduced, and quickly began to decimate the cockle stocks and threaten the beach's use as an airport – as a result it has now been banned, in favour of traditional hand-raking.

To the north of the airport, connected by a thin strip of land, is the coastal village of **EOLIGARRY** (Eolaigearraidh), with a passenger ferry link to Ludag on South Uist and several sheltered sandy bays close by. To the west of the village is **Cille-Bharra**, burial ground of the MacNeils (and Compton MacKenzie). The ground lies beside the ruins of a medieval church and two chapels, one of which has been reroofed to provide shelter for several carved graveslabs, some rather bizarre religious and secular objects and a replica of an eleventh-century rune-inscribed cross, the original of which is in the National Museum of Scotland in Edinburgh (see p.86).

Vatersay (Bhatarsaigh)

To the south of Barra, the island of **Vatersay** (Bhatarsaigh), shaped rather like an apple core, is now linked to the main island by a causeway – a mile or so southwest of Castlebay – to try and stem the depopulation which has brought the current head count down to just over seventy. The main settlement (also known as Vatersay) is on the south coast, and to get to it you must cross a narrow isthmus, with the golden sands of Vatersay Bay to the east, and the stones and sands of Bàgh Siar a few hundred yards to the west. Above, on the dunes of the latter, is the **Annie Jane Monument**, a granite needle erected to commemorate the 350 emigrants who lost their lives when the *Annie Jane* ran aground off Vatersay in 1853 en route to Canada.

Practicalities

If you're arriving at Eoligarry, on the passenger **ferry** from South Uist, you can hire **bikes** from Barra Cycle Hire (☎01871/810284), who will meet you at the ferry. There's also a fairly decent **bus/postbus** service which does the rounds of the island (Mon–Sat). Arriving in Castlebay by **car ferry** from Lochboisdale, Oban or Mallaig is more straightforward, and you can rent **bikes** from Castlebay Cycle Hire (☎01871/810284), half a mile east of the town centre. **Car hire** is available from Barra Car Hire (☎01871/810243), who will deliver vehicles to the airport or either ferry terminal. Barra's **tourist office** (April to mid-Oct Mon–Sat 9am–5pm; also open to greet the ferry; ☎01871/810336), is situated on Main Street in Castlebay just round from the pier, and can help book accommodation, though it's as well to book in advance for B&Bs and hotels. Those interested in a **boat trip** to the sea cliffs on the island of **Mingulay**, south of Barra, whose last two inhabitants were evacuated in 1934, should phone Mr Campbell (☎01871/810303) or enquire at the *Castlebay Hotel*.

In Castlebay itself, the *Castlebay Hotel* (☎01871/810223; ④) is the most comfortable **place to stay**, followed by *Tigh-na-Mara* (☎01871/810304; ②; April–Oct), a guest house a couple of minutes' walk from the pier by the sea; another good choice is *Grianamul* (☎01871/810416, *ronnie.macneil@virgin.net*; ③; April–Oct). Although architecturally something of a 1970s monstrosity, the *Isle of Barra Hotel* (☎01871/810383, *barrahotel@aol.com*; ⑥; late-April to early Sept) enjoys a classic location overlooking Halaman Bay. The best option outside the Castlebay are is *Northbay House* (☎01871/890255; ②), which is a converted school in Buaile nam Bodach

(Balnabodach). There's a new GHHT **hostel** (no phone) in Breibhig (Brevig), a couple of miles east of Castlebay, where you can also **camp**; if you're camping rough you can use the toilets and shower in the CalMac office on the pier.

In contrast to the rest of the Western Isles, Castlebay is positively buzzing on a Sunday morning when all the shops open for the folk coming out of Mass. The *Kisimul Galley* **café** serves breakfast all day every day, and specializes in cheap- and- cheerful Scottish fry-ups – try the stovies and the bridies. For more fancy fare, head to the *Castlebay Hotel*'s cosy **bar** which regularly has cockles, crabs and scallops on its menu, and good views out over the bay. If the *Castlebay* isn't serving food, try the bar at the neighbouring *Craigard Hotel*, which serves food whenever it's open. There are two bars at the *Isle of Barra Hotel*, one of which is the locals' pub, while the other is more of a cocktail bar, and lies within the hotel itself; the food here also features excellent local fish and seafood and the hotel runs an oriental take-away. The only two watering holes in the north of the island are the airport terminal café, and the lively bar of the *Heathbank Hotel* in Bagh a Tuath (Northbay). **Films** are occasionally shown on Saturday evenings at the local school – look out for the posters – where there is also a swimming pool, library and sports centre, all of which are open to the general public.

In Vatersay, the friendly community centre is open daily in season for soups, snacks, tea and cakes.

travel details

Trains

Aberdeen to: Kyle of Lochalsh (Mon–Sat 1 daily; 5hr).

Edinburgh to: Kyle of Lochalsh (Mon–Sat 1 daily; 6hr 50min).

Fort William to: Mallaig (Mon–Sat 6 daily, Sun 3 daily; 1hr 25min).

Glasgow (Queen St) to: Mallaig (Mon–Sat 3 daily, Sun 2 daily; 5hr 10min); Oban (Mon–Sat 3 daily, Sun 2 daily; 3hr).

Inverness to: Kyle of Lochalsh (Mon–Sat 3 daily, Sun 1 daily; 2hr 30min).

Buses

Mainland

Edinburgh to: Broadford (1 daily; 6hr 30min); Oban (1 daily; 4hr); Portree (1 daily; 7hr 40min).

Glasgow to: Broadford (3 daily; 5hr 30min); Oban (Mon–Sat 4 daily, Sun 2 daily; 3hr); Portree (3 daily; 6hr 10min); Uig (2 daily; 7hr 40min).

Inverness to: Broadford (Mon–Sat 3 daily, Sun 2 daily; 2hr 50min); Portree (Mon–Sat 3 daily, Sun 2 daily; 3hr 15min).

Kyle of Lochalsh to: Broadford (7 daily; 30min); Portree (7daily; 1hr).

Skye

Armadale to: Broadford (Mon–Sat 5 daily, Sun 2 daily; 45min); Portree (Mon–Sat 6 daily, Sun 1 daily; 1hr 20min); Sligachan (Mon–Sat 4 daily, Sun 1 daily; 1hr 10min).

Broadford to: Portree (10–12 daily; 40min).

Dunvegan to: Glendale (Mon–Sat 1–4 daily; 30min).

Kyleakin to: Broadford (Mon–Sat 12–14 daily, Sun 7 daily; 15min); Portree (Mon–Sat 6–7 daily, Sun 5 daily; 1hr); Sligachan (Mon–Sat 7–8 daily, Sun 5 daily; 45min); Uig (Mon–Sat 2 daily; 1hr 20min).

Portree to: Carbost (Mon–Fri 2–3 daily, Sat 1 daily; 35min); Duntulm (Mon–Sat 2–3 daily; 1hr); Dunvegan (Mon–Sat 4 daily; 50min); Fiskavaig (Mon–Fri 2 daily, Sat 1 daily; 50min); Staffin (Mon–Sat 3 daily; 40min); Uig (Mon–Sat 4–5 daily; 30min).

Lewis/Harris

Stornoway to: Barabhas (Mon–Fri 11–13 daily, Sat 8 daily; 25min); Calanais (Mon–Sat 5–7 daily; 40min); Carlabhagh (Mon–Sat 4–6 daily; 1hr); Leverburgh (Mon–sat 4–5 daily; 2hr); Point (Mon–Sat hourly; 40min); Port Nis (Mon–Sat 6–9 daily; 1hr); Siabost (Mon–Sat 6 daily; 45min); Tarbert (Mon–Sat 4–5 daily; 1hr 10min); Timsgearraidh (Mon–Sat 1–2 daily; 1hr–1hr 30min); Tolastadh (Mon–Sat every 1hr 30min; 40min).

Tarbert to: Huisinis (Tues, Fri & schooldays 3–4 daily; 45min); Leverburgh (Mon–Sat 8 daily; 50min); Leverburgh via the Bays (Mon–Sat 3–4 daily; 1hr 10min); Scalpay (Mon–Fri 5 daily, Sat 3 daily; 20min).

Uists/Benbecula

Lochboisdale to: Ludag (Mon–Sat 6–7 daily; 30–45min).

Lochmaddy to: Balivanich (Mon–Sat 4–5 daily; 45min–2hr); Balranald (Mon–Sat 4–5 daily; 50min); Berneray (Mon–Sat 5–6 daily; 30min); Lochboisdale (Mon–Sat 2–3 daily; 2hr).

Otternish to: Balivanich (Mon–Sat 3–4 daily; 1hr–2hr 20min); Lochmaddy (Mon–Sat 6–7 daily; 20–50min).

Barra

Castlebay to: Airport/Eoligarry (Mon–Sat hourly; 35min/45min); Vatersay (Mon–Sat 8 daily; 20min).

Ferries (summer timetable)

To Barra: Mallaig–Castlebay (Sun; 3hr 45min); Oban–Castlebay (Mon, Wed, Thurs & Sat; 5hr); Lochboisdale–Castlebay (Tues, Thurs, Fri & Sun; 1hr 40min).

To Canna: Eigg–Canna (Mon & Sat; 2hr 45min–3hr); Mallaig–Canna (Mon, Wed, Fri & Sat; 2hr 30min–4hr 15min); Muck–Canna (Sat; 2hr 15min); Rùm–Canna (Mon, Wed & Sat; 1hr–1hr 15min).

To Eriskay: Ludag–Eriskay (at least 2 daily; 20min).

To Eigg: Canna–Eigg (Fri & Sat; 2hr 15min–3hr); Mallaig–Eigg (Mon, Tues, Thurs & Sat; 1hr 30–1hr 50min); Muck–Eigg (Tues, Thurs & Sat; 45–50min); Rùm–Eigg (Fri & Sat; 1hr 15min–2hr).

To Harris: Lochmaddy–Tarbert via Uig (Mon–Sat 1–2 daily; 4hr); Otternish–Leverburgh (Mon–Sat 4 daily; 1hr 10min); Uig–Tarbert (Mon–Sat 1–2 daily; 1hr 45min).

To Lewis: Ullapool–Stornoway (Mon–Sat 2 daily; 2hr 40min).

To Muck: Eigg–Muck (Tues, Thurs & Sat; 1hr); Canna–Muck (Sat; 2hr 15min); Mallaig–Muck (Tues, Thurs & Sat; 2hr 40min–4hr 45min); Rùm–Muck (Sat; 1hr 15min).

To North Uist: Leverburgh–Otternish (Mon–Sat 4 daily; 1hr 10min); Tarbert–Lochmaddy via Uig (Mon–Sat 1–2 daily; 4hr); Uig–Lochmaddy (1–2 daily; 1hr 50min).

To Raasay: Sconser–Raasay (Mon–Sat 9–10 daily; 15min).

To Rùm: Canna–Rùm (Wed, Fri & Sat; 1hr–1hr 15min); Eigg–Rùm (Mon & Sat; 1hr 30min–2hr); Mallaig–Rùm (Mon, Wed, Fri & Sat; 1hr 45min–3hr 30min); Muck–Rùm (Sat; 1hr 15min).

To Skye: Glenelg–Kylerhea (frequently daily; 15min); Mallaig–Armadale (Mon–Sat 6–7 daily; June to mid-Sept also Sun; 30min).

To South Uist: Castlebay–Lochboisdale (Mon, Wed, Thurs & Sat; 1hr 40min); Mallaig–Lochboisdale (Tues; 3hr 30min); Oban–Lochboisdale (daily except Tues & Sun; 5hr–6hr 50min).

Flights

Benbecula to: Barra (Mon–Fri 2daily; 20min); Stornoway (Mon–Fri 2 daily; 35min).

Glasgow to: Barra (Mon–Fri 2 daily, Sat 1 daily; 1hr 5min); Benbecula (Mon–Sat 1 daily; 1hr); Stornoway (Mon–Sat 2 daily; 1hr);

Inverness to: Stornoway (Mon–Fri 2 daily, Sat 1 daily; 20min).

CHAPTER SEVEN

NORTHEAST SCOTLAND

Alarge triangle of land thrusting into the North Sea, the **northeast of Scotland** comprises the area east of a line drawn roughly from Perth up to Forres, on the fringe of the Moray Firth. The area takes in the county of Angus and the city of Dundee to the south and, beyond the **Grampian Mountains**, the counties of Aberdeenshire and Moray and the city of Aberdeen. Geographically diverse, the landscape in the south is made up predominantly of undulating farmland, but, north of the Firth of Tay, this gives way to wooded glens, mountains and increasingly harsh land fringed by a dramatic coast of cliffs and long sandy beaches.

The northeast was the southern kingdom of the **Picts**, reminders of whom are scattered throughout the region in the form of numerous symbolic and beautifully carved stones found in fields, churchyards and museums – such as the one at **Meigle**. Remote, self-contained and cut off from the centres of major power in the south, the area never grew particularly prosperous, and a few feuding and intermarrying families, such as the Gordons, the Keiths and the Irvines, grew to wield disproportionate influence, building many of the region's **castles** and religious buildings and developing and planning its towns.

While the fishing industry is but a fondly held memory in many parts, a number of the northeast's ports have been transformed by the discovery of **oil** in the North Sea in the 1960s, particularly **Aberdeen**, Scotland's third-largest city. Aberdeen is the region's most stimulating urban centre, a fast, relatively sophisticated city which, for the time being, still rides a diminishing wave of oil-based prosperity. At the same time, **Dundee**, the next largest metropolis in the northeast, is making a valiant effort to emerge from a depressed post-industrial period with a reinvigorated arts scene and some heavily marketed tourist attractions, including Scott of the Antarctic's ship, *Discovery*. A little way up the Angus coast lie the historically important towns of **Arbroath** and **Montrose**, while, inland, the picturesque **Angus glens** cut into the Grampian mountains, offering a readily accessible taste of wild Highland scenery to both hikers and skiers.

North of the glens, **Deeside** is a fertile yet ruggedly attractive area made famous by the royal family, who have favoured the estate at **Balmoral** as a summer holiday retreat ever since Queen Victoria fell in love with it back in the 1840s. Beyond, the **Don Valley** is similarly endowed although less visited, while tranquil **Speyside**, a little way northwest, is best known as Scotland's premier whisky-producing region, where **malt whisky trails**, both official and unofficial, can be followed. The route around the northeast coast offers yet another aspect of a diverse region, with rugged cliffs, empty beaches and historic fishing villages tucked into coves and bays.

Northeast Scotland is well-served by an extensive **road** network, with fast links between Dundee and Aberdeen, while the area north and east of Aberdeen is dissected by a series of efficient routes. **Trains** from the south connect with Dundee, Aberdeen and other coastal towns, while an inland line from Aberdeen heads northwest to Elgin and on to Inverness. A reasonably comprehensive scheduled **bus service** is complemented by a network of **postbuses** in the Angus glens. Only in the most remote and mountainous parts does public transport disappear altogether.

DUNDEE AND ANGUS

The predominantly agricultural county of **Angus**, east of the A9 and north of the Firth of Tay, holds some of the northeast's greatest scenery and is relatively free of tourists, who tend to head further west for the Highlands proper. The coast from **Montrose** to **Arbroath** is especially inviting, with scarlet cliffs and sweeping bays, then, further south towards Dundee, gentler dunes and long sandy beaches. **Dundee** itself, although not the most obvious tourist destination, has in recent years become a more dynamic and progressive city, and makes for a less snooty alternative to Aberdeen.

In the north of the county, the long fingers of the **Angus glens** – heather-covered hills tumbling down to rushing rivers – are overlooked by the southern peaks of the Grampian Mountains. Each has its own feel and devotees, **Glen Clova** being, deservedly, one of the most popular, along with **Glen Shee**, which attracts large numbers of people to its ski slopes. Handsome market towns like **Brechin**, **Kirriemuir** and **Blairgowrie** are good bases for the area. Angus is also liberally dotted with **Pictish remains**.

Dundee

At first sight, **DUNDEE** can seem a grim place. In the nineteenth century it was Britain's main processor of jute – the world's most important vegetable fibre after cotton. Today, though economically depressed and somewhat overshadowed by its northerly neighbour, Aberdeen, it's still a refreshingly unpretentious and welcoming city, wonderfully placed on the banks of the Tay, with some good museums, a lively arts scene and useful transport connections throughout Angus.

Even prior to its Victorian heyday, Dundee was a town of considerable importance. It was here in 1309 that Robert the Bruce was proclaimed the lawful King of Scots, and during the Reformation it earned itself a reputation for tolerance, sheltering leading figures such as George Wishart and John Knox. During the Civil War, the town was destroyed by the Royalists and Cromwell's army. Later, prior to the Battle of Killiecrankie, the city was razed to the ground once more by Jacobite Viscount Dundee, who had been granted the place for his services to the Crown by James II. The city

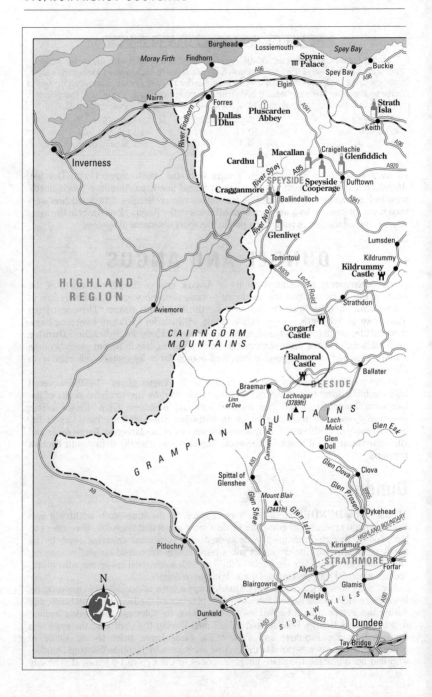

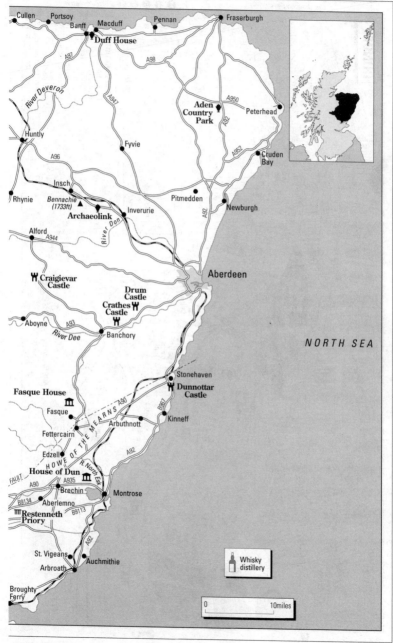

Cullen Portsoy Banff Macduff Pennan Fraserburgh
Duff House
A97 A98
River Deveron
A947
A950
Aden Country Park Peterhead
Huntly Fyvie
A96
A92
A952
Cruden Bay
Insch Pitmedden Newburgh
Rhynie *Bennachie (1733ft)*
Archaeolink Inverurie
River Don
Alford A944 River Dee
Aberdeen
♈ **Craigievar Castle**
Drum Castle
Crathes Castle
Aboyne A93 River Dee Banchory

NORTH SEA

Stonehaven
Fasque House **Dunnottar Castle**
Fasque A90 B967
Fettercairn Arbuthnott Kinneff
Edzell A92
House of Dun R. North Esk
A90 A935
B9134 Brechin Montrose
Aberlemno B9113
Restenneth Priory

St. Vigeans Auchmithie
Arbroath
Broughty Ferry

HOWE OF THE MEARNS
FAULT

🍾 Whisky distillery

0   10miles

© Crown copyright

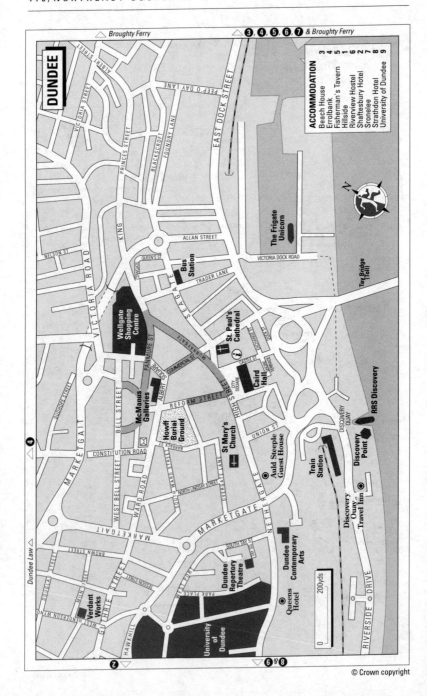

DUNDEE

△ Broughty Ferry △ ❸ ❹ ❺ ❻ ❼ & Broughty Ferry

ALBERT STREET
VICTORIA STREET
PRINCES STREET
PEEP O'DAY LANE
EAST DOCK STREET
BLACKSCROFT
FOUNDRY LANE
NELSON ST
KING STREET
VICTORIA ROAD
QUEEN'S ST
COWGATE
ALLAN STREET
VICTORIA DOCK ROAD
TRADER LANE
SEAGATE
PANMURE ST
COMMERCIAL ST
MURRAYGATE
DUDHOPE STREET
BELL STREET
ALBERT SQUARE
REFORM STREET
HIGH STREET
CASTLE ST
SEAGATE
EXCHANGE ST
CITY SQUARE
DOCK ST
WHITEHALL ST
SOUTH TAY ST
UNION ST
NETHERGATE
MARKETGATE
CONSTITUTION ROAD
WEST BELL STREET
WARD ROAD
WESTHALL STREET
BARRACK STREET
SOUTH WARD ROAD
NORTH LINDSAY STREET
OVERGATE LANE
MARKETGATE
BROWN STREET
SOUTH TAY ST
SOUTH UNION ST
HAWKHILL
WEST MARKETGAIT
PARK PLACE
WEST HENDERSON'S WYND
GUTHRIE STREET
SESSION STREET
JOHNSTON STREET
BROWN STREET
PERTH ROAD
RIVERSIDE DRIVE
DISCOVERY QUAY

ACCOMMODATION

Beach House	3
Errolbank	4
Fisherman's Tavern	5
Hillside	1
Riverview Hostel	6
Shaftesbury Hotel	2
Sronelee	7
Strathdon Hotel	8
University of Dundee	9

The Frigate Unicorn

Tay Bridge (Toll)

Bus Station

Wellgate Shopping Centre

St. Paul's Cathedral

Caird Hall

McManus Galleries

Howff Burial Ground

St Mary's Church

Auld Steeple Guest House

Train Station

Discovery Point

RRS Discovery

Discovery Quay Travel Inn

Dundee Contemporary Arts

Dundee Repertory Theatre

Verdant Works

University of Dundee

Queens Hotel

△ Dundee Law ◁ ❹ ◁ ❷ ◁ ❻ & ❽

200yds
0

© Crown copyright

picked itself up in the 1800s, its train and harbour links making it a major centre for shipbuilding, whaling and the manufacture of jute. Today, however, there's little left of Dundee's former glory, and its self-image hasn't been helped by the imposition of a couple of garish central shopping malls and the seemingly endless spread of 1970s housing estates around the city edges.

Many of Dundee's populace still depend on D.C. Thomson, the local publishing giant that produces the timelessly popular *Beano* and *Dandy* comics, as well as the *Sunday Post*, for their dwindling employment prospects. Although they have now all closed down, the city's many jam factories used to be a further major source of employment, hence the saying that Dundee was built on three Js – jam, jute and journalism. In terms of tourist sights, the most impressive is Captain Scott's Antarctic explorer ship, **RRS Discovery**, docked underneath the Tay Road Bridge, while a recreated jute mill, **Verdant Works**, has an engaging exhibition on the city's distinctive industrial heritage which has recently picked up tourism awards. However, for many visitors it is museums like the **McManus Art Galleries** and the upbeat atmosphere of the new **Dundee Contemporary Arts** building, along with the city's setting on the banks of the Tay with road and rail bridges reaching over to Fife, that make the most lasting impression.

Arrival, information and city transport

Dundee's **airport** (☎01382/643242; see p.471 for flight details) is five minutes' drive west from the city centre. There are no buses but a taxi will only set you back about £2. By **train**, you'll arrive at Taybridge Station on South Union Street (☎0345/484950), about 300yd south of the city centre near the river. Long-distance **buses** arrive at the Seagate bus station (☎01382/228054), a couple of hundred yards east of the centre.

Dundee's very helpful **tourist office** is right in the centre of things at 21 Castle St (June–Sept Mon–Sat 9am–6pm, Sun noon–4pm; Oct–May Mon–Sat 9am–5pm; ☎01382/527527), and sells bus tickets as well as booking accommodation. You can also pick up the free *Accent* listings magazine here, which details local theatre, music and exhibitions. The city's two daily newspapers are the morning *Courier & Advertiser* and the *Evening Telegraph & Post*, available at any newsagent.

Dundee's centre is reasonably compact and you can walk to most sights; **local buses** leave from the High Street or from Albert Square, one block to the north (for bus information, call ☎01382/201121). There are **taxi** ranks on Nethergate, or you could call City Cabs (☎01382/566666), Handy Taxis (☎01382/225825) or, in Broughty Ferry, Discovery Taxis (☎01382/732111).

Accommodation

In a city that's only just getting used to tourists, **accommodation** isn't plentiful, but it is comparatively cheap and there are some excellent guest houses. You'll find plenty of rooms out by the suburb of Broughty Ferry if you don't mind a twenty-minute bus ride into the city; Travel Dundee buses #8, #10 and #12 and Strathtay buses #73 and #76 leave from outside Littlewoods in the centre of town – the journey costs 90p. The **tourist office** charges ten percent of the first night's tariff for booking accommodation, which is then reimbursed by the hotel.

Hotels

Discovery Quay Travel Inn, Riverside Drive (☎01382/203240). Bland, modern chain hotel which has cornered the only waterfront spot in the city centre, right beside Discovery Point and the railway station. ②.

Queens Hotel, 160 Nethergate (☎01382/322515). Friendly old hotel which has seen better days but has a grand sweeping staircase and fine views of the Tay. Its location is good too, right in the heart of the action between the city and the University, and it has discount rates at the weekend. ⑤.

Shaftesbury Hotel, 1 Hyndford St (☎01382/669216). A converted jute merchant's house in a residential area very near town. Has a good and pleasantly informal restaurant. ④.

Strathdon Hotel, 277 Perth Rd (☎01382/665648). Family-run hotel in the west end of Dundee. The rooms are good, and the food is even better – breakfast is included and dinner is also available. ②.

Guest houses and B&Bs

Auld Steeple, 94 Nethergate (☎01382/200302). Unglamorous but simple, neat guest house in an old tenement block right in the city centre. ①.

Beach House, 22 Esplanade, Broughty Ferry (☎01382/776614). Fairly upmarket guest house fronting the Tay. ②.

Errolbank, 9 Dalgleish Rd (☎01382/462118). Victorian villa with good views of the Tay; all rooms have private bathrooms. ②.

Fisherman's Tavern, 12 Fort St, Broughty Ferry (☎01382/775941). Rooms above a cosy pub with decent food, great real ales and malt whiskies. ②.

Hillside, 43 Constitution St (☎01382/223443, *tildab@aol.com*). Homely, central B&B with four comfortable rooms. ②.

Stonelee, 69 Monifieth Rd, Broughty Ferry (☎01382/737812). The best option on a street filled with B&Bs. All rooms have en-suite bathrooms. ①.

Campus and hostel accommodation

Riverview Hostel, 127 Broughty Ferry Rd (☎01382/450565). Student residence with two small dorms and two twins on the upper level for backpackers. Open all year. Catch #75 bus from the High Street.

University of Dundee (☎01382/344039). Self-catering flats for weekly rental (from £220 a week for four-bedroom flat; July to mid-Sept), including use of the University swimming pool and sports centre. Short-term B&B is also available in student residences at 319 Perth Rd (☎01382/647171; ③).

The City

The best approach to Dundee is across the mile-and-a-half-long **Tay Road Bridge** from Fife. Offering a spectacular panorama of the city on the northern bank of the Tay, the bridge, opened in 1966, has a central walkway for pedestrians. An 80p toll is levied on cars leaving the city, but you can enter from the south for free. Running parallel is the **Tay Rail Bridge**, opened in 1887 to replace the spindly structure which collapsed in a storm only eighteen months after it was built in May 1878: the crew and 75 passengers on a train passing over the bridge at the time died. At over a mile and a half long, the present construction is the longest rail bridge in Europe.

Dundee's city centre is focused on **City Square**, a couple of hundred yards north of the Tay. The square and its surrounding streets have been much spruced up in recent years, with fountains, benches and extensive pedestrianization making for a relaxing environment, though the grand old buildings and churches have been rather overwhelmed by large shopping malls filled with a mundane mass of chain stores.

The main street, which is pedestrianized as it passes City Square, starts as Nethergate in the west, becomes High Street in the centre, then divides into Murraygate (which is also pedestrianized) and Seagate. Opposite this junction is the mottled spire of **St Paul's Episcopal Cathedral** (not open to the public), a rather gaudy George Gilbert Scott Gothic Revival structure, notable for its vividly sentimental stained glass. A hundred yards north of City Square, at the top of Reform Street, is the attractive **Albert Square**, home of the imposing D.C. Thomson building, Dundee High School and, on its eastern side, the **McManus Art Galleries and Museum** (Mon–Sat 10am–5pm, Sun 12.30–4pm, Thurs till 7pm; free). Designed by Gilbert Scott, the museum is Dundee's most impressive Victorian structure, with a delightful sweep of outside curved stone staircases and elaborate Gothic touches. Inside, the museum gives an excellent overview of the city's past, with displays ranging from Pictish stones to the Tay Bridge disaster. On the ground floor, the most impressive exhibit is the skeleton of a whale, washed up on a nearby beach in 1883 and eulogized in a poem by William McGonagall, a strong contender for world's worst poet. Upstairs, the magnificent **Albert Hall** – crowned by a roof of 480 pitch-pine panels in a Gothic arch – houses antique musical instruments, decorative glass, gold, silver, sculpture and some exquisite furniture. Don't miss the table at which the Duke of Cumberland signed the death warrants of captured Jacobites after the Battle of Culloden. On the same floor, the barrel-roofed **Victoria Gallery**'s red walls are heaving with nineteenth- and twentieth-century paintings, including some notable Pre-Raphaelite and Scottish collections (William McTaggart's seascapes being a particular highlight).

Across Ward Road from the museum, the **Howff Burial Ground** on Meadowside (daily 9am–5pm or dusk) has some great carved tombstones dating from the sixteenth to nineteenth centuries. Originally gardens belonging to a monastery, the land was given to Dundee for burials in 1564 by Mary, Queen of Scots. Five minutes' walk west of here, on West Henderson Wynd in Blackness, an award-winning museum, **Verdant Works**, tells the story of jute from its harvesting in India to its arrival in Dundee on clipper ships (April–Oct Mon–Sat 10am–5pm, Sun 11am–5pm; Nov–March Mon–Sat 10am–4pm, Sun 11am–4pm; £5 or £8.75 joint ticket with Discovery Point). In the nineteenth century, Dundee's jute mills employed 50,000 people and were responsible for the rapid industrialization and development of the city as a trading port. The museum, set in an old jute mill, recreates the turn-of-the-century factory floor, where you can watch jute being processed on fully operational quarter-size machines originally used for training workers.

Immediately west of the city centre, High Street becomes Nethergate and then Perth Road, which passes the University and as result has the best concentration of pubs, cafés and arts venues in the city. Principal among these is the exciting new **Dundee Contemporary Arts** (daily 10am–11pm; galleries open Tues–Sun 11.30am–7.30pm; ☎01382/432000) at 152 Nethergate, a stunningly-designed centre which incorporates galleries, a print studio, two art-cinema screens and an airy café-bar. The centre, opened in 1999, was designed by Richard Murphy, who converted an old brick building which had been a garage and car showroom into an inspiring new space, given energy and confidence by its bright, sleek interior and distinctive ship-like exterior. The café-bar, with large windows looking out over the industrial wasteland and railways lines which line the Tay, has quickly established itself as *the* place to hang out in Dundee, but the centre is also worth visiting for its stimulating temporary exhibitions and eclectic programme of arthouse films and cult classics.

Just south of the city centre, at the water's edge alongside the Tay Road Bridge, **Discovery Point** is an impressive development centring on the Royal Research Ship *Discovery* (same hours as Verdant Works; £5). A three-mast steam-assisted vessel built in Dundee in 1901 to take Captain Scott on his polar expeditions, it has been elegantly restored, with polished wood panels and brass trimmings giving scant indication of the privations suffered by the crew. Temperatures on board would plummet to –28°C in the Antarctic, and turns at having a bath came round every 47 days. Enthusiastic guides spin some fascinating yarns about the boat's colourful history, and the audio-visual spectacular you experience before boarding is compelling, if overhyped. The most recent addition, "Polarama", a hands-on gallery which recreates some of the conditions on the polar ice caps, was opened in 1999 by present-day Antarctic explorer Sir Ranulph Fiennes.

In total contrast is the endearingly simple wooden frigate **Unicorn** (mid-March to Oct daily 10am–5pm; Nov–March Mon–Fri 10am–4pm; £3.50), moored in Victoria Dock on the other side of the road bridge (there is a pathway between them). Built in 1824, it's the oldest British warship still afloat and was in active service up until 1968. During its service years, over 300 men would have lived and worked aboard. The fact that its 46 guns – eighteen-pounder cannons are still on display – were never fired in aggression probably accounts for its survival. Although the interior is sparse, the cannons, the splendid figureheads and the wonderful model of the ship in its fully rigged glory (23.5 miles of rope would have been used) are fascinating.

Out from the centre

A mile or so north of town, **Dundee Law** is the plug of an extinct volcano and, at 571ft, the city's highest point. Once the site of a seventh-century defensive hillfort, it is now an impressive lookout, with great views across the whole city and the Tay –the climb is steep and often windy. It takes thirty minutes to walk to the foot of the Law from the city centre, or you can take buses #3 or #4 from Albert Square.

The city's other volcanic plug of rock sits a mile to the west of Dundee Law. **Balgay Hill** is skirted by the wooded **Lochee Park**, while on its summit sits the **Mills Observatory** (April–Sept Tues–Fri 11am–5pm, Sat & Sun 12.30–4pm; Oct–March Mon–Fri 4–10pm, Sat & Sun 12.30–4pm; free), Britain's only full-time public observatory with a resident astronomer. The best time to go is after dark on winter nights; in summer there's little to be seen through the telescope, but well-explained, quirky exhibits and displays chart the history of space exploration and astronomy, and on sunny days you can play at being a human sundial and take in the fantastic views over the city through little telescopes. The observatory also has special opening times to coincide with eclipses and other astronomic events (details on ☎01382/435846). Buses #2, #36 and #37 drop you in Balgay Road, at the entrance to the park.

In the north of the city, at 34 Mains Loan between Clepington Road and the A90 ringroad, is the cheery **Shaws Dundee Sweet Factory** (June–Sept Mon–Fri 10.30am–5pm; Oct–Dec & March–May Wed only 1.30–4.30pm; 50p), situated in one part of the old Keiller's marmalade factory. It's nothing glamorous, but you'll find yourself rapt with child-like wonder at someone grappling with a five-foot slab of toffee in the small factory on the other side of a large viewing window. Bus #55 goes to the factory gate.

Four miles east of Dundee's city centre lies the seaside settlement of **BROUGHTY FERRY**, now engulfed by the city as a reluctant suburb. An eclectic mix of big villas built by jute barons up the hillside and small fishermen's cottages along the shoreline, "The Ferry" (as it's called by locals) has experienced a recent resurgence in popularity. Now a pleasant and relaxing spot with some good restaurants and pubs, it's far more unspoilt than Dundee, though the pollution level on the beach itself is pretty dire – all the city's sewage seems to end up here. The striking **Broughty Castle and Museum**, right by the seashore (April–Sept Mon–Sat 11am–5pm, Sun 12.30–4pm; Oct–March same hours except closed Mon; free), is worth a look. Built in the fifteenth century to protect the estuary, its four floors now house local-history exhibits, covering the story of Broughty Ferry as a fishing village and the history of whaling, as well as details of local geology and wildlife.

Just north of Broughty Ferry, at the junction of the A92 and B978, the chunky bricks of **Claypotts Castle** (July–Sept Sat & Sun 9.30am–6pm; £2.50) constitute one of Scotland's most complete Z-shaped tower houses. Built from 1569 to 1588, its two round towers have stepped projections to support extra rooms – a sixteenth-century architectural practice that makes Claypotts look like it's about to topple.

Eating, drinking and nightlife

The West End of Dundee, around the principal University and Perth Road, is the best area for **eating and drinking**, while the city centre, though good for a few pubs, is a bit of a non-starter for decent food. Broughty Ferry is a pleasant spot with a good selection of pubs and restaurants, which get particularly busy on summer evenings.

Restaurants

Agacan, 113 Perth Rd (☎01382/644227). Tiny Turkish restaurant with colourful paintings on the rough walls; they serve up decent kebabs and stuffed pittas, and also do takeaways. Open Tues–Sun evenings. Moderate.

Cul de Sac, 10 South Tay St (☎01382/202070). A branch of the successful Glasgow chain, well located between the Rep and DCA, serving inexpensive pasta and crepe dishes in the restaurant and snacks in the bar area. Three-course set menu for £10 (5–6.45pm) available in the restaurant.

Deep Sea, 81 Nethergate (☎01382/224449). The best of Dundee's fish'n'chip restaurants and takeaways, serving huge and tasty portions, but closes early (6.40pm).

Nawab, 43a Gray St, Broughty Ferry (☎01382/731800). An excellent and busy balti and tandoori restaurant, with a good reputation among locals. Moderate.

Le Bouquet Garni, 15 Shore Terrace (☎01382/202077). Roomy brasserie situated in the old Exchange Coffee House building just down from City Square, serving decent French, Italian and Mexican meals and filling home-made desserts. Set price three-course menus available for both lunch (£5) and dinner (£9). Moderate. Closed Sun evenings.

Raffles, 18 Perth Rd (☎01382/226344). Stylish bar/café serving wraps, inexpensive steaks and vegetarian meals until 7pm.

Jute Café-bar, Dundee Contemporary Arts Centre, 152 Nethergate. A large open-plan space on the lower level of the new arts centre, with views towards the Tay, offering table service and a decent range of sandwiches and inexpensive light meals. Open daily 10am–11pm.

Visocchi's, 40 Gray St, Broughty Ferry. Authentic and inexpensive Italian fare served in an informal, popular ice-cream café.

Pubs

Drouthie Neebours, 142–146 Perth Rd. A cheerful bar with a Robbie Burns theme, lavish painted murals and a lively student clientele.

Laing's, 8 Roseangle, off Perth Road. Usually packed on warm summer nights, thanks to its beer garden and great views over the Tay.

Mercantile, 100 Commercial St. Popular with the grey-suit brigade, but worth persevering for the excellent range of beers and quality pub snacks.

Nosey Parkers, 160 Nethergate. Recently smartened-up bar and bistro on the ground floor of the *Queen's Hotel*, between the DCA and the University.

O' Neill's, 80 North Lindsay Street. Beery Irish bar, with frequent live Celtic music.

Ship Inn, 121 Fisher St, Broughty Ferry. A narrow pub with a warm atmosphere right on the waterfront. The bistro upstairs has views over Tay and serves great food.

Nightlife

When it comes to post-pub nightlife, Dundee is muted, to say the least. There are three **nightclubs** on top of each other along South Ward Road, midway between the centre and the University precincts – *Fat Sam's*, *Enigma* and the *Mardi Gras* – all of which have a regular student following. Other places which might be worth checking out – keep an eye on posters or flyers for details – include *The Mission* on Ward Road and *The Cooler* on Session Street.

The opening of Dundee Contemporary Arts has not only provided the city with an impressive and exciting venue for exhibitions and cinema, but it has served as a reminder of Dundee's energy and ambition on the cultural front. Just up the road from DCA on Tay Square, north of Nethergate, is the prodigious Dundee Repertory Theatre (☎01382/223530), an excellent place for indigenously produced contemporary **theatre** and the home of the only permanent repertory company in Scotland. The best venue for **classical** music, including visits by the Royal Scottish Orchestra and other bigwigs, is Caird Hall (☎01382/434451), whose bulky frontage dominates City Square. For **movies**, the Odeon multiplex, in the Stack Leisure Park off Harefield Road (☎01382/400855), is predictably mainstream, while Dundee Contemporary Arts (☎01382/432000) has two comfy auditoriums showing an appealing range of foreign and art movies alongside the more challenging mainstream releases.

Listings

Airport Riverside Drive, Dundee (☎01382/643242).

American Express DP&L Travel Agents, 11 Albert St (☎01382/227232).

Banks Bank of Scotland, 2 West Marketgate (☎01382/317500); Clydesdale Bank, 96 High St (☎01382/203344); Royal Bank of Scotland, 3 High St (☎01382/228111); TSB, Meadowside (☎01382/228801).

Bike rental Just Bikes, 57 Grey St, Broughty Ferry (☎01382/732100); Nicholson's, 2 Forfar Rd (☎01382/461212).

Bookshop James Thin, 7 High St; Waterstone's, 34 Commercial St.

Car rental Arnold Clark, East Dock St (☎01382/225382); National, 45–53 Gellatly St (☎01382/224037); Hertz, 18 West Marketgait (☎01382/223711).

Bus enquiries National Express (☎0990 808080); Scottish Citylink (☎0990 505050); Strathtay Scottish for regional buses (☎01382/228345); Travel Dundee (☎01382/201121).

Currency exchange Thomas Cook, City Square (Mon–Fri 9am–5.30pm, Sat 9am–5pm; ☎01382/372500).

Football Dundee has two leading football clubs, which face each other across Tannadice Street in the north of the city. Tickets for both the premier-league Dundee United (ticket sales and information on ☎1382/833166) and first-division Dundee FC (ticket sales and information on ☎1382/826104) cost around £12.

Gay, lesbian and bisexual Switchboard ☎01382/202620.

Genealogical research Tay Valley History Society, 179 Princes St (☎1382/461845).

Golf Public courses at Ashludie, Golf Avenue, Monifieth (☎1382/532967); Caird Park (☎1382/434706); and Camperdown Country Park (☎1382/432688). Other courses along the Angus coast include Carnoustie (☎01241/853789), venue for the British Open in 1999.

Internet You can log onto the World Wide Web or send email from The Webgate Internet (☎01382/434332) at the Central Library in the Wellgate Shopping Centre.

Hospital Dundee Royal Infirmary (with 24hr accident and emergency), Barrack Road (☎01382/660111).

Library The Central Library is in the Wellgate Shopping Centre.

Pharmacy Boots, 49–53 High St (Mon–Wed, Fri & Sat 8.30am–5.45pm, Thurs 8.30am–7pm); Sunday opening is done on a rota basis.

Police Tayside Police HQ, West Bell St (☎01382/223200).

Post office GPO, 4 Meadowside (Mon–Fri 9am–5.30pm, Sat 9am–7pm; ☎0345 223344).

Rape crisis centre ☎01382/201291.

Swimming pools Olympia leisure complex (Mon–Fri 10am–8pm, Sat & Sun 10am–5pm; ☎1382/434888) beside Discovery Point.

Taxis City Cabs (☎01382/566666); Handy Taxis (☎01382/225825).

Travel agents USIT/Campus Travel, Airlie Place (☎01382/200412); Ramsay Travel, 14 Crichton St (☎01382/200394).

The Angus coast

Two roads link Dundee to Aberdeen and the northeast coast of Scotland – by far the more pleasant option is the slightly longer A92 coast road which joins the inland A90 at Stonehaven, just south of Aberdeen. Intercity **buses** follow both main routes, while the coast-hugging train line from Dundee is one of the most picturesque in Scotland, passing attractive beaches and impressive cliffs, and stopping in the old seaports of **Arbroath** and **Montrose**.

Arbroath and around

Since it was settled in the twelfth century, local fishermen have been landing their catches at **ARBROATH**, situated on the Angus coast where it starts to curve in from the North Sea towards the Firth of Tay. The **Arbroath smokie** – line-caught haddock, smoke-cured over smouldering oak chips and then poached in milk – is one of Scotland's best-known dishes, and should be eaten the original way, with a knob of butter, rather than in the more fancy pâtés and mousses that are now becoming popular. Although it has a great location, with long sandy beaches and stunning sandstone cliffs on either side of town as well as a lively harbour area, Arbroath, like Dundee, has suffered from short-sighted development, its historical associations all but subsumed by pedestrian walkways, a mess of one-way systems and ugly shopping centres.

Chiefly due to its harbour, Arbroath had, by the late eighteenth century, become a trading and manufacturing centre, famed for boot-making and sail-making (the *Cutty Sark*'s sails were made here). The town's real glory days, however, came much earlier in the thirteenth century with the completion of **Arbroath Abbey** in 1233 (April–Sept daily 9.30am–6pm; Oct–March Mon–Sat 9.30am–4pm, Sun 2–4pm; HS; £1.80), whose rose-pink sandstone ruins, described by Dr Johnson as "fragments of magnificence", stand on Abbey Street. Founded in 1178 but not granted abbey status until 1285, it was the scene of one of the most significant events in Scotland's history when, on April 6, 1320, a group of Scottish barons drew up the **Declaration of Arbroath**, asking the Pope to reverse his excommunication of Robert the Bruce and recognize him as king of a Scottish nation independent from England. The wonderfully resonant language of the document still makes for a stirring expression of Scottish nationhood: "For so long as one hundred of us remain alive, we will never in any degree be subject to the dominion of the English, since it is not for glory, riches or honour that we do fight, but for freedom alone, which no honest man loses but with his life." It was duly despatched to Pope John XXII in Avignon, who in 1324 agreed to Robert's claim.

The abbey was dissolved during the Reformation, and by the eighteenth century it was little more than a source of red sandstone for local houses. However, there is still enough left to get a good idea of how vast the place must have been: the semicircular west doorway is more or less intact, complete with medieval mouldings, and the south transept has a beautiful round window, once lit with a beacon to guide ships. In the early 1950s, the Stone of Destiny had a brief sojourn here when it was stolen from London by a group of Scottish nationalists and appeared, wrapped in a Scottish flag, at the High Altar. It was duly returned to Westminster Abbey, where it stayed until its recent move to Edinburgh Castle (see p.73).

Down by the harbour, the elegant Regency **Signal House Museum** (Mon–Sat 10am–5pm, July & Aug also Sun 2–5pm; free) stands sentinel as it has since 1813. The interior is now given over to some excellent local-history displays. A school room, fisherman's cottage and lighthouse kitchen have all been carefully re-created, with the addition of realistic smells.

WALKS AROUND ARBROATH

There's not much to see in Arbroath besides the abbey, but there are some great **walks** in the vicinity. From the Signal House, you can wander through the huddled cottages of the **Fit o' the Toon**, the harbour district where the smell of Arbroath smokies usually hangs heavy in the air. Beyond it, the seafront road heads into Victoria Park; at the far end of the road, a path climbs up over the red sandstone cliffs of **Whiting Ness**, stretching endlessly onto the horizon and eroded into a multitude of inlets, caves and arches that warrant hours of leisurely exploration. *The Arbroath Cliffs Nature Trail Guide*, available free from the tourist office, picks out twenty good viewing points along the first one and a half miles, and also gives details on the local fauna, flora and birds – you may even see puffins. After four miles the path comes to the foot of the neat little fishing village of **Auchmithie** (see below); a further four (very windy) miles north is the crest of **Lunan Bay**, a classic sweep of glorious sand crowned by the eerie ruins of Red Castle at the mouth of the Lunan Water.

St Vigeans and Auchmithie

Although now little more than a northwestern dormitory of Arbroath, the pristine and peaceful hamlet of **ST VIGEANS** is a fine example of a Pictish site colonized by Christians – the church is set defiantly on a pre-Christian mound at the centre of the village. Many Pictish and earlier remains are housed in the wonderful little **museum** (April–Sept Mon–Sat 9.30am–5.30pm, Sun 2–5.30pm; collect the key from cottage no. 7 if closed; free), including the Drosten Stone, presumed to be a memorial. One side depicts a hunt, laced with an abundance of Pictish symbolism, while the other side bears a cross, which dates it to around 850 AD.

Four miles north of Arbroath by road or coastal footpath, the clifftop village of **AUCHMITHIE** is the true home of the Arbroath smokie. However, the village didn't have a proper harbour until last century – local fishermen, apparently, were carried to their boats by their wives to avoid getting wet feet – so Arbroath became the more important port and laid claim to the delicacy. Now an attractive little fishing village, Auchmithie's main attraction is the *But'n'Ben* restaurant (☎01241/877223; closed Tues), one of the best along this coast, which specializes in delicious Scottish dishes and seafood.

Practicalities

Arbroath's helpful **tourist office**, at Market Place right in the middle of town (April, May & Sept Mon–Fri 9am–5pm, Sat 10am–5pm; June–Aug Mon–Sat 9.30am–5.30pm, Sun 10am–3pm; Oct–March Mon–Fri 9am–5pm, Sat 10am–5pm; ☎01241/872609), can recommend local walks and book accommodation. **Buses** stop at the station on Catherine Street (☎01241/870646), about a five-minute walk south of the tourist office, while **trains** (☎0345/484950) arrive at the station just across the road on Keptie Street.

The best place **to stay** is at the excellent *Five Gables Guest House* (☎01241/871632; ①), above the golf course a mile south of town on the A92: formerly the golf clubhouse, it has a great position overlooking the sea. Alternatively, try the *Harbour House Guest House*, 4 The Shore (☎01241/878047; ①), down by the harbour, which is also where you'll find the best **restaurants** and **pubs**. The best place to sample Arbroath smokies is at *The Old Brewhouse* (☎01241/879945), a convivial and moderately priced restaurant-cum-pub by the harbour wall at the end of High Street, or check out some of the 180 varieties of rum on offer at the *Smugglers Tavern*, on The Shore.

Montrose and around

"Here's the Basin, there's Montrose, shut your een and haud your nose." As the old rhyme indicates, **MONTROSE**, a seaport and market town since the thirteenth century, can sometimes smell a little rich, mostly because of its position on the edge of a virtually landlocked two-mile-square lagoon of mud known as the Basin. But with the wind in the right direction, Montrose is a great little town to visit, with a pleasant old centre and an interesting museum. The Basin too is of interest: flooded and emptied twice daily by the tides, it is a rich nature reserve for the host of geese, swans and waders who frequent the ooze to look for food. On the south side of the Basin, a mile out of Montrose along the A92, the **Montrose Basin Wildlife Centre** (daily: April–Oct 10.30am–5pm; Nov–March 10.30am–4pm; £2.50) has binoculars, high-powered telescopes, bird hides and remote-control video cameras to check out the diverse bird- and wildlife. In addition, the centre's resident ranger takes regular guided walks around the reserve.

Montrose locals are known as Gable Endies, because of the unusual way in which the town's eighteenth- and nineteenth-century merchants, influenced by architectural styles they had seen on the Continent, built their houses gable-end to the street. The few remaining original gabled houses line the wide **High Street**, off which are numerous tiny alleyways and quiet courtyards.

Two blocks behind the soaring kirk steeple at the lower end of High Street, the **Montrose Museum and Art Gallery** (Mon–Sat 10am–5pm; free) in Panmure Place on the western side of **Mid Links** park, is one of Scotland's oldest museums, dating from 1842. For a small-town museum, it has some particularly unusual exhibits, among them the so-called Samson Stone, a Pictish relic dating from 900 AD, and bearing a carving of Samson slaying the Philistines. In the local history section, look out for the mechanical paper sculpture of the town of Montrose, with a green train running along the top and yachts sailing by. On the upper floor, the maritime history exhibits include a cast of Napoleon's death mask and a model of a British man-of-war, sculpted out of bone by Napoleonic prisoners at Portsmouth. Most intriguing, however, is the enigmatic message on a scrap of paper found in a bottle at nearby Ferryden beach in 1857, written by the chief mate of a brigantine eighty years earlier: "Blowing a hurricane lying to with close-reefed main topsails ship waterlogged. Cargo of wood from Quebec. No water on board, provisions all gone. Ate the dog yesterday, three men left alive. Lord have mercy on our souls. Amen."

Outside the entrance of the museum stands a winsome study of a boy by local sculptor William Lamb (1893–1951). More of his work can be seen in the moving **William Lamb Memorial Studio** on Market Street (July to mid-Sept daily 2–5pm; for entry at other times ask at the museum; ☎01674/673232; free), including bronze heads of the Queen, Princess Margaret and the Queen Mother. The earnings from these pieces enabled him to buy the studio in the 1930s, which he donated to the town of Montrose on his death. A superbly talented but largely unheralded artist, Lamb's work is made the more impressive by the fact that he taught himself to sculpt with his left hand, having suffered a war wound in his right.

After the impressive wildlife of Montrose Basin, it's easy to ignore the town's fabulous golden **seashore**. The beach road, Marine Avenue, across from the town museum, heads down through sand dunes and golf links to car parks fringing the fine, wide beach overlooked by a slender white lighthouse.

Around Montrose: the House of Dun

Across the Basin, four miles west of Montrose, is the Palladian **House of Dun** (Easter weekend & May–Sept daily 1.30–5pm; Oct Sat & Sun 1.30–5pm; NTS; £3.90, grounds only £1), accessible on the regular Montrose–Brechin bus (#30) – ask the driver to let you off outside. Built in 1730 for David Erskine, Laird of Dun, to designs by William Adam, the house was opened to the public in 1989 after extensive restoration, and is crammed full of period furniture and objets d'art. Inside, the ornate relief plasterwork is the most impressive feature, extravagantly emblazoned with Jacobite symbolism.

You can also see some gorgeous pieces of intricate needlework, stitched by the illegitimate child of King William IV, Lady Augusta, who married into the Dun family in 1827.

The buildings in the courtyard – a hen house, gamekeeper's workshop and potting shed – have been renovated, and include a tearoom and a shop where local weavers give displays of their traditional skills.

Practicalities

The Montrose **tourist office** is squeezed into a former public toilet next to the library, at the point where Bridge Street merges into the lower end of High Street (April–June & Sept Mon–Sat 10am–5pm; July & Aug Mon–Sat 9.30am–5.30pm; ☎01674/672000). Most **buses** stop in the High Street, while the **train** station lies a block back on Western Road (hourly trains from Dundee and Aberdeen). For B&B **accommodation**, try *Oaklands*, over the river bridge at 10 Rossie Island Rd (☎01674/672018, *oaklands12@aol.com*; ①), or the friendly *Murray Lodge Hotel*, 2–8 Murray St, the northern continuation of High Street (☎01674/678880; ③). A nearby alternative is *Kirkside* (☎01674/830780; ②), an isolated converted fishing bothy situated on the edge of the sand dunes by St Cyrus Nature Reserve, just over two miles north of Montrose at the mouth of the North Esk River.

For **eating**, the liveliest place in Montrose is unquestionably *Roo's Leap*, a sports bar and restaurant by the golf club off the northern end of Traill Drive. The food is an unlikely, but excellent, mix of Scottish, American and Australian. If you want a **drink**, the vitality of *Roo's Leap* is matched by her sister café-bar, *Sharky's*, on George Street, which serves coffee and light snacks, while on High Street the more traditional *Cornerhouse Hotel* hosts folk nights on Tuesdays. The *Salutation Inn*, 69–71 Bridge St, serves good, cheap food and has a beer garden.

Strathmore and the Angus glens

Immediately north of Dundee, the low-lying Sidlaw Hills divide the city from the rich agricultural region of **Strathmore**, whose string of tidy market towns lies on a fertile strip along the southernmost edge of the heather-covered lower slopes of the Grampian Mountains. These towns act as gateways to the **Angus glens** – or "Braes o' Angus", a series of tranquil valleys penetrated by few roads and offering some of the most rugged and majestic landscapes of northeast Scotland. It's a rain-swept, wind-blown, sparsely populated area, whose roads become impassable with the first snows, sometimes as early as October, and in the summer there are ferocious midges to contend with. Nevertheless, most of the glens, particularly **Glen Clova**, are well and truly on the tourist circuit, with the rolling hills and dales attracting hikers, birdwatchers and botanists in the summer, grouse shooters and deerhunters in autumn and a growing number of skiers in winter. The most useful road through the glens is the A93, which cuts through **Glen Shee** to Braemar on Deeside (see p.454). It's pretty dramatic stuff,

---

SKIING IN THE ANGUS GLENS

For information on **skiing** in the Angus glens, call Ski Glenshee (☎013397/41320), who also offer ski rental and lessons. In addition, lessons, skis and boards are available from Cairnwell Mountain Sports (☎01250/885255), at the Spittal of Glenshee. **Ski rental** starts at around £12 a day, while lessons are around £10 for two hours. **Lift passes** cost £17.50 per day or £70 for a five-day (Mon–Fri) ticket. For the latest snow and weather conditions, phone the Ski Hotline (☎0891/654656).

threading its way over Britain's highest main road pass – the **Cairnwell Pass** (2199ft). Public transport in the region is limited: to get up the glens you'll have to rely on the **postbuses** from Blairgowrie (for Glen Shee) and Kirriemuir (for glens Clova and Prosen).

Glen Shee

The most dramatic and best known of the Angus glens, **Glen Shee** is dominated by its ski fields, ranged over four mountains above the Cairnwell mountain pass. During the winter season – December to March – skiers, predominantly from central Scotland, brave the ridiculously cold temperatures and bitter winds. Ski lifts and tows give access to gentle beginners' slopes, while experienced skiers can try the more intimidating Tiger run. In summer it's all a bit sad, with lifeless chair lifts and bare, scree-covered slopes, although hang-gliders take advantage of the crosswinds between the mountains and there are some excellent hiking and mountain-biking routes.

The well-heeled town of **BLAIRGOWRIE** (officially Blairgowrie and Rattray), little more than one main road set among raspberry fields on the glen's southernmost tip, is as good a place as any to base yourself – and is particularly useful in winter if you plan to ski. Set right on the river, the town's only claim to fame is that St Ninian once camped at Wellmeadow, a pleasant grassy triangle in the town centre. If you've time to kill here, wander up the leafy river bank to **Keathbank Mill** (daily May–Oct 10.30am–5pm; £3.50), a huge old jute mill with an 1862 steam turbine driven by the largest working water wheel in Scotland. Also housed within the complex are some absorbing workshops where the country's largest heraldic crests are carved.

Blairgowrie **tourist office** (Easter–June, Sept & Oct Mon–Sat 9.30am–5.30pm, Sun 11am–4pm; July & Aug Mon–Sat 9am–7pm, Sun 10am–6pm; Nov–Easter Mon–Fri 9.30am–5.30pm, Sat 10am–2pm; ☎01250/872960), on the high side of the Wellmeadow, can help with **accommodation**. Over the bridge spanning the fast-flowing River Ericht, Blairgowrie melts into its twin community of **Rattray**, where, on the main street (Boat Brae), you'll find the excellent *Ivy Bank House* B&B (☎01250/873056; ③), offering sweeping views of the river and surrounding hills, as well as use of a floodlit tennis court. Alternatively, there's the opulent, ivy-covered *Kinloch House* (☎01250/884237; ⑦), one of the area's most prestigious hotels, set in its own vast grounds three miles west of town on the A923, while, at the other end of the scale, **camping** is available at the year-round *Blairgowrie Holiday Park* on Rattray's Hatton Road (☎01250/872941). The town boasts plenty of places to **eat**: *Cargills* by the river on Lower Mill Street (☎01250/876735; closed Mon) is the best bet for a formal meal, while, for lighter meals and takeaways, there's the *Dome Restaurant*, just behind the tourist office, which has been run by two local Italian families since the 1920s. For good **pub** grub try the *Brig o'Blair* on the Wellmeadow, or head six miles out of town on the A93 to the delightfully situated *Bridge of Cally Hotel* (☎01250/886231; ③), which also has rooms. **Bikes** can be rented from the *Blairgowrie Holiday Park* (see above), and from Mountains and Glens (☎01250/874206), 300yd from the tourist office on Railway Road.

Nearly twenty miles north of Blairgowrie, the **SPITTAL OF GLENSHEE**, though ideally situated for skiing, is little more than a tacky service area, only worth stopping at for a quick drink or bite to eat. However, it does boast an excellent bunkhouse run by Cairnwell Mountain Sports, on the A93 (☎01250/885255), which rents out skis, bikes and even offers hang-gliding lessons. In addition, it's handily close to one of the nicest places to stay in the area, *Dalmunzie House* (☎01250/885224; ⑥), a gorgeous, turreted, Highland sporting lodge, reflecting the peace and tranquillity of the rugged scenery. From the Spittal the road climbs another five miles or so to the ski centre at the crest of the Cairnwell Pass.

Blairgowrie is well linked by **bus** to both Perth and Dundee by the hourly #57; to get up Glen Shee, however, you'll have to rely on the **postbus**, which leaves town (Mon–Sat) at 9.05am and returns from the Spittal of Glenshee at 2.15pm.

Glen Isla and Meigle

Running parallel to Glen Shee, and linked to it via the A926, is **Glen Isla**, dominated by Mount Blair (2441ft). A lot less dramatic than its sister glens, it suffers from an excess of angular conifers alongside great bald chunks of hillside waiting to be planted. At the mouth of the glen, on the B954, lies the tiny village of **MEIGLE**, fifteen miles north of Dundee and home to Scotland's most important collection of early Christian and Pictish inscribed stones. Housed in a modest former schoolhouse, the **Meigle Museum** (April–Sept daily 9.30am–6pm; HS; £1.80) displays some thirty pieces dating from the seventh to the tenth centuries, all found in and around the nearby churchyard. The majority are either gravestones that would have lain flat, or cross slabs, inscribed with the sign of the cross and usually standing. Most impressive is the 7ft-tall great cross slab, said to be Guinevere's gravestone, carved on one side with a portrayal of Daniel surrounded by lions, a beautifully executed equestrian group, and mythological creatures including a dragon and a centaur. On the other side various beasts are surmounted by the "ring of glory" – a wheel containing a cross carved and decorated in high relief. The exact meaning and purpose of the stones and their enigmatic symbols is obscure, and why so many of the stones were found at Meigle is also a mystery. The most likely theory suggests that Meigle was once an important ecclesiastical centre which attracted secular burials of prominent Picts.

Heading north into Glen Isla along the B954, the River Isla narrows and then plunges some 60ft into a deep gorge to produce the classically pretty waterfall of **Reekie Linn**, or "smoking fall", so called because of the water mist produced when the fall hits a ledge and bounces a further 20ft into a deep pool known as the Black Dub. The glen cheers up enormously north of the tiny hamlet of **KIRKTON OF GLENISLA**, ten miles or so up the glen. Here, the cosy *Glenisla Hotel* (☎01575/582223; ④) is great for eating and drinking, as well as being a good base for walking. In the nearby Glenisla forest there are some trails for hiking, while, just before Kirkton, a turnoff on the right-hand side leads to the Glenmarkie Riding Centre (☎01575/582341), which offers pony trekking and wonderfully isolated B&B (②).

Transport connections into the glen are limited: the plain Strathmore town of Alyth, three miles north of Meigle, is on the main bus routes linking Blairgowrie with Dundee and Kirriemuir, while the hourly #57 bus from Dundee to Perth passes through Meigle. The only transport up to Kirkton is a postbus which leaves Alyth at 7.40am (Mon–Sat).

Forfar, Glamis and Aberlemno

Around fifteen miles north of Dundee, along the main A90, lies **FORFAR**, Angus's county town and the ancient capital of the Picts. Although hardly the most thrilling place in the district, exuding a solid conservatism, it warrants an afternoon's exploration. Old Pictish connections are still evident in Forfar's strong support for the Scottish National Party (SNP), with a profusion of Scottish flags and stirring messages on civic buildings. The wide High Street is framed by some impressive Victorian architecture and small old-fashioned shops. Midway along, at no. 20, the **Meffen Institute Museum and Art Gallery** (Mon–Sat 10am–5pm; free) exhibits Neolithic, Pictish and Celtic remains and a thoroughly enjoyable collection of re-created historical street scenes. The most disturbing examines the town's seventeenth-century passion for witch-hunting, with a taped re-creation of locals baying for blood. There is also a comprehensive interactive computer catalogue of all the Pictish stones in Angus, and an excellent art gallery.

A series of glacial lochs peter out in the west of the town at **Forfar Loch**, now surrounded by a pleasant country park with a visitors' centre and three-mile nature trail. Two miles east, high above the wooded Loch Fithie, are the impressive remains of **Restenneth Priory** (free access), approached along an easy-to-miss side road off the B9113. Built by King Nechtan of the Picts in about the eighth century, it was adapted as an Augustinian priory in the twelfth century. Still something of a Pictish shrine, it's common to find mementoes and flowers left by pilgrims. The splayed foot spire, first seen beckoning from the road, was added in the fifteenth century.

Forfar's small **tourist office** (April–June & Sept Mon–Sat 10am–5pm; July & Aug Mon–Sat 9.30am–5.30pm; ☎01307/467876) is at 45 East High St, opposite the soaring steeple of the parish church. Numerous shops and bakers stock the famous **Forfar Bridie**, a huge folded pastry-case of mince, onion and seasonings, including Saddlers, a few door down from the tourist office, and McLarens (the locals' favourite), at 8 West High St. Otherwise, all-day **food** and **drink** can be found at the *Royal Hotel* on Castle Street, by the Town Hall.

Glamis Castle

Regular buses (#125) from Forfar (4 daily; 40min) to Dundee pass the pink-sandstone **Glamis Castle** (April–Oct daily 10.30am–4.45pm; castle and grounds £5.40, grounds only £2.50), a mile north of the picturesque village of **GLAMIS** (pronounced "Glahms"). A wondrously over-the-top, L-shaped five-storey pile set in an extensive landscaped park complete with deer and pheasants, this is one of the most famous Scottish castles. Shakespeare chose it as a central location in *Macbeth* and its royal connections (as the childhood home of the Queen Mother and birthplace of Princess Margaret) make it one of the essential stops on every bus tour of Scotland, though for many visitors the Queen Mum gloss is laid on rather thick.

Approaching the castle down the long main drive, a melee of turrets, towers and conical roofs appear fantastically at the end of the sweeping avenue of trees, framed by the Grampian Mountains. The bulk of the current building dates from the fifteenth century, although many of the later additions (particularly from the seventeenth century) give it its startling Disneyesque appearance. Glamis began life as a comparatively humble hunting lodge, used in the eleventh century by the kings of Scotland. In 1372, King Robert II gave the property to his son-in-law, Sir John Lyon, who built the core of the present building. His descendants, the earls of Kinghorne and Strathmore – the fourteenth of which was the Queen Mother's father – have lived here ever since.

The guided tour starts upstairs in the Victorian **Dining Room**, notable for its fine rose and thistle ceiling. The garish silver ship that forms the centrepiece of the table display was a golden wedding gift to the thirteenth earl from his estate workers in 1903. Another present – the grandfather clock in the corner – came from their 27 grandchildren, including a three-year-old Elizabeth Bowes-Lyon, now the Queen Mother. The atmosphere changes dramatically in the fifteenth-century **Crypt**, more properly the Lower Hall of the original tower house, which you enter through a door in the wood panelling of the Dining Room. The crypt's 12ft-thick walls enclose a haunted "lost" room, reputed to be have been sealed with the red-bearded Lord of Glamis and Crawford (also known as Beardie Crawford) inside, after he dared to play cards with the Devil one Sabbath. From here, the tour passes up a seventeenth-century staircase, whose hollow central pillar provided a primitive system of central heating.

Next is the arch-roofed **Drawing Room**, with delightful wedding-cake plasterwork (dated 1621). Classical portraits line the walls, the most notable being the vast Jacob de Wet family grouping of the third earl, who was responsible for many of the castle's seventeenth-century alterations. De Wet painted the earl in Classical armour that, unfortunately, looks like a flimsy negligee. The highlight of the tour is the family **Chapel**, completed in 1688. Jacob de Wet was commissioned to produce the frescoes from the family Bible, although his depictions of Christ wearing a hat and St Peter in a pair of glasses have raised eyebrows ever since. The chapel is said to be haunted by the spectre of a grey lady, the ghost of the sixth Lady Glamis who was burnt as a witch under orders of James V. The **Billiard Room**, complete with full-sized table and a beautiful polished walnut piano that cost £199 when it was commissioned in 1866, is decorated with various species of stuffed bird and lined with paintings and tapestries, of which the vast and colourful *Fruit Market* by Flemish artist Frans Snyders draws the most attention. **King Malcolm's Room**, so called because it is believed he died nearby in 1034, is most notable for its carved wooden chimneypiece, on which many of its most decorative panels are, in fact, highly polished leather.

From here, the tour passes into the **Royal Apartments**, where you can see the Queen Mother's delicate gilt four-poster bed which was a wedding present from her mother, who embroidered the names and dates of birth of her ten children into its panels. **Duncan's Hall**, a fifteenth-century guardroom, is the traditional – but inaccurate – setting for Duncan's murder by Macbeth (it actually took place near Elgin). Finally, the tour concludes with a random display of family artefacts that include the Queen Mother's old doll's house.

Glamis' grounds are worth a few hours in their own right. Highlights include the lead statues of James VI and Charles I at the top of the main drive, the seventeenth-century Baroque sundial, the formal Italian Garden and the verdant walks out to Earl John's Bridge and through the woodland. In Glamis village the humble **Angus Folk Museum** (Easter weekend & May–Sept daily 11am–4.30pm, Oct Sat & Sun only; NTS; £2.50), housed in six low-slung cottages in Kirk Wynd, has a bewildering array of local ephemera, including bizarrely named agricultural implements, a nineteenth-century horse-drawn hearse and a section on local bothies.

Aberlemno

Five miles east of Forfar, straddling the ridge-topping B9134, the hamlet of **ABER-LEMNO** is home to a superb collection of open-air Pictish stones (Oct–April boxed out of sight in weatherproofed wood). In the churchyard, just off the main road, an eighth-century cross slab combines a swirling Christian Celtic cross with Pictish beasts on one side and an elaborate Pictish battle scene on the other, thought to commemorate victory over the Northumbrians in 685 AD. Three other stones, bristling with Pictish and early Christian symbols, sit by the main road, overlooking huge sweeps of valley and mountain, though plans are afoot to move all the stones to a nearby indoor location to prevent further erosion. Bus #21A, from Forfar to Brechin, stops in Aberlemno.

Kirriemuir and glens Prosen, Clova and Doll

The sandstone town of **KIRRIEMUIR**, known locally as Kirrie, is set on a hill six miles northwest of Forfar on the cusp of glens Clova and Prosen. Despite the influx of hunters up for the "season", it's still a pretty special place, a haphazard confection of narrow closes, twisting wynds and steep braes. The main cluster of streets have all the appeal of an old film set, with their old-fashioned bars, tiled butcher's shop, tartan outlets and haberdasheries somehow managing to avoid being contrived and quaint – although the rapid recobbling of the town centre, around a twee statue of Peter Pan, undermines this somewhat.

In the nineteenth century, as a linen manufacturing centre, it was made famous by a local handloom-weaver's son, J.M. Barrie, with his series of novels about "Thrums", in particular *A Window in Thrums* and his third novel, *The Little Minister*. The author was to become more famous still as the creator of Peter Pan, the little boy who never grew up, a story which Barrie penned in 1904 – some say as a response to a strange upbringing dominated by the memory of his older brother, who died as a child. **Barrie's birthplace**, a plain little whitewashed cottage at 9 Brechin Rd (Easter weekend & May–Sept Mon–Sat 11am–5pm, Sun 1.30–5pm; Oct Sat 11am–5pm, Sun 1.30–5pm; NTS; £2), displays his writing desk, photos and newspaper clippings. The washhouse outside – romantically billed as Barrie's first "theatre" – was apparently the model for the house built by the Lost Boys in Never-Never Land for Wendy. Barrie chose to be buried at the nearby St Mary's Episcopal Church in Kirrie, despite being offered a more prestigious plot at London's Westminster Abbey. Another local son who attracts a handful of rather different pilgrims is Bon Scott (1946–80) of the rock band AC/DC, who was born and lived here before emigrating to Australia.

High above the B957 to Brechin, Kirriemuir Hill is crowned by a **camera obscura** (contact the tourist office for opening hours) in an old cricket pavilion. This unexpected treasure was donated to the town in 1930 by Barrie, and offers splendid views of Strathmore and the glens. On the other side of the town centre, a couple of hundred yards down the A928 to Glamis, is the **Aviation Museum** (April–Sept Mon–Sat 10am–5pm, Sun 11am–5pm; free), the lifetime collection of Richard Moss, who'll invariably be your guide through the jumble of military uniforms, photos, World War II memorabilia (including British and German propaganda leaflets) and Airfix models.

Kirrie's helpful **tourist office** is in Cumberland Close (April–June & Sept Mon–Sat 10am–5pm; July & Aug Mon–Sat 9.30am–5.30pm; ☎01575/574097), in the new development behind *Visocchi's* in the main square. **Accommodation** is available at *Crepto B&B*, Kinnordy Place (☎01575/572746; ①), or the respectable *Airlie Arms*, St Malcolm's Wynd (☎01575/572487; ③). *Visocchi's* is great for daytime **snacks** and ice cream, while the *Airlie*, and *Thrums Hotel*, on Bank Street, both serve good food in the evening. Of the **pubs**, the *Kilt and Clogs*, behind the tourist office, is the most lively. **Postbuses** into glens Clova and Prosen leave from the main post office, on Reform Street, at 8.30am (Mon–Sat). A second Glen Clova bus leaves around 3pm (Mon–Fri), but only goes as far as Clova village before returning to Kirriemuir. Hourly buses connect with Forfar for onward travel.

Glen Prosen

Five miles north of Kirrie, the low-key hamlet of **DYKEHEAD** marks the point where glens **Prosen** and Clova divide. **Accommodation** is available here at the *Royal Jubilee Arms Hotel* (☎01575/540381; ③), an old inn scarred by a grim modern conversion that, nonetheless, provides excellent all-day food, drink and Sunday-night **ceilidhs**. A mile or so up Glen Prosen, you'll find the house where Captain Scott and fellow explorer Doctor Wilson planned their ill-fated trip to Antarctica in 1910–11, with a roadside **stone cairn** commemorating the expedition. From here, Glen Prosen proper unfolds before you. Little has changed since Scott's time, and it remains essentially a quiet wooded backwater, with all the wild and rugged splendour of the other glens but without the crowds. To explore the area thoroughly you need to go on foot, but a good road circuit can be made by crossing the river at the tiny village of **GLENPROSEN** and returning to Kirriemuir along the western side of the glen via Pearsie.

The best walk in the area is the reasonably easy four-mile **Minister's Path** (so called because the local minister would walk this way twice every Sunday to conduct services in both glens), connecting Prosen and Clova. Take the footpath between the kirk and the bridge in Glenprosen village, then the right fork where the track splits and continue over the colourful burnt moorland down into Clova. As there is no afternoon return service by postbus from Prosen to Kirriemuir, you either have to stay the night or follow the path to its end, **Wester Eggie**, and pick up the Clova village postbus (Mon–Fri 3.30pm).

Glen Clova and Glen Doll

Of all the Angus glens, **Glen Clova** – which in the north becomes Glen Doll – with its stunning cliffs, heather slopes and valley meadows, is the firm favourite of many. Although it can get unpleasantly congested in peak season, the area is still remote enough so that you can leave the crowds with little effort. Wildlife is abundant, with deer on the mountains, wild hares and even grouse and the occasional buzzard. The meadow flowers on the valley floor and arctic plants (including great splashes of white and purple saxifrage) on the rocks also make it something of a botanist's paradise.

The B955 from Dykehead and Kirriemuir divides at the Gella bridge over the swift-coursing River South Esk (unofficially, road traffic is encouraged to use the western branch of the road for travel up the glen, and the eastern side going down). Six miles north of Gella, the two branches of the road join up once more at the hamlet of **CLOVA**, little more than the hearty *Clova Hotel* (☎01575/550222; ③), which also has a simple outside bunkhouse (£5 per night), and hosts regular barbecues, ceilidhs and even helicopter and balloon flights. Meals and real ale are available in the lively *Climbers' Bar* at the side of the hotel. An excellent, if fairly strenuous, four-hour walk from behind the old school at the back of the hotel leads up into the mountains and around the lip of **Loch Brandy**, which legend predicts will one day flood and drown the valley below.

North from Clova village, the road turns into a rabbit-strewn lane coursing along the riverside for four miles to the car park and informal **campsite** in **Glen Doll**, a useful starting point for numerous superb **walks** (see box). From the car park, it's only a few hundred yards further to the **youth hostel** (☎01575/550236; mid-March to Oct), a cheerful restored hunting lodge that boasts a squash court along with the usual facilities.

WALKS FROM GLEN DOLL

Ordnance Survey Landranger maps nos. 43 & 44.

These walks are some of the main routes across the Grampians from the Angus glens to Deeside, many of which follow well-established old drovers' roads. A number of them cross the royal estate of Balmoral, and Prince Charles's favourite mountain – Lochnagar – can be seen from all angles. The walks should always be approached with care; make sure to follow the usual safety precautions.

Capel Mounth to Ballater (fifteen miles/7hr). Head across the bridge from the car park, turning right after a mile when the track crosses the Cald Burn. Out of the wood, the path zigzags its way up fierce slopes before levelling out on the moorland plateau. Soon descending, the path crosses a scree near the eastern end of Loch Muick. With the loch to your left, walk down along the scree till you reach the River Muick, crossing the bridge to take the quiet track along the river's northern shore to Ballater.

Capel Mounth round trip (fifteen miles/8hr). Follow the above to Loch Muick, then follow the path down to loch level and double back on yourself along the loch's southern shore. When the track crosses the Black Burn, either take the steep left fork or continue along the shore for another mile, heading up the dramatic Streak of Lightning path that follows Corrie Chash. Both paths meet at the ruined stables below Sandy Hillock. Just beyond, take the path to the left, descending rapidly to the waterfall by the bridge at Bachnagairn, where a gentle burn-side track leads the three miles back to Glen Doll car park.

Jock's Road to Braemar (fourteen miles/7hr). Take the road north from the car park past the youth hostel. After almost a mile, follow the signposted Jock's Road to the right, keeping on the northern bank of the burn. Pass a barn, Davey's Shelter, below Cairn Lunkhard and continue onto a wide ridge towards the path's summit at Crow Craigies (3018ft). From here, the path bumps down over scree slopes to the head of Loch Callater. Go either way round the loch, and follow the Callater Burn at the other end, eventually hitting the main A93 two miles short of Braemar.

Brechin

Twelve miles or so east of Kirriemuir, **BRECHIN** is a pretty if soporific town, whose chief attraction is the old **Cathedral** on Bishop's Close, off the High Street. There's been a religious building of sorts here since the arrival of evangelizing Irish missionaries in 900 AD, and the red sandstone structure has become something of a hotchpotch of architectural styles. What you see today chiefly dates from an extensive rebuilding in 1900, with the oldest surviving part of the cathedral being the 106ft round tower, one of only two in Scotland. The cathedral's doorway, built 6ft above the ground for protection against Viking raids, has some notable carvings, while inside you can see various Pictish stones, illuminated by the jewel-coloured stained-glass windows. A mile from the town centre along the Forfar road in the Brechin Castle countryside Park is **Pictavia** (April–Oct Mon–Sat 9am–6pm, Sun 10am–6pm; Nov–March Mon–Sat 9am–5pm, Sun 10am–5pm; £3.25), a recently built tourist attraction based on the history and heritage of the Picts with the increasingly familiar blend of sound-and-light entertainments and distinctively designed displays. The lingering impact of the centre is its collection of Pictish stones, which have been gathered from the hundreds found in this area; its worth stopping in here if you want some more information on the stones at nearby Aberlemno (see p.432), St Vigean's (see p.426) and elsewhere.

The library on St Ninian Square, to the north of the cathedral, houses Brechin's **museum** (Mon & Wed 9.30am–8pm, Tues & Thurs 9.30am–6pm, Fri & Sat 9.30am–5pm; free), a one-room jumble of history, civic memorabilia, geology and painting. Just off the square is the train station of the **Caledonian Railway** (talking timetable ☎01356/622992; information line ☎01561/37760), operating steam trains on summer Sundays and bank holidays along four miles of track from Brechin to the Bridge of Dun.

The **tourist office** is located in the same building as Pictavia just out of town on the Brechin Castle estate (April–Sept daily 9.30am–5.30pm; ☎01356/623050), but can organize accommodation in town and also hands out information on hiking in Glen Esk. Brechin is on the main **transport** routes – bus #30 runs hourly to Montrose, nine miles east, and it's also served by regular Citylink coaches between Dundee and Aberdeen.

Edzell and Glen Esk

Travelling around Angus, you can hardly fail to notice the difference between organic settlements and planned towns built by paranoid landowners who forcibly rehoused local people in order to keep them under control, especially after the Jacobite uprisings. One of the better examples of this phenomenon, **EDZELL**, along the B966 five miles north of Brechin (and linked to it by buses #21, #29 and #30), was cleared and rebuilt with Victorian rectitude a mile to the west of its original site in the 1840s. The long, wide and ruler-straight main street is lined with prim nineteenth-century buildings, now doing a roaring trade as genteel teashops and antique emporia.

The original village (identifiable from the cemetery and surrounding grassy mounds) lay immediately to the west of the wonderfully explorable red sandstone ruins of **Edzell Castle** (April–Sept daily 9.30am–6pm; Oct–March Mon–Wed & Sat 9.30am–4.30pm, Thurs 9.30am–noon, Sun 2–4.30pm; HS; £2.50), itself a mile west of the planned village. The main part of the old castle is a good example of a comfortable tower house, whose main priority became luxurious living rather than defence, with some intricate decorative corbelling on the roof, a vast fireplace in the first-floor hall and numerous telltale signs of building from different ages.

It is, however, the **pleasance garden** overlooked by the castle tower that makes a visit to Edzell essential, especially in late spring and early to mid-summer. The garden was built in 1604, at the height of the optimistic Renaissance, by Sir David Lindsay, and its refinement and extravagance are evident. The walls contain sculpted images of erudition: the Planetary Deities on the east side, the Liberal Arts (including a decapitated figure of Music) on the south and, under floods of lobelia, the Cardinal Virtues on the west wall. In the centre of the garden, low-cut box hedges spell out the family mottoes and enclose voluminous beds of roses.

Four miles southwest of Edzell, lying either side of the lane to Bridgend which can be reached either by carrying on along the road past the castle, or by taking the narrow road at the southern end of Edzell village, are the **Caterthuns**, twin Iron Age hillforts that were probably occupied at different times. The surviving ramparts on the White Caterthun (978ft) – easily reached from the small car park below – are the most impressive, and this is thought to be the later fort, occupied by the Picts in the first few centuries AD. Views from both, over the mountains to the north and the plains and foothills to the south, are stunning.

Just north of Edzell, a fifteen-mile road climbs alongside the River North Esk to form **Glen Esk**, the most easterly of the Angus glens and, like the others, scarcely populated. Ten miles along the Glen, the excellent **Glenesk Folk Museum** (Easter–May Mon, Sat & Sun noon–6pm; June to mid-Oct daily noon–6pm; £2), brings together records, costumes, photographs, maps and tools from the Angus glens, depicting the often harsh way of life for the inhabitants. The museum is housed in a lovely old shooting lodge known as The Retreat, and is run independently and enthusiastically by the local community. Inside there's also a craft shop and a noted tearoom – due reward for those who have endured the winding glen road. There are some excellent **hiking** routes further up the glen, including one to Queen Victoria's Well in Glen Mark and another up Mount Keen, Scotland's most easterly Munro.

If you want to stay in Edzell, there's decent **B&B** at *Elmgrove*, Inveriscandye Road (☎01356/648266; ①), while the most attractive of the hotels in town, the *Panmure Arms* (☎01356/648950; ③) at the far end of the main street near the turn-off to the castle, has recently been smartened up and offers rooms and meals. Further up the glen, you can **camp** one and a half miles north of the village at the *Glenesk Caravan Park* (☎01356/648565; April–Oct), while at Invermark, near the head of the Glen and a good jumping-off point for various hiking routes, is *The House of Mark* (☎01356/670315; ②), a former manse in a lovely setting which serves evening meals by arrangement.

ABERDEENSHIRE AND MORAY

Aberdeenshire and Moray cover some 3500 square miles of open and varied country dotted with historic and archeological sights, from neat NTS properties and eerie prehistoric rings of standing stones to quiet kirkyards, serene abbeys and a rash of dramatic castles. Geographically, the counties break down into two distinct areas: the **hinterland**, once barren and now a patchwork of farms, rising towards high mountains, sparkling rivers and gentle valleys; and the **coast**, a classic stretch of rocky cliff, remote fishing villages and long, sandy beaches.

For visitors, **Aberdeen** is of most obvious interest in the region, with its well-kept buildings (it's often voted Britain's cleanest city), museums and gorgeous parks. From here, it's a short hop west to **Deeside**, annually visited by the royal family and an easily accessed gateway to some spectacular mountain scenery. To the north lies the **Don Valley**, a quiet area which leads into the Cairngorms at the Lecht, a popular skiing area in winter, and **Speyside**, the heart of Scotland's malt whisky industry. Further north, the **coast** offers some dramatic scenery, punctuated by picturesque villages left almost unchanged by the centuries.

Aberdeen has an **airport**, and **trains** run from here to Inverness and to major points further south. **Buses** can be few and far between, often running on schooldays only, but the main centres are well-served. By car, signposted **trails** set up by the tourist board make navigation around the Speyside whisky distilleries and visiting the north-east coast and castles a bit easier.

Aberdeen

Some 120 miles from Edinburgh, on the banks of the rivers Dee and Don smack in the middle of the northeast coast, **ABERDEEN** is commonly known as the Granite City. The third-largest city in Scotland, it's a place that people either love or hate. As Lewis Grassic Gibbon, one of the northeast's most eminent novelists, summed it up: "One detests Aberdeen with the detestation of a thwarted lover. It is the one hauntingly and exasperatingly lovable city of Scotland." Certainly, while some extol the many tones and colours of Aberdeen's **granite** buildings, others see only uniform grey and find the city grim, cold and unwelcoming. The weather doesn't help: Aberdeen lies on a latitude north of Moscow and the cutting wind and driving rain (even if it does transform the buildings into sparkling silver) can be tiresome.

Since the 1970s, **oil** has made Aberdeen a hugely wealthy and self-confident place – only four percent of Scotland's population live in the city, yet it has eight percent of the country's spending power. Despite (or perhaps because of) this, it can seem a soulless city; there's a feeling of corporate sterility and sometimes, despite its long history, Aberdeen seems to exist only as a departure point and service station for the transient population of some ten to fifteen thousand who live on the 130 oil platforms out to sea.

That said, Aberdeen's **architecture** is undeniably striking: a granite cityscape created in the nineteenth century by three fine architects: Archibald Simpson and John Smith in the early years of the century and, subsequently, A. Marshall Mackenzie. Classical inspiration and Gothic Revival styles predominate, giving grace to a material

---

OIL AND ABERDEEN

When **oil** was discovered in BP's Forties Field in 1970, Aberdonians rightly viewed it as a massive financial opportunity, and – despite fierce competition from other east coast British ports, Scandinavia and Germany – the city succeeded in persuading the oil companies to base their headquarters here. Land was made available for housing and industry, millions were invested in the harbour and offshore developments, new schools opened and the airport expanded to include a heliport, which has since become the busiest in the world.

The city's **population** swelled by 60,000, and earnings escalated from fifteen percent below the national average to a figure well above it. Wealthy oil companies built prestigious offices, swish new restaurants, upmarket bars and shops. At the peak of production in the **mid-1980s**, 2.6 million barrels a day were being turned out, and the price had reached $80 a barrel – from which it plummeted to $10 during the slump of 1986. The effect was devastating – jobs vanished at the rate of a thousand a month, house prices dropped and Aberdeen soon discovered just how dependent on oil it was. The moment oil prices began to rise, crisis struck again with the loss of 167 lives in the **Piper Alpha disaster**, which precipitated an array of much-needed but very expensive safety measures.

In recent years production levels have steadily risen back up to those of the early 1980s, though with assurances that this time the dangers of boom-bust policies have been heeded. Oil remains the cornerstone of Aberdeen's economy, keeping unemployment down to one of the lowest levels in Britain and driving up house prices not just in the city itself but in an increasingly wide area of its rural hinterland. Predictions of the imminent decline in oil reserves and the end of Aberdeen's economic boom are heard regularly, as they have been since 1970, but reliable indicators suggest that the black gold will still be flowing well into the next millennium.

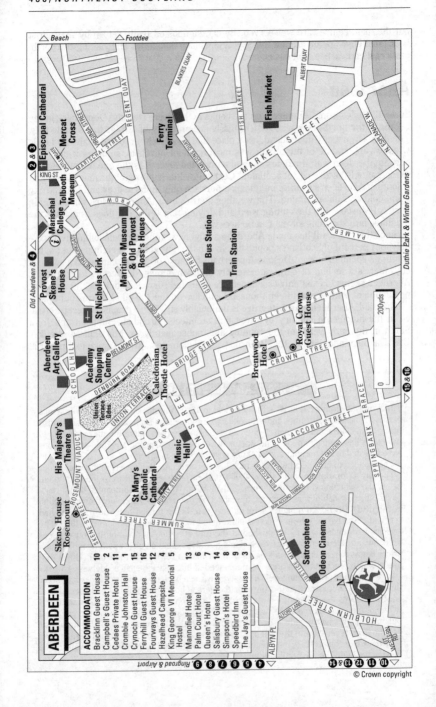

ABERDEEN

ACCOMMODATION

Bracklinn Guest House	10
Campbell's Guest House	2
Cedaes Private Hotel	11
Crombie Johnston Hall	1
Crynoch Guest House	15
Ferryhill Guest House	16
Fourways Guest House	12
Hazelhead Campsite	4
King George VI Memorial Hostel	5
Mannofield Hotel	13
Palm Court Hotel	6
Queen's Hotel	7
Salisbury Guest House	14
Simpson's Hotel	8
Speedbird Inn	9
The Jay's Guest House	3

Beach · Footdee

Episcopal Cathedral
Mercat Cross
2 & 3
KING ST
Old Aberdeen & 4
Provost Skene's House
Marischal College Tolbooth Museum
Ferry Terminal
Fish Market
Maritime Museum & Old Provost Ross's House
Bus Station
Train Station
MARKET STREET
REGENT QUAY
VIRGINIA STREET
MARISCHAL STREET
CASTLE STREET
MARISONS QUAY
BLAKES QUAY
ALBERT QUAY
FISH MARKET
PALMERSTONE ROAD
St Nicholas Kirk
Aberdeen Art Gallery
Academy Shopping Centre
SCHOOLHILL
BELMONT ST
DENBURN ROAD
Union Terrace Gdns.
UNION TERRACE
Caledonian Thistle Hotel
COLLEGE STREET
GUILD STREET
THE GREEN
BRIDGE STREET
DEE STREET
Brentwood Hotel
CROWN
Royal Crown Guest House
CROWN STREET
BON ACCORD STREET
SPRINGBANK TERRACE
15 & 16
Duthie Park & Winter Gardens
His Majesty's Theatre
Skene House Rosemount
ROSEMOUNT VIADUCT
SKENE STREET
GOLDEN SQUARE
UNION STREET
HUNTLY STREET
St Mary's Catholic Cathedral
Music Hall
SUMMER STREET
ALBYN PL
Satrosphere
Odeon Cinema
JUSTICE MILL LANE
HOLBURN STREET
ALFORD LANE
BON ACCORD CRESCENT
BON ACCORD TERRACE
ALFORD
N
200yds
0
Ringroad & Airport
9 8 7 6 5 4
15 13 12 11 10

© Crown copyright

once thought of as only good enough for tombs and paving stones. In addition, it some-times seems like every spare inch of ground has been turned into **flower gardens**, the urban parks being some of the most beautiful in Britain. This positive floral explosion – Aberdeen has been debarred from "Britain in Bloom" competitions because it kept winning – has certainly cheered up the general greyness.

Staying in such a prosperous place has its advantages. There are plenty of good restaurants and hotels, local transport is efficient and certain sights, including Aberdeen's splendid **Art Gallery**, are free. The city boasts a genuinely lively **harbour**, and stays alive at night with a thriving pub culture and a fair number of theatres, both mainstream and innovative.

Some history

In the twelfth century, Alexander I noted "Aberdon" as one of his principal towns, and by the thirteenth century it had become a centre for **trade and fishing**, a jumble of timber and wattle houses perched on three small hills, with the castle to the east and St Nicholas's kirk outside the gates to the west.

It was here that **Robert the Bruce** sought refuge during the Scottish Wars of Independence, leading to the garrison of the castle by Edward I and Balliol's sup-porters. In a night-time raid in 1306, the townspeople attacked the garrison and killed them all, an event commemorated by the city's motto "Bon Accord", the watchword for the night. The victory was not to last, however, and in 1337 Edward III stormed the city, forcing its rebuilding on a grander scale. A century later Bishop Elphinstane founded the Catholic **University** in the area north of town known today as **Old Aberdeen**, while the rest of the city developed as a mercantile centre and important port.

Industrial and economic expansion led to the Aberdeen New Streets Act in 1800, set-ting off a hectic half-century of development that almost led to financial disaster. Luckily, the city was rescued by a boom in trade: in the **shipyards** the construction of **Aberdeen Clippers** revolutionized sea transport, giving Britain supremacy in the China tea trade, and in 1882 a group of local businessmen acquired a **steam** tugboat for trawl fishing. Sail gave way to steam, and fisher families flooded in.

By the mid-twentieth century, Aberdeen's traditional industries were in decline, but the discovery of **oil** in the North Sea transformed the place from a depressed port into a boom town. Today, Aberdeen remains an extremely prosperous city, though what will happen when the oil runs out is anybody's guess.

Arrival, information and city transport

Aberdeen's Dyce **airport**, seven miles northwest of town, is served by flights from most parts of the UK and a few European cities. The #27 airport bus (Mon–Fri rough-ly every 45min until 5.20pm; £1.30) runs to Union Street and the bus station; after 6pm and at weekends, you can take the #27A (every 60–90min). The **train station** is on Guild Street, in the centre of the city (☎0345/484950), with the **bus** terminal for inter-city and regional services right beside it (☎01224/212266).

Aberdeen is also linked to Lerwick in Shetland and Stromness in Orkney by P&O **ferries** (☎01224/572615), with regular crossings from Jamieson's Quay in the harbour.

Information

From the stations it's a two-minute walk up the hill to Union Street, Aberdeen's main thoroughfare, and only a little further to the **tourist office** at St Nicholas House, Broad Street, just off the north side of Union Street at its eastern (seaward) end (June & Sept Mon–Sat 9am–5pm, Sun 10am–2pm; July & Aug Mon–Sat 9am–7pm, Sun 10am–4pm; Oct–May Mon–Fri 9am–5pm, Sat 10am–2pm; ☎01224/632727, *www.agtb.org*). They'll book accommodation for you, charging ten percent of the first night's room rate, redeemable at your hotel.

At the tourist office you can pick up the monthly **listings** magazines, *Listings Aberdeen* (an insert in the City Council's *Bon Accord* newspaper), which have details of current events and scheduled art exhibitions and theatre. The local newspapers, the morning *Press and Journal* and the *Evening Express*, are good for cinema and what's on that day. The best place for more esoteric information – anything from t'ai chi workshops to festivals and ceilidhs – is the Lemon Tree Arts Centre, 5 West North St (☎01224/642230), who produce a glossy bi-monthly programme.

City transport

Aberdeen is best explored by foot, but you might need to use **local buses**, almost all of which pass along Union Street, to reach some of the sights. There is no all-inclusive day ticket, but you can get a weekly bus pass (£12). If you plan to use the buses a lot, you should buy a **Farecard** (in £2, £5 or £10 denominations), which works rather like a phone card in that each time you travel the fare is deducted from the card. It can be bought from the main **transport office**, 395 King St, the City Council offices next to the tourist office, or the busy city-centre kiosk outside Marks & Spencer, on Union Street, which also sells decent transport **maps**. For information on local bus services, call Grampian Busline (4am–midnight; ☎01224/650065).

Taxis, which operate from ranks throughout the city centre, are rarely necessary, except late at night. If you don't manage to hail one, call Mairs Taxis (☎01224/724040).

Accommodation

As befits a high-flying business city, Aberdeen has a large choice of **accommodation**. Unfortunately, though, as most visitors *are* here on business, much of it is characterless and expensive, although it is always worth asking for cheaper weekend deals. Predictably, the best budget options are the **B&Bs** and **guest houses**, many of which are strung along Bon Accord and Crown streets (buses #6, #17 and #26 to and from Union Street), and the Great Western Road (buses #18, #19 and #24). Cheapest of all are the **youth hostel** and **student halls** left vacant for visitors in the summer months. There's also a **campsite** in the suburbs.

Hotels

Brentwood Hotel, 101 Crown St (☎01224/595440, *reservations@brentwood-hotel.demon.co.uk*). Spick-and-span refurbished old hotel south of Union Street. Popular with business people and often full during the week. ④.

Caledonian Thistle Hotel, 10–14 Union Terrace (☎01224/640233). The best of the posh hotels, in an impressive Victorian edifice just off Union Street. ⑥.

Cedars Private Hotel, 339 Great Western Rd (☎01224/583225). Small family-run hotel with friendly atmosphere. ③.

Ferryhill House Hotel, 169 Bon Accord St (☎01224/590867). One of the most historic pubs in Aberdeen, with colourful rooms and good food. ⑤.

Mannofield Hotel, 447 Great Western Rd (☎01224/315888). Charming old granite building, once a posh private house, a mile west of town. Excellent-value three-course dinners. ④.

Palm Court Hotel, 81 Seafield Rd (☎01224/310351, *info@palmcourt.co.uk*). Plush West End establishment with popular conservatory bistro-bar. ④.

Queen's Hotel, 51–53 Queen's Rd (☎01224/209999). Cheerful medium-sized city-centre hotel, recently refurbished, with a good culinary reputation. ④.

Simpson's Hotel, 59 Queen's Road (☎01224/327777, *address@simpsonshotel.com*). Highly style-conscious, terracotta-coloured modern interior to this large granite terrace house, with an excellent brasserie and good weekend rates. ⑤.

Speedbird Inn, Argyll Road, Dyce (☎01224/772884). Large, modern chain hotel at the airport. ②.

Guest houses and B&Bs

Bracklinn Guest House, 348 Great Western Rd (☎01224/317060). Welcoming Victorian house with elegant furnishings and some en-suite rooms. ②.

Campbell's Guest House, 444 King St (☎01224/625444, *cam444@zetnet.co.uk*). Highly recommended breakfasts. One mile from the city centre and handy for the beach. ②.

Crynoch Guest House, 164 Bon Accord St (☎01224/582743). A welcoming guest house in a convenient location. ①.

Fourways Guest House, 435 Great Western Rd (☎01224/310218). A converted manse in the West End of town. ②.

The Jay's Guest House, 422 King St (☎01224/638295, *jaysguesthouse@clara.net*). Well-run, non-smoking house located in Old Aberdeen, near the University. ③.

Royal Crown Guest House, 111 Crown St (☎01224/586461, *b&b@royalcrown.co.uk*). Comfortable, family-run guest house within walking distance of station and Union Street. Non-smoking. ②.

Salisbury Guest House, 12 Salisbury Terrace (☎01224/590447). Family-run, comfortable and clean guest house. ①.

Hostel, campsite, campus and self-catering accommodation

Crombie Johnstone Halls, College Bounds, Old Aberdeen (☎01224/272664). Private rooms in the best of the student halls – it's located in one of the most interesting parts of the city. Available late June–Sept.

Hazelhead Campsite, five miles west of centre on the A944 (☎01224/321268). Grassy campsite with a swimming pool nearby. Follow signs from ring road or take buses #14 or #15. April–Sept.

King George VI Memorial Hostel, 8 Queen's Rd (☎01224/646988 or central reservations ☎0541/553255). Rather soulless SYHA hostel with rooms for four to six, and a 2am curfew. Buses #14 and #15 from the train station.

Skene House Rosemount, 96 Rosemount Viaduct (☎01224/645971). Serviced apartments with 1–3 rooms, all with TVs and microwaves. Good central location. From £60 to £148 per night.

The City

Aberdeen divides neatly into five main areas. The **city centre**, roughly bounded by Broad Street, Union Street, Schoolhill and Union Terrace, features the opulent **Marischal College**, the colonnaded **Art Gallery** with its fine collection, and homes that predate Aberdeen's nineteenth-century town planning and have been preserved as **museums**. Union Street continues west to the comparatively cosmopolitan **West End**, where much of the city's decent nightlife, plus a couple of sights, can be found amid the tall grey town houses. To the south, the **harbour** still heaves with boats serving the fish and oil industries, while north of the centre lies attractive **Old Aberdeen**, a village neighbourhood presided over by **King's College** and **St Machar's Cathedral** and influenced by the large student population. The long sandy **beach** marks the city's entire eastern border.

The city centre

Any exploration of the **city centre** should begin at the east end of the mile-long **Union Street**, whose impressive architecture, sometimes lost among the shoppers and chain stores, finishes up at **Castlegate**, where Aberdeen's long-gone castle once stood. An open cobbled area, it is dominated by the late seventeenth-century **Mercat Cross**, carved with a unique gallery of Stewart sovereigns alongside some fierce gargoyles. Castlegate was once the focus of city life but nowadays is rather lifeless, with litter and pigeons easily outnumbering shoppers. However, the view up gently rising Union Street – a jumble of grey spires, turrets and jostling double-decker buses – is quintessential Aberdeen and well worth taking a moment or two to savour.

At the Union Street end of Castlegate, a discreet door on the side of the granite Town House leads into the **Tolbooth Museum** (April–Sept Tues–Sat 10am–5pm, Sun

12.30–3.30pm; £2.50 or £5 joint ticket with Maritime Museum and Provost Skene's House), quarried out of the seventeenth-century prison which lurks behind a steely-grey nineteenth-century exterior. The theme of the museum is law and imprisonment; climbing the claustrophobic staircases and squeezing into tiny, airless cells certainly gives plenty of opportunity to appreciate the harsh realities of incarceration. A suitably chilling audiovisual display featuring a talking model of a Jacobite prisoner complete with rattling chains can be seen, along with some fascinating maps and 3-D models charting Aberdeen's development from its old town beginnings.

Nearby, on King Street, the sandstone **St Andrew's Episcopal Cathedral** (mid-May to mid-Sept Mon–Sat 11am–4pm), where Samuel Seabury, America's first bishop, was ordained in 1784, offers a welcome relief from the uniform granite. Inside, its spartan whiteness is broken by florid gold ceiling bosses representing the (then) 48 states of the USA and 48 local families who remained loyal to the Episcopal Church during the eighteenth-century Penal Laws. Even more resplendent is the gilded baldachino canopy over the High Altar and the brightly coloured Seabury Centenary window in the Suther Chapel.

West down Union Street brings you to Broad Street, where Aberdeen's oldest-surviving private house, **Provost Skene's House**, dating from 1545, cowers behind modern offices at 45 Guestrow (Mon–Sat 10am–5pm, Sun 1–4pm; £2.50 or £5 joint ticket with Maritime and Tolbooth Museums). In the sixteenth century all the well-to-do houses in the area looked like this, with mellow stone and rounded turrets – yet it was only the intervention of the Queen Mother in 1938 which saved this house from the fate of its neighbours. Little has been altered since the Provost of Aberdeen lived here from 1676 to 1685, and the house is now a museum, giving an insight into the life of a rich Aberdonian merchant in the seventeenth century. Don't miss the Long Gallery, where a series of ornate tempera High Church paintings from 1622 shows a spirited defiance against the Protestant dogma of the time.

On Broad Street itself stands Aberdeen's most imposing edifice and the world's second-largest granite building after the Escorial in Madrid – the exuberant **Marischal College**, whose tall, steely-grey pinnacled neo-Gothic facade is in absolute contrast to the eyesore that houses the tourist office opposite. This spectacular architecture with all its soaring, surging lines has been painted and sketched more than any other in Aberdeen, and though not to everyone's taste – it was once described by a minor art historian as "a wedding cake covered in indigestible grey icing" – there's no escaping the fact that it is a most extraordinary feat of sculpture. The college itself was founded in 1593 by the fourth Earl Marischal, and coexisted as a separate Protestant university from Catholic King's, just up the road, for over two centuries. It was long Aberdeen's boast that their city had as many universities as the whole of England, and it wasn't until 1860 that the two were united as the University of Aberdeen. In 1893, the central tower was more than doubled in height by A. Marshall Mackenzie and the profusion of spirelets added, though the facade, which fronts an earlier quadrangle designed by Archibald Simpson in 1837–41, was not totally completed until 1906.

Behind the tower, through the college entrance, the Mitchell Hall's east window illustrates the history of the university in stained glass. The fan-vaulted lobby, once the college's old hall, now houses the wonderful **Anthropological Museum** (Mon–Fri 10am–5pm, Sun 2–5pm; free), made up of two large rooms that contain a wealth of weird exhibits, among them a series of Eskimo soapstone carvings, an outrigger canoe carved from a breadfruit tree from Papua New Guinea, a macabre Hawaiian head crafted from basketry and with real dogs' teeth, and a Tibetan prayer wheel. Most bizarre are the high-relief mummy case of an Egyptian five-year-old girl, and a stomach-churning foot, unbound and preserved in brine. The "Encyclopaedia of the Northeast" exhibition – running alphabetically from Aberdeen through to Whisky – is well labelled and amazingly varied.

Between Upperkirkgate and Union Street stands the long **St Nicholas Kirk** (May–Sept Mon–Fri noon–4pm, Sat 1–3pm, Oct–April Mon–Fri 10am–1pm; free), actually two churches in one with a solid, central bell tower rising from the middle, from where the 48-bell carillon, the largest in Britain, regularly chimes across the city. There's been a church here since at least 1157, but as the largest kirk in Scotland it was severely damaged during the Reformation and divided into the West and the East Church, separated today by the transepts and crossing; only the north transept, known as Collinson's aisle, survives from the twelfth century. The Renaissance-style **West Church**, formerly the nave of St Nicholas, was designed in the mid-eighteenth century by James Gibbs, architect of St-Martin-in-the-Fields in London's Trafalgar Square. The **East Church** was rebuilt over the groin-vaulted crypt of the restored fifteenth-century St Mary's Chapel (entered from Correction Wynd), which back in the 1600s was a place to imprison witches – you can still see the iron rings to which they were chained. Take time to explore the large peaceful churchyard, which with its green marble tombs and Baroque monuments seems a million miles from the bustling main street.

A little further west up Schoolhill, Aberdeen's engrossing **Art Gallery** (Mon–Sat 10am–5pm, Sun 2–5pm; free) was purpose-built in 1884 to a Neoclassical design by Mackenzie. You enter via the airy **Sculpture Court**, whose walls are lined with contemporary British paintings, many by Scottish artists. Highlights of the room are two Barbara Hepworth sculptures, including the central fountain, and the thick pillars running down from the upper balcony, each hewn from a different local marble. Off to one side is the Contemporary Arts and Crafts gallery, which includes work by one of the finest silversmiths in Europe, Malcolm Appleby, who lives in the nearby village of Crathes. Beyond this is the **Memorial Court**, a calming, white-walled circular room under a skylit dome that serves as the city's principal war memorial. It also houses the Lord Provost's book of condolence for the 167 people who died in the 1988 Piper Alpha oil rig disaster in the North Sea.

The **upstairs** rooms house the main body of the gallery's painting collection. The displays are changed fairly regularly, but you'll find some superb works by British Impressionists and Modernists on the balcony overlooking the central Sculpture Court; look out for Stanley Spencer's joyful portrait of the British seaside in *Southwold*, and his dramatic *Crucifixion*, as well as Robert Brough's half-dazed *View of Elgin* and Duncan Grant's haunting *Self-Portrait*. You'll also find a good selection of Scottish artists here, including various paintings by the Glasgow Boys (see p.212), and artists such as Joan Eardley, Peter Howson and Alan Davie.

Heading back towards the top of the staircase, the two-room **MacDonald collection** of nineteenth-century British art leads off to the right. At first the sheer number of Victorian landscapes crowding the walls may be disconcerting, but closer inspection will prove rewarding. Highlights include John MacWhirter's vast, sun-drenched *Morning – Isle of Arran*; the weary forms of Robert McGregor's *Les Moulières* (The Mussel Gatherers); Pre-Raphaelite canvases by Rossetti and Burne-Jones; and work by popular local artist Joseph Farquarson, known for his paintings of sheep in snow. The second MacDonald room houses 92 paintings of Victorian artists – mostly self-portraits. Local artists on display include John Phillip (1817–67), so heavily influenced by Velázquez and Murillo that he became known as "Spanish Phillip". Another Aberdonian, William Dyce (1806–64), features large, with several examples of his intensely photographic canvases.

The nineteenth-century foreign room leading off the balcony is, of course, popular for its Impressionist collection (including works by Boudin, Courbet, Sisley, Monet, Pissarro, and a deliciously bright Renoir, *La Roche Guyon*). A fabulous, sinewy cast of a Rodin male torso is the room's sculptural highlight. Off to the side, the dimly lit **Murray Room** contains prints, drawings and watercolours, pages from a fifteenth-century Flemish illuminated manuscript and Edward Lear's comically annotated view of *Boche di Cattaro*.

West of the gallery, across the rail bridge, the sunken **Union Terrace Gardens**, bordered by the sparkling light-grey granite buildings of Union Terrace, are a welcome relief from the hubbub of heavy traffic on Union Street. In summer, free brass-band concerts and orchestral performances make it a great place to have a picnic. From here there are views across to the three domes of the Central Library, St Mark's Church and His Majesty's Theatre, traditionally referred to as "Education, Salvation and Damnation". Outside the theatre stands a hulking great statue of William "Braveheart" Wallace, erected in 1888.

The West End

Tatty gentility characterizes much of the **West End**, the area around the westernmost part of Union Street, which roughly begins at the great granite columns of the city's **Music Hall**. A block north is **Golden Square** – a misnomer, as the trim houses, pubs and restaurants surrounding the statue of the Duke of Gordon are uniformly grey. The city has invested much in gentrifying the area north of Union Street, resulting in neat cobbles, old-fashioned lamps and mushrooming designer boutiques. Huntly Street, west of Golden Square, heads off towards the curiously thin spire of **St Mary's Catholic Cathedral** (daily: April–Oct 8.30am–5pm, Nov–March 8.30am–4pm), a typical example of Victorian Gothic church architecture.

On the southern side of Union Street, wedged between Bon Accord Street and Bon Accord Terrace, **Bon Accord Square** is a typical, charming Aberdeen square. In the middle, a grassy centre surrounds a great hulk of granite, commemorating **Alexander Sampson**, architect of much of nineteenth-century Aberdeen. West of Bon Accord Terrace is Justice Mill Lane, home to many of the city's favourite bars and nightclubs, and also to the **Satrosphere** (school terms Mon & Wed–Fri 10am–4pm, Sat 10am–5pm, Sun 1.30–5pm; school holidays Mon–Sat 10am–5pm, Sun 1.30–5pm; £4.50, children £2.25), Aberdeen's thoroughly entertaining hands-on science exhibition. Unassuming from the outside, the Satrosphere creates an ingenious illusion of a vast globe surrounded by numerous images of the passing visitor. Other exhibits include a superb 3-D map of northeast Scotland, examples of interactive technology and a biological section in which you can see inside beehives and an anthill.

The harbour

The old cobbled road of Shiprow winds down from Castlegate at the east end of Union Street to the north side of the harbour. Just off this steep road, peering out at the harbour through a striking modern glass facade, is the **Maritime Museum** (Mon–Sat 10am–5pm, Sun noon–3pm; £3.50 or £5 joint ticket with Provost Skene's House and Tolbooth Museums), which combines a thoroughly modern, airy museum with Aberdeen's oldest-surviving building, **Old Provost Ross's House**, laced with small rooms, low doorways and labyrinthine corridors. The marriage has been successful, and the museum is a thoroughly engrossing, imaginatively designed tribute to Aberdeen's maritime traditions.

As you walk in the front entrance, you'll see a series of blackboards, computer readouts and barometers showing everything from the time of high tide to the up-to-the-minute price of a barrel of crude oil. Suspended above the foyer and visible from five different levels is a spectacular 27ft-high model of an oil rig, which, along with terrific views over the bustling harbour, serves as a constant reminder that Aberdeen's maritime links are very much alive today. While large sections of the museum are devoted to telling the story of North Sea oil and gas production, the older industries of herring-fishing, whaling, shipbuilding and lighthouses also have their place with well-designed displays and audiovisual presentations, many of which draw heavily on personal reminiscences. Passages lead from various levels of the museum into Provost Ross's House, where intricate ship's models and a variety of nautical paintings and drawings are on display.

At the bottom of Shiprow, the cobbles meet Market Street, which runs the length of the **harbour**. Here, brightly painted oil-supply ships, sleek cruise ships and peeling fishing boats jostle for position to an ever-constant clatter and the screech of well-fed seagulls. Follow your nose down the road to the **fish market**, best visited early (7–8am) when the place is in full swing. The current market building dates from 1982, but fish has been traded here for centuries – the earliest record dating back to 1281 when an envoy of Edward I was charged for 1000 barrels of sturgeon and 5000 salt fish.

Back at the north end of Market Street, Trinity Quay runs to the shipbuilding yards and down York Street to the east corner of the harbour. Here you'll come to Aberdeen's **Footdee** or "fitee"(an easy walk or bus #14 from Union Street), a quaint nineteenth-century fishermen's village of higgledy-piggledy cottages which back onto the sea, their windows and doors facing inwards to protect from storms but also, so they say, to prevent the devil from sneaking in the back door.

From Market Street it's a twenty-minute walk or ten-minute bus ride (#6 from Market Street or #16 or #17 from Union Street) to **Duthie Park** (9.30am–dusk; free), situated on the banks of the Dee at the end of Polmuir Road. The rose garden here, known as Rose Mountain due to its profusion of blooms, can be stunning in summer, but the real treat is the Winter Gardens – a steamy jungle paradise of enormous cacti, exotic plants and tropical birds – jokingly held to be a favourite haunt with Aberdonians saving on their heating bills. From the northwestern corner of Duthie Park, a great cycle and walkway – the **Old Deeside Railway Line** – leads out of the city and past numerous old train stations.

Old Aberdeen

An independent burgh until 1891, the tranquil district of **Old Aberdeen**, a twenty-minute bus ride (#20) north of the city centre, has always maintained a separate village-like identity. Dominated by King's College and St Machar's Cathedral, its medieval cobbled streets, tiny wynds and little lanes are beautifully preserved.

The southern half of High Street is overlooked by **King's College Chapel** (Mon–Fri 9am–5pm; free), the first and finest of the college buildings, completed in 1495, with a chunky Renaissance spire. Named in honour of James IV, the chapel's west door is flanked by his coat of arms and those of his queen. It stands on the quadrangle, whose gracious buildings retain a medieval plan but were built much later; those immediately north were designed by Mackenzie early this century, with the exception of Cromwell Tower at the northeast corner, which was completed in 1658. The first thing you notice inside the chapel is that there is no aisle. Within this unusual plan, the screen, the stalls (each unique) and the ribbed arched wooden ceiling are rare and beautiful examples of medieval Scottish woodcarving. The remains of Bishop Elphinstone's tomb and the carved pulpit from nearby St Machar's are also here. A **visitor centre** (Mon–Sat 10am–5pm, Sun noon–5pm; free) in the main college buildings tells the tempestuous tale of the establishment of the University of Aberdeen, which came about finally in 1860 when Protestant Marischal College and sceptical King's College were merged, well over 200 years after the first attempt. Rivalry between the two establishments (which led to well-charted brawls in the streets) has always been intense.

From the college, the cobbled High Street leads a short way north to **St Machar's Cathedral** on the leafy Chanonry (daily 9am–5pm; free), overlooking Seaton Park and the River Don. The site was reputedly founded in 580 by Machar, a follower of Columba, when he was sent by the latter to find a grassy platform near the sea, overlooking a river shaped like the crook on a bishop's crozier. This setting fitted the bill perfectly, and the cathedral, a huge fifteenth-century fortified building, became one of the city's first great granite edifices. Inside, the stained-glass windows are a dazzling blaze of colour, and above the nave the heraldic oak ceiling from 1520 is illustrated with nearly fifty different coats of arms from Europe's royal houses and Scotland's bishops and nobles. **Guided walks** round the cathedral and University normally take place throughout the summer, leaving from King's College (June–Aug Wed 7pm; £3; contact the Tourist Information Office on ☎01224/632727 to check).

Next door to the cathedral, the **Cruickshank Botanic Gardens** (May–Sept Mon–Fri 9am–4.30pm, Sat & Sun 2–5pm; Oct–April Mon–Fri 9am–4.30pm; free), laid out in 1898, offer lovely glimpses of the cathedral through the trees. In spring and summer it's worth checking out the flowerbeds, but don't bother with the dreary zoological museum.

A wander through Seaton Park will bring you to the thirteenth-century **Brig' o' Balgownie**, which gracefully spans the River Don, nearly a mile north of the cathedral. Still standing (despite Thomas the Rhymer's prediction that it would fall were it ever to be crossed by an only son riding a mare's only foal), the bridge is best visited at sunset – Byron, who spent much of his childhood in Aberdeen, remembered it as one of his favourite places.

The beach

Of Britain's large cities, Aberdeen can surely claim to have the best **beach**. Less than a mile to the east of Union Street is a great two-mile sweep of clean sand, broken by groynes and lined all along with an esplanade, where most of the city seems to gather on a sunny day. Towards the southern end of the beach is a burgeoning concrete expanse of cinemas and fast-food outlets, a couple of fairly tatty amusement parks and a vast leisure centre. As you head further north, most of the beach's hinterland is devoted to successive golf links. The #14 bus goes along the southern esplanade.

Eating, drinking and entertainment

Aberdeen is certainly not short of good places to **eat**, though you will find it more pricey than elsewhere in northeast Scotland. Union Street and the surrounding area has a glut of attractive **restaurants** and **cafés**. As for **nightlife**, like most ports Aberdeen caters for a transient population with a lot of disposable income and a desire to get drunk as quickly as possible. Although you'll find no shortage of loud, flashy bars catering to such needs, there are still a number of more traditional old **pubs** which, though usually packed, are well worth a visit.

Restaurants and cafés

Ashvale, 46 Great Western Rd. One of Scotland's finest, and biggest, fish'n'chip shops, with seating for 300. Restaurant open daily until 11pm; takeaway until 1am. Inexpensive.

Café 52, The Green (☎01224/590094). This pleasant place serves uncomplicated but original and inexpensive food down below the south side of Union Street. Moderate. Closed Mon.

Faradays, 2 Kirk Brae, Cults (☎01224/869666). Located in an old electricity sub-station in a smart suburb a few miles west of the city, this idiosyncratic eatery specializes in designer versions of Scottish staples. Expensive. Closed all day Sun & lunchtime Mon.

Inversnecky, Beach Esplanade. Best of the beach cafés, great for big hangover breakfasts and ice-cream specials. Inexpensive.

Lemon Tree, 5 W North St. Easy-going café inside an arts centre; serves good vegetarian and vegan snacks and meals. Inexpensive.

La Lombarda, corner of Castlegate and King Street (☎01224/640916). A smart but lively trattoria which has been serving up pasta since 1922. Inexpensive–moderate.

Martha's Vineyard, 1 Alford Lane (☎01224/213795). Highly regarded West End bistro with an excellent daily-changing menu of European/Scottish cuisine. There's a more formal restaurant upstairs. Moderate. Closed all day Sun & Mon evenings.

Owlies, Unit C, Littlejohn Street (☎01224/649267). Plain French brasserie food, with plenty of vegetarian options. Closed Sun & Mon. Moderate.

Poldino's, 7 Little Belmont St (☎01224/647777). Lively, authentic Italian restaurant. Moderate. Closed Sun.

Silver Darling Restaurant, Pocra Quay, North Pier (☎01224/576229). Located at the mouth of the Dee in Footdee, this pricey restaurant serves the best seafood in town. Expensive. Closed Sat lunch & Sun.

Soul & Spice Café Bar, 15–17 Belmont St (☎01224/645200). Entertaining and colourful café serving up fantastic African and Caribbean dishes. On Thursday nights you can barter for your food. Moderate. Closed Mon.

Yu, 347 Union St (☎01224/580318). Decent, central Chinese with good fish dishes. Moderate.

Wild Boar, 19 Belmont St (☎01224/625357). Upbeat brasserie with well-priced vegetarian food, soups, salads and oriental-style noodles, as well as great cake and coffee through the day. Food served till 9pm (8pm Fri & Sat), after which DJs move in. Moderate.

Pubs and bars

Bex Bar, 44 Justice Mill Lane. A trendy spot which gets packed out at weekends: one of number of pubs and clubs along this West End street.

Café Continental, Esplanade. Large designer conservatory with windswept, rain-battered or sun-drenched views; serves more upmarket meals than the ice-cream cafés alongside.

Carriages, *Brentwood Hotel*, 101 Crown St. Unusually lively hotel cellar bar with the city's largest range of real ales and ciders. Also serves excellent bar food.

The City Bar, Netherkirkgate. One of Aberdeen's main gay bars, with live music on Fri & Sat nights. Serves cheap, plain lunches during the day.

Frankenstein Pub, 504 Union Street. The full horror theme with monsters and test-tubes lining the walls. DJs play at weekends and food served from 9am until closing time.

Ma Cameron's Inn, Little Belmont Street. Aberdeen's oldest pub, though only a section remains of the original. Serves food.

Nicky Tam's, 44 Market St. Olde-worlde-type pub, with unusual artefacts on its walls. One of the few bars in the harbourside area which feels safe to go into. Pub food served noon–8pm.

Prince of Wales, 7 St Nicholas Lane. Highly regarded Aberdeen pub with a long bar and flagstone floor. Very central and renowned for its real ales; often crowded.

RSVP, Academy Shopping Centre, Schoolhill (☎01224/625590). Stylish and busy new venue with designer furniture and live jazz on a Sunday afternoon. Open daily till midnight.

St Machar Bar, 97 High St, Old Aberdeen. The medieval quarter's only pub, a pokey, old-fashioned bar inevitably full of King's College students.

Under the Hammer, 11 N Silver St. Basement wine bar located beneath some auction rooms, popular for after-work drinks.

Clubs and live music venues

Amadeus, Queen's Links Centre, Beach Esplanade. Huge nightclub – the largest in Scotland – with all the mainstream sounds; the crowd tends to be young and raucous.

Franklyn's, Justice Mill Lane. Part of the same complex as the *Bex Bar*, with three very different rooms: a piano bar; a club bar with live bands (Fri and Sat); and crowd-pleasing chart music pumping out in the main dance area.

Lemon Tree, 5 W North St. The fulcrum of the city's arts scene with a great buzz and regular live music, comedy and folk.

Ministry of Sin, 16 Dee St. The hottest dance club for miles – Sunday nights are legendary. Occasionally has big-name guest DJs.

O'Donnaghue's, 16 Justice Mill Lane. Aberdeen's most popular Irish bar, with a large venue upstairs hosting medium-sized touring gigs.

Oh Henrys, Adelphi Close. Flash studenty club just off Union Street with regular theme nights.

Theatres and concert halls

Tickets for most of the venues below can be bought from the **box office** beside the Music Hall on Union Street (Mon–Sat 9.30am–6pm; ☎01224/641122).

Aberdeen Arts Centre, 33 King St (☎01224/635208). Hosts a variety of theatrical productions alongside a programme of lectures and exhibitions.

Aberdeen Exhibition and Conference Centre, off Ellon Road at Bridge of Don. The biggest rock and pop acts play this huge hall.

Cowdray Hall, Schoolhill (☎01224/523700). Classical music, often with visiting orchestras.

His Majesty's, Rosemount Viaduct (☎01224/637788). Aberdeen's main theatre, in a beautifully restored Edwardian building, with a programme that ranges from highbrow drama and opera to pantomime.

Lemon Tree, 5 W North St (☎01224/642230). Avant-garde events with off-the-wall comedians and plays, many coming hotfoot from the Edinburgh festivals.

Music Hall, Union Street (☎01224/632080). Big-name comedy and music acts.

Cinemas

Odeon, Justice Mill Lane (☎0800 5050007 for programme details and credit card booking). All the usual blockbusters and mainstream releases.

Virgin, Beach Esplanade (☎0541 550502) Huge, spanking-new multiscreen development by the beach.

Listings

Airport ☎01224/722331.

American Express Lunn Poly, 3–5 St Nicholas St (☎01224/633119).

Banks Bank of Scotland, 201 Union St (☎01224/804100); Clydesdale Bank, 238 Union St (☎01224/572893); Royal Bank of Scotland, 12 Golden Square (☎01224/648411).

Bike rental Alpine Bikes, 66–70 Holburn St (☎01224/211455); Cycling World, 460 George St (☎01224/632994).

Bookshops The largest are Dillons, 269–271 Union St (☎01224/210161); Waterstone's, 236b Union St (☎01224/571655); and John Smith & Son's, 195 Union St (☎01224/591157), a well-stocked store with a good Scottish section and the full range of maps.

Car rental Budget, on the Great Northern Road (☎01224/488770) and at the airport (☎01224/771777); National, 46 Summer St and at the airport (both ☎0870 4004502); Thrifty, 65 Frederick St, in the West End (☎01224/621033).

Dentist Contact the National Health Service Line (☎0800/224488) for local and emergency dentists.

Exchange Thomas Cook Bureau de Change in the Bon Accord Centre (Mon–Sat 9.30am–5.30pm; ☎01224/807100); also available at the tourist office on Broad Street.

Ferries P&O ☎01224/572615.

Football The local team, Aberdeen, plays in Scotland's Premier League and home fixtures take place at Pittodrie Stadium, between King's Road and the beach; phone ☎01224/632328 for details of forthcoming fixtures and ticket sales.

Genealogical research Aberdeen & North-East Family History Society, 164 King St (☎01224/646323).

Golf There are courses dotted all over the northeast; those in Aberdeen include the municipal King's Links (☎01224/641577) skirting the beach, and Murcar Golf Club (☎01224/704345) a testing links course five miles north of Aberdeen at Bridge of Don, which has an attractive nine-hole course, Strabathie, beside it.

Hospital The Royal Infirmary, on Foresterhill, northeast of the town centre, has a 24hr casualty department (☎01224/681818).

Internet The only public access is at the main library on Rosemount Viaduct (☎01224/652500).

Left luggage Small 24hr lockers at the train station cost £2.

Lesbian and Gay Switchboard (Wed & Fri 7–10pm; ☎01224/633500).

Libraries Main Library, Rosemount Viaduct (☎01224/652500).

Maps John Smith & Son's, 195 Union St (☎01224/591157) is an Ordnance Survey national agent.

Pharmacy Boots, 161 Union St (Mon–Sat 8am–6pm; ☎01224/211592).

Police The main police station is on Queen Street (☎01224/386000).

Post office Aberdeen's central post office is in the St Nicholas Centre, between Union Street and Upperkirkgate (Mon–Sat 9am–5.30pm; ☎0345 223344); there's also one at 489 Union St (Mon–Fri 9am–5.30pm, Sat 9am–12.30pm).

Public transport Grampian Transport Busline (☎01224/650065).

Swimming Bon Accord Baths and Leisure Centre, Justice Mill Lane (☎587920), has a 36-metre pool; Beach Leisure Centre on the Esplanade has a fun pool with flumes and slides.

Taxis Mairs Taxis (☎01224/724040).

Travel agents STA Travel, 30 Upperkirkgate (☎01224/658222); USIT/Campus Travel, 110 High St (Mon–Fri 9.30am–4.30pm; ☎273559).

Stonehaven and the Mearns

South of Aberdeen, the A92 and the main train line follow the coast to **Stonehaven**, a pretty harbour town and base for nearby **Dunnottar Castle**, a stunningly romantic ruin perched on the cliffs. The area to the south and west is known as the **Mearns**, an agricultural district of scattered population and gathering hills towards the Angus glens. **Fettercairn** is the most obvious base, for its proximity to **Fasque House**, family home of the former prime minister Gladstone.

Stonehaven is easily reached by **bus** or **train** from Aberdeen or Montrose, although public transport inland into the Mearns is virtually nonexistent.

Stonehaven and around

A busy pebble-dashed town, **STONEHAVEN** attracts hordes of holiday-makers in the summer due to its sheltered Kincardine coastline, and in mid-July in particular because of its respected **folk festival**. The town itself is split into two parts, the picturesque working harbour area being most likely to detain you. On one side of the harbour, Stonehaven's oldest building, the **Tolbooth** (June–Sept Mon & Thurs–Sat 10am–noon & 2–5pm; Wed & Sun 2–5pm; free), built as a storehouse during the construction of Dunnottar Castle (see p.450) is now a museum of local history and fishing. On calm summer evenings, you can also take **boat trips** from the harbour to the RSPB reserve at Fowlsheugh (June & July Tues & Fri 6pm).

The old High Street – lined with some fine town houses and civic buildings – connects the harbour and its surrounding old town with the late eighteenth-century planned centre on the other side of the River Carron. On New Year's Eve, High Street is the location for the ancient ceremony of **Fireballs**, when locals parade its length, swinging metal cages full of burning debris around their heads. This, it is said, wards off evil spirits for the year ahead. The **new town** focuses on the market square, overlooked by the dusky-pink granite market hall with its impressive steeple. From here, Evan Street heads inland before swinging right into Arduthie Road, which climbs up to the train station, a good fifteen-minute walk from the centre.

Practicalities

The **tourist office** is at 66 Allardice St, the main street past the square (April, May & Oct Mon–Sat 10am–1pm & 2–5pm; June & Sept Mon–Sat 10am–1pm & 2–6pm, Sun 1–6pm; July & Aug Mon–Sat 10am–7pm, Sun 1–7pm; ☎01569/762806). For **B&B** accommodation, *Arduthie House*, on Ann Street (☎01569/762381; ②), and the *Braemar*, on Evan Street (☎01569/764841; ①), are both good bets, while, a few miles south of town on the A92, *Dunnottar Mains Farm* (☎01569/762621; ①) is beautifully situated right beside Dunnottar Castle. For **food**, the *Tolbooth Seafood Restaurant* (☎01569/762287; closed Mon), above the museum on the harbour, is the place to go – it's pricey but worth it. For cheaper **pub** food or just a drink, try the entertaining *Marine Hotel* or the *Ship Inn*, both on the harbour. The most useful **buses** for Stonehaven are #107 and #117, which ply the coast road between Montrose and Aberdeen. For **bike hire** and advice about good local routes, head to Ruftrack Bikes, at 56 Barclay St, one block from the tourist office.

Dunnottar Castle, Kinneff and Arbuthnott

Two miles outside Stonehaven (the tourist office sells a walking guide for the scenic amble), **Dunnottar Castle** (Easter–Oct Mon–Sat 9am–6pm, Sun 2–5pm; Nov to Easter Mon–Fri 9am–dusk; £3) is one of the finest of Scotland's ruined castles, a huge ninth-century fortress set on a three-sided sheer cliff jutting into the sea – a setting striking enough to be chosen as the backdrop for Zeffirelli's movie version of *Hamlet*. Once the principal fortress of the northeast, the ruins are worth a good root around, and there are any number of dramatic views out to the crashing sea. Siege and bloodstained drama splatter the castle's past: in 1297 William Wallace burnt the whole English Plantagenet garrison alive here, while one of the more gruesome tales from the castle's history tells of the imprisonment and torture of 122 men and 45 women Covenanters in 1685 – an event, as it says on the Covenanters' Stone in the churchyard, "whose dark shadow is for evermore flung athwart the Castled Rock".

Four miles south of Dunnottar Castle, **CATTERLINE** is a clifftop hamlet typical of those along this stretch of coast – worth a visit for the views and the delicious, well-priced lobster at the cosy *Creel Inn*, which also offers **B&B** (☎01569/750254; ②).

Four miles further down the coast, the tiny village of **KINNEFF** lies among fields tumbling down to the sea. Its church, for the most part eighteenth-century, is a successor to the one in which the Scottish crown jewels were hidden as Cromwell marched on Scotland in 1651. Popular tradition has it that the wives of the Dunnottar garrison commander and the Kinneff parish minister hid the crown under an apron and carried the state sceptre, disguised as a distaff, with bundles of flax. The state's most precious assets were successfully hidden here for nine years. Memorials and interpretive boards inside the beautifully light and simple old church tell the story.

Some five miles inland, the straggling village of **ARBUTHNOTT** was the home of prolific local author, **Lewis Grassic Gibbon** (1901–35), whose romanticized realism perfectly encapsulates the spirit of the agricultural Mearns area. His descriptions were often quite awesome – Glasgow, for example, he neatly penned as "the vomit of a cataleptic commercialism". *Sunset Song*, his most famous work, is an essential read for those travelling in this area. The community-run **Grassic Gibbon Centre** (April–Oct daily 10am–4.30pm; £2), on the B967 through the village, is a great introduction to this fascinating and self-assured man who died so young. He is buried (under his real name of James Leslie Mitchell) in the corner of the little village graveyard, overlooking the forested banks of the Bervie Water off the main road. The parish church itself, one of the few surviving intact in Scotland that predate the Reformation, is interesting for its Norman arch, unusual fifteenth-century circular bell tower and glorious thirteenth-century chancel.

Fettercairn and Fasque House

Eight miles southeast of Arbuthnott on the tiny B9120 (and served by buses from Montrose), the village of **FETTERCAIRN** is renowned for its handsome arch, which was erected in 1861 after Queen Victoria stayed at the local pub, the *Ramsay Arms* (☎01561/340334; ③), which is still a good place to stay or to stop for a drink. One mile west, and well signposted, the **Fettercairn distillery** (May–Sept Mon–Sat 10am–4pm; free) is one of Scotland's oldest, with free tours and the customary free taster.

A short drive north on the Edzel to Banchory road, the once beautiful, but now somewhat neglected **Fasque House** (May–Sept daily 11am–5.30pm; £3.50) – family home of four-times prime minister William Ewart Gladstone – is set in grounds filled with deer, pheasants and rabbits. Built between 1789 and 1809, the house passed into the Gladstone family in 1829 when Sir John Gladstone, William's father and a rich grain broker, bought the estate, on which members of the family still live. Sir John added various extensions to the house, developing the gardens and building roads and bridges. Today, in all its intriguing decrepitude, Fasque House offers a great insight into how the affluent landowner lived in the Victorian era. Downstairs, domestic implements litter the place in a refreshingly haphazard manner, while the upstairs appears equally untouched, with a library crammed full of the Gladstones' books, a splendid Victorian bathroom complete with shower, and bedrooms looking much as the nineteenth-century maids would have left them.

Deeside

More commonly known as **Royal Deeside**, the land stretching west of the coast along the River Dee revels in its connections with the royal family, who have regularly holidayed here, at **Balmoral**, since Queen Victoria bought the estate. Eighty thousand Scots turned out to welcome her on her first visit in 1848, but some weren't so charmed – one local journalist remarked that the area was about to be "desolated by cockneys and other horrible reptiles". Today, however, most locals are fiercely protective of the royal connection.

Many of Victoria's guests weren't as enthusiastic about Deeside as she was: Count von Moltke, then aide-de-camp to Prince Frederick William of Prussia, observed, "It is very astonishing that the Royal Power of England should reside amid this lonesome, desolate, cold mountain scenery", while Tsar Nicholas II whined, "The weather is awful, rain and wind every day and on top of it no luck at all – I haven't killed a stag yet." However, the Queen adored the place, and the woods were said to remind Prince Albert of Thuringia, his homeland.

Deeside is undoubtedly handsome in a fierce, craggy Scottish way, and the royal presence has helped keep a lid on any unattractive mass development. The villages strung along the A93, the main route through the area, are well-heeled and the facilities for visitors first-class, with a number of bunkhouses and youth hostels, some outstanding hotels and plenty of castles and grounds to snoop around. It's also an excellent area for **outdoor activities**, with hiking routes into both the Grampian and Cairngorm mountains, and good mountain biking, canoeing and skiing.

Bluebird **bus** #201 from Aberdeen regularly chugs along the A93, serving most of the towns on the way to **Braemar**, past Balmoral to the west.

From Aberdeen to Banchory

West of Aberdeen is low-lying land of mixed farming, forestry and suburbs. Easily reached from the main road are the castles of **Drum** and **Crathes**, both interesting fortified houses with pleasant gardens, while the uneventful town of **Banchory** serves as gateway to the heart of Royal Deeside.

Drum and Crathes castles

Ten miles west of Aberdeen on the A93, **Drum Castle** (Easter weekend & May–Sept daily 1.30–4.45pm; Oct Sat & Sun 1.30–4.45pm; NTS; £4.40) stands in a clearing in the ancient **woods of Drum**, made up of the splendid pines and oaks that once covered this whole area before the shipbuilding industry precipitated mass forest clearance (the grounds are open 10am–6pm on the same days as the castle; £2 grounds only). The castle itself combines a 1619 Jacobean mansion with Victorian extensions and the original, huge thirteenth-century keep which has recently been restored and reopened. Given by Robert the Bruce to his armour-bearer, William de Irvine, in 1323 for services rendered at Bannockburn, the castle remained in Irvine hands for 24 generations until the NTS stepped in in 1976. To get a sense of the medieval atmosphere of the place, ascend the Turnpike Stair, above the Laigh Hall where a 700-year-old window seat gives views of the ancient forest.

Further along the A93, three and a half miles east of Banchory, **Crathes Castle** (April–Oct daily 11am–4.45pm; NTS; £2.10 or £5 including grounds and walled garden) is a splendid sixteenth-century granite tower house adorned with flourishes such as overhanging turrets, gargoyles and conical roofs. Its thick walls, narrow windows and tiny rooms loaded with heavy old furniture make Crathes rather claustrophobic, but it is saved by some wonderfully painted ceilings, either still in their original form or sensitively restored; the earliest dates from 1602. Don't miss the Room of the Nine Nobles, where great heroes of the past, among them Julius Caesar, King David and King Arthur, are skilfully painted on the beams. More intriguing still is the Green Lady's Room, where a mysterious child's skeleton was found beneath the floor and the ghost of a young girl, sometimes carrying a child, is said to have been spotted – most recently in the 1980s. The Muses Room, with portrayals of the nine muses and seven virtues, is also impressive. Beware the "trip stair", originally designed to foil seventeenth-century burglars.

By the entrance to Crathes, a cluster of restored stone cottages houses an interesting crafts shop, pottery and the *Milton Restaurant* (☎01330/844566), which serves high-class food, including a well-priced supper menu between 5pm and 7pm.

Banchory

BANCHORY, meaning "fair hollow", is really just a one-street town, and there's not much to see, though it can be a useful place to stay. The small local **museum** on Bridge Street, behind High Street (June–Sept Mon–Sat 10am–1pm & 2–5pm, Sun 2–6pm; April & May Sat only, Oct Sat only 11am–5pm; free), may warrant half an hour or so if you're a fan of local boy James Scott Skinner, renowned fiddler and composer of such tunes as *The Bonnie Lass o' Bon Accord*. Alternatively, you can watch salmon leap at the little footbridge where the Dee joins the Feugh River to the south of town.

The **tourist office**, in the museum (Easter–May & Oct Mon–Sat 10am–1pm & 2–5pm; June & Sept Mon–Sat 10am–1pm & 2–6pm, Sun 1–6pm; July & Aug Mon–Sat 9.30am–7pm, Sun 1–7pm; ☎01330/822000), can provide information on walking and fishing in the area. There are several reasonable places **to stay** here and in the surrounding countryside. In town, the *Burnett Arms Hotel*, 25 High St (☎01330/824944, *burnett@msn.com.uk*; ⑤), a friendly former coaching inn, does Banchory's best pub grub, while *Primrose Hill*, on North Deeside Road on the eastern outskirts of town (☎01330/823007; ②), is a decent B&B. Outside Banchory on the Inchmarlo road, the smart *Tor-Na-Collie Hotel* (☎01330/822242, *tornacoille@btinternet.com*; ⑥) was once a retreat for Charlie Chaplin and his family, and serves splendid Scottish salmon, venison and malt whisky in its upscale restaurant. More affordable escapism is available year-round at the *Wolf's Hearth* bunkhouse, ten miles northwest of Banchory, just outside Tornaveen on the B9119 (☎013398/83460). A converted farm building in a beautiful rural setting, it makes a great base for walking, cycling or skiing, and also offers a variety of creative activities such as painting and pottery. Evening meals are available here if you make arrangements beforehand.

Ballater and Balmoral

Heading west from Banchory on the A93, after twelve miles you'll come to the workaday town of **ABOYNE**, notable only for the excellent *Black Faced Sheep* coffee shop just off the main road, and the *White Cottage* restaurant (☎013398/86265), a couple of miles before Aboyne on the Banchory side, which specializes in high-quality Scottish cooking made with fresh local produce. Another ten miles beyond Aboyne is the neat and ordered town of **BALLATER**, attractively hemmed in by the river and fir-covered mountains. The town was dragged from obscurity in the nineteenth century when it was discovered that the local waters were useful in curing scrofula. Although scrofula is no longer a problem, Ballater spring water is back in fashion and on sale around town.

It was in Ballater that Queen Victoria first arrived in Deeside by train from Aberdeen back in 1848 – she wouldn't allow a station to be built any closer to Balmoral, eight miles further west. Although the line has long been closed, you can still visit the elegant **train station** in the centre of town, which now houses a tearoom. The local shops, having provided the royals with household basics, also flaunt their connections, sporting oversized crests above their doorways.

Ballater is an excellent base for local **walks and outdoor activities**. There are numerous hikes from Loch Muik (pronounced "Mick"), nine miles southwest of town, including the Capel Mounth drovers' route over the mountains to Glen Doll (see p.434), and a well-worn but strenuous all-day trek up and around Lochnagar (3789ft), the mountain much painted and written about by the current Prince of Wales. The starting point for all these walks is the Balmoral Rangers' **visitors' centre**, on the shores of the loch (☎013397/55059 for opening hours), which also offers a series of free guided nature walks. Good quality **bikes** can be rented from Wheels and Reels (☎013397/55864) at 2 Braemar Rd, just over the railway bridge from Station Square, while for canoeing and ski equipment and guides for a range of **outdoor activities**, contact Dave Latham (☎013308/50332). Other outdoor equipment, as well as local guide books, a full range of OS maps and good advice about heading to the local hills, is available at the friendly Lochnagar Leisure outdoor shop on Station Square (open daily 9am–5.30pm).

Ballater practicalities

The **tourist office** is opposite the station in Station Square (Easter–May & Oct Mon–Sat 10am–1pm & 2–5pm, Sun 1–5pm; June & Sept Mon–Sat 10am–1pm & 2–6pm, Sun 1–6pm; July & Aug Mon–Sat 9.30am–7pm, Sun 1–7pm; ☎013397/55306). There are plenty of reasonable **B&Bs** in town, including the excellent no-smoking *Inverdeen House*, on Bridge Square (☎013397/55759; ②), which offers a choice of six breakfasts, many involving piles of Canadian pancakes. Other places to try include two options on Braemar Road – the welcoming *Deeside Hotel* (☎013397/55420; ②), or *The Green Inn Restaurant*, 9 Victoria Rd (☎013397/55701; ⑤ for dinner, bed and breakfast), which has three very comfortable rooms. A few miles out of town on the road to Tomintoul (see p.458) is *Gairnshiel Lodge* (☎013397/55582; ②). In a remote but beautiful setting, it's a great base for walking or cycling. For **camping**, the *Anderson Road Caravan Park* (☎013397/55727; Easter–Oct) down towards the river, has around sixty tent pitches. There are numerous **places to eat**, from smart hotel restaurants to bakers and coffee shops: the award-winning *Green Inn* is pricey but excellent quality, while *Bruno's Restaurant* (☎013397/ 55346; April–Sept only; closed Mon & Tues), 34 Victoria Rd, is an unexpectedly authentic if over-the-top Italian in a family house. For **drinking** with locals, try the back bar (entrance down Golf Street) of the *Prince of Wales*, which faces the main square.

Balmoral Estate and Crathie Church

Originally a sixteenth-century tower house built for the powerful Gordon family, **Balmoral Castle** (mid-April to May Mon–Sat 10am–5pm; June & July daily 10am–5pm; £4) has been a royal residence since 1852, when it was converted to the Scottish Baronial mansion that stands today. The royal family traditionally spend their summer holidays here, but despite its fame it can be something of a disappointment even for a dedicated royalist. For the three months when the doors are nudged open, the general riffraff are permitted to view only the ballroom and the grounds; for the rest of the year it is not even visible to the paparazzi who converge en masse when the royals are in residence here in August. With so little of the castle on view, it's worth making the most of the grounds and larger estate by following some of the country walks or joining a two-hour **pony trek** (daily 10am & 2pm; for details ☎013397/42334; £20)

Opposite the castle's gates on the main road, the otherwise dull granite church of **CRATHIE**, built in 1895 with the proceeds of a bazaar held at Balmoral, is the royals' local church. A small **tourist office** operates in the car park by the church on the main road in Crathie (daily: April 10am–5pm; May–Aug 9.30am–6pm; Sept & Oct 10am–5.30pm; ☎013397/42414).

Braemar

Continuing for another few miles, the road rises to 1100ft above sea level to the upper part of Deeside and the village of **BRAEMAR**, situated where three passes meet and overlooked by an unimposing **castle** (Easter–Oct Mon–Thurs, Sat & Sun 10am–6pm; £2.50) of the same name. Signs as you enter Braemar boast that it's an "Award Winning Tourist Village", which just about sums it up, as everything seems to have been prettified to within an inch of its life or to have a price tag on it. That said, it's an invigorating, outdoor kind of place, well patronized by committed hikers, but probably best known for its Highland Games, the annual **Braemar Gathering** (first Sat of Sept). Games were first held here in the eleventh century, when Malcolm Canmore set contests for the local clans in order to pick the bravest and strongest for his army. Since Queen Victoria's day, successive generations of royals have attended, and the world's most famous Highland Games have become rather an overcrowded, overblown event. You're not guaranteed to get in if you just turn up; tickets can be bought in advance from February 1, from the Bookings Secretary, BRHS, Coilacriech, Ballater AB35 5UH (☎013397/55377).

MORRONE BRAEMAR'S BEACON

Ordnance Survey Landranger map No. 43.
Late August and through autumn, when the mountain is plush with extravagant colours, is the best time to ascend **Morrone**. In winter, it can be a spectacular viewpoint but very exposed. Allow four hours for the walk.

Make your way up Chapel Brae at the west end of Braemar, passing a car park and pond, then Mountain Cottage, and swinging left up through fine birch woods (a nature reserve). Keep right of the fences and house. The track bears right (west), and at a fork take the left branch up to the Deeside Field Club view indicator. Skirt the crags above this to the left and the path is obvious thereafter. The summit provides a fantastic sweeping view of the Cairngorms. You can descend by the upward route, but an easy continuation is to head down by the Mountain Rescue post's access path, which twists along and then down into Glen Clunie. Turn left along the minor road back to Braemar; the walk finishes by heading through the local golf course. In summer, you can take a Land Rover safari up Morrone: contact the tourist office in Braemar for details.

A pleasant diversion from Braemar is to head six miles west to the end of the road and the **Linn of Dee**, where the river plummets savagely through a narrow rock gorge. From here there are countless **walks** into the surrounding countryside or up into the heart of the Cairngorms (see p.490). There's a very basic **youth hostel** just before the falls at Inverey (mid-May to early Sept; book through the Braemar hostel on ☎013397/41659 or central reservations ☎0541/553255).

Practicalities

Braemar's **tourist office** is in the modern building known as the Mews in the middle of the village on Mar Road (Jan–May & Oct–Dec Mon–Sat 10am–1pm & 2–5pm; Sun noon–5pm; June daily 10am–6pm; July–Aug daily 9am–7pm, Sept daily 10am–1pm & 2–6pm; ☎013397/41600). **Accommodation** is scarce in Braemar in the lead-up to the Games, but at other times there's a wide choice. *Clunie Lodge Guest House*, Clunie Bank Road (☎013397/41330; ②), on the edge of town, is a good **B&B** with lovely views up Clunie Glen, and there's a large **youth hostel** at Corrie Feragie, 21 Glenshee Rd (☎013397/41659 or central reservations ☎0541/553255). Alternatively, the cheery *Rucksacks*, an easy-going bunkhouse well equipped for walkers and backpackers, is just behind the Mews complex (☎013397/41517). The *Invercauld Caravan Club Park* (☎013397/41373), just south of the village off the Glenshee Road, has fifteen **camping** pitches. Standard and fairly pricey hotel **food** is available from the bars of the various large hotels, or for some cheap stodge there's the *Braemar Takeaway* by the river bridge. For **drinking**, the *Invercauld Arms* in the middle of town is a youthful hangout with a pool table. For advice on **outdoor activities**, as well as ski, mountain-bike and climbing equipment rental, head to Braemar Mountain Sports (open daily 8.30am–7pm), opposite the *Takeaway*.

The Don Valley and the Lecht

The quiet countryside around the **Don Valley**, once renowned for its illegal whisky distilleries and smugglers, used also to be a prosperous agricultural area. As the region industrialized, however, the population drifted towards Dundee and Aberdeen, and nowadays little remains of the old farming communities except the odd deserted crofter's cottage. From Aberdeen, the River Don winds northwest through **Inverurie**, where it takes a sharp turn west to **Alford**, then continues past ruined castles through the **Upper Don Valley** and the heather moorlands of the eastern Highlands. This remote and undervisited area is positively littered with ruined castles, Pictish sites, stones and hillforts, all of which it is impossible to cover here. There are some excellent free leaflets in the Grampian Archeology series (available from all tourist offices), which give far more detail, and the well-signposted **Castle Trail** takes in the area's main castles. The Lecht Road, from Corgaff to the hilltop town of **Tomintoul**, rises steeply, making the area around it, simply known as the **Lecht**, an ideal skiing centre.

Inverurie is served by the regular Aberdeen to Inverness **train** and various **bus** services up the A96. Bluebird buses #215 and #220 link Alford with Aberdeen, but getting as far as Strathdon is much harder and public transport links with Tomintoul are all but nonexistent.

Inverurie and around

Some seventeen miles from Aberdeen, the prosperous granite farming town of **INVERURIE** makes a convenient base for visiting the numerous relics and castles in the area. The **tourist office** (July–Aug Mon–Sat 9.30am–6pm, Sun 1–5pm; Sept–June Mon–Sat 9.30am–5pm; ☎01467/625800) shares space with a bookshop at 18 High St, not far from the station, and is a good place to stop before setting off to find the local sites, many of which are tucked away and confusingly signposted. While you're in Inverurie, don't miss the **Thainstone Mart**, just off the A96 south of town, one of Europe's largest and most impressive livestock sales (Mon & Wed–Fri around 10am).

Bennachie and Archaeolink

The granite hill **Bennachie**, five miles west of Inverurie, is possibly the site of Mons Graupius, Scotland's first ever recorded battle in 84 AD when the Romans defeated the Picts. At 1733ft, this is one of the most prominent tors in the region, with tremendous views, and makes for a stiff two-hour walk. The best route starts from the Bennachie Centre (April–Oct Tues–Sun 10am–5pm, Nov–March Wed–Sun 10am–5pm), a mile past **Chapel of Garioch** (pronounced "Geery"), itself a couple of miles off the A96. Immediately west of here is one of the most notable Pictish standing stones in the region, the **Maiden Stone**, a 10ft slab inscribed with marine monsters, an elephant-like beast, and the mirror and comb for which the stone is named.

A further four miles from Chapel of Garioch, the **Archaeolink Prehistory Park**, on the B9002 at Oyne (April–Oct daily 10am–5pm; £3.90), gives an insight into the area's Pictish heritage. The brand-new park includes a reconstructed Iron Age farm, a hillside archeological site, and an innovative building containing lively audio-visual displays designed to bring prehistory (anything from six thousand years ago to the battle of Mons Graupius) to life. Although it's a clear attempt to capture the imagination of young people, adults will be just as enthralled, partly because the experience is spread across a hillside with short walks, impressive views and interesting archeological projects.

Fyvie Castle

Some thirteen miles north of Inverurie stands the huge, ochre mansion of **Fyvie Castle** (May–June & Sept daily 1.30–4.45pm; July & Aug daily 11am–4.45pm; Oct Sat & Sun 1.30–4.45pm; NTS; £4.40). Scottish Baronial to the hilt, Fyvie's fascinating roof-scape sprouts five curious steeples, one for each of the families who lived here from the thirteenth to the twentieth century. Beginning life as a typical courtyard castle, with a protective wall more than 6ft thick, over the ensuing centuries the place met with considerable architectural expansion. The Chancellor of Scotland bought Fyvie in 1596 and was probably responsible for the elaborate south front with its gables and turrets; his grandson sympathized with the Jacobites and, following his exile, the estate was confiscated and handed over to the Gordons. In 1889 the castle was sold to the Forbes-Leiths, a local family who had made a fortune in America and were responsible for the grand Edwardian interior. The exquisite dining room is nowadays rented out for corporate entertaining by oil companies who hobnob among the Flemish tapestries, Delft tiles and the fine collection of paintings that includes feathery Gainsborough portraits and twelve works by Sir Henry Raeburn.

Alford and around

ALFORD, 25 miles west of Aberdeen, only exists at all because it was chosen, in 1859, as the terminus for the Great North Scotland Railway. The best of the sights is the **Grampian Transport Museum** on Main Street (April–Oct daily 10am–5pm; £3.50), a large display of transport through the ages. Unusual exhibits include the *Craigevar Express*, a strange, three-wheeled steam-driven vehicle developed by the local postman for his rounds before the invention of the engine, and, incongruously, a beautiful Art Deco Belgian dance organ with over 400 pipes and a full set of drums.

Practically next door is the terminus for the **Alford Valley Railway** (April, May & Sept Sat & Sun 1–4.30pm; June–Aug daily 1–4.30pm; ☎019755/62326), a two-foot narrow-gauge train that runs for about a mile from Alford Station through wooded vales to the wide open space of **Murray Park**; the return journey takes an hour. The station is also home to the neat **tourist office** (April–June, Sept & Oct Mon–Sat 10am–5pm, Sun 1–5pm; July & Aug Mon–Sat 10am–6pm, Sun 1–6pm; ☎019755/62052).

Craigievar Castle

Six miles south of Alford on the A980, **Craigievar Castle** (guided tours only: May–Sept daily 1.30–4.45pm; ☎013398/83635; NTS; £6) is a fantastic pink confection of turrets, gables, balustrades and cupolas bubbling over from the top three storeys. It was built by a Baltic trader known as Willy the Merchant in 1626, who evidently allowed his whimsy to run riot. The castle's massive popularity, however – it features on everything from shortbread tins to tea towels all over Scotland – has been its undoing, and the sheer number of visitors has caused interior damage. The NTS is currently limiting the number of people entering the house by keeping the guided tours small, but in any case the best part of the castle is its external appearance, which you can see free from the well-kept **grounds** (all year 9.30am–sunset; free).

Lumsden and Rhynie

The A944 heads west from Alford, meeting the A97 just south of the tiny village of **LUMSDEN**, a surprising centre for Scottish sculpture. A contemporary **Sculpture Walk** – heralded by a fabulous skeletal black horse at its southern end – runs parallel to the main road, coming out near the premises of the **Scottish Sculpture Workshop** (Mon–Fri 9am–5pm or by arrangement; ☎01464/861372), very much an active workshop, rather than a gallery, at the northern end of village.

The village of **RHYNIE**, folded beautifully into the hills three miles further north up the A97, is for ever associated with one of the greatest Pictish memorials, the **Rhynie Man**, a remarkable 6ft boulder discovered in 1978, depicting a rare whole figure, clad in a tunic and holding what is thought to be a ceremonial axe. The original can be seen in the foyer of the regional council's headquarters at Woodhill House in Aberdeen, but there's a cast on display at the school in Rhynie, across the road from the church; if you want to see it, contact Bill Inglis on ☎01464/861398. A further claim to fame for the village is that the bedrock lying deep beneath it, known as **Rhynie Chert**, contains plant and insect fossils up to 400 million years old, making them some of the earth's oldest fossils. A mile or so from the village, along the A941 to Dufftown, a car park gives access to the **Tap O'Noth**, Scotland's second-highest Pictish hillfort (1847ft), where substantial remnants of the wall around the lip of the summit show evidence of vitrification (fierce burning), probably to fuse the rocks together.

Rhynie is a reasonable – if very quiet – place **to stay**. The cheapest and the best choice is the *Gordon Arms Hotel*, on Main Street (☎01464/861615; ①).

The Upper Don Valley

Ten miles west of Alford stand the impressive thirteenth-century stone ruins of **Kildrummy Castle** (April–Sept Mon–Sun 9.30am–6pm; HS; £1.80), site of some particularly hideous moments of conflict. During the Wars of Independence, Robert the Bruce sent his wife and children here for their own protection, but the castle blacksmith, bribed with as much gold as he could carry, set fire to the place and it fell into English hands. Bruce's immediate family survived, but his brother was executed and the entire garrison hung, drawn and quartered. Meanwhile, the duplicitous blacksmith was rewarded for his help by having molten gold poured down his throat. Other sieges took place during the subsequent centuries: Balliol's forces attacked in 1335, Cromwell took over in 1654 and the sixth Earl of Mar used the castle as the headquarters of the ill-fated Jacobite risings in 1715. Following John Erskine's withdrawal, Kildrummy became redundant and it was abandoned as a fortress and residence and fell into ruin.

Beside the ruins is a Scottish Baronial-style castle built in 1901, now the grand *Kildrummy Castle Hotel* (☎019755/71288; ⑦), superbly endowed with wood-panelled rooms, Victorian furniture and a raised terrace on which you can enjoy afternoon tea overlooking the castle.

Ten miles further west, the A944 sweeps round into the parish of **STRATHDON**, little more than a succession of occasional buildings by the roadside. However, four miles from here, up a rough track leading into Glen Nochty, lies the unexpected **Lost Gallery** (Mon & Wed–Sun 11am–5pm; ☎019756/51287), which shows work by some of Scotland's leading modern artists in a wonderfully remote and tranquil setting. Heading west again on the A944, past the much-photographed signs to the village of Lost, you'll come to **Candacraig Gardens** (May–Sept Mon–Fri 10am–5pm; Sat & Sun 10–6pm; free), the walled grounds of Candacraig House, Highland retreat of comedian Billy Connolly, who recently starred as John Brown in the award-winning film *Mrs Brown*, set at nearby Balmoral Castle (see p.454). The house is private, but the gardens, an exuberant display of colour and energy, are open to the public. In the old laundry on the other side of the main house, *No. 3 Candacraig Square* (☎019756/51472, *no3@buchanan.co.uk*; ⑦) is a stylish B&B with wooden floors, piles of books and a promise of fresh fish for breakfast.

A further eight miles on, just beyond the junction of the Ballater road, lies **Corgarff Castle** (Jan–March & Dec Sat 9.30am–4pm, Sun 2–4pm; April–Sept Mon–Sun 9.30am–6pm; Oct & Nov Mon–Wed & Sat 9.30am–4pm, Thurs 9.30am–2pm, Sun 2–4pm; HS; £2.50), an austere tower house with an unusual star-shaped curtain wall and an eventful history. Built in 1537 – the wall was added in 1748 – it was first attacked in 1571, during a religious feud between the Forbes, family of the laird of the castle, and the Gordons, who torched the place, killing the laird's wife, family and servants. In 1748, in the aftermath of Culloden, the Hanoverian government turned Corgarff into a barracks in order to track down local Jacobite rebels, and finally, in the mid-nineteenth century, the English Redcoats were stationed here with the unpopular task of trying to control whisky smuggling. Today there's little to see inside, but the place has been restored to resemble its days as a barracks, with stark rooms and rows of hard, uncomfortable beds – authentic touches which extend to graffiti on the walls and peat smoke permeating the building from a fire in the first floor. One unexpected bonus here if you're from far-flung parts is the chance to hear the history of the castle in one of the nineteen languages the keeper has recorded it in over the years, ranging from Thai to Icelandic.

Leading to the castle from the south is the old military road, which, unusually, hasn't been covered over by the present road and is fairly clear for about three miles. A mile or so along this from the castle, approached from the main road by the track beside Rowan Tree Cottage, is *Jenny's Bothy* at Dellachuper (☎019756/51449), a beautifully remote and simple **bunkhouse**, surrounded by empty scenery and wild animals. You'll have to bring your own supplies if you're coming here, but it's a great base for hiking, biking or skiing, or just detaching yourself from the madding crowd for a day or two.

Tomintoul

Just past Corgarff, at Cock Bridge, the road leaps up towards the ski slopes of the Lecht and, four miles further on, **TOMINTOUL** (pronounced "*Tom*-in-towel"), at 1150ft the highest village in the Scottish Highlands. Tomintoul owes its existence to the post-1745 landowners' panic when, as in other parts of the north, isolated inhabitants were forcibly moved to new, planted villages, where a firm eye could be kept on everybody. Its long, thin layout is reminiscent of a Wild West frontier town; Queen Victoria, passing through, wrote that it was "the most tumble-down, poor looking place I ever saw".

SKIING THE LECHT

The Lecht offers dry-ski-slope skiing all year, and the recent introduction of snow-making equipment should help extend the snow season beyond January and February. While the gentle slopes are good for beginners, experienced skiers won't find much to tax them, though there is a Snowboard Fun Park, with specially built jumps and ramps. Lift passes cost £12 a day for adults; ski and boot hire costs £12 a day from the ski school at the base station (☎019756/51440), which also provides tuition for £6 an hour.

For **information** on skiing and road conditions here, call the base station or the Ski Hotline (☎0891/654654).

That said, it makes a good base for **skiing** the Lecht area in winter, and there's some terrific **walking** hereabouts, with Tomintoul marking the end of the long-distance Speyside Way (see p.460).

Practicalities

In the central square, the **tourist office** (April, May & Oct Mon–Sat 10am–1pm & 2–5.30pm, Sun 2–5pm; June & Sept Mon–Sat 10am–1pm & 2–5.30pm, Sun 2–5.30pm; July & Aug Mon–Sat 10am–7pm, Sun 1–7pm; ☎01807/580285) also acts as the local **museum**, with mock-ups of an old farm kitchen and a smithie (same times; free). Information about the extensive Glenlivet Crown Estate, its wildlife (including reindeer) and numerous paths and bike trails is available from the **ranger's office** (☎01807/580283 for opening hours) at the far end of the long main street.

If you need a place **to stay**, the *Tomintoul Bunkhouse*, immediately beside the tourist office, is plain but friendly and useful; contact the neighbouring *Gordon Hotel* (☎01807/580206) to make bookings or call in at the hotel reception. There's also a basic SYHA hostel on Main Street (☎01807/580282 or central reservations 0541/553255). Of the B&Bs, try *Conglass Hall*, on Main Street (☎01807/580291; ①), or *Milton Farm*, half a mile out of town on the B9008 to Dufftown (☎01807/580288; ①). Of the hotels gathered around the main square, the *Glenavon* (☎01807/580218; ①) is the most convivial for a drink, and serves ale made in the local Tomintoul Brewery, while the best bet for something to **eat** is a pub meal here or at the *Gordon Hotel*.

Speyside

Strictly speaking, **Speyside** is the region surrounding the Spey River, but to most people the name is synonymous with the **whisky triangle**, stretching from just north of Craigellachie down towards Tomintoul in the south, and west to Huntly. Indeed, there are more whisky distilleries and famous brands (including Glenfiddich and Glenlivet) concentrated in this small area than in any other part of the country. Running through the heart of the region is the River Spey, whose clean clear waters play such a vital part in the whisky industry and are home to thousands of salmon. At the centre of Speyside, the quiet market town of **Dufftown** makes a good base for a tour of the distilleries, while the only other settlement of any interest is **Huntly**, being well-served by road (A96) and rail links with Aberdeen and Elgin.

Dufftown and Craigellachie

The cheery community of **DUFFTOWN**, founded in 1817 by James Duff, the fourth Earl of Fife, proudly proclaims itself "Malt Whisky Capital of the World", and indeed it exports more of the stuff than anywhere else in Britain. Approaching the town from the

---

THE SPEYSIDE WAY

The core of the 70-mile-long **Speyside Way** follows the River Spey from its mouth at Spey Bay on the Moray Firth south to Aviemore (see p.490), with branches linking it to Buckie on the Moray Firth coast, Dufftown and Tomintoul, on the edge of the Cairngorm mountains. The whole thing is a five- to seven-day walk, or a long day's cycle ride, but its proximity to main roads and small villages means that it is excellent for shorter walks, especially in the heart of distillery country between Craigellachie and Glenlivet. The path uses disused railway lines for much of its length, and there are simple campsites and good B&Bs at strategic points along the route.

---

south along the A941, you'll see the gaunt hilltop ruins of **Auchindoun Castle**. Although you can't go inside, it's enjoyable to wander along the track from the main road to this three-storey keep encircled by Pictish earthworks.

Following the A941 through the town brings you to the **Glenfiddich Distillery** (see p.461), past the old Dufftown train station, currently being restored for a steam line through to Keith. Behind the distillery, the ruin of the thirteenth-century **Balvenie Castle** (April–Sept daily 9.30am–6pm; HS; £1.20) sits on a mound overlooking vast piles of whisky barrels. The castle was a Stewart stronghold, which was abandoned after the 1745 uprising, when it was last used as a government garrison.

Four miles north of Dufftown, the small settlement of **CRAIGELLACHIE** sits above the confluence of the sparkling waters of the Fiddich and the Spey. From the village, you can look down on a beautiful iron bridge over the Spey built by Thomas Telford in 1815. By the River Fiddich on the A95 Huntly road, there's a **visitor centre** for the Speyside Way (generally open daily 9am–5pm Easter–Oct; ☎01340/881266), which sells maps of the route and gives advice on what to look for along the way.

Practicalities

Dufftown's four main streets converge on Main Square. For maps and information on the **whisky trail**, head straight to the **tourist office** inside the handsome clock tower at the centre of the square (April, May & Oct Mon–Sat 10am–1pm & 2–5pm; June & Sept Mon–Sat 10am–1pm & 2–6pm, Sun 1–6pm; July & Aug Mon–Sat 10am–7pm, Sun 1–7pm; ☎01340/820501). There's a good range of places **to stay** in Dufftown itself, as well as in the surrounding countryside. In town, *Morven*, on Main Square (☎01340/820507; ①), offers good, cheap B&B, while there's a tiny hostel, *Whisky Capital Backpackers* (☎01340/821069 or 821066), a mile out of town on the Huntly road. In Craigellachie the most comfortable option is the extremely welcoming and homely B&B attached to the *Green Hall Gallery* on Victoria Street (☎01340/871010, *stewart.johnston@dial.pippex.com*; ①). For unquestionable style and luxury, head to *Mimore House* (☎01807/590378; April–Oct; ⑥), the former home of Glenlivet owner George Smith, which sits right beside the distillery on a quiet hillside above the Livet Water, while in Archiestown, a few miles west of Craigellachie, the *Archiestown Hotel* (☎01340/810218; ⑥) is filled with an eclectic collection of odd artefacts but is a good base for walking or cycling and serves great seafood.

The *Glenfiddich Café* just beyond the tourist office on Church Street does simple **meals** and takeaways, while the popular *Taste of Speyside* on Balverie Street, just off the square, serves classier (and pricier) Scottish food. Nine miles out of town along the B9009 towards Glenlivet, the *Croft Inn* is a cosy roadside **pub** with well-priced local dishes and beautiful views over Ben Rinnes, while the best selection of malts is at the *Grouse Inn* at Cabrach, ten miles out along the A941 to Rhynie. In Craigellachie, the tiny *Fiddichside Inn*, on the A95 Huntly road, is a wonderfully original and convivial pub with a garden by the river, while the busy *Highlander Inn* (☎01340/881446; ②) on

Victoria Street serves good pub grub and also has rooms. The best place for takeaways of the liquid kind is The Whisky Shop, on Dufftown's main square, which stocks a superb range of whiskies and hosts occasional tastings. **Bikes** can be rented from Clarke's Cycle Hire (☎01340/881525), beside the *Fiddichside Inn* at Craigellachie.

Huntly

A small town set in attractive rolling farmland, the ancient burgh of **HUNTLY**, ten miles east of Dufftown and on the main train route from Aberdeen to Inverness, has little to offer the tourist other than its proximity to the Whisky Trail. It does boast, however, one of the smallest and prettiest castles in the area, albeit rather skeletal. **Huntly Castle,**

THE MALT WHISKY TRAIL

Speyside's **Malt Whisky Trail** is a clearly signposted seventy-mile meander around the region via eight distilleries, although there are others not on the official trail that you can visit by prior arrangement: The Macallan at Craigellachie (☎01340/871471), and Cragganmore at Ballindalloch (☎01807/500202) are both worth trying. Unless you're seriously interested in whisky, it's best to just pick out a couple that appeal, perhaps choosing one for the whisky and another for its setting. All the distilleries offer a guided **tour** (some are free, and some charge an entry fee, then give you a voucher which is redeemable against a bottle of whisky from the distillery shop) with a tasting to round it off – if you're driving you'll be offered a miniature to take away with you. Indeed, most people travel the route by car, though you could cycle it, or even walk using the Speyside Way (see opposite).

Cardhu, on the B9102 at Knockando (March–Nov Mon–Fri 9.30am–4.30pm; July–Sept also Sat 9.30am–4.30pm & Sun 11am–4pm; Dec–Feb 10am–4pm; £2 with voucher). This distillery was established over a century ago when the founder's wife was nice enough to raise a red flag to warn local crofters if the authorities were on the lookout for their illegal stills. Sells rich, full-bodied whisky which has distinctive peaty flavours, in an attractive bulbous bottle.

Dallas Dhu, Mannachie Road, Forres (April–Sept daily 9.30am–6pm; Oct–March Mon–Wed & Sat 9.30am–4pm, Thurs 9.30am–noon, Sun 2–4pm; £2.50). Located apart from the others, this classic Victorian distillery no longer makes whisky, but all the old equipment is in place and you can look around freely with an audioguide handset.

Glenfiddich, on the A941 just north of Dufftown (April to mid-Oct Mon–Sat 9.30am–4.30pm, Sun noon–4.30pm; mid-Oct to March Mon–Fri 9.30am–4.30pm; free). Probably the best known of the malt whiskies, and the biggest and slickest of all the distilleries. It's a lighter, sweet whisky which comes in familiar triangular shaped bottles. Uniquely, Glenfiddich is bottled on the premises – an interesting process to watch. Informative (and free) tours, though the place is thronged with tourists.

Glenlivet, on the B9008, ten miles north of Tomintoul (April–Oct Mon–Sat 10am–4pm, Sun 12.30–4pm; July & Aug last tour 5pm; £2.50 with voucher). With a famous name and a lonely hillside setting, this was the first licensed distillery in the Highlands, following the 1823 Act of Parliament which aimed to reduce illicit distilling and smuggling. The Glenlivet twelve-year-old malt is a floral, fragrant medium-bodied whisky.

Speyside Cooperage, Craigellachie, four miles north of Dufftown (all year Mon–Fri 9.30am–4.30pm, plus Easter–Sept Sat 9.30am–4pm; £2.95). Gain an insight into the ancient and skilled art of cooperage, and watch the oak casks for whisky being made and repaired.

Strathisla, Keith (Feb & March Mon–Fri 9.30am–4pm, April–Nov Mon–Sat 9.30am–4pm, Sun 12.30–4pm; £4, with a £2 voucher). A small old-fashioned distillery claiming to be Scotland's oldest (1786); it's certainly one of the most attractive, situated in a highly evocative highland location on the strath of the Isla River. The malt itself has a rich almost fruity taste and is pretty rare, but is used as the heart of the better-known Chivas Regal blend.

power centre of the Gordon family (April–Sept daily 9.30am–6pm; Oct–March Mon–Wed & Sat 9.30am–4pm, Thurs 9.30am–noon, Sun 2–4pm; HS; £2.50), sits in a peaceful clearing on the banks of the Deveron River, a ten-minute walk from the town centre down Castle Street and through an elegant arch. Built over a period of five centuries, it has sheltered the likes of Robert the Bruce and James IV (who attended a wedding here), and in 1562 became the headquarters of the Counter Reformation in Scotland. After the Battle of Corrichie, brought about by the fourth earl's third son's wish to marry Mary, Queen of Scots, and which effectively ended the Gordons' 250-year rule, the castle was pillaged and its treasures sent to St Machar's Cathedral in Aberdeen. During the Civil War the Earl of Huntly, who had supported Charles I and declared, "you can take my head off my shoulders, but not my heart from my sovereign", was shot against his castle's walls with his escort, after which the place was left to fall into ruin.

Today you can still make out the twelfth-century motte, a grassy mound on the west side of the complex, while the main castle ruin, with its splendid doorway fronted by an elaborate coat of arms, dates from the mid-fifteenth century. In the basement, a narrow passage leads to the prisons, where medieval graffiti of tents, animals and people adorn the walls.

Huntly was also the birthplace of the much-loved children's author George MacDonald, whose writing influenced Lewis Carroll, J.R.R. Tolkien and C.S. Lewis, among others. A plaque commemorates his birthplace on Duke Street, while tours of The Farm, where he grew up, can be arranged through Ian Lane (☎01466/792786). You can pick up more information in a brochure available at the tourist office which details a George MacDonald Trail through town.

Seven miles south of Huntly and served by the occasional bus, the modest chateau-style **Leith Hall** (Easter weekend & May–Sept daily 1.30–4.45pm; Oct Sat & Sun 1.30–4.45pm; NTS; £4.40) is worth visiting, even when closed, for a wander around its 286-acre grounds (daily 9.30am–dusk; £2). Home to the Leith and Leith-Hay family since 1650, the vast estate of varied farm and woodlands includes ponds, eighteenth-century stables, a bird-observation hide and signposted countryside walks. Inside, you can see personal memorabilia of the successive Leith lairds, a number of whom were in the armed services overseas, so anyone with military interests or a penchant for British imperial history will have a field day.

Three miles northwest of Huntly, between the A920 to Dufftown and the A96 to Keith (signposted from both), the **North East Falconry Centre** (daily: March–Sept 10.30am–5.30pm; Oct & Nov 10am–4pm; ☎01466/760328; £3.75) is home to some fabulous falcons, owls and eagles, with flying demonstrations four times daily.

Practicalities

Huntly's **tourist office**, 7a The Square (daily: April to late Oct 10am–5pm; July & Aug 9.30am–6pm; ☎01466/792255), will book accommodation, but charges a ten percent deposit, redeemable on the first night's stay. One of the area's best **B&Bs** is *Faitch Hill Farmhouse* (☎01466/720240; ②), four miles outside town at Gartly; in Huntly itself, the *Dunedin Guest House*, 17 Bogie St (☎01466/794162; ①), near the train station, is a good bet. One of the area's best small hotels is *The Old Manse of Marnoch* (☎01466/780873; ⑤), set on four riverside acres at Bridge of Marnoch, while for serious luxury, head for the former home of the Duke of Gordon, *The Castle Hotel* (☎01466/792696; ⑤), which stands at the end of a long driveway behind the castle ruins. The *Auld Pit* on Duke Street is a decent **pub** with regular folk music, and serves pub meals, while the home-brewed beers on offer at the *Borve Brew House* in Ruthven – four miles along the A96 to Keith and then a couple of miles along a narrow road – attract real-ale enthusiasts from across the country. **Bikes** can be rented from Huntly Cycle Centre (☎01466/793508), or from the Nordic Ski Centre near the castle (☎01466/794428), where you can also brush up your cross-country skiing skills on all-weather tracks if there's no snow.

The coast to Forres

The **coastal region** of northeast Scotland from Aberdeen to Inverness is a rugged, often bleak, landscape. Still, if the weather is good, it's well worth spending a couple of days meandering through the various little fishing villages and along the miles of deserted, unspoilt beaches. Keen walkers have the best run of the area: some of the cliffs are so steep that you have to hike considerable distances to get the best views of the coast.

Most visitors bypass **Peterhead** and **Fraserburgh**, the two largest communities, and head instead for quieter spots such as **Cruden Bay**, with its sandy beach and spooky castle, or the idyllic villages of **Pennan** and nearby **Cullen**. The other main attractions are **Duff House**, a branch of the National Gallery of Scotland, in **Banff**, the working abbey at **Pluscarden** and the **Findhorn Foundation**, near **Forres**.

The main towns and larger villages are fairly well-served by **buses**, while **trains** from Aberdeen and Inverness stop at Elgin, Forres and Nairn. Even so, it's preferable to have your own transport for reaching some of the far-flung places.

Pitmedden Gardens to Peterhead

Fourteen miles north of Aberdeen, on the outskirts of Pitmedden village, **Pitmedden Gardens** (May–Sept daily 10am–5pm; NTS; £3.90) are the creation of Alexander Seton – formerly Lord Pitmedden, before James VII removed his title as punishment for opposing his Catholicism. Seton spent his enforced retirement on perfecting an elaborate garden project he had begun in 1675, and today the utterly orderly gardens, 471 feet square, have been restored to their seventeenth-century pattern, with neat box hedges, pavilions, fountains and sundials. In the lower garden (best viewed from the terrace), the layout of three of the flowerbeds mimics those of Holyrood Abbey in Edinburgh, while the fourth flowerbed – with its crest and a weather vane, surmounted by soldiers – are tributes to Seton's father who died fighting against the Covenanters in Aberdeen. Entrance to the gardens also takes in the **Museum of Farming Life**, where you'll see old tools and a chilly, dark bothy that was once home to the workers of the 100-acre Pitmedden estate.

Tolquhon Castle

One of the area's most secluded ruins, **Tolquhon Castle** (April–Sept daily 9.30am–6pm; Oct–March Sat 9.30am–4pm, Sun 2–4pm; HS; £1.80), is tucked away off a dirt track a mile or so northwest of Pitmedden. Of the medieval remains, the gatehouse facade is the most impressive, with its handsome arched portal protected by drum towers and enriched with all manner of sculpted figures and coats of arms. You can still make out what each room was used for: the kitchen has two huge ovens gouged out of the wall, and one of the bedrooms has its own dungeon with an ominous trapdoor – at any one time there could have been eight or nine prisoners below.

Haddo House and Gardens

Four miles north of Pitmedden, the huge Palladian mansion of **Haddo House** (Easter weekend & May–Sept daily 1.30–4.45pm; Oct Sat & Sun 1.30–4.45pm; NTS; £4.40), completed to a design by William Adam in 1735, is set in 177 acres of woodland, lakes and ponds. Since 1731 Haddo has been the seat of the Gordons and several earls and marquesses of Aberdeen – the gardens, now home to otters, red squirrels, pheasants and deer, were created from a wasteland by the fourth earl in the early years of the last century. The house is now renowned for staging local music, drama and arts: check with the Haddo Arts Trust (☎01651/851770) for details of forthcoming productions.

Forvie Nature Reserve and Cruden Bay

Fifteen miles north of Aberdeen, a sideroad (signposted to Collieston) leads off the A90 past **Forvie National Nature Reserve**. This area incorporates the Sands of Forvie, one of Britain's largest and least disturbed dune systems, and boasts a rich array of birdlife. A network of trails winds along the coast and through the dunes, with one leading to a fifteenth-century village, buried by the shifting sands. Just south of here, at Newburgh, the *Udny Arms Hotel* on Mains Street (☎01358/789444, *enquiry@udny.demon.uk*; ⑥) has a superb restaurant, overlooking the mouth of the Ythan River, which is very popular with Aberdonians at the weekends.

Wonderful sandy beaches can also be found eight miles north of Forvie, at **CRUDEN BAY**, from where a pleasant fifteen-minute walk leads to the huge pink-granite ruin of **Slains Castle**. This eerie place, whose stark beauty overlooking the sea is said to have inspired Bram Stoker to write *Dracula*, was built in 1597 but remodelled in Gothic style in the nineteenth century. It is surprisingly badly signposted: from the car park at the end of Cruden Bay's Main Street, head for the sea, then along the cliffs.

A precarious three-mile walk on from Slains Castle along the cliffs brings you to the **Bullers of Buchan**, a splendid 245ft-deep sea chasm, where the ocean gushes in through a natural archway eroded by the sea. This is some of the finest cliff scenery in the country and attracts a variety of (smelly) nesting seabirds. An alternative access point is the car park just off the A975, from where a short footpath leads past some old cottages to the very edge of the chasm.

Peterhead and around

Unless you have a particular penchant for baked-bean factories and power stations, **PETERHEAD**, the easternmost mainland town in Scotland, is best avoided. The busiest white-fish port in Europe, with annual catches valued at over $75 million, its harbour is a mass of large, aggressive-looking boats, with throbbing engines and an odour of stale fish. Fishing, along with a high-security jail, used to be Peterhead's sole source of income until the arrival of the oil industry in the 1970s. The town's population increased rapidly from 13,000 to 18,000, and now the community is one of the richest in Britain, though little of the wealth seems to have found its way into civic improvement.

The oldest building in Peterhead is the 400-year-old **Ugie Salmon Fish House** on Golf Road at the mouth of the River Ugie, at the north end of town (Mon–Fri 9am–5pm, Sat 9am–noon; free), where you can watch the traditional methods of oak-smoking salmon and trout in Scotland's oldest smoke-house – the finished product is for sale at reasonable prices. In contrast, one of the town's newest buildings houses the **Peterhead Maritime Heritage Museum** (April–Oct Mon–Sat 10am–5pm, Sun noon–5pm; Nov–March Sat 10am–4pm, Sun noon–4pm; £2.50), on South Road above a clean, spacious beach. The museum tells the story of the town's fishing industry from the old herring fleet to the modern day, with a live relay of the harbourmaster's radio channel. Listen out too for the recordings of old fishermen and women, who still speak the distinctive Doric dialect.

Peterhead has no tourist office; if you need **to stay**, try *Alva House*, 128 Queen St (☎01779/477393; ③), a small centrally located B&B, or the modern and upmarket *Waterside Inn*, on Fraserburgh Road (☎01779/471121; ⑥), on the banks of the River Ugie to the north of town. For **food**, head for the town's best fish-and-chip shop, the *Dolphin*, on Alexandra Parade on the northwest side of the harbour, beside the fish market.

Aden Country Park

From Peterhead, a direct bus travels the nine miles to the 230-acre **Aden Country Park** (daily 7am–dusk; free), just beyond the town of Mintlaw. In addition to woodlands, a lake and a huge variety of wildlife, the park is home to the **Aberdeenshire**

Farming Museum (daily: March–April & Oct–Nov noon–5pm; May–Sept 11am–4.30pm; free), whose highlight is a unique semicircular farmstead built around the beginning of the nineteenth century. Despite its uninspiring title, the centre is a well-thought-out and absorbing museum with atmospheric exhibits that recall a traditional farming life.

Fraserburgh and the north coast

Ten miles or so north of Aden Park, **FRASERBURGH** is a large and fairly severe-looking town in the same vein as Peterhead, although its economy still relies on fishing alone. At the northern tip of the town, an eighteenth-century lighthouse protrudes from the top of sixteenth-century **Fraserburgh Castle**, where the highest wind speeds on mainland Britain (140mph) were recorded in 1989. The lighthouse was one of the first to be built in Scotland and now houses the **Museum of Scottish Lighthouses** (April–Oct Mon–Sat 10am–6pm, Sun noon–6pm; Nov–April closes at 4pm; £2.75), where you can see a collection of huge lenses and prisms gathered from decommissioned lighthouses, and a display on various members of the Stevenson family (including the father and grandfather of Robert Louis Stevenson), who designed many of them. Highlight of the museum is the Kinnaird Head light itself, preserved as it was when the last keeper left in 1991, with its century-old equipment still in working order.

Fraserbugh's **tourist office**, in Saltoun Square (April–June & Sept–Oct Mon–Sat 10am–1pm & 2–5pm; July & Aug Mon–Sat 10am–1pm & 2–6pm, Sun 1–6pm; ☎01346/518315), gives out information about the surrounding area, while the friendly *Coffee Shoppe*, 30 Cross St, serves great sandwiches, soup and cakes.

Pennan, Crovie and Gardenstown

The coast road between Fraserburgh and **PENNAN**, twelve miles west, is particularly attractive; it's lined with pretty churches and cottages, and countless paths lead off it to ruined castles, clifftop walks and lonely beaches. Pennan itself, a tiny fishing hamlet, lies just off the road, down a steep and hazardous hill. Consisting of little more than a single row of whitewashed stone cottages, the village leapt into the limelight when the British movie *Local Hero* was filmed here in 1982. The only place to **stay** is the *Pennan Inn* (☎01346/561201; ⑤), a convivial, lively spot with an excellent seafood **restaurant** and a cosy bar, whose customers spill out onto the sea wall on summer evenings. The tiny villages of **CROVIE** (pronounced "Crivie") and **GARDENSTOWN**, on the other side of Troup Head from Pennan, are just as appealing as their neighbour. Both are tucked in against the steep cliffs, with Crovie so narrow that its residents have to park at one end of the village and continue to their houses on foot.

Macduff and Banff

Heading west along the coast from Pennan brings you, after ten miles, to **MACDUFF**, a famous spa town during the nineteenth century and now with a thriving and pleasant harbour. The **Macduff Marine Aquarium**, 11 High Shore (daily 10am–5pm; £2.75), displaying sea creatures from the Moray Firth in Britain's deepest aquarium tank, is a fun place for kids.

Macduff more or less merges with the town of **BANFF**, whose **tourist office** (April–June & Sept Mon–Sat 10am–1pm & 2–5pm; July & Aug Mon–Sat until 6pm, Sun 1–6pm; ☎01261/812419) is housed in a Greek Doric lodge opposite the entrance to Duff House. Here, for £1 deposit, you can collect a thoroughly enjoyable **Walkman tour** of the town, which introduces both the grand Georgian upper town and, down by the harbour, the older, scruffier **Scotstown**. For sea swimming, head to Links Beach on the west side of town. The other beach, at the mouth of the Deveron, is susceptible to strong currents and is best avoided.

The town's undoubted highlight is extravagant **Duff House** (April–Oct daily 11am–5pm; Nov–March Thurs–Sun 11am–4pm; HS; £3), on the other side of the River Deveron from the aquarium, over a beautiful seven-arched bridge. Built to William Adam's design in 1730, this elegant Georgian Baroque house was originally intended for one of the northeast's richest men, William Braco, who became Earl of Fife in 1759. It was clearly built to impress, and could have been even more splendid had Adam been allowed to build curving colonnades either side; Braco's refusal to pay for carved Corinthian columns to be shipped in from Queensferry caused such bitter argument that the laird never actually came to live here and even went so far as to pull down his coach curtains whenever he passed by.

The house has been painstakingly restored and reopened as an outpost of the **National Gallery of Scotland**'s extensive collection. The first room to the left off the rococo vestibule is the **Prince of Wales' Bedroom**, so called because it was used by the future Edward VII. His mother, Queen Victoria, can be seen, looking unusually fresh-faced, in the bust under the mirror. Beyond the back of the vestibule is the dining room, hung with ponderous eighteenth-century portraits, among which Allan Ramsay's *Elizabeth, Mrs Daniel Cunyngham* leaps out for its delightfully cool composition. To the left is the **Private Drawing Room**, containing a bust of William Adam and the sweeping canvases of Welsh landscapist Richard Wilson (1714–82). On the other side of the ground floor, Countess Agnes' Boudoir, formerly Lord Macduff's dressing room, contains a riotous gilded Rococo mirror and El Greco's heartfelt *St Jerome in Penitence*, which dominates a wall of mainly religious art. This leads into the **Hunting Room**, mainly filled with treasures from Dunimarle in Fife. Magdalene Erskine, who bought the house in 1835 and bequeathed its collection to be used to found an art gallery, can be seen as a little girl, added later to the painting of the family grouping by David Allen in 1788. Oddly, all the women are shown disproportionately tiny and doll-like next to the men and boys.

Ascending the **Great Staircase**, all eyes are drawn to the enormous copy of Raphael's *Transfiguration* by Inverness's Grigor Urquhart (1797–1846). Most of the accompanying portraits are also Scottish. Upstairs, the **North Drawing Room** contains the only piece of furniture original to the house, a 1760s mirror, but more obvious is the bewilderingly bold gold and cherry-red ceiling, a not entirely successful Victorian pastiche of Adam's style. In the **Great Drawing Room**, William's son Robert Adam's symmetrical classicism meets French opulence head on, and somehow it works. The best example of this is the 1764 furniture suite of two gilded sofas and two chairs originally designed by the younger Adam and built by Chippendale, combining the Classical reference of lion's-paw feet and the Rococo influence of florid gold shells. Two chairs from the same collection recently sold at auction for £1.7 million – twice the amount previously paid for a piece of Chippendale furniture. Beyond the house there are extensive grounds with some pleasant parkland walks, notably along the River Deveron to a local beauty spot, the **Bridge of Alvah**, a couple of miles south.

A mile southwest of town along the A97, the intriguing **Colleonard Sculpture Park** (visits by arrangement only ☎01261/818284) is the world's only garden of archetypal abstractionism. Sculptor Frank Bruce, usually to be found around the site, began his outdoor collection in 1965. A man of immense talent, he carves figures and scenes of great vitality and intensity from tree trunks, which he then places around the wonderfully peaceful site.

If you want to stay, **B&Bs** include *Castlehill*, 58 Castle St, an extension of the High Street (☎01261/818372; ②), or, over the river in the heart of Macduff, Mrs Grieg's, 11 Gellymill St (☎01261/833314; ①). Four miles south of Macduff, off the A497 Turriff road, the elegant and welcoming Regency *Eden House* (☎01261/821282; ⑤) is set in extensive grounds overlooking the Deveron valley. **Camping** is best near the beach at the *Banff Links Caravan Park* (☎01261/812228; April–Sept). There are various pubs for

food and drink: the *Aul' Fife*, at 12 Low St, just along from the tourist office, serves reasonable pub grub, or try the *Market Arms*, a sixteenth-century town house on High Shore.

Cullen

Twelve miles west of Banff, past the quaint village of **Portsoy**, renowned for its green marble once shipped to Versailles and annual traditional boat festival in early July, is **CULLEN**, served by bus from Aberdeen. The town, strikingly situated beneath a superb series of arched rail viaducts, is made up of two sections – Seatown, by the harbour, and the new town on the hillside. There's a lovely stretch of sheltered sand by Seatown, where the colourful houses – confusingly numbered according to the order in which they were built – huddle end-on to the sea. Cullen's attractive old **kirk**, dating from the 1300s, lies a twenty-minute stroll south of the centre.

The town's enthusiastic **tourist office** (June–Aug daily 11am–5pm) is on the main square of the new town, and while the hotels are found in the new town, **B&Bs** are located down in Seatown. They're all much of a muchness, but no. 53 is friendly and comfortable (☎01542/840819; ①). If you want to try the local delicacy, Cullen skink – fish soup made from cream and smoked haddock – the friendly *Three Kings* **pub** on North Castle Street is your best bet, though most of the smarter hotels around town also serve it, including the grand *Seafield Arms Hotel* (☎01542/840791; ③), a seventeenth-century coaching inn which also produces expensive but delicious meals.

Elgin and around

Inland, about fifteen miles southwest of Cullen, the lively market town of **ELGIN** grew up in the thirteenth century around the River Lossie. It's an appealing place, still largely sticking to its medieval street plan, with a busy main street opening out onto an old cobbled marketplace and a tangle of wynds and pends.

On North College Street, just round the corner from the tourist office and clearly signposted, is the still lovely ruin of **Elgin Cathedral** (April–Sept daily 9.30am–6.30pm; Oct–March Mon–Wed & Sat 9.30am–4pm, Thurs 9.30am–noon, Sun 2–4pm; HS; £2, joint ticket with Spynie Palace £2.80). Once considered Scotland's most beautiful cathedral, rivalling St Andrews in importance, today it is little more than a shell, though it does retain its original facade. Founded in 1224, the three-towered cathedral was extensively rebuilt after a fire in 1270, and stood as the region's highest religious house until 1390 when the so-called Wolf of Badenoch (Alexander Stewart, Earl of Buchan and illegitimate son of Robert II) burnt the place down, along with the rest of the town, in retaliation for being excommunicated by the Bishop of Moray when he left his wife. The cathedral suffered further during the post-Reformation, when all its valuables were stripped and the building was reduced to common quarry for the locals. Unusual features include the Pictish cross slab in the middle of the ruins and the cracked gravestones with their memento mori of skulls and crossbones.

At the very top of High Street is one of the UK's oldest museums, the **Elgin Museum** (April–Sept Mon–Fri 10am–5pm, Sat 11am–4pm, Sun 2–5pm; £1.50), housed in this building since 1843. Along with the usual local exhibits, there's a weird anthropological collection including reptilian skulls, a shrunken head from Ecuador and a grinning mummy from Peru. In addition, you can see an excellent collection of fossils and well-explained Pictish relics.

The handsome, pedestrianized High Street, leading west, widens out onto the market place, the Plainstones, and the impressive Neoclassical parish **church of St Giles** (July & Aug Fri 2–5pm), built by Archibald Simpson in 1827–28.

Practicalities

Elgin is well-served by public transport, with the Aberdeen–Inverness train stopping here several times a day. The **bus station** is on Alexandra Road, a block from St Giles Church (☎01343/544222), while the **train station** is slightly less convenient, on the south side of town on Station Road (turn right out of the station, left at the island and up Moss Street to reach the centre).

The **tourist office**, 17 High St (April–Sept Mon–Sat 10am–5pm, Sun 1–5pm; July & Aug daily till 6pm, Nov–March Mon–Sat 10am–4pm; ☎01343/542666), will book **accommodation**. The *Saltire Bunkhouse*, on Pluscarden Road (☎01343/550624), offers hostel accommodation – it's a 25-minute walk from the centre of town. More central, *The Lodge*, 20 Duff Ave (☎01343/549981; ②), is a good-quality **B&B** in a house built for a former tea-plantation owner, while the castle-like *Mansion House Hotel*, The Haugh (☎01343/548811; ⑦), is one of the most exclusive in the region, and overlooks the river. Five miles out of town, *The Old Church of Urquhart* (☎01343/843063; ②) on Meft Road, Urquhart, is an unusual and comfortable B&B in a striking converted church. For **food**, a popular place is *Flanagan's Irish Pub*, 48a High St, which serves good pub grub and has regular live music; otherwise there's *Littlejohn's Brasserie*, 193 High St, a Tex-Mex and Cajun theme chain restaurant, or the *Ashvale* on Moss Street for fish and chips. The best **pubs** include *Thunderton House*, Thunderton Place, off High Street, which incorporates the seventeenth-century Great Lodge of Scottish kings, and *High Spirits*, in an old church on Moss Street. For great **picnic** foods, head to Gordon & McPhail, 58–60 South St, an Aladdin's cave of aromas, colours and delicacies, which sells one of the widest range of malt whiskies in the world.

Pluscarden Abbey

Set in attractive countryside seven miles southwest of Elgin, **Pluscarden Abbey** (daily 4.30am–8.45pm; free), looms impressively large in a peaceful clearing off an unmarked road. One of only two abbeys in Scotland with a permanent community of monks, it was founded in 1230 for a French order and, in 1390, became another of the properties burnt by the Wolf of Badenoch (see above); recovering from this, it became a priory of the Benedictine Abbey of Dunfermline in 1454 and continued as such until monastic life was suppressed in Scotland in 1560. The abbey's revival began in 1897 when the Catholic antiquarian, John, third Marquis of Bute, started to repair the building. In 1948 his son donated it to a small group of Benedictine monks from Gloucester, who established the present community. They are an active bunch, running stained glass workshops, making honey and even recording Gregorian chants on CDs – all of which is detailed on their Web site: *www.geocities.com/athens/thebes/2553/*. It is possible to stay here on retreat for a few days – apply in writing to Pluscarden Abbey, Elgin, Moray IV30 8UA or fax 01343/890258.

Lossiemouth, Spynie Palace and Duffus

Elgin's nearest seaside town, **LOSSIEMOUTH**, five miles north across the flat land of the Laich of Moray, is generally known as Lossie, a cheery golf-oriented resort, blessed with two sandy beaches. The glorious duney spit of the East Beach is reached over a footbridge across the River Lossie from the town park. In the easternmost part of the older harbour's grid of stone streets, Pitgaveny Street has the tiny **Fisheries Museum** (Easter–Sept Mon–Sat 10am–5pm; 50p), which includes some interesting scale models of fishing boats and a re-creation of the study of James Ramsay Macdonald (1866–1937), Britain's first Labour prime minister. On Prospect Terrace, above the harbour district in the airier "new" town, laid out in the nineteenth century, there's an excellent viewpoint dedicated to his memory.

Lossiemouth's development as a port came when the nearby waterways of **SPYNIE**, three miles inland, silted up and became useless to the traders of Elgin. Little remains of the settlement, although the hulking shape of **Spynie Palace** (April–Sept daily 9.30am–6.30pm; Oct–March Sat & Sun 2–4.30pm; HS; £1.80, joint ticket with Elgin Cathedral £2.80) indicates its former significance. Until 1224, Holy Trinity Church, which was part of the palace (there's no evidence of it today), was the cathedral of the Bishopric of Moray, before the honour passed to Elgin. The building remained, however, an integral part of the local ecclesiastical setup, primarily as the bishop's palace, right through until that office was abolished in the Scottish Church in 1689. The enormous rectangular David's Tower – seen looming for miles around – is the largest tower house in Scotland, and was built around a previously cylindrical corner tower during the time of Bishop David Stewart (1461–77). Views from the top over the Spynie Canal, the much-diminished sea loch and the Moray Firth, are stunning. Under the tower is a beautiful fourteenth-century beehive-roofed storage cellar. Next door, a slightly later cellar contains the wide-mouthed gun holes installed by Bishop Patrick Hepburn (1538–73), who, as a Catholic, survived the Reformation at Spynie for a full thirteen years.

Straight roads and water ditches criss-cross the flat land west of Spynie. Past the sinister shapes and frequent flights from RAF Lossiemouth is the spread-eagled settlement of **DUFFUS**, five miles west of Lossie. Old Duffus is no more than a farm or two and a motte and bailey **castle** (free access), part of which leans at a rakish angle. New Duffus, two miles northwest, is best known as the gateway to **Gordonstoun School**, the spartan (but hugely expensive) public school favoured by royalty, although Prince Charles reportedly despised its fresh-air-and-cold-showers puritanism. A quarter of a mile down the lane to Gordonstoun lie the remains of the Duffus old kirk, dating from at least 1226. A fine fourteenth-century parish cross, some beautifully inscribed graves and an 1830 watch house against grave-diggers are the highlights. Judging by the number of discarded cigarette packets, you're also likely to see a few Gordonstoun pupils at leisure.

Burghead

Windswept **BURGHEAD** was, before the imposition of the town in 1805–09 – a tightly packed grid of streets on the natural promontory – the site of an important Iron Age fort and the ancient Pictish capital of Moray. The **Burghead Bulls** were crafted here – a series of at least 25 unique Pictish stone carvings, all but six of which were destroyed when the town was built. One of these is on display in the window of the library on the main Grant Street; others can be seen in Elgin Museum, the National Museum in Edinburgh and the British Museum in London. A **well**, tucked away down King Street (key and interpretive boards are left in the porch at 69 King St), is the most remarkable surviving feature. Under a barrel roof, an impressive underground chamber fed by springs is believed to have been the water supply for the Iron Age and Pictish strongholds. The headland tip of the town is still pocked with the scant remains of early defences, including two earth ramparts, just off Bath Street, upon which an eerie burnt-out pillar sits. This is where the **Clavie** – a burning tar barrel still carried around the town on January 11, to mark the old calendar's new year – ends its annual journey. From the harbour, a wide sweep of sandy beach stretches five miles around Burghead Bay to Findhorn.

If you need to **stay** in Burghead, the *Red Craig* hotel, on the B9040 above the headland on the east side of town (☎01343/835663; ③), has B&B and camping, serves food and drink, and hosts occasional music and dances. To get to Burghead, take bus #331 from Elgin.

The Findhorn Foundation

The **Findhorn Foundation** on the B9011, about ten miles east of Elgin (Mon–Sat 9am–noon & 2–5pm, Sun 2–5pm; free), is a spiritual community and magnet for soul-searchers from around the world. Set up in 1962 by Eileen and Peter Caddy, the foundation has blossomed from its early core of three adults and three children into a full-blown community, with classes and facilities for hundreds of people. Bizarrely enough, despite its enormous growth, the Foundation is still situated on the town's caravan and camping park (☎01309/690203; April–Oct), creating an intriguing combination of people on site. Many of the original caravans have metamorphosed into more permanent structures, including some fascinating houses and community spaces employing the latest in ecological methods. It's an amazing place and, however cynical you might be, well worth at least a flying visit. Guided **tours** (Mon, Wed, Fri & Sat 2pm), residential workshops and short-term stays are all available (for details contact the visitor centre on ☎01309/690311), and there's a smart **café** and richly stocked delicatessen/general shop on site.

A mile up the road, the tidy village of **FINDHORN** has a magnificent beach, a delightful harbour, a small **Heritage Centre** (May & Sept Sat & Sun 2–5pm; June–Aug daily except Tues 2–5pm; free) and a couple of good pubs. Bus #310 from Forres runs there via the Foundation.

Forres

FORRES, one of Scotland's oldest agricultural towns, is of little note except for its pretty flower-filled parks, and the 20ft **Sueno's Stone**, on the eastern outskirts of town, one of the most remarkable Pictish stones in Scotland. Now housed in what looks like a huge glass telephone box as protection against further erosion, the stone was found buried in 1726 and mistakenly named after Swein Forkbeard, King of Denmark, though it more probably commemorates a battle between the people of Moray and the Norse settlers in Orkney. Carvings on the east face can be read as one of the earliest examples of war reportage, with the story told from the arrival of the leader at the top to the decapitated corpses of the vanquished at the bottom.

The #10 **bus** between Elgin and Inverness stops outside St Leonard's Church on High Street, further along from Forres' **tourist office** at no. 116 (Easter–June, Sept & Oct Mon–Sat 10am–1pm & 2–5pm; July & Aug Mon–Sat 10am–6pm, Sun 1–6pm; ☎01309/672938); call Bluebird in Elgin (☎01343/544222) for details of other local services. If you want **to stay** in Forres, try the *Tormhor* **B&B**, 11 High St (☎01309/673837; ①), which has large, comfortable rooms in a Victorian house overlooking some colourful gardens.

THE FINDHORN FOUNDATION

In 1962, with little money and no employment, Eileen and Peter Caddy, their three children and friend Dorothy Maclean, settled on a caravan site at Findhorn. Dorothy believed she had a special relationship with what she called the "devas" – "the archetypal formative forces of light or energy that underlie all forms in nature – plants, trees, rivers, etc", and from the uncompromising sandy soil they built a garden filled with remarkable plants and vegetables, far larger than had ever been seen in the area.

The Original Caravan – as it is marked on the site's map – still stands, surrounded by a whole host of newer timber buildings and other caravans. The Foundation is now home to a couple of hundred people, with around 8000 visitors every year. The buildings, employing solar power, earth roofs and other green initiatives, such as an ecological sewage treatment centre, show the commitment of the Findhorners to a sustainable future.

As can be expected, the Foundation is not without controversy, a local JP declaring that, "behind the benign and apparently religious front lies a hard core of New Agers experimenting with hallucinatory techniques marketed as spirituality". Findhorn, now a public company, is also accused of being overly well-heeled: a glance into the shop or a tally of the large cars parked outside the houses does give some substance to such ideas. However, most people here, although honest about the downsides of community living, are extremely positive about its benefits.

Brodie Castle

Four miles west of Forres and eight miles east of Nairn (see p.488), just off the A96, **Brodie Castle** (April–Sept Mon–Sat 11am–4.30pm, Sun 1.30–4.30pm; Oct Sat & Sun only; NTS; £4.40), dating from 1567, is a classic Z-shaped Scottish tower house set in lovely grounds (open all year; free) with drifts of daffodils in spring. Although it's now the property of the NTS, the 25th Earl of Brodie still lives here, and his presence very much contributes to the country-house atmosphere. Inside, there are all the rooms you'd expect: a panelled dining room with fabulous plasterwork, several bedrooms complete with four-posters, and a massive Victorian kitchen and servants' quarters, all linked by winding passages. The collections of furniture, porcelain and especially paintings are outstanding, with works by Jacob Cuyp and Edwin Landseer, among others. To end your trip there's a **tearoom**, where the staff dish out splendid home-baked cakes.

travel details

Trains

Aberdeen to: Arbroath (every 30min; 1hr); Dundee (every 30min; 1hr 15min); Edinburgh (1–2 hourly; 2hr 35min); Elgin (hourly; 1hr 30min); Forres (hourly; 1hr 45min); Glasgow (1–2 hourly; 2hr 35min); Huntly (hourly; 50min); Insch (hourly; 35min); Inverurie (hourly; 20min); Keith (hourly; 1hr 5min); Montrose (every 30min; 45min); Nairn (hourly; 2hr); Stonehaven (every 30min; 15min).

Dundee to: Aberdeen (every 30min; 1hr 15min); Arbroath (hourly; 20min); Montrose (hourly; 15min).

Elgin to: Forres (hourly; 15min); Nairn (hourly; 25min).

Buses

Aberdeen to: Arbroath (hourly; 1hr 20min); Ballater (hourly; 1hr 45min); Banchory (hourly; 55min); Banff (hourly; 1hr 55min); Braemar (4–6 daily; 2hr 10min); Crathie (for Balmoral) (4–6 daily; 1hr 55min); Cruden Bay (hourly; 50min); Cullen (hourly; 1hr 50min–2hr 30min); Dufftown (2 weekly; 2hr 10min); Dundee (hourly; 2hr); Elgin (hourly; 2hr 35min–3hr 40min); Forfar (2 daily; 1hr 20min); Forres (hourly; 2hr 35min); Fraserburgh (hourly; 1hr 20min); Fyvie (hourly; 1hr); Huntly (hourly; 1hr 35min); Inverurie (hourly; 45min); Macduff (hourly; 1hr 50min); Mintlaw (for Aden Park) (hourly; 50min); Montrose (hourly; 1hr); Nairn (hourly; 2hr 50min); Peterhead (every 30min; 1hr 15min); Pitmedden (hourly; 50min); Stonehaven (every 30min; 25–45min).

Ballater to: Crathie (June–Sept 1 daily; 15min).

Banchory to: Ballater (June–Sept 1 daily; 45min); Braemar (June–Sept 1 daily; 1hr 20min); Crathie (June–Sept 1 daily; 1hr); Spittal of Glenshee (June–Sept 1 daily; 2hr).

Dufftown to: Elgin (hourly; 1hr).

Dundee to: Aberdeen (hourly; 2hr); Arbroath (every 15min; 40min–1hr); Blairgowrie (every 30min; 50min–1hr); Forfar (every 30min; 30min); Glamis (2 daily; 40min); Kirriemuir (hourly; 1hr 10min); Meigle (hourly; 40min); Montrose (hourly; 1hr 15min).

Elgin to: Aberdeen (hourly; 2hr 35min–3hr 40min); Burghead (Mon–Sat hourly; 30min); Duffus (Mon–Sat hourly; 15min); Forres (hourly; 25min); Huntly (3 daily; 50min); Inverurie (3 daily; 1hr 45min); Lossiemouth (every 30min; 20min); Nairn (hourly; 40min); Pluscarden (1 daily; 20min).

Forres to: Elgin (hourly; 25min); Findhorn (Mon–Sat 8 daily; 20min).

Fraserburgh to: Banff (2 daily; 55min); Macduff (2 daily; 45min).

Montrose to: Brechin (hourly; 20min).

Peterhead to: Cruden Bay (every 30min; 20min).

Ferries

Aberdeen to: Lerwick, Shetland (6 weekly; 14hr); Stromness, Orkney (1 weekly; 10hr).

Flights

Aberdeen to: Belfast (Mon–Fri 1 daily; 2hr 45min); Birmingham (Mon–Fri 3 daily; 1hr 30min); Glasgow (1 daily; 45min); London (Heathrow 7 daily, Stansted 4 daily, Gatwick 5 daily, Luton 2 daily; 1hr 30min); Manchester (Mon–Fri 9 daily, Sat 3 daily, Sun 4 daily; 1hr 20min); Newcastle (Mon–Fri 5 daily; Sat & Sun 2 daily; 1hr); Shetland (Mon–Fri 4 daily, Sat & Sun 2 daily; 1hr).

Dundee to: London City (Mon–Fri 2 daily; 1hr 15min).

CHAPTER EIGHT

HIGHLAND REGION

he Highland region of Scotland, covering the northern two-thirds of the country, holds much of the mainland's most spectacular scenery: a classic combination of mountains, glens, lochs and rivers surrounded on three sides by a magnificently pitted and rugged coastline. The inspiring landscape and the tranquillity and space which it offers are without doubt the main attractions of the region. You may be surprised at just how remote much of it still is: the vast peat bogs in the north, for example, are among the most extensive and unspoilt wilderness areas in Europe, while a handful of the west coast's isolated crofting villages can still only be reached by boat.

Exposed to slightly different weather conditions and, to some extent, different historical and cultural influences, each of the three coastlines has its own distinct character. Along the fertile east coast, green fields and woodland run down to the sweeping sandy beaches of the **Moray**, **Cromarty** and **Dornoch firths**, while further northeast, rolling moors give way to peaty wastes and sheep country. Stretching east–west from **John O' Groats** to the wind-lashed **Cape Wrath**, the **north coast** proper, backed by the vast and ecologically unique bog lands of the **Flow Country**, is wilder and more rugged, with sheer cliffs and sand-filled bays bearing the brunt of frequently fierce Atlantic storms. Visitors with limited time tend to stick to the more scenic **west coast**, whose jagged shoreline of sea lochs, rocky headlands and white-sand coves is set against some of Scotland's most dramatic mountains, looking across to Skye, Mull and the Hebrides on the horizon.

Cutting diagonally across the heart of the southern section of the Highland region, the **Great Glen** provides an alternative focus for travel, linking the key towns of Inverness on the east coast and Fort William in the west with a chain of impressive lochs, most notably **Loch Ness**. Not far south of Inverness, the ski resort of **Aviemore** makes a convenient – if not hugely appealing – base for exploring the spectacular **Cairngorm Mountains**, while from Fort William it's possible to branch out to some fine scenery, most conveniently the beautiful expanses of **Glen Coe**, but also the remote and tranquil **Ardnamurchan peninsula**, the "Road to the Isles" to **Mallaig**, and the lochs and glens that lead up to **Kyle of Lochalsh** – the most direct route to Skye (see p.364).

ACCOMMODATION PRICE CODES

Throughout this book, accommodation **prices** have been graded with the codes below, according to the cost of the least expensive double room in high season. Price codes are not given for campsites, most of which charge under £10 per person. Almost all hostels charge less than £10 a night for a bed – the few exceptions to this rule have the prices quoted in the text. For a full account of the accommodation price codes, see p.31.

① under £40	④ £60–70	⑦ £110–150
② £40–50	⑤ £70–90	⑧ £150–200
③ £50–60	⑥ £90–110	⑨ £200 and over

SAFETY IN SCOTTISH HIGHLANDS

The mountains of the Scottish Highlands, while not as high or as steep as the Alps, are so far north that weather conditions – including blizzards and icy winds of up to 100mph – can be fatal. Every year the Scottish mountains take their toll of lives, many of them inexperienced walkers who did not realize the levels of danger involved. It's essential to take proper precautions. Always put **safety** first: never underestimate just how fast the weather can change (or how extreme the changes can be); don't venture off track if you're inexperienced; and be sure to set out properly equipped, with warm, waterproof clothing, decent footwear, a compass, all the maps you might need, and some food in case you get stuck. Make sure, too, that someone knows roughly where you have gone and when you expect to be back (and remember to contact them again on your return).

Inverness, the only major urban centre in the Highlands, is an obvious spring-board for more remote areas, with its good transport links and facilities, while on the western coast, mundane **Fort William**, backed by Ben Nevis, and the charming eighteenth-century port of **Ullapool** are both well placed for exploration of the spell-binding countryside. In the northeast, **Thurso** is a solid stone town with a regular ferry service to the Orkneys, and the old port of **Wick** was once the centre of Europe's herring industry – although it's fair to say that neither of these towns is particularly endearing in themselves. Further south lie **Dornoch**, with its sandstone fourteenth-century cathedral, and **Cromarty**, whose vernacular architecture ranks among Scotland's finest.

INVERNESS AND AROUND

Inverness, 105 miles northwest of Aberdeen on the A96 and 114 miles north of Perth on the A9, is the largest town in the Highlands – a good base for day-trips and a jump-ing-off point for many of the more remote parts of the region. While the town does boast decent shopping, one or two worthwhile museums and a striking sandstone cas-tle, it is not a compelling place to stay for long and inevitably you are drawn to the attractions of sea and mountains beyond. The approach to the town on the A9 over the barren Monadhliath Mountains from Perth and Aviemore provides a spectacular intro-duction to the district, with the **Great Glen** to the left, stretching southwestwards towards Fort William and, beyond, the massed peaks of Glen Affric. To the north is the huge, rounded form of Ben Wyvis, whilst to the east lies the **Moray Firth**, to some extent a commuter belt for Inverness, but also boasting a lovely coastline and some of the region's best castles and historic sites. The gentle, undulating green landscape is well tended and tranquil, a fertile contrast to the windswept moorland and mountains that virtually surround it.

A string of worthwhile sights punctuates the approaches to Inverness along the main route from Aberdeen. The low-key holiday resort of **Nairn**, with its long white-sand beaches and championship golf course, stands within striking distance of sever-al monuments, including the whimsical **Cawdor Castle**, featured in Shakespeare's *Macbeth*, and **Fort George**, one of several impressive Hanoverian bastions erected in the wake of the Jacobite rebellion. The infamous battle and ensuing massacre that ended Bonnie Prince Charlie's uprising took place on the outskirts of Inverness at **Culloden**, where a small visitor centre and memorial stones recall the gruesome events of 1745.

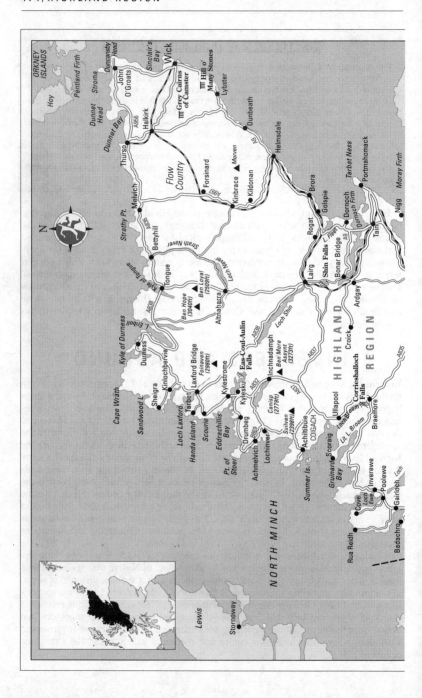

© Crown copyright

GETTING AROUND IN THE HIGHLANDS

Unless you're prepared to spend weeks on the road, the Highlands are simply too vast to see in a single trip. Most visitors, therefore, base themselves in one or two areas, exploring the coast or hills on foot, and making longer hops across the interior by car, bus or train. **Getting around** the Highlands, particularly the remoter parts, is obviously easiest if you've got your own transport, but with a little forward planning you can see a surprising amount using **buses** and **trains**, especially if you fill in with **postbuses** (timetables are available at most post offices). The A9, a modern fast **road** with some dual-carriageway sections, is the key route into the area, sweeping north from Perth through Speyside to Inverness and on to John O' Groats, with one of the Highlands' main **rail** lines following broadly the same route. In the west, the main road, the A82, runs from Glasgow to Fort William, then follows the Great Glen to Inverness, with the A87 branching off towards Skye, while the A835 links Inverness with Ullapool. Inverness can also be approached from Aberdeen by train or on the notoriously dangerous A96. However, the most romantic approach to the region has to be via the famous **West Highland Railway**, Scotland's most scenic and brilliantly engineered rail route, which crosses country that can otherwise only be seen from long-distance footpaths. From Glasgow the line travels along the Clyde River and up Loch Long, the most attractive sea loch in the Clyde Estuary, before switching to the banks of Loch Lomond on its way to Crianlaraich. After climbing around Beinn Odhar on a unique horseshoe-shaped loop of viaducts, the line traverses desolate **Rannoch Moor**, where the track had to be laid on a mattress of tree roots, brushwood and thousands of tons of earth and ashes. Skirting Loch Ossian, the train then circumnavigates Ben Nevis to enter Fort William from the northeast, through the dramatic Monessie Gorge and the southernmost part of the Great Glen. The second leg of the journey, from Fort William to Mallaig, includes the magnificent curving Glenfinnan Viaduct and views of the Small Isles and Skye as the line runs past the famous silver sands of Morar.

Inverness

Straddling a nexus of major road and rail routes, **INVERNESS** is the busy and prosperous hub of the Highlands, and an inevitable port of call if you're exploring the region by public transport. **Buses** and **trains** leave for communities right across the far north of Scotland, and it isn't uncommon for people from as far afield as Thurso, Durness and Kyle of Lochalsh to travel down for a day's shopping here – Britain's most northerly chain-store centre. Though boasting few conventional sights, the town's setting on the leafy banks of the River Ness is appealing. Crowned by a pink crenellated **castle** and lavishly decorated with flowers – for which the town has won several awards – the compact centre has retained much of its medieval street layout (although unsightly concrete blocks overshadow the period buildings in places), while the salmon-packed River Ness, which flows through the centre, is lined with leafy parks and prosperous-looking stone houses.

Some history

Inverness's sheltered **harbour** and proximity to the open sea made it an important entrepôt and shipbuilding centre during medieval times. David I, who first imposed a feudal system on Scotland, erected a **castle** on the banks of the Ness to oversee maritime trade in the early twelfth century, promoting it to royal burgh status soon after. Bolstered by receipts from the lucrative export of leather, salmon and timber, the town grew to become the kingdom's most prosperous northern outpost, and an obvious target for the marauding Highlanders who plagued this remote border area.

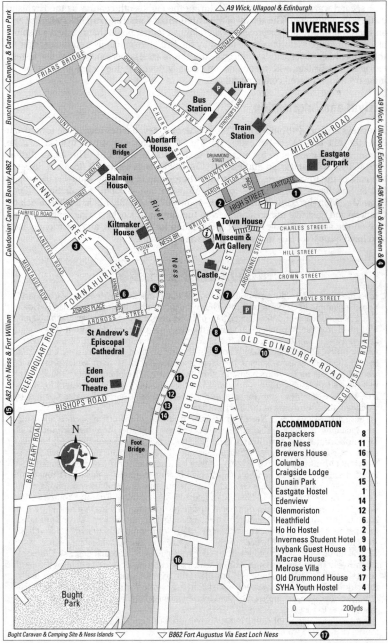

△ A9 Wick, Ullapool & Edinburgh

INVERNESS

Bunchrew △ Camping & Catavan Park

△ A9 Wick, Ullapool, Edinburgh A96 Nairn & Aberdeen △4

FRIARS BRIDGE

CHAPEL STREET

LONGMAN ROAD

Library

P

Bus Station

STROTHER'S LANE

Train Station

MILLBURN ROAD

Foot Bridge

Abertarff House

ACADEMY STREET

CHURCH STREET

Eastgate Carpark

Caledonian Canal & Beauly A862 △

HUNTLY STREET

QUEEN ST

DRUMMOND STREET

UNION STREET

BARON TAYLOR'S ST

US WYND

1

KENNETH STREET

GREIG STREET

Balnain House

BANK STREET

HUNTLY STREET

River

EASTGATE

2 **HIGH STREET**

FAIRFIELD ROAD

PLANTFIELD ROAD

Kiltmaker House

YOUNG ST

NESS BR

BRIDGE STREET

Town House

i **Museum & Art Gallery**

CHARLES STREET

HILL STREET

3

TOMNAHURICH ST

KENNETH STREET

Ness

ARDROSS ST

Castle

CASTLE STREET

ARDCONNEL STREET

CROWN STREET

6

5

ARDROSS PLACE

ARDROSS STREET

7

ARGYLE STREET

MONTAGUE ROW

A82 Loch Ness & Fort William

GLENURQUHART ROAD

St Andrew's Episcopal Cathedral ✝

ARDROSS STREET

BANK STREET

P

8

SOUTHSIDE ROAD

Eden Court Theatre

9

OLD EDINBURGH ROAD

10

15 ◁

11

HAUGH ROAD

CULDUTHEL RD

BISHOPS ROAD

NESS BANK

12

13

14

BALLIFEARY ROAD

N

Foot Bridge

LADIES WALK

NESS WALK

ACCOMMODATION

Bazpackers	**8**
Brae Ness	**11**
Brewers House	**16**
Columba	**5**
Craigside Lodge	**7**
Dunain Park	**15**
Eastgate Hostel	**1**
Edenview	**14**
Glenmoriston	**12**
Heathfield	**6**
Ho Ho Hostel	**2**
Inverness Student Hotel	**9**
Ivybank Guest House	**10**
Macrae House	**13**
Melrose Villa	**3**
Old Drummond House	**17**
SYHA Youth Hostel	**4**

16

Bught Park

0	200yds

Bught Caravan & Camping Site & Ness Islands ▽

▽ B862 Fort Augustus Via East Loch Ness

▽ **17**

A second wave of growth occurred during the eighteenth century as the Highland cattle trade flourished. The arrival of the **Caledonian Canal** and **rail** links with the east and south brought further prosperity, heralding a tourist boom that reached a fashionable zenith in the Victorian era, fostered by the British royal family's enthusiasm for all things Scottish. Over the last thirty years, the town has become one of the fastest-expanding in Britain, with its population virtually doubling due to the growing tourist industry and improved communications.

Arrival and information

Inverness **airport** (☎01463/232471) is at Dalcross, seven miles east of the town; from here the #11 **bus** (Mon–Sat every 1hr–1hr 30min; check times on ☎01343/222244; 20min; £2.50) goes into town, and a **taxi** costs around £10. The **bus station** (☎01463/233371) and **train station** (☎0345/484950) both lie just off Academy Street to the east of the town centre. The **tourist office** (June to mid-July Mon–Fri 9am–6pm, Sat & Sun 9am–5pm; mid-July to Aug Mon–Fri 9am–8.30pm, Sat & Sun 9–6pm; Sept–May Mon–Fri 9am–5pm, Sat 10am–4pm; ☎01463/234353) is in a 1960s block on Castle Wynd, just five minutes' walk from the station. It stocks a wide range of literature on the area, can book local accommodation for a £1.50 fee, and the friendly staff also hand out useful free maps of the town and environs.

TOURS AND CRUISES

Inverness is the departure point for a range of day **tours** and **cruises** to nearby attractions, including Loch Ness and the Moray Firth. Among the most popular is Guide Friday's open-topped double-decker tour of **Inverness** (May–Sept every 45min; 30min; £5), which you can hop on and off all day; the bus also goes out to **Culloden** (1hr 20min; £6.50). Tickets can be bought on the buses, which leave from Bridge Street near the tourist office, or at Guide Friday's booth in the train station (May–Oct daily except Sat 9am–5.30pm, Sat 8.30am–5.45pm, July–Sept also Mon–Fri till 8.30pm), which also acts as a booking agent for the tours below. In addition, the useful Highland County Tourist Trail bus (every two hours 10.15am–4.15pm; £4.50 for hop-on-hop-off ticket) leaves from outside the tourist office, stopping at the bus station, Fort George, Cawdor Castle and Culloden, then returning to the tourist office.

There are various **Loch Ness** tours leaving from the tourist office, such as a half-day trip including a short cruise on the loch, and visits to the **monster exhibition** at **Drumnadrochit** and **Urquhart Castle** (£8.50 excluding admission fees), or a full-day trip right round the loch, including a boat ride (£13). By far the most original tour is **Gordon's Minibus** (☎01463/731202), a history and nature tour run by a charismatic doctor of marine biology, which also goes out on a boat on the loch – a day-trip (10am–4pm) costs £8.90. Longer **boat trips** on Loch Ness are run morning and afternoon by Jacobite Cruises (April–Oct; ☎01463/233999) – a courtesy bus operates from the Tourist Office down to the dock at Tomnahurich Canal Bridge on Glenurquhart Road, a mile and a half south of the town centre. Meanwhile, an entertaining if slightly bizarre **Terror Tour** takes groups on foot around the town centre (daily 7pm from the tourist office; £5.50; ☎01463/768652), with grisly tales of ghosts, torture and witches told along the way.

Good outings further afield include the day-trips run by Stagecoach buses to **Ullapool**, **Lochinver**, **Durness** and **Smoo Cave**, which leaves from the tourist office and stops at several youth hostels en route (£15, or £19 if the trip is spread over four days). Finally, the Orkney Bus leaves Inverness bus station every day during the summer for a gruelling full-day whistle-stop tour of the **Orkney** islands (£42; advance bookings may be made at the tourist office or on ☎01955/611353).

See p.485 for details of **dolphin**-spotting cruises on the Moray Firth. Tickets for all tours are available from the tourist office.

Accommodation

Inverness is one of the few places in the Highlands where you're unlikely to have problems finding **accommodation**, although in July and August you'll have to book ahead. You can reserve a bed through the tourist office, or in the train station concourse at the Thomas Cook booth, but bear in mind that both places levy a booking fee, and charge the hotel or guest-house owner a hefty commission that is then passed on to you in your room tariff. Inverness boasts several good **hotels**, and nearly every street in the older residential areas of town has a sprinkling of **B&Bs**. Good places to look include both banks of the river south of the Ness Bridge, and Kenneth Street and its offshoots on the west side of the river. There are several budget travellers' **hostels** in town, all reasonably central, and a couple of large **campsites**, one near the Ness Islands and the other farther out to the west.

Hotels

Brae Ness, Ness Bank (☎01463/712266). A homely Georgian hotel overlooking the river and St Andrews Cathedral, with a non-smoking licensed restaurant for residents. April–Oct only. ③.

Columba, Ness Walk (☎01463/231391). Huge, central hotel opposite the castle and just over the bridge from the town centre, whose tariffs, which include breakfast, drop at weekends. Popular with bus parties and businesspeople. ④.

Dunain Park (☎01463/230512, *dunainparkhotel@btinternet.com*). Luxurious country house hotel off the A82 Fort William road, about three miles from the centre of town. Excellent food and beautiful rooms. ⑧.

Glenmoriston, 20 Ness Bank (☎01463/223777). Very classy and comfortable hotel slap on the riverside with well-appointed rooms and a topnotch Italian restaurant. ⑥.

B&Bs

Brewers House, 2 Moray Park, Island Bank Road (☎01463/235557). A welcoming B&B in a characterful old house a little further down the river than some pricier guest houses, but still an easy stroll from the centre. ①.

Craigside Lodge, 4 Gordon Terrace (☎01463/231576). Spacious rooms, great views, and close to the centre. Non-smoking. ②.

Edenview, 26 Ness Bank (☎01463/234397). Very pleasant B&B in a riverside location as good as the more expensive hotels, five minutes' walk from the centre; non-smoking. ②.

Heathfield, 2 Kenneth St (☎01463/230547). A very comfortable and friendly B&B at the quiet end of a street packed with B&Bs. All rooms have central heating and some are en suite; non-smoking. ①.

Ivybank Guest House, 28 Old Edinburgh Rd (☎01463/232796). A grand Georgian home just up the hill from the castle, with open fires and a lovely wooden interior. ②

Old Drummond House, Oak Avenue (☎01463/226301). Part of a nicely renovated 200-year-old mansion at the quiet end of a suburban avenue, a mile or so from the centre. ①.

Macrae House, 24 Ness Bank (☎01463/243658). Right on the river, friendly, and with large, comfortable rooms. Non-smoking. ②.

Melrose Villa, 35 Kenneth St (☎01463/233745). Very family-friendly, with excellent breakfasts. Three singles as well as doubles and twins, with most rooms en suite. ①.

Hostels

Bazpackers, top of Castle Street (☎01463/717663). The most homely and relaxed of the town's hostels with thirty beds including two double rooms and a twin; some dorms are mixed. Has good views and a garden, which is used for barbecues, as well as the usual cooking facilities; non-smoking.

Eastgate Hostel, Eastgate (☎01463/718756, *info@eastgatehostel.com*). Well-maintained former hotel above *Le Déja Vu* restaurant. Sleeps 38 in six-bed dorms and two twin rooms. Free tea and coffee is provided; no curfew.

Ho Ho Hostel, 23a High St (☎01463/221225). Formerly the grand Highland Club, a town base for lairds; now a large hostel with big rooms which tends to attract a partying crowd.

Inverness Student Hotel, 8 Culduthel Rd (☎01463/236556). A busy fifty-bed hostel with the usual facilities and fine views over the river. Part of the Macbackpackers group, so expect minibus tours to pull in most days.

SYHA Hostel, Victoria Drive, off Millburn Road, about three-quarters of a mile from the centre (☎01463/231771; central reservations ☎0541/553255). One of SYHA's flagship new hostels, fully equipped with large kitchens and communal areas, eco-friendly facilities and ten four-bed family rooms among the 188-bed total, but all rather soulless.

Camping

Bught Caravan and Camping Site, Bught Park (☎01463/236920). Inverness's main campsite, on the west bank of the river near the sports centre. Good facilities, but it can get very crowded at the height of the season.

Bunchrew Caravan and Camping Park, Bunchrew, three miles west of Inverness on the A862 (☎237802). Well-equipped site on the shores of the Beauly Firth, with hot water, showers, laundry and a shop. It's very popular with families, so you'll have to contend with kids as well as midges.

The Town

The logical place to begin a tour of Inverness is the central **Town House** on the High Street. Built in 1878, this Gothic pile hosted Prime Minister Lloyd George's emergency meeting to discuss the Irish crisis in September 1921, and now accommodates council offices. There's nothing of note inside, but the old **Mercat Cross** next to the main entrance is worth a look. The cross stands opposite a small square formerly used by merchants and traders and above the ancient *clach-na-cudainn*, or **"stone of tubs"** – so called because washerwomen used to rest their buckets on it on their way back from the river. A local superstition holds that as long as the stone remains in place, Inverness will continue to prosper.

Looming above the Town House and dominating the horizon is **Inverness Castle** (mid-May to Sept Mon–Sat 10am–5pm; £3), a predominantly nineteenth-century red-sandstone edifice perched picturesquely above the river. The original castle formed the core of the ancient town, which had rapidly developed as a port trading with Europe after its conversion to Christianity by St Columba in the sixth century. Two famous Scots monarchs were associated with the building: **Robert the Bruce** wrested it back from the English during the Wars of Independence, destroying it in the process, and **Mary, Queen of Scots** had the governor of the second castle hanged from its ramparts after he had refused her entry in 1562. This structure was also destined for destruction, held by the Jacobites in both the 1715 and the 1745 rebellions, and blown up by them to prevent it falling into government hands. Today's edifice houses the Sheriff Court and, in summer, the **Castle Garrison Encounter** an entertaining and noisy interactive exhibition, in which the visitor plays the role of a new recruit in the eighteenth-century Hanoverian army. Around 7.30pm during the summer, a lone piper clad in full Highland garb performs for tourists on the castle esplanade. The statue of a woman staring south from the terrace is a memorial to **Flora MacDonald**, the clanswoman who helped Bonnie Prince Charlie escape to Skye in the wake of Culloden.

Below the castle, the **Inverness Museum and Art Gallery** (Mon–Sat 9am–5pm; free) on Castle Wynd gives a good general overview of the development of the Highlands. Informative sections on geology, geography and history cover the ground floor, while upstairs you'll find a muddled selection of silver, taxidermy, weapons and bagpipes, alongside a mediocre art gallery.

Leading north from the Town House, medieval **Church Street** is home to the town's oldest-surviving buildings. On the corner with Bridge Street stands the **Steeple** (1791), whose spire had to be straightened after an earth tremor in 1816. Farther down Church Street is **Abertarff House**, reputedly the oldest complete building in Inverness and

THE TRUTH ABOUT TARTAN

Tartan is big business and an essential part of the tourist industry. Every year, hundreds of visitors return home clutching tartan monsters, foreign-made souvenirs tied with foreign-made tartan ribbon, or lengths of cloth inspiringly named Loch This, Ben That or Glen Something-Else, fondly believing that they are bringing authentic history with them. The reality is that tartan is an ancient Highland art form that romantic fiction and commercial interest have enclosed within an almost insurmountable wall of myth.

Real tartan, the kind that long ago was called **"Helande"**, was a fine, hard and almost showerproof cloth spun in Highland villages from the wool of the native sheep, dyed with preparations of local plants and with patterns woven by artist-weavers. It was worn as a huge single piece of cloth, which was belted around the waist and draped over the upper body, rather like a knee-length toga. The colours of old tartans were clear but soft, and the broken pattern gave superb camouflage, unlike modern versions, whose colours are either so strong that the pattern is swamped or so dull that it has no impact.

Tartan did not become popular in the Lowlands until the beginning of the eighteenth century, when it was adopted as the anti-Union badge of **Jacobitism**, and it was not until after 1745 that the Lowlands took it over completely. The 1747 ban on wearing tartan put an end to the making of tartan in Highland glens; instead, whole villages on the Lowland fringes devoted themselves to supplying the needs of the army and emigrant Highlanders in the colonies and, after the ban was lifted in 1782, those of the home market. The wars abated and the colonies became more self-sufficient, and what had become a major industry faced hard times. At first the remedy was sought in a proliferation of new patterns for, despite the existence of a handful with clan names, tartan was, in the main, a small-scale fashion fabric. Then Sir Walter Scott set to work glamorizing the clans, George IV visited Edinburgh in 1822 and wore a kilt, and, finally, Queen Victoria set the royal seal of approval on both the Highlands and tartan.

At about this time, the idea that every clan had its own distinguishing tartan became highly fashionable. To have the right to wear tartan, one had to belong, albeit remotely, to a clan, and so the way was paved for the "what's-my-tartan?" lists that appear in the tartan picture books and the souvenir shops. Great feats of genealogical gymnastics were performed in the concoction of these lists, but they could not include every name, so "district", "national" and "political" tartans were developed.

distinguished by its stepped gables and circular stair tower. It was erected in 1593 and is now owned by the NTS. The **Old High Church** (Fri noon–2pm & during services; tour at 12.30pm), founded by St Columba in 1171 and rebuilt on several occasions since, stands just along the street, hemmed in by a walled graveyard. Any Jacobites who survived the massacre of Culloden were brought here and incarcerated prior to their execution in the cemetery. If you take the guided tour, you'll be shown bullet holes left on gravestones by the firing squads.

Balnain House

One of Scotland's most novel museums stands over the footbridge that crosses the Ness just below the Old High Church. An immaculately restored, white-painted Georgian mansion, **Balnain House** (July–August Mon–Fri 10am–10pm, Sat–Sun 10–6pm; Sept–June Mon–Sat 10am–5pm; £2) has a modest performance space and an interactive exhibition that will appeal as much to the casual visitor as folk-music aficionados. The exhibition traces the development of Highland **music** from its prehistoric roots (ringing rocks, cast-bronze battle horns and ancient Gaelic songs) to modern electric folk-rock. CD listening posts and a short video allow you to sample snatches of numerous other musical styles from the region, including clan-gathering and spell-casting songs, complex Shetland fiddle reels and the haunting singing of the

Hebrides. You can even try to play various instruments, including the bagpipes, clarsach and fiddle. There's also a congenial café downstairs where ceilidhs, music sessions and recitals take place throughout the summer, and a shop selling traditional Highland instruments, CDs and cassettes.

Elsewhere on the west bank

A five-minute walk upstream (south) from Balnain House brings you to the **Kiltmaker Centre** on the corner of Huntly Street (mid-May to Sept Mon–Sat 9am–10pm, Sun 10am–5pm; Oct to mid-May Mon–Sat 9am–5.30pm; £2). Entered through the factory shop, a small visitor centre sets out everything you ever wanted to know about tartan. The finished products are, of course, on sale in the showroom downstairs, along with all manner of Highland knitwear, woven woollies and Harris tweed.

Rising from the west bank directly opposite the castle, **St Andrews Episcopal Cathedral** was intended by its architects to be one of the grandest buildings in Scotland. However, funds ran out before the giant twin spires of the original design could be completed, hence Inverness isn't officially a city, but a town. The interior is pretty ordinary, too, though it does claim an unusual octagonal chapterhouse.

From the cathedral, you can wander a mile or so upriver to the peaceful **Ness Islands**, an attractive, informal public park reached and linked by footbridges. Laid out with mature trees and shrubs, the islands are the favourite haunt of local anglers. Further upstream still, the river runs close to the **Caledonian Canal**, designed by Thomas Telford in the early nineteenth century as a link between the east and west coasts, joining lochs Ness, Oich, Lochy and Linnhe. Today its main use is recreational, and there are cruises through part of it to Loch Ness, while the towpath provides relaxing walks with good views.

Three miles to the west of the town, on the top of **Craig Phadrig** hill, there's a vitrified **Iron Age fort**, reputed to be where the Pictish King Brude received St Columba in the sixth century. The walls of the fort were built of stone laced with timber and, when the timber was set alight, some of the stone fused to glass – hence the term "vitrified". Waymarked forest trails start from the car parks at the bottom of the hill and lead up to the fort, though only the outline of its perimeter defences are now visible. Buses #3 and #12 from the town centre (Mon–Sat every 15min) drop you to the bottom of the hill.

Eating and drinking

Inverness has lots of **eating** places, including a few excellent-quality gourmet options, while for the budget-conscious there's no shortage of **pubs**, **cafés** and **restaurants** around the town centre. **Takeaways** cluster on Young Street, just across the river, and at the ends of Eastgate and Academy Street. Good places for **picnic food** include Crumbs on Inglis Street, The Gourmet's Lair on Union Street, and Lettuce Eat on Drummond Street.

Restaurants

Café No. 1, 75 Castle St (☎01463/226200). By far the most ambitious cooking in the town centre, with an impressive contemporary approach and good local ingredients. Moderate–expensive.

Castle Restaurant, 41 Castle St. Classic, long-established café that does a roaring trade in down-to-earth Scottish food – meat pies, chicken and fish, dished up with piles of chips. Open at 8am for breakfast; closed Sun. Inexpensive.

Le Déja Vu, 38 Eastgate (☎01463/231075). Unpretentious, relaxed place specializing in French country cooking using game, chicken, fish and shellfish. Great food, friendly service and good-value set menus. Moderate.

Dunain Park Hotel Restaurant, Dunain Park (☎01463/230512). Award-winning Scots-French restaurant in a country-house hotel set in lovely gardens just southwest of town; a good choice for a leisurely dinner. Expensive.

Girvan's, 2–4 Stephen's Brae at the eastern end of the High Street (☎01463/711900). Uncomplicated but decent restaurant – serving Scottish meat and fish dishes – and day-time patisserie.

Glen Mhor Hotel, 9 Ness Bank (☎01463/234308). *Nico's Bistro* at the back of the hotel specializes in well-presented Scottish cuisine (mainly local salmon, beef and game) at moderate prices. The *Riverview Restaurant* at the front is also good. Expensive.

Littlejohn's, Church Street (☎01463/713005). One of a chain, which serves a wide range of food, with many Mexican touches. Friendly and reasonable value. Moderate.

Rajah, Church Street end of Post Office Avenue (☎01463/237190). An excellent Indian restaurant, tucked away in a backstreet basement. Moderate.

Riva, 4–6 Ness Walk (☎01463/237377). Reasonably authentic modern Italian bistro/café beside the river with antipasta, decent mains and good coffee and cakes. Moderate. Upstairs, inexpensive pasta dishes can be had at *Pazzo's Pasta Bar* (evenings only; closed Sun & Mon).

River Café and Restaurant, 10 Bank St, near the Grieg Street footbridge (☎01463/714884). Healthy wholefood lunches and evening meals, with a great selection of freshly baked cakes and good coffee. Inexpensive–moderate.

Nightlife and entertainment

The liveliest **nightlife** in Inverness revolves around the pubs and the town's two main dance venues. The far end of Academy Street has a cluster of good **pubs**; the public bar of the *Phoenix* is the most original town-centre place, while the ersatz-Irish *Lafferty's* next door often has live music, as does the *Blackfriars* across the street. In a basement beside the river on the corner of Bank and Bridge streets, *Johnny Foxes* also drapes itself in shamrocks but draws eager crowds to its regular live music sessions. Over on Bridge Street, the *Gellions* is a legendary watering hole with several other congenial places in between.

The town's liveliest **nightclub** is *Mr G's* on Castle Street, which has queues of the town's youth forming outside on Fridays and Saturdays. On the north side of the bus station, the larger *Blue* hosts local and nationally known DJs, plus occasional bands. The basement café at Balnain House museum, on the east bank of the Ness, opposite Grieg Street footbridge, has informal **folk sessions** that sometimes turn into ceilidhs on Tuesday and Thursday nights through summer, and Thursday nights in winter. In addition, the museum stages regular recitals and workshops by Highland musicians and touring artists; details of all these are posted in the café, and the lobby upstairs. Balnain House also occasionally hosts *The Tickled Rib*, billed as the north's best comedy club – it is, in fact, the north's only comedy club. Finally, if you crave a strong infusion of tartan and **bagpipes**, the nightly "Scottish Showtime" at the *Cummings Hotel* on Church Street is the place to be; the show has been running for years and is probably the most polished of its kind you'll find.

Listings

Airport ☎01463/232471.

Bike rental Barney's, 35 Castle St (☎01463/232249).

Bookshops Leakey's, Greyfriars' Hall, Church Street (☎01463/239947), is a great spot to browse for secondhand books, with a café inside and a warming wood stove in winter; James Thin, 29 Union St (☎01463/233500), has an excellent range of Scottish books and maps; aand Waterstone's can be found at 50–52 High St (☎01463/717474).

Car rental Budget is on Railway Terrace, behind the train station (☎01463/713333); Europcar has an office at the Highlander Service Station, Millburn Road, and a desk at the airport (☎01463/235337); Hertz in the train station and at the airport (☎01463/711479); Thrifty is at 33 Harbour Rd (☎01463/224466); and Sharps Reliable Wrecks (☎01463/236684) is based at Station Square.

Cinemas The Eden Court Theatre and the attached Riverside Screen, on the banks of the Ness, host touring theatre productions, concerts and films; La Scala on Strother's Lane, just off Academy Street, has two screens; Warner Village, on the A96 Nairn road about two miles from the town centre, boasts seven screens.

Dentist V.R. Marden, 4 Fraser St (☎01463/242344).

Exchange Try American Express agents Alba Travel, 43 Church St (Mon–Sat 9am–5pm; ☎01463/239188); the tourist office's *bureau de change* (same hours as tourist office) changes cash and currency for £2.50 or 2.5 per cent; and Thomas Cook, 9–13 Inglis St (Mon–Fri 9am–5pm; ☎01463/711921).

Hospital Accident and emergency care is provided by Raigmore Hospital (☎01463/704000) on the southeastern outskirts of town close to the A9.

Internet Email access is available at MTC, 2 Grant St (Mon–Thurs 9am–5pm, Fri 9am–4.30pm).

Laundry 17 Young St (☎01463/242507).

Left luggage Train station lockers cost from £2 to £4 for 24hr; the left-luggage room in the bus station costs £1 per item (Mon–Sat 8.30am–6pm, Sun 10am–6pm).

Library Inverness library (☎01463/236463), housed in the Neoclassical building on the northeast side of the bus station, has an excellent genealogical research unit (Mon–Fri 10am–1pm & 2–5pm; ☎01463/220330). Consultations with the resident genealogist cost £12 per hour, but are free if shorter than ten minutes. An appointment is advisable.

Outdoor supplies Clive Rowland Outdoor Sports, 9 Bridge St (☎01463/238746); Graham Tiso, 41 High St (☎01463/716617).

Pharmacy Boots, Eastgate Shopping Centre (Mon–Fri 9am–5.30pm, Thurs 9am– 7pm, Sun noon–5pm; ☎01463/225167).

Post office 14–16 Queensgate (Mon–Thurs 9am–5.30pm, Fri 9.30am–5.30pm, Sat 9am–6pm; ☎0345/223344).

Public toilets Usually immaculate ones in Mealmarket Close, north side of High Street.

Sports centre Inverness sports centre and Aquadome leisure pool (Mon–Fri 7.30am–10pm, Sat & Sun 7.30am–9pm; ☎01463/667500), a mile or so south of the town centre off the A82, has a large pool, gym and other indoor sports facilities. Nearby is an ice rink (daily 2–4.30pm & 7–9.30pm).

Taxis Culloden Taxis (☎01463/790000); Rank Radio Taxis (☎01463/221111).

The Moray Firth

East of Inverness lies the fertile, sheltered coastal strip of the **Moray Firth**, its many historic sites and castles accessible on day-trips from Inverness, or en route to Aberdeen. Both the pastoral countryside and the number of attractions around here make a good contrast to the scenic splendours you'll encounter once you head further north into the Highlands. The overloaded A96 traverses this stretch and the region is well served by public transport, details of which feature in the accounts below.

Culloden

The windswept moorland of **CULLODEN** (site open all year; free; visitor centre daily: Feb, March, Nov & Dec 10am–4pm; April–Oct 9am–6pm; NTS; £3.20), five miles east of Inverness, witnessed the last ever battle on British soil when, on April 16, 1746, the Jacobite cause was finally subdued – a turning point in the history of the Scottish nation.

The second Jacobite rebellion had begun on August 19, 1745, with the raising of the Stuarts' standard at **Glenfinnan** on the west coast (see p.511). Shortly after, Edinburgh fell into Jacobite hands, and Bonnie Prince Charlie began his march on London. The English, however, had appointed the ambitious young Duke of Cumberland to command their forces, and this, together with bad weather and lack of funds, eventually forced the Jacobites to retreat north. They ended up at Culloden, where, ill-fed and exhausted after

THE DOLPHINS OF MORAY FIRTH

The **Moray Firth**, a great wedge-shaped bay forming the eastern coastline of the Highlands, is one of only three areas of UK waters that supports a resident population of **dolphins**. Just over a hundred of these beautiful, intelligent marine mammals live in the estuary, the most northerly breeding ground for this particular species – the bottle-nosed dolphin (*Tursiops truncatus*) – in Europe, and you stand a good chance of spotting a few, either from the shore or a boat.

Tursiops truncatus is the largest dolphin in the world, typically growing to a length of around 13ft and weighing between 396 and 660 pounds. The adults sport a tall, sickle-shaped dorsal fin and a distinctive beak-like "nose", and usually live for around 25 years, although a number of fifty-year-old animals have been recorded. During the summer, herds of thirty to forty dolphins have been known to congregate in the Moray Firth; no one is exactly sure why, although experts believe the annual gatherings, which take place between late June and August, may be connected to the breeding cycle. Another peculiar trait of the Moray Firth school is its habit of killing porpoises. Several porpoise corpses with serrated tooth marks have been washed ashore in the area, the dolphins tossing dead or dying porpoises around in the waves as if for fun.

Both adults and calves frequently leap out of the water, "bow riding" in front of boats and performing elegant synchronized swimming routines together. This, of course, makes them spectacular animals to watch, and dolphin-spotting has become something of a craze in the Moray Firth area. One of the best places in Scotland, if not in Europe, to look for them is **Chanonry Point**, on the Black Isle (see p.540) – a spit of sand protruding into a narrow, deep channel, where converging currents bring fish close to the surface, and thus the dolphins close to shore; the hour or so before high tide is the most likely time to see them. **Kessock Bridge**, one mile north of Inverness, is another prime dolphin-spotting location. You can go all the way down to the beach at the small village of North Cessock, underneath the road bridge, where there's a decent place to have a drink at the pub in the *North Cessock Hotel*, or you can stop above the village in a car park just off the A9 at the visitor centre and listening post (daily 10am–5pm; ☎01463/731866; £1 for the whole season) set up by a team of zoologists from Aberdeen University studying the dolphins, where hydrophones allow you to eavesdrop on the clicks and whistles of underwater conversations.

In addition, several companies run dolphin-spotting boat trips around the Moray Firth. However, researchers claim that the increased traffic is causing the dolphins unnecessary stress, particularly during the all-important breeding period, when passing vessels are thought to force calves underwater for uncomfortably long periods. They have therefore devised a code of conduct for boat operators, based on the experiences of other countries where dolphin-watching has become disruptive. So if you decide to go on a spotting cruise, make sure the operator is a member of the Dolphin Space Programme's Accreditation Scheme. Operators currently accredited include Majestic Cruises, Inverness (☎01463/731661); Karl Nielsen, 21 Great Eastern Road, Portessie, Buckie (☎01542/832289); Macaulay Charters, Inverness (☎01463/751263); Moray Firth Cruises, Shore Street, Inverness (☎01463/717900); and Dolphin Écosse, Bank House, High Street, Cromarty (☎01381/600323).

a pointless night march, they were hopelessly outnumbered by the English. The open, flat ground of Culloden Moor was also totally unsuitable for the Highlanders' style of courageous but undisciplined fighting, which needed steep hills and lots of cover to provide the element of surprise, and they were routed. After the battle, in which 1500 Highlanders were slaughtered (many of them as they lay wounded on the battlefield), Bonnie Prince Charlie fled west to the hills and islands, where loyal Highlanders sheltered and protected him. He eventually escaped to France, leaving his erstwhile supporters to their fate – and, in effect, the end of the clan system. The clans were disarmed, the wearing of tartan and playing of bagpipes forbidden, and the chiefs became landlords greedy for higher and higher rents. Culloden also unleashed an orgy of violent reprisals on Scotland, as unruly English troops raped and pillaged their way across the region; within a century, the Highland way of life had changed out of all recognition.

Today you can walk freely around the battle site; flags show the position of the two armies, and **clan graves** are marked by simple headstones. The **Field of the English**, for many years unmarked, is a mass grave for the fifty or so English soldiers who died. Half a mile east of the battlefield, just beyond the crossroads on the main road, is the **Cumberland Stone**, thought for many years to have been the point from where the Duke watched the battle. It is more likely, however, that he was much further forward and simply used the stone for shelter. Thirty Jacobites were burnt alive outside the old **Leanach cottage** next to the visitor centre; inside, it has been restored to its eighteenth-century appearance. The **visitor centre** itself provides background information through detailed displays and a film show, as well as a short play set on the day of the battle presented by local actors (June–Sept only; included in entry price), or you can take the evocative hour-long guided **walking tour** (daily June–Sept; £3). In April, on the Saturday closest to the date of the battle, there's a small commemorative service. The visitor centre has a reference library, and will check for you if you think you have an ancestor who died here. The site is served by Guide Friday **buses** from Bridge Street in Inverness (June–Sept; 10 daily from 10.30am; last bus back to town leaves Culloden at 5.45pm; 25min) and Highland Country bus #12 from Inverness post office (Mon–Sat 8 daily), as well as Highland County's Tourist Trail circular service from outside the tourist office (daily June–Sept).

The Clava Cairns

If you're visiting Culloden with your own transport, make a short detour to the **CLAVA CAIRNS**, an impressive collection of prehistoric burial chambers clustered around the south bank of the River Nairn, a mile southeast of the battlefield. Erected some time before 2000 BC, the cairns, which are encircled by standing stones in a spinney of mature beech trees, are of two different kinds: one large and one very small **ring-cairn**, and two **passage graves**, which have a narrow passageway from edge to centre. Though cremated remains have been found in both types of structure, and unburnt remains in the passage graves, little is known about the nomadic herdsmen who are thought to have built them.

Kilravock Castle

Surrounded by lawns and pine trees, **Kilravock** (pronounced "Kilrawk") **Castle** (April–Oct Wed 2–5.30pm, or by prior arrangement; ☎01667/493258; £3.50), five miles northeast of Culloden, is more like a stately home than a fortress. Dating from the fifteenth century, it is the seat of the Rose family, whose founding father, a Norman, settled here in 1190. The best-known Rose of Kilravock, however, is the one who entertained **Bonnie Prince Charlie** here on the eve of the battle of Culloden in 1745. Although not a Jacobite himself, the laird felt duty-bound by the traditional code of Highland hospitality to accommodate the rebel prince, even though he feared the consequences. According to one contemporary chronicler, the Duke of Cumberland rode out here himself on his 25th birthday to grill Rose over the affair, famously exclaiming, "I hear, sir, you've been entertaining my cousin!". He decided not to punish the Highlander, though, and for some reason left behind his knee-length **riding boots**, which are displayed in the castle, along with the bowl from which Bonnie Prince Charlie is alleged to have been served a glass of punch by his host.

Today, the Rose family maintain Kilravock as a wonderfully old-fashioned **guest house** (same number as above; ②), whose spacious, well-appointed rooms are superb value if you don't mind the ban on alcohol and cigarettes, or grace being said before meals (the establishment is run according to strict Christian principles). In addition, garden enthusiasts should not miss the opportunity to visit the castle **grounds** (Mon–Sat 10am–4pm; £1.50), which harbour a tangle of woodland trails, while the castle's **restaurant** serves lunches and afternoon teas, as well as dinners (booking essential ☎01667/493258).

Cawdor Castle

The pretty, if slightly self-satisfied village of **CAWDOR**, eight miles east of Culloden, is the site of the **Cawdor Castle** (May to mid-Oct daily 10am–5.30pm; £5.40), apocryphally known as the setting for Shakespeare's *Macbeth* (the fulfilment of the witches' prediction that Macbeth was to become Thane of Cawdor sets off his tragic desire to be king). Though visitors descend here in their droves each summer because of the site's literary associations, the castle, which dates from the early fourteenth century, could not possibly have witnessed the grisly historical events on which the Bard's drama was based. However, the immaculately restored monument – a fairy-tale affair of towers, turrets, hidden passageways, dungeons, gargoyles and crenellations whimsically shooting off from the original keep – is still well worth a visit.

The Cawdors have lived here for six centuries, and the castle still feels like a family home, albeit one with tapestries, pictures and opulent furniture. As you explore, look out for the Thorn Tree Room, a vaulted chamber complete with the remains of an ancient tree – carbon-dated to 1372 and an ancient pagan fertility symbol believed to ward off fairies and evil spirits. According to Cawdor family legend, the fourteenth-century Thane of Cawdor dreamed he should build on the spot where his donkey lay down to sleep after a day's wandering – the animal chose this tree and building began immediately.

The **grounds** of the castle are possibly the best part of the visit, with an attractive walled garden, a topiarian maze, a small golf course, a putting green and nature trails. It's also worth visiting the village for a drink or meal at the traditional *Cawdor Tavern*, an old inn serving beautifully prepared local food. Highland **bus** #12 (Mon–Sat 8 daily; 35min) runs to Cawdor from Inverness post office, with the last bus back leaving the castle just after 6pm.

Fort George

Eight miles of undulating coastal farmland separate Cawdor Castle from **Fort George** (April–Sept daily 9.30am–6.30pm; Oct–March Mon–Sat 9.30am–4.30pm, Sun 2–4.30pm; £3.50), an old Hanoverian bastion considered by military architectural historians to be one of the finest fortifications in Europe. Crowning a sandy spit that juts into the middle of the Moray Firth, it was built (1747–69) as a base for George II's army, in case the Highlanders should attempt to rekindle the Jacobite flame. By the time of its completion, however, the uprising had been firmly quashed and the fort has been used ever since as a barracks; note the armed sentries at the main entrance and the periodic crack of live gunfire from the nearby firing ranges.

Apart from the sweeping panoramic **views** across the Firth from its ramparts, the main incentive to visit Fort George is the **Regimental Museum** of the Queen's Own Highlanders. Displayed in polished glass cases is a predictable array of regimental silver, coins, moth-eaten uniforms and medals, along with some macabre war trophies, ranging from blood-stained nineteenth-century Sudanese battle robes to Iraqi gas masks gleaned in the Gulf War. The heroic deeds performed by various recipients of Victoria Crosses make compelling reading. The **chapel** is also worth a look: squat and solid outside, and all light and grace within.

Walking on the northern, grass-covered casemates, which look out into the estuary, you may be lucky enough to see the school of bottle-nosed **dolphins** (see p.485) swimming in with the tide. This is also a good spot for birdwatching: a colony of kittiwakes occupies the fort's slate rooftops, while the white-sand beach and mud flats below teem with waders and seabirds.

The easiest way to get to Fort George by public transport is by Highland **bus** #11B from Inverness post office (Mon–Sat 9 daily; 25min).

Nairn

One of the driest and sunniest places in the whole of Scotland, **NAIRN**, sixteen miles east of Inverness, began its days as a peaceful community of fishermen and farmers. The former spoke Gaelic, the latter English, allowing James VI to boast that a town in his kingdom was so large that people at one end of the main street could not understand those at the other end. Nairn became popular in Victorian times, when the train line offered a convenient link to its revitalizing sea air and mild climate, and today it still relies on tourism, with all the ingredients for a traditional seaside holiday – a sandy beach, ice-cream shops and fish-and-chip stalls. Its windy, coastal **golf course**, the Links, is one of the most popular in Scotland (☎01667/462787), and Thomas Telford's **harbour** is filled with leisure rather than fishing boats. Nearby, amid the huddled streets of old Fishertown – the town centre is known as new Fishertown – is the tiny **Fishertown Museum** (June–Aug Mon–Sat 10am–5pm; free), signposted from the town centre and the harbour. The more interesting exhibits focus on the parsimonious and puritanical life of the fishing families.

With a good map to help navigate the maze of minor roads, you can explore some pleasant countryside south of Nairn, particularly in the valley of the **River Findhorn**, with **Dulsie Bridge**, on the old military road linking Perth and Fort George, being a favourite local picnic spot. A few miles farther south, the waters of **Lochindorb** surround a ruined thirteenth-century castle. The relative flatness of the land makes these roads ideal for cycling; a bike is also a great way to explore **Culbin Forest**, an unusual area of coastal forest northeast of Nairn where the trees were planted to stabilize an extensive area of sand dune. The forest, a Site of Special Scientific Interest, has a network of paths and information boards, along with picnic spots and plenty of wildlife, including an array of migrating water fowl at the adjacent RSPB reserve of Culbin Sands.

Nairn's helpful **tourist office** is at 62 King St (Easter–May, Sept & Oct Mon–Sat 10am–5pm; June–Aug daily 9am–6pm; ☎01667/452753). For **accommodation**, try *Clifton House*, Viewfield Street (☎01667/453119; ⑥), which is stacked with antiques and paintings and hosts music and arts events, or *Greenlawns*, 13 Seafield St (☎01667/452738; ②), a spacious and friendly B&B with most rooms en suite. However, the most luxurious option is the *Golf View Hotel* (☎01667/452301; ⑥), overlooking the golf course and sea, where delicious, well-priced informal meals are served in the conservatory, also with great views. The plainer *Longhouse Restaurant* (☎01667/455532) on the corner of Harbour Street and Watson's Place has moderately priced seafood and inexpensive light meals on its menu. **Bike rental** is available from Nairn Watersports (☎01667/455416) down by the harbour.

West of Inverness: the Beauly Firth

West of Inverness, the Moray Firth becomes the **Beauly Firth**, a sheltered sea loch bounded by the Black Isle in the north and the wooded hills of the Aird to the south. Most northbound traffic uses Kessock Bridge to cross the Moray Firth from Inverness, so this whole area is quieter, and the A862, which skirts the shoreline and the mud flats, offers a more scenic alternative to the faster A9.

Beauly

The sleepy stone-built village of **BEAULY** lies ten miles west of Inverness, at the point where the Beauly River – one of Scotland's most renowned salmon-fishing streams – flows into the Firth. It's ranged around a single main street that widens into a spacious marketplace, at the north end of which stand the skeletal red sandstone remains of **Beauly Priory** (daily 9.30am–6pm; HS; £1.20). Founded in 1230 by the Bisset family for the Valliscaulian order, and later becoming Cistercian, it was destroyed during the Reformation and is now in ruins.

The locals will tell you the name Beauly was bestowed on the village by Mary, Queen of Scots, who, when staying at the priory in the summer of 1564, allegedly cried, "Ah, quelle beau lieu!" (What a beautiful place!). In fact, it derives from the Lovat family, who came to the region from France with the Normans in the eleventh century. Among the more notorious members of this dynasty was Lord Simon Lovat, whose legendary mis-adventures included a kidnap attempt on a nine-year-old girl, followed by forced marriage to her mother. He was outlawed for this, but went on to play an active role in the Jacobite uprisings, expediently swapping sides whenever the one he was spying for looked likely to lose. Such chicanery earned him the nickname "The Old Fox of '45", but failed to save him from the chop: Lovat was eventually beheaded in London (ironically enough for backing the wrong side at Culloden). The Victorian **monument** in the square, opposite the Priory, commemorates the more illustrious career of one of Simon Lovat's descendants, Simon Joseph, the sixteenth Lord Lovat, who founded a fighting unit during the Boer War. If you want to find out more about the colourful Lovats and other scions of the Fraser clan, head to the restored **Wardlaw Mausoleum** at Kirkhill, about four miles east of Beauly signposted off the A862 (May–Sept Wed & Sat 2–4pm; free), which was built in 1634 but includes a fourteenth-century window from a church previously built on the site.

As a change from distilleries, you can visit a **winery** at **Moniack Castle** (March–Oct Mon–Sat 10am–5pm; Nov–Feb Mon–Sat 11am–4pm; £2), also four miles east of Beauly, just off the main Inverness road (A862), where you can taste and buy over 25 different home-made products, including silver-birch or meadowsweet wine, sloe-berry liqueur, juniper chutney and rosehip jam.

Practicalities

Beauly has a small community tourist office in a cabin beside the priory (June–Sept daily 10am–8pm), which has information on good walks in the area. The town has a sur-prising number of **places to stay**. The most comfortable is the modern *Priory Hotel* (☎01463/782309; ④) at the top of town, which also has a good restaurant. The *Lovat Arms Hotel* (☎01463/782313; ④), at the opposite end of the main street, is a more tra-ditional option and hosts occasional ceilidhs. If you're looking for cheaper accommo-dation, try the *Heathmount Guest House* (☎01463/782411; ②), one of several pleasant **B&Bs** in a row of large Victorian houses just south of the *Lovat* on the main road.

Finding somewhere to **eat** in Beauly isn't a problem, either. Both of the town's hotels sport pricey à la carte restaurants, while the *Archdale Hotel's* cosy café, at the bottom of the square, serves a range of inexpensive snacks and main meals, including several vegetarian specialities. Otherwise, head for the *Beauly Tandoori*, which dishes up mod-erately priced Indian food, or the *Friary* chippy; both are on the main square.

Muir of Ord

MUIR OF ORD, a sprawling village four miles north of Beauly, is visited in huge num-bers for the **Glen Ord Distillery** (March–Oct Mon–Fri 9.30am–5pm; July & Aug also Sat 9.30am–5pm & Sun 12.30–5pm; £2), on its northern outskirts. Its well-laid-out visi-tor centre explains the mysteries of whisky production with a tour that winds up in the cellars, where you get to sample a selection of the famously peaty Glen Ord malts, most of which find their way into well-known blends on sale in the distillery shop.

You can either visit Ord on a guided tour from Inverness (details from the tourist office), or take the infrequent Stagecoach Inverness **bus** #18 from Union Street in Inverness (Mon–Sat 3 daily); more helpfully, the **train** from Inverness stops at Muir of Ord station (Mon–Sat 6–7 daily; June–Sept also Sun, 4 daily; 15min).

STRATHSPEY AND THE CAIRNGORMS

Rising high in the heather-clad hills above Loch Laggan, forty miles due south of Inverness, the **River Spey**, Scotland's second longest river, drains northeast towards the Moray Firth through one of the Highlands' most spellbinding valleys. Famous for its **ski slopes**, **salmon fishing** and **ospreys**, Strathspey forms a broad cleft between the mighty Monadhliath mountains in the north and the ice-sculpted Cairngorm range to the south. Outdoor enthusiasts flock here year-round to take advantage of the superb hiking, watersports and winter snows, but the valley is also a major transport artery connecting Inverness and the northern highlands with the south.

Of Strathspey's scattered settlements, **Aviemore** absorbs the largest number of visitors, particularly in midwinter when it metamorphoses into the UK's busiest ski resort. The village itself isn't up to much, but the 4000ft summit plateau of the Cairngorm is often snowcapped, providing stunning mountain scenery on a grand scale. Sedate **Kingussie**, further up the valley, is an older established holiday centre, popular more with anglers and grouse hunters than canoeists and climbers, while the Georgian town of **Grantown-on-Spey**, jumping-off point for **Loch Garten**, makes another good base for exploring the area. Most of upper Strathspey is privately owned by the Glen More Forest Park and Rothiemurchus Estate, who provide between them a plethora of year-round outdoor facilities, with masses of accommodation of all types. Both bodies actively encourage the recreational use of their land, which gives you the freedom to go virtually anywhere you want.

Aviemore

AVIEMORE was first developed as a resort in the mid-1960s, as the towering concrete **Aviemore Centre** bears witness: a shabby assortment of cavernous concrete buildings and incongruous high-rise hotels presently undergoing a much-needed redevelopment. The village proper, a sprawling jumble of traditional stone houses and tacky tourist shops set in a sea of car and coach parks, isn't much better. That said, Aviemore is by far the most important service centre in the area, with a wide range of facilities, an advantage which outweighs its lack of aesthetic appeal.

Winter sports

Scottish **skiing** on a commercial scale first really took off in Aviemore. By continental European and North American standards it's all on a tiny scale, but occasionally snow, sun and lack of crowds coincide and you can have a great day. February and March are usually the best times, but in some years the snow may still be good until April. Lots of places – not just in Aviemore itself – sell or hire equipment; for a rundown of ski schools and rental facilities in the area, check out the tourist office's *Ski Scotland* brochure.

The **Cairngorm Ski Area**, about eight miles southeast of Aviemore, above Loch Morlich in Glen More Forest Park, is well served by buses from Aviemore. You can rent skis and other equipment from the Day Lodge at the foot of the ski area

WALKS AROUND AVIEMORE

Ordnance Survey Landranger Map No. 36.

Walking is an obvious attraction in the Aviemore area, but always follow the usual safety rules (see p.473). If you want to walk the high tops, take either the service road and summit path or the chair lift up from the Day Lodge (see below). However, as well as the high mountain trails, there are some lovely **low-level walks** around Aviemore. It takes an hour or so to complete the gentle circular walk around pretty **Loch an Eilean** in the Rothiemurchus Estate, beginning at the end of the backroad that turns east off the B970 two miles south of Aviemore. The estate visitor centres at the loch-side and by the roadside at Inverdruie provide more information on the many woodland trails that criss-cross this area. A longer walk starts at the near end of **Loch Morlich**. Cross the river by the bridge and follow the dirt road, turning off after about twenty minutes to follow the signs to Aviemore. The path goes through beautiful pine woods and past tumbling burns, and you can branch off to Coylumbridge and Loch an Eilean. Unless you're properly prepared for a 25-mile hike, don't take the track to the **Lairig Ghru**, which eventually brings you out near Braemar. The routes are all well marked and easy to follow and, depending on what combination you put together, can take anything from two to five hours.

Another good shortish (half-day) walk leads along well-surfaced forestry track from *Glenmore Lodge* up towards the **Ryvoan Pass**, taking in An Lochan Uaine, known as the "Green Loch" and living up to its name, with amazing colours that range from turquoise to slate grey depending on the weather. The track narrows once past the loch and leads east towards Deeside, so retrace your steps if you don't want a major trek. The Glenmore Forest Park Visitor Centre by the roadside at the turn-off to *Glenmore Lodge* has information on other trails in this section of the forest.

(☎01479/861261), which also has a shop, a bar and restaurant, and sells tickets for the year-round chair lift. A highly controversial plan to replace the chair lift with a **funicular railway** has recently been passed – while debates rage between environmentalists, developers and tourism bodies, don't expect too much to change, for even once construction begins it's likely to be a few years before the project is completed.

If there's lots of snow, the area around **Loch Morlich** and into the **Rothiemurchus Estate** provides enjoyable cross-country skiing through lovely woods, beside rushing burns and even over frozen lochs. If you really want to know about survival in a Scottish winter, you could try a week at *Glenmore Lodge* (☎01479/861276) in the heart of the Glenmore Forest Park. This superbly equipped and organized centre, run by Sports Scotland, offers winter courses in hill-walking, mountaineering, alpine ski-mountaineering, avalanche awareness and much besides, including an array of less serious recreational courses in kayaking, abseiling and the like. To add to the winter scene, there's a herd of **reindeer** at Loch Morlich, and the Siberian Husky Club holds its races in the area.

Summer sports

In summer, the main activities around Aviemore are **watersports**, and there are two centres that offer sailing, windsurfing and canoeing. The Loch Morlich Watersports Centre (☎01479/861221), five miles or so east of Aviemore at the east end of the loch, rents equipment and offers tuition in a lovely setting with a sandy beach, while, up-valley, the Loch Insh Watersports Centre (☎01540/651272) offers the same facilities in more open and less crowded surroundings. It also rents mountain bikes, boats for loch fishing, and gives ski instruction on a 164ft dry slope.

Riding and **pony trekking** are on offer up and down the valley: try Alvie Stables at Alvie near Kincraig (☎01540/651409, mobile 0831/495397), or the Carrbridge Trekking Centre, Station Road, Carrbridge, a few miles north of Aviemore (☎01479/841602).

Fishing is very much part of the local scene; you can fish for trout and salmon on the River Spey, and the Rothiemurchus Estate has a stocked trout-fishing loch at **Inverdruie**, where success is virtually guaranteed. Instruction and rod hire is available from the centre beside the loch. Fishing permits cost around £5–15 per day to fish a stocked loch and £25 on the Spey itself, and are sold at Speyside Sports in Aviemore a mile down the road toward the ski grounds from the tourist office, and at Loch Morlich Watersports Centre (see above), which also rents rods and tackle.

The area is also a great one for **mountain biking**, with both Rothiemurchus and Glenmore estates more progressive in their attitude to the sport than many. The Rothiemurchus visitor centre at Inverdruie has route maps, and you can also hire bikes here, while Bothy Bikes (☎01479/810787) in the Aviemore Shopping Centre beside the railway station on Grampian Road rents out good-quality mountain bikes with front suspension, as well as offering friendly advice on different grades of local routes.

Information, accommodation and eating

Aviemore's **tourist office** is just south of the train station on the main drag, Grampian Road (April–October Mon–Fri 9am–6pm, Sat 10am–5pm, Sun 10am–4pm, Nov–March Mon–Fri 9am–5pm, Sat 10am–5pm; ☎01479/810363). It offers an accommodation booking service, free maps and endless leaflets on local attractions. There's no shortage of **accommodation** in the area. On Grampian Road, *MacKenzies Hotel* (☎01479/810672; ②) and *Ver Mont Guest House* (☎01479/810470; ③), are both good value, and there are also plenty of **B&Bs**: try Mrs Clark at *Sonas* (☎01479/810409; ①). However, the nicest place in the area is *Corrour House Hotel* at Inverdruie, two miles southeast of Aviemore (☎01479/810220; ⑤). As for **hostel** accommodation, Aviemore's large SYHA hostel (☎01479/810345 or central reservations ☎0541/553255), is close to the tourist office, while the brand new *Aviemore Independent Bunkhouse* (☎01479/811137) on Dalfaber Road is also very central and has good facilities, including four-bed bunk rooms and a decent drying room. There are also two more low-price options near the village of Kincraig, six miles south of Aviemore: the *Loch Insh Watersports Centre* (☎01540/651272; ①), beautifully sited beside the loch, has en-suite B&B and self-catering chalets, and the *Glen Feshie Hostel* at Balachroick (☎01540/651323), where the all-in price includes bed linen and as much porridge as you like for breakfast. There's no shortage of **campsites** either: two of the best are the Campgrounds of Scotland site at Coylumbridge (☎01479/812800) and the Forestry Enterprise one at Glenmore (☎01479/861271).

All the hotels serve run-of-the-mill bar **food**, but for a more interesting option head to *The Old Bridge Inn* on the east side of the railway, below the bridge, which serves delicious meals and real ales in a mellow, cosy setting, or *Café Mambo*, in Aviemore Shopping Centre on Grampian Road, which attracts a younger crowd with its bright, funky decor and extensive, contemporary menu. Further afield, the Loch Insh Watersports Centre (see above) has a particularly pleasant restaurant overlooking the loch, with snacks available during the day and filling meals in the evening.

Kingussie

KINGUSSIE (pronounced "Kingy*oo*see") lies twelve miles south of Aviemore and is far cosier, stacked around a single main street. Beyond its usefulness as a place to stay, the chief attraction here is the excellent **Highland Folk Museum** (May–Aug Mon–Fri 9.30am–5.30pm, Sat & Sun 1–5pm; April, Sept & Oct guided tours only Mon–Fri 10.30am–4.30pm; £3.50). The museum is split into two complementary parts: the Kingussie section contains an absorbing collection of artefacts typical to traditional Highland ways of life, as well as a farming museum, an old smokehouse, a mill, a Hebridean "blackhouse", and a traditional herb and flower garden; most days in summer there's a demonstration of various traditional crafts. The larger site at **Newtonmore** (same opening hours; joint ticket), three miles south of Kingussie on the A86, tries to create more of a living history museum, with reconstructions of a working croft, a church where recitals on traditional Highland instruments are given through the summer months, and a small village of blackhouses being constructed using only authentic tools and materials.

Kingussie is also notable for the ruins of **Ruthven Barracks** (free access), standing east across the river on a hillock. The best-preserved garrison built to pacify the Highlands after the 1715 rebellion, it makes for great exploring by day and is stunningly floodlit at night. Taken by the Jacobites in 1744, Ruthven was blown up in the wake of Culloden to prevent it from falling into enemy hands. It was also the place from where clan leader Lord George Murray dispatched his acrimonious letter to Bonnie Prince Charlie, holding him personally responsible for the string of blunders that had precipitated their defeat.

At nearby **Kincraig**, between Kingussie and Aviemore on the B9152, there are a couple of unusual encounters with animals which offer a memorable diversion if you're not setting off on various strenuous outdoor pursuits. While the style of the **Highland Wildlife Park** (daily: April–May & Sept–Oct 10am–6pm, June–Aug open till 7pm, Nov–March 10am–4pm; last entry two hours before closing; entry may be restricted in snowy conditions: phone ☎01540/651270; £6.30), with its various captive animals, may not appeal to everyone, it is accredited to the Royal Zoological Society of Scotland and offers a chance to see exotic foreigners such as wolves and bison, as well as many rarely seen natives, including pine martens, capercaillie, wildcat and eagles. Nearby, the excellent **Working Sheepdogs** show at Leault Farm (open daily; phone ☎01540/651310 to find out when demonstrations are being held; £3.50) offers the opportunity to see a champion shepherd demonstrate how to herd a flock of sheep with up to eight dogs, using whistles and other commands. The hour-long display also includes geese-herding, a chance to see traditional hand-shearing, and displays on how collie pups are trained.

Practicalities

Kingussie's **tourist office** is in the same building as the entrance to the Highland Folk Museum, on Duke Street (same hours as museum; ☎01540/661297). If you want to base yourself here, try *Greystones* (☎01540/661052, *greystones@lineone.net*; ③) on Acres Road, off Ardbroilach Road, which has good facilities for walkers and cyclists and serves meals. Other good options are *Ruthven Farm House* (☎01540/661226; ③), a pleasant **B&B** overlooking the barracks, *St Helens* (☎01540/661430; ②), on Ardbroilach Road, noted for its great breakfasts, and the very central *Bhuna Monadh* (☎01540/661186; ②), 85 High St. Of the **hotels**, *Scot House* on Newtonmore Road (☎01540/661351; ④) is a comfortable place, where you can get imaginative meals at reasonable prices. There are also a couple of decent **hostels** in the area: *The Laird's Bothy* (☎01540/661334) is right on the High Street beside the *Tipsy Laird* pub, while the *Pottery Bunkhouse* (☎01528/544231), is attached to Caoldair Pottery at Laggan Bridge, eleven miles west of Kingussie on the A86.

The most ambitious **food** in the area is served at *The Cross* restaurant, in a converted tweed mill on Tweed Mill Brae (☎01540/661166; March–Nov & Christmas; closed Tues). Its pricey meals make interesting use of local ingredients and there's a vast wine list; they also have several rooms (⑨ including dinner). Cheaper food is available at several cafés and pubs on the High Street. The *Royal Hotel* serves standard bar meals, with some vegetarian options, a good choice of cask ales and some 250 malts, while *The Tipsy Laird* also does real ales as well as bistro-style meals. *Café Volante* does great cheap-and-cheerful fish and chips and, during the day *La Cafetière* has excellent coffee, with good home baking, soup, toasties and baked potatoes; it closes at 5pm.

Carrbridge

Worth considering as an alternative to Aviemore – particularly as a skiing base –
CARRBRIDGE is a pleasant, quiet village about seven miles northeast. Its
Landmark Heritage Park (daily: April to mid-July 9.30am–6pm; mid-July to Aug
9.30am–8pm; Sept–Oct 9.30am–5.30pm; Nov–March 10am–5pm; £6.40, families from
£20.10) combines multimedia presentations on history and natural history with forest walks, nature trails, a maze and fun rides; it's more tastefully done than some
places of this kind and an excellent place for children to let off steam. There are some
decent accommodation options, including the friendly *Cairn Hotel* (☎01479/841212;
②), the immaculate *Fairwinds Hotel* (☎01479/841240; ③) and, more basic, the tiny
but cosy *Carrbridge Bunkhouse* (☎01479/841250, *christian.j@virgin.net*), half a mile
or so north of the village on the Inverness road.

Grantown-on-Spey

Buses run from Aviemore and Inverness to the tiny Georgian town of **GRANTOWN-
ON-SPEY**, about fifteen miles northeast of Aviemore, which, if you've got your own
transport, makes another good base for exploring Strathspey and the Cairngorm area.
Activity is concentrated around the attractive central square, including a small **museum** (Tues–Sat 10am–4pm; £3) on Burnfield Avenue which tells the story of the people
and the building of the town. The **tourist office** is on the High Street (April–Oct daily
9am–6pm; ☎01479/872773) and there's a wide choice of **accommodation**: *Speyside
Backpackers* (☎01479/873514) at 16 The Square has dorms and basic double rooms
(①), while, if you're after something more upmarket, head for the large seventeenth-
century *Garth Hotel*, at the north end of the square (☎01479/872836; ③), or the slightly less pricey *Tyree House Hotel* (☎01479/872615; ③) on its west side. Both are open all
year round and have good **restaurants** that serve Scottish specialities.

Loch Garten

The **Abernethy Forest RSPB Reserve** on the shore of **LOCH GARTEN**, eight miles
south of Grantown-on-Spey (or seven miles north of Aviemore), is famous as the nesting site of one of Britain's rarest birds. A little over fifty years ago, the **osprey**, known
in North America as the "fish hawk", had completely disappeared from the British
Isles. Then, in 1954, a single pair of these exquisite white-and-brown raptors mysteriously reappeared and built a nest in a tree half a mile or so from the loch. Although
efforts were made to keep the exact location secret, one year's eggs fell victim to a gang
of thieves, and thereafter the area became the centre of an effective high-security operation. Now the birds are well established not only here but elsewhere, and there are
believed to be up to 130 pairs nesting across the Highlands. The best time to visit is during the nesting season, between late April and August, when the RSPB opens an **observation centre** (daily 10am–6pm; £2.50) complete with powerful telescopes and television monitoring of the nest. This is the place to come to get a glimpse of osprey chicks
in their nest; you'll be luckier to see the birds perform their trademark swoop over
water to pluck a fish out with their talons, though nearby Loch Garten, as well as Loch
Morlich and Loch Insh, are good places to stake out in the hope of a sighting, while one
of the best spots is the Rothiemurchus trout loch at Inverdruie. The reserve is also
home to several other species of rare birds and animals, including the Scottish crossbill, capercaillie, whooper swan and red squirrel – **guided walks** leave from the observation centre at 9.30am on Wednesdays.

Loch Garten can be difficult to reach without your own transport; check with one of
the tourist offices in the area about inclusive tours combining a trip on the popular

Strathspey Steam Railway from Aviemore to Boat of Garten, with a bus journey to the reserve. If you want to stay in Boat of Garten there are a couple of good options: *Fraoch Lodge* (☎01479/831331, *info@scotmountain.co.uk*; ③) at 15 Deshar Rd, is run by mountaineers and has a bunkhouse as well as comfortable B&B, along with good facilities and local advice for outdoor enthusiasts; alternatively, *Glenavon House* (☎01479/831213; ④) is a smarter but still charming guest house with five rooms.

THE GREAT GLEN

The **Great Glen**, cutting diagonally across the Highlands from Fort William to Inverness, follows a major geological fault-line. This huge rift valley was formed when the northwestern and southeastern sides slid against each other along the fault for more than sixty miles, and were later smoothed by glaciers that only retreated around 8000 BC. The glen is impressive more for its sheer scale than its great beauty, but is an obvious and rewarding route between the east and west coast.

Of the Great Glen's four elongated lochs, the most famous is **Loch Ness**, home to the mythical beast and linked to the other three, **lochs Oich**, **Lochy** and **Linnhe** (a sea loch) by the **Caledonian Canal**. Surveyed by James Watt in 1773, this famous waterway was completed in the early 1800s by Thomas Telford to enable ships to pass between the North Sea and the Atlantic without having to navigate Scotland's treacherous northern coast. However, only 22 miles of it are bona fide canal – the other 38 exploit the Glen's natural lochs and rivers flowing west to reach the Atlantic.

The traditional and most rewarding way to travel through the glen is by **boat**. A flotilla of kayaks, small yachts and pleasure vessels take advantage of the canal and its old wooden locks during the summer, among them Jacobite Cruises (see p.478 for details). Forest Enterprise has also established an excellent **cycle path** through the Glen, divided into twelve manageable stages that make a tranquil alternative to the hazardous A82. A leaflet outlining the route, through winding timber trails, towpaths and stretches of minor roads, is available at most tourist offices, or direct from Forest Enterprise, Strathoich, Fort Augustus PH32 4BT (☎01320/366322). Following a broadly similar route is a long-distance footpath, the seventy-mile **Great Glen Way**, which takes five to seven days to walk in full – details of this can be obtained from tourist offices or Scottish Natural Heritage (☎01463/712221). In addition, the Great Glen is reasonably well served by **buses**, with several daily services between Inverness and Fort William, and a couple of extra buses covering the section between Fort William and Invergarry during school terms.

Loch Ness

Loch Ness is long and undeniably scenic, with rugged heather-clad mountains rising steeply from a wooded shoreline and attractive valleys opening up on either side, though the tree-lined A82 along its western side gives restricted views. Its fame, however, is based overwhelmingly on its legendary inhabitant, Nessie, the Loch Ness monster, whose fame ensures a steady flow of hopeful visitors to the settlements dotted along the loch, in particular **Drumnadrochit**. Nearby, the impressive ruins of **Castle Urquhart** – a favourite monster-spotting location – perch atop a rock on the loch-side and attract a deluge of bus parties during the summer. Almost as busy in high season is **Fort Augustus**, at the more scenic southwest tip of Loch Ness, where you can watch queues of boats tackling one of the Caledonian Canal's longest flight of **locks**.

Although most visitors travel along the west shore of Loch Ness, on the A82, the opposite, eastern side, skirted by the sinuous single-track B862/852 (originally a military road built to link Fort Augustus and Fort George) is quieter and affords far more spectacular views. However, buses from Inverness only run as far south as **Foyers**, so – unless you take a bus tour from Inverness (see p.478) – you'll need your own transport to complete the whole loop around the Loch, taking in the most impressive stretch between Fort Augustus and the high, hidden Loch Mhor, where the imposing Monadhliath range looms to the south.

Drumnadrochit

Situated above a verdant, sheltered bay fifteen miles from Inverness, **DRUMNADRO-CHIT**, practically the first chance to draw breath as you head down the A82, is the epicentre of Nessie hype, sporting a rash of tacky souvenir shops and two rival monster exhibitions whose head-to-head scramble for punters occasionally erupts into acrimonious exchanges – detailed with relish by the local press. Of the pair, the **Original Loch Ness Monster Exhibition** (daily: April–June & Sept–Nov 10am–6pm; July & Aug 9am–9pm; Dec–March 10am–4pm; £3.50) is the least worthwhile – basically a gift shop with a shoddy audiovisual show tacked on the side. If you're genuinely interested in "Nessie" lore, the **Official Loch Ness Monster Exhibition** (daily: April–June 9.30am–5.30pm; July–Aug 9am–8pm; Sept–Oct 9am–6.30pm; Nov–March 10am–4pm; £5.95), though more expensive (and no more "official" than the other), is a much better bet, offering an in-depth rundown of eyewitness accounts through the ages and mock-ups of the various research projects carried out in the loch. A recent upgrade has attempted to offer something to sceptics as well as believers by offering more scientific background to set against the various myths and sightings. **Cruises** on the loch aboard the *Nessie Hunter* can be booked at the Original Loch Ness Visitor Centre (Easter–Oct hourly 9.30am–6pm; 50min; £8), though a more relaxing alternative is to head out **fishing** with a local ghillie – the boat can take 5–8 people and costs £25 for two hours; contact Bruce on ☎01456/450279 to book. If you want to turn your back on all the hype and enjoy the surrounding scenery, well-run **pony-trekking** is available at the Highland Riding Centre (☎01456/450220), at Borlum Farm, just before you get to Castle Urquhart.

NESSIE

The world-famous Loch Ness monster, affectionately known as **"Nessie"** (and by serious aficionados as *Nessiteras rhombopteryx*), has been around a long time. The first mention of her crops up in St Adamnan's seventh-century biography of **St Columba**. While on his way to evangelize the pagan inhabitants of Inverness, the saint allegedly calmed the monster after she attacked one of his monks. Present-day interest, however, is probably greater outside Scotland than in, dating from the 1930s when the A82 was built along the loch's western shore. Recent encounters range from glimpses of ripples by anglers, to the famous occasion in 1961 when thirty hotel guests saw a pair of humps break the water's surface and cruise for about half a mile before submerging.

Photographic evidence is showcased in the two "Monster Exhibitions" at Drumnadrochit, but the most impressive of these exhibits – including the renowned black-and-white movie footage of Nessie's humps moving across the water, and the photo of her neck and head – have been exposed as fakes. Hi-tech sonar surveys carried out over the past two decades have failed to come up with conclusive evidence, but it's hard to dismiss Nessie as pure myth. Too many locals have mysterious tales to tell, which they invariably keep to themselves for fear of ridicule by incredulous outsiders. Loch Ness also has an undeniably enigmatic air; even the most hardened cynics rarely resist the temptation to scan the waters for signs of life, just in case . . .

Castle Urquhart

Most photographs allegedly showing the monster have been taken a couple of miles further south, around the fourteenth-century ruined loch-side **Castle Urquhart** (daily: April–June & Sept 9.30am–6.30pm; July & Aug 9.30am–8.30pm; Oct–March 9.30am–4.30pm; last admission 45min before closing; £3.80). Built as a strategic base to guard the Great Glen, the castle played an important role in the Wars of Independence. It was taken by Edward I of England and later held by Robert the Bruce against Edward III, only to be blown up in 1692 to prevent it from falling to the Jacobites. It's pretty dilapidated today, but looks particularly splendid floodlit at night when all the crowds have gone. The castle receives more visitors each year than any other historic site in the Highlands, and the pressures are inevitably taking their toll: a major project is underway to create a larger car park and visitor centre built into the hillside between the main road and the castle.

Practicalities

There's a good range of accommodation around Drumnadrochit, and in the adjoining village of Lewiston. Two very welcoming **B&Bs** are *Gilliflowers* (☎01456/450641, *gillyflowers@cali.co.uk*; ①), a renovated farmhouse tucked away down a country lane in Lewiston, or the modern *Drumbuie* (☎01456/450634; ①), on the northern approach to Drumnadrochit, which has great views and a resident herd of Highland cattle. **Hotels** include the pleasant and secluded *Benleva* (☎01456/450288; ③) between Lewiston and the loch. Two miles west from Drumnadrochit along the Cannich road is a particularly relaxed country-house hotel, *Polmailly House* (☎01456/450343, *polmaillyhousehotel@btinternet.com*; ⑤); it's very family-friendly and there's acres of space, a swimming pool, sauna, riding, and sailing on Loch Ness. For **hostel** beds, head to the immaculate and friendly *Loch Ness Backpackers Lodge* (☎01456/450807, *hostel@lochnessbackpackers.freeserve.co.uk*), at Coiltie Farmhouse in Lewiston; follow the sign to the left when coming from Drumnadrochit. As well as dorm beds, it has one double room (①), and excellent facilities, including boat trips and recommended walks.

All the hotels in the area serve good bar **food**; in Drumnadrochit the *Glen Café* has a short and simple menu with basic grills, while the slightly more upmarket *Fiddlers' Café Bar*, next door to the *Glen* on the village green, offers local steaks, salmon and appetizing home-baked pizza; it also rents out good quality **mountain bikes** (☎01456/450223), and provides maps and rain capes on request.

Glen Urquhart and Glen Affric

You can head west from Drumnadrochit on the A831 through **Glen Urquhart**, a fairly open valley with farmland giving way to scrubby woodland and heather as you near **CANNICH**. The **youth hostel** here (☎01456/415244 or central reservations ☎0541/553255; April–Oct) makes a good base for exploring **Glen Affric**, claimed by many to be Scotland's loveliest valley. It's real calendar stuff, with a rushing river and Caledonian pine and birch woods opening out onto an island-studded loch that was considerably enlarged after the building of the dam, one of many hydroelectric schemes around here. Hemmed in by a string of Munros, the glen is great for picnics and pottering, particularly on a calm and sunny day, when the still loch reflects the islands and surrounding hills.

The area also offers some tremendous **hiking**. Among the most popular routes is the one winding west through Kintail to Shiel Bridge, on the west coast near Kyle of Lochalsh (about 25 miles), which takes at least two full days; a remote but recently revamped **youth hostel** (no phone; April–Oct) makes a convenient stopover halfway into the walk on the banks of the burn above Loch Affric. The trail is easy to follow, but can get horrendously boggy if there's been a lot of rain, so allow plenty of time and take adequate wet-weather gear, as well as the relevant Ordnance Survey map.

Invermoriston and Glen Moriston to Glen Shiel

Heading south, **INVERMORISTON** is a tiny, attractive village just above Loch Ness, from where you can follow well-marked woodland trails past a series of grand water-falls. Dr Johnson and Boswell spent a couple of nights here planning their journey to the Hebrides; you, too, could stay at the *Glenmoriston Arms Hotel* (☎01320/351206; ⑤), an old-fashioned inn with more than a hundred malt whiskies at the bar. Alternatively, the SYHA *Loch Ness Hostel* (☎01320/351274 or central reservations ☎0541 553255; April–Oct), three and a half miles north of Invermoriston and overlooking the loch, is a more economical base.

If you're driving on from Invermoriston to the **west coast**, the roads (A887–A87) are good, as it's the main commercial and tourist route to the Skye Bridge. Rugged and somewhat awesome, the stretch through **Glen Moriston**, beside **Loch Cluanie**, has serious peaks at either side and little sign of human habitation as the road climbs. At the western end of the loch, you'll find the isolated *Cluanie Inn* (☎01463/798200; ⑤), a cosy wayside place with a very busy craft centre attached. From here, the road drops gradually down **Glen Shiel** into the superb mountainscape of **Kintail** (see p.516).

Fort Augustus

FORT AUGUSTUS, the tiny village at the more scenic southwestern tip of Loch Ness, was named after George II's son, the chubby lad who later became the "Butcher" Duke of Cumberland of Culloden fame; it was built as a barracks after the 1715 Jacobite rebel-lion. Today, it's dominated by comings and goings along the Caledonian Canal, which leaves Loch Ness here, and by its large former **Benedictine Abbey**, a campus of grey Victorian buildings founded on the site of the original fort in 1876. The abbey formerly housed a Catholic boys school and until recently was home to a small but active com-munity of monks, but this broke up due to financial pressures and the building now lies empty.

Traditional Highland culture is the subject of **The Clansmen Centre**'s lively and informative exhibition (Easter to mid-Oct daily 10am–6pm; £3), on the banks of the canal. Guides sporting sporrans and rough woollen plaids talk you through the daily life of the region's seventeenth-century inhabitants inside a mock-up of a turf-roofed stone croft, followed by demonstrations of weaponry in the back garden, where you can be photographed in traditional Highland garb. Most of the young staff work here for fun, donning kilts on their free weekends to fight mock battles with enthusiasts from other parts of the Highlands, which must be why they are so unnervingly adept at wielding broadswords. Rather more sedate is the small **Caledonian Canal Heritage Centre** (Easter–Oct daily 10am–6pm; free) in Ardchattan House on the northern bank of the canal, where you can view old photographs and records about the building and history of the canal, and watch a black-and-white film of the days when paddle boats and large barges passed through the locks every day.

Practicalities

Fort Augustus's small **tourist office** (April–June Mon–Sat 10am–5pm; July–Aug 9am–6pm; Sept–Oct 10am–5pm; ☎01320/366367) hands out useful free maps detailing popular walks in the area. They'll also help sort out fishing permits if you fancy trying your luck in the loch or nearby river.

The only **hostel** accommodation in town is at *Morag's Lodge* (☎01320/366289) above the petrol station on the Loch Ness side of town, where the atmosphere livens up with the daily arrival of backpackers' minibus tours. The *Old Pier* (☎01320/366418; ③) is a particularly appealing B&B, right on the loch at the north side of the village; there are log fires in the evenings – often very welcome even in summer – and boats and horse riding are available to guests. Of the **hotels**, try the small, friendly *Caledonian* (☎01320/366256; ②), overlooking the Abbey, or the *Brae* (☎01320/366289; ④), just off the main road as you approach the village from the north, surrounded by woodland.

Eating places include the *Gondolier*, on the southern side of the village, which serves ambitious Scottish food at reasonable prices, or you can try the *Bothy Bite* beside the canal for Scottish specialities with a good range of moderately priced fish, steak and pies. The village has a lively **pub**, drawing a mixed clientele of locals, yachties and backpackers, as does *Poachers* on the main road. There's some good **cycling** routes locally, along the Great Glen cycle route and elsewhere, and you can hire mountain bikes from Scottish Voyageurs (☎01320/366666), based in the last building beside the canal on the southern side, heading towards Fort William. If you're keen to paddle rather than pedal, the same company also offer guided ten-seater Canadian canoe trips, and rent out canoes and other boats.

North from Fort Augustus: East Loch Ness

The tranquil and scenic **east side of Loch Ness** is skirted by General Wade's old military highway, now the B862/852. From Fort Augustus, this narrow single-track road swings inland through the near-deserted **Stratherrick** valley, dotted with tiny lochans and flocks of shaggy sheep, before dropping down to rejoin the loch at **FOYERS**, where there are numerous marked forest trails and an impressive waterfall. In the village, the friendly *Foyers House* (☎01456/486623; ①) makes a good place to **stay** and **eat**, with a bunkhouse offering dorms and doubles, a terrace with great views over the loch, and a restaurant serving up local salmon, venison and rabbit, as well as vegetarian options.

Three miles further north at **INVERFARIGAIG** – where a road up the beautiful, steep-sided river valley leads over to Loch Mhor – stands **Boleskine House**, former residence of the infamous Satanist and occult guru, Alastair Crowley. The self-styled "Great Beast" of Black Magic lived here between 1900 and 1918, amid rumours of Devil worship and human sacrifice. In the 1970s, Led Zeppelin's Jimmy Page bought the place, but sold it after the tragic death of his daughter some years later. Set back in its own grounds, the house still has a gloomy air about it, and is not open to the public.

A much warmer welcome awaits visitors at the sleepy village of **DORES**, nestled at the top end of Loch Ness, where the *Dores Inn* makes a pleasant pit stop. Only nine miles from Inverness, the old pub, which serves an excellent pint of 80 Shilling and inexpensive bar food, is popular with Invernessians, who trickle out here on summer evenings for a stroll along the grey-pebble beach, and some monster-spotting.

THE NEVIS RANGE SKI STATION

The **Nevis Range Ski Range** (☎01397/705825), seven miles northeast of Fort William on the A82, boasts Scotland's only cable-car system (daily: July & Aug 9.30am–8pm; Sept to mid-Nov & mid-Dec to June 10am–5pm; £6.50 return), in the **AONACH MHOR** ski area – a popular attraction during both winter and the summer off-season period. Built in 1989 with a hefty grant from the regional council, the one-and-a-half mile gondola ride (15min) gives an easy approach to some high-level walking, but for most tourists it simply provides an effortless means to rise 2000ft and enjoy the spectacular views from the terrace of the self-service restaurant at the top. In July and August, you can also ski on the Nevis Range's 246-foot **dry slope** (July & Aug Sun–Thurs 11.30am–1pm; £9 including ski rental and group instruction), while a three-kilometre championship-grade **downhill mountain bike course** starting from the top gondola station is presently under construction. Highland County bus #41 from Fort William runs here four times a day (June–Oct).

Fort Augustus to Gairlochy

The fast A82 runs south from Fort Augustus along the shores of **Loch Oich**, where, at Invergarry, the A87 strikes westwards towards Kyle of Lochalsh and the Skye Bridge. Continuing south towards Spean Bridge and Fort William, there are fine views across Loch Lochy to the Glengarry mountains, including Ben Tee, on its northern side. The road comes into more open country near the **Commando Memorial**, a group of bronze soldiers, sculpted in 1952 by Scott Sutherland in memory of the men who trained in the area and lost their lives during World War II. The statue stands on a raised promontory that overlooks an awesome sweep of moor and mountain, taking in Lochaber and the Ben Nevis massif.

Beside the memorial, the minor B8004 branches down to **GAIRLOCHY**, at Loch Lochy's southern tip, where you once more encounter the Caledonian Canal – you can easily walk anywhere along this stretch of the canal, although the best access point is where the B8004 crosses it. It's worth a detour round the northwest side of Loch Lochy to lonely Loch Arkaig, a twenty-minute drive that takes you through a pass, ablaze with rhododendrons in early summer, into country that feels a hundred miles from anywhere. From the eastern end of the loch you can retrace an interesting bit of local history by **walking** around the "Dark Mile" training course used by the commandos based at nearby Achnacarry Castle during World War II – a leaflet describing the trail is available from local tourist offices.

Glen Roy and Loch Laggan

Shortly after the Commando Memorial, the A82 dips into the village of Spean Bridge, where it's met by the A86 trunk road to Dalwhinnie on the A9 (see p.299) and Kingussie in Speyside (see p.492). The countryside here is attractive but relatively untrammelled, with some good hiking routes leading to a generous sprinkling of pretty glens and Munros. At **Roy Bridge**, three miles along the road from Spean Bridge, a minor road turns off which runs up **Glen Roy**. A couple of miles along the glen, you'll see the so-called "parallel roads": not roads at all, but ancient beaches at various levels along the valley sides which mark the shorelines of a loch confined here by a glacial dam in the last Ice Age. Back on the A86, two miles beyond Roy Bridge, *Aite Cruinnichidh*, 1 Achluachrach (☎01397/712315, *gavin@achluachrach.prestel.co.uk*), is a comfortable bunkhouse in a beautiful setting, with good facilities and local advice for climbers, walkers and cyclists. The West Highland Railway line runs right past the hostel, fringing the river Spean and the spectacular Monassie Gorge, which you can view from a footpath leading down from the roadside.

The railway line and road part company at Tulloch, a few miles further east, where trains swing south to pass Loch Treig and cross Rannoch Moor (see p.298). The station building at Tulloch is a brand-new bunkhouse, *Station Lodge* (☎01397/732333, *stationlodge@ renwscot.demon.co.uk*), again with good facilities for walkers and climbers. Further east, the A86 runs alongside the artificial **Loch Laggan**, raised in 1934 to provide water for the aluminium works at Fort William; the water travels in tunnels of up to 15ft in diameter carved through miles of solid rock. To the north of the loch is the **Creag Meagaidh National Nature Reserve**, where a hill track leads up through changing bands of mountain vegetation to **Lochan a Choire**. Right by the nature reserve car park, you can see several small herds of red deer, kept here for scientific study.

Fort William and around

The area around **Fort William** is a blend of rugged mountain terrain and tranquil sea loch. To the north, gentle rounded hills give way to altogether more dramatic scenes, while to the south **Ben Nevis** – at 4406ft Britain's highest peak – looms over **Loch Linnhe**, a long sea loch at the southern end of the Great Glen from whose western shore rise the peaks of **Ardgour**.

Fort William and the surrounding area has a turbulent and bloody **history**. Founded in 1655 and named in honour of William III, it was successfully held by government troops during both of the Jacobite risings; the country to the southwest is inextricably associated with Bonnie Prince Charlie's flight after Culloden. **Glen Coe**, half an hour's drive south of Fort William, is another historic site with a violent past, renowned as much for the infamous **massacre** of 1692 as for its magnificent scenery. Nowadays the whole area is unashamedly given over to tourism, and Fort William is swamped by bus tours throughout the summer, but, as ever in the Highlands, within a thirty-minute drive you can be totally alone.

Fort William

With its stunning position on Loch Linnhe and the snow-streaked bulk of Ben Nevis rising behind, **FORT WILLIAM**, known by the many walkers and climbers that come here as "Fort Bill", should be a gem. Sadly, the same lack of taste that nearly saw the town renamed "Abernevis" in the 1950s is evident in the ribbon bungalow development and an ill-advised dual carriageway complete with a grubby pedestrian underpass, which have wrecked the waterfront. The main street and the little squares off it are more appealing, though occupied by some decidedly tacky tourist gift shops.

Arrival and information

Fort William is easily reached by **bus** from Inverness, and by **train** (the stations are next door to each other at the north end of the High Street) direct from Glasgow via the famous, scenic **West Highland Railway** (see p.476). If you're driving, parking can be a nightmare: a free shuttle bus (mid-May to Sept) runs the short distance into town from both the West End Car Park down beside the loch, at the southwest end of town, and the An Aird Car Park beside the railway station. The **tourist office**, Cameron Square, just off High Street (April–May Mon–Sat 9am–5pm, Sun 10am–4pm; June & Sept–Oct Mon–Sat 9am–6pm, Sun 10am–5pm; July–Aug Mon–Sat 9am–8.30pm, Sun 9am–6pm; Nov–March Mon–Fri 9am–5pm, Sat 10am–4pm; ☎01397/703781), hands out free town maps and can help arrange onward transport to many of the less-visited areas of the west coast. **Mountain bikes** are available for rent at Off Beat Bikes (☎01397/704008) on the High Street; they also have a branch open at the Nevis Range lower gondola station during July and August – good for exploring forest tracks in that area.

Accommodation

Fort William's plentiful **accommodation** ranges from large luxury hotels to budget hostels and bunkhouses. Numerous B&Bs are also scattered across the town, many of them in the suburb of Corpach, where there are also a couple of good hostels; it's on the other side of Loch Linnhe, three miles along the Mallaig road, and served by a regular bus service from Fort William. Note that a wide array of places to stay in this area may be reserved through the tourist office for a £1 booking fee, or you can ask for its free *Visitors Guide* and phone around yourself.

HOTELS AND B&BS

Alexandra Hotel, The Parade (☎01397/702241, *sales@miltonhotels.com*). Established hotel right in the town centre, with well-appointed rooms and a restaurant. ⑤.

Bank Street Lodge, Bank Street (☎01397/700070). New and slightly characterless lodge with neat doubles, twin and family rooms, all with TVs, and a very central location. Also has a couple of rooms used as four or eight-bed dorms (£11 per night). ①.

Distillery House, North Road, just north of the town centre near the junction for Glen Nevis (☎01397/700103). Very comfortable and well-equipped upper-range B&B. ③.

Glenloy Lodge Hotel, about six miles from Fort William on the minor road running north from Banavie (☎01397/712700). Comfortable, friendly and secluded small hotel with views across to Ben Nevis. ④.

The Grange, Grange Road (☎01397/705516). Top-grade accommodation in a striking old stone house, with four luxurious en-suite doubles and a spacious garden. Vegetarian breakfasts on request; non-smoking. April–Oct. ⑤.

Inverlochy Castle, two miles north of Fort William on the A82 (☎01397/702177). A grand country house hotel set in wooded parkland, two miles north of Fort William; exceptional levels of service and outstanding food – but at a price. ⑨.

Rhiw Goch, beside Neptune's Staircase, Banavie (☎01397/772373). Non-smoking modern villa with three twin rooms in a great situation beside the canal looking over to Ben Nevis. ①

Rhu Mhor, 42 Alma Road (☎01397/702213). Congenial B&B ten minutes' walk from the town centre, offering good breakfasts; vegetarians and vegans are catered for by arrangement. ①.

St Andrews West, Fassifern Road (☎01397/703038). Comfortable and extremely central B&B in an attractive converted granite church with various inscriptions and stained-glass windows remaining. ①

HOSTELS AND CAMPSITES

Ben Nevis Bunkhouse, Achintee Farm, Glen Nevis (☎01397/702240, *achintee.accom@glennevis.com*). A more civilized option than the nearby SYHA place, with hot showers, self-catering kitchen and TV room. Located just over the river from the Ben Nevis Visitor Centre – get to it by following the Ben path across the river or by taking Achintee Road along the north side of the river Nevis from Claggan.

Calluna, Heathcroft (☎01397/700451, *mountain@guide.u-net.com*). Central, small family-run budget self-catering flat with standard facilities, but tricky to find: head up Lundavra Road from the roundabout, then double back left along Connochie Road. The owner is one of the area's top mountain guides, so there's plenty of good outdoor advice available.

Farr Cottage, main A830 as it goes through Corpach (☎01397/772315, *farrcottage@sol.co.uk*). One of the liveliest of the local backpacker hostels, with everything from pizza feasts to whisky tastings going on in the evenings. Accommodation, in medium-sized dorms, is slightly more expensive than others locally.

Fort William Backpackers, Alma Road (☎01397/700711). A big house five minutes' walk up the hill from town, with great views and large communal areas, though some of the facilites are a bit ropey. Part of the Macbackpackers chain, so minibus tours pull in at regular intervals.

Glen Nevis SYHA Hostel, two and a half miles up the Glen Nevis road (☎01397/702336 or central reservations ☎0541 553255). Large but best avoided in mid-summer, when it's chock-full of teenagers. Handy for the Ben Nevis path but a long walk from town.

Glen Nevis Caravan and Camping Park, two miles up the Glen Nevis road (☎01397/702191). Good facilities include hot showers, a shop and restaurant.

The Smiddy Bunkhouse, Station Road (☎01397/772467, *smiddy@snowgoose.prestel.co.uk*). A cosy twelve-bed hostel right next to Corpach train station at the entrance to the Caledonian Canal. Part of the Snowgoose Mountain Centre, offering year-round mountaineering, kayaking and other outdoor activities.

The Town

Fort William's downfall started in the nineteenth century, when the original fort, which gave the town its name, was demolished to make way for the train line. Today, the town is a sprawl of dual carriageways, and there's little to detain you except the splendid and idiosyncratic **West Highland Museum**, on Cameron Square, just off the High Street (April–Oct Mon–Sat 10am–5pm; July & Aug also Sun 2–5pm; Nov–March Mon–Sat 10am–4pm; £2). Its collections cover virtually every aspect of Highland life and the presentation is traditional, but very well done, making a refreshing change from state-of-the-art heritage centres. There's a good section on Highland clans and tartans and, among interesting Jacobite relics, a secret portrait of Bonnie Prince Charlie, seemingly just a blur of paint that resolves itself into a portrait when viewed against a cylindri-

GLEN NEVIS WALKS AND HIKES

Harvey's Ben Nevis Walkers Map and Guide

The above **map** is available in the the Fort William tourist office and several shops around town. Anyone keen to do some serious **planned walking** should contact Donald Watt (☎01397/704340), the leader of the Lochaber Mountain Rescue Team, who organizes half- and whole-day walks.

Of all the walks in and around **Glen Nevis**, the ascent of **Ben Nevis**, Britain's highest summit, inevitably attracts the most attention. In high summer, the trail is teeming with hikers, whatever the weather. However, this doesn't mean the mountain should be treated casually. It can snow round the summit any day of the year and more people perish here annually than on Everest, so take the necessary precautions (see p.473); in winter, of course, the mountain should be left to the experts.

The most obvious **route** to the summit, a Victorian pony path up the whaleback south side of of the mountain, built to service the observatory that once stood on the top, starts from the Ionad Nibheis visitor centre (daily Easter–Oct 9am–5pm; free),a mile and a half southeast of Fort William along the Glen Nevis road (bus number 42 from An Aird in Fort William). From the helpful centre, cross the footbridge over the River Nevis, then follow the path (20mins) which connects with the path down to the youth hostel. Continue upwards over two aluminium footbridges, swinging onto a wide saddle with a small loch before veering right to cross the Red Burn. A series of seemingly endless zigzags rises from here over boulderfields on to a plateau, which you cross to reach the summit, marked by cairns, a shelter and a trig point. Return via the same route or, if the weather is settled and you're confident enough, make the side trip from the saddle mentioned earlier into the **Allt a'Mhuilinn glen** for spectacular views of the great cliffs on Ben Nevis' north face. The Allt a'Mhuilinn may be followed right down to valley level as an alternative route off the mountain, reaching the distillery on the A82 a mile north of Fort William. Allow a full day for the climb (8hr).

If you don't fancy a hike up the mountain, a great **low-level walk** runs from the end of the road at the top of the glen. The good but very rocky path leads through a dramatic gorge with impressive falls and rapids, then opens out into a secret hanging valley, carpeted with wild flowers, with a high waterfall at the far end. It's a pretty place for a picnic and if you're really energetic you can walk on over **Rannoch Moor** to **Corrour Station**, where you can pick up one of four daily trains to take you back to Fort William.

cal mirror. Look out, too, for the long Spanish rifle used in the assassination of a local factor (the landowner's tax-collector-cum-bailiff) – the murder that subsequently inspired Robert Louis Stevenson's novel, *Kidnapped*. You'll also see a 550kg slab of aluminium, the stuff that's processed locally into silver foil.

Excursions from town include the popular day-trip to Mallaig (see p.512) on the **Jacobite Steam Train** (mid-June to Sept Mon–Fri, also Sun during Aug; depart Fort William 10.20am, depart Mallaig 2.10pm; day return £19.75; bookings ☎01463/239026). Heading along the north shore of Loch Eil to the west coast via historic Glenfinnan (see p.511), the journey takes in some of the region's most spectacular scenery. Several **cruises** also leave from the town pier every day, offering the chance to spot the marine life of Loch Linnhe, including seals, otters and seabirds.

Glen Nevis

A ten-minute drive out of town, **Glen Nevis** is indisputably among the Highlands' most impressive glens: a classic U-shaped glacial valley hemmed in by steep bracken-covered slopes and swaths of blue-grey scree. Herds of shaggy Highland cattle graze the valley floor, where a sparkling river gushes through glades of trees. With the forbidding mass of Ben Nevis rising steeply to the north, it's not surprising this valley has been chosen as the location for scenes in several **movies**, such as *Rob Roy* and *Braveheart*. Apart from its natural beauty, Glen Nevis is also the starting point for the ascent of Scotland's highest peak, and you can rent **mountain equipment** and **mountain bikes** at the trailhead. Highland Country **bus** #42 runs from An Aird, Fort William, approximately hourly through the day as far as the youth hostel; less frequently the service carries on another two and a half miles up the glen to the car park by the Lower Falls (mid-May to Sept only; 10–20 min).

Neptune's Staircase and Corpach

Three miles from the centre of Fort William along the A830 to Mallaig at the suburb of Benavie, the Caledonian Canal climbs 64ft in less than half a mile via a punishing but picturesque series of eight locks known as **Neptune's Staircase**. There are stunning views from here of Ben Nevis and its neighbours, and it's a popular point from which to walk or cycle along the canal towpath. Bikes can be hired from Caledonian Activity Breaks (☎01397/772373), based at Rhiw Goch, one of the cottages backing onto the canal at the top of the sequence of locks.

Another mile along the road is the suburb of **Corpach**, the point where the canal enters from Loch Linnhe. The site of a mothballed paper mill, the main event here is the unexpectedly absorbing **Treasures of the Earth** exhibition (Feb–Dec daily 10am–5pm, July & Aug 9.30am–7pm; £3), which has a dazzling array of rocks, crystals, gemstones and fossils, with detailed explanations about where they come from and how they get their different colours. Some of the displays are quite entertaining, with a recreated mine showing how the stones are discovered and a UV-lit chamber revealing the psychedelic colours hidden inside different gemstones.

Eating

Fort William has a reasonable range of places **to eat**. On the High Street, the *Grog and Gruel* serves an eclectic mix of pizzas, pasta and Mexican dishes with real ale, while the *Great Food Stop* at the *Alexandra Hotel* does inexpensive grills, fish and pasta dishes. *McTavish's Kitchen*, an American/Scottish restaurant on High Street, has a predictable menu of moderately priced steaks and seafood, with several vegetarian options; in summer, it also hosts nightly Scottish entertainment sessions (8.30–11.30pm). The pick of the bunch, though, is the *Crannog Seafood Restaurant*, an elegantly converted bait store on the pier, where oysters, langoustines, prawns and salmon are cooked with flair. The wine list is also excellent, although the prices make it best kept for a treat. Out of town, the *Old Pines* near Spean Bridge (☎01397/712324) is worth trying, or you can dine very well indeed in the more formal setting of *Inverlochy Castle* (☎01397/702177), though here the bill for two will probably run into three figures. A good place for **picnic food** as well as a snack is the *Café Chardon*, up a lane off High Street next to AT Mays; they do excellent baguettes, croissants and pastries to eat in or take away.

Glen Coe

Breathtakingly beautiful, **Glen Coe** (literally "Valley of Weeping"), sixteen miles south of Fort William on the A82, is one of the best-known Highland glens: a spectacular mountain valley between velvety-green conical peaks, their tops often wreathed in cloud, and cascades of rock and scree. In 1692 it was the site of a notorious **massacre**, in which the MacDonalds were victims of a long-standing government desire to suppress the clans. Fed up with what they regarded as unacceptable lawlessness, and a groundswell of Jacobitism and Catholicism, the government offered a general pardon to all those who signed an oath of allegiance to William III by January 1, 1692. When clan chief **Alastair MacDonald** missed the deadline, a plot was hatched to make an example of "that damnable sept", and **Campbell of Glenlyon** was ordered to billet his

WALKS AROUND GLEN COE

Ordnance Survey Landranger Map No. 41.

Flanked by sheer-sided Munros, Glen Coe offers some of the Highlands' most challenging **hiking** routes, with long steep ascents over rough trails and notoriously unpredictable weather conditions that claim lives every year. The walks outlined below number among the glen's less ambitious routes, but still require a map. It's essential that you take the proper precautions (see p.473), and stick to the paths, both for your own safety and the sake of the soil, which has become badly eroded in places.

A good introduction to the splendours of Glen Coe is the half-day hike over the **Devil's Staircase**, which follows part of the old military road that once ran between Fort William and Stirling. The trail, a good option for families and less experienced hikers, starts at the village of **Kinlochleven**, due north across the mountains from Glen Coe at the far eastern tip of Loch Leven (take the B863): head along the single-track road from the British Aluminium Heritage Centre to a wooden bridge, from where a gradual climb on a dirt jeep track winds up to Penstock Farm. The path, a section of the **West Highland Way**, is marked from here onwards by thistle signs, and is therefore easy to follow uphill to the 1804ft pass and down the other side into Glen Coe. The Devil's Staircase was named by 400 soldiers who endured severe hardship to build it in the seventeenth century, but in fine settled weather the trail is safe and affords stunning views of Loch Eilde and Buachaille Etive Mhor. A more detailed account of this hike features in *Great Walks: Kinlochleven* leaflet (No. 4), on sale at most tourist offices in the area.

Another leaflet in the Great Walks series (*No. 5: Glen Coe*) gives a good description of the **Allt Coire Gabhail** hike, another old favourite. The trailhead for this half-day route is in Glen Coe itself, at the car park opposite the distinctive Three Sisters massif on the main A82 (look for the giant boulder). From the road, drop down to the floor of the glen and cross the River Coe via the wooden bridge, where you have a choice of two onward paths; the easier route, the less worn one, peels off to the right. Follow this straight up the Allt Coire Gabhail for a couple of miles until you rejoin the other (lower) path, which has ascended the valley beside the burn via a series of rock pools and lively scrambles. Cross the river here via the stepping stones and press on to the false summit directly ahead – actually the rim of the so-called "Lost Valley" which the Clan MacDonald used to flee to and hide their cattle in when attacked. Once in the valley, there are superb views of Bidean, Gearr Aonach and Beinn Fhada, which improve as you continue on to its head, another twenty- to thirty-minute walk. Unless you're well equipped and experienced, turn around at this point, as the trail climbs to some of the glen's high ridges and peaks.

Undoubtedly one of the finest walks in the Glen Coe area not entailing the ascent of a Munro is the **Buachaille Etive Beag** (BEB) circuit, for which you should check out the Ordnance Survey Pathfinder Guide: *Fort William and Glen Coe Walks*. Following the textbook glacial valleys of Lairig Eilde and Lairig Gartain, the route entails a 1968ft climb in only nine miles of rough trail, and should only be attempted by relatively fit hikers. Park near the waterfall at **The Study** – the gorge part of the A82 through Glen Coe – and walk up the road until you see a sign pointing south to "Loch Etiveside". The path angles up from here, criss-crossing the Allt Lairig Eilde before the final pull to the top of the pass, a rise of 787ft from the road. The burn flowing through Glen Etive to Dalness is, confusingly, also called the Allt Lairig Eilde; follow its west bank path until you reach a fenced-off area, and then cross the stream, using the trail that then ascends Stob Dubh (the "black peat") directly from Glen Etive to gain some height. Next, pick a traverse line across the side of the valley to the col of the Lairig Gartain, and onwards to the top of the pass – a haul of around 984ft that is the last steep ascent of this circuit. The drop down the other side towards the estate lodge of Dalness is easy. When you reach the single-track road, follow the path signposted as the "Lairig Gartain", northeast to a second pass, from where an intermittent trail descends the west (left) side of the River Coupall valley, eventually rejoining the A82. Much the most enjoyable path back northeast down the glen from here is the roughly parallel route of the old military road, which offers a gentler and safer return with superb views of the Three Sisters – finer than those ever seen by drivers.

soldiers in the homes of the MacDonalds, who for ten days entertained them with traditional Highland hospitality. In the early morning of February 13, the soldiers turned on their hosts, slaying between 38 and 45 and causing more than 300 to flee in a blizzard, some to die of exposure.

Today, the glen, a property of the NTS since the 1930s, is virtually uninhabited, and provides outstanding climbing and walking. A small **NTS visitor centre** (April–Oct 9.30am–5.30pm; 50p), in the middle of the glen just off the main road, shows a short video about the massacre, and has a gift shop selling the usual books, postcards and Highland kitsch; for information about the area, the **tourist office** at Ballachulish is more useful. There is a shortish walk from the centre through the forest to Signal Rock, which unsurprisingly offers good views up and down the glen. More substantial are the informative ranger-led **guided walks** which leave from the centre (May–Aug): a high-level hike leaves at 10.30am on Thursdays (£10) and a low-level walk at 2.30pm on Tuesdays (£2).

At the eastern end of Glen Coe beyond the demanding Buachaille Etive Mhor, the landscape opens out onto the vast Rannoch Moor, dotted with small lochs and crossed by the West Highland Way, the A82 and, farther east, the West Highland Railway. From the **Glen Coe Ski Centre**, a ski lift climbs 2400ft to Meall a Bhuiridh, giving spectacular views over Rannoch Moor and to Ben Nevis (all year; 15min; £3.75 return). At the base station, there's a tiny **Museum of Mountaineering** (daily 8.30am–5pm), where the rescue statistics make cautionary reading, and a simple but pleasant café. At the western end of the glen, **Glen Coe village** lies on the shore of Loch Leven, an inlet of Loch Linnhe.

Practicalities

There's a good selection of **accommodation** in Glen Coe and the surrounding area. Basic options include an SYHA **hostel** (☎01855/811219 or central reservations ☎0541/553255) on a back road half-way between Glen Coe village and the *Clachaig Inn*; the year-round *Red Squirrel* **campsite** (☎01855/811256) nearby; and a grassier NTS campsite (April–Oct; ☎01855/811397) on the main road. Glen Coe village has a few comfortable **B&Bs**, such as the secluded *Scorry Breac* (☎01855/811354, *john@tajones.demon.co.uk*; ①), and the *Glen Coe Guest House* (☎01855/811244; ①), while the best-known **hotel** in the area is the stark *Clachaig Inn* (☎01855/811252, *inn@glencoe-scotland.co.uk*; ③), a great place to swap stories with fellow climbers, and to reward your exertions with pints of beer and heaped platefuls of food; it's up Glen Coe, on the minor road from the Glen Coe village. At the other end of the glen, close to the Glen Coe ski area, is another well-established climber's watering hole, the *Kingshouse Hotel* (☎01855/851259; ②), a classic wayfarers' inn which always proves a welcome sight after the wide emptiness of Rannoch Moor. **Mountain bikes** and **tandems** can be rented from the *Clachaig Inn*.

Ballachulish and Kinlochleven

Two miles west of Glen Coe village, **Ballachulish village** was a major centre for the production of roofing slates, from 1693 to 1955, while North and South Ballachulish were once the terminals for the ferry across the mouth of Loch Leven, now crossed by a bridge. On the seaward side of the main road, the pricey **Highland Mysteryworld** (Easter–Oct daily 10am–6pm; £4.95), aimed mainly at families, attempts to conjure up some of the myths and legends of the Highlands, with the help of a crew of enthusiastic actors, animatronics and lots of smoke; it has a reasonable café and relatively kitsch-free gift shop. Much more genuine mystery is stirred up on **boat trips** (☎01855/811658 for details) which leave from the West Pier at Ballachulish and take you out to Eilean Munde, an island in Loch Leven where clan chiefs are buried; needless to say, the cruise is also a great way to take in the surrounding scenery.

At the eastern end of Loch Leven, at the foot of the spectacular mountains known as the Mamores, is the rather lifeless settlement of Kinlochleven, which has felt rather ignored ever since the bridge at Ballachulish ended the flow of northbound traffic detouring around the loch in preference to waiting in long ferry queues. Kinlochleven was the site of a huge aluminium smelter, established in 1904 and powered by a hydro-electric scheme that dammed the Blackwater valley above the village and which at the time it was built was the largest in Europe. The tale is told in **The Aluminium Story** (April–Oct Tues–Fri 10.30am–6pm, Sat & Sun 11am–3pm; free), a small series of displays in the same building as the town library; the final chapter of the tale is that the factory is now all but closed, and despite large amounts of aid money the town is being left to its fate.

The real activity here comes from climbers heading into the Mamores, and from walkers strolling in on the **West Highland Way**, for whom the town is a convenient overnight stop a day's walk from Fort William. The two hostels in town are the inexpensive *West Highland Lodge Bunkhouse* (☎01855/831471, *whl@cqm.co.uk*), a traditional bunkhouse with a great setting up on the hill, and the newer *Blackwater Hostel* (☎01855/831253) beside the river, decidedly upmarket, with TVs and en-suite facilities in four-bed dorms, but no communal lounge. You can also camp here, and hire mountain bikes. Welcoming B&B is available at *Edencoille Guest House* (☎01855/831358; ①), while there are two good hotels in town: *MacDonald Hotel* (☎01855/831539, *martin@macdonaldhotel.demon.co.uk*; ④), whose *Bothy Bar* is popular with walkers, and the spectacularly situated *Mamore Lodge* (☎01855/831213; ③), an old hunting lodge with attractive wood-panelled rooms and great views from the bar and restaurant.

Practicalities

Ballachulish has a useful **tourist office**, on Albert Road (April & May Mon–Sat 9am–5pm, Sun noon–4pm; June–Aug Mon–Sat 9am–6pm, Sun 10am–5pm; Sept & Oct Mon–Sat 10am–5pm, Sun 10am–4pm; ☎01855/811296), though most of the best accommodation is across the bridge in North Ballachulish and Onich. For a cheap bed head to the elderly but inexpensive *Inchree Bunkhouse* (☎01855/821287) at Onich, where accommodation is also available in chalets and there's a decent real-ale pub and bistro. In Ballachulish village, *Fern Villa* (☎01855/811393; ②) is a welcoming **B&B**, while *Cuildorag House* (☎01855/821529; ②) in Onich is a particularly pleasant vegetarian and vegan B&B, renowned for its great breakfasts. **Hotels** include the *Ballachulish* (☎01855/821582; ⑥) in South Ballachulish, a grand but welcoming old place with good food, while the *Onich Hotel* (☎01855/821214; ⑤) is smart and friendly. Enthusiastic Havoc Bikes, located in a shed by the main road at Onich, is a good place to **hire a mountain bike** with all the trimmings, including helmet, rucksack and water bottle.

THE WEST COAST

For many people, the Highlands' starkly beautiful **west coast** – stretching from the **Morvern** peninsula (opposite Mull) in the south, to wind-lashed Cape Wrath in the far north – is the epitome of "Bonnie Scotland". Serrated by long blue sea lochs, deep glens and rugged green mountains that sweep from the shoreline, its myriad islets, occasional white-sand beaches and turquoise bays can, on sunny days, look like a picture postcard of the Mediterranean. This also is the least populated part of Britain, with just two small towns, and yawning tracts of moorland and desolate peat bog between crofting settlements.

The **Vikings**, who ruled the region in the ninth century, called it the "South Land", from which the modern district of Sutherland takes its name. After Culloden, the Clearances emptied most of the inland glens of the far north, however, and left the population clinging to the coastline, where a herring-fishing industry developed. Today, tourism, crofting, fishing and salmon farming are the mainstay of the local economy, supplemented by EU construction grants and subsidies for the sheep you'll encounter everywhere.

For visitors, **cycling** and **walking** are the obvious ways to make the most of the superb scenery, and countless lochans and crystal-clear rivers offer superlative trout and salmon **fishing**. The shattered cliffs of the far northwest are an ornithologist's dream, harbouring some of Europe's largest and most diverse **seabird colonies**, and the area's craggy mountaintops are the haunt of the elusive golden eagle.

The most visited part of the west coast is the stretch between Kyle of Lochalsh and Ullapool. Lying within easy reach of Inverness, this area boasts the region's more obvious highlights: the awesome mountainscape of **Torridon**, **Gairloch**'s sandy beaches, the famous botanic gardens at **Inverewe**, and **Ullapool** itself, a picturesque and bustling fishing town from where ferries leave for the Outer Hebrides. However, press on further north, or south, and you'll get a truer sense of the isolation that makes the west coast so special. Traversed by few roads, the remote northwest corner of Scotland is wild and bleak, receiving the full force of the north Atlantic's frequently ferocious weather. The scattered settlements of the far southwest, meanwhile, tend to be more sheltered, but they are separated by some of the most extensive wilderness areas in Britain – lonely peninsulas with evocative Gaelic names like **Ardnamurchan**, **Knoydart** and **Glenelg**.

Tempered by the Gulf Stream, the west coast's weather ranges from stupendous to diabolical. Never count on a sunny morning meaning a fine day; it can rain here at any time, and go on raining for days. Beware, too, as always in this part of the world, of the dreaded **midge**, which drives even the hardiest of locals to distraction on warm summer evenings.

Without your own vehicle, **getting around** the west coast can be a problem. There's a reasonable **train** service from Inverness to Kyle of Lochalsh and from Fort William to Mallaig, and a useful **summer bus** service connects Inverness to Ullapool, Lochinver, Scourie and Durness. However, services peter out as you venture further afield, and you'll have to rely on **postbuses**, which go just about everywhere, albeit slowly and at odd times of day. **Driving** is a lot less problematic: the roads aren't busy, though they are frequently single-track and scattered with sheep. On such routes, re-fuel whenever you can, as pumps are few and far between, and make sure your vehicle is in good condition because, even if you manage to reach the nearest garage, spares may well have to be sent over from Inverness.

Morvern to Morar: the "Rough Bounds"

The remote and sparsely-populated southwest corner of the Highlands, from the **Morvern** peninsula to the busy fishing and ferry port of **Mallaig**, is a dramatic, lonely region of mountain, moorland and almost deserted glens fringed by a coast of stunning white beaches, with wonderful views to Mull and Skye. Its Gaelic name translates as the "**Rough Bounds**", implying a region geographically and spiritually apart. Even if you have got a car, you should spend a few days here exploring by foot – there are so few roads that some determined hiking is almost inevitable.

The southwest Highlands' main road is the A830, which winds in tandem with the rail line through the glens from **Fort William** to Mallaig. Along the way, the road passes **Glenfinnan**, the much photographed spot at the head of stunning Loch Shiel where Bonnie Prince Charlie gathered the clans to start the doomed Jacobite uprising of 1745. There are regular buses and trains along the main road; elsewhere in the region you'll usually have to rely on daily post- or school buses. If you have your own transport, the five-minute ferry crossing at **Corran Ferry** (every 15min; foot passengers and bicycles go free), a nine-mile drive south of Fort William down Loch Linnhe, provides a more direct point of entry for Morvern and the rugged **Ardnamurchan** peninsula.

Morvern

Bounded on three sides by sea lochs and, in the north, by desolate Glen Tarbet, the remote southwest part of the Rough Bounds region, known as **Morvern**, is unremittingly bleak and empty. Most visitors only travel through here to get to **LOCHALINE** (pronounced "Loch*aa*lin"), a remote community on the **Sound of Mull**, from where a small ferry chugs to **Fishnish** – the shortest crossing from the mainland. The village, little more than a scattering of houses and a diving school (☎01967/421627) around a small pier, is a popular anchorage for yachts cruising the west coast, but holds little else to detain you. However, the easy stroll to the nearby fourteenth-century ruins of **Ardtornish Castle**, reached via a track that turns east off the main road one and a half miles north of Lochaline, makes an enjoyable detour. A further walk takes you to see the Loch Tearnait **crannog**, a defensive island dating back about 1500 years; this walk and others are detailed in the *Great Walks* series available from tourist offices in the area. If you're looking for somewhere to **stay**, try the tiny *Lochaline Hotel* (☎01967/421657; ③), which serves reasonable bar food and has a couple of small but comfortable **rooms**.

Sunart and Ardgour

The predominantly roadless regions of **Sunart** and **Ardgour** make up the country between Loch Shiel, Loch Sunart and Loch Linnhe, north of Morvern: the heart of Jacobite support in the mid-eighteenth century, and a Catholic stronghold to this day. The area's only real village is sleepy **STRONTIAN**, grouped around a green on an inlet of Loch Sunart. In 1722, lead mines here yielded the first ever traces of the element **strontium**, named after the village. Worked by French POWs, the same mines also furnished shot for the Napoleonic wars. Strontian's other claim to fame is the **"Floating Church"**, which was moored nearby in Loch Sunart in 1843. After being refused permission by the local laird to found their own "kirk", or chapel, on the estate, members of the Free Presbyterian Church (see p.389) bought an old boat on the River Clyde, converted it into a church and then had it towed up the west coast to Loch Sunart.

Travelling by **public transport**, you can get to Strontian (Mon–Sat) on the 8am bus from Kilchoan (see below), or on a bus that leaves Fort William at 12.15pm and Ardgour at 12.50pm. Strontian's **tourist office** (Easter–Oct Mon–Sat 9am–5pm, Sun 10am–3pm; ☎01967/402131) will book accommodation for a small fee. *Loch View* **B&B** (☎01967/402465; ①) is excellent value, with large rooms in a fine loch-side Victorian house, while *Sea View* (☎01967/402060; ②), a small and very traditional cottage next door, is friendly but more basic; it welcomes dogs. The modern *Kinloch House* (☎01967/402138; ②) is very comfortable, with stunning views down the loch. Strontian also has a couple of good **hotels**, including the *Strontian Hotel* (☎01967/402029; ②), in a splendid position near the water, and the luxurious *Kilcamb Lodge* (☎01967/402257; ⑤ including dinner; March–Nov), a restored country house set in its own grounds on the loch-side, whose restaurant serves excellent food.

The Ardnamurchan peninsula

A tortuous single-track road (the B8007) winds west from **Salen** along the northern shore of Loch Sunart to the wild **Ardnamurchan peninsula**, the most westerly point on the British mainland. The unspoilt landscape is relatively gentle and wooded at the eastern end, but as you travel west the trees disappear and are replaced by a wild, salt-sprayed moorland. The peninsula, which lost most of its inhabitants during the infamous Clearances (see p.632), is today virtually deserted apart from the handful of tiny crofting settlements clinging to its jagged coastline. Ardnamurchan remains a naturalist's paradise, harbouring a huge variety of birds, animals and wildflowers like thrift and wild iris.

Glenborrodale and the Glenmore Natural History Centre

An inspiring introduction to the diverse flora, fauna and geology of Ardnamurchan is the superb **Glenmore Natural History Centre** (April–Oct 10.30am–5.30pm; £2.50), nestled near the shore just west of the hamlet of **GLENBORRODALE**. Brainchild of local photographer Michael MacGregor (whose stunning work enlivens postcard stands along the west coast), the centre is housed in a sensitively designed timber building, complete with turf roof and wildlife ponds. TV cameras relay live pictures of the comings and goings of the surrounding wildlife, from a pine marten's nest, a heronry and from underwater pools in the nearby river, while an excellent audiovisual show features MacGregor's photographs of the area accompanied by specially composed music. The small **café** serves sandwiches and good home-baked cakes and there's a useful bookshop. The nearby **RSPB reserve**, a mile to the east, is rich in wildlife too, being home to tree creepers, golden eagles, otters and seals, while for coastal wildlife-spotting – or trips to Tobermory on Mull or Fingal's Cave – contact Ardnamurchan Charters at Glenborrodale (☎01972/500208).

Kilchoan and Ardnamurchan Point

KILCHOAN, nine miles west of the Glenmore Centre, is Ardnamurchan's main village – a straggling but appealing crofting township overlooking the Sound of Mull. Between Easter and mid-October, a **car ferry** runs from here to Tobermory (7 daily; 35min), while in the winter a passenger ferry plies the route for schoolchildren and shoppers. The new community centre in the village houses a **tourist office** (Easter–Oct daily 10am–6pm; ☎01972/510222), who will help with and book accommodation, though year-round the community centre will act as an informal source of local advice and assistance.

Accommodation isn't plentiful in Kilchoan, but both the *Meall mo Chridhe Hotel* (☎01972/510328; ⑤, with dinner ⑦; April–Oct), a converted eighteenth-century manse set among trees above the road, and *Doirlinn House* (☎01972/510209; ②; March–Oct), a B&B with great views, are very pleasant. Further afield, *Feorag House* (☎01972/500248; ⑦ including dinner) at Glenborrodale is an acclaimed upmarket B&B, while a couple of miles before the Ardnamurchan Point lighthouse (see below), there's the *Sonachan Hotel* (☎01972/510211; ②), a cosy and friendly haven also offering good bar meals, and *Hillview* (☎01972/510322; ①), a traditional cottage about four miles north of Kilchoan at Achnaha (you'll need your own transport). The only direct bus to Kilchoan leaves from Corran Ferry at 12.35pm, arriving two hours later.

Beyond Kilchoan the road continues to rocky, windy **Ardnamurchan Point**, with its unmanned **lighthouse** and spectacular views west to Coll, Tiree and across to the north of Mull. You can't normally get up the tower, but the lighthouse buildings house a café and an enthusiastically run **visitor centre** (April–Oct 9.30am–6pm; £2.50; ☎01972/510210), whose main theme is lighthouses, their construction and the people who lived in them. About three miles north of the point, the shell-strewn sandy beach of **Sanna Bay** offers truly unforgettable vistas of the Small Isles to the north, circled by gulls, terns and guillemots.

Acharacle

Back on the A861 towards the district of Moidart, the main settlement is **ACHARA-CLE**, an ancient crofting village lying at the seaward end of Loch Shiel. Surrounded by gentle hills, it's an attractive place whose scattered houses form a real community, with several shops, a post office, and plenty of places to stay. The informal *Loch Shiel House Hotel* (☎01967/431224; ②) has nice rooms and simple but good food including local salmon and haddock. *Belmont* (☎01967/431266; ②) is a comfortable and central B&B, as is Mrs Crisp's (☎01967/431318; ①), just across the road. On the south side of the village, *Ardshealach Lodge* (☎01967/431301; ②) is secluded and welcoming. You can get to Acharacle by **boat** with Loch Shiel Cruises on Wednesdays (☎01397/722235), or by **bus** on the infrequent links with Mallaig and Fort William. There are plenty of untaxing and attractive **walks** in the local area – for a book detailing these call in at Out of Doors, a shop opposite the hotel. Beside this is the *Burger Bite*, a takeaway and bakery with good picnic fodder. Acharacle's village hall is often used for ceilidhs: look out for notices in the shops.

If you're determined to be a bit more adventurous, the Achananellan Centre (☎01967/431265) on the remote south shore of Loch Shiel has self-catering bunkhouse accommodation available, as well as bikes, canoes and sailing dinghies for hire. Bookings must be made in advance. The easiest way to get there is to arrange to be picked up by boat at the pier at Dalilea, a few miles east of Acharacle.

Loch Moidart and Castle Tioram

A mile north of Acharacle, a side road running north off the A861 winds for three miles or so past a secluded estuary lined with rhododendron thickets and fishing platforms to **Loch Moidart**, a calm and sheltered sea loch. Perched atop a rocky promontory in the middle of the loch is **CASTLE TIORAM** (pronounced "cheerum"), one of Scotland's most atmospheric historic monuments. Reached via a sandy causeway, the thirteenth-century fortress, whose Gaelic name means "dry land", was the seat of the MacDonalds of Clanranald until it was destroyed by their chief in 1715 to prevent it from falling into Hanoverian hands while he was away fighting for the Jacobites. Today, the surviving walls and tower enclose an inner courtyard and a couple of empty chambers.

Glenfinnan

Approaching Moidart from the north by train, or via the fast Fort William–Mallaig road (the A830), you pass a historic site with great resonance for many Scots. **GLENFINNAN**, nineteen miles west of Fort William at the head of Loch Shiel, was where Bonnie Prince Charlie raised his standard to signal the start of the Jacobite uprising of 1745. Surrounded by no more than 200 loyal clansmen, the young rebel prince waited to see if the Cameron of Loch Shiel would join his army. The drone of this powerful chief's pipers drifting up the glen was eagerly awaited, for without him the Stuarts' attempt to claim the English throne would have been sheer folly. Despite strong misgivings, Cameron did decide to support the uprising, and arrived at Glenfinnan on a sunny August 19 with 800 men, thereby encouraging other less-convinced clan leaders to follow suit. Assured of adequate backing, the prince raised his red-and-white silk colour, proclaimed his father King James III of England, and set off on the long march to London from which only a handful of the soldiers gathered at Glenfinnan would return. The spot is marked by a column, crowned with a clansman in full battle dress, erected as a tribute by Alexander Macdonald of Glenaladale in 1815.

MICHAEL JENNER

Glenfinnan Monument, Loch Shiel, the Highlands

JOHN NOBLE

Winter in the Cairngorms

Aberdeen Castlegate and Mercat Cross

Loch Duich

Puffin on Shetland

Scottish primrose

The Italian Chapel, Lamb Holm, Orkney

The Knoydart peninsula

To get to the heart of the **Knoydart peninsula**, you have to catch a boat from Mallaig or Glenelg, or else hike for a couple of days across rugged moorland and mountains and sleep rough in old stone bothies (most of which are marked on Ordnance Survey maps). Either way, you'll soon appreciate why many regard this as Britain's most dramatic and unspoilt wilderness area. Flanked by Loch Nevis ("Loch of Heaven") in the south and the fjord-like inlet of Loch Hourn ("Loch of Hell") to the north, Knoydart's nobbly green peaks (three of them Munros) sweep straight out of the sea, shrouded for much of the time in a pall of grey mist. Unsurprisingly, the peninsula tends to attract walkers, lured by the network of well-maintained **trails** that wind east into the wild interior, where Bonnie Prince Charlie is rumoured to have hidden out after Culloden.

At the end of the eighteenth century, around a thousand people eked out a living from this inhospitable terrain through crofting and fishing. Evictions in 1853 began a dramatic decrease in the population which continued to dwindle through the twentieth century as a succession of landowners ran the estate as a hunting and shooting playground, prompting a famous land raid in 1948 by a group of crofters known as the "Seven Men of Knoydart", who staked out and claimed ownership of portions of the estate. Although their bid failed, the memory of their cause was invoked when the crofters of Knoydart finally achieved control over the land they lived on in a community buy-out in 1998. These days the peninsula supports around seventy people, most of whom live in the tiny hamlet of **INVERIE**. Nestled beside a sheltered bay on the south side of the peninsula, it has a pint-sized post office, a shop and mainland Britain's most remote pub, the *Old Forge*.

Practicalities

Bruce Watt Cruises' **boat** chugs into Inverie from Mallaig (Mon, Wed & Fri 10.15am & 2.15pm, also Sat June–Aug 10.30am; ☎01687/462320 or 462233). To arrange for a boat crossing from Arnsdale on Loch Hourn, contact Len Morrison (☎01599/522352) or Mr MacTavish (☎01599/522211); it costs between £8 and £25 depending on passenger numbers.

There are two main **hiking routes** into Knoydart: the trailhead for the first is Kinloch Hourn, a crofting hamlet at the far east end of Loch Hourn which you can get to by road (turn south off the A87 six miles west of Invergarry), from where a well-marked path winds around the coast to Barrisdale and on to Inverie; you can also pick up this trail by taking a boat from Arnsdale, on the north shore of Loch Hourn. The second path into Knoydart starts at the west side of Loch Arkaig, approaching the peninsula via Glen Dessary. These are both long hard slogs over rough, desolate country, so take wet-weather gear, plenty of food, warm clothes and a good sleeping bag, and leave your name and expected time of arrival with someone when you set off.

Most of Knoydart's **accommodation** is concentrated in and around Inverie. *Torrie Shieling* (☎01687/462669, *torrreidh@aol.com*; £15 per person per night), an upmarket independent **hostel** located three-quarters of a mile east of the village on the side of the mountain, is popular with hikers and families, offering top-notch self-catering facilities, comfy wooden beds in four-person rooms, and superb views across the bay. They also have a Land Rover and boat for ferrying guests around the peninsula, and to neighbouring lochs and islands. In Inverie village itself, *Pier House* (☎01687/462347; ②, including dinner ④), a pleasant **B&B**, serves à la carte evening meals to non-residents (three courses for around £16). If you want total isolation and all the creature comforts book into the beautiful *Doune Stone Lodges* (☎01687/462667; ⑤ includes dinner and packed lunch), on the remote north side of the peninsula. Rebuilt from ruined crofts, this place has pine-fitted en-suite double rooms right on the shore, near the ruins of an ancient Pictish fort. They'll pick you up by boat from Mallaig if you book ahead. Most visitors **eat** at *Pier House* while in Knoydart; alternatively try the *Old Forge*'s generous bar meals, served indoors beside an open fire. You can hire **mountain bikes** from *Pier House*; they've organized various mountain bike trails in the area, and offer mountain walks for groups of four or more

The Glenelg peninsula

Further north, the **Glenelg peninsula**, jutting out into the Sound of Sleat, is the isolated and little-known crofting area featured in Gavin Maxwell's otter novel, **Ring of Bright Water**. Maxwell disguised the identity of this pristine stretch of coast by calling it "Camusfearnà", and it has remained a tranquil backwater in spite of the traffic that trickles through during the summer for the Kylerhea ferry to Skye. You can also approach the peninsula from the east by turning off the fast A87 at Shiel Bridge on Loch Duich, from where a narrow single-track road climbs a tortuous series of switchbacks to the Mam Ratagan Pass (1115ft), affording spectacular views over the awesome Five Sisters massif. Following the route of an old military highway and drovers' trail, the road, covered each morning by the postbus from Kyle (departs 9.45am), drops down the other side through Glen More, with the magnificent Kintail Ridge visible to the southeast, towards the peninsula's main settlement, **GLENELG**, strewn along a pebbly bay on the Sound of Sleat. A row of little whitewashed houses surrounded by trees, the village is dominated by the rambling, weed-choked ruins of Fort Bernera, an eighteenth-century garrison for English government troops, but now little more than a shell. The *Glenelg Inn* (☎01599/522273; ⑤) has luxurious, cosy rooms overlooking the bay and an excellent à la carte restaurant, which also serves cream teas, cakes and quality coffee during the day.

The six-car **Glenelg–Kylerhea ferry** (April–Oct frequent; 5min; for more details call ☎01599/511302) shuttles across the Sound of Sleat from a jetty northwest of the village. In former times, this choppy channel used to be an important drovers' crossing: 8000 cattle each year were herded head to tail across from Skye to the mainland.

One and a half miles south of Glenelg village, a left turn up Glen Beag leads to the **Glenelg Brochs**, some of the best-preserved Iron Age monuments in the country. Standing in a sheltered stream valley, the circular towers – Dun Telve and Dun Troddan – are thought to have been erected around 2000 years ago to protect the surrounding settlements from raiders. About a third of each main structure remains, with the curving drystone walls and internal passages still impressively intact.

A narrow backroad snakes its way southwest beyond Glenelg village through a scattering of old crofting hamlets and timber forests. The views across the Sound of Sleat to Knoydart grow more spectacular at each bend, reaching a high point at a windy pass that takes in a vast sweep of sea, loch and islands. Below the road at **Sandaig** is where Gavin Maxwell and his otters lived in the 1950s: the site of his house is now marked by a cairn. Swinging east, the road winds down to the waterside again, following the north shore of Loch Hourn as far as **ARNISDALE**, departure point for the boat to Knoydart (see p.514). Arnisdale is made up of the two hamlets of **CAMUSBANE** and **CORRAN**, the former consisting of a single row of old cottages ranged behind a long pebble beach, with a massive scree slope behind, while the latter, a mile along the road, is a minuscule whitewashed fishing hamlet at the water's edge. Aside from the arrival of electricity and a red telephone box, the only major addition to this gorgeous hamlet in the last hundred years has been Mrs Nash's homely **B&B** and tea hut (☎01599/522336; ③), where you can enjoy hot drinks and home-baked cake in a "shell garden", with breathtaking views on all sides. You can get to Arnisdale on the **postbus** from Kyle of Lochalsh (daily 9.45am; 3hr 40min; the return bus leaves Arnisdale at 7.10am), or use the Diversions Glenelg service between Kyle, Ratagan Youth Hostel and Glenelg post office (Mon, Wed & Fri 11.20am; 1hr 5min; ☎01599/522233) which will also go on to Arnisdale and Corran, or meet the Inverness or Glasgow buses at Kyle, by request.

Loch Duich

Skirted on its northern shore by the A87, **Loch Duich**, the boot-shaped inlet that forms the northern shoreline of the Glenelg peninsula, features prominently on the tourist trail, with buses from all over Europe thundering down the sixteen miles from **SHIEL BRIDGE** to Kyle of Lochalsh on their way to Skye. The most dramatic approach to the loch, however, is from the east through Glen Shiel, where the mountains known as the Five Sisters of Kintail surge up to heights of 3000ft – a familiar sight from countless tourist brochures, but an impressive one nonetheless. With steep-sided hills hemming in both sides of the loch, it's sometimes hard to remember that this is, in fact, the sea. There's a congenial **SYHA hostel** just outside Shiel Bridge at **RATAGAN** (☎01599/511243 or central reservations ☎0541/553255; Feb–Dec), popular with walkers newly arrived off the Glen Affric trek from Cannich (see p.497).

Eilean Donan Castle

After Edinburgh's hilltop fortress, **Eilean Donan Castle** (April–Oct daily 10am–5.30pm; £3.75), ten miles north of Shiel Bridge on the A87, has to be Scotland's most photographed monument. Presiding over the once strategically important confluence of lochs Alsh, Long and Duich, the forbidding crenellated tower rises from the water's edge, joined to the shore by a narrow stone bridge and with sheer mountains as a backdrop.

The original castle was established in 1230 by Alexander II to protect the area from the Vikings. Later, during a Jacobite uprising in 1719, it was occupied by troops dispatched by the King of Spain to help the "**Old Pretender**", James Stuart. However, when King George heard of their whereabouts, he sent frigates to weed the Spaniards out, and the castle was blown up with their stocks of gunpowder. Thereafter, it lay in ruins until John Macrae-Gilstrap had it rebuilt between 1912 and 1932. Eilean Donan has also been the setting of several major **movies**, including *Highlander*, starring Christopher Lambert, and a more recent James Bond adventure (numerous film stills

---

HIKING IN GLEN SHIEL

Ordnance Survey Map No. 33.

The mountains of **Glen Shiel**, sweeping southeast from Loch Duich, offer some of the best hiking routes in Scotland. Rising dramatically from sea level to over 3000ft in less than a couple of miles, they are also exposed to the worst of the west coast's notoriously fickle weather. Don't underestimate either of these two routes. Tracing the paths on a map, they can appear short and easy to follow; however, unwary walkers die here every year, often because they failed to allow enough time to get off the mountain by nightfall, or because of a sudden change in the weather. Neither of the routes outlined below should be attempted by inexperienced walkers, nor without a map, a compass and a detailed trekking guide – the SMC's *Hill Walks in Northwest Scotland* is recommended. Also make sure to follow the usual safety precautions outlined on p.473.

Taking in a bumper crop of Munros, the **Five Sisters traverse** is deservedly the most popular trek in the area. Allow a full day to complete the whole route, which begins at the first fire break on the left-hand side as you head southeast down the glen on the A87. Strike straight up from here and follow the ridge north along to Scurr na Moraich (2874ft), dropping down the other side to Morvich on the valley floor.

The distinctive chain of mountains across the glen from the Five Sisters is the **Kintail Ridge**, crossed by another famous hiking route that begins at the *Cluanie Inn* on the A87. From here, follow the well-worn path south around the base of the mountain until it meets up with a stalkers' trail, which winds steeply up Creag a' Mhaim (3108ft) and then west along the ridgeway, with breathtaking views south across Knoydart and the Hebridean Sea.

are sold at the ticket office). Three floors, including the banqueting hall, the bedrooms and the troops' quarters are open to the public, with various Jacobite and clan relics also on display, though the large numbers of people passing through make it hard to appreciate them.

There are several **places to stay** less than a mile away in the hamlet of **DORNIE**, including the *Silver Fir Bunkhouse* (☎01599/555264), little more than a simple hut with two bunkbeds and a woodburning stove, but friendly and characterful. Otherwise, the *Dornie Hotel*, Francis Street (☎01599/555205; ④), boasts comfortable rooms, while the *Loch Duich Hotel* (☎01599/555213; ③), has splendid doubles overlooking the loch and a small restaurant serving upmarket bar snacks and evening meals. Another good place for a bar meal is the popular *Clachan*, just along from the *Dornie Hotel*.

Kyle of Lochalsh to Scoraig peninsula

KYLE OF LOCHALSH, seven miles northeast of Eilean Donan Castle, is a busy town, a transit point on the route to Skye and an important train terminal. Straggling down the hill towards the pier and train station, it's not particularly attractive – concrete buildings, rail junk and myriad signs of the fishing industry abound – and is ideally somewhere to pass through rather than linger in. Since the **Skye road bridge** was opened in 1995, traffic has little reason to stop in town before rumbling over the channel a mile to the north, leaving its shopkeepers bereft of the passing trade they used to enjoy. The new bridge, built with private sector money, has also sparked controversy over its high tolls (£5.70 for cars), with local protesters doing battle in Dingwall Sheriff Court and Edinburgh's Court of Session.

Practicalities

Buses run to the harbour in Kyle of Lochalsh from Glasgow via Fort William and Invergarry (3 daily; 5hr 30min–6hr 15min), and from Inverness via Invermoriston (4 daily; 2hr); there's also a summer service from Edinburgh (1 daily; 7hr 15min). These routes can become very crowded, so it's wise to book in advance (☎0990/505050). All these services continue at least as far as Portree, on Skye, and a shuttle service runs across the bridge to Kyleakin every thirty minutes or so. Three or four **trains** run daily, with one or two on summer Sundays, from Inverness (2hr 30min). Curving north through Achnasheen and Glen Carron, the train line is a rail enthusiast's dream, even if scenically it doesn't quite match the West Highland line to Mallaig.

The **tourist office** (April, May & Sept–Oct Mon–Sat 9am–5pm; June & Aug Mon–Sat 9am–7pm, Sun 10am–4pm; ☎01599/534276), on top of the small hill near the old ferry jetty, will book accommodation for you, which is useful as there are surprisingly few places to stay, particularly in high summer. If you're feeling flush, splash out at the *Lochalsh Hotel* (☎01599/534202; ⑤), a wonderfully located place looking out at Skye, with fabulous seafood and an air of dated luxury. For **B&B**, try Mrs Henderson at *Glenview* (☎01599/534119; ①), five minutes' walk from the train station, or *Crowlin View* (☎01599/534286; ①), a traditional house with views to Skye, one and a half miles north of Kyle on the Plockton road. There's a simple but neat and clean backpackers in town, *Cúchulainn's* (☎01599/534492), above a pub across the main street from the tourist information. Between Kyle and Plockton, the *Old Schoolhouse* at Erbusaig (☎01599/534369; ②) is a good-quality restaurant with inexpensive and comfortable rooms. The *Seagreen Restaurant and Bookshop* (☎01599/534388), also on the Plockton road on the edge of Kyle of Lochalsh, has excellent fresh seafood and vegetarian meals in a pleasant, unfussy setting, while the *Seafood Restaurant* at the train station is also recommended, if a little pricier.

Plockton

A fifteen-minute train ride north of Kyle at the seaward end of islet-studded Loch Carron lies unbelievably picturesque **PLOCKTON**: a chocolate-box row of neatly painted cottages ranged around the curve of a tiny harbour and backed by a craggy landscape of heather and pine. Originally known as Am Ploc, the settlement was a crofting hamlet until the end of the eighteenth century, when a local laird transformed it into a prosperous fishery, renaming it "Plocktown". Its fifteen minutes of fame came in the mid-1990s, when the BBC chose the village as the setting for three series of the television drama *Hamish Macbeth*. Though the resulting spin-off has quietened down a little, in high season it's still packed full of tourists, yachtsmen and second-home owners. The unique brilliance of Plockton's light has also made it something of an artists' hangout, and during the summer the waterfront, with its row of shaggy palm trees, even shaggier Highland cattle, flower gardens and pleasure boats, is invariably punctuated by painters dabbing at their easels.

If you want **to stay**, the friendly, cosy *Haven Hotel*, on Innes Street (☎01599/544223; ⑤), is renowned for its excellent food, while the *Plockton Inn*, also on Innes Street (☎01599/544222; ③), makes an informal and comfortable alternative. The *Plockton Hotel*, Harbour Street (☎01599/544274; ④), overlooking the harbour with some rooms in a nearby cottage, has a friendly bar and serves good seafood. Of the fifteen or so **B&Bs**, *The Shieling* (☎01599/544282; ②) has a great location on a tiny headland at the top of the harbour, the nearby *Heron's Flight* (☎01599/544220; ②) has uninterrupted views across the loch from its upstairs bedrooms, while *The Manse* on Innes Street (☎01599/544442; ②) features beautifully furnished rooms and serves generous breakfasts. There's also the attractive new *Station Bunkhouse* (☎01599/544235), built in the shape of a signal box next to the railway station, which has four- and six-person dorms and a cosy open-plan kitchen and living area. An interesting **self-catering** option is to stay at the *Craig Rare Breeds Farm*, midway between Plockton and Stromeferry, where you can rub shoulders with ancient breeds of Scottish farm animals, llamas and peacocks; ask for one of the cottages on the beach (sleeping two, £250 per week; other sleeping six, £380 per week; ☎01599/544205).

You should have little difficulty finding somewhere good **to eat** in Plockton: both the *Haven* and the *Plockton Inn* have excellent seafood restaurants, while *Off the Rails*, in the train station, serves good-value, imaginative snacks by day and dinner. *The Buttery*, part of Plockton Stores on the seafront, is also open all day for snacks and inexpensive meals. For **fishing** or **seal-spotting** boat trips from Plockton, try Leisure Marine (☎01599/544306) or Sea Trek Marine (☎01599/544356).

The Applecross peninsula

The most dramatic approach to the **Applecross peninsula** (the English-sounding name is actually a corruption of the Gaelic *Apor Crosan*, meaning "estuary") is from the south, along the infamous **Bealach na Ba** (literally "Pass of the Cattle"). Crossing the forbidding hills behind Kishorn and rising to 2053ft, with a gradient and switchback bends worthy of the Alps, this route, the highest road in Scotland and a popular cycling piste, is hair-raising in places, but the panoramic views across the Minch to Raasay and Skye more than compensate. The other way in is from the north: a beautiful coast road that meanders slowly from Shieldaig on Loch Torridon, with tantalizing glimpses of the Cuillins to the south.

The sheltered, fertile coast around **APPLECROSS** village, where the Irish missionary monk Maelrhuba founded a monastery in 673 AD, comes as a surprise after the bleakness of the moorland approach. It's an idyllic place: you can wander along lanes banked with wild iris and orchids, and explore beaches and rock pools on the shore.

It's also quite an adventure to get here by **public transport**. The nearest railhead is seventeen miles northeast at Strathcarron Station, near Achnasheen, which you have to reach by 9.50am to catch the postbus to Shieldaig, on Loch Torridon. From here, a second postie leaves for Applecross at 11.30am (90min). No buses of any kind run over the Bealach na Ba. The old *Applecross Inn* (☎01520/744262; ②), right beside the sea, is the focal point of the community, with rooms upstairs and a lively bar serving snacks and tasty platefuls of local seafood. A couple of friendly **B&Bs** lie south of here towards Toscaig, with its pier and inquisitive seals: try Mrs Thompson (☎01520/744260; ①) at *Camusteel*, or Mrs Dickens (☎01520/744206; ①) at *Camusterrach*. **Camping** (☎01520/744268) is provided at the *Flowertunnel*, as you come into the village from the pass. There are a couple of options if you want to explore the area: Applecross Peninsula Visitor Services (☎01520/744262) offer half- or full-day Landrover or walking trips seeking out local history, wildlife and geology, while Applecross Mountain & Sea (☎01520/744393) have more rugged mountain expeditions and kayaking around the coast.

Loch Torridon

Loch Torridon marks the northern boundary of the Applecross peninsula, its awe-inspiring setting backed by the appealingly rugged mountains of **Liathach** and **Beinn Eighe**, tipped by streaks of white quartzite. The greater part of this area is composed of the reddish 750-million-year-old Torridonian sandstone, and some 15,000 acres of the massif are under the protection of the National Trust for Scotland. They run a **Countryside Centre** (May–Sept Mon–Sat 10am–5pm, Sun 2–5pm) at Torridon village at the east end of the

---

WALKING AROUND TORRIDON

Ordnance Survey Outdoor Leisure map No. 8.

There are difficult and unexpected conditions on virtually all hiking routes around Torridon, and the weather can change very rapidly. If you're relatively inexperienced but want to do the magnificent ridge walk along the **Liathach** (pronounced "*Lee*-a-gach", or "*Lee*-ach") massif, or the strenuous traverse of **Beinn Eighe** (pronounced "Ben *Ay*"), join a National Trust Ranger Service guided hike (details from the Torridon Countryside Centre on ☎01445/791221).

For those confident to go it alone (using the above map), one of many possible routes takes you behind Liathach and down the pass, Coire Dubh, to the main road in Glen Torridon. This is a great, straightforward walk if you're properly equipped (see p.473), covering thirteen miles and taking in superb landscapes. Allow yourself the whole day. Start at the stone bridge on the Diabaig road along the north side of Loch Torridon. Follow the Abhainn Coire Mhic Nobuil burn up to the fork at the wooden bridge and take the track east to the pass (a rather indistinct watershed) between Liathach and Beinn Eighe. The path becomes a little lost in the boggy area studded with lochans at the top of the pass, but the route is clear and, once over the watershed, the path is easy to follow. At this point you can, weather permitting, make the rewarding diversion up to the Coire Mhic Fhearchair, widely regarded as the most spectacular corrie in Scotland; otherwise continue down the Coire Dubh stream, ford the burn and follow its west bank down to the Torridon road, from where it's about four miles back to Loch Torridon.

A rewarding walk even in rough weather is the seven-mile hike up the coast from **Lower Diabaig**, ten miles northwest of Torridon village, to **Redpoint**. On a clear day, the views across to Raasay and Applecross from this gentle undulating path are superlative, but you'll have to return along the same trail, or else make your way back via Loch Maree on the A832. If you're staying in Shieldaig, the track that winds up the peninsula running north from the village makes a pleasant ninety-minute round walk.

loch, where you can call in and learn a bit more about the local geology, flora and fauna. The trust also look after **Shieldaig Island**, which lies off the pretty village of Shieldaig on the southern shore of Loch Torridon, where a heronry has been established among the tall Scots pines which cover the island; you might also have a chance of spotting a kestrel or an otter. There's an attractive small hotel by the shore in the village, *Tigh-an-Eilean* (☎01520/755251; ⑥), and also a simple campsite a little way up the hill.

The road which runs along the northern shore of the loch from **TORRIDON** village is scenic and dramatic, winding first along the shore then climbing and twisting past lochans, cliffs and gorges to the green wooded slopes of **DIABAIG**. There's a modern **youth hostel** at Torridon (☎01445/791284 or central reservations ☎0541/553255; Feb–Oct, Christmas & New Year), and one of the area's top hotels, the rambling Victorian *Loch Torridon Hotel* (☎01445/791242; ⑧), set amid well-tended loch-side grounds. Next door, *Ben Damph Lodge* (☎01445/791242, *ben@ochtorridnhotel.com*; ③) is a modern conversion of an old farmstead with neat if characterless rooms and a large climber's bar. Also in Diabaig, Miss Ross (☎01445/790240; ①) has comfortable accommodation overlooking the rocky bay, and there's a good B&B, *Tigh Fada* (☎01520/755248; ①), at **DOIREANOR**, on the southwest side of Loch Shieldaig.

Loch Maree

About eight miles north of Loch Torridon, **Loch Maree**, dotted with Caledonian pine-covered islands, is one of the west's scenic highlights, best viewed from the road (A832) that drops down to its southeastern tip through Glen Docherty. It's also surrounded by some of Scotland's finest deerstalking country: the remote, privately owned *Letterewe Lodge* on the north shore, accessible only by helicopter or boat, lies at the heart of a famous deer forest. **Queen Victoria** stayed a few days here in 1877 at the wonderfully sited *Loch Maree Hotel* (☎01445/760288, *lochmaree@easynet.co.uk*; ⑤), which is comfortable and less formal than in her day.

At the southeastern end of the loch, at the junction of the A896 from Torridon and the A832 from Achnasheen, on the road from Inverness to Kyle of Lochalsh, is the small settlement of **Kinlochewe**, another good base if you're heading into the hills. There is a bunkhouse as well as B&B at the *Kinlochewe Hotel* (☎01445/760253; bunkhouse ①, B&B ②), but for little extra you're much better off heading a mile along the road towards Torridon to *Cromasaig* B&B (☎01455/760234, *cromasaig@msn.com*; ①), a great place for hill-walkers set in the forest right at the foot of the track up Beinn Eighe. In Kinlochewe itself, MORU outdoor shop at the old petrol station opposite the hotel will furnish you with maps and guidebooks, as well as equipment and sound local advice.

The A832 skirts the southern shore of Loch Maree, passing the **Beinn Eighe Nature Reserve**, the UK's oldest wildlife sanctuary. Parts of the Beinn Eighe reserve are forested with Caledonian pinewood, which once covered the whole of the country, and it is home to pine marten, wildcat, fox, badger, Scottish crossbill, buzzards and golden eagles. There's also a wide range of flora, with the higher rocky slopes producing spectacular natural alpine rock gardens. A mile north of Kinlochewe, the **Beinn Eighe Visitor Centre** (Easter & May–Sept daily 10am–5pm) on the A832, gives details of the area's rare species and sells pamphlets describing two excellent **walks** in the reserve: a woodland trail through loch-side forest, and a more strenuous half-day hike around the base of Beinn Eighe. Both start from the car park a mile north of the visitor centre.

Gairloch

Mostly scattered around the sheltered northeastern shore of the loch of the same name, the crofting township of **GAIRLOCH** thrives during the summer as a low-key holiday resort with several tempting sandy beaches and some excellent coastal walks within easy reach. The **Gairloch Heritage Museum** (April, May & Oct Mon–Sat 11am–4pm; June–Sept Mon–Sat 10am–5pm; for winter times phone ☎01445/712287; £2.50) has eclectic, appealing displays covering geology, archeology, fishing and farming that range from a mock-up of a croft house to an early knitting machine. Probably the most interesting section is the archive – an array of photographs, maps, genealogies, lists of place names and taped recollections, mostly in Gaelic – made by elderly locals.

The area's real attraction, however, is its beautiful **coastline**. To get to one of the most impressive stretches, head around the north side of the bay and follow the single-track B8021 beyond Big Sand (a cleaner and quieter beach than the one in Gairloch) to the tiny crofting hamlet of **Melvaig** (reachable by the 9.05am Gairloch postbus), from where a narrow surfaced track winds out to **Rua Reidh** (pronounced "Roo-a Ree") Point. The converted **lighthouse** here, which looks straight out to Harris in the Outer Hebrides, serves slap-up afternoon teas and home-baked cakes (Easter–Oct Tues, Thurs & Sun noon–5pm). You can also stay in its comfortable and relaxed **bunkhouse**, or **double rooms** (book ahead in high season on ☎01445/771263, *ruareidh@netcomuk.co.uk*; ①), or use it as a base for one of the popular walking or activity holidays organized by the folk who run the bunkhouse. Around the headland from Rua Reidh lies the secluded and beautiful **Camas Mor** beach. For a great half-day walk, follow the marked footpath inland (southeast) from here along the base of a sheer scarp slope, and past a string of lochans, ruined crofts and a remote wood to Midtown on the east side of the peninsula, five miles north of Poolewe on the B8057. However, unless you leave a car at the end of the trail or arrange to be picked up, you'll have to walk or hitch back to Gairloch, as the only transport along this road is an early-morning post van.

A more leisurely way to explore the coast is on a wildlife-spotting cruise: Gairloch Marine Life Centre & Cruises (Easter–Oct ☎01445/712636) at the pier run informative and enjoyable boat trips across the bay in search of dolphins, porpoises, seals and even the odd whale. You can also rent a boat for the day through Gairloch's chandlery shop (☎01445/712458), popular with sea anglers.

Badachro and beyond

Three miles south of Gairloch, a narrow single-track lane (built with the Destitution Funds raised during the nineteenth-century potato famine) winds west from the main A832, past wooded coves and inlets on its way south of the loch to **BADACHRO**, a sleepy former fishing village in a very attractive setting with a wonderful pub, the *Badachro Inn*, right by the water's edge.

Beyond Badachro, the road winds for five more miles along the shore to **Redpoint**, a minuscule hamlet with beautiful beaches of peach-coloured sand and great views to Raasay, Skye and the Western Isles. It also marks the trailhead for the wonderful coast walk to Lower Diabaig, described on p.519. Even if you don't fancy a full-blown hike, follow the path a mile or so to the exquisite beach hidden on the south side of the headland, which you'll probably have all to yourself. Redpoint is served by the Gairloch postbus (see below).

Gairloch practicalities

There's a late afternoon bus (Mon–Sat) from Inverness to **Gairloch**, though the route and arrival time varies. Without your own transport, you'll have to depend upon postbuses to get around once there. Two postbus services (one for each side of the loch) leave from in front of the post office: one at 8.20am for Melvaig, and the other at 10.35am for Redpoint.

There's a good choice of **accommodation** in Gairloch, most of it mid-range; the central **tourist office** (April–May, mid-Sept to Oct Mon–Fri 10am–5pm, Sat 11–4pm; June Mon–Fri 9.30am–5.30pm, Sat 10am–5pm; July to mid-Sept Mon–Sat 9am–6pm, Sun noon–5pm; ☎01445/712130) will help if you have problems finding a vacancy. If you're looking for a **hotel**, try the family-run *Myrtle Bank Hotel* (☎01445/712004; ⑨), which has a good restaurant and is just above the loch. **B&Bs** are scattered throughout the area. In the village, options include the bright and pleasant *Newton Cottage* (☎01445/712007; ③), a little way up Mihol Road, and the friendly *Bains House* (☎01445/712472; ①), on the main street near the bus stop. A few hundred yards north on the Melvaig road, Gaelic-speaking Miss Mackenzie's *Duisary* (☎01445/712252; ①) is a good choice. Continuing towards Melvaig for about five miles, a little past the North Erradale junction, *Little Lodge* (☎01445/771237; ⑥ includes dinner) is outstanding, with immaculately furnished rooms, a log-burning stove, cashmere goats and dramatic sea views, as well as superb food. At Badachro, the recently built *Lochside* (☎01445/741295; ③) is spacious with a great view over the harbour and the Torridons. For **hostel** accommodation, there's a pleasant SYHA place at **Carn Dearg** two miles up the Melvaig road (☎01445/712219 or central reservations ☎0541 553255; mid-May to Sept), and the reasonable if often quiet *Badachro Bunkhouse* (☎01445/741255) overlooking Badachro harbour. **Camping** is possible at Big Sand or at Redpoint.

For **food**, Myrtle Bank's restaurant serves good meals at reasonable prices, while the fact that the chef at the *Scottish Seafood Restaurant* next to the petrol station near the pier is also the harbourmaster means that the fish and shellfish served up will be the pick of the catch. Another seafood option is *The Steading* beside the Heritage Museum. Inexpensive pasta and pricier seafood and meat are on offer at *Gino's* in the *Millcroft Hotel*, though service can be slow. For **snacks**, the *Serendipity Coffee Shop*, up the lane off the square, is a good bet, while the *Old Inn*, opposite the harbour, is a good real-ale **pub**.

Poolewe

It's a fifteen-minute hop by bus over the headland from Gairloch to the trim little village of **POOLEWE** on the sheltered south side of Loch Ewe, at the mouth of the River Ewe as it rushes down from Loch Maree. One of the area's best **walks** begins near here, signposted from the lay-by-cum-viewpoint on the main A832, a mile south of the village. It takes a couple of hours to follow the easy trail across open craggy moorland to the shores of Loch Maree, and thence to the car park at **Slatterdale**, seven miles southeast of Gairloch. If you reach Slatterdale just before 7pm on a Tuesday, Thursday or Friday, you should be able to pick up the Westerbus from Inverness back to Poolewe or Aultbea (confirm times on ☎01445/712255). Also worthwhile is the drive along the small side road running along the west shore of Loch Ewe to **COVE**. Here you'll find an atmospheric cave that was used by the "Wee Frees" as a church into this century; it's quite a perilous scramble up, however, and there's little to see once you're there. The route is also covered by a Poolewe **postbus** (1.55pm).

If you want **to stay** in the area, try the *Poolewe Hotel* (☎01445/781241; ③), on the Cove road; it's old-fashioned but very pleasant and serves straightforward food. From September until April they also have a bunkhouse available for hillwalkers. Rather more upscale is the *Pool House Hotel* (☎01445/781272, *poolhouse@inverewe.co.uk*; ⑨) which belonged to Osgood MacKenzie (see below); it has lovely views out over the loch and serves up tasty, if pricey, bar and restaurant meals. For **B&B** in Poolewe, *The Creagan* (☎01445/781424; ①), up the track on the village side of the campsite, is a welcoming modern house wreathed with honeysuckle. Up the Cove road, four miles north at **Inverasdale**, *Bruach Ard* (☎01445/781214; ②; April–Oct) has mostly en-suite rooms and great views to Assynt. At Cove, Mrs MacDonald (☎01445/781354; ②; April–Oct) offers upscale **B&B** with fine loch views. There's also an excellent **campsite** between the village and Inverewe Gardens (☎01445/781229; April–Oct). *The Bridge Cottage Coffee Shop*, just up the Cove road from the village crossroads, serves good coffee and home-baked cakes (March–Oct Mon–Sat 10.30am–5pm).

Inverewe Gardens

Half a mile across the bay from Poolewe on the A832, **Inverewe Gardens** (daily: Mid-March to Oct 9.30am–9pm; Nov to mid-March 9.30am–5pm; NTS; £5), a verdant oasis of foliage and riotously colourful flower collections, form a vivid contrast to the wild, heathery crags of the adjoining coast. They were the brainchild of **Osgood Mackenzie**, who inherited the surrounding 12,000-acre estate from his stepfather, the laird of Gairloch, in 1862. Taking advantage of the area's famously temperate climate (a consequence of the Gulf Stream, which draws a warm water current from Mexico to within a stone's throw of these shores), Mackenzie collected plants from all over the world for his walled garden, still the nucleus of the complex. Protected from Loch Ewe's corrosive salt breezes by a dense brake of Scots pine, rowan, oak, beech and birch trees, the fragile plants flourished on rich soil, brought here as ballast on Irish ships to overlay the previously infertile beach gravel and sea grass. By the time Mackenzie died in 1922, his garden sprawled over the whole peninsula, surrounded by 100 acres of woodland. Today the NTS strives to develop the place along the lines envisaged by its founder.

Around 180,000 visitors pour through here annually, but they are easily absorbed. Interconnected by a labyrinthine network of twisting paths and walkways, more than a dozen gardens feature exotic plant collections from as far afield as Chile, China, Tasmania and the Himalayas. Strolling around the lotus ponds, palm trees, and borders ablaze with exotic blooms, it's amazing to think you're at the same latitude as Hudson's Bay. Mid-May to mid-June is the best time to see the rhododendrons and azaleas, while the herbaceous garden reaches its peak in July and August, as does the wonderful Victorian vegetable and flower garden beside the sea. Look out, too, for the grand old eucalyptus in the Peace Plot, which is the largest in the northern hemisphere, and the nearby Ghost Tree (Davidia involucrata), representing the earliest evolutionary stages of flowering trees. You'll need at least a couple of hours to do the whole lot justice, and leave time for the **visitor centre** (mid-March to Oct daily 9.30am–5.30pm), which houses an informative display on the history of the garden. Guided walks (April–Oct Mon–Fri) leave from here every weekday at 1.30pm. The **restaurant** at the top of the car park does good snacks and lunches.

Gruinard Bay and the Scoraig peninsula

Three buses each week (Mon, Wed & Sat; eastwards in the morning, westwards in the evening) run the twenty-mile stretch along the A832 from Poolewe past **Aultbea**, a small NATO naval base, to the head of **Little Loch Broom**, surrounded by a salt marsh that is covered with flowers in early summer. From **Laide**, the road skirts the shores of **Gruinard Bay**, offering fabulous views and, at the inner end of the bay, some excellent sandy beaches. During World War II, **Gruinard Island**, in the bay, was used as a testing ground for biological warfare, and for years was ringed by huge signs warning the public not to land. The anthrax spores released during the testing can live in the soil for up to a thousand years, but in 1987, after much protest, the Ministry of Defence had the island decontaminated and it was finally declared "safe" in 1990.

The road heads inland before joining the A835 at **Braemore Junction** (three Inverness–Ullapool buses stop here daily) above the head of **Loch Broom**. Just nearby, and easily accessible from the A835, are the spectacular 164ft **Falls of Measach**, which plunge through the mile-long **Corrieshalloch Gorge**. You can overlook the cascades from a special observation platform, or from the impressive suspension bridge that spans the chasm, whose 197ft vertical sides are draped in a rich array of plant life, with thickets of wych elm, goat willow and bird cherry miraculously thriving on the cliffs. North from the head of Loch Broom to Ullapool is one of the so-called **Destitution Roads**, built to give employment to local people during the nineteenth-century potato famines.

Hotels along here include the excellent *Old Smiddy* (☎01445/731425; ③, with dinner ⑥; April–Oct) on the main road in Laide, on the western shore of Guinard Bay and linked with Braemore and Achnasheen on the Kyle of Lochalsh railway by postbus. Crammed with travel trophies, family memorabilia, books and paintings by local artists (some on sale), the hotel has fine mountain views to the east, and serves outstanding food. Another option is *Cul-na-Mara* (☎01445/731295; ①), up the turning just past the *Sand Hotel*. At the head of Little Loch Broom, the *Dundonnell Hotel* (☎01854/633204, *selbie@dundonnellhotel.co.uk*; ⑤) is smart and comfortable and serves bar meals, while *Sail Mhor Croft* (☎01854/633224, *sailmhor@btinternet.com*) is a small independent hostel in a lovely location on the loch-side a couple of miles before the *Dundonnell Hotel*.

The Scoraig peninsula

The outer part of the rugged **Scoraig peninsula**, dividing Little Loch Broom and Loch Broom, is one of the remotest places on the British mainland, accessible only by boat or on foot. Formerly dotted with crofting townships, it is now deserted apart from tiny **SCORAIG** village, where a mostly self-sufficient community has established itself, complete with windmills, organic vegetable gardens and a thriving primary school. Understandably, Scoraig's inhabitants would rather not be regarded as tourist curiosities, so only venture out here if you're sympathetic to such a community. To reach **Scoraig**, you have three main options: you can drive to Badrallach and walk from there, catch the occasional ferry from Ullapool to the *Altnaharrie Hotel* (see p.526) then walk, or phone the Scoraig **boat** operator (☎01854/633226), who serves the area two days a week. **Accommodation** on the Scoraig peninsula is limited to a small and particularly pleasant **campsite** at Badrallach, on the northeast shore of Little Loch Broom and a good bothy available if you've an airbed or sleeping mat (☎01854/633281).

Ullapool

ULLAPOOL, the northwest's principal centre of population, was founded at the height of the herring boom in 1788 by the **British Fisheries Society**, on a sheltered arm of land jutting into Loch Broom. The grid-plan town is still an important fishing centre, though the ferry link to Stornoway on Lewis (see p.387) means that in high season its personality is practically swamped by visitors. Even so, it's still a hugely appealing place and a good base for exploring the northwest Highlands – especially if you are relying on public transport. Regular **buses** run from here to Inverness, Durness and (from May to early Oct) to the railhead at Lairg. Accommodation is plentiful and Ullapool is an obvious hideaway if the weather is bad, with cosy pubs, a new swimming pool and a lively arts centre, the *Ceilidh Place*.

Arrival and information

Forming the backbone of its grid plan, Ullapool's two main arteries are the loch-side **Shore Street** and, parallel to it, **Argyle Street**, further inland. **Buses** stop at the pier, in the town centre near the ferry dock, from where it's easy to get your bearings. The well-run **tourist office** (April–July & Sept–Nov Mon–Fri 9am–5.30pm, Sat 10am–5pm, Sun noon–5pm; Aug Mon–Sat 9am–6pm, Sun noon–6pm; Oct Mon–Fri 9am–5pm, Sat noon–4pm; Nov & Dec Mon–Fri 11am–4pm; ☎01854/612135), on Argyle Street, offers an accommodation booking service. If you're heading onto the Outer Hebrides, there are two or three daily **ferries** (Mon–Sat; 2hr 30min); for precise timings, contact CalMac on ☎01854/612358.

ULLAPOOL WALKS, HIKES AND CYCLE RIDES

Ordnance Survey Maps nos. 15, 19 & 20.

Ullapool is at the start of several excellent **hiking trails**, ranging from sedate shoreside ambles to long and strenuous ascents of Munros. However, the weather here can change very quickly, so take the necessary precautions (see p.473). More detailed descriptions of the routes outlined below are available from the **youth hostel** on Shore Street (30p), and are recommended; hostellers can also rent the relevant up-to-date OS maps – essential for the hill walks.

An easy half-day ramble begins at the north end of Quay Street: cross the river here and follow its bank left towards the sea until you reach a second river and cross the bridge. A single-track road leads to a hilltop lighthouse from where you gain fine views across the sea to the Summer Isles. Return the same way or via the main road (A835).

For a harder half-day hike, head north along Mill Street on the east edge of town to Broom Court retirement home – trailhead for the Ullapool hill walk (look for the sign next to the electricity substation). A rocky path zigzags steeply up from the roadside to the summit of **Meall Mor**, where there are great views of the area's major peaks. This is also a prime spot for botanists, with a rich array of plants and flowers, including two insect-eating species: sundew and butterwort. The path then drops sharply down the heather-clad north side of Meall Mor into **Glen Achall**, where you turn left onto the surfaced road running past the limestone quarry; the main road back to Ullapool lies a further thirty minutes' walk west. A right turn where the path meets the road will take you up to Loch Achall and the start of an old drovers' trail across the middle of the Highlands to **Croick** (see p.546). A well-maintained bothy at **Knockdamph**, eleven miles further on, marks the midway point of this long-distance hike, which should not be undertaken alone or without proper gear.

If you're reasonably experienced and can use a map and compass, a day-walk well worth tackling is the rock path to **Achininver**, near Achiltiebuie. The route, which winds along one of the region's most beautiful and unspoilt stretches of coastline to a small **youth hostel** (book ahead on ☎01854/622254; mid-May to Sept), is easy to follow in good weather, but gets very boggy and slippery when wet. Sound footwear, a light pack and a route guide are essential.

The warden and assistants at Ullapool hostel can also give advice on more serious mountain hikes in the area. Among the most popular is the walk to **Scoraig** (see p.524), following the old coast route over the pass to Badrallach, on the south side of the peninsula, and then northwest to Scoraig village itself. The only drawback with this rewarding route is that to get back to Ullapool you have to rely on the *Altnaharrie Hotel's* pricey and sporadic ferry boat (May–Sept; to check times, call ☎01854/633230); miss the boat and the only accommodation for miles is the ultra-expensive hotel or the bothy and campsite over at Badrallach (see p.524). If you have a **mountain bike**, the return trip to Scoraig via Badrallach can be completed in a single day.

Alternatively, try the **Rhidorroch** estate track, which turns right off the A835 just past the *Mercury Hotel* (two miles out of Ullapool), and then heads past the limestone quarry mentioned earlier to Loch Achall and beyond. At the East Rhidorroch Lodge, ignore the suspension bridge and strike up the steep hill ahead onto open moorland and secluded **Loch Damph**, where there's a small bothy. A much easier but no less scenic cycle route is the tour of Loch Broom, taking in the hamlets of **Letters** and **Loggie** on the tranquil western shore, which you can get to via a quiet single-track road (off the A832 once you've cycled south and round the loch from Ullapool). At the end of this, a jeep track heads for the vitrified Iron Age fort at **Dun Lagaidh**; you have to return by the same route.

Accommodation

Ullapool, a popular holiday centre in summer, has all kinds of **accommodation**, ranging from one of Scotland's most expensive hotels, the *Altnaharrie*, to innumerable guest houses and B&Bs, plus a well-situated **campsite** (up the hill from the pier and turn left) and an excellent **youth hostel** on Shore Street (☎01854/612254 or central reservations ☎0541 553255; Feb–Dec).

Altnaharrie Hotel (☎01854/633230). A world-famous, select hotel with a very highly regarded restaurant, located across the loch from town – you're collected by launch. ⑨.

Brae Guest House, Shore Street (☎01854/612421). A great guest house in a beautifully maintained traditional building right on the loch-side. ②.

The Ceilidh Place, W Argyle Street (☎01854/612103, *reservations@ceilidh.demon.co.uk*). Tasteful and popular hotel, with the west coast's best bookshop, a relaxing first-floor lounge, a great bar-restaurant, sea views, and a laid-back atmosphere. Also has a good-value bunkhouse (May–Oct), for £15 per person in family rooms. ⑥.

Ferry Boat Inn, Shore Street (☎01854/612366). Traditional inn right on the waterfront with a friendly atmosphere and reasonable food. ③.

Point Cottage, 22 West Shore St (☎01854/612494). Very well-equipped rooms and good showers, at the quieter end of the seafront. Guests can borrow OS maps already marked up with walking routes. ②.

The Shieling, Garve Road (☎01854/612947). Outstandingly comfortable guest house overlooking the loch with immaculate, spacious rooms (rooms 4 and 5 have the best views), superb breakfasts (try their home-made venison and leek sausages) and a sauna. ②.

Tigh Na Mara, Ardinrean (☎01854/655282). Twelve miles from Ullapool on the opposite (west) shore of Loch Broom, but worth the trip. One of Scotland's most renowned vegetarian places, offering gourmet veggie/vegan breakfasts and simple rooms in a romantic setting. The price includes dinner. ⑥.

Waterside House, 6 West Shore Street (☎01854/612140). Very appealing rooms in an outstandingly pleasant, friendly B&B on the seafront. ②.

West House, West Argyle St (☎01854/613126, *r.lindsay@btinternet.com*). Busy independent backpackers' hostel with four- to six-bed dorms and more civilized B&B on offer in a nearby house. Minibus day-tours organized and bike hire available.

The Town

Day or night, most of the action in Ullapool centres on the **harbour**, which has an authentic and salty air, especially when the boats are in. By day, attention focuses on the comings and goings of the ferry, fishing boats and smaller craft, while in the evening, yachts swing on the current, the shops stay open late, and customers from the *Ferry Boat Inn* line the sea wall. During summer, booths advertise trips to the **Summer Isles** – a cluster of uninhabited islets two to three miles offshore – to view seabird colonies, dolphins and porpoises, but if you're lucky you'll spot marine life from the waterfront. Otters occasionally nose around the rocks near the *Ferry Boat Inn*, and seals swim past begging scraps from the boats moored in the middle of the loch.

The only conventional "sight" in town is the **museum**, West Argyle Street (April–Oct Mon–Sat 9.30am–5.30pm plus mid-July to mid-Aug Mon–Sat till 8pm; Nov–March, Wed & Sat 11am–3pm; £2), in the old parish church, with displays on crofting, fishing, local religion and emigration. During the Clearances, Ullapool was one of the ports through which evicted crofters left to start new lives in Canada, Australia and New Zealand.

Eating and drinking

Ullapool has a wide array of places to eat and drink, ranging from the cheap-and-cheerful chippies on the harbour front to one of Scotland's most expensive gourmet restaurants, at the *Altnaharrie Hotel*. The two best **pubs** are the *Arch Inn*, home of the Ullapool football team, and the *Ferry Boat Inn* (known as the "FBI"), where you can enjoy a pint of real ale at the loch-side – midges permitting. The slightly less characterful *Seaforth* by the pier is the place to catch middle-of-the-road live **music**, while live folk music is a regular occurrence at *The Ceilidh Place* or on Thursday nights at the *FBI*.

Altnaharrie Hotel (☎01854/633230). World-class cuisine by the renowned chef Gun Eriksen; superb, but steep at around £75 for dinner, and it's hard to get a table if you're a non-resident.

The Ceilidh Place, W Argyle Street (☎01854/612286). Filling snacks are served at the excellent bar, while full meals, including imaginative seafood and vegetarian dishes, are on offer in the spacious restaurant, accompanied by occasional live music. The good coffee shop does great cakes and home-made ice cream.

John MacLean's, Shore Street. A wholefood shop/deli where you can stock up on picnic-style fare, as well as a selection of freshly baked cakes.

Morefield, Morefield Lane off North Road (☎01854/612161). Huge portions of succulent seafood, easily Ullapool's best-value, are served in the restaurant, while the bar has good fish at lower prices. It's not so great for vegetarians, and is hard to find, being improbably hidden in a modern housing estate beyond the bridge on the north side of the town.

The Scottish Larder, Ladysmith Street (☎01854/612185). Reasonably priced and filling food from local sources, specializing in interesting pies, open for lunch and dinner.

North of Ullapool

North of Ullapool, the landscape changes to consist not of mountain ranges but of extraordinary peaks rising individually from the moorland. As you head further north, the peaks become more widely spaced and settlements smaller and fewer, linked by twisting single-track roads and shore-side footpaths that make excellent hiking trails. You can easily sidestep what little tourist traffic there is by heading down the peaceful backroads, which, after twisting through idyllic crofts, invariably end up at a deserted beach or windswept headland with superb views west to the Outer Hebrides.

Ten miles north of Ullapool, a single-track road winds west off the A835 to squeeze between the northern shore of Loch Lurgainn and the lower slopes of **Cul Beag** (2523ft) and craggy Stac Pollaidh (2012ft) to reach the **Coigach** peninsula. To the southeast, the awesome bulk of **Ben More Coigach** (2439ft) presides over the district, which contains some spectacular coastal scenery including a string of sandy beaches and the Summer Isles, scattered just offshore.

Coigach's main settlement is **ACHILTIBUIE**, an old crofting village stretched above a series of white-sand coves and rocks tapering into the Atlantic, from where a fleet of small fishing boats carries sheep, and tourists, to the island pastures during the summer. The village also attracts gardening enthusiasts, thanks to the space-station-like structure overlooking its main beach. Dubbed "The Garden of the Future", the **Hydroponicum** (Easter–Sept 10am–5pm; £4; tours hourly on the hour) is a kind of glorified greenhouse that concentrates the sun's heat, while protecting the plants inside from winter cold and acidic soil. The results – exotic plants, fruit, fragrant flowers and herbs thriving in four separate "climate rooms" – speak for themselves; you can also taste its famous strawberries and other produce in the subtropical setting of the *Lily Pond Café*, which serves meals, desserts and snacks. Also worth a visit is the **Achiltibuie Smokehouse** (April–Sept Mon–Sat 9.30am–5pm; free), three miles north of the Hydroponicum at **Altandhu**, where you can see meat, fish and game being cured in the traditional way and can buy some afterwards.

The wonderful *Summer Isles Hotel* (☎01854/622282; ⑨; April–Oct), just up the road from the Achiltibuie school, enjoys a near-perfect setting above a sandy beach with views over the islands, and is virtually self-sufficient. The hotel buys in Hydroponicum fruit and vegetables, but has its own dairy, poultry, and even runs a small smokehouse, so the food in its excellent restaurant (open to non-residents) is about as fresh as it comes. A set dinner costs about £35, while superb bar snacks and lunches feature crab, langoustines and smoked mackerel starting from £5. Of Achiltibuie's several **B&Bs**, *Dornie House* (☎01854/622271; ①) in the north of the settlement is welcoming and has particularly fine views. There's also a beautifully situated twenty-bed SYHA **hostel**

(☎01854/622254 or central reservations ☎0541 553255; mid-May to Sept), three miles down the coast at Achininver, which is handy for Coigach's many mountain hikes.

Lochinver

The narrow road north from Coigach through Inverkirkaig is unremittingly spectacular, threading its way through a tumultuous landscape of secret valleys, moorland and bare rock, past the startling shapes of **Cul Beag** (2523ft), **Cul Mor** (2785ft) and the distinctive sugar-loaf **Suilven** (2398ft). A scattering of pebble-dashed bungalows around a sheltered bay heralds your arrival at **LOCHINVER**, the last sizeable village before Thurso, also with the last cash machine. It's a workaday place, with a huge fish market, from where large trucks head off to the rest of Britain. There's a better-than-average **tourist office** (April–Oct Mon–Sat 10am–5pm, July & Aug also Sun 11am–4pm; ☎01571/844330), whose **visitor centre** gives an interesting rundown on the area's geology, wildlife and history; a countryside ranger is available to advise on walks. The area is popular with **fishing** enthusiasts, and fly rods and other equipment are available for rent from the newsagent on the main road. You can get hold of permits at the tourist office, while for boat trips for sea fishing contact Badnaban Cruises on ☎01571/844358. **Mountain bikes** are available in the village from Assynt Adventures, on the main road near the police station.

Lochinver has a range of good **B&Bs**: on the north side of the harbour, *Ardglas* (☎01571/844257; ③) has superb views, though no en-suite rooms, while nearby *Davar* (☎01571/844501; ②) is better-equipped. More central, just above the tourist office, the comfortable *Polcraig* (☎01571/844429; ②) can arrange fishing. If you're looking for **hotel** accommodation, a pleasant and relaxing option is the *Albannach* (☎01571/844407; ⑦ includes dinner; March–Dec) at Baddidarroch, an attractive nineteenth-century building set in a walled garden, and renowned for its excellent seafood, caught locally and served in a lovely wood-panelled dining room. Lochinver's most imaginative **food** can be found in the *Larder Riverside Bistro* on the main street: it has local seafood, venison and several vegetarian choices at reasonable prices. Decent bar meals are available at the *Caberfeidh* next door, which is also the most convivial place to head for a drink, while the *Seamens' Mission*, down at the harbour, is a good option for filling meals (some vegetarian) if you're on a tight budget.

Inverkirkaig Falls

Approaching Lochinver from the south, the road bends sharply through a wooded valley where a signpost for **Inverkirkaig Falls** marks the start of a long but gentle **walk** to the base of **Suilven** – the most distinctive mountain in Scotland, its huge sandstone dome rising above the heather boglands of Assynt. Serious hikers use the path to approach the mighty peak, but you can follow it for an easy three-to-four-hour ramble, taking in a waterfall and a tour of a secluded loch. If you're travelling by vehicle, use the car park below the excellent Achins Bookshop near the trailhead, which is well stocked with titles on the Highlands, and has a café serving cream teas, cakes and good coffee.

East of Lochinver

The area to the **east of Lochinver**, traversed by the A837 and bounded by the gnarled peaks of the Ben More Assynt massif, is a wilderness of mountains, moorland, mist and scree. Dotted with lochs and lochans, it's also an angler's paradise, home to the only non-migratory fish in northern Scotland, the brown trout, and numerous other sought-after species, including the Atlantic salmon, sea trout, Arctic char and a massive prize strain of cannibal ferox. **Fishing** permits for the rivers in this area are like gold dust during the summer, snapped up months in advance by exclusive hunting-lodge hotels, but you can sometimes obtain last-minute cancellations (try the *Inver Lodge* on ☎01571/844496); permits for fishing lochs are easier to get hold of.

Although most of the land here is privately owned, nearly 27,000 acres are managed as the **Inverpolly National Nature Reserve**, whose visitor centre (April–Oct daily 10am–5pm; ☎01854/666254) at Knockan Cliff, twelve miles north of Ullapool on the A835, gives a thorough overview of the diverse flora and wildlife in the surrounding habitats. The theory of thrust faults was developed here in 1859 by eminent geologist James Nicol, and an interpretive **Geological Trail** shows you how to detect the movement of rock plates in the nearby cliffs. A few miles further on in the village of Knockan, the *Birchbank Holiday Lodge* (☎01854/666215; ②) is an excellent base if you're planning to hike or fish in the area; it's on a working sheep farm run by one of the area's top outdoor guides, who has a wealth of information on the best routes and places to explore.

Further north, on the rocky promontory synt, stand the jagged remnants of **Ardveck Castle** (free access), a MacLeod stronghold from 1597 that fell to the Seaforth Mackenzies after a siege in 1691. Previously, the Marquis of Montrose had been imprisoned here after his defeat at Carbisdale in 1650. The rebel duke, whom the local laird had betrayed to the government for £20,000 and 400 bowls of sour meal, was eventually led away to be executed in Edinburgh, lashed back to front on his horse.

The *Inchnadamph Hotel* (☎01571/822202; ④), on Loch Assynt, is a wonderfully traditional Highland retreat; inside, the walls are covered with the stuffed catches of its past guests. The hotel offers fine old-fashioned cooking, usually with good vegetarian options, in its moderately priced restaurant and bar. It's popular with anglers, who get free fishing rights to Loch Assynt, as well as several hill lochs backing onto Ben More, haunts of the infamous ferox trout. Just along the road, the Assynt Field Centre at *Inchnadamph Lodge* (☎01571/822218; ①) has basic but comfortable bunk rooms, as well as more spacious B&B accommodation. Through the year, the centre offers a variety of outdoor activity breaks and holidays, ranging from the obvious hill walking to dry-stone dyke building and cookery courses focusing on local products.

North from Lochinver: the coast road

Heading **north from Lochinver**, there are two possible routes: the fast A837, which runs eastwards along the shore of Loch Assynt to join the northbound A894, or the narrow **coastal road** (the B869) that locals dub "The Breakdown Zone" because its ups and downs claim so many victims during summer. Hugging the indented shoreline, this route is the more scenic, offering superb views of the Summer Isles, as well as a number of rewarding side-trips to beaches and dramatic cliffs. **Postbuses** from Lochinver cover the route as far as Ardvar or Drumbeg (Mon–Sat). Unusually, most of the land and lochs around here are owned by local crofters rather than wealthy landlords. Helped by grants and private donations, the **Assynt Crofters' Trust** made history in 1993 when it pulled off the first ever community buyout of estate land in Scotland, and it's now pursuing a number of projects aimed at strengthening the local economy and conserving the environment. The Trust owns the lucrative fishing rights to the area, too, selling permits for £5 per day (£25 per week) through local post offices and the tourist office in Lochinver. An alternative outdoor activity is **pony trekking**, which is available through Clachtoll Trekking Centre (☎01571/855364), at Clachtoll on the road between Achmelvich and Stoer.

Heading north, the first village worthy of a detour is **ACHMELVICH**, a couple of miles along a side road, whose tiny bay cradles the whitest beach and most stunning turquoise water you'll encounter this side of the Seychelles. There's a noisy **campsite** and a basic forty-bed **youth hostel** (☎01571/844480 or central reservations ☎0541/553255; April–Sept) just behind the largest beach. However, for total peace and quiet there are other equally seductive beaches beyond the headlands.

The side road that branches north off the B869 between **Stoer** and **Clashnessie**, both of which have sandy beaches, ends abruptly by the automatic **lighthouse** at **Raffin** – built in 1870 by the Stevenson brothers (one of whom was the author Robert Louis Stevenson's dad) – but you can continue for two miles along a well-worn track to Stoer Point, named after the colossal rock pillar that stands offshore known as "The Old Man of Stoer". Surrounded by sheer cliffs and splashed with guano from the seabird colonies that nest on its 200ft sides, it was climbed for the first time in 1961.

DRUMBEG, nine miles further on, is a major target for trout anglers, lying within reach of countless lochans. Permits to fish them are sold at the post office, but you'll need a detailed map and a compass to find your way in and out of this area without getting hopelessly lost. There's a lot of self-catering accommodation in the area, but few **B&Bs**. A good choice, however, is *Taigh Druimbeag* (☎01571/833209; ③; April–Oct), a comfortable old Edwardian house with period furniture and a large garden; to find it, turn off the main road at the primary school and follow the signs.

Kylesku to Kinlochbervie

KYLESKU, 33 miles north of Ullapool and around six miles east of Drumbeg, is the site of the award-winning road bridge spanning the mouth of lochs Glencoul and Glendhu. It's a pleasant place for a short stay, with plenty of good walks and a congenial hotel by the water's edge above the old ferry slipway. The family-run *Kylesku Hotel* (☎01971/502231; ④; March–Oct) has en-suite rooms, a welcoming bar popular with locals, and an excellent restaurant serving fresh seafood, including lobster, crab, mussels and local salmon (you can watch the fish being landed on the pier). Alternatively, *Newton Lodge* (☎01971/502070; ③, including dinner ⑤) is a modern, friendly and comfortable small hotel a few hundred yards up the road towards Ullapool. Cheaper accommodation is available at *Kylesku Lodges and Backpackers* (☎01971/502003), with twin rooms in a series of reasonable A-frame lodges and, inevitably, a great setting. Statesman Cruises runs entertaining boat trips (March–Oct daily 11am & 2pm; round trip 2hr; £10; ☎01571/844446) from the jetty below the hotel to the 650ft **Eas-Coul-Aulin**, Britain's highest waterfall, at the head of Loch Glencoul; otters, seals, porpoises and minke whales can occasionally be spotted along the way.

It's also possible to reach Eas-Coul-Aulin on foot: a rough trail (3hr) leaves the A894 three miles south of Kylesku, skirting the south shore of **Loch na Gainmhich** (known locally as the "sandy loch") to approach the falls from above. Great care should be taken here as the path above the cliffs can get very slippery when wet; the rest of the route is also difficult to follow, particularly in bad weather, and should only be attempted by experienced, properly equipped and compass-literate hikers. However, there are several less demanding walks around Kylesku if you just fancy a gentle amble: one of the most popular is the half-day low-level route along the north side of Loch Glendhu, beginning at **Kylestrome**, on the opposite side of the bridge from the hotel. Follow the surfaced jeep track east from the trailhead and turn left onto a footpath that leads through the woods. This eventually emerges on to the open mountainside, dropping down to cross a burn from where it then winds to a boarded-up old house called Glendhu, where there's a picturesque pebble beach. Several interesting side-trips and variations to this walk may be undertaken with the help of the detailed *Ordnance Survey Landranger Map No. 15*, but you'll need a compass and wet-weather gear in case of bad weather.

Ten miles north of Kylesku, the widely scattered crofting community of **SCOURIE**, on a bluff above the main road, surrounds a beautiful sandy beach whose safe bathing has made it a popular holiday destination for families; there's plenty to do for walkers and trout anglers, too. Scourie itself has some good accommodation: try the charming *Scourie Lodge* (☎01971/502248; ②; March–Oct), an old shooting retreat with a lovely garden; the welcoming owners also do great evening meals. **UPPER BADCALL** village, three miles south of Scourie and even more remote, has a couple of **B&Bs**, including *Stoer View* (☎01971/502411; ①), whose clean and comfortable rooms look over Eddrachillis Bay to Stoer Point. For a little more luxury, try the nearby old-established *Eddrachillis Hotel* (☎01971/502080; ⑤, with dinner ⑥), which enjoys a spectacular situation on the bay, and serves reasonable bar food. There's also a good **campsite**, the *Scourie Caravan and Camping Park* (☎01971/502060) near the centre of the village.

Handa Island

Visible just offshore to the north of Scourie is **Handa Island**, a huge chunk of red Torridon sandstone surrounded by sheer cliffs and carpeted with machair and purple-tinged moorland. Teeming with seabirds, it's an internationally important wildlife reserve and a real treat for ornithologists, with vast colonies of razorbills and guillemots breeding on its guano-splashed cliffs during summer. From late May to mid-July, large numbers of puffins waddle comically over the turf-covered clifftops where they dig their burrows.

Apart from a solitary warden, Handa is deserted. Until midway through the last century, however, it supported a thriving, if somewhat eccentric, community of crofters. Surviving on a diet of fish, potatoes and seabirds, the islanders, whose ruined cottages still cling to the slopes by the jetty, devised their own system of government, with a "queen" (Handa's oldest widow) and "parliament" (a council of men who met each morning to discuss the day's business). Uprooted by the 1846 potato famine, most of the villagers eventually emigrated to Canada's Cape Breton; today, Handa is private property, administered as a nature sanctuary by the Scottish Wildlife Trust. If you're landing on the island, you're encouraged to make a donation of around £1.50 towards its upkeep.

You'll need about three hours to follow the footpath around the island – an easy and enjoyable walk taking in the north shore's Great Stack rock pillar and some fine views across the Minch: a detailed route guide is featured in the SWT's free leaflet available from the warden's office when you arrive. Weather permitting, boats (☎01971/502347; £7) leave for Handa throughout the day (until around 4pm) from the tiny cove of **TARBET**, three miles northwest of the main road and accessible by postbus from Scourie (Mon–Sat 1 daily; 1.50pm), where there's a small car park and jetty. Alternatively, if you want to see the island and the local coastline, with its attendant sea- and bird-life, from the sea, Laxford Cruises (☎01971/502251) offer two-hour boat trips from **FANAGMORE** (May–Sept Mon–Sat 10am, noon & 2pm; July & Aug also 4pm; £8), a mile further up the coast from Tarbet (reached by the same postbus as above). Camping is not allowed on the island, but the SWT maintains a **bothy** for birdwatchers (reservations must be made on ☎0131/312 7765, or with the warden on the island), while in Tarbet, Rex and Liz Norris (☎01971/502098; ①) run a comfortable little **B&B** overlooking the bay. For food, Tarbet's unexpected *Seafood Restaurant* (Mon–Sat noon–7pm) serves delicious, moderately priced fish and vegetarian dishes, and a good selection of home-made cakes and desserts, in its airy conservatory just above the jetty.

Kinlochbervie and beyond

North of Scourie, the road sweeps inland through the starkest part of the Highlands; rocks piled on rocks, bog and water create an almost alien landscape, and the astonishingly bare, stony coastline looks increasingly inhospitable. After about eight miles, at **Rhiconich**, you can branch off the main road to **KINLOCHBERVIE**, a major fishing port set in a rugged, rocky inlet. Trucks from all over Europe pick up cod and shellfish from the trawlers here, crewed mainly by east coast fishermen. *The Old Schoolhouse Restaurant and Guest House* (☎01971/521383; ③) provides comfortable accommodation and home-cooked meals.

Beyond Kinlochbervie, a single-track road takes you through isolated **Oldshoremore**, a working crofters' village scattered above a stunning white-sand beach, to **BLAIRMORE**, where you can park for the four-mile walk across peaty moorland to deserted **Sandwood Bay**. Few visitors make this half-day detour north, but the beach at the end of the rough track is one of the most beautiful in Scotland. Flanked by rolling dunes and lashed by fierce gales for much of the year, the shell-white sands are said to be haunted by a bearded mariner – one of many sailors to have perished on this notoriously dangerous stretch of coast since the Vikings first navigated it over a millennium ago. Around the turn of the last century, the beach, whose treacherous undercurrents make it unsuitable for swimming, also witnessed Britain's most recent recorded sighting of a mermaid. Plans are afoot to bulldoze a motorable road up here, so enjoy the tranquillity while you can. Cape Wrath, the most northwesterly point in mainland Britain, lies a day's hike north. However, most people approach the headland from Durness on the north coast (see below). If you want **to camp** in the area, try the well-equipped site at Oldshoremore (☎01971/521281), or continue through Blairmore to **Sheigra**, where the road ends, for informal camping behind the beach.

THE NORTH COAST

Though a constant stream of sponsored walkers, caravans and tour groups makes it to **John O' Groats**, surprisingly few visitors travel the whole length of the Highlands' wild **north coast**. Those that do, however, rarely return disappointed. Pounded by one of the world's most ferocious seaways, Scotland's rugged northern shore is backed by barren mountains in the west, and in the east by lochs and open rolling grasslands. Between its far ends, mile upon mile of crumbling cliffs and sheer rocky headlands shelter bays whose perfect white beaches are nearly always deserted, even in the height of summer, though, somewhat incongruously, they're also home to Scotland's best **surfing** waves. This is a great area for **birdwatching**, with huge seabird colonies clustered in clefts and on remote stacks at regular intervals along the coast; **seals** also bob around in the surf offshore, and in winter **whales** put in the odd appearance in the more sheltered estuaries of the northwest.

Getting around this stretch of coast without your own transport can be a slow and frustrating business: **Thurso**, the area's main town and springboard for Orkney, is well connected by bus and train with Inverness, but further west, after the main A836 peters into a single-track road, you have to rely on a convoluted series of postbus connections or, in peak season, a single Highland Country bus (#387).

Durness and around

Scattered around a string of sheltered sandy coves and grassy clifftops, **DURNESS**, the most northwesterly village on the British mainland, straddles the turning point on the main road as it swings east from the inland peat bogs of the interior to the north coast's fertile strip of limestone machair. First settled by the Picts around 400 BC, the area has been farmed ever since, its crofters being among the few not cleared off estate land during the nineteenth century. Today, Durness is the centre of several crofting communities and a good base for a couple of days, with some good walks. Even if you're only passing through, it's worth pausing here to see the **Smoo Cave**, a gaping hole in a sheer limestone cliff, and to visit beautiful **Balnakiel beach**, to the west. In addition, Durness is the jumping-off point for roadless and rugged **Cape Wrath**, the windswept promontory at the Scotland's northwest tip, which has retained an end-of-the-world mystique lost long ago by John O' Groats.

The Smoo Cave

A mile or so east of Durness village lies the 200ft-long **Smoo Cave**, a natural wonder, formed partly by the action of the sea, and partly by the small burn that flows through it. Tucked away at the end of a narrow sheer-sided sea cove, guides will show you the illuminated interior, although the much-hyped rock formations are less memorable than the short rubber-dinghy trip you have to make in the second of three caverns, where the whole experience is enlivened after wet weather by a **waterfall** that crashes through the middle of the cavern. A boat trip leaves from Smoo Cave on a wildlife tour of the coast around Durness, taking in stretches of the shoreline only accessible by sea. The trip (May–Sept daily, times depending on weather and tide – ☎01971/511365 or ☎01971/511284; 90min; £6.50) takes a close look at **seabird colonies**, and sightings of seals, puffins and porpoises are common.

Balnakiel

A narrow road winds northwest of Durness to tiny **BALNAKIEL**, whose name derives from the Gaelic *Baile ne Cille* (Village of the Church). The ruined **chapel** that today overlooks this remote hamlet was built in the seventeenth century, but a church has stood here for at least 1200 years. A skull-and-crossbones stone set in the south wall marks the grave of Donald MacMurchow, a seventeenth-century highwayman and con-tract killer who murdered eighteen people for his clan chief (allegedly by throwing them from the top of the Smoo Cave). The "half-in, half-out" position of his grave was apparently a compromise between his grateful employer and the local clergy, who ini-tially refused to allow such an evil man to be buried on church ground. Balnakiel is also known for its **golf course**, whose ninth and final hole involves a 155-yard drive over the Atlantic; you can rent equipment from the clubhouse. The **Balnakiel Craft Village** (daily 10am–6pm; free), back towards Durness, is worth a visit. Housed in an imagina-tively converted 1950s military base, the campus consists of a dozen or so workshops where you can watch painters, potters, leather workers, candle makers, woodworkers, stone carvers, knitters and weavers in action.

The white-sand beach on the east side of Balnakiel Bay is a stunning sight in any weather, but most spectacular on sunny days when the water turns to brilliant turquoise. For the best views, walk along the path that winds north through the dunes behind it; this eventually leads to **Faraid Head** – from the Gaelic Fear Ard (High Fellow) – where you stand a good chance of spotting puffins from late May until mid-July. The fine views over the mouth of Loch Eriboll and west to Cape Wrath make this round walk (3–4hr) the best in the Durness area.

Cape Wrath

An excellent day-trip from Durness begins three miles southwest of the village at **Keoldale**, where a foot-passenger ferry (June–Aug hourly 9.30am–4.30pm; May & Sept approximately 4 daily; no motorcycles; ☎01971/511376) crosses the Kyle of Durness estuary to link up with a minibus (☎01971/511287; May–Sept) that runs the eleven miles out to **Cape Wrath**. The UK mainland's most northwesterly point, the headland takes its name not from the stormy seas that crash against it for most of the year, but from the Norse word *hvarf*, meaning "turning place" – a throwback to the days when Viking warships used it as a navigation point during raids on the Scottish coast. These days, a lighthouse (another of those built by Robert Louis Stevenson's father) warns ships away from the treacherous rocks. Looking east to Orkney and west to the Outer Hebrides, it stands above the famous **Clo Mor cliffs**, the highest sea cliffs in Britain and a prime breeding site for seabirds. You can walk from here to remote Sandwood

Bay (see p.532), visible to the south, although the route, which cuts inland across lochan-dotted moorland, is hard to follow in places. Hikers generally continue south from Sandwood to the trail end at Blairmore; if you hitch or walk the six miles from here to Kinlochbervie you can, with careful planning, catch a bus back to Durness. Don't attempt this route from south to north, as, if the weather closes in, the Cape Wrath minibus stops running. Note also that much of the land bordering the headland is a military firing range and the area is sometimes closed – check with Durness tourist office before you set off.

Durness practicalities

Public transport in the area is sparse; the key service on the north coast is the Highland Country link (#387) to Thurso (June to mid-Sept Mon–Sat) leaving Thurso at 11.30am and Durness at 3pm. This connects at Durness with the daily Inverness Traction link (June to mid-Sept) from Inverness via Ullapool and Lochinver. Postbuses provide a more complicated year-round alternative; check at the post office, tourist office or youth hostel.

Durness has an enthusiastic **tourist office** (April–Oct Mon–Sat 10am–5pm, July & Aug also Sun 11am–4pm; Oct–March Mon–Fri 10am–1.30pm; ☎01971/511259), in the village centre, which can help with accommodation and arranges ranger-guided walks; its small visitor centre also features excellent interpretive panels detailing the area's history, geology, flora and fauna, with some good insights into the day-to-day life of the community. **Accommodation** is fairly limited in Durness itself, but there are further options along nearby Loch Eriboll (see below). Durness's best offering is the *Cape Wrath Hotel* (☎01971/511212; main hotel ④, annex ②), which has a beautiful setting near the ferry jetty at Keoldale. Popular with walkers and fishermen, its rather austere character is offset by friendly service and a stunning view from the dining room. Of the **B&Bs**, *Puffin Cottage* (☎01971/511208; ①) is small but pleasant, while the friendly **youth hostel** (☎01971/511244 or central reservations ☎0541/553255; mid-March to Sept), beside the Smoo Cave car park, a mile and a half east of the village, also rents out mountain bikes. There's **camping** at *Sango Sands Caravan and Camping Site*, Harbour Road (☎01971/511262), which has the added advantage of a good bar and restaurant. The other good **eating** option is the restaurant at Loch Eriboll's *Port-Na-Con* guest house – you should book in advance.

Loch Eriboll

Ringed by ghost-like limestone mountains, deep and sheltered **Loch Eriboll**, six miles east of Durness, is the north coast's most spectacular sea loch. Servicemen stationed here during World War II to protect passing Russian convoys nicknamed it "Loch 'Orrible", but if you're looking for somewhere wild and unspoilt, you'll find this a perfect spot. Porpoises and otters are a common sight along the rocky shore, and minke whales occasionally swim in from the open sea.

Overlooking its own landing stage at the water's edge, *Port-Na-Con* (☎01971/511367, *shm@capetech.co.uk*; ②; mid-March to Oct), seven miles from Durness on the west side of the loch, is a wonderful **B&B**, popular with anglers and divers (it'll refill air tanks for £2.50). Top-notch food is served in its small restaurant (open all year, including Christmas), with a choice of vegetarian haggis, local kippers, fruit compote and home-made croissants for breakfast, and adventurous three-course evening meals for around £12; the menu always includes a gourmet vegetarian dish. Non-residents are welcome, although you'll need to book. Another good option, half a mile further south, is *Rowan House* (☎01971/511347; ①), a child-friendly place overlooking the loch with a tiny eighteen-hole golf course; fresh local oysters often feature on its menu. A further half a mile south, *Choraidh Croft* (☎01971/511235; ①; Easter–Nov), offers B&B and has a rare-breeds collection (£2), as well as a good café.

Tongue

It's a long slog around Loch Eriboll and east over the top of A Mhùine moor to the pretty crofting township of **TONGUE**. Dominated by the ruins of **Varick Castle**, the village, an eleventh-century Norse stronghold, is strewn over the east shore of the **Kyle of Tongue**, which you can either cross via a new causeway, or by following the longer and more scenic single-track road around its southern side. When the tide recedes, this shallow estuary becomes a mass of golden sand flats, superb on sunny days, with the sharp profiles of **Ben Hope** (3040ft) and **Ben Loyal** (2509ft) looming large to the south.

In 1746, the Kyle of Tongue was the scene of a naval engagement reputed to have sealed the fate of Bonnie Prince Charlie's **Jacobite rebellion**. In response to a plea for help from the prince, the king of France dispatched a sloop and £13,600 in gold coins to Scotland. However, the Jacobite ship *Hazard* was spotted by the English frigate, *Sheerness*, and fled into the Kyle, hoping that the larger enemy vessel would not be able to follow. It did, though, and soon forced the *Hazard* aground. Pounded by English cannon fire, its Jacobite crew slipped ashore under cover of darkness in an attempt to smuggle the treasure to Inverness, but they were followed by scouts of the local Mackay clan, who were not of the Jacobite persuasion. The next morning, a larger platoon of Mackays waylaid the rebels, who, hopelessly outnumbered and outgunned, began throwing the gold into **Lochan Hakel**, southwest of Tongue (most of it was recovered later). The Prince, meanwhile, had sent 1500 of his men north to rescue the treasure, but these too were defeated en route; historians debate whether the missing men might have altered the outcome of the Battle of Culloden three weeks later.

If you want **to stay** in Tongue, try *Rhian Cottage* (☎01847/611257; ②, with dinner ④), a pretty whitewashed house with an attractive garden, about a mile down the road past the post office, while *Cloisters* (☎01847/601286; ②), two miles out of town at Talmire on the west side of the Kyle, has great views out towards the Orkney Islands and is well worth heading out of town for. The *Ben Loyal Hotel* (☎01847/611216; ④) and *Tongue Hotel* (☎01847/611206; ④; March–Oct) are more luxurious, and both do excellent food. There's also a beautifully situated and friendly SYHA **hostel** (☎01847/611301 or central reservations ☎0541/553255; mid-March to Oct), right beside the causeway a mile north of the village centre on the east shore of the Kyle, and two **campsites**: *Kincraig Camping and Caravan Site* (☎01847/611218) just south of Tongue post office, and *Talmine Camping and Caravan Site* (☎01847/601225), just behind a sandy beach at Talmine, five miles north of Tongue on the western side of the Kyle.

Bettyhill to Dounreay

BETTYHILL, a major crofting village, straggles along the side of a narrow tidal estuary, and down the coast to two splendid beaches. Forming an unbroken arc of pure white sand between the Naver and Borgie rivers, **Torrisdale beach** is the more impressive of the pair, ending in a smooth white spit that forms part of the **Invernaver Nature Reserve**. During summer, arctic terns nest here on the river banks, dotted with clumps of rare Scottish primroses, and you stand a good chance of spotting an otter or two. The delightful and loyally maintained **Strathnaver Museum** (April–Oct Mon–Sat 10am–1pm & 2–5pm; £1.90), housed in the old church set apart from the village near the sea, is full of locally donated bits and pieces, and includes panels by local school children telling the story of the Strathnaver Clearances. You can also see some

Pictish stones and a 3800-year-old early Bronze Age beaker found in Strathnaver, the river valley south of the village, whose numerous prehistoric sites are mapped on an excellent pamphlet sold at the entrance desk.

Bettyhill's small **tourist office** (April–May Mon–Sat 1–5pm; June Mon–Sat 11am–5pm; July & July Mon–Sat 10am–5pm; Aug Mon–Sat 10am–6pm, Sun noon–5pm; ☎01641/521342) can book **accommodation** for you. The *Bettyhill Hotel* (☎01641/521230; ③), at the top of the hill, has character, and does good bar food. There are also several good-value B&Bs, including *Shenley* (☎01641/521421; ③; April–Oct), a grand but homely detached house in an elevated spot in the middle of the village, and *Bruachmhor* (☎01641/521265; ③; April–Oct), a small but comfortable croft house, facing south over the village.

As you move east from Bettyhill, the north coast changes dramatically as the hills on the horizon recede to be replaced by fields fringed with flagstone walls. At the hamlet of **MELVICH**, twelve miles from Bettyhill, the A897 cuts south through Strath Halladale, the Flow Country (see below) and the Strath of Kildonan to Helmsdale on the east coast (see p.549). Melvich has some good accommodation, including the excellent *Sheiling Guesthouse* (☎01641/531256; ②; April–Oct) by the main road, whose impressive breakfast menu features locally smoked haddock and fresh herring.

Five miles further east, **Dounreay Nuclear Power Station**, a surreal collection of stark domes and chimney stacks marooned in the middle of nowhere, is still a fairly major local employer, though its three fast-breeder reactors were decommissioned in April 1994 and it now reprocesses spent nuclear fuel rather than generating electricity. A permanent **exhibition** (Easter–Sept daily 10am–5pm; free) in the old aircraft control tower details the processes (and, unsurprisingly, the benefits) of nuclear power, and does at least make an attempt to address issues such as the area's "leukemia cluster", and the high levels of radiation reported over the years on the nearby beaches. Free tours of the site are run from the centre, though you're not allowed out of the bus.

South from Melvich: the Flow Country

From Melvich, you can head forty miles or so south towards Helmsdale (see p.549) on the A897, through the **Flow Country**. This huge expanse of bog land came into the news a few years ago when ecology experts, responding to plans to transform the area into forest, drew attention to the threat to this fragile landscape, described by one contemporary commentator as of "unique and global importance, equivalent to the African Serengeti or Brazil's rainforest". Some forest was planted, but the environmentalists won the day, and the forestry syndicates have had to pull out. There's an excellent RSPB Flow Country **visitor centre** (Easter–Oct daily 9am–6pm; ☎01641/571225), based in the train station at Forsinard, fifteen miles south of Melvich, which is easily accessible from Thurso, Wick and the south by train. Guided walks through the RSPB **nature reserve** leave from the visitor centre (May–Aug Tues & Thurs) and illuminate the importance of the area and its wildlife.

Thurso

Approached from the isolation of the west, **THURSO** feels like a metropolis. In reality, it's a relatively small service centre visited mostly by people passing through to the nearby port of **Scrabster** to catch the ferry to Stromness in Orkney. The town's name derives from the Norse word *Thorsa*, literally "River of the God Thor", and in Viking times this was a major gateway to the mainland. Later, ships set sail from here for the Baltic and Scandinavian ports loaded with meal, beef, hides and fish. Much of the town, however, dates from the 1790s, when Sir John Sinclair built a large new extension to the old fishing port, "according to the most regular plan that could be contrived and in a manner not only ornamental but also positively well adapted for preserving the health and promoting the convenience of the inhabitants". The nearby Dounreay Nuclear Power Station ensured continuing prosperity after World War II, when workers from the plant (dubbed "Atomics" by the locals) settled in Thurso in large numbers. Its gradual rundown over recent years has cast a shadow over the local economy, but investment in new industries such as telecommunications has improved matters.

Traill Street is the main drag, turning into the pedestrianized Rotterdam Street and High Street precinct at its northern end. However, the shops are uninspiring, and you're better off heading to the old part of town near the harbour, to see **Old St Peter's Church**, a substantial ruin with origins in the thirteenth century, but which has been much altered over the years. Alternatively, you could visit the **Thurso Heritage Museum**, High Street (Mon–Sat 10am–1pm, 2–5pm; 50p) whose most intriguing exhibit is the Pictish **Skinnet Stone**, intricately carved with enigmatic symbols and a runic cross.

Practicalities

It's a ten-minute walk from the **train station**, with services to Inverness and Wick, down Princes Street and Sir George Street, to the **tourist office** on Riverside Road (April–Oct Mon–Sat 9am–5pm; July & Aug also Sun 11am–4pm; ☎01847/892371). The bus station, close by, runs regular **buses** to John O' Groats, Wick and Inverness and a summer service to Durness. **Ferries** operate daily from adjoining Scrabster to Orkney, which has less frequent links to Shetland and Aberdeen. You can book ahead through P&O Scottish Ferries, Aberdeen (☎01224/572615) or through any local tourist office. If you fancy a day-trip to Orkney, see "John O' Groats" (p.538). The local bus services aren't much help if you're connecting with the ferry at Scrabster – the walk is just over a mile long, or a **taxi** (☎01847/892868) will set you back £3.

Thurso is well-stocked with **accommodation**, including a decent if tight-fitting hostel, *Sandra's* (☎01847/894575, *sandra's-hostel@carson.softnet.co.uk*), 24 Princes St, with four-bed bunkrooms and drying and self-catering facilities above the lively local café. Inexpensive if tatty dorms and doubles are also available at *Ormlie Lodge* (☎01847/896888), a block of student accommodation on Ormlie Road, close to the station. Of the **B&Bs**, *Murray House*, 1 Campbell St (☎01847/895759; ①), is central, comfortable and friendly, or you could try the welcoming Mrs Oag, 9 Couper St (☎01847/894529; ①), east of the High Street near the town hall, or Mrs Budge (☎01847/893205; ①), 6 Pentland Crescent, next to the beach front. The recently refurbished *Royal Hotel* (☎01847/893191; ④) on Traill Street is the main **hotel** in town and is a reasonable choice. The nearest **campsite** (☎01847/805503) is out towards Scrabster alongside the main road.

Food options include *Le Bistro*, 2 Traill St, with a reasonable-value menu of lunchtime snacks and more ambitious evening meals, and *Upper Deck*, by the harbour at Scrabster, serving large, moderately priced steaks and seafood dishes. There are several **cafés** in the town centre which offer standard, filling snacks, including *Johnston's* on Traill Street and *Sandra's* on Princes Street, while the most enjoyably rowdy **pub** is the *Central*, on Traill Street. After the pub, head to *Skinandi's Nightclub* on Sir Georges Street.

You can **hire bikes** at the Bike and Camping shop on the extension of the High Street, beyond its junction with Couper Street, while a little further along at 57 High St, Harper's fishing shop (☎01847/893179) is the place to hire wetsuits or boards, or get hold of other **surfing** supplies, before you take on the mighty north-coast breaks.

Dunnet Head to Duncansby Head

Despite the plaudits that John O' Groats customarily receives, Britain's northernmost mainland point is in fact **Dunnet Head**. The headland is at the far side of Dunnet Bay, a vast sandy beach backed by huge dunes about six miles east of Thurso. The bay is popular with surfers, and even in the winter you can usually spot intrepid figures far out in the Pentland Firth's breakers. There's a **Ranger Centre** (April–Sept Tues–Fri 2–5pm, Sat & Sun 2–6pm) beside the campsite at the east end of the bay, where you can pick up information on good local history and nature walks, including a short self-guided trail into Dunnet Forest, a failed plantation which has been left to go – literally – to seed, allowing a rich range of plant and animal life to thrive. Nearby is the small village of **DUNNET**, where it's worth stopping in at **Mary-Ann's Cottage** (June–Sept Tues–Sun 2–4.30pm; £1), a farming croft vacated in 1990 by 93-year-old Mary-Ann Calder, whose grandfather had built the cottage, and maintained just as she left it, full of reminders of the three generations who lived and worked there over the last 150 years.

For Dunnet Head, turn off at Dunnet onto the B855, which runs for four miles over windy heather and bog to the tip of the headland, crowned with a Victorian lighthouse. The red cliffs below are startling, with weirdly eroded rock stacks and a huge variety of seabirds; on a clear day you can see the whole northern coastline from Cape Wrath to Duncansby Head, and across the Pentland Firth to Orkney.

John O' Groats

Familiar from endless postcards, **JOHN O' GROATS** comes as something of an anticlimax. The views north to Orkney are fine enough, but the village itself turns out to be little more than a windswept grassy slope leading down to the sea, dominated by an enormous car park that is jammed throughout the summer with tour buses. The village gets its name from the Dutchman, Jan de Groot, who obtained the ferry contract for the crossing to Orkney in 1496. The eight-sided house he built for his eight quarrelling sons (so that each one could enter by his own door) is echoed in the octagonal tower of the much-photographed *John O' Groats Hotel*, which is fast falling into disrepair but remains a good stop-off for a quick drink.

Aside from the frequent if irregular links with Land's End, maintained by a succession of walkers, cyclists, vintage-car drivers and pushers of baths, John O' Groats is connected by regular **buses** to Wick (4–5 daily; 50min) and Thurso (Mon–Fri 5 daily, Sat 2 daily; 1hr). John O' Groats Ferries (☎01955/611353) operates a daily passenger ferry across to Burwick in the Orkney Islands (May & Sept 1 daily; June–Aug 4 daily; 45min; £24 return): officially this is a foot-passenger service, but it will take bicycles and motorbikes if it isn't too busy. The company also offers a couple of whistle-stop day-tours of Orkney, as well as a more leisurely afternoon wildlife cruise round the Stacks of Duncansby and the seabird colonies of Stroma (1hr 30min; £12). The **tourist office** (April–Oct Mon–Sat 9am–5pm; ☎01955/611373) by the car park can help sort out **accommodation**: alternatively, try *Swona View* B&B (☎01955/611297; ①; April–Oct) on the road to Duncansby Head, or *Creag-Na-Mara* (☎01847/851713; ①), a welcoming B&B serving tasty evening meals at East Mey, west along the Thurso road. *Bencorragh House* (☎01955/611449; ②, with dinner ④; March–Oct) has very pleasant farmhouse accommodation at Upper Gills in Canisbay. If you're on a tight budget, head for the small **youth hostel** (☎01955/611424 or central reservations ☎0541/553255; April–Oct) at Canisbay, or one of the two local **campsites** – *Stroma View* (☎01955/611313), one mile along the Thurso road, is the more pleasant.

Duncansby Head

If you're disappointed by John O' Groats, press on a couple of miles further east to **Duncansby Head**, which, with its lighthouse, dramatic cliffs and well-worn coastal path, has a lot more to offer. The birdlife here is prolific, and south of the headland lie some spectacular 200ft cliffs, cut by sheer-sided clefts known locally as *geos*. This is also a good place to view from which to view Orkney. Dividing the islands from the mainland is the infamous **Pentland Firth**, one of the world's most treacherous waterways. Only seven miles across, it forms a narrow channel between the Atlantic Ocean and North Sea, and for fourteen hours each day the tide rips through here from west to east at a rate of ten knots or more, flooding back in the opposite direction for the remaining ten hours. Combined with the rocky sea bed and a high wind, this can cause deep whirlpools and terrifying 30–40ft towers of water to form when the ebbing tide crashes across the reefs offshore. The latter, known as the "Bores of Duncansby", are the subject of many old mariners' myths from the time of the Vikings onwards.

THE EAST COAST

The **east coast** of the Highlands, between Inverness and Wick, is nowhere near as spectacular as the west, with gentle undulating moors, grassland and low cliffs where you might expect to find sea lochs and mountains. Washed by the cold waters of the North Sea, it's markedly cooler, too, although less prone to spells of permadrizzle, and midges. Although the Inverness–Thurso train line is twice forced by topography to head inland, the region's main transport artery, the A9 – slower here than in the south – follows the coast, which veers sharply northeast exactly parallel with the Great Glen, formed by the same geological fault.

From around the ninth century AD onwards, the **Norse** influence was more keenly felt here than in any other part of mainland Britain, and dozens of Scandinavian-sounding names recall the era when this was a Viking kingdom. Culturally and scenically, much of the east coast is more lowland than highland and Caithness in particular evolved more or less separately from the Highlands, avoiding the bloody tribal feuds that wrought such havoc further south and west. Later, however, the nineteenth-century **Clearances** hit the region hard, as countless ruined cottages and empty glens show. Hundreds of thousands of crofters were evicted, and forced to emigrate to New Zealand, Canada and Australia, or else take up fishing in one of the numerous herring ports established on the coast. The oil boom has brought a transient prosperity to one or two places over the past two decades, but the area remains one of the country's poorest, reliant on sheep farming, fishing and tourism.

The one stretch of the east coast that's always been relatively rich is the **Black Isle**, whose main village, **Cromarty**, is the region's undisputed highlight, with a crop of elegant mansions and appealing fishermen's cottages clustered near the entrance to the Cromarty Firth. In late medieval times, pilgrims including James IV of Scotland poured through here en route to the red-sandstone town of **Tain** to worship at the shrine of St Duthac, where the former sacred enclave has now been converted into one of the many "heritage centres" that punctuate the route north. Beyond **Dornoch**, a famous golfing resort renowned for its salubrious climate and sweeping beach, the ersatz-Loire chateau, **Dunrobin Castle**, is the main tourist attraction, a monument as much to the iniquities of the Clearances as to the eccentricity of Victorian taste. The award-winning **Timespan Heritage Centre** further north at Helmsdale recounts the human cost of the landlords' greed, while the area around the port of **Lybster** is littered with the remains of more ancient civilizations. **Wick**, the largest town on this section of coast, has an interesting past inevitably entwined with the fishing industry, whose story is told in another good heritage centre, but is otherwise uninspiring. The relatively flat landscapes of this northeast corner – windswept peat bog and farmland dotted with lochans and grey and white crofts – are a surprising contrast to the more rugged country south and west of here.

The Black Isle and around

Sandwiched between the Cromarty Firth to the north and the Moray and Beauly firths to the south, the **Black Isle** is not an island at all, but a fertile peninsula whose rolling hills, prosperous farms and stands of deciduous woodland make it more reminiscent of Dorset or Sussex than the Highlands. It probably gained its name because of its mild climate: there's rarely frost, which leaves the fields "black" all winter; another explanation is that the name derives from the Gaelic word for black, *dubh* – a possible corruption of St Duthus (see p.544).

The Black Isle is littered with dozens of **prehistoric sites**, but the main incentive to make the detour east from the A9 is to visit the picturesque eighteenth-century town of **Cromarty**, huddled at the northeast tip of the peninsula. A string of villages along the south coast is also worth stopping off in en route, and one of them, Rosemarkie, has an outstanding small museum devoted to **Pictish culture**. Chanonry Point is among the best **dolphin-spotting** sites in Europe.

Avoch, Fortrose and Rosemarkie

The most rewarding approach to Cromarty is along the south side of the Black Isle, on the A832 past the **Clootie Well**, just north of Munlochy, where coloured rags are hung on a fence to bring luck and health. Next comes the attractive harbourside fishing village of **AVOCH** (pronounced "Och"), where the *Station Hotel* serves good bar meals and real ale; there's a tiny heritage centre in the basement at the back. **FORTROSE**, a few miles further east, is another quiet village dominated by the ruins of an early thirteenth-century **cathedral**. Founded by King David I, it now languishes on a lovely yew-studded green bordered by red-sandstone and colourwashed houses, where a horde of gold coins dating from the time of Robert III was unearthed in 1880. There's also a memorial to the Seaforth family, whose demise the Brahan Seer famously predicted (see below).

There's a memorial plaque to the seer at nearby **Chanonry Point**, reached by a backroad from the north end of Fortrose; the thirteenth hole of the golf course here marks the spot where he met his death. Jutting into a narrow channel in the Moray Firth (deepened to allow warships into the estuary during the last war), the point, fringed on one side by a beach of golden sand and shingle, is an excellent place to look for **dolphins** (see p.485). Come here around high tide, and you stand a good chance of spotting a couple leaping through the surf in search of fish brought to the surface by converging currents.

ROSEMARKIE, a one-street village north of Fortrose at the opposite (northwest) end of the beach, is thought to have been evangelized by St Boniface in the early eighth century. **Groam House Museum** (May–Sept Mon–Sat 10am–5pm, Sun 2–4.30pm; Oct–April Sat & Sun 2–4pm; £1.50), at the bottom of the village, displays a bumper crop of intricately carved standing stones (among them the famous Rosemarkie Cross Slab), and shows an informative video highlighting Pictish sites in the region. A lovely mile-and-a-half **woodland walk**, along the banks of a sparkling burn to Fairy Glen, begins at the car park just beyond the village on the road to Cromarty. Inexpensive bar food is also available at the wonderfully old-fashioned *Plough Inn*, just down the main street from the museum.

Cromarty

An ancient legend recalls that the twin headlands flanking the entrance to the Cromarty Firth, known as The Sutors (from the Gaelic word for shoemaker), were once a pair of

THE BRAHAN SEER

Legend has it that the seventeenth-century visionary **Cùinneach Odhar** (Kenneth Mackenzie, from Uig on Skye), who lived and worked on the Seaforths' estate, derived his powers from a small white divination stone passed on to him, through his mother, from a Viking princess. With the pebble pressed against his eye, Cùinneach foretold everything from outbreaks of measles in the village to the building of the Caledonian Canal, the Clearances and World War II. His visions brought him widespread fame, but also resulted in his untimely death. In 1660, Countess Seaforth, wife of the local laird, summoned the seer after her husband was late home from a trip to France. Reluctantly – when pressurized – he told the Countess that he had seen the earl "on his knees before a fair lady, his arm round her waist and her hand pressed to his lips". At this, she flew into a rage, accused him of sullying the family name and ordered him to be thrown head first into a barrel of boiling tar. However, just before the gruesome execution, which took place near Brahan Castle on Chanonry Point, Cùinneach made his last prediction: when a deaf and dumb earl inherited the estate, the Seaforth line would end. His prediction finally came true in 1815 when the last earl died.

giant cobblers who used to protect the Black Isle from pirates. Nowadays, however, the only giants in the area are Nigg and Invergordon's colossal oil rigs, marooned in the estuary like metal monsters marching out to sea. Built and serviced here for the Forties North Sea oil field, they form a surreal counterpoint to the web of tiny streets and chocolate-box workers' cottages of **CROMARTY**, the Black Isle's main settlement. Sheltered by The Sutors at the northeast corner of the peninsula, the town, an ancient ferry crossing point on the pilgrimage trail to St Duthac's shrine in Tain, lost much of its trade during the nineteenth century to places served by the railway; a branch line to the town was begun but never completed. Although a royal burgh since the fourth century, Cromarty didn't became a prominent port until 1772 when the entrepreneurial local landlord, George Ross, founded a hemp mill here. Imported Baltic hemp was spun into cloth and rope in the mill, fuelling a period of prosperity during which Cromarty acquired some of Scotland's finest Georgian houses; these, together with the terraced fishers' cottages of the nineteenth-century herring boom, have earned the town somewhat corny epithet, "the jewel in the crown of Scottish vernacular architecture".

To get a sense of Cromarty's past, head straight for the award-winning **museum** housed in the old **Courthouse** on Church Street (daily: April–Oct 10am–5pm; Nov–Dec & March noon–4pm; £3), which tells the history of the town using audiovisuals and animated figures (not as dreadful as they sound, and children love them). You are also issued with a personal stereo, a tape and a map for a walking tour around the town. **Hugh Miller** (1802–52) a stonemason turned author, geologist, folklorist and Free Church campaigner, was born in Cromarty, and his **birthplace** (May–Sept Mon–Sat 11am–1pm & 2–5pm, Sun 2–5pm; NTS; £2), a modest thatched cottage on Church Street, has been restored to give an idea of what Cromarty must have been like in his day. Aside from any formal sights, Cromarty is a pleasant place just to wander around, and there's an excellent **walk** out to the south Sutor stacks. You can pick up the path by leaving town on Miller Road, and turning right when the lane becomes "The Causeway"; follow this through the woods and past eighteenth-century Cromarty House until you reach the junction at Mains Farm; a left turn here takes you across open fields and through woods to the top of the headland, from where there are superb views across the Moray Firth.

Before you move on, bear in mind that Bill Fraser of the widely respected Dolphin Écosse will take you out on half- or full-day **boat trips** to see seals, porpoises, bottlenosed dolphins and occasionally minke whales just off the coast; you can contact him on ☎01381/600323, or visit their Dolphin Centre in Bank House on High Street, which has all sorts of background information on dolphins and whales, along with some spectacular photographs of the animals taken by clients while out on the boat. The tiny two-car Nigg–Cromarty **ferry** (May–Sept daily 9am–6pm), Scotland's smallest, also doubles up as a cruiser on summer evenings; you can catch it from the jetty near the lighthouse.

Practicalities

Nine **buses** each day run to Cromarty from Inverness (55min), returning from the stop near the playing fields on the western outskirts of town. During summer, **accommodation** is in short supply, so book ahead. Most upmarket is the traditional *Royal Hotel* (☎01381/600217; ⑥), down at the harbour, which has rather small but richly furnished rooms overlooking the Firth, and a good bar/restaurant. For **B&B**, try one of the attractive old houses on Church Street, such as Mrs Robertson's at no. 7 (☎01381/600488; ①). Above the town, Mrs Ricketts (☎01381/600308; ①) offers well-equipped rooms and good views.

The most down-to-earth place **to eat** is the *Cromarty Arms*, which serves basic, inexpensive bar meals, and a good selection of ales and malts. It also hosts a lively karaoke night and occasional country and western bands on Fridays. If you're after something a little more sophisticated, you could try the *Thistle Restaurant*, on Church Street, or the *Royal Hotel*'s restaurant, which features Scottish specialities. Cheaper meals are available in the cosy public bar or, on fine nights, on the terrace outside with great views over the firth.

Strathpeffer

STRATHPEFFER, a Victorian spa town surrounded by wooded hills, is a congenial place to stop over. During its heyday, this was a renowned European **health resort** complete with a Pump Room, where visitors could chat while they sipped the water. Today, sadly, some of its buildings are in a sorry state, including several huge faded hotels, though plans are afoot to restore the Pavilion Ballroom to its former glory. Activity is concentrated around the main square, in the middle of which the **Water Sampling Pavilion** rekindles some of the atmosphere of the Victorian days with bath chairs nestling against the wall and four taps carrying sulphur-laden water from various nearby sources – you are free to sample them although for most people the rank smell more than offsets any possible benefit.

Also making the most of the Victorian theme is the **Highland Museum of Childhood** (mid-March to Oct Mon–Sat 10am–5pm, Sun 2–5pm, open till 7pm Mon–Fri during July & Aug; £1.50), located at the restored Victorian railway station half a mile east of the main square. An attraction aimed at families, the museum looks at growing up in the Highlands, from home- and school-life to folklore and festivals, with some well-displayed black-and-white photographs, display cabinets with toys and games, and a colourful series of commissioned murals. In other parts of the station are a pleasant café and craft workshops.

Within striking distance of the bleak **Ben Wyvis**, Strathpeffer is also a popular base for walkers. One of the best hikes in the area begins from the SYHA **hostel**, at the west end of the village, from where a forestry track leads through dense woodland towards the hill of Cnoc Mor. Rather less than a mile farther on, you can turn up onto the ridge on the right and follow it to reach the vitrified Pictish hill fort of **Knock Farril**, which affords superb panoramic views to the Cromarty Firth and the surrounding mountains. From here, you can pick up a minor road and continue along the ridge to Dingwall, from where there are buses back to Strathpeffer. A shorter route drops back down from Knock Farril to the main road and then on to the village. Allow a full day for the longer route, a half-day for the shorter.

Practicalities

Buses run regularly between Dingwall and Strathpeffer (Mon–Sat), dropping passengers in the square, where you'll find a small **tourist office** (April, May & Sept Mon–Fri 10am–5pm, Sat 11am–4pm; June to mid-Oct Mon–Sat 10am–5pm, Sun 11am–4pm; ☎01997/421415) with information on points west as well as local areas. The **hotels** in the village are very popular with bus tours, but often have room: the vast *Ben Wyvis* (☎01997/421323; ④) is adequate, in nice grounds east of the main square on the Dingwall road, while north of the main square a converted Victorian villa, complete with turrets, houses the *Holly Lodge Hotel* (☎01997/421254; ②). The *Inver Lodge*, west of the main square (☎01997/421392; ①), and *Francisville*, just past the church (☎01997/421345; ①), both offer good **B&B**. If you don't mind dorms, head for the rambling fifty-bed **youth hostel** (☎01997/421532 or central reservations ☎0541 553255; April–Sept), a mile southwest of the main square up the hill towards Jameston, while those keen on tackling a broader range of outdoor pursuits, including canoeing, mountain biking and assault courses, should head to the excellent Fairburn Activity Centre (☎01997/433397; ②), set in the grounds of a magnificent country estate about three miles outside the village of Marybank, south of Strathpeffer and northwest of Muir of Ord.

Dingwall and the Cromarty Firth

Most traffic nowadays takes the upgraded A9 north from Inverness, bypassing the small provincial town of **DINGWALL** (from the Norse *thing*, "parliament", and *vollr*, "field"), a royal burgh since 1226 and former port that was left high and dry when the river receded during the last century. Today, it's a tidy but dull service and market town with one long main street that's bustling all day and moribund by dinner time. Dingwall's only real claim to fame is that it was the birthplace of Macbeth, whose family occupied the now ruined castle on Castle Street.

If you need **to stay**, Castle Street is a good place to look for B&Bs: try *The Croft* (☎01349/863319; ①) at no. 25, or *St Clements* (☎01349/862172; ①) at no. 17. The smartest hotel is the stylish *Tulloch Castle*, Castle Drive (☎01349/861325; ⑤), a former Highland clan headquarters, or there's the central *Royal Hotel*, High Street (☎01349/862130; ④).

Northeast of Dingwall, the **Cromarty Firth** has always been recognized as a perfect natural harbour. During World War I it was a major **naval base**, and today its sheltered waters are used as a centre for repairing North Sea oil rigs. The A862 road from Dingwall rejoins the A9 just after the main road crosses the firth on a long causeway; shortly after this, perched on a spit between the road and the firth is the recently established **Clanland and Sealpoint** (daily 9.30am–5.30pm, open till 8pm July–Sept; £3.50), another of the heritage centres which crop up with almost monotonous regularity throughout the Highland region. Each has its story to tell, however, and this one looks at the Munro Clan, along with the traditional fishing industry and some of the local wildlife, particularly the seals of the firth. Predictably, large amounts of space are given over to the café and souvenir shop, and the family-oriented exhibits mean that it can be boisterous inside.

Rather quirkier attractions can be found not far away, notably the extraordinary edifice on the hill behind **EVANTON**, a few miles further along the A9 from Clanland. This is the **Fyrish Monument**, built by a certain Sir Hector Munro, partly to give employment to the area and partly to commemorate his own capture of the Indian town of Seringapatam in 1781 – hence the design, resembling an Indian gateway. If you want to get a close-up look, it's a tough two-hour walk through pine woods to the top. An easier, but no less dramatic walk from the village, is to follow the Allt Graad river to the mile-long **Black Rock** gorge, an unexpected chasm formed when glacial meltwaters cut a deep furrow in a band of softer sandstone. The gorge, a giddy 100ft deep in places but only 12–15ft wide, was reputedly once jumped by a local man, but the proximity of the surrounding wood, as well as the curtain of damp ferns and mosses which cling to the rocks, would make a repeat of this, or any close inspection of the gorge, pretty dangerous. The best approach to the gorge is along a track which leaves from *Evanton Caravan Park*, where there's also a simple but neat bunkhouse (☎01349/830917; *mlb@blackrockscot.freeserve.co.uk*), one of only two hostels on this entire stretch between Inverness and Thurso.

Around the Tain peninsula

Bounded in the south by the Cromarty Firth, and in the north by the Dornoch Firth, the hammer-shaped **Tain peninsula** can still be approached by the ancient ferry crossing from Cromarty to Nigg. The peninsula's largest settlement is **TAIN**, a small town of grand whisky-coloured sandstone buildings, and the birthplace of **St Duthus**, a missionary who inspired great devotion in the Middle Ages. His miracle-working relics were enshrined in a sanctuary here in the eleventh century, and in 1360 St Duthus Collegiate Church was built, visited annually by James IV, who usually arrived here fresh from the arms of his mistress, Janet Kennedy, whom he had conveniently installed in nearby Moray. A good place to get to grips with the peninsula's past is the **Tain Through Time** exhibition (April–Oct daily 10am–6pm; Nov–March Mon–Fri noon–4pm; £3.50), which makes creative use of three old buildings around the church and a graveyard, guiding you round using an audio guide with headphones. The ticket price also includes a tour of the church and neighbouring **museum** on Castle Brae (just off the High Street), housing an interesting display of the famous Tain silver, along with mediocre archeological finds and clan memorabilia. There's not a great deal more to see in Tain, but check out the High Street's castellated sixteenth-century **Tolbooth**, with its stone turrets and old curfew bell. Tain's only other attraction, the **whisky distillery** where the highly rated **Glenmorangie** malt is produced (shop open Mon–Fri 9am–5pm; June–Oct also Sat 10am–4pm; tours Mon–Fri 10.30am–3.30pm, Sat 10.30am–2.30pm; £2), lies just off the A9 on the north side of town.

For **accommodation**, the *Mansfield House Hotel* (☎01862/892052; *mansfield@cali.co.uk*; ⑤), a modernized mansion-hotel in the Scots-Baronial mould, is renowned for its cooking, while the more modest *Golf View House* (☎01862/892856; ②), three minutes' drive from the town centre on Knockbreck Road, offers comfortable B&B. Good quality but still moderately priced **food** is available at the *Morangie House Hotel* to the north of town, while *Harry Gow* on the High Street (open all day) serves typical Scottish food, and classic Italian is dished up at *Café Volante*, also on the High Street, beside the Post Office.

Portmahomack

Although few people bother to explore the Tain area as far east as **Tarbat Ness** on the tip of the peninsula, if you're driving it's well worth setting aside a couple of hours to make the detour. The green, windswept village of **PORTMAHOMACK** sprawls downhill to a sandy beach and round a bay full of sailing boats. On top of the hill, a Pictish archeological site is being excavated next to the pretty whitewashed **Tarbat Old Church**, with its odd tower and balustraded entrance at the back. There's also a **lighthouse** (one of the highest in Britain) at the gorse-covered point, reached along narrow roads running through fertile farmland. A good seven-mile walk starts here (2–3hr round-trip): head south from Tarbat Ness for three miles, following the narrow passage between the foot of the cliffs and the foreshore, until you get to the hamlet of Rockfield. A path leads past a row of fishermen's cottages from here to Portmahomack, then joins the tarmac road running northeast back to the lighthouse.

Back in Portmahomack, the *Oystercatcher* on Main Street is one of the eating highlights of this stretch of the east coast, serving delicious seafood, home-made soups and salads (open Tues–Sun 11am–6pm; also Fri & Sat evenings); they also have a few very-good-value **rooms** (☎01862/871560; ①). Otherwise, if you want to stay, you could try the *Caledonian Hotel* (☎01862/871345; ②) further along Main Street, which looks over the beach to the Dornoch Firth.

Bonar Bridge and around

Before the causeway was built across the Dornoch Firth, traffic heading along the coast used to skirt around the estuary, crossing the Kyle of Sutherland at **BONAR BRIDGE**. In the fourteenth and fifteenth centuries, the village harboured a large **iron foundry**. Ore was brought across the peat moors of the central Highlands from the west coast on sledges, and fuel for smelting came from the oak forest draped over the northern shores of the nearby kyle. However, James IV, passing through here on his way to Tain, was shocked to find the forest virtually clear-felled and ordered that oak saplings be planted in the gaps. Although now hemmed in by spruce plantations, the beautiful ancient woodland east of Bonar Bridge dates from this era.

These days there's little of note in Bonar Bridge other than the bridge itself, which has had three incarnations up to the present steel construction of 1973, all recalled on a stone plinth on the north side. However, you may want to check out the unusual **airboat** trips (book on ☎01863/766839; 30min–1hr; £8/£15), run from the *Caledonian Hotel*. The unlikely looking craft, with a huge fan mounted on the back of a flat-bottomed launch, previously saw service in the Everglade swamps of Florida, and is used in similar fashion on the kyle to skim over shallow water and mud flats to get a closer look at the local wildlife and scenery.

Carbisdale Castle

Towering high above the River Shin, three miles northwest of Bonar Bridge, the daunting neo-Gothic profile of **Carbisdale Castle** (not open to the public) overlooks the **Kyle of Sutherland**, as well as the battlefield where the gallant Marquis of Montrose was defeated in 1650, finally forcing Charles II – if he wanted to be received as king (see p.631) – to accede to the Scots demand for Presbyterianism. It was erected between 1906 and 1917 for the dowager **Duchess of Sutherland**, following a protracted family feud. After the death of her husband, the late Duke of Sutherland, the will leaving her the lion's share of the vast estate was contested by his stepchildren from his first marriage. In the course of the ensuing legal battle, the Duchess was found in contempt of court for destroying important documents pertinent to the case, and locked up in Holloway prison for six weeks. However, the Sutherlands eventually recanted (although there was no personal reconciliation) and, by way of compensation, built their stepmother a castle worthy of her rank. Designed in three distinct styles (to give the impression it was added to over a long period of time), Carbisdale was eventually acquired by a Norwegian shipping magnate in 1933, and finally gifted, along with its entire contents and estate, to the SYHA, which has turned it into what must be one of the most opulent **hostels** in the world, full of white Italian marble sculptures, huge gilt-framed portraits, sweeping staircases and magnificent drawing rooms alongside standard facilities such as self-catering kitchens, games rooms, TV rooms and thirty dorms, including some recently upgraded four-bed family rooms (☎01549/421232; March–Oct except first two weeks in May). The best way to get here by public transport is to take a train to nearby **Culrain** station, which lies within easy walking distance of the castle. **Buses** from Inverness (3 daily; 1hr 30min) and Tain (4 daily; 25min) only run as far as **Ardgay**, three miles south.

Croick Church

A mile or so southwest of Bonar Bridge, the scattered village of **ARDGAY** stands at the mouth of Strath Carron, a wooded river valley winding west into the heart of the Highlands. It's worth heading ten miles up the strath to **Croick Church**, which harbours one of Scotland's most poignant and emotive reminders of the **Clearances**. Huddled behind a brake of wind-bent trees, the graveyard surrounding the tiny grey chapel sheltered eighteen families (92 individuals) evicted from nearby Glen Calvie during the spring of 1845 to make way for flocks of Cheviot sheep, introduced by the Duke of Sutherland as a quick money earner (see p.548). A reporter from the *Times* described the "wretched spectacle" as the villagers filed out of the glen " . . . in a body, two or three carts filled with children, many of them infants". An even more evocative written record of the event is preserved on the diamond-shaped panes of the chapel windows, where the villagers scratched **graffiti memorials** still legible today: "Glen Calvie people was in the churchyard May 24th 1845", "Glen Calvie people the wicked generation", and "This place needs cleaning".

Lairg

North of Bonar Bridge, the A836 parallels the River Shin for eleven miles, to **LAIRG**, a bleak and scattered place at the eastern end of lonely **Loch Shin**. On fine days, the vast wastes of heather and deergrass surrounding the village can be beautiful, but in the rain it can be a deeply depressing landscape. This workaday village is predominantly a **transport hub** and the railhead for a huge area to the northwest, and there's nothing much to see in town. However, a mile southeast on the A839, there are signs of early settlement at nearby **Ord Hill**, where archeological digs have recently yielded traces of human habitation dating back to Neolithic times. The Ferrycroft Countryside Centre and **tourist office**, on the west side of the river (April–Oct Mon–Sat 9.30am–5.30pm, Sun 10am–5pm; ☎01549/402160), hands out leaflets detailing the locations of hut circles and other sites and is the starting point for forest walks and an archeological trail to Ord Hill. Four miles south of Lairg, on the opposite side of the river – along the A836, then the B864 – the **Falls of Shin** is one of the best places in Scotland to see **salmon** leaping on their upstream migration; there's a viewing platform, and the café by the car park does good snacks and meals. The season for salmon returning to spawn is from June to September. Every August, Lairg hosts an annual lamb sale, the biggest one-day livestock market in Europe, when sheep from all over the north of Scotland are bought and sold.

Practicalities

Lairg, at the centre of the region's **road system**, is distinctly hard to avoid: the A838, traversing some of the loneliest country in the Highlands, is the quickest route for Cape Wrath; the A836 heads up to Tongue on the north coast; and the A839 links up to the A837 to push west through lovely Strath Oykel, to Lochinver on the west coast. For non-drivers, Lairg is on the **train line** connecting Inverness to Wick and Thurso and is the nexus of several **postbus routes** around the northwest Highlands, including one which links Lairg with Ledmore, on the Ullapool–Durness road. Trains arrive north of the main road along the loch; buses stop right on the loch. Should you want to stay, *Carnbren* (☎01549/402259; ①), just south of the bridge on the Bonar Bridge road, is comfortable, as is the *Old Coach House* (☎01549/402378; ①; May–Oct), three miles south of Lairg on the B864 at Achany. *Park House* (☎01549/402208; ②) on Station Road, overlooking Loch Shin, is a welcoming spot if you're planning on doing some walking, fishing or cycling in the area.

Dornoch

DORNOCH, eight miles north of Tain, lies on a flattish headland overlooking the **Dornoch Firth**. Surrounded by sand dunes and blessed with an exceptionally sunny climate by Scottish standards, it's something of a middle-class holiday resort, with solid Edwardian hotels, trees and flowers in profusion, and miles of sandy beaches giving good views across the estuary to the Tain peninsula. The town is also renowned for its championship **golf course**, ranked eleventh in the world and the most northerly first-class course in the world.

Dating from the twelfth century, Dornoch became a royal burgh in 1628. Among its oldest buildings, which are all grouped round the spacious square, the tiny **Cathedral** was founded in 1224 and built of local sandstone. The original building was horribly damaged by marauding Mackays in 1570, and much of what you see today was restored by the Countess of Sutherland in 1835, though her worst Victorian excesses were removed this century, when the interior stonework was returned to its original state. A later addition were the stained-glass windows in the north wall, which were endowed by the expat American-based Andrew Carnegie (see p.271). Opposite, the fortified six-teenth-century Bishop's Palace, a fine example of vernacular architecture, with stepped gables and towers, has been refurbished as an upmarket hotel (see below). Next door, the **Old Town Jail** (Mon–Sat 10am–5pm; free) contains a mock-up of a nineteenth-cen-tury cell accessed through a gift and crafts shop.

In 1722, Dornoch saw the last burning of a **witch** in Scotland. The unfortunate old woman, accused of turning her daughter into a pony and riding her around town, ruined her chances of acquittal by misquoting the Gaelic version of the Lord's Prayer during the trial, and was sentenced to burn alive in a barrel of boiling tar – an event commemorated by the **Witch's Stone**, just south of the Square on Carnaig Street.

Practicalities

Buses from Tain and Inverness stop in the Square, where you'll also find a **tourist office** (Mon–Fri 9am–5pm; May–Oct also Sat 9am–4pm; July–Aug also Sun 11am–5pm; ☎01862/810400). There's no shortage of **accommodation**: the *Trentham Hotel* (☎01862/810551; ①), near the golf course on the northeast edge of town, is friendly and comfortable if a bit staid, while the characterful *Dornoch Castle Hotel* (☎01862/810216; April–Oct; ④), in the Bishop's Palace on the Square, has a cosy old-style bar and relax-ing tea garden. Of the B&Bs, try *Trevose* (☎01862/810269; March–Sept; ①), on the Square, which is swathed in roses, or, a couple of miles out on the A949, *Evelix Farmhouse* (☎01862/810271; June–Sept; ①). Those with a tent may choose to head for the *Caravan Park* (☎01862/810423; April–Oct), attractively set between the manicured golf course and the uncombed vegetation of the sand dunes which fringe the beach, although the site does get busy with caravans in July and August. Expensive gourmet **meals** are available at the *2 Quail* restaurant (Tues–Sat ☎01862/811811) on Castle Street, which also has tasteful rooms available (③), while both the hotels do good bar and restaurant meals and the *Cathedral Café* is open until 9pm in summer and serves delicious soup and snacks.

Golspie to Wick

Ten miles north of Dornoch on the A9 lies the straggling red-sandstone town of **GOL-SPIE**, whose status as an administrative centre does little to relieve its dullness. It does, however, boast an eighteen-hole **golf course** and a sandy beach, while half a mile further up the coast the **Big Burn** has several rapids and waterfalls that can be seen from an attractive **woodland trail** (beginning at the *Sutherland Arms Hotel*).

Dunrobin Castle

The main reason to stop in Golspie, though, is to look around **Dunrobin Castle** (May–Oct Mon–Sat 10.30am–4.30pm, Sun noon–4.30pm plus June–Sept daily till

5.30pm; £4.80), overlooking the sea a mile north of town. Approached via a long tree-lined drive, this fairy-tale confection of turrets and pointed roofs – modelled by the architect Sir Charles Barry (designer of the Houses of Parliament) on a Loire chateau – is the seat of the infamous Sutherland family, at one time Europe's biggest landowners, with a staggering 1.3 million acres, and the principal driving force behind the **Clearances** in this area. The castle is on a correspondingly vast scale, boasting 189 furnished rooms, of which the tour only takes in seventeen. Staring up at the pile from the midst of its elaborate **formal gardens**, it's worth remembering that such extravagance was paid for by uprooting literally thousands of crofters from the surrounding glens. Much of the extra income generated by the evictions was lavished on the castle's opulent **interior**, which is crammed full of fine furniture, paintings (including works by Landseer, Allan Ramsay and Sir Joshua Reynolds), tapestries and objets d'art.

Set aside at least an hour for Dunrobin's amazing **museum**, housed in an eighteenth-century building at the edge of the garden. Inside, hundreds of disembodied animals' heads and horns peer down from the walls, alongside other more macabre appendages, from elephants' toes to rhinos' tails. Bagged mainly by the fifth Duke and Duchess of Sutherland, the trophies vie for space with other fascinating family memorabilia, including one of John O' Groat's bones, Chinese opium pipes, and such curiosities as a "picnic gong from the South Pacific". There's also an impressive collection of ethnographic artefacts acquired by the Sutherlands on their frequent hunting jaunts, ranging from an Egyptian sarcophagus to some finely carved Pictish stones.

The Sutherland Monument

You can't miss the 100ft **Monument** to the first Duke of Sutherland, which peers proprietorially down from the summit of the 1293ft **Beinn a'Bhragaidh**, a mile northwest of Golspie. An inscription cut into its base recalls that the statue was erected in 1834 by ". . . a mourning and grateful tenantry [to] . . . a judicious, kind and liberal landlord . . . [who would] open his hands to the distress of the widow, the sick and the traveller". Unsurprisingly, there's no reference to the fact that the duke, widely regarded as Scotland's own Josef Stalin, forcibly evicted 15,000 crofters from his million-acre estate – a fact which, in the words of one local historian, makes the monument ". . . a grotesque representation of the many forces that destroyed the Highlands". Campaigners are lobbying, so far unsuccessfully, to have the monument broken into pieces and scattered over the hillside, so that visitors can walk over the remains to a new, more appropriate memorial. However, the Sutherland estate and local council have continually resisted moves to replace it.

It's worth the wet, rocky **climb** (round-trip 90min) to the top of the hill for the wonderful views south along the coast past Dornoch to the Moray Firth and west towards Lairg and Loch Shin. It's a steep and strenuous walk, however, and there's no view until you're out of the trees, about ten minutes from the top. Take the road opposite Munro's TV Rentals in Golspie's main street, which leads up the hill, past a fountain, under the railway and through a farmyard – from here, follow the Beinn a'Bhragaidh footpath (BBFP) signs along the path into the woods. You can go back the way you came, or follow a clear track which initially goes north from the monument and then winds down through Benvraggie Wood to meet a tarred road; turn left here to link into the path of the Big Burn Glen walk (see above).

Loch Fleet

Just to the south of Golspie, the A9 fringes a tidal estuary on a causeway that was constructed in 1816 by Thomas Telford. The inlet, **Loch Fleet** (open access; free), is part of a large nature reserve harbouring some delicate coastal and woodland vegetation, including Britain's greatest concentration of one-flowered wintergreen, also known as

St Olaf's candlestick, as well as a range of birdlife including greylag geese and arctic terns, and sealife such as seals and otters. You can walk in the reserve by following the minor road south out of Golspie for three miles – from Balblair Bay a path leads into pine-forested Balblair Wood, while from Littleferry there are walks along the coastal heathland to the Moray Firth beaches.

Four miles northwest of Loch Fleet on the A839 to Lairg is one of Scotland's most unusual and imaginative **hostels**, *Rogat Railway Carriage* (☎01408/641343, *rograil@globalnet.co.uk*), where you can stay in one of two old railway carriages parked in a siding beside the station on the Inverness–Thurso line in the tiny settlement of Rogat. Each of the first-class compartments has a bunk bed on one side and the original seats on the other, while the two end compartments are used as a kitchen and common room. The owners have mountain bikes available so that you can explore the local countryside, the convivial local pub serves evening meals, and a small reduction is even offered to those arriving by train or bicycle.

Brora

BRORA, on the coast six miles north of Golspie, once boasted the only bridge in the region – thus the name, which means "River of the Bridge" in Norse. Until the 1960s, it was the only coal-mining village in the Highlands, having played host to the industry for four hundred years. These days, however, the small grey town harbours little of interest, although it's accessible by bus and train and does have *Capaldi's* on High Street, which sells brilliant homemade Italian ice cream. Three miles south of the town is the remarkably well-preserved Iron Age broch of Carn Liath, with great twelve-foot thick walls and a number of obvious features intact, such as a staircase and entrance passage. The car park for the site is on the inland side of the A9, just before the broch if you're travelling north. A more interesting way to reach it is by walking along the coastal path which links Golspie and Brora. A mile or so north of town, the **Clynelish Distillery** (March–Nov Mon–Fri 9.30am–4.30pm; Dec–Feb by appointment ☎01408/623000; £2), will give you a guided tour and a sample dram.

The best **B&B** in the area is *Clynelish Farm* (☎01408/621265; ②) – turn left after the BP garage – a working Victorian stone farmhouse with en-suite rooms, built to provide employment for dispossessed crofters after the Clearances. The rooms here are spacious, with views over the fields to the Moray Firth, and evening meals are available by arrangement. Also worth considering for B&B is *Seaforth* (☎01408/621793; ①), a working croft on ten acres of land looking towards the sea.

Helmsdale

Eleven miles up the A9 from Golspie, **HELMSDALE** is an old herring port, founded in the nineteenth century to house the evicted inhabitants of Strath Kildonan, which lies behind it. Today, the sleepy-looking grey village attracts thousands of tourists, most of them to see the attractively designed **Timespan Heritage Centre**, beside the river (Easter–Oct Mon–Sat 9.30am–5pm, Sun 2–5pm; £3.50). It's a remarkable venture for a place of this size, telling the local story of Viking raids, witch-burning, Clearances, fishing and gold-prospecting through hi-tech displays, sound effects and an audiovisual programme. The centre also has an art gallery, which often has a decent show of works by Scottish artists. For a spot of light relief after the exhibition, head across the road to the sugary pink and frilly *Mirage Restaurant*. The proprietor has become something of a Scottish celebrity, modelling herself on the romantic novelist Barbara Cartland, whose shooting lodge is nearby. Photographs proudly displayed on the walls show the peroxide-blonde restaurateuse posing with her heroine, while the fittings and furnishings reflect her predilection for all things pink and kitsch, with fish tanks, fake-straw parasols, and plastic seagulls set off by the country and western soundtrack. She also dishes up great fish and chips, grills and puddings.

Helmsdale's **tourist office** (April–Sept Mon–Sat 10.30am–4pm; ☎01431/821640) in the Timespan centre will book accommodation for you. Most of the **B&Bs** are on the outskirts of town: *Broomhill House*, Navidale Road (☎01431/821259; ③), is the best of the bunch, with bedrooms in a turret added to the former croft by a miner who struck it lucky in the Kildonan gold rush (see below). Alternatively, try *Torbuie* (☎01431/821424; ③), in Navidale, on the A9 less than a mile from the village, or *Eastdale*, half a mile up the A897 (☎01431/821334; ③), both of which offer comfortable rooms. There's also a small **youth hostel** (☎01431/821577; mid-May to Sept), about half a mile north of the harbour.

BAILE AN OR

From Helmsdale the single-track A897 runs up Strath Kildonan and across the Flow Country (see p.536) to the north coast, at first following the River Helmsdale river, a strictly controlled and exclusive salmon river frequented by the royals. Some eight miles up the Strath at **BAILE AN OR** (Gaelic for "goldfield"), gold was discovered in the bed of the Kildonan Burn in 1869; a gold rush ensued, hardly on the scale of the Yukon, but quite bizarre in the Scottish Highlands. A tiny amount of gold is still found by some hardy prospectors every year: if you fancy **gold-panning** yourself, you can hire the relevant equipment for £2.50 from Helmsdale's gift and fishing-tackle shop, Strath Ullie, opposite the Timespan Heritage Centre, which also sells a booklet with a few basic tips.

Dunbeath and Lybster

Just north of Helmsdale, the A9 begins its long haul up the **Ord of Caithness**. This steep hill used to form a pretty impregnable obstacle, and the desolate road still gets blocked during winter snowstorms. Once over the pass, the landscape changes dramatically as heather-clad moors give way to miles of treeless green grazing lands, peppered with derelict crofts and latticed by long drystone walls. This whole area was devastated during the Clearances; the ruined village of **BADBEA**, reached via a footpath running east off the main road a short way after the pass, is a poignant monument to this cruel era. Built by tenants evicted from nearby Ousdale, the settlement now lies deserted, although its ruined hovels show what hardship the crofters had to endure: the cottages stood so near the windy cliff edge that children had to be tethered to prevent them from being blown into the sea.

DUNBEATH, hidden at the mouth of a small strath, twelve miles north of Ord of Caithness, was another village founded to provide work in the wake of the Clearances. The local landlord built a harbour here in 1800, at the start of the herring boom, and the settlement briefly flourished. Today it's a sleepy place, with lobster pots stacked at the quayside and views of windswept Dunbeath Castle (closed to the public) on the opposite side of the bay. The novelist Neil Gunn was born here, in one of the terraced houses under the flyover that now swoops above the village; you can find out more about him at the **Dunbeath Heritage Centre** (Easter–Oct daily 10am–5pm; £1.50), signposted from the road. The best of the handful of modest **B&Bs** here is *Tormore Farm* (☎01593/731240; ③), a large farmhouse with four comfortable rooms, half a mile north of the harbour on the A9. Just north of Dunbeath is the simple but moving **Laidhay Croft Museum** (Easter to mid-Nov daily 10am–6pm; £1), which offers a useful perspective on the sometimes over-romanced life of the Highlander before the Clearances. A little further up the coast, obvious from the A9 between the villages of Latheron and Lybster, is the **Clan Gunn Heritage Centre and Museum** (June–Sept Mon–Sat 11am–5pm; July & Aug also Sun 2–5pm; £1.50), housed in an old white church surrounded by a graveyard, set against green fields and the precipitous coastline. It's mainly a place for members of the Clan Gunn and its septs – which include the more common surnames of Johnson, Thomson and Wilson, although it also doles out a bit more local history and a few tidbits for those on the trail of Neil Gunn, whose most famous novels, *Highland River* and *The Silver Darlings*, were set along this coastline.

The final stretch of road before Wick gives great views over the cliffs and out to sea to the oil rigs perched on the horizon. The planned village of **LYBSTER**, established at the height of the nineteenth-century herring boom, once had 200-odd boats working out of its harbour. Today, although still a busy fishing port, it's a grim collection of grey pebble-dashed bungalows centred on a broad main street. Most visitors head straight for the nearby **Grey Cairns of Camster**, seven miles due north and one of the most memorable sights on the northeast coast. Surrounded by bleak moorland, these two enormous prehistoric burial chambers, constructed 4000–5000 years ago, were immaculately designed, with corbelled drystone roofs in their hidden chambers, which you can crawl into through narrow passageways. More extraordinary ancient remains lie at **East Clyth**, two miles north of Lybster on the A99, where a path leads to the "**Hill o' Many Stanes**". Some 200 boulders stand in the ground here, forming 22 parallel rows that run north to south; no one has yet worked out what they were used for, although archeological studies have shown there were once 600 stones in place. A fourteen-mile track waymarked as a cycle path leads between the two sites, entering the forest at a car park half a mile south of the Camster Cairns and emerging near the single-track road which passes the Hill O' Many Stanes and connects with the A99. Another relatively unknown historic site in the area is the **Whaligoe staircase**, ten miles north of Lybster on the A99 at the north end of the village of Ulbster. The stairway, which has 365 steps constructed out of the distinctive local slab stone, leads steeply down from the side of the house beside the car park to a natural harbour surrounded by cliffs. At the bottom you'll see a few remnants of the harbour used by herring fishermen in the last century, as well as vast numbers of seabirds, including cormorants, skuas and puffins; the daunting climb back up is made a little bit easier by the thought that, unlike the fishermen, you don't have a creel full of herring to carry all the way to the top. The stairway is steep and uneven for much of the way down, so be particularly careful if the steps are wet. To get to the stairway, turn off towards the sea at the junction signposted on its landward side to the "Cairn o'Get".

Wick

Originally a Viking settlement named *Vik* (meaning "bay"), **WICK** has been a royal burgh since 1589. It's actually two towns: Wick proper, and **Pultneytown**, immediately south across the river, a messy, rather run-down community planned by Thomas Telford in 1806 for the British Fisheries Society, to encourage evicted crofters to take up fishing.

Wick's heyday was in the mid-nineteenth century, when it was the busiest herring port in Europe, exporting tons of fish to Russia, Scandinavia and the West Indian slave plantations. Robert Louis Stevenson described it as " . . . the meanest of man's towns, situated on the baldest of God's bays", and it's still a pretty grim place, in spite of a bustling shopping centre and some solid Victorian civic architecture. Pultneytown, lined with rows of fishermen's cottages, is the area most worth a wander, with the acres of largely derelict net-mending sheds, stores and cooperages around the harbour giving some idea of the former scale of the fishing trade. The town's story is told in the excellent **Wick Heritage Centre** in Bank Row, Pultneytown (June–Sept Mon–Sat 10am–5pm; £2), which contains a fascinating array of artefacts from the old fishing days, including fully-rigged boats, original boat models, the old Noss Head lighthouse light and a great photographic collection dating from the 1880s.

Rising steeply from a needle-thin promontory three miles north of Wick are the dramatic fifteenth- to seventeenth-century ruins of **Sinclair** and **Girnigoe castles**, which functioned as a single stronghold for the earls of Caithness. In 1570 the fourth earl, suspecting his son of trying to murder him, imprisoned him in the dungeon here until he died of starvation. There's a good clifftop walk (2hr 30min) to the castles from the tiny fishing village of **Staxigoe**: head north from the harbour to Field of Noss farm and follow the line of the cliffs, where you'll encounter all sorts of seabirds, including puffins, negotiating various gates and stiles along the way. When you reach Noss Head lighthouse, head along the access road to a car park, where a path leads out to the castles on the north-facing coastline.

Practicalities

The **train** station and **bus** stops are next to each other behind the hospital. Frequent local buses run to Thurso and up the coast to John O' Groats. Wick also has an **airport** (☎01955/602215), a couple of miles north of the town, with direct flights from Edinburgh, and Aberdeen, and connections further south. From the train station, head across the river down Bridge Street to the **tourist office**, just off the High Street (Mon–Sat 10am–5pm, July–Sept also Sun 10am–5pm; ☎01955/602596), which can organize local **accommodation**. The best value **B&B** in town is the welcoming *Greenvoe* on George Street (☎01955/603942; ①), looking over the river. *Wellington Guest House*, just behind the station at 41–43 High St (☎01955/603287; ②; March–Oct), is reasonable value, as is *The Clachan* B&B, South Road (☎01955/605384; ②), while The *Harbour Guest House*, on Rose Street, Pultneytown (☎01955/603276; ①) is friendly but more basic. The best of the hotels is *Mackay's*, by the river in the town centre (☎01955/602323, *mackays.hotel@caithness-mm.co.uk*; ③). Good quality **bikes** can be hired from Wheels Cycle Shop (Easter–Sept Mon–Sat; ☎01955/603636) on Glamis Road.

As for **eating**, the good-value *Lamplighter Restaurant*, High Street, serves enormous helpings of imaginative food; downstairs in the same building, *Houston's Café* cheerfully churns out good burgers. *Cabrelli's*, at the east end of the High Street, opposite the bridge over to Pultneytown, is a real find, trapped in a time warp, and serving piles of fish and chips, along with authentic pizza. A few doors further on, *Carter's* serves unremarkable pub grub, while the adjoining *Camps* is among the liveliest of the **pubs** in the evenings, with occasional live music.

travel details

Trains

Aviemore to: Edinburgh (Mon–Sat 8 daily, Sun 3 daily; 3hr); Inverness (Mon–Sat 8 daily, Sun 4 daily; 40min); Newtonmore (Mon–Sat 6 daily, Sun 4 daily; 20min).

Dingwall to: Helmsdale (Mon–Sat 3 daily, plus Sun 2 daily in summer; 2hr); Inverness (Mon–Sat 6–7 daily, plus Sun 4 daily in summer; 25min); Kyle of Lochalsh (Mon–Sat 3–4 daily, plus Sun 2 daily in summer; 2hr); Lairg (Mon–Sat 3 daily, plus Sun 2 daily in summer; 1hr 10min); Thurso (Mon–Sat 3 daily, plus Sun 2 daily in summer; 3hr 20min); Wick (Mon–Sat 3 daily, plus Sun 2 daily in summer; 3hr 20min).

Fort William to: Arisaig (Mon–Sat 4 daily, plus Sun 3 daily in summer; 1hr 10min); Crianlarich (Mon–Sat 3–4 daily, Sun 1–3 daily; 1hr 40min); Glasgow (Mon–Sat 3 daily, Sun 1–2 daily; 4hr); Glenfinnan (4 daily; 35min); London (1 nightly; 12hr); Mallaig (Mon–Sat 4 daily, Sun 1–3 daily; 1hr 25min).

Inverness to: Aviemore (Mon–Sat 8 daily, Sun 4 daily; 40min); Dingwall (Mon–Sat 6–7 daily, plus Sun 4 daily in summer; 25min); Edinburgh (Mon–Sat 8 daily, Sun 3 daily; 3hr 30min); Helmsdale (Mon–Sat 3 daily, plus Sun 2 daily in summer; 2hr 20min); Kyle of Lochalsh (Mon–Sat 3–4 daily, plus Sun 2 daily in summer; 2hr 40min);

Lairg (Mon–Sat 3 daily, plus Sun 2 daily in summer; 1hr 40min); London (Mon–Fri & Sun 2 daily, Sat 1 daily; 8hr 35min); Plockton (Mon–Sat 3–4 daily, plus Sun 2 daily in summer; 2hr 15min); Thurso (Mon–Sat 3 daily, plus Sun 2 daily in summer; 3hr 45min); Wick (Mon–Sat 3 daily, plus Sun 2 daily in summer; 3hr 45min).

Kyle of Lochalsh to: Dingwall (Mon–Sat 3–4 daily, plus Sun 2 daily in summer; 2hr); Inverness (Mon–Sat 3–4 daily, plus Sun 2 daily in summer; 2hr 40min); Plockton (Mon–Sat 3–4 daily, plus Sun 2 daily in summer; 20min).

Lairg to: Dingwall (Mon–Sat 3 daily, plus Sun 2 daily in summer; 1hr 10min); Inverness (Mon–Sat 3 daily, plus Sun 2 daily in summer; 1hr 40min); Thurso (Mon–Sat 3 daily, plus Sun 2 daily in summer; 2hr 5min); Wick (Mon–Sat 3 daily, plus Sun 2 daily in summer; 2hr 5min).

Mallaig to: Arisaig (Mon–Sat 4 daily, plus Sun 3 daily in summer; 15min); Fort William (Mon–Sat 4 daily, plus Sun 3 daily in summer; 1hr 25min); Glasgow (Mon–Sat 3 daily, Sun 1–2 daily; 5hr 20min); Glenfinnan (Mon–Sat 4 daily, plus Sun 3 daily in summer; 35 min).

Newtonmore to: Aviemore (Mon–Sat 6 daily, Sun 4 daily; 20min); Inverness (Mon–Sat 6 daily, Sun 4 daily; 55min).

Thurso to: Dingwall (Mon–Sat 3 daily, plus Sun 2 daily in summer; 3hr 20min); Inverness (Mon–Sat 3 daily, plus Sun 2 daily in summer; 3hr 45min); Lairg (Mon–Sat 3 daily, plus Sun 2 daily in summer; 2hr 5min).

Wick to: Dingwall (Mon–Sat 3 daily, plus Sun 2 daily in summer; 3hr 20min); Inverness (Mon–Sat 3 daily, plus Sun 2 daily in summer; 3hr 45min); Lairg (Mon–Sat 3 daily, plus Sun 2 daily in summer; 2hr 5min).

Buses

Aviemore to: Grantown-on-Spey (6–9 daily; 35min); Inverness (15 daily; 40min); Newtonmore (8 daily; 20min).

Brora to: Thurso (4–5 daily; 1hr 50min); Wick (5–6 daily; 1hr 15min).

Dornoch to: Brora (5 daily; 35min); Inverness (10 daily; 1hr 10min).

Fort William to: Acharacle (Mon–Sat 2–4 daily; 1hr 30min); Drumnadrochit (6 daily; 1hr 30min); Fort Augustus (6 daily; 1hr); Inverness (6 daily; 2hr); Mallaig (1–2 daily; 2hr).

Gairloch to: Dingwall (3 weekly; 2hr); Inverness (3 weekly; 2hr 20min); Redpoint (1 daily; 1hr 35min).

Inverness to: Aberdeen (hourly; 3hr 40min); Aviemore (Mon–Sat 15 daily, Sun 12 daily; 40min); Cromarty (4 daily; 45min); Drumnadrochit (6 daily; 25min); Durness (May to early Oct 1 daily; 5hr); Fort Augustus (6 daily; 1hr); Fort William (6 daily; 2hr); Gairloch (1 daily; 2hr 20min); Glasgow (7 daily; 3hr 35min–4hr 25min); John O' Groats (1–2 daily; 3hr 40min); Kirkwall (April–Sept 2 daily; 5hr 20min); Kyle of Lochalsh (3–4 daily; 2hr); Lairg (Mon–Sat 2 daily; 2hr); Lochinver (May to early Oct 1 daily; 3hr 10min); Nairn (Mon–Sat hourly; 35min); Newtonmore (8 daily; 1hr 10min); Oban (Mon–Sat 2 daily; 4hr); Perth (10 daily; 2hr 35min); Portree (3–4 daily; 3hr 20min); Tain (hourly; 1hr 15min); Thurso (Mon–Sat 5 daily, Sun 4 daily; 3hr 30 min); Ullapool (2–4 daily; 1hr 25min); Wick (Mon–Sat 3 daily; 1hr 55min).

Kyle of Lochalsh to: Fort William (3 daily; 1hr 50min); Glasgow (3 daily; 5hr); Inverness (3–4 daily; 2hr).

Lochinver to: Inverness (May to early Oct 1 daily; 3hr 10min).

Mallaig to: Acharacle (1–3 daily; 1hr 45min); Fort William (1–2 daily; 2hr).

Thurso to: Bettyhill (2 daily; 1hr 20min); Inverness (Mon–Sat 5 daily, Sun 4 daily; 3hr 30min); Wick (Mon–Sat 2–4 daily, Sun 1 daily; 35min).

Wick to: Inverness (Mon–Sat 3 daily; 1hr 55min); Thurso (Mon–Sat 2–4 daily, Sun 1 daily; 35min).

Ferries

To Lewis: Ullapool–Stornoway, see p.413.

To Mull: Kilchoan–Tobermory, see p.363.

To Orkney: Scrabster–Stromness, see p.621.

To Skye: Mallaig–Armadale; Glenelg–Kylerhea, see p.413.

To the Small Isles: Mallaig–Eigg, Rum, Muck and Canna, see p.413.

Flights

Inverness to: Amsterdam (1 daily; 1hr 35min); Edinburgh (Mon–Fri 1 daily; 50min); Glasgow (Mon–Fri 2 daily; 50min); Kirkwall (Mon–Fri 2 daily; 40min); London (4 daily; 1hr 25min); Shetland (Mon–Fri 1 daily; 1hr 50min); Stornoway (Mon–Sat 2 daily; 40min).

CHAPTER NINE

ORKNEY AND SHETLAND

R eaching up towards the Arctic Circle, and totally exposed to turbulent Atlantic weather systems, the Orkney and Shetland islands gather neatly into two distinct and very different clusters. Often referring to themselves first as Orcadians or Shetlanders, and with unofficial but widely displayed flags, their inhabitants regard Scotland as a separate entity; the mainland to them is the one in their own archipelago, not the Scottish mainland. This feeling of detachment arises from their distinctive geography, history and culture, in which they differ not only from Scotland but also from each other.

To the south, just a short step from the Scottish mainland, are the seventy or so **Orkney Islands**. With the major exception of Hoy, which is high and rugged, these islands are mostly low-lying, gently sloping and richly fertile, and for centuries have provided a reasonably secure living for their inhabitants from farming and, to a much lesser extent, fishing. In spring and summer the days are long, the skies enormous, the sandy beaches dazzling and the meadows thick with wild flowers. There is a peaceful continuity to Orcadian life reflected not only in the well-preserved treasury of Stone Age settlements, such as **Skara Brae**, and standing stones, most notably the **Stones of Stenness**, but also in the rather conservative nature of society here today.

Another sixty miles north, the **Shetland Islands** are in nearly all respects a complete contrast. Dramatic cliffs, teeming with thousands of seabirds, rise straight out of the water to rugged, heather-coated hills, while ice-sculpted sea inlets cut deep into the land, offering memorable coastal walks in Shetland's endless summer evenings. With little fertile ground, Shetlanders have traditionally been crofters rather than farmers, often looking to the sea for an uncertain living in fishing and whaling or the naval and merchant services. Today islanders enthusiastically embrace new opportunities such as fish farming and computing. Nevertheless, the past isn't forgotten; the Norse heritage is clear in every road sign and there are many well-preserved prehistoric sites, such as **Broch of Mousa** and **Jarlshof**.

Since people first began to explore the North Atlantic, Orkney and Shetland have been stepping stones on routes between Britain, Ireland and Scandinavia, and both groups have a long history of settlement, certainly from around 3500–4000 BC. The **Norse settlers**, who began to arrive from about 800 AD, with substantial migration from around 900 AD, left the islands with a unique cultural character. Orkney was a powerful Norse earldom, and Shetland (at first part of the same earldom) was ruled directly from Norway for nearly 300 years after 1195. The Norse legacy is clearly evident today in place names and in dialect words; neither group was ever part of the Gaelic-speaking culture of Highland Scotland, and the later Scottish influence is essentially a Lowland one.

Orkney and Shetland may share a common Norse heritage, but the modern **transport links** between the two are surprisingly poor. In the winter, there is just one ferry a week between the two, and only two a week in the height of summer. And while it's fairly common to meet a fellow visitor who's visiting both sets of islands, it's rare to find an Orcadian who's been to Shetland, or vice versa. When leaving their homeland, for whatever reason, Shetlanders tend to go to Aberdeen, while Orcadians pop over to Caithness on the

Scottish mainland. Public transport is not bad, and the council-run inter-island ferries on Shetland are very cheap; Orkney's inter-island ferries, by contrast, are expensive. If you're thinking of bringing your own vehicle, it might be worth looking into hiring one locally instead, given the time and cost of the car ferries from the mainland.

It's impossible to underestimate the influence of the **weather** in these parts. The one thing you can say about it is that it's interesting, frequently dramatic. More often than not, it will be windy and rainy, though, as they say in the nearby Faroes, you can have all four seasons in one day. The wind-chill factor is not to be taken lightly, and there is often a dampness or drizzle in the air, even when it's not actually raining. Even in late spring and summer, when there can be long dry spells with lots of sunshine, you still need to come prepared for wind, rain and, most frustrating of all, the occasional sea fog. The one good thing about the almost constant presence of the wind is that midges are less of a problem, except on Hoy.

ORKNEY

Just a short step from John O' Groats, the **Orkney Islands** are a unique and fiercely independent grouping. In spring and summer the meadows and clifftops are a brilliant green, shining with wild flowers, while long days pour light onto the land and sea. For an Orcadian, the "Mainland" invariably means the largest island in Orkney, rather than the rest of Scotland, and throughout their history they've been linked to lands much further afield, principally Scandinavia. In the words of the late Orcadian poet George Mackay Brown:

> *Orkney lay athwart a great sea-way*
> *from Viking times onwards, and its lore*
> *is crowded with sailors, merchants, adventurers,*
> *pilgrims, smugglers, storms and sea-changes.*
> *The shores are strewn with wrack, jetsam,*
> *occasional treasure.*

Small communities began to settle in the islands around 4000 BC, and the village at **Skara Brae** on the Mainland is one of the best-preserved Stone Age settlements in Europe. This and many of the other older archeological sites, including the **Stones of Stenness** and **Maes Howe**, are concentrated in the central and western parts of the Mainland. Elsewhere the islands are scattered with chambered tombs and stone circles, a tribute to the well-developed religious and ceremonial practices taking place here from around 2000 BC. More sophisticated **Iron Age** inhabitants built fortified villages incorporating stone towers known as brochs, protected by walls and ramparts, many of which are still in place. Later, Pictish culture spread to Orkney and the remains of several of their early Christian settlements can still be seen, the best at the **Brough of Birsay** in the West Mainland, where a group of small houses is clustered around the remains of an early church. In around the ninth century, **Norse** settlers from Scandinavia arrived and the islands became Norse earldoms, forming an outpost of a powerful, expansive culture which was gradually forcing its way south. The last of the Norse earls was killed in 1231, but they had a lasting impact on the islands, leaving behind not only their language but also the great **St Magnus Cathedral** in Kirkwall, one of Scotland's outstanding examples of medieval architecture.

After the end of Norse rule, the islands became the preserve of **Scottish earls**, who exploited and abused the islanders, although a steady increase in sea trade did offer

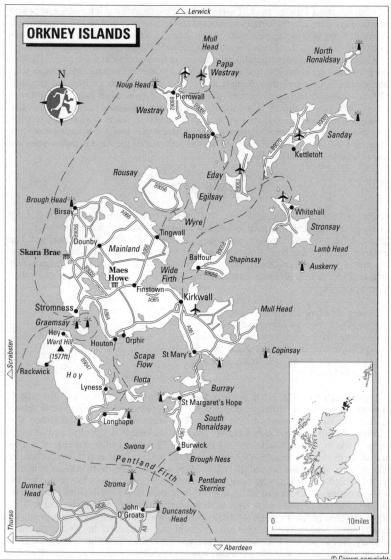

ORKNEY ISLANDS

N

Lerwick

Mull Head

Papa Westray

North Ronaldsay

Noup Head

Pierowall

Westray

B9066

B9065

Rapness

Sanday

B9069

B9070

B9063

Kettletoft

Rousay

Eday

Egilsay

B9056

Whitehall

Brough Head

Birsay

Stronsay

B9055

Wyre

Tingwall

Lamb Head

A966

Dounby

Mainland

Balfour

Shapinsay

Skara Brae

B9058

Auskerry

Maes Howe

A965

Wide Firth

B9059

Finstown

Kirkwall

A965

Mull Head

Stromness

A964

Graemsay

A961

Hoy

Ward Hill

(1577ft)

Houton

Orphir

Scapa Flow

St Mary's

Copinsay

B9047

Rackwick

Hoy

Lyness

Flotta

Burray

St Margaret's Hope

South Ronaldsay

A961

Longhope

Swona

Burwick

Brough Ness

Pentland Firth

Pentland Skerries

Dunnet Head

Stroma

Thurso

John O'Groats

A9

Duncansby Head

Scrabster

Aberdeen

0   10miles

© Crown copyright

some chance of escape. French and Spanish ships sheltered here in the sixteenth century, and the ships of the **Hudson Bay Company** recruited hundreds of Orcadians to work in the Canadian fur trade. The islands were also an important staging post in the **whaling industry** and the herring boom, which drew great numbers of small Dutch, French and Scottish boats. More recently, the naval importance of **Scapa Flow**

ISLAND WILDLIFE

Orkney and Shetland support huge numbers of **seabirds**, particularly during the breeding season from April to August, when cliffs and coastal banks are alive with thousands of guillemots, razorbills, puffins, fulmars and, particularly in Shetland, gannets. Arctic terns are often to be found on small offshore islets or gravelly spits. On coastal heathland or moorland you should see arctic skuas, great skuas, curlews and occasionally whimbrel or golden plover, while in remoter meadows in Orkney, a corncrake may be heard. Many kinds of wild duck are present, especially in winter, but eiders are particularly common. In spring and autumn, large numbers of migrants drop in on their way north or south and very rare specimens may turn up at any time of year. Fair Isle, in particular, has a long list of rarities, and Shetland's isolation has produced its own distinctive subspecies of wren. Some of the best or most accessible bird sites have been noted in the text.

The separation of the islands from the mainland has also meant that some species of **land mammal** are absent and others have developed subspecies. For instance, Shetland has no voles but Orkney boasts its own distinctive type. However, both groups have considerable populations of seals, and Shetland is probably the best place in the whole of Europe to get to see an otter. Further offshore you may well see porpoises, dolphins and several species of whale including minke, pilot, sperm and killer. Shetland is also home to the famous Shetland Pony, whose diminutive form can be seen all over the islands; now mostly domesticated, there are a few places where the ponies still run wild.

Neither of the island groups supports many **trees**, and very few are native. However, the clifftops and meadows of both Orkney and Shetland are rich with beautiful **wild flowers**, including pink thrift, the pale-pink heather-spotted orchid, red campion and, in wetter areas, golden marsh marigolds, yellow iris and insect-eating sundew. Notable **smaller plants** include the purple Scottish primrose, which grows only in Orkney and the far north of Scotland, and the Shetland (or Edmondston's) mouse-eared chickweed with its delicate white flower streaked with yellow, which grows only on the island of Unst.

brought plenty of money and activity during both world wars, and left the clifftops dotted with gun emplacements and the seabed scattered with wrecks, making for wonderful diving opportunities. Since the war, things have quietened down somewhat, although in the last two decades the large **oil terminal** on the island of Flotta, combined with EU funding, has brought surprise windfalls, stemming the exodus of young people. Meanwhile, many disenchanted southerners have become "ferryloupers" (incomers), moving north in search of peace and the apparent simplicity of island life.

The **Mainland** has two main settlements: the ferry port of **Stromness**, an attractive old fishing town on the far southwestern shore, and the central capital of **Kirkwall**, which stands at the dividing point between East and West Mainland. The whole of Mainland is relatively heavily populated and farmed throughout, and is joined by causeways to a string of southern islands, the largest of which is **South Ronaldsay**. The southern island of **Hoy**, the second largest in the archipelago, presents a superbly dramatic landscape, with some of the highest seacliffs in the country. Hoy, however, is atypical of Orkney's smaller, much quieter **northern islands** (linked to the Mainland by regular ferries), which are low-lying, elemental but fertile outcrops of rock and sand, scattered across the ocean.

Rolling out of the sea "like the backs of sleeping whales" (Mackay Brown again), the Orkney Isles offer excellent coastal **walking** and beautiful sweeping white-sand beaches. There is also some good **fishing** to be had in both salt and fresh water, with the rivers and lochs providing some of the best trout and sea-trout fishing in Britain. A lively cultural life includes the **Orkney Folk Festival** in May, and a science festival in

September, both of which have events throughout the islands. June sees the **St Magnus Festival**, an arts festival based in Kirkwall, while July is peppered with several island regattas, followed by numerous agricultural shows culminating in the County Show held in the middle of August. To find out what's on (and what the weather's going to be like), tune in to Radio Orkney on 93.7FM (Mon–Fri 7.30–8am), and buy yourself a copy of *The Orcadian*, which comes out on a Thursday.

Getting around

Bus services on the Orkney Mainland are fairly infrequent, and virtually non-existent on a Sunday, with some of the most interesting areas not served at all; on the islands, there's usually a bus service to and from the ferry terminal and that's all. However,

---

DIALECT AND PLACE NAMES

Between the tenth and seventeenth centuries the chief language of Orkney and Shetland was **Norn**, a Scandinavian tongue close to modern Faroese and Icelandic. After the end of Norse rule and with the transformation of the church, the law, commerce and education, Norn gradually lost out to Scots and English, eventually petering out completely in the eighteenth century. Today, Orkney and Shetland have their own dialects, and individual islands and communities within each group have local variations. The **dialects** have a Scots base, with some Old Norse words; however, they don't sound strongly Scottish, with the Orkney accent – which has been likened to the Welsh one – especially distinctive. Listed below are some of the words you're most likely to hear, including some birds' names and common elements in place names. In most cases, the Shetland form is given; the Orkney terms are very similar, if not identical.

aak	guillemot	*neesick*	porpoise
alan	storm petrel	*noost*	hollow place where a
ayre	beach		boat is drawn up
böd	fisherman's store	*norie*	puffin
bonxie	great skua	(or *tammie-norie*)	
bruck	rubbish	*noup*	steep headland
burra	heath rush	*peerie* (in Orkney,	small
corbie	raven	often *peedie*)	
crö	sheepfold	*plantiecrub*	small drystone
du	familiar form of "you"	(or *plantiecrö*)	enclosure for
dunter	eider duck		growing cabbages
eela	rod-fishing from	*quoy*	enclosed, cultivated
	small boats		common land
ferrylouper	incomer (Orkney)	*reestit*	cured (as in *reestit*
fourareen	four-oared boat		mutton)
foy	party or festival	*roost*	tide race
geo	coastal inlet	*scattald*	common grazing land
haa	laird's house	*scootie alan*	arctic skua
hap	hand-knitted shawl	*scord*	gap or pass in a
kame	ridge of hills		ridge of hills
kishie	basket	*shaela*	dark grey
maa	seagull	*shalder*	oystercatcher
mallie (Shetland) or	fulmar petrel	*simmer dim*	summer twilight
mallimak (Orkney)		*sixern*	six-oared boat
mool	headland	*solan*	gannet
moorit	brown	*soothmoother*	incomer (Shetland)
mootie	tiny	*tystie*	black guillemot
muckle	large	*voe*	sea inlet

GETTING TO ORKNEY

Orkney is connected to the Scottish mainland by several **ferry** routes. P&O Scottish Ferries (☎01856/850655) runs car ferries to **Stromness** once a week (June–Aug twice weekly) from **Aberdeen** (8hr) and daily services on the much shorter and cheaper crossing (2hr) from **Scrabster**, linked by shuttle bus to the nearby town of Thurso on the north coast, which has train and bus connections from Inverness. There's also the little-known option of hopping aboard one of the Orcargo vessels (☎01856/873838) that sail into **Kirkwall** from **Invergordon** (9hr), on the Tain peninsula, just north of Inverness. As the name suggests, the ships are primarily for cargo, so facilities are basic; prices are competitive, however, and there are six sailings a week, though they arrive and leave from Invergordon at an ungodly hour in the morning. A new vehicle ferry service is also in the pipeline between St Margaret's Hope on South Ronaldsay, and Gills, east of Thurso, on the north coast (ring the tourist board for the latest).

A passenger ferry runs between **John O' Groats** and **Burwick** on South Ronaldsay (May–Sept 2–4 daily; 45min), with which the Orkney Bus service from Inverness connects; there's also a free bus service from Thurso. A day-trip is available from Inverness or John O' Groats, with a tour of some of the major sights on Orkney; details of both ferry and bus are available from John O' Groats Ferries (☎01955/611353 or ☎0800/731 7872). There's also a weekly (June–Aug twice weekly; 8hr) P&O service between Stromness and **Lerwick** in Shetland.

Direct **flights** connect Kirkwall airport with Shetland, Wick, Inverness, Aberdeen, Edinburgh and Glasgow, with good connections from Birmingham, London and Manchester. All these services can be booked through British Airways (☎0345/222111).

cycling is cheap and, with few steep hills and modest distances, relatively easy, though the wind can make it hard going. Bikes can be rented in Kirkwall, Stromness and on most of the smaller islands. Bringing a **car** to Orkney is straightforward, if not exactly cheap; alternatively, you can rent one in Kirkwall, Stromness or on several of the islands. Especially if time is limited, it may be worth considering one of the informative bus or minibus **tours**: Wildabout Orkney Tours (☎01856/851011, *wildabout@orknet.co.uk*) offer good-value tours of the chief sights on the Mainland and Hoy.

Getting to the other islands from the Mainland isn't difficult, though it is relatively expensive: Orkney Ferries (☎01856/872044) operates several **ferries** daily to Hoy, Shapinsay and Rousay, and between one and three, depending on route and season, to all the others except North Ronaldsay, which has a weekly boat on Fridays. If you're taking a car on any of the ferries, it is sensible to book your ticket well in advance. There are also **flights** to Eday, North Ronaldsay, Westray, Papa Westray, Sanday and Stronsay, operated by Loganair (☎01856/872420), using a tiny eight-seater plane. In July and August, Loganair even offer sightseeing flights over Orkney,

ACCOMMODATION PRICE CODES

Throughout this book, accommodation **prices** have been graded with the codes below, according to the cost of the least expensive double room in high season. Price codes are not given for campsites, most of which charge under £10 per person. Almost all hostels charge less than £10 a night for a bed – the few exceptions to this rule have the prices quoted in the text. For a full account of the accommodation price codes, see p.31.

① under £40	④ £60–70	⑦ £110–150
② £40–50	⑤ £70–90	⑧ £150–200
③ £50–60	⑥ £90–110	⑨ £200 and over

which are spectacular in fine weather, as well as a discounted Orkney Adventure Ticket, which allows you to visit three islands. Travel between individual islands by sea or air isn't so straightforward, but careful study of timetables can sometimes reduce the need to come all the way back to Kirkwall. It's worth enquiring from Orkney Ferries about the additional sailings on summer Sundays that often make useful inter-island connections.

Stromness

STROMNESS has to be one of the most enchanting ports at which to arrive by boat, its picturesque waterfront a procession of tiny sandstone jetties and slate roofs nestling below the green hill of Brinkie's Brae. As Orkney's main point of arrival, Stromness is a great introduction, and one that's well worth spending a day exploring, or using as a base, in preference to Kirkwall. Despite looking considerably older than Kirkwall, Stromness was actually something of a late starter, even though the natural sheltered harbour of Hamnavoe must have been used since Viking times. The town really only took off in the eighteenth century, when European conflicts made it safer for ships heading across the Atlantic to travel around the top of Scotland rather than through the English Channel, many of them calling in to Stromness to take on food, water and crew. The Hudson's Bay Company made Stromness its main base from which to make the long journey across the north Atlantic, and crews from Stromness were also hired for herring and whaling expeditions, and, of course, press-ganged into the Royal Navy.

By 1842, the town boasted forty or so pubs and reports were made of "outrageous and turbulent proceedings of seamen and others who frequent the harbour". The herring boom brought large numbers of small boats to the town, along with thousands of young women who gutted and pickled the fish before they were packed in barrels. Today Stromness remains an important harbour town and fishing port, serving as Orkney's main ferry terminal and as the headquarters of the Northern Lighthouse Board.

Information and accommodation

Arriving by ferry, you'll disembark at the new ferry terminal, which also houses the **tourist office** (April–Oct Mon–Sat 8am–6pm, Sun 9am–4pm; Nov–March Mon–Fri 9am–5pm; ☎01856/850716), where you can pick up the excellent free *Stromness Heritage Guide*, which takes you through all the buildings of interest. Unfortunately, Stromness has a fairly poor selection of **hotels**, with the venerable Victorian *Stromness Hotel* (☎01856/850610, *stromnesshotel@compuserve.com*; ⑤) – the town's first – probably your best bet. As for **B&Bs**, there's a traditional end-on waterfront house next to the museum at 2 South End (☎01856/850215; ②; April–Oct), or, further south still, *Stenigar* (☎01856/850438; ②; April–Oct), a converted boatyard which has lots of character and is situated just before the campsite on the Ness Road. Two **self-catering** options worth considering are *Pier House* (☎01856/850415; 6 people; £350 per week), a traditional end-on house at 34 Dundas Street that does weekend lets in the low season as well as week-long summer lets, or, for complete isolation, you can rent out the farmhouse on the Holms of Stromness (☎01224/587278; 8 people; £390 per week), the tidal islands in Stromness harbour (a rowing boat comes with the house).

Stromness has an SYHA **hostel** in a converted school on Hellichole Road (☎01856/850589; mid-March to Oct), signposted off the main street; it has a curfew and single-sex dorms. More laid-back is the family-run *Brown's Hostel*, 45–47 Victoria St (☎01856/850661), with bunk beds in shared rooms and kitchen facilities; it's open all year and all day, and there's no curfew. There's also a **campsite** (May to mid-Sept; ☎01856/873535) in a superb setting a mile south of the ferry terminal at Point of Ness, with views out to Hoy; it's well-equipped and even has its own lounge, but is extremely exposed, especially if a southwesterly is blowing.

The Town

Stromness still has a few reminders of the town's trading heyday, most notably the **Warehouse**, situated diagonally opposite the new ferry terminal – though it may not look like it, the building was constructed in the 1760s, too late to catch the trade in American rice. More eye-catching is the **Stromness Hotel**, a tall and imposing sandstone building behind the Warehouse; during the Second World War Gracie Fields sang from its balcony, when it served as the headquarters of the Orkney and Shetland Defence (OS Def).

Unlike Kirkwall, the old town of Stromness – famously described by Sir Walter Scott as "a dirty, straggling town" – still hugs the shoreline, its one and only street, a narrow winding affair, built long before the advent of the motor car, still paved with great flagstones and fed by a tight network of alleyways or closes. The central section, which begins at the Stromness Hotel, is known as **Victoria Street**, though in fact it takes on several other names – Graham Place, Dundas Street, Alfred Street and South End – as it threads its way southwards. On the east side of the street the houses are gable end on to the waterfront, and originally each one would have had their own pier, from which merchants would trade with passing ships.

You can visit the first of the old jetties, to the south of the modern harbour, as it now houses the **Pier Arts Centre** (Tues–Sat 10.30am–12.30pm & 1.30–5pm; July & Aug also Sun 2–5pm; free). The art gallery is spread over two buildings, divided by a lovely flagstone sun-trap courtyard (access is down an alleyway off the main street): the first building hosts temporary exhibitions, often featuring painting and sculpture by local artists, while the warehouse has a remarkable permanent display of twentieth-century British art. At first it comes as a shock to see abstract works executed by members of the Cornish art scene such Barbara Hepworth, Ben Nicholson, Terry Frost and Patrick Heron, but the marine themes of many of the works, and in particular the primitive scenes by Alfred Wallis, have a special resonance in this seaport.

Ten minutes' walk down the main street, at the junction of Alfred Street and South End, is the newly refurbished **Stromness Museum** (May–Sept daily 10am–5pm; Oct–April Mon–Sat 10.30am–12.30pm & 1.30–5pm; £2), built in 1858, partly to house the collections of the local natural history society. The natural history collection is still there – don't miss the pull-out drawers of birds' eggs, butterflies and moths – and has since been joined by a whole range of salty artefacts gathered from shipwrecks and Arctic expeditions, including barnacle-encrusted crockery from the German High Seas Fleet that sank in Scapa Flow, beaver fur hats, Cree Indian cloth and part of the torpedo that sunk the HMS *Royal Oak*. As a plaque recalls, the Stromness-born poet **George Mackay Brown** (1921–1996) lived out the last twenty years of his life in the house diagonally opposite the museum.

The **cannon**, further south down South End by the shore, was fired to announce the arrival of a ship from the Hudson's Bay Company. Today the trade in American rice and Canadian fur has gone, but the site of the cannon still gives magnificent views of the harbour. Further south along Ness Road is **The Doubles**, a large pair of houses on a raised platform that were built as a home by Mrs Christian Robertson with the proceeds of her shipping agency, which sent as many as 800 men on whaling expeditions in one year.

Eating and drinking

Stromness has a couple of decent **places to eat** on and off the main street. The moderately expensive *Hamnavoe Restaurant,* at 35 Graham Place (☎01856/850606; Thurs–Sun eves only), offers the town's most ambitious cooking, using local produce of its prehistoric monuments, the Neolithic village of Skara Brae. Less well known is that the cliffs to the north and south of the Bay of Skaill, where Skara Brae lies, provide some of the most spectacularly rugged coastal walks on Orkney's Mainland. The best place to head for is **Yesnaby**, to the south of the Bay of Skaill, where the sandstone cliffs have been savagely eroded into stacks and *geos* by the force of the Atlantic. Come here during a westerly gale and you'll see the waves sending sea spray shooting over the wartime buildings and the neighbouring fields. As a result, the clifftops support a unique plantlife, which thrives on the salt spray, including the rare and very small Scottish Primrose, which flowers in May and from July to late September. The walk south along the coast from here is exhilarating: the Old Man of Hoy is visible in the distance, and, after a mile and a half, you come to West Mainland's own version, known as **Yesnaby Castle**.

Skara Brae and Skaill House

The beautiful white curve of the Bay of Skaill is home to **Skara Brae** (April–Sept daily 9.30am–6.30pm; Oct–March Mon–Sat 9.30am–4.30pm, Sun 2–4.30pm; £4 in summer; £3.20 in winter), where the extensive remains of a small Neolithic fishing and farming village, dating back to 3000 BC, were discovered in 1850 after a fierce storm ripped off the dunes covering them. The village is very well preserved, its houses huddled together and connected by narrow passages which would originally have been covered over with turf. The houses themselves consist of a single, spacious living room, surrounded by a vast array of domestic detail, including dressers, fireplaces, built-in cupboards, beds and boxes, all carefully put together from slabs of stone.

Unfortunately, the sheer numbers now visiting Skara Brae mean that you can no longer explore the site properly, but only look down from the outer walls. Sadly, too, the best-preserved example, House 6, now sports a perspex roof to protect it from the elements; however, House 1, which also contains a dresser, as yet does not. Before you reach the site you must buy a ticket from the new visitor centre, which also contains a small introductory exhibition that begins with a short video. That, a few replica finds, and some hands-on stuff for kids, helps put the site in context. You then proceed to a full-scale replica of House 6, complete with a fake wood-and-skin roof. It's all a tad neat and tidy, with fetching up-lighting, rather than dark, smoky and smelly, but it'll give you the general idea.

In the summer months, your ticket to Skara Brae also covers entry to nearby **Skaill House**, a vast range of buildings 300 yards inland, that was once the home of the laird of Skaill. The original house was a simple two-storey block with a small courtyard, built for Bishop George Graham in the 1620s, but it has since been much extended. Guided tours are available at no extra charge, or you can simply stroll round. The house's prize possession is Captain Cook's dinner service from the *Resolution*, which was delivered after Cook's death when the *Resolution* and the *Discovery* sailed into Stromness in 1780. The last occupant of the house was Mrs Kathleen Scarth, who died in 1991; her bedroom has been left as it was, and is filled with old frocks, an ostrich feather fan and a "twist and slim exerciser".

Practicalities

With no bus service to speak of, you really need your own transport to reach Sandwick. There's no main settlement as such, though you'll find a couple of inexpensive, modern **B&Bs** in the vicinity. On the A967, overlooking the Loch of Harray, there's *Dencraigon* (☎01856/841647; ①), while northeast of the Bay of Skaill in a more secluded location is *Netherstove* (☎01856/841625; ①), with a great view over the bay, comfortable rooms and self-catering cottages available; the Georgian former manse of *Flotterston House*

(☎01856/841700; ②) also enjoys great views, and does very good breakfasts. Closer to Yesnaby (and Stromness), at Kirbister, *Brettobreck Farm* (☎01856/850373; ①) is a traditional and homely Orcadian farmhouse and working dairy farm.

Birsay

Occupying the northwest corner of the Mainland, the parish of **BIRSAY** was the centre of Norse power in Orkney for several centuries, before the earls moved to Kirkwall some time after the construction of the cathedral. Today a tiny cluster of homes is gathered around the sandstone ruins of the **Earl's Palace**, which was built in the second half of the sixteenth century by Robert Stewart, Earl of Orkney, using the forced labour of the islanders, who weren't even given food and drink for their work. By all accounts, it was a "sumptuous and stately dwelling", built in four wings around a central courtyard, its upper rooms decorated with painted ceilings and rich furnishings; surrounding the palace were flower and herb gardens, a bowling green and archery butts. The palace appears to have lasted barely a century before falling into rack and ruin; the crumbling walls and turrets retain much of their grandeur, although inside there is little remaining domestic detail. By comparison, the Earl's Palace in Kirkwall seems almost humble.

Half a mile southeast of the palace, up the burn, is the **Barony Mills** (April–Sept daily 10am–1pm & 2–5pm; £1.50), Orkney's only working nineteenth-century water mill to survive into the modern era. The mill specializes in producing traditional stoneground beremeal, essential for making bere bannocks. Bere is a four-kernel barley crop with a very short growing season perfectly suited for the local climate and was once the staple diet in these parts. The miller on duty will give you a guided tour and show you the machinery going through its paces, though milling only takes place in the autumn.

Brough of Birsay

Just over half a mile northwest of the palace is the **Brough of Birsay**, a substantial Pictish settlement on a small tidal island that is only accessible during the two hours each side of high tide. Stromness and Kirkwall tourist offices have the tide times and Radio Orkney broadcasts them (93.7 FM; Mon–Fri 7.30–8am). Once you reach the island, there's a small ticket office where you must pay your entrance fee (£1), and where you can see a few artefacts gathered from the site, including a game made from whalebone and an antler pin. Coastal erosion over the last eight centuries means that some of the site has disappeared off the side of the low cliffs, and concrete sea defences are currently in place to try and stem the tide.

The focus of the village was – and still is – the sandstone-built twelfth-century **St Peter's Church**, which stands higher than the surrounding buildings; the stone seating along the walls is still in place, and there are a couple of semi-circular recesses for altars, and a semi-circular apse. The church is thought to have stood at the centre of a monastic complex of some sort – the foundations of a courtyard and outer buildings can be made out to the west. Close by is a large complex of Viking-era buildings, including several houses, a sauna and some sophisticated stone drains.

The Brough of Birsay is a popular day-trip, partly due to the fun of dodging the tides, but few folk bother to explore the rest of the island, whose gentle green slopes, when viewed from the mainland, belie the dramatic, rugged cliffs that characterize the rest of the coastline. In winter, sea spray from the waves crashing against the cliffs can envelop the entire island. In summer the cliffs are home to various seabirds, including a fair few puffin, making the half-mile walk to the island's castellated **lighthouse**, and back along the northern coastline, well worth the effort. If you make it

Orphir

The southern shores of the West Mainland, overlooking Scapa Flow, are much gentler than the rest of the coastline, and have fewer of Orkney's premier league sights. However, if you've time to spare, or you're heading for Hoy from the car ferry terminal at Houton, there are a couple of points of interest in the neighbouring parish of **ORPHIR**. Here, beside the parish cemetery, the council have built a new **Orkneyinga Saga Centre** (daily 9am–5pm; free), where a small exhibition and a fifteen-minute audiovisual attempts to give you a brief rundown of the plot of the *Orkneyinga Saga*, the bloodthirsty Viking tale written around 1200 AD by an unnamed Icelandic author, which described the conquest of the Northern Isles by the Norsemen. The Earl's Bu at Orphir features in the saga as the home of Earl Thorfinn the Mighty, Earl Paul and his son, Haakon, who ordered the murder of Earl (later Saint) Magnus on Egilsay (see p.581). The foundations of what is presumed to have been the Earl's Bu have been uncovered just outside the cemetery gates, while inside the cemetery is a section of the round church, built by Haakon after his pilgrimage to Jerusalem.

Further along the A954 towards Kirkwall lies the **Hobbister RSPB reserve**, a mixture of moorland, sea cliffs, saltmarsh and sandflats that's great for spotting a wide variety of birdlife, and, at the sandy Waulkmill Bay, a relatively warm place in which to swim.

Kirkwall

Initial impressions of **KIRKWALL** are not always favourable. It has nothing to match the picturesque harbour of Stromness, and its urban sprawl is far less appealing. However, it does have one great redeeming feature, and that is its sandstone cathedral, without doubt the finest medieval building in the north of Scotland. In any case, if you're staying any length of time in Orkney, you're more or less bound to find yourself in Kirkwall at some point, as the town is also home to the island's better-stocked shops, including the islands' only large supermarket, and is the departure point for most of the ferries to Orkney's northern isles.

Part of the reason for Kirkwall's disappointing waterfront is that today's harbour is a largely modern invention; in the mid-nineteenth century, the shoreline ran along Junction Road, and before that it was flush with the west side of main street. Nowadays, the town is very much divided into two main focal points: the busy **harbour**, at the north end of the town, where ferries come and go all year round, and where, during the summer, launches offload smartly dressed holidaymakers from the numerous cruise ships that weigh anchor in the Bay of Kirkwall; and the flagstoned **main street**, which changes its name four times as it twists its way south from the harbour past the cathedral.

Arrival, information and accommodation

Car **ferries** docking at Stromness are met by buses to Kirkwall (40min), and there are also bus connections (45min) from the Burwick terminal on South Ronaldsay, served by passenger ferry from John O' Groats. The **bus station** is five minutes' walk west of the town centre. Kirkwall **airport** is about three miles southeast of Kirkwall on the A960; it's not served by buses, but a taxi into town should only set you back about £6.

Kirkwall itself is an easy place in which to orientate yourself, despite its **main street** taking four different names – Bridge Street, Albert Street, Broad Street and Victoria Street – as it winds through the town, and the prominent spire of St Magnus Cathedral clearly marks the town centre. The helpful **tourist office**, on Broad Street beside the cathedral graveyard (April–Sept daily 8.30am–8pm; Oct–March Mon–Sat 9.30am–5pm; ☎01856/872856), books accommodation, changes money and gives out an excellent free leaflet, the *Kirkwall Heritage Guide*, which takes you through all the buildings of interest. Most events are advertised in *The Orcadian*, which comes out on Thursdays, and there's a *What's on Diary* on BBC Radio Orkney (93.7 FM; Mon–Fri 7.30–8am).

As for **accommodation**, Kirkwall has plenty of small rooms in ordinary B&Bs, and a host of blandly refurbished hotels, but nothing exceptional, so unless you're reliant on public transport, or have business in town, there's really no strong reason to base yourself here, rather than out in Orkney's wonderful countryside. The SYHA **hostel** (☎01856/872243) on the road to Orphir is a good ten minutes' walk from the centre of town – it's no beauty from the outside, but its comfortable enough inside. A more central option is the small *Peedie Hostel* (☎01856/875477), on the waterfront next door to the *Ayre Hotel*. There's also a **campsite** (☎01856/873535; mid-May to mid-Sept) behind the new Pickaquoy Leisure Centre, five minutes' walk west of the bus station; the site is well-equipped with laundry facilities, but it's hardly what you'd call picturesque.

Hotels and B&Bs

Albert Hotel, Mounthoolie Lane (☎01856/876000). Great central location, lively bar (with disco attached), and completely refurbished inside, this is a comfortable option. ③.

Ayre Hotel, Ayre Road (☎01856/873001, *reception@ayrehotel.co.uk*) Despite outside appearances, this is probably the best option in town: smart, friendly and on the waterfront, with a good reputation for traditional live music. ⑤.

Briar Lea, 10 Dundas Crescent (☎01856/872747). Attractive nineteenth-century stone-built B&B, with its own walled garden, within easy walking distance of the town centre. ①.

Foveran Hotel, two miles out on the A964 to Orphir (☎01856/872389). Suitable if you've got your own transport, this is a pleasant modern hotel, with comfortable rooms, a good restaurant, and great views over Scapa Flow. ④.

West End Hotel, 14 Main St (☎01856/872368). Comfortable and welcoming hotel in an old, characterful building; serves huge breakfasts. ③.

Whiteclett, St Catherine's Place (☎01856/874193). Reliable, comfortable B&B in a listed house right by the waterfront. ①.

The Town

Standing at the very heart of Kirkwall, **St Magnus Cathedral** (April–Sept Mon–Sat 9am–6pm, Sun 2–6pm; Oct–March Mon–Sat 9am–1pm & 2–5pm; Sunday service at 11.15am) is the town's most compelling sight. This beautiful red sandstone building was begun in 1137 by the Orkney Earl Rognvald, who decided to make full use of a growing cult surrounding the figure of his uncle Magnus, killed on the orders of his cousin Haakon in 1115 (see p.581). When Magnus's body was buried in Birsay a heavenly light was said to have shone overhead, and his grave soon became a place of pilgrimage attributed with miraculous powers and attracting pilgrims from as far afield as Shetland. When Rognvald finally took over the earldom he built the cathedral in his uncle's honour, moving the centre of religious and secular power from Birsay to Kirkwall.

The first version of the cathedral, built using yellow sandstone from Eday and red sandstone from the Mainland, was somewhat smaller than today's structure, which has been added to over the centuries, with a new east window in the thirteenth century, the extension of the nave in the fifteenth century and a new west window to mark the building's 850th anniversary in 1987. Today the soft sandstone is badly eroded – the capitals around the main doors are reduced to gnarled stumps – but it's still an immensely impressive building, its shape and style echoing the great cathedrals of Europe. Inside, the atmosphere is surprisingly intimate, the bulky sandstone columns drawing you up to the exposed brickwork arches, while around the walls is a series of mostly seventeenth-century tombstones, many carved with a skull and crossbones and other emblems of mortality, alongside chilling inscriptions calling on the reader to "remember death waits us all, the hour none knows". In the southeastern corner of the cathedral lies the tomb of the Stromness-born Arctic explorer John Rae, who went off to try and find Sir John Franklin's expedition; he is depicted asleep, dressed in moleskins and furs, his rifle and Bible by his side. Beside Rae's tomb is Orkney's own poets' corner, with memorials to, among others, George Mackay Brown, Eric Linklater, Robert Rendall and Edwin Muir. Another poignant monument is the one to the dead of HMS *Royal Oak*, which was torpedoed in Scapa Flow in 1939 with the loss of 833 men (see p.573).

To the south of the church are the ruined remains of the **Bishop's Palace** (April–Sept daily 9.30am–6.30pm; HS; £1.80), residence of the Bishop of Orkney since the twelfth century. It was here that the Norwegian King Haakon died in 1263 on his return from defeat at the Battle of Largs. Most of what you see now, however, dates from the time of Bishop Robert Reid, the founder of Edinburgh University, in the mid-sixteenth century. The walls still stand, as does the tall round tower in which the bishop had his private chambers; a narrow spiral staircase takes you to the top for a good view of the cathedral and across Kirkwall's rooftops. If you're planning on visiting any of Orkney's other Historic Scotland sights, it might be worth buying the joint ticket, which costs £9 and covers entry to Skara Brae, the Broch of Gurness, and Maes Howe.

The neighbouring **Earl's Palace**, built by the infamous Earl Patrick Stewart around 1600, using forced labour, is rather better preserved, and a lot more fun to explore. With its grand entrance, fancy oriel windows, dank dungeons, massive fireplaces and magnificent central hall, it has a confident solidity, and is reckoned to be one of the finest examples of Renaissance architecture in Scotland. The roof may be missing, but many domestic details remain, including a set of toilets and the stone shelves used by the clerk to do his filing. Earl Patrick enjoyed his palace for only a very short time before he was imprisoned. The earl ordered his son, Robert, to organize an insurrection; he held out four days in the palace against the Earl of Caithness, but eventually shared the same fate as his father (see p.606).

Opposite the cathedral stands the sixteenth-century **Tankerness House**, a former home for the clergy. It has been renovated countless times over the years, most recently in the 1960s in order to provide a home for the **Orkney Museum** (Mon–Sat 10.30am–5pm; May–Sept also Sun 2–5pm; free). Among its more unusual artefacts are a collection of balls used in a traditional Orkney street game, The Ba', played at Christmas and New Year; other exhibits to look out for include a witch's spell box, and a lovely whalebone plaque from a Viking boat grave discovered on Sanday. In addition, there are a couple of rooms which have been restored as they would have been in 1820, when the building was a private home for the Baikie family. On a warm summer afternoon, the gardens (which can be entered either from the house itself or from a gate on Tankerness Lane) are thick with the buzz of bees and brilliant blooms.

At the harbour end of Junction Road, at Kiln Corner, you can browse around the tiny **Orkney Wireless Museum** (April–Sept Mon–Sat 10am–4.30pm, Sun 2–4.30pm; £2), which is packed to the roof with every sort of radio equipment, but is particularly strong on technical flotsam from the two world wars.

Highland Park, Scapa and the Grain Earth House

Further afield, a mile or so south of the town centre on the A961 to South Ronaldsay, is the **Highland Park distillery** (Easter–Oct Mon–Fri 10am–4pm; July & Aug also Sat 10am–4pm & Sun noon–4pm; Nov–March Mon–Fri tours at 2pm; ☎01856/874619; £3), billed as "the most northerly legal distillery in Scotland". It's been in operation for more than 200 years, and still has its own maltings, although it was closed during World War

II, when the army used it as a food store and the huge vats served as communal baths. You can decide for yourself whether the taste still lingers by partaking of the customary dram after one of the regular guided tours of the beautiful old buildings.

If the weather happens to be unusually good and you're moved to consider taking the plunge but are stuck in Kirkwall, do as the locals do and head one mile south of town on the B9148 to **Scapa Bay**, Kirkwall's very own sandy beach. Briefly a naval headquarters at the outbreak of World War I, Scapa's pier is now used by the council tugs and pilot launches servicing the oil tankers out in Scapa Flow. Visible from the beach is the green Admiralty wreck buoy marking the position of HMS *Royal Oak*, which was torpedoed by a German U-Boat on October 14, 1939, with the loss of 833 men (out of a total crew of around 1400). A small display shed at the eastern end of the bay tells the full story, and has photos of the wreck (still an official war grave) as it looks today.

If you've time to kill and the weather's not so good, you could search out one of Kirkwall's more unusual sights, the **Grain Earth House**, a food cellar dating back to the first millennium BC, now hidden in the industrial estate, northwest of the town centre. Collect the key (and a torch) from Ortak jewellers, at the entrance to the estate, and head round the corner. Steep steps lead down to a long, dark, curving passageway which ends at a stone-clad cellar held up by large stone pillars – now you know what it felt like to be an Iron Age bere bannock.

Eating, drinking and entertainment

Given the quality of Orkney beef, and the quantity of shellfish caught in the vicinity, Kirkwall's **food** options are pretty disappointing. *Trenabies* and the *Pomona Café*, both on Albert Street, are both venerable institutions, but the nicest **café** is the *Strynd* tearoom up the alleyway by the tourist office. For something more substantial, there's nothing for it but to head for one of the town's hotels – the *Albert*, and the *West End* are probably the best options, offering both **bar meals** and à la carte – or opt for Orkney's Indian restaurant, the *Mumtaz*, on Bridge Street. The best **fish and chips** are from *Raeburn's* at the corner of Union Street and Junction Road.

The **nightlife** scene in Kirkwall is a lot more animated. The liveliest **pub** is the *Torvhaug Inn* at the harbour end of Bridge Street; another good place to try is the *Bothy Bar* in the *Albert Hotel*, which sometimes has live music and is attached to *Matchmakers* **disco** (Thurs, Fri & Sat only). The *Ayre Hotel* has a good reputation for **traditional live music**, especially the regular Orkney Accordion and Fiddle Club nights on Wednesdays. There's also sometimes live music at the *Quoyburray Inn*, a couple of miles beyond the airport on the A960 – check *The Orcadian* entertainment listings for the latest.

Kirkwall's new Pickaquoy Leisure Centre – known locally as the "Picky" – is a short walk from the town centre, up Pickaquoy Road, past Safeways supermarket. It now serves as one of the town's main large-scale venues, and also contains the New Phoenix **cinema** (☎01856/879900). It does not, however, have a swimming pool: this is located on the other side of town on Thomas Street.

Listings

Airport ☎01856/872421.
Banks There are branches of the big Scottish banks on the main street, all with their own cashpoints.
Bike rental Bobby's Cycle Hire, Tankerness Lane (☎01856/875777).
Bookshops Leonard's at the corner of Bridge Street and Albert Street are the best stocked.
Camping gear & outdoor sports Eric Kemp, 31–33 Bridge St (☎872137).
Car rental Peace's Car Hire, Junction Road (☎01856/872866); John G. Shearer, Ayre Service Station (☎01856/872950); W. R. Tullock, Castle Street and Kirkwall Airport (☎01856/876262).

car ferries arrive at Stromness, but there is still a small passenger ferry between John O' Groats and Burwick, on the southernmost tip of the island (see p.559 for details).

St Margaret's Hope

The main settlement on South Ronaldsay is **ST MARGARET'S HOPE**, which local tradition says takes its name from Margaret, the Maid of Norway, who is thought to have died here in November 1290 while on her way to marry the English King Edward II (then Prince Edward). Margaret had already been proclaimed the Queen of Scotland, and the marriage was intended to unify the two countries. Today, St Margaret's Hope – or "The Hope", as it's known locally – is a pleasing little gathering of stone-built houses overlooking a sheltered bay, and is by far the best base from which to explore the area. As is obvious from the architecture, and the piers, The Hope was once a thriving port, and local hopes are pinned on the new car ferry service link with Caithness that is due to start in the near future – in the meantime, it remains a very peaceful place in which to chill out.

The village smithy on Cromarty Square has been turned into a **Smiddy Museum** (May & Sept daily 2–4pm; June–Aug noon–4pm; Oct Sun 2–4pm; free), which is particularly fun for kids, who enjoy getting hands-on with the old tools, drills and giant bellows. There's also a small exhibition on the annual **Boys' Ploughing Match**, in which local boys compete with miniature hand-held ploughs. The competition, which is taken extremely seriously by all those involved, happens on the third Saturday in August, at the beautiful golden beach at the **Sands O'Right** in Hoxa, a couple of miles west of The Hope.

St Margaret's Hope has some very good **accommodation** options. First choice is the *Creel Restaurant and Rooms* (☎01856/831311; ④) on Front Road, one of the best restaurants in Scotland and winner of all sorts of awards for its superb **food** featuring local produce. It's expensive, but friendly and relaxed, and the rooms are comfortable too. More modest bar meals are available in the popular bar of the nearby *Murray Arms Hotel* (☎01856/831205; ②), and from the *Galley Inn* of *The Anchorage* B&B (☎01856/831456; ③), also on the seafront. Among the Hope's **B&Bs**, *West End House* (☎01856/831495; ②) is outstanding, with appealing rooms and a pleasant garden, as is *Bellevue Guest House* (☎01856/831294; ②), on a hill just east of the village. For more basic accommodation, head for *Wheems* **hostel**, about a mile and a half from the War Memorial in Eastside (☎01856/831537). Mattresses and ingredients for a wholesome breakfast are provided, and organic produce from the croft is on sale.

Tomb of the Eagles

One of the most enjoyable archeological sights to visit on Orkney is the ancient chambered burial cairn, at the southeastern corner of South Ronaldsay, known as the **Tomb of the Eagles** (daily: April–Oct 10am–8pm; Nov–March 10am–noon; £2.50). Discovered, excavated and still owned by a local farmer, Ronald Simpson of Liddel, a visit here makes a refreshing change from the usual interpretive centre. First off, you get to look round the family's private museum of prehistoric artefacts – this is the original "hands-on" museum, so visitors can actually touch and admire the painstaking craftsmanship of Neolithic folk, and examine a skull. Next you get a brief guided tour of a nearby Bronze Age **burnt mound**, which is basically a Neolithic rubbish dump, beside which there was a large trough, where joints of meat were boiled by throwing in rocks from the fire. Finally you get to walk out to the **chambered cairn**, by the cliff's edge, where human remains were found alongside talons and carcasses of sea eagles. To enter the cairn you must lie on a trolley and pull yourself in using an overhead rope – something that's guaranteed to put a smile on every visitor's face. The cairn's clifftop location is spectacular, and walking along the coast in either direction is rewarding:

south to the sea inlet of Ham Geo, or north to Halcro Head, and beyond to Wind Wick Bay, where seals and their pups can be seen in the autumn.

Hoy

Hoy, Orkney's second-largest island, rises sharply out of the sea to the southwest of the Mainland. The least typical of the islands, but certainly the most dramatic, its north and west sides are made up of great glacial valleys and mountainous moorland rising to the 1577ft mass of Ward Hill, dropping into the sea off the enormous cliffs of St John's Head, and, to the south, forming the sea stack known as the **Old Man of Hoy**. This part of the island, though a huge expanse, is virtually uninhabited, with just the cluster of houses at **Rackwick** nestling dramatically in a bay between the cliffs. Meanwhile, most of Hoy's 400 or so residents live on the gentler, more fertile land in the southeast in and around the villages of **Lyness** and **Longhope**. This part of the island is littered with buildings dating from the two world wars, when Scapa Flow served as the main base for the British Navy.

Two **ferry services** run to Hoy: a passenger ferry from Stromness to the village of Hoy (2–4 daily; 25min; ☎01856/850624), which also serves the small island of Graemsay; and the roll-on/roll-off car ferry from Houton on the Mainland to Lyness (2–5 daily; 30min–1hr; ☎01856/811397), which sometimes calls in at the oil terminal island of Flotta, and begins and ends its daily schedule at Longhope. There's no bus service on Hoy, but those arriving on the passenger ferry from Stromness should find a **minibus** waiting to take them to Rackwick.

North Hoy

Much of Hoy's magnificent landscape is embraced by the **North Hoy RSPB Reserve** (which covers most of the northwest end of the island), in which the rough grasses and heather harbour a cluster of arctic plants and a healthy population of mountain hares, as well as numerous great skuas, plus a few merlins, kestrels and peregrine falcons, while the more sheltered valleys are nesting sites for snipe and arctic skua. Walkers, arriving by passenger ferry from Stromness at Moaness Pier, near the tiny village of **HOY**, and heading for Rackwick, can either catch the minibus or take the well-marked footpath that passes Sandy Loch, and along the large open valley beyond. On the western side of this valley is the narrow gully of **Berriedale**, which supports Britain's most northerly native woodland, a huddle of birch, hazel and honeysuckle.

The minibus route to Rackwick is via the single-track road along another valley to the south. En route, duck boards head across the heather to the **Dwarfie Stane**, Orkney's most unusual chambered tomb, cut from a solid block of sandstone and dating back to 3000 BC. The sheer effort of carving out this tomb, with its two side-cells, is staggering, and as you crawl inside the marks of the tools used by the Neolithic builders on the ceiling are still visible. The tomb is also decorated with copious Victorian graffiti, the most interesting of which is to be found on the northern exterior, where Major Mouncey, a former British spy in Persia and a confirmed eccentric who dressed in Persian garb, carved his name in Latin backwards, and also in Persian the words "I have sat two nights and so learnt patience".

RACKWICK is an old crofting and fishing village squeezed between towering sandstone cliffs on the west coast. Once quite extensively cultivated, Rackwick went into a steady decline in the middle of this century: its school closed in 1953 and the last fishing boat put to sea in 1963. These days only a few of the houses are inhabited all year round (the rest serve as holiday homes), though the savage isolation of the place has provided inspiration to a number of artists and writers, including Orkney's George

Mackay Brown, who wrote that "when Rackwick weeps, its grief is long and forlorn and utterly desolate". A small farm building beside the hostel serves as a tiny **museum** (open any time; free), with a few old photos and a brief rundown of Rackwick's rough history. Take the time, too, to stroll down to the beach, comprised mostly of giant sandstone pebbles washed smooth by the sea, which make a thunderous noise when the wind gets up.

Despite its isolation, Rackwick has a steady stream of walkers and climbers passing through it en route to the **Old Man of Hoy**, a great sandstone column some 450ft high, perched on an old lava flow which protects it from the erosive power of the sea. The Old Man is a popular challenge for rock climbers, and a 1966 ascent, led by Chris Bonnington, was the first televised climb in Britain. The well-trodden footpath from Rackwick is an easy three-mile walk (3hr return) – the great skuas will only divebomb you during the nesting season – and rewards you with a great view of the stack. The surrounding cliffs provide ideal rocky ledges for the nests of thousands of seabirds, including guillemots, kittiwakes, razorbills, puffins and shags. Continuing north along the clifftops, the path peters out before **St John's Head** which, at 1136ft, is one of the highest sea cliffs in the country and mostly too sheer even for nesting seabirds.

Practicalities

There are very few places to stay in North Hoy, other than the two council-run, SYHA-affiliated **hostels**, which are housed in converted schools; to book ahead, you must contact the council (☎01856/873535 ext 2404). The *Hoy Hostel* (May to mid-Sept) in Hoy village is the larger of the two, but the *Rackwick Hostel* enjoys an even better location. You can **camp** in Rackwick, either behind the hostel, down by the new, unusually attractive public toilets, or beside *Burnside Cottage* (☎01856/791316), the heather-thatched **bothy** in a beautiful setting right by the beach, which has no mattresses or kitchen facilities. **Bike rental** is available from Moaness Pier (☎01856/791225). However, there's no shop in Rackwick, so take all your supplies with you; the post office shop in Hoy only sells chocolate, but the *Hoy Inn* (closed Mon), near the post office, serves very good **bar meals**. Be warned, too, that North Hoy is probably the worst place on Orkney for midges.

Lyness and South Walls

On the opposite side of Hoy, along the sheltered eastern shore, high moorland gives way to a gentler environment similar to that on the rest of Orkney. Hoy marks the western boundary of Scapa Flow, and **LYNESS** played a major role for the British Navy during both world wars. Many of the old wartime buildings have been cleared away over the last few decades, but the harbour and hills around Lyness are still scarred with the scattered remains of concrete structures which once served as hangars and storehouses during the war, and are now used as barns and cowsheds. Among these are the remains of what was – incredibly – the largest cinema in Europe, but perhaps the most unusual remaining building is the monochrome Art Deco facade of the old **Garrison Theatre**, on the main road to the south of Lyness. Formerly the grandiose façade and foyer of a huge Nissen hut, which disappeared long ago, it's now a private home. Lyness also has a large **naval cemetery**, where many of the victims of the various disasters that have occurred in the Flow, such as the sinking of the *Royal Oak* (see opposite) now lie, alongside a handful of German graves.

The old oil pump house, which still stands opposite the new Lyness ferry terminal, has been turned into the **Scapa Flow Visitor Centre** (mid-May to mid-Sept Mon–Sat 9am–4.30pm, Sun 10.30am–3.45pm; July & Aug Mon–Sat 9am–4.30pm, Sun 9.45am–6pm; mid-Sept to mid-May Mon–Fri 9am–4.30pm; £2), a fascinating insight into wartime Orkney. As well as the usual old photos, torpedoes, flags, guns and propellers,

SCAPA FLOW

Apart from a few oil tankers, there's generally very little activity in the great natural harbour of **Scapa Flow**. Yet for the first half of the twentieth century, the Flow served as the main base of the British Navy, with over a hundred warships anchored here at any one time. The coastal defences required to make Scapa Flow safe to use as the country's chief naval headquarters were considerable and many are still visible all over Orkney, ranging from half-sunk blockships to the Churchill Barriers (see p.573) and the gun batteries that pepper the coastline; the barriers were erected following the torpedoing of **HMS Royal Oak** by a German U-Boat in October 1939, and withstood several heavy German air raids during the course of 1940. Ironically, the worst disaster the Flow has ever witnessed was self-inflicted, when **HMS Vanguard** sank, on July 9, 1917, after suffering an internal explosion, taking over 1000 of her crew with her.

Scapa Flow's most celebrated moment in naval history, however, was when the entire **German High Seas Fleet** was interned here immediately after the end of World War I. A total of 74 ships was anchored off the island of Cava awaiting the outcome of the Versailles Peace Conference. At 10.30am, on Midsummer's Day, 1919, having learned that the German Navy was to be reduced to just 24 ships, the German in command, Admiral von Reuter, ordered all ships to be scuttled – by 5pm, every ship was beached or had sunk. Some still argue that the British government knew full well what von Reuter planned to do, but declined to intervene, so as to avoid the diplomatic nightmare of dividing up the fleet between the Allies.

Between the wars, the largest **salvage operation** in history took place in Scapa Flow, with the firm of Cox & Danks alone raising 24 destroyers and two huge battleships. Despite this, seven large German ships – three battleships and four light cruisers – remain on the seabed of Scapa Flow, along with four destroyers and a U-Boat. As a result, it is considered one of the world's greatest dive sites. Scapa Scuba (☎01856/851218), based in Stromness, offers one-to-one **scuba diving** tuition for beginners, lasting three hours, diving on one of the blockships sunk by the Churchill Barriers; they also offer wreck diving for those with more experience. If you don't want to get your feet wet, Roving Eye Enterprises (☎01856/811360) run a boat fitted with an underwater camera, which does the diving for you, while you sit back and watch the video screen. The trip leaves from Houton Pier at 1.20pm, takes three hours, and includes a visit to the Scapa Flow Visitor Centre in Lyness (see below).

there's a paratrooper's folding bicycle, and a whole section devoted to the scuttling of the German High Seas Fleet and the sinking of the *Royal Oak* (see above). The pump house itself retains much of its old equipment – you can even ask for a working demo of one of the oil-fired boilers – used to pump oil off tankers moored at Lyness into sixteen tanks, and from there into underground reservoirs cut into the neighbouring hillside. Every hour on the half hour, an audio-visual on the history of Scapa Flow is shown in the sole surviving tank, which has the most incredible acoustics.

Melsetter House

The finest architecture on Hoy is to be found at **Melsetter House** (Thurs, Sat & Sun by appointment; ☎01856/791352), four miles southwest of Lyness, overlooking the deep inlet of North Bay. Originally built in 1738, it was bought by Thomas Middlemore, heir to a Birmingham leather tycoon, who commissioned the Arts and Crafts architect William Lethaby to transform the house in 1898. The charming owners will happily take you round a handful of the thoroughly lived-in rooms in the house itself, all of which are simply decorated with white wood-panelling, floral plasterwork and William Morris-style fabrics, and leave you to wander freely around the house's very beautiful grounds. Don't miss the little **Chapel of St Margaret & St Colm** that Lethaby fashioned from the house's outhouses, which features some characteristic symbolic touches, and four tiny, stained-glass windows, by, among others, Ford Maddox Brown and Burne-Jones. The walk back along the cliffs of the west coast to Rackwick is spectacular and takes about six hours.

South Walls

To the east, a narrow spit of sand connects the rest of Hoy with **South Walls**, a fertile peninsula which is more densely populated, with farms and homes. On the north side of South Walls is the main settlement of **LONGHOPE**, an important safe anchorage during the Napoleonic Wars and the First World War, but since then overshadowed by Lyness and Flotta. Longhope remains a lifeboat station, and it was the **Longhope Lifeboat** which capsized in strong gale force winds in 1969, on its way to the aid of a Liberian freighter. The entire eight-man crew was killed, leaving seven widows and ten fatherless children; the crew of the freighter, by contrast, survived. There's a gut-wrenching memorial to the men – six of whom came from just two families – in **Kirkhope Churchyard** on the road to Cantick Head Lighthouse.

Evidence of Longhope's strategic importance during the Napoleonic Wars lies to the east of the village at the Point of Hackness, where the **Hackness Martello Tower** stands guard over the entrance to the bay, with a matching tower on the opposite promontory of Crockness. Built in 1815, these two circular sandstone Martello Towers are the northernmost in Britain, and were built to protect merchant ships waiting for a Royal Navy escort from American and French privateers. You can visit Hackness Tower – if it's locked, a sign will tell you where to get the key from – via a steep ladder connected to the first floor, where nine men and one officer shared the circular room. Originally a portable ladder would have been used and retracted, making the place pretty much impregnable: the walls are up to nine feet on the seaward side, and the tower even had its own water supply. Overlooking the bay at the nearby **Hackness Battery**, positioned closer to the shore, yet more cannon were trained on the horizon.

Practicalities

There are a handful of very good, friendly **B&Bs**: *Stonequoy Farm* (☎01856/791234; ①) is a lovely 200-acre farm south of Lyness, overlooking Longhope, and the *Old Custom House* (☎01856/701358; ①) is a historic building distinguished by the miniature lions that sit atop the columns flanking the doorway, situated on the other side of the bay in Longhope. Also on this side is *Burnhouse* (☎01856/701263; ①), which also has a self-catering cottage available for rent. Other outstanding self-catering options include a beautifully converted outbuilding at Melsetter House (☎01856/791352; 4 people; £350 per week), and the lighthouse keepers' cottages at Cantick Head (☎01856/701255; 4–6 people; £210 per week). For **food**, there's little choice other than B&Bs, which will often provide an ample and delicious evening meal. Otherwise, the *Anchor Bar*, round the back of the ugly *Hoy Hotel* in Lyness, dishes up typical pub food; the *Scapa Flow Visitor Centre* café serves tea, coffee and snacks. There are two shops, one round the back of the *Hoy Hotel*, and one by the pier in Longhope. **Car and bike rental** is available from Halyel Car Hire in Lyness (☎01856/791240).

Shapinsay

Just a few miles northeast of Kirkwall, **Shapinsay** is the most accessible of Orkney's northern isles. A gently undulating gridplan patchwork of rich farmland, it's a bit like an island suburb of Kirkwall. Its chief attraction for visitors is **Balfour Castle** (May–Sept Wed & Sun guided tours 3pm), the imposing Baronial pile designed by David Bryce and completed in 1848 by the Balfour family of Westray, who had made a small fortune in India the previous century. The Balfours died out in 1960 and the castle was bought by a Polish Cavalry Officer, Captain Tadeusz Zawadski, whose family now run the place as a hotel. The guided tours are great fun, and go down very well with children too, as they finish off with complimentary tea and home-made cakes in the servants' quarters. Before you enter the castle, you get to walk through the wooded grounds and view the vast kitchen gardens, which are surrounded by 15ft-high walls, and once had coal-fired greenhouses to produce fruit and vegetables out of season. The castle itself is not that magnificent inside, though it has a nice lived-in feel and is pretty grand for Orkney; otters feature prominently as they appear in the Balfour family crest.

The Balfours also reformed the island's agricultural system and built **BALFOUR** village, a neat and disciplined cottage development, to house their estate workers. The family's grandiose efforts in estate management have left some appealingly eccentric relics. Melodramatic fortifications around the harbour include the huge and ornate, if not exactly beautiful **Gatehouse**, which is now a pub. There's also a stone-built coal-fired **Gasometer**, which once supplied castle and harbour with electricity and, southwest of the pier, the castellated **Dishan Tower**, a seventeenth-century doocot that was converted into a cold, salt-water shower in Victorian times. The old village **Smithy** (Mon, Tues & Thurs–Sat noon–4.30pm, Wed & Sun noon–5.30pm; free) on the main street now serves as a museum of local history, with a tearoom upstairs.

Most folk visit Shapinsay on a day-trip, but if you're staying here for a few days there are one or two points of interest beyond the castle and village. One mile north of Balfour village there's the small **Mill Dam RSPB reserve**, with a hide to the west, from which you can look down on the pintail, widgeon and shovelers that breed on the wetlands. The east coast from the Foot northwards has the most interesting cliffs and sea caves, and will eventually bring you to the fairly well-preserved **Broch of Burroughston**, which is also a good spot for watching seals sunning themselves on the nearby rocks. The best stretch of sand is at the sweeping curve of **Veantro Bay** in the north.

Practicalities

Less than thirty minutes from Kirkwall by **ferry**, Shapinsay is an easy day-trip. If you want to visit the castle, before you set out you must buy an all-inclusive ticket from Kirkwall tourist office (£14.50), which includes a return ferry ticket and castle entry. The ferry for the guided tour leaves at 2.15pm, but you can catch an earlier ferry if you want to have some time to explore the rest of the island. It's also possible **to stay** in opulent style in *Balfour Castle* (☎01856/711282; *balfourcastle@btinternet.com*; ⑧); room prices include dinner, bed and breakfast, and you get use of the library and the other public rooms. More modest accommodation is available at *Girnigoe* (☎01856/711256; ①, full board ③), a very comfortable B&B close to the north shore of Veantro Bay. The only food option is the **café** in the old smithy (May–Sept), which serves teas and sandwiches.

Rousay, Egilsay and Wyre

Just over half a mile away from the Mainland's northern shore, the hilly island of **Rousay** is one of the most interesting of the smaller isles, home to a number of intriguing prehistoric sites, as well as being one of the more accessible. The group of a dozen or so houses above the ferry terminal is the only settlement of any size, but a single road runs around the edge of the island, connecting a string of small farms which make use of the more cultivable coastal fringes. Many visitors come on a day-trip, as it's easy enough to reach the main points of archeological interest on the south coast by foot from the ferry terminal. Rousay's diminutive neighbours, **Egilsay** and **Wyre**, contain a few medieval attractions of their own, which can either be visited on a day-trip from Rousay itself, or from the mainland.

Trumland House to the Knowe of Yarso

Despite its long history of settlement, Rousay is today home to little more than 200 people (many of them incomers), as this was one of the few parts of Orkney to suffer Highland-style clearances, initially by George William Traill at Quandale in the northwest. His successor, Lt-General Traill-Burroughs, built the unlovely **Trumland House**, a forbidding Jacobean-style pile designed by David Bryce in 1873, hidden in the trees half a mile from the ferry terminal. Continuing to substitute sheep for people, he built a wall to force crofters onto a narrow coastal strip and eventually provoked so much distress and anger that a gunboat had to be sent to restore order. You can learn a little more about the history and wildlife of the island from the well-laid-out **Trumland Orientation Centre** (Mon–Sat 7.30am–7pm; mid-May to mid-Sept also Sun), housed in a modern bungalow by the pier that doubles as a sort of waiting room for the ferry.

The first trio of archeological sights are spread out over the next couple of miles, on and off the road that leads west from the ferry terminal. **Taversoe Tuick**, the nearest chambered cairn, lies just beyond Trumland House, and was discovered by workers during the building of a Victorian viewpoint. Dating back to 3500 BC, it's unusual in that it exploits its sloping site by having two storeys, one entered from the upper side and one from the lower. A little further west is the **Blackhammer Cairn**, which is more promising inside than it looks from the outside. You enter through the roof via a ladder; the long interior is divided into "stalls" by large flagstones, rather like the more famous cairn at Midhowe (see below). Finally, there's the **Knowe of Yarso**, another stalled cairn dating from the same period that's a stiff climb up the hill from the road but worth it, if only for the magnificent view. The remains of 29 individuals were found inside, with the skulls neatly arranged around the walls; the bones of 36 deer were also buried here.

A footpath sets off from beside the Taversoe Tuick tomb off into the **RSPB reserve** that encompasses a large section of the nearby heather-backed hills, the highest of which is **Blotchnie Fiold** (821ft). This high ground offers good hill-walking, with superb panoramic views of the surrounding islands, as well as excellent birdwatching. If you're lucky, you may well catch a glimpse of merlins, hen harriers, peregrine falcons and red-throated divers, although the latter are more widespread just outside the reserve on one of the island's three lochs, which also offer good trout fishing.

Midhowe Cairn and Broch

The southwestern side of Rousay is home to the most significant of the island's archeological remains, strung out along the shores of the tide races of Eynhallow Sound, which run between the island and the Mainland. Most lie on the **Westness Walk**, a mile-long heritage trail that begins at Westness Farm, four miles northwest of the ferry terminal. **Midhowe Cairn**, about a mile on from the farm, comes as something of a surprise, both for its immense size – it's known as "the great ship of death" and measures nearly 100ft in length – and for the fact that it's now entirely surrounded by a stone-walled barn with a corrugated roof. Unfortunately, you can't actually explore the roofless communal burial chamber, dating back to 3500 BC, but only look down from the overhead walkway. The central corridor is partitioned with slabs of rock, with twelve compartments on each side, where the remains of 25 people were discovered in a crouched position with their backs to the wall.

A couple of hundred yards beyond Midhowe Cairn is perhaps Rousay's finest archeological site, **Midhowe Broch**, whose compact layout suggests that it was originally built as a sort of fortified family house, surrounded by a complex series of ditches and ramparts. These are now partially obscured by later houses, many of which have shelving and stairs still intact. The broch itself looks as though it's about to collapse – it was obviously shored up with flagstone buttresses back in the Iron Age, and has more recently been given extra sea defences by Historic Scotland. The interior of the broch is divided into two separate rooms, each with their own hearth, water tank and quern stone, all of which date from the final phase of occupation around the second century AD.

From Midhowe Broch you get a good view of the nearby small island of **Eynhallow**, which is surrounded by the most ferocious tides. The island was cleared in 1851, at which point it was discovered that one of the houses was in fact a converted church, possibly part of a monastery, dating back to at least the twelfth century. Beyond Midhowe, a walk along the coast will take you past the impressive cliff scenery around **Scabra Head**, where numerous seabirds nest in summer. Inland, the heathland of Quandale and Brings provides yet more birdwatching, with arctic terns and arctic skuas in abundance.

Egilsay and Wyre

Egilsay, the largest of the low-lying islands sheltering close to the eastern shore of Rousay, makes for an easy day-trip. The island is dominated by the ruins of **St Magnus Church**, with its distinctive round tower. Built around the twelfth century in a prominent position in the middle of the island, probably on the site of a much earlier version, the roofless church is the only surviving example of the traditional round-towered churches of Orkney and Shetland. It is possible that it was built as a shrine to Earl (later Saint) Magnus, who arranged to meet his cousin Haakon here in 1117, only to be treacherously killed by the latter's cook, Lifolf. A cenotaph marks the spot where the murder took place, about a quarter of a mile southeast of the church. Egilsay is almost entirely inhabited by incomers, and a large slice of the island's farmland is managed by the RSPB in order to encourage corncrakes, which you may be lucky enough to hear.

The tiny, neighbouring island of **Wyre**, to the southwest, is another possible day-trip, and is best known for **Cubbie Roo's Castle**, the "fine stone fort" and "really solid stronghold" mentioned in the *Orkneyinga Saga*, and built around 1150 by local farmer Kolbein Hruga. The castle gets another mention in *Haakon's Saga*, when those inside successfully withstood all attacks. The outer defences have survived well on three sides of the castle, which has a central keep, with walls to a height of around six feet, its central water tank still intact. Close by the castle stands **St Mary's Chapel**, a roofless twelfth-century church founded either by Kolbein or his son, Bjarni the Poet, who was Bishop of Orkney. Kolbein's permanent residence or Bu is recalled in the name of the nearby farm, the Bu of Wyre, where the poet **Edwin Muir** (1887–1959) spent his childhood, described in detail in his autobiography. If you walk to the very western tip of Wyre, known as **The Taing**, you're pretty much guaranteed to see large numbers of grey and common seals basking on the rocks.

Practicalities

Rousay makes a good day-trip from the Mainland, with regular **car ferry** sailings from Tingwall (20min) which has bus connections to and from Kirkwall. Most ferries call in at Egilsay and Wyre, but some need to be booked the day before at the Tingwall ferry terminal (☎01856/751360). Alternatively, you can join one of the very informative **minibus tours** run by Rousay Traveller (June–Aug Tues–Fri; ☎01856/821234), which connect with ferries and last between two and six hours, the longer ones allowing extended walks. **Bike rental** is available from Arts, Bikes & Crafts on Pier Road (☎01856/821398).

Accommodation on Rousay is extremely limited. The only hotel is the *Taversoe* (☎01856/821325; ②), a modern extension added onto an old croft, a couple of miles

By the twelfth-century, the chapel had become a place of pilgrimage for those suffering from eye complaints.

The island's visual focus is **Holland House**, occupying the high central point of the island and once seat of the local lairds, the Traill family, who ruled over Papay for three centuries. The main house, with its crowstepped gables, is still in private hands, but the current owners are perfectly happy for visitors to explore the old buildings of the home farm, on the west side of the road, which include a kiln, a doocot and a horse-powered threshing mill. An old bothy for single male servants, decorated with red horse yokes, has even been restored and made into a small **museum** (open at any time; free), filled with bygone bits and bobs from a wooden flea trap to a box bed.

A road leads down from Holland House to the western shore, where Papay's prime prehistoric site, the **Knap of Howar**, stands overlooking Westray. Dating from around 3500 BC, this Neolithic farm building makes a fair claim to being the oldest-standing house in Europe. It's made up of two roofless buildings, linked by a little passageway; one has a hearth and copious stone shelves, and is thought to have been some kind of storehouse. Half a mile north along the coast from the Knap of Howar is **St Boniface Kirk**, a pre-Reformation church that has recently been restored. Inside, it's beautifully simple, with a bare flagstone floor, drystone walls, a little wooden gallery and just a couple of surviving box pews. The church is known to have seated at least 220, which meant they would have been squashed in 14 to a pew. In the surrounding graveyard there's a Viking **hogback grave**, decorated with carvings in imitation of the wooden shingles on the roof of a Viking longhouse.

The northern tip of the island around **North Hill** (157ft) is now an **RSPB reserve**. During the breeding season, you're asked to keep to the coastal fringe, where razorbills, guillemots, fulmar, kittiwakes and puffin nest, particularly around Fowl Craig on the east coast, where you can also view the rare Scottish primrose which flowers in May and from July to late September. If you want to explore the interior of the reserve, which plays host to one of the largest arctic tern colonies in Europe as well as numerous arctic skuas, contact the warden at Rose Cottage (☎01857/644240), who does regular escorted walks.

If you're here for more than a day, it's worth considering hiring a boat to take you over to the **Holm of Papay**, an even smaller island off the east coast. Despite its tiny size, the Holm boasts several Neolithic chambered cairns, one of which, occupying the highest point, is extremely impressive. Descending into the tomb via a ladder, you enter the main rectangular chamber which is nearly seventy feet in length, with no fewer than twelve side-cells, each with its own lintelled entrance. To arrange a boat, contact the Community Co-op (see below).

Practicalities

With a regular **passenger ferry** service from Pierowall (3–6 daily; 25min), Papa Westray is an easy day-trip from Westray. However, it's just as easy to stay on Papay and take a day-trip to Westray instead. On Tuesdays and Fridays, the **car ferry** from Kirkwall to Westray continues on to Papa Westray; at other times, you can catch the bus from Rapness to Pierowall to connect with the passenger ferry. Papay is also connected to Westray by the **world's shortest scheduled flight** – two minutes in duration, less with a following wind. Tickets from Loganair cost around £15 one-way; you can also fly direct from Kirkwall to Papa Westray (Mon–Sat 1–2 daily). The island's Community Co-operative (☎01857/644267) has a **minibus** which will take you from the pier to wherever you want on the island. It also runs a shop, a sixteen-bed SYHA-affiliated **hostel**, a **guest house** (②; full board ⑤) and a **self-catering cottage** (6 people; £160 per week), all housed within the old estate workers' cottages at Beltane, to the east of Holland House.

Eday

A long, thin island at the centre of Orkney's northern isles, **Eday** shares more characteristics with Rousay and Hoy than with its immediate neighbours, dominated as it is by a great block of heather-covered upland, with farmland confined to a narrow strip of coastal ground. However, Eday's hills have proved useful in their own way, providing huge quantities of peat which has been exported to the other peatless northern isles for fuel, and was even, for a time, exported to various whisky distillers. Eday's yellow sandstone has also been extensively quarried, and was used to build the St Magnus Cathedral in Kirkwall.

The island is very sparsely inhabited, has no real village as such, and is almost divided in two by the thin waist, where the island's airfield (known as London Airport) lies. The chief points of interest are all in the northern half of the island, beyond the post office, petrol pump and Eday Community Enterprises shop on the main road. This marks the beginning of the signposted **Eday Heritage Walk**, which covers all the main sights, and takes about three hours to complete. The walk initially follows the road heading northwest, past the RSPB bird hide overlooking **Mill Loch**, where several pairs of red-throated divers regularly breed.

Clearly visible to the north of the road is the fifteen-foot **Stone of Setter**, Orkney's most distinctive standing stone, weathered into three thick, lichen-encrusted fingers. The stone clearly held centre stage in the Neolithic landscape, and is visible from the other nearby prehistoric sites. From here, passing the less spectacular Braeside and Huntersquoy chambered cairns en route, climb the hill to reach Eday's finest, the **Vinquoy Chambered Cairn**, which has a similar structure to that of Maes Howe. You can crawl into the tomb through the narrow entrance – a skylight inside lets light into the main, beehive chamber, now home to some lovely ferns, but not into the four side-cells. From the cairn, continue north to the viewpoint on the summit of **Vinquoy Hill** (248ft), and on to the very northernmost tip of the island, and the dramatic red sandstone sea cliffs of **Red Head**, where guillemots, razorbills, puffins and other seabirds nest in summer.

Alternatively, simply head straight down to the east coast and **Carrick House**, the grandest home on Eday (mid-June to mid-Sept Sun 2pm; £2; ☎01857/622260). Built by the Laird of Eday in 1633, it was extended in the original style by successive owners, but is best known for its associations with the pirate **John Gow** – on whom Sir Walter Scott's novel *The Pirate* is based – who attempted to attack the house in 1725, only for his ship *The Revenge* to run aground on the Calf of Eday. He asked for help from the local laird, but was taken prisoner in Carrick House, before eventually being sent off to London where he was tortured and executed.

From Carrick House, the uninhabited island of the **Calf of Eday** is only a stone's throw away. If you're staying on Eday, it's easy enough to organize a boat to take you over to the island: try J&H Thomson (☎01857/622256). The island features several chambered cairns, and is home to some massive bird colonies along its eastern cliffs, including a large colony of great black-backed gulls and numerous black guillemots, as well as all the usual suspects.

Practicalities

Eday's **ferry** terminal is at Backaland pier in the south, not ideal for visiting the more interesting northern section of the island, although if you haven't got your own transport you should find it fairly easy to get a lift with someone off the ferry (2 daily; 1hr 15min–2hr). Alternatively, rent a **taxi** from Mr A. Stewart by the pier (☎01857/622206), or **bicycles** from Martin Burkett at Hamarr, in the valley below the post office (☎01857/622331). Orkney Ferries also run an **Eday Heritage Tour** every Sunday (mid-June to mid-Sept), which costs just under £30 per person, and includes return ferry tickets and a guided minibus tour around the island (including Carrick House). It's also possible to do a day-trip on the Loganair **flight** from Kirkwall to Eday on Wednesdays (☎01856/872494).

The best option when it comes to **accommodation** is the new self-catering cottages set in the hacienda-style complex around the local pub, *Priate Gow's Inn* (Fri–Sun only), in Calfsound (☎01700/505357; ①). All six cottages are well equipped, and can be hired out for anything from one night to a week. Friendly **B&B** is available at *Skaill Farm*, a traditional farmhouse just south of the airport (☎01857/622271; full board ③; closed April & May). The SYHA-affiliated **hostel**, situated in an exposed spot just north of the airport, is very basic and is run by Eday Community Association (☎01857/622206; April–Sept).

Stronsay

A low-lying, three-legged island to the southeast of Eday, **Stronsay** is strongly agricultural, its interior an almost uninterrupted patchwork of green pastures. Stronsay features few real sights, but the coastline has enormous appeal: a beguiling combination of sandstone cliffs, home to several seabird colonies, interspersed with wide white sands and (in fine weather) clear turquoise bays. Stronsay has seen two economic booms in the last three hundred years. The first took place in the eighteenth century, and employed as many as 3000 people; it was built on collecting vast quantities of seaweed and exporting the **kelp** for use in the chemical industry, particularly in making iodine, soap and glass. In the following century, **fishing** on a grand scale came to dominate life here, as Whitehall harbour became one of the main Scottish centres for the curing of herring caught by French, Dutch and Scottish boats. By the 1840s, up to four hundred boats were working out of the port, attracting hundreds of women herring gutters. By the 1930s, however, the herring stocks had been severely depleted and the industry began a long decline.

WHITEHALL, in the north of the island, remains the only real village on Stronsay, made up of a couple of rows of stone-built fishermen's cottages set between two large piers. Wandering along the tranquil, rather forlorn harbour front today, you'll find it hard to believe that the village once supported 5000 people in the fishing industry during the summer season, as well as a small army of coopers, coal merchants, butchers, bakers, several Italian ice-cream parlours and a cinema. It was said that on a Sunday, you could walk across the decks of the boats all the way to **Papa Stronsay**, the tiny island that shelters Whitehall from north, on which you can still see some of the old herring curing stations. Several houses in Whitehall are roofless and others lie empty, but the old fish market by the pier now houses a **Heritage Centre** (May–Sept daily 11am–5pm; free), with a few photos and artefacts from the herring days; it also has a small café.

If the weather's fine, you can choose which of the island's many arching, dazzlingly white beaches to relax on. The most dramatic section of coastline, featuring great layered slices of sandstone, lies in the southeast corner of the island. Signposts show the way to Orkney's biggest and most dramatic natural arch, the **Vat of Kirbuster**. Before you reach the arch there's a seaweedy, shallow pool in a natural sandstone amphitheatre, where the water is warmed by the sun and kids and adults can safely wallow: close by is a rocky inlet for those who prefer colder, more adventurous swimming. You'll find progressively more nesting seabirds, including a few puffin, as you approach **Burgh Head**, further along down the coast. Meanwhile, at the promontory of **Lamb Head**, there are usually loads of seals, a large colony of arctic terns, and good views out to the lighthouse on the outlying island of **Auskerry**, to the south.

Practicalities

Stronsay is served by a regular car **ferry** service from Kirkwall to Whitehall (twice daily; 1hr 35min–2hr), and weekday Loganair **flights** from Kirkwall. There's no bus service, but D.S. Peace (☎01857/616335) operates taxis and **rents cars**. Of the few **accommodation** options available, a good choice is the new **hostel** in the old fish market by the pier, with a well-equipped kitchen, washing machine and comfortable bunkbedded rooms. It's run by the folk at the *Stronsay Hotel* opposite (☎01857/616213; ①), which has seen better days – it once boasted the longest bar in the north of Scotland – but is currently undergoing a long overdue refurbishment. There's even more basic accommodation at *Torness Camping Barn* in Holland Farm (☎01857/616314), beyond Dishes, in the south of the island. Alternatively, the *Stronsay Bird Reserve* (☎01857/616363; ①) is a nicely positioned **B&B**, which also offers camping on the shores of Mill Bay. The bar in the *Stronsay Hotel* does pub **food**, and there's a takeaway along the street at *Woodlea* that's open sporadically (☎01857/616337); otherwise, you'll need to bring your own supplies and make use of the island's two shops. There's a **swimming pool** behind the school which is available for public use, but it's operated on a voluntary basis so check first at the heritage centre.

Sanday

Sanday, though the largest of the northern isles, is also the most insubstantial, a great low-lying, drifting dune strung out between several rocky points. The island's sweeping aquamarine bays and vast stretches of clean white sand are the finest in Orkney, and in dry, clear weather it's a superb place to spend a day or two. The sandy soil is, in fact, very fertile, and the island remains predominantly agricultural even today, holding its very own agricultural show each year at the beginning of August.

The island has a long history as a shipping hazard, with many wrecks smashed against its shores, although the construction of the **Start Point Lighthouse** in 1802 on the island's exposed eastern tip reduced the risk for seafarers. Shipwrecks were, in fact, not an unwelcome sight on Sanday, as the island has no peat, and driftwood was the only source of fuel other than cow dung – it's even said that the locals used to pray for shipwrecks in church. The present Stevenson lighthouse, which dates from 1870, now sports very natty vertical black and white stripes. It actually stands on a tidal island, which is only accessible on either side of low tide, so ask locally for the tide times before setting out (it takes an hour to walk there and back); phone the lighthouse keeper (☎01857/600385) in advance if you want to see inside.

The shoreline supports a healthy seal, otter and wading bird population, and behind the splendid sandy beaches are stretches of beautiful open machair and grassland, thick with wild flowers during the spring and summer. The entire coastline presents the opportunity for superb walks, with particularly spectacular sand dunes to the south of Cata Sand. Sanday is also rich in archeology, with hundreds of mostly unexcavated sites including cairns, brochs and burnt mounds. The most impressive is **Quoyness Chambered Cairn**, on the fertile farmland of Els Ness peninsula. The tomb, which dates from before 2000 BC, has been partially reconstructed, and rises to a height of around 13ft. The imposing, narrow entrance, flanked by high drystone walls would originally have been roofed for the whole of the way into the 13ft-long main chamber, where bones and skulls were discovered in the six small side-cells.

Unfortunately, the island's knitting factory recently closed down, but you can still visit Sanday's unusual **Orkney Angora** craft shop (☎01857/600421), in Upper Breckan in the parish of Burness. The owner will usually oblige with a quick look and a stroke of one of the comically long-haired albino rabbits who supply the wool. Close by is the stone tower of an old windmill, which belonged to the neighbouring farmstead and house of **Scar**, where you can still see the chimney of the farm's old steam-powered meal mill.

Practicalities

Ferries to Sanday arrive at the new terminal at the southern tip of the island and are met by the **minibus** (book on ☎01857/600467), which will take you to most points. The airfield is in the centre of the island and there are Loganair **flights** to Kirkwall twice daily on weekdays, and once on Saturdays. The fishing port of Kettletoft is where the ferry used to dock, and where you'll find the island's two **hotels**, neither of which is spectacularly good. Of the two, the *Belsair Hotel* (☎01857/600206; ②) has the slightly more adventurous restaurant menu, while the *Kettletoft Hotel* (☎01857/600217; ①) has a lively bar that's popular with the locals. Of the handful of **B&Bs**, try *Quivals* (☎01857/600418; ①), who can also organize car and bike rental. For a wonderful, reasonably-priced **self-catering cottage** over by Start Point, contact Richard Corser (☎01857/600403; 3–4 people; £150 per week).

North Ronaldsay

North Ronaldsay – or "North Ron" as it's fondly known – is Orkney's most northerly island. Separated from Sanday by the treacherous waters of the North Ronaldsay Firth, it has a unique outpost atmosphere, brought about by its extreme isolation. Measuring just three miles by one and rising only 66ft above sea level, the island is almost overwhelmed by the enormity of the sky, the strength of wind and, of course, the ferocity of the sea – so much so that its very existence seems an act of tenacious defiance. Despite these adverse conditions, North Ronaldsay has been inhabited for centuries, and continues to be heavily farmed, from old-style crofts whose roofs are made from huge local flagstones. With no natural harbours and precious little farmland, the islanders have been forced to make the most of what they have and **seaweed** has played an important role in the local economy. During the eighteenth century kelp was gathered here, burnt in pits and sent south for use in the chemicals industry.

The island's **sheep** are a unique, tough, goat-like breed, who feed mostly on seaweed, giving their flesh a dark tone and a rich, gamey taste, and making their thick wool highly prized. A high **drystone dyke**, completed in the mid-nineteenth century and running the thirteen miles around the edge of the island, keeps them off the farmland, except during lambing season when the ewes are allowed onto the pastureland. North Ronaldsay sheep are also unusual in that they can't be rounded up by sheepdogs like ordinary sheep, but scatter far and wide at some considerable speed. Instead, once a year the islanders herd the sheep communally into a series of **drystone "punds"** near Dennis Head, for clipping and dipping, in what is one of the last acts of communal farmi ng practised in Orkney.

There are very few real sights on the island, and the most frequent visitors are ornithologists, who come in considerable numbers to catch a glimpse of the rare migrants who land here briefly on their spring and autumn migrations. The peak times of year for migrants is from late March to early June, and from mid-August to early November, although there are also many breeding species which spend the spring and summer here, including gulls, terns, waders, black guillemots, cormorants and even the odd corncrake. As on Fair Isle, there's now a permanent **Bird Observatory**, situated in the southwest corner of the island, which can give advice as to what birds have recently been sighted. The observatory was established in 1987 by adapting a croft to wind and solar power.

Holland House – built by the Traill family who bought the island in 1727 – and the island's two lighthouses at Dennis Head, are the only features to interrupt the flat horizon. The attractive, stone-built **Old Beacon** was first lit in 1789, but the lantern was replaced by the huge bauble of masonry you now see as long ago as 1809. The **New**

Lighthouse, half a mile to the north, is the tallest land-based lighthouse in Britain, rising to a height of over 100ft. On a clear day you can see Fair Isle, and even Sumburgh and Fitful Head on Shetland.

Practicalities

The **ferry** from Kirkwall to North Ronaldsay only runs once a week (usually on Fridays; 2hr 40min–3hr), though day-trips are possible on occasional Sundays between late May and early September (phone ☎01856/872044 for details). Probably your best bet is to catch a Loganair **flight** from Kirkwall (Mon–Sat 2 daily), which allows between five and seven hours on the island. You can **stay** overnight, either at the *North Ronaldsay Bird Observatory* (☎01857/633200; *alison@nrbo.prestel.co.uk*; ①–③), which offers full-board either in private guest rooms or in dorms. Full-board accommodation is also available at *Garso*, in the northeast (☎01857/633244; *christine.muir@virgin.net*; ③), which also has a self-catering cottage. The *Burrian Inn*, to the southeast of the war memorial, is the island's small **pub**, and does hot food. **Camping** is possible; for further information, phone ☎01857/633222.

ONWARDS TO NORWAY, THE FAROE ISLANDS AND ICELAND

Thanks to the historical ties and the attraction of a short hop to continental Europe, **Norway** is a popular destination for Shetlanders and Orcadians. Norwegians often think of Shetland and Orkney as their western isles and, particularly in west Norway, old wartime bonds with Shetland are still strong. Norwegian yachts and sail training vessels are frequent visitors to Lerwick and Kirkwall. Shetlanders can also go by ferry to the **Faroe Islands** – steep, angular shapes rising out of the North Atlantic – and from Faroe on to **Iceland**.

There are weekly **flights** between June and September from Kirkwall in Orkney (1hr 45min) and twice-weekly from Sumburgh in Shetland (1hr) to Bergen in Norway. Short inclusive breaks are available by air from Shetland (book through Hay & Co; ☎01950/460661). From June to August the large, comfortable and fast Faroese car **ferry** *Nörrona* makes weekly return trips from her home port in Faroe to Shetland, Norway, Iceland and Denmark. From Shetland, Bergen in Norway and Torshavn in Faroe are 13 hours away; to Iceland the journey takes 33 hours including a brief stop in Faroe; on the way back there's a two-day stopover in Faroe while the ship makes a return trip to Denmark.

SHETLAND

Many maps place the **Shetland Islands** in a box somewhere off Aberdeen, but in fact Bergen in Norway is a lot closer than Edinburgh, and the Arctic Circle nearer than Manchester. The Shetland **landscape** is a product of the struggle between rock and the forces of water and ice that have, over millennia, tried to break it to pieces. Smoothed by the last glaciation, the surviving land has been exposed to the most violent weather experienced in the British Isles; it isn't for nothing that Shetlanders call the place "the Old Rock", and the coastline, a crust of cliffs with caves, blowholes and stacks, testifies to the continuing battle. Inland (a relative term, since you're never more than three miles from the sea), the terrain is a barren mix of moorland, often studded with peaty lochs of a brilliant blue (when the sun shines), and the occasional patch of green farmland, dotted with hardy, multi-coloured sheep and diminutive

---

GETTING TO SHETLAND

The **car ferry** from **Aberdeen**, P&O Scottish Ferries (☎01224/572615 or 01595/695252, *passenger@poscottishferries.co.uk*), operates a direct overnight service four or five times a week to Lerwick (14hr). There's also a once-weekly daytime service from **Stromness** in Orkney (8–10hr), which increases to twice weekly in summer (June–Aug), one overnight, one daytime. If you're visiting both Orkney and Shetland, be sure to check out the discounted **round-trip fares** advertised in the P&O brochure.

From mid-May to mid-September, Shetland is also directly connected to **Bergen** in Norway (13hr), **Tórshavn** in Faroe (13hr) and, via Faroe, with **Seydisfjördur** in Iceland (33hr) and **Hanstholm** in Denmark (50hr) on Smyril Line (details from P&O Scottish Ferries).

By **air**, British Airways (☎0345/222111) flies from **Edinburgh**, **Glasgow**, **Aberdeen**, **Inverness**, **Kirkwall** and **Wick**, with connections from **Birmingham**, **Manchester** and **London**. The main airport is at **Sumburgh**, 25 miles south of Lerwick, with connecting bus services to the latter. Standard fares are high, but various cheaper tickets and special offers are sometimes available if you can meet the booking conditions.

Supporting an impressive array of **birds and wildlife**, the islands offer excellent birdwatching and coastal walking. The **fishing** is good, too, with lochs well stocked with brown trout, sea trout in the voes and the chance to go sea angling for ling, mackerel or even shark and halibut. **Camping** rough isn't discouraged in Shetland if done considerately and the landowner is asked first. However, make sure you're fully equipped to cope with the Shetland wind, which tests the most resilient of tents to the limit: pick a sheltered site, if possible, and use all the guy-ropes you have.

Getting around

Public transport is pretty good in Shetland, with **buses** fanning out from Lerwick to just about every corner of Mainland, and even via ferries across to Yell and Unst: you can buy the full timetable (70p; includes all ferries and flights) from Lerwick Tourist Office. Various **tours** by bus, minibus or private car are also available; operators include John Leask & Son (☎01595/693162), Island Trails (☎01950/422408), run by Elizabeth Johnson, or the more specialist Shetland Wildlife Tours (☎01950/460254, *shetland.wildllife.tours@zetnet.co.uk*). Shetland Field Studies Trust organizes the occasional nature walk (book through the tourist office), while the Shetland Tourist Guides Association (☎01595/696671) offers tailor-made tours for groups or individuals. If you want to **rent a car** once on the islands there are several firms to choose from (see "Listings" on p.599). **Hitching** is viable and pretty safe and **cycling** is a reasonable choice in summer, given the low level of traffic, though the wind can make some journeys very hard going.

Inter-island travel is very straightforward: the larger islands have frequent **car ferry** services throughout the day; journey times are mostly less than 25 minutes; and fares are much cheaper than those in Orkney or the Hebrides. Adults are charged around £2.50 return on most routes (around £5 to Foula, Fair Isle, Papa Stour and Out Skerries) and a car and driver cross for around £9 return. There are also British Airways **flights** linking Tingwall Airstrip (☎01595/840246), five miles west of Lerwick, to Unst and Fair Isle and less frequent Loganair flights to Whalsay, Out Skerries, Papa Stour and Foula. Some Unst and Fair Isle flights leave from Sumburgh Airport. Sample fares for these flights are £20 single Tingwall–Foula or £36 single to Fair Isle; be sure to book well in advance, however, as the planes only take eight passengers, and be prepared to be flexible, as flights are often cancelled due to the weather. It's also possible to take **boat trips** for pleasure, to explore the coastline and spot birds, seals, porpoises, dolphins and whales; operators include the aforementioned Shetland Wildlife Tours (see above), and Tom Jamieson from Sandwick (for the Broch of Mousa) (☎01950/431367). Specialist services for **diving** or **sea angling** can be tracked down through the Lerwick tourist office (see below).

Lerwick

For Shetlanders, there's only one place to stop, meet and do business and that's "da toon", **LERWICK**. Very much the focus of Shetland's commercial life, Lerwick is home to about 7500 people, roughly a third of the islands' population. All year, its sheltered **harbour** at the heart of the town is busy with ferries, fishing boats, oil-rig supply vessels and a variety of more specialized craft including seismic survey and naval vessels from all round the North Sea. In summer, the quaysides come alive with local pleasure craft, visiting yachts, cruise liners, historic vessels such as the restored *Swan*, and the

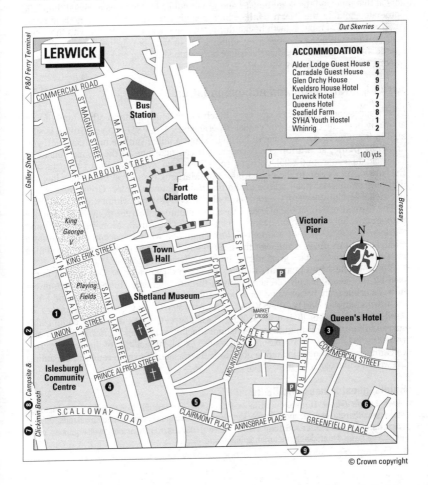

LERWICK

ACCOMMODATION

Alder Lodge Guest House	5
Carradale Guest House	4
Glen Orchy House	9
Kveldsro House Hotel	6
Lerwick Hotel	7
Queens Hotel	3
Seafield Farm	8
SYHA Youth Hostel	1
Whinrig	2

© Crown copyright

occasional tall sailing ship. Behind the old harbour is the compact town centre, made up of one long main street, Commercial Street; from here, narrow lanes, known as "**closses**", rise westwards to the late-Victorian "**new town**".

Lerwick began life as a **temporary settlement**, catering to the Dutch herring fleet in the seventeenth century, which brought in as many as 20,000 men. During the nineteenth century, with the presence of ever larger Scottish, English and Scandinavian boats, it became a major fishing centre, and whalers called to pick up crews on their way to the northern hunting grounds. In 1839, the visiting Danish governor of Faroe declared that "everything made me feel that I had come to the land of opulence". Business was conducted largely from buildings known as **lodberries**, each typically having a store, a house and small yard on a private jetty. **Smuggling** was part of the daily routine, and secret tunnels – some of which still exist – connected the lodberries to illicit stores. During the late nineteenth century, the construction of the Esplanade along the shore isolated several lodberries from the sea, but further south beyond the *Queen's Hotel* are some that still show their original form. Lerwick expanded considerably at this time and the large houses and grand public buildings established then still dominate, notably the **Town Hall**, which remains the most prominent landmark. Another period of rapid growth began during the oil boom of the 1970s, with the farmland to the southwest disappearing under a suburban sprawl, the town's northern approaches becoming an industrial estate and some shopping and office development moving to new, car-friendly sites.

Arrival, information and accommodation

First impressions of Lerwick are very much dependent on the weather (and, if you arrive by boat, the crossing you've just experienced). The P&O **ferry terminal** is situated in the unprepossessing north harbour, about a mile from the town centre. If you arrive by **plane**, at **Sumburgh Airport**, you can take one of the regular buses to Lerwick; taxis (around £25) and car rental are also available. Buses stop on the Esplanade, very close to the old harbour and Market Cross, or at the Viking bus station on Commercial Road a little to the north of the town centre. Orientation within Lerwick is straightforward: the town is small and everything is within walking distance.

The **tourist office**, at the Market Cross on Commercial Street (May–Sept Mon–Fri 8am–6pm, Sat 8am–4pm, Sun 10am–1pm; Oct–April Mon–Fri 9am–5pm; ☎01595/693434), is a good source of information, and will book accommodation for a small fee. In July, August and over the Folk Festival weekend in April, accommodation is in short supply, so it's a good idea to book in advance if possible.

Shetland's best **hotels** are not to be found in Lerwick, which has been spoilt in the past by the steady supply of clientele from the oil business. The upper-range **guest houses** are usually better value for money, though you'll get closer to Shetland life in the town's simpler **B&Bs**. The SYHA hostel (☎01595/692114, *islesburgh@zetnet.co.uk*; April–Sept) at Isleburgh House on King Harald Street, offers unusually comfortable surroundings, and has mightily useful laundry facilities. Lerwick's *Clickimin* **campsite** (☎01595/694555; late April to Sept), enjoys the excellent facilities of the neighbouring Clickimin leisure centre, including good hot showers, but it's sheltered location, amidst Lerwick's suburbs, is far from idyllic.

Hotels, guest houses and B&Bs

Alder Lodge Guest House, 6 Clairmont Place (☎01595/695705). Converted former Victorian bank, recently refurbished, and probably the best middle-range accommodation available. ③.

Carradale Guest House, 36 King Harald St (☎01595/692251). Spacious, well-equipped guest house in a large, comfortable Victorian family home. ①.

BÖDS

With only one official SYHA hostel in the whole of Shetland, it's worth knowing about the islands' unique network of **camping böds**, which are open from April to September. Traditionally, a böd (pronounced "burd") was a small building beside the shore, where fishermen used to house their gear and occasionally sleep; the word was also applied to trading posts established by merchants of the Hanseatic League. The tourist board uses the term pretty loosely, however, as none of the places they run is strictly speaking a böd: they range from stone-built cottages to weatherboarded sail lofts. In order to stay at a böd, you can't simply turn up on spec, but must book in advance through Lerwick Tourist Office (☎01595/693434), as there are no live-in wardens. All the böds have some form of (primitive) heating system, cold water, toilets, a kitchen (though no stove or cooking utensils), and bunk beds, but (as yet) no mattresses, so a sleeping bag and bedding mat are pretty much essential. If you're camping anyway, they're a great way to escape the wind and rain for a night or two; they're also remarkably good value, at around £3 per person per night. Except in June, July and August, it's even possible to pay for exclusive use of any of the böds; prices range from £35 to £90 per night depending on the size of the böd.

Glen Orchy House, 20 Knab Rd (☎01595/692031). A particularly comfortable, fully modernized guest house that's almost a hotel, licensed and with good home cooking. ④.

Kvelsdro House Hotel, Greenfield Place (☎01595/692195). Lerwick's smartest and most luxurious place, with immaculate bedrooms and a good harbour view from the bar. It's hard to find, but locals will usually oblige (note: it's pronounced "Kelro"). ⑥.

Lerwick Hotel, 15 South Rd (☎01595/692166). Modern hotel, with some good sea views, particularly favoured by business travellers. ⑤.

Queen's Hotel, Commercial Street (☎01595/692826). Right on the waterfront by the old harbour, with its feet in the sea; a beautiful old building that's undergoing badly needed refurbishment. ⑤.

Seafield Farm, off Sea Road (☎01595/693853). A very friendly B&B in a huge modern farmhouse overlooking the sea, a mile or so southwest of the town centre and therefore best for those with their own transport. ①.

Whinrig, 12 Burgh Rd (☎01595/693554). Reasonably central B&B, very comfortable and secluded. ①.

The Town

Lerwick's attractive, flagstone-clad **Commercial Street**, universally known to locals as "da Street", is still very much the core of the town. Its narrow, winding form, set back one block from the Esplanade, provides shelter from the elements even on the worst days, and is where locals meet, shop, exchange news and gossip and bring in the New Year to the sound of a harbourful of ships' sirens. The buildings exhibit a mixed bag of architectural styles, from the powerful neo-Baroque of the Bank of Scotland at no. 117 to the plainer houses and old lodberries at the south end, beyond the *Queen's Hotel*. Here, you'll find **Bain's Beach**, a small, hidden stretch of golden sand that's one of the prettiest spots in Lerwick. Further south lie the Victorian Anderson Homes and the Anderson High School, the latter's ornate, Franco-Scottish towers and dormers now unfortunately rather lost among later additions. Both were the gift of **Arthur Anderson** (1792–1868), co-founder of the Peninsular and Oriental Steam Navigation Company (P&O), for more on whom, see p.596.

The Street's northern end is marked by the towering walls of **Fort Charlotte** (daily: June–Sept 9am–10pm; Oct–May 9am–4pm; free), which would once have stood directly above the beach. Begun for Charles II in 1665, during the war with the Dutch, the fort was attacked and burnt down by the latter in August 1673. In the 1780s it was

Monty's Bistro and Deli, 5 Mounthooly St (☎01595/696555). Upstairs, an unpretentious bistro offers accomplished contemporary cooking – the best in Lerwick – with friendly service and moderately expensive dishes. The downstairs deli serves inexpensive and delicious snacks, soups, salads and baked potatoes (also does takeaways). Closed Sun.

Osla's Café, Mounthooly Street. Snug, basement café with outdoor seating, decked out in bright Aztec colours, below Westwood Pine, specializing in savoury and sweet pancakes. Closed Sun.

Peerie Café, Esplanade. Funky new designer shop/gallery/café in an old lodberry, with imaginative cakes and sandwiches, and what is probably Britain's northernmost latté. Closed Sun.

Raba Indian Restaurant, 26 Commercial Rd (☎01595/695585). A consistently excellent curry house, with cheerful, efficient service and reasonable prices.

Drinking, nightlife and entertainment

At weekends or whenever the fishing fleet is confined to harbour, Lerwick's **pubs** are great social centres, packed full and brimming with atmosphere. The downstairs bar in the *Thule* on the Esplanade, is an archetypal seaport pub, usually heaving with serious drinkers. The friendliest place in town, however, is the upstairs bar in the *Lounge*, up Mounthooly Street, where local musicians usually play Saturday lunchtime and some evenings. If you're desperate to keep going until the early hours, head for the town's main dance venue, *Posers*, a small, lively and smartish nightclub at the back of the *Grand Hotel* on Commerical Street.

Music features very strongly in Shetland life and every style has an enthusiastic following. The emphasis in traditional music is firmly instrumental, not vocal, with substantial numbers of young people learning the fiddle. In late April, musicians from all over the world converge on Shetland for the excellent **Shetland Folk Festival**, which embraces a wider range of musical styles than the title might suggest; there are concerts and dances in every corner of the islands. For details, telephone the Folk Festival office (☎01595/694757) or write to them at 5 Burns Lane, Lerwick. In mid-October, there's an **Accordion and Fiddle Festival**: similar format, same mailing address, but a different musical focus. Throughout the year, there are traditional dances in local halls all over Shetland; the whole community turns up and you can watch, or join in with, dances like the Boston Two-Step, Quadrilles or the Foula Reel. There are also gigs featuring a surprising number of accomplished local groups; rock-tinged folk styles are particularly strong. Names to catch live or recorded include Hom Bru, Drop the Box, Filska and Fiddlers' Bid. Legendary local fiddler Aly Bain (see p.653) makes occasional appearances on the islands. For details of what's on, listen in to *Good Evening Shetland* (BBC Radio Shetland, 92.7MHz FM, Mon–Fri 5.30pm), buy the *Shetland Times* on Fridays, or visit their Web site: *www.shetland-times.co.uk*. Some events are also advertised on Shetland's independent radio station, SIBC (96.2MHz FM, 24 hours). If you want to pick up a CD or cassette of traditional Shetland music, head for High Level Music on the Market Cross.

Not surprisingly, another Shetland passion is **boating and yachting**, and regattas take place most summer weekends, in different venues throughout the islands. Lately, the sport of **yoal racing** has caught on in a big way and teams from different districts compete passionately in large six-oared boats which used to serve as the backbone of Shetland's fishing industry.

Listings

Airports Tingwall Airport (☎01595/840246); Sumburgh Airport (☎01950/460654).

Banks Clydesdale, Bank of Scotland and Royal Bank of Scotland are all on Commercial Street; the Trustee Savings Bank is the gleaming and locally controversial structure on the Esplanade.

Bike rental Grantfield Garage, Commercial Road (Mon–Sat 8am–1pm & 2–5pm; ☎01595/692709).

Bookshops Shetland Times Bookshop, 73–79 Commercial St (Mon–Sat 9am–5pm; ☎01595/695531).

Bus companies Leask (Sandwick, Sumburgh Airport; Yell, Unst and Fetlar; ☎01856/693162); Shalder Coaches (Walls and Sandness; Scalloway; ☎01595/880217); White's Coaches (Brae and Hillswick; Vidlin and Laxo for Whalsay and Out Skerries; Walls and Sandness; ☎809443).

Car rental Bolts Car Hire, 26 North Rd (☎01595/693636); John Leask & Sons, Esplanade (☎01595/693162); Star Rent-a-Car, 22 Commercial Rd (☎01595/692075). All of these have offices at Sumburgh Airport.

Consulates Denmark, Iceland, Netherlands and Sweden at Hay and Company, 66 Commercial Rd (☎01595/692533); Finland, France, Norway and Germany at Shearer Shipping Services, Garthspool (☎01595/692556).

Laundry There is no self-service laundry in Shetland. Lerwick Laundry, 36 Market St (☎01595/693043; closed Sun), does washes, but charges individually for each item.

Medical care The Gilbert Bain Hospital (☎01595/743000) and the Lerwick Health Centre (☎01595/693201) are opposite each other on Scalloway Road.

Newspapers Daily newspapers arrive in Lerwick around noon (weather permitting); the *Shetland Times* comes out every Friday.

Post office Commercial Street (Mon–Fri 9am–5pm, Sat 9am–noon); there's a sub-post office in the Toll Clock Shopping Centre, 26 North Rd.

Sports There is a large, modern sports centre incorporating a superb leisure pool at the Clickimin Leisure Centre, Lochside, on the west side of town by Clickimin Loch (☎01595/694555). There's also a café and bar.

Travel agents John Leask & Son, Esplanade (☎01595/693162); Shetland Travelscope, Toll Clock Shopping Centre, 26 North Rd (☎01595/696644).

Bressay and Noss

Shielding Lerwick from the full force of the North Sea is the island of **Bressay**, dominated at its southern end by the conical Ward Hill (744ft) – "Da Wart" – and accessible on an hourly car and passenger ferry from Lerwick (5min). At the end of the nineteenth century, Bressay had a population of around 800, due mostly to the prosperity brought by the Dutch herring fleet; now about 350 people live here. To find out more on the history of the island, visit the **Bressay Heritage Centre** (Tues & Fri–Sun 11am–5.30pm; ☎01595/820368), by the ferry terminal in **MARYFIELD**. A short distance to the north lies **Gardie House**, built in 1724 and, in its Neoclassical detail, one of the finest of Shetland's laird houses, where the likes of Sir Walter Scott and minor royalty once stayed.

In 1917, convoys of merchant ships would gather in Bressay Sound before travelling by naval escort across the Atlantic. Huge World War I gun batteries at Score Hill on Aith Ness in the north, and on Bard Head in the south, were constructed, and now provide a focus for a couple of interesting cliff and coastal walks. Another fine walk can be made to **Bressay Lighthouse**, three miles south of the ferry terminal at Kirkibuster Ness, built by the Stevensons in the 1850s. There are plans to turn the lighthouse and its shore station into a Marine Heritage Centre and camping böd (☎01595/694688 for the latest). Until the camping böd is open, your best bet for **accommodation** is the *Maryfield House Hotel* (☎01595/820207; ③), near the ferry terminal, which is friendly and serves good-value meals in the restaurant and cosy bar.

Noss

The chief reason most visitors pass through Bressay is in order to visit the tiny but spectacular island of **Noss** – the name means "a point of rock" – just off Bressay's eastern shore. Sloping gently into the sea at its western end, and plunging vertically from

The **lighthouse**, on the top of the cliff, designed by Robert Stevenson, was built in 1821, and the keepers' cottages are now rented out as self-catering accommodation (☎01387/372240). The lighthouse itself is not open to the public, but its grounds offer great views to Noss in the north and Fair Isle to the south, as well as the perfect site for watching nesting seabirds such as kittiwakes, fulmars, shags and guillemots, not to mention gannets diving for fish. This is also the easiest place in Shetland to get close to **puffins**. During the nesting season (May to mid-Aug), you simply need to look over the western wall, just before you enter the lighthouse complex, to see them arriving at their burrows a few yards below with beakfuls of sand eels or giving flying lessons to their offspring; on no account should you try to climb over the wall.

Fair Isle

Halfway between Shetland and Orkney and very different from both, **Fair Isle** supports a vibrant community of around seventy people. The north end of the island rises like a wall; the Sheep Rock, a sculpted stack of rock and grass on the east side, is one of the island's most dramatic features. The croft land and the island's scattered houses are concentrated in the east and south. Measuring just three miles by one and a half, being on Fair Isle feels a bit like being on an aircraft carrier in the middle of the Atlantic, and the weather reflects its isolated position. You can almost guarantee that it'll be windy, and most probably wet, though if you're lucky, your visit might coincide with fine weather, what the islanders call "a given day".

At one time Fair Isle's population was not far short of four hundred, but Clearances forced emigration from the middle of the nineteenth century. By the 1950s, the population had shrunk to just 44, a point at which evacuation and abandonment of the island was seriously considered. **George Waterston**, who'd bought the island and set up a bird observatory in 1948, passed it into the care of the NTS in 1954 and rejuvenation began. Since then, islanders, the Trust and the Shetland Islands Council have invested in many improvements to housing, the harbour and basic services, including an advanced electricity system integrating wind and diesel generation, and crafts including boat-building, the making of fiddles, felt and stained glass have been developed.

The focus for many visitors is the **Bird Observatory**, built in 1969 just above the sandy bay of North Haven where the ferry from Shetland Mainland arrives. It's one of the major European centres for ornithology and its work in watching, trapping, recording and ringing birds goes on all year. Fair Isle is a landfall for a huge number and range of migrant birds during the spring and autumn passages. Migration routes converge here and more than 345 species, including many rarities, have been noted. As a result, Fair Isle is a haven for twitchers; for more casual bird watchers, however, there's also plenty of resident birdlife to enjoy. The high-pitched screeching that fills the sky above the airstrip comes from hundreds of arctic terns, and arctic skuas can also be seen here. Those in search of puffins should head for the cliffs around Furse, while for gannets, go for the spectacular stacks of Scroo and Dronger.

Fair Isle is, of course, even better known for its **knitting** patterns, still produced with as much skill as ever by the local knitwear co-operative, though not in the quantities which you might imagine from a walk around city department stores; there are demonstrations at the Community Hall, by the island school, from time to time (usually on a Monday, or when a cruise ship calls by). If the Hall is closed, then you'll have to make do with the samples on display at the island's **museum** (opening times vary and are advertised locally; ☎01595/760244; free), which is named after George Waterston, and situated next door to the island's Methodist Chapel. Particularly memorable are stories of shipwrecks; in 1868 the islanders undertook a heroic rescue of all

465 German emigrants aboard the *Lessing*. More famously the *El Gran Grifon*, part of the retreating Spanish Armada, was lost here in 1588 and 300 Spanish seamen were washed up on the island. Food was in such short supply that fifty died of starvation before help could be summoned from Shetland. The idea that the islanders borrowed all their patterns from the shipwrecked Spanish seamen is nowadays regarded as a patronizing myth.

Fair Isle has two **lighthouses**, one at either end of the island, both designed by the Stevenson family and erected in 1892. Before that, the Vikings used to light beacons to signal an enemy fleet advancing, and in the nineteenth century a semaphore consisting of a tall wooden pole was used – it can still be seen on the hill above South Lighthouse. The North Lighthouse was considered to be on such an exposed spot that the fog horn was operated from inside the lighthouse. Both lighthouses were automated in 1998, and the South Lighthouse had the distinction of being the last manned lighthouse in the country.

Practicalities

Administratively, Fair Isle is connected to Shetland, as are most of its transport links. The passenger **ferry** connects Fair Isle with either Lerwick (on alternate Thurs; 4hr 30min) or Grutness, in Sumburgh (Tues, Sat & alternate Thurs; 2hr 40min); for bookings contact J.W. Stout (☎01595/760222) in advance. The crossing can be very rough at times, so if you're at all susceptible to seasickness, it might be worth considering catching a **flight** from Tingwall (Mon, Wed, Fri & Sat) or Sumburgh (Tues, Thurs & Sat); a one-way ticket costs £36, and day-trips are possible on Mondays and Wednesdays.

Camping is not permitted on Fair Isle, but if you want **to stay**, the *Fair Isle Lodge & Bird Observatory* (☎01595/760258, *birdobs@zetnet.co.uk*; ③, full board ⑤), offers full board, B&B and hostel-style dorm beds for £25 per person. Even if you're staying elsewhere, or visiting on a day-trip, the bird observatory offers tea, coffee and good home cooking for lunch and dinner; you might even be able to lend a hand with the observatory's research programme. The only other B&B options are *Schoolton* (☎01595/760250; ①, full board ③), or *Upper Lough* (☎01595/760248; ①, full board ③), both in the south of the island. There is a shop/post office in the south of the island (closed Thurs & Sun).

Central Mainland

The districts of Tingwall and Weisdale, plus the old capital of Scalloway, make up the **Central Mainland**, an area of minor interest in the grand scheme of things, but one which is very easy to reach from Lerwick (and vice versa). In fine weather, it's a captivating mix of farms, moors, lochs and includes Shetland's only significant woodland; the scale of the scenery ranges from the intimate to the vast, with particularly spectacular views from high points above Whiteness and Weisdale. The area also holds strong historical associations, with the Norse parliament at **Lawting Holm** and unhappy memories of Earl Patrick Stewart's harsh rule at Scalloway, and nineteenth-century clearances at Weisdale.

Scalloway

Approaching **SCALLOWAY** from the shoulder of the **Scord**, there's a dramatic view over the town and the islands to the south and west. Once the capital of Shetland, Scalloway's importance waned through the eighteenth century as Lerwick, just six miles to the east, grew in trading success and status. Nowadays, Scalloway is very

If you're flying from **Tingwall Airstrip** (☎01595/840246), it's easy enough to get to the airstrip by taxi or car from either Lerwick or Scalloway; check-in is a laid-back affair, so if you're getting an early flight and arrive half an hour before your flight, you'll have ample time. One of the best places **to stay**, within easy striking distance of the airstrip, is at *South Haven* (☎01595/840350; ③), in Nesbister, overlooking Whiteness Voe; the proprietor couldn't be more accommodating and helpful. You can also **camp** in a tiny site beside the *Westings Hotel* (☎01595/840242; open all year) in nearby Wormadale. If you want to stay even closer to the airstrip, the modern *Herrislea House Hotel* (☎01595/840208; ④) overlooks the airstrip by the main crossroads. Its spacious **bar**, the heavily themed *Starboard Tack*, doubles as Tingwall's social centre, serves simple pub food and features occasional live traditional music.

Weisdale

WEISDALE, to the northwest of Tingwall, is notable primarily for **Weisdale Mill** (Wed–Sat 10.30am–4.30pm, Sun noon–4.30pm; free), situated up the B9075 from the head of Weisdale Voe. Built for milling grain in 1855, it is now an attractively converted arts centre, housing the small, beautifully designed **Bonhoga Gallery**, in which touring and local exhibitions of painting, sculpture and other media are shown. Don't miss the small but fascinating **Shetland Textile Working Museum** (Wed–Sat 10.30am–4pm, Sun noon–4pm; £1), in the basement, which puts on temporary exhibitions, and has pull-out drawers showing the knitted patterns unique to Shetland and Fair Isle. There's also a very pleasant café, serving soup, scones and snacks in the south-facing conservatory overlooking the stream.

Weisdale is an evocative name in Shetland, for in this valley some of the cruellest Clearances of people in favour of sheep took place in the middle of the nineteenth century. The perpetrator was David Dakers Black, a farmer from the county of Angus who began buying land in 1843. Hundreds of tenants were dispossessed and in 1850 the large **Kergord House**, then called Flemington, was built towards the northern end of the valley from the stones of some of the older houses. The ruined shells of some of the rest still stand on the valley sides; local writers, particularly John J. Graham, have recounted the period in novels (notably his *Shadowed Valley*) and drama.

Around Kergord House and on the upper valley sides there are several **tree plantations** dating mainly from around 1920 but with a later experimental addition by the Forestry Commission. An amazing range of species is present, from the sycamores and willows which thrive in many Shetland gardens to examples of chestnut, copper beech, monkey puzzle and much else besides. Along with the trees comes a woodland ecosystem, with foxgloves, Britain's most northerly rookery and a reliable cuckoo. During the war, Kergord House played a role in the Shetland Bus operation (see p.606); the saboteurs who trained here are said to have amused visitors by demonstrating booby traps and incendiary devices in the garden.

South of Kergord House and Weisdale Mill around the head of Weisdale Voe, it's possible to turn southwards along the west shore where, among trees near the voe's narrowest point, is the ruined house once occupied by **John Cluness Ross** (1786–1853). He settled in the Cocos Islands in the Indian Ocean, went into coconut farming and appointed himself king, the first of three in a family dynasty which ruled (some would say oppressed) the islanders for decades.

The Westside

The western Mainland of Shetland – known as the **Westside** – stretches west from Weisdale and Voe to Sandness. Although there are some important archeological remains and wildlife in the area, the Westside's greatest appeal lies in its outstanding **coastal scenery** and walks. At its heart, the Westside's rolling brown and purple moorland, dotted with patches of bright-green reseeded land, glistens with dozens of small, picturesque blue or silver lochs. On the west coast the rounded form of Sandness Hill (750ft) falls steeply away into the Atlantic. The coastal scenery, cut by several deep voes, is very varied; aside from dramatic cliffs, there are intimate coves and some fine beaches.

Bixter and around

The chief crossroads for the area is effectively **BIXTER**, a place of no particular consequence from where you can travel south to Skeld and Reawick, west to Walls, West Burrafirth and Sandness, or northwest along a scenic winding road towards **AITH** and eventually Voe (see p.612). There isn't a lot here either, except a shop and school, and an attractive little harbour that serves as the base for the west of Shetland lifeboat, but you can **stay** in the refurbished *Aith Hall Camping Barn* (☎01595/810327; June–Aug), where you can either crash inside the community hall, or pitch your own tent outside and simply use the facilities. Northwest of Aith, the road ends at the farm of **Vementry**, also, confusingly, the name of the nearby island that boasts the best-preserved **heelshaped cairn** in Shetland, right on top of the highest hill, Muckle Ward (298ft). There are also two excellently preserved **six-inch guns** from the First World War on Swarbucks Head, in the north of the island. To reach the island, enquire locally or through Lerwick tourist office.

Southwest of Bixter, on the picturesque Sandsting peninsula, there are two beautiful terracotta-coloured **sandy bays** at Reawick, and excellent **coastal walks** to be had along the coast around Westerwick and Culswick, past red granite cliffs, caves and stacks. Three miles southwest of Bixter lies the finest Neolithic structure in the Westside, dubbed the **Staneydale Temple** by the archeologist who excavated it because it resembled one on Malta. Whatever its true function, it was twice as large as the surrounding oval-shaped houses (now in ruins) and was certainly of great importance, perhaps as some kind of community centre. The horseshoe-shaped foundations measure more than 40ft by 20ft internally with immensely thick walls, still around 4ft high, whose roof would have been supported by spruce posts (two postholes can still be clearly seen). To reach the temple, take the path marked out by black-and-white poles across the moorland for half a mile from the road. There's another significant prehistoric sight, the **Scord of Brouster**, near the Brig of Waas, where the Walls and Sandness roads divide. A helpful information board provides an explanation of the layout of various ruined houses and field boundaries, making it easier to imagine what life might have been like for the people who lived on this hillside between 3000 and 1500 BC.

Walls and Sandness

Once an important fishing port, **WALLS** (pronounced "Waas"), appealingly set round its harbour, is now a quiet village, which comes alive once a year in the middle of August for the Walls Agricultural Show, the biggest farming bash on the island. At other times, you can visit the small **Walls Museum** (Thurs–Sun 2–6pm; free), mostly of knitwear, but also displaying a typical croft interior from the turn of the century, and sundry bits of nauticalia. Walls also boasts by far the best **accommodation** options on the Westside. The beautifully restored *Voe House* (April–Oct; book through Lerwick tourist office) is the largest camping böd on Shetland; the modest price includes peat for the fires. The best B&B around is the wonderfully welcoming *Skeoverick*

(☎01595/809349; ①), a lovely modern crofthouse which lies a mile or so north of Walls. The only hotel in the area is *Burrastow House* (☎01595/809307; ⑥), beautifully situated about three miles southwest of Walls; the house itself dates back to 1759, and has real character, with wood-panelling, a traditional Victorian sit-down bath tub, and a conservatory. *Burrastow House* is also one of the best places **to eat** in the whole of Shetland, offering distinguished cooking in idyllic surroundings; meals, though expensive, are fantastic, and booking ahead is pretty much essential.

A short distance across the sea lies the island of **Vaila**, from where in 1837 Lerwick philanthropist Arthur Anderson operated a fishing station in an unsuccessful attempt to break down the system of fishing tenures under which tenants were forced to fish for the landlords under pain of eviction. The ruins of Anderson's fishing station still stand on the shore, but the most conspicuous monument is **Vaila Hall**, the largest laird's house on Shetland, originally built in 1696, but massively enlarged by a wealthy Yorkshire mill-owner, Herbert Anderton, who bought the island in 1893. Anderton also restored the island's ancient watchtower of Mucklaberry Castle, built a Buddhist temple (now sadly in ruins), and had a cannon fired whenever he arrived on the island. The island is currently owned by an eccentric young Polish woman and her partner; if you wish to visit, enquire at *Burrastow House.*

The end of the road as far as the Westside is concerned is the scattered crofting settlement of **SANDNESS** (pronounced "*Saa*ness"), which you can reach by road or by walking the coast from Walls past the dramatic Deepdale and across Sandness Hill. It's an oasis of green meadows in the peat moorland, with a nice beach, too. The modern Jamieson's **woollen spinning mill** (Mon–Fri 8am–5pm; free), at Sandness, is the only one on Shetland producing pure Shetland wool; it welcomes visitors, and you can watch how they spin the exceptionally fine Shetland wool into yarn.

Papa Stour

A mile offshore from Sandness is the quintessentially peaceful island of **Papa Stour**, created out of volcanic lava and ash which has subsequently been eroded into some of the most impressive coastal scenery in Shetland. In good weather, it makes for a perfect day-trip, but in foul weather or a sea mist, it can certainly appear pretty bleak. Its name, which means "big island of the priests", derives from its early Celtic Christian connections, and it was home, in the eighteenth century, to people who were mistakenly believed to have been lepers, though in fact were suffering from a hereditary skin disease caused by severe malnutrition. The land is, in fact, very fertile, and in the nineteenth century, Papa Stour supported around three hundred inhabitants, but by the early 1970s there was a population crisis: the island's school closed, and the remaining sixteen inhabitants were all past child-bearing age; worse still, it looked like the post office would close and the mailboat be withdrawn. The islanders made appeals for new blood to revive the fragile economy and managed to stage a dramatic recovery, releasing croft land to young settlers from Britain and overseas. Papa Stour was briefly dubbed "the hippie isle", but it wasn't long before some newcomers moved on, to other parts of Shetland or elsewhere, making a further appeal necessary in the early 1990s. Today the island supports a community of thirty or so.

The island's main settlement, **BIGGINGS**, lies in the west near the pier, and it was here that excavation in the early 1980s revealed the remains of a thirteenth-century Norse house, which is thought to have belonged to Duke Haakon, heir to the Norwegian throne. There's an explanatory panel, but nothing much to see – in any case, the chief reason to come to Papa Stour is to go walking; to reach the best of the coastal scenery, head for the far west of the island. From **Virda Field** (285ft), the highest point on the island, in the far northwest, you can see the treacherous rocks of Ve

Skerries, three miles or so northwest off the coast, where a lighthouse was erected as recently as 1979. The couple of miles of coastline from here southeast to Hamna Voe has some of the island's best stacks, blowholes and natural arches. Probably the most spectacular formation of all is the **Christie's Hole**, a gloup or partly roofed cleft, which extends far inland from the cliff line, and where shags nest on precipitous ledges. Other points of interest include a couple of defunct horizontal click-mills (see p.567), below Dutch Loch, and the remains of a "meal road", so called because the workmen were paid in oatmeal or flour. Several pairs of red-throated divers breed on inland lochs such as Gorda Water.

Practicalities

In summer, the passenger **ferry** runs from West Burrafirth on the Westside to Papa Stour (Mon, Wed & Fri–Sun). Always book in advance and reconfirm the day before departure (☎01595/810460); day-trips are only possible on Friday, Saturday and Sunday. There's also a **flight** from Tingwall airport every Tuesday, and again a day-trip is feasible; tickets cost just £15 one-way and the airstrip is southwest of Biggings, by the school. The only accommodation on the island is *North House* **B&B** (☎01595/873238; ①, full board ③), who can arrange boat trips around the stacks and sea caves. There's no shop, so even day-trippers should bring their own picnic with them.

Foula

Southwest of Walls, at "the edge of the world", **Foula** is without a doubt the most iso-lated inhabited island in the British Isles, separated from the nearest point on Mainland Shetland by about fourteen miles of often turbulent ocean. Seen from the Mainland, its distinctive mountainous form changes subtly, depending upon the vantage point, but the outline is unforgettable. Its western **cliffs**, the second highest in Britain after those of St Kilda, rise at the Kame to some 1220ft above sea level; a clear day offers a mag-nificent panorama stretching from Unst to Fair Isle. On a bad day, the exposure is com-plete and the cliffs generate turbulent blasts of wind known in Shetland as "flans" which tear down the hills with tremendous force.

The island has been inhabited since prehistoric times, and the people here take pride in their separateness from Shetland, cherishing local traditions such as the observance of the **Julian calendar**, officially dropped in Britain in 1752, where Old Yule is cele-brated on January 6 and the New Year doesn't arrive until January 13. The folk of Foula were still using Norse udal law in the late seventeenth century, seemingly unaware that it had been superseded by Scots law in the rest of the country. Foula was also the last place that Norn, the old Norse language of Orkney and Shetland, was spoken as a first language in the eighteenth century. Likewise, the island's isolation also meant that more of the Shetland dialect survived here than elsewhere; in the late nineteenth cen-tury, Foula's people provided an enormous amount of information on the dialect and its roots in Norn for a study undertaken by the Faroese philologist Jakob Jakobsen. Foula's population, which peaked at around two hundred at the end of the nineteenth century, has fluctuated wildly over the years, dropping to three in 1720 following an epi-demic of "muckle fever" or smallpox; today, the community numbers around forty.

Arriving on Foula, you can't help but be amazed by the sheer size of the island's immense, bare mountain summits. However, the gentler eastern slopes provide good crofting land, plentiful peat, and it is along this "green belt" that the island's population are scattered. The island, whose name is derived from the Old Norse for "bird island", also provides a home for a quarter of a million **birds**. Arctic terns wheel overhead at the airstrip, red-throated divers can usually be seen on Mill Loch, while fulmars, guille-mots and gannets cling to the rock ledges, but it is the island's colony of **great skuas** or "bonxies" whom you can't fail to notice. From the edge of extinction a hundred years ago, the bonxies are now thriving, with an estimated 3000 pairs on Foula, making it the largest colony in Britain. Sadly, the skuas, who eat the eggs and young of other birds, have devastated the puffin population, and, during the nesting season, they attack anyone who comes near. Although their dive-bombing antics are primarily meant as a threat, they can make walking across the island's moorland interior fairly stressful – the best advice is to stick to the coast.

Practicalities

A day-trip by **ferry** isn't possible, as the summer passenger service to Foula from Walls only runs on Tuesdays, Saturdays and alternate Thursdays (2hr 30min), with a sailing from Scalloway on remaining Thursdays (3hr); it's essential to book and reconfirm (☎01595/753232). The boat arrives at Ham, in the middle of the east coast, and has to be winched up on to the pier to protect it. There are also **flights** from Tingwall, to Foula (Mon–Wed & Fri; ☎01595/840226), with day-trips possible except on Tuesdays; tickets cost around £20 one-way. If you want to stay on the island, the only **B&B** is *Leraback* (☎01595/753226; ②), near Ham, which does full-board only. Even if you go to the island just for the day, bear in mind that there's no shop, so you'll need to take all your supplies with you. There's just one road, which runs along the eastern side of the island, and is used by Foula's remarkable fleet of unroadworthy vehicles.

North Mainland

The **North Mainland**, stretching more than thirty miles north from the central belt around Lerwick, is wilder than much of Shetland, with almost relentlessly bleak moorland and some rugged and dramatic coastal scenery. It is all but split in two by the isthmus of Mavis Grind: to the south are the districts of Delting, home to Shetland's oil terminal, Lunnasting, gateway to the islands of Whalsay and Out Skerries, and Nesting; to the north is the remote region of Northmavine, which boasts some of the most scenic cliffs in Shetland.

Voe and around

If you're travelling north, you're bound to pass by **VOE**, as it sits at the main crossroads of the North Mainland: to the east, the road leads to Vidlin and Laxo, ferry terminals for Whalsay and Outskerries; to the northeast the road cuts across to Toft, where the ferry departs for Yell (see p.617); to the northwest, it continues on to Brae and Northmaven. If you stay on the main road, it's easy to miss the picturesque old village, a tight huddle of homes and workshops down below the road around the pier. Set at the head of a deep, sheltered, sea loch, Voe has a Scandinavian appearance helped by the presence of the **Sail Loft**, painted in a rich, deep red. The building was originally used by fishermen and whalers for storing their gear; later, it became a knitwear workshop, and it was here that woollen jumpers were knitted for the 1953 Mount Everest expedition. Today, the building has been converted into a large **camping böd** (April–Oct; book through Lerwick tourist office); it has hot showers, a kitchen, and a solid-fuel heater in the smaller of the bedrooms. There's a handy bakery across the road, and the *Pierhead Restaurant & Bar*, a cosy wood-panelled **pub** with a real fire and occasional live music, which offers a good bar menu and à la carte including the odd catch from the local fishing boats; phone ahead to check if the restaurant is open (☎01806/588332).

Beyond Laxo, the ferry terminal for Whalsay (see p.615), and Vidlin, the departure point for the Out Skerries (see p.616), nine miles northeast of Voe, lies **Lunna House**, with its distinctive red window surrounds, set above a sheltered harbour. The house was originally built in 1660 by the Hunter family, but is best known as the initial headquarters from which the Shetland Bus resistance operation was conducted during World War II (see p.606). Down the hill lies the little whitewashed **Lunna Kirk**, built in 1753, with a beautiful tiny interior including a carved hexagonal pulpit. Among its more peculiar features is a "lepers' squint" on the outside wall, through which those believed to have the disease could participate in the service without risk of infecting the congregation; there was, however, no leprosy here, the outcasts in fact suffering from a hereditary, non-infectious skin condition, brought on by malnutrition. In the graveyard, several unidentified Norwegian sailors, torpedoed by the Nazis, are buried.

Brae and Sullom Voe

BRAE, a sprawling settlement that still has the feel of a frontier town, was one of four expanded in some haste in the 1970s to accommodate the workforce for the huge **Sullom Voe Oil Terminal**, just to the northeast. The longest sea loch in Shetland, Sullom Voe has always attracted the interest of outsiders in search of a deep-water harbour. During World War II it was home to the Norwegian Air Force and a base for RAF seaplanes. Although the oil terminal, built between 1975 and 1982, has passed its production peak, it is still the largest of its kind in Europe. Its size, however, isn't obvious from beyond the site boundary and few clues remain to the extraordinary scale of the construction effort, which for several years involved a workforce of 6000 accommodated in two large "construction villages" and two ships. It is still a huge source of employment, but its long-term future depends partly on whether it obtains the contracts for exploiting the new oilfields west of Shetland.

Brae may not, at first sight, appear to be somewhere to spend the night, but it does boast one of Shetland's finest **hotels**, *Busta House* (☎01806/522506; ⑤), a lovely laird's house with stepped gables, that has been enlarged tastefully over the last four hundred years and which sits across the bay of Busta Voe from the modern sprawl of Brae. Even if you're not staying the night here, it's worth coming for afternoon tea in the Long Room, a stroll around the lovely wooded grounds, or for a drink and a superb bar meal in the hotel's pub-like bar. A cheaper alternative is the modern crofthouse **B&B** of *Westayre* (☎01806/522368; ①), beyond Busta, overlooking a red sandy bay on the peaceful island of Muckle Roe, which is linked to the mainland by a bridge. The nearest **campsite** (☎01806/522563), by the unattractive *Valleyfield Guest House*, on the main road a mile or so south of Brae, has all the facilities you could want, but a pitiable location.

Northmavine

Mavis Grind, the narrow ithsmus at which it's said you can throw a stone from the Atlantic to the North Sea, or at least to Sullom Voe, marks the start of **Northmavine**, the northwest peninsula of North Mainland, and unquestionably one of the most picturesque areas of Shetland with its often rugged scenery, magnificent coastline and wide open spaces. Three miles north of the isthmus, it's worth abandoning the main road to explore the remoter corners; the twisting sideroad west to Gunnister and Nibon travels through a wonderful tumbled landscape of pink and grey rock where abandoned fields and broken shells of croft houses provide abundant evidence of past human struggles to make a living. Where the road ends, at Nibon, you can view a jigsaw of islands and rocky headlands which, even on a relatively calm day, smash the Atlantic into streams of white foam.

Hillswick

HILLSWICK, the main settlement in the area, was once served by the steamboats of the North of Scotland, Orkney & Shetland Steam Navigation Company, and in the early 1900s the firm built the **St Magnus Hotel** to house their customers, importing it in the form of a timber kit from Norway. Despite various alterations over the years, it still stands overlooking St Magnus Bay, rather magnificently clad in black timber-framing and white weatherboarding. Nearer the shore is the much older Hillswick House and, attached to it, **Da Böd**, once the oldest pub in Shetland, said to have been founded by a German merchant in 1684, but now a rather unpredictable hippy café called *The Booth*.

It is possible **to stay** at the *St Magnus Hotel* (☎01806/503372; ②), whose foyer, dining room and bedrooms retain their original pine walls, but you can't help feeling that the place has seen better days – and the food is very ordinary. For a decent **B&B** in the vicinity of Hillswick, look no further than *Almara* (☎01806/503261; ①), a mile or two back down the road in Upper Urafirth, which will present you with good food, a family welcome and excellent views. If you're looking for a **beach** to collapse on, the nicest sandiest one is on the west side of the Hillswick isthmus, overlooking Dore Holm (see below), a short walk across the fields from the hotel.

Esha Ness

Just outside Hillswick, a sideroad leads west to the exposed headland of **Esha Ness** (pronounced "*Ay*sha Ness"), celebrated for its splendid coastline views. Spectacular red granite **cliffs**, eaten away to form fantastic shapes by the elements, are spread out before you as the road climbs away from Hillswick: in the foreground are the stacks known as **The Drongs** off the Ness of Hillswick, while in the distant the Westside and Papa Stour are visible.

A mile or so south off the main road is the **Tangwick Haa Museum** (May–Sept Mon–Fri 1–5pm, Sat & Sun 11am–7pm; free), which, through photographs, old documents and fishing gear, tells the often moving story of this remote corner of Shetland and its role in the dangerous trade of deep-sea fishing and whaling. Kids and adults alike will also enjoy the shells, the Shetland wool and sand samples, and the prize exhibit, the Gunnister Man, who was found preserved in peat in 1951. Over 250 years old now, he's down to his bones, for the most part, but his clothes are in good condition, as is his knitted purse, which contained three coins: two Dutch and one Swedish.

Just before it finally peters out, the road divides, with the southern branch leading to the remains of **Stenness fishing station**, which was once one of the most important deep-sea or haaf-fishing stations in Shetland. The remains of a few of the böds used by the fishermen are still visible along the sloping pebbly beach where they would dry their catch. At the peak of operations in the early nineteenth century, as many as eighteen trips a year were made in up to seventy open six-oared boats, or "sixareens", to the fishing grounds thirty or forty miles to the west. A Shetland folk song, *Rowin' Foula Doon*, recalls how the crews rowed so far west that the island of Foula began to sink below the eastern horizon. Visible half a mile offshore to the south is **Dore Holm** or the "Drinking Horse", an impressive island with a natural arch.

The northern branch of the road ends at the **Esha Ness Lighthouse**, a great place to view the red sandstone cliffs, stacks and blowholes of this stretch of coast. A useful information board at the lighthouse details some of the dramatic geological features here, and, if the weather's a bit rough, you should be treated to some spectacular crashing waves. One of the features to beware of at Esha Ness are the blowholes, some of which are hidden far inland. The best example is the **Holes of Scraada**, a partly roofed cleft where the sea suddenly appears 300 yards inland from the cliff line. The incredible power of the sea can be seen in the various giant boulder fields above the cliffs – these **storm beaches** are formed by rocks torn from the cliffs in storms and deposited inland.

One of the few places to stay in Esha Ness is *Johnnie Notions* **camping böd** (April–Oct; book through Lerwick tourist office; no electricity), up a turning north off the main road, in the hamlet of Hamnavoe. The house was originally the birthplace of **Johnnie "Notions" Williamson** (1740–1803). A man of many talents, including blacksmithing and weaving, his fame rests on his work in protecting several thousand of the population against **smallpox** using a serum and a method of inoculation he'd invented himself, to the amazement of the medical profession. He used a scalpel to lift a flap of skin without drawing blood, then placed the serum he'd prepared underneath, dressing it with a cabbage leaf and a bandage.

Ronas Hill

North of Ronas Voe, by the shores of Colla Firth, an unmarked road leads up **Collafirth Hill**, at the top of which are the crumbling remains of a NATO radio station. However, the natural landscape is much more impressive, with tremendous views on a clear day, and a foreground of large, scattered stones with hardly any vegetation. Though the walk isn't quite as straightforward as it looks, scale and distance being hard to judge in this setting, Collafirth Hill is the easiest place from which to approach the rounded contours of **Ronas Hill**, Shetland's highest point (1475ft). The climb, with no obvious path, is exhausting but rewarding (4hr return; see also the safety precautions on p.473): from the top you can look west to one of the most beautifully sculptured parts of the Shetland coast, as the steep slope of the hill drops down to the arching sand and shingle beach called the **Lang Ayre**, south and east over all of the Mainland, north along the coast of Yell, or out into the daunting expanse of the Atlantic. Also at the summit, among sub-Arctic vegetation and blockfields of granite boulders formed by intense frost and wind, is a Neolithic or Bronze Age **chambered cairn**, one of the best-preserved in Shetland and useful as a shelter from the wind.

Whalsay and Out Skerries

The island of **Whalsay**, known in Shetland as the "Bonnie Isle", is a thriving and extremely friendly community of over one thousand, devoted almost entirely to fishing. The islands' crews operate a fleet of immense super trawlers and have coped with the change and uncertainty that characterize the industry by investing huge sums in fishing further afield and catching a wider range of species, and have thus sustained a remarkable level of prosperity. The island is, in addition, extremely fertile, but crofting takes second place to fishing here; there are also plentiful supplies of peat, which can be seen in spring and summer, stacked neatly to dry out above huge peat banks, ready to be bagged for the winter.

Ferries from the Mainland arrive at the island's chief town, **SYMBISTER**, in the southwest, whose harbour is usually dominated by the presence of several of the island's sophisticated, multi-million-pound purse-netters, some over 180ft long; you'll also see smaller fishing boats and probably a few "fourareens", which the locals race regularly in the summer months. Across the busy harbour from the ferry berth stands the tiny grey granite **Pier House** (Mon–Sat 9am–1pm & 2–5pm, Sun 2–4pm; 50p), the key for which resides in the shop opposite. This picturesque little building, with a hoist built into one side, is thought to have been a Hanseatic merchants' store, and contains a good display on how the Germans traded salt, tobacco, spirits and cloth for Whalsay's salted fish from medieval times until the eighteenth century. Close by is the Harbour View house that is thought to have been a Hanseatic storehouse or booth (and is now a private house and hairdressers). On a hill overlooking the town is the imposing Georgian mansion of **Symbister House**, built in grey granite and boasting a Neoclassical portico. It was built in 1830s at great expense by Robert Bruce, not because he wanted to live on Whalsay, but, so the story goes, because he wanted to deprive his heirs of his fortune. Since 1940 it has served as the local school and, in the process, has lost some of its grandeur.

At the hamlet of **SODOM** – an anglicized version of Sudheim, meaning "South House" – about half a mile east of Symbister, is **Grieve House** (now a camping böd, see below), the modest former home of celebrated Scots poet, writer and republican **Hugh MacDiarmid** (1892–1978), born Christopher Grieve in the Borders town of Langholm (see p.157). He stayed here from 1933 until 1942, writing about half of his output, including much of his best work: lonely, contemplative poems honouring fishing and fishermen, with whom he sometimes went out to sea. Estranged from his first wife and family and with a drink problem, MacDiarmid, practically broken, had sought temporary relief in Shetland. At first, he seems to have fallen in love with the islands, but poor physical and mental health exacerbated (if not caused) by chronic poverty, dogged him. Eventually, unwillingly conscripted to work in a Glasgow munitions factory, he left with his new wife and young son, never to return.

Although the majority of folk live in or around Symbister, the rest of the island – which measures roughly two miles by eight – is quite evenly and fairly densely populated. Of the prehistoric remains on Whalsay, the most notable are the two **Bronze Age houses** on the northeastern coast of the island, half a mile south of Skaw, respectively as the "Benie Hoose", and "Yoxie Biggins". The latter is also known as the "Standing Stones of Yoxie", due to the use of megaliths to form large sections of the walls, many of which still stand. The houses were clearly used over a very long period, as over 1800 tools were discovered in the Benie Hoose – the community also built the nearby chambered tomb.

Car ferries between Laxo and Whalsay (30min) run roughly every 45 minutes from early morning until late evening; if you have a car, however, it's an idea to book ahead (☎01806/566259). In bad weather, especially southeasterly gales, the service operates from Vidlin. There are also regular **flights** from Tingwall (Mon & Wed–Fri), but these are request only so you must book ahead; day-trips are only possible on Thursdays. A few locals do **B&B** for the odd visitor who turns up: try Mrs Jamieson (☎01806/566496; ①) in Symbister, or enquire at the post office; Mrs Simpson also has a few inexpensive self-catering options on the island (☎01806/566429). Alternatively, you can stay at the **camping böd** of *Grieve House* (April–Oct; book through Lerwick tourist office; no electricity), in Sodom. The house has lovely views overlooking Linga Sound, but is hidden from the main road, so ask for directions at the shop on the brow of the hill along the road to Huxter Loch. The island also has an eighteen-hole **golf course**, near the airstrip in Skaw, in the northeast, several shops, and a **leisure centre** with an excellent swimming pool close to the school in Symbister.

Out Skerries

Lying four miles out to sea, off the northeast tip of Whalsay, the **Out Skerries** (or Skerries as the locals call them), consist of three tiny low-lying rocky islands – Housay, Bruray and Grunay – the first two linked by a bridge. That people live here at all is remarkable, and that it is one of Shetland's most dynamic communities is astonishing, its affluence based on fishing from a superb, small natural harbour sheltered by all three islands, and on salmon farming in a nearby inlet. There are good, if short, walks, with a few prehistoric remains, but the majority of visitors to Skerries are divers exploring the wreck-strewn coastline, and ornithologists who come here when the wind is in the east, in the hope of catching a glimpse of rare migrants.

The Skerries' jetty and airstrip are both on the middle island of **Bruray**, which also boasts the Skerries highest point, Bruray Wart (173ft), an easy climb, and one which brings you up close to the islands' ingenious spiral channel collection system for rainwater, which can become scarce in summer. The easternmost island, **Grunay**, is now uninhabited, though you can clearly see the abandoned lighthouse keepers' cottages on the island's chief hill; despite appearances, the lighthouse itself sits on the outlying islet of Bound Skerry. The largest of the Skerries' trio, **Housay**, has the most indented and intriguing coastline, to which you should head if the weather's fine. En route, make sure you wander through the Battle Pund stone circle, a wide ring of boulders in the southeastern corner of the island.

Ferries to and from Skerries leave from Vidlin (Mon & Fri–Sun; 1hr 30min), and Lerwick (Tues & Thurs; 2hr 30min), but day-trips are only possible from Vidlin on Fridays, Saturdays and Sundays. Make sure you book your journey by 5pm the previous evening (☎01806/515226), or the ferry might not run. You can take your car over, but, with less than a mile of road to drive along, it's hardly worth it. There are also regular flights from Tingwall (Mon & Wed–Fri), though a day-trip by plane is only possible on Thursdays. There is a shop, and a shower/toilet block by the pier, and **camping** is permitted, with permission. Alternatively, you can stay in *Rocklea* (☎01806/515228; ①, full board ②), a friendly **B&B** on Bruray run by Mrs Johnson.

Yell

Historically, **Yell**, the largest of Shetland's North Isles, hasn't had good write-ups. The writer, Eric Linklater, described it as "dull and dark", while the Scottish historian Buchanan claimed it was "so uncouth a place that no creature can live therein, except such as are born there". Certainly, if you keep to the fast main road which links the island's two ferry terminals of Ulsta and Gutcher, you'll pass a lot of uninspiring peat moorland, but the landscape is relieved by several voes which cut deeply into it, providing superb natural harbours used as hiding places by German submarines during World War II. Yell's coastline, too, is gentler and greener than the interior and provides an ideal habitat for a large population of **otters**; locals will point out the best places to watch for them.

At **BURRAVOE**, in the southeastern corner of Yell, there's a lovely whitewashed laird's house dating from 1672, with crowstepped gables, that now houses the **Old Haa Museum** (late April to Sept Tues–Thurs & Sat 10am–4pm, Sun 2–5pm; free), which is stuffed with artefacts, and has lots of material on the history of the local herring and whaling industry; there's a very pleasant wood-panelled café on the ground floor, too. Across the road is **St Colman's Kirk**, completed in 1900 featuring three Gothic-windowed bays surmounted by a tiny little spire.

The island's largest village, **MID YELL**, has a couple of shops, a pub and a leisure centre with a good swimming pool. A mile or so to the northwest of the village, on an exposed hill above the main road, stands the spooky, abandoned **Windhouse**, dating in part from the early eighteenth century; skeletons were found under the floor and in its wood-panelled walls, and the house is now believed by many to be haunted (its unhaunted lodge is a camping böd; see below). North of Windhouse, around the Loch of Lumbister, there's an **RSPB reserve** that's home to merlins, skuas and red-throated divers, and is scattered with wild flowers in summer. A pleasant walk leads along the nearby narrow gorge known as **Daal of Lumbister**, where you can see a lush growth of honeysuckle, wild thyme and moss campion.

In the north of Yell, the area around **CULLIVOE** has relatively gentle, but attractive, coastal scenery. The **Sands of Breckon** are made from crushed shells, and are beautifully sheltered in a cove a mile or two north of Cullivoe. A couple of miles to the west, the road ends at **GLOUP**, with its secretive, narrow voe. In the nineteenth century, this was one of the largest haaf-fishing stations in Shetland; a memorial commemorates the 58 men who were lost when a great storm overwhelmed six of their "sixerns" (six-oared, open rowing boats) in July 1881. This area provides some excellent walking, as does the Atlantic coast further west, where there's an Iron Age fort and field system at **Burgi Geos**.

Practicalities

Ferries to Yell are frequent and inexpensive, and taking a car over is easy, too; the Mainland ferry terminal is at Toft (daily every 30min; 20min). One of the best **B&Bs** on Yell is *Hillhead* (☎01957/722274; ①) in Burravoe; you can also stay with the Tullochs at Gutcher's post office (☎01957/744201; ①). A cheaper alternative is to stay in the **camping böd** at *Windhouse Lodge* (April–Oct; book through Lerwick tourist office), the (unhaunted) gatehouse on the main road near Mid Yell; it has a small wood-and peat-fired heater and hot showers. There isn't a great range of **food** options on the island but the non-smoking café in the *Old Haa Museum* (closed Mon & Fri) at Burravoe has soup, snacks and delicious home baking. The *Hilltop Bar* in Mid Yell offers standard bar meals, while the *Seaview Café* at the Gutcher ferry terminal has filled rolls, snacks, soup, teas and coffees.

Fetlar

Known as "the garden of Shetland", **Fetlar** is the most fertile of the North Isles, much of it grassy moorland and lush green meadows with masses of summer flowers. Around 900 people once lived here and there might well be more than 100 now were it not for the activities of **Sir Arthur Nicolson**, who in the first half of the nineteenth century cleared many of the people at forty days' notice to make room for sheep. Nicolson's architectural tastes were rather more eccentric than some other local tyrants; his rotting but still astonishing **Brough Lodge**, a rambling castellated composition built in stone and brick in the 1820s, can be seen a mile or so south of the ferry terminal, and owes something – perhaps an apology – to Gothic, Classical and maybe even Tudor styles. Nicolson is also responsible for the nearby round tower folly, which was built with stone taken from the abandoned crofthouses.

Today Fetlar's population live on the southern and eastern sides of the island. At the main settlement, **HOUBIE**, in the centre of the island on the south coast, there's a rather less adventurously styled laird's house called Leagarth, built by Fetlar's most famous son, Sir William Watson Cheyne, who with Lord Lister pioneered antiseptic surgery. Nearby is the excellent **Fetlar Interpretive Centre** (May–Sept Tues–Sun noon–5pm; free) presenting the island's history and offering information on Fetlar's outstanding birdlife through the Internet as well as by more conventional means.

Much of the northern half of the island around Fetlar's highest point, Vord Hill 522ft), is now the **RSPB North Fetlar Reserve**, which is closed from mid-May to mid-July, during which time visits are only possible with permission from the warden at Baelan, the house signposted off the main road from Brough Lodge to Houbie (☎01957/733246). As well as harbouring important colonies of arctic skuas and whimbrels, the reserve is perhaps best known for Britain's only breeding pair of **snowy owls**, which bred on Stackaberg, to the southwest of Vord Hill, from 1967 to 1975. Around twenty chicks were raised before the old male died, and since then only the female has been seen. The warden can advise you on the latest, and occasionally conducts guided walks in search of the snowy owl (phone as above). Fetlar is also one of very few places you'll see graceful **red-necked phalarope** (late May to July): the birds are unusual in that the female does the courting and then leaves the male in charge of incubation. The island boasts 95 percent of the UK population, and an RSPB hide has been provided overlooking the marshes (or mires), to the east of the **Loch of Funzie** (which, incidentally, is pronounced "Finnie"); the loch itself is a good place to look out for red-throated divers.

Of the archeological remains on Fetlar, perhaps the most remarkable is the **Funzie Girt** or Finnigirt, an ancient stone boundary of uncertain date, which divides the island into two. Its southern end has been destroyed, but it is well preserved on the western and northern slopes of Vord Hill, within the RSPB reserve (see above). Elsewhere on Fetlar, particularly along the remoter north coast and on Lamb Hoga, the higher moorland peninsula to the southwest, there is excellent walking. At Tresta, on the south coast, is a beautiful, sheltered, sandy beach and the loch behind it, Papil Water, is good for fishing.

Practicalities

Ferries to Fetlar (5–6 daily; 25min) depart from both Gutcher (on Yell) and Belmont (on Unst), though they are by no means as frequent as the ferries between the Mainland, Yell and Unst. The ferry docks at Oddsta, three miles northwest of Houbie; the only public transport is an infrequent **post car** (Mon, Wed & Fri), so if you don't have a car you should try to negotiate a lift on the ferry. If you do have a car, bear in mind that there's no petrol station on Fetlar, so fill up before you come across. Accommodation is in short supply and booking is advisable, if you wish to stay the night. Fetlar's most comfortable **B&B** is the modern *Gord* (☎01957/733227; ①), behind the island shop in Houbie, followed by *The Glebe* (☎01957/733242; ②), which is non-smoking, and is hidden among the trees above Papil Water; both will provide an evening meal. *The Garths* **campsite** (☎01957/733227; May–Sept) is in a field just to the west of Houbie, with toilets, showers and drying facilities. There's a post office, shop and **café** (closed Mon) in the middle of Houbie.

Unst

Unst has a population of around 1000, of whom 300 to 400 are connected to the RAF radar base at Saxa Vord, listening out for uninvited intruders. Much of the interior is rolling grassland – a blessed relief after the peaty moorland of Yell – but the coast is more dramatic: a fringe of cliffs relieved by some beautiful sandy beaches. As Britain's most northerly inhabited island, there is a surfeit of "most northerly" sights, which is fair enough, given that many visitors only come here in order to head straight for Hermaness, to look out over Muckle Flugga and the northernmost tip of Britain, to the North Pole beyond.

On the south coast of the island, not far from the ferry terminal, is **UYEASOUND**, with the stone-built Greenwell's Booth, an old Hanseatic merchants' warehouse by the pier. The house on the island of Uyea, which protects the harbour, was once the home of Sir Basil Neven-Spence, the local MP (1935–50). Further east lie the ruins of **Muness Castle**, a dinky little defensive structure, with matching bulging bastions and corbelled turrets at opposite corners. The castle was built in 1598 by the Scots incomer, Laurence Bruce, step-brother and chief bully boy of the infamous Earl Robert Stewart, and probably designed by Andrew Crawford, who shortly afterwards built Scalloway Castle for Robert's son Patrick. The inscription above the entrance asks visitors "not to hurt this vark aluayis", but the castle was sacked by Danish pirates in 1627 and never really re-roofed. A little to the north is a vast sandy beach, backed by the deserted crofting settlement of Sandwick.

Unst's main settlement is **BALTASOUND**, where the remains of old jetties around the bay testify to a bygone herring industry, which saw the local population of around 500 swell to as much as 10,000 during the fishing season. Nowadays, Baltasound boasts an airport, a hotel with a pub, a shop, a post office, a leisure centre with a pool, and also Britain's most northerly brewery, the **Valhalla Brewery**, which opened in 1997 and welcomes visits by appointment (☎01957/711348; £2).

From Baltasound, the main road crosses what appears to be a giant boulder field. What you see is, in fact, serpentine rock, found widely on Unst; most often it's greyish green, but it weathers to rusty orange, and in some stone walls there are pieces which are of an extraordinary deep turquoise hue. The serpentine soil is so poor it produces unusual vegetation, turning the grass bluish-grey. At the **Keen of Hamar** National Nature Reserve, east of Baltasound, numerous rare plants, including Norwegian sandwort and the unique mouse-eared Edmondston's chickweed, grow in an almost lunar landscape.

Britain's most northerly post office is over the hill to the north, at **HAROLDSWICK**, smart and eminently photogenic in its red weatherboarding. Down near the shore the **Unst Boat Haven** (May–Sept daily 2–5pm; otherwise a key is available from the adjacent shop; free), displays a beautifully presented collection of historic boats with many tools of the trade and information on fishing; most of the boats are from Shetland, with one from Norway. A little to the northeast, next door to the Methodist chapel on the road to Norwick, stands an old crofthouse that now houses the **Unst Heritage Centre** (May–Sept daily 2–5pm; free), where you can find out about other aspects of Unst life. The road ends at Skaw, with a beautiful beach and the very last house in Britain.

The road that heads off northwest from Haroldswick leads to the head of **Burra Firth**, a north-facing inlet surrounded by cliffs and home to Britain's most northerly golf course and rugby pitch. It is guarded to the east by the hills of **Saxa Vord** (936ft), Unst's highest point, topped by several MoD installations. It was here that the country's unofficial wind speed record of 177mph was recorded in 1962, before the anemometer was blown away. To the west of Burra Firth lies the bleak headland of **Hermaness**, now a National Nature Reserve and home to more than 100,000 nesting seabirds. There's an excellent **visitor centre** in the former lighthouse keepers' shore station, where you can pick up a leaflet showing the marked routes across the heather, which allow you access into the reserve. Whatever you do, stick to the path so as to avoid annoying the vast numbers of nesting great skuas.

From Hermaness Hill, you can look down over the jagged rocks of the wonderfully-named Vesta Skerry, Rumblings, Tipta Skerry and **Muckle Flugga**. There are few more dramatic settings for a lighthouse, and few sites could ever have presented as great a challenge to the builders, who erected it in 1858. Beyond the lighthouse is **Out Stack**, the most northerly bit of Britain, where Lady Franklin landed in 1849 in order to pray (in vain as it turned out) for the safe return for her husband from his expedition to discover the North West Passage, undertaken four years previously. The views from here are inevitably marvellous, as is the birdlife; there's a huge gannetry on one of the stacks, and puffins burrow all along the clifftops. The walk down the west side of Unst towards Westing is one of the finest in Shetland and, if the wind's blowing hard, the seascape should be pretty dramatic.

Practicalities

Ferries leave regularly from Gutcher on Yell for Belmont on Unst (every 15–30min; 10min); booking in advance is wise (☎01957/722259). **Flights** to Unst depart from Sumburgh Airport (Mon–Fri only), and arrive at the airport near Baltasound. By far the best **accommodation** on Unst is historic *Buness House* (☎01957/711315, *buness@zetnet.co.uk*; ③), a lovely old Haa in Baltasound. Another very good bet is *Prestagaard* (☎01957/755234; ①), a more modest Victorian B&B in Uyeasound, where there's also the very handy, independent *Gardiesfauld Hostel* (☎01957/755259; April–Sept), which allows **camping**, and offers **bike rental**. The *Baltasound Hotel* serves **food** and drink to non-residents, and snacks and teas can be had at the tearoom in NorNova Knitwear just north of Muness Castle, or, often on a help-yourself basis, at the Haroldswick Shop. Shetland Wildlife Tours (☎01950/460254) offer a very popular, though expensive **boat trip** around Muckle Flugga, though you need good sea legs to enjoy it even in calm weather; the boats leave from Mid Yell, on the neighbouring island of Yell (May–Aug Wed 10am; £70).

travel details

ORKNEY

Mainland Buses

Kirkwall to: Burwick (4 daily; 45min); Houton (Mon–Sat 3–5 daily; 30min); St Margaret's Hope (Mon–Fri 4 daily, Sat 2 daily; 40min); Stromness (Mon–Sat 6–8 daily; 40min); Tingwall (Mon–Sat 3 daily; 25min).

Ferries to Orkney (summer only)

Aberdeen–Stromness (2 weekly; 8–10hr); Invergordon–Kirkwall (6 weekly; 9hr); John O' Groats–Burwick (passengers only; 2–4 daily; 45min); Lerwick–Stromness (2 weekly; 8hr); Scrabster–Stromness (1–3 daily; 2hr).

Inter-Island Ferries (summer only)

Eday: Kirkwall–Eday (2 daily; 1hr 15min–2hr).
Egilsay: Tingwall–Egilsay (3–4 daily; 50min–1hr 45min).
Flotta: Houton–Flotta (2–5 daily; 45min)
Hoy: Houton–Hoy (2–5 daily; 30min–1hr); Stromness–Hoy (passenger-only; 2–4 daily; 25min).
North Ronaldsay: Kirkwall–North Ronaldsay (Fri; 2hr 40min)
Papa Westray: Kirkwall–Papa Westray (Tues & Fri; 2hr 15min); Pierowall (Westray)–Papa Westray (passenger-only; 3–6 daily; 25min).
Rousay: Tingwall–Rousay (6 daily; 30min).
Sanday: Kirkwall–Sanday (1–3 daily; 1hr 25min).
Shapinsay: Kirkwall–Shapinsay (5–6 daily; 45min).
Stronsay: Kirkwall–Stronsay (2 daily; 1hr 35min–2hr).
Westray: Kirkwall–Westray (2–3 daily; 1hr 25min).
Wyre: (4–5 daily; 45min–2hr 5min).

Flights to Orkney (Mon–Sat only)

Aberdeen–Kirkwall (3 daily; 45min); Edinburgh–Kirkwall (1 daily; 1hr 30min); Glasgow–Kirkwall (1–2 daily; 1hr 20min–2hr 10min); Inverness–Kirkwall (2 daily; 50min).

Inter-Island Flights (Mon–Sat only)

Kirkwall to: Eday (Wed 3 daily; 8–36min); North Ronaldsay (1–2 daily; 15min); Papa Westray (2 daily; 12min); Sanday (1–2 daily; 20min); Stronsay (Mon–Fri 2 daily; 25min); Westray (1–2 daily; 12min).

SHETLAND

Mainland Buses

Lerwick to: Aith (Mon–Sat 1–3 daily; 45min); Brae (Mon–Fri 4–5 daily, Sat 2 daily; 45min); Hamnavoe (Mon–Sat 1–2 daily; 30min); Hillswick (1 daily except Wed & Sun; 1hr 15min); Laxo (1 daily; 40min); Sandwick (Mon–Sat 5–6 daily, Sun 3 daily; 25min); Scalloway (Mon–Sat 5–6 daily; 15min); Sumburgh (2–4 daily; 45min); Toft (Mon–Sat 1 daily; 55min); Vidlin (Mon–Sat 2 daily; 45min); Walls (Mon–Sat 1–3 daily, 45min).

Unst

Baltasound–Haroldswick (2–4 daily; 5–10min); Belmont–Baltasound (Mon–Fri school term only 1 daily; 1hr); Belmont–Uyeasound (Mon–Sat 1–3 daily; 5min).

Yell

Mid-Yell–Gutcher (1–3 daily, Sun 1 daily in school term; 25min); Ulsta–Burravoe (Mon–Sat 1 daily; 10min); Ulsta–Gutcher (Mon–Sat (1–2 daily, Sun 1 daily in school term; 30min).

Ferries to Shetland (summer only)

Aberdeen–Lerwick (4–5 weekly; 14hr); Stromness–Lerwick (2 weekly; 8–10hr).

Inter-Island Ferries (summer only)

Bressay: Lerwick–Bressay (every 30min–1hr; 5min).
Fair Isle: Lerwick–Fair Isle (alternate Thurs 4hr 30min); Sumburgh–Fair Isle (Tues, Sat & alternate Thurs 2hr 40min).
Fetlar: Belmont (Unst)–Oddsta (2–3 daily; 25min); Gutcher (Yell)–Oddsta (5–6 daily; 25min).

Foula: Scalloway–Foula (alternate Thus; 3hr); Walls–Foula (Tues & alternate Thurs; 2hr 30min).

Out Skerries: Lerwick–Skerries (Tues & Thurs; 2hr 30min); Vidlin–Skerries (Mon 1 daily, Fri–Sun 3 daily; 1hr 30min);

Papa Stour: West Burrafirth–Papa Stour (Mon, Wed & Sun 1 daily, Fri–Sat 2 daily; 45min).

Unst: Gutcher (Yell)–Belmont (every 15–45min; 10min).

Whalsay: Laxo–Symbister (14–16 daily; 30min).

Yell: Toft–Ulsta (every 20–40min; 20min).

Flights to Shetland (summer only)

Aberdeen–Sumburgh (Mon–Fri 4 daily, Sat & Sun 2 daily; 1hr); Edinburgh–Sumburgh (Mon–Sat 1 daily; 1hr 50min); Glasgow–Sumburgh (Mon–Fri 2 daily, Sat & Sun 1 daily; 2hr 25min); Inverness–Sumburgh (Mon–Sat 1 daily; 1hr 35min); Kirkwall–Sumburgh (Mon–Sat 1–2 daily; 35min); Wick–Sumburgh (Mon–Sat 1 daily; 40min).

Inter-island flights (summer only)

Sumburgh: Fair Isle (Tues, Thurs & Sat; 15min); Unst (Mon–Fri 1 daily; 35min);

Tingwall: Fair Isle (Mon, Wed & Fri 2 daily, Sat 1 daily; 25min); Foula (Mon & Wed 2 daily, Tues & Fri 1 daily; 15min); Out Skerries, calling at Whalsay on request (Mon, Wed & Fri 1 daily, Thurs 2 daily; 20min); Papa Stour (Tues 2 daily; 10min); Unst (Mon–Fri 1 daily; 25min).

THE HISTORICAL
FRAMEWORK

PREHISTORIC SCOTLAND

Scotland, like the rest of prehistoric Britain, was settled by successive waves of peoples arriving from the east. These first inhabitants were **hunter-gatherers**, whose heaps of animal bones and shells have been excavated, amongst other places, in the caves along the coast near East Wemyss in Fife. Around 4500 BC, **Neolithic farming peoples** from the European mainland began moving into Scotland. To provide themselves with land for their cereal crops and grazing for their livestock, they cleared large areas of upland forest, usually by fire, and in the process created the characteristic moorland landscapes of much of modern Scotland. These early farmers established permanent settlements, some of which, like the well-preserved village of **Skara Brae** on Orkney, were near the sea, enabling them to supplement their diet by fishing and develop their skills as boat-builders. The Neolithic settlements were not as isolated as was once imagined: geological evidence has, for instance, revealed that the stone used to make axe-heads found in the Hebrides was quarried in Northern Ireland.

Settlement spurred the development of more complex forms of religious belief. The Neolithic peoples built large chambered burial mounds or **cairns**, such as Maes Howe in Orkney. This reverence for human remains suggests a belief in some form of afterlife, a concept that the next wave of settlers, the **Beaker people**, certainly believed in. They placed pottery beakers filled with drink in the tombs of their dead to assist the passage of the deceased on their journey to, or their stay in, the next world. The Beaker people also built the mysterious **stone circles**, thirty of which have been discovered in Scotland. Such monuments were a massive commitment in terms of time and energy, with many of the stones carried from miles away, just as they were at Stonehenge in England, the most famous stone circle of all. One of the best-known Scottish circles is that of **Callanish** on the Isle of Lewis, where a dramatic series of monoliths (single standing stones) form avenues leading towards a circle made up of thirteen standing stones. The exact function of the circles is still unknown, but many of the stones are aligned with the position of the sun at certain points in its annual cycle, suggesting that the monuments are related to the changing of the seasons.

The Beaker people also brought the **Bronze Age** to Scotland. Bronze, an alloy of copper and tin, was stronger and more flexible than its predecessor, flint, which had long been used for axe-heads and knives. New materials led directly to the development of more effective weapons, and the sword and the shield made their first appearance around 1000 BC. Agricultural needs plus new weaponry added up to a state of endemic warfare as villagers raided their neighbours to steal livestock and grain. The Bronze Age peoples responded to the danger by developing a range of defences, among them the spectacular **hillforts**, great earthwork defences, many of which are thought to have been occupied from around 1000 BC and remained in use throughout the Iron Age, sometimes far longer. Less spectacular but equally practical were the **crannogs**, smaller settlements built on artificial islands constructed of logs, earth, stones and brush, such as Cherry Island in Loch Ness.

Conflict in Scotland intensified in the first millennium BC as successive waves of **Celtic** settlers, arriving from the south, increased competition for land. Around 400 BC, the Celts brought the technology of **iron** with them and, as Winston Churchill put it, "Men armed with iron entered Britain and killed the men of bronze". These fractious times witnessed the construction of hundreds of **brochs** or fortified towers. Concentrated along the Atlantic coast and in the northern and western isles, the brochs were drystone fortifications (that is, built without mortar or cement) often over 40ft in height. Some historians claim they provided protection for small coastal settlements from the attentions of Roman slave traders. Much the best-preserved broch is on the Shetland island of **Mousa**; its double walls rise to about 40ft, only a little short of their original height. The Celts continued to migrate north almost up until Julius Caesar's first incursion into Britain in 55 BC.

At the end of the prehistoric period, immediately prior to the arrival of the Romans, Scotland was divided among a number of warring Iron Age tribes, who, apart from the raiding, were preoccupied with wresting a living from the land, growing barley and oats, rearing sheep, hunting deer and fishing for salmon. The Romans were to write these people into history under the collective name Picti, or **Picts**, meaning painted people, after their body tattoos.

THE ROMANS

The **Roman conquest** of Britain began in 43 AD, almost a century after Caesar's first invasion. By 80 AD the Roman governor, Agricola, felt secure enough in the south of Britain to begin an invasion of the north, building a string of forts across the Clyde–Forth line and defeating a large force of Scottish tribes at Mons Graupius. The long-term effect of his campaign, however, was slight. Work on a major fort – to be the base for 5000 – at Inchtuthill, on the Tay, was abandoned before it was finished, and the legions withdrew south. In 123 AD the **Emperor Hadrian** decided to seal the frontier against the northern tribes and built **Hadrian's Wall**, which stretched from the Solway Firth to the Tyne and was the first formal division of the island of Britain. Twenty years later, the Romans again ventured north and built the **Antonine Wall** between the Clyde and the Forth. This was occupied for about forty years, but thereafter the Romans, frustrated by the inhospitable terrain of the Highlands, largely gave up their attempt to subjugate the north, and instead adopted a policy of containment.

It was the Romans who produced the first written accounts of the peoples of Scotland. In the second century AD, the Greco-Egyptian geographer Ptolemy drew up the first-known map of Scotland, which identified seventeen tribal territories. Other descriptions were less scientific, compounding the mixture of fear and contempt with which the Romans regarded their Pictish neighbours. Dio Cassius, a Roman commentator writing in 197 AD, informed his readers that:

> *They live in huts, go naked and unshod. They mostly have a democratic government, and are much addicted to robbery. They can bear hunger and cold and all manner of hardship; they will retire into their marshes and hold out for days with only their heads above water, and in the forest they will subsist on barks and roots.*

THE DARK AGES

In the years following the departure of the Romans, traditionally put at 450 AD, the population of Scotland changed considerably. By 500 AD the **Picts** occupied the northern isles, and the north and the east as far south as Fife. Today their settlements can be generally identified by place names with a "Pit" prefix, such as Pitlochry, and by the existence of carved symbol stones, like those found at Aberlemno in Angus. To the west, between Dumbarton and Carlisle, was a population of **Britons**. Many of the Briton leaders had Roman names, which suggests that they were a Romanized Celtic people, possibly a combination of tribes maintained by the Romans as a buffer between the Wall and the northern tribes, and peoples pushed west by the Anglo-Saxon invaders landing on the east coast. Both the Britons and the Picts spoke variations of P-Celtic, from which Welsh, Cornish and Breton developed.

On the west coast, to the north and west of the Britons, lived the **Scotti**, Irish-Celtic invaders who would eventually give their name to the whole country. The first Scotti arrived in the Western Isles from Ireland in the fourth century AD, and about a century later their great king, Fergus Mor, moved his base from Antrim to Dunadd, near Lochgilphead, where he founded the kingdom of Dalriada. The Scotti spoke Q-Celtic, the precursor of modern Gaelic. On the east coast, the Germanic Angles had sailed north along the coast to carve out an enclave around Dunbar in East Lothian. The final addition to the ethnic mix was also non-Celtic; from around 800 AD, **Norse** invaders began to arrive, settling mainly in the northern isles (see box

THE NORTHERN ISLES

With their sophisticated ships and navigational skills, the **Vikings**, who began their expansion in the eighth century, soon gained supremacy over the Pictish peoples in Shetland, Orkney, the extreme northeast corner of the mainland and the Western Isles. In 872, the King of Norway set up an earldom in **Orkney** from which **Shetland** was also governed: for the next six centuries the northern isles took a path distinct from the rest of what is now called Scotland, becoming a base for raiding and colonization in much of the rest of Britain and Ireland, and a link in the chain that connected Faroe, Iceland, Greenland and, more tenuously, North America. Norse culture flourished, and buildings such as St Magnus Cathedral in Kirkwall, Orkney, begun in 1137, give some idea of its energy (see

p.569). However, there were bouts of unrest, and finally Shetland was brought under direct rule from Norway at the end of the twelfth century.

When Norway united with Sweden under the Danish crown in the fourteenth century, Norse power began to wane and Scottish influence to increase. In 1469, a marriage was arranged between Margaret, daughter of the Danish King Christian I, and the future King James III of Scotland. Short of cash for her dowry, Christian mortgaged Orkney to Scotland in 1468, followed by Shetland in 1469; neither pledge was ever successfully redeemed. The laws, religion and administration of the northern isles became Scottish, though their Norse heritage is still very evident in place names, dialect and culture.

above) and the northeast of the mainland.

The next few centuries saw almost constant warfare among the different groups. The main issue was land, but this was frequently complicated by the need of the warrior castes, who dominated all of these cultures, to exhibit martial prowess. Military conquests did play their part in bringing the peoples of Scotland together, but the most persuasive force was **Christianity**. Many of the Britons had been Christians since Roman times and it had been a Briton, St Ninian, who conducted the first missionary work among the Picts at the end of the fourth century. Attempts to convert the Picts were resumed in the sixth century by St Columba, who, as a Gaelic-speaking Scotti, demonstrated that Christianity could provide a bridge between the different tribes.

Christianity proved attractive to pagan kings because it seemed to offer them extra supernatural powers. As St Columba declared, when he inaugurated his cousin Aidan as king of Dalriada in 574, "Believe firmly, O Aidan, that none of your enemies will be able to resist you unless you first deal falsely against me and my successors." This combination of spiritual and political power, when taken with Columba's establishment of the island of **Iona** as a centre of Christian culture, opened the way for many peaceable contacts between the Picts and Scotti. Intermarriage became commonplace, and the Scotti king Kenneth MacAlpine, who united Dalriada and Pictland in 843, was the son of a Pictish princess – the Picts traced succes-

sion through the female line. Similarly, MacAlpine's creation of the united kingdom of **Alba**, later known as **Scotia**, was part of a process of integration rather than outright conquest. Kenneth and his successors gradually extended the frontiers of their kingdom by marriage and force of arms until, by 1034, almost all of what we now call Scotland was under their rule.

THE MIDDLE AGES

By the time of his death in 1034, **Malcolm II** was recognized as the king of Scotia. He was not, though, a national king in the sense that we understand the term, as under the Gaelic system kings were elected from the *derbfine*, a group made up of those whose great-grandfathers had been kings. The chosen successor, supposedly the fittest to rule, was known as the *tanist*. By the eleventh century, however, Scottish kings had become familiar with the principle of heredity, and were often tempted to bend the rules of *tanistry*. Thus, the childless Malcolm secured the succession of his grandson **Duncan** by murdering a potential rival *tanist*. Duncan, in turn, was killed by **Macbeth** in 1040. Macbeth was not, therefore, the villain of Shakespeare's imagination, but simply an ambitious Scot of royal blood acting in a relatively conventional way.

The victory of **Malcolm III**, known as Canmore (bighead), over Macbeth in 1057, marked the beginning of a period of fundamental

KINGS AND QUEENS OF SCOTLAND

Kenneth I 842–858	**Malcolm II** 1005–1034	**Margaret** 1286–1290
Donald I 858–862	**Duncan I** 1034–1040	**John Balliol** 1292–1296
Constantine I 862–876	**Macbeth** 1040–1057	**Robert I** (the Bruce)
Aed 876–878	**Malcolm III** (Canmore)	1306–1329
Giric 878–889	1057–1093	**David II** 1329–1371
Donald II 889–900	**Donald III** 1093–1094	**Robert II** 1371–1390
Constantine II 900–943	**Duncan II** 1094	**Robert III** 1390–1406
Malcolm I 943–954	**Donald III** 1094–1097	**James I** 1406–1437
Indulf 954–962	**Edgar** 1097–1107	**James II** 1437–1460
Duf 962–966	**Alexander I** 1107–1124	**James III** 1460–1488
Culén 966–971	**David I** 1124–1153	**James IV** 1488–1513
Kenneth II 971–995	**Malcolm IV** 1153–1165	**James V** 1513–1542
Constantine III 995–997	**William the Lion** 1165–1214	**Mary (Queen of Scots)**
Kenneth III 997–1005	**Alexander II** 1214–1249	1542–1567
	Alexander III 1249–1286	**James VI** 1567–1625

change in Scottish society. Having avenged his father Duncan, Malcolm III, who had spent the previous seventeen years at the English court, sought to apply to Scotland a range of ideas he had brought back with him. He and his heirs established a secure dynasty based on succession through the male line and introduced **feudalism** into Scotland, a system that was diametrically opposed to the Gaelic system, which rested on blood ties: the followers of a Gaelic king were his kindred, whereas the followers of a feudal king were vassals bought with land. The Canmores successfully feudalized much of southern and eastern Scotland by making grants to their Norman, Breton and Flemish followers but, beyond that, traditional clan-based forms of social relations persisted.

The Canmores, independent of the local nobility, who remained a military threat, also began to reform the **Church**. This development started with the efforts of Margaret, Malcolm III's English wife, who brought Scottish religious practices into line with those of the rest of Europe and was eventually canonized. **David I** (1124–53) continued the process by importing monks to found a series of monasteries, principally along the border at Kelso, Melrose, Jedburgh and Dryburgh. By 1200 the entire country was covered by a network of eleven bishoprics, although church organization remained weak within the Highlands. Similarly, the dynasty founded a series of **royal burghs**, towns such as Edinburgh, Stirling and Berwick, and bestowed upon them charters recognizing

them as centres of trade. The charters usually granted a measure of self-government, vested in the town corporation or guild, and the monarchy hoped this liberality would both encourage loyalty and increase the prosperity of the kingdom. Scotland's Gaelic-speaking clans had little influence within the burghs, and, by 1550, Scots – a northern version of Anglo-Saxon – had become the main language throughout the Lowlands.

The policies of the Canmores laid the basis for a cultural rift in Scotland between the Highland and Lowland communities. Before that became an issue, however, the Scots had to face a major threat from the south. In 1286 **Alexander III** died, and a hotly disputed succession gave Edward I, the king of England, an opportunity to subjugate Scotland. In 1291 Edward presided over a conference where the rival claimants to the Scottish throne presented their cases. Edward chose John Balliol in preference to Robert the Bruce, his main rival, and obliged John to pay him homage, thus turning Scotland into a vassal kingdom. Bruce refused to accept the decision, thereby continuing the conflict, and in 1295 Balliol renounced his allegiance to Edward and formed an alliance with France – the beginning of what is known as the "Auld Alliance". In the conflict that followed, the Bruce family sided with the English, Balliol was defeated and imprisoned, and Edward seized control of almost all of Scotland.

Edward had shown little mercy during his conquest of Scotland – he had, for example, had most of the population of Berwick massacred – and his cruelty seems to have provoked a truly national resistance. This focused on **William Wallace**, a man of relatively lowly origins who forged an army of peasants, lesser knights and townsmen that was fundamentally different to the armies raised by the nobility. Figures like Balliol, holding lands in England, France and Scotland, were part of an international aristocracy for whom warfare was merely the means by which they struggled for power. Wallace, by contrast, led proto-nationalist forces determined to expel the English from their country. Probably for that very reason Wallace never received the support of the nobility and, after a bitter ten-year campaign, he was betrayed and executed in London in 1305.

With Wallace out of the way, feudal intrigue resumed. In 1306 Robert the Bruce, the erstwhile ally of the English, defied Edward and had himself crowned king of Scotland. Edward died the following year, but the unrest dragged on until 1314, when Bruce decisively defeated a huge English army under Edward II at the Battle of Bannockburn. At last Bruce was firmly in control of his kingdom, and in 1320 the Scots asserted their right to independence in a successful petition to the pope, now known as the **Declaration of Arbroath**.

In the years following Bruce's death in 1329, the Scottish monarchy gradually declined in influence. The last of the Bruce dynasty died in 1371, to be succeeded by the "Stewards", hence **Stewarts**, but thereafter a succession of Scottish rulers, culminating with James VI in 1567, came to the throne when still children. The power vacuum was filled by the nobility, whose key members exercised control as Scotland's regents while carving out territories where they ruled with the power, if not the title, of kings. At the close of the fifteenth century, the Douglas family alone controlled Galloway, Lothian, Stirlingshire, Clydesdale and Annandale. The more vigorous monarchs of the period, notably **James I** (1406–37), did their best to curb the power of such dynasties, but their efforts were usually nullified at the next regency. **James IV** (1488–1513), the most talented of the early Stewarts, might have restored the authority of the crown, but his invasion of England ended in a terrible defeat for the Scots – and his own death – at the battle of Flodden Field.

The reign of **Mary, Queen of Scots** (1542–67) typified the problems of the Scottish monarchy. Mary came to the throne when just one week old, and immediately caught the attention of the English king, Henry VIII, who sought, first by persuasion and then by military might, to secure her hand in marriage for his five-year-old son, Edward. Beginning in 1544, the English launched a series of devastating attacks on Scotland, an episode Sir Walter Scott later called the "Rough Wooing", until, in the face of another English invasion in 1548, the Scots – or at least those not supporting Henry – turned to the "Auld Alliance". The French king proposed marriage between Mary and the Dauphin Francis, promising in return military assistance against the English. The six-year-old queen sailed for France in 1548, leaving her loyal nobles and their French allies in control, and her husband succeeded to the French throne in 1559. When she returned thirteen years later, following the death of Francis, she had to pick her way through the rival ambitions of her nobility and deal with something entirely new – the religious Reformation.

THE REFORMATION

The **Reformation** in Scotland was a complex social process, whose threads are often hard to unravel. Nevertheless, it is quite clear that, by the end of the sixteenth century, the established Church was held in general contempt. Many members of the higher clergy regarded their relationship with the Church purely in economic terms, and forty percent of known illegitimate births (ie those subsequently legitimized) were the product of the "celibate" clergy's liaisons.

Another spur to the Scottish Reformation was the identification of Protestantism with anti-French feeling. In 1554, Mary of Guise, the French mother of the absent Queen Mary, had become regent, and her habit of appointing Frenchmen to high office was seen as part of an attempt to subordinate Scotland's interests to those of France. There was considerable resentment, and in 1557 a group of nobles banded together to form the **Lords of the Congregation**, whose dual purpose was to oppose French influence and promote the reformed religion. With English military backing, the Protestant lords succeeded in deposing the French regent in 1560, and, when the

Scottish Parliament assembled shortly afterwards, it asserted the primacy of Protestantism by forbidding the Mass and abolishing the authority of the pope. The nobility proceeded to confiscate two-thirds of Church lands, a huge prize that did much to bolster their new beliefs.

Even without the economic incentives, Protestantism was a highly charged political doctrine. Luther had argued that each individual's conscience was capable of discerning God's will. This meant that a hierarchical priesthood, existing to interpret God's will, was unnecessary and that the people themselves might conclude their rulers were breaking God's laws, in which case the monarch should be opposed or even deposed. This point was made very clearly to Queen Mary by the Protestant reformer **John Knox** at their first meeting in 1561. Subjects, he told her, were not bound to obey an ungodly monarch.

Knox, a Protestant exile who had returned to Scotland in 1559, was a follower of the Genevan reformer Calvin, who combined Luther's views on individual conscience with a belief in predestination. He argued that an omnipotent God must know everything, including the destinies of every human being. Consequently, it was determined before birth who was to be part of the Elect, bound for heavenly glory, and who was not, a doctrine that placed enormous pressure on its adherents to demonstrate by their godly behaviour that they were of the Elect. This was the doctrine that Knox brought back to Scotland and laid out in his Articles of Confession of Faith, better known as the **Scot's Confession**, which was to form the basis of the reformed faith for over seventy years.

Mary ducked and weaved, trying to avoid an open breach with her Protestant subjects. The fires of popular displeasure were kept well-stoked by Knox, however, who declared "one Mass was more fearful than if ten thousand enemies were landed in any part of the realm, of purpose to suppress the whole religion". At the same time, Mary was engaged in a balancing act between the factions of the Scottish nobility. Her difficulties were exacerbated by her disastrous second marriage to **Lord Darnley**, a cruel and politically inept character, whose jealousy led to his involvement in the murder of Mary's favourite, David Rizzio, who was dragged from the queen's supper room at Holyrood and stabbed 56 times. The incident caused the Scottish Protestants more than a little unease, but they were entirely scandalized in 1567, when Darnley himself was murdered and Mary promptly married the **Earl of Bothwell**, widely believed to be the murderer. This was too much to bear, and the Scots rose in rebellion, driving Mary into exile in England at the age of just 25. The queen's illegitimate half-brother, the Earl of Moray, became regent, and her son, the infant James, was left behind to be raised a Protestant prince. Mary, meanwhile, became perceived as such a threat to the English throne that Queen Elizabeth I had her executed in 1587.

Knox could now concentrate on the organization of the reformed Church, or **Kirk**, which he envisaged as a body empowered to intervene in the daily lives of the people. **Andrew Melville**, another leading reformer, wished to push this theocratic vision further. He proposed the abolition of all traces of Episcopacy – the rule of the bishops in the Church – and that the Kirk should adopt a **Presbyterian** structure, administered by a hierarchy of assemblies, part-elected and part-appointed. At the bottom of the chain, beneath the General Assembly, Synod and Presbytery, would be the Kirk session, responsible for church affairs, the performance of the minister and the morals of the parish. In 1592, the Melvillian party achieved a measure of success when presbyteries and synods were accepted as legal church courts and the office of bishop was suspended.

James VI (1567–1625) disliked Presbyterianism because its quasi-democratic structure – particularly the lack of royally appointed bishops – appeared to threaten his authority. He was, however, unable to resist the reformers until 1610, when, strengthened by his installation as James I of England after Elizabeth's death in 1603, he restored the Scottish bishops. The argument about the nature of Kirk organization would lead to bloody conflict in the years after James's death.

THE RELIGIOUS WARS

Raised in Episcopalian England, **Charles I** (1625–49) had little understanding of Scottish reformism. He believed in the Divine Right of Kings, an authoritarian creed that claimed the monarch was God's representative on earth and, therefore, his authority had divine sanction, a concept entirely counter to Protestant thought. In 1637, Charles attempted to impose a new prayer book on the Kirk, laying down forms of worship in line with those favoured by the High Anglican Church. The reformers denounced these changes as "Popery" and organized the **National Covenant**, a religious pledge that committed the signatories to "Labour by all means lawful to recover the purity and liberty of the Gospel as it was established and professed".

Charles declared all the "**Covenanters**" to be rebels, a proclamation endorsed by his Scottish bishops. Consequently, when the king backed down from military action and called a General Assembly of the Kirk, the assembly promptly abolished the Episcopacy. Charles pronounced the proceedings illegal, but lack of finance stopped him from mounting an effective military campaign – whereas the Covenanters, well-financed by the Kirk, assembled a proficient army under Alexander Leslie. In desperation, Charles summoned the English Parliament, the first for eleven years, hoping it would pay for an army. But, like the calling of the General Assembly, the decision was a disaster and Parliament was much keener to criticize his policies than to raise taxes. In response Charles declared war on Parliament in 1642.

Until 1650, Scotland was ruled by the Covenanters and the power of the Presbyterian Kirk grew considerably. Laws were passed establishing schools in every parish and, less usefully, banning trade with Catholic countries. The only effective opposition to the theocratic state came from the **Marquis of Montrose**, who had initially supported the Covenant but lined up with the king when war broke out. His army was drawn from the Highlands and Islands, where the Kirk's influence was weakest. Montrose was a gifted campaigner who won several notable victories against the Covenanters, but the reluctance of his troops to stay south of the Highland Line made it impossible for him to capitalize on his successes, and he was eventually captured and executed in 1650.

Largely confined to the peripheries of Scotland, Montrose's campaigns were a sideshow to the **Civil War** being waged further south. Here, the Covenanters and the English Parliamentarians faced the same royal enemy and in 1643 formed an alliance. Indeed, it was

the Scots army that captured Charles at Newark in Nottinghamshire, in 1646. There was, however, friction between the allies. Many of the Parliamentarians, including Cromwell, were **Independents**, who favoured a looser form of doctrinal control within the state Church than did the Presbyterians, and were inclined towards religious toleration for the law-abiding sects outside the state Church. In addition, the Scots believed the English were tainted with **Erastianism** – a belief in placing the secular authority of Parliament over the spiritual authority of the Church.

The Parliamentarians in turn suspected the Scots of hankering for the return of the monarchy, a suspicion confirmed when, at the invitation of the Earl of Argyll, the future Charles II came back to Scotland in 1650. To regain his Scottish kingdom, Charles was obliged to renounce his father and sign the Covenant, two bitter pills taken to impress the population. In the event, the "Presbyterian restoration" was short-lived. Cromwell invaded, defeated the Scots at Dunbar and forced Charles into exile. Until the Restoration of 1660, Scotland was united with England and governed by seven commissioners.

Although the restoration of **Charles II** (1660–85) brought bishops back to the Kirk, they were integrated into an essentially Presbyterian structure of Kirk sessions and presbyteries, and the General Assembly, which had been abolished by Cromwell, was not re-established. Over 300 clergymen, a third of the Scottish ministry, refused to accept the reinstatement of the bishops and were edged out of the Church, forced to hold open-air services, called **Conventicles**, which Charles did his best to suppress. Religious opposition inspired military resistance and the Lowlands witnessed scenes of brutal repression as the king's forces struggled to keep control in what was known as "The Killing Time". In the southwest, a particular stronghold of the Covenanters, the government imported Highlanders, the so-called "Highland Host", to root out the opposition, which they did with great barbarity.

Charles II was succeeded by his brother **James VII** (James II of England), whose ardent Catholicism caused a Protestant backlash in England. In 1689, he was forced into exile in France and the throne passed to **Mary**, his Protestant daughter, and her Dutch husband,

William of Orange. In Scotland, William and Mary restored the full Presbyterian structure and abolished bishops, though they chose not to restore the political and legal functions of the Kirk, which remained subject to parliamentary control. This settlement ended Scotland's religious wars and completed its reformation.

THE UNION

Although the question of Kirk organization was settled in 1690, the political issue of the relationship between the Crown and the Scottish Parliament was not. From 1689 to 1697, William was at war with France, partly financed by Scottish taxes and partly fought by Scottish soldiers. Yet many Scots, mindful of the Auld Alliance, disapproved of the war and others suffered financially from the disruption to trade

with France. There were other economic irritants too, principally the legally sanctioned monopoly that English merchants had over trade with the English colonies. This monopoly inspired the **Darien Scheme**, a plan to establish a Scottish colony in Panama. The colonists set off in 1698, but, thwarted by the opposition of both William and the English merchants, the scheme proved a miserable failure. The colony collapsed with the loss of £200,000 – an amount equal to half the value of the entire coinage in Scotland – and an angry Scottish Parliament threatened to refuse the king taxes as rioting broke out in the cities.

Meanwhile, in the north, the Highlanders blamed William for the massacre of the **MacDonalds of Glen Coe**. In 1691, William had offered pardons to those Highland chiefs

---

THE HIGHLANDS

The country that was united with England in 1707 contained three distinct cultures: in south and east Scotland, they spoke Scots; in Shetland, Orkney and much of the northeast the local dialect, though Scots-based, contained elements of Norn (Old Norse); in the rest of north and west Scotland, including the Western Isles, Gaelic was spoken. These linguistic differences were paralleled by different forms of social organization and customs. The people of north and west Scotland were mostly pastoralists, moving their sheep and cattle to Highland pastures in the summer, and returning to the glens in the winter. They lived in single-room dwellings, heated by a central peat fire and sometimes shared with livestock, and in hard times they would subsist on cakes made from the blood of their live cattle mixed with oatmeal. **Highlanders** supplemented their meagre income by raiding their clan neighbours and the prosperous Lowlands, whose inhabitants regarded their northern compatriots with a mixture of fear and contempt. In the early seventeenth century, Montgomerie, a Lowland poet, suggested that God had created the first Highlander out of horseshit. When God asked his creation what he would do, the reply was "I will doun to the Lowland, Lord, and thair steill a kow".

It would be a mistake, however, to infer from the primitive nature of Highland life that the institutions of this society had existed from time immemorial. This is especially true of the "**clan**", a term that only appears in its modern usage in the sixteenth century. In theory, the clan bound together blood relatives who shared a common

ancestor, a concept clearly derived from the ancient Gaelic notion of kinship. But in practice many of the clans were of non-Gaelic origin – such as the Frasers, Sinclairs and Stewarts, all of Anglo-Norman descent – and it was the mythology of a common ancestor, rather than the actuality, that cemented the clans together. Furthermore, clans were often made up of people with a variety of surnames, and there are documented cases of individuals changing their names when they swapped allegiances.

At the upper end of Highland society was the **clan chief** (who might have been a minor figure, like MacDonald of Glen Coe, or a great lord, like the Duke of Argyll, head of the Campbells), who provided protection for his followers: they would, in turn, fight for him when called upon to do so. Below the clan chief were the **chieftains of the septs**, or subunits of the clan, and then came the **tacksmen**, major tenants of the chief to whom they were frequently related. The tacksmen sublet their land to **tenants**, who were at the bottom of the social scale. The Highlanders wore a simple belted plaid wrapped around the body – rather than the kilt – and not until the late seventeenth century were certain **tartans** roughly associated with particular clans. The detailed codification of the tartan was produced by the Victorians, whose romantic vision of Highland life originated with George IV's visit to Scotland in 1822, when he appeared in an elaborate version of Highland dress, complete with flesh-coloured tights (for more on tartan, see p.481).

who had opposed his accession, on condition that they took an oath of allegiance by New Year's Day 1692. Alasdair MacDonald of Glen Coe had turned up at the last minute, but his efforts to take the oath were frustrated by the king's officials, who were determined to see his clan, well-known for their support of the Stewarts, destroyed. In February 1692, Captain Robert Campbell quartered his men in Glen Coe and, two weeks later, in the middle of the night, his troops acted on their secret orders and slaughtered as many MacDonalds as they could. Thirty-eight died, and the massacre caused a national scandal, especially among the clans, where "Murder under Trust" – killing those offering you shelter – was considered a particularly heinous crime.

The situation in Scotland was further complicated by the question of the succession. Mary died without leaving an heir and, on William's death in 1702, the crown passed to her sister **Anne**, who was also childless. In response, the English Parliament secured the Protestant succession by passing the Act of Settlement, which named the Electress Sophia of Hanover as the next in line to the throne. The Act did not, however, apply in Scotland, and the English feared that the Scots would invite James Edward Stewart back from France to be their king. Consequently, Parliament appointed commissioners charged with the consideration of a union with "proper methods towards attaining a union with Scotland". The project seemed doomed to failure when the Scottish Parliament passed the **Act of Security** in 1703, stating that Scotland would not accept a Hanoverian monarch unless they had first received guarantees protecting their religion and their trade.

Nevertheless, despite the strength of anti-English feeling, the Scottish Parliament passed the **Act of Union** by 110 votes to 69 in January 1707. Some historians have explained the vote in terms of bribery and corruption. This certainly played a part (the Duke of Hamilton, for example, switched sides at a key moment and was subsequently rewarded with an English dukedom), but there were other factors. Scottish politicians were divided between the Cavaliers – Jacobites (supporters of the Stewarts) and Episcopalians – and the Country party, whose Presbyterian members dreaded the return of the Stewarts more than they disliked the Hanoverians. There were commercial consider-

ations too. In 1705, the English Parliament had passed the Alien Act, which threatened to impose severe penalties on cross-border trade, whereas the Union gave merchants of both countries free access to each other's markets. The Act of Union also guaranteed the Scottish legal system and the Presbyterian Kirk, and offered compensation to those who had lost money in the Darien Scheme.

Under the terms of the Act, both parliaments were to be replaced by a new British Parliament based in London, with the Scots apportioned 45 MPs and 16 peers. There were riots when the terms became known, but no sustained opposition.

THE JACOBITE RISINGS

When James VII/II was deposed he had fled to France, where he planned the reconquest of his kingdom with the support of the French king. In 1702, James's successor, William, died, and the hopes of the Stewarts passed to his cousin James, the "Old Pretender" (Pretender in the sense of having pretensions to the throne; Old to distinguish him from his son Charles, the "Young Pretender"). The British crown passed to Anne, however, and after her death and the accession of the Hanoverian George I, the first major **Jacobite uprising** occurred in 1715. Its timing appeared perfect. Scottish opinion was moving against the Union, which had failed to bring Scotland any tangible economic benefits. The English had also been accused of bad faith when, contrary to their pledges, they attempted to impose their legal practices on the Scots. Neither were Jacobite sentiments confined to Scotland. There were many in England who toasted the "King across the water" and showed no enthusiasm for the new German ruler. In September 1715, the fiercely Jacobite John Erskine, Earl of Mar, raised the Stewart standard at Braemar Castle. Just eight days later, he captured Perth, where he gathered an army of over 10,000 men, drawn mostly from the Episcopalians of northeast Scotland and from the Highlands. Mar's rebellion took the government by surprise. They had only 4000 soldiers in Scotland, under the command of the Duke of Argyll, but Mar dithered until he lost the military advantage. There was an indecisive battle at Sheriffmuir in November, but by the time the Old Pretender arrived the following month 6000 veteran Dutch troops had reinforced Argyll. The rebellion disintegrated rapidly and James slunk back to exile in France in February 1716.

The **Jacobite uprising of 1745**, led by James's dashing son, Charles Edward Stewart (Bonnie Prince Charlie), had little chance of success. The Hanoverians had consolidated their hold on the English throne, Lowland society was uniformly loyalist, and even among the Highlanders Charles only attracted just over a half of the 20,000 clansmen who could have marched with him. Nevertheless, after a decisive victory over government forces at Prestonpans, Charles made a spectacular advance into England, getting as far as Derby. London was in a state of panic: its shops were closed and the Bank of England, fearing a run on sterling, slowed withdrawals by paying out in sixpences. But Derby was as far south as Charles got. On December 6, threatened by superior forces, the Jacobites decided to retreat to Scotland. The Duke of Cumberland was sent in pursuit and the two armies met on **Culloden Moor**, near Inverness, in April 1746. Outnumbered and outgunned, the Jacobites were swept from the field, losing over 1200 men compared to Cumberland's 300 plus. After the battle, many of the wounded Jacobites were slaughtered, an atrocity that earned Cumberland the nickname "Butcher". Jacobite hopes died at Culloden and the prince lived out the rest of his life in drunken exile.

In the aftermath of the uprising, the wearing of tartan, the bearing of arms and the playing of bagpipes were all banned. Rebel chiefs lost their land and the Highlands were placed under military occupation. Most significantly, the government prohibited the private armies of the chiefs, thereby effectively destroying the clan system.

THE HIGHLAND CLEARANCES

Once the clan chief was forbidden his own army, he had no need of the large tenantry that had previously been a vital military asset. Conversely, the second half of the eighteenth century saw the Highland population increase dramatically after the introduction of the easy-to-grow and nutritious potato. Between 1745 and 1811, the population of the Outer Hebrides, for example, rose from 13,000 to 24,500. The clan chiefs adopted different policies to deal with the new situation. Some encouraged emigration, and as many as 6000 Highlanders left for the Americas between 1800 and 1803 alone.

Other landowners developed alternative forms of employment for their tenantry: mainly fishing and kelping. **Kelp** (brown seaweed) was gathered and burnt to produce soda ash, which was used in the manufacture of soap, glass and explosives. There was a rising market for soda ash until the 1810s, with the price increasing from £2 a ton in 1760 to £20 in 1808, making a fortune for some landowners and providing thousands of Highlanders with temporary employment. Other landowners developed **sheep runs** on the Highland pastures, introducing hardy breeds like the black-faced Linton and the Cheviot. But extensive sheep farming proved incompatible with a high peasant population, and many landowners decided to clear their estates of tenants, some of whom were forcibly moved to tiny plots of marginal land, where they were to farm as **crofters**.

The pace of the **Highland Clearances** accelerated after the end of the Napoleonic Wars in 1815, when the market price for kelp, fish and cattle declined, leaving sheep as the only profitable Highland product. The most notorious Clearances took place on the estates of the Countess of Sutherland, who owned a million acres in northern Scotland. Between 1807 and 1821, around 15,000 people were thrown off her land, evictions carried out by Patrick Sellar, the estate factor, with considerable brutality. Those who failed to leave by the appointed time had their homes burnt in front of them, and one elderly woman, who failed to get out of her home after it was torched, subsequently died from burns. The local sheriff charged Sellar with her death, but a jury of landowners acquitted him – and the sheriff was sacked. As the dispossessed Highlanders scratched a living from the acid soils of some tiny croft, they learnt through bitter experience the limitations of the clan. Famine followed, forcing large-scale emigration to America and Canada and leaving the huge uninhabited areas found in the region today.

The crofters eked out a precarious existence, but they hung on throughout the nineteenth century, often by taking seasonal employment away from home. In the 1880s, however, a sharp downturn in agricultural prices made it difficult for many crofters to pay their rent. This time, inspired by the example of the Irish Land League, they resisted eviction, forming the **Highland Land Reform Association** and the **Crofters' Party**. In 1886, in response to the social unrest, Gladstone's Liberal government passed the **Crofters' Holdings Act**, which conceded three of the crofters' demands: security of tenure, fair rents to be decided independently, and the right to pass on crofts by inheritance. But Gladstone did not attempt to increase the amount of land available for crofting, and shortage of land remained a major problem until the **Land Settlement Act** of 1919 made provision for the creation of new crofts. Nevertheless, the population of the Highlands has continued to decline during the twentieth century, with many of the region's young people finding city life more appealing.

INDUSTRIALIZATION

Glasgow was the powerhouse of Scotland's **Industrial Revolution**. The passage from Glasgow to the Americas was much shorter than that from rival English ports and a lucrative transatlantic trade in tobacco had developed as early as the seventeenth century. This in turn stimulated Scottish manufacturing, since, under the terms of the Navigation Acts, the Americans were not allowed to trade manufactured goods. Scottish-produced linen, paper and wrought iron were exchanged for Virginia tobacco, and when the American Revolution disrupted the trade in the 1770s and 1780s, the Scots successfully turned to trade with the West Indies and, most important of all, to the production of cotton textiles.

Glasgow's west coast location gave it ready access to the sources of raw cotton in the Americas, while the rapid growth of the British Empire provided an expanding market for its finished cloth. Initially, the city's **cotton industry**, like the earlier linen industry, was organized domestically, with spinners and weavers working in their homes, but increased demand required mass production and a need for factories. In 1787, Scotland had only nineteen mills; by 1840 there were nearly 200.

The growth of the textile industry spurred the development of other industries. In the mid-eighteenth century, the **Carron Ironworks** was founded near Falkirk, specializing in the production of military munitions. Here, the capital and expertise were English, but the location was determined by Scottish coal reserves, and by 1800 it was the largest ironworks in Europe. The basis of Scotland's **shipbuilding** industry was laid as early as 1802, when the steam vessel

Charlotte Dundas was launched on the Forth–Clyde canal. Within thirty years, 95 steam vessels had been built in Scotland, most of them on Clydeside. The growth of the iron and shipbuilding industries, plus the extensive use of steam power, created a massive demand for coal, and pit shafts were sunk across the coalfields of southern Scotland.

Industrialization led to a concentration of Scotland's **population** in the central Lowlands. In 1840, one-third of the country's industrial workers lived in Lanarkshire alone, and Glasgow's population grew from 17,000 in the 1740s to over 200,000 a century later. Such sudden growth created urban overcrowding on a massive scale and, as late as 1861, 64 percent of the entire Scottish population lived in one- or two-room houses. For most Clydesiders, "house" meant a couple of small rooms in a grim tenement building, where many of the poorest families were displaced Highlanders and Irish immigrants, with the Irish arriving in Glasgow at the rate of one thousand a week during the potato famine of the 1840s.

By the late nineteenth century a measure of prosperity had emerged from industrialization, and the well-paid Clydeside engineers went to their forges wearing bowler hats and starched collars. They were confident of the future, but their optimism was misplaced. Scotland's industries were very much geared to the export market, and after **World War I** they found conditions much changed. During the war years, when exports had been curtailed by a combination of U-boat activity and war production, new industries had developed in India and Japan, and the eastern market for Scottish goods never recovered. The postwar world also witnessed a contraction of world trade, which hit the shipbuilding industry very hard and, in turn, damaged the steel and coal industries. By 1931, for instance, pig-iron production was at less than 25 percent of its 1920 output.

These difficulties were compounded by the financial collapse of the early 1930s, and by 1932 28 percent of the Scottish workforce was unemployed. Four hundred thousand Scots emigrated between 1921 and 1931, and those who stayed endured some of the worst social conditions in the British Isles. By the late 1930s, Scotland had the highest infant mortality rate in Europe, while some thirty percent of homes had no toilet or bath. There was a partial economic recovery in the mid-1930s, but high unemployment remained until the start of **World War II**.

THE LABOUR MOVEMENT

In the late eighteenth century, conditions for the labouring population varied enormously. At one extreme, the handloom weavers, working from home, were well-paid and much in demand, whereas the coal miners remained serfs, bought and sold with the pits they worked in, until 1799. During this period, the working class gave some support to the **radical movement**, those loosely connected groups of reformers, led by the lower middle class, who took their inspiration from the French Revolution. One of these groups, "The Friends of the People", campaigned for the extension of the right to vote, and such apparently innocuous activities earned one member, Thomas Muir, a sentence of fourteen years' transportation to Australia.

In 1820, the radicals called for a national strike and an insurrection to "show the world that we are . . . determined to be free". At least 60,000 workers downed tools for a week, and one group set off for the Carron Ironworks to seize arms. The government was, however, well prepared. It slammed radical leaders into prison and a heavy military presence kept control of the streets. The strike fizzled out and three leading radicals, all weavers, were later executed.

The 1832 Scottish Reform Act extended the franchise to include a large proportion of the middle class and thereafter political radicalism assumed a more distinctive working-class character, though its ideals still harked back to the American and French revolutions. In the 1840s, the **Chartists** led the campaign for working-class political rights by sending massive petitions to Parliament and organizing huge demonstrations. When Parliament rejected the petitions, the more determined Chartists – the "physical-force men" – urged insurrection. This call to arms was not taken up by the Scottish working class, however, and support for the Chartists fell away. The insurrectionary phase of Scottish labour was over.

During the next thirty years, as Scotland's economy prospered, skilled workers organized themselves into **craft unions**, such as the Amalgamated Society of Engineers, dedicated to negotiating improvements for their members within the status quo. Politically, the trade unions gave their allegiance to the Liberal Party, but the first major crack in the Liberal-Union alliance came in 1888, when **Keir Hardie** left the Liberals to form the Scottish Socialist Party, which was later merged with the Independent Labour Party, founded in Bradford in 1893. Scottish socialism as represented by the ILP was ethical rather than Marxist in orientation, owing a great deal to the Kirk background of many of its members. But electoral progress was slow, partly because the Roman Catholic priesthood consistently preached against socialism.

In the early years of the twentieth century, two small Marxist groups established themselves on Clydeside: the **Socialist Labour Party**, which concentrated on workplace militancy, and the party-political **British Socialist Party**, whose most famous member was the Marxist lecturer John MacLean. During World War I, the local organizers of the SLP gained considerable influence by playing on the fears of the skilled workers, who felt their status was being undermined by the employment of unskilled workers. After the war, the influence of the shop stewards culminated in a massive campaign for the forty-hour working week. The strikes and demonstrations of the campaign, including one of 100,000 people in St George's Square in Glasgow, panicked the government into sending in the troops. But this was no Bolshevik Revolution – as Emmanuel Shinwell, the seamen's leader and future Labour Party politician, observed, "[the troops] had nothing much to do but chat to the local people and drink their cups of tea". The rank-and-file may have had little interest in revolution, but many of the activists did go on to become leaders within the newly formed Communist Party of Great Britain.

The ILP, now an affiliated part of the socialist **Labour Party**, made its electoral breakthrough in 1922, when it sent 29 Scottish MPs to Westminster. They set out with high hopes of social progress and reform, aspirations that were dashed, like trade union militancy, by the 1930s Depression. At the 1945 general election, Labour won forty seats in Scotland and, in more recent times, the party has dominated Scottish politics with its gradual eclipse of the Scottish Conservatives. In 1955 the Conservatives held 36 Scottish seats, by 1995 they had just ten, and the 1997 general election left them with none at all.

The ILP MPs of the 1920s combined their socialism with a brand of Scottish nationalism.

In 1924, for instance, the MP James Maxton had declared his intentions to "make English-ridden, capitalist-ridden Scotland into the Scottish socialist Commonwealth". The Labour Party maintained an official policy of self-government for Scotland, endorsing home rule in 1945 and 1947, but these endorsements were made with less and less enthusiasm. In 1958, Labour abandoned the commitment altogether and adopted a unionist vision of Scotland, much to the chagrin of many Scottish activists.

In 1971, **Upper Clyde Shipbuilders** stood on the brink of closure, its demise symbolizing the failure of traditional Labour politicians to revive Scotland's industrial base, which had resumed its decline after the end of World War II. In the event, UCS was partly saved by the work-in organized by two Communist shop stewards, Jimmy Reid and Jimmy Airlie. After fourteen months, the work-in finally succeeded in winning government support to keep part of the shipyard open, and Scots saw the broadly based campaign waged on its behalf as a national issue – Scottish industries set against an indifferent London government. Many socialist Scots, like James Jack, General Secretary of the Scottish TUC, moved towards some form of nationalism. Twenty-one years later, the closure of the steelworks at **Ravenscraig**, Motherwell, revived many of the same emotions.

TOWARDS DEVOLUTION

The **National Party of Scotland** was formed in 1928, its membership averaging about 7000 people, mostly drawn from the non-industrial parts of the country. Very much a mixture of practical politicians and left-leaning eccentrics, such as the poet Hugh MacDiarmid, in 1934 it merged with the right-wing Scottish Party to create the **Scottish National Party**. The SNP, after years in the political wilderness, achieved its electoral breakthrough in 1967 when Winnie Ewing won Hamilton from Labour in a by-election. The following year the SNP won 34 percent of the vote in local government elections and gained control of Cumbernauld, successes that had repercussions within both the Labour and Conservative parties. Both parties, wishing to head off the Nationalists, began to work on schemes to give Scotland a measure of self-government, and the term **"Devolution"** was coined. However, when the Conservatives came to power in 1970, Edward Heath, the prime minister, shelved plans

for devolution because the SNP had only secured a twelve percent share of the Scottish vote.

The situation changed dramatically in 1974, when Labour were returned to power with a wafer-thin majority. The SNP held seven seats, which gave them considerable political leverage, and devolution was back on the agenda. The SNP had also run an excellent election campaign, concentrating on North Sea oil, which was now being piped ashore in significant quantities. Their two most popular slogans, "England expects.... Scotland's oil" and "Rich Scots or Poor Britons?", seemed to have caught the mood of Scotland.

In 1979, the Labour government, struggling to hold onto office after a "winter of discontent", put its devolution proposals before the Scottish people in a **referendum**. The "yes" vote gained 33 percent, the "no" vote 31 percent; although a majority was in favour, it was not by the required 40 percent. Not for the first time, Scottish opinion had shifted away from home rule; the reluctance to embrace it was based on uncertainty about what might follow, a concern about too many layers of government and, in some areas, a fear that the resulting assembly might be dominated by the Clydeside conurbation. The incoming Conservative government of Margaret Thatcher set its face against any form of devolution. It argued that the majority of Scots had voted for parties committed to the Union – namely Labour, the Liberal Democrats and themselves – and that only a minority supported the separation advocated by the SNP. At the same time, the government asserted that any form of devolution must lead inevitably to the break-up of the United Kingdom and, therefore, that the devolution solutions put forward by other parties could not be what the Scottish people wanted, because the inescapable result would be separation.

As the Thatcher years rolled on, growing evidence from opinion polls and central and local government elections suggested that few Scottish voters accepted either this reasoning or the implication that Scots did not know what was good for them. The Conservatives' support in Scotland was further eroded by their introduction of the deeply unpopular Community Charge – universally nicknamed the **Poll Tax** – a form of local taxation that was charged essentially on a per capita basis and took little account of income. The fact that it had been imposed in Scotland a year earlier than in England and Wales was the source of further resentment.

In 1992, having largely rejected Conservative ideology and all but a few of the party's candidates, Scots found themselves still under a Tory government, this time with John Major at the helm. Though some Scottish Conservatives quietly supported devolution, their limited influence in the party as a whole was evident in the appointment of Michael Forsyth, one of the most articulate advocates of Thatcherite policy, as Secretary of State for Scotland.

Throughout the 1980s and early 1990s, the case for devolution had been made consistently by both Labour and the Liberal Democrats. In 1989, they, together with a cross-section of Scottish organizations, including local government, churches and trade unions, co-operated in the establishment of the **Scottish Constitutional Convention**, a standing conference which developed detailed proposals for the introduction of a devolved Scottish legislature. Initially, the SNP saw the Convention as a diversion from their aim of an independent Scotland firmly attached to the European Union and did not join. Later, however, nationalists began to argue that devolution might after all offer a stepping stone to independence.

By the mid-1990s the promise of change was in the air, but without their hands directly on the levers of power, none of the main players could make it happen. The start gun on Scotland's new political era came in May 1997 with the UK general election, won by Tony Blair's Labour party by a landslide: the Tories lost every single one of their Scottish seats. Under the stewardship of Scottish Secretary Donald Dewar, the new Labour government moved swiftly to publish its proposals for devolution and a **referendum** was organized for that September. Scottish voters were asked whether or not they agreed with two propositions: first, that a Scottish parliament should be established; and second, that it should have the power to vary income tax by up to three pence in the pound. Labour, the Liberal Democrats and the Scottish National Party united in calling for a "Yes, Yes" vote, and the electorate responded with a clear endorsement: 75 percent of voters in favour of a Scottish Parliament and 64 percent supporting tax-varying powers.

The excitement generated in Scotland by the referendum helped imbue the subsequent setting up of the Parliament with a palpable sense of destiny – something it had to cling to as many of the fears voiced in 1979 again resurfaced:

that there were too many layers of government, and that the whole process was so costly. By and large, however, the optimistic mood was carried through to Scotland's **general election** – the first ever, given that the last elected Scottish parliament in 1707 had not been under universal suffrage – which took place in May 1999 to significant media interest from around the world. The form of proportional representation adopted for the election made it unlikely that any one party would achieve an overall majority in the 129-seat assembly, and indeed the final result left the Labour party, with 56 seats, needing to enter into a coalition with the Liberal Democrats (with 17 seats) to achieve a governing majority. The leader of the Labour group, **Donald Dewar**, became Scotland's First Minister, with **Jim Wallace**, leader of the Scottish Liberal Democrats, as his deputy. The SNP, led by **Alex Salmond**, won 35 seats with just under thirty percent of the vote, making them the second largest party, while proportional representation ensured that the Conservatives regained a presence in Scottish politics once more with 18 seats. Joining the main parties in the assembly were the first Green politician to be elected in a national vote in the UK, a left-wing socialist, and a maverick former Labour member who stood as an independent. The new MSPs (Members of the Scottish Parliament) voted **Sir David Steel**, former leader of the British Liberal Party, to be the Presiding Officer.

In a **ceremony** deliberately mixing pomp with down-to-earth, populist touches, the Queen came to the Parliament's temporary home in the Church of Scotland Assembly Hall in Edinburgh to officially open the Parliament on July 1, 1999. Her blessing marked the official transfer of power to the new assembly over education, health, law and order, social work, local government, planning and the environment, economic development, agriculture and fisheries, sport and the arts. Meanwhile, Westminster will retain control over defence, foreign affairs, major economic and tax issues and social security. The new Parliament has the power to initiate new legislation, and to pass bills without the endorsement of Westminster.

Early indications are that while certain issues, for instance **land reform**, display the new priorities a parliament focused on Scotland allows, others, such as the volatile question of higher education tuition fees, have highlighted the strains inherent in coalition government, at the same time putting pressure on Labour to break with policies being pursued by the government in Westminster. The implications of this are, of course, profound, and a constant theme of the early period of the Parliament has been the need for the Labour/Liberal Democrat coalition, along with the pro-Unionist Conservatives, to prove that devolved government can still offer distinctive Scottish solutions within a broader British outlook, while the SNP insist that such solutions are consistently hobbled by their need to tie into London-led policies, and that the only way for Scotland to govern itself properly is to be fully independent.

However, many questions have yet to be resolved, not least the issue of the consequences for the British parliament and **constitution**. For years, outspoken Labour MP for West Lothian, Tam Dalyell, has criticized his own party for its failure to answer what has become known as the West Lothian Question. Simply put, should Scottish MPs at Westminster continue to have the same amount of influence over the affairs of the rest of Britain now that a Scottish parliament is looking after the same affairs in Scotland? This is a tricky issue for the government, since, although it currently enjoys a huge majority, any reduction in Scottish MPs at Westminster could, in the future, threaten its ability to form a British government.

THE FUTURE

Expectations are high in Scotland, not only that the Parliament will stimulate a vitality and originality in the way Scottish issues are tackled, but also that it can cement a credible, effective and accountable power structure within the country. Scots are proud of the recognition the Parliament has brought their nation, and many hope it will both reflect and sustain the recent flourishing the country has seen in a number of fields, notably the arts, science and technology, and sport.

An early test for the new government is whether the **economy** can keep pace with the raised expectations and sustain its recent prosperity. There have been hard times, particularly in central Scotland, where the decline of the heavy industries, including deep coal-mining, steelmaking, shipbuilding and engineering, has been all but total, and unemployment has produced profound social problems in parts of Glasgow, Edinburgh and smaller towns.

However, there has been a notable growth in service industries; for example, financial services and insurance have had a substantial impact in Edinburgh, Glasgow and various towns across the Central Belt. In northeast Scotland, particularly around Aberdeen, the oil industry – although past its boom – continues to underpin an economy which might otherwise have struggled to cope with the uncertainties of agriculture and, especially, fishing.

Though there have been encouraging signs of recent progress, the **Highlands and Islands** remain an economically fragile area that needs special measures – distance from markets being an obvious and fundamental problem. Prosperity of a temporary sort has been provided in some areas by oil, but the best options for the future are likely to lie in selective, high-quality development in fishing, fish farming and other food-based industries, activities which use the Internet and other advanced telecommunications technology, primary industries such as forestry and quarrying and, last but certainly not least, tourism. Increasingly, the local environment is seen as a major asset for the attraction and success of most kinds of employment. One of the keys to Highland development, some would say the most important of all, is the ownership and control of land. Some of the largest Highland estates continue to be owned and managed from afar, with little regard to local needs or priorities; the success of groups of crofters in buying estates in Assynt and Knoydart, as well as the purchase of the island of Eigg by its inhabitants, hints at a broadening of land ownership which many hope the land reforms brought in early on by the Scottish Parliament will do more to promote.

Unquestionably the most striking change in Scotland in the last decade has been a **cultural renaissance**. Especially notable has been the revival of Gaelic, supported by large investments in broadcasting and publishing, and demonstrated by the popularity among young audiences – few of them Gaels – of bands like Runrig and Capercaillie. But the transformation goes beyond that: old inhibitions about writing in Scots or in Shetland dialect have been laid to rest too, and much of Glasgow's recent success is attributed to the city's focus on the arts. It remains to be seen whether Scotland's new cultural confidence and political life will act as the catalysts for the country's potential in a new century.

WILDLIFE

A comprehensive account of Scotland's wildlife would fill a whole book: what follows is a general overview of the effects of climate and human activity on the country's flora and fauna.

CLIMATE

Scotland's mountains are high enough to impose harsh conditions, especially in the Highlands, and the **Cairngorm plateau** (the largest area of high ground in the whole of Britain) is almost arctic even in summer. Despite this, however, since the easing of the Ice Age about 10,000 years ago, Scotland has developed a rather complex climate, and some areas of the country are quite mild.

The warmish water of the Gulf Stream tempers conditions on the west coast, so that at **Inverewe**, for example, you'll find incongruously lush gardens blooming with subtropical plants. Inland, the weather becomes more extreme, but what restricts plant life on many Scottish hills is not the cold so much as the stress of wind and gloomy cloud cover. **Ben Nevis**, for example, is clouded and whipped by 50mph gales for more than two-thirds of the year, and as a result, the tree line – the height to which trees grow up the slopes – may be only 150ft above sea level near the west coast, but up to over 2000ft on some of the sheltered hillsides inland.

A BRIEF HISTORY

After the Ice Age, "arctic" and "alpine" plants abounded, eventually giving way to woody shrubs and trees, notably the **Scots pine**. Oak and other hardwood trees followed in some places, but the Scots pine remained the distinctive tree, spreading expansively to form the great **Caledonian Forest**. Parts of this ancient forest still remain, miraculously surviving centuries of attack, but it is only comparatively recently that attempts at positive conservation have been made.

Early **settlement**, from the Picts to the Norsemen, led to clearance of large areas of forest, and huge areas were burnt during the clan wars. When centuries of unrest ended with the Jacobite defeat at Culloden in 1745, the glens were ransacked for timber, which was floated downriver to fuel iron smelting and other industries. The clansmen had had a free-booting cattle economy, but during the infamous **Clearances** both the cattle and the defeated Highlanders were replaced by the more profitable sheep of the new landlords. As also happened on the English downland and moorland, intensive sheep grazing kept the land open, eventually destroying much woodland by preventing natural regeneration.

In Victorian times, **red deer** herds, which also graze heavily, provided stalking, and when rapid-firing breech-loading guns came into general use around the 1850s, **grouse shooting** became a passion. It's strange to think of birds changing the scenery, but grouse graze heather and thus large areas are burnt to encourage fresh green growth. No tree saplings survive and the open moorland is maintained.

The flatter **lowlands** are now dominated by mechanized farming; barley, beef, turnips and potatoes conspire against wildlife, and pollution and development are as damaging here as elsewhere. Even the so-called **"wilderness"** is under threat. Its own popularity obviously holds dangers, and the unique flora of the Cairngorm peaks, for example, is in danger of being stamped out under the feet of the summer visitors using the ski lifts. But even more damaging than tourism is **conifer planting**. In recent decades, boosted (if not caused) by generous grant aid and tax dodges, large areas of open moorland have been planted with tightly packed monocultural ranks of foreign conifers, forbidding to much wildlife. Coniferization is particularly threatening to large areas of bogland in the "Flow Country" of Caithness and elsewhere, areas that are as unique a natural environment as the tropical rainforests. For these and other similar habitats, registration as an **SSSI** – a Site of Special Scientific Interest – has proved barely adequate, and the only real safeguard is for such areas to be owned or managed by organizations such as Scottish Natural Heritage (the national agency) or the Scottish Wildlife Trust, the Royal Society for the Protection of Birds and similar voluntary groups.

WILD FLOWERS

Relic patches of the Scots pine Caledonian Forest, such as the Black Wood of Rannoch and Rothiemurchus Forest below the Cairngorms, are often more open than an oak wood, the pines, interspersed with birch and juniper, spaced out in hilly heather. These woods feature some wonderful wild flowers, such as the **wintergreens** which justify their name, unobtrusive **orchids** in the shape of creeping lady's tresses and lesser twayblade and, in parts of the northeast especially, the rare beauty of the **twinflower**, holding its paired heads over the summer needle litter.

You'll also find old oak woods in some places, especially in the lower coastward lengths of the southern glens. Here the Atlantic influence encourages masses of spring flowers including **wood anemone** and **wild hyacinth**, the Scottish term for what in England is called a bluebell. (In Scotland the name "bluebell" describes the summer-flowering English harebell that grows on more open ground.) Scotland, or at least lowland Scotland, has many flowers found further south in Britain – **maiden pink**, orchids, **cowslip** and others in grassy areas. Roadside flowers, such as **meadowsweet** and **meadow buttercup**, **dog rose**, **primrose** and **red campion**, extend widely up through Scotland, but others, such as the **white field rose** and **mistletoe**, **red valerian**, **small scabious**, **cuckoo pint** and **traveller's joy** (and the elm tree), reach the end of their range in the Scottish central lowlands.

Scotland's mountains, especially where the rock is limey or basic in character, as on Ben Lawers, for example, are dotted with arctic-alpine plants, such as mountain **avens**, with their white flowers and glossy oak-like leaves, and handsome **purple saxifrage**, both of which favour a soil rich in calcium. Here as elsewhere, the flowers are to be found on ledges and rock-faces out of reach of the sheep and deer. Other classic mountain plants are **alpine lady's mantle** and **moss campion**, which grows in a tight cushion, set with single pink flowers.

Higher up on the bleak wind-battered mountain tops, there may be nothing much more than a low "heath" of mosses and maybe some tough low grasses or rushes between the scatterings of rubble. Because this environment encourages few insects, such plants are generally self-fertilizing and some even produce small plants or "bulbils" in their flower heads instead of seed.

A variety of ferns shelter in the slopes amid the tumbled rock screes or in cracks in the rock alongside streams. In Scotland's damp climate, you'll also see many ferns on lower ground, but some, the **holly fern** for one, are true mountain species. **Lichens**, too, are common on exposed rocks, and in the woods bushy and bearded lichens can coat the branches and trunks.

Bogs are a natural feature of much of the flatter ground in the Highlands, often extending for miles. Scottish bogland comprises an intricate mosaic of domes of living bog moss (sometimes bright green or a striking orange or yellow), domes of drier, heathery peat, and pools dotted in between. The wettest areas give rise to specialized plants such as **cranberry**, **bearberry** and also the **sundews**, which gain nutrients in these poor surroundings by trapping and absorbing midges with the sticky hairs on their flat leaves.

At sea level, the rivers spawn estuaries; these and some sea lochs are edged with **salt marshes**, which in time dry out into "meadows" colourful with **sea aster** and other flowers. The west coast, especially the cliffs of Galloway, shimmers blue with **spring squill** as soon as the winter eases, while the Galloway shore marks the southernmost limit of **Scots lovage**, a celery-scented member of the cow parsley family. A relic of arctic times, the **oysterplant**, with blue-grey leaves and pink bell flowers, also grows here, as it does on the shores of Iceland and Scandinavia.

Scotland has some wonderful **sand dune** systems, which on the back shores harden into grassy patches often grazed by rabbits to create a fine turf.

BIRDLIFE

It might seem unexpected to find birds nesting at over 3000ft, but in Scotland the wind is strong enough to blow patches of icy ground clear of snow, enabling birds to make their homes on the mountains. The **dotterel**, a small wader with a chestnut stomach, is a rare summer visitor to the Cairngorms and other heights – in the Arctic it nests down to sea level. Even rarer is the **snow bunting**, the male black and white, the female brownish – perhaps only ten pairs nest on Scotland's mountains, although they are seen much more widely around the coasts in winter, when the male also becomes brown. The **snowy owl**, at the southern limit of its range, is a regular visitor to Shetland.

More common on the heights is the **ptarmigan**, shy and almost invisible in its summer coat, as it plays hide and seek amongst the lichen-patched boulders – you're most likely to see it on the Cairngorms, as it ventures out for the sandwich crusts left by the summer visitors using the ski lifts. It is resident up here, and moults from mottled in summer to pure white in winter.

The ptarmigan's camouflage helps protect it from the **golden eagle**. This magnificent bird ranges across many Highland areas – there are perhaps three hundred nesting pairs on Skye, the Outer Hebrides, above Aviemore and Deeside, and in the northwest Highlands, each needing a territory of thousands of acres over which to hunt hares, grouse and ptarmigan. The **raven** also has strong links with the mountains, tumbling in crazy acrobatics past the rockfaces. After nearly seventy years' absence, the **white-tailed (sea) eagle**, whose wing span is even greater than that of the golden eagle, has been successfully re-introduced to Rùm. The resident breeding population is still very small, however, and the exact location of the eyries is kept secret.

Where the slopes lessen to moorland, the domain of the **red grouse** begins. This game bird not only affects the landscape but also, via the persecution of gamekeepers, threatens eagles and other birds of prey, although they are all theoretically protected. The **cuckoo** can be heard as far north as Shetland – one of its favourite dupes, the **meadow pipit**, is fairly widespread on any rough ground up to 3000ft. Dunlin and other waders nest on the wet moorlands and boglands, where the soft land allows

them to use their delicate bills to probe for insects and other food.

You'll come across many notable birds where pine woods encroach onto open moor. One such is the **black grouse**, with its bizarre courtship rituals, where both sexes come together for aggressive, ritualistic display in a small gathering area known as a "lek". The **capercaillie**, found deeper in the forest and perhaps floundering amongst the branches, is an unexpectedly large, turkey-like bird, about 3ft from bill to end of tail, which also has a flamboyant courting display. A game bird, it was shot to extinction but reintroduced into Scotland from Europe in 1837. Other birds that favour the pine woods are the **long-eared owl**, many of the tit family (including the **crested tit** in the Spey Valley), the **siskin** and the **goldcrest**. The Speyside woods, especially, are a stronghold of the **crossbill**, which uses its overlapping bill to prise open pine cones.

Scottish **lochs** are as rich in birdlife as the moorlands that embrace them. After fifty years of absence, the **osprey** returned and more than a hundred pairs now breed; the best site to see them is near Loch Garten on Speyside. In addition to common species such as **mallard** and **tufted duck**, you might also see **goosander**, **red-breasted merganser** and other wildfowl. The superbly streamlined fish-eating **red-** and **black-throated divers** nest in the northwest, while the **great northern diver**, with its shivery wailing call, is largely a winter visitor on the coasts, although one or two pairs may occasionally nest.

Scotland is also strong on **coastal birds**. **Eider duck** gather in their thousands at the mouth of the Tay, and the estuaries are also a magnet for **waders** and **wild geese** in winter: the total population of barnacle geese from the Arctic island of Spitsbergen winters in the Solway estuary and on the farmland alongside. Other areas to head for if you're interested in seabirds are remote cliffs such as St Abb's Head in the Borders, and the many offshore "**bird islands**", which, although often little more than bare rock, attract vast colonies that fish the sea around them. Some have their own speciality – **Manx shearwaters** have vast colonies on Rùm, for example, while the Shetland isle of Foula has about a third (three thousand pairs) of all the **great skuas** breeding in the northern hemisphere. Remote St Kilda is also stunning, with snowstorms of **gannets, puffins, guillemots, petrels** and **shearwaters**.

In addition to Scotland's resident bird population, and the winter and spring migrants, the western coasts and islands often see transatlantic "accidentals" blown far off course, which give rise to inbred **subspecies**. St Kilda is of particular interest to specialists, not only for its sheer numbers of resident birds but also for the St Kilda wren, a distinct subspecies. Fair Isle also sees large numbers of migrant and vagrant birds from both sides of the Atlantic. In northern and parts of eastern Scotland, the English all-black carrion crow is replaced by the "hoodie" or **hooded crow**, also found around the Mediterranean, with its distinctive grey back and underparts. Where the ranges of carrion crow and hoodie overlap, they interbreed, producing offspring with some grey patches of plumage.

MAMMALS

By the mid-eighteenth century, much of Scotland's wild animal life – including the Scottish **wolf**, **beaver**, **wild boar** and **elk** – had already disappeared (though the beaver is now being re-introduced). The indigenous **reindeer** was wiped out in the twelfth century, but more recently a semi-wild herd of Swedish stock was reintroduced to the slopes of the Cairngorms above Aviemore. Of two other semi-wild species, **Highland cattle** and **Shetland ponies**, the former is a classic case of breeding fitting conditions (they can survive in snowy conditions for fifty days a year), while the latter, the smallest British native pony, probably arrived in the later stages of the Ice Age when the ice was retreating but still gave a bridge across the salt water. There are feral goats in some places, but probably the most interesting of such animals is the Soay sheep of St Kilda. This, Britain's only truly wild sheep, notable for its soft brown fleece, can be seen as a farm pet and in wildlife parks – and is even used to graze some nature reserves in the south of Britain.

Although there are **sika** and **fallow deer** in places, and **roe deer** are widespread, Scotland is the stronghold of wild **red deer** herds, which, despite culling, stalking for sport and harsh winters, still number more than quarter of a million head. By origin a woodland animal, they might graze open ground – of necessity when the forest has been cleared – but they also move up to high ground in summer to avoid the biting flies and the tourists, and to graze on heather and lichens. They're most obvious in the snowy depths of winter, when, forced downhill in search of food, large numbers may be seen by road or rail travellers on Rannoch Moor or between Blair Atholl and Drumochter Pass.

The **fox** is widespread, as are the **mole** and **hedgehog**, but the **badger** is rather more rare. The **wild cat** and **pine marten** live in remote areas, hiding away in the moors and forests. The former, despite its initial resemblance to the family pet, is actually quite different – larger, with longer, striped fur, and a blunt-ended bushy tail that is also striped. The agile cat-sized pine marten, although hunted by gamekeepers, is maintaining reduced numbers, preying on squirrels and other small animals.

Native red **squirrels** are predominantly found in the Highlands, where they are still largely free from competition from the greys, which began to establish themselves about a century ago and now have a strong presence in many lowland areas. **Rabbit** and **brown hare** are widespread, as are the **blue** or **mountain hare** in the Highlands, usually adopting a white or patchy white coat in winter. The north Scottish **stoat** also dons a white winter coat, its tail tipped with black, when it is known as ermine. Although Scotland is too far north for the dormouse and the harvest mouse, **shrews, voles** and **field mice** abound and, though there are few bats, the related **pipistrelle** is quite widely seen.

You may also be lucky enough to encounter the **otter**, endangered in the rest of Britain. In Scotland, the otter is found not only in the rushing streams but more often along the west coast and in the northern and western isles, where it hunts the seashore for crabs and inshore fish. The otter is not to be confused with the feral **mink**, escaped from fur farms to take up life in the wild; these mink are a scourge in some areas, destroying birds.

Whales and their kin are frequent visitors to coastal waters and **seals**, including the shy grey seal, are quite common. However, in the hitherto virgin sea lochs of the west coast, both the seals and the coastal otters are under threat from the spread of **fish farms** (for salmon and sea trout). Not only are they poisoned by the chemicals used to keep the trapped fish vermin-free, but they also face the threat of being shot by the fish-farm owners when they raid what is to them simply a natural larder.

FISH, REPTILES AND INSECTS

Quite apart from the Loch Ness monster, Scotland has a rich water life. The Dee and other rivers are fished when **salmon** swim upstream to breed in their ancestral gravel headwaters. The fish leap waterfalls on the way, and many rivers which have been dammed for hydroelectric power generation have "salmon ladders" to help them – these make great tourist attractions. The **sea trout** is also strongly migratory, the **brown** or **mountain trout** less so, although river or stream dwellers do move upstream and loch dwellers move up the incoming rivers to spawn. Related to these game fish is the **powan** or **freshwater herring**, found only in the poorer northern basins of Loch Lomond, and possibly a relic from Ice Age arctic conditions. The richer southern waters of Loch Lomond and similar lakes contain **roach**, **perch** and other "coarse" fish.

Although the **adder** is common, the grass snake is not found in Scotland. Both **lizards** and the snake-like **slowworm** (in fact a legless lizard) are widespread, as are the **frog** and **toad**; the natterjack toad, however, is rarely seen this far north.

Scottish boglands are notable for their **dragon flies**, which prefer acid water, and **hawkers, darters** and **damselflies** feature in the south. One Scottish particular is the **blue hawker**, common in parts of the western Highlands. As for **butterflies**, some of the familiar types from further south – common blue, hairstreaks and others – are scattered in areas where conditions are not too harsh. One species with a liking for the heights is the **mountain ringlet**, only seen elsewhere in the English Lake District and in the Alps, which flies above 1500ft in the Grampians. Adapted to quite harsh conditions, it is clearly a relic of early post-glacial times. Another mountain butterfly, the **Scotch argus**, no longer found in England or Wales, is widespread in Scotland, and the **elephant hawk moth** can be seen in the Insh marshes below the Cairngorms.

ARCHITECTURE

From crofts to castles, the Victorian grand residence to the "new towns", Scotland has a rich legacy of strong, unique buildings. Stonework predominates, from the long houses of the Western Isles to the soft red sandstone that fills the streets of Glasgow. Surrounding countries have also had a substantial influence: some settlements in Orkney and Shetland evoke links with the Norse kingdoms, while the ruined church architecture of the central belt is testimony to a long history of battles with the marauding English.

PREHISTORIC TIMES TO THE THIRTEENTH CENTURY

One morning in 1850, after a ferocious storm, the villagers of Orkney woke to find **Skara Brae** (see p.564 – one of the earliest prehistoric sites in Scotland) revealed beneath the beautiful white sands. Situated nineteen miles northwest of Kirkwall, this **Neolithic** stone village is so well preserved that you can still see domestic details, typical of the age, such as flagstone box beds, built due to the lack of timber on the islands. Small passages unite what must have been quite a large and intricate settlement of stock farmers, who originally came to Scotland from mainland Europe; a turf roof provided insulation from wind and cold. The chambered tombs at **Maes Howe** (Orkney; see p.563) are another great architectural achievement, dating from 2750 BC and

complete with Viking graffiti from later raids on the islands. These tombs are remarkably well constructed, incorporating monoliths into the fine masonry that supports the narrow passages and small tomb cells. A fairly large community also existed at the **Jarlshof** prehistoric and Norse settlement on Shetland (see p.603), where small stone cells grouped around a central hearth provided the main accommodation, with now ruined outhouses used for bronze work and sheltering cattle. The survival of a number of ritual sites, including many **stone circles**, suggests some form of religious activity in Scotland at this time. One of the most beautiful and well-preserved stands at **Callanish** (Lewis; see p.396), where a circle of megaliths rise majestically from the ground with radiating lines of stone in a mysteriously symbolic form. The central stone is nearly 16ft high and sits next to a small chambered cairn, which may have once contained human remains.

During the **Bronze Age**, from around 1000 BC, the two predominant types of defensive settlements, made from earth and timber, were spectacular **hillforts**, and artificial islands built in the middle of lochs, called **crannogs**; little now remains of either of these. It wasn't until the **Iron Age** (from around 400 BC) that the next significant architectural development was to occur. For residents of the northwest mainland and the northern islands, the need for protection from attack or invasion and from the harshness of the weather was particularly extreme, and so it's here that most of Scotland's 400 or so **brochs,** the majority in ruins, can be found. Circular, windowless and tall – some over 40ft high – these drystone buildings were sturdily built to protect the inhabitants who lived inside, sheltered underneath wooden constructions. Broad at the bottom and narrow at the top, the unusual shape was due to the necessity for a thick base to support the high walls and provide storage and guard rooms. Brochs also had two walls and a spiral staircase leading up to a timber roof – a very useful vantage point. Some were inhabited for several centuries; the finest example is the **Broch of Mousa** from c.100 BC in Shetland (see p.626), which is remarkably well preserved due to its isolated position on a small island, free from the stone stealing that plagued subsequent settlements.

In 83 AD, the Scottish border came under threat from the **Romans**. Their success was limited, however, and the civilizing influence of Rome was to have barely any effect on the life and tribes of Scotland, who continued to live in brochs and crannogs, or erect primitive buildings of timber, wattle and clay, regardless. Of the Roman structures that have survived, the most impressive are the remnants of the **Antonine Wall**, a 36-mile-long construction that stretched from Kilpatrick to Bo'ness. Less substantial than the great Hadrian's Wall, it was originally built as a temporary measure to aid the overthrow of the fierce Pictish tribes, but was soon abandoned.

The subsequent introduction of **Christianity** left a much greater architectural legacy in Scotland. The primitive church of 397 AD at **Whithorn** (see p.176) marks one of the earliest Christian sites in Scotland and, with the arrival of St Columba at Iona in 563, the Celtic Christian community really came to dominate the country's religious matters. Evidence of this can be seen in the characteristic **round towers** at **Brechin** (Angus; see p.435) and **Egilsay** (Orkney; see p.581). Places of refuge for the monastic fellowship during times of attack, these were well defended, with a raised entrance and few windows. The simple and basic structures of the Irish Celtic church conveyed their ascetic religious beliefs, while artistic and creative energies were poured into the making of sculpted crosses and illuminated manuscripts. Fine carving survives at the monastic foundation on **Iona** (see p.331), a religious community that still thrives today. Few other such buildings remain, indicating that they were constructed from materials like timber, clay and turf.

The marriage of Malcolm III to the Saxon princess Margaret, in 1070, signified a dramatic upsurge in Scottish architecture. Malcolm created a feudal society based on agriculture and, more importantly, his wife orchestrated the reintroduction of Latin Christianity to the central areas of Scotland, founding many ecclesiastical buildings and finally bringing a European influence to this region – while the Highlands and Islands continued to build in the vernacular tradition. The **Romanesque** (or Norman) style can be seen at its best in **Dalmeny Church** (see p.105). This simple, thick-walled three-cell church has narrow window openings and a round arched doorway crowned by typically Romanesque wall arcading. The Anglo-Norman influence also created larger buildings, cruciform in plan with aisled naves and three-storey elevations; these were not actual physical levels but would consist of arches, a middle storey, usually formed by blind arches or decorative wall hangings but sometimes and, at the top, stained-glass windows. The thick piers and semicircular arches of **Dunfermline Abbey** (Fife; see p.270) are typically Norman. However, it was the Cistercians who brought the significant pointed arch and lancet window to Scotland and introduced the **Gothic** style to the country's craftsmen. As buildings were either reconstructed or modified in future centuries, the church at **Dunstaffnage** (Argyll; see p.318), with its simple rectangular plan and lancet windows, is a rare example of Early Gothic design. The twelfth-century abbey at **Jedburgh** in the Borders (see p.154) was just one of the abbeys that housed the religious communities being imported from England and France to southern and central parts of the country. Now in ruins, this church is very much in the transitional style between Romanesque and Gothic, as the west front contains a Romanesque round-arched doorway with a thirteenth-century rose window in the main gable. One of the most complete of the ruined Border Abbeys, **Dryburgh Abbey** (see p.146), in beautiful red sandstone, has an unusual vertical emphasis in the main arcade. **Melrose Abbey** (see p.144) contains examples of High Gothic detail, such as delicate tracery and flying buttresses, while **Kelso Abbey** (see p.141) stands out for its simplicity and massive proportions. These great Scottish abbeys, with the exception of the austere Cistercian communities, would have been richly decorated with tapestries, murals and carved furnishings. Unfortunately, their position in the southeast of Scotland left them vulnerable to attack from the English and they suffered badly as a result.

In the thirteenth century, the Norman kings brought a more settled period, establishing their authority through a network of loyal nobles who controlled parts of the country but recognized the king as overall ruler. This allowed for the building of great cathedrals, notably those of Glasgow and Elgin. **Glasgow Cathedral** (see p.205) is Scotland's only complete medieval cathedral to survive the Reformation; the verticality of the interior and the elegance of the clustered piers are monuments to the power of the Gothic tradition. The building itself is an amalgam of influences, from the Early Pointed style of the east end of the choir to the magnificent Late Gothic vaulting of the lower church, and is a poignant reminder of the wealth of architecture that has been lost to the nation over the years. **Elgin Cathedral** (see p.467), once "the ornament of the realm", with its unusual double aisles and rich furnishings, was an extravagant Anglo-Saxon statement of refinement and power, built to impress the Highland clans. It is in ruins, having been destroyed in 1390 by an earl angry at being excommunicated for leaving his wife.

The popular image of the great Scottish **castle**, the stuff of myth and legend, perched on a rocky crag and often surrounded by woodlands, heather and deer, is remarkably different from the cold reality of daily castle living. Rising in stone above the small peasant dwellings of turf and timber, the castle was a centre of administrative and judicial control, as well as a secure place in times of conflict. **Castle Sween** on Loch Sween (see p.343) is the earliest stone castle in Scotland, built in the eleventh century with a Norman-style round-arched doorway leading into the centre of the quadrangular building, once roofed with timber. With its origins in the twelfth century, **Edinburgh Castle** (see p.70) stands out as the archetypal royal Scottish castle. Built on an extinct volcano, it commanded a strong strategic position and served throughout much of its history as a resonant symbol of power and protection. The epitome of the romantic Highland castle, on the other hand, is the beautifully picturesque **Eilean Donan** on Loch Duich (see p.516), ten miles south of the Kyle of Lochalsh. Originally a small thirteenth-century castle of enclosure, it was used to garrison Spanish troops as part of the Jacobite Rising, and was destroyed by English warships in 1719. The present building is predominantly a reconstruction, initiated at the beginning of the twentieth century, an immaculate three-storey keep perched on a rocky outcrop with a dramatic arched bridge.

Developments in warfare and architecture marched hand in hand, and thirteenth-century castles employed a number of defensive techniques: the use of catapults and assault towers, the strengthening of outer walls, and construction of round towers to allow for a better view of the base. Two miles north of Oban, the tall, thick walls of **Dunstaffnage** (see p.318) are topped with a crenellated wall walk and contain few windows but many well-placed firing slits; an outer defence like the moat at **Rothesay** (Isle of Bute; see p.308), which was established c.1204, was also common. Natural defences such as rocky outcrops were particularly impenetrable; **Dirleton Castle** (near North Berwick; see p.133) uses one to great advantage, its weaker side protected by three towers forcing outwards in an aggressive manner, and **Stirling Castle** is similarly well defended (see p.247). Situated on a grassy hilltop, the reinforced tower at **Bothwell Castle** (near Blantyre; see p.237) provided an effective last refuge in an attack.

THE FOURTEENTH AND FIFTEENTH CENTURIES

With the power of the monarch declining and the nobility fighting for territory and power, the **fourteenth century** was a time of great strife and warfare in Scotland; consequently, law and order were overthrown and few buildings constructed. The destruction predominantly affected the Lowlands, the Highlanders being a law unto themselves within their own social system, strategically using the mountains to defend their proud autonomy. Castles continued to be strengthened, often growing in size to accommodate larger buildings. The impressive fourteenth-century castles of **Tantallon** (near North Berwick; see p.134) and **Doune** (Perthshire; see p.252) both contain a massive gatehouse employed to protect the entrance, and provide the lord with accommodation. This gave him full control of the castle's defences, necessary at a time when hired mercenaries were commonly used in private armies. For lesser nobles, the **tower house** was the perfect solution to the conflicting problems of comfort and defence. The tower house became a popular high-security residence, being smaller and cheaper than a great castle. Tall and narrow with smooth walls and few windows, these buildings featured a raised entrance and crenellated parapet as the main elements of passive defence – relying on thick walls and great height for effect. Being of a simple yet flexible design, the majority were expanded and decorated in later centuries, and none exist in their original form (see "Sixteenth and Seventeenth Centuries" for examples).

The **fifteenth century**, fluctuating between periods of war and peace, allowed tower houses to retain their popularity among the lesser nobles, being secure, yet comfortable enough for everyday living. High Gothic principles became established in ecclesiastical buildings, and the construction of the great royal residences introduced the spirit of the **Early Renaissance** to Scotland. In the 1420s, James I began to rebuild **Linlithgow Palace** (see p.262) and by 1500 it had become a large and symmetrical structure, in contrast to the random organization of medieval castles. Designed as a quadrangle with an open central court, it was primarily a domestic royal residence with a system of corridors and stairwells and large, regularly placed windows. This hint of Renaissance order and elegance was markedly different from the usual defensive principles of high walls and small window openings. Once considered the finest in the realm, the central chambers would have been luxuriously decorated with painted plaster and wall hangings.

The Gothic style was still favoured in ecclesiastical architecture, most apparent in **Melrose Abbey** (see p.143). Twice destroyed in the fourteenth century, the rebuilding left excellent examples of High Gothic, the east window being the work of the York school of masons, and the richly carved south transept by a French master mason, which accounts for the lavish use of decoration. The flying buttresses are of particular note, being structural, not merely decorative. Due to an increase in trade with other countries, wealthy landowners could afford to construct small churches, staffed by secular clergy to pray for the soul of the benefactor. Many small collegiate buildings were built at this time, predominantly with a Late Gothic flavour: the most unusual and extreme is the mid-fifteenth-century **Rosslyn Chapel** (Edinburgh; see p.107), with its elaborate carving and decorative flying buttresses. Also around this time, the castellated features of castles and towers began to creep into church architecture, seen in the use of crow-stepped gables at **St Michael's Church** (Linlithgow; see p.262), or the crenellated parapet at **King's College Chapel** (Aberdeen; see p.445).

THE SIXTEENTH AND SEVENTEENTH CENTURIES

The massacre of the Scots at Flodden in 1513 set the tone for unrest in the early part of the **sixteenth century**, leaving little opportunity for new buildings or styles. However, the Stewart dynasty continued to breathe the Renaissance spirit into their opulent palaces. A royal holiday home for the Stewart monarchs, **Falkland Palace** (Fife; see p.275), with its reconstructed south range, is an excellent example of **French Renaissance** design, the solid buttresses transformed into Classical columns. This courtly look is also apparent at **Stirling Castle** (see p.247), a true amalgam of styles, perched high up on a rocky outcrop. Here, the Renaissance facade of the Royal Palace, completed in 1540, is merely tacked onto the Gothic structure, with a line of restless statues perched on elegant wall shafts. Ultimately, this fashion did not catch on, as nobles preferred security and comfort over elegance.

The Reformation of 1560 released a tragic wave of wholesale destruction of sculptural and other decorative items in church buildings. The tower house, however, regained popularity, as a considerable amount of church land had been sold off to nobles, who then wanted to create mini-castles as emblems of power and prestige. These buildings developed right through to the seventeenth century, often changing dramatically in plan, for example at **Drum Castle** (Aberdeen; see p.451). Originally built in the late thirteenth century, the dignified tower was extended to its full Jacobean glory in the seventeenth century, when the desire for greater comfort and space called for a larger building. The **Scottish Baronial** style, characterized by crow-stepped gables and conical roofs, lightened the austerity of the original tower form and took these buildings to their peak. Excellent examples include **Claypotts Castle** (near Dundee; see p.422), where defensive features have been subsumed to the need for extra accommodation, which is corbelled out at the top of the Z-plan towers. Other castles of note are **Crathes** (Deeside; see p.422), **Fyvie** (near Inverurie; see p.456) and **Glamis Castle** (north of Dundee; see p.431), which was constructed in the early seventeenth century. A later, even more decorative approach can be found at the absurdly pink-hued **Craigievar Castle**, 26 miles west of Aberdeen (see p.457). Built in 1626 and hailed as the finest tower house in Scotland, the crenellation serves to enhance the top-heavy accommodation area, but the beautifully preserved interior contains excellent stucco work. In all of these examples, useful defensive elements have been manipulated for effective decorative purposes.

The religious Wars of the Covenant (1639–44) and invasion of Cromwell (1650) initially discouraged contemporary building in the **seventeenth century**. However, it did see the final development of the **Early Scottish Renaissance**, marked by regular, symmetrical plans, the use of pediments and other decorative details of Classical origin, and an ordered dignified facade. Initiated in 1628, the elaborate **George Heriot's Hospital** in Edinburgh, which is now a school, is an excellent example. Here, Renaissance ideas are not merely decorative items tacked onto the front but are incorporated by the architect, **William Wallace**, into the overall design. The quadrangular plan with a tower at each corner is a feast of turrets, chimneys and cupolas that top the symmetrical facade. As the century progressed, the landed classes, having travelled and become more aware of the cultural conditions in England and Europe, began to take a serious interest in the design of their mansions, led by the influential figure of Sir William Bruce, who essentially founded the **Classical** school in Scotland. He undertook the major reconstruction of the **Palace of Holyrood** (Edinburgh; see p.81) in 1671–79, creating a delicate and restrained courtyard frontage of fine proportion and exacting detail. **Drumlanrig Castle** (Dumfries; see p.168), built between 1679 and 1690, is an extravagant mansion, more obviously Classical with a balanced plan and a sweeping double staircase at the entrance.

THE EIGHTEENTH CENTURY

In the early years after the Act of Union (1707), the Scottish economy was at a low ebb. Gradually conditions began to improve as trade, encouraged by the union, began to take off, further enhanced by the agricultural revolution. By mid-century, the industrial age had ignited an architectural explosion. The towns of Edinburgh and Glasgow were to receive the best in **Neoclassical** architecture, as steadily increasing industrial production called for more housing, warehouses and municipal buildings. In line with the rationality and order of the Enlightenment, symmetry and proportion in design came into stride with the English Classicism of Sir Christopher Wren and Inigo Jones. Edinburgh's **New Town**, designed by **James Craig** in 1767, is characterized by symmetrical wide streets and large tree-filled squares, with service lanes that follow the main axis of the roads. Amongst this sandstone glory lies **Charlotte Square** (see p.94), the north side of which was designed by the renowned Classicist **Robert Adam** in 1791. The Venetian windows and restrained use of decoration create a unified facade, the main rooms clearly defined by angular stonework in comparison to the smooth sandstone of the other storeys. Compared with the medieval High Street that descends from the Castle, and the narrow lanes that run from it, these formal squares reflect a new approach to civilized urban living, allowing the upper classes to dwell in their own spacious areas away from the huddle of the Old Town. Adam was the shining light in a talented family of architects, who modified elegant **Hopetoun House** (Edinburgh; see p.106) in c.1721–60. Set in an excellent position overlooking the Forth, this delicate and symmetrically designed building makes full use of triangular pediments and round-headed windows to recall the noble spirit of Classical times.

Concurrently, an interest in medieval architecture, encouraged by romantic fiction and the cult of the picturesque, led to **Gothic Revivalism**. Here, the pointed arch took over from the geometric rigours of Classicism. **Inveraray Castle** (Argyll; see p.311), built between 1745 and 1761, is one of the first Georgian castles to recreate itself in this neo-Gothic style. Although the interior is inspired by Classicism, the exterior makes use of pointed arches and crenellated parapets, the conical roofs being a later addition. Another neo-Gothic building is **Culzean Castle** (1771–92), attractively situated on a clifftop south of Ayr (see p.180) and extensively remodelled by Robert Adam in the latter part of the century. He designed every detail, from the fine interior plasterwork, complete with swags and urns, to the castellated exterior with mock arrow slits, to give a romantically medieval touch to the dramatic setting.

THE NINETEENTH CENTURY

By the turn of the century, Scotland had changed dramatically, climbing from a poor backwater to become one of the Empire's leading industrial centres. Furthermore, after Queen Victoria "discovered" Scotland in 1842, it became highly fashionable, fuelled by the image of wild clans and rugged, lonely landscapes – a far cry from the bitter reality of life within the rapidly industrializing central belt, populated increasingly by families left homeless by the Highland Clearances. The major cities of Glasgow, Edinburgh and Dundee were expanding at great speed, filling up with warehouses, municipal buildings and workers' accommodation. This ushered in the **Victorian Age** of architecture. Marked by a continuation of the Romantic and Classical idioms established in the eighteenth century, grand buildings celebrated the pride and self-confidence of the industrial giants. A fusion of historical styles became common, and architects increasingly looked for novel ways to decorate their buildings. For instance, the Tudor-Gothic **Donaldson's Hospital** in Edinburgh, designed by **William Playfair** in 1851, fuses a symmetrical plan with elaborate turrets and a central decorated tower. Playfair was also responsible for creating the rich facade at **Floors Castle** (near Kelso; see p.142), in 1838, cloaking the building in a new fashionable guise without changing the basic structural design.

Inspired by simple proportion and logical harmony, the followers of the **Greek Revival** created buildings of massive serenity, using little decoration. In Glasgow, **Alexander "Greek" Thomson** brought a unique interpretation to this style. He created buildings from warehouses to tenements and churches, such as Glasgow's impressive **St Vincent Street Church** (see p.203), an imposing construction that mixes the massive solidity of Greek design with exotic motifs and decoration. In Edinburgh, it was **William Playfair** who created the city's icons of Greek Revivalism: the **Royal Scottish Academy** of 1836 (see p.91), and the **National Gallery of Scotland** of 1857 (see p.91), are both well proportioned with precise detail, the former making more use of scrolls and wreaths, the latter slightly less ponderous and more elegant. With the Gothic style no longer restricted to ecclesiastical architecture, the majestic

Glasgow University building of 1870, designed by George Gilbert Scott, dominates the skyline of the West End in pseudo-medieval splendour. Similarly, in Edinburgh, the **Scottish National Portrait Gallery** of 1885–90, designed by Sir R. Rowand Anderson, is richly detailed with pointed arches and turrets.

New materials of the industrial age, such as cast iron, were being used to great effect, in buildings such as **Kibble Palace** in the Botanic Gardens (Glasgow; see p.214) and the interior of the **Royal Museum of Scotland** (Edinburgh; see p.88), which was based on London's Crystal Palace. The industrial age also gave birth to such great figures of **engineering** as **William Telford**, **Sir Benjamin Baker** and **Sir John Fowler**, who constructed roads and bridges throughout Scotland. Baker and Fowler were responsible for the pinnacle of Scottish engineering that straddles the Firth of Forth in cantilevered steel glory – the **Forth Railway Bridge** spans more than a mile, took seven years to build and employed more than 5000 men at a time, rivalling the Eiffel Tower in its complexity.

THE TWENTIETH CENTURY

At the turn of the century, Scotland was riding on the crest of a wave, with a healthy economy and solid industrial base, but a long period of postwar depression was to destroy this security. In any case, while the Victorian well-to-do had been luxuriating in their fine buildings, the workers had lived in slums, a situation that was to result in mass demolition later in the century.

Despite many financial difficulties, Glasgow's **Charles Rennie Mackintosh** began to design exciting new buildings, motivated by the desire for complete organic unity of structure and decoration. Associated with the Art Nouveau school and their push for change after the conservatism of the previous century, he produced some buildings of excellent quality and form. The **Glasgow School of Art** (see p.207) is the archetypal Mackintosh work, fusing the curvilinear shapes of Art Nouveau with the crow-stepped gables and conical roofs of the Scots Baronial tradition. The interior effectively combines practicality with decorative beauty; and the library, in particular, promotes his forward-thinking style as it makes use of a strong vertical motif for its columns, lighting and furnishing (for more on Mackintosh, see p.208). Outside the bustling city at **Hill House** in Helensburgh (see p.301), Mackintosh created a domestic building in 1902 that unites the turrets and chimney stack of the Baronial tradition with a modern interior. In the drawing room he creates two "zones", the wide bay window overlooking the Firth, for summer, and a cosy fireplace with a bookcase as a backdrop for winter evenings.

World War I brought a dramatic shift in scientific and artistic sensibilities; with the old ways undermined, people looked more and more to the future. This new atmosphere was represented in the **Art Deco** style, celebrating speed and technology. Typical features include modern, flat roofs, soaring geometric motifs and the use of reinforced concrete, which allowed semicircular glazed bays to project out from the building. However, due to financial constraints, few buildings were actually being erected; some gems that were include Glasgow's **Baird Hall of Residence** in Sauchiehall Street, built in 1938. The architect W. Beresford Inglis used two soaring projecting towers with bay windows to give a dynamic prominence to the general bulk of the building. In contrast, the large, brick-covered planes of the **Glasgow Film Theatre** (see p.230), constructed one year later and designed by James McKissack, enhance the squat flat-roofed building. **The Maybury**, on the outskirts of Edinburgh, is a typical "roadhouse" built to cater for the new car-bound tourist, who could gaze up into the regularly spaced windows of the tower, designed to emulate the radiator of a huge limousine.

Despite the innovative ideas for town planning after World War I and the great rehousing plans set in motion after World War II, few public or private buildings of note were produced. Instead, vast **suburban sprawls** were constructed in the most economical manner, resulting in their bland architectural character. More recently, the development of housing associations has allowed residents to have some influence over their living space, and tower blocks have been replaced with small brick buildings laid out in crescents and tree-lined streets. In the public realm, the possibilities of modern technology continued to be explored, for example at the **Exhibition Plant Houses** at Edinburgh's Royal Botanic Garden (see p.214). Built in 1967, the glass skin is held in place by an outside structure of steel and iron to provide the maximum use of space inside. The manipulation of glass to enhance space is also apparent at the **Burrell Collection** (Pollok Park, Glasgow; see p.215), built in 1983 to house the great collection of Sir William Burrell. The architect Barry Gasson effectively fused nature and art, employing large panes of glass to take advantage of the surrounding woodland light, while the geometric use of red sandstone contrasts well with the wildness of the parkland.

The current trend for conservation and renovation has produced some fine work: the glass-fronted **Festival Theatre** in Edinburgh and **The Lighthouse** in Glasgow, now Scotland's Centre for Architecture, Design and the City, are both successful and dynamic conversions of older buildings. Glasgow's year as **City of Architecture and Design** in 1999, of which The Lighthouse was the showpiece, tended to focus on Glasgow's rich architectural heritage, but it did strive to remind Scots of the importance of the buildings around them. And the futuristic **Homes for the Future** beside Glasgow Green, and the prominence of work such as Sir Norman Foster's **"Armadillo"** building on the banks of the Clyde, prove that the city still has an appetite for innovative modern design. Edinburgh, meanwhile, waits with baited breath for the new **Scottish Parliament** building, designed by Catalan Enric Miralles, to rise from the building site opposite the Palace of Holyroodhouse at the bottom of the Royal Mile. Encouraged by the enthusiastic reception for the innovative and beautiful **National Museum of Scotland**, which has been described as the finest post-war building in the capital, expectations are high that the new Parliament will offer the Scots an architectural icon to help define their aspirations in a new century.

MUSIC

Scottish music is in better health than for decades, with a bedrock of Celtic groups – the likes of Boys of the Lough, Silly Wizard, Tannahill Wavers and Runrig – storming through traditional material in a blaze of bagpipes and flying fiddles. This new roots culture seems to have finally shaken off the image of Andy Stewart and Jimmy Shand, with their accordions and sentimental songs of the Highlands.

Scotland through the 1980s and 1990s saw an explosion of roots and dance music, and, at the same time, a renewal and revisiting of traditions that had seemed perilously close to the edge. As the 1990s close, there are a half a dozen Scottish labels devoted entirely to local music; there's a monthly roots magazine, the aptly titled **Living Tradition**, and a real sense of a scene – from Glasgow right up to the Shetlands. A new generation of bands and musicians can wear their Scottishness on their sleeves, confident that this is a music at last commanding as much respect as the traditions of Ireland.

That Scots music had been troubled in the years of English pop and rock dominance was in part, perhaps, due to its nature. A precision is required in traditional Scottish performance – especially in piping – that irons out much of the individual flair of a solo player. But the broadening of the music in the new roots scene, with "non-traditional" influences coming from Ireland in particular, and from the folk scene in general, has allowed the virtuosity of individual artists to come through.

THE CELTIC FOLK BAND ARRIVES

As in much of northern Europe, the story of Scotland's roots scene begins amid the **"folk revival"** of the 1960s – a time when folk song and traditional music engaged people who did not have strong family links with an ongoing tradition. For many in Scotland, traditional music had skipped a generation and they had to make a conscious effort to learn about it. At first, the main influences were largely American – skiffle music and people like Pete Seeger – but soon people started to look to their own traditions, taking inspiration from the Gaelic songs of **Cathy-Ann McPhee**, then still current in rural outposts, or the old **travelling singers** – people like the **Stewarts of Blairgowrie**, **Isla Cameron**, **Lizzie Higgins**, and the greatest of them all, Lizzie's mother, **Jeannie Robertson**.

On the instrumental front, there were fewer obvious role models despite the continued presence of a great many people playing in **Scottish dance bands**, **pipe bands** and **Strathspey and Reel Societies** (fiddle orchestras). In the 1960s the action was coming out of Ireland and the recorded repertoire of bands like The Chieftains became the core of many a pub session in Scotland. Even in the early 1970s, folk fiddle players were rare, although **Aly Bain** (see box opposite) made a huge impression when he came down from Shetland and, soon after, Shetland Reels started to creep into the general folk repertoire.

The "Celtic Folk Band" was a creation of the 1960s. Previously the art of a traditional musician was essentially a solo one. These days, however, there is a more or less standard formula with a melody lead – usually fiddle or pipes – plus guitar, bouzouki and a singer. The singer is often just another sound in the band whereas before it was the song that was the focus. Instrumental in these developments was a Glasgow folk group, **The Clutha**, who in a folk scene dominated by singers and guitarists, boasted not one but two fiddlers, along with a concertina, and four strong singers – including the superb **Gordeanna McCulloch**.

The Clutha were hugely influential and became even more successful when **Jimmy Anderson** introduced a set of chamber pipes into the line-up. Jimmy was not only a great piper but was also a pipe maker and he "invented" a set of pipes to be played in the key of D

ALY BAIN AND SHETLAND MAGIC

Aly Bain has been a minor deity among Scottish musicians for three decades. A fiddle player of exquisite technique and individuality, he has been the driving force of one of Scotland's all-time great bands, Boys of the Lough, throughout that time, while latterly diversifying roles as a TV presenter and author. In these guises, he has been instrumental in spreading the wings of Scottish music to an even greater extent. First and foremost, though, Bain is a Shetlander and his greatest legacy is the inspiration he has provided for a thriving revival of fortunes for Shetland's own characteristic tradition.

Aly was brought up in the capital of Shetland, Lerwick, and was enthused to play the fiddle by Bob Duncan – who endlessly played him records by the Strathspey king Scott Skinner – and later the old maestro, Tom Anderson. Duncan and Anderson were the last of an apparently dying breed, and the youthful Aly was an odd sight dragging his fiddle along to join in with the old guys at the Shetland Fiddlers Society. Players like Willie Hunter Jnr and Snr, Willie Pottinger and Alex Hughson were legends locally, but they belonged to another age and the magic of Shetland fiddle playing – one inflected with the eccentricity of the isolated environment and the influence of nearby Scandinavia.

By the time the teenage Aly was persuaded to leave for the mainland, Shetland was changing by the minute, and the discovery of North Sea oil altered it beyond redemption, as the new industri-al riches trampled its unique community spirit and sense of tradition. The old fiddlers gradually faded and died, and Shetland music seemed destined to disappear too.

That it didn't was largely down to Aly. After a spell with Billy Connolly (then a folk artist) on the Scottish folk circuit, Aly found himself working with blues iconoclast Mike Whellans, and then the two of them tumbled into a link-up with two Irishmen, Robin Morton and Cathal McConnell, in a group they called Boys of the Lough. The last thing Aly Bain imagined was that he'd spend the next quarter of a century answering to this name. But he did, and his joyful artistry, unwavering integrity and unquenchable appetite and commitment to the music of his upbringing kept Shetland music alive in a manner he could never have imagined. Even more importantly, it stung the imagination of the generation that followed.

These days, Shetland music is buzzing again, with its own annual festival a treat of music-making and drinking. There are young musicians pouring out of the place, and a plethora of bands of all styles, including pop-oriented groups such as Rock, Salt & Nails and more recently Red Vans. The pick of the roots players, currently, is Catriona MacDonald – who was also taught by Tom Anderson, in his last days. She is adept at classical music, and is fast becoming an accomplished mistress of Norwegian music, and her mum went to school with Aly Bain – which in Shetland these days counts for an awful lot.

---

which sounded much quieter than the Highland pipes. This was essential at that time, as virtually all the venues were acoustic and sound systems were not up to the job of balancing out the sounds of pipes, fiddle and voices. Such a development was to come later, in the late 1970s, with bands like Battlefield Band, The Tannahill Weavers and Ossian.

Key, too, to developments were **The Boys of the Lough**, a Scots-Irish group led by the Shetland fiddler **Aly Bain** (see box) and **The Whistlebinkies**. Developing in the Glasgow folk scene alongside The Clutha, both these groups took a strong instrumental line, rather than The Clutha's song-based approach. These two bands were in many ways Scotland's equivalent of The Chieftains and through their musical ability and recognition outside the folk clubs, played an important part in breaking down musical barriers.

The Whistlebinkies were notable for employing only traditional instruments, including fine clarsach (Celtic harp) from **Judith Peacock**. However, the most important, and definingly Scottish, element of all three of these bands was the presence of **bagpipes**. Clutha had piper **Jimmy Anderson**, the Whistlebinkies featured **Rab Wallace**, who had a firm background in the Scots piping scene, while The Boys also had an experienced piper in **Robin Morton**. They were pioneers for what was to become a revolution.

PIBROCH: SCOTS PIPES

Bagpipes are synonymous with Scotland yet they are not a specifically Scots instrument. The pipes were once to be found right across Europe, and pockets remain, across the English border in Northumbria, all over Ireland, in Spain and Italy, and in eastern Europe, where bagpipe festivals are still held in rural areas. In Scotland, bagpipes seem to have made their appearance around the fifteenth century, and over the next hundred years or so they took on several forms, including quieter varieties (small pipes), both bellows and mouth blown, which allowed a diversity of playing styles.

The Highland bagpipe form known as **pibroch** (*piobaireachd* in Gaelic) evolved around this time, created by clan pipers for military, gathering, lamenting and marching purposes. Legend among the clan pipers of this era were the MacCrimmons (they of the famous *MacCrimmon's Lament*, composed during the Jacobite rebellion), although they were but one of several important piping clans, among which were the MacArthurs, MacKays and MacDonalds, and others. In the seventeenth and eighteenth centuries, through the influence of the British army, reels and strathspeys joined the repertoire and a tradition of military pipe bands emerged. After World War II they were joined by civilian bands, alongside whom developed a network of piping competitions.

The bagpipe tradition has continued uninterrupted, although for much of this century under the domination of the military and the folklorists Piobaireachd Society. Recently, however, a number of Scottish musicians have revived the pipes in new and innovative forms. Following the lead of Clutha, The Boys of the Lough, and The Whistlebinkies, a new wave of young bands began to feature pipers, notably **Alba** with the then-teenage **Alan McLeod**, the **Battlefield Band**, whose arrangements involve the beautifully measured piping of **Duncan McGillivray**, and **Ossian** with **Iain MacDonald**. These players redefined the boundaries of pipe music using notes and finger movements outside of the traditional range. They also showed the influence of Irish Uillean pipe players (particularly Paddy Keenan of the Bothy Band) and Cape Breton styles which many claim is the original, pre-military Scottish style.

In 1983 Robin Morton released **A Controversy of Pipers** on his Temple Records label, an album featuring six pipers from folk bands who were also top competitive players in the piping world. Up until this point, pipers in a folk band could be considered second class by some in the piping establishment. This record-ing made a statement and soon the walls began to crumble . . .

Alongside all this came a revived interest in traditional piping, and in particular the strathspeys, slow airs and reels, which had tended to get submerged beneath the familiar military territory of marches and laments. The century's great bagpipe players, notably **John Burgess**, received a belated wider exposure. His legacy includes a masterful album and a renowned teaching career to ensure that the old piping tradition marches proudly into the next century.

FOLK SONG AND THE CLUB SCENE

Whilst the folk bands were starting to catch up on the Irish and integrating bagpipes, **folk song** was also flourishing. The song tradition in Scotland is one of the strongest in Europe and in all areas of the country there were pockets of great singers and characters. In the 1960s the common ground was the folk club network and the various festivals dotted around the country.

The great modern pioneer of Scots folk song, and a man who it is perhaps no exaggeration to say rescued the whole British tradition, was the great singer and songwriter **Ewan MacColl**, born in Perthshire in 1915. He recorded the seminal **Scottish Popular Ballads** as early as 1956, and founded the first folk club in Britain. After MacColl, another of the building blocks of the 1960s folk revival were the Aberdeen group, **The Gaugers**. Song was the heart of this group – Tam Speirs, Arthur Watson and Peter Hall were all good singers – though they were also innovative in using instrumentation (fiddle, concertina and whistle) without a guitar or other rhythm instrument to tie the sound together.

Other significant Scots groups on the 1960s scene included the **Ian Campbell Folk Group**, Birmingham-based but largely Scots in character (and including future Fairport Daves, Swarbrick and Pegg, as well as Ian's sons, Ali and Robin, who went on to form UB40). They flirted with commercialism and pop sensibilities – as virtually every folk group of the era was compelled to do – and were too often unfairly bracketed with England's derided Spinners as a result. So too were **The Corries**, although they laced their blandness with enterprise, inventing their own instrumentation and writing the new unofficial national anthem, *Flower of Scotland*.

Other more adventurous experiments grew out of the folk and acoustic club scene in mid-1960s

Glasgow and Edinburgh. It was at *Clive's Incredible Folk Club*, in Glasgow, that **The Incredible String Band** made their debut, led by **Mike Heron** and **Robin Williamson**. They took an unfashionable glance back into their own past on the one hand, while plunging headlong into psychedelia and other uncharted areas on the other. Their success broke down significant barriers, both in and out of Scotland, and in their wake came a succession of Scottish folk-rock crossover musicians. Glasgow-born **Bert Jansch** launched folk super-group Pentangle with Jacqui McShee, John Renbourn and Danny Thompson, and the flute-playing **Ian Anderson** found rock success with Jethro Tull. Meanwhile, a more traditional Scottish sound was promoted by the likes of **Archie**, **Ray** and **Cilla Fisher**, who sang new and traditional ballads, individually and together.

The great figure, however, along with MacColl, was the singer and guitarist **Dick Gaughan**, whose passionate artistry towers like a colossus above three decades. He started out in the Edinburgh folk club scene with an impenetrable accent, a deep belief in the socialist commitment of traditional song, and a guitar technique that had old masters of the art hanging on to the edge of their seats. For a couple of years in the early 1970s, he played with Aly Bain in The Boys of the Lough, knocking out fiery versions of trad Celtic material. Gaughan became frustrated, however, by the limitations of a primarily instrumental (and fiddle-dominated) group and subsequently formed **Five Hand Reel**. Again playing Scots-Irish traditional material, they might have been the greatest folk-rock band of them all if they hadn't just missed the Fairport/Steeleye Span boat.

Leaving to pursue an independent career, Gaughan became a fixture on the folk circuit and made a series of albums exploring Scots and Irish traditional music and re-interpreting the material for guitar. His **Handful of Earth** (1981) was perhaps the single best solo folk album of the decade, a record of stunning intensity with enough contemporary relevance and historical belief to grip all generations of music fans. And though sparing in his output, and modest about his value in the genre, he's also become one of the best songwriters of his generation.

Crucial contributions to folk song came, too, from two giants of the Scottish folk scene who were probably more appreciated throughout Europe than at home – the late **Hamish Imlach** and **Alex Campbell** – and from **song collectors** and academics such as **Norman Buchan**, with his hugely influential songbook, *101 Scottish Songs*, and **Peter Hall**, with *The Scottish Folksinger*.

GAELIC ROCKING AND FUSIONS

Scottish music took an unexpected twist in 1978 with the low-key release of an album called **Play Gaelic**. It was made by a little-known ceilidh group called **Runrig**, who took their name from the old Scottish oil field system of agriculture, and worked primarily in the backwaters of the Highlands and Islands. The thing, though, that stopped people in their tracks was the fact that they were writing original material in Gaelic. This was the first time any serious Scottish working band had achieved any sort of attention with Gaelic material, although Ossian were touching on it around a similar time, as were Nah-Oganaich.

Runrig have since marched on to unprecedented heights, appearing in front of rock audiences at concert halls around the world where only a partial proportion of the audience are jocks in exile. Their Gaelic input is marginal these days, but they started a whole new ball rolling, chipping away at prejudices, adopting accordions and bagpipes, ever sharper arrangements, electric instruments, full-blown rock styles, surviving the inevitable personnel changes and the continuous carping of critics accusing them of selling out with every new market conquered. They even made a concept album, *Recovery*, which related the history of the Gael in one collection, provoking unprecedented interest in the Gaelic language after years of it being regarded in Scotland as moribund and defunct.

Of course, not everyone applauds. Critics point out that many singers using the language are not native Gaelic speakers and only learn the words phonetically, while further controversy has been caused by the "sampling" of archive recordings for use in backing tracks. For many people these songs are important and personal, and in the case of some of the religious singing, they felt very strongly that this use was in bad taste.

Nonetheless, the popularity of Gaelic roots bands undeniably paved the way for "purer" Scots musicians and singers: clarsach player

CEILIDHS, FESTIVALS AND CONTACTS

Scottish dances thrived for years under the auspices of the RSCDS, the Royal Scottish County Dance Society. Their events tended to be fairly formal, with dancers who were largely skilled, but in the 1970s and 1980s more and more Scottish dances, or ceilidhs, adopted the (English barn dance) practice of a "caller" to call out the moves. Nowadays there are two types of traditional dance events: **ceilidh** dances, usually with a caller and perhaps a more folky band, and **Scottish Country Dances**, usually with a more traditional Scottish dance band line-up and an expectation that the dancers will know the dance forms.

Scottish **music festivals** range from the Celtic Connections Festival (January at The Glasgow Royal Concert Hall) where you can catch many of the top names in the Celtic music world in a comfortable concert setting, to lots of smaller festivals which offer a mix of concert, ceilidh and informal sessions. In recent years there has been an increase in the number of festivals where teaching takes a central role. Many of these are in the Highlands and Islands where the Feisean movement has introduced thousands of people to traditional music-making.

Scottish bands such as Capercaillie and Runrig feed the notion that folk music can be exciting, electric and diverse, without losing sight of its roots. However, the survival of traditional music depends on support from young players: they need to play it,

listen to it, and take it forward. In Scotland, change is coming from a grass-roots **Feisean Movement** (*feis* is Gaelic for festival). These festivals, held during summer months and school holidays, involve children receiving tuition in traditional music, drama, art, dance and Gaelic singing, with evening gigs in local venues. The teachers (and performers) are often leading musicians.

The idea began on the island of Barra, in the southern Hebrides, in 1981 and has spread to many parts of the Highlands and Islands. Its results have been remarkable. Beginners on the fiddle, clarsach, guitar, tin whistle or accordion have now begun to form bands and teach others. And the sheer numbers of young people coming through the Feis throughout the Highlands has resulted in more and more communities holding workshops and ceilidhs. In small communities there are great economic spin-offs for instrument makers, music shops and for teachers of traditional music.

Tuition projects have not been limited to the Highlands. In Edinburgh, Stan Reeves has made remarkable progress with the **Scots Music Group** within The Adult Learning Project, leading to several hundred people learning traditional instruments and an annual festival of fiddle music. In Glasgow, the **Glasgow Fiddle Workshop**, under the guidance of Ian Fraser, has made similar progress and is starting to widen its brief beyond fiddle tuition.

CONTACTS

Adult Learning Project/Scots Music Group 184 Dalry Road, Edinburgh, EH11 2EP (☎ 0131/337 5442, fax 337 9316).

Feisean Nan Gaidheal Nicolson House, Somerled Square, Portree, Isle of Skye IV51 9EJ (☎01478/613355, fax 613399).

The Living Tradition PO Box 1026, Kilmarnock, Ayrshire KA2 0LG (☎ 01563 571220, *living.tradition @almac.co.uk*). A traditional music magazine pub-

lished from Ayrshire. It covers music from Britain and Ireland, with a focus, obviously, on Scotland. They also run a mail order service for traditional recordings.

The Piping Centre 32 McPhater St, Glasgow (☎ 0141 353 0220, fax 353 1570). The place to visit for anybody with an interest in piping. They have an exhibition, a teaching programme, concert space, café and even a hotel.

Alison Kinnaird, for instance; singers **Savourna Stevenson**, **Christine Primrose**, **Flora McNeill**, **Cathy-Ann MacPhee**, **Heather Heywood**, and **Jock Duncan**; and the **Wrigley sisters** from Orkney – who started out as teenagers playing traditional music with technical accomplishment and attitude and are now the core of the band **Seelyhoo**.

And among the ranks of the roots or fusion bands, each with their own agendas and styles,

have passed many – perhaps most – of Scotland's finest contemporary musicians. **Silly Wizard**, especially, featured a singer of cutting quality in **Andy M. Stewart** (and did he need that M.), while **Phil and Johnny Cunningham** have gone on to display a pioneering zeal in their efforts to use their skills on accordion and fiddle to knit Scottish traditional music with other cultures.

Mouth Music, too, were innovative: a Scots-origin (but recently Canadian) duo of

Martin Swan and Talitha MacKenzie, who mixed Gaelic vocals (including the traditional "mouth music" techniques of sung rhythms) with African percussion and dance sounds. Talitha MacKenzie later went solo, radically transforming traditional Scottish songs, which she clears from the dust of folklore with wonderful multitracked vocals and the characteristic Mouth Music African rhythms.

Another development was the fusion of traditional music and **jazz** by bands such as **The Easy Club** and the duo of piper **Hamish Moore** and jazz saxophonist **Dick Lee**. Moore has since come full circle, now taking his inspiration from a parallel Scottish culture which has developed in **Cape Breton**. Scottish interest in Cape Breton music has also led to the more or less lost tradition of Scottish step dancing being reintroduced.

At the beginning of the new century, however, the two most interesting Scottish roots groups are surely **Capercaillie** and Shooglenifty. The former, based on the arrangements of **Manus Lunny** and the gorgeous singing of **Karen Mattheson**, rose from Argyll pub sessions to flirt with mass commercial appeal, reworking Gaelic and traditional songs from the West Highlands. **Shooglenifty** meanwhile captured the imagination of a new audience with a style they described with their tongues in their cheeks as "acid croft".

DISCOGRAPHY

In addition to the discs reviewed below, see the box overleaf for details of the remarkable Scottish Tradition Series of CDs and cassettes. For more information, check out the "Scottish Music Links" at *www.netreal.co.uk* – a wonderful site with links to many label and artist pages.

GENERAL COMPILATIONS

The Caledonian Companion (Greentrax, Scotland). A 1975 live recording of four of Scotland's most respected northeast musicians – Alex Green, Willie Fraser, Charlie Bremner and John Grant – featuring solo fiddle, mouthorgan, whistle and diddling.

The Rough Guide to Scottish Music (World Music Network, UK). A terrific compilation, this is strongest on the new roots bands – with good selections from Battlefield Band, Capercaillie and Wolfstone, among others – but it also

delves into folk (Dick Gaughan) and traditional singing (Catherine-Ann McPhee, Heather Heyward).

The Nineties Collection (Greentrax, Scotland). Sixteen artists, including four pipers and well-known names such as Aly Bain and Phil Cunningham play all-new tunes in a traditional style. Also available is a companion book containing over 200 tunes (Canongate Books, Scotland).

TRADITIONAL SINGERS

Jock Duncan Duncan is an authentic bothy ballad singer from Pitlochry who gets to the heart of any song. He made his recording debut aged seventy on the album below, backed by musicians including his son, the piper Gordon Duncan.

Ye Shine Whar Ye Stan' (Springthyme, Scotland). Some of the traditional singing on this album is truly remarkable and the production from Battlefield Band founder Brian McNeill is impressive, too, creating an atmosphere that only falls a little short of the experience of a live performance.

Heather Heywood Heywood, from Ayrshire, is reckoned by many Scotland's foremost traditional singer of her generation. She performs largely core Scottish ballads and songs.

By Yon Castle Wa' (Greentrax, Scotland). A 1993 disc of epic ballads and contemporary songs, produced by Battlefield Band founder Brian McNeill. Heywood's forte is traditional song which she usually sings *a cappella*. McNeill makes the album accessible, without compromising the basic style, with the addition of accompaniment, including pipes – something which is difficult to do in live performance. This was a landmark recording in the traditional area.

Catherine-Ann MacPhee
Catherine-Ann MacPhee, from Barra, has a warm yet strong voice and her Gaelic has the soft pronunciation of the southern islands of the Outer Hebrides.

Canan Nan Gaidheal (*The Language of the Gael*; Greentrax, Scotland). This superb 1980s recording, re-released on CD, shows mature traditional singing from one of the best of the current generation of Gaelic singers.

Gordeanna McCulloch
The lead singer of seminal 1960s band, The Clutha, Gordeanna McCulloch is another of the

THE SCOTTISH TRADITIONS SERIES

Scottish traditional music – in its deepest, darkest manifestations – has been superbly documented in a series of archive recordings produced by Peter Cooke and others at Edinburgh University's School of Scottish Studies. The highlights of this collection have found their way onto a series of a couple of dozen cassettes and/or CDs, which, if you're seriously interested in the roots of many of the musicians covered in this article, are nothing less than a treasure trove.

The first volume in the series, **Bothy Ballads**, is one of the most important and fascinating. These narrative songs were composed, sung and passed around the unmarried farmworkers accommodated in bothies or outhouses in late-Victorian and Edwardian days. The songs were often comic or satirical, such as warnings about skinflint farmers to be avoided at the hiring markets. Under the bothy system, workers would move on from farm to farm after six-month "fees", so the songs were in constant circulation and re-invention. They include some gorgeous ballads and instrumentals.

Music from the Western Isles (Volume 2) is another intriguing disc: **Gaelic songs** recorded in the Hebrides, including some great examples of "**mouth music**", the vocal dance music where sung rhythms are employed to take the place of instruments. There are *pibroch* songs on this disc, too – the vocal equivalent of the pipers' airs and laments. On Volume 3, *Waulking Songs from Barra*, you enter another extraordinary domain,

that of Gaelic **washing songs**, thumped out by women to the rhythms of their cloth pounding. If you were played this blind, you could imagine yourself to be thousands of miles from Scotland. More amazing vocal traditions are unleashed on Volume 6, *Gaelic Psalms from Barra*, with their slow, fractured unison singing.

An equally compelling vocal tradition is that of the Scottish **Travelling Singers**, showcased on Volume 5, *The Muckle Sangs*. This is a delight, including virtually all the greats, Jeannie Robertson, Lizzie Higgins and the Stewarts of Blairgowrie among them.

Fiddle music is also outstandingly represented in the series, with several volumes devoted to the art. Volume 4, *Shetland Fiddle Music*, features classic players such as Tom Anderson and George Sutherland, who were to exert such influence on the likes of Aly Bain and Catriona MacDonald. Volume 9, *The Fiddler and His Art*, is a fine overall compilation, showing the different styles prevalent around the country.

Finally, as you'd expect, the Scottish Tradition has recordings of some of the finest **pibroch pipers**, among them George Moss (volume 15), and pipe majors William MacLean, Robert Brown and R.B. Nicol (volumes 10, 11 and 12).

The Scottish Tradition Series recordings are available on CD and cassette from the Scottish label Greentrax (Cockenzie Business Centre, Edinburgh Rd, Cockenzie, East Lothian EH32 0HL; ☎01875/814155).

great voices of the Scottish Folk revival.
In Freenship's Name (Greentrax, Scotland). Gordeanna's voice is a strong, sweet and flexible instrument, capable of a variety of tones. Here, she is at home among some great Scots songs, all traditional, bar one, and backed by some of Scotland's top musicians.

Jim Reid

With Arbroath's Foundry Bar band, Jim Reid was for many years a well-known face at festivals and ceilidhs throughout Scotland. One of the country's finest singers.
I Saw the Wild Geese Flee (Springthyme, Scotland). A selection of songs ranging from his own compositions to traditional ballads. Just Jim's version of *I Saw the Wild Geese Flee* makes this re-issued album a classic.

Margaret Stewart and Allan MacDonald

Lewis-born Margaret Stewart is a talented

Gaelic singer; Allan MacDonald is one of the famous piping family from Glenuig – his brother was the piper with Ossian and Battlefield Band. *Fhuair Mi Pog* (Greentrax, Scotland). This is a fascinating CD of music and Gaelic song that works as terrific entertainment; lovely singing and great tunes, some of the best written by Allan himself.

Jane Turriff

Jane Turriff is a legendary song carrier. Born into the Aberdeenshire Stewart family in 1915, she grew up in a travelling family.
Singin is Ma Life (Springthyme, Scotland). A must for anyone interested in traditional song style. Content ranges from the "big" ballads such as *Dowie Dens of Yarrow* through to the classic C&W song *Empty Saddles*.

Sheena Wellington

Broadcaster and radio presenter, Sheena

Wellington is Fife Council's Traditional Arts development officer and one of Scotland's leading traditional singers.

Strong Women (Greentrax, Scotland). A live recording showing off what Sheena does best: communicating traditional song to an audience.

Mick West

Well-known as a session singer, West is now rated at home and abroad as one of the country's finest traditional singers.

Fine Flowers & Foolish Glances (KRL, Scotland). One of the most successful albums using jazz musicians with a strong traditional singer. It may prove to be a classic.

INSTRUMENTALISTS

Aly Bain

Shetland-born Aly Bain (see box on p.655) is one of the great movers in Scottish music's revival, through his band Boys of the Lough (see p.655), and a panoply of solo and collaborative ventures.

Aly Bain and Friends (Greentrax, Scotland). One of the bestselling Scottish albums of modern times, compiled from a TV series Bain produced on traditional Scottish music. The friends include Boys of the Lough, Capercaillie, Hamish Moore and Dick Lee, and zydeco star Queen Ida and her Bonne Temps band.

TOM ANDERSON AND ALY BAIN

The Silver Bow: The Fiddle Music of Shetland (Topic, UK). This collection of Shetland fiddle tunes was notable for bringing together Bain with his old teacher, Tom Anderson. They played both individually and together on the album and the effect is never less than enthralling.

WITH PHIL CUNNINGHAM

The Pearl (Whirlie, Scotland). Bain teams up with Scotland's finest accordion player for some fabulous tunes, from slow airs to Shetland reels, reflecting the incredible range of styles which this duo have mastered. Phil composed almost half of the tracks and he plays five of the six instruments featured.

John Burgess

The century's greatest exponent of traditional bagpipes.

King of the Highland Pipers (Topic, UK). The maestro demonstrates his art to devastating effect through *piobaireachd*, strathspeys, hornpipes, reels and marches. Not for the fainthearted!

Pete Clarke

A great fiddle player whose skills with slow air

playing also makes him in great demand as a song accompanist.

Fiddle Case (Smiddymade, Scotland). An hour of top-notch traditional music – not all Scottish fiddle though – there are tunes from Europe and the US and even a couple of songs. There's a classical feel to some of the pieces which works well, with cello and flute parts.

Gordon Duncan

Gordon Duncan, the son of bothy singer Jock, is one of Scotland's younger generation of pipers who is stretching the boundaries with some breathtaking solo piping.

The Circular Breath (Greentrax, Scotland). As well as performing on the Great Highland Bagpipe, Gordon plays the practice chanter and low whistle. He is joined by banjo-player Gerry O'Connor, Ian Carr on guitar, Ronald MacArthur on bass guitar, Jim Sutherland playing clay pots and Andy Cook on Ugandan harp.

Alasdair Fraser

A master fiddler, renowned for his slow airs and now for his leading of The Skyedance Band, whose members provided music for the film *Braveheart*.

Dawn Dance (Culburnie, Scotland). An album of completely self-penned tunes in the traditional style which bounces along, defying you to sit still while you listen. Fraser has a rare clarity of playing, without sacrificing the feel and enthusiasm essential to traditional music.

Mac-Talla

In 1994 this "Gaelic supergroup" made a small number of concert appearances and one spectacular recording before settling back into their own individual paths having "made the statement". Mac-Talla's members included singers Arthur Cormack, Christine Primrose and Eilidh MacKenzie plus Alison Kinnaird on clarsach, and ex-Runrig musician Blair Douglas.

Mairidh Gaol is Ceol (Temple, Scotland). Glorious harmony and solo singing, accordion and harp – you can hear the spirit even if you don't understand the language.

Willie Hunter and Violet Tulloch

Willie Hunter was one of the all-time greats of the Shetland fiddle and Violet Tulloch is one of Shetland's leading piano accompanists.

The Willie Hunter Sessions (Greentrax, Scotland). A set of recordings made over several years including Scots and Shetland strathspeys, reels and slow airs. "Traditional chamber music" of the highest order.

William Jackson

Billy Jackson is one of Scotland's best-known traditional composers. He wrote some – and arranged most – of the music for folk band Ossian, and now works solo.

Inchcolm (Linn Records, Scotland). This album brings Billy's harp playing to centre stage. It is a collection of largely unrelated tracks with some orchestral interludes and forays into Early and Eastern musics.

Hamish Moore

One of Scotland's finest contemporary pipers, Hamish Moore plays Border pipes, Scottish Small pipes and the great Highland Bagpipe.

Stepping on the Bridge (Greentrax, Scotland). Inspired by the Scottish culture he discovered in Cape Breton, Moore plays Scottish pipes with Cape Breton accompanists to produce a lively glimpse of what piping may have been like before it became regimented.

Iain McLachlan

Iain McLachlan is a well-known and respected accordion player who also plays fiddle and melodeon.

An Island Heritage (Springthyme, Scotland). From the writer of *The Dark Island*, real traditional music from the Western Isles played on accordion, fiddle, melodeon and pipes.

Scott Skinner

Skinner was a legendary, Victorian era fiddler – formidably kilted and moustachioed.

Music Of Scott Skinner (Topic, UK). An essential roots album, featuring rare and authentic recordings by the elusive genius of the fiddle – and the weird strathspey style in particular – dating from 1908. Some of the quality is understandably distorted, though the collection is supplemented by modern interpretations by Bill Hardie.

"NEW ROOTS" GROUPS

Battlefield Band

The Battlefield Band have been one of the enduring top groups of the last thirty years. Evolving line-up changes have kept a continued freshness, with the constant being skilled musicianship and excellent songwriting.

Rain, Hail or Shine (Temple, Scotland). All the Battlefield Band trademarks are here in force – distinctive keyboard playing, well-chosen pipe tunes, guitar and bouzouki injecting excitement and tension, fine singing – and John McCusker's sharp fiddle-playing is a joy throughout.

Boys of the Lough

With the virtuoso talents of Shetland fiddler Aly Bain and singer/flautist Cathal McConnell at the heart of the band, The Boys have been a benchmark of taste for thirty years.

The Boys of the Lough (Shanachie, US). This was the group's 1973 debut – and remains one of their strongest sets, powered by contributions from Dick Gaughan and piper Robin Morton.

The Day Dawn (Lough Records, Scotland). Quality, taste, superb singing and the relaxed easy style that comes from skilled musicians with years of experience. Along with the concertina and mandola of Dave Richardson, Aly on fiddle and Cathal on flute, whistle and vocals, this album features singer and *uillean* piper Christy O'Leary.

Capercaillie

The hugely influential and successful Capercaillie have taken Gaelic music to a worldwide audience in a modern contemporary style from a traditional base. They have in Karen Mattheson one of the best singers around today.

Beautiful Wasteland (Survival Records, Scotland/GreenLinnet, US). Flute, whistle and *uillean* pipes pop up all over the place and a whole host of things are happening with fiddles, bouzoukis, keyboards and percussion, too.

Ceolbeg

Ceolbeg were not a full-time band but produced some of the finest albums of the genre, featuring some fabulous songs from their singer, Davy Steele.

An Unfair Dance (Greentrax, Scotland). An impressive collection of tunes played on a huge variety of instruments, with a great sense of light and shade.

Deaf Shepherd

Following in the footsteps of the Battlefield Band, Deaf Shepherd are a passionate 1990s band, rooted in the Scottish tradition, and getting more skilled all the time.

Synergy (Greentrax, Scotland). A really varied album, including traditional and new material, and jumps from reels to jigs and back, involving vigorous fiddle playing and powerful bouzouki. Poignant guitar, fiddle and whistle countermelodies blend smoothly with the vocals.

The Easy Club

An admirably ambitious and sadly underrated group, the Easy Club took the baton from the

more thoughtful Scots bands of the 1970s and ran with it at a pace, injecting traditional rhythms with a jazz sense.
Essential (Eclectic, Scotland). Essential it is. MacColl's *First Time Ever I Saw Your Face* never sounded like this before.

Mouth Music

Gaelic nonsense songs – *puirt-a-beul* – met ambient dance, funk keyboards and African sampling in Talitha MacKenzie and Martin Swan's Mouth Music.
Mouth Music (Cooking Vinyl, UK). Talitha MacKenzie has gone on to a solo career but this first Mouth Music disc remains her finest hour – one of the best Celtic fusions committed to disc, featuring stunning rhythms, funk, Gaelic sea shanties and *puirt-a-beul*.

Ossian

This groundbreaking band, formed in the mid-1970s, have recently reformed with a new line-up featuring Iain MacInnes on pipes and Stuart Morison on fiddle alongside founder members Billy Jackson on harp and Billy Ross on guitar and dulcimer.
The Carrying Stream (Greentrax, Scotland). A fine album, signalling the welcome return of Ossian's quintessentially Scottish sound. This is a collection of terrific tunes – first rate jigs and reels, both traditional and contemporary, blended with songs in English, Scots and Gaelic.

Runrig

This band of Gaelic rock pioneers were formed in North Uist, Outer Hebrides in 1973 by brothers Rory (bass/vocals) and Calum MacDonald (drums/vocals), with singer Donnie Munro joining the following year. They worked their way up, over fifteen years, from ceilidhs to stadiums, going Top 10 in the UK charts in 1991. They are perhaps at their very best live, with memorable tunes and vocals and well-honed, subtle musicianship.
Alba (Pinnacle, UK). An excellent "best of" compilation of this most dynamic Gaelic band.

Seelyhoo

The Wrigley sisters from Orkney have made their own statement with their own recordings. On this album they are joined by several other musicians in a band which came out of the Edinburgh session scene.
Leetera (Greentrax, Scotland). A really fresh approach to traditional tunes and Gaelic song using fiddle, guitar, bass guitar, accordion,

whistle, keyboard and percussion. Vibrant music from some of Scotland's young rising stars.

Shooglenifty

Shooglenifty are a brilliant, innovative band who have made their mark well beyond the Scottish roots scene with their grafting of Scottish trad motifs and club culture trance-dance. Live, they are unstoppable.
A Whisky Kiss (Greentrax, Scotland). The album that coined the term "acid croft", with elements of traditional music and house. A sound here, a strange sound there, a sequence played in an odd way. There's nothing else like it.

Silly Wizard

Silly Wizard were a key roots band, featuring Andy M. Stewart (vocals, bouzouki, guitar), Phil (accordion, etc) and Johnny Cunningham (fiddle). Their albums are full of fresh, lively takes on the whole traditional repertoire.
Live Wizardry (Green Linnet, US). The band at their zenith in 1988, playing traditional and self-composed dance tunes and narrative ballads.

Andy M. Stewart, Phil Cunningham and Manus Lunny

Fire In The Glen (Shanachie, US). Two former members of Silly Wizard combine with an Irishman in a formidable celebration of Scottish traditional music. Phil Cunningham's brilliance as an accordion player is demonstrated on any number of albums, but it's especially impressive placed against the wonderful, wonderful singing of Andy M. Stewart.

The Whistlebinkies

One of the founding folk groups in Scotland – often dubbed the "Scottish Chieftains" – the Binkies are still playing music with a difference.
A Wanton Fling (Greentrax, Scotland). An album that has all the freshness of early Whistlebinkies recordings – a combination of lowland pipes, clarsach, flute, concertina and fiddle.

Wolfstone

Wolfstone play folk-rock from the Highlands – "stadium rock meets village-hall ceilidh" said one reviewer – full of passion and fire.
The Half Tail (Green Linnet, Scotland). This is a more subdued progressive sound than usual for Wolfstone, featuring amongst other tracks, a classic whaling song *Bonnie Ship the Diamond*, *The Last Leviathan* and catchy instrumental sets.

FOLK SINGER-SONGWRITERS
Eric Bogle
Bogle emigrated from Scotland to work in Australia as an accountant but when he returned home he was hailed for writing one of the great modern folk songs, *The Band Played Waltzing Matilda*.

Something of Value (Sonet, UK/Philo, US). Bogle's singing doesn't quite match his songwriting, but he has all-star support. Includes the number above.

Archie and Cilla Fisher
The Fisher family – Archie, Ray and Cilla – were mainstays of the 1960s/70s Scottish folk club scene, reviving old ballads and creating new ones.

ARCHIE FISHER

The Man With A Rhyme (Folk Legacy, US). Archie's finest hour – fourteen tracks from 1976 with the Fisher voice and guitar backed by concertina, banjo, dulcimers, cello, fiddle and flute.

CILLA FISHER AND ARTIE TREZISE

Cilla and Artie (Greentrax, Scotland). Released in 1979, this still retains an ease and freshness – and Cilla's imperious rendition of the late Stan Rogers' *The Jeannie C* is in itself worth the acquisition.

Dick Gaughan
Singer/guitarist/songwriter, Gaughan is one of the most charismatic Scottish performers – an artist who can make you laugh, cry and explode with anger with every twist and nuance of delivery. His new material is still up there with his classic albums of the 1980s.

Handful of Earth (Sonet, UK/Philo, US). This is the Gaughan classic: a majestic album of traditional and modern songs, still formidable a decade on. When *Folk Roots* magazine asked its readers to nominate the album of the 1980s, it won by a street – and deservedly so.

Robin Laing
Robin Laing is one of the best songwriters and performers to emerge out of the Scottish folk scene in the 1990s.

Walking In Time (Greentrax, Scotland). Includes four re-workings of traditional songs, three by other writers and seven of Laing's own songs, accompanied by his own Spanish guitar.

Producer Brian McNeill's multi-instrumental talents are also in evidence on most of the tracks.

Ewan MacColl
MacColl was, simply, one of the all-time greats of British folk song.

In Black and White (Cooking Vinyl, UK/Green Linnet, US). This posthumous compilation, lovingly compiled by his family, showcases MacColl's superb technique as a singer, his gift for choruses (*Dirty Old Town*), his colourful observation as a lyricist (*The Driver's Song*), and his raging sense of injustice (*Black And White*), written after the Sharpeville Massacre of 1963. A fitting epitaph.

Dougie MacLean
One-time member of The Tannahill Weavers, Dougie MacLean is now carving out a successful solo career as a singer-songwriter.

The Dougie MacLean Collection (Putumayo, US). A good selection from Dougie's extensive recorded output including perhaps his most famous song, *Caledonia*.

Adam McNaughtan
Adam McNaughtan has written many songs rich in Glasgow wit including one which has travelled the world, *Oor Hamlet*, a condensed version of Shakespeare's *Hamlet* to the tune of *The Mason's Apron*. He has a deep understanding of the tradition and is one of Scotland's national treasures.

Last Stand At Mount Florida (Greentrax, Scotland). Adam's comic songs are masterpieces and here he is in excellent voice, accompanied by fellow Stramash members – Finlay Allison, Bob Blair and John Eaglesham.

Brian McNeill
A man of amazing talents, the one time fiddling founder of the Battlefield Band is a multi-instrumentalist and a songwriter of some substance.

No Gods (Greentrax, Scotland). An album showing the broadening of McNeill's writing talent both in song and tunes. He is joined by ten backing musicians including masterful guitarist Tony MacManus.

by Pete Heywood and Colin Irwin
(Taken from the *Rough Guide to World Music*)

SCOTTISH ROCK, POP AND DANCE

Over the last fifty years, **Scottish rock** has tossed out seminal acts, global success stories, overlooked hopefuls and over-rated hype, in equal measure. Yet as late as the end of the 1970s, commercial success was very much dependent upon the London marketing scene – that is until, in the DIY spirit fomented by punk, a small independent record label, **Postcard**, was set up in Glasgow, a hotbed of burgeoning rock talent. The label was to have a crucial and long-lasting effect on the Scottish music industry. Starting out by signing up virtually unknown acts such as Aztec Camera and Orange Juice, the nationwide popularity of these bands gave other independent Scottish labels and bands the confidence to challenge international markets.

THE BEST OF TIMES, THE WORST OF TIMES

Ironically, the first "rock" star from Scotland was the first of many who would come to be regarded as inherently British, rather than Scottish. In the 1950s, London-based Glaswegian **Lonnie Donegan** gave the world his hugely influential new style of **skiffle** (his version of US blues and country). The UK loved it, and his single *Rock Island Line* (1955) sold three million copies within six months. It was also a hit in the States (quite a feat for the time), but it was British teenagers who sat up, listened and learned – not least The Quarrymen, led by one John Lennon.

It wasn't until the mid-1960s, long after skiffle had merged into a peculiarly British brand of rock'n'roll (which then mutated into rock), that more serious chart action from Scottish talent would be seen. As the "British Invasion" of the US steamed ahead, **folk** singer-songwriter **Donovan** (born in Glasgow, raised mostly in Hertfordshire) rolled with the times with *Catch The Wind* (1965), which saw him labelled as Dylan-lite (it was released at the same time as *The Times They Are A-Changin*). He subsequently scooted through styles and their attendant dress codes, from folk to pop, from flower power to rock – always lagging, it seemed, slightly behind the creative leaders. Elsewhere the folk influence also held sway, though with increasingly untraditional results, as Glaswegian **The Incredible String Band** (see p.657) began fusing multi-ethnic styles, blues and psychedelia, the results of which produced their classic album *The Hangman's Beautiful Daughter* (1968). And in 1967, down in London, Edinburgh-born **Ian Anderson** began his career as the charismatic frontman for the mighty Jethro Tull (see p.657).

At the close of the 1960s, **Gerry Rafferty** and the folky **Humblebums**, who also numbered future comedian Billy Connolly, were having little impact. When the band split, Rafferty relocated to London and formed **Stealer's Wheel**; if the glorious pop-folk of *Stuck In The Middle With You* (1973) failed to reserve a place in the public consciousness as the decades passed, then Quentin Tarantino's use of it in *Reservoir Dogs* made sure it wouldn't be forgotten by a 1990s audience. The group's success petered out, but in 1978 Rafferty's solo *Baker Street* – either classic **MOR** sheen or banal dirge according to taste – imprinted its mournful sax riff upon pop history, and the album *City to City* (1978) went platinum in the States. Wildly contrasting in style, 1975's *Pick Up The Pieces* was the **Average White Band** pumping out tightly played **funk** to an appreciative, loosened-up audience, and in 1974, a bunch of Glaswegian ex-pats in Australia formed the hard rock/**heavy metal** beast **AC/DC** that would spawn *Back In Black* (1980).

The 1970s also saw phenomenal success for the scourge of every serious musician, the **teeny-bop** band. Between 1974 and 1976, Edinburgh's tartan-sporting pin-ups the **Bay City Rollers** inspired besotted victims to scream at them loudly and buy enough records to give them nine Top 10 hits. And this despite the songs including a surfeit of covers and the band's admittance that they hadn't played on some tracks. Thankfully, for non-fans, they went abroad to crack the US market, at which point home interest began to wane and the posters began to come down from countless bedroom walls.

SALVAGING THE SEVENTIES

It was, of course, partly the corpse of such perceived musical bad taste that **punk** came to pogo up and down upon. Of Scotland's very own clenched-fist malcontents, Glasgow's **Johnny and the Self Abusers** would split on the release of their first single. Slightly longer-term shoutiness was provided by Dunfermline's **The Skids**, whose anthemic top-ten *Into The Valley* (1979) posited the group as musical warriors in full charge, an image that slotted in neatly beside the urban guerrilla approach of punk rockers south of the border. And in London itself, new wave group **The Tourists**, with vocals from Aberdeen's Annie Lennox, enjoyed a couple of hits before disbanding in 1980. Although short lived, all three groups were nurturing 1980s rock stars – members of Simple Minds, Big Country and the Eurythmics respectively.

Continued overleaf

SCOTTISH ROCK, POP AND DANCE (continued)

Arty post-punkers **Simple Minds** discovered grandiose synth-driven **rock** with *Once Upon A Time* (1985), typifying both the best and worst of 1980s stadium rock. Tellingly, their only US single to chart well was *Don't You (Forget About Me)* (1985), the decade's ultimate arena singalong. **Big Country's** debut album *The Crossing* (1983) boasted a soaring swirl of Celtic guitars, which proved popular both in the UK and the US; their second, *Steeltown* (1984), was bleaker but notable for dealing with Scottish economic and industrial decline. The **Eurythmics** got off to a shaky start, but in 1983 their startling image was adorning many an MTV screen as the pop-video generation embraced *Sweet Dreams (Are Made Of This)*. By 1990 they'd split, with **Annie Lennox** going on to enjoy solo success, though they reformed in 1999.

A KICK UP THE EIGHTIES
While Simple Minds et al had been busy imploding and then resurrecting themselves as rock, Glasgow's independent Postcard label had kick-started a Scottish **pop** revolution. **Orange Juice's** clean, soulful music reached its greatest audience with the finger-clicking *Rip It Up* (1982), and singer-songwriter **Edwyn Collins** maintains an intermittent career as both producer and solo artist (the resonant, 1950s-inflected *A Girl Like You* was a worldwide hit in 1995). Postcard also discovered the **Bluebells** (who included Lonnie Donnegan's son), whose breezy *Young At Heart* charted in 1980 and 1993, and a fifteen-year-old **Roddy Frame**, whose group **Aztec Camera** later achieved success with the acoustic pop of the sublime singles *Oblivious* (1982) and *Somewhere In My Heart* (1988); like Collins, Frame continues to produce solo material.

Complimenting this poppy exuberance, rather more sedate American influences were evident in the underrated **Love And Money**, who doled out a few biting lyrics plus the neglected torch-song *You're Beautiful*, and also in **Hipsway**, who scored on both sides of the Atlantic with *The Honey Thief* (1986). **Wet Wet Wet's** *Wishing I Was Lucky* (1987), was superb recession pop mixed with blue-eyed soul; subsequent material was somewhat restrained and slicker – terminally so for some tastes – and the hits continued, though in 1999 singer Marti Pellow left the band. Slide-guitar slithered all over **Texas'** hit *I Don't Want A Lover* (1989), after which things went quiet until the stylistic magpie of an album that was *White On Blonde* (1997) hauled them onto the

international stage. Less successful in the long term were Dundee boys **Danny Wilson**, who briefly tickled the top thirty with *Mary's Prayer* (1987) but reserved their best for *Second Summer of Love* (1989), a pithy ditty about acid house culture, and if you wanted political lyrics sung in a broad Scots accent, **The Proclaimers** briefly provided, strumming their way through the hugely enjoyable *Sunshine On Leith* (1986). A more consistent presence has been maintained by **Del Amitri** (and their sideburns) who announced their trad-rock blueprint with *Waking Hours* in 1990.

More original were Glasgow's rather mournful **Blue Nile**, who have thus far produced three shimmering albums at a snail's pace: *A Walk Across The Rooftops* (1984), *Hats* (1989) and *Peace At Last* (1996). While the critics continue to lavish praise on the songs – effortless, minimalist paeans to love – the public mostly manage to ignore them. Following the success of *Sulk* (1982), a cult following was also to be the largest reward for Dundee's eclectic **Associates** and the solo work of frontman **Billy Mackenzie**; **The Silencers** too, whose second album *A Blues For Buddha* (1988) showcased a knack for cinematic tunes and hypnotic rhythms, managed to garner a small following. Greater commercial success eventually went to Edinburgh man **Mike Scott**, who gathered together the **Waterboys** in London in 1982 and began the quest for his Big Music, which resulted in some heartlifting singles like *The Whole of the Moon* (1985). Such lofty ambition was reduced in scope for the excellent *Fisherman's Blues* (1988), and his more acoustic solo work continues to delight.

Throughout the mainstream-dominated mid-1980s, the **alternative scene** was brewing a heady concoction that would have far-reaching effects. **The Jesus and Mary Chain's** rock'n'roll hedonism – sex, drugs, a truckload of biking imagery and antisocial volume levels – stomped into disaffected teenagers' record collections with the benchmark debut *Psychocandy* (1984), whose clanging feedback and West Coast melodies gave a pretty good impression of sonic claustrophobia. Memories of bubblegum and the Velvet Underground would also surface in **The Pastels**, who appeared on *NME's* seminal *C86* compilation, though they were never to scale the commercial heights of the Mary Chain. Similarly, Bathgate's **Goodbye Mr Mackenzie** featured a certain Shirley Manson on vocals, whose success with Garbage in the 1990s has rather eclipsed her former band's fine album *The*

Rattler (1986). For a while, however, it seemed that the Glasgow suburb of Bellshill was to be music's Mecca. From here came the closely related **The Vaselines**, **BMX Bandits**, and **Captain America** (who would become **Eugenius**), who between them produced several rough gems that would resurface in the grunge years when Kurt Cobain paid them homage, plus several band members for **Teenage Fanclub**, whose own *Bandwagonesque* (1991) is every bit as essential as Nirvana's *Nevermind*.

MUSIC FOR THE MILLENNIUM

Until the late 1980s, Scotland's most obvious contribution to **dance music** had been the hi-NRG disco of **Bronski Beat**, formed in London, whose album *Age of Consent* (1984), armed with the falsetto of Glaswegian **Jimmy Sommerville**, took on various gay issues, including homophobia. But as the house scene became difficult to ignore and the Ecstasy-fuelled dance-rock crossover of "Madchester" stormed the charts with a vengeance, Scottish outfits were present and correct. As the **JAMMS**, Jimmy Cauty and Bill Drummond had already hit disco paydirt with *Doctorin' The Tardis* (1988), but as **The KLF**, their 1990 "Stadium House Trilogy" brought the cash rolling in (£1 million of which they would later burn – literally – in an act of art-terrorism/publicity stunt). They were also a huge influence on ambient music when *Chill Out* (1990) became the scene's very own *Dark Side Of The Moon*, and when Jimmy Cauty co-founded **The Orb**. Initially an indie guitar band, **The Shamen** were to have clubbers chanting "E's are good" to the chorus of *Ebeneezer Goode* (1992), while the **Soup Dragons** adopted the Rolling Stones' *I'm Free* and gave it a baggy beat. And high above, **Primal Scream** (formed by Bobby Gillespie, ex-drummer for the Jesus And Mary Chain) floated around in

yet more Stonesy, chemical inspired dubbed-out bliss with the timeless *Screamadelica* (1989).

Scotland's own dance scene has since flowered to become one of the liveliest in Europe. Independent labels such as **Soma** – who signed French dance-groovers Daft Punk – **Bellboy Records** and **Hook Records** have all released top-quality dance tracks. DJs **Stuart MacMillan** and **Orde Meikle**, creators of Slam, perform globally, returning with world-class DJs to pack out Glasgow clubs. DJ **Howie B** helped break the boundaries of performance by mixing U2 live on their 1997 tour, while the camera-shy **Blue Boy** is a club favourite with his fantastic fusion of dance and funky soul, and the **Glasgow Underground** label ensures that deep house maintains a presence worthy of its influence. Edinburgh-raised **Finlay Quaye**'s laid-back and eternally summery *Maverick A Strike* (1997) mixes up reggae and dance-rock, for which he received a Brit award in 1998.

The indie tradition trundles on apace, with Glasgow once again apparently stuffed full of musos, many of them signed to guitar group **The Delgados**' label Chemikal Underground. If there's a particular theme to the moment, lo-fi might just about encapsulate the folk-tinged wispiness of **Belle and Sebastian**'s hushed tones, the minimalism of **Arab Strap** and the sonic experimentalism of noisniks **Mogwai**. But punk too continues to thrash about in various guises, from **Idlewild** to **Bis** (who made pop history in 1996 by being the first unsigned band to appear on *Top of the Pops*, as they squeaked out *Candy Pop*), and is funked up a little by **Urusei Yatsura**. And to prove that Scottish acts aren't just watching from the commercial sidelines, **Travis** have moved on from their early stomp-along glam-rockers to produce the best selling *The Man Who* (1999), brimming with tasteful angst.

BOOKS

Wherever a book is in print, the UK publisher is given first in each listing, separated, where applicable, from the US publisher by an oblique slash. Where books are published in only one of these countries we have specified which one; when the same company publishes the book in both, its name appears just once. Out of print titles are indicated as o/p – these should be easy to track down in secondhand bookshops.

FICTION

Iain Banks *The Bridge* (Abacus/HarperCollins); *Complicity* (Little, Brown/Bantam); *The Crow Road* (UK Abacus); *Espedair Street* (UK Abacus); *Song of Stone* (Little, Brown/Simon and Schuster); *The Wasp Factory* (Little, Brown/Simon and Schuster); *Whit* (UK Little, Brown). Just a few titles by this astonishingly prolific author, who also writes sci-fi as Iain M. Banks. His work can be funny, pacy, thought-provoking, imaginative and downright disgusting. It is never dull.

J.M. Barrie. Born and educated in Scotland, Barrie moved to London to work as a journalist. He wrote a series of short stories and other works set in Kirriemuir where he was born. He's best known, of course, for *Peter Pan*.

M.C. Beaton *Death of a Snob* (Transworld/Mysterious Press). Crime novels with Hamish Macbeth as the offbeat policeman in a small Highland town. Black comedy.

D. K. Broster *The Jacobite Trilogy* (UK Mandarin). Tear-jerking trilogy centred round the tribulations of the Jacobite supporters.

George Mackay Brown *Beside the Ocean of Time* (UK Flamingo). A child's journey through the history of an Orkney island, and an adult's effort to make sense of the place's secrets in the late twentieth century. *Magnus* (Canongate)

is his retelling of the death of St Magnus with parallels for modern times.

John Buchan *The Complete Richard Hannay* (Penguin/Godine). This single volume includes *The 39 Steps*, *Greenmantle*, *Mr Standfast*, *The Three Hostages* and *The Island of Sheep*. Good gung-ho stories with a great feel for Scottish landscape. In the US, both Oxford University Press and Godine publish various editions of the Hannay stories. Less well-known, but better, are Buchan's historical romances such as *Midwinter* (UK B&W Publishing), a Jacobite thriller, and *Witchwood* (Canongate), a tale of religious strife in the seventeenth century.

Isla Dewar *Women Talking Dirty* (UK Headline Review). Set in Edinburgh suburbia, the outrageous, funny and poignant soul-bearing of two women who become fast friends over a bottle of vodka and detailed post-match analysis. *Keeping up with Magda* (Review/Trafalgar Square) and *Giving up on Ordinary* (UK Headline Review) are in a similar style.

Dorothy Dunnett, *Caprice and Rondo* (Penguin/Vintage). Dunnett is a popular writer of crime novels and a series of historical novels, the first featuring a Scottish mercenary in the sixteenth century.

Christine Marion Fraser, *Kinvara* (UK Hodder & Stoughton). Glasgow-born Fraser's family sagas are set in the Hebrides and in Argyll; her latest novel is centred on a lighthouse keeper on the west coast of Scotland.

George MacDonald Fraser *The General Danced at Dawn* (Fontana/Acacia); *McAuslain in the Rough* (Fontana/HarperCollins); *The Sheikh and the Dustbin* (Fontana/HarperCollins). Touching and very funny collections of short stories detailing life in a Highland regiment after World War II.

Janice Galloway *The Trick is to Keep Breathing* (Minerva Dalkey Archive). The story of a woman's mind as she slowly spirals into madness. Almost unwittingly readers are drawn into the vortex and suddenly find themselves empathizing with the heroine's confusion. A brilliantly written, intense book. Her latest, much acclaimed novel *Foreign Parts* (Vintage) explores the friendship of two women.

Lewis Grassic Gibbon *A Scots Quair* (Penguin/Schocken o/p). A landmark trilogy set in northeast Scotland during and after World War I, the events seen through the eyes of Chris Guthrie, "torn between her love for the land and her desire to escape a peasant culture". Strong, seminal work.

Alasdair Gray *Lanark: A Life in Four Books* (Picador/Harvest). A postmodern blend of social realism and labyrinthine fantasy. Gray's extraordinary debut as a novelist, featuring his own allegorical illustrations, takes invention and comprehension to their limits.

Neil M. Gunn *The Silver Darlings* (UK Faber). Probably Gunn's most representative and best-known book, evocatively set on the northeast coast and telling the story of the herring fishermen during the great years of the industry. Other examples of his romantic, symbolic works include *The Lost Glen, The Silver Bough* and *Wild Geese Overhead* (UK Chambers).

James Hogg *The Private Memoirs and Confessions of a Justified Sinner* (Penguin/Canongate). Complex, dark mid-nineteenth-century novel dealing with possession, myth and folklore, as it looks at the confession of an Edinburgh murderer from three different points of view.

Joyce Holmes *Foreign Body* (UK Headline). An attractive amateur duo of detectives solve murders in closely-observed small community in the Highlands. Welcome newcomer to the crime scene.

Jackie Kay The protagonist of Kay's first novel, *Trumpet* (Picador/Random House), is dead before the story begins. He was a black Scottish jazz trumpeter, who has left a wife in mourning and a son in deep shock. For the posthumous medical report has revealed handsome Joss Moody, revered in the jazz world, to be a woman. A humane and multi-layered work.

James Kelman *The Busconductor Hines* (UK Phoenix). The wildly funny story of a young Glasgow bus conductor with an intensely boring job and a limitless imagination. *How Late it Was, How Late* (Vintage/Delta) is Kelman's Booker Prize winning and disturbing look at life as seen through the eyes of a foul-mouthed, blind Glaswegian drunk.

A.L. Kennedy *Looking for the Possible Dance* (UK Vintage). Young Scottish writer dissects the difficulties of human relationships on a personal and wider social level. More recent novels *So I Am Glad* and *Original Bliss* (both UK Minerva) have the same deft touch.

Eric Linklater *The Dark of Summer* (Canongate). Set on the Faroes, Shetland, Orkney (where the author was born) and in theatres of war, this novel exhibits the best of Linklater's compelling narrative style, although his comic *Private Angelo* (Canongate) is better known.

Alexander MacArthur and Kingsley Long *No Mean City* (UK Corgi). Classic story of razor gangs in 1935 Glasgow.

William McIlvanney *Docherty* (UK Sceptre). Tale of a hard, poverty-wracked Scottish coal-mining community by one of the country's most-respected contemporary authors.

Compton Mackenzie *Whisky Galore* (UK Penguin). Comic novel based on a true story of the wartime wreck of a cargo of whisky on a Hebridean island. Full of predictable stereotypes but still funny.

Naomi Mitchison *Lobster on the Agenda* (UK House of Lochar). Recently republished, Mitchison's novel written in 1952 about contemporary life in the West Highlands precisely captures a community which, shaken by the war, is trying to look forward while hampered by the prejudices of the past.

Neil Munro *The Complete Edition of the Para Handy Tales* (UK Pan). Engaging and witty stories relating the adventures of a Clyde puffer captain as he more or less legally steers his grubby ship up and down the west coast. Despite a fond – if slightly patronizing – view of the Gaelic mind, they are enormous fun.

Ian Rankin *The Hanging Garden* (UK Orion). Best known of modern Scottish crime writers, Rankin deals with the underside of Edinburgh, which can be very bleak. Not for the faint-hearted.

Sir Walter Scott *The Waverley Novels* (Penguin). The books that did much to create the romanticized version of Scottish life and history. A series of critical hardback editions have been published by Edinburgh University Press: *Kenilworth, Tale of Old Mortality, Black Dwarf, St Ronan's Well* and *The Antiquary*. For more on Scott, see p.147.

Iain Crichton Smith *Consider the Lilies* (UK Canongate). Poetic lament about the Highland Clearances by Scotland's finest bilingual (English and Gaelic) writer.

Muriel Spark *The Prime of Miss Jean Brodie* (Penguin/NAL Dutton). Wonderful evocation of middle-class Edinburgh life and aspirations, still apparent in that city today.

Alan Spence *The Stone Garden* (UK Phoenix). Perceptive, gently humorous and well-crafted short stories based on childhood experiences in Glasgow.

R. L. Stevenson *Dr Jekyll and Mr Hyde* (Penguin/Vintage); *Kidnapped* (Penguin/Signet); *The Master of Ballantrae* (Penguin/Oxford University Press); *Weir of Hermiston* (UK Penguin). Nineteenth-century tales of intrigue and adventure. For more on Stevenson, see p.101.

Nigel Tranter *The Bruce Trilogy* (Hodder & Stoughton). Massive tome about Robert the Bruce by a prolific and hugely popular author on Scottish themes. *The Flockmasters* (B & W) deals with the Clearances and *Kettle of Fish* (B & W) with salmon poaching in the Tweed.

Alan Warner *Morvern Callar* (Vintage/Anchor). Story of a supermarket shelf-packer from Oban who follows her vision to the rave clubs of Ibiza and the quiet beauty of the West Highlands. The sequel is *These Demented Lands* (Vintage), and his latest, *The Sopranos* (Jonathan Cape), follows a Catholic girls' choir to Edinburgh where they meet Life.

Irvine Welsh *Irvine Welsh Omnibus* (Vintage/Norton). A compendium including *Trainspotting*, *The Acid House* and *Marabou Stork Nightmares*, all of which can also be found as separate titles. Welsh trawls through the horrors of drug addiction, sexual fantasy, urban decay and hopeless youth, making you either rejoice at an authentic and unapologetic new voice for the dispossessed, or throw up. Thankfully, his unflinching attention is not without humour.

Kevin Williamson, ed. *Children of Albion Rovers* (Canongate/Overlook Press). A fast-track introduction to some of the best Scottish writers of the drug-culture generation, with novellas by the likes of Irvine Welsh, Alan Warner, Gordon Legge and Laura J. Hird.

CHILDREN'S FICTION

Eleanor Atkinson *Greyfriars Bobby* (Puffin/Buccaneer Books). Part of Edinburgh folklore, this is the tear-jerking true story of a faithful dog who nightly visited his master's grave. Suitable for ten-year-olds and over.

George Mackay Brown *Pictures in the Cave* (UK Kelpie). A collection of stories based on folk tales, told by a master poet. Suitable for nine-year-olds and over.

Kathleen Fidler *Desperate Journey* (UK Kelpie). Story of a family driven from Scotland in

the Sutherland Clearances across the Atlantic to Canada. *The Droving Lad* (UK Kelpie). A thriller about a boy and his first experience of herding cattle from the Highlands to the Lowlands. Suitable for nine-year-olds and over.

Mairi Hedderwick *Katie Morag and the Two Grandmothers* (Collins/Trafalgar Square). One of the many delightful stories of a little girl and the trouble she gets in on the west-coast island of Struay, beautifully illustrated by the author. Suitable for reading to under-fives.

Ted Hughes *Nessie the Mannerless Monster* (Faber). A verse story about the famous monster who goes to London to see the queen. Suitable for five- to eight-year-olds.

Mollie Hunter *A Stranger Came Ashore* (UK Kelpie). Set in Shetland, this a tragic and gripping historical tale. Suitable for ten-year-olds and over.

Gavin Maxwell *Ring of Bright Water* (UK Penguin). Heart-warming true tale of the author's relationship with three otters. Suitable for five- to eight-year-olds.

Aileen Paterson *Maisie Goes to Glasgow* (UK Amaising). There are lots of adventures of this mischievous cat, mostly set in Scotland. Suitable for five- to eight-year-olds.

Robert Louis Stevenson *Kidnapped* (Puffin Classic/Bantam Classic). A thrilling historical adventure set in eighteenth-century Scotland. Every bit as exciting as the better known *Treasure Island* (Puffin Classic/Scholastic Paperbacks).

POETRY

George Mackay Brown *Selected Poems 1954–1983* (John Murray). Brown's work is as haunting, beautiful and gritty as the Orkney islands which inspire it.

Robert Burns *Selected Poems*. (Penguin). Scotland's most famous bard. Immensely popular all over the world, his best known works are his earlier ones, including "Auld Lang Syne" and "My Love Is Like A Red, Red Rose".

Carol Anne Duffy *Selected Poems* (Penguin). Some of her work reflects her early childhood in Glasgow, all of it is personal and packed with striking images.

William Dunbar *The Poems of William Dunbar* (UK Mercat Press). An important literary figure in his time, his poetry reveals the concerns and attitudes to life at the court of James IV.

Douglas Dunn *Selected Poems, 1964–83* (Faber). A writer of delicately-wrought poetry, ranging from the intensely private to those involved with Scottish issues. He also edited *The Faber Book of Twentieth-Century Scottish Poetry* (Faber & Faber). All the big names (except for Dunn himself) and some lesser-known works.

Kathleen Jamie *The Queen of Sheba; The Way We Live* (Bloodaxe UK). Although often set in Scotland, her work has a wider significance; its tone is strong, almost angry, and its themes both personal and universal.

Jackie Kay *The Adoption Papers* and *Other Lovers* (Bloodaxe UK). Her poetry explores being black, Scottish and gay and deals with personal relationships in an accessibly intimate way.

Liz Lochhead *Bagpipe Muzak* (Penguin); *Dreaming Frankenstein and Other Poems* (Polygon). A strong straightforward style, coupled with shrewd observations, Lochhead speaks with immediacy on personal relationships.

Norman MacCaig *Selected Poems* (Chatto & Windus). Justly celebrated for its keen observation of the natural world, MacCaig's work remains intellectually challenging without being arid. His poetry, rooted in the Highlands, uses detail to explore a universal landscape. *Norman MacCaig; A Celebration* (Chapman) is an anthology written for his 85th birthday, and includes work by more than ninety writers, including Ted Hughes and Seamus Heaney.

Hugh MacDiarmid *Selected Poems* (Penguin). Immensely influential, not least for his nationalist views and his use of Scots, MacDiarmid's poetry is richly challenging. *A Drunk Man Looks at a Thistle* (UK S.A.P.) is acknowledged as a masterpiece of Scottish literature.

MacCaig, Morgan, Lochhead *Three Scottish Poets* (Canongate). A representative selection from the work of three well-known poets. Differing perspectives – natural, metaphysical, urban, political and feminist – reflect the complexity of the modern Scottish experience.

Sorley Maclean (Somhairle Macgill-Eain) *From Wood to Ridge: Collected Poems* (Vintage). Written in Gaelic, his poems have been translated into bilingual editions all over the world; they deal with the sorrows of poverty, war and love.

William McGonagall *McGonagall: A Selection* (ed Colin Walker; UK Birlinn). Verse so bad you have to read it – or perhaps not.

John McQueen and Tom Scott, eds *The Oxford Book of Scottish Verse* (UK Oxford University Press). Claims to be the most comprehensive anthology of Scottish poetry ever published.

Edwin Morgan *Selected Poems* (Carcanet). A love of words and their sounds is evident in his poems, which are refreshingly varied and often experimental. He comments on the Scottish scene with shrewdness and humour.

Edwin Muir *Collected Poems* (Faber). Muir's childhood on Orkney remained with him as a dream of paradise from which he was banished to Glasgow. His poems are passionately concerned with Scotland.

Don Paterson *God's Gift to Women* and *Nil Nil* (Faber). A young writer whose work examines the working class, sex and drink with a wry sense of humour and an exciting, innovative voice.

Tom Scott, ed. *The Penguin Book of Scottish Verse* (UK Penguin). Good general selection.

Iain Crichton Smith *Collected Poems* (Carcanet UK). Born on the Isle of Lewis, Iain Crichton Smith wrote with feeling and sometimes bitterness, in both Gaelic and English, of the life of the rural communities, the iniquities of the Free Church, the need to revive Gaelic culture and the glory of the Scottish landscape.

Roderick Watson, ed *The Poetry of Scotland* (UK Edinburgh University Press). An accessible anthology of poems in English, Scots and Gaelic (with notes and translations) from the fourteenth century to the present day.

FOLKLORE AND LEGEND

Margaret Bennett *Scottish Customs from the Cradle to the Grave* (Polygon). Fascinating and sympathetic extensive oral history.

Michael Brander *Tales of the Borders* (UK Mainstream). Part social history and part guidebook, a collection of romantic nineteenth-century Border tales retold and put into historical context.

Alan J. Bruford and Donald Archie McDonald, eds *Scottish Traditional Tales* (Polygon). A huge collection of folk stories from all over Scotland, taken from tape archives.

Steuart Campbell *The Loch Ness Monster: The Evidence* (UK Birlinn). For those curious as to whether Nessie is folklore or fact, this book contains all the evidence and leaves the reader to decide.

Neil Philip, ed *The Penguin Book of Scottish Folk Tales* (UK Penguin). A collection of over a hundred folk tales from all over Scotland.

Nigel Tranter *Tales and Traditions of Scottish Castles* (UK Neil Wilson). The myths and legends of some of Scotland's more famous castles.

HISTORY, POLITICS AND CULTURE

Adamnan (trans. by John Marsden) *The Illustrated Life of Columba* (UK Floris Books). The original story of the life of St Columba, annotated and accompanied by beautiful photos of the places associated with him, in particular the Hebridean island of Iona.

Ian Adams and Meredith Somerville *Cargoes of Despair and Hope* (UK John Donald Publishing). Riveting mixture of contemporary documents and letters telling the story of Scottish emigration to North America from 1603 to 1803.

Colin Bell *Scotland's Century – An Autobiography of the Nation* (HarperCollins). Richly illustrated and readable account of the social history of Scotland, based on radio interviews with people from all walks of life.

Bella Bathurst *The Lighthouse Stevensons* (HarperCollins). Fascinating account of the lives and amazing achievements of Robert Louis Stevenson's family, who built many of the island lighthouses round Scotland.

David Daiches, ed *The New Companion to Scottish Culture* (Polygon/Subterranean). A dense, wide-ranging tome with more than 300 articles on Scottish culture in its widest sense, from eating to marriage customs to the Scottish Enlightenment.

G. Donaldson & R.S. Morpeth, ed *A Dictionary of Scottish History* (UK John Donald). A user-friendly volume listing dates, facts and potted biographies.

Ninian Dunnett *Out on the Edge* (Canongate). A readable series of interviews with Scots, probing the national psyche.

Antonia Fraser *Mary, Queen of Scots* (UK Mandarin). An acclaimed biography of Scotland's most tragic queen, capturing the essence of both the period and the woman.

George MacDonald Fraser *The Steel Bonnets* (HarperCollins). Immensely enjoyable and erudite account of sixteenth-century cattle-rustling, feud, blackmail, murder and mayhem in the border country between England and Scotland.

Rosemary Goring *Chambers Scottish Biographical Dictionary* (UK Chambers). More than 2000 mini-biographies of important Scots, both well-known and obscure, in fields such as law, medicine, education, the Church, music and the stage.

Historic Scotland (UK Stationery Office). A series of books covering many aspects of Scotland's history and prehistory, including the Picts, Vikings, Romans and Celts. All are colourful, accessible and well-presented. Available at many Historic Scotland properties as well as bookshops.

Michael Lynch *Scotland: A New History* (UK Pimlico). Probably the best available overview of Scottish history, taking the story up to 1992.

James MacKay *William Wallace* (Mainstream). An authoritative biography, and the best of a rash of books capitalizing on the success of the movie *Braveheart* – the book is more of a stickler for historical fact than the film.

Fitzroy Maclean *Bonnie Prince Charlie* (Canongate). Very readable and more or less definitive biography of Scotland's most romanticized historical figure, written by the "real" James Bond.

John McLeod *No Great Mischief If You Fall* (Mainstream/Trafalgar). Gloom and doom on the rape of the Highlands; an enraging, bleak but stimulating book debunking some of the myths upheld by the Highland industry.

Ann McSween and Mick Sharp *Prehistoric Scotland* (Batsford o/p/New Amsterdam Books). Thematic introductory guide to many of Scotland's prehistoric sites, with atmospheric black-and-white photographs and imaginative illustrations.

John Prebble *Glen Coe* (Penguin); *Culloden* (Penguin); *The Highland Clearances* (Penguin). Emotive, subjective and accessible accounts of key events in Highland history.

John Purser *Scotland's Music* (Mainstream). Comprehensive overview of traditional and classical music in Scotland – thorough and scholarly but readable.

Scotland's Past in Action *Building Railways; Feeding Scotland; Fishing and Whaling.* Some of the titles in an attractive series of small illustrated books, produced by the National Museums of Scotland.

T.C. Smout *A History of the Scottish People 1560–1830* (HarperCollins); *A Century of the*

Scottish People 1830–1950 (HarperCollins). Widely acclaimed books, brimful of interest for those keen on social history. Smout combines enormous learning with a clear and entertaining style.

Martin Wallace *A Little Book of Celtic Saints* (UK Appletree Press). A small but informative volume.

Andy Wightman *Who Owns Scotland* (Canongate). A detailed and revealing breakdown of the patterns of land ownership and use in Scotland, but rather dry for general reading.

ART, ARCHITECTURE AND HISTORIC SITES

Lesley Astaire, Roddy Martine and Fritz von Schulenburg *Living in Scotland* (Thames & Hudson). A fascinating, if rather intense, photographic tour of the interiors of the main country homes, inhabited castles and grand town houses of Scotland.

Roger Billcliffe *The Scottish Colourists* (UK John Murray). An impressive, perhaps definitive study of a group of artists reckoned by many to be Scotland's finest.

Jude Burkhauser *Glasgow Girls: Women in Art and Design 1880–1920* (Canongate). The lively contribution of women to the development of the Glaswegian Art Nouveau movement is recognized in this authoritative account.

Alan Crawford *Charles Rennie Mackintosh* (Thames & Hudson). Part of the World of Art series, describing the major contribution of Scotland's premier architect.

Kitty Cruft and Andrew Fraser, eds *James Craig 1744–95* (UK Mercat Press). Distinguished authors offer reassessments of Craig's achievement in designing Edinburgh's New Town.

Miles Glendinning, ed *A History of Scottish Architecture from the Renaissance to the Present Day* (UK EUP). The most comprehensive work on the history of Scottish architecture.

Exploring Scotland's Heritage (UK The Stationery Office). Detailed, beautifully illustrated series with the emphasis on historic buildings and archeological sites. Recently updated titles cover Orkney, Shetland, the Highlands, Aberdeen and Northeast Scotland, Fife, Perthshire and Angus, and Argyll and the Western Isles.

Bill Hare *Contemporary Painting in Scotland* (UK Craftsman House). Features the work of 48 contemporary artists – including John Bellany,

Bruce McLean and Elizabeth Blackadder – and gives special attention to the "New Painting" that emerged in the 1980s and developed into a distinctive Scottish style. Expensive and serious.

Charles McKean, David Walker and Frank Walker *Central Glasgow* (UK Rutland Press). An architectural romp through the city centre and West End, with plenty of photographs and informed comment, *Central Glasgow* is part of the Rutland Press series of illustrated guides to Scottish architecture. Whilst authoritative, they are not at all stuffy and are conveniently pocket-sized. In addition, the Press has produced studies of such notable figures as James Miller, Basil Spence and Peter Womersley.

Duncan MacMillan *Scottish Art 1460–1990* (Mainstream). Lavish overview of Scottish painting with good sections on landscape, portraiture and the Glasgow Boys.

Colin McWilliam, ed *The Buildings of Scotland* (UK Penguin). There are volumes on various regions of Scotland, including Fife, Edinburgh and Lothian, all of which provide comprehensive and scholarly coverage of every building of importance. Though easy to follow, they would best suit visitors intending to spend more than a couple of weeks in Scotland.

Steven Parissien *Adam Style* (Phaidon). A well-illustrated account of the birth of the Neoclassical style named for the two Scottish Adam brothers, Robert and James.

Andrew Gibbon Williams and Andrew Brown *The Bigger Picture: A History of Scottish Art* (UK BBC Books). Originally published to accompany a TV series, this is a richly illustrated survey of Scottish art from 1603 to the present day. Suitable for the lay reader.

GUIDES AND PICTURE BOOKS

Colin Baxter *Scotland from the Air* (UK Lomond); **Colin Baxter and Jim Crumley** *Portrait of Edinburgh* (UK Colin Baxter Photography); **Colin Baxter** *Scotland* (UK Colin Baxter); and **Baxter and Jack McLean** *The City of Glasgow* (UK Colin Baxter Photography). Best known for his ubiquitous postcards, Baxter's photographs succeed in capturing the grandeur of Scotland's moody landscapes and characterful cityscapes.

Laurie Campbell & Roy Dennis *Golden Eagles* (UK Colin Baxter). Second only to the stag as a symbol of Scotland, the eagle is captured in this book in magnificent photographs.

Collins Gem *Scots Dictionary* (UK HarperCollins). Handy, pocket-sized guide to the mysteries of Scottish vocabulary and idiom.

Collins Guide *Scottish Wild Flowers; Scottish Birds* (UK HarperCollins). Well-illustrated and informative small guides. Also in the guide series are *Clans and Tartans* and *Scottish Surnames* which are a first step on the road to genealogy.

Joe Fisher *The Glasgow Encyclopedia* (Mainstream). The essential Glasgow reference book, covering nearly every facet of this complex urban society.

Hamish Haswell-Smith *The Scottish Islands* (UK Canongate). An exhaustive and impressive gazetteer with maps and absorbing information on all the Scottish islands. Filled with attractive sketches and paintings, the book is breathtaking in its thoroughness and lovingly gathered detail.

Magnus Magnusson and Graham White, eds *The Nature of Scotland – Landscape, Wildlife and People* (Canongate). Glossy picture-based book on Scotland's natural heritage, from geology to farming and conservation. Good section on crofting.

Andrew Murray Scott *Discovering Dundee: The Story of a City* (UK Mercat Press). A good popular history of the city and some of its famous citizens.

Donald Omand *The Borders Book* (UK Birlinn). An entertaining history of the much disputed land between England and Scotland, from prehistory to its present passion for rugby.

Paul Ramsay *Lochs & Glens of Scotland* (UK Collins & Brown). Informative text and stunning photographs of the Highlands that make you want to book a holiday immediately.

Anne Shade *Scotland for Kids* (Mainstream). Indispensable advice on where to go and what to do with children in Scotland, written by a mother of two.

Cecil Sinclair *Tracing your Scottish Ancestors* (UK The Stationery Office). Probably the best guide to ancestry research in the Scottish Record Office – definitely worth reading before visiting General Register House.

David Williams *The Glasgow Guide* (UK Canongate). Thirteen walks round Glasgow, with the emphasis on historical points of interest: buildings, graveyards, museums and architecture.

Michael and Elspeth Wills *Walks in Edinburgh's Old Town* (UK Mercat Press). A small guide which takes you into the nooks and crannies of Scotland's most historically intense city centre. Also *Walks in Edinburgh's New Town* (UK Mercat Press) to get you up to date.

MEMOIRS AND TRAVELOGUES

David Craig *On the Crofter's Trail* (UK Pimlico). Using anecdotes and interviews with descendants, Craig conveys the hardship and tragedy of the Highland Clearances without being mawkish.

Jim Crumley *Gulfs of Blue Air – A Highland Journey* (Mainstream). Recent travelogue mixed with nature notes and references to Scottish poets such as MacCaig and Mackay Brown.

David Duff ed *Queen Victoria's Highland Journals* (UK Hamlyn). The daily diary of the Scottish adventures of "Mrs Brown" – Victoria's writing is detailed and interesting without being twee, and she lovingly conveys her affection for Deeside and the Highlands.

Elizabeth Grant of Rothiemurchus *Memoirs of a Highland Lady* (Canongate). Hugely readable recollections written with wit and perception at the turn of the eighteenth century, charting social changes in Edinburgh, London and particularly Speyside.

James Hunter *Scottish Highlanders* (Mainstream). Attempts to explain the strong sense of blood ties held by people of Scottish descent all over the world; lots of history and good photographs.

Samuel Johnson and James Boswell *A Journey to the Western Isles of Scotland* and *The Journal of a Tour to the Hebrides* (UK Penguin). Lively accounts of a famous journey around the islands taken by the famous lexicographer, Dr Samuel Johnson, and his biographer and friend.

Tom Morton *Spirit of Adventure: A Journey Beyond the Whisky Trails* (Mainstream). Offbeat and funny view of Scotland's whisky industry as seen from the back of a motorcycle in appalling weather.

Edwin Muir *Highland Journey* (Mainstream). A classic travelogue written in 1935 by the Orcadian writer on his return to Scotland from London.

Robert Louis Stevenson *Edinburgh: Picturesque Notes* (Barnes and Noble). Charming evocation of Stevenson's birthplace – its moods, curiosities and influences on his work.

Mike Tomkies *A Last Wild Place* (UK Jonathan Cape). Written by a journalist who lived in a derelict croft in northwest Scotland for twenty years, this is a perceptive and loving account of the natural world around him.

WILDLIFE AND OUTDOOR PURSUITS

Bartholomew Walks Series (UK Bartholomew). The series covers individual areas of Scotland, including Perthshire, Loch Lomond and the Trossachs, Oban, Mull and Lochaber, and Skye and Wester Ross. Each booklet has a range of walks of varying lengths with clear maps and descriptions.

Donald Bennet *The Munros*; **Scott Johnstone et al**. *The Corbetts* (UK Scottish Mountaineering Trust). Authoritative and attractively illustrated hillwalkers' guides to the Scottish peaks. SMT also publishes guides to districts and specific climbs.

Hamish Brown *Hamish's Mountain Walk and Climbing the Corbetts* (Bâton Wicks). The best of the travel narratives about walking in the Scottish Highlands.

Andrew Dempster *Classic Mountain Scrambles in Scotland* (UK Mainstream). Guide to hill walks in Scotland that combine straightforward walking with some rock-climbing.

Derek Douglas *The Thistle: A Chronicle of Scottish Rugby* (Mainstream). History of the game for enthusiasts, from Victorian times to the present day, with some good photos.

Richard Fitter, Alastair Fitter and Marhorie Blanney *Collins Pocket Guide to the Wild Flowers of Britain and Northern Europe* (UK HarperCollins). An excellent, easy-to-use field guide.

Muriel Gray *The First Fifty* (UK Corgi). Scottish TV presenter Gray takes an enthusiastic and irreverent tour of her favourite Scottish peaks, described as "Munro bagging without a beard".

David Hamilton *The Scottish Golf Guide* (Canongate). An inexpensive paperback with descriptions of and useful information about 84 of Scotland's best courses.

John Hancox *Collins Pocket Reference – Cycling in Scotland* (UK HarperCollins). Spiralbound edition with over fifty road routes of all grades up and down the country, each with a useful route map. For more off-road mountain bike routes, try **Derek Purdy** *Scotland: The Central Valley* (UK Haynes Publishers) in the *Ride Your Bike* series, or **Harry Henniker** *101*

Bike Routes in Scotland (UK Mainstream).

Philip Lusby & Jenny Wright *Scottish Wild Plants* (UK The Stationery Office). Beautifully produced book about the rarer plants of Scotland, their discovery and conservation, produced in conjunction with the Royal Botanic Gardens of Edinburgh.

Michael Madders and Julia Welstead *Where to Watch Birds in Scotland* (UK Christopher Helm). Region-by-region guide with maps, details on access and habitat, and notes on what to see when.

Kenny MacDonald, ed *Scottish Football Quotations* (UK Mainstream). Shows you the humour that prevents Scottish football fans from losing heart.

Ian Mitchell *Mountain Days and Bothy Nights* (UK Luath Press). A slim but highly entertaining volume describing the characters and experiences of modern-day hill climbing.

Jenny Parke *Ski & Snowboard: Scotland* (UK Luath Press). Informative book about where to find the best slopes, with loads of useful advice.

Ordnance Survey Pathfinder Series (Jarrold Publishing/Seven Hills Book Distribution). Top-quality maps, colour pictures and clear text. Titles include: *Loch Lomond and the Trossachs*, *Fort William and Glen Coe* and *Perthshire*.

Robert Price *Scotland's Golf Courses* (UK Mercat Press o/p). A thorough lowdown on Scottish courses for serious golfers, with good photographs.

Pastime Publications *Scotland for Game, Sea and Coarse Fishing* (UK Pastime Publications). General guide on what to fish, where and for how much, along with notes on records, regulations and convenient accommodation. Published in association with the Scottish Tourist Board.

Roger Smith *The West Highland Way*; *The Southern Upland Way* (both The Stationery Office o/p). Comprehensive guides to long-distance paths, containing information on sights, history, nature and help on planning your trek, as well as specially oriented maps. The Stationery Office also publishes a series called *Twenty-Five Walks*, each volume covering a particular city or region of Scotland with colour pictures and excellent maps.

Ralph Storer *100 Best Routes on Scottish Mountains* (UK David and Charles). A compilation of the best day-walks in Scotland, including some of the classics overlooked by the Munroing guides.

FOOD AND DRINK

Annette Hope *A Caledonian Feast* (UK Mainstream). Authoritative and entertaining history of Scottish food and social life from the ninth to the twentieth centuries. Lots of recipes.

Michael Jackson *Malt Whisky Companion* (UK Dorling Kindersley). An attractively put together tome, considered by many to be the "bible" on malt whisky tasting.

Ralph Kenna *The Glasgow Pub Companion* (UK Neil Wilson). Covers about 200 pubs, traditional and trendy.

G.W. Lockhart *The Scots and Their Fish* (UK Birlinn). Tells the history of fish and fishing in Scotland, and ends with a selection of traditional recipes.

Claire Macdonald *The Claire Macdonald Cookbook* (UK Bantam). Lady Claire Macdonald of Macdonald has become widely known in Scottish cookery circles. She promotes the use of native food and runs a successful hotel on Skye.

Charles McLean *Pocket Guides: Scotch Whisky*; **Charles McLean and Jason Lowe** *Malt Whisky* (UK Mitchell Beazley o/p). The first is a small, thorough, fact-filled book covering malt, grain and blended whiskies, plus whisky-based liqueurs. The second is an attractive coffee-table book with inspiring photographs of the places whisky comes from, as well as detailed background information.

Nick Nairn *Wild Harvest*; *Wild Harvest 2* (UK BBC Books). Glossy TV tie-ins by an engaging young Scottish chef, who takes up the challenge of gathering and eating from the wild. Both books feature fascinating, if difficult to recreate, recipes. His latest addition is *Island Harvest* (UK BBC Books).

J. Redding & T. Weston *Rainbows and Wellies* (UK Findhorn Press). Scotland is not noted for its vegetarianism but this is a vegan book with some great gourmet recipes which has gained wide popularity.

LANGUAGE

Language is a thorny, complex and often highly political issue in Scotland. If you're not from Scotland yourself, you're most likely to be addressed in a variety of English, spoken in a Scottish accent. Even then, you're likely to hear phrases and words that are part of what is known as Lowland Scottish or Scots, which is now officially recognized as a distinct language in its own right. To a lesser extent, Gaelic, too, remains a living language, particularly in the *Gàidhealtachd* or Gaelic-speaking areas of the Western Isles, parts of Skye and a few scattered Hebridean islands. In Orkney and Shetland, the local dialect of Scots contains many words carried over from Norn, the Norse language spoken in the Northern Isles from the time of the Vikings until the eighteenth century (for more on this, see p.558).

Lowland Scottish or **Scots** is spoken by thirty percent of the Scottish population, according to the latest survey. It began life as a northern branch of Anglo-Saxon, and emerged as a distinct language in the Middle Ages. From the 1370s until the Union in 1707, it was the country's main literary and documentary language. Since the eighteenth century, however, it has been systematically repressed in preference to English. Robbie Burns is the most obvious literary exponent of the Scots language, but there has been a revival this century led by poets such as Hugh MacDiarmid. (For examples of the works of both writers, see "Books".) Only very recently has Scots enjoyed something of a renaissance, getting itself on the Scottish school curriculum in 1996, and achieving official

recognition as a distinct language in 1998. Despite these enormous political achievements, many people (rightly or wrongly) still regard Scots as a dialect of English.

Scottish **Gaelic** (*Gàidhlig*, pronounced "Gallic") is one of only four Celtic languages to survive into the modern age (Welsh, Breton and Irish Gaelic are the other three). Manx, the old language of the Isle of Man, died out earlier this century, while Cornish was finished as a community language way back in the eighteenth century. Scottish Gaelic is most closely related to Irish Gaelic and Manx – hardly surprising since Gaelic was introduced to Scotland from Ireland around the third century BC. Some folk still argue that Scottish Gaelic is merely a dialect of its parent language, Irish Gaelic, and indeed the two languages remain more or less mutually intelligible. From the fifth to the twelfth centuries, Gaelic enjoyed an expansionist phase, gradually becoming the national language, thanks partly to the backing of the Celtic church in Iona. At the end of this period, Gaelic was spoken throughout virtually all of what is now Scotland – the main exceptions being Orkney and Shetland.

From that high point onwards Gaelic began a steady decline over the next few centuries. Even before Union with England, power, religious ideology and wealth gradually passed into non-Gaelic hands. The royal court was transferred to Edinburgh and an Anglo-Norman legal system was put in place. The Celtic church was Romanized by the introduction of foreign clergy, and, most importantly of all, English and Flemish merchants colonized the new trading towns of the east coast. In addition, the pro-English attitudes held by the Covenanters led to strong anti-Gaelic feeling within the Church of Scotland from its inception.

The two abortive Jacobite rebellions of 1715 and 1745 furthered the language's decline, as did the Clearances that took place in the Gaelic-speaking Highlands from the 1770s to the 1820s, which forced thousands to migrate to central Scotland's new industrial belt or emigrate to North America. Although efforts were made to halt the decline in the first half of the nineteenth century, the 1872 Education Act gave no official recognition to Gaelic, and children were severely punished if they were caught speaking the language in school.

Current estimates put the number of Gaelic speakers at 86,000 (about two percent of the population), the majority of whom live in the *Gàidhealtachd*, with an extended Gaelic community of perhaps 250,000 who have some understanding of the language. In the last two decades the language has stabilized and even recovered, thanks to the introduction of bilingual primary and nursery schools, and a huge increase in the amount of broadcasting time given to Gaelic-language programmes. The success of rock bands such as Runrig has shown that it is possible to combine traditional Gaelic culture with popular entertainment and reach a mass audience.

GAELIC GRAMMAR AND PRONUNCIATION

Gaelic is a highly complex tongue, with a fiendish, antiquated grammar and, with only eighteen letters, an intimidating system of spelling. Pronunciation is actually easier than it appears at first glance – one general rule to remember is that the **stress** always falls on the first syllable of a word. The general rule of syntax is that the verb starts the sentence whether it's a question or not, followed by the subject and then the object; adjectives generally follow the word they are describing.

SHORT AND LONG VOWELS

Gaelic has both short and long vowels, the latter being denoted by an acute or grave accent.
a as in c**a**t; before nn and ll, like the *ow* in b**ow** (of a boat)
à as in b**a**r
e as in p**e**t
é like the *ai* in r**ai**n
i like the *ee* in str**ee**t, but shorter
í like the *ee* in fr**ee**
o as in p**o**t
ò like the *a* in the enthr**a**l
ó like the *ow* in b**ow** (of a boat)
u like the *oo* in sc**oo**t
ù like the *oo* in l**oo**

VOWEL COMBINATIONS

Gaelic is littered with diphthongs, which, rather like in English, can be pronounced in several different ways depending on the individual word.
ai like the *a* in c**a**t, or the *e* in p**e**t; before dh or

gh, like the *ee* in str**ee**t
ao like the *ur* in s**ur**ly
ei like the *a* in m**a**te
ea like the *e* in p**e**t, or the *a* in c**a**t, and sometimes like the *a* in m**a**te; before ll or nn like the *ow* in b**ow** (of a boat)
èa as in h**ea**r
eu like the *ai* in tr**ai**n, or the *ea* in f**ea**r
ia like the *ea* in f**ea**r
io like the *ea* in f**ea**r, or the *ee* in str**ee**t, but shorter
ua like the *ooe* in w**ooe**r

CONSONANTS

The consonants listed below are those that differ substantially from the English.
b at the beginning of a word as in **b**ig; in the middle or at the end of a word like the *p* in **p**air
bh at the beginning of a word like the *v* in **v**an; elsewhere it is silent
c as in **c**at; after a vowel it has aspiration *before* it
ch always as in lo**ch**, never as in **ch**urch
cn like the *cr* in **cr**owd
d like the *d* in **d**og, but with the tongue pressed against the back of the upper teeth; at the beginning of a word before e or i, like the *j* in **j**am; in the middle or at the end of a word like the *t* in cat; after i like the *ch* in **ch**urch
dh before and after a, o or u an aspirated *g*, rather like someone gargling; before e or i like the *y* in **y**es; elsewhere silent
fh usually silent; somtimes like the *h* in **h**ouse
g at the beginning of a word as in **g**et; before e like the *y* in **y**es; in the middle or end of a word like the *ck* in so**ck**; after i like the *ch* in lo**ch**
gh at the beginning of a word as in **g**et; before or after a, o or u rather like someone gargling; after i sometimes like the *y* in ga**y**, but often silent
l after i and sometimes before e like the *l* in **l**ot; elsewhere a peculiarly Gaelic sound produced by flattening the front of the tongue against the palate
mh like the *v* in **v**an
p at the beginning of a word as in **p**et; elsewhere it has aspiration *before* it
rt pronounced as **sht**
s before e or i like the *sh* in **sh**ip; otherwise as in English
sh before a, o or u like the *h* in **h**ouse; before e like the *ch* in lo**ch**
t before e or i like the *ch* in **ch**urch; in the middle or at the end of a word it has aspiration *before* it; otherwise as in English
th at the beginning of a word, like the *h* in **h**ouse; elsewhere, and in the word *thu*, silent

GAELIC PHRASES AND VOCABULARY

The choice is limited when it comes to **teach-yourself Gaelic** courses, but the BBC *Can Seo* cassette and book is perfect for starting you off. Drier and more academic is *Teach Yourself Gaelic* (Hodder & Stoughton), which is aimed at bringing beginners to Scottish "O" grade standard. *Everyday Gaelic* by Morag MacNeill (Gairm) is the best phrasebook around.

BASIC WORDS AND GREETINGS

yes	tha	night	oidhche	music	ceòl
no	chan eil	here	an seo	book	leabhar
hello	hallo	there	an sin	tired	sgìth
how are you?	ciamar a tha thu?	this way	mar seo	food	lòn
OK	tha gu math	that way	mar sin	bread	aran
thank you	tapadh leat	pound/s	not/aichean	water	uisge
welcome	fàilte	tomorrow	a-màireach	milk	bainne
come in	thig a-staigh	tonight	a-nochd	beer	leann
goodbye	mar sin leat	cheers	slàinte	wine	fion
goodnight	oidhche mhath	yesterday	an-dé	whisky	uisge beatha
who?	cò?	today	an-diugh	post office	post oifis
where is...?	càit a bheil...?	tomorrow	maireach	Edinburgh	Dun Eideann
when?	cuine?	now	a-nise	Glasgow	Glaschu
what is it?	dé tha ann?	hotel	taigh-òsda	America	Ameireaga
morning	madainn	house	taigh	Ireland	Eire
evening	feasgar	story	sgeul	England	Sasainn
day	là	song	òran	London	Lunnain

SOME USEFUL PHRASES

It's a nice day	tha latha math ann	Do you speak Gaelic?	a bheil Gàidhlig agad?
How much is that?	dè tha e 'cosg?	What is the Gaelic for?	Dé a' Ghàidhlig a tha
What's your name?	dè 'n t-ainm a th'ort?		. air?
Excuse me	gabh mo leisgeul	I don't understand	chan eil mi 'tuigsinn
What time is it?	dé am uair a tha e?	I don't know	chan eil fhios agam
I'm thirsty	tha am pathadh orm	That's good	's math sin
I'd like a double room	'se rùm dùbailte tha	It doesn't matter	's coma
	mi 'giarraigh	I'm sorry	Tha mi duilich

NUMBERS AND DAYS

1	aon	10	deich	1000	mìle
2	dà/dhà	11	aon deug	Monday	Diluain
3	trì	20	fichead	Tuesday	Dimàirt
4	ceithir	21	aon ar fhichead	Wednesday	Diciadain
5	còig	30	deug ar fhichead	Thursday	Diardaoin
6	sia	40	dà fhichead	Friday	Dihaoine
7	seachd	50	lethcheud	Saturday	Disathurna
8	ochd	60	trì fichead	Sunday	Didòmhnaich/
9	naoi	100	ceud		. La na Sàbaid

SURNAMES

The prefix **Mac** or **Mc** in Scottish surnames derives from the Gaelic, meaning "son of". In Scots, Mac is used for both sexes; but in Gaelic, women are referred to as Nic. For example:

Donnchadh Mac Aodh   Duncan MacKay   *Iseabail Nic Aodh*   Isabel MacKay

GAELIC GEOGRAPHICAL AND PLACE-NAME TERMS

The purpose of the list below is to help with place-name derivations (from Gaelic) and with more detailed map reading. For a list of place-names derived from the Norse, see p.558)

abhainn	river
ach or **auch**, from **achadh**	field
ail, **aileach**	rock
Alba	Scotland
ardan or **arden**, from **àird**	a point of land or height
aros	dwelling
ault, from **allt**	stream
bal or **bally**, from **baile**	town, village
balloch, from **bealach**	mountain pass
bad	clump of trees
bagh	bay
ban	white, fair
bàrr	summit
beg, from **beag**	small
ben, from **beinn**	mountain
blair, from **blàr**	field or battlefield
camas	bay, harbour
cairn, from **càrn**	pile of stones
craig, from **creag**	rock
cnoc	hill
coll or **colly**, from **coille**	wood
corran	a point jutting into the sea
corrie, from **coire**	round hollow in mountainside, whirlpool
craig, from **creag**	rock, crag
cruach	bold hill
drum, from **druim**	ridge
dubh	black
dun or **dum**, from **dùn**	fort
eilean	island
ess, from **eas**	waterfall
fin, from **fionn**	white
gair or **gare**, from **geàrr**	short
garv, from **garbh**	rough
geodha	cove
glen, from **gleann**	valley
gower or **gour**, from **gabhar**	goat
inch, from **innis**	meadow or island
inver, from **inbhir**	rivermouth
ken or **kin**, from **ceann**	head
knock, from **cnoc**	hill
kyle, from **caolas**	narrow strait
lag	hollow
larach	site of an old ruin
liath	grey
loch	lake
meall	round hill
mon, from **monadh**	hill
more, from **mór**	large, great
rannoch, from **raineach**	bracken
ross, from **ros**	promontory
rubha	promontory
sgeir	sea rock
sgurr	sharp point
sron	**nose**, prow or promontory
strath, from **srath**	broad valley
tarbet, from **tairbeart**	isthmus
tigh	house
tir or **tyre**, from **tìr**	land
torr	hill, castle
tràigh	shore
uig	shelter
uisge	water

GLOSSARY

Auld Old.

Aye Yes.

Bairn Baby.

Blackhouse Thick-walled traditional dwelling.

Bonnie Pretty.

Bothy Primitive cottage or hut; farmworker's or shepherd's mountain shelter.

Brae Slope; hill.

Brig Bridge.

Broch Circular prehistoric stone fort.

Burn Small stream or brook.

Byre Shelter for cattle; cottage.

Cairn Mound of stones.

Carse Riverside area of flat alluvium.

Ceilidh Social gathering involving dancing, drinking, singing and storytelling.

Clan Extended family.

Covenanters Supporter of the Presbyterian Church in the seventeenth century.

Corbett Mountain between 2500ft and 3000ft high.

Corbie-stepped Architectural term; any set of steps on a gable.

Crannog Celtic lake or bog dwelling.

Croft Small plot of farmland with house, common in the Highlands.

Crow-stepped Same as *corbie-stepped*.

Dolmen Grave chamber.

Dram Literally, one-sixteenth of an ounce. Usually refers to a small measure of whisky.

Dun Fortified mound.

First-foot The first person to enter a household on *Hogmanay* (see below).

Firth Narrow inlet.

Gillie Personal guide used on hunting or fishing trips.

Glen Deep, narrow mountain valley.

Harling Limestone and gravel mix used to cover buildings.

Hogmanay New Year's Eve.

Howe Valley.

Howff Meeting place; pub.

HS Historic Scotland

Ken Knowledge; understanding.

Kilt Knee-length tartan skirt worn by Highland men.

Kirk Church.

Laird Landowner; aristocrat.

Law Rounded hill.

Links Grassy coastal land; coastal golf course.

Lochan Little loch or lake.

Machair Sandy, grassy, lime-rich coastal land, generally used for grazing.

Manse Official home of a Presbyterian minister.

Munro Mountain over 3000ft high.

Munro-bagging Sport of trying to climb as many Munros as possible.

Peel Fortified tower, built to withstand Border raids.

Pend Archway or vaulted passage.

Presbyterian The official (Protestant) Church of Scotland, established by John Knox during the Reformation.

Sassenach English.

Shinty Simple form of hockey.

SNH Scottish Natural Heritage

SNP Scottish National Party.

Sporran Leather purse worn in front of a kilt.

Tartan Check-patterned woollen cloth, particular patterns being associated with particular clans.

Thane A landowner of high rank; the chief of a clan.

Trews Tartan trousers.

Wee Small.

Wynd Narrow lane.

Yett Gate or door.

INDEX

ROUGH GUIDES: Travel

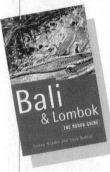

ROUGH GUIDES:
Reference and Music CDs

REFERENCE
Classical Music
Classical:
  100 Essential CDs
Drum'n'bass
House Music
Jazz
Music USA

Opera
Opera:
  100 Essential CDs
Reggae
Reggae:
  100 Essential CDs
Rock
Rock:
  100 Essential CDs
Techno
World Music
World Music:
  100 Essential CDs
English Football
European Football

Internet
Millennium

ROUGH GUIDE MUSIC CDs
Music of the
  Andes
Australian
  Aboriginal
Brazilian Music
Cajun & Zydeco

Classic Jazz
Music of
  Colombia
Cuban Music
Eastern Europe

Music of Egypt
English Roots
  Music
Flamenco
India & Pakistan
Irish Music
Music of Japan
Kenya & Tanzania
Native American
North African
Music of Portugal

Reggae
Salsa
Scottish Music
South African
  Music
Music of Spain
Tango
Tex-Mex
West African
  Music
World Music
World Music Vol 2
Music of
  Zimbabwe

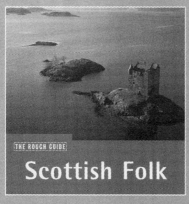

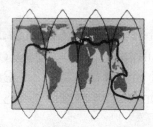